The Oxford German Dictionary and Grammar

The Oxford German Dictionary and Grammar

Second Edition

Dictionary
Gunhild Prowe
Jill Schneider

Second edition edited by
Roswitha Morris
Robin Sawers

Grammar
William Rowlinson

OXFORD
UNIVERSITY PRESS

OXFORD
UNIVERSITY PRESS

Great Clarendon Street, Oxford OX2 6DP

Oxford University Press is a department of the University of Oxford.
It furthers the University's objective of excellence in research, scholarship,
and education by publishing worldwide in

Oxford New York

Athens Auckland Bangkok Bogotá Buenos Aires Calcutta
Cape Town Chennai Dar es Salaam Delhi Florence Hong Kong Istanbul
Karachi Kolkata Kuala Lumpur Madrid Melbourne Mexico City Mumbai
Nairobi Paris São Paulo Shanghai Singapore Taipei Tokyo Toronto Warsaw

with associated companies in Berlin Ibadan

Oxford is a registered trade mark of Oxford University Press
in the UK and in certain other countries

British Library Cataloguing in Publication Data
Data available

Library of Congress Cataloging in Publication Data
Data available
ISBN 0-19-860389-4

10 9 8 7 6 5 4 3 2 1

Typeset by Morton Word Processing Ltd
Printed in Great Britain by
Mackays of Chatham plc
Chatham, Kent

General Contents

Dictionary

Contents

Proprietary terms

This dictionary includes some words which are, or are asserted to be, proprietary names or trademarks. Their inclusion does not imply that they have acquired for legal purposes a non-proprietary or general significance, nor is any other judgement implied concerning their legal status. In cases where the editor has some evidence that a word is used as a proprietary name or trademark this is indicated by the letter (P), but no judgement concerning the legal status of such words is made or implied thereby.

Contents

Proprietary terms

Introduction

This dictionary reflects recent changes to the spelling of German ratified in July 1996. The symbol * has been introduced to refer from the old spelling to the new, preferred one:

> **As*** *nt* -ses, -se *s.* Ass
> **dasein*** *vi sep* (*sein*) da sein, *s.* da
> **Schiffahrt*** *f s.* Schifffahrt

Where both the old and new forms are valid, an equals sign = is used to refer to the preferred form:

> **aufwändig** *a* = aufwendig
> **Tunfisch** *m* = Thunfisch

When such forms follow each other alphabetically, they are given with commas, with the preferred form in first place:

> **Panther, Panter** *m* -s, - panther

In phrases, *od* (oder) is used:

> …**deine(r,s)** *poss pron* yours;
> die D~en *od* d~en *pl* your family *sg*

On the English–German side, only the preferred German form is given.

- A swung dash ~ represents the headword or that part of the headword preceding a vertical bar |. The initial letter of a German headword is given to show whether or not it is a capital.
- The vertical bar | follows the part of the headword which is not repeated in compounds or derivatives.
- Square brackets [ ] are used for optional material.
- Angled brackets < > are used after a verb translation to indicate the object; before a verb translation to indicate the subject; before an adjective to indicate a typical noun which it qualifies.

- Round brackets ( ) are used for field or style labels
  (see list on pages xvii–xix), and for explanatory matter.

- A box □ indicates a new part of speech within an entry.

- *od* (oder) and *or* denote that words or portions of a phrase are
  synonymous. An oblique stroke / is used where there is a
  difference in usage or meaning.

- ≈ is used where no exact equivalent exists in the other language.

- A dagger † indicates that a German verb is irregular and that the
  parts can be found in the verb table on pages 499–503. Compound
  verbs are not listed there as they follow the pattern of the basic
  verb.

- The stressed vowel is marked in a German headword by _ (long) or .
  (short). A phonetic transcription is only given for words which do
  not follow the normal rules of pronunciation. These rules can be
  found on page xiii.

- German headword nouns are followed by the gender and, with the
  exception of compound nouns, by the genitive and plural. These
  are only given at compound nouns if they present some difficulty.
  Otherwise the user should refer to the final element.

- Nouns that decline like adjectives are entered as follows: **-e(r)** *m/f*,
  -e(s) *nt*.

- Adjectives which have no undeclined form are entered
  in the feminine form with the masculine and neuter in brackets
  -e(r,s).

- The reflexive pronoun **sich** is accusative unless marked (*dat*).

Phonetic symbols used for German words

a	Hand	hant	ŋ	lang	laŋ
a:	Bahn	ba:n	o	Moral	mo'ra:l
ɐ	Ober	'o:bɐ	o:	Boot	bo:t
ɐ̯	Uhr	u:ɐ̯	o̯	loyal	lo̯a'ja:l
ã	Conférencier	kõferã'si̯e:	õ	Konkurs	kõ'kʊrs
ã:	Abonnement	abɔnə'mã:	õ:	Ballon	ba'lõ:
ai̯	weit	vai̯t	ɔ	Post	pɔst
au̯	Haut	hau̯t	ø	Ökonom	øko'no:m
b	Ball	bal	ø:	Öl	ø:l
ç	ich	ɪç	œ	göttlich	'gœtliç
d	dann	dan	ɔy	heute	'hɔytə
dʒ	Gin	dʒɪn	p	Pakt	pakt
e	Metall	me'tal	r	Rast	rast
e:	Beet	be:t	s	Hast	hast
ɛ	mästen	'mɛstən	ʃ	Schal	ʃa:l
ɛ:	wählen	'vɛ:lən	t	Tal	ta:l
ɛ̃	Cousin	ku'zɛ̃:	ts	Zahl	tsa:l
ə	Nase	'na:zə	tʃ	Couch	kau̯tʃ
f	Faß	fas	u	Kupon	ku'põ:
g	Gast	gast	u:	Hut	hu:t
h	haben	'ha:bən	u̯	aktuell	ak'tu̯ɛl
i	Rivale	ri'va:lə	ʊ	Pult	pʊlt
i:	viel	fi:l	v	was	vas
i̯	Aktion	ak'tsi̯o:n	x	Bach	bax
ɪ	Birke	'bɪrkə	y	Physik	fy'zi:k
j	ja	ja:	y:	Rübe	'ry:bə
k	kalt	kalt	ỹ	Nuance	'nỹã:sə
l	Last	last	ʏ	Fülle	'fʏlə
m	Mast	mast	z	Nase	'na:zə
n	Naht	na:t	ʒ	Regime	re'ʒi:m

ʔ Glottal stop, e.g. Koordination / koʔɔrdina'tsi̯on /.

: Length sign after a vowel, e.g. Chrom / kro:m /.

' Stress mark before stressed syllable, e.g. Balkon / bal'kõ:/.

Guide to German pronunciation

Consonants

Pronounced as in English with the following exceptions:

b	as	p	
d	as	t	*at the end of a word or syllable*
g	as	k	

ch	as in Scottish lo<u>ch</u>	*after a, o, u, au*
	like an exaggerated h as in <u>h</u>uge	*after i, e, ä, ö, ü, eu, ei*

-chs	as	x	(as in bo<u>x</u>)
-ig	as	-ich / ɪç /	*when a suffix*
j	as	y	(as in <u>y</u>es)

ps		
pn		the p is pronounced

qu	as	k + v	

s	as	z	(as in <u>z</u>ero) *at the beginning of a word*
	as	s	(as in bu<u>s</u>) *at the end of a word or syllable, before a consonant, or when doubled*

sch	as	sh	
sp	as	shp	*at the beginning of a word*
st	as	sht	*at the beginning of a word*

v	as	f	(as in <u>f</u>or)
	as	v	(as in <u>v</u>ery) *within a word*

w	as	v	(as in <u>v</u>ery)
z	as	ts	

Vowels

Approximately as follows:

a	short	as	u	(as in b<u>u</u>t)
	long	as	a	(as in c<u>a</u>r)
e	short	as	e	(as in p<u>e</u>n)
	long	as	a	(as in p<u>a</u>per)
i	short	as	i	(as in b<u>i</u>t)
	long	as	ee	(as in qu<u>ee</u>n)
o	short	as	o	(as in h<u>o</u>t)
	long	as	o	(as in p<u>o</u>pe)
u	short	as	oo	(as in f<u>oo</u>t)
	long	as	oo	(as in b<u>oo</u>t)

Vowels are always short before a double consonant, and long when followed by an h or when double

ie	is pronounced	ee	(as in k<u>ee</u>p)

Diphthongs

au		as	ow	(as in h<u>ow</u>)
ei		as	y	(as in m<u>y</u>)
ai				
eu		as	oy	(as in b<u>oy</u>)
äu				

Pronunciation of the alphabet

English/Englisch		German/Deutsch
eɪ	a	a:
biː	b	be:
siː	c	tse:
diː	d	de:
iː	e	e:
ef	f	ɛf
dʒiː	g	ge:
eɪtʃ	h	ha:
aɪ	i	i:
dʒeɪ	j	jɔt
keɪ	k	ka:
el	l	ɛl
em	m	ɛm
en	n	ɛn
əʊ	o	o:
piː	p	pe:
kjuː	q	ku:
aː(r)	r	ɛr
es	s	ɛs
tiː	t	te:
juː	u	u:
viː	v	faʊ
ˈdʌbljuː	w	ve:
eks	x	ɪks
waɪ	y	ˈʏpsilɔn
zed	z	tsɛt
eɪ umlaut	ä	ɛ:
əʊ umlaut	ö	ø:
juː umlaut	ü	y:
esˈzed	ß	ɛsˈtsɛt

Abbreviations

adjective	*a*	Adjektiv
abbreviation	*abbr*	Abkürzung
accusative	*acc*	Akkusativ
Administration	*Admin*	Administration
adverb	*adv*	Adverb
American	*Amer*	amerikanisch
Anatomy	*Anat*	Anatomie
Archaeology	*Archaeol*	Archäologie
Architecture	*Archit*	Architektur
Astronomy	*Astr*	Astronomie
attributive	*attrib*	attributiv
Austrian	*Aust*	österreichisch
Motor vehicles	*Auto*	Automobil
Aviation	*Aviat*	Luftfahrt
Biology	*Biol*	Biologie
Botany	*Bot*	Botanik
Chemistry	*Chem*	Chemie
collective	*coll*	Kollektivum
Commerce	*Comm*	Handel
conjunction	*conj*	Konjunktion
Cookery	*Culin*	Kochkunst
dative	*dat*	Dativ
definite article	*def art*	bestimmter Artikel
demonstrative	*dem*	Demonstrativ-
dialect	*dial*	Dialekt
Electricity	*Electr*	Elektrizität
something	*etw*	etwas
feminine	*f*	Femininum
figurative	*fig*	figurativ
genitive	*gen*	Genitiv
Geography	*Geog*	Geographie
Geology	*Geol*	Geologie
Geometry	*Geom*	Geometrie
Grammar	*Gram*	Grammatik
Horticulture	*Hort*	Gartenbau
impersonal	*impers*	unpersönlich
indefinite article	*indef art*	unbestimmter Artikel
indefinite pronoun	*indef pron*	unbestimmtes Pronomen
infinitive	*inf*	Infinitiv
inseparable	*insep*	untrennbar
interjection	*int*	Interjektion
invariable	*inv*	unveränderlich
irregular	*irreg*	unregelmäßig
someone	*jd*	jemand
someone	*jdm*	jemandem
someone	*jdn*	jemanden
someone's	*jds*	jemandes
Journalism	*Journ*	Journalismus

Law	*Jur*	Jura
Language	*Lang*	Sprache
literary	*liter*	dichterisch
masculine	*m*	Maskulinum
Mathematics	*Math*	Mathematik
Medicine	*Med*	Medizin
Meteorology	*Meteorol*	Meteorologie
Military	*Mil*	Militär
Mineralogy	*Miner*	Mineralogie
Music	*Mus*	Musik
noun	*n*	Substantiv
Nautical	*Naut*	nautisch
North German	*N Ger*	Norddeutsch
nominative	*nom*	Nominativ
neuter	*nt*	Neutrum
or	*od*	oder
Proprietary term	*P*	Warenzeichen
pejorative	*pej*	abwertend
Photography	*Phot*	Fotografie
Physics	*Phys*	Physik
plural	*pl*	Plural
Politics	*Pol*	Politik
possessive	*poss*	Possessiv-
past participle	*pp*	zweites Partizip
predicative	*pred*	prädikativ
prefix	*pref*	Präfix
preposition	*prep*	Präposition
present	*pres*	Präsens
present participle	*pres p*	erstes Partizip
pronoun	*pron*	Pronomen
Psychology	*Psych*	Psychologie
past tense	*pt*	Präteritum
Railway	*Rail*	Eisenbahn
reflexive	*refl*	reflexiv
regular	*reg*	regelmäßig
relative	*rel*	Relativ-
Religion	*Relig*	Religion
see	*s.*	siehe
School	*Sch*	Schule
separable	*sep*	trennbar
singular	*sg*	Singular
South German	*S Ger*	Süddeutsch
someone	*s.o.*	jemand
something	*sth*	etwas
Technical	*Techn*	Technik
Telephone	*Teleph*	Telefon
Textiles	*Tex*	Textilien
Theatre	*Theat*	Theater
Television	*TV*	Fernsehen
Typography	*Typ*	Typographie
University	*Univ*	Universität
auxiliary verb	*v aux*	Hilfsverb
intransitive verb	*vi*	intransitives Verb
reflexive verb	*vr*	reflexives Verb
transitive verb	*vt*	transitives Verb

vulgar	*vulg*	vulgär
Zoology	*Zool*	Zoologie
familiar	ⓕ	familiär
slang	⊠	Slang
old spelling	*	alte Schreibung

German–English Dictionary

Aa

Aal *m* -[e]s, -e eel

Aas *nt* -es carrion; ⊠ swine

ab *prep* (+ *dat*) from ● *adv* off; (*weg*) away; (*auf Fahrplan*) departs; **ab und zu** now and then; **auf und ab** up and down

abändern *vt sep* alter; (*abwandeln*) modify

Abbau *m* dismantling; (*Kohlen-*) mining. **a~en** *vt sep* dismantle; mine <*Kohle*>

abbeißen† *vt sep* bite off

abbeizen *vt sep* strip

abberufen† *vt sep* recall

abbestellen *vt sep* cancel; **jdn a~** put s.o. off

abbiegen† *vi sep* (*sein*) turn off; **[nach] links a~** turn left

Abbildung *f* -, -en illustration

abblättern *vi sep* (*sein*) flake off

abblend|en *vt/i sep* (*haben*) [**die Scheinwerfer**] **a~en** dip one's headlights. **A~licht** *nt* dipped headlights *pl*

abbrechen† *v sep* ● *vt* break off; (*abreißen*) demolish ● *vi* (*sein/haben*) break off

abbrennen† *v sep* ● *vt* burn off; (*niederbrennen*) burn down ● *vi* (*sein*) burn down

abbringen† *vt sep* dissuade (**von** from)

Abbruch *m* demolition; (*Beenden*) breaking off

abbuchen *vt sep* debit

abbürsten *vt sep* brush down; (*entfernen*) brush off

abdanken *vi sep* (*haben*) resign; <*Herrscher:*> abdicate

abdecken *vt sep* uncover; (*abnehmen*) take off; (*zudecken*) cover; **den Tisch a~** clear the table

abdichten *vt sep* seal

abdrehen *vt sep* turn off

Abdruck *m* (*pl* ̈-e) impression. **a~en** *vt sep* print

abdrücken *vt/i sep* (*haben*) fire; **sich a~** leave an impression

Abend *m* -s, -e evening; **am A~** in the evening; **heute A~** this evening, tonight; **gestern A~** yesterday evening, last night. **A~brot** *nt* supper. **A~essen** *nt* dinner; (*einfacher*) supper. **A~mahl** *nt* (*Relig*) [Holy] Communion. **a~s** *adv* in the evening

Abenteuer *nt* -s,- adventure; (*Liebes-*) affair. **a~lich** *a* fantastic

aber *conj* but; **oder a~** or else ● *adv* (*wirklich*) really

Aber|glaube *m* superstition. **a~gläubisch** *a* superstitious

abfahr|en† *v sep* ● *vi* (*sein*) leave; <*Auto:*> drive off ● *vt* take away; (*entlangfahren*) drive along; use <*Fahrkarte*>; **abgefahrene Reifen** worn tyres. **A~t** *f* departure; (*Talfahrt*) descent; (*Piste*) run; (*Ausfahrt*) exit

Abfall *m* refuse, rubbish; (*auf der Straße*) litter; (*Industrie-*) waste

abfallen† *vi sep* (*sein*) drop, fall; (*übrig bleiben*) be left (**für** for); (*sich neigen*) slope away. **a~d** *a* sloping

Abfallhaufen *m* rubbish-dump

abfällig *a* disparaging

abfangen† *vt sep* intercept

abfärben *vi sep* (*haben*) <*Farbe:*> run; <*Stoff:*> not be colour-fast

abfassen *vt sep* draft

abfertigen *vt sep* attend to; (*zollamtlich*) clear; **jdn kurz a~** ▯ give s.o. short shrift

abfeuern *vt sep* fire

abfind|en† *vt sep* pay off; (*entschädigen*) compensate; **sich a~en mit** come to terms with. **A~ung** *f* -, -en compensation

abfliegen† *vi sep* (*sein*) fly off; (*Aviat*) take off

abfließen† *vi sep* (*sein*) drain *or* run away

Abflug *m* (*Aviat*) departure

Abfluss m drainage; *(Öffnung)* drain. **A~rohr** nt drain-pipe

abfragen vt sep jdn od jdm Vokabeln a~ test s.o. on vocabulary

Abfuhr f - removal; *(fig)* rebuff

abführ|en vt sep take or lead away. **A~mittel** nt laxative

abfüllen vt sep auf od in Flaschen a~ bottle

Abgase ntpl exhaust fumes

abgeben† vt sep hand in; *(abliefern)* deliver; *(verkaufen)* sell; *(zur Aufbewahrung)* leave; *(Fußball)* pass; *(ausströmen)* give off; *(abfeuern)* fire; *(verlauten lassen)* give; cast <Stimme>; jdm etw a~ give s.o. a share of sth

abgehen† v sep ● vi (sein) leave; *(Theat)* exit; *(sich lösen)* come off; *(abgezogen werden)* be deducted ● vt walk along

abgehetzt a harassed. **abgelegen** a remote. **abgeneigt** a etw *(dat)* nicht abgeneigt sein not be averse to sth. **abgenutzt** a worn. **Abgeordnete(r)** m/f deputy; *(Pol)* Member of Parliament. **abgepackt** a pre-packed

abgeschieden a secluded

abgeschlossen a *(fig)* complete; <Wohnung> self-contained.

abgesehen prep apart (from von). **abgespannt** a exhausted. **abgestanden** a stale. **abgestorben** a dead; <Glied> numb. **abgetragen** a worn. **abgewetzt** a threadbare

abgewinnen† vt sep win (jdm from s.o.); etw *(dat)* Geschmack a~ get a taste for sth

abgewöhnen vt sep jdm/sich das Rauchen a~ cure s.o. of/ give up smoking

abgießen† vt sep pour off; drain <Gemüse>

Abgott m idol

abgöttisch adv a~ lieben idolize

abgrenz|en vt sep divide off; *(fig)* define. **A~ung** f - demarcation

Abgrund m abyss; *(fig)* depths pl

abgucken vt sep 🔲 copy

Abguss m cast

abhacken vt sep chop off

abhaken vt sep tick off

abhalten† vt sep keep off; *(hindern)* keep, prevent (von from); *(veranstalten)* hold

abhanden adv a~ kommen get lost

Abhandlung f treatise

Abhang m slope

abhängen¹ vt sep *(reg)* take down; *(abkuppeln)* uncouple

abhäng|en²† vi sep *(haben)* depend (von on). **a~ig** a dependent (von on). **A~igkeit** f - dependence

abhärten vt sep toughen up

abheben† v sep ● vt take off; *(vom Konto)* withdraw; sich a~ stand out (gegen against) ● vi *(haben)* <Cards> cut [the cards]; *(Aviat)* take off; <Rakete:> lift off

abheften vt sep file

Abhilfe f remedy

abholen vt sep collect

abhör|en vt sep listen to; *(überwachen)* tap; jdn od jdm Vokabeln a~en test s.o. on vocabulary. **A~gerät** nt bugging device

Abitur nt -s ≈ A levels pl

abkaufen vt sep buy *(dat* from)

abklingen† vi sep *(sein)* die away; *(nachlassen)* subside

abkochen vt sep boil

abkommen† vi sep *(sein)* a~ von stray from; *(aufgeben)* give up. **A~** nt -s,- agreement

Abkömmling m -s, -e descendant

abkratzen vt sep scrape off

abkühlen vt/i sep *(sein)* cool; sich a~ cool [down]

Abkunft f - origin

abkuppeln vt sep uncouple

abkürz|en vt sep shorten; abbreviate <Wort>. **A~ung** f short cut; *(Wort)* abbreviation

abladen† vt sep unload

Ablage f shelf; *(für Akten)* tray

ablager|n *vt sep* deposit. **A~ung** *f* -, -en deposit

ablassen† *vt sep* drain [off]; let off <*Dampf*>

Ablauf *m* drain; (*Verlauf*) course; (*Ende*) end; (*einer Frist*) expiry. **a~en†** *v sep* ● *vi* (*sein*) run *or* drain off; (*verlaufen*) go off; (*enden*) expire; <*Zeit:*> run out; <*Uhrwerk:*> run down ● *vt* walk along; (*absuchen*) scour (**nach** for)

ableg|en *v sep* ● *vt* put down; discard <*Karte*>; (*abheften*) file; (*ausziehen*) take off; sit, take <*Prüfung*>; **abgelegte Kleidung** cast-offs *pl* ● *vi* (*haben*) take off one's coat; (*Naut*) cast off. **A~er** *m* -s,- (*Bot*) cutting; (*Schössling*) shoot

ablehn|en *vt sep* refuse; (*missbilligen*) reject. **A~ung** *f* -, -en refusal; rejection

ableit|en *vt sep* divert; **sich a~en** be derived (**von/aus** from). **A~ung** *f* derivation; (*Wort*) derivative

ablenk|en *vt sep* deflect; divert <*Aufmerksamkeit*>. **A~ung** *f* -, -en distraction

ablesen† *vt sep* read

ablicht|en *vt sep* photocopy. **A~ung** *f* photocopy

abliefern *vt sep* deliver

ablös|en *vt sep* detach; (*abwechseln*) relieve; **sich a~en** come off; (*sich abwechseln*) take turns. **A~ung** *f* relief

abmach|en *vt sep* remove; (*ausmachen*) arrange; (*vereinbaren*) agree. **A~ung** *f* -, -en agreement

abmager|n *vi sep* (*sein*) lose weight. **A~ungskur** *f* slimming diet

abmelden *vt sep* cancel; (*im Hotel*) check out

abmessen† *vt sep* measure

abmühen (sich) *vr sep* struggle

Abnäher *m* -s,- dart

abnehm|en† *v sep* ● *vt* take off, remove; pick up <*Hörer*>; **jdm etw a~en** take/(*kaufen*) buy sth from s.o. ● *vi* (*haben*) decrease; (*nachlassen*) decline; <*Person:*> lose weight; <*Mond:*> wane. **A~er** *m* -s,- buyer

Abneigung *f* dislike (**gegen** of)

abnorm *a* abnormal

abnutz|en *vt sep* wear out. **A~ung** *f* - wear [and tear]

Abon|nement /abɔnə'mã:/ *nt* -s, -s subscription. **A~nent** *m* -en, -en subscriber. **a~nieren** *vt* take out a subscription to

Abordnung *f* -, -en deputation

abpassen *vt sep* wait for; **gut a~** time well

abraten† *vi sep* (*haben*) **jdm von etw a~** advise s.o. against sth

abräumen *vt/i* (*haben*) clear away

abrechn|en *v sep* ● *vt* deduct ● *vi* (*haben*) settle up. **A~ung** *f* settlement; (*Rechnung*) account

Abreise *f* departure. **a~n** *vi sep* (*sein*) leave

abreißen† *v sep* ● *vt* tear off; (*demolieren*) pull down ● *vi* (*sein*) come off

abrichten *vt sep* train

Abriss *m* demolition; (*Übersicht*) summary

abrufen† *vt sep* call away; (*Computer*) retrieve

abrunden *vt sep* round off

abrüst|en *vi sep* (*haben*) disarm. **A~ung** *f* disarmament

abrutschen *vi sep* (*sein*) slip

Absage *f* -, -n cancellation; (*Ablehnung*) refusal. **a~n** *v sep* ● *vt* cancel ● *vi* (*haben*) [jdm] a~n cancel an appointment [with s.o.]; (*auf Einladung*) refuse [s.o.'s invitation]

Absatz *m* heel; (*Abschnitt*) paragraph; (*Verkauf*) sale

abschaffen *vt sep* abolish; get rid of <*Auto, Hund*>

abschalten *vt/i sep* (*haben*) switch off

Abscheu *m* - revulsion

abscheulich *a* revolting

abschicken *vt sep* send off

Abschied *m* -[e]s, -e farewell; (*Trennung*) parting; **A~ nehmen** say goodbye (**von** to)

abschießen† *vt sep* shoot down; (*abfeuern*) fire; launch <*Rakete*>

abschirmen *vt sep* shield

abschlagen† *vt sep* knock off; (*verweigern*) refuse

Abschlepp|dienst *m* breakdown service. **a~en** *vt sep* tow away. **A~seil** *nt* tow-rope

abschließen† *v sep* ● *vt* lock; (*beenden, abmachen*) conclude; make <*Wette*>; balance <*Bücher*> ● *vi* (*haben*) lock up; (*enden*) end. **a~d** *adv* in conclusion

Abschluss *m* conclusion. **A~zeugnis** *nt* diploma

abschmecken *vt sep* season

abschmieren *vt sep* lubricate

abschneiden† *v sep* ● *vt* cut off ● *vi* (*haben*) gut/schlecht a~ do well/badly

Abschnitt *m* section; (*Stadium*) stage; (*Absatz*) paragraph

abschöpfen *vt sep* skim off

abschrauben *vt sep* unscrew

abschreck|en *vt sep* deter; (*Culin*) put in cold water <*Ei*>. **a~end** *a* repulsive. **A~ungsmittel** *nt* deterrent

abschreib|en† *v sep* ● *vt* copy; (*Comm & fig*) write off ● *vi* (*haben*) copy. **A~ung** *f* (*Comm*) depreciation

Abschrift *f* copy

Abschuss *m* shooting down; (*Abfeuern*) firing; (*Raketen-*) launch

abschüssig *a* sloping; (*steil*) steep

abschwellen† *vi sep* (*sein*) go down

abseh|bar *a* in a~barer Zeit in the foreseeable future. **a~en**† *vt/i sep* (*haben*) copy; (*voraussehen*) foresee; a~en von disregard; (*aufgeben*) refrain from

abseits *adv* apart; (*Sport*) offside ● *prep* (+ *gen*) away from. **A~** *nt* - (*Sport*) offside

absend|en† *vt sep* send off. **A~er** *m* sender

absetzen *v sep* ● *vt* put *or* set down; (*ablagern*) deposit; (*abnehmen*) take off; (*abbrechen*) stop; (*entlassen*) dismiss; (*verkaufen*) sell; (*abziehen*) deduct ● *vi* (*haben*) pause

Absicht *f* -, -en intention; mit A~ intentionally, on purpose

absichtlich *a* intentional

absitzen† *v sep* ● *vi* (*sein*) dismount ● *vt* ⚠ serve <*Strafe*>

absolut *a* absolute

absolvieren *vt* complete; (*bestehen*) pass

absonder|n *vt sep* separate; (*ausscheiden*) secrete. **A~ung** *f* -, -en secretion

absorbieren *vt* absorb

abspeisen *vt sep* fob off (mit with)

absperr|en *vt sep* cordon off; (*abstellen*) turn off; (*SGer*) lock. **A~ung** *f* -, -en barrier

abspielen *vt sep* play; (*Fußball*) pass; sich a~ take place

Absprache *f* agreement

absprechen† *vt sep* arrange; sich a~ agree

abspringen† *vi sep* (*sein*) jump off; (*mit Fallschirm*) parachute; (*abgehen*) come off

Absprung *m* jump

abspülen *vt sep* rinse

abstamm|en *vi sep* (*haben*) be descended (von from). **A~ung** *f* - descent

Abstand *m* distance; (*zeitlich*) interval; A~ halten keep one's distance

abstatten *vt sep* jdm einen Besuch a~ pay s.o. a visit

Abstecher *m* -s,- detour

abstehen† *vi sep* (*haben*) stick out

absteigen† *vi sep* (*sein*) dismount; (*niedersteigen*) descend; (*Fußball*) be relegated

abstell|en *vt sep* put down; (*lagern*) store; (*parken*) park; (*abschalten*) turn off. **A~gleis** *nt* siding. **A~raum** *m* box-room

absterben† *vi sep* (*sein*) die; (*gefühllos werden*) go numb

Abstieg *m* -[e]s, -e descent; (*Fußball*) relegation

---

*old spelling

abstimm|en *v sep* ● *vi* (*haben*) vote (**über** + *acc* on). ● *vt* coordinate (**auf** + *acc* with). **A~ung** *f* vote

Abstinenzler *m* -s, - teetotaller

abstoßen† *vt sep* knock off; (*verkaufen*) sell; (*fig: ekeln*) repel. **a~d** *a* repulsive

abstreiten† *vt sep* deny

Abstrich *m* (*Med*) smear

abstufen *vt sep* grade

Absturz *m* fall; (*Aviat*) crash

abstürzen *vi sep* (*sein*) fall; (*Aviat*) crash

absuchen *vt sep* search

absurd *a* absurd

Abszess *m* -es, -e abscess

Abt *m* -[e]s,⸚e abbot

abtasten *vt sep* feel; (*Techn*) scan

abtauen *vt/i sep* (*sein*) thaw; (*entfrosten*) defrost

Abtei *f* -, -en abbey

Abteil *nt* compartment

Abteilung *f* -, -en section; (*Admin, Comm*) department

abtragen† *vt sep* clear; (*einebnen*) level; (*abnutzen*) wear out

abträglich *a* detrimental (*dat* to)

abtreib|en† *vt sep* (*Naut*) drive off course; **ein Kind a~en lassen** have an abortion. **A~ung** *f* -, -en abortion

abtrennen *vt sep* detach; (*abteilen*) divide off

Abtreter *m* -s,- doormat

abtrocknen *vt/i sep* (*haben*) dry; **sich a~** dry oneself

abtropfen *vi sep* (*sein*) drain

abtun† *vt sep* (*fig*) dismiss

abwägen† *vt sep* (*fig*) weigh

abwandeln *vt sep* modify

abwarten *v sep* ● *vt* wait for ● *vi* (*haben*) wait [and see]

abwärts *adv* down[wards]

Abwasch *m* -[e]s washing-up; (*Geschirr*) dirty dishes *pl.* **a~en†** *v sep* ● *vt* wash; wash up <*Geschirr*>; (*entfernen*) wash off ● *vi* (*haben*) wash up. **A~lappen** *m* dishcloth

Abwasser *nt* -s,⸚ sewage. **A~kanal** *m* sewer

abwechseln *vi/r sep* (*haben*) [sich] **a~** alternate; <*Personen:*> take turns. **a~d** *a* alternate

Abwechslung *f* -, -en change; **zur A~** for a change

abwegig *a* absurd

Abwehr *f* - defence; (*Widerstand*) resistance; (*Pol*) counter-espionage. **a~en** *vt sep* ward off. **A~system** *nt* immune system

abweich|en† *vi sep* (*sein*) deviate/ (*von Regel*) depart (**von** from); (*sich unterscheiden*) differ (**von** from). **a~end** *a* divergent; (*verschieden*) different. **A~ung** *f* -, -en deviation

abweis|en† *vt sep* turn down; turn away <*Person*>. **a~end** *a* unfriendly. **A~ung** *f* rejection

abwenden† *vt sep* turn away; (*verhindern*) avert

abwerfen† *vt sep* throw off; throw <*Reiter*>; (*Aviat*) drop; (*Kartenspiel*) discard; shed <*Haut, Blätter*>; yield <*Gewinn*>

abwert|en *vt sep* devalue. **A~ung** *f* -, -en devaluation

Abwesenheit *f* - absence; absent-mindedness

abwickeln *vt sep* unwind; (*erledigen*) settle

abwischen *vt sep* wipe

abzahlen *vt sep* pay off

abzählen *vt sep* count

Abzahlung *f* instalment

Abzeichen *nt* badge

abzeichnen *vt sep* copy

Abzieh|bild *nt* transfer. **a~en†** *v sep* ● *vt* pull off; take off <*Laken*>; strip <*Bett*>; (*häuten*) skin; (*Phot*) print; run off <*Kopien*>; (*zurückziehen*) withdraw; (*abrechnen*) deduct ● *vi* (*sein*) go away, <*Rauch:*> escape

Abzug *m* withdrawal; (*Abrechnung*) deduction; (*Phot*) print (*Korrektur-*) proof; (*am Gewehr*) trigger; (*A~söffnung*) vent; **A~e** *pl* deductions

abzüglich *prep* (+ *gen*) less

Abzugshaube *f* [cooker] hood

abzweig|en *v sep* ● *vi* (*sein*) branch off ● *vt* divert. **A~ung** *f* -, -en junction; (*Gabelung*) fork

ach *int* oh; **a~ je!** oh dear! **a~ so** I see

Achse *f* -, -n axis; (*Rad-*) axle

Achsel *f* -, -n shoulder. **A~höhle** *f* armpit. **A~zucken** *nt* -s shrug

acht *inv a*, **A~** *f* -, -en eight

Acht *f* **A~ geben** be careful; **A~ geben auf** (+ *acc*) look after; **außer A~ lassen** disregard; **sich in A~ nehmen** be careful

acht|e(r,s) *a* eighth. **a~eckig** *a* octagonal. **A~el** *nt* -s,- eighth

achten *vt* respect ● *vi* (*haben*) **a~ auf** (+ *acc*) pay attention to; (*aufpassen*) look after

Achterbahn *f* roller-coaster

achtlos *a* careless

achtsam *a* careful

Achtung *f* - respect (**vor** + *dat* for); **A~!** look out!

acht|zehn *inv a* eighteen. **a~zehnte(r,s)** *a* eighteenth. **a~zig** *a inv* eighty. **a~zigste(r,s)** *a* eightieth

Acker *m* -s,- field. **A~bau** *m* agriculture. **A~land** *nt* arable land

addieren *vt/i* (*haben*) add

Addition /-'tsi̯oːn/ *f* -, -en addition

ade *int* goodbye

Adel *m* -s nobility

Ader *f* -, -n vein

Adjektiv *nt* -s, -e adjective

Adler *m* -s,- eagle

adlig *a* noble. **A~e(r)** *m* nobleman

Administration /-'tsi̯oːn/ *f* - administration

Admiral *m* -s,-e admiral

adop|tieren *vt* adopt. **A~tion** /-'tsi̯oːn/ *f* -, -en adoption. **A~tiveltern** *pl* adoptive parents. **A~tivkind** *nt* adopted child

Adrenalin *nt* -s adrenalin

Adres|se *f* -, -n address. **a~sieren** *vt* address

Adria *f* - Adriatic

---

*alte Schreibung

Adverb *nt* -s, -ien /-i̯ən/ adverb

Affäre *f* -, -n affair

Affe *m* -n, -n monkey; (*Menschen-*) ape

affektiert *a* affected

affig *a* affected; (*eitel*) vain

Afrika *nt* -s Africa

Afrikan|er(in) *m* -s,- (*f* -, -nen) African. **a~isch** *a* African

After *m* -s,- anus

Agen|t(in) *m* -en, -en (*f* -, -nen) agent. **A~tur** *f* -, -en agency

Aggres|sion *f* -, -en aggression. **a~siv** *a* aggressive

Agnostiker *m* -s,- agnostic

Ägypt|en /ɛ'ɡʏptən/ *nt* -s Egypt. **Ä~er(in)** *m* -s,- (*f* -, -nen) Egyptian. **ä~isch** *a* Egyptian

ähneln *vi* (*haben*) (+ *dat*) resemble; **sich ä~** be alike

ahnen *vt* have a presentiment of; (*vermuten*) suspect

Ahnen *mpl* ancestors. **A~forschung** *f* genealogy

ähnlich *a* similar; **jdm ä~ sehen** resemble s.o. **Ä~keit** *f* -, -en similarity; resemblance

Ahnung *f* -, -en premonition; (*Vermutung*) idea, hunch

Ahorn *m* -s, -e maple

Ähre *f* -, -n ear [of corn]

Aids /eːts/ *nt* - Aids

Akademie *f* -, -n academy

Akadem|iker(in) *m* -s,- (*f* -, -nen) university graduate. **a~isch** *a* academic

akklimatisieren (sich) *vr* become acclimatized

Akkord *m* -[e]s, -e (*Mus*) chord. **A~arbeit** *f* piece-work

Akkordeon *nt* -s, -s accordion

Akkumulator *m* -s, -en /-'toːrən/ (*Electr*) accumulator

Akkusativ *m* -s, -e accusative. **A~objekt** *nt* direct object

Akrobat|(in) *m* -en, -en (*f* -, -nen) acrobat. **a~isch** *a* acrobatic

Akt *m* -[e]s, -e act; (*Kunst*) nude

Akte *f* -, -n file; **A~n** documents. **A~ntasche** *f* briefcase

Aktie /ˈakts:iə/ f -, -n (*Comm*) share.
A∼ngesellschaft f joint-stock
company

Aktion /akˈts:io:n/ f -, -en action.
A∼är m -s, -e shareholder

aktiv a active

aktuell a topical; (*gegenwärtig*)
current

Akupunktur f - acupuncture

Akustik f - acoustics pl

akut a acute

Akzent m -[e]s, -e accent

akzept|abel a acceptable.
a∼ieren vt accept

Alarm m -s alarm; (*Mil*) alert.
a∼ieren vt alert; (*beunruhigen*)
alarm

Albdruck m nightmare

albern a silly ● vi (*haben*) play the
fool

Albtraum m nightmare

Album nt -s, -ben album

Algebra f - algebra

Algen fpl algae

Algerien /-iən/ nt -s Algeria

Alibi nt -s, -s alibi

Alimente pl maintenance sg

Alkohol m -s alcohol. a∼frei a
non-alcoholic

Alkohol|iker(in) m -s,- (f -, -nen)
alcoholic. a∼isch a alcoholic

all inv pron all das/mein Geld all the/
my money; all dies all this

All nt -s universe

alle pred a finished

all|e(r,s) pron all; (*jeder*) every;
a∼es everything, all; (*alle Leute*)
everyone; a∼e pl all; a∼es Geld all
the money; a∼e beide both [of
them/us]; a∼e Tage every day; a∼e
drei Jahre every three years; ohne
a∼en Grund without any reason; vor
a∼em above all; a∼es in a∼em all
in all; a∼es aussteigen! all change!

Allee f -, -n avenue

allein adv alone; (*nur*) only; a∼
stehend single; a∼ der Gedanke the
mere thought; von a∼[e] of its/
<*Person*> one's own accord;
(*automatisch*) automatically ● conj

but. A∼erziehende(r) m/f single
parent. a∼ig a sole. A∼stehende
pl single people

allemal adv every time; (*gewiss*)
certainly

allenfalls adv at most; (*eventuell*)
possibly

aller|beste(r,s) a very best; am
a∼besten best of all. a∼dings adv
indeed; (*zwar*) admittedly.
a∼erste(r,s) a very first

Allergie f -, -n allergy

allergisch a allergic (gegen to)

Aller|heiligen nt -s All Saints Day.
a∼höchstens adv at the very
most. a∼lei inv a all sorts of ● pron
all sorts of things. a∼letzte(r,s) a
very last. a∼liebste(r,s) a
favourite ● adv am a∼liebsten for
preference; am a∼liebsten haben
like best of all. a∼meiste(r,s) a
most ● adv am a∼meisten most of
all. A∼seelen nt -s All Souls Day.
a∼wenigste(r,s) a very least
● adv am a∼wenigsten least of all

allgemein a general, adv -ly; im
A∼en (a∼en) in general. A∼heit f -
community; (*Öffentlichkeit*) general
public

Allianz f -, -en alliance

Alligator m -s, -en /-ˈtoːrən/
alligator

alliiert a allied; die A∼en pl the
Allies

all|jährlich a annual. a∼mählich
a gradual

Alltag m working day; der A∼ (*fig*)
everyday life

alltäglich a daily; (*gewöhnlich*)
everyday; <*Mensch*> ordinary

alltags adv on weekdays

allzu adv [far] too; a∼ oft all too
often; a∼ vorsichtig over-cautious

Alm f -, -en alpine pasture

Almosen ntpl alms

Alpdruck m = Albdruck

Alpen pl Alps

Alphabet nt -[e]s, -e alphabet.
a∼isch a alphabetical, adv -ly

Alptraum m = Albtraum

als *conj* as; (*zeitlich*) when; (*mit Komparativ*) than; **nichts als** nothing but; **als ob** as if *or* though

also *adv & conj* so; **a~ gut** all right then; **na a~!** there you are!

alt *a* old; (*gebraucht*) second-hand; (*ehemalig*) former; **alt werden** grow old

Alt *m* -s (*Mus*) contralto

Altar *m* -s,⁻e altar

Alt|e(r) *m/f* old man/woman; **die A~en** old people. **A~eisen** *nt* scrap iron. **A~enheim** *nt* old people's home

Alter *nt* -s,- age; (*Bejahrtheit*) old age; **im A~** at the age of

älter *a* older; **mein ä~er Bruder** my elder brother

altern *vi* (*sein*) age

Alternative *f* -, -n alternative

Alters|grenze *f* age limit. **A~heim** *nt* old people's home. **A~rente** *f* old-age pension. **a~schwach** *a* old and infirm

Alter|tum *nt* -s,⁻er antiquity. **a~tümlich** *a* old; (*altmodisch*) old-fashioned

altklug *a* precocious

alt|modisch *a* old-fashioned. **A~papier** *nt* waste paper. **A~warenhändler** *m* second-hand dealer

Alufolie *f* [aluminium] foil

Aluminium *nt* -s aluminium, (*Amer*) aluminum

am *prep* = **an dem**; **am Montag** on Monday; **am Morgen** in the morning; **am besten** [the] best

Amateur /-'tøːɐ/ *m* -s, -e amateur

Ambition /-'tsi̯oːn/ *f* -, -en ambition

Amboss *m* -es, -e anvil

ambulan|t *a* out-patient ... ● *adv* **a~t behandeln** treat as an out-patient. **A~z** *f* -, -en out-patients' department

Ameise *f* -, -n ant

amen *int*, **A~** *nt* -s amen

Amerika *nt* -s America

Amerikan|er(in) *m* -s,- (*f* -, -nen) American. **a~isch** *a* American

Ammoniak *nt* -s ammonia

Amnestie *f* -, -n amnesty

amoralisch *a* amoral

Ampel *f* -, -n traffic lights *pl*

Amphitheater *nt* amphitheatre

Amput|ation /-'tsi̯oːn/ *f* -, -en amputation. **a~ieren** *vt* amputate

Amsel *f* -, -n blackbird

Amt *nt* -[e]s,⁻er office; (*Aufgabe*) task; (*Teleph*) exchange. **a~lich** *a* official. **A~szeichen** *nt* dialling tone

Amulett *nt* -[e]s, -e [lucky] charm

amüs|ant *a* amusing. **a~ieren** *vt* amuse; **sich a~ieren** be amused (**über** + *acc* at); (*sich vergnügen*) enjoy oneself

··

an
● *preposition* (+ *dative*)

❗ Note that **an** plus **dem** can become **am**

····▶ (*räumlich*) on; (*Gebäude, Ort*) at. **an der Wand** on the wall. **Frankfurt an der Oder** Frankfurt on [the] Oder. **an der Ecke** at the corner. **am Bahnhof** at the station. **an ... vorbei** past

····▶ (*zeitlich*) on. **am Montag** on Monday. **an jedem Sonntag** every Sunday. **am 24. Mai** on May 24th

····▶ (*sonstige Verwendungen*) **arm/reich an Vitaminen** low/rich in vitamins. **jdn an etw erkennen** recognize s.o. by sth. **an etw leiden** suffer from sth. **an einer Krankheit sterben** die of a disease. **an [und für] sich** actually

● *preposition* (+ *accusative*)

❗ Note that **an** plus **das** can become **ans**

····▶ to. **schicke es an deinen Bruder** send it to your brother. **er ging ans Fenster** he went to the window

····▶ (*auf, gegen*) on. **etw an die Wand hängen** to hang sth on the wall. **lehne es an den Baum** lean it on *or* against the tree

····▶ (*sonstige Verwendungen*) **an etw/ jdn glauben** believe in sth/s.o. **an etw denken** think of sth. **sich an etw erinnern** remember sth

---

*old spelling

● *adverb*

····▸ (*auf Fahrplan*) Köln an: 9.15 arriving Cologne 09.15

····▸ (*angeschaltet*) on. die Waschmaschine/der Fernseher/das Licht/das Gas ist an the washing machine/television/light/gas is on

····▸ (*ungefähr*) around; about. an [die] 20 000 DM around *or* about 20,000 DM

····▸ (*in die Zukunft*) von heute an from today (onwards)

analog *a* analogous; (*Computer*) analog. **A∼ie** *f* -, -n analogy

Analphabet *m* -en, -en illiterate person. **A∼entum** *nt* -s illiteracy

Analy|se *f* -, -n analysis. **a∼sieren** *vt* analyse. **A∼tiker** *m* -s,- analyst. **a∼tisch** *a* analytical

Anämie *f* - anaemia

Ananas *f* -, -[se] pineapple

Anatomie *f* - anatomy

Anbau *m* cultivation; (*Gebäude*) extension. **a∼en** *vt sep* build on; (*anpflanzen*) cultivate, grow

anbei *adv* enclosed

anbeißen† *v sep* ● *vt* take a bite of ● *vi* (*haben*) <*Fisch:*> bite

anbeten *vt sep* worship

Anbetracht *m* in A∼ (+ *gen*) in view of

anbieten† *vt sep* offer; sich a∼ offer (zu to)

anbinden† *vt sep* tie up

Anblick *m* sight. **a∼en** *vt sep* look at

anbrechen† *v sep* ● *vt* start on; break into <*Vorräte*> ● *vi* (*sein*) begin; <*Tag:*> break; <*Nacht:*> fall

anbrennen† *v sep* ● *vt* light ● *vi* (*sein*) burn

anbringen† *vt sep* bring [along]; (*befestigen*) fix

Anbruch *m* (*fig*) dawn; bei A∼ des Tages/der Nacht at daybreak/ nightfall

Andacht *f* -, -en reverence; (*Gottesdienst*) prayers *pl*

andächtig *a* reverent; (*fig*) rapt

andauern *vi sep* (*haben*) last; (*anhalten*) continue. **a∼d** *a* persistent; (*ständig*) constant

Andenken *nt* -s,- memory; (*Souvenir*) souvenir

ander|e(r,s) *a* other; (*verschieden*) different; (*nächste*) next; ein a∼er, eine a∼e another ● *pron* der a∼e/ die a∼en the other/others; ein a∼er another [one]; (*Person*) someone else; kein a∼er no one else; einer nach dem a∼en one after the other; alles a∼e/nichts a∼es everything/nothing else; unter a∼em among other things. **a∼enfalls** *adv* otherwise. **a∼erseits** *adv* on the other hand. **a∼mal** *adv* ein a∼mal another time

ändern *vt* alter; (*wechseln*) change; sich ä∼ change

andernfalls *adv* otherwise

anders *pred a* different; a∼ werden change ● *adv* differently; <*riechen, schmecken*> different; (*sonst*) else; jemand a∼ someone else

anderseits *adv* on the other hand

andersherum *adv* the other way round

anderthalb *inv a* one and a half; a∼ Stunden an hour and a half

Änderung *f* -, -en alteration; (*Wechsel*) change

andeut|en *vt sep* indicate; (*anspielen*) hint at. **A∼ung** *f* -, -en indication; hint

Andrang *m* rush (nach for); (*Gedränge*) crush

androhen *vt sep* jdm etw a∼ threaten s.o. with sth

aneignen *vt sep* sich (*dat*) a∼ appropriate; (*lernen*) learn

aneinander *adv & pref* together; <*denken*> of one another; a∼ vorbei past one another; a∼ geraten quarrel

Anekdote *f* -, -n anecdote

anerkannt *a* acknowledged

anerkenn|en† *vt sep* acknowledge, recognize; (*würdigen*) appreciate. **a∼end** *a* approving. **A∼ung** *f* - acknowledgement, recognition; appreciation

anfahren† *v sep* ● *vt* deliver; (*streifen*) hit ● *vi* (*sein*) start

Anfall *m* fit, attack. **a~en**† *v sep* ● *vt* attack ● *vi* (*sein*) arise; <*Zinsen:*> accrue

anfällig *a* susceptible (**für** to); (*zart*) delicate

Anfang *m* -s,-̈e beginning, start; **zu** *od* **am A~** at the beginning; (*anfangs*) at first. **a~en**† *vt/i sep* (*haben*) begin, start; (*tun*) do

Anfänger(in) *m* -s,- (*f* -, -nen) beginner

anfangs *adv* at first. **A~buchstabe** *m* initial letter. **A~gehalt** *nt* starting salary

anfassen *vt sep* touch; (*behandeln*) treat; tackle <*Arbeit*>; **sich a~** hold hands

anfechten† *vt sep* contest

anfertigen *vt sep* make

anfeuchten *vt sep* moisten

anflehen *vt sep* implore, beg

Anflug *m* (*Avia*) approach

anforder|n *vt sep* demand; (*Comm*) order. **A~ung** *f* demand

Anfrage *f* enquiry. **a~n** *vi sep* (*haben*) enquire, ask

anfreunden (sich) *vr sep* make friends (**mit** with)

anfügen *vt sep* add

anfühlen *vt sep* feel; **sich weich a~** feel soft

anführ|en *vt sep* lead; (*zitieren*) quote; (*angeben*) give. **A~er** *m* leader. **A~ungszeichen** *ntpl* quotation marks

Angabe *f* statement; (*Anweisung*) instruction; (*Tennis*) service; **nähere A~n** particulars

angeb|en† *v sep* ● *vt* state; give <*Namen, Grund*>; (*anzeigen*) indicate; set <*Tempo*> ● *vi* (*haben*) (*Tennis*) serve; (🔲 *protzen*) show off. **A~er(in)** *m* -s,- (*f* -, -nen) 🔲 show-off. **A~erei** *f* - 🔲 showing-off

angeblich *a* alleged

angeboren *a* innate; (*Med*) congenital

---
*alte Schreibung

Angebot *nt* offer; (*Auswahl*) range; **A~ und Nachfrage** supply and demand

angebracht *a* appropriate

angeheiratet *a* <*Onkel, Tante*> by marriage

angeheitert *a* 🔲 tipsy

angehen† *v sep* ● *vi* (*sein*) begin, start; <*Licht, Radio:*> come on; (*anwachsen*) take root; **a~ gegen** fight ● *vt* attack; tackle <*Arbeit*>; (*bitten*) ask (**um** for); (*betreffen*) concern

angehör|en *vi sep* (*haben*) (+ *dat*) belong to. **A~ige(r)** *m/f* relative

Angeklagte(r) *m/f* accused

Angel *f* -, -n fishing-rod; (*Tür-*) hinge

Angelegenheit *f* matter

Angel|haken *m* fish-hook. **a~n** *vi* (*haben*) fish (**nach** for); **a~n gehen** go fishing ● *vt* (*fangen*) catch. **A~rute** *f* fishing-rod

angelsächsisch *a* Anglo-Saxon

angemessen *a* commensurate (*dat* with); (*passend*) appropriate

angenehm *a* pleasant; (*bei Vorstellung*) **a~!** delighted to meet you!

angeregt *a* animated

angesehen *a* respected; <*Firma*> reputable

angesichts *prep* (+ *gen*) in view of

angespannt *a* intent; <*Lage*> tense

Angestellte(r) *m/f* employee

angewandt *a* applied

angewiesen *a* dependent (**auf** + *acc* on); **auf sich selbst a~** on one's own

angewöhnen *vt sep* **jdm etw a~** get s.o. used to sth; **sich** (*dat*) **etw a~** get into the habit of doing sth

Angewohnheit *f* habit

Angina *f* - tonsillitis

angleichen† *vt sep* adjust (*dat* to)

anglikanisch *a* Anglican

Anglistik *f* - English [language and literature]

Angorakatze *f* Persian cat

angreif|en† *vt sep* attack; tackle
<*Arbeit*>; (*schädigen*) damage. **A~er**
m -s,- attacker; (*Pol*) aggressor

angrenzen *vi sep* (*haben*) adjoin
(an etw *acc* sth). **a~d** *a* adjoining

Angriff *m* attack; **in A~ nehmen**
tackle. **a~slustig** *a* aggressive

Angst *f* -,-̈e fear; (*Psych*) anxiety;
(*Sorge*) worry (**um** about); **A~ haben**
be afraid (**vor** + *dat* of); (*sich sorgen*)
be worried (**um** about); **jdm A~**
machen frighten s.o.

ängstigen *vt* frighten; (*Sorge*
machen) worry; **sich ä~** be
frightened; be worried (**um** about)

ängstlich *a* nervous; (*scheu*) timid;
(*verängstigt*) frightened, scared;
(*besorgt*) anxious

angucken *vt sep* 🔲 look at

angurten (sich) *vr sep* fasten one's
seat-belt

anhaben† *vt sep* have on; **er/es**
kann mir nichts a~ (*fig*) he/it cannot
hurt me

anhalt|en† *v sep* ● *vt* stop; hold
<*Atem*>; **jdn zur Arbeit a~en** urge
s.o. to work ● *vi* (*haben*) stop;
(*andauern*) continue. **a~end** *a*
persistent. **A~er(in)** *m* -s,- (*f* -,
-nen) hitchhiker; **per A~er fahren**
hitchhike. **A~spunkt** *m* clue

anhand *prep* (+ *gen*) with the aid of

Anhang *m* appendix

anhängen¹ *vt sep* (*reg*) hang up;
(*befestigen*) attach

anhäng|en²† *vi* (*haben*) be a
follower of. **A~er** *m* -s,- follower;
(*Auto*) trailer; (*Schild*) [tie-on] label;
(*Schmuck*) pendant. **A~erin** *f* -, -nen
follower. **a~lich** *a* affectionate

anhäufen *vt sep* pile up

Anhieb *m* **auf A~** straight away

Anhöhe *f* hill

anhören *vt sep* listen to; **sich gut**
a~ sound good

animieren *vt* encourage (**zu** to)

Anis *m* -es aniseed

Anker *m* -s,- anchor; **vor A~ gehen**
drop anchor. **a~n** *vi* (*haben*)
anchor; (*liegen*) be anchored

anketten *vt sep* chain up

Anklage *f* accusation; (*Jur*) charge;
(*Ankläger*) prosecution. **A~bank** *f*
dock. **a~n** *vt sep* accuse (*gen* of);
(*Jur*) charge (*gen* with)

Ankläger *m* accuser; (*Jur*)
prosecutor

anklammern *vt sep* clip on; **sich**
a~ cling (**an** + *acc* to)

ankleben *v sep* ● *vt* stick on ● *vi*
(*sein*) stick (**an** + *dat* to)

anklopfen *vi sep* (*haben*) knock

anknipsen *vt sep* 🔲 switch on

ankommen† *vi sep* (*sein*) arrive;
(*sich nähern*) approach; **gut a~**
arrive safely; (*fig*) go down well (**bei**
with); **nicht a~ gegen** (*fig*) be no
match for; **a~ auf** (+ *acc*) depend on;
das kommt darauf an it [all] depends

ankreuzen *vt sep* mark with a
cross

ankündig|en *vt sep* announce.
A~ung *f* announcement

Ankunft *f* - arrival

ankurbeln *vt sep* (*fig*) boost

anlächeln *vt sep* smile at

anlachen *vt sep* smile at

Anlage *f* -, -n installation;
(*Industrie-*) plant; (*Komplex*)
complex; (*Geld-*) investment; (*Plan*)
layout; (*Beilage*) enclosure;
(*Veranlagung*) aptitude; (*Neigung*)
predisposition; [öffentliche] **A~n**
[public] gardens; **als A~** enclosed

Anlass *m* -es,-̈e reason; (*Gelegenheit*)
occasion; **A~ geben zu** give cause
for

anlass|en† *vt sep* (*Auto*) start; 🔲
leave on <*Licht*>; keep on <*Mantel*>.
A~er *m* -s,- starter

anlässlich *prep* (+ *gen*) on the
occasion of

Anlauf *m* (*Sport*) run-up; (*fig*)
attempt. **a~en†** *v sep* ● *vi* (*sein*)
start; (*beschlagen*) mist up; <*Metall:*>
tarnish; **rot a~en** blush ● *vt* (*Naut*)
call at

anlegen *v sep* ● *vt* put (**an** + *acc*
against); put on <*Kleidung,*
Verband>; lay back <*Ohren*>; aim
<*Gewehr*>; (*investieren*) invest;
(*ausgeben*) spend (**für** on); draw up

<Liste>; **es darauf a~** *(fig)* aim (**zu** to) ● *vi (haben) <Schiff:>* moor; **a~ auf** (+ *acc*) aim at

anlehnen *vt sep* lean (**an** + *acc* against); **sich a~** lean (**an** + *acc* on)

Anleihe *f -, -n* loan

anleit|en *vt sep* instruct. **A~ung** *f* instructions *pl*

anlernen *vt sep* train

Anliegen *nt -s,-* request; *(Wunsch)* desire

anlieg|en† *vi sep (haben)* [eng] **a~en** fit closely; [eng] **a~end** close-fitting. **A~er** *mpl* residents; '**A~er frei**' 'access for residents only'

anlügen† *vt sep* lie to

anmachen *vt sep* 🔲 fix; *(anschalten)* turn on; dress *<Salat>*

anmalen *vt sep* paint

Anmarsch *m (Mil)* approach

anmeld|en *vt sep* announce; *(Admin)* register; **sich a~en** say that one is coming; *(Admin)* register; *(Sch)* enrol; *(im Hotel)* check in; *(beim Arzt)* make an appointment. **A~ung** *f* announcement; *(Admin)* registration; *(Sch)* enrolment; *(Termin)* appointment

anmerk|en *vt sep* mark; **sich** *(dat)* **etw a~en lassen** show sth. **A~ung** *f -, -en* note

Anmut *f -* grace; *(Charme)* charm

anmutig *a* graceful

annähen *vt sep* sew on

annäher|nd *a* approximate. **A~ungsversuche** *mpl* advances

Annahme *f -, -n* acceptance; *(Adoption)* adoption; *(Vermutung)* assumption

annehm|bar *a* acceptable. **a~en†** *vt sep* accept; *(adoptieren)* adopt; acquire *<Gewohnheit>*; *(sich zulegen, vermuten)* assume; **angenommen, dass** assuming that. **A~lichkeiten** *fpl* comforts

Anno *adv* **A~ 1920** in the year 1920

Annon|ce /a'nõ:sə/ *f -, -n* advertisement. **a~cieren** /-'si:-/ *vt/i (haben)* advertise

annullieren *vt* annul; cancel

Anomalie *f -, -n* anomaly

anonym *a* anonymous

Anorak *m -s, -s* anorak

anordn|en *vt sep* arrange; *(befehlen)* order. **A~ung** *f* arrangement; order

anorganisch *a* inorganic

anormal *a* abnormal

anpass|en *vt sep* try on; *(angleichen)* adapt *(dat* to); **sich a~** adapt *(dat* to). **A~ung** *f -* adaptation. **a~ungsfähig** *a* adaptable. **A~ungsfähigkeit** *f* adaptability

Anpfiff *m (Sport)* kick-off

Anprall *m -[e]s* impact. **a~en** *vi sep (sein)* strike (**an etw** *acc* sth)

anpreisen† *vt sep* commend

Anprob|e *f* fitting. **a~ieren** *vt sep* try on

anrechnen *vt sep* count (**als** as); *(berechnen)* charge for; *(verrechnen)* allow *<Summe>*

Anrecht *nt* right (**auf** + *acc* to)

Anrede *f* [form of] address. **a~n** *vt sep* address; speak to

anreg|en *vt sep* stimulate; *(ermuntern)* encourage (**zu** to); *(vorschlagen)* suggest. **a~end** *a* stimulating. **A~ung** *f* stimulation; *(Vorschlag)* suggestion

Anreise *f* journey; *(Ankunft)* arrival. **a~n** *vi sep (sein)* arrive

Anreiz *m* incentive

Anrichte *f -, -n* sideboard. **a~n** *vt sep (Culin)* prepare; *(garnieren)* garnish (**mit** with); *(verursachen)* cause

anrüchig *a* disreputable

Anruf *m* call. **A~beantworter** *m -s,-* answering machine. **a~en†** *v sep* ● *vt* call to; *(bitten)* call on (**um** for); *(Teleph)* ring ● *vi (haben)* ring (**bei jdm** s.o.)

ans *prep* = **an das**

Ansage *f* announcement. **a~n** *vt sep* announce

ansamm|eln *vt sep* collect; *(anhäufen)* accumulate; **sich a~eln**

collect; (*sich häufen*) accumulate; <*Leute:*> gather. **A~lung** *f* collection; (*Menschen-*) crowd

ansässig *a* resident

Ansatz *m* beginning; (*Versuch*) attempt

anschaffen *vt sep* [*sich dat*] etw a~ acquire/(*kaufen*) buy sth

anschalten *vt sep* switch on

anschau|en *vt sep* look at. **a~lich** *a* vivid, *adv* -ly. **A~ung** *f* -, -en (*fig*) view

Anschein *m* appearance. **a~end** *adv* apparently

anschirren *vt sep* harness

Anschlag *m* notice; (*Vor-*) estimate; (*Überfall*) attack (auf + *acc* on); (*Mus*) touch; (*Techn*) stop. **a~en†** *v sep* ● *vt* put up <*Aushang*>; strike <*Note, Taste*>; cast on <*Masche*>; (*beschädigen*) chip ● *vi* (*haben*) strike/(*stoßen*) knock (an + *acc* against); (*wirken*) be effective ● *vi* (*sein*) knock (an + *acc* against)

anschließen† *v sep* ● *vt* connect (an + *acc* to); (*zufügen*) add; **sich a~ an** (+ *acc*) (*anstoßen*) adjoin; (*folgen*) follow; (*sich anfreunden*) become friendly with; **sich jdm a~** join s.o. ● *vi* (*haben*) a~ an (+ *acc*) adjoin; (*folgen*) follow. **a~d** *a* adjoining; (*zeitlich*) following ● *adv* afterwards

Anschluss *m* connection; (*Kontakt*) contact; **A~ finden** make friends; **im A~ an** (+ *acc*) after

anschmiegsam *a* affectionate

anschmieren *vt sep* smear

anschnallen *vt sep* strap on; **sich a~** fasten one's seat-belt

anschneiden† *vt sep* cut into; broach <*Thema*>

anschreiben† *vt sep* write (an + *acc* on); (*Comm*) put on s.o.'s account; (*sich wenden*) write to

Anschrift *f* address

anschuldig|en *vt sep* accuse. **A~ung** *f* -, -en accusation

anschwellen† *vi sep* (*sein*) swell

ansehen† *vt sep* look at; (*einschätzen*) regard (als as); [*sich dat*] etw a~ look at sth; (*TV*) watch

sth. **A~** *nt* -s respect; (*Ruf*) reputation

ansehnlich *a* considerable

ansetzen *v sep* ● *vt* join (an + *acc* to); (*veranschlagen*) estimate ● *vi* (*haben*) (*anbrennen*) burn; **zum Sprung a~** get ready to jump

Ansicht *f* view; **meiner A~ nach** in my view; **zur A~** (*Comm*) on approval. **A~s[post]karte** *f* picture postcard. **A~ssache** *f* matter of opinion

ansiedeln (sich) *vr sep* settle

ansonsten *adv* apart from that

anspannen *vt sep* hitch up; (*anstrengen*) strain; tense <*Muskel*>

Anspielung *f* -, -en allusion; hint

Anspitzer *m* -s,- pencil-sharpener

Ansprache *f* address

ansprechen† *v sep* ● *vt* speak to; (*fig*) appeal to ● *vi* (*haben*) respond (auf + *acc* to)

anspringen† *v sep* ● *vt* jump at ● *vi* (*sein*) (*Auto*) start

Anspruch *m* claim/(*Recht*) right (auf + *acc* to); **A~ haben** be entitled (auf + *acc* to); **in A~ nehmen** make use of; (*erfordern*) demand; take up <*Zeit*>; occupy <*Person*>; **hohe A~e stellen** be very demanding. **a~slos** *a* undemanding. **a~svoll** *a* demanding; (*kritisch*) discriminating; (*vornehm*) upmarket

anstacheln *vt sep* (*fig*) spur on

Anstalt *f* -, -en institution

Anstand *m* decency; (*Benehmen*) [good] manners *pl*

anständig *a* decent; (*ehrbar*) respectable; (*richtig*) proper

anstandslos *adv* without any trouble

anstarren *vt sep* stare at

anstatt *conj & prep* (+ *gen*) instead of

ansteck|en *v sep* ● *vt* pin (an + *acc* to/on); put on <*Ring*>; (*anzünden*) light; (*in Brand stecken*) set fire to; (*Med*) infect; **sich a~en** catch an infection (bei from) ● *vi* (*haben*) be infectious. **a~end** *a* infectious. **A~ung** *f* -, -en infection

anstehen† *vi sep* (*haben*) queue

anstelle *prep* (+ *gen*) instead of

anstell|en *vt sep* put, stand (**an** + *acc* against); (*einstellen*) employ; (*anschalten*) turn on; (*tun*) do; **sich a~en** queue [up]. **A~ung** *f* employment; (*Stelle*) job

Anstieg *m* -[e]s, -e climb; (*fig*) rise

anstiften *vt sep* cause; (*anzetteln*) instigate

Anstoß *m* (*Anregung*) impetus; (*Stoß*) knock; (*Fußball*) kick-off; **A~ erregen** give offence (**an** + *dat* at). **a~en** *v sep* ● *vt* knock; (*mit dem Ellbogen*) nudge ● *vi* (*sein*) knock (**an** + *acc* against) ● *vi* (*haben*) adjoin (**an** etw *acc* sth); **a~en auf** (+ *acc*) drink to; **mit der Zunge a~en** lisp

anstößig *a* offensive

anstrahlen *vt sep* floodlight

anstreichen† *vt sep* paint; (*anmerken*) mark

anstreng|en *vt sep* strain; (*ermüden*) tire; **sich a~en** exert oneself; (*sich bemühen*) make an effort (**zu** to). **a~end** *a* strenuous; (*ermüdend*) tiring. **A~ung** *f* -, -en strain; (*Mühe*) effort

Anstrich *m* coat [of paint]

Ansturm *m* rush; (*Mil*) assault

Ansuchen *nt* -s,- request

Antarktis *f* - Antarctic

Anteil *m* share; **A~ nehmen** take an interest (**an** + *dat* in). **A~nahme** *f* - interest (**an** + *dat* in); (*Mitgefühl*) sympathy

Antenne *f* -, -n aerial

Anthologie *f* -, -n anthology

Anthropologie *f* - anthropology

Anti|alkoholiker *m* teetotaller. **A~biotikum** *nt* -s, -ka antibiotic

antik *a* antique. **A~e** *f* - [classical] antiquity

Antikörper *m* antibody

Antilope *f* -, -n antelope

Antipathie *f* - antipathy

Antiquariat *nt* -[e]s, -e antiquarian bookshop

Antiquitäten *fpl* antiques. **A~händler** *m* antique dealer

Antrag *m* -[e]s,̈-e proposal; (*Pol*) motion; (*Gesuch*) application. **A~steller** *m* -s,- applicant

antreffen† *vt sep* find

antreten† *v sep* ● *vt* start; take up <*Amt*> ● *vi* (*sein*) line up

Antrieb *m* urge; (*Techn*) drive; **aus eigenem A~** of one's own accord

Antritt *m* start; **bei A~ eines Amtes** when taking office

antun† *vt sep* **jdm etw a~** do sth to s.o.; **sich** (*dat*) **etwas a~** take one's own life

Antwort *f* -, -en answer, reply (**auf** + *acc* to). **a~en** *vt/i* (*haben*) answer (**jdm** s.o.)

anvertrauen *vt sep* entrust/ (*mitteilen*) confide (**jdm** to s.o.)

Anwalt *m* -[e]s,̈-e, **Anwältin** *f* -, -nen lawyer; (*vor Gericht*) counsel

Anwandlung *f* -, -en fit (**von** of)

Anwärter(in) *m*(*f*) candidate

anweis|en† *vt sep* assign (*dat* to); (*beauftragen*) instruct. **A~ung** *f* instruction; (*Geld-*) money order

anwend|en *vt sep* apply (**auf** + *acc* to); (*gebrauchen*) use. **A~ung** *f* application; use

anwerben† *vt sep* recruit

Anwesen *nt* -s,- property

anwesen|d *a* present (**bei** at); **die A~den** those present. **A~heit** *f* - presence

anwidern *vt sep* disgust

Anwohner *mpl* residents

Anzahl *f* number

anzahl|en *vt sep* pay a deposit on. **A~ung** *f* deposit

anzapfen *vt sep* tap

Anzeichen *nt* sign

Anzeige *f* -, -n announcement; (*Inserat*) advertisement; **A~ erstatten gegen jdn** report s.o. to the police. **a~n** *vt sep* announce; (*inserieren*) advertise; (*melden*) report [to the police]; (*angeben*) indicate

anzieh|en† *vt sep* ● *vt* attract; (*festziehen*) tighten; put on <*Kleider*,

Bremse>; *(ankleiden)* dress; **sich a~en** get dressed. **a~end** *a* attractive. **A~ungskraft** *f* attraction; *(Phys)* gravity

Anzug *m* suit

anzüglich *a* suggestive

anzünden *vt sep* light; *(in Brand stecken)* set fire to

anzweifeln *vt sep* question

apart *a* striking

Apathie *f* - apathy

apathisch *a* apathetic

Aperitif *m* -s, -s aperitif

Apfel *m* -s,- apple

Apfelsine *f* -, -n orange

Apostel *m* -s,- apostle

Apostroph *m* -s, -e apostrophe

Apotheke *f* -, -n pharmacy. **A~er(in)** *m* -s,- (*f* -, -nen) pharmacist, [dispensing] chemist

Apparat *m* -[e]s, -e device; *(Phot)* camera; *(Radio, TV)* set; *(Teleph)* telephone; **am A~!** speaking!

Appell *m* -s, -e appeal; *(Mil)* roll-call. **a~ieren** *vi (haben)* appeal (**an** + *acc* **to**)

Appetit *m* -s appetite; **guten A~!** enjoy your meal! **a~lich** *a* appetizing

Applaus *m* -es applause

Aprikose *f* -, -n apricot

April *m* -[s] April

Aquarell *nt* -s, -e water-colour

Aquarium *nt* -s, -ien aquarium

Äquator *m* -s equator

Ära *f* - era

Araber(in) *m* -s,- (*f* -, -nen) Arab

arabisch *a* Arab; *(Geog)* Arabian; *<Ziffer>* Arabic

Arbeit *f* -, -en work; *(Anstellung)* employment, job; *(Aufgabe)* task; *(Sch)* [written] test; *(Abhandlung)* treatise; *(Qualität)* workmanship; **sich an die A~ machen** set to work; **sich** *(dat)* **viel A~ machen** go to a lot of trouble. **a~en** *v sep ● vi (haben)* work (**an** + *dat* **on**) **● vt** make. **A~er(in)** *m* -s,- (*f* -, -nen) worker; *(Land-, Hilfs-)* labourer. **A~erklasse** *f* working class

Arbeit|geber *m* -s,- employer. **A~nehmer** *m* -s,- employee

Arbeits|amt *nt* employment exchange. **A~erlaubnis, A~genehmigung** *f* work permit. **A~kraft** *f* worker. **a~los** *a* unemployed; **~los sein** be out of work. **A~lose(r)** *m/f* unemployed person; **die A~losen** the unemployed *pl.* **A~losenunterstützung** *f* unemployment benefit. **A~losigkeit** *f* - unemployment

arbeitsparend *a* labour-saving

Arbeitsplatz *m* job

Archäo|loge *m* -n, -n archaeologist. **A~logie** *f* - archaeology

Arche *f* - **die A~** Noah Noah's Ark

Architek|t(in) *m* -en, -en (*f* -, -nen) architect. **a~tonisch** *a* architectural. **A~tur** *f* - architecture

Archiv *nt* -s, -e archives *pl*

Arena *f* -, -nen arena

arg *a* bad; *(groß)* terrible

Argentin|ien /-iən/ *nt* -s Argentina. **a~isch** *a* Argentinian

Ärger *m* -s annoyance; *(Unannehmlichkeit)* trouble. **ä~lich** *a* annoyed; *(leidig)* annoying; **ä~lich sein** be annoyed. **ä~n** *vt* annoy; *(necken)* tease; **sich ä~n** get annoyed (**über jdn/etw** with s.o./ about sth). **Ä~nis** *nt* -ses, -se annoyance; **öffentliches Ä~nis** public nuisance

Arglist *f* - malice

arglos *a* unsuspecting

Argument *nt* -[e]s, -e argument. **a~ieren** *vi (haben)* argue (**dass** that)

Arie /'a:riə/ *f* -, -n aria

Aristo|krat *m* -en, -en aristocrat. **A~kratie** *f* - aristocracy. **a~kratisch** *a* aristocratic

Arkt|is *f* - Arctic. **a~isch** *a* Arctic

arm *a* poor

Arm *m* -[e]s, -e arm; **jdn auf den Arm nehmen** 🖲 pull s.o.'s leg

Armaturenbrett *nt* instrument panel; *(Auto)* dashboard

Armband nt (pl -bänder) bracelet; (Uhr-) watch-strap. **A~uhr** f wristwatch

Arm|e(r) m/f poor man/woman; **die A~en** the poor pl

Armee f -, -n army

Ärmel m -s,- sleeve. **Ä~kanal** m [English] Channel. **ä~los** a sleeveless

Arm|lehne f arm. **A~leuchter** m candelabra

ärmlich a poor; (elend) miserable

armselig a miserable

Armut f - poverty

Arran|gement /arãʒə'mã:/ nt -s, -s arrangement. **a~gieren** /-'ʒi:rən/ vt arrange

arrogant a arrogant

Arsch m -[e]s,-̈e (vulg) arse

Arsen nt -s arsenic

Art f -, -en manner; (Weise) way; (Natur) nature; (Sorte) kind; (Biol) species; **auf diese Art** in this way

Arterie /-iə/ f -, -n artery

Arthritis f - arthritis

artig a well-behaved

Artikel m -s,- article

Artillerie f - artillery

Artischocke f -, -n artichoke

Arznei f -, -en medicine

Arzt m -[e]s,-̈e doctor

Ärzt|in f -, -nen [woman] doctor. **ä~lich** a medical

As* nt -ses, -se s. Ass

Asbest m -[e]s asbestos

Asche f - ash. **A~nbecher** m ashtray. **A~rmittwoch** m Ash Wednesday

Asiat|(in) m -en, -en (f -, -nen) Asian. **a~isch** a Asian

Asien /'a:ziən/ nt -s Asia

asozial a antisocial

Aspekt m -[e]s, -e aspect

Asphalt m -[e]s asphalt. **a~ieren** vt asphalt

Ass nt -es, -e ace

Assistent(in) m -en, -en (f -, -nen) assistant

Ast m -[e]s,-̈e branch

asthetisch a aesthetic

Asth|ma nt -s asthma. **a~matisch** a asthmatic

Astro|loge m -n, -n astrologer. **A~logie** f - astrology. **A~naut** m -en, -en astronaut. **A~nomie** f - astronomy

Asyl nt -s, -e home; (Pol) asylum. **A~ant** m -en, -en asylum-seeker

Atelier /-'lie:/ nt -s, -s studio

Atem m -s breath. **a~los** a breathless. **A~zug** m breath

Atheist m -en, -en atheist

Äther m -s ether

Athiopien /-iən/ nt -s Ethiopia

Athlet|(in) m -en, -en (f -, -nen) athlete. **a~isch** a athletic

Atlant|ik m -s Atlantic. **a~isch** a Atlantic; **der A~ische Ozean** the Atlantic Ocean

Atlas m -lasses, -lanten atlas

atmen vt/i (haben) breathe

Atmosphäre f -, -n atmosphere

Atmung f - breathing

Atom nt -s, -e atom. **A~bombe** f atom bomb. **A~krieg** m nuclear war

Atten|tat nt -[e]s, -e assassination attempt. **A~täter** m assassin

Attest nt -[e]s, -e certificate

Attrak|tion /-'tsio:n/ f -, -en attraction. **a~tiv** a attractive

Attribut nt -[e]s, -e attribute

ätzen vt corrode; (Med) cauterize; (Kunst) etch. **ä~d** a corrosive; <Spott> caustic

au int ouch; **au fein!** oh good!

Aubergine /obɛr'ʒi:nə/ f -, -n aubergine

auch adv & conj also, too; (außerdem) what's more; (selbst) even; **a~ wenn** even if; **sie weiß es a~ nicht** she doesn't know either; **wer/wie/was a~ immer** whoever/ however/whatever

Audienz f -, -en audience

audiovisuell a audio-visual

Auditorium nt -s, -ien (Univ) lecture hall

---
*old spelling

auf

●*preposition (+ dative)*

····▶ *(nicht unter)* on. **auf dem Tisch** on the table. **auf Deck** on deck. **auf der Erde** on earth. **auf der Welt** in the world. **auf der Straße** in the street

····▶ *(bei Institution, Veranstaltung usw.)* at; *(bei Gebäude, Zimmer)* in. **auf der Schule/Uni** at school/ university. **auf einer Party/Hochzeit** at a party/wedding. **Geld auf der Bank haben** have money in the bank. **sie ist auf ihrem Zimmer** she's in her room. **auf Urlaub** on holiday

●*preposition (+ accusative)*

····▶ *(nicht unter)* on[to]. **er legte das Buch auf den Tisch** he laid the book on the table. **auf eine Mauer steigen** climb onto a wall. **auf die Straße gehen** go [out] into the street

····▶ *(bei Institution, Veranstaltung usw.)* to. **auf eine Party/die Toilette gehen** go to a party/the toilet. **auf die Schule/Uni gehen** go to school/ university. **auf Urlaub schicken** send on holiday

····▶ *(bei Entfernung)* **auf 10 km [Entfernung] zu sehen/hören** visible/ audible for [a distance of] 10 km

····▶ *(zeitlich) (wie lange)* for; *(bis)* until; *(wann)* on. **auf Jahre [hinaus]** for years [to come]. **auf ein paar Tage** for a few days. **etw auf nächsten Mittwoch verschieben** postpone sth until next Wednesday. **das fällt auf einen Montag** it falls on a Monday

····▶ *(Art und Weise)* in. **auf diese [Art und] Weise** in this way. **auf Deutsch/Englisch** in German/ English

····▶ *(aufgrund)* **auf Wunsch** on request. **auf meine Bitte** on *or* at my request. **auf Befehl** on command

····▶ *(Proportion)* to. **ein Teelöffel auf einen Liter Wasser** one teaspoon to one litre of water. **auf die Sekunde/ den Millimeter [genau]** [precise] to the nearest second/millimetre

····▶ *(Toast)* to. **auf deine Gesundheit!** your health!

●*adverb*

····▶ *(aufgerichtet, aufgestanden)* up. **auf!** *(steh auf!)* up you get! **auf und ab** *(hin und her)* up and down

····▶ *(aufsetzen)* **Helm/Hut/Brille auf!** helmet/hat/glasses on!

····▶ *(geöffnet, offen)* open. **Fenster/ Mund auf!** open the window/your mouth!

aufatmen *vi sep (haben)* heave a sigh of relief

aufbahren *vt sep* lay out

Aufbau *m* construction; *(Struktur)* structure. **a∼en** *v sep* ● *vt* construct, build; *(errichten)* erect; *(schaffen)* build up; *(arrangieren)* arrange; **sich a∼en** *(fig)* be based (**auf** + *dat* on) ● *vi (haben)* be based (**auf** + *dat* on)

aufbauschen *vt sep* puff out; *(fig)* exaggerate

aufbekommen† *vt sep* get open; *(Sch)* be given [as homework]

aufbessern *vt sep* improve; *(erhöhen)* increase

aufbewahr|en *vt sep* keep; *(lagern)* store. **A∼ung** *f* - safe keeping; storage; *(Gepäck-)* left-luggage office

aufblas|bar *a* inflatable. **a∼en†** *vt sep* inflate

aufbleiben† *vi sep (sein)* stay open; *<Person>* stay up

aufblenden *vt/i sep (haben) (Auto)* switch to full beam

aufblühen *vi sep (sein)* flower

aufbocken *vt sep* jack up

aufbrauchen *vt sep* use up

aufbrechen† *v sep* ● *vt* break open ● *vi (sein) <Knospe>* open; *(sich aufmachen)* set out, start

aufbringen† *vt sep* raise *<Geld>*; find *<Kraft>*

Aufbruch *m* start, departure

aufbrühen *vt sep* make *<Tee>*

aufbürden *vt sep* **jdm etw a∼** *(fig)* burden s.o. with sth

aufdecken *vt sep (auflegen)* put on; *(abdecken)* uncover; *(fig)* expose

aufdrehen *vt sep* turn on

aufdringlich *a* persistent

aufeinander *adv* one on top of the other; *<schießen>* at each other; *<warten>* for each other; **a~ folgend** successive; *<Tage>* consecutive.

Aufenthalt *m* stay; **10 Minuten A~ haben** *<Zug:>* stop for 10 minutes. **A~serlaubnis, A~sgenehmigung** *f* residence permit. **A~sraum** *m* recreation room; *(im Hotel)* lounge

Auferstehung *f* - resurrection

aufessen† *vt sep* eat up

auffahr|en† *vi sep (sein)* drive up; *(aufprallen)* crash, run (**auf** + *acc* into). **A~t** *f* drive; *(Autobahn-)* access road, slip road; *(Bergfahrt)* ascent

auffallen† *vi sep (sein)* be conspicuous; **unangenehm a~** make a bad impression

auffällig *a* conspicuous

auffangen† *vt sep* catch; pick up

auffass|en *vt sep* understand; *(deuten)* take. **A~ung** *f* understanding; *(Ansicht)* view

aufforder|n *vt sep* ask; *(einladen)* invite. **A~ung** *f* request; invitation

auffrischen *v sep* ● *vt* freshen up; revive *<Erinnerung>*; **seine Englischkenntnisse a~** brush up one's English

aufführ|en *vt sep* perform; *(angeben)* list; **sich a~en** behave. **A~ung** *f* performance

auffüllen *vt sep* fill up

Aufgabe *f* task; *(Rechen-)* problem; *(Verzicht)* giving up; **A~n** *(Sch)* homework *sg*

Aufgang *m* way up; *(Treppe)* stairs *pl*; *(Astr)* rise

aufgeben† *v sep* ● *vt* give up; post *<Brief>*; send *<Telegramm>*; place *<Bestellung>*; register *<Gepäck>*; put in the paper *<Annonce>*; **jdm eine Aufgabe a~** set s.o. a task; **jdm Suppe a~** serve s.o. with soup ● *vi (haben)* give up

Aufgebot *nt* contingent (**an** + *dat* of); *(Relig)* banns *pl*

aufgedunsen *a* bloated

aufgehen† *vi sep (sein)* open; *(sich lösen)* come undone; *<Teig, Sonne:>* rise; *<Saat:>* come up; *(Math)* come out exactly; **in Flammen a~** go up in flames

aufgelegt *a* **gut/schlecht a~ sein** be in a good/bad mood

aufgeregt *a* excited; *(erregt)* agitated

aufgeschlossen *a (fig)* openminded

aufgeweckt *a (fig)* bright

aufgießen† *vt sep* pour on; *(aufbrühen)* make *<Tee>*

aufgreifen† *vt sep* pick up; take up *<Vorschlag, Thema>*

aufgrund *prep* (+ *gen*) on the strength of

Aufguss *m* infusion

aufhaben† *v sep* ● *vt* have on; **den Mund a~** have one's mouth open; **viel a~** *(Sch)* have a lot of homework ● *vi (haben)* be open

aufhalten† *vt sep* hold up; *(anhalten)* stop; *(abhalten)* keep; *(offenhalten)* hold out *<Hand>*; **sich a~** stay; *(sich befassen)* spend one's time (**mit** on)

aufhäng|en *vt/i sep (haben)* hang up; *(henken)* hang; **sich a~en** hang oneself. **A~er** *m* -s,- loop

aufheben† *vt sep* pick up; *(hochheben)* raise; *(aufbewahren)* keep; *(beenden)* end; *(rückgängig machen)* lift; *(abschaffen)* abolish; *(Jur)* quash *<Urteil>*; repeal *<Gesetz>*; *(ausgleichen)* cancel out; **gut aufgehoben sein** be well looked after

aufheitern *vt sep* cheer up; **sich a~** *<Wetter:>* brighten up

aufhellen *vt sep* lighten; **sich a~** *<Himmel:>* brighten

aufhetzen *vt sep* incite

aufholen *v sep* ● *vt* make up ● *vi (haben)* catch up; *(zeitlich)* make up time

aufhören *vi sep (haben)* stop

aufklappen *vt/i sep (sein)* open

aufklär|en *vt sep* solve; **jdn a~en** enlighten s.o.; **sich a~en** be solved; <*Wetter:*> clear up. **A~ung** *f* solution; enlightenment; (*Mil*) reconnaissance; **sexuelle A~ung** sex education

aufkleb|en *vt sep* stick on. **A~er** *m* **-s,-** sticker

aufknöpfen *vt sep* unbutton

aufkochen *v sep* ● *vt* bring to the boil ● *vi* (*sein*) come to the boil

aufkommen† *vi sep* (*sein*) start; <*Wind:*> spring up; <*Mode:*> come in

aufkrempeln *vt sep* roll up

aufladen† *vt sep* load; (*Electr*) charge

Auflage *f* impression; (*Ausgabe*) edition; (*Zeitungs-*) circulation

auflassen† *vt sep* leave open; leave on <*Hut*>

Auflauf *m* crowd; (*Culin*) ≈ soufflé

auflegen *v sep* ● *vt* apply (**auf** + *acc* to); put down <*Hörer*>; **neu a~** reprint ● *vi* (*haben*) ring off

auflehn|en (sich) *vr sep* (*fig*) rebel. **A~ung** *f* - rebellion

auflesen† *vt sep* pick up

aufleuchten *vi sep* (*haben*) light up

auflös|en *vt sep* dissolve; close <*Konto*>; **sich a~en** dissolve; <*Nebel:*> clear. **A~ung** *f* dissolution; (*Lösung*) solution

aufmach|en *v sep* ● *vt* open; (*lösen*) undo; **sich a~en** set out (**nach** for) ● *vi* (*haben*) open; **jdm a~en** open the door to s.o. **A~ung** *f* -, **-en** get-up

aufmerksam *a* attentive; **a~ werden auf** (+ *acc*) notice; **jdn a~ machen auf** (+ *acc*) draw s.o.'s attention to. **A~keit** *f* -, **-en** attention; (*Höflichkeit*) courtesy

aufmuntern *vt sep* cheer up

Aufnahme *f* -, **-n** acceptance; (*Empfang*) reception; (*in Klub, Krankenhaus*) admission; (*Einbeziehung*) inclusion; (*Beginn*) start; (*Foto*) photograph; (*Film-*) shot; (*Mus*) recording; (*Band-*) tape recording. **a~fähig** *a* receptive. **A~prüfung** *f* entrance examination

aufnehmen† *vt sep* pick up; (*absorbieren*) absorb; take <*Nahrung, Foto*>; (*fassen*) hold; (*annehmen*) accept; (*leihen*) borrow; (*empfangen*) receive; (*in Klub, Krankenhaus*) admit; (*beherbergen, geistig erfassen*) take in; (*einbeziehen*) include; (*beginnen*) take up; (*niederschreiben*) take down; (*filmen*) film, shoot; (*Mus*) record; **auf Band a~** tape[-record]

aufopfer|n *vt sep* sacrifice; **sich a~n** sacrifice oneself. **A~ung** *f* self-sacrifice

aufpassen *vi sep* (*haben*) pay attention; (*sich vorsehen*) take care; **a~ auf** (+ *acc*) look after

Aufprall *m* **-[e]s** impact. **a~en** *vi sep* (*sein*) **a~en auf** (+ *acc*) hit

aufpumpen *vt sep* pump up, inflate

aufputsch|en *vt sep* incite. **A~mittel** *nt* stimulant

aufquellen† *vi sep* (*sein*) swell

aufraffen *vt sep* pick up; **sich a~** pick oneself up; (*fig*) pull oneself together

aufragen *vi sep* (*sein*) rise [up]

aufräumen *vt/i sep* (*haben*) tidy up; (*wegräumen*) put away

aufrecht *a & adv* upright. **a~erhalten†** *vt sep* (*fig*) maintain

aufreg|en *vt* excite; (*beunruhigen*) upset; (*ärgern*) annoy; **sich a~en** get excited; (*sich erregen*) get worked up. **a~end** *a* exciting. **A~ung** *f* excitement

aufreiben† *vt sep* chafe; (*fig*) wear down. **a~d** *a* trying

aufreißen† *v sep* ● *vt* tear open; dig up <*Straße*>; open wide <*Augen, Mund*> ● *vi* (*sein*) split open

aufrichtig *a* sincere. **A~keit** *f* - sincerity

aufrollen *vt sep* roll up; (*entrollen*) unroll

aufrücken *vi sep* (*sein*) move up; (*fig*) be promoted

Aufruf *m* appeal (**an** + *dat* to). **a~en†** *vt sep* call out <*Namen*>; **jdn a~en** call s.o.'s name

Aufruhr *m* -s, -e turmoil;
(*Empörung*) revolt

aufführ|en *vt sep* stir up. **A~er** *m*
-s,- rebel. **a~erisch** *a*
inflammatory; (*rebellisch*) rebellious

aufrunden *vt sep* round up

aufrüsten *vi sep* (*haben*) arm

aufsagen *vt sep* recite

aufsässig *a* rebellious

Aufsatz *m* top; (*Sch*) essay

aufsaugen† *vt sep* soak up

aufschauen *vi sep* (*haben*) look up
(zu at/(*fig*) to)

aufschichten *vt sep* stack up

aufschieben† *vt sep* slide open;
(*verschieben*) put off, postpone

Aufschlag *m* impact; (*Tennis*)
service; (*Hosen-*) turn-up; (*Ärmel-*)
upturned cuff; (*Revers*) lapel; (*Comm*)
surcharge. **a~en**† *v sep* ● *vt* open;
crack <*Ei*>; (*hochschlagen*) turn up;
(*errichten*) put up; (*erhöhen*)
increase; cast on <*Masche*>; **sich**
(*dat*) **das Knie a~en** cut [open] one's
knee ● *vi* (*haben*) hit (**auf etw** *acc/dat*
sth); (*Tennis*) serve; (*teurer werden*)
go up

aufschließen† *v sep* ● *vt* unlock
● *vi* (*haben*) unlock the door

aufschlussreich *a* revealing;
(*lehrreich*) informative

aufschneiden† *v sep* ● *vt* cut
open; (*in Scheiben*) slice ● *vi* (*haben*)
🄸 exaggerate

Aufschnitt *m* sliced sausage, cold
meat [and cheese]

aufschrauben *vt sep* screw on;
(*abschrauben*) unscrew

Aufschrei *m* [sudden] cry

aufschreiben† *vt sep* write down;
jdn a~ <*Polizist:*> book s.o.

Aufschrift *f* inscription; (*Etikett*)
label

Aufschub *m* delay; (*Frist*) grace

aufschürfen *vt sep* **sich** (*dat*) **das
Knie a~** graze one's knee

aufschwingen† **(sich)** *vr sep* find
the energy (**zu** for)

Aufschwung *m* (*fig*) upturn

aufsehen† *vi sep* (*haben*) look up
(**zu** at/(*fig*) to). **A~** *nt* -s **A~ erregen**
cause a sensation; **A~ erregend**
sensational

Aufseher(in) *m* -s,- (*f* -, -nen)
supervisor; (*Gefängnis-*) warder

aufsetzen *vt sep* put on; (*verfassen*)
draw up; (*entwerfen*) draft; **sich a~**
sit up

Aufsicht *f* supervision; (*Person*)
supervisor. **A~srat** *m* board of
directors

aufsperren *vt sep* open wide

aufspielen *v sep* ● *vi* (*haben*) play
● *vr* **sich a~** show off

aufspießen *vt sep* spear

aufspringen† *vi sep* (*sein*) jump
up; (*aufprallen*) bounce; (*sich öffnen*)
burst open

aufspüren *vt sep* track down

aufstacheln *vt sep* incite

Aufstand *m* uprising, rebellion

aufständisch *a* rebellious

aufstehen† *vi sep* (*sein*) get up;
(*offen sein*) be open; (*fig*) rise up

aufsteigen† *vi sep* (*sein*) get on;
<*Reiter:*> mount; <*Bergsteiger:*>
climb up; (*hochsteigen*) rise [up]; (*fig:
befördert werden*) rise (**zu** to); (*Sport*)
be promoted

aufstell|en *vt sep* put up; (*Culin*)
put on; (*postieren*) post; (*in einer
Reihe*) line up; (*nominieren*)
nominate; (*Sport*) select
<*Mannschaft*>; make out <*Liste*>; lay
down <*Regel*>; make <*Behauptung*>;
set up <*Rekord*>. **A~ung** *f*
nomination; (*Liste*) list

Aufstieg *m* -[e]s, -e ascent; (*fig*)
rise; (*Sport*) promotion

Aufstoßen *nt* -s burping

aufstrebend *a* (*fig*) ambitious

Aufstrich *m* [sandwich] spread

aufstützen *vt sep* rest (**auf** + *acc*
on); **sich a~** lean (**auf** + *acc* on)

Auftakt *m* (*fig*) start

auftauchen *vi sep* (*sein*) emerge;
(*fig*) turn up; <*Frage:*> crop up

auftauen *vt/i sep* (*sein*) thaw

aufteil|en *vt sep* divide [up].
A~ung *f* division

auftischen *vt sep* serve [up]

Auftrag *m* -[e]s,-̈e task; (*Kunst*) commission; (*Comm*) order; **im A~** (+ *gen*) on behalf of. **a~en†** *vt sep* apply; (*servieren*) serve; (*abtragen*) wear out; **jdm a~en** instruct s.o. (**zu** to). **A~ geber** *m* -s,- client

auftrennen *vt sep* unpick, undo

auftreten† *vi sep* (*sein*) tread; (*sich benehmen*) behave, act; (*Theat*) appear; (*die Bühne betreten*) enter; (*vorkommen*) occur

Auftrieb *m* buoyancy; (*fig*) boost

Auftritt *m* (*Theat*) appearance; (*auf die Bühne*) entrance; (*Szene*) scene

aufwachen *vi sep* (*sein*) wake up

aufwachsen† *vi sep* (*sein*) grow up

Aufwand *m* -[e]s expenditure; (*Luxus*) extravagance; (*Mühe*) trouble; **A~ treiben** be extravagant

aufwändig *a* = aufwendig

aufwärmen *vt sep* heat up; (*fig*) rake up; **sich a~** warm oneself; (*Sport*) warm up

Aufwartefrau *f* cleaner

aufwärts *adv* upwards; (*bergauf*) uphill; **es geht a~ mit jdm/etw** s.o./ sth is improving

Aufwartung *f* - cleaner

aufwecken *vt sep* wake up

aufweichen *v sep* ● *vt* soften ● *vi* (*sein*) become soft

aufweisen† *vt sep* have, show

aufwend|en† *vt sep* spend; **Mühe a~en** take pains. **a~ig** *a* lavish; (*teuer*) expensive

aufwert|en *vt sep* revalue. **A~ung** *f* revaluation

aufwickeln *vt sep* roll up; (*auswickeln*) unwrap

Aufwiegler *m* -s,- agitator

aufwisch|en *vt sep* wipe up; wash <*Fußboden*>. **A~lappen** *m* floorcloth

aufwühlen *vt sep* churn up

aufzähl|en *vt sep* enumerate, list. **A~ung** *f* list

aufzeichn|en *vt sep* record; (*zeichnen*) draw. **A~ung** *f* recording; **A~ungen** notes

aufziehen† *v sep* ● *vt* pull up; hoist <*Segel*>; (*öffnen*) open; draw <*Vorhang*>; (*großziehen*) bring up; rear <*Tier*>; mount <*Bild*>; thread <*Perlen*>; wind up <*Uhr*>; (🔲 *necken*) tease ● *vi* (*sein*) approach

Aufzug *m* hoist; (*Fahrstuhl*) lift, (*Amer*) elevator; (*Prozession*) procession; (*Theat*) act

Augapfel *m* eyeball

Auge *nt* -s, -n eye; (*Punkt*) spot; **vier A~n werfen** throw a four; **gute A~n** good eyesight; **unter vier A~n** in private; **im A~ behalten** keep in sight; (*fig*) bear in mind

Augenblick *m* moment; **A~!** just a moment! **a~lich** *a* immediate; (*derzeitig*) present ● *adv* immediately; (*derzeit*) at present

Augen|braue *f* eyebrow. **A~höhle** *f* eye socket. **A~licht** *nt* sight. **A~lid** *nt* eyelid

August *m* -[s] August

Auktion /-'tsịo:n/ *f* -, -en auction

Aula *f* -, -len (*Sch*) [assembly] hall

Au-pair-Mädchen /o'pɛ:r-/ *nt* aupair

aus *prep* (+ *dat*) out of; (*von*) from; (*bestehend*) [made] of; **aus Angst** from *or* out of fear; **aus Spaß** for fun ● *adv* out; <*Licht, Radio*> off; **aus sein auf** (+ *acc*) be after; **aus und ein** in and out; **von sich aus** of one's own accord; **von mir aus** as far as I'm concerned

ausarbeiten *vt sep* work out

ausarten *vi sep* (*sein*) degenerate (**in** + *acc* into)

ausatmen *vt/i sep* (*haben*) breathe out

ausbauen *vt sep* remove; (*vergrößern*) extend; (*fig*) expand

ausbedingen† *vt sep* sich (*dat*) a~ insist on; (*zur Bedingung machen*) stipulate

ausbesser|n *vt sep* mend, repair. **A~ung** *f* repair

ausbeulen *vt sep* remove the dents from; (*dehnen*) make baggy

ausbild|en *vt sep* train; (*formen*) form; (*entwickeln*) develop; **sich**

a∼en train (**als/zu** as); (*entstehen*) develop. **A∼ung** *f* training; (*Sch*) education

ausbitten† *vt sep* **sich** (*dat*) **a∼** ask for; (*verlangen*) insist on

ausblasen† *vt sep* blow out

ausbleiben† *vi sep* (*sein*) fail to appear/ <*Erfolg:*> materialize; (*nicht heimkommen*) stay out

Ausblick *m* view

ausbrech|en *vi sep* (*sein*) break out; <*Vulkan:*> erupt; (*fliehen*) escape; **in Tränen a∼en** burst into tears. **A∼er** *m* runaway

ausbreit|en *vt sep* spread [out]. **A∼ung** *f* spread

Ausbruch *m* outbreak; (*Vulkan-*) eruption; (*Wut-*) outburst; (*Flucht*) escape, break-out

ausbrüten *vt sep* hatch

Ausdauer *f* perseverance; (*körperlich*) stamina. **a∼nd** *a* persevering; (*unermüdlich*) untiring

ausdehnen *vt sep* stretch; (*fig*) extend; **sich a∼** stretch; (*Phys & fig*) expand; (*dauern*) last

ausdenken† *vt sep* **sich** (*dat*) **a∼** think up; (*sich vorstellen*) imagine

Ausdruck *m* expression; (*Fach-*) term; (*Computer*) printout. **a∼en** *vt sep* print

ausdrücken *vt sep* squeeze out; squeeze <*Zitrone*>; stub out <*Zigarette*>; (*äußern*) express

ausdrucks|los *a* expressionless. **a∼voll** *a* expressive

auseinander *adv* apart; (*entzwei*) in pieces; **a∼ falten** unfold; **a∼ gehen** part; <*Linien, Meinungen:*> diverge; <*Ehe:*> break up; **a∼ halten** tell apart; **a∼ nehmen** take apart *or* to pieces; **a∼ setzen** explain (**jdm** to s.o.); **sich a∼ setzen** sit apart; (*sich aussprechen*) have it out (**mit jdm** with s.o.); come to grips (**mit einem Problem** with a problem). **A∼setzung** *f* -, -en discussion; (*Streit*) argument

auserlesen *a* select, choice

Ausfahrt *f* drive; (*Autobahn-, Garagen-*) exit

Ausfall *m* failure; (*Absage*) cancellation; (*Comm*) loss. **a∼en**† *vi sep* (*sein*) fall out; (*versagen*) fail; (*abgesagt werden*) be cancelled; **gut/ schlecht a∼en** turn out to be good/ poor

ausfallend, ausfällig *a* abusive

ausfertig|en *vt sep* make out. **A∼ung** *f* -, -en **in doppelter A∼ung** in duplicate

ausfindig *a* **a∼ machen** find

Ausflug *m* excursion, outing

Ausflügler *m* -s,- [day-]tripper

Ausfluss *m* outlet; (*Abfluss*) drain; (*Med*) discharge

ausfragen *vt sep* question

Ausfuhr *f* -, -en (*Comm*) export

ausführ|en *vt sep* take out; (*Comm*) export; (*erklären*) explain. **a∼lich** *a* detailed ● *adv* in detail. **A∼ung** *f* execution; (*Comm*) version; (*äußere*) finish; (*Qualität*) workmanship; (*Erklärung*) explanation

Ausgabe *f* issue; (*Buch-*) edition; (*Comm*) version

Ausgang *m* way out, exit; (*Flugsteig*) gate; (*Ende*) end; (*Ergebnis*) outcome. **A∼spunkt** *m* starting-point. **A∼ssperre** *f* curfew

ausgeben† *vt sep* hand out; issue <*Fahrkarten*>; spend <*Geld*>; **sich a∼ als** pretend to be

ausgebildet *a* trained

ausgebucht *a* fully booked; <*Vorstellung*> sold out

ausgefallen *a* unusual

ausgefranst *a* frayed

ausgeglichen *a* [well-]balanced

ausgeh|en† *vi sep* (*sein*) go out; <*Haare:*> fall out; <*Vorräte, Geld:*> run out; (*verblassen*) fade; **gut/ schlecht a∼en** end well/badly; **davon a∼en, dass** assume that. **A∼verbot** *nt* curfew

ausgelassen *a* high-spirited

ausgemacht *a* agreed

ausgenommen *conj* except; **a∼ wenn** unless

ausgeprägt *a* marked

ausgeschlossen *pred a* out of the question

ausgeschnitten *a* low-cut

ausgesprochen *a* marked ● *adv* decidedly

ausgestorben *a* extinct; **[wie] a~** *<Straße:>* deserted

Ausgestoßene(r) *m/f* outcast

ausgezeichnet *a* excellent

ausgiebig *a* extensive; (*ausgedehnt*) long; **a~ Gebrauch machen von** make full use of

ausgießen† *vt sep* pour out

Ausgleich *m* -[e]s balance; (*Entschädigung*) compensation. **a~en†** *v sep* ● *vt* balance; even out *<Höhe>*; (*wettmachen*) compensate for; **sich a~en** balance out ● *vi* (*haben*) (*Sport*) equalize. **A~streffer** *m* equalizer

ausgrab|en† *vt sep* dig up; (*Archaeol*) excavate. **A~ung** *f* -, -en excavation

Ausguss *m* [kitchen] sink

aushaben† *vt sep* have finished *<Buch>*

aushalten† *vt sep* bear, stand; hold *<Note>*; (*Unterhalt zahlen für*) keep; **nicht auszuhalten, nicht zum A~** unbearable

aushändigen *vt sep* hand over

aushängen¹ *vt sep* (*reg*) display; take off its hinges *<Tür>*

aushäng|en²† *vi sep* (*haben*) be displayed. **A~eschild** *nt* sign

ausheben† *vt sep* excavate

aushecken *vt sep* (*fig*) hatch

aushelfen† *vi sep* (*haben*) help out (**jdm** s.o.)

Aushilf|e *f* [temporary] assistant; **zur A~e** to help out. **A~skraft** *f* temporary worker. **a~sweise** *adv* temporarily

aushöhlen *vt sep* hollow out

auskennen† (sich) *vr sep* know one's way around; **sich mit/in etw** (*dat*) **a~** know all about sth

auskommen† *vi sep* (*sein*) manage (**mit/ohne** with/without); (*sich vertragen*) get on (**gut** well)

auskugeln *vt sep* **sich** (*dat*) **den Arm a~** dislocate one's shoulder

auskühlen *vt/i sep* (*sein*) cool

auskundschaften *vt sep* spy out

Auskunft *f* -,-̈e information; (*A~sstelle*) information desk/ (*Büro*) bureau; (*Teleph*) enquiries *pl*; **eine A~** a piece of information

auslachen *vt sep* laugh at

Auslage *f* [window] display; **A~n** expenses

Ausland *nt* im/ins **A~** abroad

Ausländ|er(in) *m* -s,- (*f* -, -nen) foreigner. **a~isch** *a* foreign

Auslandsgespräch *nt* international call

auslass|en† *vt sep* let out; let down *<Saum>*; (*weglassen*) leave out; (*versäumen*) miss; (*Culin*) melt; (*fig*) vent *<Ärger>* (**an** + *dat* on). **A~ungszeichen** *nt* apostrophe

Auslauf *m* run. **a~en†** *vi sep* (*sein*) run out; *<Farbe:>* run; (*Naut*) put to sea; *<Modell:>* be discontinued

ausleeren *vt sep* empty [out]

ausleg|en *vt sep* lay out; display *<Waren>*; (*auskleiden*) line (**mit** with); (*bezahlen*) pay; (*deuten*) interpret. **A~ung** *f* -, -en interpretation

ausleihen† *vt sep* lend; **sich** (*dat*) **a~** borrow

Auslese *f* - selection; (*fig*) pick; (*Elite*) elite

ausliefer|n *vt sep* hand over; (*Jur*) extradite. **A~ung** *f* handing over; (*Jur*) extradition; (*Comm*) distribution

ausloggen *vi sep* log off *or* out

auslosen *vt sep* draw lots for

auslös|en *vt sep* set off, trigger; (*fig*) cause; arouse *<Begeisterung>*; (*einlösen*) redeem; pay a ransom for *<Gefangene>*. **A~er** *m* -s,- trigger; (*Phot*) shutter release

Auslosung *f* draw

auslüften *vt/i sep* (*haben*) air

ausmachen *vt sep* put out; (*abschalten*) turn off; (*abmachen*) arrange; (*erkennen*) make out;

(*betragen*) amount to; (*wichtig sein*) matter

Ausmaß *nt* extent; **A~e** dimensions

Ausnahm|e *f* -, -n exception. **A~ezustand** *m* state of emergency. **a~slos** *adv* without exception. **a~sweise** *adv* as an exception

ausnehmen† *vt sep* take out; **gut** <*Fisch*>; **sich gut a~** look good. **a~d** *adv* exceptionally

ausnutz|en, ausnütz|en *vt sep* exploit. **A~ung** *f* exploitation

auspacken *vt sep* unpack; (*auswickeln*) unwrap

ausplaudern *vt sep* let out, blab

ausprobieren *vt sep* try out

Auspuff *m* -s exhaust [system]. **A~gase** *ntpl* exhaust fumes. **A~rohr** *nt* exhaust pipe

auspusten *vt sep* blow out

ausradieren *vt sep* rub out

ausrauben *vt sep* rob

ausräuchern *vt sep* smoke out; fumigate <*Zimmer*>

ausräumen *vt sep* clear out

ausrechnen *vt sep* work out

Ausrede *f* excuse. **a~n** *v sep* ● *vi* (*haben*) finish speaking ● *vt* **jdm etw a~n** talk s.o. out of sth

ausreichen *vi sep* (*haben*) be enough. **a~d** *a* adequate

Ausreise *f* departure. **a~n** *vi sep* (*sein*) leave the country. **A~visum** *nt* exit visa

ausreißen† *v sep* ● *vt* pull *or* tear out ● *vi* (*sein*) 🔲 run away

ausrenken *vt sep* dislocate

ausrichten *vt sep* align; (*bestellen*) deliver; (*erreichen*) achieve; **jdm a~** tell s.o. (**dass** that); **ich soll Ihnen Grüße von X a~** X sends [you] his regards

ausrotten *vt sep* exterminate; (*fig*) eradicate

Ausruf *m* exclamation. **a~en**† *vt sep* exclaim; call out <*Namen*>; (*verkünden*) proclaim; **jdn a~en lassen** have s.o. paged. **A~ezeichen** *nt* exclamation mark

ausruhen *vt/i sep* (*haben*) rest; **sich a~** have a rest

ausrüst|en *vt sep* equip. **A~ung** *f* equipment; (*Mil*) kit

ausrutschen *vi sep* (*sein*) slip

Aussage *f* -, -n statement; (*Jur*) testimony, evidence; (*Gram*) predicate. **a~n** *vt/i sep* (*haben*) state; (*Jur*) give evidence, testify

ausschalten *vt sep* switch off

Ausschank *m* sale of alcoholic drinks; (*Bar*) bar

Ausschau *f* - **A~ halten nach** look out for

ausscheiden† *vi sep* (*sein*) leave; (*Sport*) drop out; (*nicht in Frage kommen*) be excluded

ausschenken *vt sep* pour out

ausscheren *vi sep* (*sein*) (*Auto*) pull out

ausschildern *vt sep* signpost

ausschimpfen *vt sep* tell off

ausschlafen† *vi/r sep* (*haben*) [**sich**] **a~** get enough sleep; (*morgens*) sleep late

Ausschlag *m* (*Med*) rash; **den A~ geben** (*fig*) tip the balance. **a~gebend** *a* decisive

ausschließ|en† *vt sep* lock out; (*fig*) exclude; (*entfernen*) expel. **a~lich** *a* exclusive

ausschlüpfen *vi sep* (*sein*) hatch

Ausschluss *m* exclusion; expulsion; **unter A~ der Öffentlichkeit** in camera

ausschneiden† *vt sep* cut out

Ausschnitt *m* excerpt, extract; (*Zeitungs-*) cutting; (*Hals-*) neckline

ausschöpfen *vt sep* ladle out; (*Naut*) bail out; exhaust <*Möglichkeiten*>

ausschreiben† *vt sep* write out; (*ausstellen*) make out; (*bekanntgeben*) announce; put out to tender <*Auftrag*>

Ausschreitungen *fpl* riots; (*Exzesse*) excesses

Ausschuss *m* committee; (*Comm*) rejects *pl*

ausschütten *vt sep* tip out; (*verschütten*) spill; (*leeren*) empty

*old spelling

aussehen† vi sep (haben) look; **wie sieht er/es aus?** what does he/it look like? **A~** nt -s appearance

außen adv [on the] outside; **nach a~** outwards. **A~bordmotor** m outboard motor. **A~handel** m foreign trade. **A~minister** m Foreign Minister. **A~politik** f foreign policy. **A~seite** f outside. **A~seiter** m -s,- outsider; (fig) misfit. **A~stände** mpl outstanding debts

außer prep (+ dat) except [for], apart from; (außerhalb) out of; **a~ sich** (fig) beside oneself ● conj except; **a~ wenn** unless. **a~dem** adv in addition, as well ● conj moreover

äußer|e(r,s) a external; <Teil, Schicht> outer. **Ä~e(s)** nt exterior; (Aussehen) appearance

außer|ehelich a extramarital. **a~gewöhnlich** a exceptional. **a~halb** prep (+ gen) outside ● adv **a~halb wohnen** live outside town

äußer|lich a external; (fig) outward. **ä~n** vt express; **sich ä~n** comment; (sich zeigen) manifest itself

außerordentlich a extraordinary

äußerst adv extremely

äußerste|(r,s) a outermost; (weiteste) furthest; (höchste) utmost, extreme; (letzte) last; (schlimmste) worst. **Ä~(s)** nt das **Ä~** the limit; (Schlimmste) the worst; **sein Ä~s tun** do one's utmost; **aufs Ä~** extremely

Äußerung f -, -en comment; (Bemerkung) remark

aussetzen v sep ● vt expose (dat to); abandon <Kind>; launch <Boot>; offer <Belohnung>; **etwas auszusetzen haben an** (+ dat) find fault with ● vi (haben) stop; <Motor> cut out

Aussicht f -, -en view/(fig) prospect (auf + acc of); **weitere A~en** (Meteorol) further outlook sg. **a~slos** a hopeless

ausspannen v sep ● vt spread out; unhitch <Pferd> ● vi (haben) rest

aussperren vt sep lock out

ausspielen v sep ● vt play <Karte>; (fig) play off (gegen against) ● vi (haben) (Kartenspiel) lead

Aussprache f pronunciation; (Gespräch) talk

aussprechen† vt sep pronounce; (äußern) express; **sich a~** talk; come out (für/gegen in favour of/against)

Ausspruch m saying

ausspucken v sep ● vt spit out ● vi (haben) spit

ausspülen vt sep rinse out

ausstatt|en vt sep equip. **A~ung** f -, -en equipment; (Innen-) furnishings pl; (Theat) scenery and costumes pl

ausstehen† v sep ● vt suffer; **Angst a~** be frightened; **ich kann sie nicht a~** I can't stand her ● vi (haben) be outstanding

aussteigen† vi sep (sein) get out; (aus Bus, Zug) get off; **alles a~!** all change!

ausstell|en vt sep exhibit; (Comm) display; (ausfertigen) make out; issue <Pass>. **A~ung** f exhibition; (Comm) display

aussterben† vi sep (sein) die out; (Biol) become extinct

Aussteuer f trousseau

Ausstieg m -[e]s, -e exit

ausstopfen vt sep stuff

ausstoßen† vt sep emit; utter <Fluch>; heave <Seufzer>; (ausschließen) expel

ausstrahl|en vt/i sep (sein) radiate, emit; (Radio, TV) broadcast. **A~ung** f radiation

ausstrecken vt sep stretch out; put out <Hand>

ausstreichen† vt sep cross out

ausströmen v sep ● vi (sein) pour out; (entweichen) escape ● vt emit; (ausstrahlen) radiate

aussuchen vt sep pick, choose

Austausch m exchange. **a~bar** a interchangeable. **a~en** vt sep exchange; (auswechseln) replace

austeilen vt sep distribute

Auster f -, -n oyster

austragen† vt sep deliver; hold <Wettkampf>; play <Spiel>

Austral|ien /-iən/ *nt* -s Australia.
A~ier(in) *m* -s,- (*f* -, -nen)
Australian. **a~isch** *a* Australian

austreiben† *vt sep* drive out;
(*Relig*) exorcize

austreten† *v sep* ● *vt* stamp out;
(*abnutzen*) wear down ● *vi* (*sein*)
come out; (*ausscheiden*) leave (**aus**
etw sth); [mal] **a~** 🚽 go to the loo

austrinken† *vt/i sep* (*haben*) drink
up; (*leeren*) drain

Austritt *m* resignation

austrocknen *vt/i sep* (*sein*) dry out

ausüben *vt sep* practise; carry on
<*Handwerk*>; exercise <*Recht*>;
exert <*Druck, Einfluss*>

Ausverkauf *m* [clearance] sale.
a~t *a* sold out

Auswahl *f* choice, selection; (*Comm*)
range; (*Sport*) team

auswählen *vt sep* choose, select

Auswander|er *m* emigrant. **a~n**
vi sep (*sein*) emigrate. **A~ung** *f*
emigration

auswärt|ig *a* non-local;
(*ausländisch*) foreign. **a~s** *adv*
outwards; (*Sport*) away. **A~sspiel**
nt away game

auswaschen† *vt sep* wash out

auswechseln *vt sep* change;
(*ersetzen*) replace; (*Sport*) substitute

Ausweg *m* (*fig*) way out

ausweichen† *vi sep* (*sein*) get out
of the way; **jdm/etw a~en** avoid/
(*sich entziehen*) evade s.o./sth

Ausweis *m* -es, -e pass; (*Mitglieds-,
Studenten-*) card. **a~en†** *vt sep*
deport; **sich a~en** prove one's
identity. **A~papiere** *ntpl*
identification papers. **A~ung** *f*
deportation

auswendig *adv* by heart

auswerten *vt sep* evaluate

auswickeln *vt sep* unwrap

auswirk|en (sich) *vr sep* have an
effect (**auf** + *acc* on). **A~ung** *f* effect;
(*Folge*) consequence

auswringen *vt sep* wring out

auszahlen *vt sep* pay out;
(*entlohnen*) pay off; (*abfinden*) buy
out; **sich a~** (*fig*) pay off

auszählen *vt sep* count; (*Boxen*)
count out

Auszahlung *f* payment

auszeichn|en *vt sep* (*Comm*) price;
(*ehren*) honour; (*mit einem Preis*)
award a prize to; (*Mil*) decorate; **sich
a~en** distinguish oneself. **A~ung** *f*
honour; (*Preis*) award; (*Mil*)
decoration; (*Sch*) distinction

ausziehen† *v sep* ● *vt* pull out;
(*auskleiden*) undress; take off
<*Mantel, Schuhe*> ● *vi* (*sein*) move
out; (*sich aufmachen*) set out

Auszug *m* departure; (*Umzug*) move;
(*Ausschnitt*) extract; (*Bank-*)
statement

Auto *nt* -s, -s car; **A~ fahren** drive;
(*mitfahren*) go in the car. **A~bahn** *f*
motorway

Autobiographie *f* autobiography

Auto|bus *m* bus. **A~fahrer(in)**
m(f) driver, motorist. **A~fahrt** *f*
drive

Autogramm *nt* -s, -e autograph

Automat *m* -en, -en automatic
device; (*Münz-*) slot-machine;
(*Verkaufs-*) vending-machine;
(*Fahrkarten-*) machine; (*Techn*)
robot. **A~ik** *f* - automatic
mechanism; (*Auto*) automatic
transmission

automatisch *a* automatic

Autonummer *f* registration
number

Autopsie *f* -, -n autopsy

Autor *m* -s, -en /-'to:rən/ author

Auto|reisezug *m* Motorail.
A~rennen *nt* motor race

Autorin *f* -, -nen author[ess]

Autori|sation /-'tsːioːn/ *f* -
authorization. **A~tät** *f* -, -en
authority

Auto|schlosser *m* motor
mechanic. **A~skooter** /-skuːtɐ/ *m*
-s,- dodgem. **A~stopp** *m* -s per
A~stopp fahren hitch-hike.
A~verleih *m* car hire [firm].
A~waschanlage *f* car wash

---

autsch *int* ouch
Axt *f* -,⁻e axe

Bb

B, b /be:/ *nt* - (*Mus*) B flat
Baby /'be:bi/ *nt* -s, -s baby.
 B∼ausstattung *f* layette. **B∼-
 sitter** /-sɪtɐ/ *m* -s,- babysitter
Bach *m* -[e]s,⁻e stream
Backbord *nt* -[e]s port [side]
Backe *f* -, -n cheek
backen *vt/i*† (*haben*) bake; (*braten*)
 fry
Backenzahn *m* molar
Bäcker *m* -s,- baker. **B∼ei** *f* -, -en,
 B∼laden *m* baker's shop
Back|obst *nt* dried fruit. **B∼ofen**
 m oven. **B∼pfeife** *f* ⚇ slap in the
 face. **B∼pflaume** *f* prune.
 B∼pulver *nt* baking-powder.
 B∼stein *m* brick
Bad *nt* -[e]s,⁻er bath; (*Zimmer*)
 bathroom; (*Schwimm-*) pool; (*Ort*)
 spa
Bade|anstalt *f* swimming baths *pl*.
 B∼anzug *m* swim-suit. **B∼hose** *f*
 swimming trunks *pl*. **B∼kappe** *f*
 bathing-cap. **B∼mantel** *m*
 bathrobe. **b∼n** *vi* (*haben*) have a
 bath; (*im Meer*) bathe ● *vt* bath;
 (*waschen*) bathe. **B∼ort** *m* seaside
 resort. **B∼wanne** *f* bath.
 B∼zimmer *nt* bathroom
Bagger *m* -s,- excavator; (*Nass-*)
 dredger. **B∼see** *m* flooded gravel-
 pit
Bahn *f* -, -en path; (*Astr*) orbit;
 (*Sport*) track; (*einzelne*) lane; (*Rodel-*)
 run; (*Stoff-*) width; (*Eisen-*) railway;
 (*Zug*) train; (*Straßen-*) tram.
 b∼brechend *a* (*fig*) pioneering.
 B∼hof *m* [railway] station.
 B∼steig *m* -[e]s, -e platform.
 B∼übergang *m* level crossing

Bahre *f* -, -n stretcher
Baiser /bɛ'ze:/ *nt* -s, -s meringue
Bake *f* -, -n (*Naut, Aviat*) beacon
Bakterien /-iən/ *fpl* bacteria
Balanc|e /ba'lã:sə/ *f* - balance.
 b∼ieren *vt/i* (*haben/sein*) balance
bald *adv* soon; (*fast*) almost
Baldachin /-xi:n/ *m* -s, -e canopy
bald|ig *a* early; <*Besserung*> speedy.
 b∼möglichst *adv* as soon as
 possible
Balg *nt* & *m* -[e]s,⁻er ⚇ brat
Balkan *m* -s Balkans *pl*
Balken *m* -s,- beam
Balkon /bal'kõ:/ *m* -s, -s balcony;
 (*Theat*) circle
Ball¹ *m* -[e]s,⁻e ball
Ball² *m* -[e]s,⁻e (*Tanz*) ball
Ballade *f* -, -n ballad
Ballast *m* -[e]s ballast. **B∼stoffe**
 mpl roughage *sg*
Ballen *m* -s,- bale; (*Anat*) ball of the
 hand/(*Fuß-*) foot; (*Med*) bunion
Ballerina *f* -, -nen ballerina
Ballett *nt* -s, -e ballet
Ballon /ba'lõ:/ *m* -s, -s balloon
Balsam *m* -s balm
Balt|ikum *nt* -s Baltic States *pl*.
 b∼isch *a* Baltic
Bambus *m* -ses, -se bamboo
banal *a* banal
Banane *f* -, -n banana
Banause *m* -n, -n philistine
Band¹ *nt* -[e]s,⁻er ribbon; (*Naht-,
 Ton-, Ziel-*) tape; **am laufenden B∼** ⚇
 non-stop
Band² *m* -[e]s,⁻e volume
Band³ *nt* -[e]s, -e (*fig*) bond
Band⁴ /bɛnt/ *f* -, -s [jazz] band
Bandag|e /ban'da:ʒə/ *f* -, -n
 bandage. **b∼ieren** *vt* bandage
Bande *f* -, -n gang
bändigen *vt* control, restrain;
 (*zähmen*) tame
Bandit *m* -en, -en bandit
Band|maß *nt* tape-measure.
 B∼scheibe *f* (*Anat*) disc.
 B∼wurm *m* tapeworm

Bang|e f B~e haben be afraid; jdm B~e machen frighten s.o. **b~en** vi (haben) fear (**um** for)

Banjo nt -s, -s banjo

Bank¹ f -,˙-e bench

Bank² f -, -en (Comm) bank. **B~einzug** m direct debit

Bankett nt -s, -e banquet

Bankier /baŋ'kie:/ m -s, -s banker

Bankkonto nt bank account

Bankrott m -s, -s bankruptcy. **b~** a bankrupt

Bankwesen nt banking

Bann m -[e]s, -e (fig) spell. **b~en** vt exorcize; (abwenden) avert; [wie] gebannt spellbound

Banner nt -s,- banner

bar a (rein) sheer; <Gold> pure; **b~es Geld** cash; [in] bar bezahlen pay cash

Bar f -, -s bar

Bär m -en, -en bear

Baracke f -, -n (Mil) hut

Barb|ar m -en, -en barbarian. **b~arisch** a barbaric

bar|fuß adv barefoot. **B~geld** nt cash

barmherzig a merciful

barock a baroque. **B~** nt & m -[s] baroque

Barometer nt -s,- barometer

Baron m -s, -e baron. **B~in** f -, -nen baroness

Barren m -s,- (Gold-) bar, ingot; (Sport) parallel bars pl. **B~gold** nt gold bullion

Barriere f -, -n barrier

Barrikade f -, -n barricade

barsch a gruff

Barsch m -[e]s, -e (Zool) perch

Bart m -[e]s,˙-e beard; (der Katze) whiskers pl

bärtig a bearded

Barzahlung f cash payment

Basar m -s, -e bazaar

Base¹ f -, -n [female] cousin

Base² f -, -n (Chem) alkali, base

Basel nt -s Basle

basieren vi (haben) be based (**auf** + dat on)

Basilikum nt -s basil

Basis f -,Basen base; (fig) basis

basisch a (Chem) alkaline

Bask|enmütze f beret. **b~isch** a Basque

Bass m -es,˙-e bass

Bassin /ba'sɛ̃:/ nt -s, -s pond; (Brunnen-) basin; (Schwimm-) pool

Bassist m -en, -en bass player; (Sänger) bass

Bast m -[e]s raffia

basteln vt make ● vi (haben) do handicrafts

Batterie f -, -n battery

Bau¹ m -[e]s, -e burrow; (Fuchs-) earth

Bau² m -[e]s, -ten construction; (Gebäude) building; (Auf-) structure; (Körper-) build; (B~stelle) building site. **B~arbeiten** fpl building work sg; (Straßen-) road-works

Bauch m -[e]s, Bäuche abdomen, belly; (Magen) stomach; (Bauchung) bulge. **b~ig** a bulbous. **B~nabel** m navel. **B~redner** m ventriloquist. **B~schmerzen** mpl stomach-ache sg. **B~speicheldrüse** f pancreas

bauen vt build; (konstruieren) construct ● vi (haben) build (**an etw** dat sth); **b~ auf** (+ acc) (fig) rely on

Bauer¹ m -s, -n farmer; (Schach) pawn

Bauer² nt -s,- [bird]cage

bäuerlich a rustic

Bauern|haus nt farmhouse. **B~hof** m farm

bau|fällig a dilapidated. **B~genehmigung** f planning permission. **B~gerüst** nt scaffolding. **B~jahr** nt year of construction. **B~kunst** f architecture. **b~lich** a structural

Baum m -[e]s, Bäume tree

baumeln vi (haben) dangle

bäumen (sich) vr rear [up]

Baum|schule f [tree] nursery. **B~wolle** f cotton

---

*old spelling

Bausch *m* -[e]s, **Bäusche** wad; **in B~ und Bogen** (*fig*) wholesale. **b~en** *vt* puff out

Bau|sparkasse *f* building society. **B~stein** *m* building brick. **B~stelle** *f* building site; (*Straßen-*) roadworks *pl*. **B~unternehmer** *m* building contractor

Bayer|(in) *m* -s, -n (*f* -, -nen) Bavarian. **B~n** *nt* -s Bavaria

bay[e]risch *a* Bavarian

Bazillus *m* -, -len bacillus

beabsichtig|en *vt* intend. **b~t** *a* intended; intentional

beacht|en *vt* take notice of; (*einhalten*) observe; (*folgen*) follow; **nicht b~en** ignore. **b~lich** *a* considerable. **B~ung** *f* - observance; **etw** (*dat*) **keine B~ung schenken** take no notice of sth

Beamte(r) *m*, **Beamtin** *f* -, -nen official; (*Staats-*) civil servant; (*Schalter-*) clerk

beanspruchen *vt* claim; (*erfordern*) demand

beanstand|en *vt* find fault with; (*Comm*) make a complaint about. **B~ung** *f* -, -en complaint

beantragen *vt* apply for

beantworten *vt* answer

bearbeiten *vt* work; (*weiter-*) process; (*behandeln*) treat (**mit** with); (*Admin*) deal with; (*redigieren*) edit; (*Theat*) adapt; (*Mus*) arrange

Beatmungsgerät *nt* ventilator

beaufsichtig|en *vt* supervise. **B~ung** *f* - supervision

beauftragen *vt* instruct; commission <*Künstler*>

bebauen *vt* build on; (*bestellen*) cultivate

beben *vi* (*haben*) tremble

Becher *m* -s,- beaker; (*Henkel-*) mug; (*Joghurt-, Sahne-*) carton

Becken *nt* -s,- basin; pool; (*Mus*) cymbals *pl*; (*Anat*) pelvis

bedacht *a* careful; **darauf b~** anxious (**zu** to)

bedächtig *a* careful; slow

bedanken (sich) *vr* thank (**bei jdm** s.o.)

Bedarf *m* -s need/(*Comm*) demand (**an** + *dat* for); **bei B~** if required. **B~shaltestelle** *f* request stop

bedauer|lich *a* regrettable. **b~licherweise** *adv* unfortunately. **b~n** *vt* regret; (*bemitleiden*) feel sorry for; **bedaure!** sorry! **b~nswert** *a* pitiful; (*bedauerlich*) regrettable

bedeckt *a* covered; <*Himmel*> overcast

bedenken† *vt* consider; (*überlegen*) think over. **B~** *pl* misgivings; **ohne B~** without hesitation

bedenklich *a* doubtful; (*verdächtig*) dubious; (*ernst*) serious

bedeut|en *vi* (*haben*) mean. **b~end** *a* important; (*beträchtlich*) considerable. **B~ung** *f* -, -en meaning; (*Wichtigkeit*) importance. **b~ungslos** *a* meaningless; (*unwichtig*) unimportant. **b~ungsvoll** *a* significant; (*vielsagend*) meaningful

bedien|en *vt* serve; (*betätigen*) operate; **sich [selbst] b~en** help oneself. **B~ung** *f* -, -en service; (*Betätigung*) operation; (*Kellner*) waiter; (*Kellnerin*) *f* waitress. **B~ungsgeld** *nt* service charge

Bedingung *f* -, -en condition; **B~en** conditions; (*Comm*) terms. **b~slos** *a* unconditional

bedroh|en *vt* threaten. **b~lich** *a* threatening. **B~ung** *f* threat

bedrücken *vt* depress

bedruckt *a* printed

bedürf|en† *vi* (*haben*) (+ *gen*) need. **B~nis** *nt* -ses, -se need

Beefsteak /'bi:fste:k/ *nt* -s, -s steak; **deutsches B~** hamburger

beeilen (sich) *vr* hurry; hasten (**zu** to)

beeindrucken *vt* impress

beeinflussen *vt* influence

beeinträchtigen *vt* mar; (*schädigen*) impair

beengen *vt* restrict

beerdig|en *vt* bury. **B~ung** *f* -, -en funeral

Beere *f* -, -n berry

Beet *nt* -[e]s, -e (*Hort*) bed
Beete *f* -, -n rote B~ beetroot
befähig|en *vt* enable; (*qualifizieren*) qualify. **B~ung** *f* - qualification; (*Fähigkeit*) ability
befahrbar *a* passable
befallen† *vt* attack; <*Angst:*> seize
befangen *a* shy; (*gehemmt*) self-conscious; (*Jur*) biased. **B~heit** *f* - shyness; self-consciousness; bias
befassen (sich) *vr* concern oneself/(*behandeln*) deal (**mit** with)
Befehl *m* -[e]s, -e order; (*Leitung*) command (**über** + *acc* of). **b~en**† *vt* jdm etw b~en order s.o. to do sth ● *vi* (*haben*) give the orders. **B~sform** *f* (*Gram*) imperative. **B~shaber** *m* -s,- commander
befestigen *vt* fasten (**an** + *dat* to); (*Mil*) fortify
befeuchten *vt* moisten
befinden† (**sich**) *vr* be. **B~** *nt* -s [state of] health
beflecken *vt* stain
befolgen *vt* follow
beförder|n *vt* transport; (*im Rang*) promote. **B~ung** *f* -, -en transport; promotion
befragen *vt* question
befrei|en *vt* free; (*räumen*) clear (**von** of); (*freistellen*) exempt (**von** from); **sich b~en** free oneself. **B~er** *m* -s,- liberator. **B~ung** *f* - liberation; exemption
befreunden (sich) *vr* make friends; **befreundet sein** be friends
befriedig|en *vt* satisfy. **b~end** *a* satisfying; (*zufrieden stellend*) satisfactory. **B~ung** *f* - satisfaction
befrucht|en *vt* fertilize. **B~ung** *f* - fertilization; **künstliche B~ung** artificial insemination
Befugnis *f* -, -se authority
Befund *m* result
befürcht|en *vt* fear. **B~ung** *f* -, -en fear
befürworten *vt* support
begab|t *a* gifted. **B~ung** *f* -, -en gift, talent

begeben† (**sich**) *vr* go; **sich in Gefahr b~** expose oneself to danger
begegn|en *vi* (*sein*) jdm/etw b~en meet s.o./sth. **B~ung** *f* -, -en meeting
begehr|en *vt* desire. **b~t** *a* sought-after
begeister|n *vt* jdn b~n arouse s.o.'s enthusiasm. **b~t** *a* enthusiastic; (*eifrig*) keen. **B~ung** *f* - enthusiasm
Begierde *f* -, -n desire
Beginn *m* -s beginning. **b~en**† *vt/i* (*haben*) start, begin
beglaubigen *vt* authenticate
begleichen† *vt* settle
begleit|en *vt* accompany. **B~er** *m* -s, - companion; (*Mus*) accompanist. **B~ung** *f* -, -en company; (*Mus*) accompaniment
beglück|en *vt* make happy. **b~wünschen** *vt* congratulate (**zu** on)
begnadig|en *vt* (*Jur*) pardon. **B~ung** *f* -, -en (*Jur*) pardon
begraben† *vt* bury
Begräbnis *n* -ses, -se burial; (*Feier*) funeral
begreif|en† *vt* understand; **nicht zu b~en** incomprehensible. **b~lich** *a* understandable
begrenz|en *vt* form the boundary of; (*beschränken*) restrict. **b~t** *a* limited. **B~ung** *f* -, -en restriction; (*Grenze*) boundary
Begriff *m* -[e]s, -e concept; (*Ausdruck*) term; (*Vorstellung*) idea
begründ|en *vt* give one's reason for. **b~et** *a* justified. **B~ung** *f* -, -en reason
begrüß|en *vt* greet; (*billigen*) welcome. **b~enswert** *a* welcome. **B~ung** *f* - greeting; welcome
begünstigen *vt* favour
begütert *a* wealthy
behaart *a* hairy
behäbig *a* portly
behag|en *vi* (*haben*) please (jdm s.o.). **B~en** *nt* -s contentment; (*Genuss*) enjoyment. **b~lich** *a* comfortable. **B~lichkeit** *f* - comfort

behalten† *vt* keep; (*sich merken*) remember

Behälter *m* -s,- container

behand|eln *vt* treat; (*sich befassen*) deal with. **B~lung** *f* treatment

beharr|en *vi* (*haben*) persist (**auf** + *dat* in). **b~lich** *a* persistent

behaupt|en *vt* maintain; (*vorgeben*) claim; (*sagen*) say; (*bewahren*) retain; **sich b~en** hold one's own. **B~ung** *f* -, -en assertion; claim; (*Äußerung*) statement

beheben† *vt* remedy

behelf|en (**sich**) *vr* make do (**mit** with). **b~smäßig** *a* makeshift ● *adv* provisionally

beherbergen *vt* put up

beherrsch|en *vt* rule over; (*dominieren*) dominate; (*meistern, zügeln*) control; (*können*) know. **b~t** *a* self-controlled. **B~ung** *f* - control

beherzigen *vt* heed

behilflich *a* jdm **b~** sein help s.o.

behinder|n *vt* hinder; (*blockieren*) obstruct. **b~t** *a* handicapped; (*schwer*) disabled. **B~te(r)** *m/f* handicapped/disabled person. **B~ung** *f* -, -en obstruction; (*Med*) handicap; disability

Behörde *f* -, -n [public] authority

behüte|n *vt* protect. **b~t** *a* sheltered

behutsam *a* careful; (*zart*) gentle

bei
● *preposition* (+ *dative*)

❗ Note that **bei** plus **dem** can become **beim**

····▸ (*nahe*) near; (*dicht an, neben*) by; (*als Begleitung*) with. **wer steht da bei ihm?** who is standing there next to *or* with him? **etw bei sich haben** have sth with *or* on one. **bleiben Sie beim Gepäck/bei den Kindern** stay with the luggage/with the children. **war heute ein Brief für mich bei der Post?** was there a letter for me in the post today?

····▸ (*an*) by. **jdn bei der Hand nehmen** take s.o. by the hand

····▸ (*in der Wohnung von*) at …'s home *or* house/flat. **bei mir [zu Hause]** at my home *or* 🏠 place. **bei seinen Eltern leben** live with one's parents. **wir sind bei Ulrike eingeladen** we have been invited to Ulrike's. **bei Schmidt** at the Schmidts'; (*Geschäft*) at Schmidts'; (*auf Briefen*) c/o Schmidt. **bei jdm/einer Firma arbeiten** work for s.o./a firm. **bei uns tut man das nicht** we don't do that where I come from.

····▸ (*gegenwärtig*) at; (*verwickelt*) in. **bei einer Hochzeit/einem Empfang** at a wedding/reception. **bei einem Unfall** in an accident

····▸ (*im Falle von*) in the case of, with; (*bei Wetter*) in. **wie bei den Römern** as with the Romans. **bei Nebel** in fog, if there is fog. **bei dieser Hitze** in this heat

····▸ (*angesichts*) with; (*trotz*) in spite of. **bei deinen guten Augen** with your good eyesight. **bei all seinen Bemühungen** in spite of *or* despite all his efforts

····▸ (*Zeitpunkt*) at, on. **bei diesen Worten errötete er** he blushed at this *or* on hearing this. **bei seiner Ankunft** on his arrival. **bei Tag/Nacht** by day/night

····▸ (*Gleichzeitigkeit, mit Verbalsubstantiv*) **beim …en** while *or* when …ing. **beim Spazierengehen im Walde** while walking in the woods. **beim Überqueren der Straße** when crossing the road. **sie war beim Lesen** she was reading. **wir waren beim Frühstück** we were having breakfast

beibehalten† *vt sep* keep

beibringen† *vt sep* jdm etw **b~** teach s.o. sth; (*mitteilen*) break sth to s.o.; (*zufügen*) inflict sth on s.o.

Beicht|e *f* -, -n confession. **b~en** *vt/i* (*haben*) confess. **B~stuhl** *m* confessional

beide *a & pron* both; **b~s** both; **dreißig b~** (*Tennis*) thirty all. **b~rseitig** *a* mutual. **b~rseits** *adv & prep* (+ *gen*) on both sides (of)

beieinander *adv* together

Beifahrer(in) *m(f)* [front-seat] passenger; (*Motorrad*) pillion passenger

Beifall *m* -[e]s applause; (*Billigung*) approval; **B~ klatschen** applaud

beifügen *vt sep* add; (*beilegen*) enclose

beige /beːʒ/ *inv a* beige

beigeben† *vt sep* add

Beihilfe *f* financial aid; (*Studien-*) grant; (*Jur*) aiding and abetting

Beil *nt* -[e]s, -e hatchet, axe

Beilage *f* supplement; (*Gemüse*) vegetable

beiläufig *a* casual

beilegen *vt sep* enclose; (*schlichten*) settle

Beileid *nt* condolences *pl*. **B~sbrief** *m* letter of condolence

beiliegend *a* enclosed

beim *prep* = **bei dem**; **b~ Militär** in the army; **b~ Frühstück** at breakfast

beimessen† *vt sep* (*fig*) attach (*dat* to)

Bein *nt* -[e]s, -e leg; **jdm ein B~ stellen** trip s.o. up

beinah[e] *adv* nearly, almost

Beiname *m* epithet

beipflichten *vi sep* (*haben*) agree (*dat* with)

Beirat *m* advisory committee

beisammen *adv* together; **b~ sein** be together

Beisein *nt* presence

beiseite *adv* aside; (*abseits*) apart; **b~ legen** put aside; (*sparen*) put by

beisetz|en *vt sep* bury. **B~ung** *f* -, -en funeral

Beispiel *nt* example; **zum B~** for example. **b~sweise** *adv* for example

beißen† *vt/i* (*haben*) bite; (*brennen*) sting; **sich b~** <*Farben:*> clash

Bei|stand *m* -[e]s help. **b~stehen**† *vi sep* (*haben*) **jdm b~stehen** help s.o.

beistimmen *vi sep* (*haben*) agree

Beistrich *m* comma

Beitrag *m* -[e]s,̈-e contribution; (*Mitglieds-*) subscription; (*Versicherungs-*) premium; (*Zeitungs-*) article. **b~en**† *vt/i sep* (*haben*) contribute

bei|treten† *vi sep* (*sein*) (+ *dat*) join. **B~tritt** *m* joining

Beize *f* -, -n (*Holz-*) stain

beizeiten *adv* in good time

beizen *vt* stain <*Holz*>

bejahen *vt* answer in the affirmative; (*billigen*) approve of

bejahrt *a* aged, old

bekämpf|en *vt* fight. **B~ung** *f* fight (*gen* against)

bekannt *a* well-known; (*vertraut*) familiar; **jdn b~ machen** introduce s.o.; **etw b~ machen** *od* **geben** announce sth; **b~ werden** become known. **B~e(r)** *m/f* acquaintance; (*Freund*) friend. **B~gabe** *f* announcement. **b~lich** *adv* as is well known. **B~machung** *f* -, -en announcement; (*Anschlag*) notice. **B~schaft** *f* - acquaintance; (*Leute*) acquaintances *pl*; (*Freunde*) friends *pl*

bekehr|en *vt* convert. **B~ung** *f* -, -en conversion

bekenn|en† *vt* confess, profess <*Glauben*>; **sich [für] schuldig b~en** admit one's guilt. **B~tnis** *nt* -ses, -se confession; (*Konfession*) denomination

beklag|en *vt* lament; (*bedauern*) deplore; **sich b~en** complain. **b~enswert** *a* unfortunate. **B~te(r)** *m/f* (*Jur*) defendant

bekleid|en *vt* hold <*Amt*>. **B~ung** *f* clothing

Beklemmung *f* -, -en feeling of oppression

bekommen† *vt* get; have <*Baby*>; catch <*Erkältung*> ● *vi* (*sein*) **jdm gut b~** do s.o. good; <*Essen:*> agree with s.o.

beköstig|en *vt* feed. **B~ung** *f* - board; (*Essen*) food

bekräftigen *vt* reaffirm

bekreuzigen (sich) *vr* cross oneself

bekümmert *a* troubled; (*besorgt*) worried

bekunden *vt* show

Belag *m* -[e]s,-̈e coating; (*Fußboden-*) covering; (*Brot-*) topping; (*Zahn-*) tartar; (*Brems-*) lining

belager|n *vt* besiege. **B∼ung** *f* -, -en siege

Belang *m* von B∼ of importance; **B∼e** *pl* interests. **b∼los** *a* irrelevant; (*unwichtig*) trivial

belassen† *vt* leave; **es dabei b∼** leave it at that

belasten *vt* load; (*fig*) burden; (*beanspruchen*) put a strain on; (*Comm*) debit; (*Jur*) incriminate

belästigen *vt* bother; (*bedrängen*) pester; (*unsittlich*) molest

Belastung *f* -, -en load; (*fig*) strain; (*Comm*) debit. **B∼smaterial** *nt* incriminating evidence. **B∼szeuge** *m* prosecution witness

belaufen† (sich) *vr* amount (**auf** + *acc* to)

belauschen *vt* eavesdrop on

beleb|en *vt* (*fig*) revive; (*lebhaft machen*) enliven. **b∼t** *a* lively; <*Straße*> busy

Beleg *m* -[e]s, -e evidence; (*Beispiel*) instance (**für** of); (*Quittung*) receipt. **b∼en** *vt* cover/(*garnieren*) garnish (**mit** with); (*besetzen*) reserve; (*Univ*) enrol for; (*nachweisen*) provide evidence for; **den ersten Platz b∼en** (*Sport*) take first place. **B∼schaft** *f* -, -en work-force. **b∼t** *a* occupied; <*Zunge*> coated; <*Stimme*> husky; **b∼te Brote** open sandwiches

belehren *vt* instruct

beleidig|en *vt* offend; (*absichtlich*) insult. **B∼ung** *f* -, -en insult

belesen *a* well-read

beleucht|en *vt* light; (*anleuchten*) illuminate. **B∼ung** *f* -, -en illumination

Belg|ien /-iən/ *nt* -s Belgium. **B∼ier(in)** *m* -s,- (*f* -, -nen) Belgian. **b∼isch** *a* Belgian

belicht|en *vt* (*Phot*) expose. **B∼ung** *f* - exposure

Belieb|en *nt* -s **nach B∼en** [just] as one likes. **b∼ig** *a* **eine b∼ige Zahl** any number you like ● *adv* **b∼ig oft** as often as one likes. **b∼t** *a* popular

bellen *vi* (*haben*) bark

belohn|en *vt* reward. **B∼ung** *f* -, -en reward

belustig|en *vt* amuse. **B∼ung** *f* -, -en amusement

bemalen *vt* paint

bemängeln *vt* criticize

bemannt *a* manned

bemerk|bar *a* **sich b∼bar machen** attract attention. **b∼en** *vt* notice; (*äußern*) remark. **b∼ enswert** *a* remarkable. **B∼ung** *f* -, -en remark

bemitleiden *vt* pity

bemüh|en *vt* trouble; **sich b∼en** try (**zu** to; **um etw** to get sth); (*sich kümmern*) attend (**um** to); **b∼t sein** endeavour (**zu** to). **B∼ung** *f* -, -en effort

benachbart *a* neighbouring

benachrichtig|en *vt* inform; (*amtlich*) notify. **B∼ung** *f* -, -en notification

benachteiligen *vt* discriminate against; (*ungerecht sein*) treat unfairly

benehmen† (sich) *vr* behave. **B∼** *nt* -s behaviour

beneiden *vt* envy (**um etw** sth)

Bengel *m* -s,- boy; (*Rüpel*) lout

benötigen *vt* need

benutz|en, (*SGer*) **benütz|en** *vt* use; take <*Bahn*> **B∼ung** *f* use

Benzin *nt* -s petrol

beobacht|en *vt* observe. **B∼er** *m* -s,- observer. **B∼ung** *f* -, -en observation

bequem *a* comfortable; (*mühelos*) easy; (*faul*) lazy. **b∼en (sich)** *vr* deign (**zu** to). **B∼lichkeit** *f* -, -en comfort; (*Faulheit*) laziness

berat|en† *vt* advise; (*überlegen*) discuss; **sich b∼en confer** ● *vi* (*haben*) discuss (**über etw** *acc* sth); (*beratschlagen*) confer. **B∼er(in)** *m* -s,-, (*f* -, -nen) adviser. **B∼ung** *f* -, -en guidance; (*Rat*) advice;

(*Besprechung*) discussion; (*Med, Jur*) consultation

berechn|en *vt* calculate; (*anrechnen*) charge for; (*abfordern*) charge. **B∼ung** *f* calculation

berechtig|en *vt* entitle; (*befugen*) authorize; (*fig*) justify. **b∼t** *a* justified, justifiable. **B∼ung** *f* -, -en authorization; (*Recht*) right; (*Rechtmäßigkeit*) justification

bered|en *vt* talk about; sich b∼en talk. **B∼samkeit** *f* - eloquence

beredt *a* eloquent

Bereich *m* -[e]s, -e area; (*fig*) realm; (*Fach-*) field

bereichern *vi* enrich

bereit *a* ready. **b∼en** *vt* prepare; (*verursachen*) cause; give <*Überraschung*>. **b∼halten**† *vt sep* have/(*ständig*) keep ready. **b∼legen** *vt sep* put out [ready]. **b∼machen** *vt sep* get ready. **b∼s** *adv* already

Bereitschaft *f* -, -en readiness; (*Einheit*) squad. **B∼sdienst** *m* B∼sdienst haben (*Mil*) be on stand-by; <*Arzt:*> be on call. **B∼spolizei** *f* riot police

bereit|stehen† *vi sep* (*haben*) be ready. **b∼stellen** *vt sep* put out ready; (*verfügbar machen*) make available. **B∼ung** *f* - preparation. **b∼willig** *a* willing

bereuen *vt* regret

Berg *m* -[e]s, -e mountain; (*Anhöhe*) hill; in den B∼en in the mountains. **b∼ab** *adv* downhill. **B∼arbeiter** *m* miner. **b∼auf** *adv* uphill. **B∼bau** *m* -[e]s mining

bergen† *vt* recover; (*Naut*) salvage; (*retten*) rescue

Berg|führer *m* mountain guide. **b∼ig** *a* mountainous. **B∼kette** *f* mountain range. **B∼mann** *m* (*pl* -leute) miner. **B∼steiger(in)** *m* -s,- (*f* -, -nen) mountaineer, climber

Bergung *f* - recovery; (*Naut*) salvage; (*Rettung*) rescue

Berg|wacht *f* mountain rescue service. **B∼werk** *nt* mine

Bericht *m* -[e]s, -e report; (*Reise-*) account. **b∼en** *vt/i* (*haben*) report; (*erzählen*) tell (von of). **B∼erstatter(in)** *m* -s,- (*f* -, -nen) reporter

berichtigen *vt* correct

beriesel|n *vt* irrigate. **B∼ungsanlage** *f* sprinkler system

Berlin *nt* -s Berlin. **B∼er** *m* -s,- Berliner

Bernhardiner *m* -s,- St Bernard

Bernstein *m* amber

berüchtigt *a* notorious

berücksichtig|en *vt* take into consideration. **B∼ung** *f* - consideration

Beruf *m* profession; (*Tätigkeit*) occupation; (*Handwerk*) trade. **b∼en**† *vt* appoint; sich b∼en refer (auf + *acc* to); (*vorgeben*) plead (auf etw *acc* sth); ● *a* competent; b∼en sein be destined (zu to). **b∼lich** *a* professional; <*Ausbildung*> vocational ● *adv* professionally; b∼lich tätig sein work, have a job. **B∼sberatung** *f* vocational guidance. **b∼smäßig** *adv* professionally. **B∼sschule** *f* vocational school. **B∼ssoldat** *m* regular soldier. **b∼stätig** *a* working; b∼stätig sein work, have a job. **B∼stätige(r)** *m/f* working man/woman. **B∼ung** *f* -, -en appointment; (*Bestimmung*) vocation; (*Jur*) appeal; B∼ung einlegen appeal. **B∼ungsgericht** *nt* appeal court

beruhen *vi* (*haben*) be based (auf + *dat* on)

beruhig|en *vt* calm [down]; (*zuversichtlich machen*) reassure. **b∼end** *a* calming; (*tröstend*) reassuring; (*Med*) sedative. **B∼ung** *f* - calming; reassurance; (*Med*) sedation. **B∼ungsmittel** *nt* sedative; (*bei Psychosen*) tranquillizer

berühmt *a* famous. **B∼heit** *f* -, -en fame; (*Person*) celebrity

berühr|en *vt* touch; (*erwähnen*) touch on. **B∼ung** *f* -, -en touch; (*Kontakt*) contact

---

besänftigen *vt* soothe

Besatz *m* -es,⸚e trimming

Besatzung *f* -, -en crew; (*Mil*) occupying force

beschädig|en *vt* damage. **B~ung** *f* -, -en damage

beschaffen *vt* obtain, get ● *a* so b~ sein, dass be such that. **B~heit** *f* - consistency

beschäftig|en *vt* occupy; <*Arbeitgeber:*> employ; sich b~en occupy oneself. **b~t** *a* busy; (*angestellt*) employed (bei at). **B~ung** *f* -, -en occupation; (*Anstellung*) employment

beschämt *a* ashamed; (*verlegen*) embarrassed

beschatten *vt* shade; (*überwachen*) shadow

Bescheid *m* -[e]s information; jdm B~ sagen *od* geben let s.o. know; B~ wissen know

bescheiden *a* modest. **B~heit** *f* - modesty

bescheinen† *vt* shine on; von der Sonne beschienen sunlit

bescheinig|en *vt* certify. **B~ung** *f* -, -en [written] confirmation; (*Schein*) certificate

beschenken *vt* give a present/ presents to

Bescherung *f* -, -en distribution of Christmas presents

beschildern *vt* signpost

beschimpf|en *vt* abuse, swear at. **B~ung** *f* -, -en abuse

beschirmen *vt* protect

Beschlag *m* in B~ nehmen monopolize. **b~en†** *vt* shoe ● *vi* (*sein*) steam *or* mist up ● *a* steamed *or* misted up. **B~nahme** *f* -, -n confiscation; (*Jur*) seizure. **b~nahmen** *vt* confiscate; (*Jur*) seize

beschleunig|en *vt* hasten; (*schneller machen*) speed up <*Schritt*> ● *vi* (*haben*) accelerate. **B~ung** *f* - acceleration

beschließen† *vt* decide; (*beenden*) end ● *vi* (*haben*) decide (über + *acc* about)

Beschluss *m* decision

beschmutzen *vt* make dirty

beschneid|en† *vt* trim; (*Hort*) prune; (*Relig*) circumcise. **B~ung** *f* - circumcision

beschnüffeln *vt* sniff at

beschönigen *vt* (*fig*) gloss over

beschränken *vt* limit, restrict; sich b~ auf (+ *acc*) confine oneself to

beschrankt *a* <*Bahnübergang*> with barrier[s]

beschränk|t *a* limited; (*geistig*) dull-witted. **B~ung** *f* -, -en limitation, restriction

beschreib|en† *vt* describe. **B~ung** *f* -, -en description

beschuldig|en *vt* accuse. **B~ung** *f* -, -en accusation

beschummeln *vt* 🔲 cheat

Beschuss *m* (*Mil*) fire; (*Artillerie-*) shelling

beschütz|en *vt* protect. **B~er** *m* -s,- protector

Beschwer|de *f* -, -n complaint; **B~den** (*Med*) trouble *sg*. **b~en** *vt* weight down; sich b~en complain. **b~lich** *a* difficult

beschwindeln *vt* cheat (um out of); (*belügen*) lie to

beschwipst *a* 🔲 tipsy

beseitig|en *vt* remove. **B~ung** *f* - removal

Besen *m* -s,- broom

besessen *a* obsessed (von by)

besetz|en *vt* occupy; fill <*Posten*>; (*Theat*) cast <*Rolle*>; (*verzieren*) trim (mit with). **b~t** *a* occupied; <*Toilette, Leitung*> engaged; <*Zug, Bus*> full up; der Platz ist b~t this seat is taken. **B~tzeichen** *nt* engaged tone. **B~ung** *f* -, -en occupation; (*Theat*) cast

besichtig|en *vt* look round <*Stadt*>; (*prüfen*) inspect; (*besuchen*) visit. **B~ung** *f* -, -en visit; (*Prüfung*) inspection; (*Stadt-*) sightseeing

besiedelt *a* dünn/dicht b~ sparsely/densely populated

besiegen *vt* defeat

besinn|en† (sich) *vr* think, reflect; (*sich erinnern*) remember (auf jdn/

etw s.o./sth). **B~ung** *f* - reflection; (*Bewusstsein*) consciousness; **bei/ ohne B~ung** conscious/unconscious. **b~ungslos** *a* unconscious

Besitz *m* possession; (*Eigentum, Land-*) property; (*Gut*) estate. **b~en**† *vt* own, possess; (*haben*) have. **B~er(in)** *m* -s,- (*f* -, -nen) owner; (*Comm*) proprietor

besoffen *a* ☒ drunken; **b~ sein** be drunk

besonder|e(r,s) *a* special; (*bestimmt*) particular; (*gesondert*) separate. **b~s** *adv* [e]specially, particularly; (*gesondert*) separately

besonnen *a* calm

besorg|en *vt* get; (*kaufen*) buy; (*erledigen*) attend to; (*versorgen*) look after. **b~t** *a* worried/(*bedacht*) concerned (um about). **B~ung** *f* -, -en errand; **B~ungen machen** do shopping

bespitzeln *vt* spy on

besprech|en† *vt* discuss; (*rezensieren*) review. **B~ung** *f* -, -en discussion; review; (*Konferenz*) meeting

besser *a* & *adv* better. **b~n** *vt* improve; **sich b~n** get better. **B~ung** *f* - improvement; **gute B~ung!** get well soon!

Bestand *m* -[e]s,ᵉe existence; (*Vorrat*) stock (**an** + *dat* of)

beständig *a* constant; <*Wetter*> settled; **b~ gegen** resistant to

Bestand|saufnahme *f* stocktaking. **B~teil** *m* part

bestätig|en *vt* confirm; acknowledge <*Empfang*>; **sich b~en** prove to be true. **B~ung** *f* -, -en confirmation

bestatt|en *vt* bury. **B~ung** *f* -, -en funeral

Bestäubung *f* - pollination

bestaunen *vt* gaze at in amazement; (*bewundern*) admire

best|e(r,s) *a* best; **b~en Dank!** many thanks! **B~e(r,s)** *m/f/nt* best; **sein B~es tun** do one's best

bestech|en† *vt* bribe; (*bezaubern*) captivate. **b~end** *a* captivating. **b~lich** *a* corruptible. **B~ung** *f* - bribery. **B~ungsgeld** *nt* bribe

Besteck *nt* -[e]s, -e [set of] knife, fork and spoon; (*coll*) cutlery

bestehen† *vi* (*haben*) exist; (*fortdauern*) last; (*bei Prüfung*) pass; **~ aus** consist/(*gemacht sein*) be made of; **~ auf** (+ *dat*) insist on ● *vt* pass <*Prüfung*>

besteig|en† *vt* climb; (*aufsteigen*) mount; ascend <*Thron*>. **B~ung** *f* ascent

bestell|en *vt* order; (*vor-*) book; (*ernennen*) appoint; (*bebauen*) cultivate; (*ausrichten*) tell; **zu sich b~en** send for; **b~t sein** have an appointment; **kann ich etwas b~en?** can I take a message? **B~schein** *m* order form. **B~ung** *f* order; (*Botschaft*) message; (*Bebauung*) cultivation

besteuer|n *vt* tax. **B~ung** *f* - taxation

Bestie /'bɛstiə/ *f* -, -n beast

bestimm|en *vt* fix; (*entscheiden*) decide; (*vorsehen*) intend; (*ernennen*) appoint; (*ermitteln*) determine; (*definieren*) define; (*Gram*) qualify ● *vi* (*haben*) be in charge (**über** + *acc* of). **b~t** *a* definite; (*gewiss*) certain; (*fest*) firm,. **B~ung** *f* fixing; (*Vorschrift*) regulation; (*Ermittlung*) determination; (*Definition*) definition; (*Zweck*) purpose; (*Schicksal*) destiny. **B~ungsort** *m* destination

Bestleistung *f* (*Sport*) record

bestraf|en *vt* punish. **B~ung** *f* -, -en punishment

Bestrahlung *f* radiotherapy

Bestreb|en *nt* -s endeavour; (*Absicht*) aim. **B~ung** *f* -, -en effort

bestreiten† *vt* dispute; (*leugnen*) deny; (*bezahlen*) pay for

bestürz|t *a* dismayed; (*erschüttert*) stunned. **B~ung** *f* - dismay, consternation

Bestzeit *f* (*Sport*) record [time]

Besuch *m* -[e]s, -e visit; (*kurz*) call; (*Schul-*) attendance; (*Gast*) visitor;

---

*old spelling

(Gäste) visitors *pl*; **B∼ haben** have a visitor/visitors; **bei jdm zu** *od* **auf B∼ sein** be staying with s.o. **b∼en** *vt* visit; *(kurz)* call on; *(teilnehmen)* attend; go to <*Schule, Ausstellung*>. **B∼er(in)** *m* -s,- (*f* -, -nen) visitor; caller. **B∼szeit** *f* visiting hours *pl*

betagt *a* aged, old

betätig|en *vt* operate; **sich b∼en** work **(als** as). **B∼ung** *f* -, -en operation; *(Tätigkeit)* activity

betäub|en *vt* stun; <*Lärm:*> deafen; *(Med)* anaesthetize; *(lindern)* ease; deaden <*Schmerz*>; **wie b∼t** dazed. **B∼ung** *f* - daze; *(Med)* anaesthesia. **B∼ungsmittel** *nt* anaesthetic

Bete *f* -, -n Rote B∼ beetroot

beteilig|en *vt* give a share to; **sich b∼en** take part **(an** + *dat* in); *(beitragen)* contribute **(an** + *dat* to). **b∼t** *a* **b∼t sein** take part/(*an Unfall*) be involved/(*Comm*) have a share **(an** + *dat* in); **alle B∼ten** all those involved. **B∼ung** *f* -, -en participation; involvement; *(Anteil)* share

beten *vi (haben)* pray

Beton /be'tɔŋ/ *m* -s concrete

betonen *vt* stressed, emphasize

beton|t *a* stressed; *(fig)* pointed. **B∼ung** *f* -, -en stress

Betracht *m* **in B∼ ziehen** consider; **außer B∼ lassen** disregard; **nicht in B∼ kommen** be out of the question. **b∼en** *vt* look at; *(fig)* regard **(als** as)

beträchtlich *a* considerable

Betrachtung *f* -, -en contemplation; *(Überlegung)* reflection

Betrag *m* -[e]s, ̈-e amount. **b∼en†** *vt* amount to; **sich b∼en** behave. **B∼en** *nt* -s behaviour; *(Sch)* conduct

betreff|en† *vt* affect; *(angehen)* concern. **b∼end** *a* relevant. **b∼s** *prep* (+ *gen*) concerning

betreiben† *vt (leiten)* run; *(ausüben)* carry on

betreten† *vt* step on; *(eintreten)* enter; 'B∼ verboten' 'no entry'; *(bei Rasen)* 'keep off [the grass]'

betreu|en *vt* look after. **B∼er(in)** *m* -s,- (*f* -, -nen) helper; *(Kranken-)* nurse. **B∼ung** *f* - care

Betrieb *m* business; *(Firma)* firm; *(Treiben)* activity; *(Verkehr)* traffic; **außer B∼** not in use; *(defekt)* out of order

Betriebs|anleitung, B∼anweisung *f* operating instructions *pl*. **B∼ferien** *pl* firm's holiday. **B∼leitung** *f* management. **B∼rat** *m* works committee. **B∼störung** *f* breakdown

betrinken† (sich) *vr* get drunk

betroffen *a* disconcerted; **b∼ sein** be affected **(von** by)

betrüb|en *vt* sadden. **b∼t** *a* sad

Betrug *m* -[e]s deception; *(Jur)* fraud

betrüg|en† *vt* cheat, swindle; *(Jur)* defraud; *(in der Ehe)* be unfaithful to. **B∼er(in)** *m* -s,- (*f* -, -nen) swindler. **B∼erei** *f* -, -en fraud

betrunken *a* drunken; **b∼ sein** be drunk. **B∼e(r)** *m* drunk

Bett *nt* -[e]s, -en bed. **B∼couch** *f* sofa-bed. **B∼decke** *f* blanket; *(Tages-)* bedspread

Bettel|ei *f* - begging. **b∼n** *vi (haben)* beg

Bettler(in) *m* -s,- (*f* -, -nen) beggar

Bettpfanne *f* bedpan

Betttuch (Bettuch) *nt* sheet

Bett|wäsche *f* bed linen. **B∼zeug** *nt* bedding

betupfen *vt* dab **(mit** with)

beug|en *vt* bend; *(Gram)* decline; conjugate <*Verb*>; **sich b∼en** bend; *(lehnen)* lean; *(sich fügen)* submit *(dat* to). **B∼ung** *f* -, -en *(Gram)* declension; conjugation

Beule *f* -, -n bump; *(Delle)* dent

beunruhig|en *vt* worry; **sich b∼en** worry. **B∼ung** *f* - worry

beurlauben *vt* give leave to

beurteil|en *vt* judge. **B∼ung** *f* -, -en judgement; *(Ansicht)* opinion

Beute *f* - booty, haul; *(Jagd-)* bag; *(eines Raubtiers)* prey

Beutel *m* -s,- bag; *(Tabak- & Zool)* pouch. **B∼tier** *nt* marsupial

Bevölkerung *f* -, -en population

bevollmächtigen *vt* authorize

bevor *conj* before; **b~ nicht** until

bevormunden *vt* treat like a child

bevorstehen† *vi sep* (*haben*) approach; (*unmittelbar*) be imminent. **b~d** approaching, forthcoming; **unmittelbar b~d** imminent

bevorzug|en *vt* prefer; (*begünstigen*) favour. **b~t** *a* privileged; <*Behandlung*> preferential

bewachen *vt* guard

Bewachung *f* - guard; **unter B~** under guard

bewaffn|en *vt* arm. **b~et** *a* armed. **B~ung** *f* - armament; (*Waffen*) arms *pl*

bewahren *vt* protect (**vor** + *dat* from); (*behalten*) keep; **die Ruhe b~** keep calm

bewähren (sich) *vr* prove one's/ <*Ding:*> its worth; (*erfolgreich sein*) prove a success

bewähr|t *a* reliable; (*erprobt*) proven. **B~ung** *f* - (*Jur*) probation. **B~ungsfrist** *f* [period of] probation. **B~ungsprobe** *f* (*fig*) test

bewältigen *vt* cope with; (*überwinden*) overcome

bewässer|n *vt* irrigate. **B~ung** *f* - irrigation

bewegen¹ *vt* (*reg*) move; **sich b~** move; (*körperlich*) take exercise

bewegen²† *vt* **jdn dazu b~, etw zu tun** induce s.o. to do sth

Beweg|grund *m* motive. **b~lich** *a* movable, mobile; (*wendig*) agile. **B~lichkeit** *f* - mobility; agility. **B~ung** *f* -, -en movement; (*Phys*) motion; (*Rührung*) emotion; (*Gruppe*) movement; **körperliche B~ung** physical exercise. **b~ungslos** *a* motionless

Beweis *m* -es, -e proof; (*Zeichen*) token; **B~e** evidence *sg*. **b~en†** *vt* prove; (*zeigen*) show; **sich b~en**

prove oneself/<*Ding:*> itself. **B~material** *nt* evidence

bewerb|en† (**sich**) *vr* apply (**um** for; **bei** to). **B~er(in)** *m* -s,- (*f* -, -nen) applicant. **B~ung** *f* -, -en application

bewerten *vt* value; (*einschätzen*) rate; (*Sch*) mark, grade

bewilligen *vt* grant

bewirken *vt* cause; (*herbeiführen*) bring about

bewirt|en *vt* entertain. **B~ung** *f* - hospitality

bewohn|bar *a* habitable. **b~en** *vt* inhabit, live in. **B~er(in)** *m* -s,- (*f* -, -nen) resident, occupant; (*Einwohner*) inhabitant

bewölk|en (sich) *vr* cloud over; **b~t** cloudy. **B~ung** *f* - clouds *pl*

bewunder|n *vt* admire. **b~nswert** *a* admirable. **B~ung** *f* - admiration

bewusst *a* conscious (*gen* of); (*absichtlich*) deliberate. **b~los** *a* unconscious. **B~losigkeit** *f* - unconsciousness; **B~sein** *nt* -s consciousness; (*Gewissheit*) awareness; **bei B~sein** conscious

bezahl|en *vt/i* (*haben*) pay; pay for <*Ware, Essen*>. **B~ung** *f* - payment; (*Lohn*) pay. **B~fernsehen** *nt* pay television; pay TV

bezaubern *vt* enchant

bezeichn|en *vt* mark; (*bedeuten*) denote; (*beschreiben, nennen*) describe (**als** as). **b~end** *a* typical. **B~ung** *f* marking; (*Beschreibung*) description (**als** as); (*Ausdruck*) term; (*Name*) name

bezeugen *vt* testify to

bezichtigen *vt* accuse (*gen* of)

bezieh|en† *vt* cover; (*einziehen*) move into; (*beschaffen*) obtain; (*erhalten*) get; (*in Verbindung bringen*) relate (**auf** + *acc* to); **sich b~en** (*bewölken*) cloud over; **sich b~en auf** (+ *acc*) refer to; **das Bett frisch b~en** put clean sheets on the bed. **B~ung** *f* -, -en relation; (*Verhältnis*) relationship; (*Bezug*) respect; **B~ungen haben** have

connections. **b~ungsweise** *adv*
respectively; (*vielmehr*) or rather

Bezirk *m* -[e]s, -e district

Bezug *m* cover; (*Kissen-*) case;
(*Beschaffung*) obtaining; (*Kauf*)
purchase; (*Zusammenhang*)
reference; **B~e** *pl* earnings; **B~**
nehmen refer (**auf** + *acc* to); **in B~**
auf (+ *acc*) regarding

bezüglich *prep* (+ *gen*) regarding
● *a* relating (**auf** + *acc* to)

bezwecken *vt* (*fig*) aim at

bezweifeln *vt* doubt

BH /beː'haː/ *m* -[s], -[s] bra

Bibel *f* -, -n Bible

Biber *m* -s,- beaver

Biblio|thek *f* -, -en library.
B~thekar(in) *m* -s,- (*f* -, -nen)
librarian

biblisch *a* biblical

bieg|en† *vt* bend; **sich b~en** bend
● *vi* (*sein*) curve (**nach** to); **um die**
Ecke b~en turn the corner. **b~sam**
a flexible, supple. **B~ung** *f* -, -en
bend

Biene *f* -, -n bee. **B~nstock** *m*
beehive. **B~nwabe** *f* honeycomb

Bier *nt* -s, -e beer. **B~deckel** *m*
beer-mat. **B~krug** *m* beer-mug

bieten† *vt* offer; (*bei Auktion*) bid

Bifokalbrille *f* bifocals *pl*

Bigamie *f* - bigamy

bigott *a* over-pious

Bikini *m* -s, -s bikini

Bilanz *f* -, -en balance sheet; (*fig*)
result; **die B~ ziehen** (*fig*) draw
conclusions (**aus** from)

Bild *nt* -[e]s, -er picture; (*Theat*)
scene

bilden *vt* form; (*sein*) be; (*erziehen*)
educate

Bild|erbuch *nt* picture-book.
B~fläche *f* screen. **B~hauer** *m*
-s,- sculptor. **b~lich** *a* pictorial;
(*figurativ*) figurative. **B~nis** *nt* -ses,
-se portrait. **B~schirm** *m* (*TV*)
screen. **B~schirmgerät** *nt* visual
display unit, VDU. **b~schön** *a* very
beautiful

Bildung *f* - formation; (*Erziehung*)
education; (*Kultur*) culture

Billard /'bɪljart/ *nt* -s billiards *sg*.
B~tisch *m* billiard table

Billett /bɪl'jɛt/ *nt* -[e]s, -e & -s ticket

Billiarde *f* -, -n thousand million
million

billig *a* cheap; (*dürftig*) poor; **recht**
und b~ right and proper. **b~en** *vt*
approve. **B~ung** *f* - approval

Billion /bɪlio:n/ *f* -, -en million
million, billion

Bimsstein *m* pumice stone

Binde *f* -, -n band; (*Verband*)
bandage; (*Damen-*) sanitary towel.
B~hautentzündung *f*
conjunctivitis. **b~n†** *vt* tie (**an** + *acc*
to); make <*Strauß*>; bind <*Buch*>;
(*fesseln*) tie up; (*Culin*) thicken; **sich**
b~n commit oneself. **B~strich** *m*
hyphen. **B~wort** *nt* (*pl* -wörter)
(*Gram*) conjunction

Bind|faden *m* string. **B~ung** *f* -,
-en (*fig*) tie; (*Beziehung*) relationship;
(*Verpflichtung*) commitment; (*Ski-*)
binding; (*Tex*) weave

binnen *prep* (+ *dat*) within.
B~handel *m* home trade

Bio- *pref* organic

Bio|chemie *f* biochemistry.
b~dynamisch *m* organic.
B~graphie, B~grafie *f* -, -n
biography

Bio|hof *m* organic farm. **B~laden**
m health-food store

Biolog|e *m* -n, -n biologist. **B~ie** *f* -
biology. **b~isch** *a* biological;
b~ischer Anbau organic farming;
b~isch angebaut organically grown

Birke *f* -, -n birch [tree]

Birm|a *nt* -s Burma. **b~anisch** *a*
Burmese

Birn|baum *m* pear-tree. **B~e** *f* -, -n
pear; (*Electr*) bulb

bis *prep* (+ *acc*) as far as, [up] to;
(*zeitlich*) until, till; (*spätestens*) by;
bis zu up to; **bis auf** (+ *acc*)
(*einschließlich*) [down] to;
(*ausgenommen*) except [for]; **drei bis**
vier Mark three to four marks; **bis**
morgen! see you tomorrow! ● *conj*
until

Bischof *m* -s,-̈e bishop

bisher *adv* so far, up to now

Biskuit|rolle /bɪsˈkviːt-/ *f* Swiss roll. **B~teig** *m* sponge mixture

Biss *m* -es, -e bite

bisschen *inv pron* **ein b~** a bit, a little; **kein b~** not a bit

Biss|en *m* -s,- bite, mouthful. **b~ig** *a* vicious; (*fig*) caustic

bisweilen *adv* from time to time

bitt|e *adv* please; (*nach Klopfen*) come in; (*als Antwort auf 'danke'*) don't mention it, you're welcome; **wie b~e?** pardon? **B~e** *f* -, -n request/(*dringend*) plea (**um** for). **b~en†** *vt/i* (*haben*) ask/(*dringend*) beg (**um** for); (*einladen*) invite, ask. **b~end** *a* pleading

bitter *a* bitter. **B~keit** *f* - bitterness. **b~lich** *adv* bitterly

Bittschrift *f* petition

bizarr *a* bizarre

bläh|en *vt* swell; <*Vorhang, Segel:*> billow ● *vi* (*haben*) cause flatulence. **B~ungen** *fpl* flatulence *sg*, 🔲 wind *sg*

Blamage /blaˈmaːʒə/ *f* -, -n humiliation; (*Schande*) disgrace

blamieren *vt* disgrace; **sich b~** disgrace oneself; (*sich lächerlich machen*) make a fool of oneself

blanchieren /blɑ̃ˈʃiːrən/ *vt* (*Culin*) blanch

blank *a* shiny. **B~oscheck** *m* blank cheque

Blase *f* -, -n bubble; (*Med*) blister; (*Anat*) bladder. **b~n†** *vt/i* (*haben*) blow; play <*Flöte*>. **B~nentzündung** *f* cystitis

Blas|instrument *nt* wind instrument. **B~kapelle** *f* brass band

blass *a* pale; (*schwach*) faint

Blässe *f* - pallor

Blatt *nt* -[e]s,–̈er (*Bot*) leaf; (*Papier*) sheet; (*Zeitung*) paper

Blattlaus *f* greenfly

blau *a*, **B~** *nt* -s,- blue; **b~er Fleck** bruise; **b~es Auge** black eye; **b~ sein** 🔲 be tight; **Fahrt ins B~e**

mystery tour. **B~beere** *f* bilberry. **B~licht** *nt* blue flashing light

Blech *nt* -[e]s, -e sheet metal; (*Weiß-*) tin; (*Platte*) metal sheet; (*Back-*) baking sheet; (*Mus*) brass; (🔲 *Unsinn*) rubbish. **B~schaden** *m* (*Auto*) damage to the bodywork

Blei *nt* -[e]s lead

Bleibe *f* - place to stay. **b~n†** *vi* (*sein*) remain, stay; (*übrig-*) be left; **ruhig b~n** keep calm; **bei etw b~n** (*fig*) stick to sth; **b~n Sie am Apparat** hold the line; **etw b~n lassen** not to do sth. **b~nd** *a* permanent; (*anhaltend*) lasting

bleich *a* pale. **b~en†** *vi* (*sein*) bleach; (*ver-*) fade ● *vt* (*reg*) bleach. **B~mittel** *nt* bleach

blei|ern *a* leaden. **b~frei** *a* unleaded. **B~stift** *m* pencil. **B~stiftabsatz** *m* stiletto heel. **B~stiftspitzer** *m* -s,- pencil sharpener

Blende *f* -, -n shade, shield; (*Sonnen-*) [sun] visor; (*Phot*) diaphragm; (*Öffnung*) aperture; (*an Kleid*) facing. **b~n** *vt* dazzle, blind

Blick *m* -[e]s, -e look; (*kurz*) glance; (*Aussicht*) view; **auf den ersten B~** at first sight. **b~en** *vi* (*haben*) look/ (*kurz*) glance (**auf** + *acc* at). **B~punkt** *m* (*fig*) point of view

blind *a* blind; (*trübe*) dull; **b~er Alarm** false alarm; **b~er Passagier** stowaway. **B~darm** *m* appendix. **B~darmentzündung** *f* appendicitis. **B~e(r)** *m/f* blind man/woman; **die B~en** the blind *pl*. **B~enhund** *m* guidedog. **B~enschrift** *f* braille. **B~gänger** *m* -s,- (*Mil*) dud. **B~heit** *f* - blindness

blink|en *vi* (*haben*) flash; (*funkeln*) gleam; (*Auto*) indicate. **B~er** *m* -s,- (*Auto*) indicator. **B~licht** *nt* flashing light

blinzeln *vi* (*haben*) blink

Blitz *m* -es, -e [flash of] lightning; (*Phot*) flash. **B~ableiter** *m* lightning-conductor. **b~artig** *a* lightning ... ● *adv* like lightning. **b~en** *vi* (*haben*) flash; (*funkeln*) sparkle; **es hat geblitzt** there was a flash of lightning. **B~licht** nt (Phot) flash. **b~sauber** a spick and span. **b~schnell** a lightning ... ● adv like lightning

Block m -[e]s,⁻e block ● -[e]s, -s & ⁻e pad; (Häuser-) block

Blockade f -, -n blockade

Blockflöte f recorder

blockieren vt block; (Mil) blockade

Blockschrift f block letters pl

blöd[e] a feeble-minded; (dumm) stupid

Blödsinn m -[e]s idiocy; (Unsinn) nonsense

blöken vi (haben) bleat

blond a fair-haired; <Haar> fair

bloß a bare; (alleinig) mere ● adv only, just

bloß|legen vt sep uncover. **b~stellen** vt sep compromise

Bluff m -s, -s bluff. **b~en** vt/i (haben) bluff

blühen vi (haben) flower; (fig) flourish. **b~d** a flowering; (fig) flourishing, thriving

Blume f -, -n flower; (vom Wein) bouquet. **B~nbeet** nt flower-bed. **B~ngeschäft** nt flower-shop, florist's. **B~nkohl** m cauliflower. **B~nmuster** nt floral design. **B~nstrauß** m bunch of flowers. **B~ntopf** m flowerpot; (Pflanze) pot plant. **B~nzwiebel** f bulb

blumig a (fig) flowery

Bluse f -, -n blouse

Blut nt -[e]s blood. **b~arm** a anaemic. **B~bahn** f blood-stream. **B~bild** nt blood count. **B~druck** m blood pressure. **b~dürstig** a bloodthirsty

Blüte f -, -n flower, bloom; (vom Baum) blossom; (B~zeit) flowering period; (Baum-) blossom time; (Höhepunkt) peak, prime

Blut|egel m -s,- leech. **b~en** vi (haben) bleed

Blüten|blatt nt petal. **B~staub** m pollen

Blut|er m -s,- haemophiliac. **B~erguss** m bruise. **B~gefäß** nt

blood-vessel. **B~gruppe** f blood group. **b~ig** a bloody. **B~körperchen** nt -s,- corpuscle. **B~probe** f blood test. **b~rünstig** a (fig) bloody, gory. **B~schande** f incest. **B~spender** m blood donor. **B~sturz** m haemorrhage. **B~transfusion, B~übertragung** f blood transfusion. **B~ung** f -, -en bleeding; (Med) haemorrhage; (Regel-) period. **b~unterlaufen** a bruised; <Auge> bloodshot. **B~vergiftung** f blood-poisoning. **B~wurst** f black pudding

Bö f -, -en gust; (Regen-) squall

Bob m -s, -s bob[-sleigh]

Bock m -[e]s,⁻e buck; (Ziege) billy goat; (Schaf) ram; (Gestell) support. **b~ig** a 🔲 stubborn. **B~springen** nt leap-frog

Boden m -s,⁻ ground; (Erde) soil; (Fuß-) floor; (Grundfläche) bottom; (Dach-) loft, attic. **B~satz** m sediment. **B~schätze** mpl mineral deposits. **B~see** (der) Lake Constance

Bogen m -s,- & ⁻ curve; (Geom) arc; (beim Skilauf) turn; (Archit) arch; (Waffe, Geigen-) bow; (Papier) sheet; **einen großen B~ um jdn/etw machen** 🔲 give s.o./sth a wide berth. **B~schießen** nt archery

Bohle f -, -n [thick] plank

Böhm|en nt -s Bohemia. **b~isch** a Bohemian

Bohne f -, -n bean; **grüne B~n** French beans

bohner|n vt polish. **B~wachs** nt floor-polish

bohr|en vt/i (haben) drill (nach for); drive <Tunnel>; sink <Brunnen>; <Insekt:> bore. **B~er** m -s,- drill. **B~insel** f [offshore] drilling rig. **B~turm** m derrick

Boje f -, -n buoy

Böllerschuss m gun salute

Bolzen m -s,- bolt; (Stift) pin

bombardieren vt bomb; (fig) bombard (mit with)

Bombe f -, -n bomb. **B~nangriff** m bombing raid. **B~nerfolg** m huge success

Bon /bɔŋ/ m -s, -s voucher; (Kassen-) receipt

Bonbon /bɔŋ'bɔŋ/ m & nt -s, -s sweet

Bonus m -[sses], -[sse] bonus

Boot nt -[e]s, -e boat. **B~ssteg** m landing-stage

Bord[1] nt -[e]s, -e shelf

Bord[2] m (Naut) **an B~** aboard, on board; **über B~** overboard. **B~buch** nt log[-book]

Bordell nt -s, -e brothel

Bordkarte f boarding-pass

borgen vt borrow; **jdm etw b~** lend s.o. sth

Borke f -, -n bark

Börse f -, -n purse; (Comm) stock exchange. **B~nmakler** m stockbroker

Borst|e f -, -n bristle. **b~ig** a bristly

Borte f -, -n braid

Böschung f -, -en embankment

böse a wicked, evil; (unartig) naughty; (schlimm) bad; (zornig) cross; **jdm** od **auf jdn b~ sein** be cross with s.o.

bos|haft a malicious, spiteful. **B~heit** f -, -en malice; spite; (Handlung) spiteful act/(Bemerkung) remark

böswillig a malicious

Botani|k f - botany. **B~ker(in)** m -s,- (f -, -nen) botanist

Bot|e m -n, -n messenger. **B~engang** m errand. **B~schaft** f -, -en message; (Pol) embassy. **B~schafter** m -s,- ambassador

Bouillon /bʊl'jɔŋ/ f -, -s clear soup. **B~würfel** m stock cube

Bowle /'boːlə/ f -, -n punch

box|en vi (haben) box ● vt punch. **B~en** nt -s boxing. **B~er** m -s,- boxer

brachliegen† vi sep (haben) lie fallow

Branche /'brã:ʃə/ f -, -n [line of] business. **B~nverzeichnis** nt (Teleph) classified directory

Brand m -[e]s,-̈e fire; (Med) gangrene; (Bot) blight; **in B~ geraten** catch fire; **in B~ setzen** od **stecken** set on fire. **B~bombe** f incendiary bomb

Brand|stifter m arsonist. **B~stiftung** f arson

Brandung f - surf

Brand|wunde f burn. **B~zeichen** nt brand

Branntwein m spirit; (coll) spirits pl. **B~brennerei** f distillery

bras|ilianisch a Brazilian. **B~ilien** /-iən/ nt -s Brazil

Brat|apfel m baked apple. **b~en**† vt/i (haben) roast; (in der Pfanne) fry. **B~en** m -s,- roast; (B~stück) joint. **b~fertig** a oven-ready. **B~hähnchen** nt roasting chicken. **B~kartoffeln** fpl fried potatoes. **B~pfanne** f frying-pan

Bratsche f -, -n (Mus) viola

Bratspieß m spit

Brauch m -[e]s,Bräuche custom. **b~bar** a usable; (nützlich) useful. **b~en** vt need; (ge-, verbrauchen) use; take <Zeit>; **er b~t es nur zu sagen** he only has to say

Braue f -, -n eyebrow

brau|en vt brew. **B~er** m -s,- brewer. **B~erei** f -, -en brewery

braun a, **B~** nt -s,- brown; **b~ werden** <Person:> get a tan; **b~ [gebrannt] sein** be [sun-]tanned

Bräune f - [sun-]tan. **b~n** vt/i (haben) brown; (in der Sonne) tan

Braunschweig nt -s Brunswick

Brause f -, -n (Dusche) shower; (an Gießkanne) rose; (B~limonade) fizzy drink

Braut f -,-̈e bride; (Verlobte) fiancée

Bräutigam m -s, -e bridegroom; (Verlobter) fiancé

Brautkleid nt wedding dress

Brautpaar nt bridal couple; (Verlobte) engaged couple

brav a good; (redlich) honest ● adv dutifully; (redlich) honestly

bravo *int* bravo!

BRD *abbr* (Bundesrepublik Deutschland) FRG

Brech|eisen *nt* jemmy; (*B∼stange*) crowbar. **b∼en**† *vt* break; (*Phys*) refract <*Licht*>; (*erbrechen*) vomit; **sich b∼en** <*Wellen:*> break; <*Licht:*> be refracted; **sich** (*dat*) **den Arm b∼en** break one's arm ● *vi* (*sein*) break ● *vi* (*haben*) vomit, be sick. **B∼reiz** *m* nausea. **B∼stange** *f* crowbar

Brei *m* -[e]s, -e paste; (*Culin*) purée; (*Hafer-*) porridge

breit *a* wide; <*Schultern, Grinsen*> broad. **B∼e** *f* -, -n width; breadth; (*Geog*) latitude. **b∼en** *vt* spread (**über** + *acc* over). **B∼engrad** *m* [degree of] latitude. **B∼enkreis** *m* parallel

Bremse[1] *f* -, -n horsefly

Bremse[2] *f* -, -n brake. **b∼n** *vt* slow down; (*fig*) restrain ● *vi* (*haben*) brake

Bremslicht *nt* brake-light

brenn|bar *a* combustible; **leicht b∼bar** highly [in]flammable. **b∼en**† *vi* (*haben*) burn; <*Licht:*> be on; <*Zigarette:*> be alight; (*weh tun*) smart, sting ● *vt* burn; (*rösten*) roast; (*im Brennofen*) fire; (*destillieren*) distil. **b∼end** *a* burning; (*angezündet*) lighted; (*fig*) fervent **B∼erei** *f* -, -en distillery

Brennessel* *f s.* Brennnessel

Brenn|holz *nt* firewood. **B∼ofen** *m* kiln. **B∼nessel** *f* stinging nettle. **B∼punkt** *m* (*Phys*) focus. **B∼spiritus** *m* methylated spirits. **B∼stoff** *m* fuel

Bretagne /bre'tanjə/ (die) - Brittany

Brett *nt* -[e]s, -er board; (*im Regal*) shelf; **schwarzes B∼** notice board. **B∼spiel** *nt* board game

Brezel *f* -, -n pretzel

Bridge /brɪtʃ/ *nt* - (*Spiel*) bridge

Brief *m* -[e]s, -e letter. **B∼beschwerer** *m* -s,- paperweight. **B∼freund(in)** *m(f)* penfriend. **B∼kasten** *m* letter-box. **B∼kopf** *m* letter-head. **b∼lich** *a &*

adv by letter. **B∼marke** *f* [postage] stamp. **B∼öffner** *m* paper-knife. **B∼papier** *nt* notepaper. **B∼tasche** *f* wallet. **B∼träger** *m* postman. **B∼umschlag** *m* envelope. **B∼wahl** *f* postal vote. **B∼wechsel** *m* correspondence

Brikett *nt* -s, -s briquette

Brillant *m* -en, -en [cut] diamond

Brille *f* -, -n glasses *pl*, spectacles *pl*; (*Schutz-*) goggles *pl*; (*Klosett-*) toilet seat

bringen† *vt* bring; (*fort-*) take; (*ein-*) yield; (*veröffentlichen*) publish; (*im Radio*) broadcast; show <*Film*>; **ins Bett b∼** put to bed; **jdn nach Hause b∼** take/(*begleiten*) see s.o. home; **um etw b∼** deprive of sth; **jdn dazu b∼, etw zu tun** get s.o. to do sth; **es weit b∼** (*fig*) go far

Brise *f* -, -n breeze

Brit|e *m* -n, -n, **B∼in** *f* -, -nen Briton. **b∼isch** *a* British

Bröck|chen *nt* -s,- (*Culin*) crouton. **b∼elig** *a* crumbly; <*Gestein*> friable. **b∼eln** *vt/i* (*haben/sein*) crumble

Brocken *m* -s,- chunk; (*Erde, Kohle*) lump

Brokat *m* -[e]s, -e brocade

Brokkoli *pl* broccoli *sg*

Brombeere *f* blackberry

Bronchitis *f* - bronchitis

Bronze /'brõːsə/ *f* -, -n bronze

Brosch|e *f* -, -n brooch. **b∼iert** *a* paperback. **B∼üre** *f* -, -n brochure; (*Heft*) booklet

Brösel *mpl* (*Culin*) breadcrumbs

Brot *n* -[e]s, -e bread; **ein B∼** a loaf [of bread]; (*Scheibe*) a slice of bread

Brötchen *n* -s,- [bread] roll

Brotkrümel *m* breadcrumb

Bruch *m* -[e]s, ̈-e break; (*Brechen*) breaking; (*Rohr-*) burst; (*Med*) fracture; (*Eingeweide-*) rupture, hernia; (*Math*) fraction; (*fig*) breach; (*in Beziehung*) break-up

brüchig *a* brittle

Bruch|landung *f* crash-landing. **B∼rechnung** *f* fractions *pl*.

B~stück nt fragment. **B~teil** m fraction

Brücke f -, -n bridge; (Teppich) rug

Bruder m -s,- brother

brüderlich a brotherly, fraternal

Brügge nt -s Bruges

Brüh|e f -, -n broth, stock. **B~würfel** m stock cube

brüllen vt/i (haben) roar

brumm|eln vt/i (haben) mumble. **b~en** vi (haben) <Insekt:> buzz; <Bär:> growl; <Motor:> hum; (murren) grumble **B~er** m -s,- ☐ bluebottle. **b~ig** a ☐ grumpy

brünett a dark-haired

Brunnen m -s,- well; (Spring-) fountain; (Heil-) spa water

brüsk a brusque

Brüssel nt -s Brussels

Brust f -,-̈e chest; (weibliche, Culin: B~stück) breast. **B~bein** nt breastbone

brüsten (sich) vr boast

Brust|fellentzündung f pleurisy. **B~schwimmen** nt breaststroke

Brüstung f -, -en parapet

Brustwarze f nipple

Brut f -, -en incubation

brutal a brutal

brüten vi (haben) sit (on eggs); (fig) ponder (über + dat over)

Brutkasten m (Med) incubator

brutto adv, **B~-** pref gross

Bub m -en, -en (SGer) boy. **B~e** m -n, -n (Karte) jack, knave

Buch nt -[e]s,-̈er book; **B~ führen** keep a record (über + acc of); **die B~-̈er führen** keep the accounts

Buche f -, -n beech

buchen vt book; (Comm) enter

Bücher|ei f -,-en library. **B~regal** nt bookcase, bookshelves pl. **B~schrank** m bookcase

Buchfink m chaffinch

Buch|führung f bookkeeping. **B~halter(in)** m -s,- (f -, -nen) bookkeeper, accountant. **B~haltung** f bookkeeping,

accountancy; (Abteilung) accounts department. **B~handlung** f bookshop

Büchse f -, -n box; (Konserven-) tin, can

Buch|stabe m -n, -n letter. **b~stabieren** vt spell [out]. **b~stäblich** adv literally

Bucht f -, -en (Geog) bay

Buchung f -, -en booking, reservation; (Comm) entry

Buckel m -s,- hump; (Beule) bump; (Hügel) hillock

bücken (sich) vr bend down

bucklig a hunchbacked

Bückling m -s, -e smoked herring

Buddhis|mus m - Buddhism. **B~t(in)** m -en, -en (f -, -nen) Buddhist. **b~tisch** a Buddhist

Bude f -, -n hut; (Kiosk) kiosk; (Markt-) stall; (☐ Zimmer) room

Budget /by'dʒe:/ nt -s, -s budget

Büfett nt -[e]s, -e sideboard; (Theke) bar; **kaltes B~** cold buffet

Büffel m -s,- buffalo

Bügel m -s,- frame; (Kleider-) coathanger; (Steig-) stirrup; (Brillen-) sidepiece. **B~brett** nt ironing-board. **B~eisen** nt iron. **B~falte** f crease. **b~frei** a non-iron. **b~n** vt/i (haben) iron

Bühne f -, -n stage. **B~nbild** nt set. **B~neingang** m stage door

Buhrufe mpl boos

Bukett nt -[e]s, -e bouquet

Bulgarien /-iən/ nt -s Bulgaria

Bull|auge nt (Naut) porthole. **B~dogge** f bulldog. **B~dozer** /-do:zɐ/ m -s,- bulldozer. **B~e** m -n, -n bull; (☒ Polizist) cop

Bummel m -s,- ☐ stroll. **B~lei** f - ☐ dawdling

bummel|ig a ☐ slow; (nachlässig) careless. **b~n** vi (sein) ☐ stroll ● vi (haben) ☐ dawdle. **B~streik** m go-slow. **B~zug** m ☐ slow train

Bums m -es, -e ☐ bump, thump

Bund[1] nt -[e]s, -e bunch

Bund[2] m -[e]s,-̈e association; (Bündnis) alliance; (Pol) federation;

(*Rock-, Hosen-*) waistband; der B∼ the Federal Government

Bündel *nt* -s,- bundle. **b∼n** *vt* bundle [up]

Bundes|- *pref* Federal. **B∼genosse** *m* ally. **B∼kanzler** *m* Federal Chancellor. **B∼land** *nt* [federal] state; (*Aust*) province. **B∼liga** *f* German national league. **B∼rat** *m* Upper House of Parliament. **B∼regierung** *f* Federal Government. **B∼republik** *f* die B∼republik Deutschland the Federal Republic of Germany. **B∼tag** *m* Lower House of Parliament. **B∼wehr** *f* [Federal German] Army

bünd|ig *a & adv* kurz und b∼ig short and to the point. **B∼nis** *nt* -sses, -sse alliance

Bunker *m* -s,- bunker; (*Luftschutz-*) shelter

bunt *a* coloured; (*farbenfroh*) colourful; (*grell*) gaudy; (*gemischt*) varied; (*wirr*) confused; **b∼e Platte** assorted cold meats. **B∼stift** *m* crayon

Bürde *f* -, -n (*fig*) burden

Burg *f* -, -en castle

Bürge *m* -n, -n guarantor. **b∼n** *vi* (*haben*) b∼n für vouch for; (*fig*) guarantee

Bürger|(in) *m* -s,- (*f* -, -nen) citizen. **B∼krieg** *m* civil war. **b∼lich** *a* civil; <*Pflicht*> civic; (*mittelständisch*) middle-class. **B∼liche(r)** *m/f* commoner. **B∼meister** *m* mayor. **B∼rechte** *npl* civil rights. **B∼steig** *m* -[e]s, -e pavement

Bürgschaft *f* -, -en surety

Burgunder *m* -s,- (*Wein*) Burgundy

Büro *nt* -s, -s office. **B∼angestellte(r)** *m/f* office-worker. **B∼klammer** *f* paper-clip. **B∼kratie** *f* -, -n bureaucracy. **b∼kratisch** *a* bureaucratic

Bursche *m* -n, -n lad, youth

Bürste *f* -, -n brush. **b∼n** *vt* brush. **B∼nschnitt** *m* crew cut

Bus *m* -ses, -se bus; (*Reise-*) coach

Busch *m* -[e]s,-̈e bush

Büschel *nt* -s,- tuft

buschig *a* bushy

Busen *m* -s,- bosom

Bussard *m* -s, -e buzzard

Buße *f* -, -n penance; (*Jur*) fine

Bußgeld *nt* (*Jur*) fine

Büste *f* -, -n bust; (*Schneider-*) dummy. **B∼nhalter** *m* -s,- bra

Butter *f* - butter. **B∼blume** *f* buttercup. **B∼brot** *nt* slice of bread and butter. **B∼milch** *f* buttermilk. **b∼n** *vt* butter

b.w. *abbr* (**bitte wenden**) P.T.O.

Cc

ca. *abbr* (**circa**) about

Café /ka'fe:/ *nt* -s, -s café

camp|en /'kɛmpən/ *vi* (*haben*) go camping. **C∼ing** *nt* -s camping. **C∼ingplatz** *m* campsite

Caravan /'ka[:]ravan/ *m* -s, -s (*Auto*) caravan; (*Kombi*) estate car

CD /ts:e:'de:/ *f* -, -s compact disc, CD. **CD-ROM** /ts:e:de:'rɔm/ *f* -,-(s) CD-ROM

Cell|ist(in) /tʃɛ'lɪst(ɪn)/ *m* -en, -en (*f* -, -nen) cellist. **C∼o** /'tʃɛlo/ *nt* -, -los & -li cello

Celsius /'tsɛlzɪʊs/ *inv* Celsius, centigrade

Champagner /ʃam'panjɐ/ *m* -s champagne

Champignon /'ʃampɪnjɔŋ/ *m* -s, -s [field] mushroom

Chance /'ʃãːs[ə]/ *f* -, -n chance

Chaos /'kaːɔs/ *nt* - chaos

Charakter /ka'raktɐ/ *m* -s, -e /-'teːrə/ character. **c∼isieren** *vt* characterize. **c∼istisch** *a* characteristic (für of)

charm|ant /ʃar'mant/ *a* charming. **C∼e** /ʃarm/ *m* -s charm

Charter|flug /'tʃ-, 'ʃartɐ-/ *m* charter flight. **c∼n** *vt* charter

Chassis /ʃa'si:/ *nt* -,- /-'si:[s], -'si:s/ chassis

Chauffeur /ʃɔ'føːɐ/ *m* -s, -e chauffeur; (*Taxi-*) driver

Chauvinist /ʃovi'nɪst/ *m* -en, -en chauvinist

Chef /ʃɛf/ *m* -s, -s head; 🄵 boss

Chemie /çe'mi:/ *f* - chemistry

Chem|iker(in) /'çe:-/ *m* -s,- (*f* -, -nen) chemist. **c∼isch** *a* chemical; **c∼ische Reinigung** dry-cleaning; (*Geschäft*) dry-cleaner's

Chicorée /'ʃɪkore:/ *m* -s chicory

Chiffre /'ʃɪfɐ, 'ʃɪfrə/ *f* -, -n cipher

Chile /'çi:le/ *nt* -s Chile

Chin|a /'çi:na/ *nt* -s China. **C∼ese** *m* -n, -n, **C∼esin** *f* -, -nen Chinese. **c∼esisch** *a* Chinese. **C∼esisch** *nt* -[s] (*Lang*) Chinese

Chip /tʃɪp/ *m* -s, -s [micro]chip. **C∼s** *pl* crisps

Chirurg /çi'rʊrk/ *m* -en, -en surgeon. **C∼ie** /-'gi:/ *f* - surgery

Chlor /kloːɐ/ *nt* -s chlorine

Choke /tʃoːk/ *m* -s, -s (*Auto*) choke

Cholera /'koːlera/ *f* - cholera

cholerisch /koˈleːrɪʃ/ *a* irascible

Cholesterin /ço-, kolɛste'riːn/ *nt* -s cholesterol

Chor /koːɐ/ *m* -[e]s,⁓e choir

Choreographie, Choreografie /koreogra'fi:/ *f* -, -n choreography

Christ /krɪst/ *m* -en, -en Christian. **C∼baum** *m* Christmas tree. **C∼entum** *nt* -s Christianity **c∼lich** *a* Christian

Christus /'krɪstʊs/ *m* -ti Christ

Chrom /kroːm/ *nt* -s chromium

Chromosom /kromo'zoːm/ *nt* -s, -en chromosome

Chronik /'kroːnɪk/ *f* -, -en chronicle

chronisch /'kroːnɪʃ/ *a* chronic

Chrysantheme /kryzan'teːmə/ *f* -, -n chrysanthemum

circa /'tsɪrka/ *adv* about

Clique /'klɪkə/ *f* -, -n clique

Clou /klu:/ *m* -s, -s highlight, 🄵 high spot

Clown /klauːn/ *m* -s, -s clown

Club /klʊp/ *m* -s, -s club

Cocktail /'kɔkteːl/ *m* -s, -s cocktail

Code /'koːt/ *m* -s, -s code

Comic-Heft /'kɔmɪk-/ *nt* comic

Computer /kɔm'pjuːtɐ/ *m* -s,- computer. **c∼isieren** *vt* computerize. **C∼spiel** *nt* computer game

Conférencier /kõ'feræ'sie:/ *m* -s,- compère

Cord /kɔrt/ *m* -s, **C∼samt** *m* corduroy

Couch /kautʃ/ *f* -, -es settee

Cousin /ku'zɛ̃:/ *m* -s, -s [male] cousin. **C∼e** /-'ziːnə/ *f* -, -n [female] cousin

Creme /kreːm/ *f* -s, -s cream; (*Speise*) cream dessert

Curry /'kari, 'kœri/ *nt & m* -s curry powder ● *nt* -s, -s (*Gericht*) curry

Dd

da *adv* there; (*hier*) here; (*zeitlich*) then; (*in dem Fall*) in that case; **von da an** from then on; **da sein** be there/(*hier*) here; (*existieren*) exist; **wieder da sein** be back ● *conj* as, since

dabei (*emphatic*: **dabei**) *adv* nearby; (*daran*) with it; (*eingeschlossen*) included; (*hinsichtlich*) about it; (*währenddem*) during this; (*gleichzeitig*) at the same time; (*doch*) and yet; **dicht d∼** close by; **d∼ sein** be present; (*mitmachen*) be involved; **d∼ sein, etw zu tun** be just doing sth

Dach *nt* -[e]s,⁓er roof. **D∼boden** *m* loft. **D∼luke** *f* skylight. **D∼rinne** *f* gutter

Dachs *m* -es, -e badger

Dachsparren *m* -s,- rafter

Dackel *m* -s,- dachshund

dadurch (*emphatic:* **da**durch) *adv* through it/them; (*Ursache*) by it; (*deshalb*) because of that; **d~, dass** because

dafür (*emphatic:* **da**für) *adv* for it/ them; (*anstatt*) instead; (*als Ausgleich*) but [on the other hand]; **d~, dass** considering that; **ich kann nichts dafür** it's not my fault

dagegen (*emphatic:* **da**gegen) *adv* against it/them; (*Mittel, Tausch*) for it; (*verglichen damit*) by comparison; (*jedoch*) however; **hast du was d~?** do you mind?

daheim *adv* at home

daher (*emphatic:* **da**her) *adv* from there; (*deshalb*) for that reason; **das kommt d~, weil** that's because ● *conj* that is why

dahin (*emphatic:* **da**hin) *adv* there; **bis d~** up to there; (*bis dann*) until/ (*Zukunft*) by then; **jdn d~bringen, dass er etw tut** get s.o. to do sth

dahinten *adv* back there

dahinter (*emphatic:* **da**hinter) *adv* behind it/them; **d~ kommen** (*fig*) get to the bottom of it

Dahlie /-iə/ *f* -, -n dahlia

dalassen† *vt sep* leave there

daliegen† *vi sep* (*haben*) lie there

damalig *a* at that time; **der d~e Minister** the then minister

damals *adv* at that time

Damast *m* -es, -e damask

Dame *f* -, -n lady; (*Karte, Schach*) queen; (*D~spiel*) draughts *sg*. **d~nhaft** *a* ladylike

damit (*emphatic:* **da**mit) *adv* with it/ them; (*dadurch*) by it; **hör auf d~!** stop it! ● *conj* so that

Damm *m* -[e]s,~e dam

dämmer|ig *a* dim. **D~licht** *nt* twilight. **d~n** *vi* (*haben*) <*Morgen:*> dawn; **es d~t** it is getting light/(*abends*) dark. **D~ung** *f* dawn; (*Abend-*) dusk

Dämon *m* -s, -en /-'mo:nən/ demon

Dampf *m* -es,~e steam; (*Chem*) vapour. **d~en** *vi* (*haben*) steam

dämpfen *vt* (*Culin*) steam; (*fig*) muffle <*Ton*>; lower <*Stimme*>

Dampf|er *m* -s,- steamer. **D~kochtopf** *m* pressure-cooker. **D~maschine** *f* steam engine. **D~walze** *f* steamroller

danach (*emphatic:* **da**nach) *adv* after it/them; <*suchen*> for it/them; <*riechen*> of it; (*später*) afterwards; (*entsprechend*) accordingly; **es sieht d~ aus** it looks like it

Däne *m* -n, -n Dane

daneben (*emphatic:* **da**neben) *adv* beside it/them; (*außerdem*) in addition; (*verglichen damit*) by comparison

Dän|emark *nt* -s Denmark. **D~in** *f* -, -nen Dane. **d~isch** *a* Danish

Dank *m* -es thanks *pl*; **vielen D~!** thank you very much! **d~** *prep* (+ *dat or gen*) thanks to. **d~bar** *a* grateful; (*erleichtert*) thankful; (*lohnend*) rewarding. **D~barkeit** *f* - gratitude. **d~e** *adv* **d~e** [schön *od* sehr]! thank you [very much]! **d~en** *vi* (*haben*) thank (**jdm** s.o.); (*ablehnen*) decline; **nichts zu d~en!** don't mention it!

dann *adv* then; **selbst d~, wenn** even if

daran (*emphatic:* **da**ran) *adv* on it/ them; at it/them; <*denken*> of it; **nahe d~** on the point (etw zu tun of doing sth). **d~setzen** *vt sep* alles d~setzen do one's utmost (zu to)

darauf (*emphatic:* **da**rauf) *adv* on it/ them; <*warten*> for it; <*antworten*> to it; (*danach*) after that; (*d~hin*) as a result. **d~hin** *adv* as a result

daraus (*emphatic:* **da**raus) *adv* out of or from it/them; **er macht sich nichts d~** he doesn't care for it

darlegen *vt sep* expound; (*erklären*) explain

Darlehen *nt* -s,- loan

Darm *m* -[e]s,~e intestine

darstell|en *vt sep* represent; (*bildlich*) portray; (*Theat*) interpret; (*spielen*) play; (*schildern*) describe. **D~er** *m* -s,- actor. **D~erin** *f* -, -nen actress. **D~ung** *f* representation; interpretation; description

darüber (*emphatic:* **darüber**) *adv* over it/them; (*höher*) above it/them; <*sprechen, lachen, sich freuen*> about it; (*mehr*) more; **d∼ hinaus** beyond [it]; (*dazu*) on top of that

darum (*emphatic:* **darum**) *adv* round it/them; <*bitten, kämpfen*> for it; (*deshalb*) that is why; **d∼, weil** because

darunter (*emphatic:* **darunter**) *adv* under it/them; (*tiefer*) below it/them; (*weniger*) less; (*dazwischen*) among them

das *def art & pron s.* **der**

dasein* *vi sep* (*sein*) **da sein,** *s.* **da. D∼** *nt* **-s** existence

dass *conj* that

dasselbe *pron s.* **derselbe**

Daten|sichtgerät *nt* visual display unit, VDU. **D∼verarbeitung** *f* data processing

datieren *vt/i* (*haben*) date

Dativ *m* **-s, -e** dative. **D∼objekt** *nt* indirect object

Dattel *f* **-, -n** date

Datum *nt* **s, -ten** date; **Daten** dates; (*Angaben*) data

Dauer *f* **-** duration, length; (*Jur*) term; **auf die D∼** in the long run. **D∼auftrag** *m* standing order. **d∼haft** *a* lasting, enduring; (*fest*) durable. **D∼karte** *f* season ticket. **d∼n** *vi* (*haben*) last; **lange d∼n** take a long time. **d∼nd** *a* lasting; (*ständig*) constant. **D∼welle** *f* perm

Daumen *m* **-s,-** thumb; **jdm den D∼ drücken** *od* **halten** keep one's fingers crossed for s.o.

Daunen *fpl* down *sg.* **D∼decke** *f* [down-filled] duvet

davon (*emphatic:* **davon**) *adv* from it/them; (*dadurch*) by it; (*damit*) with it/them; (*darüber*) about it; (*Menge*) of it/them; **das kommt d∼!** it serves you right! **d∼kommen†** *vi sep* (*sein*) escape (**mit dem Leben** with one's life). **d∼laufen†** *vi sep* (*sein*) run away. **d∼machen** (**sich**) *vr sep* Ⓘ make off. **d∼tragen†** *vt sep*

carry off; (*erleiden*) suffer; (*gewinnen*) win

davor (*emphatic:* **davor**) *adv* in front of it/them; <*sich fürchten*> of it; (*zeitlich*) before it/them

dazu (*emphatic:* **dazu**) *adv* to it/them; (*damit*) with it/them; (*dafür*) for it; **noch d∼** in addition to that; **jdn d∼ bringen, etw zu tun** get s.o. to do sth; **ich kam nicht d∼** I didn't get round to [doing] it. **d∼kommen†** *vi sep* (*sein*) arrive [on the scene]; (*hinzukommen*) be added. **d∼rechnen** *vt sep* add to it/them

dazwischen (*emphatic:* **dazwischen**) *adv* between them; in between; (*darunter*) among them. **d∼kommen†** *vi sep* (*sein*) (*fig*) crop up; **wenn nichts d∼kommt** if all goes well

Debat|te *f* **-, -n** debate; **zur D∼te stehen** be at issue. **d∼tieren** *vt/i* (*haben*) debate

Debüt /de'by:/ *nt* **-s, -s** début

Deck *nt* **-[e]s, -s** (*Naut*) deck; **an D∼** on deck. **D∼bett** *nt* duvet

Decke *f* **-, -n** cover; (*Tisch-*) tablecloth; (*Bett-*) blanket; (*Reise-*) rug; (*Zimmer-*) ceiling; **unter einer D∼stecken** Ⓘ be in league

Deckel *m* **-s,-** lid; (*Flaschen-*) top; (*Buch-*) cover

decken *vt* cover; tile <*Dach*>; lay <*Tisch*>; (*schützen*) shield; (*Sport*) mark; meet <*Bedarf*>; **jdn d∼** (*fig*) cover up for s.o.; **sich d∼** (*fig*) cover oneself (**gegen** against); (*übereinstimmen*) coincide

Deckname *m* pseudonym

Deckung *f* **-** (*Mil*) cover; (*Sport*) defence; (*Mann-*) marking; (*Boxen*) guard; (*Sicherheit*) security; **in D∼ gehen** take cover

defin|ieren *vt* define. **D∼ition** /-'tsio:n/ *f* **-, -en** definition

Defizit *nt* **-s, -e** deficit

deformiert *a* deformed

deftig *a* Ⓘ <*Mahlzeit*> hearty; <*Witz*> coarse

Degen *m* **-s,-** sword; (*Fecht-*) épée

degeneriert *a* (*fig*) degenerate

---

degradieren vt (Mil) demote; (fig) degrade

dehn|bar a elastic. **d~en** vt stretch; lengthen <Vokal>; sich **d~en** stretch

Deich m -[e]s, -e dike

dein poss pron your. **d~e(r,s)** poss pron yours; **die D~en** od **d~en** pl your family sg. **d~erseits** adv for your part. **d~etwegen** adv for your sake; (wegen dir) because of you, on your account. **d~etwillen** adv um **d~etwillen** for your sake. **d~ige** poss pron der/die/das **d~ige** yours. **d~s** poss pron yours

Dekan m -s, -e dean

Deklin|ation /-'tsio:n/ f -, -en declension. **d~ieren** vt decline

Dekolleté, Dekolletee /dekɔl'te:/ nt -s, -s low neckline

Dekor m & nt -s decoration. **D~ateur** /-'tø:ɐ/ m -s, -e interior decorator; (Schaufenster-) window-dresser. **D~ation** /-'tsio:n/ f -, -en decoration; (Schaufenster-) window-dressing; (Auslage) display. **d~ativ** a decorative. **d~ieren** vt decorate; dress <Schaufenster>

Deleg|ation /-'tsio:n/ f -, -en delegation. **D~ierte(r)** m/f delegate

delikat a delicate; (lecker) delicious; (taktvoll) tactful. **D~essengeschäft** nt delicatessen

Delikt nt -[e]s, -e offence

Delinquent m -en, -en offender

Delle f -, -n dent

Delphin m -s, -e dolphin

Delta nt -s, -s delta

dem def art & pron s. der

dementieren vt deny

dem|entsprechend a corresponding; (passend) appropriate ● adv accordingly; (passend) appropriately. **d~nächst** adv soon; (in Kürze) shortly

Demokrat m -en, -en democrat. **D~ie** f -, -n democracy. **d~isch** a democratic

demolieren vt wreck

Demonstr|ant m -en, -en demonstrator. **D~ation** /-'tsio:n/ f

-, -en demonstration. **d~ieren** vt/i (haben) demonstrate

demontieren vt dismantle

Demoskopie f - opinion research

Demut f - humility

den def art & pron s. der. **d~en** pron s. der

denk|bar a conceivable. **d~en†** vt/i (haben) think (**an** + acc of); (sich erinnern) remember (**an etw** acc sth); **das kann ich mir d~en** I can imagine [that]; **ich d~e nicht daran** I have no intention of doing it. **D~mal** nt memorial; (Monument) monument. **d~würdig** a memorable

denn conj for; **besser/mehr d~ je** better/more than ever ● adv **wie/wo d~?** but how/where? **warum d~ nicht?** why ever not? **es sei d~ [, dass]** unless

dennoch adv nevertheless

Denunz|iant m -en, -en informer. **d~ieren** vt denounce

Deodorant nt -s, -s deodorant

deplaciert, deplatziert /-'tsi:ɐt/ a (fig) out of place

Deponie f -, -n dump. **d~ren** vt deposit

deportieren vt deport

Depot /de'po:/ nt -s, -s depot; (Lager) warehouse; (Bank-) safe deposit

Depression f -, -en depression

deprimieren vt depress

---

der, die, das, pl **die**

● definite article

(acc **den, die, das,** pl **die**; gen **des, der, des,** pl **der**; dat **dem, der, dem,** pl **den**)

····▸ the. **der Mensch** the person; (als abstrakter Begriff) man. **die Natur** nature. **das Leben** life. **das Lesen/ Tanzen** reading/dancing. **sich** (dat) **das Gesicht/die Hände waschen** wash one's face/hands. **5 Mark das Pfund** 5 marks a pound

● pronoun

(acc **den, die, das,** pl **die**; gen **dessen, deren, dessen,** pl **deren**; dat **dem, der, dem,** pl **denen**)

● *demonstrative pronoun*
····▸ that; (*pl*) those
····▸ (*attributiv*) **der Mann war es** it
was 'that man
····▸ (*substantivisch*) he, she, it; (*pl*)
they. **der war es** it was 'him. **die da**
(*person*) that woman/girl; (*thing*)
that one

● *relative pronoun*
····▸ (*Person*) who. **der Mann, der/
dessen Sohn hier arbeitet** the man
who/whose son works here. **die Frau,
mit der ich Tennis spiele** the woman
with whom I play tennis, the woman
I play tennis with. **das Mädchen, das
ich gestern sah** the girl I saw
yesterday
····▸ (*Ding*) which, that. **ich sah ein
Buch, das mich interessierte** I saw a
book that interested me. **die CD, die
ich mir anhöre** the CD I am listening
to. **das Auto, mit dem wir nach
Deutschland fahren** the car we are
going to Germany in *or* in which we
are going to Germany

derb *a* tough; (*kräftig*) strong; (*grob*)
coarse; (*unsanft*) rough

deren *pron s.* der

dergleichen *inv a* such ● *pron*
such a thing/such things

der-/die-/dasselbe, *pl*
dieselben *pron* the same; **ein- und
dasselbe** one and the same thing

derzeit *adv* at present

des *def art s.* der

Desert|eur /-ˈtøːɐ̯/ *m* -s, -e deserter.
d~ieren *vi* (*sein/haben*) desert

desgleichen *adv* likewise ● *pron*
the like

deshalb *adv* for this reason; (*also*)
therefore

Designer(in) /diˈzaɪnɐ, -nərɪn/ *m*
-s,- (*f*, -, -nen) designer

Desin|fektion /dɛsʔɪnfɛkˈtsi̯oːn/ *f*
disinfecting. **D~fektionsmittel** *nt*
disinfectant. **d~fizieren** *vt* disinfect

dessen *pron s.* der

Destill|ation /-ˈtsi̯oːn/ *f* -
distillation. **d~ieren** *vt* distil

desto *adv* **je mehr d~ besser** the
more the better

deswegen *adv* = deshalb

Detektiv *m* -s, -e detective

Deton|ation /-ˈtsi̯oːn/ *f* -, -en
explosion. **d~ieren** *vi* (*sein*) explode

deut|en *vt* interpret; predict
<*Zukunft*> ● *vi* (*haben*) point (**auf** +
acc at/(*fig*) to). **d~lich** *a* clear;
(*eindeutig*) plain

deutsch *a* German. **D~** *nt* -[s]
(*Lang*) German; **auf D~** in German.
D~e(r) *m/f* German. **D~land** *nt* -s
Germany

Deutung *f* -, -en interpretation

Devise *f* -, -n motto. **D~n** *pl* foreign
currency *or* exchange *sg*

Dezember *m* -s,- December

dezent *a* unobtrusive; (*diskret*)
discreet

Dezernat *nt* -[e]s, -e department

Dezimalzahl *f* decimal

d.h. *abbr* (*das heißt*) i.e.

Dia *nt* -s, -s (*Phot*) slide

Diabet|es *m* - diabetes. **D~iker** *m*
-s,- diabetic

Diadem *nt* -s, -e tiara

Diagnose *f* -, -n diagnosis

diagonal *a* diagonal. **D~e** *f* -, -n
diagonal

Diagramm *nt* -s, -e diagram;
(*Kurven-*) graph

Diakon *m* -s, -e deacon

Dialekt *m* -[e]s, -e dialect

Dialog *m* -[e]s, -e dialogue

Diamant *m* -en, -en diamond

Diapositiv *nt* -s, -e (*Phot*) slide

Diaprojektor *m* slide projector

Diät *f* -, -en (*Med*) diet; **D~ leben** be
on a diet

dich *pron* (*acc of* du) you; (*refl*)
yourself

dicht *a* dense; (*dick*) thick;
(*undurchlässig*) airtight; (*wasser-*)
watertight ● *adv* densely; (*nahe*)
close (**bei** to). **D~e** density. **d~en¹**
vt make watertight

dicht|en² *vi* (*haben*) write poetry.
● *vt* write. **D~er(in)** *m* -s,- (*f* -, -en)

poet. **d~erisch** *a* poetic. **D~ung¹** *f* -, -en poetry; (*Gedicht*) poem

Dichtung² *f* -, -en seal; (*Ring*) washer; (*Auto*) gasket

dick *a* thick; (*beleibt*) fat; (*geschwollen*) swollen; (*fam; eng*) close; **d~ machen** be fattening. **d~flüssig** *a* thick; (*Phys*) viscous. **D~kopf** *m* 🄴 stubborn person; **einen D~kopf haben** be stubborn

die *def art & pron s.* **der**

Dieb|(in) *m* -[e]s, -e (*f* -, -nen) thief. **d~isch** *a* thieving; <*Freude*> malicious. **D~stahl** *m* -[e]s,-̈e theft

Diele *f* -, -n floorboard; (*Flur*) hall

dien|en *vi* (*haben*) serve. **D~er** *m* -s,- servant; (*Verbeugung*) bow. **D~erin** *f* -, -nen maid, servant

Dienst *m* -[e]s, -e service; (*Arbeit*) work; (*Amtsausübung*) duty; **außer D~** off duty; (*pensioniert*) retired; **D~ haben** work; <*Soldat, Arzt:*> be on duty

Dienstag *m* Tuesday. **d~s** *adv* on Tuesdays

Dienst|bote *m* servant. **d~frei** *a* **d~freier Tag** day off; **d~frei haben** have time off; <*Soldat, Arzt:*> be off duty. **D~grad** *m* rank. **D~leistung** *f* service. **d~lich** *a* official ● *adv* **d~lich verreist** away on business. **D~mädchen** *nt* maid. **D~reise** *f* business trip. **D~stelle** *f* office. **D~stunden** *fpl* office hours

dies *inv pron* this. **d~bezüglich** *a* relevant ● *adv* regarding this matter. **d~e(r,s)** *pron* this; (*pl*) these; (*substantivisch*) this [one]; (*pl*) these; **d~e Nacht** tonight; (*letzte*) last night

dieselbe *pron s.* **derselbe**

Dieselkraftstoff *m* diesel [oil]

diesmal *adv* this time

Dietrich *m* -s, -e skeleton key

Diffamation /-'tsːioːn/ *f* - defamation

Differential* /-'tsːiaːl/ *nt* -s, -e *s.* **Differenzial**

Differenz *f* -, -en difference. **D~ial** *nt* -s, -e differential. **d~ieren** *vt/i*

(*haben*) differentiate (**zwischen** + *dat* between)

Digital- *pref* digital. **D~uhr** *f* digital clock/watch

Dikt|at *nt* -[e]s, -e dictation. **D~ator** *m* -s, -en /-'toːrən/ dictator. **D~atur** *f* -, -en dictatorship. **d~ieren** *vt/i* (*haben*) dictate

Dill *m* -s dill

Dimension *f* -, -en dimension

Ding *nt* -[e]s, -e & 🄴 -er thing; **guter D~e sein** be cheerful; **vor allen D~en** above all

Dinosaurier /-iɐ̯/ *m* -s,- dinosaur

Diözese *f* -, -n diocese

Diphtherie *f* - diphtheria

Diplom *nt* -s, -e diploma; (*Univ*) degree

Diplomat *m* -en, -en diplomat

dir *pron* (*dat of* **du**) [to] you; (*refl*) yourself; **ein Freund von dir** a friend of yours

direkt *a* direct ● *adv* directly; (*wirklich*) really. **D~ion** /-'tsːioːn/ *f* - management; (*Vorstand*) board of directors. **D~or** *m* -s, -en /-'toːrən/, **D~orin** *f* -, -nen director; (*Bank-, Theater-*) manager; (*Sch*) head; (*Gefängnis*) governor. **D~übertragung** *f* live transmission

Dirig|ent *m* -en, -en (*Mus*) conductor. **d~ieren** *vt* direct; (*Mus*) conduct

Dirndl *nt* -s,- dirndl [dress]

Diskette *f* -, -n floppy disc

Disko *f* -, -s 🄴 disco. **D~thek** *f* -, -en discothèque

diskret *a* discreet

Diskus *m* -, -se & **Disken** discus

Disku|ssion *f* -, -en discussion. **d~tieren** *vt/i* (*haben*) discuss

disponieren *vi* (*haben*) make arrangements; **d~ [können] über** (+ *acc*) have at one's disposal

Disqualifi|kation /-'tsːioːn/ *f* disqualification. **d~zieren** *vt* disqualify

Dissertation /-'tsːioːn/ *f* -, -en dissertation

Dissident *m* -en, -en dissident

Distanz f -, -en distance. **d~ieren (sich)** vr dissociate oneself (von from). **d~iert** a aloof

Distel f -, -n thistle

Disziplin f -, -en discipline. **d~arisch** a disciplinary. **d~iert** a disciplined

dito adv ditto

diverse attrib a pl various

Divid|ende f -, -en dividend. **d~ieren** vt divide (**durch** by)

Division f -, -en division

DJH abbr (Deutsche Jugendherberge) [German] youth hostel

DM abbr (Deutsche Mark) DM

doch conj & adv but; (dennoch) yet; (trotzdem) after all; **wenn d~** ...! if only ...! **nicht d~**! don't!

Docht m -[e]s, -e wick

Dock nt -s, -s dock. **d~en** vt/i (haben) dock

Dogge f -, -n Great Dane

Dogm|a nt -s, -men dogma. **d~atisch** a dogmatic

Dohle f -, -n jackdaw

Doktor m -s, -en /-'to:rən/ doctor. **D~arbeit** f [doctoral] thesis

Dokument nt -[e]s, -e document. **D~arbericht** m documentary. **D~arfilm** m documentary film

Dolch m -[e]s, -e dagger

Dollar m -s,- dollar

dolmetsch|en vt/i (haben) interpret. **D~er(in)** m -s,- (f -, -nen) interpreter

Dom m -[e]s, -e cathedral

Domino nt -s, -s dominoes sg. **D~stein** m domino

Dompfaff m -en, -en bullfinch

Donau f - Danube

Donner m -s thunder. **d~n** vi (haben) thunder

Donnerstag m Thursday. **d~s** adv on Thursdays

doof a ▣ stupid

Doppel nt -s,- duplicate; (Tennis) doubles pl. **D~bett** nt double bed. **D~decker** m -s,- doubledecker

[bus]. **d~deutig** a ambiguous. **D~gänger** m -s,- double. **D~kinn** nt double chin. **D~name** m double-barrelled name. **D~punkt** m (Gram) colon. **D~stecker** m two-way adaptor. **d~t** a double; <Boden> false; **in d~ter Ausfertigung** in duplicate; **die d~te Menge** twice the amount ● adv doubly; (zweimal) twice; **d~t so viel** twice as much. **D~zimmer** nt double room

Dorf nt -[e]s,"-er village. **D~bewohner** m villager

dörflich a rural

Dorn m -[e]s, -en thorn. **d~ig** a thorny

Dorsch m -[e]s, -e cod

dort adv there. **d~ig** a local

Dose f -, -n tin, can

dösen vi (haben) doze

Dosen|milch f evaporated milk. **D~öffner** m tin or can opener

dosieren vt measure out

Dosis f -, Dosen dose

Dot-com-Firma f dot-com (company)

Dotter m & nt -s,- [egg] yolk

Dozent(in) m -en, -en (f -, -nen) (Univ) lecturer

Dr. abbr (Doktor) Dr

Drache m -n, -n dragon. **D~n** m -s,- kite. **D~nfliegen** nt hang-gliding

Draht m -[e]s,"-e wire; **auf D~** ▣ on the ball. **D~seilbahn** f cable railway

Dram|a nt -s, -men drama. **D~atik** f - drama. **D~atiker** m -s,- dramatist. **d~atisch** a dramatic

dran adv ▣ = daran; **gut/schlecht d~ sein** be well off/in a bad way; **ich bin d~** it's my turn

Drang m -[e]s urge; (Druck) pressure

dräng|eln vt/i (haben) push; (bedrängen) pester. **d~en** vt push; (bedrängen) urge; **sich d~en** crowd (um round) ● vi (haben) push; (eilen) be urgent; **d~en auf** (+ acc) press for

dran|halten† (sich) vr sep hurry. **d~kommen†** vi sep (sein) have one's turn

drauf *adv* 🔲 = darauf; d∼ und dran sein be on the point (etw zu tun of doing sth). **D∼gänger** *m* -s,- daredevil

draußen *adv* outside; (*im Freien*) out of doors

drechseln *vt* (*Techn*) turn

Dreck *m* -s dirt; (*Morast*) mud

Dreh *m* -s 🔲 knack; den D∼ heraushaben have got the hang of it. **D∼bank** *f* lathe. **D∼bleistift** *m* propelling pencil. **D∼buch** *nt* screenplay, script. **d∼en** *vt* turn; (*im Kreis*) rotate; (*verschlingen*) twist; roll <*Zigarette*>; shoot <*Film*>; lauter/leiser d∼en turn up/down; sich d∼en turn; (*im Kreis*) rotate; (*schnell*) spin; <*Wind:*> change; sich d∼en um revolve around; (*sich handeln*) be about ● *vi* (*haben*) turn; <*Wind:*> change; an etw (*dat*) d∼en turn sth. **D∼stuhl** *m* swivel chair. **D∼tür** *f* revolving door. **D∼ung** *f* -, -en turn; (*im Kreis*) rotation. **D∼zahl** *f* number of revolutions

drei *inv a*, **D∼** *f* -, -en three; (*Sch*) ≈ pass. **D∼eck** *nt* -[e]s, -e triangle. **d∼eckig** *a* triangular. **d∼erlei** *inv a* three kinds of ● *pron* three things. **d∼fach** *a* triple. **d∼mal** *adv* three times. **D∼rad** *nt* tricycle

dreißig *inv a* thirty. **d∼ste(r,s)** *a* thirtieth

dreiviertel* *inv a* drei viertel, *s.* viertel. **D∼stunde** *f* three-quarters of an hour

dreizehn *inv a* thirteen **d∼te(r,s)** *a* thirteenth

dreschen† *vt* thresh

dress|ieren *vt* train. **D∼ur** *f* - training

dribbeln *vi* (*haben*) dribble

Drill *m* -[e]s (*Mil*) drill. **d∼en** *vt* drill

Drillinge *mpl* triplets

dringlich *a* urgent

Drink *m* -[s], -s [alcoholic] drink

drinnen *adv* inside

dritt *adv* zu d∼ in threes; wir waren zu d∼ there were three of us. **d∼e(r,s)** *a* third; ein D∼er a third person. **d∼el** *inv a* a third. **D∼el** *nt*

-s,- third. **d∼ens** *adv* thirdly. **d∼rangig** *a* third-rate

Drog|e *f* -, -n drug. **D∼enabhängige(r)** *m/f* drug addict. **D∼erie** *f* -, -n chemist's shop. **D∼ist** *m* -en, -en chemist

drohen *vi* (*haben*) threaten (jdm s.o.)

dröhnen *vi* (*haben*) resound; (*tönen*) boom

Drohung *f* -, -en threat

drollig *a* funny; (*seltsam*) odd

Drops *m* -,- [fruit] drop

Drossel *f* -, -n thrush

drosseln *vt* (*Techn*) throttle; (*fig*) cut back

drüben *adv* over there

Druck¹ *m* -[e]s,-̈e pressure; unter D∼ setzen (*fig*) pressurize

Druck² *m* -[e]s, -e printing; (*Schrift, Reproduktion*) print. **D∼buchstabe** *m* block letter

drucken *vt* print

drücken *vt/i* (*haben*) press; (*aus-*) squeeze; <*Schuh:*> pinch; (*umarmen*) hug; Preise d∼ force down prices; (*an Tür*) d∼ push; sich d∼ 🔲 make oneself scarce; sich d∼ vor (+ *dat*) 🔲 shirk. **d∼d** *a* heavy; (*schwül*) oppressive

Drucker *m* -s,- printer

Druckerei *f* -, -en printing works

Druck|fehler *m* misprint. **D∼knopf** *m* press-stud. **D∼luft** *f* compressed air. **D∼sache** *f* printed matter. **D∼schrift** *f* type; (*Veröffentlichung*) publication; in D∼schrift in block letters *pl*

Druckstelle *f* bruise

Drüse *f* -, -n (*Anat*) gland

Dschungel *m* -s,- jungle

du *pron* (*familiar address*) you; auf Du und Du on familiar terms

Dübel *m* -s,- plug

Dudelsack *m* bagpipes *pl*

Duell *nt* -s, -e duel

Duett *nt* -s, -e [vocal] duet

Duft *m* -[e]s,-̈e fragrance, scent; (*Aroma*) aroma. **d∼en** *vi* (*haben*) smell (nach of)

dulden vt tolerate; (erleiden) suffer ● vi (haben) suffer

dumm a stupid; (unklug) foolish; (🛈 lästig) awkward; **wie d~!**. **d~erweise** adv stupidly; (leider) unfortunately. **D~heit** f -, -en stupidity; (Torheit) foolishness; (Handlung) folly. **D~kopf** m 🛈 fool.

dumpf a dull

Düne f -, -n dune

Dung m -s manure

Düng|emittel nt fertilizer. **d~en** vt fertilize. **D~er** m -s,- fertilizer

dunk|el a dark; (vage) vague; (fragwürdig) shady; **d~les Bier** brown ale; **im D~eln** in the dark

Dunkel|heit f - darkness. **D~kammer** f dark-room. **d~n** vi (haben) get dark

dünn a thin; <Buch> slim; (spärlich) sparse; (schwach) weak

Dunst m -es,ˉe mist, haze; (Dampf) vapour

dünsten vt steam

dunstig a misty, hazy

Duo nt -s, -s [instrumental] duet

Duplikat nt -[e]s, -e duplicate

Dur nt - (Mus) major [key]

durch prep (+ acc) through; (mittels) by; [geteilt] **d~** (Math) divided by ● adv **die Nacht d~** throughout the night; **d~ und d~ nass** wet through

durchaus adv absolutely; **d~ nicht** by no means

durchblättern vt sep leaf through

durchblicken vi sep (haben) look through; **d~ lassen** (fig) hint at

Durchblutung f circulation

durchbohren vt insep pierce

durchbrechen[1]† vt/i sep (haben) break [in two]

durchbrechen[2]† vt insep break through; break <Schallmauer>

durchbrennen† vi sep (sein) burn through; <Sicherung:> blow

Durchbruch m breakthrough

durchdrehen v sep ● vt mince ● vi (haben/sein) 🛈 go crazy

durchdringen† vi sep (sein) penetrate; (sich durchsetzen) get one's way. **d~d** a penetrating; <Schrei> piercing

durcheinander adv in a muddle; <Person> confused; **d~ bringen** muddle [up]; confuse <Person>; **d~ geraten** get mixed up; **d~ reden** all talk at once. **D~** nt -s muddle

durchfahren vi sep (sein) drive through; <Zug:> go through

Durchfahrt f journey/drive through; **auf der D~** passing through; 'D~ verboten' 'no thoroughfare'

Durchfall m diarrhoea. **d~en**† vi sep (sein) fall through; (🛈 versagen) flop; (bei Prüfung) fail

Durchfuhr f - (Comm) transit

durchführ|bar a feasible. **d~en** vt sep carry out

Durchgang m passage; (Sport) round; 'D~ verboten' 'no entry' . **D~sverkehr** m through traffic

durchgeben† vt sep pass through; (übermitteln) transmit; (Radio, TV) broadcast

durchgebraten a gut **d~** well done

durchgehen† vi sep (sein) go through; (davonlaufen) run away; <Pferd:> bolt; **jdm etw d~ lassen** let s.o. get away with sth. **d~d** a continuous; **d~d geöffnet** open all day; **d~der Zug** through train

durchgreifen† vi sep (haben) reach through; (vorgehen) take drastic action. **d~d** a drastic

durchhalte|n† v sep (fig) ● vi (haben) hold out ● vt keep up. **D~vermögen** nt stamina

durchkommen† vi sep (sein) come through; (gelangen, am Telefon) get through

durchlassen† vt sep let through

durchlässig a permeable; (undicht) leaky

Durchlauferhitzer m -s,- geyser

durchlesen† vt sep read through

durchleuchten vt insep X-ray

durchlöchert a riddled with holes

durchmachen vt sep go through; (*erleiden*) undergo

Durchmesser m -s,- diameter

durchnässt a wet through

durchnehmen† vt sep (*Sch*) do

durchnummeriert a numbered consecutively

durchpausen vt sep trace

durchqueren vt insep cross

Durchreiche f -, -n hatch

Durchreise f journey through; **auf der D~** passing through. **d~n** vi sep (*sein*) pass through

durchreißen† vt/i sep (*sein*) tear

Durchsage f -, -n announcement. **d~n** vt sep announce

Durchschlag m carbon copy; (*Culin*) colander. **d~en**† v sep ● vt (*Culin*) rub through a sieve; **sich d~en** (*fig*) struggle through ● vi (*sein*) <*Sicherung:*> blow

durchschlagend a (*fig*) effective; <*Erfolg*> resounding

durchschneiden† vt sep cut

Durchschnitt m average; **im D~** on average. **d~lich** a average ● adv on average. **D~s-** pref average

Durchschrift f carbon copy

durchsehen† v sep ● vi (*haben*) see through ● vt look through

durchseihen vt sep strain

durchsetzen vt sep force through; **sich d~** assert oneself; <*Mode:*> catch on

Durchsicht f check

durchsichtig a transparent

durchsickern vi sep (*sein*) seep through; <*Neuigkeit:*> leak out

durchstehen† vt sep (*fig*) come through

durchstreichen† vt sep cross out

durchsuch|en vt insep search. **D~ung** f -, -en search

durchwachsen a <*Speck*> streaky; (Ⓔ *gemischt*) mixed

durchwählen vi sep (*haben*) (*Teleph*) dial direct

durchweg adv without exception

durchwühlen vt insep rummage through; ransack <*Haus*>

Durchzug m through draught

dürfen†
● *transitive & auxiliary verb*
····▸ (*Erlaubnis haben zu*) be allowed; may, can. **etw [tun] dürfen** be allowed to do sth. **darf ich das tun?** may or can I do that? **nein, das darfst du nicht** no you may not or cannot [do that]. **er sagte mir, ich dürfte sofort gehen** he told me I could go at once. **hier darf man nicht rauchen** smoking is prohibited here. **sie darf/durfte es nicht sehen** she must not/was not allowed to see it.
····▸ (*in Höflichkeitsformeln*) may. **darf ich rauchen?** may I smoke? **darf/dürfte ich um diesen Tanz bitten?** may/might I have the pleasure of this dance?
····▸ **dürfte** (*sollte*) should, ought. **jetzt dürften sie dort angekommen sein** they should or ought to be there by now. **das dürfte nicht allzu schwer sein** that should not be too difficult. **ich hätte es nicht tun/sagen dürfen** I ought not to have done/said it
● *intransitive verb*
····▸ (*irgendwohin gehen dürfen*) be allowed to go; may go; can go. **darf ich nach Hause?** may or can I go home? **sie durfte nicht ins Theater** she was not allowed to go the theatre

dürftig a poor; <*Mahlzeit*> scanty

dürr a dry; <*Boden*> arid; (*mager*) skinny. **D~e** f -, -n drought

Durst m -[e]s thirst; **D~ haben** be thirsty. **d~ig** a thirsty

Dusche f -, -n shower. **d~n** vi/r (*haben*) [sich] **d~n** have a shower

Düse f -, -n nozzle. **D~nflugzeug** nt jet

Dutzend nt -s, -e dozen. **d~weise** adv by the dozen

duzen vt jdn **d~** call s.o. 'du'

Dynam|ik f - dynamics sg; (*fig*) dynamism. **d~isch** a dynamic; <*Rente*> index-linked

Dynamit nt -es dynamite

Dynamo m -s, -s dynamo

Dynastie f -, -n dynasty

D-Zug /'de:-/ *m* express [train]

Ee

Ębbe *f* -, -n low tide

eben *a* level; (*glatt*) smooth; **zu e~er Erde** on the ground floor ● *adv* just; (*genau*) exactly; **e~ noch** only just; (*gerade vorhin*) just now; **das ist es e~!** that's just it! **E~bild** *nt* image

Ebene *f* -, -n (*Geog*) plain; (*Geom*) plane; (*fig: Niveau*) level

eben|falls *adv* also; **danke, e~falls** thank you, [the] same to you. **E~holz** *nt* ebony. **e~so** *adv* just the same; (*ebenso sehr*) just as much; **e~so gut** just as good; *adv* just as well; **e~so sehr** just as much; **e~so viel** just as much/many; **e~so wenig** just as little/few; (*noch*) no more

Eber *m* -s,- boar

ebnen *vt* level; (*fig*) smooth

Ęcho *nt* -s, -s echo

ęcht *a* genuine, real; authentic ● *adv* ⚿ really; typically. **E~heit** *f* - authenticity

Ęck|ball *m* (*Sport*) corner. **E~e** *f* -, -n corner; **um die E~e bringen** ⚿ bump off. **e~ig** *a* angular; <*Klammern*> square; (*unbeholfen*) awkward. **E~zahn** *m* canine tooth

Ecu, ECU /e'ky:/ *m* -[s], -[s] ecu

edel *a* noble; (*wertvoll*) precious; (*fein*) fine. **e~mütig** *a* magnanimous. **E~stahl** *m* stainless steel. **E~stein** *m* precious stone

Efeu *m* -s ivy

Effękt *m* -[e]s, -e effect. **E~en** *pl* securities. **e~iv** *a* actual, *adv* -ly; (*wirksam*) effective

EG *f* - *abbr* (Europäische Gemeinschaft) EC

egal *a* **das ist mir e~** ⚿ it's all the same to me ● *adv* **e~ wie/wo** no matter how/where

Ęgge *f* -, -n harrow

Ego|ismus *m* - selfishness. **E~ịst(in)** *m* -en, -en (*f* -, -nen) egoist. **e~ịstisch** *a* selfish

eh *adv* (*Aust, fam*) anyway

ehe *conj* before; **ehe nicht** until

Ehe *f* -, -n marriage. **E~bett** *nt* double bed. **E~bruch** *m* adultery. **E~frau** *f* wife. **e~lich** *a* marital; <*Recht*> conjugal; <*Kind*> legitimate

ehemalig *a* former. **e~s** *adv* formerly

Ehe|mann *m* (*pl* -männer) husband. **E~paar** *nt* married couple

eher *adv* earlier, sooner; (*lieber, vielmehr*) rather; (*mehr*) more

Ehering *m* wedding ring

Ehr|e *f* -, -n honour. **e~en** *vt* honour. **e~enamtlich** *a* honorary ● *adv* in an honorary capacity. **E~engast** *m* guest of honour. **e~enhaft** *a* honourable. **E~ensache** *f* point of honour. **E~enwort** *nt* word of honour. **e~erbietig** *a* deferential. **E~furcht** *f* reverence; (*Scheu*) awe. **e~fürchtig** *a* reverent. **E~gefühl** *nt* sense of honour. **E~geiz** *m* ambition. **e~geizig** *a* ambitious. **e~lich** *a* honest; **e~lich gesagt** to be honest. **E~lichkeit** *f* - honesty. **e~los** *a* dishonourable. **e-würdig** *a* venerable; (*als Anrede*) Reverend

Ei *nt* -[e]s, -er egg

Eibe *f* -, -n yew

Eiche *f* -, -n oak. **E~l** *f* -, -n acorn

eichen *vt* standardize

Eichhörnchen *nt* -s,- squirrel

Eid *m* -[e]s, -e oath

Eidechse *f* -, -n lizard

eidlich *a* sworn ● *adv* on oath

Eidotter *m & nt* egg yolk

Eier|becher *m* egg-cup. **E~kuchen** *m* pancake; (*Omelett*) omelette. **E~schale** *f* eggshell. **E~schnee** *m* beaten egg-white. **E~stock** *m* ovary

---

Eifer *m* -s eagerness. **E~sucht** *f* jealousy. **e~süchtig** *a* jealous

eifrig *a* eager

Eigelb *nt* -[e]s, -e [egg] yolk

eigen *a* own; (*typisch*) characteristic (*dat* of); (*seltsam*) odd; (*genau*) particular. **E~art** *f* peculiarity. **e~artig** *a* peculiar. **e~händig** *a* personal; <*Unterschrift*> own. **E~heit** *f* -, -en peculiarity. **E~name** *m* proper name. **e~nützig** *a* selfish. **e~s** *adv* specially. **E~schaft** *f* -, -en quality; (*Phys*) property; (*Merkmal*) characteristic; (*Funktion*) capacity. **E~schaftswort** *nt* (*pl* -wörter) adjective. **E~sinn** *m* obstinacy. **e~sinnig** *a* obstinate

eigentlich *a* actual, real; (*wahr*) true ● *adv* actually, really; (*streng genommen*) strictly speaking

Eigen|tor *nt* own goal. **E~tum** *nt* -s property. **E~tümer(in)** *m* -s,- (*f* -, -nen) owner. **E~tumswohnung** *f* freehold flat. **e~willig** *a* self-willed; <*Stil*> highly individual

eignen (sich) *vr* be suitable

Eil|brief *m* express letter. **E~e** *f* - hurry; **E~e haben** be in a hurry; <*Sache:*> be urgent. **e~en** *vi* (*sein*) hurry ● (*haben*) (*drängen*) be urgent. **e~ig** *a* hurried; (*dringend*) urgent; **es e~ig haben** be in a hurry. **E~zug** *m* semi-fast train

Eimer *m* -s,- bucket; (*Abfall-*) bin

ein
● *indefinite article*
····▸ a, (*vor Vokal*) an. **ein Kleid/Apfel/ Hotel/Mensch** a dress/an apple/a[n] hotel/a human being. **so ein** such a. **was für ein ...** (*Frage*) what kind of a ...? (*Ausruf*) what a ...!
● *adjective*
····▸ (*Ziffer*) one. **eine Mark** one mark. **wir haben nur eine Stunde** we only have an/(*betont*) one hour. **eines Tages/Abends** one day/evening
····▸ (*derselbe*) the same. **einer Meinung sein** be of the same opinion. **mit jdm in einem Zimmer schlafen** sleep in the same room as s.o.

einander *pron* one another

Einäscherung *f* -, -en cremation

einatmen *vt/i sep* (*haben*) inhale, breathe in

Einbahnstraße *f* one-way street

einbalsamieren *vt sep* embalm

Einband *m* binding

Einbau *m* installation; (*Montage*) fitting. **e~en** *vt sep* install; (*montieren*) fit. **E~küche** *f* fitted kitchen

einbegriffen *pred a* included

Einberufung *f* call-up

Einbettzimmer *nt* single room

einbeulen *vt sep* dent

einbeziehen† *vt sep* [mit] e~ include; (*berücksichtigen*) take into account

einbiegen† *vi sep* (*sein*) turn

einbild|en *vt sep* **sich** (*dat*) **etw e~en** imagine sth; **sich** (*dat*) **viel e~en** be conceited. **E~ung** *f* imagination; (*Dünkel*) conceit. **E~ungskraft** *f* imagination

einblenden *vt sep* fade in

Einblick *m* insight

einbrech|en† *vi sep* (*haben/sein*) break in; **bei uns ist eingebrochen worden** we have been burgled. **E~er** *m* burglar

einbringen† *vt sep* get in; bring in <*Geld*>

Einbruch *m* burglary; **bei E~ der Nacht** at nightfall

einbürger|n *vt sep* naturalize. **E~ung** *f* - naturalization

einchecken /-tʃɛkən/ *vt/i sep* (*haben*) check in

eindecken (sich) *vr sep* stock up

eindeutig *a* unambiguous; (*deutlich*) clear

eindicken *vt sep* (*Culin*) thicken

eindringen† *vi sep* (*sein*) **e~en in** (+ *acc*) penetrate into; (*mit Gewalt*) force one's/<*Wasser:*> its way into; (*Mil*) invade

Eindruck *m* impression

eindrücken *vt sep* crush

eindrucksvoll *a* impressive

ein|e(r,s) *pron* one; *(jemand)* someone; *(man)* one, you

einebnen *vt sep* level

eineiig *a* <Zwillinge> identical

eineinhalb *inv a* one and a half; **e~ Stunden** an hour and a half

Einelternfamilie *f* one-parent family

einengen *vt sep* restrict

Einer *m* -s,- *(Math)* unit. **e~** *pron s.* **eine(r,s). e~lei** *inv a* ● *attrib a* one kind of; *(eintönig, einheitlich)* the same ● *pred a* 🛈 immaterial; **es ist mir e~lei** it's all the same to me. **e~seits** *adv* on the one hand

einfach *a* simple; <Essen> plain; <Faden, Fahrt> single; **e~er Soldat** private. **E~heit** *f* - simplicity

einfädeln *vt sep* thread; *(fig; arrangieren)* arrange

einfahr|en† *v sep* ● *vi (sein)* arrive; <Zug:> pull in ● *vt (Auto)* run in. **E~t** *f* arrival; *(Eingang)* entrance, way in; *(Auffahrt)* drive; *(Autobahn-)* access road; **keine E~t** no entry

Einfall *m* idea; *(Mil)* invasion. **e~en†** *vi sep (sein)* collapse; *(eindringen)* invade; **jdm e~en** occur to s.o.; **was fällt ihm ein!** what does he think he is doing!

Einfalt *f* - naïvety

einfarbig *a* of one colour; <Stoff, Kleid> plain

einfass|en *vt sep* edge; set <Edelstein>. **E~ung** *f* border, edging

einfetten *vt sep* grease

Einfluss *m* influence. **e~reich** *a* influential

einförmig *a* monotonous. **E~keit** *f* - monotony

einfrieren† *vt/i sep (sein)* freeze

einfügen *vt sep* insert; *(einschieben)* interpolate; **sich e~** fit in

einfühlsam *a* sensitive

Einfuhr *f* -, -en import

einführ|en *vt sep* introduce; *(einstecken)* insert; *(einweisen)* initiate; *(Comm)* import. **e~end** *a*

introductory. **E~ung** *f* introduction; *(Einweisung)* initiation

Eingabe *f* petition; *(Computer)* input

Eingang *m* entrance, way in; *(Ankunft)* arrival

eingebaut *a* built-in; <Schrank> fitted

eingeben† *vt sep* hand in; *(Computer)* feed in

eingebildet *a* imaginary; *(überheblich)* conceited

Eingeborene(r) *m/f* native

eingehen† *v sep* ● *vi (sein)* come in; *(ankommen)* arrive; *(einlaufen)* shrink; *(sterben)* die; <Zeitung, Firma:> fold; **auf etw** *(acc)* **e~** go into sth; *(annehmen)* agree to sth ● *vt* enter into; contract <Ehe>; make <Wette>; take <Risiko>

eingemacht *a (Culin)* bottled

eingenommen *pred a (fig)* taken **(von** with); prejudiced **(gegen** against)

eingeschneit *a* snowbound

eingeschrieben *a* registered

Einge|ständnis *nt* admission. **e~stehen†** *vt sep* admit

eingetragen *a* registered

Eingeweide *pl* bowels, entrails

eingewöhnen (sich) *vr sep* settle in

eingießen† *vt sep* pour in; *(einschenken)* pour

eingleisig *a* single-track

einglieder|n *vt sep* integrate. **E~ung** *f* integration

eingravieren *vt sep* engrave

eingreifen† *vi sep (haben)* intervene. **E~** *nt* -s intervention

Eingriff *m* intervention; *(Med)* operation

einhaken *vt/r sep* **jdn e~** *od* **sich bei jdm e~** take s.o.'s arm

einhalten† *v sep* ● *vt* keep; *(befolgen)* observe ● *vi (haben)* stop

einhändigen *vt sep* hand in

einhängen *vt sep* hang; put down <Hörer>

---

einheimisch *a* local; (*eines Landes*) native; (*Comm*) home-produced. **E~e(r)** *m/f* local native

Einheit *f* -, -en unity; (*Maß-, Mil*) unit. **e~lich** *a* uniform. **E~spreis** *m* standard price; (*Fahrpreis*) flat fare

einholen *vt sep* catch up with; (*aufholen*) make up for; (*erbitten*) seek; (*einkaufen*) buy

einhüllen *vt sep* wrap

einhundert *inv a* one hundred

einig *a* united; [sich (*dat*)] **e~** **sein** be in agreement

einig|e(r,s) *pron* some; (*ziemlich viel*) quite a lot of; (*substantivisch*) **e~e** *pl* some; (*mehrere*) several; (*ziemlich viele*) quite a lot; **e~es** *sg* some things; **vor e~er Zeit** some time ago

einigen *vt* unite; unify <*Land*>; **sich e~** come to an agreement

einigermaßen *adv* to some extent; (*ziemlich*) fairly; (*ziemlich gut*) fairly well

Einigkeit *f* - unity; (*Übereinstimmung*) agreement

einjährig *a* one-year-old; **e~e** **Pflanze** annual

einkalkulieren *vt sep* take into account

einkassieren *vt sep* collect

Einkauf *m* purchase; (*Einkaufen*) shopping; **Einkäufe machen** do some shopping. **e~en** *vt sep* buy; **e~en** **gehen** go shopping. **E~swagen** *m* shopping trolley

einklammern *vt sep* bracket

Einklang *m* harmony; **in E~ stehen** be in accord (**mit** with)

einkleben *vt sep* stick in

einkleiden *vt sep* fit out

einklemmen *vt sep* clamp

einkochen *v sep* ● *vi* (*sein*) boil down ● *vt* preserve, bottle

Einkommen *nt* -s income. **E~[s]steuer** *f* income tax

Einkünfte *pl* income *sg*; (*Einnahmen*) revenue *sg*

einlad|en† *vt sep* load; (*auffordern*) invite; (*bezahlen für*) treat. **E~ung** *f* invitation

Einlage *f* enclosure; (*Schuh-*) arch support; (*Programm-*) interlude; (*Comm*) investment; (*Bank-*) deposit; **Suppe mit E~** soup with noodles/ dumplings

Ein|lass *m* -es admittance. **e~lassen†** *vt sep* let in; run <*Bad, Wasser*>; **sich auf etw** (*acc*) **e~lassen** get involved in sth

einleben (sich) *vr sep* settle in

Einlege|arbeit *f* inlaid work. **e~n** *vt sep* put in; lay in <*Vorrat*>; lodge <*Protest*>; (*einfügen*) insert; (*Auto*) engage <*Gang*>; (*Culin*) pickle; (*marinieren*) marinade; **eine Pause e~n** have a break. **E~sohle** *f* insole

einleit|en *vt sep* initiate; (*eröffnen*) begin. **E~ung** *f* introduction

einleuchten *vi sep* (*haben*) be clear (*dat* to). **e~d** *a* convincing

einliefer|n *vt sep* take (**ins** **Krankenhaus** to hospital). **E~ung** *f* admission

einlösen *vt sep* cash <*Scheck*>; redeem <*Pfand*>; (*fig*) keep

einmachen *vt sep* preserve

einmal *adv* once; (*eines Tages*) one or some day; **noch/schon e~** again/ before; **noch e~ so teuer** twice as expensive; **auf e~** at the same time; (*plötzlich*) suddenly; **nicht e~** not even. **E~eins** *nt* - [multiplication] tables *pl*. **e~ig** *a* (*einzigartig*) unique; (Ⅰ *großartig*) fantastic

einmarschieren *vi sep* (*sein*) march in

einmisch|en (sich) *vr sep* interfere. **E~ung** *f* interference

Einnahme *f* -, -n taking; (*Mil*) capture; **E~n** *pl* income *sg*; (*Einkünfte*) revenue *sg*; (*Comm*) receipts; (*eines Ladens*) takings

einnehmen† *vt sep* take; have <*Mahlzeit*>; (*Mil*) capture; take up <*Platz*>

einordnen *vt sep* put in its proper place; (*klassifizieren*) classify; **sich e~** fit in; (*Auto*) get in lane

einpacken *vt sep* pack

einparken *vt sep* park

einpflanzen *vt sep* plant; implant <*Organ*>

einplanen *vt sep* allow for

einprägen *vt sep* impress (jdm [up]on s.o.); **sich** (*dat*) **etw e~en** memorize sth.

einrahmen *vt sep* frame

einrasten *vi sep* (*sein*) engage

einräumen *vt sep* put away; (*zugeben*) admit; (*zugestehen*) grant

einrechnen *vt sep* include

einreden *v sep* ● *vt* **jdm/sich** (*dat*) **etw e~** persuade s.o./oneself of sth.

einreiben† *vt sep* rub (**mit** with)

einreichen *vt sep* submit; **die Scheidung e~** file for divorce

Einreih|er *m* **-s,-** single-breasted suit. **e~ig** *a* single-breasted

Einreise *f* entry. **e~n** *vi sep* (*sein*) enter (**nach Irland** Ireland)

einrenken *vt sep* (*Med*) set

einricht|en *vt sep* fit out; (*möblieren*) furnish; (*anordnen*) arrange; (*Med*) set <*Bruch*>; (*eröffnen*) set up; **sich e~en** furnish one's home; (*sich einschränken*) economize; (*sich vorbereiten*) prepare (**auf** + *acc* for). **E~ung** *f* furnishing; (*Möbel*) furnishings *pl*; (*Techn*) equipment; (*Vorrichtung*) device; (*Eröffnung*) setting up; (*Institution*) institution; (*Gewohnheit*) practice

einrosten *vi sep* (*sein*) rust; (*fig*) get rusty

eins *inv a & pron* one; **noch e~** one other thing; **mir ist alles e~** 🔢 it's all the same to me. **E~** *f* **-,-en** one; (*Sch*) ≈ A

einsam *a* lonely; (*allein*) solitary; (*abgelegen*) isolated. **E~keit** *f* **-** loneliness; solitude; isolation

einsammeln *vt sep* collect

Einsatz *m* use; (*Mil*) mission; (*Wett-*) stake; (*E~teil*) insert; **im E~** in action

einschalt|en *vt sep* switch on; (*einschieben*) interpolate; (*fig:*

beteiligen) call in; **sich e~en** (*fig*) intervene. **E~quote** *f* (*TV*) viewing figures *pl*; ≈ ratings *pl*

einschätzen *vt sep* assess; (*bewerten*) rate

einschenken *vt sep* pour

einscheren *vi sep* (*sein*) pull in

einschicken *vt sep* send in

einschieben† *vt sep* push in; (*einfügen*) insert

einschiff|en (sich) *vr sep* embark. **E~ung** *f* **-** embarkation

einschlafen† *vi sep* (*sein*) go to sleep; (*aufhören*) peter out

einschläfern *vt sep* lull to sleep; (*betäuben*) put out; (*töten*) put to sleep. **e~d** *a* soporific

Einschlag *m* impact. **e~en**† *v sep* ● *vt* knock in; (*zerschlagen*) smash; (*drehen*) turn; take <*Weg*>; take up <*Laufbahn*> ● *vi* (*haben*) hit/ <*Blitz:*> strike (**in etw** *acc* sth); (*Erfolg haben*) be a hit

einschleusen *vt sep* infiltrate

einschließ|en† *vt sep* lock in; (*umgeben*) enclose; (*einkreisen*) surround; (*einbeziehen*) include; **sich e~en** lock oneself in; **Bedienung eingeschlossen** service included. **e~lich** *adv* inclusive ● *prep* (+ *gen*) including

einschneiden† *vt/i sep* (*haben*) [**in**] **etw** *acc* **e~** cut into sth. **e~d** *a* (*fig*) drastic

Einschnitt *m* cut; (*Med*) incision; (*Lücke*) gap; (*fig*) decisive event

einschränk|en *vt sep* restrict; (*reduzieren*) cut back; **sich e~en** economize. **E~ung** *f* **-, -en** restriction; (*Reduzierung*) reduction; (*Vorbehalt*) reservation

Einschreib|[e]brief *m* registered letter. **e~en**† *vt sep* enter; register <*Brief*>; **sich e~en** put one's name down; (*sich anmelden*) enrol. **E~en** *nt* registered letter/packet; **als** *od* **per E~en** by registered post

einschüchtern *vt sep* intimidate

Einsegnung *f* **-, -en** confirmation

einsehen† *vt sep* inspect; (*lesen*) consult; (*begreifen*) see

---

einseitig *a* one-sided; (*Pol*) unilateral ● *adv* on one side; (*fig*) one-sidedly; (*Pol*) unilaterally

einsenden† *vt sep* send in

einsetzen *v sep* ● *vt* put in; (*einfügen*) insert; (*verwenden*) use; put on <*Zug*>; call out <*Truppen*>; (*Mil*) deploy; (*ernennen*) appoint; (*wetten*) stake; (*riskieren*) risk ● *vi* (*haben*) start; <*Winter, Regen:*> set in

Einsicht *f* insight; (*Verständnis*) understanding; (*Vernunft*) reason. **e~ig** *a* understanding

Einsiedler *m* hermit

einsinken† *vi sep* (*sein*) sink in

einspannen *vt sep* harness; **jdn e~** 🔢 rope s.o. in

einsparen *vt sep* save

einsperren *vt sep* shut/(*im Gefängnis*) lock up

einsprachig *a* monolingual

einspritzen *vt sep* inject

Einspruch *m* objection; **E~ erheben** object; (*Jur*) appeal

einspurig *a* single-track; (*Auto*) single-lane

einst *adv* once; (*Zukunft*) one day

Einstand *m* (*Tennis*) deuce

einstecken *vt sep* put in; post <*Brief*>; (*Electr*) plug in; (🔢 *behalten*) pocket; (🔢 *hinnehmen*) take; suffer <*Niederlage*>; **etw e~** put sth in one's pocket

einsteigen† *vi sep* (*sein*) get in; (*in Bus/Zug*) get on

einstell|en *vt sep* put in; (*anstellen*) employ; (*aufhören*) stop; (*regulieren*) adjust, set; (*Optik*) focus; tune <*Motor, Zündung*>; tune to <*Sender*>; **sich e~en** turn up; <*Schwierigkeiten:*> arise; **sich e~en auf** (+ *acc*) adjust to; (*sich vorbereiten*) prepare for. **E~ung** *f* employment; (*Regulierung*) adjustment; (*TV, Auto*) tuning; (*Haltung*) attitude

einstig *a* former

einstimmig *a* unanimous. **E~keit** *f* - unanimity

einstöckig *a* single-storey

einstudieren *vt sep* rehearse

einstufen *vt sep* classify

Ein|sturz *m* collapse. **e~stürzen** *vi sep* (*sein*) collapse

einstweilen *adv* for the time being; (*inzwischen*) meanwhile

eintasten *vt sep* key in

eintauchen *vt/i sep* (*sein*) dip in

eintauschen *vt sep* exchange

eintausend *inv a* one thousand

einteil|en *vt sep* divide (**in** + *acc* into); (*Biol*) classify; **sich** (*dat*) **seine Zeit gut e~en** organize one's time well. **e~ig** *a* one piece. **E~ung** *f* division

eintönig *a* monotonous. **E~keit** *f* - monotony

Eintopf *m*, **E~gericht** *nt* stew

Eintracht *f* - harmony

Eintrag *m* -[e]s,⸚e entry. **e~en**† *vt sep* enter; (*Admin*) register; **sich e~en** put one's name down

einträglich *a* profitable

Eintragung *f* -, -en registration

eintreffen† *vi sep* (*sein*) arrive; (*fig*) come true

eintreiben† *vt sep* drive in; (*einziehen*) collect

eintreten† *v sep* ● *vi* (*sein*) enter; (*geschehen*) occur; **in einen Klub e~** join a club; **e~ für** (*fig*) stand up for ● *vt* kick in

Eintritt *m* entrance; (*zu Veranstaltung*) admission; (*Beitritt*) joining; (*Beginn*) beginning. **E~skarte** *f* [admission] ticket

einüben *vt sep* practise

einundachtzig *inv a* eighty-one

Einvernehmen *nt* -s understanding; (*Übereinstimmung*) agreement

einverstanden *a* **e~ sein** agree

Einverständnis *nt* agreement; (*Zustimmung*) consent

Einwand *m* -[e]s,⸚e objection

Einwander|er *m* immigrant. **e~n** *vi sep* (*sein*) immigrate. **E~ung** *f* immigration

einwandfrei *a* perfect

einwärts *adv* inwards

einwechseln *vt sep* change

einwecken *vt sep* preserve, bottle

Einweg- *pref* non-returnable

einweichen *vt sep* soak

einweih|en *vt sep* inaugurate; (*Relig*) consecrate; (*einführen*) initiate; **in ein Geheimnis e~en** let into a secret. **E~ung** *f* -, -en inauguration; consecration; initiation

einweisen† *vt sep* direct; (*einführen*) initiate; **ins Krankenhaus e~** send to hospital

einwerfen† *vt sep* insert; post <*Brief*>; (*Sport*) throw in

einwickeln *vt sep* wrap [up]

einwillig|en *vi sep* (*haben*) consent, agree (**in** + *acc* to). **E~ung** *f* - consent

Einwohner|(in) *m* -s,- (*f* -, -nen) inhabitant. **E~zahl** *f* population

Einwurf *m* interjection; (*Einwand*) objection; (*Sport*) throw-in; (*Münz-*) slot

Einzahl *f* (*Gram*) singular

einzahl|en *vt sep* pay in. **E~ung** *f* payment; (*Einlage*) deposit

einzäunen *vt sep* fence in

Einzel *nt* -s,- (*Tennis*) singles *pl*. **E~bett** *nt* single bed. **E~gänger** *m* -s,- loner. **E~haft** *f* solitary confinement. **E~handel** *m* retail trade. **E~händler** *m* retailer. **E~haus** *nt* detached house. **E~heit** *f* -, -en detail. **E~karte** *f* single ticket. **E~kind** *nt* only child

einzeln *a* single; (*individuell*) individual; (*gesondert*) separate; odd <*Handschuh, Socken*>; **e~e Fälle** some cases. **E~e(r,s)** *pron* der/die E~e the individual; **E~e** *pl* some; **im E~en** in detail

Einzel|teil *nt* [component] part. **E~zimmer** *nt* single room

einziehen† *v sep* ● *vt* pull in; draw in <*Atem, Krallen*>; (*Zool, Techn*) retract; indent <*Zeile*>; (*aus dem Verkehr ziehen*) withdraw; (*beschlagnahmen*) confiscate;

(*eintreiben*) collect; make <*Erkundigungen*>; (*Mil*) call up ● *vi* (*sein*) enter; (*umziehen*) move in; (*eindringen*) penetrate

einzig *a* only; (*einmalig*) unique; **eine e~e Frage** a a single question ● *adv* only; **e~ und allein** solely. **E~e(r,s)** *pron* der/die/das E~e the only one; **ein/kein E~er** a/not a single one; **das E~e, was mich stört** the only thing that bothers me

Eis *nt* -es ice; (*Speise-*) ice-cream; **Eis am Stiel** ice lolly; **Eis laufen** skate. **E~bahn** *f* ice rink. **E~bär** *m* polar bear. **E~becher** *m* ice-cream sundae. **E~berg** *m* iceberg. **E~diele** *f* ice-cream parlour

Eisen *nt* -s,- iron. **E~bahn** *f* railway

eisern *a* iron; (*fest*) resolute; **e~er Vorhang** (*Theat*) safety curtain; (*Pol*) Iron Curtain

Eis|fach *nt* freezer compartment. **e~gekühlt** *a* chilled. **e~ig** *a* icy. **E~kaffee** *m* iced coffee. **E~lauf** *m* skating. **E~läufer(in)** *m(f)* skater. **E~pickel** *m* ice-axe. **E~scholle** *f* ice-floe. **E~vogel** *m* kingfisher. **E~würfel** *m* ice-cube. **E~zapfen** *m* icicle. **E~zeit** *f* ice age

eitel *a* vain; (*rein*) pure. **E~keit** *f* - vanity

Eiter *m* -s pus. **e~n** *vi* (*haben*) discharge pus

Eiweiß *nt* -es, -e egg-white

Ekel *m* -s disgust; (*Widerwille*) revulsion. **e~haft** *a* nauseating; (*widerlich*) repulsive. **e~n** *vt/i* (*haben*) **mich** *od* **mir e~t** [es] **davor** it makes me feel sick ● *vr* **sich e~n vor** (+ *dat*) find repulsive

eklig *a* disgusting, repulsive

elastisch *a* elastic; (*federnd*) springy; (*fig*) flexible

Elch *m* -[e]s, -e elk

Elefant *m* -en, -en elephant

elegan|t *a* elegant. **E~z** *f* - elegance

Elektri|ker *m* -s,- electrician. **e~sch** *a* electric

---
*alte Schreibung

Elektrizität *f* - electricity.
E∼swerk *nt* power station
Elektr|oartikel *mpl* electrical
appliances. **E∼ode** *f* -, -n electrode.
E∼onik *f* - electronics *sg*.
e∼onisch *a* electronic
Elend *nt* -s misery; (*Armut*) poverty.
e∼ *a* miserable; (*krank*) poorly;
(*gemein*) contemptible. **E∼sviertel**
nt slum
elf *inv a*, **E∼** *f* -, -en eleven
Elfe *f* -, -n fairy
Elfenbein *nt* ivory
Elfmeter *m* (*Fußball*) penalty
elfte(r,s) *a* eleventh
Ell[en]bogen *m* elbow
Ellip|se *f* -, -n ellipse. **e∼tisch** *a*
elliptical
Elsass *nt* - Alsace
elsässisch *a* Alsatian
Elster *f* -, -n magpie
elter|lich *a* parental. **E∼n** *pl*
parents. **e∼nlos** *a* orphaned.
E∼nteil *m* parent
Email /e'mai:/ *nt* -s, -s, **E∼le**
/e'maljə/ *f* -, -n enamel
E-Mail /'i:meɪl/ *f* -, -s e-mail; e-mail
message
Emanzi|pation /-'tsio:n/ *f* -
emancipation. **e∼piert** *a*
emancipated
Embargo *nt* -s, -s embargo
Embryo *m* -s, -s embryo
Emigr|ant(in) *m* -en, -en (*f* -, -nen)
emigrant. **E∼ation** /-'tsio:n/ *f* -
emigration. **e∼ieren** *vi* (*sein*)
emigrate
Empfang *m* -[e]s,ˉe reception;
(*Erhalt*) receipt; **in E∼ nehmen**
receive; (*annehmen*) accept. **e∼en**†
vt receive; (*Biol*) conceive
Empfäng|er *m* -s,- recipient; (*Post-*)
addressee; (*Zahlungs-*) payee; (*Radio*,
TV) receiver. **E∼nis** *f* - (*Biol*)
conception
Empfängnisverhütung *f*
contraception. **E∼smittel** *nt*
contraceptive
Empfangs|bestätigung *f*
receipt. **E∼dame** *f* receptionist.
E∼halle *f* [hotel] foyer

empfehl|en† *vt* recommend.
E∼ung *f* -, -en recommendation;
(*Gruß*) regards *pl*
empfind|en† *vt* feel. **e∼lich** *a*
sensitive (**gegen** to); (*zart*) delicate.
E∼lichkeit *f* - sensitivity; delicacy;
tenderness; touchiness. **E∼ung** *f* -,
-en sensation; (*Regung*) feeling
empor *adv* (*liter*) up[wards]
empören *vt* incense; **sich e∼** be
indignant; (*sich auflehnen*) rebel
Emporkömmling *m* -s, -e upstart
empör|t *a* indignant. **E∼ung** *f* -
indignation; (*Auflehnung*) rebellion
Ende *nt* -s, -n end; (*eines Films*,
Romans) ending; (**E** *Stück*) bit; **zu**
E∼ sein be finished; **etw zu E∼**
schreiben finish writing sth; **am E∼**
at the end; (*schließlich*) in the end;
(**E** *vielleicht*) perhaps; (**E** *erschöpft*)
at the end of one's tether
end|en *vi* (*haben*) end. **e∼gültig** *a*
final; (*bestimmt*) definite
Endivie /-iə/ *f* -, -n endive
end|lich *adv* at last, finally;
(*schließlich*) in the end. **e∼los** *a*
endless. **E∼station** *f* terminus.
E∼ung *f* -, -en (*Gram*) ending
Energie *f* - energy
energisch *a* resolute;
(*nachdrücklich*) vigorous
eng *a* narrow; (*beengt*) cramped;
(*anliegend*) tight; (*nah*) close; **e∼**
anliegend tight-fitting
Engagement /āgaʒə'mā:/ *nt* -s, -s
(*Theat*) engagement; (*fig*)
commitment
Engel *m* -s,- angel
England *nt* -s England
Engländer *m* -s,- Englishman;
(*Techn*) monkey-wrench; **die E∼** the
English *pl*. **E∼in** *f* -, -nen
Englishwoman
englisch *a* English. **E∼** *nt* -[s]
(*Lang*) English; **auf E∼** in English
Engpass *m* (*fig*) bottle-neck
en gros /ã'gro:/ *adv* wholesale
Enkel *m* -s,- grandson; **E∼** *pl*
grandchildren. **E∼in** *f* -, -nen
granddaughter. **E∼kind** *nt*

grandchild. **E~sohn** *m* grandson.
E~tochter *f* granddaughter

Ensemble /ã'sã:bəl/ *nt* **-s, -s**
ensemble; (*Theat*) company

entart|en *vi* (*sein*) degenerate.
e~et *a* degenerate

entbehren *vt* do without;
(*vermissen*) miss

entbind|en† *vt* release (**von** from);
(*Med*) deliver (**von** of) ● *vi* (*haben*)
give birth. **E~ung** *f* delivery.
E~ungsstation *f* maternity ward

entdeck|en *vt* discover. **E~er** *m*
-s,- discoverer; (*Forscher*) explorer.
E~ung *f* -, -en discovery

Ente *f* -, -n duck

entehren *vt* dishonour

enteignen *vt* dispossess;
expropriate <*Eigentum*>

enterben *vt* disinherit

Enterich *m* -s, -e drake

entfallen† *vi* (*sein*) not apply; **auf**
jdn e~ be s.o.'s share

entfern|en *vt* remove; **sich e~en**
leave. **e~t** *a* distant; (*schwach*)
vague; **2 Kilometer e~t** 2 kilometres
away; **e~t verwandt** distantly
related. **E~ung** *f* -, -en removal;
(*Abstand*) distance; (*Reichweite*)
range

entfliehen† *vi* (*sein*) escape

entfremden *vt* alienate

entfrosten *vt* defrost

entführ|en *vt* abduct, kidnap;
hijack <*Flugzeug*>. **E~er** *m*
abductor, kidnapper; hijacker.
E~ung *f* abduction, kidnapping;
hijacking

entgegen *adv* towards ● *prep* (+
dat) contrary to. **e~gehen**† *vi sep*
(*sein*) (+ *dat*) go to meet; (*fig*) be
heading for. **e~gesetzt** *a* opposite;
(*gegensätzlich*) opposing.
e~kommen† *vi sep* (*sein*) (+ *dat*)
come to meet; (*zukommen auf*) come
towards; (*fig*) oblige. **E~kommen**
nt **-s** helpfulness; (*Zugeständnis*)
concession. **e~kommend** *a*
approaching; <*Verkehr*> oncoming;

(*fig*) obliging. **e~nehmen**† *vt sep*
accept. **e~wirken** *vi sep* (*haben*) (+
dat) counteract; (*fig*) oppose

entgegn|en *vt* reply (**auf** + *acc* to).
E~ung *f* -, -en reply

entgehen† *vi sep* (*sein*) (+ *dat*)
escape; **jdm e~** (*unbemerkt bleiben*)
escape s.o.'s notice; **sich** (*dat*) **etw**
e~ lassen miss sth

Entgelt *nt* -[e]s payment; **gegen E~**
for money

entgleis|en *vi* (*sein*) be derailed;
(*fig*) make a gaffe. **E~ung** *f* -, -en
derailment; (*fig*) gaffe

entgräten *vt* fillet, bone

Enthaarungsmittel *nt* depilatory

enthalt|en† *vt* contain; **in etw** (*dat*)
e~en sein be contained/
(*eingeschlossen*) included in sth; **sich**
der Stimme e~en (*Pol*) abstain.
e~sam *a* abstemious. **E~ung** *f*
(*Pol*) abstention

enthaupten *vt* behead

entheben† *vt* **jdn seines Amtes e~**
relieve s.o. of his post

Enthüllung *f* -, -en revelation

Enthusias|mus *m* - enthusiast.
E~t *m* -en, -en enthusiast

entkernen *vt* stone; core <*Apfel*>

entkleiden *vt* undress; **sich e~en**
undress

entkommen† *vi* (*sein*) escape

entkorken *vt* uncork

entladen† *vt* unload; (*Electr*)
discharge; **sich e~** discharge;
<*Gewitter:*> break; <*Zorn:*> explode

entlang *adv* & *prep* (+ *preceding acc*
or following dat) along; **die Straße**
e~ along the road; **an etw** (*dat*) **e~**
along sth. **e~fahren**† *vi sep* (*sein*)
drive along. **e~gehen**† *vi sep* (*sein*)
walk along

entlarven *vt* unmask

entlass|en† *vt* dismiss; (*aus*
Krankenhaus) discharge; (*aus der*
Haft) release. **E~ung** *f* -, -en
dismissal; discharge; release

entlast|en *vt* relieve the strain on;
ease <*Gewissen, Verkehr*>; relieve
(**von** of); (*Jur*) exonerate. **E~ung** *f* -
relief; exoneration

---

*old spelling

entlaufen† *vi* (*sein*) run away

entleeren *vt* empty

entlegen *a* remote

entlohnen *vt* pay

entlüft|en *vt* ventilate. **E~er** *m* **-s,-** extractor fan. **E~ung** *f* ventilation

entmündigen *vt* declare incapable of managing one's own affairs

entmutigen *vt* discourage

entnehmen† *vt* take (*dat* from); (*schließen*) gather (*dat* from)

entpuppen (sich) *vr* (*fig*) turn out (**als etw** to be sth)

entrahmt *a* skimmed

entrichten *vt* pay

entrinnen† *vi* (*sein*) escape

entrüst|en *vt* fill with indignation; **sich e~en** be indignant (**über** + *acc* at). **e~et** *a* indignant. **E~ung** *f* - indignation

entsaft|en *vt* extract the juice from. **E~er** *m* **-s,-** juice extractor

entsagen *vi* (*haben*) (+ *dat*) renounce

entschädig|en *vt* compensate. **E~ung** *f* -, **-en** compensation

entschärfen *vt* defuse

entscheid|en† *vt/i* (*haben*) decide; **sich e~en** decide; <*Sache:*> be decided. **e~end** *a* decisive; (*kritisch*) crucial. **E~ung** *f* decision

entschließen† **(sich)** *vr* decide, make up one's mind; **sich anders e~** change one's mind

entschlossen *a* determined; (*energisch*) resolute; **kurz e~** without hesitation. **E~heit** *f* - determination

Entschluss *m* decision

entschlüsseln *vt* decode

entschuld|bar *a* excusable. **e~igen** *vt* excuse; **sich e~igen** apologize (**bei** to); **e~igen Sie [bitte]!** sorry! (*bei Frage*) excuse me. **E~igung** *f* -, **-en** apology; (*Ausrede*) excuse; **um E~igung bitten** apologize

entsetz|en *vt* horrify. **E~en** *nt* **-s** horror. **e~lich** *a* horrible; (*schrecklich*) terrible

Entsorgung *f* - waste disposal

entspann|en *vt* relax; **sich e~en** relax; <*Lage:*> ease. **E~ung** *f* - relaxation; easing; (*Pol*) détente

entsprech|en† *vi* (*haben*) (+ *dat*) correspond to; (*übereinstimmen*) agree with. **e~end** *a* corresponding; (*angemessen*) appropriate; (*zuständig*) relevant ● *adv* correspondingly; appropriately; (*demgemäß*) accordingly ● *prep* (+ *dat*) in accordance with

entspringen† *vi* (*sein*) <*Fluss:*> rise; (*fig*) arise, spring (*dat* from)

entstammen *vi* (*sein*) come/ (*abstammen*) be descended (*dat* from)

entsteh|en† *vi* (*sein*) come into being; (*sich bilden*) form; (*sich entwickeln*) develop; <*Brand:*> start; (*stammen*) originate. **E~ung** *f* - origin; formation; development

entstell|en *vt* disfigure; (*verzerren*) distort. **E~ung** *f* disfigurement; distortion

entstört *a* (*Electr*) suppressed

enttäusch|en *vt* disappoint. **E~ung** *f* disappointment

entwaffnen *vt* disarm

entwässer|n *vt* drain. **E~ung** *f* - drainage

entweder *conj* & *adv* either

entwerfen† *vt* design; (*aufsetzen*) draft; (*skizzieren*) sketch

entwert|en *vt* devalue; (*ungültig machen*) cancel. **E~er** *m* **-s,-** ticket-cancelling machine. **E~ung** *f* devaluation; cancelling

entwick|eln *vt* develop; **sich e~eln** develop. **E~lung** *f* -, **-en** development; (*Biol*) evolution. **E~lungsland** *nt* developing country

entwöhnen *vt* wean (*gen* from); cure <*Süchtige*>

entwürdigend *a* degrading

Entwurf *m* design; (*Konzept*) draft; (*Skizze*) sketch

entwurzeln *vt* uproot

entzie|hen† *vt* take away (*dat* from); **jdm den Führerschein e~hen** disqualify s.o. from driving; **sich**

e~hen (+ *dat*) withdraw from.
E~hungskur *f* treatment for drug/
alcohol addiction

entziffern *vt* decipher

Entzug *m* withdrawal;
(*Vorenthaltung*) deprivation

entzünd|en *vt* ignite; (*anstecken*)
light; (*fig: erregen*) inflame; **sich**
e~en ignite; (*Med*) become inflamed.
e~et *a* (*Med*) inflamed. e~lich *a*
inflammable. **E~ung** *f* (*Med*)
inflammation

entzwei *a* broken

Enzian *m* -s, -e gentian

Enzyklo|pädie *f* -, -en
encyclopaedia. e~pädisch *a*
encyclopaedic

Enzym *nt* -s, -e enzyme

Epidemie *f* -, -n epidemic

Epi|lepsie *f* - epilepsy.
E~leptiker(in) *m* -s,- (*f* -, -nen)
epileptic. e~leptisch *a* epileptic

Epilog *m* -s, -e epilogue

Episode *f* -, -n episode

Epoche *f* -, -n epoch

Epos *nt* -/Epen epic

er *pron* he; (*Ding, Tier*) it

erachten *vt* consider (**für nötig**
necessary). **E~** *nt* -s **meines E~s** in
my opinion

erbarmen (sich) *vr* have pity/
<*Gott:*> mercy (*gen* on). **E~** *nt* -s
pity; mercy

erbärmlich *a* wretched

erbauen *vt* build; (*fig*) edify; **nicht**
erbaut von [!] not pleased about

Erbe[1] *m* -n, -n heir

Erbe[2] *nt* -s inheritance; (*fig*)
heritage. e~n *vt* inherit

erbeuten *vt* get; (*Mil*) capture

Erbfolge *f* (*Jur*) succession

erbieten† (**sich**) *vr* offer (**zu to**)

Erbin *f* -, -nen heiress

erbitten† *vt* ask for

erbittert *a* bitter; (*heftig*) fierce

erblassen *vi* (*sein*) turn pale

erblich *a* hereditary

erblicken *vt* catch sight of

erblinden *vi* (*sein*) go blind

erbrechen† *vt* vomit ● *vi/r* [**sich**]
e~ vomit. **E~** *nt* -s vomiting

Erbschaft *f* -, -en inheritance

Erbse *f* -, -n pea

Erb|stück *nt* heirloom. **E~teil** *nt*
inheritance

Erd|apfel *m* (*Aust*) potato.
E~beben *nt* -s,- earthquake.
E~beere *f* strawberry

Erde *f* -, -n earth; (*Erdboden*) ground;
(*Fußboden*) floor. e~n *vt* (*Electr*)
earth

erdenklich *a* imaginable

Erd|gas *nt* natural gas.
E~geschoss *nt* ground floor.
E~kugel *f* globe. **E~kunde** *f*
geography. **E~nuss** *f* peanut. **E~öl**
nt [mineral] oil

erdrosseln *vt* strangle

erdrücken *vt* crush to death

Erd|rutsch *m* landslide. **E~teil** *m*
continent

erdulden *vt* endure

ereignen (sich) *vr* happen

Ereignis *nt* -ses, -se event. e~los
a uneventful. e~reich *a* eventful

Eremit *m* -en, -en hermit

erfahr|en† *vt* learn, hear; (*erleben*)
experience ● *a* experienced. **E~ung**
f -, -en experience; in **E~ung bringen**
find out

erfassen *vt* seize; (*begreifen*) grasp;
(*einbeziehen*) include; (*aufzeichnen*)
record

erfind|en† *vt* invent. **E~er** *m* -s,-
inventor. e~erisch *a* inventive.
E~ung *f* -, -en invention

Erfolg *m* -[e]s, -e success; (*Folge*)
result; **E~ haben** be successful.
e~en *vi* (*sein*) take place;
(*geschehen*) happen. e~los *a*
unsuccessful. e~reich *a* successful

erforder|lich *a* required,
necessary. e~n *vt* require, demand

erforsch|en *vt* explore;
(*untersuchen*) investigate. **E~ung** *f*
exploration; investigation

erfreu|en *vt* please. e~lich *a*
pleasing. e~licherweise *adv*
happily. e~t *a* pleased

erfrier|en† *vi* (*sein*) freeze to death; <*Glied:*> become frostbitten; <*Pflanze:*> be killed by the frost. **E~ung** *f* -, -en frostbite

erfrisch|en *vt* refresh. **E~ung** *f* -, -en refreshment

erfüll|en *vt* fill; (*nachkommen*) fulfil; serve <*Zweck*>; discharge <*Pflicht:*> sich e~en come true. **E~ung** *f* fulfilment

erfunden *a* invented

ergänz|en *vt* complement; (*hinzufügen*) add. **E~ung** *f* complement; supplement; (*Zusatz*) addition

ergeben† *vt* produce; (*zeigen*) show, establish; sich e~en result; <*Schwierigkeit:*> arise; (*kapitulieren*) surrender; (*sich fügen*) submit ● *a* devoted; (*resigniert*) resigned

Ergebnis *nt* -ses, -se result. **e~los** *a* fruitless

ergiebig *a* productive; (*fig*) rich

ergreifen† *vt* seize; take <*Maßnahme, Gelegenheit*>; take up <*Beruf*>; (*rühren*) move; **die Flucht e~** flee. **e~d** *a* moving

ergriffen *a* deeply moved. **E~heit** *f* - emotion

ergründen *vt* (*fig*) get to the bottom of

erhaben *a* raised; (*fig*) sublime

Erhalt *m* -[e]s receipt. **e~en**† *vt* receive, get; (*gewinnen*) obtain; (*bewahren*) preserve, keep; (*instand halten*) maintain; (*unterhalten*) support; **am Leben e~en** keep alive ● *a* **gut/schlecht e~en** in good/bad condition; **e~en bleiben** survive

erhältlich *a* obtainable

Erhaltung *f* - preservation; maintenance

erhängen (sich) *vr* hang oneself

erheb|en† *vt* raise; levy <*Steuer*>; charge <*Gebühr*>; **Anspruch e~en** lay claim (**auf** + *acc* to); **Protest e~en** protest; **sich e~en** rise; <*Frage:*> arise. **e~lich** *a* considerable. **E~ung** *f* -, -en elevation; (*Anhöhe*) rise; (*Aufstand*) uprising; (*Ermittlung*) survey

erheiter|n *vt* amuse. **E~ung** *f* - amusement

erhitzen *vt* heat

erhöh|en *vt* raise; (*fig*) increase; **sich e~en** rise, increase. **E~ung** *f* -, -en increase

erhol|en (sich) *vr* recover (**von** from); (*nach Krankheit*) convalesce; (*sich ausruhen*) have a rest. **e~sam** *a* restful. **E~ung** *f* - recovery; (*Ruhe*) rest

erinner|n *vt* remind (**an** + *acc* of); **sich e~n** remember (**an jdn/etw** s.o./ sth). **E~ung** *f* -, -en memory; (*Andenken*) souvenir

erkält|en (sich) *vr* catch a cold; **e~et sein** have a cold. **E~ung** *f* -, -en cold

erkenn|bar *a* recognizable; (*sichtbar*) visible. **e~en**† *vt* recognize; (*wahrnehmen*) distinguish. **E~tnis** *f* -, -se recognition; realization; (*Wissen*) knowledge; **die neuesten E~tnisse** the latest findings

Erker *m* -s,- bay

erklär|en *vt* declare; (*erläutern*) explain; **sich bereit e~en** agree (**zu** to). **e~end** *a* explanatory. **e~lich** *a* explicable; (*verständlich*) understandable. **e~licherweise** *adv* understandably. **E~ung** *f* -, -en declaration; explanation; **öffentliche E~ung** public statement

erkrank|en *vi* (*sein*) fall ill; be taken ill (**an** + *dat* with). **E~ung** *f* -, -en illness

erkundig|en (sich) *vr* enquire (**nach jdm/etw** after s.o./about sth). **E~ung** *f* -, -en enquiry

erlangen *vt* attain, get

Erlass *m* -es,⁻e (*Admin*) decree; (*Befreiung*) exemption; (*Straf-*) remission

erlassen† *vt* (*Admin*) issue; **jdm etw e~** exempt s.o. from sth; let s.o. off <*Strafe*>

erlauben *vt* allow, permit; **ich kann es mir nicht e~** I can't afford it

Erlaubnis *f* - permission. **E~schein** *m* permit

erläutern *vt* explain

Erle *f* -, -n alder

erleb|en *vt* experience; (*mit-*) see; have <*Überraschung*>. **E~nis** *nt* -ses, -se experience

erledigen *vt* do; (*sich befassen mit*) deal with; (*beenden*) finish; (*entscheiden*) settle; (*töten*) kill

erleichter|n *vt* lighten; (*vereinfachen*) make easier; (*befreien*) relieve; (*lindern*) ease. **e~t** *a* relieved. **E~ung** *f* - relief

erleiden† *vt* suffer

erleuchten *vt* illuminate; **hell erleuchtet** brightly lit

erlogen *a* untrue, false

Erlös *m* -es proceeds *pl*

erlöschen† *vi* (*sein*) go out; (*vergehen*) die; (*aussterben*) die out; (*ungültig werden*) expire; **erloschener Vulkan** extinct volcano

erlös|en *vt* save; (*befreien*) release (*von* from); (*Relig*) redeem. **e~t** *a* relieved. **E~ung** *f* release; (*Erleichterung*) relief; (*Relig*) redemption

ermächtig|en *vt* authorize. **E~ung** *f* -, -en authorization

Ermahnung *f* exhortation; admonition

ermäßig|en *vt* reduce. **E~ung** *f* -, -en reduction

ermessen† *vt* judge; (*begreifen*) appreciate. **E~** *nt* -s discretion; (*Urteil*) judgement; **nach eigenem E~** at one's own discretion

ermitt|eln *vt* establish; (*herausfinden*) find out ● *vi* (*haben*) investigate (*gegen jdn* s.o.). **E~lungen** *fpl* investigations. **E~lungsverfahren** *nt* (*Jur*) preliminary inquiry

ermöglichen *vt* make possible

ermord|en *vt* murder. **E~ung** *f* -, -en murder

ermüd|en *vt* tire ● *vi* (*sein*) get tired. **E~ung** *f* - tiredness

ermutigen *vt* encourage. **e~d** *a* encouraging

ernähr|en *vt* feed; (*unterhalten*) support, keep; **sich e~en von** live/ <*Tier:*> feed on. **E~er** *m* -s,- breadwinner. **E~ung** *f* - nourishment; nutrition; (*Kost*) diet

ernenn|en† *vt* appoint. **E~ung** *f* -, -en appointment

erneu|ern *vt* renew; (*auswechseln*) replace; change <*Verband*>; (*renovieren*) renovate. **E~erung** *f* renewal; replacement; renovation. **e~t** *a* renewed; (*neu*) new ● *adv* again

ernst *a* serious; **e~ nehmen** take seriously. **E~** *m* -es seriousness; **im E~** seriously; **mit einer Drohung E~ machen** carry out a threat; **ist das dein E~?** are you serious? **e~haft** *a* serious. **e~lich** *a* serious

Ernte *f* -, -n harvest; (*Ertrag*) crop. **E~dankfest** *nt* harvest festival. **e~n** *vt* harvest; (*fig*) reap, win

ernüchter|n *vt* sober up; (*fig*) bring down to earth. **e~nd** *a* (*fig*) sobering

Erober|er *m* -s,- conqueror. **e~n** *vt* conquer. **E~ung** *f* -, -en conquest

eröffn|en *vt* open; **jdm etw e~en** announce sth to s.o. **E~ung** *f* opening; (*Mitteilung*) announcement

erörter|n *vt* discuss. **E~ung** *f* -, -en discussion

Erot|ik *f* - eroticism. **e~isch** *a* erotic

Erpel *m* -s,- drake

erpicht *a* **e~auf** (+ *acc*) keen on

erpress|en *vt* extort; blackmail <*Person*>. **E~er** *m* -s,- blackmailer. **E~ung** *f* - extortion; blackmail

erprob|en *vt* test. **e~t** *a* proven

erraten† *vt* guess

erreg|bar *a* excitable. **e~en** *vt* excite; (*hervorrufen*) arouse; **sich e~en** get worked up. **e~end** *a* exciting. **E~er** *m* -s,- (*Med*) germ. **e~t** *a* agitated; (*hitzig*) heated. **E~ung** *f* - excitement

erreich|bar *a* within reach; <*Ziel*> attainable; <*Person*> available. **e~en** *vt* reach; catch <*Zug*>; live to <*Alter*>; (*durchsetzen*) achieve

---

*old spelling

errichten vt erect

erringen† vt gain, win

erröten vi (sein) blush

Errungenschaft f -, -en achievement; (☐ Anschaffung) acquisition

Ersatz m -es replacement, substitute; (Entschädigung) compensation. **E~reifen** m spare tyre. **E~teil** nt spare part

erschaffen† vt create

erschein|en† vi (sein) appear; <Buch:> be published. **E~ung** f -, -en appearance; (Person) figure; (Phänomen) phenomenon; (Symptom) symptom; (Geist) apparition

erschieß|en† vt shoot [dead]. **E~ungskommando** nt firing squad

erschlaffen vi (sein) go limp

erschlagen† vt beat to death; (tödlich treffen) strike dead; **vom Blitz e~ werden** be killed by lightning

erschließen† vt develop

erschöpf|en vt exhaust. **e~t** a exhausted. **E~ung** f - exhaustion

erschrecken vi (sein) get a fright ● vt (reg) startle; (beunruhigen) alarm; **du hast mich erschreckt** you gave me a fright

erschrocken a frightened; (erschreckt) startled

erschütter|n vt shake; (ergreifen) upset deeply. **E~ung** f -, -en shock

erschwinglich a affordable

ersehen† vt (fig) see (aus from)

ersetzen vt replace; make good <Schaden>; refund <Kosten>; **jdm etw e~** compensate s.o. for sth

ersichtlich a obvious, apparent

erspar|en vt save. **E~nis** f -, -se saving; **E~nisse** savings

erst adv (zuerst) first; (noch nicht mehr als) only; (nicht vor) not until; **e~ dann** only then; **eben e~** [only] just

erstarren vi (sein) solidify; (gefrieren) freeze; (steif werden) go stiff; (vor Schreck) be paralysed

erstatten vt (zurück-) refund; **Bericht e~** report (jdm to s.o.)

Erstaufführung f first performance, première

erstaun|en vt amaze, astonish. **E~en** nt amazement, astonishment. **e~lich** a amazing

Erst|ausgabe f first edition. **e~e(r,s)** a first; (beste) best; **e~e Hilfe** first aid. **E~e(r)** m/f first; (Beste) best; **fürs E~e** for the time being; **als E~es** first of all; **er kam als E~er** he arrived first

erstechen† vt stab to death

ersteigern vt buy at an auction

erstens adv firstly, in the first place. **e~ere(r,s)** a the former; **der/die/das E~ere** the former

ersticken vt suffocate; smother <Flammen> ● vi (sein) suffocate. **E~** nt -s suffocation; **zum E~** stifling

erstklassig a first-class

ersuchen vt ask, request. **E~** nt -s request

ertappen vt ☐ catch

erteilen vt give (jdm s.o.)

ertönen vi (sein) sound; (erschallen) ring out

Ertrag m -[e]s,-̈e yield. **e~en**† vt bear

erträglich a bearable; (leidlich) tolerable

ertränken vt drown

ertrinken† vi (sein) drown

erübrigen (sich) vr be unnecessary

erwachsen a grown-up. **E~e(r)** m/f adult, grown-up

erwäg|en† vt consider. **E~ung** f -, -en consideration; **in E~ung ziehen** consider

erwähn|en vt mention. **E~ung** f -, -en mention

erwärmen vt warm; **sich e~** warm up; (fig) warm (für to)

erwart|en vt expect; (warten auf) wait for. **E~ung** f -, -en expectation

erweisen† vt prove; (bezeigen) do <Gefallen, Dienst, Ehre>; **sich e~ als** prove to be

erweitern vt widen; dilate <Pupille>; (fig) extend, expand

Erwerb m -[e]s acquisition; (Kauf) purchase; (Brot-) livelihood; (Verdienst) earnings pl. **e~en†** vt acquire; (kaufen) purchase. **e~slos** a unemployed. **e~stätig** a employed

erwider|n vt reply; return <Besuch, Gruß>. **E~ung** f -, -en reply

erwirken vt obtain

erwürgen vt strangle

Erz nt -es, -e ore

erzähl|en vt tell (jdm s.o.) ● vi (haben) talk (von about). **E~er** m -s,- narrator. **E~ung** f -, -en story, tale

Erzbischof m archbishop

erzeug|en vt produce; (Electr) generate. **E~er** m -s,- producer. **E~nis** nt -ses, -se product; landwirtschaftliche **E~nisse** farm produce sg.

erzieh|en† vt bring up; (Sch) educate. **E~er** m -s,- [private] tutor. **E~erin** f -, -nen governess. **E~ung** f - upbringing; education

erzielen vt achieve; score <Tor>

erzogen a gut/schlecht **e~** well/ badly brought up

es
● pronoun
····▸ (Sache) it; (weibliche Person) she/ her; (männliche Person) he/him. **ich bin es** it's me. **wir sind traurig, ihr seid es auch** we are sad, and so are you. **er ist es, der ...** he is the one who .... **es sind Studenten** they are students
····▸ (impers) it. **es hat geklopft** there was a knock. **es klingelt** someone is ringing. **es wird schöner** the weather is improving. **es geht ihm gut/ schlecht** he is well/unwell. **es lässt sich aushalten** it is bearable. **es gibt** there is or (pl) are
····▸ (als formales Objekt) **er hat es gut** he has it made; he's well off. **er**

meinte es gut he meant well. **ich hoffe/glaube es** I hope/think so

Esche f -, -n ash

Esel m -s,- donkey; (🅵 Person) ass

Eskimo m -[s], -[s] Eskimo

Eskort|e f -, -n (Mil) escort. **e~ieren** vt escort

essbar a edible

essen† vt/i (haben) eat; **zu Mittag Abend e~** have lunch/supper; **e~ gehen** eat out. **E~** nt -s,- food; (Mahl) meal; (festlich) dinner

Esser(in) m -s,- (f -, -nen) eater

Essig m -s vinegar. **E~gurke** f [pickled] gherkin

Esslöffel m ≈ dessertspoon. **Essstäbchen** ntpl chopsticks. **Esstisch** m dining-table. **Esswaren** fpl food sg; (Vorräte) provisions. **Esszimmer** nt dining-room

Estland nt -s Estonia

Estragon m -s tarragon

etablieren (sich) vr establish oneself/<Geschäft:> itself

Etage /e'taːʒə/ f -, -n storey. **E~nbett** nt bunk-beds pl. **E~nwohnung** f flat

Etappe f -, -n stage

Etat /e'taː/ m -s, -s budget

Eth|ik f - ethic; (Sittenlehre) ethics sg. **e~isch** a ethical

ethnisch a ethnic; **e~e Säuberung** ethnic cleansing

Etikett nt -[e]s, -e[n] label; (Preis-) tag. **e~ieren** vt label

Etui /e'tviː/ nt -s, -s case

etwa adv (ungefähr) about; (zum Beispiel) for instance; (womöglich) perhaps; **nicht e~, dass ...** not that ...; **denkt nicht e~ ...** don't imagine ...

etwas pron something; (fragend/ verneint) anything; (ein bisschen) some, a little; **sonst noch e~?** anything else? **so e~ Ärgerliches!** what a nuisance! ● adv a bit

Etymologie f - etymology

euch *pron* (*acc of* **ihr** *pl*) you; (*dat*) [to] you; (*refl*) yourselves; (*einander*) each other

euer *poss pron pl* your. e~e, e~t- *s.* eure, euret-

Eule *f* -, -n owl

Euphorie *f* - euphoria

eur|e *poss pron pl* your. e~e(r,s) *poss pron* yours. e~etwegen *adv* for your sake; (*wegen euch*) because of you, on your account. e~etwillen *adv* um e~etwillen for your sake. e~ige *poss pron* der/die/das e~ige yours

Euro *m* -[s], -[s] Euro. E~- *pref* Euro-

Europa *nt* -s Europe. E~- *pref* European

Europä|er(in) *m* -s,- (*f* -, -nen) European. e~isch *a* European

Euter *nt* -s,- udder

evakuier|en *vt* evacuate. E~ung *f* - evacuation

evan|gelisch *a* Protestant. E~gelium *nt* -s, -ien gospel

eventuell *a* possible ● *adv* possibly; (*vielleicht*) perhaps

Evolution /-'tsjo:n/ *f* - evolution

ewig *a* eternal; (*endlos*) never-ending; e~ dauern 🔢 take ages. E~keit *f* - eternity

Examen *nt* -s,- & -mina (*Sch*) examination

Exemplar *nt* -s, -e specimen; (*Buch*) copy. e~isch *a* exemplary

exerzieren *vt/i* (*haben*) (*Mil*) drill; (*üben*) practise

exhumieren *vt* exhume

Exil *nt* -s exile

Existenz *f* -, -en existence; (*Lebensgrundlage*) livelihood

existieren *vi* (*haben*) exist

exklusiv *a* exclusive. e~e *prep* (+ *gen*) excluding

exkommunizieren *vt* excommunicate

Exkremente *npl* excrement *sg*

Expedition /-'tsjo:n/ *f* -, -en expedition

Experiment *nt* -[e]s, -e experiment. e~ieren *vi* (*haben*) experiment

Experte *m* -n, -n expert

explo|dieren *vi* (*sein*) explode. E~sion *f* -, -en explosion

Expor|t *m* -[e]s, -e export. E~teur /-'tø:ɐ/ *m* -s, -e exporter. e~tieren *vt* export

extra *adv* separately; (*zusätzlich*) extra; (*eigens*) specially; (🔢 *absichtlich*) on purpose

extravagan|t *a* flamboyant; (*übertrieben*) extravagant

extravertiert *a* extrovert

extrem *a* extreme. E~ist *m* -en, -en extremist

Exzellenz *f* - (*title*) Excellency

Exzentr|iker *m* -s,- eccentric. e~isch *a* eccentric

Fabel *f* -, -n fable. f~haft *a* 🔢 fantastic

Fabrik *f* -, -en factory. F~ant *m* -en, -en manufacturer. F~at *nt* -[e]s, -e product; (*Marke*) make. F~ation /-'tsjo:n/ *f* - manufacture

Fach *nt* -[e]s, ̈-er compartment; (*Schub-*) drawer; (*Gebiet*) field; (*Sch*) subject. F~arbeiter *m* skilled worker. F~arzt *m*, F~ärztin *f* specialist. F~ausdruck *m* technical term

Fächer *m* -s,- fan

Fach|gebiet *nt* field. f~kundig *a* expert. f~lich *a* technical; (*beruflich*) professional. F~mann *m* (*pl* -leute) expert. f~männisch *a* expert. F~schule *f* technical college. F~werkhaus *nt* half-timbered house. F~wort *nt* (*pl* -wörter) technical term

Fackel *f* -, -n torch

fade *a* insipid; (*langweilig*) dull

Faden *m* -s,⁻ thread; (*Bohnen-*) string; (*Naut*) fathom

Fagott *nt* -[e]s, -e bassoon

fähig *a* capable (**zu**/*gen* of); (*tüchtig*) able, competent. **F~keit** *f* -, -en ability; competence

fahl *a* pale

fahnd|en *vi* (*haben*) search (**nach** for). **F~ung** *f* -, -en search

Fahne *f* -, -n flag; (*Druck-*) galley [proof]; **eine F~ haben** 🛈 reek of alcohol. **F~nflucht** *f* desertion

Fahr|ausweis *m* ticket. **F~bahn** *f* carriageway; (*Straße*) road. **f~bar** *a* mobile

Fähre *f* -, -n ferry

fahr|en† *vi* (*sein*) go, travel; <*Fahrer:*> drive; <*Radfahrer:*> ride; (*verkehren*) run, (*ab-*) leave; <*Schiff:*> sail; **mit dem Auto/Zug f~en** go by car/train; **was ist in ihn gefahren?** 🛈 what has got into him? ● *vt* drive; ride <*Fahrrad*>; take <*Kurve*>. **f~end** *a* moving; (*f~bar*) mobile; (*nicht sesshaft*) travelling. **F~er** *m* -s,- driver. **F~erflucht** *f* failure to stop after an accident. **F~erhaus** *nt* driver's cab. **F~erin** *f* -, -nen woman driver. **F~gast** *m* passenger. **F~geld** *nt* fare. **F~gestell** *nt* chassis; (*Aviat*) undercarriage. **F~karte** *f* ticket. **F~kartenschalter** *m* ticket office. **f~lässig** *a* negligent. **F~lässigkeit** *f* - negligence. **F~lehrer** *m* driving instructor. **F~plan** *m* timetable. **f~planmäßig** *a* scheduled ● *adv* according to/(*pünktlich*) on schedule. **F~preis** *m* fare. **F~prüfung** *f* driving test. **F~rad** *nt* bicycle. **F~schein** *m* ticket. **F~schule** *f* driving school. **F~schüler(in)** *m(f)* learner driver. **F~stuhl** *m* lift

Fahrt *f* -, -en journey; (*Auto*) drive; (*Ausflug*) trip; (*Tempo*) speed

Fährte *f* -, -n track; (*Witterung*) scent

Fahr|tkosten *pl* travelling expenses. **F~werk** *nt*

undercarriage. **F~zeug** *nt* -[e]s, -e vehicle; (*Wasser-*) craft, vessel

fair /fɛːɐ̯/ *a* fair

Fakultät *f* -, -en faculty

Falke *m* -n, -n falcon

Fall *m* -[e]s,⁻e fall; (*Jur, Med, Gram*) case; **im F~[e]** in case (*gen* of); **auf jeden F~** in any case; (*bestimmt*) definitely; **für alle F~e** just in case; **auf keinen F~** on no account

Falle *f* -, -n trap

fallen† *vi* (*sein*) fall; (*sinken*) go down; [**im Krieg**] **f~** be killed in the war; **f~ lassen** drop <*etw, fig: Plan, jdn*>; make <*Bemerkung*>

fällen *vt* fell; (*fig*) pass <*Urteil*>

fällig *a* due; <*Wechsel*> mature; **längst f~** long overdue. **F~keit** *f* - (*Comm*) maturity

falls *conj* in case; (*wenn*) if

Fallschirm *m* parachute. **F~jäger** *m* paratrooper. **F~springer** *m* parachutist

Falltür *f* trapdoor

falsch *a* wrong; (*nicht echt, unaufrichtig*) false; (*gefälscht*) forged; <*Geld*> counterfeit; <*Schmuck*> fake ● *adv* wrongly; falsely; <*singen*> out of tune; **f~ gehen** <*Uhr:*> be wrong

fälschen *vt* forge, fake

Falschgeld *nt* counterfeit money

fälschlich *a* wrong; (*irrtümlich*) mistaken

Falsch|meldung *f* false report; (*absichtlich*) hoax report. **F~münzer** *m* -s,- counterfeiter

Fälschung *f* -, -en forgery, fake

Falte *f* -, -n fold; (*Rock-*) pleat; (*Knitter-*) crease; (*im Gesicht*) line; wrinkle

falten *vt* fold

Falter *m* -s,- butterfly; moth

faltig *a* creased; <*Gesicht*> lined; wrinkled

familiär *a* family ...; (*vertraut, zudringlich*) familiar; (*zwanglos*) informal

Familie /-iə/ *f* -, -n family. **F~nforschung** *f* genealogy. **F~nname** *m* surname

---

F~nplanung f family planning.
F~nstand m marital status
Fan /fɛn/ m -s, -s fan
Fana|tiker m -s,- fanatic. **f~tisch**
a fanatical
Fanfare f -, -n trumpet; (*Signal*)
fanfare
Fang m -[e]s,-̈e capture; (*Beute*)
catch; F~e (*Krallen*) talons; (*Zähne*)
fangs. **F~arm** m tentacle. **f~en†** vt
catch; (*ein-*) capture; **gefangen
nehmen** take prisoner. **F~en** nt -s
F~en spielen play tag. **F~frage** f
catch question
Fantasie f -, -n = Phantasie
Farb|aufnahme f colour
photograph. **F~band** nt (*pl* -bänder)
typewriter ribbon. **F~e** f -, -n
colour; (*Maler-*) paint; (*zum Färben*)
dye; (*Karten*) suit. **f~echt** a colour-
fast
färben vt colour; dye <*Textilien,
Haare*> ● vi (*haben*) not be colour-
fast
farb|enblind a colour-blind.
f~enfroh a colourful. **F~film** m
colour film. **f~ig** a coloured ● adv
in colour. **F~ige(r)** m/f coloured
man/woman. **F~kasten** m box of
paints. **f~los** a colourless. **F~stift**
m crayon. **F~stoff** m dye;
(*Lebensmittel-*) colouring. **F~ton** m
shade
Färbung f -, -en colouring
Farn m -[e]s, -e fern
Färse f -, -n heifer
Fasan m -[e]s, -e[n] pheasant
Faschierte(s) nt (*Aust*) mince
Fasching m -s (*SGer*) carnival
Faschis|mus m - fascism. **F~t** m
-en, -en fascist. **f~tisch** a fascist
Faser f -, -n fibre
Fass nt -es,-̈er barrel, cask; **Bier vom
F~** draught beer
Fassade f -, -n façade
fassbar a comprehensible;
(*greifbar*) tangible
fassen vt take [hold of], grasp;
(*ergreifen*) seize; (*fangen*) catch; (*ein-*)
set; (*enthalten*) hold; (*fig: begreifen*)
take in, grasp; conceive <*Plan*>;

make <*Entschluss*>; **sich f~** compose
oneself; **sich kurz f~** be brief; **nicht
zu f~** (*fig*) unbelievable ● vi (*haben*)
f~ an (+ *acc*) touch
Fassung f -, -en mount; (*Edelstein-*)
setting; (*Electr*) socket; (*Version*)
version; (*Beherrschung*) composure;
aus der F~ bringen disconcert.
f~slos a shaken; (*erstaunt*)
flabbergasted. **F~svermögen** nt
capacity
fast adv almost, nearly; **f~ nie**
hardly ever
fast|en vi (*haben*) fast. **F~enzeit** f
Lent. **F~nacht** f Shrovetide;
(*Karneval*) carnival.
F~nachtsdienstag m Shrove
Tuesday
fatal a fatal; (*peinlich*) embarrassing
Fata Morgana f - -/- -nen mirage
fauchen vi (*haben*) spit, hiss ● vt
snarl
faul a lazy; (*verdorben*) rotten, bad;
<*Ausrede*> lame
faul|en vi (*sein*) rot; <*Zahn:*> decay;
(*verwesen*) putrefy. **f~enzen** vi
(*haben*) be lazy. **F~enzer** m -s,-
lazy-bones *sg.* **F~heit** f - laziness
Fäulnis f - decay
Fauna f - fauna
Faust f -,Fäuste fist; **auf eigene F~**
(*fig*) off one's own bat.
F~handschuh m mitten.
F~schlag m punch
Fauxpas /fo'pa/ m -,- /-[s], -s/ gaffe
Favorit(in) /favo'ri:t(m)/ m -en, -en
(f -, -nen) (*Sport*) favourite
Fax nt -, -[e] fax. **f~en** vt fax
Faxen fpl ⚀ antics; **F~ machen** fool
about
Faxgerät nt fax machine
Februar m -s, -e February
fecht|en† vi (*haben*) fence. **F~er** m
-s,- fencer
Feder f -, -n feather; (*Schreib-*) pen;
(*Spitze*) nib; (*Techn*) spring. **F~ball**
m shuttlecock; (*Spiel*) badminton.
F~busch m plume. **f~leicht** a as
light as a feather. **f~n** vi (*haben*) be
springy; (*nachgeben*) give; (*hoch-*)
bounce. **f~nd** a springy; (*elastisch*)

elastic. **F~ung** f - (*Techn*) springs pl; (*Auto*) suspension

Fee f -, -n fairy

Fegefeuer nt purgatory

fegen vt sweep

Fehde f -, -n feud

fehl a **f~ am Platze** out of place. **F~betrag** m deficit. **f~en** vi (*haben*) be missing/(*Sch*) absent; (*mangeln*) be lacking; **mir f~t die Zeit** I haven't got the time; **was f~t ihm?** what's the matter with him? **das hat uns noch gefehlt!** that's all we need! **f~end** a missing; (*Sch*) absent

Fehler m -s,- mistake, error; (*Sport & fig*) fault; (*Makel*) flaw. **f~frei** a faultless. **f~haft** a faulty. **f~los** a flawless

Fehl|geburt f miscarriage. **F~griff** m mistake. **F~kalkulation** f miscalculation. **F~schlag** m failure. **f~schlagen†** vi sep (*sein*) fail. **F~start** m (*Sport*) false start. **F~zündung** f (*Auto*) misfire

Feier f -, -n celebration; (*Zeremonie*) ceremony; (*Party*) party. **F~abend** m end of the working day; **F~abend machen** stop work. **f~lich** a solemn; (*förmlich*) formal. **f~n** vt celebrate; hold <*Fest*> ● vi (*haben*) celebrate. **F~tag** m [public] holiday; (*kirchlicher*) feast-day; **erster/zweiter F~tag** Christmas Day / Boxing Day. **f~tags** adv on public holidays

feige a cowardly; **f~ sein** be a coward ● adv in a cowardly way

Feige f -, -n fig

Feig|heit f - cowardice. **F~ling** m -s, -e coward

Feile f -, -n file. **f~n** vt/i (*haben*) file

feilschen vi (*haben*) haggle

fein a fine; (*zart*) delicate; <*Strümpfe*> sheer; <*Unterschied*> subtle; (*scharf*) keen; (*vornehm*) refined; (*prima*) great; **sich f~ machen** dress up. **F~arbeit** f precision work

---

Feind(in) m -es, -e (f -, -nen) enemy. **f~lich** a enemy; (*f~selig*) hostile. **F~schaft** f -, -en enmity

fein|fühlig a sensitive. **F~gefühl** nt sensitivity; (*Takt*) delicacy. **F~heit** f -, -en fineness; delicacy; subtlety; refinement; **F~heiten** subtleties. **F~kostgeschäft** nt delicatessen [shop]

feist a fat

Feld nt -[e]s, -er field; (*Fläche*) ground; (*Sport*) pitch; (*Schach-*) square; (*auf Formular*) box. **F~bett** nt camp-bed. **F~forschung** f fieldwork. **F~herr** m commander. **F~stecher** m -s,- field-glasses pl. **F~webel** m -s,-(*Mil*) sergeant. **F~zug** m campaign

Felge f -, -n [wheel] rim

Fell nt -[e]s, -e (*Zool*) coat; (*Pelz*) fur; (*abgezogen*) skin, pelt

Fels m -en, -en rock. **F~block** m boulder. **F~en** m -s,- rock

Femininum nt -s, -na (*Gram*) feminine

Feminist|(in) m -en, -en (f -, -nen) feminist. **f~isch** a feminist

Fenchel m -s fennel

Fenster nt -s,- window. **F~brett** nt window-sill. **F~scheibe** f [window-]pane

Ferien /'fe:riən/ pl holidays; (*Univ*) vacation sg; **F~ haben** be on holiday. **F~ort** m holiday resort

Ferkel nt -s,- piglet

fern a distant; **der F~e Osten** the Far East; **sich f~ halten** keep away ● adv far away; **von f~** from a distance ● prep (+ dat) far [away] from. **F~bedienung** f remote control. **F~e** f - distance; **in weiter F~e** far away; (*zeitlich*) in the distant future. **f~er** a further ● adv (*außerdem*) furthermore; (*in Zukunft*) in future. **f~gelenkt** a remote-controlled; <*Rakete*> guided. **F~gespräch** nt long-distance call. **F~glas** nt binoculars pl. **F~kurs[us]** m correspondence course. **F~licht** nt (*Auto*) full beam. **F~meldewesen** nt

---

telecommunications *pl.* **F~rohr** *nt*
telescope. **F~schreiben** *nt* telex

Fernseh|apparat *m* television
set. **f~en**† *vi sep* (*haben*) watch
television. **F~en** *nt* **-s** television.
F~er *m* **-s,-** [television] viewer;
(*Gerät*) television set

Fernsprech|amt *nt* telephone
exchange. **F~er** *m* telephone

Fernsteuerung *f* remote control

Ferse *f* **-, -n** heel

fertig *a* finished; (*bereit*) ready;
(*Comm*) ready-made; <*Gericht*>
ready-to-serve; **f~ werden mit** finish;
(*bewältigen*) cope with; **f~ sein** have
finished; (*fig*) be through (**mit jdm**
with s.o.); (🔲 *erschöpft*) be all in/
(*seelisch*) shattered; **etw f~ bringen**
manage to do sth; (*beenden*) finish
sth; **etw/jdn f~ machen** finish sth;
(*bereitmachen*) get sth/s.o. ready; (🔲
erschöpfen) wear s.o. out; (*seelisch*)
shatter s.o.; **sich f~ machen** get
ready; **etw f~ stellen** complete sth
● *adv* **f~ essen/lesen** finish eating/
reading. **F~bau** *m* (*pl* **-bauten**)
prefabricated building. **f~en** *vt*
make. **F~gericht** *nt* ready-to-serve
meal. **F~haus** *nt* prefabricated
house. **F~keit** *f* **-, -en** skill.
F~stellung *f* completion. **F~ung** *f*
- manufacture

fesch *a* 🔲 attractive

Fessel *f* **-, -n** ankle

fesseln *vt* tie up; tie (**an** + *acc* to);
(*fig*) fascinate

fest *a* firm; (*nicht flüssig*) solid;
(*erstarrt*) set; (*haltbar*) strong; (*nicht
locker*) tight; (*feststehend*) fixed;
(*ständig*) steady; <*Anstellung*>
permanent; <*Schlaf*> sound; <*Blick,
Stimme*> steady; **f~ werden** harden;
<*Gelee:*> set; **f~e Nahrung** solids *pl*
● *adv* firmly; tightly; steadily;
soundly; (*kräftig, tüchtig*) hard; **f~
schlafen** be fast asleep; **f~ angestellt**
permanent

Fest *nt* **-[e]s, -e** celebration; (*Party*)
party; (*Relig*) festival; **frohes F~!**
happy Christmas!

fest|binden† *vt sep* tie (**an** + *dat*
to). **f~bleiben**† *vi sep* (*sein*) (*fig*)

remain firm. **f~halten**† *v sep* ● *vt*
hold on to; (*aufzeichnen*) record; **sich
f~halten** hold on ● *vi* (*haben*)
f~halten an (+ *dat*) (*fig*) stick to;
cling to <*Tradition*>. **f~igen** *vt*
strengthen. **F~iger** *m* **-s,-** styling
lotion/(*Schaum-*) mousse. **F~igkeit**
f **-** firmness; solidity; strength;
steadiness. **F~land** *nt* mainland;
(*Kontinent*) continent. **f~legen** *vt
sep* (*fig*) fix, settle; lay down
<*Regeln*>; tie up <*Geld*>; **sich
f~legen** commit oneself

festlich *a* festive **F~keiten** *fpl*
festivities

fest|liegen† *vi sep* (*haben*) be fixed,
settled. **f~machen** *v sep* ● *vt*
fasten/(*binden*) tie (**an** + *dat* to);
(*f~legen*) fix, settle ● *vi* (*haben*)
(*Naut*) moor. **F~mahl** *nt* feast.
F~nahme *f* **-, -n** arrest.
f~nehmen† *vt sep* arrest.
f~setzen *vt sep* fix, settle;
(*inhaftieren*) gaol; **sich f~setzen**
collect. **f~sitzen**† *vi sep* (*haben*) be
firm/<*Schraube:*> tight; (*haften*)
stick; (*nicht weiterkommen*) be stuck.
F~spiele *npl* festival *sg.*
f~stehen† *vi sep* (*haben*) be
certain. **f~stellen** *vt sep* fix;
(*ermitteln*) establish; (*bemerken*)
notice; (*sagen*) state. **F~tag** *m*
special day

Festung *f* **-, -en** fortress

Festzug *m* [grand] procession

Fete /'fe:tə, 'fɛ:tə/ *f* **-, -n** party

fett *a* fat; fatty; (*fettig*) greasy;
rich; <*Druck*> bold. **F~** *nt* **-[e]s, -e**
fat; (*flüssig*) grease. **f~arm** *a* low-
fat. **f~en** *vt* grease ● *vi* (*haben*) be
greasy. **F~fleck** *m* grease mark.
f~ig *a* greasy

Fetzen *m* **-s,-** scrap; (*Stoff*) rag

feucht *a* damp, moist; <*Luft*>
humid. **F~igkeit** *f* **-** dampness;
(*Nässe*) moisture; (*Luft-*) humidity.
F~igkeitscreme *f* moisturizer

Feuer *nt* **-s,-** fire; (*für Zigarette*)
light; (*Begeisterung*) passion; **F~
machen** light a fire. **F~alarm** *m*
fire alarm. **f~gefährlich** *a*
[in]flammable. **F~leiter** *f* fire-

escape. **F∼löscher** *m* -s,- fire
extinguisher. **F∼melder** *m* -s,- fire
alarm. **f∼n** *vi* (*haben*) fire (auf + *acc*
on). **F∼probe** *f* (*fig*) test. **f∼rot** *a*
crimson. **F∼stein** *m* flint.
F∼stelle *f* hearth. **F∼treppe** *f*
fire-escape. **F∼wache** *f* fire station.
F∼waffe *f* firearm. **F∼wehr** *f* -,
-en fire brigade. **F∼wehrauto** *nt*
fire-engine. **F∼wehrmann** *m* (*pl*
-männer & -leute) fireman. **F∼werk**
nt firework display, fireworks *pl*.
F∼zeug *nt* lighter

feurig *a* fiery; (*fig*) passionate

Fiaker *m* -s,- (*Aust*) horse-drawn cab

Fichte *f* -, -n spruce

Fieber *nt* -s [raised] temperature;
F∼ haben have a temperature. **f∼n**
vi (*haben*) be feverish.
F∼thermometer *nt* thermometer

fiebrig *a* feverish

Figur *f* -, -en figure; (*Roman-, Film-*)
character; (*Schach-*) piece

Filet /fi'le:/ *nt* -s, -s fillet

Filiale *f* -, -n (*Comm*) branch

Filigran *nt* -s filigree

Film *m* -[e]s, -e film; (*Kino-*) film;
(*Schicht*) coating. **f∼en** *vt/i* (*haben*)
film. **F∼kamera** *f* cine-/(*für
Kinofilm*) film camera

Filt|er *m* & (*Techn*) *nt* -s,- filter;
(*Zigaretten-*) filter-tip. **f∼ern** *vt*
filter. **F∼erzigarette** *f* filter-tipped
cigarette. **f∼rieren** *vt* filter

Filz *m* -es felt. **F∼stift** *m* felt-tipped
pen

Fimmel *m* -s,- 🔲 obsession

Finale *nt* -s,- (*Mus*) finale; (*Sport*)
final

Finanz *f* -, -en finance. **F∼amt** *nt*
tax office. **f∼iell** *a* financial.
f∼ieren *vt* finance. **F∼minister** *m*
minister of finance

find|en† *vt* find; (*meinen*) think; den
Tod f∼en meet one's death; **wie
f∼est du das?** what do you think of
that? **es wird sich f∼en** it'll turn up;
(*fig*) it'll be all right ● *vi* (*haben*) find
one's way. **F∼er** *m* -s,- finder.

F∼erlohn *m* reward. **f∼ig** *a*
resourceful

Finesse *f* -, -n (*Kniff*) trick; **F∼n**
(*Techn*) refinements

Finger *m* -s,- finger; die **F∼** lassen
von 🔲 leave alone. **F∼abdruck** *m*
finger-mark; (*Admin*) fingerprint.
F∼hut *m* thimble. **F∼nagel** *m*
finger-nail. **F∼spitze** *f* fingertip.
F∼zeig *m* -[e]s, -e hint

Fink *m* -en, -en finch

Finn|e *m* -n, -n, **F∼in** *f* -, -nen Finn.
f∼isch *a* Finnish. **F∼land** *nt* -s
Finland

finster *a* dark; (*düster*) gloomy;
(*unheildrohend*) sinister. **F∼nis** *f* -
darkness; (*Astr*) eclipse

Firma *f* -, -men firm, company

Firmen|wagen *m* company car.
F∼zeichen *nt* trade mark, logo

Firmung *f* -, -en (*Relig*) confirmation

Firnis *m* -ses, -se varnish. **f∼sen** *vt*
varnish

First *m* -[e]s, -e [roof] ridge

Fisch *m* -[e]s, -e fish; **F∼e** (*Astr*)
Pisces. **F∼dampfer** *m* trawler.
f∼en *vt/i* (*haben*) fish. **F∼er** *m* -s,-
fisherman. **F∼erei** *f* - fishing.
F∼händler *m* fishmonger.
F∼reiher *m* heron

Fiskus *m* - der **F∼** the Treasury

fit *a* fit. **Fitness** *f* - fitness

fix *a* 🔲 quick; (*geistig*) bright; **f∼e
Idee** obsession; **fix und fertig** all
finished; (*bereit*) all ready; (🔲
erschöpft) shattered. **F∼er** *m* -s,- ✖
junkie

fixieren *vt* stare at; (*Phot*) fix

Fjord *m* -[e]s, -e fiord

flach *a* flat; (*eben*) level; (*niedrig*)
low; (*nicht tief*) shallow

Fläche *f* -, -n area; (*Ober-*) surface;
(*Seite*) face. **F∼nmaß** *nt* square
measure

Flachs *m* -es flax. **f∼blond** *a*
flaxen-haired; <*Haar*> flaxen

flackern *vi* (*haben*) flicker

Flagge *f* -, -n flag

Flair /flɛːɐ̯/ *nt* -s air, aura

Flak *f* -, -[s] anti-aircraft artillery/
(*Geschütz*) gun

flämisch *a* Flemish

Flamme *f* -, -n flame; (*Koch-*) burner

Flanell *m* -s (*Tex*) flannel

Flank|e *f* -, -n flank. **f~ieren** *vt* flank

Flasche *f* -, -n bottle. **F~nbier** *nt* bottled beer. **F~nöffner** *m* bottle-opener

flatter|haft *a* fickle. **f~n** *vi* (*sein/ haben*) flutter; <*Segel:*> flap

flau *a* (*schwach*) faint; (*Comm*) slack

Flaum *m* -[e]s down. **f~ig** *a* downy; **f~ig rühren** (*Aust Culin*) cream

flauschig *a* fleecy; <*Spielzeug*> fluffy

Flausen *fpl* 🗉 silly ideas

Flaute *f* -, -n (*Naut*) calm; (*Comm*) slack period; (*Schwäche*) low

fläzen (sich) *vr* 🗉 sprawl

Flechte *f* -, -n (*Med*) eczema; (*Bot*) lichen; (*Zopf*) plait. **f~n†** *vt* plait; weave <*Korb*>

Fleck *m* -[e]s, -e[n] spot; (*größer*) patch; (*Schmutz-*) stain, mark; **blauer F~** bruise. **f~en** *vi* (*haben*) stain. **f~enlos** *a* spotless. **F~entferner** *m* -s,- stain remover. **f~ig** *a* stained

Fledermaus *f* bat

Flegel *m* -s,- lout. **f~haft** *a* loutish

flehen *vi* (*haben*) beg (**um** for)

Fleisch *nt* -[e]s flesh; (*Culin*) meat; (*Frucht-*) pulp; **F~ fressend** carnivorous. **F~er** *m* -s,- butcher. **F~fresser** *m* -s,- carnivore. **f~ig** *a* fleshy. **f~lich** *a* carnal. **F~wolf** *m* mincer

Fleiß *m* -es diligence; **mit F~** diligently; (*absichtlich*) on purpose. **f~ig** *a* diligent; (*arbeitsam*) industrious

fletschen *vt* **die Zähne f~** <*Tier:*> bare its teeth

flex|ibel *a* flexible; <*Einband*> limp. **F~ibilität** *f* - flexibility

flicken *vt* mend; (*mit Flicken*) patch. **F~** *m* -s,- patch

Flieder *m* -s lilac

Fliege *f* -, -n fly; (*Schleife*) bow-tie. **f~n†** *vi* (*sein*) fly; (*geworfen werden*) be thrown; (🗉 *fallen*) fall; (🗉 *entlassen werden*) be fired/(*von der Schule*) expelled; **in die Luft f~n** blow up ● *vt* fly. **f~nd** *a* flying. **F~r** *m* -s,- airman; (*Pilot*) pilot; (🗉 *Flugzeug*) plane. **F~rangriff** *m* air raid

flieh|en† *vi* (*sein*) flee (**vor** + *dat* from); (*entweichen*) escape ● *vt* shun. **f~end** *a* fleeing; <*Kinn, Stirn*> receding

Fliese *f* -, -n tile

Fließ|band *nt* assembly line. **f~en†** *vi* (*sein*) flow; (*aus Wasserhahn*) run. **f~end** *a* flowing; <*Wasser*> running; <*Verkehr*> moving; (*geläufig*) fluent

flimmern *vi* (*haben*) shimmer; (*TV*) flicker

flink *a* nimble; (*schnell*) quick

Flinte *f* -, -n shotgun

Flirt /flœrt/ *m* -s, -s flirtation. **f~en** *vi* (*haben*) flirt

Flitter *m* -s sequins *pl*. **F~wochen** *fpl* honeymoon *sg*

flitzen *vi* (*sein*) 🗉 dash

Flock|e *f* -, -n flake; (*Wolle*) tuft. **f~ig** *a* fluffy

Floh *m* -[e]s,¨e flea. **F~spiel** *nt* tiddly-winks *sg*

Flora *f* - flora

Florett *nt* -[e]s, -e foil

florieren *vi* (*haben*) flourish

Floskel *f* -, -n [empty] phrase

Floß *nt* -es,¨e raft

Flosse *f* -, -n fin; (*Seehund-, Gummi-*) flipper; (🗷 *Hand*) paw

Flöt|e *f* -, -n flute; (*Block-*) recorder. **f~en** *vi* (*haben*) play the flute/ recorder; (🗉 *pfeifen*) whistle ● *vt* play on the flute/recorder. **F~ist(in)** *m* -en, -en (*f* -, -nen) flautist

flott *a* quick; (*lebhaft*) lively; (*schick*) smart

Flotte *f* -, -n fleet

flottmachen *vt sep* **wieder f~** (*Naut*) refloat; get going again <*Auto*>; put back on its feet <*Unternehmen*>

Flöz *nt* -es, -e [coal] seam

Fluch *m* -[e]s,¨e curse. **f~en** *vi* (*haben*) curse, swear

Flucht f - flight; (*Entweichen*) escape; die F~ ergreifen take flight. **f~artig** a hasty

flücht|en vi (*sein*) flee (**vor** + *dat* from); (*entweichen*) escape ● *vr* **sich f~en** take refuge. **f~ig** a fugitive; (*kurz*) brief; <*Blick*> fleeting; <*Bekanntschaft*> passing; (*oberflächlich*) cursory; (*nicht sorgfältig*) careless. **f~ig kennen** know slightly. **F~igkeitsfehler** m slip. **F~ling** m -s, -e fugitive; (*Pol*) refugee

Fluchwort nt (*pl* -wörter) swear-word

Flug m -[e]s,¨e flight. **F~abwehr** f anti-aircraft defence

Flügel m -s,- wing; (*Fenster-*) casement; (*Mus*) grand piano

Fluggast m [air] passenger

flügge a fully-fledged

Flug|gesellschaft f airline. **F~hafen** m airport. **F~lotse** m air-traffic controller. **F~platz** m airport; (*klein*) airfield. **F~preis** m air fare. **F~schein** m air ticket. **F~schneise** f flight path. **F~schreiber** m -s,- flight recorder. **F~schrift** f pamphlet. **F~steig** m -[e]s, -e gate. **F~zeug** nt -[e]s, -e aircraft, plane

Flunder f -, -n flounder

flunkern vi (*haben*) 🔟 tell fibs

Flur m -[e]s, -e [entrance] hall; (*Gang*) corridor

Fluss m -es,¨e river; (*Fließen*) flow; im F~ (*fig*) in a state of flux. **f~abwärts** adv downstream. **f~aufwärts** adv upstream

flüssig a liquid; <*Lava*> molten; (*fließend*) fluent; <*Verkehr*> freely moving. **F~keit** f -, -en liquid; (*Anat*) fluid

Flusspferd nt hippopotamus

flüstern vt/i (*haben*) whisper

Flut f -, -en high tide; (*fig*) flood

Föderation /-'tsːioːn/ f -, -en federation

Fohlen nt -s,- foal

Föhn m -s föhn [wind]; (*Haartrockner*) hair-drier. **f~en** vt [blow-]dry

Folg|e f -, -n consequence; (*Reihe*) succession; (*Fortsetzung*) instalment; (*Teil*) part. **f~en** vi (*sein*) follow (jdm/etw s.o./sth); (*zuhören*) listen (dat to); **wie f~t** as follows ● (*haben*) (*gehorchen*) obey (jdm s.o.). **f~end** a following; F~endes the following

folger|n vt conclude (**aus** from). **F~ung** f -, -en conclusion

folg|lich adv consequently. **f~sam** a obedient

Folie /'foːliə/ f -, -n foil; (*Plastik-*) film

Folklore f - folklore

Folter f -, -n torture. **f~n** vt torture

Fön (P) m -s, -e hair-drier

Fonds /fõː/ m -,- /-[s], -s/ fund

fönen* vt s. föhnen

Förder|band nt (*pl* -bänder) conveyor belt. **f~lich** a beneficial

fordern vt demand; (*beanspruchen*) claim; (*zum Kampf*) challenge

fördern vt promote; (*unterstützen*) encourage; (*finanziell*) sponsor; (*gewinnen*) extract

Forderung f -, -en demand; (*Anspruch*) claim

Förderung f - promotion; encouragement; (*Techn*) production

Forelle f -, -n trout

Form f -, -en form; (*Gestalt*) shape; (*Culin, Techn*) mould; (*Back-*) tin; [gut] in F~ in good form

Formalität f -, -en formality

Format nt -[e]s, -e format; (*Größe*) size; (*fig: Bedeutung*) stature

formatieren vt format

Formel f -, -n formula

formen vt shape, mould; (*bilden*) form; sich f~ take shape

förmlich a formal

form|los a shapeless; (*zwanglos*) informal. **F~sache** f formality

Formular nt -s, -e [printed] form

formulier|en vt formulate, word. **F~ung** f -, -en wording

---

forsch|en vi (haben) search (**nach** for). **f~end** a searching. **F~er** m -s,- research scientist; (Reisender) explorer. **F~ung** f -, -en research

Forst m -[e]s, -e forest

Förster m -s,- forester

Forstwirtschaft f forestry

Fort nt -s, -s (Mil) fort

fort adv away; **f~ sein** be away; (gegangen/verschwunden) have gone; **und so f~** and so on; **in einem f~** continuously. **F~bewegung** f locomotion. **F~bildung** f further education/training. **f~bleiben†** vi sep (sein) stay away. **f~bringen†** vt sep take away. **f~fahren†** vi sep (sein) go away ● (haben/sein) continue (**zu** to). **f~fallen†** vi sep (sein) be dropped/(ausgelassen) omitted; (entfallen) no longer apply; (aufhören) cease. **f~führen** vt sep continue. **f~gehen†** vi sep (sein) leave, go away; (ausgehen) go out; (andauern) go on. **f~geschritten** a advanced; (spät) late. **F~geschrittene(r)** m/f advanced student. **f~lassen†** vt sep let go; (auslassen) omit. **f~laufen†** vi sep (sein) run away; (sich f~setzen) continue. **f~laufend** a consecutive. **f~pflanzen (sich)** vr sep reproduce; <Ton, Licht> travel. **F~pflanzung** f - reproduction. **F~pflanzungsorgan** nt reproductive organ. **f~schicken** vt sep send away; (abschicken) send off. **f~schreiten†** vi sep (sein) continue; (Fortschritte machen) progress, advance. **f~schreitend** a progressive; <Alter> advancing. **F~schritt** m progress; **F~schritte machen** make progress. **f~schrittlich** a progressive. **f~setzen** vt sep continue; **sich f~setzen** continue. **F~setzung** f -, -en continuation; (Folge) instalment; **F~setzung folgt** to be continued. **F~setzungsroman** m serialized novel, serial. **f~während** a constant. **f~ziehen†** v sep ● vt pull away ● vi (sein) move away

Fossil nt -, -ien /-iən/ fossil

Foto nt -s, -s photo. **F~apparat** m camera. **f~gen** a photogenic

Fotograf|(in) m -en, -en (f -, -nen) photographer. **F~ie** f -, -n photography; (Bild) photograph. **f~ieren** vt take a photo[graph] of ● vi (haben) take photographs. **f~isch** a photographic

Fotokopie f photocopy. **F~ren** vt photocopy. **F~rgerät** nt photocopier

Fötus m -, -ten foetus

Foul /faul/ nt -s, -s (Sport) foul. **f~en** vt foul

Fracht f -, -en freight. **F~er** m -s,- freighter. **F~gut** nt freight. **F~schiff** nt cargo boat

Frack m -[e]s,ˉe & -s tailcoat

Frage f -, -n question; **nicht in F~ kommen** s. infrage. **F~bogen** m questionnaire. **f~n** vt (haben) ask; **sich f~n** wonder (**ob** whether). **f~nd** a questioning. **F~zeichen** nt question mark

frag|lich a doubtful; <Person, Sache> in question. **f~los** adv undoubtedly

Fragment nt -[e]s, -e fragment

fragwürdig a questionable; (verdächtig) dubious

Fraktion /-'tsiːoːn/ f -, -en parliamentary party

Franken¹ m -s,- (Swiss) franc

Franken² nt -s Franconia

frankieren vt stamp, frank

Frankreich nt -s France

Fransen fpl fringe sg

Franz|ose m -n, -n Frenchman; **die F~osen** the French pl. **F~ösin** f -, -nen Frenchwoman. **f~ösisch** a French. **F~ösisch** nt -[s] (Lang) French

Fraß m -es feed; (pej: Essen) muck

Fratze f -, -n grotesque face; (Grimasse) grimace

Frau f -, -en woman; (Ehe-) wife; **F~Thomas** Mrs Thomas; **Unsere Liebe F~** (Relig) Our Lady

Frauen|arzt m, **F~ärztin** f gynaecologist. **F~rechtlerin** f -, -nen feminist

Fräulein *nt* -s,- single woman; (*jung*) young lady; (*Anrede*) Miss

frech *a* cheeky; (*unverschämt*) impudent. **F∼heit** *f* -, -en cheekiness; impudence; (*Äußerung*) impertinence

frei *a* free; (*freischaffend*) freelance; <*Künstler*> independent; (*nicht besetzt*) vacant; (*offen*) open; (*bloß*) bare; **f∼er Tag** day off; **sich** (*dat*) **f∼nehmen** take time off; **f∼ machen** (*räumen*) clear; vacate <*Platz*>; (*befreien*) liberate; **f∼ lassen** leave free; **ist dieser Platz f∼?** is this seat taken? '**Zimmer f∼**' 'vacancies' ● *adv* freely; (*ohne Notizen*) without notes; (*umsonst*) free

Frei|bad *nt* open-air swimming pool. **f∼beruflich** *a & adv* freelance. **F∼e** *nt* **im F∼en** in the open air, out of doors. **F∼gabe** *f* release. **f∼geben†** *v sep* ● *vt* release; (*eröffnen*) open; **jdm einen Tag f∼geben** give s.o. a day off ● *vi* (*haben*) **jdm f∼geben** give s.o. time off. **f∼gebig** *a* generous. **F∼gebigkeit** *f* - generosity. **f∼haben†** *v sep* ● *vt* **eine Stunde f∼haben** have an hour off; (*Sch*) have a free period ● *vi* (*haben*) be off work/(*Sch*) school; (*beurlaubt sein*) have time off. **f∼händig** *adv* without holding on

Freiheit *f* -, -en freedom, liberty. **F∼sstrafe** *f* prison sentence

Frei|herr *m* baron. **F∼körperkultur** *f* naturism. **F∼lassung** *f* - release. **F∼lauf** *m* free-wheel. **f∼legen** *vt sep* expose. **f∼lich** *adv* admittedly; (*natürlich*) of course. **F∼lichttheater** *nt* open-air theatre. **f∼machen** *vt sep* (*frankieren*) frank; (*entkleiden*) bare; **einen Tag f∼machen** take a day off. **F∼maurer** *m* Freemason. **f∼schaffend** *a* freelance. **f∼schwimmen† (sich)** *v sep* pass one's swimming test. **f∼sprechen†** *vt sep* acquit. **F∼spruch** *m* acquittal. **f∼stehen†** *vi sep* (*haben*) stand empty; **es steht ihm f∼** (*fig*) he

is free (**zu** to). **f∼stellen** *vt sep* exempt (**von** from); **jdm etw f∼stellen** leave sth up to s.o. **F∼stil** *m* freestyle. **F∼stoß** *m* free kick

Freitag *m* Friday. **f∼s** *adv* on Fridays

Frei|tod *m* suicide. **F∼umschlag** *m* stamped envelope. **f∼weg** *adv* freely; (*offen*) openly. **f∼willig** *a* voluntary. **F∼willige(r)** *m/f* volunteer. **F∼zeichen** *nt* ringing tone; (*Rufzeichen*) dialling tone. **F∼zeit** *f* free *or* spare time; (*Muße*) leisure. **F∼zeit-** *pref* leisure ... **F∼zeitbekleidung** *f* casual wear. **f∼zügig** *a* unrestricted; (*großzügig*) liberal

fremd *a* foreign; (*unbekannt*) strange; (*nicht das eigene*) other people's; **ein f∼er Mann** a stranger; **f∼e Leute** strangers; **unter f∼em Namen** under an assumed name; **ich bin hier f∼** I'm a stranger here. **F∼e** *f* - in der **F∼e** away from home; (*im Ausland*) in a foreign country. **F∼e(r)** *m/f* stranger; (*Ausländer*) foreigner; (*Tourist*) tourist. **F∼enführer** *m* [tourist] guide. **F∼enverkehr** *m* tourism. **F∼enzimmer** *nt* room [to let]; (*Gäste-*) guest room. **f∼gehen†** *vi sep* (*sein*) Ⓘ be unfaithful. **F∼sprache** *f* foreign language. **F∼wort** *nt* (*pl* -wörter) foreign word

Freske *f* -, -n, **Fresko** *nt* -s, -ken fresco

Fresse *f* -, -n ⊠ (*Mund*) gob; (*Gesicht*) mug. **f∼n†** *vt/i* (*haben*) eat. **F∼n** *nt* -s feed; (⊠ *Essen*) grub

Fressnapf *m* feeding bowl

Freud|e *f* -, -n pleasure; (*innere*) joy; **mit F∼en** with pleasure; **jdm eine F∼e machen** please s.o. **f∼ig** *a* joyful

freuen *vt* please; **sich f∼** be pleased (**über** + *acc* about); **sich f∼ auf** (+ *acc*) look forward to; **es freut mich** I'm glad (**dass** that)

Freund *m* -es, -e friend; (*Verehrer*) boyfriend. **F∼in** *f* -, -nen friend; (*Liebste*) girlfriend. **f∼lich** *a* kind; (*umgänglich*) friendly; (*angenehm*)

pleasant. **f~licherweise** *adv*
kindly. **F~lichkeit** *f* -, **-en**
kindness; friendliness; pleasantness
Freund|schaft *f* -, **-en** friendship;
F~schaft schließen become friends.
f~lich *a* friendly

Frieden *m* -s peace; **F~ schließen**
make peace; **im F~** in peace-time;
lass mich in F~! leave me alone!
F~svertrag *m* peace treaty

Fried|hof *m* cemetery. **f~lich** *a*
peaceful

frieren† *vi* (*haben*) <*Person:*> be
cold; *impers* **es friert/hat gefroren** it
is freezing/there has been a frost;
frierst du? are you cold? ● (*sein*)
(*gefrieren*) freeze

Fries *m* -es, -e frieze

frisch *a* fresh; (*sauber*) clean;
(*leuchtend*) bright; (*munter*) lively;
(*rüstig*) fit; **sich f~ machen** freshen
up ● *adv* freshly, newly; **ein Bett f~
beziehen** put clean sheets on a bed;
f~ gestrichen! wet paint! **F~e** *f* -
freshness; brightness; liveliness;
fitness. **F~haltepackung** *f*
vacuum pack

Fri|seur /fri'zø:ɐ̯/ *m* -s, -e
hairdresser; (*Herren-*) barber.
F~seursalon *m* hairdressing
salon. **F~seuse** /-'zø:zə/ *f* -, -n
hairdresser

frisier|en *vt* jdn/sich f~en do s.o.'s/
one's hair; **die Bilanz/einen Motor
f~en** ⓘ fiddle the accounts/soup up
an engine

Frisör *m* -s, -e = **Friseur**

Frist *f* -, **-en** period; (*Termin*)
deadline; (*Aufschub*) time; **drei Tage
F~** three days' grace. **f~los** *a*
instant

Frisur *f* -, **-en** hairstyle

frittieren *vt* deep-fry

frivol /fri'vo:l/ *a* frivolous

froh *a* happy; (*freudig*) joyful;
(*erleichtert*) glad

fröhlich *a* cheerful; (*vergnügt*)
merry. **F~keit** *f* - cheerfulness;
merriment

fromm *a* devout; (*gutartig*) docile

Frömmigkeit *f* - devoutness

Fronleichnam *m* Corpus Christi

Front *f* -, **-en** front. **f~al** *a* frontal;
<*Zusammenstoß*> head-on ● *adv*
from the front; <*zusammenstoßen*>
head-on. **F~alzusammenstoß** *m*
head-on collision

Frosch *m* -[e]s,⸚e frog. **F~laich** *m*
frog-spawn. **F~mann** *m* (*pl*
-männer) frogman

Frost *m* -[e]s,⸚e frost. **F~beule** *f*
chilblain

frösteln *vi* (*haben*) shiver

frost|ig *a* frosty. **F~schutzmittel**
nt antifreeze

Frottee *nt* & *m* -s towelling

frottier|en *vt* rub down.
F~[hand]tuch *nt* terry towel

Frucht *f* -,⸚e fruit; **F~ tragen** bear
fruit. **f~bar** *a* fertile; (*fig*) fruitful.
F~barkeit *f* - fertility

früh *a* early ● *adv* early; (*morgens*) in
the morning; **heute f~** this morning;
von f~ an *od* **auf** from an early age.
F~aufsteher *m* -s,- early riser.
F~e *f* - **in aller F~e** bright and
early; **in der F~e** (*SGer*) in the
morning. **f~er** *adv* earlier; (*eher*)
sooner; (*ehemals*) formerly; (*vor
langer Zeit*) in the old days; **f~er
oder später** sooner or later; **ich
wohnte f~er in X** I used to live in X.
f~ere(r,s) *a* earlier; (*ehemalig*)
former; (*vorige*) previous; **in f~eren
Zeiten** in former times. **f~estens**
adv at the earliest. **F~geburt** *f*
premature birth/(*Kind*) baby.
F~jahr *nt* spring. **F~ling** *m* -s, -e
spring. **f~morgens** *adv* early in
the morning. **f~reif** *a* precocious

Frühstück *nt* breakfast. **f~en** *vi*
(*haben*) have breakfast

frühzeitig *a* & *adv* early; (*vorzeitig*)
premature

Frustr|ation /-'tsi̯o:n/ *f* -, **-en**
frustration. **f~ieren** *vt* frustrate

Fuchs *m* -es,⸚e fox; (*Pferd*) chestnut.
f~en *vt* ⓘ annoy

Füchsin *f* -, **-nen** vixen

Fuge[1] *f* -, -n joint

Fuge[2] *f* -, -n (*Mus*) fugue

füg|en *vt* fit (in + *acc* into); (*an-*) join (an + *acc* on to); (*dazu-*) add (zu to); **sich f~en** fit (in + *acc* into); adjoin/ (*folgen*) follow (an etw *acc* sth); (*fig: gehorchen*) submit (*dat* to). **f~sam** *a* obedient. **F~ung** *f* -, -en eine F~ung des Schicksals a stroke of fate

fühl|bar *a* noticeable. **f~en** *vt/i* (*haben*) feel; **sich f~en** feel (krank/ einsam ill/lonely); (⚠ *stolz sein*) fancy oneself. **F~er** *m* -s,- feeler. **F~ung** *f* - contact

Fuhre *f* -, -n load

führ|en *vt* lead; guide <*Tourist*>; (*geleiten*) take; (*leiten*) run; (*befehligen*) command; (*verkaufen*) stock; bear <*Namen*>; keep <*Liste, Bücher*> ● *vi* (*haben*) lead; (*verlaufen*) go, run; **zu etw f~en** lead to sth. **f~end** *a* leading. **F~er** *m* -s,- leader; (*Fremden-*) guide; (*Buch*) guide[book]. **F~erhaus** *nt* driver's cab. **F~erschein** *m* driving licence; **den F~erschein machen** take one's driving test. **F~erscheinentzug** *m* disqualification from driving. **F~ung** *f* -, -en leadership; (*Leitung*) management; (*Mil*) command; (*Betragen*) conduct; (*Besichtigung*) guided tour; (*Vorsprung*) lead; in **F~ung gehen** go into the lead

Fuhr|unternehmer *m* haulage contractor. **F~werk** *nt* cart

Fülle *f* -, -n abundance, wealth (an + *dat* of); (*Körper-*) plumpness. **f~n** *vt* fill; (*Culin*) stuff

Füllen *nt* -s,- foal

Füll|er *m* -s,- ⚠, **F~federhalter** *m* fountain pen. **F~ung** *f* -, -en filling; (*Braten-*) stuffing

fummeln *vi* (*haben*) fumble (an + *dat* with)

Fund *m* -[e]s, -e find

Fundament *nt* -[e]s, -e foundations *pl.* **f~al** *a* fundamental

Fundbüro *nt* lost-property office

fünf *inv a*, **F~** *f* -, -en five; (*Sch*) ≈ fail mark. **F~linge** *mpl* quintuplets. **f~te(r,s)** *a* fifth. **f~zehn** *inv a* fifteen. **f~zehnte(r,s)** *a* fifteenth. **f~zig** *inv a* fifty. **f~zigste(r,s)** *a* fiftieth

fungieren *vi* (*haben*) act (als as)

Funk *m* -s radio. **F~e** *m* -n, -n spark. **f~eln** *vi* (*haben*) sparkle; <*Stern:*> twinkle. **F~en** *m* -s,- spark. **f~en** *vt* radio. **F~sprechgerät** *nt* walkie-talkie. **F~spruch** *m* radio message. **F~streife** *f* [police] radio patrol

Funktion /-'tsːioːn/ *f* -, -en function; (*Stellung*) position; (*Funktionieren*) working; **außer F~** out of action. **F~är** *m* -s, -e official. **f~ieren** *vi* (*haben*) work

für *prep* (+ *acc*) for; **Schritt für Schritt** step by step; **was für [ein]** what [a]! (*fragend*) what sort of [a]? **Für** *nt* **das Für und Wider** the pros and cons *pl*

Furche *f* -, -n furrow

Furcht *f* - fear (vor + *dat* of); **F~ erregend** terrifying. **f~bar** *a* terrible

fürcht|en *vt/i* (*haben*) fear; **sich f~en** be afraid (vor + *dat* of). **f~erlich** *a* dreadful

füreinander *adv* for each other

Furnier *nt* -s, -e veneer. **f~t** *a* veneered

Fürsorg|e *f* care; (*Admin*) welfare; (⚠ *Geld*) ≈ social security. **F~er(in)** *m* -s,- (*f* -, -nen) social worker. **f~lich** *a* solicitous

Fürst *m* -en, -en prince. **F~entum** *nt* -s, ̈-er principality. **F~in** *f* -, -nen princess

Furt *f* -, -en ford

Furunkel *m* -s,- (*Med*) boil

Fürwort *nt* (*pl* -wörter) pronoun

Furz *m* -es, -e (*vulg*) fart

Fusion *f* -, -en fusion; (*Comm*) merger

Fuß *m* -es, ̈-e foot; (*Aust: Bein*) leg; (*Lampen-*) base; (*von Weinglas*) stem; **zu Fuß** on foot; **zu Fuß gehen** walk; **auf freiem Fuß** free. **F~abdruck** *m*

---

footprint. **F~abtreter** *m* -s,-
doormat. **F~ball** *m* football.
F~ballspieler *m* footballer.
F~balltoto *nt* football pools *pl.*
F~bank *f* footstool. **F~boden** *m*
floor

Fussel *f* -, -n & *m* -s, -[n] piece of
fluff; **F~n** fluff *sg.* **f~n** *vi* (*haben*)
shed fluff

fußen *vi* (*haben*) be based (**auf** + *dat*
on)

Fußgänger|(in) *m* -s,- (*f* -, -nen)
pedestrian. **F~brücke** *f* footbridge.
F~zone *f* pedestrian precinct

Fuß|geher *m* -s,- (*Aust*) =
F~gänger. F~gelenk *nt* ankle.
F~hebel *m* pedal. **F~nagel** *m*
toenail. **F~note** *f* footnote.
F~pflege *f* chiropody. **F~rücken**
m instep. **F~sohle** *f* sole of the
foot. **F~tritt** *m* kick. **F~weg** *m*
footpath; **eine Stunde F~weg** an
hour's walk

futsch *pred a* ⊞ gone

Futter¹ *nt* -s feed; (*Trocken-*) fodder

Futter² *nt* -s,- (*Kleider-*) lining

Futteral *nt* -s, -e case

füttern¹ *vt* feed

füttern² *vt* line

Futur *nt* -s (*Gram*) future

Gg

Gabe *f* -, -n gift; (*Dosis*) dose

Gabel *f* -, -n fork. **g~n (sich)** *vr*
fork. **G~stapler** *m* -s,- fork-lift
truck. **G~ung** *f* -, -en fork

gackern *vi* (*haben*) cackle

gaffen *vi* (*haben*) gape, stare

Gage /'gaːʒə/ *f* -, -n (*Theat*) fee

gähnen *vi* (*haben*) yawn

Gala *f* - ceremonial dress

Galavorstellung *f* gala
performance

Galerie *f* -, -n gallery

Galgen *m* -s,- gallows *sg.* **G~frist** *f*
⊞ reprieve

Galionsfigur *f* figurehead

Galle *f* - bile; (*G~nblase*) gall-
bladder. **G~nblase** *f* gall-bladder.
G~nstein *m* gallstone

Galopp *m* -s gallop; **im G~** at a
gallop. **g~ieren** *vi* (*sein*) gallop

gammel|n *vi* (*haben*) ⊞ loaf
around. **G~ler(in)** *m* -s,- (*f* -, -nen)
drop-out

Gams *f* -, -en (*Aust*) chamois

Gämse *f* -, -n chamois

Gang *m* -[e]s,ṅe walk; (*G~art*) gait;
(*Boten-*) errand; (*Funktionieren*)
running; (*Verlauf, Culin*) course;
(*Durch-*) passage; (*Korridor*)
corridor; (*zwischen Sitzreihen*) aisle,
gangway; (*Anat*) duct; (*Auto*) gear; **in
G~ bringen** get going; **im G~e sein**
be in progress; **Essen mit vier G~en**
four-course meal

gängig *a* common; (*Comm*) popular

Gangschaltung *f* gear change

Gangster /'gɛnstɐ/ *m* -s,- gangster

Ganove *m* -n, -n ⊞ crook

Gans *f* -,ṅe goose

Gänse|blümchen *nt* -s,- daisy.
G~füßchen *ntpl* inverted commas.
G~haut *f* goose-pimples *pl.*
G~rich *m* -s, -e gander

ganz *a* whole, entire; (*vollständig*)
complete; (⊞ *heil*) undamaged,
intact; **die g~e Zeit** all the time, the
whole time; **eine g~e Weile/Menge**
quite a while/lot; *inv* **g~
Deutschland** the whole of Germany;
wieder g~ machen ⊞ mend; **im
Großen und G~en** on the whole
● *adv* quite; (*völlig*) completely,
entirely; (*sehr*) very; **nicht g~** not
quite; **g~ allein** all on one's own; **g~
und gar** completely, totally; **g~ und
gar nicht** not at all. **G~e(s)** *nt*
whole. **g~jährig** *adv* all the year
round. **g~tägig** *a & adv* full-time;
<*geöffnet*> all day. **g~tags** *adv* all
day; <*arbeiten*> full-time

gar¹ *a* done, cooked

gar² *adv* gar nicht/nichts/niemand not/nothing/no one at all

Garage /ga'ra:ʒə/ *f -, -n* garage

Garantie *f -, -n* guarantee. **g~ren** *vt/i (haben)* [für] etw g~ren guarantee sth. **G~schein** *m* guarantee

Garderobe *f -, -n (Kleider)* wardrobe; *(Ablage)* cloakroom; *(Künstler-)* dressing-room. **G~nfrau** *f* cloakroom attendant

Gardine *f -, -n* curtain

garen *vt/i (haben)* cook

gären† *vi (haben)* ferment; *(fig)* seethe

Garn *nt -[e]s, -e* yarn; *(Näh-)* cotton

Garnele *f -, -n* shrimp; prawn

garnieren *vt* decorate; *(Culin)* garnish

Garnison *f -, -en* garrison

Garnitur *f -, -en* set; *(Möbel-)* suite

Garten *m -s,-̈* garden. **G~arbeit** *f* gardening. **G~bau** *m* horticulture. **G~haus** *nt*, **G~laube** *f* summerhouse. **G~schere** *f* secateurs *pl*

Gärtner|(in) *m -s,- (f -, -nen)* gardener. **G~ei** *f -, -en* nursery

Gärung *f -* fermentation

Gas *nt -es, -e* gas; Gas geben 🚗 accelerate. **G~maske** *f* gas mask. **G~pedal** *nt (Auto)* accelerator

Gasse *f -, -n* alley; *(Aust)* street

Gast *m -[e]s,-̈e* guest; *(Hotel-)* visitor; *(im Lokal)* patron; zum Mittag G~̃e haben have people to lunch; bei jdm zu G~ sein be staying with s.o. **G~arbeiter** *m* foreign worker. **G~bett** *nt* spare bed

Gäste|bett *nt* spare bed. **G~buch** *nt* visitors' book. **G~zimmer** *nt* [hotel] room; *(privat)* spare room

gast|freundlich *a* hospitable. **G~freundschaft** *f* hospitality. **G~geber** *m -s,-* host. **G~geberin** *f -, -nen* hostess. **G~haus** *nt*, **G~hof** *m* inn, hotel

gastlich *a* hospitable

Gastronomie *f -* gastronomy

Gast|spiel *nt* guest performance. **G~spielreise** *f (Theat)* tour. **G~stätte** *f* restaurant. **G~wirt** *m* landlord. **G~wirtin** *f* landlady. **G~wirtschaft** *f* restaurant

Gas|werk *nt* gasworks *sg*. **G~zähler** *m* gas-meter

Gatte *m -n, -n* husband

Gattin *f -, -nen* wife

Gattung *f -, -en* kind; *(Biol)* genus; *(Kunst)* genre

Gaudi *f - (Aust, fam)* fun

Gaumen *m -s,-* palate

Gauner *m -s,-* crook, swindler. **G~ei** *f -, -en* swindle

Gaze /'ga:zə/ *f -* gauze

Gazelle *f -, -n* gazelle

Gebäck *nt -s* [cakes and] pastries *pl*; *(Kekse)* biscuits *pl*

Gebälk *nt -s* timbers *pl*

geballt *a <Faust>* clenched

Gebärde *f -, -n* gesture

gebär|en† *vt* give birth to, bear; geboren werden be born. **G~mutter** *f* womb, uterus

Gebäude *nt -s,-* building

Gebeine *ntpl* [mortal] remains

Gebell *nt -s* barking

geben† *vt* give; *(tun, bringen)* put; *(Karten)* deal; *(aufführen)* perform; *(unterrichten)* teach; etw verloren g~ give sth up as lost; viel/wenig g~ auf (+ acc) set great/little store by; sich g~ *(nachlassen)* wear off; *(besser werden)* get better; *(sich verhalten)* behave ● *impers* es gibt there is/are; was gibt es Neues/zum Mittag/im Kino? what's the news/for lunch/on at the cinema? es wird Regen g~ it's going to rain ● *vi (haben) (Karten)* deal

Gebet *nt -[e]s, -e* prayer

Gebiet *nt -[e]s, -e* area; *(Hoheits-)* territory; *(Sach-)* field

gebieten† *vt* command; *(erfordern)* demand ● *vi (haben)* rule

Gebilde *nt -s,-* structure

gebildet *a* educated; *(kultiviert)* cultured

Gebirg|e *nt -s,-* mountains *pl*. **g~ig** *a* mountainous

Gebiss nt -es, -e teeth pl; (künstliches) false teeth pl; dentures pl, (des Zaumes) bit

geblümt a floral, flowered

gebogen a curved

geboren a born; g~er Deutscher German by birth; Frau X, g~e Y Mrs X, née Y

Gebot nt -[e]s, -e rule

gebraten a fried

Gebrauch m use; (Sprach-) usage; Gebräuche customs; in G~ in use; G~ machen von make use of. **g~en** vt use; zu nichts zu g~en useless

gebräuchlich a common; <Wort> in common use

Gebrauch|sanleitung, G~sanweisung f directions pl for use. **g~t** a used; (Comm) secondhand. **G~twagen** m used car

gebrechlich a frail, infirm

gebrochen a broken ● adv g~ Englisch sprechen speak broken English

Gebrüll nt -s roaring

Gebühr f -, -en charge, fee; über G~ excessively. **g~end** a due; (geziemend) proper. **g~enfrei** a free ● adv free of charge. **g~enpflichtig** a & adv subject to a charge; g~enpflichtige Straße toll road

Geburt f -, -en birth; von G~ by birth. **G~enkontrolle, G~enregelung** f birth-control. **G~enziffer** f birth-rate

gebürtig a native (aus of); g~er Deutscher German by birth

Geburts|datum nt date of birth. **G~helfer** m obstetrician. **G~hilfe** f obstetrics sg. **G~ort** m place of birth. **G~tag** m birthday. **G~urkunde** f birth certificate

Gebüsch nt -[e]s, -e bushes pl

Gedächtnis nt -ses memory; aus dem G~ from memory

Gedanke m -ns, -n thought (an + acc of); (Idee) idea; sich (dat) G~n machen worry (über + acc about).

g~nlos a thoughtless; (zerstreut) absent-minded. **G~nstrich** m dash

Gedärme ntpl intestines; (Tier-) entrails

Gedeck nt -[e]s, -e place setting; (auf Speisekarte) set meal

gedeihen† vi (sein) thrive, flourish

gedenken† vi (haben) propose (etw zu tun to do sth); jds g~ remember s.o. **G~** nt -s memory

Gedenk|feier f commemoration. **G~gottesdienst** m memorial service

Gedicht nt -[e]s, -e poem

Gedräng|e nt -s crush, crowd. **g~t** a (knapp) concise ● adv g~t voll packed

Geduld f - patience; **G~ haben** be patient. **g~en (sich)** vr be patient. **g~ig** a patient. **G~[s]spiel** nt puzzle

gedunsen a bloated

geehrt a honoured; Sehr g~er Herr X Dear Mr X

geeignet a suitable; im g~en Moment at the right moment

Gefahr f -, -en danger; in G~ in danger; auf eigene G~ at one's own risk; G~ laufen run the risk (etw zu tun of doing sth)

gefähr|den vt endanger; (fig) jeopardize. **g~lich** a dangerous

gefahrlos a safe

Gefährt nt -[e]s, -e vehicle

Gefährte m -n, -n, **Gefährtin** f -, -nen companion

gefahrvoll a dangerous, perilous

Gefälle nt -s,- slope; (Straßen-) gradient

gefallen† vi (haben) jdm g~ please s.o.; er/es gefällt mir I like him/it; sich (dat) etw g~ lassen put up with sth

Gefallen[1] m -s,- favour

Gefallen[2] nt -s pleasure (an + dat in); dir zu G~ to please you

Gefallene(r) m soldier killed in the war

gefällig a pleasing; (hübsch) attractive; (hilfsbereit) obliging; noch etwas g~? will there be anything

else? **G~keit** *f* -, -en favour;
(*Freundlichkeit*) kindness

Gefangen|e(r) *m/f* prisoner.
G~nahme *f* - capture.
g~nehmen* *vt sep* g~ nehmen, *s.*
fangen. **G~schaft** *f* - captivity

Gefängnis *nt* -ses, -se prison;
(*Strafe*) imprisonment. **G~strafe** *f*
imprisonment; (*Urteil*) prison
sentence. **G~wärter** *m* [prison]
warder

Gefäß *nt* -es, -e container; (*Blut-*)
vessel

gefasst *a* composed; (*ruhig*) calm;
g~ sein auf (+ *acc*) be prepared for

gefedert *a* sprung

gefeiert *a* celebrated

Gefieder *nt* -s plumage

gefleckt *a* spotted

Geflügel *nt* -s poultry. **G~klein** *nt*
-s giblets *pl.* **g~t** *a* winged

Geflüster *nt* -s whispering

Gefolge *nt* -s retinue, entourage

gefragt *a* popular

Gefreite(r) *m* lance-corporal

gefrier|en† *vi* (*sein*) freeze.
G~fach *nt* freezer compartment.
G~punkt *m* freezing point.
G~schrank *m* upright freezer.
G~truhe *f* chest freezer

gefroren *a* frozen

gefügig *a* compliant; (*gehorsam*)
obedient

Gefühl *nt* -[e]s, -e feeling;
(*Empfindung*) sensation;
(*G~sregung*) emotion; im G~ haben
know instinctively. **g~los** *a*
insensitive; (*herzlos*) unfeeling;
(*taub*) numb. **g~smäßig** *a*
emotional; (*instinktiv*) instinctive.
G~sregung *f* emotion. **g~voll** *a*
sensitive; (*sentimental*) sentimental

gefüllt *a* filled; (*voll*) full

gefürchtet *a* feared, dreaded

gefüttert *a* lined

gegeben *a* given; (*bestehend*)
present; (*passend*) appropriate.
g~enfalls *adv* if need be

gegen *prep* (+ *acc*) against; (*Sport*)
versus; (*g~über*) to[wards];
(*Vergleich*) compared with;
(*Richtung, Zeit*) towards; (*ungefähr*)
around; **ein Mittel g~** a remedy for
● *adv* **g~ 100 Leute** about 100
people. **G~angriff** *m* counter-attack

Gegend *f* -, -en area, region;
(*Umgebung*) neighbourhood

gegeneinander *adv* against/
(*gegenüber*) towards one another

Gegen|fahrbahn *f* opposite
carriageway. **G~gift** *nt* antidote.
G~maßnahme *f* countermeasure.
G~satz *m* contrast; (*Widerspruch*)
contradiction; (*G~teil*) opposite; im
G~satz zu unlike. **G~seitig** *a*
mutual; **sich g~seitig hassen** hate
one another. **G~stand** *m* object;
(*Gram, Gesprächs-*) subject.
G~stück *nt* counterpart; (*G~teil*)
opposite. **G~teil** *nt* opposite,
contrary; **im G~teil** on the contrary.
g~teilig *a* opposite

gegenüber *prep* (+ *dat*) opposite;
(*Vergleich*) compared with; **jdm g~
höflich sein** be polite to s.o. ● *adv*
opposite. **G~** *nt* -s person opposite.
g~liegend *a* opposite.
g~stehen† *vi sep* (*haben*) (+ *dat*)
face; **feindlich g~stehen** (+ *dat*) be
hostile to. **g~stellen** *vt sep*
confront; (*vergleichen*) compare

Gegen|verkehr *m* oncoming
traffic. **G~vorschlag** *m* counter-
proposal. **G~wart** *f* - present;
(*Anwesenheit*) presence. **g~wärtig**
a present ● *adv* at present.
G~wehr *f* - resistance. **G~wert** *m*
equivalent. **G~wind** *m* head wind.
g~zeichnen *vt sep* countersign

geglückt *a* successful

Gegner|(in) *m* -s,- (*f* -, -nen)
opponent. **g~isch** *a* opposing

Gehabe *nt* -s affected behaviour

Gehackte(s) *nt* mince

Gehalt *nt* -[e]s,-er salary.
G~serhöhung *f* rise

gehässig *a* spiteful

gehäuft *a* heaped

Gehäuse *nt* -s,- case; (*TV, Radio*)
cabinet; (*Schnecken-*) shell

Gehege *nt* -s,- enclosure

geheim *a* secret; **g~ halten** keep secret; **im G~en** secretly.
G~dienst *m* Secret Service.
G~nis *nt* -ses, -se secret.
g~nisvoll *a* mysterious

gehemmt *a* (*fig*) inhibited

gehen†
● *intransitive verb* (*sein*)
••••► (*sich irgendwohin begeben*) go; (*zu Fuß*) walk. **tanzen/schwimmen/ einkaufen gehen** go dancing/ swimming/shopping. **schlafen gehen** go to bed. **zum Arzt gehen** go to the doctor's. **in die Schule gehen** go to school. **auf und ab gehen** walk up and down. **über die Straße gehen** cross the street
••••► (*weggehen; fam: abfahren*) go; leave. **ich muss bald gehen** I must go soon. **Sie können gehen** you may go. **der Zug geht um zehn Uhr 🚂** the train leaves *or* goes at ten o'clock
••••► (*funktionieren*) work. **der Computer geht wieder/nicht mehr** the computer is working again/has stopped working. **meine Uhr geht falsch/richtig** my watch is wrong/ right
••••► (*möglich sein*) be possible. **ja, das geht ja,** I *or* we can manage that. **das geht nicht** that can't be done; (🚂 *ist nicht akzeptabel*) it's not good enough, it's not on 🚂. **es geht einfach nicht, dass du so spät nach Hause kommst** it simply won't do for you to come home so late
••••► (🚂 *gerade noch angehen*) **es geht [so]** it is all right. **Wie war die Party? — Es ging so** How was the party? — Not bad *or* So-so
••••► (*sich entwickeln*) do; go. **der Laden geht gut** the shop is doing well. **es geht alles nach Wunsch** everything is going to plan
••••► (*impers*) **wie geht es Ihnen?** how are you? **es geht ihm gut/schlecht** (*gesundheitlich*) he is well/not well; (*geschäftlich*) he is doing well/badly; **ein gut g~des Geschäft** a thriving business

••••► (*impers; sich um etw handeln*) **es geht um** it concerns. **worum geht es hier?** what is this all about? **es geht ihr nur ums Geld** she is only interested in money

Geheul *nt* -s howling

Gehilfe *m* -n, -n, **Gehilfin** *f* -, -nen trainee; (*Helfer*) assistant

Gehirn *nt* -s brain; (*Verstand*) brains *pl* **G~erschütterung** *f* concussion. **G~hautentzündung** *f* meningitis. **G~wäsche** *f* brainwashing

gehoben *a* (*fig*) superior

Gehöft *nt* -[e]s, -e farm

Gehör *nt* -s hearing

gehorchen *vi* (*haben*) (+ *dat*) obey

gehören *vi* (*haben*) belong (*dat* to); **dazu gehört Mut** that takes courage; **es gehört sich nicht** it isn't done

gehörlos *a* deaf

Gehörn *nt* -s, -e horns *pl*; (*Geweih*) antlers *pl*

gehorsam *a* obedient. **G~** *m* -s obedience

Geh|steig *m* -[e]s, -e pavement. **G~weg** *m* = Gehsteig; (*Fußweg*) footpath

Geier *m* -s,- vulture

Geig|e *f* -, -n violin. **g~en** *vi* (*haben*) play the violin ● *vt* play on the violin. **G~er(in)** *m* -s,- (*f* -, -nen) violinist

geil *a* lecherous; randy; (🚂 *toll*) great

Geisel *f* -, -n hostage

Geiß *f* -, -en (*SGer*) [nanny-]goat. **G~blatt** *nt* honeysuckle

Geist *m* -[e]s, -er mind; (*Witz*) wit; (*Gesinnung*) spirit; (*Gespenst*) ghost; **der Heilige G~** the Holy Ghost *or* Spirit

geistes|abwesend *a* absent-minded. **G~blitz** *m* brainwave. **g~gegenwärtig** *adv* with great presence of mind. **g~gestört** *a* [mentally] deranged. **g~krank** *a* mentally ill. **G~krankheit** *f* mental illness. **G~wissenschaften** *fpl* arts. **G~zustand** *m* mental state

geist|ig *a* mental; (*intellektuell*) intellectual. **g~lich** *a* spiritual; (*religiös*) religious; <*Musik*> sacred;

<Tracht> clerical. **G~liche(r)** *m* clergyman. **G~lichkeit** *f* - clergy. **g~reich** *a* clever; (*witzig*) witty

Geiz *m* -es meanness. **g~en** *vi* (*haben*) be mean (mit with). **G~hals** *m* 🔽 miser. **g~ig** *a* mean, miserly. **G~kragen** *m* 🔽 miser

Gekicher *nt* -s giggling

geknickt *a* 🔽 dejected

gekonnt *a* accomplished ● *adv* expertly

gekränkt *a* offended, hurt

Gekritzel *nt* -s scribble

Gelächter *nt* -s laughter

geladen *a* loaded

gelähmt *a* paralysed

Geländer *nt* -s,- railings *pl*; (*Treppen-*) banisters

gelangen *vi* (*sein*) reach/(*fig*) attain (zu etw/an etw *acc* sth)

gelassen *a* composed; (*ruhig*) calm. **G~heit** *f* - equanimity; (*Fassung*) composure

Gelatine /ʒela-/ *f* - gelatine

geläufig *a* common, current; (*fließend*) fluent; jdm g~ sein be familiar to s.o.

gelaunt *a* gut/schlecht g~ sein be in a good/bad mood

gelb *a* yellow; (*bei Ampel*) amber; das G~e vom Ei the yolk of the egg. **G~** *nt* -s,- yellow. **g~lich** *a* yellowish. **G~sucht** *f* jaundice

Geld *nt* -es, -er money; öffentliche G~er public funds. **G~beutel** *m*, **G~börse** *f* purse. **G~geber** *m* -s,- backer. **g~lich** *a* financial. **G~mittel** *ntpl* funds. **G~schein** *m* banknote. **G~schrank** *m* safe. **G~strafe** *f* fine. **G~stück** *nt* coin

Gelee /ʒe'le:/ *nt* -s, -s jelly

gelegen *a* situated; (*passend*) convenient

Gelegenheit *f* -, -en opportunity, chance; (*Anlass*) occasion; (*Comm*) bargain; bei G~ some time. **G~sarbeit** *f* casual work. **G~skauf** *m* bargain

gelegentlich *a* occasional ● *adv* occasionally; (*bei Gelegenheit*) some time

Gelehrte(r) *m/f* scholar

Geleit *nt* -[e]s escort; freies G~ safe conduct. **g~en** *vt* escort

Gelenk *nt* -[e]s, -e joint. **g~ig** *a* supple; (*Techn*) flexible

gelernt *a* skilled

Geliebte(r) *m/f* lover

gelingen† *vi* (*sein*) succeed, be successful. **G~** *nt* -s success

gellend *a* shrill

geloben *vt* promise [solemnly]; das Gelobte Land the Promised Land

Gelöbnis *nt* -ses, -se vow

gelöst *a* (*fig*) relaxed

gelten† *vi* (*haben*) be valid; *<Regel:>* apply; g~ als be regarded as; etw nicht g~ lassen not accept sth; wenig/viel g~ be worth/(*fig*) count for little/a lot; jdm g~ be meant for s.o.; das gilt nicht that doesn't count. **g~d** *a* valid; *<Preise>* current; *<Meinung>* prevailing; g~d machen assert *<Recht, Forderung>*; bring to bear *<Einfluss>*

Geltung *f* - validity; (*Ansehen*) prestige; zur G~ bringen set off

Gelübde *nt* -s,- vow

gelungen *a* successful

Gelüst *nt* -[e]s, -e desire

gemächlich *a* leisurely ● *adv* in a leisurely manner

Gemahl *m* -s, -e husband. **G~in** *f* -, -nen wife

Gemälde *nt* -s,- painting. **G~galerie** *f* picture gallery

gemäß *prep* (+ *dat*) in accordance with

gemäßigt *a* moderate; *<Klima>* temperate

gemein *a* common; (*unanständig*) vulgar; (*niederträchtig*) mean; g~er Soldat private

Gemeinde *f* -, -n [local] community; (*Admin*) borough; (*Pfarr-*) parish; (*bei Gottesdienst*) congregation. **G~rat** *m* local council/(*Person*) councillor. **G~wahlen** *fpl* local elections

gemein|gefährlich *a* dangerous.
  G~heit *f* -, -en commonness;
  vulgarity; meanness; (*Bemerkung,*
  Handlung) mean thing [to say/do];
  so eine G~heit! how mean!
  G~kosten *pl* overheads.
  g~nützig *a* charitable. **g~sam** *a*
  common ● *adv* together

Gemeinschaft *f* -, -en community.
  g~lich *a* joint; <*Besitz*> communal
  ● *adv* jointly; (*zusammen*) together.
  G~sarbeit *f* team-work

Gemenge *nt* -s,- mixture

Gemisch *nt* -[e]s, -e mixture. **g~t**
  a mixed

Gemme *f* -, -n engraved gem

Gemse* *f* -, -n *s.*Gämse

Gemurmel *nt* -s murmuring

Gemüse *nt* -s,- vegetable; (*coll*)
  vegetables *pl.* **G~händler** *m*
  greengrocer

gemustert *a* patterned

Gemüt *nt* -[e]s, -er nature,
  disposition; (*Gefühl*) feelings *pl*

gemütlich *a* cosy; (*gemächlich*)
  leisurely; (*zwanglos*) informal;
  <*Person*> genial; **es sich** (*dat*) **g~**
  machen make oneself comfortable.
  G~keit *f* - cosiness

Gen *nt* -s, -e gene

genau *a* exact, precise; <*Waage,*
  Messung> accurate; (*sorgfältig*)
  meticulous; (*ausführlich*) detailed;
  nichts G~es wissen not know any
  details; **g~ genommen** strictly
  speaking; **g~!** exactly! **G~igkeit** *f* -
  exactitude; precision; accuracy;
  meticulousness

genauso *adv* just the same;
  (*g~sehr*) just as much; **g~ teuer** just
  as expensive; **g~ gut** just as good;
  adv just as well; **g~ sehr** just as
  much; **g~ viel** just as much/many;
  g~ wenig just as little/few; (*noch*) no
  more

Gendarm /ʒãˈdarm/ *m* -en, -en
  (*Aust*) policeman

Genealogie *f* - genealogy

genehmig|en *vt* grant; approve
  <*Plan*>. **G~ung** *f* -, -en permission;
  (*Schein*) permit

geneigt *a* sloping, inclined; (*fig*)
  well-disposed (*dat* towards)

General *m* -s, -̈e general.
  G~direktor *m* managing director.
  G~probe *f* dress rehearsal.
  G~streik *m* general strike

Generation /-ˈtsi̯oːn/ *f* -, -en
  generation

Generator *m* -s, -en /-ˈtoːrən/
  generator

generell *a* general

genes|en† *vi* (*sein*) recover.
  G~ung *f* - recovery; (*Erholung*)
  convalescence

Genetik *f* - genetics *sg*

Genf *nt* -s Geneva. **G~er** *a* Geneva
  ...; **G~er See** Lake Geneva

genial *a* brilliant. **G~ität** *f* genius

Genick *nt* -s, -e [back of the] neck;
  sich (*dat*) **das G~ brechen** break
  one's neck

Genie /ʒeˈniː/ *nt* -s, -s genius

genieren /ʒeˈniːrən/ *vt* embarrass;
  sich g~ feel *or* be embarrassed

genieß|bar *a* fit to eat/drink.
  g~en† *vt* enjoy; (*verzehren*) eat/
  drink

Genitiv *m* -s, -e genitive

Genosse *m* -n, -n (*Pol*) comrade.
  G~nschaft *f* -, -en cooperative

genug *inv a & adv* enough

Genüge *f* zur G~ sufficiently. **g~n**
  vi (*haben*) be enough. **g~nd** *inv a*
  sufficient, enough; (*Sch*) fair ● *adv*
  sufficiently, enough

Genuss *m* -es,-̈e enjoyment;
  (*Vergnügen*) pleasure; (*Verzehr*)
  consumption

geöffnet *a* open

Geo|graphie, G~grafie *f* -
  geography. **g~graphisch,**
  g~grafisch *a* geographical.
  G~logie *f* - geology. **g~logisch** *a*
  geological. **G~meter** *m* -s,-
  surveyor. **G~metrie** *f* - geometry.
  g~metrisch *a* geometric[al]

geordnet *a* well-ordered; (*stabil*)
  stable; **alphabetisch g~** in
  alphabetical order

Gepäck *nt* -s luggage, baggage.
  G~ablage *f* luggage-rack.

G~aufbewahrung f left-luggage office. **G~schein** m left-luggage ticket; (*Aviat*) baggage check. **G~träger** m porter; (*Fahrrad-*) luggage carrier; (*Dach-*) roof-rack

Gepard m -s, -e cheetah

gepflegt a well-kept; <*Person*> well-groomed; <*Hotel*> first-class

gepunktet a spotted

gerade a straight; (*direkt*) direct; (*aufrecht*) upright; (*aufrichtig*) straightforward; <*Zahl*> even ● adv straight; directly; (*eben*) just; (*genau*) exactly; (*besonders*) especially; **g~ sitzen/stehen** sit/stand [up] straight; **g~ erst** only just. **G~** f -, -n straight line. **g~aus** adv straight ahead/on. **g~heraus** adv (*fig*) straight out. **g~so** adv just the same; **g~so gut** just as good; adv just as well. **g~stehen†** vi sep (*haben*) (*fig*) accept responsibility (**für** for). **g~zu** adv virtually; (*wirklich*) absolutely

Geranie /-iə/ f -, -n geranium

Gerät nt -[e]s, -e tool; (*Acker-*) implement; (*Küchen-*) utensil; (*Elektro-*) appliance; (*Radio-, Fernseh-*) set; (*Turn-*) piece of apparatus; (*coll*) equipment

geraten† vi (*sein*) get; **in Brand g~** catch fire; **in Wut g~** get angry; **gut g~** turn out well

Geratewohl nt **aufs G~** at random

geräuchert a smoked

geräumig a spacious, roomy

Geräusch nt -[e]s, -e noise. **g~los** a noiseless

gerben vt tan

gerecht a just; (*fair*) fair. **g~fertigt** a justified. **G~igkeit** f - justice; fairness

Gerede nt -s talk

geregelt a regular

gereizt a irritable

Geriatrie f - geriatrics sg

Gericht¹ nt -[e]s, -e (*Culin*) dish

Gericht² nt -[e]s, -e court [of law]; **vor G~** in court; **das Jüngste G~** the Last Judgement. **g~lich** a

judicial; <*Verfahren*> legal ● adv **g~lich vorgehen** take legal action. **G~shof** m court of justice. **G~smedizin** f forensic medicine. **G~ssaal** m court-room. **G~svollzieher** m -s,- bailiff

gerieben a grated; (🛈 *schlau*) crafty

gering a small; (*niedrig*) low; (*g~fügig*) slight. **g~fügig** a slight. **g~schätzig** a contemptuous; <*Bemerkung*> disparaging. **g~ste(r,s)** a least; **nicht im G~sten** not in the least

gerinnen† vi (*sein*) curdle; <*Blut:*> clot

Gerippe nt -s,- skeleton; (*fig*) framework

gerissen a 🛈 crafty

Germ m -[e]s & (*Aust*) f - yeast

German|e m -n, -n [ancient] German. **g~isch** a Germanic. **G~istik** f - German [language and literature]

gern[e] adv gladly; **g~ haben** like; (*lieben*) be fond of; **ich tanze g~** I like dancing; **willst du mit?—g~!** do you want to come?—I'd love to!

Gerste f - barley. **G~nkorn** nt (*Med*) stye

Geruch m -[e]s, ̈-e smell (**von/nach** of). **g~los** a odourless. **G~ssinn** m sense of smell

Gerücht nt -[e]s, -e rumour

gerührt a (*fig*) moved, touched

Gerümpel nt -s lumber, junk

Gerüst nt -[e]s, -e scaffolding; (*fig*) framework

gesammelt a collected; (*gefasst*) composed

gesamt a entire, whole. **G~ausgabe** f complete edition. **G~eindruck** m overall impression. **G~heit** f - whole. **G~schule** f comprehensive school. **G~summe** f total

Gesandte(r) m/f envoy

Gesang m -[e]s, ̈-e singing; (*Lied*) song; (*Kirchen-*) hymn. **G~verein** m choral society

Gesäß nt -es buttocks pl

---

*alte Schreibung

Geschäft nt -[e]s, -e business; (*Laden*) shop, store; (*Transaktion*) deal; **schmutzige G~e** shady dealings; **ein gutes G~machen** do very well (**mit** out of). **g~ig** a busy; <*Treiben*> bustling. **G~igkeit** f - activity. **g~lich** a business ... ● adv on business

Geschäfts|brief m business letter. **G~führer** m manager; (*Vereins-*) secretary. **G~mann** m (pl -leute) businessman. **G~stelle** f office; (*Zweigstelle*) branch. **g~tüchtig** a **g~tüchtig sein** be a good businessman/-woman. **G~zeiten** fpl hours of business

geschehen† vi (sein) happen (*dat* to); **das geschieht dir recht!** it serves you right! **gern g~!** you're welcome! **G~** nt -s events pl

gescheit a clever

Geschenk nt -[e]s, -e present, gift

Geschicht|e f -, -n history; (*Erzählung*) story; (🄓 *Sache*) business. **g~lich** a historical

Geschick nt -[e]s fate; (*Talent*) skill. **G~lichkeit** f - skilfulness, skill. **g~t** a skilful; (*klug*) clever

geschieden a divorced

Geschirr nt -s, -e (*coll*) crockery; (*Porzellan*) china; (*Service*) service; (*Pferde-*) harness; **schmutziges G~** dirty dishes pl. **G~spülmaschine** f dishwasher. **G~tuch** nt tea-towel

Geschlecht nt -[e]s, -er sex; (*Gram*) gender; (*Generation*) generation. **g~lich** a sexual. **G~skrankheit** f venereal disease. **G~steile** ntpl genitals. **G~sverkehr** m sexual intercourse. **G~swort** nt (pl -wörter) article

geschliffen a (*fig*) polished

Geschmack m -[e]s, -̈e taste; (*Aroma*) flavour; (*G~ssinn*) sense of taste; **einen guten G~ haben** (*fig*) have good taste. **g~los** a tasteless; **g~los sein** (*fig*) be in bad taste. **g~voll** a (*fig*) tasteful

Geschoss nt -es, -e missile; (*Stockwerk*) storey, floor

Geschrei nt -s screaming; (*fig*) fuss

Geschütz nt -es, -e gun, cannon

geschützt a protected; <*Stelle*> sheltered

Geschwader nt -s,- squadron

Geschwätz nt -es talk

geschweige conj **g~ denn** let alone

Geschwindigkeit f -, -en speed; (*Phys*) velocity. **G~sbegrenzung, G~sbeschränkung** f speed limit

Geschwister pl brother[s] and sister[s]; siblings

geschwollen a swollen; (*fig*) pompous

Geschworene|(r) m/f juror; **die G~n** the jury sg

Geschwulst f -, -̈e swelling; (*Tumor*) tumour

geschwungen a curved

Geschwür nt -s, -e ulcer

gesellig a sociable; (*Zool*) gregarious; (*unterhaltsam*) convivial; **g~er Abend** social evening

Gesellschaft f -, -en company; (*Veranstaltung*) party; **die G~** society; **jdm G~ leisten** keep s.o. company. **g~lich** a social. **G~sspiel** nt party game

Gesetz nt -es, -e law. **G~entwurf** m bill. **g~gebend** a legislative. **G~gebung** f - legislation. **g~lich** a legal. **g~mäßig** a lawful; (*gesetzlich*) legal. **g~widrig** a illegal

gesichert a secure

Gesicht nt -[e]s, -er face; (*Aussehen*) appearance. **G~sfarbe** f complexion. **G~spunkt** m point of view. **G~szüge** mpl features

Gesindel nt -s riff-raff

Gesinnung f -, -en mind; (*Einstellung*) attitude

gesondert a separate

Gespann nt -[e]s, -e team; (*Wagen*) horse and cart/carriage

gespannt a taut; (*fig*) tense; <*Beziehungen*> strained; (*neugierig*) eager; (*erwartungsvoll*) expectant; **g~ sein, ob** wonder whether; **auf etw g~ sein** look forward eagerly to sth

Gespenst nt -[e]s, -er ghost. **g~isch** a ghostly; (*unheimlich*) eerie

Gespött *nt* -[e]s mockery; **zum G∼ werden** become a laughing-stock

Gespräch *nt* -[e]s-e conversation; (*Telefon-*) call; **ins G∼ kommen** get talking; **im G∼ sein** be under discussion. **g∼ig** *a* talkative, **G∼sthema** *nt* topic of conversation

Gestalt *f* -, -en figure; (*Form*) shape, form; **G∼ annehmen** (*fig*) take shape. **g∼en** *vt* shape; (*organisieren*) arrange; (*schaffen*) create; (*entwerfen*) design; **sich g∼en** turn out

Geständnis *nt* -ses, -se confession

Gestank *m* -s stench, [bad] smell

gestatten *vt* allow, permit; **nicht gestattet** prohibited; **g∼ Sie?** may I?

Geste /'gɛ-, 'ge:stə/ *f* -, -n gesture

Gesteck *nt* -[e]s, -e flower arrangement

gestehen† *vt/i* (*haben*) confess; confess to <*Verbrechen*>

Gestein *nt* -[e]s, -e rock

Gestell *nt* -[e]s, -e stand; (*Flaschen-*) rack; (*Rahmen*) frame

gesteppt *a* quilted

gestern *adv* yesterday; **g∼ Nacht** last night

gestrandet *a* stranded

gestreift *a* striped

gestrichelt *a* <*Linie*> dotted

gestrichen *a* **g∼er Teelöffel** level teaspoon[ful]

gestrig /'gɛstrɪç/ *a* yesterday's; **am g∼en Tag** yesterday

Gestrüpp *nt* -s, -e undergrowth

Gestüt *nt* -[e]s, -e stud [farm]

Gesuch *nt* -[e]s, -e request; (*Admin*) application. **g∼t** *a* sought-after

gesund *a* healthy; **g∼ sein** be in good health; <*Sport, Getränk:*> be good for one; **wieder g∼ werden** get well again

Gesundheit *f* - health; **G∼!** (*bei Niesen*) bless you! **g∼lich** *a* a health ...; **g∼licher Zustand** state of health ● *adv* **es geht ihm g∼lich gut**/

schlecht he is in good/poor health. **g∼sschädlich** *a* harmful

getäfelt *a* panelled

Getöse *nt* -s racket, din

Getränk *nt* -[e]s, -e drink. **G∼ekarte** *f* wine-list

getrauen *vt* sich (*dat*) etw **g∼** dare [to] do sth; **sich g∼** dare

Getreide *nt* -s (*coll*) grain

getrennt *a* separate; **g∼ leben** live apart; **g∼ schreiben** write as two words

getreu *a* faithful ● *prep* (+ *dat*) true to. **g∼lich** *adv* faithfully

Getriebe *nt* -s,- bustle; (*Techn*) gear; (*Auto*) transmission; (*Gehäuse*) gearbox

getrost *adv* with confidence

Getto *nt* -s, -s ghetto

Getue *nt* -s 🔟 fuss

Getümmel *nt* -s tumult

geübt *a* skilled

Gewächs *nt* -es, -e plant

gewachsen *a* jdm **g∼ sein** be a match for s.o.

Gewächshaus *nt* greenhouse

gewagt *a* daring

gewählt *a* refined

gewahr *a* **g∼ werden** become aware (*acc/gen* of)

Gewähr *f* - guarantee

gewähr|en *vt* grant; (*geben*) offer. **g∼leisten** *vt* guarantee

Gewahrsam *m* -s safekeeping; (*Haft*) custody

Gewalt *f* -, -en power; (*Kraft*) force; (*Brutalität*) violence; **mit G∼** by force. **G∼herrschaft** *f* tyranny. **g∼ig** *a* powerful; (🔟 *groß*) enormous; (*stark*) tremendous. **g∼sam** *a* forcible; <*Tod*> violent. **g∼tätig** *a* violent. **G∼tätigkeit** *f* -, -en violence; (*Handlung*) act of violence

Gewand *nt* -[e]s, ⁻er robe

gewandt *a* skilful. **G∼heit** *f* - skill

Gewebe *nt* -s,- fabric; (*Anat*) tissue

Gewehr *nt* -s, -e rifle, gun

Geweih *nt* -[e]s, -e antlers *pl*

---

*old spelling

Gewerb|e *nt* -s,- trade. **g~lich** *a* commercial. **g~smäßig** *a* professional

Gewerkschaft *f* -, -en trade union. **G~ler(in)** *m* -s,- (*f* -, -nen) trade unionist

Gewicht *nt* -[e]s, -e weight; (*Bedeutung*) importance. **G~heben** *nt* -s weight-lifting

Gewinde *nt* -s,- [screw] thread

Gewinn *m* -[e]s, -e profit; (*fig*) gain, benefit; (*beim Spiel*) winnings *pl*; (*Preis*) prize; (*Los*) winning ticket. **G~beteiligung** *f* profit-sharing. **g~en†** *vt* win; (*erlangen*) gain; (*fördern*) extract ● *vi* (*haben*) win; **g~en an** (+ *dat*) gain in. **g~end** *a* engaging. **G~er(in)** *m* -s,- (*f* -, -nen) winner

Gewirr *nt* -s, -e tangle; (*Straßen-*) maze

gewiss *a* certain

Gewissen *nt* -s,- conscience. **g~haft** *a* conscientious. **g~los** *a* unscrupulous. **G~sbisse** *mpl* pangs of conscience

gewissermaßen *adv* to a certain extent; (*sozusagen*) as it were

Gewissheit *f* - certainty

Gewitt|er *nt* -s,- thunderstorm. **g~rig** *a* thundery

gewogen *a* (*fig*) well-disposed (*dat* towards)

gewöhnen *vt* jdn/sich **g~ an** (+ *acc*) get s.o. used to/get used to; [an] jdn/etw gewöhnt sein be used to s.o./ sth

Gewohnheit *f* -, -en habit. **G~srecht** *nt* common law

gewöhnlich *a* ordinary; (*üblich*) usual; (*ordinär*) common

gewohnt *a* customary; (*vertraut*) familiar; (*üblich*) usual; etw (*acc*) **g~ sein** be used to sth

Gewölbe *nt* -s,- vault

Gewühl *nt* -[e]s crush

gewunden *a* winding

Gewürz *nt* -es, -e spice. **G~nelke** *f* clove

gezackt *a* serrated

gezähnt *a* serrated; (*Säge*) toothed

Gezeiten *fpl* tides

gezielt *a* specific; (*Frage*) pointed

geziert *a* affected

gezwungen *a* forced. **g~ermaßen** *adv* of necessity

Gicht *f* - gout

Giebel *m* -s,- gable

Gier *f* - greed (nach for). **g~ig** *a* greedy

gieß|en† *vt* pour; water <*Blumen, Garten*>; (*Techn*) cast ● *v impers* es **g~t** it is pouring [with rain]. **G~kanne** *f* watering-can

Gift *nt* -[e]s, -e poison; (*Schlangen-*) venom; (*Biol, Med*) toxin. **g~ig** *a* poisonous; <*Schlange*> venomous; (*Med, Chem*) toxic; (*fig*) spiteful. **G~müll** *m* toxic waste. **G~pilz** *m* toadstool

Gilde *f* -, -n guild

Gin /dʒɪn/ *m* -s gin

Ginster *m* -s (*Bot*) broom

Gipfel *m* -s,- summit, top; (*fig*) peak. **G~konferenz** *f* summit conference. **g~n** *vi* (*haben*) culminate (**in** + *dat* in)

Gips *m* -es plaster. **G~verband** *m* (*Med*) plaster cast

Giraffe *f* -, -n giraffe

Girlande *f* -, -n garland

Girokonto /'ʒiːro-/ *nt* current account

Gischt *m* -[e]s & *f* - spray

Gitar|re *f* -, -n guitar. **G~rist(in)** *m* -en, -en (*f* -, -nen) guitarist

Gitter *nt* -s,- bars *pl*; (*Rost*) gratting, grid; (*Geländer, Zaun*) railings *pl*; (*Fenster-*) grille; (*Draht-*) wire screen

Glanz *m* -es shine; (*von Farbe, Papier*) gloss; (*Seiden-*) sheen; (*Politur*) polish; (*fig*) brilliance; (*Pracht*) splendour

glänzen *vi* (*haben*) shine. **g~d** *a* shining, bright; <*Papier*> glossy; (*fig*) brilliant

glanz|los *a* dull. **G~stück** *nt* masterpiece

Glas *nt* -es, ̈-er glass; (*Brillen-*) lens; (*Fern-*) binoculars *pl*; (*Marmeladen-*) [glass] jar. **G~er** *m* -s,- glazier

glasieren *vt* glaze; ice <*Kuchen*>

glas|ig *a* glassy; (*durchsichtig*) transparent. **G~scheibe** *f* pane

Glasur *f* -, -en glaze; (*Culin*) icing

glatt *a* smooth; (*eben*) even; <*Haar*> straight; (*rutschig*) slippery; (*einfach*) straightforward; <*Absage*> flat; **g~ streichen** smooth out; **g~ rasiert** clean-shaven; **g~ gehen** go off smoothly; **das ist g~ gelogen** it's a downright lie

Glätte *f* -, smoothness; (*Rutschigkeit*) slipperiness

Glatt|eis *nt* [black] ice. **g~weg** *adv* 🎵 outright

Glatz|e *f* -, -n bald patch; (*Voll-*) bald head; **eine G~e bekommen** go bald. **g~köpfig** *a* bald

Glaube *m* -ns belief (**an** + *acc* in); (*Relig*) faith; **G~n schenken** (+ *dat*) believe. **g~n** *vt/i* (*haben*) believe (**an** + *acc* in); (*vermuten*) think; **jdm g~n** believe s.o; **nicht zu g~n** unbelievable, incredible. **G~nsbekenntnis** *nt* creed

gläubig *a* religious; (*vertrauend*) trusting. **G~e(r)** *m/f* (*Relig*) believer; **die G~en** the faithful. **G~er** *m* -s,- (*Comm*) creditor

glaub|lich *a* **kaum g~lich** scarcely believable. **g~würdig** *a* credible; <*Person*> reliable

gleich *a* same; (*identisch*) identical; (*g~wertig*) equal; **g~ bleibend** constant; **2 mal 5 [ist] g~ 10** two times 5 equals 10; **das ist mir g~** it's all the same to me; **ganz g~, wo/wer** no matter where/who ● *adv* equally; (*übereinstimmend*) identically, the same; (*sofort*) immediately; (*in Kürze*) in a minute; (*fast*) nearly; (*direkt*) right. **g~altrig** *a* [of] the same age. **g~bedeutend** *a* synonymous. **g~berechtigt** *a* equal. **G~berechtigung** *f* equality

gleichen† *vi* (*haben*) **jdm/etw g~** be like *or* resemble s.o./sth

gleich|ermaßen *adv* equally. **g~falls** *adv* also, likewise; **danke g~falls** thank you, the same to you. **G~gewicht** *nt* balance; (*Phys* &

fig) equilibrium. **g~gültig** *a* indifferent; (*unwichtig*) unimportant. **G~gültigkeit** *f* indifference. **g~machen** *vt sep* make equal; **dem Erdboden g~machen** raze to the ground. **g~mäßig** *a* even, regular; (*beständig*) constant. **G~mäßigkeit** *f* - regularity

Gleichnis *nt* -ses, -se parable

Gleich|schritt *m* **im G~schritt** in step. **g~setzen** *vt sep* equate/ (*g~stellen*) place on a par (*dat*/**mit** with). **g~stellen** *vt sep* place on a par (*dat* with). **G~strom** *m* direct current

Gleichung *f* -, -en equation

gleichwertig *adv a* of equal value. **g~zeitig** *a* simultaneous

Gleis *nt* -es, -e track; (*Bahnsteig*) platform; **G~ 5** platform 5

gleiten† *vi* (*sein*) glide; (*rutschen*) slide. **g~d** *a* sliding; **g~de Arbeitszeit** flexitime

Gleitzeit *f* flexitime

Gletscher *m* -s,- glacier

Glied *nt* -[e]s, -er limb; (*Teil*) part; (*Ketten-*) link; (*Mitglied*) member; (*Mil*) rank. **g~ern** *vt* arrange; (*einteilen*) divide. **G~maßen** *fpl* limbs

glitschig *a* slippery

glitzern *vi* (*haben*) glitter

globalisier|en *vt* globalize. **G~ung** *f* -, -en globalization

Globus *m* - & -busses, -ben & -busse globe

Glocke *f* -, -n bell. **G~nturm** *m* bell-tower, belfry

glorreich *a* glorious

Glossar *nt* -s, -e glossary

Glosse *f* -, -n comment

glotzen *vi* (*haben*) stare

Glück *nt* -[e]s [good] luck; (*Zufriedenheit*) happiness; **G~ bringend** lucky; **G~/kein G~ haben** be lucky/unlucky; **zum G~** luckily, fortunately; **auf gut G~** on the off chance; (*wahllos*) at random. **g~en** *vi* (*sein*) succeed

glücklich *a* lucky, fortunate; (*zufrieden*) happy; (*sicher*) safe ● *adv* happily; safely. **g~erweise** *adv* luckily, fortunately

Glücksspiel *nt* game of chance; (*Spielen*) gambling

Glückwunsch *m* good wishes *pl*; (*Gratulation*) congratulations *pl*; herzlichen G~! congratulations! (*zum Geburtstag*) happy birthday! **G~karte** *f* greetings card

Glüh|birne *f* light-bulb. **g~en** *vi* (*haben*) glow. **g~end** *a* glowing; (*rot-*) red-hot; <*Hitze*> scorching; (*leidenschaftlich*) fervent. **G~faden** *m* filament. **G~wein** *m* mulled wine. **G~würmchen** *nt* **-s,-** glow-worm

Glukose *f* - glucose

Glut *f* - embers *pl*; (*Röte*) glow; (*Hitze*) heat; (*fig*) ardour

Glyzinie /-iə/ *f* -, **-n** wisteria

GmbH *abbr* (Gesellschaft mit beschränkter Haftung) ≈ plc

Gnade *f* - mercy; (*Gunst*) favour; (*Relig*) grace. **G~nfrist** *f* reprieve

gnädig *a* gracious; (*mild*) lenient; **g~e Frau** Madam

Gnom *m* **-en, -en** gnome

Gobelin /gobəˈlɛ̃:/ *m* **-s, -s** tapestry

Gold *nt* **-[e]s** gold. **g~en** *a* gold ...; (*g~farben*) golden. **G~fisch** *m* goldfish. **g~ig** *a* sweet, lovely. **G~lack** *m* wallflower. **G~regen** *m* laburnum. **G~schmied** *m* goldsmith

Golf[1] *m* **-[e]s, -e** (*Geog*) gulf

Golf[2] *nt* **-s** golf. **G~platz** *m* golf-course. **G~schläger** *m* golf-club. **G~spieler(in)** *m(f)* golfer

Gondel *f* -, **-n** gondola; (*Kabine*) cabin

gönnen *vt* jdm etw g~ not begrudge s.o. sth; jdm etw nicht g~ begrudge s.o. sth

Gör *nt* **-s, -en, Göre** *f* -, **-n** 🛈 kid

Gorilla *m* **-s, -s** gorilla

Gosse *f* -, **-n** gutter

Got|ik *f* - Gothic. **g~isch** *a* Gothic

Gott *m* **-[e]s,** ⁻er God; (*Myth*) god

Götterspeise *f* jelly

Gottes|dienst *m* service. **G~lästerung** *f* blasphemy

Gottheit *f* -, **-en** deity

Göttin *f* -, **-nen** goddess

göttlich *a* divine

gottlos *a* ungodly; (*atheistisch*) godless

Grab *nt* **-[e]s,** ⁻er grave

graben† *vi* (*haben*) dig

Graben *m* **-s,** ⁻ ditch; (*Mil*) trench

Grab|mal *nt* tomb. **G~stein** *m* gravestone, tombstone

Grad *m* **-[e]s, -e** degree

Graf *m* **-en, -en** count

Grafik *f* -, **-en** graphics *sg*; (*Kunst*) graphic arts *pl*; (*Druck*) print

Gräfin *f* -, **-nen** countess

grafisch *a* graphic; **g~e Darstellung** diagram

Grafschaft *f* -, **-en** county

Gram *m* **-s** grief

grämen (sich) *vr* grieve

Gramm *nt* **-s, -e** gram

Gram|matik *f* -, **-en** grammar. **g~matikalisch** *a* grammatical

Granat *m* **-[e]s, -e** (*Miner*) garnet. **G~e** *f* -, **-n** shell; (*Hand-*) grenade

Granit *m* **-s, -e** granite

Gras *nt* **-es,** ⁻er grass. **g~en** *vi* (*haben*) graze. **G~hüpfer** *m* **-s,-** grasshopper

grässlich *a* dreadful

Grat *m* **-[e]s, -e** [mountain] ridge

Gräte *f* -, **-n** fishbone

Gratifikation /-ˈtsi̯o:n/ *f* -, **-en** bonus

gratis *adv* free [of charge]. **G~probe** *f* free sample

Gratu|lant(in) *m* **-en, -en** (*f* -, **-nen**) well-wisher. **G~lation** /-ˈtsi̯o:n/ *f* -, **-en** congratulations *pl*; (*Glückwünsche*) best wishes *pl*. **g~lieren** *vi* (*haben*) jdm g~lieren congratulate s.o. (**zu** on); (*zum Geburtstag*) wish s.o. happy birthday

grau *a*, **G~** *nt* **-s,-** grey

Gräuel *m* **-s,-** horror

grauen *v impers* mir graut [es] davor I dread it. **G~** *nt* **-s** dread. **g~haft** *a* gruesome; (*grässlich*) horrible

gräulich *a* horrible

grausam a cruel. **G~keit** f -, -en cruelty

graus|en v impers mir graust davor I dread it. **G~en** nt -s horror, dread. **g~ig** a gruesome

gravieren vt engrave. **g~d** a (fig) serious

graziös a graceful

greifen† vt take hold of; (fangen) catch ● vi (haben) reach (nach for); um sich g~ (fig) spread

Greis m -es, -e old man. **G~in** f -, -nen old woman

grell a glaring; <Farbe> garish; (schrill) shrill

Gremium nt -s, -ien committee

Grenze|e f -, -n border; (Staats-) frontier; (Grundstücks-) boundary; (fig) limit. **g~en** vi (haben) border (an + acc on). **g~enlos** a boundless; (maßlos) infinite

Griech|e m -n, -n Greek. **G~enland** nt -s Greece. **G~in** f -, -nen Greek woman. **g~isch** a Greek. **G~isch** nt -[s] (Lang) Greek

Grieß m -es semolina

Griff m -[e]s, -e grasp, hold; (Hand-) movement of the hand; (Tür-, Messer-) handle; (Schwert-) hilt. **g~bereit** a handy

Grill m -s, -s grill; (Garten-) barbecue

Grille f -, -n (Zool) cricket

grill|en vt grill; (im Freien) barbecue ● vi (haben) have a barbecue. **G~fest** nt barbecue

Grimasse f -, -n grimace; **G~n** schneiden pull faces

grimmig a furious; <Kälte> bitter

grinsen vi (haben) grin

Grippe f -, -n influenza, ⚕ flu

grob a coarse; (unsanft, ungefähr) rough; (unhöflich) rude; (schwer) gross; <Fehler> bad; **g~ geschätzt** roughly. **G~ian** m -s, -e brute

Groll m -[e]s resentment. **g~en** vi (haben) be angry (dat with); <Donner:> rumble

Grönland nt -s Greenland

Gros nt -ses,- (Maß) gross

Groschen m -s,- (Aust) groschen; ⚕ ten-pfennig piece

groß a big; <Anzahl, Summe> large; (bedeutend, stark) great; (g~artig) grand; <Buchstabe> capital; **g~e Ferien** summer holidays; **der größte Teil** the majority or bulk; **g~ werden** <Person:> grow up; **g~ in etw** (dat) **sein** be good at sth; **G~ und Klein** young and old; **im G~en und Ganzen** on the whole ● adv <feiern> in style; (⚕ viel) much

groß|artig a magnificent. **G~aufnahme** f close-up. **G~britannien** nt -s Great Britain. **G~buchstabe** m capital letter. **G~e(r)** m/f unser G~er our eldest; **die G~en** the grown-ups; (fig) the great pl

Größe f -, -n size; (Ausmaß) extent; (Körper-) height; (Bedeutsamkeit) greatness; (Math) quantity; (Person) great figure

Großeltern pl grandparents

Groß|handel m wholesale trade. **G~händler** m wholesaler. **G~macht** f superpower. **g~mütig** a magnanimous. **G~mutter** f grandmother. **G~schreibung** f capitalization. **g~spurig** a pompous; (überheblich) arrogant. **G~stadt** f [large] city. **g~städtisch** a city ... **G~teil** m large proportion; (Hauptteil) bulk

größtenteils adv for the most part

groß|tun† (sich) vr sep brag. **G~vater** m grandfather. **g~ziehen**† vt sep bring up; rear <Tier>. **g~zügig** a generous. **G~zügigkeit** f - generosity

Grotte f -, -n grotto

Grübchen nt -s,- dimple

Grube f -, -n pit

grübeln vi (haben) brood

Gruft f -,-e [burial] vault

grün a green; im G~en out in the country; die G~en the Greens

Grund m -[e]s,-e ground; (Boden) bottom; (Hinter-) background; (Ursache) reason; aus diesem G~e for this reason; im G~e [genommen] basically; auf G~ laufen (Naut) run aground; **zu G~e richten/gehen** *s.* zugrunde. **G~begriffe** *mpl* basics. **G~besitzer** *m* landowner

gründ|en *vt* found, set up; start <*Familie*>; (*fig*) base (**auf** + *acc* on); **sich g~en** be based (**auf** + *acc* on). **G~er(in)** *m* -s,- (*f* -, -nen) founder

Grund|farbe *f* primary colour. **G~form** *f* (*Gram*) infinitive. **G~gesetz** *nt* (*Pol*) constitution. **G~lage** *f* basis, foundation

gründlich *a* thorough. **G~keit** *f* - thoroughness

Gründonnerstag *m* Maundy Thursday

Grund|regel *f* basic rule. **G~riss** *m* ground-plan; (*fig*) outline. **G~satz** *m* principle. **g~sätzlich** *a* fundamental; (*im Allgemeinen*) in principle; (*prinzipiell*) on principle; **G~schule** *f* primary school. **G~stück** *nt* plot [of land]

Gründung *f* -, -en foundation

Grün|span *m* verdigris. **G~streifen** *m* grass verge; (*Mittel-*) central reservation

grunzen *vi* (*haben*) grunt

Gruppe *f* -, -n group; (*Reise-*) party

gruppieren *vt* group

Grusel|geschichte *f* horror story. **g~ig** *a* creepy

Gruß *m* -es,ᵉe greeting; (*Mil*) salute; **einen schönen G~ an X** give my regards to X; **viele/herzliche G~e** regards; **Mit freundlichen G~en** Yours sincerely/faithfully

grüßen *vt/i* (*haben*) say hallo (**jdn** to s.o.); (*Mil*) salute; **g~Sie X von mir** give my regards to X; **grüß Gott!** (*SGer, Aust*) good morning/ afternoon/evening!

gucken *vi* (*haben*) 🔲 look

Guerilla /geˈrɪlja/ *f* - guerrilla warfare. **G~kämpfer** *m* guerrilla

Gulasch *nt & m* -[e]s goulash

gültig *a* valid

Gummi *m & nt* -s, -[s] rubber; (*Harz*) gum. **G~band** *nt* (*pl* -bänder) elastic *or* rubber band

gummiert *a* gummed

Gummi|knüppel *m* truncheon. **G~stiefel** *m* gumboot, wellington. **G~zug** *m* elastic

Gunst *f* - favour

günstig *a* favourable; (*passend*) convenient

Gurgel *f* -, -n throat. **g~n** *vi* (*haben*) gargle

Gurke *f* -, -n cucumber; (*Essig-*) gherkin

Gurt *m* -[e]s, -e strap; (*Gürtel*) belt; (*Auto*) safety-belt. **G~band** *nt* (*pl* -bänder) waistband

Gürtel *m* -s,- belt. **G~linie** *f* waistline. **G~rose** *f* shingles *sg*

Guss *m* -es,ᵉe (*Techn*) casting; (*Strom*) stream; (*Regen-*) downpour; (*Torten-*) icing. **G~eisen** *nt* cast iron

gut *a* good; <*Gewissen*> clear; (*gütig*) kind (**zu** to); **jdm gut sein** be fond of s.o.; **im G~en** amicably; **schon gut** that's all right ● *adv* well; <*schmecken, riechen*> good; (*leicht*) easily; **gut zu sehen** clearly visible; **gut drei Stunden** a good three hours

Gut *nt* -[e]s,ᵉer possession, property; (*Land-*) estate; **Gut und Böse** good and evil; **Güter** (*Comm*) goods

Gutacht|en *nt* -s,- expert's report. **G~er** *m* -s,- expert

gutartig *a* good-natured; (*Med*) benign

Gute|(s) *nt* **etwas/nichts G~s** something/nothing good; **G~s tun** do good; **G~s tun** do good; **alles G~!** all the best!

Güte *f* -, -n goodness, kindness; (*Qualität*) quality

Güterzug *m* goods train

gut|gehen* *vi sep* (*sein*) **gut gehen**, *s.* gehen. **g~gehend*** *a* gut gehend, *s.* gehen. **g~gläubig** *a* trusting. **g~haben†** *vt sep* **fünfzig Mark g~haben** have fifty marks credit (**bei** with). **G~haben** *nt* -s,- [credit] balance; (*Kredit*) credit

gut|machen *vt sep* make up for; make good <*Schaden*>. **g~mütig** *a* good-natured. **G~mütigkeit** *f* - good nature. **G~schein** *m* credit note; (*Bon*) voucher; (*Geschenk-*) gift

token. **g~schreiben**† *vt sep* credit.
G~schrift *f* credit

Guts|haus *nt* manor house

gut|tun* *vi sep* (*haben*) gut tun, *s.*
tun. **g~willig** *a* willing

Gymnasium *nt* -s, -ien ≈ grammar
school

Gymnastik *f* - [keep-fit] exercises
pl; (*Turnen*) gymnastics *sg*

Gynäko|loge *m* -n, -n
gynaecologist. **G~logie** *f* -
gynaecology

H, h /ha:/ *nt*, -,- (*Mus*) B, b

Haar *nt* -[e]s, -e hair; sich (*dat*) die
Haare *od* das H~ waschen wash
one's hair; um ein H~ 🔲 very
nearly. **H~bürste** *f* hairbrush.
h~en *vi* (*haben*) shed hairs; <*Tier:*>
moult ● *vr* sich h~en moult. **h~ig**
a hairy; 🔲 tricky. **H~klemme** *f*
hair-grip. **H~nadelkurve** *f* hairpin
bend. **H~schnitt** *m* haircut.
H~spange *f* slide.
H~waschmittel *nt* shampoo

Habe *f* - possessions *pl*

haben†
● *transitive verb*
⋯▸ have; (*im Präsens*) have got 🔲. er
hat kein Geld he has no money *or* 🔲
he hasn't got any money. ich habe/
hatte die Grippe I've got flu/had flu.
was haben Sie da? what have you
got there? wenn ich die Zeit hätte if I
had the time
⋯▸ (*empfinden*) Angst/Hunger/Durst
haben be frightened/hungry/thirsty.
was hat er? what's wrong with him?
⋯▸ (+ *Adj., es*) es gut/schlecht haben
be well/badly off. es schwer haben
be having a difficult time

⋯▸ (+ *zu*) (*müssen*) du hast zu
gehorchen you must obey
● *auxiliary verb*
⋯▸ have. ich habe/hatte ihn eben
gesehen I have *or* I've/I had *or* I'd
just seen him. er hat es gewusst he
knew it. er hätte ihr geholfen he
would have helped her
● *reflexive verb*
⋯▸ (🔲 sich aufregen) make a fuss.
hab dich nicht so! don't make such a
fuss!

Habgier *f* greed. **h~ig** *a* greedy

Habicht *m* -[e]s, -e hawk

Hachse *f* -, -n (*Culin*) knuckle

Hackbraten *m* meat loaf

Hacke¹ *f* -, -n hoe; (*Spitz-*) pick

Hacke² *f* -, -n, **Hacken** *m* -s,- heel

hack|en *vt* hoe; (*schlagen,
zerkleinern*) chop; <*Vogel:*> peck.
H~fleisch *nt* mince

Hafen *m* -s,- harbour; (*See-*) port.
H~arbeiter *m* docker. **H~stadt** *f*
port

Hafer *m* -s oats *pl*. **H~flocken** *fpl*
[rolled] oats

Haft *f* - (*Jur*) custody; (*H~strafe*)
imprisonment. **h~bar** *a* (*Jur*)
liable. **H~befehl** *m* warrant

haften *vi* (*haben*) cling; (*kleben*)
stick; (*bürgen*) vouch/(*Jur*) be liable
(*für* for)

Häftling *m* -s, -e detainee

Haftpflicht *f* (*Jur*) liability.
H~versicherung *f* (*Auto*) third-
party insurance

Haftung *f* - (*Jur*) liability

Hagebutte *f* -, -n rose-hip

Hagel *m* -s hail. **h~n** *vi* (*haben*) hail

hager *a* gaunt

Hahn *m* -[e]s,- cock; (*Techn*) tap

Hähnchen *nt* -,-s- (*Culin*) chicken

Hai[fisch] *m* -[e]s, -e shark

Häkchen *nt* -s,- tick

häkel|n *vt/i* (*haben*) crochet.
H~nadel *f* crochet-hook

Haken *m* -s,- hook; (*Häkchen*) tick;
(🔲 *Schwierigkeit*) snag. **h~** *vt* hook
(*an* + *acc* to). **H~kreuz** *nt* swastika

halb *a* half; **auf h~em Weg** half-way
● *adv* half; **h~drei** half past two; **fünf
[Minuten] vor/nach h~vier** twenty-
five [minutes] past three/to four.
H~e(r,s) *f*/*m*/*nt* half [a litre]

halber *prep* (+ *gen*) for the sake of;
Geschäfte h~ on business

Halbfinale *nt* semifinal

halbieren *vt* halve, divide in half;
(*Geom*) bisect

Halb|insel *f* peninsula. **H~kreis** *m*
semicircle. **H~kugel** *f* hemisphere.
h~laut *a* low ● *adv* in an
undertone. **h~mast** *adv* at half-
mast. **H~mond** *m* half moon.
H~pension *f* half-board. **h~rund**
a semicircular. **H~schuh** *m* [flat]
shoe. **h~tags** *adv* [for] half a day;
h~tags arbeiten ≈ work part-time.
H~ton *m* semitone. **h~wegs** *adv*
half-way; (*ziemlich*) more or less.
h~wüchsig *a* adolescent. **H~zeit**
f (*Sport*) half-time; (*Spielzeit*) half

Halde *f* -, -n dump, tip

Hälfte *f* -, -n half; **zur H~** half

Halfter *f* -, -n & *nt* -s,- holster

Halle *f* -, -n hall; (*Hotel*-) lobby;
(*Bahnhofs*-) station concourse

hallen *vi* (*haben*) resound; (*wider*-)
echo

Hallen- *pref* indoor

hallo *int* hallo

Halluzination /-'ts:io:n/ *f* -, -en
hallucination

Halm *m* -[e]s, -e stalk; (*Gras*-) blade

Hals *m* -es, ̈e neck; (*Kehle*) throat;
aus vollem H~e at the top of one's
voice; <*lachen*> out loud. **H~band**
nt (*pl* -bänder) collar.
H~schmerzen *mpl* sore throat *sg*

halt *int* stop! (*Mil*) halt! 🔲 wait a
minute!

Halt *m* -[e]s, -e hold; (*Stütze*) support;
(*innerer*) stability; (*Anhalten*) stop;
H~ machen stop. **h~bar** *a* durable;
(*Tex*) hard-wearing; (*fig*) tenable;
h~bar bis ... (*Comm*) use by ...

halten† *vt* hold; make <*Rede*>; give
<*Vortrag*>; (*einhalten, bewahren*)
keep; [*sich* (*dat*)] **etw h~** keep
<*Hund*>; take <*Zeitung*>; **h~ für**

regard as; **viel h~ von** think highly
of; **sich links h~** keep left; **sich h~
an** (+ *acc*) (*fig*) keep to ● *vi* (*haben*)
hold; (*haltbar sein, bestehen bleiben*)
keep; <*Freundschaft, Blumen:*> last;
(*Halt machen*) stop; **auf sich** (*acc*) **h~**
take pride in oneself; **zu jdm h~** be
loyal to s.o.

Halte|stelle *f* stop. **H~verbot** *nt*
waiting restriction; '**H~verbot**' 'no
waiting'

Haltung *f* -, -en (*Körper*-) posture;
(*Verhalten*) manner; (*Einstellung*)
attitude; (*Fassung*) composure;
(*Halten*) keeping

Hammel *m* -s,- ram; (*Culin*) mutton.
H~fleisch *nt* mutton

Hammer *m* -s, ̈- hammer

hämmern *vt/i* (*haben*) hammer

Hamster *m* -s,- hamster. **h~n** *vt/i*
🔲 hoard

Hand *f* -, ̈e hand; **jdm die H~ geben**
shake hands with s.o.; **rechter/linker
H~** on the right/left; **zweiter H~**
second-hand; **unter der H~**
unofficially; (*geheim*) secretly; **H~
und Fuß haben** (*fig*) be sound.
H~arbeit *f* manual work;
(*handwerklich*) handicraft;
(*Nadelarbeit*) needlework;
(*Gegenstand*) handmade article.
H~ball *m* [German] handball.
H~bewegung *f* gesture.
H~bremse *f* handbrake. **H~buch**
nt handbook, manual

Händedruck *m* handshake

Handel *m* -s trade, commerce;
(*Unternehmen*) business; (*Geschäft*)
deal; **H~ treiben** *vi* **h~n** *vi*
(*haben*) act; (*Handel treiben*) trade
(**mit** in); **von etw** *od* **über etw** (*acc*)
h~n deal with sth; **sich h~n um** be
about, concern. **H~smarine** *f*
merchant navy. **H~sschiff** *nt*
merchant vessel. **H~sschule** *f*
commercial college. **H~sware** *f*
merchandise

Hand|feger *m* -s,- brush.
H~fläche *f* palm. **H~gelenk** *nt*
wrist. **H~gemenge** *nt* -s,- scuffle.
H~gepäck *nt* hand-luggage.
h~geschrieben *a* hand-written.

h∼greiflich *a* tangible; **h∼greiflich werden** become violent. **H∼griff** *m* handle

handhaben *vt insep* (*reg*) handle

Handikap /'hɛndikɛp/ *nt* -s, -s handicap

Handkuss *m* kiss on the hand

Händler *m* -s,- dealer, trader

handlich *a* handy

Handlung *f* -, -en act; (*Handeln*) action; (*Roman-*) plot; (*Geschäft*) shop. **H∼sweise** *f* conduct

Hand|schellen *fpl* handcuffs. **H∼schlag** *m* handshake. **H∼schrift** *f* handwriting; (*Text*) manuscript. **H∼schuh** *m* glove. **H∼stand** *m* handstand. **H∼tasche** *f* handbag. **H∼tuch** *nt* towel

Handwerk *nt* craft, trade. **H∼er** *m* -s,- craftsman; (*Arbeiter*) workman

Handy /'hɛndi/ *nt* -s, -s mobile phone

Hanf *m* -[e]s hemp

Hang *m* -[e]s,ẹe slope; (*fig*) inclination

Hänge|brücke *f* suspension bridge. **H∼matte** *f* hammock

hängen[1] *vt* (*reg*) hang

hängen[2]† *vi* (*haben*) hang; **h∼ an** (+ *dat*) (*fig*) be attached to; **h∼ lassen** leave

Hannover *nt* -s Hanover

hänseln *vt* tease

hantieren *vi* (*haben*) busy oneself

Happen *m* -s,- mouthful; **einen H∼ essen** have a bite to eat

Harfe *f* -, -n harp

Harke *f* -, -n rake. **h∼n** *vt/i* (*haben*) rake

harmlos *a* harmless; (*arglos*) innocent

Harmonie *f* -, -n harmony

Harmonika *f* -, -s accordion; (*Mund-*) mouth-organ

harmonisch *a* harmonious

Harn *m* -[e]s urine. **H∼blase** *f* bladder

Harpune *f* -, -n harpoon

hart *a* hard; (*heftig*) violent; (*streng*) harsh

Härte *f* -, -n hardness; (*Strenge*) harshness; (*Not*) hardship. **h∼n** *vt* harden

Hart|faserplatte *f* hardboard. **h∼näckig** *a* stubborn; (*ausdauernd*) persistent. **H∼näckigkeit** *f* - stubbornness; persistence

Harz *nt* -es, -e resin

Haschee *nt* -s, -s (*Culin*) hash

Haschisch *nt & m* -[s] hashish

Hase *m* -n, -n hare

Hasel *f* -, -n hazel. **H∼maus** *f* dormouse. **H∼nuss** *f* hazel-nut

Hass *m* -es hatred

hassen *vt* hate

hässlich *a* ugly; (*unfreundlich*) nasty. **H∼keit** *f* - ugliness; nastiness

Hast *f* - haste. **h∼ig** *a* hasty, hurried

hast, hat, hatte, hätte *s.* haben

Haube *f* -, -n cap; (*Trocken-*) drier; (*Kühler-*) bonnet

Hauch *m* -[e]s breath; (*Luft-*) breeze; (*Duft*) whiff; (*Spur*) tinge. **h∼dünn** *a* very thin

Haue *f* -, -n pick; (Ⓐ *Prügel*) beating. **h∼n**† *vt* beat; (*hämmern*) knock; (*meißeln*) hew; **sich h∼n** fight; **übers Ohr h∼n** Ⓐ cheat ● *vi* (*haben*) bang (**auf** + *acc* on); **jdm ins Gesicht h∼n** hit s.o. in the face

Haufen *m* -s,- heap, pile; (*Leute*) crowd

häufen *vt* heap *or* pile [up]; **sich h∼** pile up; (*zunehmen*) increase

häufig *a* frequent

Haupt *nt* -[e]s, Häupter head. **H∼bahnhof** *m* main station. **H∼fach** *nt* main subject. **H∼gericht** *nt* main course

Häuptling *m* -s, -e chief

Haupt|mahlzeit *f* main meal **H∼mann** *m* (*pl* -leute) captain. **H∼post** *f* main post office. **H∼quartier** *nt* headquarters *pl*. **H∼rolle** *f* lead; (*fig*) leading role. **H∼sache** *f* main thing; **in der**

---
*old spelling

H∼sache in the main. **h∼sächlich**
a main. **H∼satz** *m* main clause.
H∼stadt *f* capital.
H∼verkehrsstraße *f* main road.
H∼verkehrszeit *f* rush-hour.
H∼wort *nt* (*pl* -wörter) noun
Haus *nt* -es, Häuser house; (*Gebäude*)
building; (*Schnecken-*) shell; **zu H∼e**
at home; **nach H∼e** home.
H∼arbeit *f* housework; (*Sch*)
homework. **H∼arzt** *m* family
doctor. **H∼aufgaben** *fpl* homework
sg. **H∼besetzer** *m* -s,- squatter
hausen *vi* (*haben*) live; (*wüten*)
wreak havoc
Haus|frau *f* housewife.
h∼gemacht *a* home-made.
H∼halt *m* -[e]s, -e household; (*Pol*)
budget. **h∼halten**† *vi sep* (*haben*)
h∼halten mit manage carefully;
conserve <*Kraft*>. **H∼hälterin** *f* -,
-nen housekeeper. **H∼haltsgeld** *nt*
housekeeping [money].
H∼haltsplan *m* budget. **H∼herr**
m head of the household; (*Gastgeber*)
host
Hausierer *m* -s,- hawker
Hauslehrer *m* [private] tutor.
H∼in *f* governess
häuslich *a* domestic, <*Person*>
domesticated
Haus|meister *m* caretaker.
H∼ordnung *f* house rules *pl.*
H∼putz *m* cleaning. **H∼rat** *m* -[e]s
household effects *pl.* **H∼schlüssel**
m front-door key. **H∼schuh** *m*
slipper. **H∼suchung** *f* [police]
search. **H∼suchungsbefehl** *m*
search-warrant. **H∼tier** *nt* domestic
animal; (*Hund, Katze*) pet. **H∼tür** *f*
front door. **H∼wirt** *m* landlord.
H∼wirtin *f* landlady
Haut *f* -,Häute skin; (*Tier-*) hide.
H∼arzt *m* dermatologist
häuten *vt* skin; **sich h∼** moult
haut|eng *a* skin-tight. **H∼farbe** *f*
colour; (*Teint*) complexion
Hebamme *f* -, -n midwife
Hebel *m* -s,- lever
heben† *vt* lift; (*hoch-, steigern*) raise;
sich h∼ rise; <*Nebel:*> lift; (*sich
verbessern*) improve

hebräisch *a* Hebrew
hecheln *vi* (*haben*) pant
Hecht *m* -[e]s, -e pike
Heck *nt* -s, -s (*Naut*) stern; (*Aviat*)
tail; (*Auto*) rear
Hecke *f* -, -n hedge
Heck|fenster *nt* rear window.
H∼tür *f* hatchback
Heer *nt* -[e]s, -e army
Hefe *f* - yeast
Heft *nt* -[e]s, -e booklet; (*Sch*)
exercise book; (*Zeitschrift*) issue.
h∼en *vt* (*nähen*) tack; (*stecken*) pin/
(*klammern*) clip/(*mit Heftmaschine*)
staple (**an** + *acc* to). **H∼er** *m* -s,- file
heftig *a* fierce, violent; <*Regen*>
heavy; <*Schmerz, Gefühl*> intense
Heft|klammer *f* staple; (*Büro-*)
paper-clip. **H∼maschine** *f* stapler.
H∼zwecke *f* -, -n drawing-pin
Heide[1] *m* -n, -n heathen
Heide[2] *f* -, -n heath; (*Bot*) heather.
H∼kraut *nt* heather
Heidelbeere *f* bilberry
Heidin *f* -, -nen heathen
heikel *a* difficult, tricky
heil *a* undamaged, intact; <*Person*>
unhurt; **mit h∼er Haut** 🔲 unscathed
Heil *nt* -s salvation
Heiland *m* -s (*Relig*) Saviour
Heil|anstalt *f* sanatorium;
(*Nerven-*) mental hospital. **H∼bad**
nt spa. **h∼bar** *a* curable
Heilbutt *m* -[e]s, -e halibut
heilen *vt* cure; heal <*Wunde*> ● *vi*
(*sein*) heal
Heilgymnastik *f* physiotherapy
heilig *a* holy; (*geweiht*) sacred; **der
H∼e Abend** Christmas Eve; **die h∼e
Anna** Saint Anne; **h∼ sprechen**
canonize. **H∼abend** *m* Christmas
Eve. **H∼e(r)** *m/f* saint.
H∼enschein *m* halo. **H∼keit** *f* -
sanctity, holiness. **H∼tum** *nt* -s,-̈er
shrine
heil|kräftig *a* medicinal.
H∼kräuter *ntpl* medicinal herbs.
H∼mittel *nt* remedy.
H∼praktiker *m* -s,- practitioner of
alternative medicine. **H∼sarmee** *f*
Salvation Army. **H∼ung** *f* - cure

Heim *nt* -[e]s, -e home; (*Studenten-*) hostel. **h~** *adv* home

Heimat *f* -, -en home; (*Land*) native land. **H~stadt** *f* home town

heim|begleiten *vt sep* see home. **H~computer** *m* home computer. **h~fahren**† *v sep* ● *vi* (*sein*) go/drive home ● *vt* take/drive home. **H~fahrt** *f* way home. **h~gehen**† *vi sep* (*sein*) go home

heimisch *a* native, indigenous; (*Pol*) domestic

Heim|kehr *f* - return [home]. **h~kehren** *vi sep* (*sein*) return home. **h~kommen**† *vi sep* (*sein*) come home

heimlich *a* secret; **etw h~ tun** do sth secretly. **H~keit** *f* -, -en secrecy; **H~keiten** secrets

Heim|reise *f* journey home. **H~spiel** *nt* home game. **h~suchen** *vt sep* afflict. **h~tückisch** *a* treacherous; (*Krankheit*) insidious. **h~wärts** *adv* home. **H~weg** *m* way home. **H~weh** *nt* -s homesickness; **H~weh haben** be homesick. **H~werker** *m* -s,- [home] handyman. **h~zahlen** *vt sep* **jdm etw h~zahlen** (*fig*) pay s.o. back for sth

Heirat *f* -, -en marriage. **h~en** *vt/i* (*haben*) marry. **H~santrag** *m* proposal; **jdm einen H~santrag machen** propose to s.o.

heiser *a* hoarse. **H~keit** *f* - hoarseness

heiß *a* hot; (*hitzig*) heated; (*leidenschaftlich*) fervent

heißen† *vi* (*haben*) be called; (*bedeuten*) mean; **ich heiße** ... my name is ...; **wie h~Sie?** what is your name? **wie heißt** ... **auf Englisch?** what's the English for ...? ● *vt* call; **jdn etw tun h~** tell s.o. to do sth

heiter *a* cheerful; (*Wetter*) bright; (*amüsant*) amusing; **aus h~em Himmel** (*fig*) out of the blue

Heiz|anlage *f* heating; (*Auto*) heater. **H~decke** *f* electric blanket.

h~en *vt* heat; light <*Ofen*> ● *vi* (*haben*) put the heating on; <*Ofen:*> give out heat. **H~gerät** *nt* heater. **H~kessel** *m* boiler. **H~körper** *m* radiator. **H~lüfter** *m* -s,- fan heater. **H~material** *nt* fuel. **H~ung** *f* -, -en heating; (*Heizkörper*) radiator

Hektar *nt* & *m* -s,- hectare

Held *m* -en, -en hero. **h~enhaft** *a* heroic. **H~entum** *nt* -s heroism. **H~in** *f* -, -nen heroine

helf|en† *vi* (*haben*) help (**jdm** s.o.); (*nützen*) be effective; **sich** (*dat*) **nicht zu h~en wissen** not know what to do; **es hilft nichts** it's no use. **H~er(in)** *m* -s,- (*f* -, -nen) helper, assistant

hell *a* light; (*Licht ausstrahlend, klug*) bright; <*Stimme*> clear; (🇮 *völlig*) utter; **h~es Bier** ≈ lager ● *adv* brightly

Hell|igkeit *f* - brightness. **H~seher(in)** *m* -s,- (*f* -, -nen) clairvoyant

Helm *m* -[e]s, -e helmet

Hemd *nt* -[e]s, -en vest; (*Ober-*) shirt

Hemisphäre *f* -, -n hemisphere

hemm|en *vt* check; (*verzögern*) impede; (*fig*) inhibit. **H~ung** *f* -, -en (*fig*) inhibition; (*Skrupel*) scruple; **H~ungen haben** be inhibited. **h~ungslos** *a* unrestrained

Hendl *nt* -s, -[n] (*Aust*) chicken

Hengst *m* -[e]s, -e stallion

Henkel *m* -s,- handle

Henne *f* -, -n hen

her *adv* here; (*zeitlich*) ago; **her mit** ...! give me ...! **von Norden/weit her** from the north/far away; **vom Thema her** as far as the subject is concerned; **her sein** come (**von** from); **es ist schon lange her** it was a long time ago

herab *adv* down [here]; **von oben h~** from above; (*fig*) condescending

herablassen† *vt sep* let down; **sich h~** condescend (**zu** to)

herab|sehen† *vi sep* (*haben*) look down (**auf** + *acc* on). **h~setzen** *vt sep* reduce, cut; (*fig*) belittle

---

Heraldik f - heraldry

heran adv near; [bis] h~ an (+ acc) up to. **h~kommen†** vi sep (sein) approach; h~kommen an (+ acc) come up to; (erreichen) get at; (fig) measure up to. **h~machen (sich)** vr sep sich h~machen an (+ acc) approach; get down to <Arbeit>. **h~wachsen†** vi sep (sein) grow up. **h~ziehen†** v sep ● vt pull up (an + acc to); (züchten) raise; (h~bilden) train; (hinzuziehen) call in ● vi (sein) approach

herauf adv up [here]; die Treppe h~ up the stairs. **h~setzen** vt sep raise, increase

heraus adv out (aus of); h~ damit od mit der Sprache! out with it! **h~bekommen†** vt sep get out; (ausfindig machen) find out; (lösen) solve; Geld h~bekommen get change. **h~finden†** v sep ● vt find out ● vi (haben) find one's way out. **h~fordern** vt sep provoke; challenge <Person>. **H~forderung** f provocation; challenge. **H~gabe** f handing over; (Admin) issue; (Veröffentlichung) publication. **h~geben†** vt sep hand over; (Admin) issue; (veröffentlichen) publish; edit <Zeitschrift>; jdm Geld h~geben give s.o. change ● vi (haben) give change (auf + acc for). **H~geber** m -s,- publisher; editor. **h~halten† (sich)** vr sep (fig) keep out (aus of). **h~kommen†** vi sep (sein) come out; (aus Schwierigkeit, Takt) get out; auf eins od dasselbe h~kommen Ⓘ come to the same thing. **h~lassen†** vt sep let out. **h~nehmen†** vt sep take out; sich zu viel h~nehmen (fig) take liberties. **h~reden (sich)** vr sep make excuses. **h~rücken** v sep ● vt move out; (hergeben) hand over ● vi (sein) h~rücken mit hand over; (fig: sagen) come out with. **h~schlagen†** vt sep knock out; (fig) gain. **h~stellen** vt sep put out; sich h~stellen turn out (als to be; dass that). **h~ziehen†** vt sep pull out

herb a sharp; <Wein> dry; (fig) harsh

herbei adv here. **h~führen** vt sep (fig) bring about. **h~schaffen** vt sep get. **h~sehnen** vt sep long for

Herberg|e f -, -n [youth] hostel; (Unterkunft) lodging. **H~svater** m warden

herbestellen vt sep summon

herbitten† vt sep ask to come

herbringen† vt sep bring [here]

Herbst m -[e]s, -e autumn. **h~lich** a autumnal

Herd m -[e]s, -e stove, cooker

Herde f -, -n herd; (Schaf-) flock

herein adv in [here]; h~! come in! **h~bitten†** vt sep ask in. **h~fallen†** vi sep (sein) Ⓘ be taken in (auf + acc by). **h~kommen†** vi sep (sein) come in. **h~lassen†** vt sep let in. **h~legen** vt sep Ⓘ take for a ride

Herfahrt f journey/drive here

herfallen† vi sep (sein) ~ über (+ acc) attack; fall upon <Essen>

hergeben† vt sep hand over; (fig) give up

hergehen† vi sep (sein) h~ vor (+ dat) walk along in front of; es ging lustig her Ⓘ there was a lot of merriment

herholen vt sep fetch; weit hergeholt (fig) far-fetched

Hering m -s, -e herring; (Zeltpflock) tent-peg

her|kommen† vi sep (sein) come here; wo kommt das her? where does it come from? **h~kömmlich** a traditional. **H~kunft** f - origin

herleiten vt sep derive

hermachen vt sep viel/wenig h~ be impressive/unimpressive; (wichtig nehmen) make a lot of/little fuss (von of); sich h~ über (+ acc) fall upon; tackle <Arbeit>

Hermelin[1] nt -s, -e (Zool) stoat

Hermelin[2] m -s, -e (Pelz) ermine

Hernie /'hɛrniə/ f -, -n hernia

Heroin nt -s heroin

heroisch a heroic

Herr m -n, -en gentleman; (Gebieter) master (über + acc of); [Gott,] der H~ the Lord [God]; H~ Meier Mr Meier;

Sehr geehrte H~en Dear Sirs.
H~enhaus nt manor [house].
h~enlos a ownerless; <Tier> stray

Herrgott m der H~ the Lord

herrichten vt sep prepare; **wieder**
h~ renovate

Herrin f -, -nen mistress

herrlich a marvellous; (großartig)
magnificent

Herrschaft f -, -en rule; (Macht)
power; (Kontrolle) control; **meine**
H~en! ladies and gentlemen!

herrsch|en vi (haben) rule;
(verbreitet sein) prevail; **es h~te**
Stille there was silence. **H~er(in)** m
-s,- (f -, -nen) ruler

herrühren vi sep (haben) stem (**von**
from)

herstammen vi sep (haben) come
(**aus/von** from)

herstell|en vt sep establish;
(Comm) manufacture, make. **H~er**
m -s,- manufacturer, maker.
H~ung f - establishment;
manufacture

herüber adv over [here]

herum adv im Kreis h~ [round] in a
circle; **falsch h~** the wrong way
round; **um ... h~** round ...;
(ungefähr) [round] about ...; **h~ sein**
be over. **h~drehen** vt sep turn
round/(wenden) over; turn
<Schlüssel>. **h~gehen** vi sep (sein)
walk around; <Zeit:> pass; **h~gehen**
um go round. **h~kommen**† vi sep
(sein) get about; **h~kommen um** get
round; come round <Ecke>; **um etw**
[nicht] h~kommen (fig) [not] get out
of sth. **h~sitzen**† vi sep (haben) sit
around; **h~sitzen um** sit round.
h~sprechen† (sich) vr sep
<Gerücht:> get about. **h~treiben**†
(sich) vr sep hang around.
h~ziehen† vi sep (sein) move
around; (ziellos) wander about

herunter adv down [here]; **die**
Treppe h~ down the stairs.
h~fallen† vi fall off.
h~gekommen a (fig) run-down;
<Gebäude> dilapidated; <Person>

down-at-heel. **h~kommen**† vi sep
(sein) come down; (fig) go to rack
and ruin; <Firma, Person:> go
downhill; (gesundheitlich) get run
down. **h~lassen**† vt sep let down,
lower. **h~machen** vt sep 🛇
reprimand; (herabsetzen) run down.
h~spielen vt sep (fig) play down

hervor adv out (aus of).
h~bringen† vt sep produce; utter
<Wort>. **h~gehen** vi sep (sein)
come/(sich ergeben) emerge/(folgen)
follow (aus from). **h~heben** vt sep
(fig) stress, emphasize. **h~ragen** vi
sep (haben) jut out; (fig) stand out.
h~ragend a (fig) outstanding.
h~rufen† vt sep (fig) cause.
h~stehen† vi sep (haben) protrude.
h~treten† vi sep (sein) protrude,
bulge; (fig) stand out. **h~tun**†
(sich) vr sep (fig) distinguish
oneself; (angeben) show off

Herweg m way here

Herz nt -ens, -en heart; (Kartenspiel)
hearts pl; **sich** (dat) **ein H~ fassen**
pluck up courage. **H~anfall** m
heart attack

herzhaft a hearty; (würzig) savoury

herziehen† v sep ● vt **hinter sich**
(dat) **h~** pull along [behind one] ● vi
(sein) **hinter jdm h~** follow along
behind s.o.; **über jdn h~** 🛇 run s.o.
down

herz|ig a sweet, adorable.
H~infarkt m heart attack.
H~klopfen nt -s palpitations pl

herzlich a cordial; (warm) warm;
(aufrichtig) sincere; **h~en Dank!**
many thanks! **h~e Grüße** kind
regards

herzlos a heartless

Herzog m -s,⸚e duke. **H~in** f -, -nen
duchess. **H~tum** nt -s,⸚er duchy

Herzschlag m heartbeat; (Med)
heart failure

Hessen nt -s Hesse

heterosexuell a heterosexual

Hetze f - rush; (Kampagne) virulent
campaign (**gegen** against). **h~n** vt
chase; **sich h~n** hurry

Heu nt -s hay

Heuchelei f - hypocrisy

heuch|eln *vt* feign ● *vi* (*haben*) pretend. **H~ler(in)** *m* -s,- (*f* -, -nen) hypocrite. **h~lerisch** *a* hypocritical

heuer *adv* (*Aust*) this year

heulen *vi* (*haben*) howl; (国 *weinen*) cry

Heu|schnupfen *m* hay fever. **H~schober** *m* -s,- haystack. **H~schrecke** *f* -, -n grasshopper

heut|e *adv* today; (*heutzutage*) nowadays; **h~e früh** *od* **Morgen** this morning; **von h~e auf morgen** from one day to the next. **h~ig** *a* today's ...; (*gegenwärtig*) present; **der h~ige Tag** today. **h~zutage** *adv* nowadays

Hexe *f* -, -n witch. **h~n** *vi* (*haben*) work magic. **H~nschuss** *m* lumbago

Hieb *m* -[e]s, -e blow; (*Peitschen-*) lash; **H~e** hiding *sg*

hier *adv* here; **h~ sein/bleiben/ lassen/behalten** be/stay/leave/keep here; **h~ und da** here and there; (*zeitlich*) now and again

hier|auf *adv* on this/these; (*antworten*) to this; (*zeitlich*) after this. **h~aus** *adv* out of *or* from this/these. **h~durch** *adv* through this/these; (*Ursache*) as a result of this. **h~her** *adv* here. **h~hin** *adv* here. **h~in** *adv* in this/these. **h~mit** *adv* with this/these; (*Comm*) herewith; (*Admin*) hereby. **h~nach** *adv* after this/these; (*demgemäß*) according to this/these. **h~über** *adv* over/(*höher*) above this/these; (*sprechen, streiten*) about this/these. **h~von** *adv* from this/these; (*h~über*) about this/these; (*Menge*) of this/these. **h~zu** *adv* to this/ these; (*h~für*) for this/these. **h~zulande** *adv* here

hiesig *a* local. **H~e(r)** *m/f* local

Hilf|e *f* -, -n help, aid; **um H~e rufen** call for help. **h~los** *a* helpless. **H~losigkeit** *f* - helplessness. **h~reich** *a* helpful

Hilfs|arbeiter *m* unskilled labourer. **h~bedürftig** *a* needy; **h~bedürftig sein** be in need of help. **h~bereit** *a* helpful. **H~kraft** *f*

helper. **H~mittel** *nt* aid. **H~verb** *nt* auxiliary verb

Himbeere *f* raspberry

Himmel *m* -s,- sky; (*Relig & fig*) heaven; (*Bett-*) canopy; **unter freiem H~** in the open air. **H~bett** *nt* four-poster [bed]. **H~fahrt** *f* Ascension

himmlisch *a* heavenly

hin *adv* there; **hin und her** to and fro; **hin und zurück** there and back; (*Rail*) return; **hin und wieder** now and again; **an** (+ *dat*) ... **hin** along; **auf** (+ *acc*) ... **hin** in reply to <*Brief, Anzeige*>; on <*jds Rat*>; **zu** *od* **nach** ... **hin** towards; **hin sein** 国 be gone; **es ist noch lange hin** it's a long time yet

hinauf *adv* up [there]. **h~gehen†** *vi sep* (*sein*) go up. **h~setzen** *vt sep* raise

hinaus *adv* out [there]; (*nach draußen*) outside; **zur Tür h~** out of the door; **auf Jahre h~** for years to come; **über etw** (*acc*) **h~** beyond sth; (*Menge*) [over and] above sth; **über etw** (*acc*) **h~ sein** (*fig*) be past sth. **h~gehen†** *vi sep* (*sein*) go out; <*Zimmer:*> face (**nach Norden** north); **h~gehen über** (+ *acc*) go beyond, exceed. **h~laufen†** *vi sep* (*sein*) run out; **h~laufen auf** (+ *acc*) (*fig*) amount to. **h~lehnen (sich)** *vr sep* lean out. **h~schieben†** *vt sep* push out; (*fig*) put off. **h~werfen†** *vt sep* throw out; (国 *entlassen*) fire. **h~wollen†** *vi sep* (*haben*) want to go out; **h~wollen auf** (+ *acc*) (*fig*) aim at. **h~ziehen†** *v sep* ● *vt* pull out; (*in die Länge ziehen*) delay; **sich h~ziehen** drag on; be delayed ● *vi* (*sein*) move out. **h~zögern** *vt* delay; **sich h~zögern** be delayed

Hinblick *m* **im H~ auf** (+ *acc*) in view of; (*hinsichtlich*) regarding

hinder|lich *a* awkward; **jdm h~lich sein** hamper s.o. **h~n** *vt* hamper; (*verhindern*) prevent. **H~nis** *nt* -ses, -se obstacle. **H~nisrennen** *nt* steeplechase

Hindu *m* -s, -s Hindu. **H~ismus** *m*
- Hinduism

hindurch *adv* through it/them

hinein *adv* in [there]; (*nach drinnen*)
inside; **h~ in** (+ *acc*) into.
h~fallen† *vi sep* (*sein*) fall in.
h~gehen† *vi sep* (*sein*) go in;
h~gehen in (+ *acc*) go into.
h~reden *vi sep* (*haben*) jdm
h~reden interrupt s.o.; (*sich
einmischen*) interfere in s.o.'s affairs.
h~versetzen (sich) *vr sep* sich in
jds Lage h~versetzen put oneself in
s.o.'s position. **h~ziehen**† *vt sep*
pull in; **h~ziehen in** (+ *acc*) pull into;
in etw (*acc*) h~gezogen werden (*fig*)
become involved in sth

hin|fahren† *v sep* ● *vi* (*sein*) go/
drive there ● *vt* take/drive there.
H~fahrt *f* journey/drive there;
(*Rail*) outward journey. **h~fallen**†
vi sep (*sein*) fall. **h~fliegen**† *v sep*
● *vi* (*sein*) fly there; 🔲 fall ● *vt* fly
there. **H~flug** *m* flight there;
(*Admin*) outward flight

Hingeb|ung *f* - devotion.
h~ungsvoll *a* devoted

hingehen† *vi sep* (*sein*) go/(*zu Fuß*)
walk there; (*vergehen*) pass; **h~ zu**
go up to; **wo gehst du hin?** where are
you going?

hingerissen *a* rapt; **h~ sein** be
carried away (**von** by)

hinhalten† *vt sep* hold out; (*warten
lassen*) keep waiting

hinken *vi* (*haben*/*sein*) limp

hin|knien (sich) *vr sep* kneel down.
h~kommen† *vi sep* (*sein*) get there;
(*h~gehören*) belong, go; (🔲
auskommen) manage (**mit** with); (🔲
stimmen) be right. **h~laufen**† *vi sep*
(*sein*) run/(*gehen*) walk there.
h~legen *vt sep* lay *or* put down;
sich h~legen lie down.
h~nehmen† *vt sep* (*fig*) accept

hinreichen *v sep* ● *vt* hand (*dat* to)
● *vi* (*haben*) extend (**bis** to);
(*ausreichen*) be adequate. **h~d** *a*
adequate

Hinreise *f* journey there; (*Rail*)
outward journey

hinreißen† *vt sep* (*fig*) carry away;
sich **h~ lassen** get carried away.
h~d *a* ravishing

hinricht|en *vt sep* execute. **H~ung**
f execution

hinschreiben† *vt sep* write there;
(*aufschreiben*) write down

hinsehen† *vi sep* (*haben*) look

hinsetzen *vt sep* put down; sich **h~**
sit down

Hinsicht *f* - in dieser **H~** in this
respect; in finanzieller **H~**
financially. **h~lich** *prep* (+ *gen*)
regarding

hinstellen *vt sep* put *or* set down;
park <*Auto*>

hinstrecken *vt sep* hold out; sich
h~ extend

hinten *adv* at the back; dort **h~**
back there; nach/von **h~** to the
back/from behind. **h~herum** *adv*
round the back; 🔲 by devious means

hinter *prep* (+ *dat*/*acc*) behind;
(*nach*) after; **h~ jdm/etw herlaufen**
run after s.o./sth; **h~ etw** (*dat*)
stecken (*fig*) be behind sth; **h~ etw**
(*acc*) kommen (*fig*) get to the bottom
of sth; etw **h~ sich** (*acc*) bringen get
sth over [and done] with

Hinterbliebene *pl* (*Admin*)
surviving dependants; die **H~n** the
bereaved family *sg*

hintere|(r,s) *a* back, rear; **h~s**
Ende far end

hintereinander *adv* one behind/
(*zeitlich*) after the other; dreimal **h~**
three times in succession

Hintergedanke *m* ulterior motive

hintergehen† *vt* deceive

Hinter|grund *m* background.
H~halt *m* -[e]s, -e ambush.
h~hältig *a* underhand

hinterher *adv* behind, after;
(*zeitlich*) afterwards

Hinter|hof *m* back yard. **H~kopf**
m back of the head

hinterlassen† *vt* leave [behind];
(*Jur*) leave, bequeath (*dat* to).
H~schaft *f* -, -en (*Jur*) estate

hinterlegen *vt* deposit

Hinter|leib *m* (*Zool*) abdomen.
H∼list *f* deceit. **h∼listig** *a*
deceitful. **H∼n** *m* -s,- Ⓔ bottom,
backside. **H∼rad** *nt* rear *or* back
wheel. **h∼rücks** *adv* from behind.
h∼ste(r,s) *a* last; **h∼ste Reihe**
back row. **H∼teil** *nt* Ⓔ behind.
H∼treppe *f* back stairs *pl*

hinterziehen† *vt* (*Admin*) evade

hinüber *adv* over *or* across [*there*];
h∼ sein (Ⓔ *unbrauchbar, tot*) have
had it. **h∼gehen**† *vi sep* (*sein*) go
over *or* across; **h∼gehen über** (+ *acc*)
cross

hinunter *adv* down [*there*].
h∼gehen† *vi sep* (*sein*) go down.
h∼schlucken *vt sep* swallow

Hinweg *m* way there

hinweg *adv* away, off; **h∼ über** (+
acc) over; **über eine Zeit h∼** over a
period. **h∼kommen**† *vt sep* (*sein*)
h∼kommen über (+ *acc*) (*fig*) get
over. **h∼sehen**† *vi sep* (*haben*)
h∼sehen über (+ *acc*) see over; (*fig*)
overlook. **h∼setzen** (sich) *vr sep*
sich **h∼setzen über** (+ *acc*) ignore

Hinweis *m* -es, -e reference;
(*Andeutung*) hint; (*Anzeichen*)
indication; **unter H∼ auf** (+ *acc*) with
reference to. **h∼en**† *v sep* ● *vi*
(*haben*) point (**auf** + *acc* to) ● *vt* **jdn**
auf etw (*acc*) **h∼en** point sth out to
s.o.

hinwieder *adv* on the other hand

hin|zeigen *vi sep* (*haben*) point (**auf**
+ *acc* to). **h∼ziehen**† *vt sep* pull;
(*fig: in die Länge ziehen*) drag out;
(*verzögern*) delay; **sich h∼ziehen**
drag on

hinzu *adv* in addition. **h∼fügen** *vt*
sep add. **h∼kommen**† *vt sep* (*sein*)
be added; (*ankommen*) arrive [on the
scene]; join (**zu jdm** s.o.).
h∼ziehen† *vt sep* call in

Hiobsbotschaft *f* bad news *sg*

Hirn *nt* -s brain; (*Culin*) brains *pl*.
H∼hautentzündung *f* meningitis

Hirsch *m* -[e]s, -e deer; (*männlich*)
stag; (*Culin*) venison

Hirse *f* - millet

Hirt *m* -en, -en, **Hirte** *m* -n, -n
shepherd

hissen *vt* hoist

Histor|iker *m* -s,- historian.
h∼isch *a* historical; (*bedeutend*)
historic

Hitz|e *f* - heat. **h∼ig** *a* (*fig*) heated;
<*Person*> hot-headed; (*jähzornig*)
hot-tempered. **H∼schlag** *m* heat-
stroke

H-Milch /'ha:-/ *f* long-life milk

Hobby *nt* -s, -s hobby

Hobel *m* -s,- (*Techn*) plane; (*Culin*)
slicer. **h∼n** *vt/i* (*haben*) plane.
H∼späne *mpl* shavings

hoch *a* (*attrib* hohe(r,s)) high;
<*Baum, Mast*> tall; <*Offizier*> high-
ranking; <*Alter*> great; <*Summe*>
large; <*Strafe*> heavy; **hohe Schuhe**
ankle boots ● *adv* high; (*sehr*)
highly; **h∼ gewachsen** tall; **h∼**
begabt highly gifted; **h∼ gestellte**
Persönlichkeit important person; **die**
Treppe h∼ up the stairs; **sechs Mann**
h∼ six of us/them. **H∼** *nt* -s, -s
cheer; (*Meteorol*) high

Hoch|achtung *f* high esteem.
H∼achtungsvoll *adv* Yours
faithfully. **H∼betrieb** *m* great
activity; **in den Geschäften herrscht**
H∼betrieb the shops are terribly
busy. **H∼deutsch** *nt* High German.
H∼druck *m* high pressure.
H∼ebene *f* plateau. **h∼fahren**† *vi*
sep (*sein*) go up; (*auffahren*) start up;
(*aufbrausen*) flare up. **h∼gehen**† *vi*
sep (*sein*) go up; (*explodieren*) blow
up; (*aufbrausen*) flare up.
h∼gestellt *attrib a* <*Zahl*>
superior; (*fig*) ***h∼ gestellt**, *s.* **hoch**.
H∼glanz *m* high gloss. **h∼gradig**
a extreme. **h∼hackig** *a* high-
heeled. **h∼halten**† *vt sep* hold up;
(*fig*) uphold. **H∼haus** *nt* high-rise
building. **h∼heben**† *vt sep* lift up;
raise <*Hand*>. **h∼kant** *adv* on end.
h∼kommen† *vi sep* (*sein*) come up;
(*aufstehen*) get up; (*fig*) get on [in the
world]. **H∼konjunktur** *f* boom.
h∼krempeln *vt sep* roll up.
h∼leben *vi sep* (*haben*) **h∼leben**
lassen give three cheers for;
H∼mut *m* pride, arrogance.

h~näsig a 🔲 snooty. **H~ofen** m blast-furnace. **h~ragen** vi sep rise [up]; <Turm:> soar. **H~ruf** m cheer. **H~saison** f high season. **h~schlagen†** vt sep turn up <Kragen>. **H~schule** f university; (Musik-, Kunst-) academy. **H~sommer** m midsummer. **H~spannung** f high/(fig) great tension. **h~spielen** vt sep (fig) magnify. **H~sprung** m high jump

höchst adv extremely, most

Hochstapler m -s,- confidence trickster

höchst|e(r,s) a highest; <Baum, Turm> tallest; (oberste, größte) top; **es ist h~e Zeit** it is high time. **h~ens** adv at most; (es sei denn) except perhaps. **H~geschwindigkeit** f top or maximum speed. **H~maß** nt maximum. **h~persönlich** adv in person. **H~preis** m top price. **H~temperatur** f maximum temperature

Hoch|verrat m high treason. **H~wasser** nt high tide; (Überschwemmung) floods pl. **H~würden** m -s Reverend; (Anrede) Father

Hochzeit f -, -en wedding. **H~skleid** nt wedding dress. **H~sreise** f honeymoon [trip]. **H~stag** m wedding day/(Jahrestag) anniversary

Hocke f - in der **H~sitzen** squat. **h~n** vi (haben) squat ● vr sich **h~n** squat down

Hocker m -s,- stool

Höcker m -s,- bump; (Kamel-) hump

Hockey /hɔki/ nt -s hockey

Hode f -, -n, **Hoden** m -s,- testicle

Hof m -[e]s,¨e [court]yard; (Bauern-) farm; (Königs-) court; (Schul-) playground; (Astr) halo

hoffen vt/i (haben) hope (auf + acc for). **h~tlich** adv I hope, let us hope

Hoffnung f -, -en hope. **h~slos** a hopeless. **h~svoll** a hopeful

höflich a polite. **H~keit** f -, -en politeness, courtesy

hohe(r,s) a s. hoch

Höhe f -, -n height; (Aviat, Geog) altitude; (Niveau) level; (einer Summe) size; (An-) hill

Hoheit f -, -en (Staats-) sovereignty; (Titel) Highness. **H~sgebiet** nt [sovereign] territory. **H~szeichen** nt national emblem

Höhe|nlinie f contour line. **H~nsonne** f sun-lamp. **H~punkt** m (fig) climax, peak. **h~r** a & adv higher; **h~re Schule** secondary school

hohl a hollow; (leer) empty

Höhle f -, -n cave; (Tier-) den; (Hohlraum) cavity; (Augen-) socket

Hohl|maß nt measure of capacity. **H~raum** m cavity

Hohn m -s scorn, derision

höhnen vt deride

holen vt fetch, get; (kaufen) buy; (nehmen) take (aus from)

Holland nt -s Holland

Holländ|er m -s,- Dutchman; die **H~er** the Dutch pl. **H~erin** f -, -nen Dutchwoman. **h~isch** a Dutch

Höll|e f - hell. **h~isch** a infernal; (schrecklich) terrible

Holunder m -s (Bot) elder

Holz nt -es,¨er wood; (Nutz-) timber. **H~blasinstrument** nt woodwind instrument

hölzern a wooden

Holz|hammer m mallet. **h~ig** a woody. **H~kohle** f charcoal. **H~schnitt** m woodcut. **H~wolle** f wood shavings pl

Homöopathie f - homoeopathy

homosexuell a homosexual. **H~e(r)** m/f homosexual

Honig m -s honey. **H~wabe** f honeycomb

Hono|rar nt -s, -e fee. **h~rieren** vt remunerate; (fig) reward

Hopfen m -s hops pl; (Bot) hop

hopsen vi (sein) jump

horchen vi (haben) listen (auf + acc to); (heimlich) eavesdrop

---

hören vt hear; (an-) listen to ● vi (haben) hear; (horchen) listen; (gehorchen) obey; h~ **auf** (+ acc) listen to

Hör|er m -s,- listener; (Teleph) receiver. **H~funk** m radio. **H~gerät** nt hearing-aid

Horizon|t m -[e]s horizon. **h~tal** a horizontal

Hormon nt -s, -e hormone

Horn nt -s,̈-er horn. **H~haut** f hard skin; (Augen-) cornea

Hornisse f -, -n hornet

Horoskop nt -[e]s, -e horoscope

Horrorfilm m horror film

Hör|saal m (Univ) lecture hall. **H~spiel** nt radio play

Hort m -[e]s, -e (Schatz) hoard; (fig) refuge. **h~en** vt hoard

Hortensie /-iə/ f -, -n hydrangea

Hose f -, -n, **Hosen** pl trousers pl. **H~nrock** m culottes pl. **H~nschlitz** m fly, flies pl. **H~nträger** mpl braces

Hostess f -, -tessen hostess; (Aviat) air hostess

Hostie /'hɔstiə/ f -, -n (Relig) host

Hotel nt -s, -s hotel

hübsch a pretty; (nett) nice

Hubschrauber m -s,- helicopter

Huf m -[e]s, -e hoof. **H~eisen** nt horseshoe

Hüft|e f -, -n hip. **H~gürtel** m -s,- girdle

Hügel m -s,- hill. **h~ig** a hilly

Huhn nt -s,̈-er chicken; (Henne) hen

Hühn|chen nt -s,- chicken. **H~erauge** nt corn **H~erstall** m henhouse

Hülle f -, -n cover; (Verpackung) wrapping; (Platten-) sleeve. **h~n** vt wrap

Hülse f -, -n (Bot) pod; (Etui) case. **H~nfrüchte** fpl pulses

human a humane. **H~ität** f - humanity

Hummel f -, -n bumble-bee

Hummer m -s,- lobster

Hum|or m -s humour; **H~or haben** have a sense of humour. **h~orvoll** a humorous

humpeln vi (sein/haben) hobble

Humpen m -s,- tankard

Hund m -[e]s, -e dog; (Jagd-) hound. **H~ehütte** f kennel

hundert inv a one/a hundred. **H~** nt -s, -e hundred; **H~e** od **h~e von** hundreds of. **H~jahrfeier** f centenary. **h~prozentig** a & adv one hundred per cent. **h~ste(r,s)** a hundredth. **H~stel** nt -s,- hundredth

Hündin f -, -nen bitch

Hüne m -n, -n giant

Hunger m -s hunger; **H~ haben** be hungry. **h~n** vi (haben) starve. **H~snot** f famine

hungrig a hungry

Hupe f -, -n (Auto) horn. **h~n** vi (haben) sound one's horn

hüpfen vi (sein) skip; <Frosch:> hop; <Grashüpfer:> jump

Hürde f -, -n (Sport & fig) hurdle; (Schaf-) pen, fold

Hure f -, -n whore

hurra int hurray

husten vi (haben) cough. **H~** m -s cough. **H~saft** m cough mixture

Hut¹ m -[e]s,̈-e hat; (Pilz-) cap

Hut² f - auf der **H~sein** be on one's guard (vor + dat against)

hüten vt watch over; tend <Tiere>; (aufpassen) look after; **das Bett h~ müssen** be confined to bed; **sich h~** be on one's guard (vor + dat against); **sich h~, etw zu tun** take care not to do sth

Hütte f -, -n hut; (Hunde-) kennel; (Techn) iron and steel works. **H~nkäse** m cottage cheese. **H~nkunde** f metallurgy

Hyäne f -, -n hyena

hydraulisch a hydraulic

Hygien|e /hy'giːnə/ f - hygiene. **h~isch** a hygienic

Hypno|se f - hypnosis. **h~tisch** a hypnotic. **H~tiseur** /-'zøːɐ/ m -s, -e hypnotist. **h~tisieren** vt hypnotize

Hypochonder /hypoˈxɔndɐ/ *m* -s,- hypochondriac

Hypothek *f* -, -en mortgage

Hypothese *f* -, -n hypothesis

Hys|terie *f* - hysteria. **h~terisch** *a* hysterical

I i

ich *pron* I; **ich bins** it's me. **Ich** *nt* -[s], -[s] self; (*Psych*) ego

IC-Zug /iˈtseː-/ *m* inter-city train

ideal *a* ideal. **I~** *nt* -s, -e ideal. **I~ismus** *m* - idealism. **I~ist(in)** *m* -en, -en (*f* -, -nen) idealist. **i~istisch** *a* idealistic

Idee *f* -, -n idea; **fixe I~** obsession

identifizieren *vt* identify

identisch *a* identical

Ideo|logie *f* -, -n ideology. **i~logisch** *a* ideological

idiomatisch *a* idiomatic

Idiot *m* -en, -en idiot. **i~isch** *a* idiotic

idyllisch /iˈdʏlɪʃ/ *a* idyllic

Igel *m* -s,- hedgehog

ihm *pron* (*dat of* **er, es**) [to] him; (*Ding, Tier*) [to] it

ihn *pron* (*acc of* **er**) him; (*Ding, Tier*) it. **i~en** *pron* (*dat of* **sie** *pl*) [to] them. **I~en** *pron* (*dat of* **Sie**) [to] you

ihr *pron* (*2nd pers pl*) you ● (*dat of* **sie** *sg*) [to] her; (*Ding, Tier*) [to] it ● *poss pron* her; (*Ding, Tier*) its; (*pl*) their. **Ihr** *poss pron* your. **i~e(r,s)** *poss pron* hers; (*pl*) theirs. **I~e(r,s)** *poss pron* yours. **i~erseits** *adv* for her/(*pl*) their part. **I~erseits** *adv* on your part. **i~etwegen** *adv* for her/(*Ding, Tier*) its/(*pl*) their sake; (*wegen*) because of her/it/them, on her/its/their account. **I~etwegen**

adv for your sake; (*wegen*) because of you, on your account. **i~ige** *poss pron* **der/die/das i~ige** hers; (*pl*) theirs. **I~ige** *poss pron* **der/die/das I~ige** yours. **i~s** *poss pron* hers; (*pl*) theirs. **I~s** *poss pron* yours

Ikone *f* -, -n icon

illegal *a* illegal

Illus|ion *f* -, -en illusion. **i~orisch** *a* illusory

Illustr|ation /-ˈtsi̯oːn/ *f* -, -en illustration. **i~ieren** *vt* illustrate. **I~ierte** *f* -n, -[n] [illustrated] magazine

Iltis *m* -ses, -se polecat

im *prep* = in dem

Imbiss *m* snack. **I~stube** *f* snackbar

Imit|ation /-ˈtsi̯oːn/ *f* -, -en imitation. **i~ieren** *vt* imitate

Imker *m* -s,- bee-keeper

Immatrikul|ation /-ˈtsi̯oːn/ *f* - (*Univ*) enrolment. **i~ieren** *vt* (*Univ*) enrol; **sich i~ieren** enrol

immer *adv* always; **für i~** for ever; (*endgültig*) for good; **i~ noch** still; **i~ mehr** more and more; **was i~** whatever. **i~hin** *adv* (*wenigstens*) at least; (*trotzdem*) all the same; (*schließlich*) after all. **i~zu** *adv* all the time

Immobilien /-i̯ən/ *pl* real estate *sg*. **I~makler** *m* estate agent

immun *a* immune (**gegen** to)

Imperialismus *m* - imperialism

impf|en *vt* vaccinate, inoculate. **I~stoff** *m* vaccine. **I~ung** *f* -, -en vaccination, inoculation

imponieren *vi* (*haben*) impress (**jdm** s.o.)

Impor|t *m* -[e]s, -e import. **I~teur** /-ˈtøːɐ/ *m* -s, -e importer. **i~tieren** *vt* import

impoten|t *a* (*Med*) impotent. **I~z** *f* - (*Med*) impotence

imprägnieren *vt* waterproof

Impressionismus *m* - impressionism

improvisieren *vt/i* (*haben*) improvise

imstande *pred a* able (**zu** to);
capable (**etw zu tun** of doing sth)

in *prep* (+ *dat*) in; (+ *acc*) into, in; (*bei
Bus, Zug*) on; **in der Schule** at school;
in die Schule to school ● *a* **in sein**
be in

Inbegriff *m* embodiment

indem *conj* (*während*) while;
(*dadurch*) by (+ -*ing*)

Inder(in) *m* -s,- (*f* -, -**nen**) Indian

indessen *conj* while ● *adv*
(*unterdessen*) meanwhile

Indian|er(in) *m* -s,- (*f* -, -**nen**)
(American) Indian. **i∼isch** *a* Indian

Indien /'ɪndiən/ *nt* -s India

indirekt *a* indirect

indisch *a* Indian

indiskret *a* indiscreet

indiskutabel *a* out of the question

Individu|alist *m* -en, -en
individualist. **I∼alität** *f* -
individuality. **i∼ell** *a* individual

Indizienbeweis /m'di:ts:iən-/ *m*
circumstantial evidence

industr|ialisiert *a* industrialized.
I∼ie *f* -, -n industry. **i∼iell** *a*
industrial

ineinander *adv* in/into one another

Infanterie *f* - infantry

Infektion /-'ts:io:n/ *f* -, -en
infection. **I∼skrankheit** *f*
infectious disease

infizieren *vt* infect; **sich i∼** become/
<*Person.*> be infected

Inflation /-'ts:io:n/ *f* - inflation.
i∼är *a* inflationary

infolge *prep* (+ *gen*) as a result of.
i∼dessen *adv* consequently

Inform|atik *f* - information science.
I∼ation /-'ts:io:n/ *f* -, -en
information; **I∼ationen** information
sg. **i∼ieren** *vt* inform; **sich i∼ieren**
find out (**über** + *acc* about)

infrage *adv* **etw i∼ stellen** question
sth; (*ungewiss machen*) make sth
doubtful; **nicht i∼ kommen** be out of
the question

infrarot *a* infra-red

Ingenieur /ɪnʒe'niɔ̃:ɐ/ *m* -s, -e
engineer

Ingwer *m* -s ginger

Inhaber(in) *m* -s,- (*f* -, -**nen**) holder;
(*Besitzer*) proprietor; (*Scheck-*) bearer

inhaftieren *vt* take into custody

inhalieren *vt/i* (*haben*) inhale

Inhalt *m* -[e]s, -e contents *pl*;
(*Bedeutung, Gehalt*) content;
(*Geschichte*) story. **I∼sangabe** *f*
summary. **I∼sverzeichnis** *nt* list/
(*in Buch*) table of contents

Initiative /inits:ia'ti:və/ *f* -, -n
initiative

inklusive *prep* (+ *gen*) including
● *adv* inclusive

inkonsequent *a* inconsistent

inkorrekt *a* incorrect

Inkubationszeit /-'ts:io:ns-/ *f*
(*Med*) incubation period

Inland *nt* -[e]s home country;
(*Binnenland*) interior.
I∼sgespräch *nt* inland call

inmitten *prep* (+ *gen*) in the middle
of; (*unter*) amongst

innen *adv* inside; **nach i∼** inwards.
I∼architekt(in) *m(f)* interior
designer. **I∼minister** *m* Minister of
the Interior; (*in UK*) Home
Secretary. **I∼politik** *f* domestic
policy. **I∼stadt** *f* town centre

inner|e(r,s) *a* inner; (*Med, Pol*)
internal. **I∼e(s)** *nt* interior; (*Mitte*)
centre; (*fig: Seele*) inner being.
I∼eien *fpl* (*Culin*) offal *sg*. **i∼halb**
prep (+ *gen*) inside; (*zeitlich & fig*)
within; (*während*) during ● *adv*
i∼halb von within. **i∼lich** *a*
internal

innig *a* sincere

innovativ *a* innovative

Innung *f* -, -en guild

ins *prep* = **in das**

Insasse *m* -n, -n inmate; (*im Auto*)
occupant; (*Passagier*) passenger

insbesondere *adv* especially

Inschrift *f* inscription

Insekt *nt* -[e]s, -en insect.
I∼envertilgungsmittel *nt*
insecticide

Insel *f* -, -n island

Inser|at nt -[e]s, -e [newspaper] advertisement. **i~ieren** vt/i (haben) advertise

insge|heim adv secretly. **i~samt** adv [all] in all

insofern, insoweit adv /-'zo:-/ in this respect; **i~ als** in as much as

Insp|ektion /ɪnspɛk'tsi̯o:n/ f -, -en inspection. **I~ektor** m -en, -en /-'to:rən/ inspector

Install|ateur /ɪnstala'tø:ɐ̯/ m -s, -e fitter; (Klempner) plumber. **i~ieren** vt install

instand adv **i~ halten** maintain; (pflegen) look after. **I~haltung** f - maintenance, upkeep

Instandsetzung f - repair

Instanz /-st-/ f -, -en authority

Instinkt /-st-/ m -[e]s, -e instinct. **i~iv** a instinctive

Institut /-st-/ nt -[e]s, -e institute

Instrument /-st-/ nt -[e]s, -e instrument. **I~almusik** f instrumental music

Insulin nt -s insulin

inszenier|en vt (Theat) produce. **I~ung** f -, -en production

Integr|ation /-'tsi̯o:n/ f - integration. **i~ieren** vt integrate; **sich i~ieren** integrate

Intellekt m -[e]s intellect. **i~uell** a intellectual

intelligen|t a intelligent. **I~z** f - intelligence

Intendant m -en, -en director

Intensivstation f intensive-care unit

interaktiv a interactive

inter|essant a interesting. **I~esse** nt -s, -n interest; **I~esse haben** be interested (**an** + dat in). **I~essengruppe** f pressure group. **I~essent** m -en, -en interested party; (Käufer) prospective buyer. **i~essieren** vt interest; **sich i~essieren** be interested (**für** in)

Inter|nat nt -[e]s, -e boarding school. **i~national** a international. **I~nist** m -en, -en specialist in

internal diseases. **I~pretation** /-'tsi̯o:n/ f -, -en interpretation. **i~pretieren** vt interpret. **I~vall** nt -s, -e interval. **I~vention** /-'tsi̯o:n/ f -, -en intervention

Internet nt -s, -s Internet; **im I~** on the Internet

Interview /'ɪntɐvju:/ nt -s, -s interview. **i~en** /-'vju:ən/ vt interview

intim a intimate

intoleran|t a intolerant. **I~z** f - intolerance

intravenös a intravenous

Intrige f -, -n intrigue

introvertiert a introverted

Invalidenrente f disability pension

Invasion f -, -en invasion

Inven|tar nt -s, -e furnishings and fittings pl; (Techn) equipment; (Bestand) stock; (Liste) inventory. **I~tur** f -, -en stock-taking

investieren vt invest

inwie|fern adv in what way. **i~weit** adv how far, to what extent

Inzest m -[e]s incest

inzwischen adv in the meantime

Irak (der) -[s] Iraq. **i~isch** a Iraqi

Iran (der) -[s] Iran. **i~isch** a Iranian

irdisch a earthly

Ire m -n, -n Irishman; **die I~n** the Irish pl

irgend adv **wenn i~ möglich** if at all possible. **i~ein** indef art some/any; **i~ein anderer** someone/anyone else. **i~eine(r,s)** pron any one; (jemand) someone/anyone. **i~etwas** pron something; anything. **i~jemand** pron someone; anyone. **i~wann** pron at some time [or other]/at any time. **i~was** pron 🗍 something [or other]/anything. **i~welche(r,s)** pron any. **i~wer** pron someone/ anyone. **i~wie** adv somehow [or other]. **i~wo** adv somewhere/ anywhere

Irin f -, -nen Irishwoman

irisch a Irish

Irland nt -s Ireland

Ironie f - irony

ironisch *a* ironic

irre *a* mad, crazy; (🔲 *gewaltig*)
incredible. **I∼(r)** *m/f* lunatic.
i∼führen *vt sep* (*fig*) mislead

irre|machen *vt sep* confuse. **i∼n**
vi/r (*haben*) [sich] **i∼n** be mistaken
● *vi* (*sein*) wander. **I∼nanstalt** *f*,
I∼nhaus *nt* lunatic asylum.
i∼werden† *vi sep* (*sein*) get
confused

Irrgarten *m* maze

irritieren *vt* irritate

Irr|sinn *m* madness, lunacy.
i∼sinnig *a* mad; (🔲 *gewaltig*)
incredible. **I∼tum** *m* -s,ⁿer mistake

Ischias *m* & *nt* - sciatica

Islam (der) -[s] Islam. **islamisch** *a*
Islamic

Island *nt* -s Iceland

Isolier|band *nt* insulating tape.
i∼en *vt* isolate; (*Phys*, *Electr*)
insulate; (*gegen Schall*) soundproof.
I∼ung *f* - isolation; insulation;
soundproofing

Israel /'israe:l/ *nt* -s Israel. **I∼eli** *m*
-[s], -s & *f* -, -[s] Israeli. **i∼elisch** *a*
Israeli

ist *s.* sein; er ist he is

Ital|ien /-iən/ *nt* -s Italy.
I∼iener(in) *m* -s,- (*f* -, -nen) Italian.
i∼ienisch *a* Italian. **I∼ienisch** *nt*
-[s] (*Lang*) Italian

Jj

ja *adv*, **Ja** *nt* -[s] yes; **ich glaube ja** I
think so; **ja nicht!** not on any
account! **da seid ihr ja!** there you are!

Jacht *f* -, -en yacht

Jacke *f* -, -n jacket; (*Strick-*)
cardigan

Jackett /ʒa'kɛt/ *nt* -s, -s jacket

Jade *m* -[s] & *f* - jade

Jagd *f* -, -en hunt; (*Schießen*) shoot;
(*Jagen*) hunting; shooting; (*fig*)
pursuit (**nach** of); **auf die J∼** gehen
go hunting/shooting. **J∼gewehr** *nt*
sporting gun. **J∼hund** *m* gun-dog;
(*Hetzhund*) hound

jagen *vt* hunt; (*schießen*) shoot;
(*verfolgen*, *wegjagen*) chase; (*treiben*)
drive; **sich j∼** chase each other; **in
die Luft j∼** blow up ● *vi* (*haben*)
hunt, go hunting/shooting; (*fig*)
chase (**nach** after) ● *vi* (*sein*) race,
dash

Jäger *m* -s,- hunter

Jahr *nt* -[e]s, -e year. **j∼elang** *adv*
for years. **J∼eszahl** *f* year.
J∼eszeit *f* season. **J∼gang** *m*
year; (*Wein*) vintage. **J∼hundert** *nt*
century

jährlich *a* annual, yearly

Jahr|markt *m* fair. **J∼tausend** *nt*
millennium. **J∼zehnt** *nt* -[e]s, -e
decade

Jähzorn *m* violent temper. **j∼ig** *a*
hot-tempered

Jalousie /ʒalu'zi:/ *f* -, -n venetian
blind

Jammer *m* -s misery

jämmerlich *a* miserable; (*Mitleid
erregend*) pitiful

jammern *vi* (*haben*) lament ● *vt* jdn
j∼n arouse s.o.'s pity

Jänner *m* -s,- (*Aust*) January

Januar *m* -s, -e January

Jap|an *nt* -s Japan. **J∼aner(in)** *m*
-s,- (*f* -, -nen) Japanese. **j∼anisch** *a*
Japanese. **J∼anisch** *nt* -[s] (*Lang*)
Japanese

jäten *vt/i* (*haben*) weed

jaulen *vi* (*haben*) yelp

Jause *f* -, -n (*Aust*) snack

jawohl *adv* yes

Jazz /jats:, dʒɛs/ *m* - jazz

je *adv* (*jemals*) ever; (*jeweils*) each;
(*pro*) per; **je nach** according to; **seit
eh und je** always ● *conj* **je mehr,
desto besser** the more the better
● *prep* (+ *acc*) per

Jeans /dʒi:ns/ *pl* jeans

jed|e(r,s) *pron* every; (*j∼er
Einzelne*) each; (*j∼er Beliebige*) any;

(*substantivisch*) everyone; each one; anyone; **ohne j~en Grund** without any reason. **j~enfalls** *adv* in any case; (*wenigstens*) at least.
j~ermann *pron* everyone.
j~erzeit *adv* at any time.
j~esmal *adv* every time

jedoch *adv & conj* however

jemals *adv* ever

jemand *pron* someone, somebody; (*fragend, verneint*) anyone, anybody

jen|e(r,s) *pron* that; (*pl*) those; (*substantivisch*) that one; (*pl*) those. **j~seits** *prep* (+ *gen*) [on] the other side of

jetzt *adv* now

jiddisch *a*, **J~** *nt* -[s] Yiddish

Job /dʒɔp/ *m* -s, -s job. **j~ben** *vi* (*haben*) 🄴 work

Joch *nt* -[e]s, -e yoke

Jockei, Jockey /'dʒɔki/ *m* -s, -s jockey

Jod *nt* -[e]s iodine

jodeln *vi* (*haben*) yodel

Joga *m & nt* -[s] yoga

joggen /'dʒɔgən/ *vi* (*haben/sein*) jog

Joghurt, Jogurt *m & nt* -[s] yoghurt

Johannisbeere *f* redcurrant

Joker *m* -s,- (*Karte*) joker

Jolle *f* -, -n dinghy

Jongleur /ʒõ'gløːɐ/ *m* -s, -e juggler

Jordanien /-iən/ *nt* -s Jordan

Journalis|mus /ʒʊrnaˈlɪsmʊs/ *m* - journalism. **J~t(in)** *m* -en, -en (*f* -, -nen) journalist

Jubel *m* -s rejoicing, jubilation. **j~n** *vi* (*haben*) rejoice

Jubiläum *nt* -s,-äen jubilee; (*Jahrestag*) anniversary

jucken *vi* (*haben*) itch; **sich j~en** scratch; **es j~t mich** I have an itch

Jude *m* -n, -n Jew. **J~ntum** *nt* -s Judaism; (*Juden*) Jewry

Jüd|in *f* -, -nen Jewess. **j~isch** *a* Jewish

Judo *nt* -[s] judo

Jugend *f* - youth; (*junge Leute*) young people *pl*. **J~herberge** *f* youth hostel. **J~kriminalität** *f* juvenile delinquency. **j~lich** *a* youthful. **J~liche(r)** *m/f* young man/woman. **J~liche** *pl* young people. **J~stil** *m* art nouveau

Jugoslaw|ien /-iən/ *nt* -s Yugoslavia. **j~isch** *a* Yugoslav

Juli *m* -[s], -s July

jung *a* young; <*Wein*> new ● *pron* **J~ und Alt** young and old. **J~e** *m* -n, -n boy. **J~e(s)** *nt* young animal/bird; (*Katzen-*) kitten; (*Bären-*) cub; (*Hunde-*) pup; **die J~en** the young *pl*

Jünger *m* -s,- disciple

Jung|frau *f* virgin; (*Astr*) Virgo. **J~geselle** *m* bachelor

Jüngling *m* -s, -e youth

jüngst|e(r,s) *a* youngest; (*neueste*) latest; **in j~er Zeit** recently

Juni *m* -[s], -s June

Jura *pl* law *sg*

Jurist|(in) *m* -en, -en (*f* -, -nen) lawyer. **j~isch** *a* legal

Jury /ʒy'riː/ *f* -, -s jury; (*Sport*) judges *pl*

Justiz *f* - **die J~** justice

Juwel *nt* -s, -en & (*fig*) -e jewel. **J~ier** *m* -es, -e jeweller

Jux *m* -es, -e 🄴 joke; **aus Jux** for fun

Kk

Kabarett *nt* -s, -s & -e cabaret

Kabel *nt* -s,- cable. **K~fernsehen** *nt* cable television

Kabeljau *m* -s, -e & -s cod

Kabine *f* -, -n cabin; (*Umkleide-*) cubicle; (*Telefon-*) booth; (*einer K~nbahn*) car. **K~nbahn** *f* cable-car

Kabinett *nt* -s, -e (*Pol*) Cabinet

Kabriolett nt -s, -s convertible

Kachel f -, -n tile. **k~n** vt tile

Kadenz f -, -en (Mus) cadence

Käfer m -s,- beetle

Kaffee /'kafe:, ka'fe:/ m -s, -s coffee. **K~kanne** f coffee-pot. **K~maschine** f coffee-maker. **K~mühle** f coffee-grinder

Käfig m -s, -e cage

kahl a bare; (haarlos) bald; **k~ geschoren** shaven

Kahn m -s,-̈e boat; (Last-) barge

Kai m -s, -s quay

Kaiser m -s,- emperor. **K~in** f -, -nen empress. **k~lich** a imperial. **K~reich** nt empire. **K~schnitt** m Caesarean [section]

Kajüte f -, -n (Naut) cabin

Kakao /ka'kau:/ m -s cocoa

Kakerlak m -s & -en, -en cockroach

Kaktus m -, -teen /-'te:ən/ cactus

Kalb nt -[e]s,-̈er calf. **K~fleisch** nt veal

Kalender m -s,- calendar; (Termin-) diary

Kaliber nt -s,- calibre; (Gewehr-) bore

Kalium nt -s potassium

Kalk m -[e]s, -e lime; (Kalzium) calcium. **k~en** vt whitewash. **K~stein** m limestone

Kalkulation /-'ts:io:n/ f -, -en calculation. **k~ieren** vt/i (haben) calculate

Kalorie f -, -n calorie

kalt a cold; **mir ist k~** I am cold

Kälte f - cold; (Gefühls-) coldness; **10 Grad K~** 10 degrees below zero

Kalzium nt -s calcium

Kamel nt -s, -e camel

Kamera f -, -s camera

Kamerad(in) m -en, -en (f -, -nen) companion; (Freund) mate; (Mil, Pol) comrade

Kameramann m (pl -männer & -leute) cameraman

Kamille f - camomile

Kamin m -s, -e fireplace; (SGer: Schornstein) chimney

Kamm m -[e]s,-̈e comb; (Berg-) ridge; (Zool, Wellen-) crest

kämmen vt comb; **jdn/sich k~** comb s.o.'s/one's hair

Kammer f -, -n small room; (Techn, Biol, Pol) chamber. **K~musik** f chamber music

Kammgarn nt (Tex) worsted

Kampagne /kam'panjə/ f -, -n (Pol, Comm) campaign

Kampf m -es,-̈e fight; (Schlacht) battle; (Wett-) contest; (fig) struggle

kämpfen vi (haben) fight; **sich k~en durch** fight one's way through. **K~er(in)** m -s,- (f -, -nen) fighter

Kampfrichter m (Sport) judge

Kanada nt -s Canada

Kanad|ier(in) /-iɐ, -iərɪn/ m -s,- (f -, -nen) Canadian. **k~isch** a Canadian

Kanal m -s,-̈e canal; (Abfluss-) drain, sewer; (Radio, TV) channel; **der K~** the [English] Channel

Kanalisation /-'ts:io:n/ f - sewerage system, drains pl

Kanarienvogel /-iən-/ m canary

Kanarisch a **K~e Inseln** Canaries

Kandidat(in) m -en, -en (f -, -nen) candidate

kandiert a candied

Känguru nt -s, -s kangaroo

Kaninchen nt -s,- rabbit

Kanister m -s,- canister; (Benzin-) can

Kännchen nt -s,- [small] jug; (Kaffee-) pot

Kanne f -, -n jug; (Tee-) pot; (Öl-) can; (große Milch-) churn

Kannibal|e m -n, -n cannibal. **K~ismus** m - cannibalism

Kanon m -s, -s canon; (Lied) round

Kanone f -, -n cannon, gun

kanonisieren vt canonize

Kantate f -, -n cantata

Kante f -, -n edge

Kanten m -s,- crust [of bread]

Kanter m -s,- canter

kantig a angular

Kantine f -, -n canteen

Kanton m -s, -e (Swiss) canton

Kanu nt -s, -s canoe

Kanzel f -, -n pulpit; (*Aviat*) cockpit

Kanzler m -s,- chancellor

Kap nt -s, -s (*Geog*) cape

Kapazität f -, -en capacity

Kapelle f -, -n chapel; (*Mus*) band

kapern vt (*Naut*) seize

kapieren vt ☐ understand

Kapital nt -s capital. **K~ismus** m - capitalism. **K~ist** m -en, -en capitalist. **k~istisch** a capitalist

Kapitän m -s, -e captain

Kapitel nt -s,- chapter

Kaplan m -s, -e curate

Kappe f -, -n cap

Kapsel f -, -n capsule; (*Flaschen-*) top

kaputt a ☐ broken; (*zerrissen*) torn; (*defekt*) out of order; (*ruiniert*) ruined; (*erschöpft*) worn out. **k~gehen**† vi sep (*sein*) ☐ break; (*zerreißen*) tear; (*defekt werden*) pack up; <*Ehe, Freundschaft:*> break up. **k~lachen (sich)** vr sep ☐ be in stitches. **k~machen** vt sep ☐ break; (*zerreißen*) tear; (*defekt machen*) put out of order; (*erschöpfen*) wear out; **sich k~machen** wear oneself out

Kapuze f -, -n hood

Kapuzinerkresse f nasturtium

Karaffe f -, -n carafe; (*mit Stöpsel*) decanter

Karamell m -s caramel. **K~bonbon** m & nt ≈ toffee

Karat nt -[e]s, -e carat

Karawane f -, -n caravan

Kardinal m -s,-e cardinal. **K~zahl** f cardinal number

Karfreitag m Good Friday

karg a meagre; (*frugal*) frugal; (*spärlich*) sparse; (*unfruchtbar*) barren; (*gering*) scant

Karibik f - Caribbean

kariert a check[ed]; <*Papier*> squared; **schottisch k~** tartan

Karik|atur f -, -en caricature; (*Journ*) cartoon. **k~ieren** vt caricature

Karneval m -s, -e & -s carnival

Kärnten nt -s Carinthia

Karo nt -s, -s (*Raute*) diamond; (*Viereck*) square; (*Muster*) check (*Kartenspiel*) diamonds pl

Karosserie f -, -n bodywork

Karotte f -, -n carrot

Karpfen m -s,-, carp

Karren m -s,- cart; (*Hand-*) barrow. **k~** vt cart

Karriere /ka'rie:rə/ f -, -n career; **K~ machen** get to the top

Karte f -, -n card; (*Eintritts-, Fahr-*) ticket; (*Speise-*) menu; (*Land-*) map

Kartei f -, -en card index

Karten|spiel nt card-game; (*Spielkarten*) pack of cards. **K~vorverkauf** m advance booking

Kartoffel f -, -n potato. **K~brei** m nt mashed potatoes

Karton /kar'tɔŋ/ m -s, -s cardboard; (*Schachtel*) carton

Karussell nt -s, -s & -e roundabout

Käse m -s,- cheese

Kaserne f -, -n barracks pl

Kasino nt -s, -s casino

Kasperle nt & m -s,- Punch. **K~theater** nt Punch and Judy show

Kasse f -, -n till; (*Registrier-*) cash register; (*Zahlstelle*) cash desk; (*im Supermarkt*) check-out; (*Theater-*) box-office; (*Geld*) pool [of money], ☐ kitty; (*Kranken-*) health insurance scheme; **knapp bei K~ sein** ☐ be short of cash. **K~nwart** m -[e]s, -e treasurer. **K~nzettel** m receipt

Kasserolle f -, -n saucepan

Kassette f -, -n cassette; (*Film-, Farbband-*) cartridge. **K~nrekorder** /-rəkɔrdɐ/ m -s,- cassette recorder

kassier|en vi (*haben*) collect the money/(*im Bus*) the fares ● vt collect. **K~er(in)** m -s,- (f -, -nen) cashier

Kastanie /kas'ta:niə/ f -, -n [horse] chestnut, ☐ conker

Kasten *m* -s,- box; (*Brot-*) bin; (*Flaschen-*) crate; (*Brief-*) letter-box; (*Aust: Schrank*) cupboard

kastrieren *vt* castrate; neuter

Katalog *m* -[e]s, -e catalogue

Katalysator *m* -s, -en /-'to:rən/ catalyst; (*Auto*) catalytic converter

Katapult *nt* -[e]s, -e catapult

Katarrh, Katarr *m* -s, -e catarrh

Katastrophe *f* -, -n catastrophe

Katechismus *m* - catechism

Kategorie *f* -, -n category

Kater *m* -s,- tom-cat; (🔢 *Katzenjammer*) hangover

Kathedrale *f* -, -n cathedral

Kath|olik(in) *m* -en, -en (*f* -, -nen) Catholic. **k~olisch** *a* Catholic. **K~olizismus** *m* - Catholicism

Kätzchen *nt* -s,- kitten; (*Bot*) catkin

Katze *f* -, -n cat. **K~njammer** *m* 🔢 hangover. **K~nsprung** *m* ein K~nsprung 🔢 a stone's throw

Kauderwelsch *nt* -[s] gibberish

kauen *vt/i* (*haben*) chew; bite <*Nägel*>

Kauf *m* -[e]s, Käufe purchase; **guter K~** bargain; **in K~nehmen** (*fig*) put up with. **k~en** *vt/i* (*haben*) buy; **k~en bei** shop at

Käufer(in) *m* -s,- (*f* -, -nen) buyer; (*im Geschäft*) shopper

Kauf|haus *nt* department store. **K~laden** *m* shop

käuflich *a* saleable; (*bestechlich*) corruptible; **k~ erwerben** buy

Kauf|mann *m* (*pl* -leute) businessman; (*Händler*) dealer; (*dial*) grocer. **K~preis** *m* purchase price

Kaugummi *m* chewing-gum

Kaulquappe *f* -, -n tadpole

kaum *adv* hardly

Kaution /-'tsjo:n/ *f* -, -en surety; (*Jur*) bail; (*Miet-*) deposit

Kautschuk *m* -s rubber

Kauz *m* -es, Käuze owl

Kavalier *m* -s, -e gentleman

Kavallerie *f* - cavalry

Kaviar *m* -s caviare

keck *a* bold; cheeky

Kegel *m* -s,- skittle; (*Geom*) cone. **K~bahn** *f* skittle-alley. **k~n** *vi* (*haben*) play skittles

Kehl|e *f* -, -n throat; **aus voller K~e** at the top of one's voice. **K~kopf** *m* larynx. **K~kopfentzündung** *f* laryngitis

Kehr|e *f* -, -n [hairpin] bend. **k~en** *vi* (*haben*) (*fegen*) sweep ● *vt* sweep; (*wenden*) turn; **sich nicht k~en an** (+ *acc*) not care about. **K~icht** *m* -[e]s sweepings *pl*. **K~reim** *m* refrain. **K~seite** *f* (*fig*) drawback. **k~tmachen** *vi sep* (*haben*) turn back; (*sich umdrehen*) turn round

Keil *m* -[e]s, -e wedge

Keilriemen *m* fan belt

Keim *m* -[e]s, -e (*Bot*) sprout; (*Med*) germ. **k~en** *vi* (*haben*) germinate; (*austreiben*) sprout. **k~frei** *a* sterile

kein *pron* no; not a; **k~e fünf Minuten** less than five minutes. **k~e(r,s)** *pron* no one, nobody; (*Ding*) none, not one. **k~esfalls** *adv* on no account. **k~eswegs** *adv* by no means. **k~mal** *adv* not once. **k~s** *pron* none, not one

Keks *m* -[es], -[e] biscuit

Kelch *m* -[e]s, -e goblet, cup; (*Relig*) chalice; (*Bot*) calyx

Kelle *f* -, -n ladle; (*Maurer*) trowel

Keller *m* -s,- cellar. **K~ei** *f* -, -en winery. **K~wohnung** *f* basement flat

Kellner *m* -s,- waiter. **K~in** *f* -, -nen waitress

keltern *vt* press

keltisch *a* Celtic

Kenia *nt* -s Kenya

kenn|en† *vt* know; **k~en lernen** get to know; (*treffen*) meet; **sich k~en lernen** meet; (*näher*) get to know one another. **K~er** *m* -s,-, **K~erin** *f* -, -nen connoisseur; (*Experte*) expert. **k~tlich** *a* recognizable; **k~tlich machen** mark. **K~tnis** *f* -, -se knowledge; **zur K~tnis nehmen** take note of; **in K~tnis setzen** inform (**von** of). **K~wort** *nt* (*pl* -wörter) reference; (*geheimes*) password. **K~zeichen** *nt* distinguishing mark or feature; (*Merkmal*) characteristic,

(*Markierung*) marking; (*Auto*) registration. **k~zeichnen** *vt* distinguish; (*markieren*) mark

kentern *vi* (*sein*) capsize

Keramik *f* -, -en pottery

Kerbe *f* -, -n notch

Kerker *m* -s,- dungeon; (*Gefängnis*) prison

Kerl *m* -s, -e & -s ▣ fellow, bloke

Kern *m* -s, -e pip; (*Kirsch-*) stone; (*Nuss-*) kernel; (*Techn*) core; (*Atom-, Zell- & fig*) nucleus; (*Stadt-*) centre; (*einer Sache*) heart. **K~energie** *f* nuclear energy. **K~gehäuse** *nt* core. **k~los** *a* seedless. **K~physik** *f* nuclear physics *sg*

Kerze *f* -, -n candle. **K~nhalter** *m* -s,- candlestick

kess *a* pert

Kessel *m* -s,- kettle

Kette *f* -, -n chain; (*Hals-*) necklace. **k~n** *vt* chain (**an** + *acc* to). **K~nladen** *m* chain store

Ketze|r(in) *m* -s,- (*f* -, -nen) heretic. **K~rei** *f* - heresy

keuch|en *vi* (*haben*) pant. **K~husten** *m* whooping cough

Keule *f* -, -n club; (*Culin*) leg; (*Hühner-*) drumstick

keusch *a* chaste

Khaki *nt* - khaki

kichern *vi* (*haben*) giggle

Kiefer¹ *f* -, -n pine[-tree]

Kiefer² *m* -s,- jaw

Kiel *m* -s, -e (*Naut*) keel

Kiemen *fpl* gills

Kies *m* -es gravel. **K~el** *m* -s,-, **K~elstein** *m* pebble

Kilo *nt* -s, -[s] kilo. **K~gramm** *nt* kilogram. **K~hertz** *nt* kilohertz. **K~meter** *m* kilometre. **K~meterstand** *m* ≈ mileage. **K~watt** *nt* kilowatt

Kind *nt* -es, -er child; **von K~ auf** from childhood

Kinder|arzt *m*, **K~ärztin** *f* paediatrician. **K~bett** *nt* child's cot. **K~garten** *m* nursery school. **K~geld** *nt* child benefit.

K~lähmung *f* polio. **k~leicht** *a* very easy. **k~los** *a* childless. **K~mädchen** *nt* nanny. **K~reim** *m* nursery rhyme. **K~spiel** *nt* children's game. **K~tagesstätte** *f* day nursery. **K~teller** *m* children's menu. **K~wagen** *m* pram. **K~zimmer** *nt* child's/children's room; (*für Baby*) nursery

Kind|heit *f* - childhood. **k~isch** *a* childish. **k~lich** *a* childlike

kinetisch *a* kinetic

Kinn *nt* -[e]s, -e chin. **K~lade** *f* jaw

Kino *nt* -s, -s cinema

Kiosk *m* -[e]s, -e kiosk

Kippe *f* -, -n (*Müll-*) dump; (▣ *Zigaretten-*) fag-end. **k~n** *vt* tilt; (*schütten*) tip (**in** + *acc* into) ● *vi* (*sein*) topple

Kirch|e *f* -, -n church. **K~enbank** *f* pew. **K~endiener** *m* verger. **K~enlied** *nt* hymn. **K~enschiff** *nt* nave. **K~hof** *m* churchyard. **k~lich** *a* church ... ● *adv* **k~lich** getraut werden be married in church. **K~turm** *m* church tower, steeple. **K~weih** *f* -, -en [village] fair

Kirmes *f* -, -sen = **Kirchweih**

Kirsche *f* -, -n cherry

Kissen *nt* -s,- cushion; (*Kopf-*) pillow

Kiste *f* -, -n crate; (*Zigarren-*) box

Kitsch *m* -es sentimental rubbish; (*Kunst*) kitsch

Kitt *m* -s [adhesive] cement; (*Fenster-*) putty

Kittel *m* -s,- overall, smock

Kitz *nt* -es, -e (*Zool*) kid

Kitz|el *m* -s,- tickle; (*Nerven-*) thrill. **k~eln** *vt/i* (*haben*) tickle. **k~lig** *a* ticklish

kläffen *vi* (*haben*) yap

Klage *f* -, -n lament; (*Beschwerde*) complaint; (*Jur*) action. **k~n** *vi* (*haben*) lament; (*sich beklagen*) complain; (*Jur*) sue

Kläger(in) *m* -s,- (*f* -, -nen) (*Jur*) plaintiff

klamm *a* cold and damp; (*steif*) stiff. **K~** *f* -, -en (*Geog*) gorge

---

Klammer f -, -n (Wäsche-) peg; (Büro-) paper-clip; (Heft-) staple; (Haar-) grip; (für Zähne) brace; (Techn) clamp; (Typ) bracket. **k~n (sich)** vr cling (an + acc to)

Klang m -[e]s,-̈e sound; (K~farbe) tone

Klapp|e f -, -n flap; (⚠ Mund) trap. **k~en** vt fold; (hoch-) tip up ● vi (haben) ⚠ work out

Klapper f -, -n rattle. **k~n** vi (haben) rattle. **K~schlange** f rattlesnake

klapp|rig a rickety; (schwach) decrepit. **K~stuhl** m folding chair

Klaps m -es, -e pat, smack

klar a clear; **sich** (dat) **k~ werden** make up one's mind; (erkennen) realize (**dass** that); **sich** (dat) **k~** od **im K~en sein** realize (**dass** that) ● adv clearly; (⚠ natürlich) of course

klären vt clarify; **sich k~** clear; (fig: sich lösen) resolve itself

Klarheit f -,- clarity

Klarinette f -, -n clarinet

klar|machen vt sep make clear (dat to); **sich** (dat) **etw k~machen** understand sth. **k~stellen** vt sep clarify

Klärung f - clarification

Klasse f -, -n class; (Sch) class, form; (Zimmer) classroom. **k~** inv a ⚠ super. **K~narbeit** f [written] test. **K~nzimmer** nt classroom

Klass|ik f - classicism; (Epoche) classical period. **K~iker** m -s,- classical author; (Mus) composer. **k~isch** a classical; (typisch) classic

Klatsch m -[e]s gossip. **K~base** f ⚠ gossip. **k~en** vt slap; Beifall **k~en** applaud ● vi (haben) make a slapping sound; (im Wasser) splash; (tratschen) gossip; (applaudieren) clap. **k~nass** a ⚠ soaking wet

klauen vt/i (haben) ⚠ steal

Klausel f -, -n clause

Klaustrophobie f - claustrophobia

Klausur f -, -en (Univ) paper

Klavier nt -s, -e piano. **K~spieler(in)** m(f) pianist

kleb|en vt stick/(mit Klebstoff) glue (an + acc to) ● vi (haben) stick (an + dat to). **k~rig** a sticky. **K~stoff** m adhesive, glue. **K~streifen** m adhesive tape

Klecks m -es, -e stain; (Tinten-) blot; (kleine Menge) dab. **k~en** vi (haben) make a mess

Klee m -s clover

Kleid nt -[e]s, -er dress; K~er dresses; (Kleidung) clothes. **k~en** vt dress; (gut stehen) suit. **K~erbügel** m coat-hanger. **K~erbürste** f clothes-brush. **K~erhaken** m coat-hook. **K~erschrank** m wardrobe. **k~sam** a becoming. **K~ung** f - clothes pl, clothing. **K~ungsstück** nt garment

Kleie f - bran

klein a small, little; (von kleinem Wuchs) short; **k~ schneiden** cut up small. **von k~ auf** from childhood. **K~arbeit** f painstaking work. **K~e(r,s)** m/f/nt little one. **K~geld** nt [small] change. **K~handel** m retail trade. **K~heit** f - smallness; (Wuchs) short stature. **K~holz** nt firewood. **K~igkeit** f -, -en trifle; (Mahl) snack. **K~kind** nt infant. **k~laut** a subdued. **k~lich** a petty

klein|schreiben† vt sep write with a small [initial] letter. **K~stadt** f small town. **k~städtisch** a provincial

Kleister m -s paste. **k~n** vt paste

Klemme f -, -n [hair-]grip. **k~n** vt jam; **sich** (dat) **den Finger k~n** get one's finger caught ● vi (haben) jam, stick

Klempner m -s,- plumber

Klerus (der) - the clergy

Klette f -, -n burr

kletter|n vi (sein) climb. **K~pflanze** f climber

Klettverschluss m Velcro (P) fastening

klicken vi (haben) click

Klient(in)/ kli'ɛnt(ɪn)/ m -en, -en (f -, -nen) (Jur) client

Kliff *nt* -[e]s, -e cliff

Klima *nt* -s climate. **K~anlage** *f* air-conditioning

klimat|isch *a* climatic. **k~isiert** *a* air-conditioned

klimpern *vi* (*haben*) jingle; **k~** auf (+ *dat*) tinkle on <*Klavier*>; strum <*Gitarre*>

Klinge *f* -, -n blade

Klingel *f* -, -n bell. **k~n** *vi* (*haben*) ring; es **k~t** there's a ring at the door

klingen† *vi* (*haben*) sound

Klinik *f* -, -en clinic

Klinke *f* -, -n [door] handle

Klippe *f* -, -n [submerged] rock

Klips *m* -es, -e clip; (*Ohr-*) clip-on ear-ring

klirren *vi* (*haben*) rattle <*Glas:*> chink

Klo *nt* -s, -s ⊞ loo

klopfen *vi* (*haben*) knock; (*leicht*) tap; <*Herz:*> pound; es **k~te** there was a knock at the door

Klops *m* -es, -e meatball

Klosett *nt* -s, -s lavatory

Kloß *m* -es,̈-e dumpling

Kloster *nt* -s,̈- monastery; (*Nonnen-*) convent

klösterlich *a* monastic

Klotz *m* -es,̈-e block

Klub *m* -s, -s club

Kluft *f* -,̈-e cleft; (*fig: Gegensatz*) gulf

klug *a* intelligent; (*schlau*) clever. **K~heit** *f* - cleverness

Klump|en *m* -s,- lump

knabbern *vt/i* (*haben*) nibble

Knabe *m* -n, -n boy. **k~nhaft** *a* boyish

Knäckebrot *nt* crispbread

knack|en *vt/i* (*haben*) crack. **K~s** *m* -es, -e crack

Knall *m* -[e]s, -e bang. **K~bonbon** *m* cracker. **k~en** *vi* (*haben*) go bang; <*Peitsche:*> crack ● *vt* (⊞ *werfen*) chuck; jdm eine **k~en** ⊞ clout s.o. **k~ig** *a* ⊞ gaudy

---

*old spelling

knapp *a* (*gering*) scant; (*kurz*) short; (*mangelnd*) scarce; (*gerade ausreichend*) bare; (*eng*) tight. **K~heit** *f* - scarcity

knarren *vi* (*haben*) creak

Knast *m* -[e]s ⊞ prison

knattern *vi* (*haben*) crackle; <*Gewehr:*> stutter

Knäuel *m & nt* -s,- ball

Knauf *m* -[e]s, Knäufe knob

knauserig *a* ⊞ stingy

knautschen *vt* ⊞ crumple ● *vi* (*haben*) crease

Knebel *m* -s,- gag. **k~n** *vt* gag

Knecht *m* -[e]s, -e farm-hand; (*fig*) slave

kneif|en† *vt* pinch ● *vi* (*haben*) pinch; (⊞ *sich drücken*) chicken out. **K~zange** *f* pincers *pl*

Kneipe *f* -, -n ⊞ pub

knet|en *vt* knead; (*formen*) mould. **K~masse** *f* Plasticine(P)

Knick *m* -[e]s, -e bend; (*Kniff*) crease. **k~en** *vt* bend; (*kniffen*) fold; **geknickt sein** ⊞ be dejected

Knicks *m* -es, -e curtsy. **k~en** *vi* (*haben*) curtsy

Knie *nt* -s,- /'kni:ə/ knee

knien /'kni:ən/ *vi* (*haben*) kneel ● *vr* **sich k~** kneel [down]

Kniescheibe *f* kneecap

Kniff *m* -[e]s, -e pinch; (*Falte*) crease; (⊞ *Trick*) trick. **k~en** *vt* fold

knipsen *vt* (*lochen*) punch; (*Phot*) photograph ● *vi* (*haben*) take a photograph/photographs

Knirps *m* -es, -e ⊞ little chap; (P) (*Schirm*) telescopic umbrella

knirschen *vi* (*haben*) grate; <*Schnee, Kies:*> crunch

knistern *vi* (*haben*) crackle; <*Papier:*> rustle

Knitter|falte *f* crease. **k~frei** *a* crease-resistant. **k~n** *vi* (*haben*) crease

knobeln *vi* (*haben*) toss (um for)

Knoblauch *m* -s garlic

Knöchel *m* -s,- ankle; (*Finger-*) knuckle

Knochen *m* -s,- bone. **K∼mark** *nt* bone marrow

knochig *a* bony

Knödel *m* -s,- (*SGer*) dumpling

Knoll|e *f* -, -n tuber

Knopf *m* -[e]s,ːe button; (*Griff*) knob

knöpfen *vt* button

Knopfloch *nt* buttonhole

Knorpel *m* -s gristle; (*Anat*) cartilage

Knospe *f* bud

Knoten *m* -s,- knot; (*Med*) lump; (*Haar-*) bun, chignon. **k∼** *vt* knot. **K∼punkt** *m* junction

knüll|en *vt* crumple ● *vi* (*haben*) crease. **K∼er** *m* -s,- 🔔 sensation

knüpfen *vt* knot; (*verbinden*) attach (**an** + *acc* to)

Knüppel *m* -s,- club; (*Gummi-*) truncheon

knurren *vi* (*haben*) growl; <*Magen:*> rumble

knusprig *a* crunchy, crisp

knutschen *vi* (*haben*) 🔔 smooch

k.o. /ka'ʔoː/ *a* **k.o. schlagen** knock out; **k.o. sein** 🔔 be worn out

Koalition /koali'tsːioːn/ *f* -, -en coalition

Kobold *m* -[e]s, -e goblin, imp

Koch *m* -[e]s,ːe cook; (*im Restaurant*) chef. **K∼buch** *nt* cookery book. **k∼en** *vt* cook; (*sieden*) boil; make <*Kaffee, Tee*>; **hart gekochtes Ei** hard-boiled egg ● *vi* (*haben*) cook; (*sieden*) boil; 🔔 seethe (**vor** + *dat* with). **K∼en** *nt* -s cooking; (*Sieden*) boiling. **k∼end** *a* boiling. **K∼herd** *m* cooker, stove

Köchin *f* -, -nen [woman] cook

Koch|löffel *m* wooden spoon. **K∼nische** *f* kitchenette. **K∼platte** *f* hotplate. **K∼topf** *m* saucepan

Köder *m* -s,- bait

Koffein /kɔfe'iːn/ *nt* -s caffeine. **k∼frei** *a* decaffeinated

Koffer *m* -s,- suitcase. **K∼kuli** *m* luggage trolley. **K∼raum** *m* (*Auto*) boot

Kognak /'kɔnjak/ *m* -s, -s brandy

Kohl *m* -[e]s cabbage

Kohle *f* -, -n coal. **K∼[n]hydrat** *nt* -[e]s, -e carbohydrate. **K∼nbergwerk** *nt* coal-mine, colliery. **K∼ndioxid** *nt* carbon dioxide. **K∼nsäure** *f* carbon dioxide. **K∼nstoff** *m* carbon

Koje *f* -, -n (*Naut*) bunk

Kokain /koka'iːn/ *nt* -s cocaine

kokett *a* flirtatious. **k∼ieren** *vi* (*haben*) flirt

Kokon /ko'kõː/ *m* -s, -s cocoon

Kokosnuss (*f*) coconut

Koks *m* -es coke

Kolben *m* -s,- (*Gewehr-*) butt; (*Mais-*) cob; (*Techn*) piston; (*Chem*) flask

Kolibri *m* -s, -s humming-bird

Kolik *f* -, -en colic

Kollaborateur /-'tøːɐ̯/ *m* -s, -e collaborator

Kolleg *nt* -s, -s & -ien /-jən/ (*Univ*) course of lectures

Kolleg|e *m* -n, -n, **K∼in** *f* -, -nen colleague. **K∼ium** *nt* -s, -ien staff

Kollekt|e *f* -, -n (*Relig*) collection. **K∼tion** /-'tsːioːn/ *f* -, -en collection

Köln *nt* -s Cologne. **K∼ischwasser, K∼isch Wasser** *nt* eau-de-Cologne

Kolonie *f* -, -n colony

Kolonne *f* -, -n column; (*Mil*) convoy

Koloss *m* -es, -e giant

Koma *nt* -s, -s coma

Kombi *m* -s, -s = **K∼wagen**. **K∼nation** /-'tsːioːn/ *f* -, -en combination; (*Folgerung*) deduction; (*Kleidung*) co-ordinating outfit. **k∼nieren** *vt* combine; (*fig*) reason; (*folgern*) deduce. **K∼wagen** *m* estate car

Kombüse *f* -, -n (*Naut*) galley

Komet *m* -en, -en comet

Komfort /kɔm'foːɐ̯/ *m* -s comfort; (*Luxus*) luxury

Komik *f* - humour. **K∼er** *m* -s,- comic, comedian

komisch *a* funny; <*Oper*> comic; (*sonderbar*) odd, funny. **k∼erweise** *adv* funnily enough

Komitee *nt* -s, -s committee

Komma *nt* -s, -s & -ta comma; (*Dezimal-*) decimal point; **drei K~ fünf** three point five

Kommando *nt* -s, -s order; (*Befehlsgewalt*) command; (*Einheit*) detachment. **K~brücke** *f* bridge

kommen† *vi* (*sein*) come; (*eintreffen*) arrive; (*gelangen*) get (nach to); **k~ lassen** send for; **auf/ hinter etw** (*acc*) **k~** think of/find out about sth; **um/zu etw k~** lose/ acquire sth; **wieder zu sich k~** come round; **wie kommt das?** why is that? **k~d** *a* coming; **k~den Montag** next Monday

Kommen|tar *m* -s, -e commentary; (*Bemerkung*) comment. **k~tieren** *vt* comment on

kommerziell *a* commercial

Kommissar *m* -s, -e commissioner; (*Polizei-*) superintendent

Kommission *f* -, -en commission; (*Gremium*) committee

Kommode *f* -, -n chest of drawers

Kommunalwahlen *fpl* local elections

Kommunion *f* -, -en [Holy] Communion

Kommun|ismus *m* - Communism. **K~ist(in)** *m* -en, -en (*f* -, -nen) Communist. **k~istisch** *a* Communist

kommunizieren *vi* (*haben*) receive [Holy] Communion

Komödie /ko'mø:diə/ *f* -, -n comedy

Kompagnon /'kɔmpanjõ:/ *m* -s, -s (*Comm*) partner

Kompanie *f* -, -n (*Mil*) company

Komparse *m* -n, -n (*Theat*) extra

Kompass *m* -es, -e compass

komplett *a* complete

Komplex *m* -es, -e complex

Komplikation /-'ts̷io:n/ *f* -, -en complication

Kompliment *nt* -[e]s, -e compliment

Komplize *m* -n, -n accomplice

komplizier|en *vt* complicate. **k~t** *a* complicated

Komplott *nt* -[e]s, -e plot

kompo|nieren *vt*/*i* (*haben*) compose. **K~nist** *m* -en, -en composer

Kompost *m* -[e]s compost

Kompott *nt* -[e]s, -e stewed fruit

Kompromiss *m* -es, -e compromise; **einen K~ schließen** compromise. **k~los** *a* uncompromising

Konden|sation /-'ts̷io:n/ *f* - condensation. **k~sieren** *vt* condense

Kondensmilch *f* evaporated/ (*gesüßt*) condensed milk

Kondition /-'ts̷io:n/ *f* - (*Sport*) fitness; **in K~** in form

Konditor *m* -s, -en /-'to:rən/ confectioner. **K~ei** *f* -, -en patisserie

Kondo|lenzbrief *m* letter of condolence. **k~lieren** *vi* (*haben*) express one's condolences

Kondom *nt* & *m* -s, -e condom

Konfekt *nt* -[e]s confectionery; (*Pralinen*) chocolates *pl*

Konfektion /-'ts̷io:n/ *f* - ready-to-wear clothes *pl*

Konferenz *f* -, -en conference; (*Besprechung*) meeting

Konfession *f* -, -en [religious] denomination. **k~ell** *a* denominational

Konfetti *nt* -s confetti

Konfirm|and(in) *m* -en, -en (*f* -, -nen) candidate for confirmation. **K~ation** /-'ts̷io:n/ *f* -, -en (*Relig*) confirmation. **k~ieren** *vt* (*Relig*) confirm

Konfitüre *f* -, -n jam

Konflikt *m* -[e]s, -e conflict

Konföderation /-'ts̷io:n/ *f* confederation

konfus *a* confused

Kongress *m* -es, -e congress

König *m* -s, -e king. **K~in** *f* -, -nen queen. **k~lich** *a* royal; (*hoheitsvoll*) regal; (*großzügig*) handsome. **K~reich** *nt* kingdom

---

*alte Schreibung

Konjunktiv *m* -s, -e subjunctive

Konjunktur *f* - economic situation; (*Hoch-*) boom

konkret *a* concrete

Konkurren|t(in) *m* -en, -en (*f* -, -nen) competitor, rival. **K~z** *f* - competition; **jdm K~z machen** compete with s.o. **K~zkampf** *m* competition, rivalry

konkurrieren *vi* (*haben*) compete

Konkurs *m* -es, -e bankruptcy

können†
● *auxiliary verb*
····▶ (*vermögen*) be able to; (*Präsens*) can; (*Vergangenheit, Konditional*) could. **ich kann nicht schlafen** I cannot *or* can't sleep. **kann ich Ihnen helfen?** can I help you? **kann/könnte das explodieren?** can/could it explode? **es kann sein, dass er kommt** he may come

! Distinguish **konnte** and **könnte** (both can be 'could'): **er konnte sie nicht retten** he couldn't *or* was unable to rescue them. **er konnte sie noch retten** he was able to rescue them. **er könnte sie noch retten, wenn …** he could still rescue them if …

····▶ (*dürfen*) can, may. **kann ich gehen?** can *or* may I go? **können wir mit[kommen]?** can *or* may we come too?
● *transitive verb*
····▶ (*beherrschen*) know <language>; be able to play <game>. **können Sie Deutsch?** do you know any German? **sie kann das [gut]** she can do that [well]. **ich kann nichts dafür** I can't help that, I'm not to blame
● *intransitive verb*
····▶ (*fähig sein*) **ich kann [heute] nicht** I can't [today]. **er kann nicht anders** there's nothing else he can do; (*es ist seine Art*) he can't help it. **er kann nicht mehr** 🔲 he can't go on; (*nicht mehr essen*) he can't eat any more
····▶ (*irgendwohin gehen können*) be able to go; can go. **ich kann nicht ins Kino** I can't go to the cinema. **er**

konnte endlich nach Florenz at last he was able to go to Florence

konsequen|t *a* consistent; (*logisch*) logical. **K~z** *f* -, -en consequence

konservativ *a* conservative

Konserv|en *fpl* tinned or canned food *sg.* **K~endose** *f* tin, can. **K~ierungsmittel** *nt* preservative

Konsonant *m* -en, -en consonant

Konstitution /-'tsio:n/ *f* -, -en constitution. **k~ell** *a* constitutional

konstruieren *vt* construct; (*entwerfen*) design

Konstruk|tion /-'tsio:n/ *f* -, -en construction; (*Entwurf*) design. **k~tiv** *a* constructive

Konsul *m* -s, -n consul. **K~at** *nt* -[e]s, -e consulate

Konsum *m* -s consumption. **K~güter** *npl* consumer goods

Kontakt *m* -[e]s, -e contact. **K~linsen** *fpl* contact lenses. **K~person** *f* contact

kontern *vt/i* (*haben*) counter

Kontinent /'kɔn-, kɔnti'nɛnt/ *m* -[e]s, -e continent

Konto *nt* -s, -s account. **K~auszug** *m* [bank] statement. **K~nummer** *f* account number. **K~stand** *m* [bank] balance

Kontrabass *m* double-bass

Kontroll|abschnitt *m* counterfoil. **K~e** *f* -, -n control; (*Prüfung*) check. **K~eur** /-'løːɐ̯/ *m* -s, -e [ticket] inspector. **k~ieren** *vt* check; inspect <Fahrkarten>; (*beherrschen*) control

Kontroverse *f* -, -n controversy

Kontur *f* -, -en contour

konventionell *a* conventional

Konversationslexikon *nt* encyclopaedia

konvert|ieren *vi* (*haben*) (*Relig*) convert. **K~it** *m* -en, -en convert

Konzentration /-'tsio:n/ *f* -, -en concentration. **K~slager** *nt* concentration camp

konzentrieren *vt* concentrate; **sich k~** concentrate (**auf** + *acc* on)

Konzẹpt nt -[e]s, -e [rough] draft; jdn aus dem K~bringen put s.o. off his stroke

Konzẹrn m -s, -e (Comm) group [of companies]

Konzẹrt nt -[e]s, -e concert; (Klavier-) concerto

Konzession f -, -en licence; (Zugeständnis) concession

Konzil nt -s, -e (Relig) council

Kooperation /koʔɔpəraˈtsɪoːn/ f co-operation

Koordin|ation /koʔɔrdinaˈtsɪoːn/ f - co-ordination. **k~ieren** vt co-ordinate

Kopf m -[e]s,̈-e head; ein K~ Kohl/ Salat a cabbage/lettuce; aus dem K~ from memory; (auswendig) by heart; auf dem K~ (verkehrt) upside down; K~ stehen stand on one's head; sich (dat) den K~ waschen wash one's hair; sich (dat) den K~ zerbrechen rack one's brains. **K~ball** m header

köpfen vt behead; (Fußball) head

Kopf|ende nt head. **K~haut** f scalp. **K~hörer** m headphones pl. **K~kissen** nt pillow. **k~los** a panic-stricken. **K~rechnen** nt mental arithmetic. **K~salat** m lettuce. **K~schmerzen** mpl headache sg. **K~sprung** m header, dive. **K~stand** m headstand. **K~steinpflaster** nt cobble-stones pl. **K~tuch** nt headscarf. **k~über** adv head first; (fig) headlong. **K~wäsche** f shampoo. **K~weh** nt headache

Kopie f -, -n copy. **k~ren** vt copy

Koppel¹ f -, -n enclosure; (Pferde-) paddock

Koppel² nt -s,- (Mil) belt. **k~n** vt couple

Koralle f -, -n coral

Korb m -[e]s,̈-e basket; jdm einen K~ geben (fig) turn s.o. down. **K~ball** m [kind of] netball

Kord m -s (Tex) corduroy

Kordel f -, -n cord

Korinthe f -, -n currant

Kork m -s,- cork. **K~en** m -s,- cork. **K~enzieher** m -s,- corkscrew

Korn nt -[e]s,̈-er grain, (Samen-) seed; (am Visier) front sight

Körn|chen nt -s,- granule. **k~ig** a granular

Körper m -s,- body; (Geom) solid. **K~bau** m build, physique. **k~behindert** a physically disabled. **k~lich** a physical; <Strafe> corporal. **K~pflege** f personal hygiene. **K~schaft** f -, -en corporation, body

korrẹkt a correct. **K~or** m -s, -en /-ˈtoːrən/ proof-reader. **K~ur** f -, -en correction. **K~urabzug** m proof

Korrespon|dẹnt(in) m -en, -en (f -, -nen) correspondent. **K~dẹnz** f -, -en correspondence

Korridor m -s, -e corridor

korrigieren vt correct

Korrosion f - corrosion

korrup|t a corrupt. **K~tion** /-ˈtsɪoːn/ f - corruption

Korsẹtt nt -[e]s, -e corset

koscher a kosher

Kosename m pet name

Kosmet|ik f - beauty culture. **K~ika** ntpl cosmetics. **K~ikerin** f -, -nen beautician. **k~isch** a cosmetic; <Chirurgie> plastic

kosm|isch a cosmic. **K~onaut(in)** m -en, -en (f -, -nen) cosmonaut

Kosmos m - cosmos

Kost f - food; (Ernährung) diet; (Verpflegung) board

kostbar a precious. **K~keit** f -, -en treasure

kosten¹ vt/i (haben) [von] etw k~ taste sth

kosten² vt cost; (brauchen) take; wie viel kostet es? how much is it? **K~** pl expense sg, cost sg; (Jur) costs; auf meine K~ at my expense. **K~[vor]anschlag** m estimate. **k~los** a free ● adv free [of charge]

köstlich a delicious; (entzückend) delightful

Kostprobe f taste; (fig) sample

Kostüm nt -s, -e (Theat) costume; (Verkleidung) fancy dress; (Schneider-) suit. **k~iert** a k~iert sein be in fancy dress

Kot m -[e]s excrement

Kotelett /kɔt'lɛt/ nt -s, -s chop, cutlet. **K~en** pl sideburns

Köter m -s,- (pej) dog

Kotflügel m (Auto) wing

kotzen vi (haben) 🗵 throw up

Krabbe f -, -n crab, shrimp

krabbeln vi (sein) crawl

Krach m -[e]s,⸚e din, racket; (Knall) crash; (🗓 Streit) row; (🗓 Ruin) crash. **k~en** vi (haben) crash; **es hat gekracht** there was a bang/(🗓 Unfall) a crash ● (sein) break, crack; (auftreffen) crash (gegen into)

krächzen vi (haben) croak

Kraft f -,⸚e strength; (Gewalt) force; (Arbeits-) worker; **in/außer K~** in/no longer in force. **K~fahrer** m driver. **K~fahrzeug** nt motor vehicle. **K~fahrzeugbrief** m [vehicle] registration document

kräftig a strong; (gut entwickelt) sturdy; (nahrhaft) nutritious; (heftig) hard

kraft|los a weak. **K~probe** f trial of strength. **K~stoff** m (Auto) fuel. **K~wagen** m motor car. **K~werk** nt power station

Kragen m -s,- collar

Krähe f -, -n crow

krähen vi (haben) crow

Kralle f -, -n claw

Kram m -s 🗓 things pl, 🗓 stuff; (Angelegenheiten) business. **k~en** vi (haben) rummage about (**in** + dat in; **nach** for)

Krampf m -[e]s,⸚e cramp. **K~adern** fpl varicose veins. **k~haft** a convulsive; (verbissen) desperate

Kran m -[e]s,⸚e (Techn) crane

Kranich m -s, -e (Zool) crane

krank a sick; <Knie, Herz> bad; **k~ sein/werden** be/fall ill. **K~e(r)** m/f sick man/woman, invalid; **die K~en** the sick pl

kränken vt offend, hurt

Kranken|bett nt sick-bed. **K~geld** nt sickness benefit. **K~gymnast(in)** m -en, -en (f -, -nen) physiotherapist. **K~gymnastik** f physiotherapy. **K~haus** nt hospital. **K~kasse** f health insurance scheme/(Amer) office. **K~pflege** f nursing. **K~saal** m [hospital] ward. **K~schein** m certificate of entitlement to medical treatment. **K~schwester** f nurse. **K~versicherung** f health insurance. **K~wagen** m ambulance

Krankheit f -, -en illness, disease

kränklich a sickly

krank|melden vt sep jdn k~melden report s.o. sick; **sich k~melden** report sick

Kranz m -es,⸚e wreath

Krapfen m -s,- doughnut

Krater m -s,- crater

kratzen vt/i (haben) scratch. **K~er** m -s,- scratch

Kraul nt -s (Sport) crawl. **k~en¹** vi (haben/sein) (Sport) do the crawl

kraulen² vt tickle; **sich am Kopf k~** scratch one's head

kraus a wrinkled; <Haar> frizzy; (verworren) muddled. **K~e** f -, -n frill

kräuseln vt wrinkle; frizz <Haar->; gather <Stoff>; **sich k~** wrinkle; (sich kringeln) curl; <Haar:> go frizzy

Kraut nt -[e]s, Kräuter herb; (SGer) cabbage; (Sauer-) sauerkraut

Krawall m -s, -e riot; (Lärm) row

Krawatte f -, -n [neck]tie

kreativ /krea'ti:f/ a creative. **K~tur** f -, -en creature

Krebs m -es, -e crayfish; (Med) cancer; (Astr) Cancer

Kredit m -s, -e credit; (Darlehen) loan; **auf K~** on credit. **K~karte** f credit card

Kreid|e f - chalk. **k~ig** a chalky

kreieren /kre'i:rən/ vt create

Kreis m -es, -e circle; (Admin) district

kreischen *vt/i (haben)* screech; (*schreien*) shriek

Kreisel *m* -s,- [spinning] top

kreis|en *vi (haben)* circle; revolve (um around). **k~förmig** *a* circular. **K~lauf** *m* cycle; (*Med*) circulation. **K~säge** *f* circular saw. **K~verkehr** *m* [traffic] roundabout

Krem *f* -,-s & *m* -s, -e cream

Krematorium *nt* -s, -ien crematorium

Krempe *f* -, -n [hat] brim

krempeln *vt* turn (nach oben up)

Krepp *m* -s, -s & -e crêpe

Krepppapier *nt* crêpe paper

Kresse *f* -, -n cress; (*Kapuziner-*) nasturtium

Kreta *nt* -s Crete

Kreuz *nt* -es, -e cross; (*Kreuzung*) intersection; (*Mus*) sharp; (*Kartenspiel*) clubs *pl*; (*Anat*) small of the back; über K~ crosswise; das K~ schlagen cross oneself. **k~en** *vt* cross; sich k~en cross; <*Straßen:*> intersect; <*Meinungen:*> clash ● *vi (haben/sein)* cruise. **K~fahrt** *f* (*Naut*) cruise. **K~gang** *m* cloister

kreuzig|en *vt* crucify. **K~ung** *f* -, -en crucifixion

Kreuz|otter *f* adder, common viper. **K~ung** *f* -, -en intersection; (*Straßen-*) crossroads *sg*. **K~verhör** *nt* cross-examination. **k~weise** *adv* crosswise. **K~worträtsel** *nt* crossword [puzzle]. **K~zug** *m* crusade

kribbel|ig *a* 🔟 edgy. **k~n** *vi (haben)* tingle; (*kitzeln*) tickle

kriech|en† *vi (sein)* crawl; (*fig*) grovel (vor + *dat* to). **K~spur** *f* (*Auto*) crawler lane. **K~tier** *nt* reptile

Krieg *m* -[e]s, -e war

kriegen *vt* 🔟 get; ein Kind k~ have a baby

kriegs|beschädigt *a* war-disabled. **K~dienstverweigerer** *m* -s,- conscientious objector. **K~gefangene(r)** *m* prisoner of war. **K~gefangenschaft** *f* captivity. **K~gericht** *nt* court martial. **K~list** *f* stratagem. **K~rat** *m* council of war. **K~recht** *nt* martial law

Krimi *m* -s, -s 🔟 crime story/film. **K~nalität** *f* - crime; (*Vorkommen*) crime rate. **K~nalpolizei** *f* criminal investigation department. **K~nalroman** *m* crime novel. **k~nell** *a* criminal

Krippe *f* -, -n manger; (*Weihnachts-*) crib; (*Kinder-*) crèche. **K~nspiel** *nt* Nativity play

Krise *f* -, -n crisis

Kristall *nt* -s crystal; (*geschliffen*) cut glass

Kritik *f* -, -en criticism; (*Rezension*) review; unter aller K~ 🔟 abysmal

Kriti|ker *m* -s,- critic; (*Rezensent*) reviewer. **k~sch** *a* critical. **k~sieren** *vt* criticize; review

kritzeln *vt/i (haben)* scribble

Krokodil *nt* -s, -e crocodile

Krokus *m* -, -[se] crocus

Krone *f* -, -n crown; (*Baum-*) top

krönen *vt* crown

Kronleuchter *m* chandelier

Krönung *f* -, -en coronation; (*fig: Höhepunkt*) crowning event

Kropf *m* -[e]s,̈-e (*Zool*) crop; (*Med*) goitre

Kröte *f* -, -n toad

Krücke *f* -, -n crutch

Krug *m* -[e]s,̈-e jug; (*Bier-*) tankard

Krümel *m* -s,- crumb. **k~ig** *a* crumbly. **k~n** *vt* crumble ● *vi (haben)* be crumbly

krumm *a* crooked; (*gebogen*) curved; (*verbogen*) bent

krümmen *vt* bend; crook <*Finger*>; sich k~ bend; (*sich winden*) writhe; (*vor Lachen*) double up

Krümmung *f* -, -en bend, curve

Krüppel *m* -s,- cripple

Kruste *f* -, -n crust; (*Schorf*) scab

Kruzifix *nt* -es, -e crucifix

Kub|a *nt* -s Cuba. **k~anisch** *a* Cuban

Kübel _m_ -s,- tub; (_Eimer_) bucket; (_Techn_) skip

Küche _f_ -, -n kitchen; (_Kochkunst_) cooking; **kalte/warme K~** cold/hot food

Kuchen _m_ -s,- cake

Küchen|herd _m_ cooker, stove. **K~maschine** _f_ food processor, mixer. **K~schabe** _f_ -, -n cockroach

Kuckuck _m_ -s, -e cuckoo

Kufe _f_ -, -n [sledge] runner

Kugel _f_ -, -n ball; (_Geom_) sphere; (_Gewehr-_) bullet; (_Sport_) shot. **k~förmig** _a_ spherical. **K~lager** _nt_ ball-bearing. **k~n** _vt/i_ (_haben_) roll; **sich k~n** (_vor Lachen_) fall about. **K~schreiber** _m_ -s,-, ballpoint [pen]. **k~sicher** _a_ bullet-proof. **K~stoßen** _nt_ -s shot-putting

Kuh _f_ -,-̈e cow

kühl _a_ cool; (_kalt_) chilly. **K~box** _f_ -, -en cool-box. **K~e** _f_ - coolness; chilliness. **k~en** _vt_ cool; refrigerate <_Lebensmittel_>; chill <_Wein_>. **K~er** _m_ -s,-; (_Auto_) radiator. **K~erhaube** _f_ bonnet. **K~fach** _nt_ frozen-food compartment. **K~raum** _m_ cold store. **K~schrank** _m_ refrigerator. **K~truhe** _f_ freezer. **K~wasser** _nt_ [radiator] water

kühn _a_ bold

Kuhstall _m_ cowshed

Küken _nt_ -s,- chick; (_Enten-_) duckling

Kulissen _fpl_ (_Theat_) scenery _sg;_ (_seitlich_) wings; **hinter den K~** (_fig_) behind the scenes

Kult _m_ -[e]s, -e cult

kultivier|en _vt_ cultivate. **k~t** _a_ cultured

Kultur _f_ -, -en culture. **K~beutel** _m_ toiletbag. **k~ell** _a_ cultural. **K~film** _m_ documentary film

Kultusminister _m_ Minister of Education and Arts

Kümmel _m_ -s caraway; (_Getränk_) kümmel

Kummer _m_ -s sorrow, grief; (_Sorge_) worry; (_Ärger_) trouble

kümmer|lich _a_ puny; (_dürftig_) meagre; (_armselig_) wretched. **k~n** _vt_

concern; **sich k~n um** look after; (_sich befassen_) concern oneself with; (_beachten_) take notice of

kummervoll _a_ sorrowful

Kumpel _m_ -s,- 🄸 mate

Kunde _m_ -n, -n customer. **K~ndienst** _m_ [after-sales] service

Kundgebung _f_ -, -en (_Pol_) rally

kündig|en _vt_ cancel <_Vertrag_>; give notice of withdrawal for <_Geld_>; give notice to quit <_Wohnung_>; **seine Stellung k~en** give [in one's] notice ● _vi_ (_haben_) give [in one's] notice; **jdm k~en** give s.o. notice. **K~ung** _f_ -, -en cancellation; notice [of withdrawal/dismissal/to quit]; (_Entlassung_) dismissal. **K~ungsfrist** _f_ period of notice

Kund|in _f_ -, -nen [woman] customer. **K~schaft** _f_ - clientele, customers _pl_

künftig _a_ future ● _adv_ in future

Kunst _f_ -,-̈e art; (_Können_) skill. **K~faser** _f_ synthetic fibre. **K~galerie** _f_ art gallery. **K~geschichte** _f_ history of art. **K~gewerbe** _nt_ arts and crafts _pl._ **K~griff** _m_ trick

Künstler _m_ -s,- artist; (_Könner_) master. **K~in** _f_ -, -nen [woman] artist. **k~isch** _a_ artistic

künstlich _a_ artificial

Kunst|stoff _m_ plastic. **K~stück** _nt_ trick; (_große Leistung_) feat. **k~voll** _a_ artistic; (_geschickt_) skilful

kunterbunt _a_ multicoloured; (_gemischt_) mixed

Kupfer _nt_ -s copper

Kupon /ku'põ:/ _m_ -s, -s voucher; (_Zins-_) coupon; (_Stoff-_) length

Kuppe _f_ -, -n [rounded] top

Kuppel _f_ -, -n dome

kupp|eln _vt_ couple (**an** + _acc_ to) ● _vi_ (_haben_) (_Auto_) operate the clutch. **K~lung** _f_ -, -en coupling; (_Auto_) clutch

Kur _f_ -, -en course of treatment, cure

Kür _f_ -, -en (_Sport_) free exercise; (_Eislauf_) free programme

Kurbel _f_ -, -n crank. **K~welle** _f_ crankshaft

Kürbis *m* -ses, -se pumpkin

Kurier *m* -s, -e courier

kurieren *vt* cure

kurios *a* curious, odd. **K~ität** *f* -, -en oddness; (*Objekt*) curiosity

Kurort *m* health resort; (*Badeort*) spa

Kurs *m* -es, -e course; (*Aktien-*) price. **K~buch** *nt* timetable

kursieren *vi* (*haben*) circulate

kursiv *a* italic ● *adv* in italics. **K~schrift** *f* italics *pl*

Kursus *m* -,Kurse course

Kurswagen *m* through carriage

Kurtaxe *f* visitors' tax

Kurve *f* -, -n curve; (*Straßen-*) bend

kurz *a* short; (*knapp*) brief; (*rasch*) quick; (*schroff*) curt; **k~e Hosen** shorts; **vor k~em** a short time ago; **seit k~em** lately; **den Kürzeren ziehen** get the worst of it; **k~ vor** shortly before; **sich k~ fassen** be brief; **k~ und gut** in short; **zu k~ kommen** get less than one's fair share. **k~ärmelig** *a* short-sleeved. **k~atmig** *a* **k~atmig sein** be short of breath

Kürze *f* - shortness; (*Knappheit*) brevity; **in K~** shortly. **k~n** *vt* shorten; (*verringern*) cut

kurzfristig *a* short-term ● *adv* at short notice

kürzlich *adv* recently

Kurz|meldung *f* newsflash. **K~schluss** *m* short circuit. **K~schrift** *f* shorthand. **k~sichtig** *a* short-sighted. **K~sichtigkeit** *f* - short-sightedness. **K~streckenrakete** *f* short-range missile

Kürzung *f* -, -en shortening; (*Verringerung*) cut (*gen* in)

Kurz|waren *fpl* haberdashery *sg*. **K~welle** *f* short wave

kuscheln (sich) *vr* snuggle (**an** + *acc* up to)

Kusine *f* -, -n [female] cousin

Kuss *m* -es,-̈e kiss

küssen *vt/i* (*haben*) kiss; **sich k~** kiss

Küste *f* -, -n coast

Küster *m* -s,- verger

Kutsch|e *f* -, -n [horse-drawn] carriage/(*geschlossen*) coach. **K~er** *m* -s,- coachman, driver

Kutte *f* -, -n (*Relig*) habit

Kutter *m* -s,- (*Naut*) cutter

Kuvert /ku've:ɐ/ *nt* -s, -s envelope

Ll

Labor *nt* -s, -s & -e laboratory. **L~ant(in)** *m* -en, -en (*f* -, -nen) laboratory assistant

Labyrinth *nt* -[e]s, -e maze, labyrinth

Lache *f* -, -n puddle; (*Blut-*) pool

lächeln *vi* (*haben*) smile. **L~** *nt* -s smile. **l~d** *a* smiling

lachen *vi* (*haben*) laugh. **L~** *nt* -s laugh; (*Gelächter*) laughter

lächerlich *a* ridiculous; **sich l~ machen** make a fool of oneself. **L~keit** *f* -, -en ridiculousness; (*Kleinigkeit*) triviality

Lachs *m* -es, -e salmon

Lack *m* -[e]s, -e varnish; (*Japan-*) lacquer; (*Auto*) paint. **l~en** *vt* varnish. **l~ieren** *vt* varnish; (*spritzen*) spray. **L~schuhe** *mpl* patent-leather shoes

laden† *vt* load; (*Electr*) charge; (*Jur: vor-*) summon

Laden *m* -s,-̈ shop; (*Fenster-*) shutter. **L~dieb** *m* shop-lifter. **L~schluss** *m* [shop] closing-time. **L~tisch** *m* counter

Laderaum *m* (*Naut*) hold

lädieren *vt* damage

Ladung *f* -, -en load; (*Naut, Aviat*) cargo; (*elektrische*) charge

---

Lage f -, -n position, situation; (*Schicht*) layer; **nicht in der L~ sein** not be in a position (**zu** to)

Lager nt -s,- camp; (*L~haus*) warehouse; (*Vorrat*) stock; (*Techn*) bearing; (*Erz-, Ruhe-*) bed; (*eines Tieres*) lair; **[nicht] auf L~** [not] in stock. **L~haus** nt warehouse. **l~n** vt store; (*legen*) lay; **sich l~n** settle. **L~raum** m store-room. **L~ung** f - storage

Lagune f -, -n lagoon

lahm a lame. **l~en** vi (*haben*) be lame

lähmen vt paralyse

Lähmung f -, -en paralysis

Laib m -[e]s, -e loaf

Laich m -[e]s (*Zool*) spawn

Laie m -n, -n layman; (*Theat*) amateur. **l~nhaft** a amateurish

Laken nt -s,- sheet

Lakritze f - liquorice

lallen vt/i (*haben*) mumble; <*Baby:*> babble

Lametta nt -s tinsel

Lamm nt -[e]s,-̈er lamb

Lampe f -, -n lamp; (*Decken-, Wand-*) light; (*Glüh-*) bulb. **L~nfieber** nt stage fright

Lampion /lam'piɔŋ/ m -s, -s Chinese lantern

Land nt -[e]s,-̈er country; (*Fest-*) land; (*Bundes-*) state, Land; (*Aust*) province; **auf dem L~e** in the country; **an L~ gehen** (*Naut*) go ashore. **L~arbeiter** m agricultural worker. **L~ebahn** f runway. **l~en** vt/i (*sein*) land; (🗊 *gelangen*) end up

Ländereien pl estates

Länderspiel nt international

Landesverrat m treason

Landkarte f map

ländlich a rural

Land|schaft f -, -en scenery; (*Geog, Kunst*) landscape; (*Gegend*) country[side]. **l~schaftlich** a scenic; (*regional*) regional. **L~streicher** m -s,- tramp. **L~tag** m state/(*Aust*) provincial parliament

Landung f -, -en landing

Land|vermesser m -s,- surveyor. **L~weg** m country lane; **auf dem L~weg** overland. **L~wirt** m farmer. **L~wirtschaft** f agriculture; (*Hof*) farm. **l~wirtschaftlich** a agricultural

lang[1] adv & prep (+ *preceding acc or preceding* an + *dat*) along; **den** od **am Fluss l~** along the river

lang[2] a long; (*groß*) tall; **seit l~em** for a long time; ● adv **eine Stunde l~** for an hour; **mein Leben l~** all my life. **l~ärmelig** a long-sleeved. **l~atmig** a long-winded. **l~e** adv a long time; <*schlafen*> late; **schon l~e** [for] a long time; (*zurückliegend*) a long time ago; **l~e nicht** not for a long time; (*bei weitem nicht*) nowhere near

Länge f -, -n length; (*Geog*) longitude; **der L~nach** lengthways

Läng|engrad m degree of longitude. **l~er** a & adv longer; (*längere Zeit*) [for] some time

Langeweile f - boredom; **L~ haben** be bored

lang|fristig a long-term; <*Vorhersage*> long-range. **l~jährig** a long-standing; <*Erfahrung*> long

länglich a oblong; **l~ rund** oval

längs adv & prep (+ *gen/dat*) along; (*der Länge nach*) lengthways

lang|sam a slow. **L~samkeit** f - slowness

längst adv [schon] l~ for a long time; (*zurückliegend*) a long time ago; **l~ nicht** nowhere near

Lang|strecken- pref long-distance; (*Mil, Aviat*) long-range. **l~weilen** vt bore; **sich l~weilen** be bored. **l~weilig** a boring

Lanze f -, -n lance

Lappalie /la'paːliə/ f -, -n trifle

Lappen m -s,- cloth; (*Anat*) lobe

Lärche f -, -n larch

Lärm m -s noise. **l~end** a noisy

Larve /'larfə/ f -, -n larva; (*Maske*) mask

lasch a listless; (*schlaff*) limp

Lasche f -, -n tab, flap

Laser /'leː-, 'laːzɐ/ m -s,- laser

lassen†

● *transitive verb*

····▸ (+ *inf; veranlassen*) etw tun lassen
have *or* get sth done. **jdn etw tun
lassen** make s.o. do sth.; get s.o. to
do sth. **sich** *dat* **die Haare schneiden
lassen** have *or* get one's hair cut. **jdn
warten lassen** make *or* let s.o. wait;
keep s.o. waiting. **jdn grüßen lassen**
send one's regards to s.o. **jdn
kommen/rufen lassen** send for s.o.

····▸ (+ *inf; erlauben*) let; allow;
(*hineinlassen/herauslassen*) let *or*
allow (**in** + *acc* into, **aus** + *dat* out
of). **jdn etw tun lassen** let s.o. do sth;
allow s.o. to do sth. **er ließ mich nicht
ausreden** he didn't let me finish
[what I was saying]

····▸ (*belassen, bleiben lassen*) leave.
jdn in Frieden lassen leave s.o. in
peace. **etw ungesagt lassen** leave sth
unsaid

····▸ (*unterlassen*) stop. **das Rauchen
lassen** stop smoking. **er kann es
nicht lassen, sie zu quälen** he can't
stop *or* he is forever tormenting her

····▸ (*überlassen*) jdm etw lassen let s.o.
have sth

····▸ (*als Aufforderung*) lass/lasst uns
gehen/fahren! let's go!

● *reflexive verb*

····▸ **das lässt sich machen** that can be
done. **das lässt sich nicht beweisen** it
can't be proved. **die Tür lässt sich
leicht öffnen** the door opens easily

● *intransitive verb*

····▸ 🔲 **Lass mal. Ich mache das schon**
Leave it. I'll do it

lässig *a* casual. **L~keit** *f* -
casualness

Lasso *nt* -s, -s lasso

Last *f* -, -en load; (*Gewicht*) weight;
(*fig*) burden; **L~en** charges; (*Steuern*)
taxes. **L~auto** *nt* lorry. **l~en** *vi*
(*haben*) weigh heavily/(*liegen*) rest
(**auf** + *dat* on)

Laster¹ *m* -s,- 🔲 lorry

Laster² *nt* -s,- vice

läster|n *vt* blaspheme ● *vi* (*haben*)
make disparaging remarks (**über** +
acc about). **L~ung** *f* -, -en
blasphemy

lästig *a* troublesome; **l~ sein/werden**
be/become a nuisance

Last|kahn *m* barge.
L~[kraft]wagen *m* lorry

Latein *nt* -[s] Latin. **L~amerika** *nt*
Latin America. **l~isch** *a* Latin

Laterne *f* -, -n lantern; (*Straßen-*)
street lamp. **L~npfahl** *m* lamp-post

latschen *vi* (*sein*) 🔲 traipse

Latte *f* -, -n slat; (*Tor-, Hoch-
sprung-*) bar

Latz *m* -es,-̈e bib

Lätzchen *nt* -s,- [baby's] bib

Latzhose *f* dungarees *pl*

Laub *nt* -[e]s leaves *pl*; (*L~werk*)
foliage. **L~baum** *m* deciduous tree

Laube *f* -, -n summer-house

Laub|säge *f* fretsaw. **L~wald** *m*
deciduous forest

Lauch *m* -[e]s leeks *pl*

Lauer *f* auf der **L~ liegen** lie in wait.
l~n *vi* (*haben*) lurk; **l~n auf** (+ *acc*)
lie in wait for

Lauf *m* -[e]s, Läufe run; (*Laufen*)
running; (*Verlauf*) course; (*Wett-*)
race; (*Sport: Durchgang*) heat;
(*Gewehr-*) barrel; **im L~[e]** (+ *gen*) in
the course of. **L~bahn** *f* career.
l~en† *vi* (*sein*) run; (*zu Fuß gehen*)
walk; (*gelten*) be valid; **Ski/
Schlittschuh l~en** ski/skate. **l~end**
a running; (*gegenwärtig*) current;
(*regelmäßig*) regular; **auf dem
L~enden sein** be up to date ● *adv*
continually

Läufer *m* -s,- (*Person, Teppich*)
runner; (*Schach*) bishop

Lauf|gitter *nt* play-pen.
L~masche *f* ladder. **L~zettel** *m*
circular

Lauge *f* -, -n soapy water

Laun|e *f* -, -n mood; (*Einfall*) whim;
guter L~e sein, gute L~e haben be
in a good mood. **l~isch** *a* moody

Laus *f* -,Läuse louse; (*Blatt-*) greenfly

lauschen *vi* (*haben*) listen

laut a loud; (*geräuschvoll*) noisy; l~ lesen read aloud; l~er stellen turn up ● *prep* (+ *gen/dat*) according to. L~ *m* -es, -e sound

Laute f -, -n (*Mus*) lute

lauten vi (*haben*) <*Text:*> run, read

läuten vt/i (*haben*) ring

lauter a pure; (*ehrlich*) honest; <*Wahrheit*> plain ● a inv sheer; (*nichts als*) nothing but

laut|hals adv at the top of one's voice, <*lachen*> out loud. l~los a silent, <*Stille*> hushed. L~schrift f phonetics pl. L~sprecher m loudspeaker. L~stärke f volume

lauwarm a lukewarm

Lava f -, -ven lava

Lavendel m -s lavender

lavieren vi (*haben*) manœuvre

Lawine f -, -n avalanche

Lazarett nt -[e]s, -e military hospital

leasen /'li:sən/ vt rent

Lebehoch nt cheer

leben vt/i (*haben*) live (von on); leb wohl! farewell! L~ nt -s,- life, (*Treiben*) bustle; am L~ alive. l~d a living

lebendig a live; (*lebhaft*) lively; (*anschaulich*) vivid; l~ sein be alive. L~keit f - liveliness; vividness

Lebens|abend m old age. L~alter nt age. l~fähig a viable. L~gefahr f mortal danger; in L~gefahr in mortal danger; <*Patient*> critically ill. l~gefährlich a extremely dangerous; <*Verletzung*> critical. L~haltungskosten pl cost of living sg. l~länglich a life ... ● adv for life. L~lauf m curriculum vitae. L~mittel ntpl food sg. L~mittelgeschäft nt food shop. L~mittelhändler m grocer. L~retter m rescuer; (*beim Schwimmen*) life-guard. L~unterhalt m livelihood; seinen L~unterhalt verdienen earn one's living. L~versicherung f life assurance. L~wandel m conduct. l~wichtig a vital. L~zeit f auf L~zeit for life

Leber f -, -n liver. L~fleck m mole

Lebe|wesen nt living being. L~wohl nt -s, -s & -e farewell

leb|haft a lively; <*Farbe*> vivid. L~kuchen m gingerbread. l~los a lifeless. L~zeiten fpl zu jds L~zeiten in s.o.'s lifetime

leck a leaking. L~ nt -s, -s leak. l~en¹ vi (*haben*) leak

lecken² vi (*haben*) lick

lecker a tasty. L~ bissen m delicacy

Leder nt -s,- leather

ledig a single

leer a empty; (*unbesetzt*) vacant; l~ laufen (*Auto*) idle. l~en vt empty; sich l~en empty. L~lauf m (*Auto*) neutral. L~ung f -, -en (*Post*) collection

legal a legal. l~isieren vt legalize. L~ität f - legality

Legas|thenie f - dyslexia. L~theniker m -s,- dyslexic

legen vt put; (*hin-, ver-*) lay; set <*Haare*>; sich l~ lie down; (*nachlassen*) subside

Legende f -, -n legend

leger /le'ʒe:ɐ̯/ a casual

Legierung f -, -en alloy

Legion f -, -en legion

Legislative f - legislature

legitim a legitimate. L~ität f - legitimacy

Lehm m -s clay

Lehn|e f -, -n (*Rücken-*) back; (*Arm-*) arm. l~en vt lean (an + *acc* against); sich l~en lean (an + *acc* against) ● vi (*haben*) be leaning (an + *acc* against)

Lehr|buch nt textbook. L~e f -, -n apprenticeship; (*Anschauung*) doctrine; (*Theorie*) theory; (*Wissenschaft*) science; (*Erfahrung*) lesson. l~en vt/i (*haben*) teach. L~er m -s,- teacher; (*Fahr-*) instructor. L~erin f -, -nen teacher. L~erzimmer nt staff-room. L~fach nt (*Sch*) subject. L~gang m course. L~kraft f teacher. L~ling m -s, -e apprentice; (*Auszubildender*) trainee. L~plan m

syllabus. **l∼reich** *a* instructive.
L∼stelle *f* apprenticeship.
L∼stuhl *m* (*Univ*) chair. **L∼zeit** *f*
apprenticeship

Leib *m* -es, -er body; (*Bauch*) belly.
L∼eserziehung *f* (*Sch*) physical
education. **L∼gericht** *nt* favourite
dish. **l∼lich** *a* physical;
(*blutsverwandt*) real, natural.
L∼wächter *m* bodyguard

Leiche *f* -, -n [dead] body; corpse.
L∼nbestatter *m* -s,- undertaker.
L∼nhalle *f* mortuary. **L∼nwagen**
m hearse. **L∼nzug** *m* funeral
procession, cortège

Leichnam *m* -s, -e [dead] body

leicht *a* light; <*Stoff*> lightweight;
(*gering*) slight; (*mühelos*) easy; **jdm**
l∼ fallen be easy for s.o.; **etw l∼**
machen make sth easy (**dat** for); **es**
sich (*dat*) **l∼ machen** take the easy
way out; **etw l∼ nehmen** (*fig*) take
sth lightly. **L∼athletik** *f* [track and
field] athletics *sg*. **L∼gewicht** *nt*
(*Boxen*) lightweight. **l∼gläubig** *a*
gullible. **l∼hin** *adv* casually.
L∼igkeit *f* - lightness;
(*Mühelosigkeit*) ease; (*L∼sein*)
easiness; **mit L∼igkeit** with ease.
L∼sinn *m* carelessness;
recklessness; (*Frivolität*) frivolity.
l∼sinnig *a* careless; (*unvorsichtig*)
reckless

Leid *nt* -[e]s sorrow, grief; (*Böses*)
harm; **es tut mir L∼ I** am sorry; **er**
tut mir L∼ I feel sorry for him. **l∼** *a*
jdn/etw l∼ sein/werden be/get tired
of s.o./sth

Leide|form *f* passive. **l∼n†** *vt/i*
(*haben*) suffer (**an** + *dat* from); **jdn/**
etw nicht l∼n können dislike s.o./sth.
L∼n *nt* -s,- suffering; (*Med*)
complaint; (*Krankheit*) disease.
l∼nd *a* suffering. **L∼nschaft** *f* -,
-en passion. **l∼nschaftlich** *a*
passionate

leider *adv* unfortunately; **l∼er ja/**
nicht I'm afraid so/not

Leier|kasten *m* barrel-organ. **l∼n**
vt/i (*haben*) wind; (*herunter-*) drone
out

Leih|e *f* -, -n loan. **l∼en†** *vt* lend;
sich (*dat*) **etw l∼en** borrow sth.
L∼gabe *f* loan. **L∼gebühr** *f*
rental; lending charge. **L∼haus** *nt*
pawnshop. **L∼wagen** *m* hire-car.
l∼weise *adv* on loan

Leim *m* -s glue. **l∼en** *vt* glue

Leine *f* -, -n rope; (*Wäsche-*) line;
(*Hunde-*) lead, leash

Lein|en *nt* -s linen. **L∼wand** *f*
linen; (*Kunst*) canvas; (*Film-*) screen

leise *a* quiet; <*Stimme, Berührung*>
soft; (*schwach*) faint; (*leicht*) light;
l∼r stellen turn down

Leiste *f* -, -n strip; (*Holz-*) batten;
(*Anat*) groin

leist|en *vt* achieve, accomplish; **sich**
(*dat*) **etw l∼en** treat oneself to sth;
(**!** *anstellen*) get up to sth; **ich kann**
es mir nicht l∼en I can't afford it.
L∼ung *f* -, -en achievement; (*Sport,*
Techn) performance; (*Produktion*)
output; (*Zahlung*) payment

Leit|artikel *m* leader, editorial.
l∼en *vt* run, manage; (*an-/*
hinführen) lead; (*Mus, Techn, Phys*)
conduct; (*lenken, schicken*) direct.
l∼end *a* leading; <*Posten*>
executive

Leiter¹ *f* -, -n ladder

Leit|er² *m* -s,- director; (*Comm*)
manager; (*Führer*) leader; (*Mus,*
Phys) conductor. **L∼erin** *f* -, -nen
director; manageress; leader.
L∼planke *f* crash barrier.
L∼spruch *m* motto. **L∼ung** *f* -, -en
(*Führung*) direction; (*Comm*)
management; (*Aufsicht*) control;
(*Electr: Schnur*) lead, flex; (*Kabel*)
cable; (*Telefon-*) line; (*Rohr-*) pipe;
(*Haupt-*) main. **L∼ungswasser** *nt*
tap water

Lektion /-'tsːioːn/ *f* -, -en lesson

Lekt|or *m* -s, -en /-'toːrən/, **L∼orin** *f*
-, -nen (*Univ*) assistant lecturer;
(*Verlags-*) editor. **L∼üre** *f* -, -n
reading matter

Lende *f* -, -n loin

lenk|en *vt* guide; (*steuern*) steer;
(*regeln*) control; **jds Aufmerksamkeit**
auf sich (*acc*) **l∼en** attract s.o.'s
attention. **L∼rad** *nt* steering-wheel.

L∼stange f handlebars pl. **L∼ung** f - steering

Leopard m -en, -en leopard

Lepra f - leprosy

Lerche f -, -n lark

lernen vt/i (haben) learn; (für die Schule) study

Lesbierin /'lɛsbiərɪn/ f -, -nen lesbian. **l∼isch** a lesbian

les|en† vt/i (haben) read; (Univ) lecture ● vt pick, gather. **L∼en** nt -s reading. **L∼er(in)** m -s,- (f -, -nen) reader. **l∼erlich** a legible. **L∼ezeichen** nt bookmark

lethargisch a lethargic

Lettland nt -s Latvia

letzt|e(r,s) a last; (neueste) latest; in **l∼er Zeit** recently; **l∼en Endes** in the end. **l∼ens** adv recently; (zuletzt) lastly. **l∼ere(r,s)** a the latter; **der/die/das L∼ere** the latter

Leucht|e f -, -n light. **l∼en** vi (haben) shine. **l∼end** a shining. **L∼er** m -s,- candlestick. **L∼feuer** nt beacon. **L∼rakete** f flare. **L∼reklame** f neon sign. **L∼röhre** f fluorescent tube. **L∼turm** m lighthouse

leugnen vt deny

Leukämie f - leukaemia

Leumund m -s reputation

Leute pl people; (Mil) men; (Arbeiter) workers

Leutnant m -s, -s second lieutenant

Lexikon nt -s, -ka encyclopaedia; (Wörterbuch) dictionary

Libanon (der) -s Lebanon

Libelle f -, -n dragonfly

liberal a (Pol) Liberal

Libyen nt -s Libya

Licht nt -[e]s, -er light; (Kerze) candle; **L∼ machen** turn on the light. **l∼** a bright; (Med) lucid; (spärlich) sparse. **L∼bild** nt [passport] photograph; (Dia) slide. **L∼blick** m (fig) ray of hope. **l∼en** vt thin out; **den Anker l∼en** (Naut) weigh anchor; **sich l∼en** become less dense; thin. **L∼hupe** f headlight flasher; **die L∼hupe betätigen** flash

one's headlights. **L∼maschine** f dynamo. **L∼ung** f -, -en clearing

Lid nt -[e]s, -er [eye]lid. **L∼schatten** m eye-shadow

lieb a dear; (nett) nice; (artig) good; **jdn l∼ haben** be fond of s.o.; (lieben) love s.o.; **es wäre mir l∼er** I should prefer it (wenn if)

Liebe f -, -n love. **l∼n** vt love; (mögen) like; **sich l∼n** love each other; (körperlich) make love. **l∼nd** a loving. **l∼nswert** a lovable. **l∼nswürdig** a kind. **l∼nswürdigerweise** adv very kindly

lieber adv rather; (besser) better; **l∼ mögen** like better; **ich trinke l∼ Tee** I prefer tea

Liebes|brief m love letter. **L∼dienst** m favour. **L∼kummer** m heartache. **L∼paar** nt [pair of] lovers pl

lieb|evoll a loving, affectionate. **L∼haber** m -s,- lover; (Sammler) collector. **L∼haberei** f -, -en hobby. **L∼kosung** f -, -en caress. **l∼lich** a lovely; (sanft) gentle; (süß) sweet. **L∼ling** m -s, -e darling; (Bevorzugte) favourite. **L∼lings-** pref favourite. **l∼los** a loveless; <Eltern> uncaring; (unfreundlich) unkind. **L∼schaft** f -, -en [love] affair. **l∼ste(r,s)** a dearest; (bevorzugt) favourite ● adv **am l∼sten** best [of all]; **jdn/etw am l∼sten mögen** like s.o./sth best [of all]. **L∼ste(r)** m/f beloved; (Schatz) sweetheart

Lied nt -[e]s, -er song

liederlich a slovenly; (unordentlich) untidy. **L∼keit** f - slovenliness; untidiness

Lieferant m -en, -en supplier

liefer|bar a (Comm) available. **l∼n** vt supply; (zustellen) deliver; (hervorbringen) yield. **L∼ung** f -, -en delivery; (Sendung) consignment

Liege f -, -n couch. **l∼n**† vi (haben) lie; (gelegen sein) be situated; **l∼n bleiben** remain lying [there]; (im Bett) stay in bed; <Ding:> be left; <Schnee:> settle; <Arbeit:> remain undone; (*zurückgelassen werden*) be left behind; **l~n lassen** leave; (*zurücklassen*) leave behind; (*nicht fortführen*) leave undone; **l~n an** (+ *dat*) (*fig*) be due to; (*abhängen*) depend on; **jdm [nicht] l~n** [not] suit s.o.; **mir liegt viel daran** it is very important to me. **L~stuhl** *m* deck-chair. **L~stütz** *m* -es, -e press-up, (*Amer*) push-up. **L~wagen** *m* couchette car

Lift *m* -[e]s, -e & -s lift

Liga *f* -, -gen league

Likör *m* -s, -e liqueur

lila *inv a* mauve; (*dunkel*) purple

Lilie /'li:liə/ *f* -, -n lily

Liliputaner(in) *m* -s,- (*f* -, -nen) dwarf

Limo *f* -, -[s] [!], **L~nade** *f* -, -n fizzy drink; lemonade

Limousine /limu'zi:nə/ *f* -, -n saloon

lind *a* mild

Linde *f* -, -n lime tree

linder|n *vt* relieve, ease. **L~ung** *f* - relief

Lineal *nt* -s, -e ruler

Linie /-iə/ *f* -, -n line; (*Zweig*) branch; (*Bus-*) route; **L~ 4** number 4 [bus/ tram]; **in erster L~** primarily. **L~nflug** *m* scheduled flight. **L~nrichter** *m* linesman

lin[i]iert *a* lined, ruled

Link|e *f* -n, -n left side; (*Hand*) left hand; (*Boxen*) left; **die L~e** (*Pol*) the left. **l~e(r,s)** *a* left; (*Pol*) leftwing; **l~e Masche** purl

links *adv* on the left; (*bei Stoff*) on the wrong side; (*verkehrt*) inside out; **l~ stricken** purl. **L~händer(in)** *m* -s,- (*f* -, -nen) lefthander. **l~händig** *a* & *adv* lefthanded

Linoleum /-leʊm/ *nt* -s lino, linoleum

Linse *f* -, -n lens; (*Bot*) lentil

Lippe *f* -, -n lip. **L~nstift** *m* lipstick

Liquid|ation /-'ts:io:n/ *f* -, -en liquidation. **l~ieren** *vt* liquidate

lispeln *vt*/*i* (*haben*) lisp

List *f* -, -en trick, ruse

Liste *f* -, -n list

listig *a* cunning, crafty

Litanei *f* -, -en litany

Litauen *nt* -s Lithuania

Liter *m* & *nt* -s,- litre

Literatur *f* - literature

Liturgie *f* -, -n liturgy

Litze *f* -, -n braid

Lizenz *f* -, -en licence

Lob *nt* -[e]s praise

Lobby /'lɔbi/ *f* - (*Pol*) lobby

loben *vt* praise

löblich *a* praiseworthy

Lobrede *f* eulogy

Loch *nt* -[e]s, ̈er hole. **l~en** *vt* punch a hole/holes in; punch <*Fahrkarte*>. **L~er** *m* -s,- punch

löcherig *a* full of holes

Locke *f* -, -n curl. **l~n¹** *vt* curl; **sich l~n** curl

locken² *vt* lure, entice; (*reizen*) tempt. **l~d** *a* tempting

Lockenwickler *m* -s,- curler; (*Rolle*) roller

locker *a* loose; <*Seil*> slack; <*Erde*> light; (*zwanglos*) casual; (*zu frei*) lax. **l~n** *vt* loosen; slacken <*Seil*>; break up <*Boden*>; relax <*Griff*>; **sich l~n** become loose; <*Seil*> slacken; (*sich entspannen*) relax

lockig *a* curly

Lockmittel *nt* bait

Loden *m* -s (*Tex*) loden

Löffel *m* -s,- spoon; (*L~ voll*) spoonful. **l~n** *vt* spoon up

Logarithmus *m* -, -men logarithm

Logbuch *nt* (*Naut*) log-book

Loge /'lo:ʒə/ *f* -, -n lodge; (*Theat*) box

Log|ik *f* - logic. **l~isch** *a* logical

Logo *nt* -s, -s logo

Lohn *m* -[e]s, ̈e wages *pl*, pay; (*fig*) reward. **L~empfänger** *m* wage-earner. **l~en** *vi*/*r* (*haben*) [sich] **l~en** be worth it *or* worth while ● *vt* be worth. **l~end** *a* worthwhile; (*befriedigend*) rewarding. **L~erhöhung** *f* [pay] rise. **L~steuer** *f* income tax

Lok *f* -, -s [!] = **Lokomotive**

Lokal *nt* -s, -e restaurant; (*Trink-*) bar

Lokomotiv|e *f* -, -n engine, locomotive. **L~führer** *m* engine driver

London *nt* -s London. **L~er** *a* London ... ● *m* -s,- Londoner

Lorbeer *m* -s, -en laurel. **L~blatt** *nt* (*Culin*) bay-leaf

Lore *f* -, -n (*Rail*) truck

Los *nt* -es, -e lot; (*Lotterie-*) ticket; (*Schicksal*) fate

los *pred a* los sein be loose; jdn/etw los sein be rid of s.o./sth; was ist [mit ihm] los? what's the matter [with him]? ● *adv* los! go on! Achtung, fertig, los! ready, steady, go!

lösbar *a* soluble

losbinden† *vt sep* untie

Lösch|blatt *nt* sheet of blotting-paper. **l~en** *vt* put out, extinguish; quench <*Durst*>; blot <*Tinte*>; (*tilgen*) cancel; (*streichen*) delete

Löschfahrzeug *nt* fire-engine

lose *a* loose

Lösegeld *nt* ransom

losen *vt* (*haben*) draw lots (um for)

lösen *vt* undo; (*lockern*) loosen; (*entfernen*) detach; (*klären*) solve; (*auflösen*) dissolve; cancel <*Vertrag*>; break off <*Beziehung*>; (*kaufen*) buy; sich l~ come off; (*sich trennen*) detach oneself/itself; (*lose werden*) come undone; (*sich klären*) resolve itself; (*sich auflösen*) dissolve

los|fahren† *vi sep* (*sein*) start; <*Auto:*> drive off; **l~fahren auf** (+ *acc*) head for. **l~gehen†** *vi sep* (*sein*) set off; (🆒 *anfangen*) start; <*Bombe:*> go off; **l~gehen auf** (+ *acc*) head for; (*fig: angreifen*) go for. **l~kommen†** *vi sep* (*sein*) get away (von from). **l~lassen†** *vt sep* let go of; (*freilassen*) release

löslich *a* soluble

los|lösen *vt sep* detach; sich l~lösen become detached; (*fig*) break away (von from). **l~machen** *vt sep* detach; untie. **l~reißen†** *vt sep* tear off; sich l~reißen break free; (*fig*) tear oneself away. **l~schicken** *vt*

sep send off. **l~sprechen†** *vt sep* absolve (**von** from)

Losung *f* -, -en (*Pol*) slogan; (*Mil*) password

Lösung *f* -, -en solution. **L~smittel** *nt* solvent

loswerden† *vt sep* get rid of

Lot *nt* -[e]s, -e perpendicular; (*Blei-*) plumb[-bob]. **l~en** *vt* plumb

löt|en *vt* solder. **L~lampe** *f* blow-lamp

lotrecht *a* perpendicular

Lotse *m* -n, -n (*Naut*) pilot. **l~n** *vt* (*Naut*) pilot; (*fig*) guide

Lotterie *f* -, -n lottery

Lotto *nt* -s, -s lotto; (*Lotterie*) lottery

Löw|e *m* -n, -n lion; (*Astr*) Leo. **L~enzahn** *m* (*Bot*) dandelion. **L~in** *f* -, -nen lioness

loyal /loa'ja:l/ *a* loyal. **L~ität** *f* - loyalty

Luchs *m* -es, -e lynx

Lücke *f* -, -n gap. **l~nhaft** *a* incomplete; <*Wissen*> patchy. **l~nlos** *a* complete; <*Folge*> unbroken

Luder *nt* -s,- ✖ (*Frau*) bitch

Luft *f* -,⁼e air; tief L~ holen take a deep breath; in die L~ gehen explode. **L~angriff** *m* air raid. **L~aufnahme** *f* aerial photograph. **L~ballon** *m* balloon. **L~blase** *f* air bubble. **L~druck** *m* atmospheric pressure

lüften *vt* air; raise <*Hut*>; reveal <*Geheimnis*>

Luft|fahrt *f* aviation. **L~fahrtgesellschaft** *f* airline. **L~gewehr** *nt* airgun. **l~ig** *a* airy; <*Kleid*> light. **L~kissenfahrzeug** *nt* hovercraft. **L~krieg** *m* aerial warfare. **l~leer** *a* **l~leerer Raum** vacuum. **L~linie** *f* 100 km **L~linie** 100 km as the crow flies. **L~matratze** *f* air-bed, inflatable mattress. **L~pirat** *m* hijacker. **L~post** *f* airmail. **L~röhre** *f* windpipe. **L~schiff** *nt* airship. **L~schlange** *f* [paper] streamer. **L~schutzbunker** *m* air-raid shelter

Lüftung f - ventilation

Luft|veränderung f change of air.
L~waffe f air force. **L~zug** m
draught

Lüg|e f -, -n lie. **l~en†** vt/i (haben)
lie. **L~ner(in)** m -s,- (f -, -nen) liar.
l~nerisch a untrue; <Person>
untruthful

Luke f -, -n hatch; (Dach-) skylight

Lümmel m -s,- lout

Lump m -en, -en scoundrel. **L~en** m
-s,- rag; in **L~en** in rags.
L~enpack nt riff-raff.
L~ensammler m rag-and-bone
man. **l~ig** a mean, shabby

Lunge f -, -n lungs pl; (L~nflügel)
lung. **L~nentzündung** f
pneumonia

Lupe f -, -n magnifying glass

Lurch m -[e]s, -e amphibian

Lust f -,̈-e pleasure; (Verlangen)
desire; (sinnliche Begierde) lust; **L~**
haben feel like (**auf etw** acc sth); **ich**
habe keine L~ I don't feel like it;
(will nicht) I don't want to

lustig a jolly; (komisch) funny; **sich**
l~ machen über (+ acc) make fun of

Lüstling m -s, -e lecher

lust|los a listless. **L~mörder** m
sex killer. **L~spiel** nt comedy

lutsch|en vt/i (haben) suck. **L~er**
m -s,- lollipop

Lüttich nt -s Liège

Luv f & nt - nach Luv (Naut) to
windward

luxuriös a luxurious

Luxus m - luxury

Lymph|drüse /ˈlʏmf-/ f,
L~knoten m lymph gland

lynchen /ˈlʏnçən/ vt lynch

Lyr|ik f - lyric poetry. **L~iker** m -s,-
lyric poet. **l~isch** a lyrical

Mm

Machart f style

machen

● transitive verb

····▸ (herstellen, zubereiten) make
<money, beds, music, exception, etc>.
aus Plastik/Holz gemacht made of
plastic/wood. **sich** (dat) **etw machen**
lassen have sth made. **etw aus jdm**
machen make s.o. into sth. **jdn zum**
Präsidenten machen make s.o.
president. **er machte sich** (dat) **viele**
Freunde/Feinde he made a lot of
friends/enemies. **jdm/sich** (dat)
[einen] Kaffee machen make [some]
coffee for s.o./oneself. **ein Foto**
machen take a photo

····▸ (verursachen) make, cause
<difficulties>; cause <pain, anxiety>.
jdm Arbeit machen make [extra]
work for s.o., cause s.o. extra work.
jdm Mut/Hoffnung machen give s.o.
courage/hope. **das macht Hunger/**
Durst this makes you hungry/
thirsty. **das macht das Wetter** that's
[because of] the weather

····▸ (ausführen, ordnen) do <job,
repair 🖪: room, washing, etc.>.; take
<walk, trip, exam, course>. **sie**
machte mir die Haare 🖪 she did my
hair for me. **einen Besuch [bei jdm]**
machen pay [s.o.] a visit

····▸ (tun) do <nothing, everything>.
was machst du [da]? what are you
doing? **so etwas macht man nicht**
that [just] isn't done

····▸ **was macht ...?** (wie ist es um ...
bestellt?) how is ...? **was macht die**
Gesundheit/Arbeit? how are you
keeping/how is the job [getting on]?

····▸ (Math: ergeben) be. **zwei mal zwei**
macht vier two times two is four. **das**
macht 6 Mark [zusammen] that's or
that comes to six marks [altogether]

····► (*schaden*) **was macht das schon?**
what does it matter? **[das] macht
nichts!** 🛈 it doesn't matter

····► **machs gut!** 🛈 look after yourself!;
(*auf Wiedersehen*) so long!

● *reflexive verb*

····► **sich machen** 🛈 do well

····► **sich an etw** (*acc*) **machen** get down
to sth. **sie machte sich an die Arbeit**
she got down to work

● *intransitive verb*

····► **das macht hungrig/durstig** it
makes you hungry/thirsty. **das
macht dick** it's fattening

Macht *f* -,-̈e power. **M~haber** *m* -s,-
ruler

mächtig *a* powerful ● *adv* 🛈
terribly

machtlos *a* powerless

Mädchen *nt* -s,- girl; (*Dienst-*) maid.
m~haft *a* girlish. **M~name** *m*
girl's name; (*vor der Ehe*) maiden
name

Made *f* -, -n maggot

madig *a* maggoty

Madonna *f* -, -nen madonna

Magazin *nt* -s, -e magazine; (*Lager*)
warehouse; store-room

Magd *f* -,-̈e maid

Magen *m* -s,-̈ stomach.
M~verstimmung *f* stomach upset

mager *a* thin; <*Fleisch*> lean;
<*Boden*> poor; (*dürftig*) meagre.
M~keit *f* - thinness; leanness.
M~sucht *f* anorexia

Magie *f* - magic

Mag|ier /'ma:giɐ/ *m* -s,- magician.
m~isch *a* magic

Magistrat *m* -s, -e city council

Magnet *m* -en & -[e]s, -e magnet.
m~isch *a* magnetic

Mahagoni *nt* -s mahogany

Mäh|drescher *m* -s,- combine
harvester. **m~en** *vt/i* (*haben*) mow

Mahl *nt* -[e]s,-̈er & -e meal

mahlen† *vt* grind

Mahlzeit *f* meal; **M~!** enjoy your
meal!

Mähne *f* -, -n mane

mahn|en *vt/i* (*haben*) remind
(*wegen* about); (*ermahnen*)
admonish; (*auffordern*) urge (**zu** to).
M~ung *f* -, -en reminder;
admonition

Mai *m* -[e]s, -e May; **der Erste Mai**
May Day. **M~glöckchen** *nt* -s,-
lily of the valley

Mailand *nt* -s Milan

Mais *m* -es maize; (*Culin*) sweet corn

Majestät *f* -, -en majesty. **m~isch**
a majestic

Major *m* -s, -e major

Majoran *m* -s marjoram

makaber *a* macabre

Makel *m* -s,- blemish; (*Defekt*) flaw

Makkaroni *pl* macaroni *sg*

Makler *m* -s,- (*Comm*) broker

Makrele *f* -, -n mackerel

Makrone *f* -, -n macaroon

mal *adv* (*Math*) times; (*bei Maßen*)
by; (🛈 *einmal*) once; (*eines Tages*)
one day; **nicht mal** not even

Mal *nt* -[e]s, -e time; **zum ersten/
letzten Mal** for the first/last time; **ein
für alle Mal** once and for all; **jedes
Mal** every time; **jedes Mal, wenn**
whenever

Mal|buch *nt* colouring book.
m~en *vt/i* (*haben*) paint. **M~er** *m*
-s,- painter. **M~erei** *f* -, -en
painting. **M~erin** *f* -, -nen painter.
m~erisch *a* picturesque

Mallorca /ma'lɔrka, -'jɔrka/ *nt* -s
Majorca

malnehmen† *vt sep* multiply (**mit**
by)

Malz *nt* -es malt

Mama /'mama, ma'ma:/ *f* -s, -s
mummy

Mammut *nt* -s, -e & -s mammoth

mampfen *vt* 🛈 munch

man *pron* one, you; (*die Leute*)
people, they; **man sagt** they say, it is
said

manch|e(r,s) *pron* many a; [*so*]
m~es Mal many a time; **m~e Leute**
some people ● (*substantivisch*)
m~er/m~e many a man/woman;
m~e *pl* some; (*Leute*) some people;
(*viele*) many [people]; **m~es** some

things; (*vieles*) many things.
m~erlei *inv a* various ● *pron* various things

manchmal *adv* sometimes

Mandant(in) *m* -en, -en (*f* -, -nen) (*Jur*) client

Mandarine *f* -, -n mandarin

Mandat *nt* -[e]s, -e mandate; (*Jur*) brief; (*Pol*) seat

Mandel *f* -, -n almond; (*Anat*) tonsil. **M~entzündung** *f* tonsillitis

Manege /ma'ne:ʒə/ *f* -, -n ring; (*Reit-*) arena

Mangel[1] *m* -s,⸚ lack; (*Knappheit*) shortage; (*Med*) deficiency; (*Fehler*) defect

Mangel[2] *f* -, -n mangle

mangel|haft *a* faulty, defective; (*Sch*) unsatisfactory. **m~n**[1] *vi* (*haben*) **es m~t an** (+ *dat*) there is a lack/(*Knappheit*) shortage of

mangeln[2] *vt* put through the mangle

Manie *f* -, -n mania

Manier *f* -, -en manner; **M~en** manners. **m~lich** *a* well-mannered ● *adv* properly

Manifest *nt* -[e]s, -e manifesto

Maniküre *f* -, -n manicure; (*Person*) manicurist. **m~n** *vt* manicure

Manko *nt* -s, -s disadvantage; (*Fehlbetrag*) deficit

Mann *m* -[e]s,⸚er man; (*Ehe-*) husband

Männchen *nt* -s,- little man; (*Zool*) male

Mannequin /'manəkɛ̃/ *nt* -s, -s model

männlich *a* male; (*Gram & fig*) masculine; (*mannhaft*) manly; <*Frau*> mannish. **M~keit** *f* - masculinity; (*fig*) manhood

Mannschaft *f* -, -en team; (*Naut*) crew

Manöv|er *nt* -s,- manœuvre; (*Winkelzug*) trick. **m~rieren** *vt/i* (*haben*) manœuvre

Mansarde *f* -, -n attic room; (*Wohnung*) attic flat

Manschette *f* -, -n cuff. **M~nknopf** *m* cuff-link

Mantel *m* -s,⸚ coat; overcoat

Manuskript *nt* -[e]s, -e manuscript

Mappe *f* -, -n folder; (*Akten-*) briefcase; (*Schul-*) bag

Märchen *nt* -s,- fairy-tales

Margarine *f* - margarine

Marienkäfer /ma'ri:ən-/ *m* lady-bird

Marihuana *nt* -s marijuana

Marine *f* marine; (*Kriegs-*) navy. **m~blau** *a* navy [blue]

marinieren *vt* marinade

Marionette *f* -, -n puppet, marionette

Mark[1] *f* -,- mark; **drei M~** three marks

Mark[2] *nt* -[e]s (*Knochen-*) marrow (*Bot*)pith; (*Frucht-*) pulp

markant *a* striking

Marke *f* -, -n token; (*rund*) disc; (*Erkennungs-*) tag; (*Brief-*) stamp; (*Lebensmittel-*) coupon; (*Spiel-*) counter; (*Markierung*) mark; (*Fabrikat*) make; (*Tabak-*) brand. **M~nartikel** *m* branded article

markieren *vt* mark; (ⅈ *vortäuschen*) fake

Markise *f* -, -n awning

Markstück *nt* one-mark piece

Markt *m* -[e]s,⸚e market; (*M~platz*) market-place. **M~forschung** *f* market research

Marmelade *f* -, -n jam; (*Orangen-*) marmalade

Marmor *m* -s marble

Marokko *nt* -s Morocco

Marone *f* -, -n [sweet] chestnut

Marsch *m* -[e]s,⸚e march. **m~** *int* (*Mil*) march!

Marschall *m* -s,⸚e marshal

marschieren *vi* (*sein*) march

Marter *f* -, -n torture. **m~n** *vt* torture

Märtyrer(in) *m* -s,- (*f* -, -nen) martyr

Marxismus *m* - Marxism

März *m* -, -e March

Marzipan *nt* -s marzipan

---

*alte Schreibung

Masche *f* -, -n stitch; (*im Netz*) mesh; (⊞ *Trick*) dodge. **M~ndraht** *m* wire netting

Maschin|e *f* -, -n machine; (*Flugzeug*) plane; (*Schreib-*) typewriter; **M~e schreiben** type. **m~egeschrieben** *a* typewritten, typed. **m~ell** *a* machine ... ● *adv* by machine. **M~enbau** *m* mechanical engineering. **M~engewehr** *nt* machine-gun. **M~ist** *m* -en, -en machinist; (*Naut*) engineer

Masern *pl* measles *sg*

Maserung *f* -, -en [wood] grain

Maske *f* -, -n mask; (*Theat*) make-up

maskieren *vt* mask; **sich m~** dress up (**als** as)

maskulin *a* masculine

Masochist *m* -en, -en masochist

Maß[1] *nt* -es, -e measure; (*Abmessung*) measurement; (*Grad*) degree; (*Mäßigung*) moderation; **in hohem Maße** to a high degree

Maß[2] *f* -,- (*SGer*) litre [of beer]

Massage /ma'sa:ʒə/ *f* -, -n massage

Massaker *nt* -s,- massacre

Maßband *nt* (*pl* -bänder) tape-measure

Masse *f* -, -n mass; (*Culin*) mixture; (*Menschen-*) crowd; **eine M~ Arbeit** ⊞ masses of work. **m~nhaft** *adv* in huge quantities. **M~nproduktion** *f* mass production. **m~nweise** *adv* in huge numbers

Masseu|r /ma'søːɐ̯/ *m* -s, -e masseur. **M~se** /-'søːzə/ *f* -, -n masseuse

maß|gebend *a* authoritative; (*einflussreich*) influential. **m~geblich** *a* decisive. **m~geschneidert** *a* made-to-measure

massieren *vt* massage

massig *a* massive

mäßig *a* moderate; (*mittelmäßig*) indifferent. **m~en** *vt* moderate; **sich m~en** moderate; (*sich beherrschen*) restrain oneself. **M~ung** *f* - moderation

massiv *a* solid; (*stark*) heavy

Maß|krug *m* beer mug. **m~los** *a* excessive; (*grenzenlos*) boundless; (*äußerst*) extreme. **M~nahme** *f* -, -n measure

Maßstab *m* scale; (*Norm & fig*) standard. **m~sgerecht, m~sgetreu** *a* scale ... ● *adv* to scale

Mast[1] *m* -[e]s, -en pole; (*Überland-*) pylon; (*Naut*) mast

Mast[2] *f* - fattening

mästen *vt* fatten

masturbieren *vi* (*haben*) masturbate

Material *nt* -s, -ien /-iən/ material; (*coll*) materials *pl*. **M~ismus** *m* - materialism. **m~istisch** *a* materialistic

Mathe *f* - ⊞ maths *sg*

Mathe|matik *f* - mathematics *sg*. **M~matiker** *m* -s,- mathematician. **m~matisch** *a* mathematical

Matinee *f* -, -n (*Theat*) morning performance

Matratze *f* -, -n mattress

Matrose *m* -n, -n sailor

Matsch *m* -[e]s mud; (*Schnee-*) slush

matt *a* weak; (*gedämpft*) dim; (*glanzlos*) dull; <Politur, Farbe> matt. **M~** *nt* -s (*Schach*) mate

Matte *f* -, -n mat

Mattglas *nt* frosted glass

Matura *f* - (*Aust*) ≈ A levels *pl*

Mauer *f* -, -n wall. **M~werk** *nt* masonry

Maul *nt* -[e]s, Mäuler (*Zool*) mouth; **halts M~!** ⊞ shut up! **M~korb** *m* muzzle. **M~tier** *nt* mule. **M~wurf** *m* mole

Maurer *m* -s,- bricklayer

Maus *f* -, Mäuse mouse

Maut *f* -, -en (*Aust*) toll. **M~straße** *f* toll road

maximal *a* maximum

Maximum *nt* -s, -ma maximum

Mayonnaise /majɔ'nɛːzə/ *f* -, -n mayonnaise

Mechan|ik /me'ça:nɪk/ *f* - mechanics *sg*; (*Mechanismus*) mechanism. **M~iker** *m* -s,-

mechanic. **m~isch** a mechanical.
m~isieren vt mechanize.
M~ismus m -, -men mechanism

meckern vi (haben) bleat; ([🄴]
nörgeln) grumble

Medaille /me'daljə/ f -, -n medal.
M~on /-'jō:/ nt -s, -s medallion
(Schmuck) locket

Medikament nt -[e]s, -e medicine

Meditation /-'ts:io:n/ f -, -en
meditation. **m~ieren** vi (haben)
meditate

Medium nt -s, -ien medium; die
Medien the media

Medizin f -, -en medicine. **M~er** m
-s,- doctor; (Student) medical
student. **m~isch** a medical;
(heilkräftig) medicinal

Meer nt -[e]s, -e sea. **M~busen** m
gulf. **M~enge** f strait.
M~esspiegel m sea-level.
M~jungfrau f mermaid.
M~rettich m horseradish.
M~schweinchen nt -s,- guinea-
pig

Mehl nt -[e]s flour. **M~schwitze** f
(Culin) roux

mehr pron & adv more; nicht m~ no
more; (zeitlich) no longer; nichts m~
no more; (nichtsweiter) nothing else;
nie m~ never again. **m~eres** pron
several things pl. **m~fach** a
multiple; (mehrmalig) repeated
● adv several times.
M~fahrtenkarte f book of tickets.
M~heit f -, -en majority.
m~malig a repeated. **m~mals**
adv several times. **m~sprachig** a
multilingual. **M~wertsteuer** f
value-added tax, VAT. **M~zahl** f
majority; (Gram) plural.
M~zweck- pref multi-purpose

meiden† vt avoid, shun

Meile f -, -n mile. **m~nweit** adv
[for] miles

mein poss pron my. **m~e(r,s)** poss
pron mine; die **M~en** od **m~en** pl
my family sg

Meineid m perjury

meinen vt mean; (glauben) think;
(sagen) say

mein|erseits adv for my part.
m~etwegen adv for my sake;
(wegen mir) because of me; ([🄴] von
mir aus) as far as I'm concerned

Meinung f -, -en opinion; jdm die
M~ sagen give s.o. a piece of one's
mind. **M~sumfrage** f opinion poll

Meise f -, -n (Zool) tit

Meißel m -s,- chisel. **m~n** vt/i
(haben) chisel

meist adv mostly; (gewöhnlich)
usually. **m~e** a der/die/das m~e
most; die **m~en** Leute most people;
am **m~en** [the] most ● pron das
m~e most [of it]; die **m~en** most.
m~ens adv mostly; (gewöhnlich)
usually

Meister m -s,- master craftsman;
(Könner) master; (Sport) champion.
m~n vt master. **M~schaft** f -, -en
mastery; (Sport) championship

meld|en vt report; (anmelden)
register; (ankündigen) announce;
sich m~en report (bei to); (zum
Militär) enlist; (freiwillig) volunteer;
(Teleph) answer; (Sch) put up one's
hand; (von sich hören lassen) get in
touch (bei with). **M~ung** f -, -en
report; (Anmeldung) registration

melken† vt milk

Melodie f -, -n tune, melody

melodisch a melodic; melodious

Melone f -, -n melon

Memoiren /me'mǫa:rən/ pl
memoirs

Menge f -, -n amount, quantity;
(Menschen-) crowd; (Math) set; eine
M~ Geld a lot of money. **m~n** vt
mix

Mensa f -, -sen (Univ) refectory

Mensch m -en, -en human being;
der **M~** man; die **M~en** people;
jeder/kein **M~** everybody/nobody.
M~enaffe m ape.
m~enfeindlich a antisocial.
M~enfresser m -s,- cannibal;
(Zool) man-eater. **m~enfreundlich**
a philanthropic. **M~enleben** nt
human life; (Lebenszeit) lifetime.
m~enleer a deserted.

M∼enmenge *f* crowd. **M∼enraub**
m kidnapping. **M∼enrechte** *ntpl*
human rights. **m∼enscheu** *a*
unsociable. **m∼enwürdig** *a*
humane. **M∼heit** *f* - die M∼heit
mankind, humanity. **m∼lich** *a*
human; (*human*) humane.
M∼lichkeit *f* - humanity

Menstru|ation /-ˈts:io:n/ *f* -
menstruation. **m∼ieren** *vi* (*haben*)
menstruate

Mentalität *f* -, -en mentality

Menü *nt* -s, -s menu; (*festes M∼*) set
meal

Meridian *m* -s, -e meridian

merk|bar *a* noticeable. **M∼blatt** *nt*
[explanatory] leaflet. **m∼en** *vt*
notice; **sich** (*dat*) **etw m∼en**
remember sth. **M∼mal** *nt* feature

merkwürdig *a* odd, strange

Messe[1] *f* -, -n (*Relig*) mass; (*Comm*)
[trade] fair

Messe[2] *f* -, -n (*Mil*) mess

messen† *vt/i* (*haben*) measure;
(*ansehen*) look at; **[bei jdm] Fieber
m∼** take s.o.'s temperature; **sich mit
jdm m∼ können** be a match for s.o.

Messer *nt* -s,- knife

Messias *m* - Messiah

Messing *nt* -s brass

Messung *f* -, -en measurement

Metabolismus *m* - metabolism

Metall *nt* -s, -e metal. **m∼isch** *a*
metallic

Metamorphose *f* -, -n
metamorphosis

metaphorisch *a* metaphorical

Meteor *m* -s, -e meteor. **M∼ologie**
f - meteorology

Meter *m* & *nt* -s,- metre. **M∼maß**
nt tape-measure

Method|e *f* -, -n method. **m∼isch** *a*
methodical

Metropole *f* -, -n metropolis

Metzger *m* -s,- butcher. **M∼ei** *f* -,
-en butcher's shop

Meuterei *f* -, -en mutiny

meutern *vi* (*haben*) mutiny; (⚠
schimpfen) grumble

Mexikan|er(in) *m* -s,- (*f* -, -nen)
Mexican. **m∼isch** *a* Mexican

Mexiko *nt* -s Mexico

miauen *vi* (*haben*) mew, miaow

mich *pron* (*acc of* **ich**) me; (*refl*)
myself

Mieder *nt* -s,- bodice

Miene *f* -, -n expression

mies *a* ⚠ lousy

Miet|e *f* -, -n rent; (*Mietgebühr*) hire
charge; **zur M∼e wohnen** live in
rented accommodation. **m∼en** *vt*
rent <*Haus, Zimmer*>; hire <*Auto,
Boot*>. **M∼er(in)** *m* -s,- (*f* -, -nen)
tenant. **m∼frei** *a* & *adv* rent-free.
M∼shaus *nt* block of rented flats.
M∼vertrag *m* lease. **M∼wagen** *m*
hire-car. **M∼wohnung** *f* rented flat;
(*zu vermieten*) flat to let

Migräne *f* -, -n migraine

Mikro|chip *m* microchip.
M∼computer *m* microcomputer.
M∼film *m* microfilm

Mikro|fon, M∼phon *nt* -s, -e
microphone. **M∼skop** *nt* -s, -e
microscope. **m∼skopisch** *a*
microscopic

Mikrowelle *f* microwave.
M∼nherd *m* microwave oven

Milbe *f* -, -n mite

Milch *f* - milk. **M∼glas** *nt* opal
glass. **m∼ig** *a* milky. **M∼mann** *m*
(*pl* -männer) milkman. **M∼straße** *f*
Milky Way

mild *a* mild; (*nachsichtig*) lenient.
M∼e *f* - mildness; leniency. **m∼ern**
vt make milder; (*mäßigen*) moderate;
(*lindern*) ease; **sich m∼ern** become
milder; (*sich mäßigen*) moderate;
<*Schmerz:*> ease; **m∼ernde
Umstände** mitigating circumstances

Milieu /miˈliø:/ *nt* -s, -s [social]
environment

Militär *nt* -s army; (*Soldaten*) troops
pl; **beim M∼** in the army. **m∼isch**
a military

Miliz *f* -, -en militia

Milliarde /mɪˈliardə/ *f* -, -n
thousand million, billion

Milli|gramm *nt* milligram.
M~meter *m* & *nt* millimetre.
M~meterpapier *nt* graph paper
Million /mɪˈljoːn/ *f* -, -en million.
M~är *m* -s, -e millionaire
Milz *f* - (*Anat*) spleen
mimen *vt* (🛇 *vortäuschen*) act
Mimose *f* -, -n mimosa
Minderheit *f* -, -en minority
minderjährig *a* (*Jur*) under-age.
M~e(r) *m*/*f* (*Jur*) minor
mindern *vt* diminish; decrease
minderwertig *a* inferior. **M~keit**
f - inferiority. **M~keitskomplex**
m inferiority complex
Mindest- *pref* minimum. **m~e** *a* &
pron der/die/das **M~e** *od* **m~e** the
least; **nicht im M~en** not in the least.
m~ens *adv* at least. **M~lohn** *m*
minimum wage. **M~maß** *nt*
minimum
Mine *f* -, -n mine; (*Bleistift-*) lead;
(*Kugelschreiber-*) refill.
M~nräumboot *nt* minesweeper
Mineral *nt* -s, -e & -ien /-iən/
mineral. **m~isch** *a* mineral.
M~wasser *nt* mineral water
Miniatur *f* -, -en miniature
Minigolf *nt* miniature golf
minimal *a* minimal
Minimum *nt* -s, -ma minimum
Mini|ster *m*, -s,- minister.
m~steriell *a* ministerial.
M~sterium *nt* -s, -ien ministry
minus *conj, adv* & *prep* (+ *gen*)
minus. **M~** *nt* - deficit; (*Nachteil*)
disadvantage. **M~zeichen** *nt*
minus [sign]
Minute *f* -, -n minute
mir *pron* (*dat of* ich) [to] me; (*refl*)
myself
Misch|ehe *f* mixed marriage.
m~en *vt* mix; blend <*Tee, Kaffee*>;
toss <*Salat*>; shuffle <*Karten*>; **sich**
m~en mix; <*Person;*> mingle (**unter**
+ *acc* with); **sich m~en in** (+ *acc*)
join in <*Gespräch*>; meddle in
<*Angelegenheit*> ● *vi* (*haben*) shuffle
the cards. **M~ling** *m* -s, -e half-

caste. **M~ung** *f* -, -en mixture;
blend
miserabel *a* abominable
missachten *vt* disregard
Miss|achtung *f* disregard.
M~bildung *f* deformity
missbilligen *vt* disapprove of
Miss|billigung *f* disapproval.
M~brauch *m* abuse
missbrauchen *vt* abuse;
(*vergewaltigen*) rape
Misserfolg *m* failure
Misse|tat *f* misdeed. **M~täter** *m*
🛇 culprit
missfallen† *vi* (*haben*) displease
(jdm s.o.)
Miss|fallen *nt* -s displeasure;
(*Missbilligung*) disapproval.
M~geburt *f* freak; (*fig*)
monstrosity. **M~geschick** *nt*
mishap; (*Unglück*) misfortune
miss|glücken *vi* (*sein*) fail.
m~gönnen *vt* begrudge
misshandeln *vt* ill-treat
Misshandlung *f* ill-treatment
Mission *f* -, -en mission
Missionar(in) *m* -s, -e (*f* -, -nen)
missionary
Missklang *m* discord
misslingen† *vi* (*sein*) fail; **es**
misslang ihr she failed. **M~** *nt* -s
failure
Missmut *m* ill humour. **m~ig** *a*
morose
missraten† *vi* (*sein*) turn out badly
Miss|stand *m* abuse; (*Zustand*)
undesirable state of affairs.
M~stimmung *f* discord; (*Laune*)
bad mood
misstrauen *vi* (*haben*) jdm/etw **m~**
mistrust s.o./sth; (*Argwohn hegen*)
distrust s.o./sth
Misstrau|en *nt* -s mistrust;
(*Argwohn*) distrust. **M~ensvotum**
nt vote of no confidence. **m~isch** *a*
distrustful; (*argwöhnisch*) suspicious
Miss|verständnis *nt*
misunderstanding. **m~verstehen†**
vt misunderstand. **M~wirtschaft** *f*
mismanagement
Mist *m* -[e]s manure; 🛇 rubbish

Mistel *f* -, -n mistletoe

Misthaufen *m* dungheap

mit *prep* (+ *dat*) with; <*sprechen*> to; (*mittels*) by; (*inklusive*) including; (*bei*) at; **mit Bleistift** in pencil; **mit lauter Stimme** in a loud voice; **mit drei Jahren** at the age of three ● *adv* (*auch*) as well; **mit anfassen** (*fig*) lend a hand

Mitarbeit *f* collaboration. **m~en** *vi sep* collaborate (**an** + *dat* on). **M~er(in)** *m(f)* collaborator; (*Kollege*) colleague; employee

Mitbestimmung *f* co-determination

mitbringen† *vt sep* bring [along]

miteinander *adv* with each other

Mitesser *m* (*Med*) blackhead

mitfahren† *vi sep* (*sein*) go/come along; **mit jdm m~** go with s.o.; (*mitgenommen werden*) be given a lift by s.o.

mitfühlen *vi sep* (*haben*) sympathize

mitgeben† *vt sep* **jdm etw m~** give s.o. sth to take with him

Mitgefühl *nt* sympathy

mitgehen† *vi sep* (*sein*) **mit jdm m~** go with s.o.

Mitgift *f* -, -en dowry

Mitglied *nt* member. **M~schaft** *f* -membership

mithilfe *prep* (+ *gen*) with the aid of

Mithilfe *f* assistance

mitkommen† *vi sep* (*sein*) come [along] too; (*fig: folgen können*) keep up; (*verstehen*) follow

Mitlaut *m* consonant

Mitleid *nt* pity, compassion; **M~erregend** pitiful. **m~ig** *a* pitying; (*mitfühlend*) compassionate. **m~slos** *a* pitiless

mitmachen *v sep* ● *vt* take part in; (*erleben*) go through ● *vi* (*haben*) join in

Mitmensch *m* fellow man

mitnehmen† *vt sep* take along; (*mitfahren lassen*) give a lift to; (*fig: schädigen*) affect badly; (*erschöpfen*) exhaust; **'zum M~'** 'to take away'

mitreden *vi sep* (*haben*) join in [the conversation]; (*mit entscheiden*) have a say (**bei** in)

mitreißen† *vt sep* sweep along; (*fig: begeistern*) carry away; **m~d** rousing

mitsamt *prep* (+ *dat*) together with

mitschreiben† *vt sep* (*haben*) take down

Mitschuld *f* partial blame. **m~ig** *a* **m~ig sein** be partly to blame

Mitschüler(in) *m(f)* fellow pupil

mitspielen *vi sep* (*haben*) join in; (*Theat*) be in the cast; (*beitragen*) play a part

Mittag *m* midday, noon; (*Mahlzeit*) lunch; (*Pause*) lunch-break; **heute/gestern M~** at lunch-time today/yesterday; **[zu] M~ essen** have lunch. **M~essen** *nt* lunch. **m~s** *adv* at noon; (*als Mahlzeit*) for lunch; **um 12 Uhr m~s** at noon. **M~spause** *f* lunch-hour; (*Pause*) lunch-break. **M~sschlaf** *m* after-lunch nap

Mittäter|(in) *m(f)* accomplice. **M~schaft** *f* - complicity

Mitte *f* -, -n middle; (*Zentrum*) centre; **die goldene M~** the golden mean; **M~ Mai** in mid-May; **in unserer M~** in our midst

mitteil|en *vt sep* **jdm etw m~en** tell s.o. sth; (*amtlich*) inform s.o. of sth. **M~ung** *f* -, -en communication; (*Nachricht*) piece of news

Mittel *nt* -s,- means *sg*; (*Heil*) remedy; (*Medikament*) medicine; (*M~wert*) mean; (*Durchschnitt*) average; **M~** *pl* (*Geld-*) funds, resources. **m~** *pred a* medium; (*m~mäßig*) middling. **M~alter** *nt* Middle Ages *pl*. **m~alterlich** *a* medieval. **M~ding** *nt* (*fig*) cross. **m~europäisch** *a* Central European. **M~finger** *m* middle finger. **m~los** *a* destitute. **m~mäßig** *a* middling; [nur] **m~mäßig** mediocre. **M~meer** *nt* Mediterranean. **M~punkt** *m* centre; (*fig*) centre of attention

mittels *prep* (+ *gen*) by means of

Mittel|schule *f* = Realschule. **M~smann** *m* (*pl* -männer)

intermediary, go-between.
M∼stand *m* middle class.
m∼ste(r,s) *a* middle. **M∼streifen**
m (*Auto*) central reservation.
M∼stürmer *m* centre-forward.
M∼welle *f* medium wave.
M∼wort *nt* (*pl -wörter*) participle

mitten *adv* m∼ in/auf (*dat/acc*) in
the middle of. **m∼durch** *adv* [right]
through the middle

Mitternacht *f* midnight

mittler|e(r,s) *a* middle; <*Größe,
Qualität*> medium; (*durchschnittlich*)
mean, average. **m∼weile** *adv*
meanwhile; (*seitdem*) by now

Mittwoch *m -s, -e* Wednesday.
m∼s *adv* on Wednesdays

mitunter *adv* now and again

mitwirk|en *vi sep* (*haben*) take part;
(*helfen*) contribute. **M∼ung** *f*
participation

mix|en *vt* mix. **M∼er** *m -s,-* (*Culin*)
liquidizer, blender

Möbel *pl* furniture *sg*. **M∼stück** *nt*
piece of furniture. **M∼wagen** *m*
removal van

Mobiliar *nt -s* furniture

mobilisier|en *vt* mobilize. **M∼ung**
f - mobilization

Mobil|machung *f -* mobilization.
M∼telefon *nt* mobile phone

möblier|en *vt* furnish; **m∼tes
Zimmer** furnished room

mochte, möchte *s.* mögen

Mode *f -, -n* fashion; **M∼ sein** be
fashionable

Modell *nt -s, -e* model. **m∼ieren** *vt*
model

Modenschau *f* fashion show

Modera|tor *m -s, -en* /-'to:rən/,
M∼torin *f -, -nen* (*TV*) presenter

modern *a* modern; (*modisch*)
fashionable. **m∼isieren** *vt*
modernize

Mode|schmuck *m* costume
jewellery. **M∼schöpfer** *m* fashion
designer

modisch *a* fashionable

Modistin *f -, -nen* milliner

modrig *a* musty

modulieren *vt* modulate

Mofa *nt -s, -s* moped

mogeln *vi* (*haben*) ⚠ cheat

mögen†
● *transitive verb*
····▸ like. **sie mag ihn sehr [gern]** she
likes him very much. **möchten Sie
ein Glas Wein?** would you like a
glass of wine? **lieber mögen** prefer.
ich möchte lieber Tee I would prefer
tea
● *auxiliary verb*
····▸ (*wollen*) want to. **sie mochte nicht
länger bleiben** she didn't want to
stay any longer. **ich möchte ihn
[gerne] sprechen** I'd like to speak to
him. **möchtest du nach Hause?** do
you want to go home? *or* would you
like to go home?
····▸ (*Vermutung, Möglichkeit*) may. **ich
mag mich irren** I may be wrong.
wer/was mag das sein? whoever/
whatever can it be? **[das] mag sein**
that may well be. **mag kommen, was
da will** come what may

möglich *a* possible; **alle m∼en** all
sorts of; **über alles M∼e sprechen**
talk about all sorts of things.
m∼erweise *adv* possibly. **M∼keit**
f -, -en possibility. **M∼keitsform** *f*
subjunctive. **m∼st** *adv* if possible;
m∼st viel as much as possible

Mohammedan|er(in) *m -s,-* (*f -,
-nen*) Muslim. **m∼isch** *a* Muslim

Mohn *m -s* poppy

Möhre, Mohrrübe *f -, -n* carrot

Mokka *m -s* mocha; (*Geschmack*)
coffee

Molch *m -[e]s, -e* newt

Mole *f -, -n* (*Naut*) mole

Molekül *nt -s, -e* molecule

Molkerei *f -, -en* dairy

Moll *nt -* (*Mus*) minor

mollig *a* cosy; (*warm*) warm;
(*rundlich*) plump

Moment *m -s, -e* moment; **M∼[mal]!**
just a moment! **m∼an** *a*
momentary; (*gegenwärtig*) at the
moment

---

*old spelling

Monarch *m* -en, -en monarch. **M~ie** *f* -, -n monarchy

Monat *m* -s, -e month. **m~elang** *adv* for months. **m~lich** *a* & *adv* monthly

Mönch *m* -[e]s, -e monk

Mond *m* -[e]s, -e moon

mondän *a* fashionable

Mond|finsternis *f* lunar eclipse. **m~hell** *a* moonlit. **M~sichel** *f* crescent moon. **M~schein** *m* moonlight

monieren *vt* criticize

Monitor *m* -s, -en /-'to:rən/ (*Techn*) monitor

Monogramm *nt* -s, -e monogram

Mono|log *m* -s, -e monologue. **M~pol** *nt* -s, -e monopoly. **m~ton** *a* monotonous

Monster *nt* -s,- monster

Monstrum *nt* -s, -stren monster

Monsun *m* -s, -e monsoon

Montag *m* Monday

Montage /mɔn'ta:ʒə/ *f* -, -n fitting; (*Zusammenbau*) assembly; (*Film-*) editing; (*Kunst*) montage

montags *adv* on Mondays

Montanindustrie *f* coal and steel industry

Monteur /mɔn'tøːɐ/ *m* -s, -e fitter. **M~anzug** *m* overalls *pl*

montieren *vt* fit; (*zusammenbauen*) assemble

Monument *nt* -[e]s, -e monument. **m~al** *a* monumental

Moor *nt* -[e]s, -e bog; (*Heide-*) moor

Moos *nt* es, -e moss **m~ig** *a* mossy

Moped *nt* -s, -s moped

Mopp *m* -s, -s mop

Moral *f* - morals *pl*, (*Selbstvertrauen*) morale; (*Lehre*) moral. **m~isch** *a* moral

Mord *m* -[e]s, -e murder, (*Pol*) assassination. **M~anschlag** *m* murder/assassination attempt. **m~en** *vt/i* (*haben*) murder, kill

Mörder *m* -s,- murderer, (*Pol*) assassin. **M~in** *f* -, -nen murderess. **m~isch** *a* murderous; (☐ *schlimm*) dreadful

morgen *adv* tomorrow; **m~ Abend** tomorrow evening

Morgen *m* -s,- morning; (*Maß*) ≈ acre; **am M~** in the morning; **heute/Montag M~** this/Monday morning. **M~dämmerung** *f* dawn. **M~rock** *m* dressing-gown. **M~rot** *nt* red sky in the morning. **m~s** *a* in the morning

morgig *a* tomorrow's; **der m~e Tag** tomorrow

Morphium *nt* -s morphine

morsch *a* rotten

Morsealphabet *nt* Morse code

Mörtel *m* -s mortar

Mosaik /moza'i:k/ *nt* -s, -e[n] mosaic

Moschee *f* -, -n mosque

Mosel *f* - Moselle

Moskau *nt* -s Moscow

Moskito *m* -s, -s mosquito

Moslem *m* -s, -s Muslim

Motiv *nt* -s, -e motive; (*Kunst*) motif

Motor /'mo:tɔr, mo'to:ɐ/ *m* -s, -en /-'to:rən/ engine; (*Elektro-*) motor. **M~boot** *nt* motor boat

motorisieren *vt* motorize

Motor|rad *nt* motor cycle. **M~roller** *m* motor scooter

Motte *f* -, -n moth. **M~nkugel** *f* mothball

Motto *nt* -s, -s motto

Möwe *f* -, -n gull

Mücke *f* -, -n gnat; (*kleine*) midge; (*Stech-*) mosquito

müd|e *a* tired; **es m~e sein** be tired (**etw zu tun** of doing sth). **M~igkeit** *f* - tiredness

muffig *a* musty; (☐ *mürrisch*) grumpy

Mühe *f* -, -n effort; (*Aufwand*) trouble; **sich** (*dat*) **M~ geben** make an effort; (*sich bemühen*) try; **nicht der M~ wert** not worth while; **mit M~ und Not** with great difficulty; (*gerade noch*) only just. **m~los** *a* effortless

muhen *vi* (*haben*) moo

Mühl|e *f* -, -n mill; (*Kaffee-*) grinder. **M~stein** *m* millstone

Müh|sal f -, -e (liter) toil; (Mühe) trouble. **m~sam** a laborious; (beschwerlich) difficult

Mulde f -, -n hollow

Müll m -s refuse. **M~abfuhr** f refuse collection

Mullbinde f gauze bandage

Mülleimer m waste bin; (Mülltonne) dustbin

Müller m -s,- miller

Müll|halde f [rubbish] dump. **M~schlucker** m refuse chute. **M~tonne** f dustbin

multi|national a multinational. **M~plikation** /-'ts:io:n/ f -, -en multiplication. **m~plizieren** vt multiply

Mumie /'mu:miə/ f -, -n mummy

Mumm m -s ⚔ energy

Mumps m - mumps

Mund m -[e]s,-̈er mouth; ein M~ voll Suppe a mouthful of soup; halt den M~! ⚔ shut up! **m~art** f dialect. **m~artlich** a dialect

Mündel nt & m -s,- (Jur) ward. **m~sicher** a gilt-edged

münden vi (sein) flow/<Straße:> lead (in + acc into)

Mundharmonika f mouth-organ

mündig a m~ sein/werden (Jur) become of age. **M~keit** f - (Jur) majority

mündlich a verbal; m~e Prüfung oral

Mündung f -, -en (Fluss-) mouth; (Gewehr-) muzzle

Mundwinkel m corner of the mouth

Munition /-'ts:io:n/ f - ammunition

munkeln vt/i (haben) talk (von of); es wird gemunkelt rumour has it (dass that)

Münster nt -s,- cathedral

munter a lively; (heiter) merry; m~ sein (wach) be wide awake ; gesund und m~ fit and well

Münz|e f -, -n coin; (M~stätte) mint. **M~fernsprecher** m payphone

mürbe a crumbly; <Obst> mellow; <Fleisch> tender. **M~teig** m short pastry

Murmel f -, -n marble

murmeln vt/i (haben) murmur; (undeutlich) mumble

Murmeltier nt marmot

murren vt/i (haben) grumble

mürrisch a surly

Mus nt -es purée

Muschel f -, -n mussel; [sea] shell

Museum /mu'ze:ʊm/ nt -s, -seen /-'ze:ən/ museum

Musik f - music. **m~alisch** a musical

Musiker(in) m -s,- (f -, -nen) musician

Musik|instrument nt musical instrument. **M~kapelle** f band. **M~pavillon** m bandstand

musisch a artistic

musizieren vi (haben) make music

Muskat m -[e]s nutmeg

Muskel m -s, -n muscle. **M~kater** m stiff and aching muscles pl

muskulös a muscular

muss s. müssen

Muße f - leisure

müssen†
● auxiliary verb
····▸ (gezwungen/verpflichtet/notwendig sein) have to; must. er muss es tun he must or has to do it; ⚔ he's got to do it. ich musste schnell fahren I had to drive fast. das muss 1968 gewesen sein it must have been in 1968. er muss gleich hier sein he must be here at any moment

····▸ (in negativen Sätzen; ungezwungen) sie muss es nicht tun she does not have to or ⚔ she hasn't got to do it. es musste nicht so sein it didn't have to be like that

····▸ es müsste (sollte) doch möglich sein it ought to or should be possible. du müsstest es mal versuchen you ought to or should try it

● intransitive verb

····▸ (*irgendwohin gehen müssen*) have to *or* must go. **ich muss nach Hause/ zum Arzt** I have to *or* must go home/ to the doctor. **ich musste mal [aufs Klo]** I had to go [to the loo]

müßig *a* idle

musste, müsste *s.* müssen

Muster *nt* -s,- pattern; (*Probe*) sample; (*Vorbild*) model. **M~beispiel** *nt* typical example; (*Vorbild*) perfect example. **m~gültig, m~haft** *a* exemplary. **m~n** *vt* eye; (*inspizieren*) inspect. **M~ung** *f* -, -en inspection; (*Mil*) medical; (*Muster*) pattern

Mut *m* -[e]s courage; **jdm Mut machen** encourage s.o.; **zu M~e sein** = **zumute sein**, *s.* zumute

mut|ig *a* courageous. **m~los** *a* despondent

mutmaßen *vt* presume; (*Vermutungen anstellen*) speculate

Mutprobe *f* test of courage

Mutter¹ *f* -,-̈ mother

Mutter² *f* -, -n (*Techn*) nut

Muttergottes *f* -,- madonna

Mutterland *nt* motherland

mütterlich *a* maternal; (*fürsorglich*) motherly. **m~erseits** *adv* on one's/the mother's side

Mutter|mal *nt* birthmark; (*dunkel*) mole. **M~schaft** *f* - motherhood. **m~seelenallein** *a* & *adv* all alone. **M~sprache** *f* mother tongue. **M~tag** *m* Mother's Day

Mütze *f* -, -n cap; **wollene M~** woolly hat

MwSt. *abbr* (Mehrwertsteuer) VAT

mysteriös *a* mysterious

Mystik /'mʏstɪk/ *f* - mysticism

myth|isch *a* mythical. **M~ologie** *f* - mythology

Nn

na *int* well; **na gut** all right then

Nabel *m* -s,- navel. **N~schnur** *f* umbilical cord

nach

● *preposition* (+ *dative*)

····▸ (*räumlich*) to. **nach London fahren** go to London. **der Zug nach München** (*noch nicht abgefahren*) the train for Munich; the Munich train. **nach Hause gehen** go home. **nach Osten [zu]** eastwards; towards the east

····▸ (*zeitlich*) after; (*Uhrzeit*) past. **nach fünf Minuten/dem Frühstück** after five minutes/breakfast. **zehn [Minuten] nach zwei** ten [minutes] past two

····▸ (*[räumliche und zeitliche] Reihenfolge*) after. **nach Ihnen/dir!** after you!

····▸ (*mit bestimmten Verben*) for. **greifen/streben/schicken nach** grasp/strive/send for

····▸ (*gemäß*) according to. **nach der neuesten Mode gekleidet** dressed in [accordance with] the latest fashion. **dem Gesetz nach** in accordance with the law; by law. **nach meiner Ansicht** *od* **Meinung, meiner Ansicht** *od* **Meinung nach** in my view *or* opinion. **nach etwas schmecken/ riechen** taste/smell of sth

● *adverb*

····▸ (*zeitlich*) **nach und nach** little by little; gradually. **nach wie vor** still

nachahm|en *vt sep* imitate. **N~ung** *f* -, -en imitation

Nachbar|(in) *m* -n, -n (*f* -, -nen) neighbour. **N~haus** *nt* house next door. **n~lich** *a* neighbourly; (*Nachbar-*) neighbouring. **N~schaft** *f* - neighbourhood

nachbestell|en *vt sep* reorder. **N~ung** *f* repeat order

nachbild|en *vt sep* copy, reproduce. **N~ung** *f* copy, reproduction

nachdatieren *vt sep* backdate

nachdem *conj* after; **je n~** it depends

nachdenk|en† *vi sep* (*haben*) think (**über** + *acc* about). **n~lich** *a* thoughtful

nachdrücklich *a* emphatic

nacheinander *adv* one after the other

Nachfahre *m* -n, -n descendant

Nachfolg|e *f* succession. **N~er(in)** *m* -s,- (*f* -, -nen) successor

nachforsch|en *vi sep* (*haben*) make enquiries. **N~ung** *f* enquiry

Nachfrage *f* (*Comm*) demand. **n~n** *vi sep* (*haben*) enquire

nachfüllen *vt sep* refill

nachgeben† *v sep* ● *vi* (*haben*) give way: (*sich fügen*) give in, yield ● *vt* **jdm Suppe n~** give s.o. more soup

Nachgebühr *f* surcharge

nachgehen† *vi sep* (*sein*) <*Uhr:*> be slow; **jdm/etw n~** follow s.o./sth; follow up <*Spur, Angelegenheit*>; pursue <*Angelegenheit*>

Nachgeschmack *m* after-taste

nachgiebig *a* indulgent; (*gefällig*) compliant. **N~keit** *f* - indulgence; compliance

nachgrübeln *vi sep* (*haben*) ponder (**über** + *acc* on)

nachhaltig *a* lasting

nachhelfen† *vi sep* (*haben*) help

nachher *adv* later; (*danach*) afterwards; **bis n~!** see you later!

Nachhilfeunterricht *m* coaching

Nachhinein *adv* **im N~** afterwards

nachhinken *vi sep* (*sein*) (*fig*) lag behind

nachholen *vt sep* (*später holen*) fetch later; (*mehr holen*) get more; (*später machen*) do later; (*aufholen*) catch up on

Nachkomme *m* -n, -n descendant. **n~n†** *vi sep* (*sein*) follow [later],

come later; **etw** (*dat*) **n~n** (*fig*) comply with <*Bitte*>; carry out <*Pflicht*>. **N~nschaft** *f* - descendants *pl*, progeny

Nachkriegszeit *f* post-war period

Nachlass *m* -es,⸚e discount; (*Jur*) [deceased's] estate

nachlassen† *v sep* ● *vi* (*haben*) decrease; <*Regen, Hitze:*> let up; <*Schmerz:*> ease; <*Sturm:*> abate; <*Augen, Leistungen:*> deteriorate ● *vt* **etw vom Preis n~** take sth off the price

nachlässig *a* careless; (*leger*) casual; (*unordentlich*) sloppy. **N~keit** *f* - carelessness; sloppiness

nachlesen† *vt sep* look up

nachlöse|n *vi sep* (*haben*) pay one's fare on the train/on arrival. **N~schalter** *m* excess-fare office

nachmachen *vt sep* (*später machen*) do later; (*imitieren*) imitate, copy; (*fälschen*) forge

Nachmittag *m* afternoon; **heute/gestern N~** this/yesterday afternoon. **n~s** *adv* in the afternoon

Nachnahme *f* **etw per N~ schicken** send sth cash on delivery *or* COD

Nachname *m* surname

Nachporto *nt* excess postage

nachprüfen *vt sep* check, verify

Nachricht *f* -, -en [piece of] news *sg*; **N~en** news *sg*; **eine N~ hinterlassen** leave a message; **jdm N~ geben** inform s.o. **N~endienst** *m* (*Mil*) intelligence service

nachrücken *vi sep* (*sein*) move up

Nachruf *m* obituary

nachsagen *vt sep* repeat (**jdm** after s.o.); **jdm Schlechtes/Gutes n~** speak ill/well of s.o.

Nachsaison *f* late season

nachschicken *vt sep* (*später schicken*) send later; (*hinterher-*) send after (**jdm** s.o.); send on <*Post*> (**jdm** to s.o.)

nachschlagen† *v sep* ● *vt* look up ● *vi* (*haben*) **in einem Wörterbuch n~en** consult a dictionary; **jdm n~en** take after s.o.

Nachschrift *f* transcript; (*Nachsatz*) postscript

Nachschub *m* (*Mil*) supplies *pl*

nachsehen† *v sep* ● *vt* (*prüfen*) check; (*nachschlagen*) look up; (*hinwegsehen über*) overlook ● *vi* (*haben*) have a look; (*prüfen*) check; **im Wörterbuch n~** consult a dictionary

nachsenden† *vt sep* forward <*Post*> (**jdm** to s.o.); '**bitte n~**' 'please forward'

nachsichtig *a* forbearing; lenient; indulgent

Nachsilbe *f* suffix

nachsitzen† *vi sep* (*haben*) **n~ müssen** be kept in [after school]; **jdn n~ lassen** give s.o. detention. **N~** *nt* **-s** (*Sch*) detention

Nachspeise *f* dessert, sweet

nachsprechen† *vt sep* repeat (**jdm** after s.o.)

nachspülen *vt sep* rinse

nächst /-çst/ *prep* (+ *dat*) next to. **n~beste(r,s)** *a* first [available]; (*zweitbeste*) next best. **n~e(r,s)** *a* next; (*nächstgelegene*) nearest; <*Verwandte*> closest; **in n~er Nähe** close by; **am n~en sein** be nearest *or* closest ● *pron* **der/die/das N~e** the next; **der N~e bitte** next please; **als N~es** next; **fürs N~e** for the time being. **N~e(r)** *m* fellow man

nachstehend *a* following ● *adv* below

Nächst|enliebe *f* charity. **n~ens** *adv* shortly. **n~gelegen** *a* nearest

nachsuchen *vi sep* (*haben*) search; **n~ um** request

Nacht *f* -,̈e night; **über/bei N~** overnight/at night; **morgen N~** tomorrow night; **heute N~** tonight; (*letzte Nacht*) last night; **gestern N~** last night; (*vorletzte Nacht*) the night before last. **N~dienst** *m* night duty

Nachteil *m* disadvantage; **zum N~** to the detriment (*gen* of)

Nacht|falter *m* moth. **N~hemd** *nt* night-dress; (*Männer-*) night-shirt

Nachtigall *f* -, -en nightingale

Nachtisch *m* dessert

Nachtklub *m* night-club

nächtlich *a* nocturnal, night ...

Nacht|lokal *nt* night-club. **N~mahl** *nt* (*Aust*) supper

Nachtrag *m* postscript; (*Ergänzung*) supplement. **n~en**† *vt sep* add; **jdm etw n~en** (*fig*) bear a grudge against s.o. for sth. **n~end** *a* vindictive; **n~end sein** bear grudges

nachträglich *a* subsequent, later; (*verspätet*) belated ● *adv* later; (*nachher*) afterwards; (*verspätet*) belatedly

Nacht|ruhe *f* night's rest; **angenehme N~ruhe!** sleep well! **n~s** *adv* at night; **2 Uhr n~s** 2 o'clock in the morning. **N~schicht** *f* night-shift. **N~tisch** *m* bedside table. **N~tischlampe** *f* bedside lamp. **N~topf** *m* chamber-pot. **N~wächter** *m* night-watchman. **N~zeit** *f* night-time

Nachuntersuchung *f* check-up

Nachwahl *f* by-election

Nachweis *m* -es, -e proof. **n~bar** *a* demonstrable. **n~en**† *vt sep* prove; (*aufzeigen*) show; (*vermitteln*) give details of; **jdm nichts n~en können** have no proof against s.o.

Nachwelt *f* posterity

Nachwirkung *f* after-effect

Nachwuchs *m* new generation; (Ⓘ *Kinder*) offspring. **N~spieler** *m* young player

nachzahlen *vt/i sep* (*haben*) pay extra; (*später zahlen*) pay later; **Steuern n~** pay tax arrears

nachzählen *vt/i sep* (*haben*) count again; (*prüfen*) check

Nachzahlung *f* extra/later payment; (*Gehalts-*) back-payment

nachzeichnen *vt sep* copy

Nachzügler *m* -s,- latecomer; (*Zurückgebliebener*) straggler

Nacken *m* -s,- nape *or* back of the neck

nackt *a* naked; (*bloß, kahl*) bare; <*Wahrheit*> plain. **N~heit** *f* - nakedness, nudity. **N~kultur** *f* nudism. **N~schnecke** *f* slug

Nadel *f* -, **-n** needle; (*Häkel-*) hook; (*Schmuck-, Hut-*) pin. **N∼arbeit** *f* needlework. **N∼baum** *m* conifer. **N∼stich** *m* stitch; (*fig*) pinprick. **N∼wald** *m* coniferous forest

Nagel *m* **-s,** ⁻ nail. **N∼haut** *f* cuticle. **N∼lack** *m* nail varnish. **n∼n** *vt* nail. **n∼neu** *a* brand-new

nagen *vt/i* (*haben*) gnaw (**an** + *dat* at); **n∼d** (*fig*) nagging

Nagetier *nt* rodent

nah *a, adv & prep* = nahe

Näharbeit *f* sewing

Nahaufnahme *f* close-up

nahe *a* nearby; (*zeitlich*) imminent; (*eng*) close; **der N∼ Osten** the Middle East; **in n∼r Zukunft** in the near future; **von n∼m** [from] close to; **n∼ sein** be close (*dat* to) ● *adv* near, close; **<*verwandt*>** closely; **n∼ an** (+ *acc/dat*) near [to], close to; **n∼ daran sein, etw zu tun** nearly do sth; **n∼ liegen** be close; (*fig*) be highly likely; **n∼ legen** (*fig*) recommend (*dat* to); **jdm n∼ legen, etw zu tun** urge s.o. to do sth; **jdm n∼ gehen** (*fig*) affect s.o. deeply; **jdm zu n∼ treten** (*fig*) offend s.o. ● *prep* (+ *dat*) near [to], close to

Nähe *f* - nearness, proximity; **aus der N∼** [from] close to; **in der N∼** near *or* close by

nahe|gehen* *vi sep* (*sein*) **n∼ gehen,** *s.* nahe. **n∼legen*** *vt sep* **n∼ legen,** *s.* nahe. **n∼liegen*** *vi sep* (*haben*) **n∼ liegen,** *s.* nahe

nähen *vt/i* (*haben*) sew; (*anfertigen*) make; (*Med*) stitch [up]

näher *a* closer; **<*Weg*>** shorter; **<*Einzelheiten*>** further ● *adv* closer; (*genauer*) more closely; **n∼ kommen** come closer; (*fig*) get closer (*dat* to); **sich n∼ erkundigen** make further enquiries; **n∼ an** (+ *acc/dat*) nearer [to], closer to ● *prep* (+ *dat*) nearer [to], closer to. **N∼e[s]** *nt* [further] details *pl.* **n∼n (sich)** *vr* approach

nahezu *adv* almost

Nähgarn *nt* [sewing] cotton

Nahkampf *m* close combat

Näh|maschine *f* sewing machine. **N∼nadel** *f* sewing-needle

nähren *vt* feed; (*fig*) nurture

nahrhaft *a* nutritious

Nährstoff *m* nutrient

Nahrung *f* - food, nourishment. **N∼smittel** *nt* food

Nährwert *m* nutritional value

Naht *f* -, ⁻e seam; (*Med*) suture. **n∼los** *a* seamless

Nahverkehr *m* local service

Nähzeug *nt* sewing; (*Zubehör*) sewing kit

naiv /na'iːf/ *a* naïve. **N∼ität** /-viˈtɛːt/ *f* - naïvety

Name *m* **-ns,** **-n** name; **im N∼n** (+ *gen*) in the name of; **<*handeln*>** on behalf of. **n∼nlos** *a* nameless; (*unbekannt*) unknown, anonymous. **N∼nstag** *m* name-day. **N∼nsvetter** *m* namesake. **N∼nszug** *m* signature. **n∼ntlich** *adv* by name; (*besonders*) especially

namhaft *a* noted; (*ansehnlich*) considerable; **n∼ machen** name

nämlich *adv* (*und zwar*) namely; (*denn*) because

nanu *int* hallo

Napf *m* **-[e]s,** ⁻e bowl

Narbe *f* -, **-n** scar

Narkose *f* -, **-n** general anaesthetic. **N∼arzt** *m* anaesthetist. **N∼mittel** *nt* anaesthetic

Narr *m* **-en,** **-en** fool; **zum N∼en halten** make a fool of. **n∼en** *vt* fool

Närr|in *f* -, **-nen** fool. **n∼isch** *a* foolish; (🇦 *verrückt*) crazy (**auf** + *acc* about)

Narzisse *f* -, **-n** narcissus

naschen *vt/i* (*haben*) nibble (**an** + *dat* at)

Nase *f* -, **-n** nose

näseln *vi* (*haben*) speak through one's nose; **n∼d** nasal

Nasen|bluten *nt* **-s** nosebleed. **N∼loch** *nt* nostril

Nashorn *nt* rhinoceros

nass *a* wet

Nässe *f* - wet; wetness. **n∼n** *vt* wet

Nation /na'tsːioːn/ *f* -, -en nation.
n~al *a* national. **N~alhymne** *f*
national anthem. **N~alismus** *m* -
nationalism. **N~alität** *f* -, -en
nationality. **N~alspieler** *m*
international

Natrium *nt* -s sodium

Natron *nt* -s doppeltkohlensaures
N~ bicarbonate of soda

Natter *f* -, -n snake; (*Gift-*) viper

Natur *f* -, -en nature; von N~ aus by
nature. **n~alisieren** *vt* naturalize.
N~alisierung *f* -, -en
naturalization

Naturell *nt* -s, -e disposition

Natur|erscheinung *f* natural
phenomenon. **N~forscher** *m*
naturalist. **N~kunde** *f* natural
history

natürlich *a* natural ● *adv*
naturally; (*selbstverständlich*) of
course. **N~keit** *f* - naturalness

natur|rein *a* pure. **N~schutz** *m*
nature conservation; unter N~schutz
stehen be protected.
N~schutzgebiet *nt* nature
reserve. **N~wissenschaft** *f*
[natural] science.
N~wissenschaftler *m* scientist

nautisch *a* nautical

Navigation /-'tsːioːn/ *f* - navigation

Nazi *m* -s, -s Nazi

n.Chr. *abbr* (nach Christus) AD

Nebel *m* -s,- fog; (*leicht*) mist

neben *prep* (+ *dat/acc*) next to,
beside; (+ *dat*) (*außer*) apart from.
n~an *adv* next door

Neben|anschluss *m* (*Teleph*)
extension. **N~ausgaben** *fpl*
incidental expenses

nebenbei *adv* in addition;
(*beiläufig*) casually

Neben|bemerkung *f* passing
remark. **N~beruf** *m* second job

nebeneinander *adv* next to each
other, side by side

Neben|eingang *m* side entrance.
N~fach *nt* (*Univ*) subsidiary
subject. **N~fluss** *m* tributary

nebenher *adv* in addition

nebenhin *adv* casually

Neben|höhle *f* sinus. **N~kosten**
pl additional costs. **N~produkt** *nt*
by-product. **N~rolle** *f* supporting
role; (*Kleine*) minor role. **N~sache**
f unimportant matter. **n~sächlich**
a unimportant. **N~satz** *m*
subordinate clause. **N~straße** *f*
minor road; (*Seiten-*) side street.
N~wirkung *f* side-effect.
N~zimmer *nt* room next door

neblig *a* foggy; (*leicht*) misty

neck|en *vt* tease. **N~erei** *f* -
teasing. **n~isch** *a* teasing

Neffe *m* -n, -n nephew

negativ *a* negative. **N~** *nt* -s, -e
(*Phot*) negative

Neger *m* -s,- Negro

nehmen† *vt* take (*dat* from); sich
(*dat*) etw n~ take sth; help oneself to
<*Essen*>

Neid *m* -[e]s envy, jealousy. **n~isch**
a envious, jealous (auf + *acc* of); auf
jdn n~isch sein envy s.o.

neig|en *vt* incline; (*zur Seite*) tilt;
(*beugen*) bend; sich n~en incline;
<*Boden:*> slope; <*Person:*> bend
(über + *acc* over) ● *vi* (*haben*) n~en
zu (*fig*) have a tendency towards; be
prone to <*Krankheit*>; incline
towards <*Ansicht*>; dazu n~en, etw
zu tun tend to do sth. **N~ung** *f* -, -en
inclination; (*Gefälle*) slope; (*fig*)
tendency

nein *adv*, **N~** *nt* -s no

Nektar *m* -s nectar

Nelke *f* -, -n carnation; (*Culin*) clove

nenn|en† *vt* call; (*taufen*) name;
(*angeben*) give; (*erwähnen*) mention;
sich n~en call oneself. **n~enswert**
a significant

Neon *nt* -s neon. **N~beleuchtung**
f fluorescent lighting

Nerv *m* -s, -en /-fən/ nerve; die N~en
verlieren lose control of oneself.
n~en *vt* jdn n~en 🗵 get on s.o.'s
nerves. **N~enarzt** *m* neurologist.
n~enaufreibend *a* nerve-racking.
N~enkitzel *m* 🗓 thrill.
N~ensystem *nt* nervous system.
N~enzusammenbruch *m*
nervous breakdown

nervös *a* nervy, edgy; (*Med*) nervous; **n~ sein** be on edge

Nervosität *f* - nerviness, edginess

Nerz *m* -es, -e mink

Nessel *f* -, -n nettle

Nest *nt* -[e]s, -er nest; (🔲 *Ort*) small place

nett *a* nice; (*freundlich*) kind

netto *adv* net

Netz *nt* -es, -e net; (*Einkaufs-*) string bag; (*Spinnen-*) web; (*auf Landkarte*) grid; (*System*) network; (*Electr*) mains *pl*. **N~haut** *f* retina. **N~karte** *f* area season ticket. **N~werk** *nt* network

neu *a* new; (*modern*) modern; **wie neu** as good as new; **das ist mir neu** it's news to me; **von n~em** all over again ● *adv* newly; (*gerade erst*) only just; (*erneut*) again; **etw neu schreiben** rewrite sth; **neu vermähltes Paar** newly-weds *pl*. **N~auflage** *f* new edition; (*unverändert*) reprint. **N~bau** *m* (*pl* -ten) new house/building

Neu|e(r) *m/f* new person, newcomer; (*Schüler*) new boy/girl. **N~e(s)** *nt* **das N~e** the new; **etwas N~es** something new; (*Neuigkeit*) a piece of news; **was gibts N~es?** what's the news?

neuerdings *adv* [just] recently

neuest|e(r,s) *a* newest; (*letzte*) latest; **seit n~em** just recently. **N~e** *nt* **das N~e** the latest thing; (*Neuigkeit*) the latest news *sg*

neugeboren *a* newborn

Neugier, Neugierde *f* - curiosity; (*Wissbegierde*) inquisitiveness

neugierig *a* curious (**auf** + *acc* about); (*wissbegierig*) inquisitive

Neuheit *f* -, -en novelty; newness

Neuigkeit *f* -, -en piece of news; **N~en news** *sg*

Neujahr *nt* New Year's Day; **über N~** over the New Year

neulich *adv* the other day

Neumond *m* new moon

neun *inv a*, **N~** *f* -, -en nine. **n~te(r,s)** *a* ninth. **n~zehn** *inv a* nineteen. **n~zehnte(r,s)** *a* nineteenth. **n~zig** *inv a* ninety. **n~zigste(r,s)** *a* ninetieth

Neuralgie *f* -, -n neuralgia

neureich *a* nouveau riche

Neurologe *m* -n, -n neurologist

Neurose *f* -, -n neurosis

Neuschnee *m* fresh snow

Neuseeland *nt* -s New Zealand

neuste(r,s) *a* = neueste(r,s)

neutral *a* neutral. **N~ität** *f* - neutrality

Neutrum *nt* -s, -tra neuter noun

neu|vermählt* *a* n~ vermählt, *s.* neu. **N~zeit** *f* modern times *pl*

nicht *adv* not; **ich kann n~** I cannot or can't; **er ist n~ gekommen** he hasn't come; **bitte n~!** please don't! **n~ berühren!** do not touch! **du kennst ihn doch, n~?** you know him, don't you?

Nichte *f* -, -n niece

Nichtraucher *m* non-smoker

nichts *pron* & *a* nothing; **n~ mehr** no more; **n~ ahnend** unsuspecting; **n~ sagend** meaningless; (*uninteressant*) nondescript. **N~** *nt* - nothingness; (*fig: Leere*) void

Nichtschwimmer *m* non-swimmer

nichts|nutzig *a* good-for-nothing; (🔲 *unartig*) naughty. **n~sagend*** *a* n~ sagend, *s.* nichts. **N~tun** *nt* -s idleness

Nickel *nt* -s nickel

nicken *vi* (*haben*) nod

Nickerchen *nt* -s,-. 🔲 nap

nie *adv* never

nieder *a* low ● *adv* down. **n~brennen†** *vt/i sep* (*sein*) burn down. **N~deutsch** *nt* Low German. **N~gang** *m* (*fig*) decline. **n~gedrückt** *a* (*fig*) depressed. **n~geschlagen** *a* dejected, despondent. **N~kunft** *f* -,¨-e confinement. **N~lage** *f* defeat

Niederlande (die) *pl* the Netherlands

---

*old spelling

Niederländ|er *m* -s,- Dutchman; die N~er the Dutch *pl.* **N~erin** *f* -, -nen Dutchwoman. **n~isch** *a* Dutch

nieder|lassen† *vt sep* let down; sich n~lassen settle; (*sich setzen*) sit down. **N~lassung** *f* -, -en settlement; (*Zweigstelle*) branch. **n~legen** *vt sep* put *or* lay down; resign <*Amt*>; **die Arbeit n~legen** go on strike. **n~metzeln** *vt sep* massacre. **N~sachsen** *nt* Lower Saxony. **N~schlag** *m* precipitation; (*Regen*) rainfall; (*radioaktiver*) fallout. **n~schlagen†** *vt sep* knock down; lower <*Augen*>; (*unterdrücken*) crush. **n~schmettern** *vt sep* (*fig*) shatter. **n~setzen** *vt sep* put *or* set down; sich n~setzen sit down. **n~strecken** *vt sep* fell; (*durch Schuss*) gun down. **n~trächtig** *a* base, vile. **n~walzen** *vt sep* flatten

niedlich *a* pretty; sweet

niedrig *a* low; (*fig: gemein*) base ● *adv* low

niemals *adv* never

niemand *pron* nobody, no one

Niere *f* -, -n kidney; **künstliche N~** kidney machine

niesel|n *vi* (*haben*) drizzle. **N~regen** *m* drizzle

niesen *vi* (*haben*) sneeze. **N~** *nt* -s sneezing; (*Nieser*) sneeze

Niete¹ *f* -, -n rivet; (*an Jeans*) stud

Niete² *f* -, -n blank; Ⓕ failure

nieten *vt* rivet

Nikotin *nt* -s nicotine

Nil *m* -[s] Nile. **N~pferd** *nt* hippopotamus

nimmer *adv* (*SGer*) not any more; **nie und n~** never

nirgend|s, n~wo *adv* nowhere

Nische *f* -, -n recess, niche

nisten *vi* (*haben*) nest

Nitrat *nt* -[e]s, -e nitrate

Niveau /ni'vo:/ *nt* -s, -s level; (*geistig, künstlerisch*) standard

nix *adv* Ⓕ nothing

Nixe *f* -, -n mermaid

nobel *a* noble; (Ⓕ *luxuriös*) luxurious; (Ⓕ *großzügig*) generous

noch *adv* still; (*zusätzlich*) as well; (*mit Komparativ*) even; **n~ nicht** not yet; **gerade n~** only just; **n~ immer** *od* **immer n~** still; **n~ letzte Woche** only last week; **wer n~?** who else? **n~ etwas** something else; (*Frage*) anything else? **n~ einmal** again; **n~ ein Bier** another beer; **n~ größer** even bigger; **n~ so sehr** however much ● *conj* **weder ... n~** neither ... nor

nochmals *adv* again

Nomad|e *m* -n, -n nomad. **n~isch** *a* nomadic

nominier|en *vt* nominate. **N~ung** *f* -, -en nomination

Nonne *f* -, -n nun. **N~nkloster** *nt* convent

Nonstopflug *m* direct flight

Nord *m* -[e]s north. **N~amerika** *nt* North America

Norden *m* -s north

nordisch *a* Nordic

nördlich *a* northern; <*Richtung*> northerly ● *adv & prep* (+ *gen*) **n~ [von] der Stadt** [to the] north of the town

Nordosten *m* north-east

Nord|pol *m* North Pole. **N~see** *f* - North Sea. **N~westen** *m* north-west

Nörgelei *f* -, -en grumbling

nörgeln *vi* (*haben*) grumble

Norm *f* -, -en norm; (*Techn*) standard; (*Soll*) quota

normal *a* normal. **n~erweise** *adv* normally

normen *vt* standardize

Norwe|gen *nt* -s Norway. **N~ger(in)** *m* -s,- (*f* -, -nen) Norwegian. **n~gisch** *a* Norwegian

Nost|algie *f* - nostalgia. **n~algisch** *a* nostalgic

Not *f* -,-̈e need; (*Notwendigkeit*) necessity; (*Entbehrung*) hardship; (*seelisch*) trouble; **Not leiden** be in need, suffer hardship; **Not leidende Menschen** needy people; **zur Not** if need be; (*äußerstenfalls*) at a pinch

Notar *m* -s, -e notary public

Not|arzt *m* emergency doctor.
N~ausgang *m* emergency exit.
N~behelf *m* -[e]s, -e makeshift.
N~bremse *f* emergency brake.
N~dienst *m* N~dienst haben be on
call

Note *f* -, -n note; (*Zensur*) mark;
ganze/halbe N~ (*Mus*) semi-breve/
minim; **N~n lesen** read music;
persönliche N~ personal touch.
N~nblatt *nt* sheet of music.
N~nschlüssel *m* clef

Notfall *m* emergency; **für den N~**
just in case. **n~s** *adv* if need be

notieren *vt* note down; (*Comm*)
quote; **sich** (*dat*) **etw n~** make a note
of sth

nötig *a* necessary; **n~ haben** need;
das N~ste the essentials *pl* ● *adv*
urgently. **n~enfalls** *adv* if need be.
N~ung *f* - coercion

Notiz *f* -, -en note; (*Zeitungs-*) item;
[keine] N~ nehmen von take [no]
notice of. **N~buch** *nt* notebook.
N~kalender *m* diary

Not|lage *f* plight. **n~landen** *vi*
(*sein*) make a forced landing.
N~landung *f* forced landing.
n~leidend* *a* Not leidend, *s.* Not.
N~lösung *f* stopgap

Not|ruf *m* emergency call; (*Naut,
Aviat*) distress call; (*Nummer*)
emergency services number.
N~signal *nt* distress signal.
N~stand *m* state of emergency.
N~unterkunft *f* emergency
accommodation. **N~wehr** *f* - (*Jur*)
self-defence

notwendig *a* necessary; essential
● *adv* urgently. **N~keit** *f* -, -en
necessity

Notzucht *f* - (*Jur*) rape

Nougat /'nu:gat/ *m & nt* -s nougat

Novelle *f* -, -n novella; (*Pol*)
amendment

November *m* -s,- November

Novize *m* -n, -n, **Novizin** *f* -, -nen
(*Relig*) novice

Nu *m* im Nu 🔲 in a flash

nüchtern *a* sober; (*sachlich*)
matter-of-fact; (*schmucklos*) bare;
(*ohne Würze*) bland; **auf n~en Magen**
on an empty stomach

Nudel *f* -, -n piece of pasta; **N~n**
pasta *sg*; (*Band-*) noodles. **N~holz**
nt rolling-pin

Nudist *m* -en, -en nudist

nuklear *a* nuclear

null *inv a* zero, nought; (*Teleph*) O;
(*Sport*) nil; (*Tennis*) love; **n~ Fehler**
no mistakes; **n~ und nichtig** (*Jur*)
null and void. **N~** *f* -, -en nought,
zero; (*fig: Person*) nonentity.
N~punkt *m* zero

numerieren* *vt s.* nummerieren

Nummer *f* -, -n number; (*Ausgabe*)
issue; (*Darbietung*) item; (*Zirkus-*)
act; (*Größe*) size. **n~ieren** *vt*
number. **N~nschild** *nt* number-
plate

nun *adv* now; (*na*) well; (*halt*) just;
nun gut! very well then!

nur *adv* only, just; **wo kann sie nur
sein?** wherever can she be? **er soll
es nur versuchen!** just let him try!

Nürnberg *nt* -s Nuremberg

nuscheln *vt/i* (*haben*) mumble

Nuss *f* -,̈e nut. **N~knacker** *m* -s,-
nutcrackers *pl*

Nüstern *fpl* nostrils

Nut *f* -, -en, **Nute** *f* -, -n groove

Nutte *f* -, -n 🔲 tart 🔲

nutz|bar *a* usable; **n~bar machen**
utilize; cultivate <*Boden*>.
n~bringend *a* profitable

nutzen *vt* use, utilize; (*aus-*) take
advantage of ● *vi* (*haben*) = nützen.
N~ *m* -s benefit; (*Comm*) profit; **N~
ziehen aus** benefit from; **von N~ sein**
be useful

nützen *vi* (*haben*) be useful *or* of use
(*dat* to); <*Mittel:*> be effective; **nichts
n~** be useless *or* no use; **was nützt
mir das?** what good is that to me?
● *vt* = nutzen

nützlich *a* useful. **N~keit** *f* -
usefulness

nutz|los *a* useless; (*vergeblich*) vain.
N~losigkeit *f* - uselessness.
N~ung *f* - use, utilization

Nylon /'nai:lɔn/ nt -s nylon

Nymphe /'nymfə/ f -, -n nymph

Oo

o int o ja/nein! oh yes/no!

Oase f -, -n oasis

ob conj whether; **ob reich, ob arm** rich or poor; **und ob!** 🄴 you bet!

Obacht f O∼ **geben** pay attention; O∼! look out!

Obdach nt -[e]s shelter. **o∼los** a homeless. **O∼lose(r)** m/f homeless person; **die O∼losen** the homeless pl

Obduktion /-'ts:io:n/ f -, -en post-mortem

O-Beine ntpl 🄴 bow-legs, bandy legs

oben adv at the top; (auf der Oberseite) on top; (eine Treppe hoch) upstairs; (im Text) above; **da o∼** up there; **o∼ im Norden** up in the north; **siehe o∼** see above; **o∼ auf** (+ acc/dat) on top of; **nach o∼** up[wards]; (die Treppe hinauf) upstairs; **von o∼** from above/upstairs; **von o∼ bis unten** from top to bottom/<Person> to toe; **jdn von o∼ bis unten mustern** look s.o. up and down; **o∼ erwähnt** od **genannt** above-mentioned. **o∼drein** adv on top of that

Ober m -s,- waiter

Ober|arm m upper arm. **O∼arzt** m ≈ senior registrar. **O∼deck** nt upper deck. **o∼e(r,s)** a upper; (höhere) higher. **O∼fläche** f surface. **o∼flächlich** a superficial. **O∼geschoss** nt upper storey. **o∼halb** adv & prep (+ gen) above. **O∼haupt** nt (fig) head. **O∼haus** nt (Pol) upper house; (in UK) House of Lords. **O∼hemd** nt [man's] shirt. **o∼irdisch** a surface ... ● adv above ground. **O∼kiefer** m upper jaw. **O∼körper** m upper part of the body. **O∼leutnant** m lieutenant. **O∼lippe** f upper lip

Obers nt - (Aust) cream

Ober|schenkel m thigh. **O∼schule** f grammar school. **O∼seite** f upper/(rechte Seite) right side

Oberst m -en & -s, -en colonel

oberste(r,s) a top; (höchste) highest; <Befehlshaber, Gerichtshof> supreme; (wichtigste) first

Ober|stimme f treble. **O∼teil** nt top. **O∼weite** f chest/(der Frau) bust size

obgleich conj although

Obhut f - care

obig a above

Objekt nt -[e]s, -e object; (Haus, Grundstück) property

Objektiv nt -s, -e lens. **o∼** a objective. **O∼ität** f - objectivity

Oblate f -, -n (Relig) wafer

Obmann m (pl -männer) [jury] foreman; (Sport) referee

Oboe /o'bo:ə/ f -, -n oboe

Obrigkeit f - authorities pl

obschon conj although

Observatorium nt -s, -ien observatory

obskur a obscure; dubious

Obst nt -es (coll) fruit. **O∼baum** m fruit-tree. **O∼garten** m orchard. **O∼händler** m fruiterer

obszön a obscene

O-Bus m trolley bus

obwohl conj although

Ochse m -n, -n ox

öde a desolate; (unfruchtbar) barren; (langweilig) dull. **Öde** f - desolation; barrenness; dullness

oder conj or; **du kennst ihn doch, o∼?** you know him, don't you?

Ofen m -s,⁻ stove; (Heiz-) heater; (Back-) oven; (Techn) furnace

offen a open; <Haar> loose; <Flamme> naked; (o∼herzig) frank; (o∼ gezeigt) overt; (unentschieden) unsettled; **o∼e Stelle** vacancy; **Wein o∼ verkaufen** sell wine by the glass; **o∼ bleiben** remain open; **o∼ halten**

hold open <Tör>; keep open <Mund, Augen>; o~ **lassen** leave open; leave vacant <Stelle>; o~ **stehen** be open; <Rechnung:> be outstanding; **jdm** o~ **stehen** (fig) be open to s.o.; adv o~ **gesagt** od **gestanden** to be honest. **o~bar** a obvious ● adv apparently. **o~baren** vt reveal. **O~barung** f -, -en revelation. **O~heit** f - frankness, openness. **o~sichtlich** a obvious

offenstehen* vi sep (haben) **offen stehen**, s. **offen**

öffentlich a public. **Ö~keit** f - public; **in aller Ö~keit** in public, publicly

Offerte f -, -n (Comm) offer

offiziell a official

Offizier m -s, -e (Mil) officer

öffn|en vt/i (haben) open; **sich ö~en** open. **Ö~er** m -s,- opener. **Ö~ung** f -, -en opening. **Ö~ungszeiten** fpl opening hours

oft adv often

öfter adv quite often. **ö~e(r,s)** a frequent; **des Ö~en** frequently. **ö~s** adv 🇹 quite often

oh int oh!

ohne prep (+ acc) without; **o~ mich!** count me out! **oben o~** topless ● conj o~ **zu überlegen** without thinking; **o~ dass ich es merkte** without my noticing it. **o~dies** adv anyway. **o~gleichen** pred a unparalleled. **o~hin** adv anyway

Ohn|macht f -, -en faint; (fig) powerlessness; **in O~macht fallen** faint. **o~mächtig** a unconscious; (fig) powerless; **o~mächtig werden** faint

Ohr nt -[e]s, -en ear

Öhr nt -[e]s, -e eye

Ohrenschmalz nt ear-wax. **O~schmerzen** mpl earache sg

Ohrfeige f slap in the face. **o~n** vt **jdn o~n** slap s.o.'s face

Ohr|läppchen nt -s,- ear-lobe. **O~ring** m ear-ring. **O~wurm** m earwig

oje int oh dear!

okay /o'ke:/ a & adv 🇹 OK

Öko|logie f - ecology. **ö~logisch** a ecological. **Ö~nomie** f - economy; (Wissenschaft) economics sg. **ö~nomisch** a economic; (sparsam) economical

Oktave f -, -n octave

Oktober m -s,- October

ökumenisch a ecumenical

Öl nt -[e]s, -e oil; **in Öl malen** paint in oils. **Ölbaum** m olivetree. **ölen** vt oil. **Ölfarbe** f oil-paint. **Ölfeld** nt oilfield. **Ölgemälde** nt oil-painting. **ölig** a oily

Oliv|e f -, -n olive. **O~enöl** nt olive oil

Ölmessstab m dip-stick. **Ölsardinen** fpl sardines in oil. **Ölstand** m oil-level. **Öltanker** m oil-tanker. **Ölteppich** m oil-slick

Olympiade f -, -n Olympic Games pl, Olympics pl

Olymp|iasieger(in) /o'lympia-/ m(f) Olympic champion. **o~isch** a Olympic; **O~ische Spiele** Olympic Games

Ölzeug nt oilskins pl

Oma f -, -s 🇹 granny

Omnibus m bus; (Reise-) coach

onanieren vi (haben) masturbate

Onkel m -s,- uncle

Opa m -s, -s 🇹 grandad

Opal m -s, -e opal

Oper f -, -n opera

Operation /-'tsio:n/ f -, -en operation. **O~ssaal** m operating theatre

Operette f -, -n operetta

operieren vt operate on <Patient, Herz>; **sich o~ lassen** have an operation ● vi (haben) operate

Opernglas nt opera-glasses pl

Opfer nt -s,- sacrifice; (eines Unglücks) victim; **ein O~ bringen** make a sacrifice; **jdm/etw zum O~ fallen** fall victim to s.o./sth. **o~n** vt sacrifice

Opium nt -s opium

Opposition /-'ts:io:n/ f - opposition. **O~spartei** f opposition party

Optik f - optics sg, (⚏ Objektiv) lens. **O~er** m -s,- optician

optimal a optimum

Optimis|mus m - optimism. **O~t** m -en, -en optimist. **o~tisch** a optimistic

optisch a optical; <Eindruck> visual

Orakel nt -s,- oracle

Orange /o'rã:ʒə/ f -, -n orange. **o~** inv a orange. **O~ade** /orã'ʒa:də/ f -, -n orangeade. **O~nmarmelade** f [orange] marmalade

Oratorium nt -s, -ien oratorio

Orchester /ɔr'kɛstə/ nt -s,- orchestra

Orchidee /ɔrçi'de:ə/ f -, -n orchid

Orden m -s,- (Ritter-, Kloster-) order; (Auszeichnung) medal, decoration

ordentlich a neat. tidy; (anständig) respectable; (ordnungsgemäß ⚏: richtig) proper; <Mitglied, Versammlung> ordinary; (⚏ gut) decent; (⚏ gehörig) good

Order f -, -s & -n order

ordinär a common

Ordination /-'ts:io:n/ f -, -en (Relig) ordination; (Aust) surgery

ordn|en vt put in order; tidy; (an-) arrange. **O~er** m -s,- steward; (Akten-) file

Ordnung f - order; **O~ machen** tidy up; **in O~ bringen** put in order; (aufräumen) tidy; (reparieren) mend; (fig) put right; **in O~ sein** be in order; (ordentlich sein) be tidy; (fig) be all right; **[geht] in O~!** OK! **o~sgemäß** a proper. **O~sstrafe** f (Jur) fine. **o~swidrig** a improper

Ordonnanz, Ordonanz f -, -en (Mil) orderly

Organ nt -s, -e organ; voice

Organisation /-'ts:io:n/ f -, -en organization

organisch a organic

organisieren vt organize; (⚏ beschaffen) get [hold of]

Organismus m -, -men organism; (System) system

Organspenderkarte f donor card

Orgasmus m -, -men orgasm

Orgel f -, -n (Mus) organ. **O~pfeife** f organ-pipe

Orgie /'ɔrgiə/ f -, -n orgy

Orien|t /'o:riɛnt/ m -s Orient. **o~talisch** a Oriental

orientier|en /oriɛn'ti:rən/ vt inform (über + acc about); **sich o~en** get one's bearings, orientate oneself; (unterrichten) inform oneself (über + acc about). **O~ung** f - orientation; **die O~ung verlieren** lose one's bearings

original a original. **O~** nt -s, -e original. **O~übertragung** f live transmission

originell a original; (eigenartig) unusual

Orkan m -s, -e hurricane

Ornament nt -[e]s, -e ornament

Ort m -[e]s, -e place; (Ortschaft) [small] town; **am Ort** locally; **am Ort des Verbrechens** at the scene of the crime

ortho|dox a orthodox. **O~graphie, O~grafie** f - spelling. **O~päde** m -n, -n orthopaedic specialist

örtlich a local

Ortschaft f -, -en [small] town; (Dorf) village; **geschlossene O~** (Auto) built-up area

Orts|gespräch nt (Teleph) local call. **O~verkehr** m local traffic. **O~zeit** f local time

Öse f -, -n eyelet; (Schlinge) loop; **Haken und Öse** hook and eye

Ost m -[e]s east

Osten m -s east; **nach O~** east

ostentativ a pointed

Osteopath m -en, -en osteopath

Oster|ei /'o:stə²ai:/ nt Easter egg. **O~fest** nt Easter. **O~glocke** f daffodil. **O~n** nt -,- Easter; **frohe O~n!** happy Easter!

Österreich nt -s Austria. **Ö~er** m, -s,-, **Ö~erin** f -, -nen Austrian. **ö~isch** a Austrian

östlich a eastern; <Richtung> easterly ● adv & prep (+ gen) **ö~**

[von] der Stadt [to the] east of the town

Ostsee f Baltic [Sea]

Otter[1] m -s,- otter

Otter[2] f -, -n adder

Ouverture /uvɛr'ty:rə/ f -, -n overture

oval a oval. **O∼** nt -s, -e oval

Oxid, Oxyd nt -[e]s, -e oxide

Ozean m -s, -e ocean

Ozon nt -s ozone. **O∼loch** nt hole in the ozone layer. **O∼schicht** f ozone layer

paar pron inv ein p∼ a few; ein p∼ Mal a few times; alle p∼ Tage every few days. **P∼** nt -[e]s, -e pair; (Ehe-, Liebes-) couple. **p∼en** vt mate; (verbinden) combine; **sich p∼en** mate. **P∼ung** f -, -en mating. **p∼weise** adv in pairs, in twos

Pacht f -, -en lease; (P∼summe) rent. **p∼en** vt lease

Pächter m -s,- lessee; (eines Hofes) tenant

Pachtvertrag m lease

Päckchen nt -s,- package, small packet

pack|en vt/i (haben) pack; (ergreifen) seize; (fig: fesseln) grip. **P∼en** m -s,- bundle. **p∼end** a (fig) gripping. **P∼papier** nt [strong] wrapping paper. **P∼ung** f -, -en packet; (Med) pack

Pädagog|e m -n, -n educationalist; (Lehrer) teacher. **P∼ik** f - educational science

Paddel nt -s,- paddle. **P∼boot** nt canoe. **p∼n** vt/i (haben/sein) paddle. **P∼sport** m canoeing

Page /'pa:ʒə/ m -n, -n page

Paillette /pai:'jɛtə/ f -, -n sequin

Paket nt -[e]s, -e packet; (Post-) parcel

Pakist|an nt -s Pakistan. **P∼aner(in)** m -s,- (f -, -nen) Pakistani. **p∼anisch** a Pakistani

Palast m -[e]s, -̈e palace

Paläst|ina nt -s Palestine. **P∼inenser(in)** m -s,- (f -, -nen) Palestinian. **p∼inensisch** a Palestinian

Palette f -, -n palette

Palme f -, -n palm[-tree]

Pampelmuse f -, -n grapefruit

Panier|mehl nt (Culin) breadcrumbs pl. **p∼t** a (Culin) breaded

Panik f - panic

Panne f -, -n breakdown; (Reifen-) flat tyre; (Missgeschick) mishap

Panther, Panter m -s,- panther

Pantine f -, -n [wooden] clog

Pantoffel m -s, -n slipper; mule

Pantomime[1] f -, -n mime

Pantomime[2] m -n, -n mime artist

Panzer m -s,- armour; (Mil) tank; (Zool) shell. **p∼n** vt armourplate. **P∼schrank** m safe

Papa /'papa, pa'pa:/ m -s, -s daddy

Papagei m -s & -en, -en parrot

Papier nt -[e]s, -e paper. **P∼korb** m waste-paper basket. **P∼schlange** f streamer. **P∼waren** fpl stationery sg

Pappe f - cardboard

Pappel f -, -n poplar

pappig a 🄳 sticky

Papp|karton m, **P∼schachtel** f cardboard box

Paprika m -s, -[s] [sweet] pepper; (Gewürz) paprika

Papst m -[e]s, -̈e pope

päpstlich a papal

Parade f -, -n parade

Paradies nt -es, -e paradise

Paraffin nt -s paraffin

Paragraph, Paragraf m -en, -en section

parallel a & adv parallel. **P∼e** f -, -n parallel

Paranuss f Brazil nut

Parasit m -en, -en parasite

parat a ready

Parcours /parˈkuːɐ̯/ m -,- /-[s], -s/ (*Sport*) course

Pardon /parˈdõː/ int sorry!

Parfüm nt -s, -e & -s perfume, scent. **p~iert** a perfumed, scented

parieren vi (*haben*) 🔲 obey

Park m -s, -s park. **p~en** vt/i (*haben*) park. **P~en** nt -s parking; 'P~en verboten' 'no parking'

Parkett nt -[e]s, -e parquet floor; (*Theat*) stalls pl

Park|haus nt multi-storey car park. **P~lücke** f parking space. **P~platz** m car park; parking space. **P~scheibe** f parking-disc. **P~schein** m car-park ticket. **P~uhr** f parking-meter. **P~verbot** nt parking ban; 'P~verbot' 'no parking'

Parlament nt -[e]s, -e parliament. **p~arisch** a parliamentary

Parodie f -, -n parody

Parole f -, -n slogan; (*Mil*) password

Partei f -, -en (*Pol, Jur*) party; (*Miet-*) tenant; für jdn P~ ergreifen take s.o.'s part. **p~isch** a biased

Parterre /parˈtɛr/ nt -s, -s ground floor; (*Theat*) rear stalls pl

Partie f -, -n part; (*Tennis, Schach*) game; (*Golf*) round; (*Comm*) batch; eine gute P~ machen marry well

Partikel nt -s,- particle

Partitur f -, -en (*Mus*) full score

Partizip nt -s, -ien /-iən/ participle

Partner|(in) m -s,- (f -, -nen) partner. **P~schaft** f -, -en partnership. **P~stadt** f twin town

Party /ˈpaːɐ̯ti/ f -, -s party

Parzelle f -, -n plot [of ground]

Pass m -es, ⸚e passport; (*Geog, Sport*) pass

Passage /paˈsaːʒə/ f -, -n passage; (*Einkaufs-*) shopping arcade

Passagier /pasaˈʒiːɐ̯/ m -s, -e passenger

Passant(in) m -en, -en (f -, -nen) passer-by

Passe f -, -n yoke

passen vi (*haben*) fit; (*geeignet sein*) be right (für for); (*Sport*) pass the ball; (*aufgeben*) pass; p~ zu go [well] with; (*übereinstimmen*) match; jdm p~ fit s.o.; (*gelegen sein*) suit s.o.; [ich] passe pass. **p~d** a suitable; (*angemessen*) appropriate; (*günstig*) convenient; (*übereinstimmend*) matching

passier|en vt pass; cross <Grenze>; (*Culin*) rub through a sieve ● vi (*sein*) happen (jdm to s.o.); es ist ein Unglück p~t there has been an accident. **P~schein** m pass

Passiv nt -s, -e (*Gram*) passive

Passstraße f pass

Paste f -, -n paste

Pastell nt -[e]s, -e pastel

Pastete f -, -n pie; (*Gänseleber-*) pâté

pasteurisieren /pastøriˈziːrən/ vt pasteurize

Pastor m -s, -en /-ˈtoːrən/ pastor

Pate m -n, -n godfather; (*fig*) sponsor; **P~n** godparents. **P~nkind** nt godchild

Patent nt -[e]s, -e patent; (*Offiziers-*) commission. **p~** a 🔲 clever; <Person> resourceful. **p~ieren** vt patent

Pater m -s,- (*Relig*) Father

Patholog|e m -n, -n pathologist. **p~isch** a pathological

Patience /paˈsi̯ãːs/ f -, -n patience

Patient(in) /paˈtsi̯ɛnt(ɪn)/ m -en, -en (f -, -nen) patient

Patin f -, -nen godmother

Patriot|(in) m -en, -en (f -, -nen) patriot. **p~isch** a patriotic. **P~ismus** m - patriotism

Patrone f -, -n cartridge

Patrouille /paˈtrʊljə/ f -, -n patrol

Patsch|e f in der P~e sitzen 🔲 be in a jam. **p~nass** a 🔲 soaking wet

Patt nt -s stalemate

Patz|er m -s,- 🔲 slip. **p~ig** a 🔲 insolent

Pauk|e f -, -n kettledrum; auf die P~e hauen 🔲 have a good time;

(*prahlen*) boast. **p~en** *vt/i* (*haben*)
🔟 swot

pauschal *a* all-inclusive;
(*einheitlich*) flat-rate; (*fig*) sweeping
<*Urteil*>; **p~e Summe** lump sum.
P~e *f* -, -n lump sum. **P~reise** *f*
package tour. **P~summe** *f* lump
sum

Pause¹ *f* -, -n break; (*beim Sprechen*)
pause; (*Theat*) interval; (*im Kino*)
intermission; (*Mus*) rest; **P~ machen**
have a break

Pause² *f* -, -n tracing. **p~n** *vt* trace

pausenlos *a* incessant

pausieren *vi* (*haben*) have a break;
(*ausruhen*) rest

Pauspapier *nt* tracing-paper

Pavian *m* -s, -e baboon

Pavillon /'pavɪljõ/ *m* -s, -s pavilion

Pazifi|k *m* -s Pacific [Ocean].
p~sch *a* Pacific

Pazifist *m* -en, -en pacifist

Pech *nt* -s pitch; (*Unglück*) bad luck;
P~ haben be unlucky

Pedal *nt* -s, -e pedal

Pedant *m* -en, -en pedant

Pediküre *f* -, -n pedicure

Pegel *m* -s,- level; (*Gerät*) water-
level indicator. **P~stand** *m* [water]
level

peilen *vt* take a bearing on

peinigen *vt* torment

peinlich *a* embarrassing, awkward;
(*genau*) scrupulous; **es war mir sehr
p~** I was very embarrassed

Peitsche *f* -, -n whip. **p~n** *vt* whip;
(*fig*) lash ● *vi* (*sein*) lash (**an** + *acc*
against). **P~nhieb** *m* lash

Pelikan *m* -s, -e pelican

Pell|e *f* -, -n skin. **p~en** *vt* peel;
shell <*Ei*>; **sich p~en** peel

Pelz *m* -es, -e fur

Pendel *nt* -s,- pendulum. **p~n** *vi*
(*haben*) swing ● *vi* (*sein*) commute.
P~verkehr *m* shuttle-service; (*für
Pendler*) commuter traffic

Pendler *m* -s,- commuter

penetrant *a* penetrating; (*fig*)
obtrusive

Penis *m* -, -se penis

Penne *f* -, -n 🔟 school

Pension /pã'zio:n/ *f* -, -en pension;
(*Hotel*) guest-house; **bei voller/halber
P~** with full/half board. **P~är(in)**
m -s, -e (*f* -, -nen) pensioner. **P~at**
nt -[e]s, -e boarding-school.
p~ieren *vt* retire. **P~ierung** *f* -
retirement

Pensum *nt* -s [allotted] work

Peperoni *f* -,- chilli

per *prep* (+ *acc*) by

Perfekt *nt* -s (*Gram*) perfect

Perfektion /-'ts:io:n/ *f* - perfection

perforiert *a* perforated

Pergament *nt* -[e]s, -e parchment.
P~papier *nt* grease-proof paper

Period|e *f* -, -n period. **p~isch** *a*
periodic

Perl|e *f* -, -n pearl; (*Glas-, Holz-*)
bead; (*Sekt-*) bubble. **P~mutt** *nt* -s
mother-of-pearl

Pers|ien /-iən/ *nt* -s Persia.
p~isch *a* Persian

Person *f* -, -en person; (*Theat*)
character; **für vier P~en** for four
people

Personal *nt* -s personnel, staff.
P~ausweis *m* identity card.
P~chef *m* personnel manager.
P~ien /-iən/ *pl* personal
particulars. **P~mangel** *m* staff
shortage

persönlich *a* personal ● *adv*
personally, in person. **P~keit** *f* -,
-en personality

Perücke *f* -, -n wig

pervers *a* [sexually] perverted.
P~ion *f* -, -en perversion

Pessimis|mus *m* - pessimism.
P~t *m* -en, -en pessimist. **p~tisch**
a pessimistic

Pest *f* - plague

Petersilie /-iə/ *f* - parsley

Petroleum /-leʊm/ *nt* -s paraffin

Petze *f* -, -n 🔟 sneak. **p~n** *vi*
(*haben*) 🔟 sneak

Pfad *m* -[e]s, -e path. **P~finder** *m*
-s,- [Boy] Scout. **P~finderin** *f* -,
-nen [Girl] Guide

Pfahl *m* -[e]s, ̈-e stake, post

Pfalz (die) - the Palatinate

Pfand *nt* -[e]s, ̈-er pledge; (*beim Spiel*)
forfeit; (*Flaschen-*) deposit

pfänd|en *vt* (*Jur*) seize. **P~erspiel**
nt game of forfeits

Pfandleiher *m* -s,- pawnbroker

Pfändung *f* -, -en (*Jur*) seizure

Pfann|e *f* -, -n [frying-]pan.
P~kuchen *m* pancake

Pfarr|er *m* -s,- vicar, parson;
(*katholischer*) priest. **P~haus** *nt*
vicarage

Pfau *m* -s, -en peacock

Pfeffer *m* -s pepper. **P~kuchen** *m*
gingerbread. **P~minze** *f* - (*Bot*)
peppermint. **p~n** *vt* pepper; (▣
schmeißen) chuck. **P~streuer** *m*
-s,- pepperpot

Pfeif|e *f* -, -n whistle; (*Tabak-,*
Orgel-) pipe. **p~en†** *vt/i* (*haben*)
whistle; (*als Signal*) blow the whistle

Pfeil *m* -[e]s, -e arrow

Pfeiler *m* -s,- pillar; (*Brücken-*) pier

Pfennig *m* -s, -e pfennig

Pferch *m* -[e]s, -e [sheep] pen

Pferd *nt* -es, -e horse; zu P~e on
horseback. **P~erennen** *nt* horse-
race; (*als Sport*) [horse-]racing.
P~eschwanz *m* horse's tail;
(*Frisur*) pony-tail. **P~estall** *m*
stable. **P~estärke** *f* horsepower

Pfiff *m* -[e]s, -e whistle

Pfifferling *m* -s, -e chanterelle

pfiffig *a* smart

Pfingst|en *nt* -s Whitsun. **P~rose**
f peony

Pfirsich *m* -s, -e peach

Pflanz|e *f* -, -n plant. **p~en** *vt* plant.
P~enfett *nt* vegetable fat. **p~lich**
a vegetable

Pflaster *nt* -s,- pavement; (*Heft-*)
plaster. **p~n** *vt* pave

Pflaume *f* -, -n plum

Pflege *f* - care; (*Kranken-*) nursing;
in P~ nehmen look after; (*Admin*)
foster <*Kind*>. **p~bedürftig** *a* in
need of care. **P~eltern** *pl* foster-
parents. **P~kind** *nt* foster-child.
p~leicht *a* easy-care. **p~n** *vt* look
after, care for; nurse <*Kranke*>;
cultivate <*Künste, Freundschaft*>.
P~r(in) *m* -s,- (*f* -, -nen) nurse;
(*Tier-*) keeper

Pflicht *f* -, -en duty; (*Sport*)
compulsory exercise/routine.
p~bewusst *a* conscientious.
P~gefühl *nt* sense of duty

pflücken *vt* pick

Pflug *m* -[e]s, ̈-e plough

pflügen *vt/i* (*haben*) plough

Pforte *f* -, -n gate

Pförtner *m* -s,- porter

Pfosten *m* -s,- post

Pfote *f* -, -n paw

Pfropfen *m* -s,- stopper; (*Korken*)
cork. **p~** *vt* graft (**auf** + *acc* on [to]);
(▣ *pressen*) cram (**in** + *acc* into)

pfui *int* ugh

Pfund *nt* -[e]s, -e & - pound

Pfusch|arbeit *f* ▣ shoddy work.
p~en *vi* (*haben*) ▣ botch one's
work. **P~erei** *f* -, -en ▣ botch-up

Pfütze *f* -, -n puddle

Phantasie *f* -, -n imagination; **P~n**
fantasies; (*Fieber-*) hallucinations.
p~los *a* unimaginative. **p~ren** *vi*
(*haben*) fantasize; (*im Fieber*)
delirious. **p~voll** *a* imaginative

phantastisch *a* fantastic

pharma|zeutisch *a*
pharmaceutical. **P~zie** *f* -
pharmacy

Phase *f* -, -n phase

Philologie *f* - [study of] language
and literature

Philosoph *m* -en, -en philosopher.
P~ie *f* -, -n philosophy

philosophisch *a* philosophical

Phobie *f* -, -n phobia

Phonet|ik *f* - phonetics *sg*. **p~isch**
a phonetic

Phosphor *m* -s phosphorus

Photo *nt*, **Photo-** = Foto, Foto-

Phrase *f* -, -n empty phrase

Physik *f* - physics *sg*. **p~alisch** *a*
physical

Physiker(in) *m* -s,- (*f* -, -nen)
   physicist
Physiologie *f* - physiology
physisch *a* physical
Pianist(in) *m* -en, -en (*f* -, -nen)
   pianist
Pickel *m* -s,- pimple, spot;
   (*Spitzhacke*) pick. **p~ig** *a* spotty
Picknick *nt* -s, -s picnic
piep[s]|en *vi* (*haben*) <*Vogel:*>
   cheep; <*Maus:*> squeak; (*Techn*)
   bleep. **P~er** *m* -s,- bleeper
Pier *m* -s, -s [harbour] pier
Pietät /pie'tɛːt/ *f* - reverence. **p~los**
   a irreverent
Pigment *nt* -[e]s, -e pigment.
   P~ierung *f* - pigmentation
Pik *nt* -s, -s (*Karten*) spades *pl*
pikant *a* piquant; (*gewagt*) racy
piken *vt* 🔲 prick
pikiert *a* offended, hurt
Pilger|(in) *m* -s,- (*f* -, -nen) pilgrim.
   P~fahrt *f* pilgrimage. **p~n** *vi* (*sein*)
   make a pilgrimage
Pille *f* -, -n pill
Pilot *m* -en, -en pilot
Pilz *m* -es, -e fungus; (*essbarer*)
   mushroom
pingelig *a* 🔲 fussy
Pinguin *m* -s, -e penguin
Pinie /-iə/ *f* -, -n stone-pine
pinkeln *vi* (*haben*) 🔲 pee
Pinsel *m* -s,- [paint]brush
Pinzette *f* -, -n tweezers *pl*
Pionier *m* -s, -e (*Mil*) sapper; (*fig*)
   pioneer
Pirat *m* -en, -en pirate
Piste *f* -, -n (*Ski-*) run, piste; (*Renn-*)
   track; (*Aviat*) runway
Pistole *f* -, -n pistol
pitschnass *a* 🔲 soaking wet
pittoresk *a* picturesque
Pizza *f* -, -s pizza
Pkw /'pe:kave:/ *m* -s, -s car
plädieren *vi* (*haben*) plead (**für** for);
   auf Freispruch p~ (*Jur*) ask for an
   acquittal

Plädoyer /plɛdoa'je:/ *nt* -s, -s (*Jur*)
   closing speech; (*fig*) plea
Plage *f* -, -n [hard] labour; (*Mühe*)
   trouble; (*Belästigung*) nuisance.
   p~n *vt* torment, plague; (*bedrängen*)
   pester; **sich p~n** struggle
Plakat *nt* -[e]s, -e poster
Plakette *f* -, -n badge
Plan *m* -[e]s,-̈e plan
Plane *f* -, -n tarpaulin; (*Boden-*)
   groundsheet
planen *vt/i* (*haben*) plan
Planet *m* -en, -en planet
planier|en *vt* level. **P~raupe** *f*
   bulldozer
Planke *f* -, -n plank
plan|los *a* unsystematic. **p~mäßig**
   a systematic; <*Ankunft*> scheduled
Plansch|becken *nt* paddling pool.
   p~en *vi* (*haben*) splash about
Plantage /plan'ta:ʒə/ *f* -, -n
   plantation
Planung *f* - planning
plappern *vi* (*haben*) chatter ● *vt*
   talk <*Unsinn*>
plärren *vi* (*haben*) bawl
Plasma *nt* -s plasma
Plastik¹ *f* -, -en sculpture
Plast|ik² *nt* -s plastic. **p~isch** *a*
   three-dimensional; (*formbar*) plastic;
   (*anschaulich*) graphic
Plateau /pla'to:/ *nt* -s, -s plateau
Platin *nt* -s platinum
platonisch *a* platonic
plätschern *vi* (*haben*) splash;
   <*Bach:*> babble ● *vi* (*sein*) <*Bach:*>
   babble along
platt *a & adv* flat. **P~** *nt* -[s] (*Lang*)
   Low German
Plättbrett *nt* ironing-board
Platte *f* -, -n slab; (*Druck-*) plate;
   (*Metall-, Glas-*) sheet; (*Fliese*) tile;
   (*Koch-*) hotplate; (*Tisch-*) top;
   (*Schall-*) record, disc; (*zum
   Servieren*) [flat] dish, platter; **kalte
   P~** assorted cold meats and cheeses
   pl
Plätt|eisen *nt* iron. **p~en** *vt/i*
   (*haben*) iron
Plattenspieler *m* record-player

Platt|form f -, -en platform.
  P~füße mpl flat feet

Platz m -es,⁻e place; (von Häusern
  umgeben) square; (Sitz-) seat; (Sport-)
  ground; (Fußball-) pitch; (Tennis-)
  court; (Golf-) course; (freier Raum)
  room, space; **P~ nehmen** take a seat;
  P~ machen make room; **vom P~
  stellen** (Sport) send off.
  P~anweiserin f -, -nen usherette

Plätzchen nt -s,- spot; (Culin)
  biscuit

platzen vi (sein) burst; (auf-) split;
  (🄵 scheitern) fall through;
  <Verlobung:> be off

Platz|karte f seat reservation
  ticket. **P~mangel** m lack of space.
  P~patrone f blank. **P~verweis**
  m (Sport) sending off. **P~wunde** f
  laceration

Plauderei f -, -en chat

plaudern vi (haben) chat

plausibel a plausible

pleite a 🄵 **p~ sein** be broke:
  <Firma:> be bankrupt. **P~** f -, -n 🄵
  bankruptcy; (Misserfolg) flop; **P~
  gehen** od **machen** go bankrupt

plissiert a [finely] pleated

Plomb|e f -, -n seal; (Zahn-) filling.
  p~ieren vt seal; fill <Zahn>

plötzlich a sudden

plump a plump; clumsy

plumpsen vi (sein) 🄵 fall

plündern vt/i (haben) loot

Plunderstück nt Danish pastry

Plural m -s, -e plural

plus adv, conj & prep (+ dat) plus.
  P~ nt - surplus; (Gewinn) profit
  (Vorteil) advantage, plus. **P~punkt**
  m (Sport) point; (fig) plus

Po m -s, -s 🄵 bottom

Pöbel m -s mob, rabble. **p~haft** a
  loutish

pochen vi (haben) knock, <Herz:>
  pound; **p~ auf** (+ acc) (fig) insist on

pochieren /pɔˈʃiːrən/ vt poach

Pocken pl smallpox sg

Podest nt -[e]s, -e rostrum

Podium nt -s, -ien /-iən/ platform;
  (Podest) rostrum

Poesie /poeˈziː/ f - poetry

poetisch a poetic

Pointe /ˈpoɛ̃ːtə/ f -, -n point (of a
  joke)

Pokal m -s, -e goblet; (Sport) cup

pökeln vt (Culin) salt

Poker nt -s poker

Pol m -s, -e pole. **p~ar** a polar

Polarstern m pole-star

Pole m, -n, -n Pole. **P~n** nt -s Poland

Police /poˈliːsə/ f -, -n policy

Polier m -s, -e foreman

polieren vt polish

Polin f -, -nen Pole

Politesse f -, -n [woman] traffic
  warden

Politik f - politics sg; (Vorgehen,
  Maßnahme) policy

Polit|iker(in) m -s,- (f, -, -nen)
  politician. **p~isch** a political

Politur f -, -en polish

Polizei f - police pl. **p~lich** a police
  ... ● adv by the police; <sich
  anmelden> with the police.
  P~streife f police patrol.
  P~stunde f closing time.
  P~wache f police station

Polizist m -en, -en policeman. **P~in**
  f -, -nen policewoman

Pollen m -s pollen

polnisch a Polish

Polster nt -s,- pad; (Kissen) cushion;
  (Möbel-) upholstery. **p~n** vt pad;
  upholster <Möbel>. **P~ung** f -
  padding; upholstery

Polter|abend m wedding-eve
  party. **p~n** vi (haben) thump bang

Polyäthylen nt -s polythene

Polyester m -s polyester

Polyp m -en, -en polyp. **P~en**
  adenoids pl

Pommes frites /pɔmˈfriːt/ pl
  chips; (dünner) French fries

Pomp m -s pomp

Pompon /põˈpõː/ m -s, -s pompon

pompös a ostentatious

Pony¹ nt -s, -s pony

Pony² m -s, -s fringe

Pop m -[s] pop

Popo *m* -s, -s 🄴 bottom

populär *a* popular

Pore *f* -, -n pore

Porno|graphie, Pornografie *f* - pornography. **p~graphisch, p~grafisch** *a* pornographic

Porree *m* -s leeks *pl*

Portal *nt* -s, -e portal

Portemonnaie /portmɔ'ne:/ *nt*-s, -s purse

Portier /por'tie:/ *m* -s, -s doorman, porter

Portion /-'tsi̯o:n/ *f* -, -en helping, portion

Portmonee *nt* -s, -s = Portemonnaie

Porto *nt* -s postage. **p~frei** *adv* post free, post paid

Porträ|t /por'trɛ:/ *nt* -s, -s portrait. **p~tieren** *vt* paint a portrait of

Portugal *nt* -s Portugal

Portugies|e *m* -n, -n, **P~in** *f* -, -nen Portuguese. **p~isch** *a* Portuguese

Portwein *m* port

Porzellan *nt* -s china, porcelain

Posaune *f* -, -n trombone

Position /-'tsi̯o:n/ *f* -, -en position

positiv *a* positive. **P~** *nt* -s, -e (*Phot*) positive

Post *f* - post office; (*Briefe*) mail, post; **mit der P~** by post

postalisch *a* postal

Post|amt *nt* post office. **P~anweisung** *f* postal money order. **P~bote** *m* postman

Posten *m* -s,- post; (*Wache*) sentry; (*Waren-*) batch; (*Rechnungs-*) item, entry

Poster *nt & m* -s,- poster

Postfach *nt* post-office *or* PO box

Post|karte *f* postcard. **p~lagernd** *adv* poste restante. **P~leitzahl** *f* postcode. **P~scheckkonto** *nt* ≈ National Girobank account. **P~stempel** *m* postmark

postum *a* posthumous

post|wendend *adv* by return of post. **P~wertzeichen** *nt* [postage] stamp

Potenz *f* -, -en potency; (*Math & fig*) power

Pracht *f* - magnificence, splendour

prächtig *a* magnificent; splendid

prachtvoll *a* magnificent

Prädikat *nt* -[e]s, -e rating; (*Comm*) grade; (*Gram*) predicate

prägen *vt* stamp (auf + *acc* on); emboss <*Leder*>; mint <*Münze*>; coin <*Wort*>; (*fig*) shape

prägnant *a* succinct

prähistorisch *a* prehistoric

prahl|en *vi* (*haben*) boast, brag (mit about)

Prakti|k *f* -, -en practice. **P~kant(in)** *m* -en, -en (*f* -, -nen) trainee

Prakti|kum *nt* -s, -ka practical training. **p~sch** *a* practical; (*nützlich*) handy; (*tatsächlich*) virtual; **p~scher Arzt** general practitioner ● *adv* practically; virtually; (*in der Praxis*) in practice. **p~zieren** *vt/i* (*haben*) practise; (*anwenden*) put into practice; (🄴 *bekommen*) get

Praline *f* -, -n chocolate

prall *a* bulging; (*dick*) plump; <*Sonne*> blazing ● *adv* **p~ gefüllt** full to bursting. **p~en** *vi* (*sein*) **p~ auf** (+ *acc*)/**gegen** collide with, hit; <*Sonne:*> blaze down on

Prämie /-i̯ə/ *f* -, -n premium; (*Preis*) award

präm[i]ieren *vt* award a prize to

Pranger *m* -s,- pillory

Pranke *f* -, -n paw

Präparat *nt* -[e]s, -e preparation

Präsens *nt* - (*Gram*) present

präsentieren *vt* present

Präsenz *f* - presence

Präservativ *nt* -s, -e condom

Präsident|(in) *m* -en, -en (*f* -, -nen) president. **P~schaft** *f* - presidency

Präsidium *nt* -s presidency; (*Gremium*) executive committee; (*Polizei-*) headquarters *pl*

prasseln vi (haben) <Regen:> beat down; <Feuer:> crackle

Präteritum nt -s imperfect

Praxis f -, -xen practice; (Erfahrung) practical experience; (Arzt-) surgery; **in der P~** in practice

Präzedenzfall m precedent

präzis[e] a precise

predig|en vt/i (haben) preach. **P~t** f -, -en sermon

Preis m -es, -e price; (Belohnung) prize. **P~ausschreiben** nt competition

Preiselbeere f (Bot) cowberry; (Culin) ≈ cranberry

preisen† vt praise

preisgeben† vt sep abandon (dat to); reveal <Geheimnis>

preis|gekrönt a award-winning. **p~günstig** a reasonably priced ● adv at a reasonable price. **P~lage** f price range. **p~lich** a price ... ● adv in price. **P~richter** m judge. **P~schild** nt price-tag. **P~träger(in)** m(f) prize-winner. **p~wert** a reasonable

Prell|bock m buffers pl. **p~en** vt bounce; (verletzen) bruise; (🗵 betrügen) cheat. **P~ung** f -, -en bruise

Premiere /prə'mie:rə/ f -, -n première

Premierminister(in) /prə'mie:-/ m(f) Prime Minister

Presse f -, -n press. **p~n** vt press

Pressluftbohrer m pneumatic drill

Preuß|en nt -s Prussia. **p~isch** a Prussian

prickeln vi (haben) tingle

Priester m -s,- priest

prima inv a first-class, first-rate; (🗵 toll) fantastic

primär a primary

Primel f -, -n primula

primitiv a primitive

Prinz m -en, -en prince. **P~essin** f -, -nen princess

Prinzip nt -s, -ien /-iən/ principle. **p~iell** a <Frage> of principle ● adv on principle

Prise f -, -n P~ Salz pinch of salt

Prisma nt -s, -men prism

privat a private, personal. **P~adresse** f home address. **p~isieren** vt privatize

Privileg nt -[e]s, -ien /-iən/ privilege. **p~iert** a privileged

pro prep (+ dat) per. **Pro** nt - das Pro und Kontra the pros and cons pl

Probe f -, -n test, trial; (Menge, Muster) sample; (Theat) rehearsal; **auf die P~ stellen** put to the test; **ein Auto P~ fahren** test-drive a car. **p~n** vt/i (haben) (Theat) rehearse. **p~weise** adv on a trial basis. **P~zeit** f probationary period

probieren vt/i (haben) try; (kosten) taste; (proben) rehearse

Problem nt -s, -e problem. **p~atisch** a problematic

problemlos a problem-free ● adv without any problems

Produkt nt -[e]s, -e product

Produk|tion /-'tsio:n/ f -, -en production. **p~tiv** a productive

Produ|zent m -en, -en producer. **p~zieren** vt produce

Professor m -s, -en /-'so:rən/ professor

Profi m -s, -s (Sport) professional

Profil nt -s, -e profile; (Reifen-) tread; (fig) image

Profit m -[e]s, -e profit. **p~ieren** vi (haben) profit (**von** from)

Prognose f -, -n forecast; (Med) prognosis

Programm nt -s, -e programme; (Computer-) program; (TV) channel; (Comm: Sortiment) range. **p~ieren** vt/i (haben) (Computer) program. **P~ierer(in)** m -s,- (f -, -nen) [computer] programmer

Projekt nt -[e]s, -e project

Projektor m -s, -en /-'to:rən/ projector

Prolet m -en, -en boor. **P~ariat** nt -[e]s proletariat

Prolog m -s, -e prologue

Promenade f -, -n promenade

Promille pl 🛈 alcohol level sg in the blood; **zu viel P~ haben** 🛈 be over the limit

Prominenz f - prominent figures pl

Promiskuität f - promiscuity

promovieren vi (haben) obtain one's doctorate

prompt a prompt

Pronomen nt -s,- pronoun

Propaganda f - propaganda; (Reklame) publicity

Propeller m -s,- propeller

Prophet m -en, -en prophet

prophezei|en vt prophesy. **P~ung** f -, -en prophecy

Proportion /-'tsio:n/ f -, -en proportion

Prosa f - prose

prosit int cheers!

Prospekt m -[e]s, -e brochure; (Comm) prospectus

prost int cheers!

Prostitu|ierte f -n, -n prostitute. **P~tion** /-'tsio:n/ f - prostitution

Protest m -[e]s, -e protest

Protestant|(in) m -en, -en (f -, -nen) (Relig) Protestant. **p~isch** a (Relig) Protestant

protestieren vi (haben) protest

Prothese f -, -n artificial limb; (Zahn-) denture

Protokoll nt -s, -e record; (Sitzungs-) minutes pl; (diplomatisches) protocol

protz|en vi (haben) show off (**mit etw** sth). **p~ig** a ostentatious

Proviant m -s provisions pl

Provinz f -, -en province

Provision f -, -en (Comm) commission

provisorisch a provisional, temporary

Provokation /-'tsio:n/ f -, -en provocation

provozieren vt provoke

Prozedur f -, -en [lengthy] business

Prozent nt -[e]s, -e & - per cent; 5 P~ 5 per cent. **P~satz** m percentage. **p~ual** a percentage …

Prozess m -es, -e process; (Jur) lawsuit; (Kriminal-) trial

Prozession f -, -en procession

prüde a prudish

prüf|en vt test/(über-) check (**auf +** acc for); audit <Bücher>; (Sch) examine; **p~ender Blick** searching look. **P~er** m -s,- inspector; (Buch-) auditor; (Sch) examiner. **P~ling** m -s, -e examination candidate. **P~ung** f -, -en examination; (Test) test; (Bücher-) audit; (fig) trial

Prügel m -s,- cudgel; **P~** pl hiding sg, beating sg. **P~ei** f -, -en brawl, fight. **p~n** vt beat, thrash

Prunk m -[e]s magnificence, splendour

Psalm m -s, -en psalm

Pseudonym nt -s, -e pseudonym

pst int shush!

Psychi|ater m -s,- psychiatrist. **P~atrie** f - psychiatry. **p~atrisch** a psychiatric

psychisch a psychological

Psycho|analyse f psychoanalysis. **P~loge** m -n, -n psychologist. **P~logie** f - psychology. **p~logisch** a psychological

Pubertät f - puberty

Publi|kum nt -s public; (Zuhörer) audience; (Zuschauer) spectators pl. **p~zieren** vt publish

Pudding m -s, -s blancmange; (im Wasserbad gekocht) pudding

Pudel m -s,- poodle

Puder m & 🛈 nt -s,- powder. **P~dose** f [powder] compact. **p~n** vt powder. **P~zucker** m icing sugar

Puff m & nt -s, -s ⊠ brothel

Puffer m -s,- (Rail) buffer; (Culin) pancake. **P~zone** f buffer zone

Pull|i m -s, -s jumper. **P~over** m -s,- jumper; (Herren-) pullover

Puls m -es pulse. **P~ader** f artery

Pult nt -[e]s, -e desk

Pulver nt -s,- powder. **p~ig** a powdery

Pulverkaffee *m* instant coffee

pummelig *a* 🛈 chubby

Pumpe *f* -, -n pump. **p~n** *vt/i* (*haben*) pump; (🛈 *leihen*) lend; [sich (*dat*)] etw p~n (🛈 *borgen*) borrow sth

Pumps /pœmps/ *pl* court shoes

Punkt *m* -[e]s, -e dot; (*Tex*) spot; (*Geom, Sport & fig*) point; (*Gram*) full stop, period; **P~ sechs Uhr** at six o'clock sharp

pünktlich *a* punctual. **P~keit** *f* - punctuality

Pupille *f* -, -n (*Anat*) pupil

Puppe *f* -, -n doll; (*Marionette*) puppet; (*Schaufenster-, Schneider-*) dummy; (*Zool*) chrysalis

pur *a* pure; (🛈 *bloß*) sheer

Püree *nt* -s, -s purée; (*Kartoffel-*) mashed potatoes *pl*

purpurrot *a* crimson

Purzel|baum *m* 🛈 somersault. **p~n** *vi* (*sein*) 🛈 tumble

Puste *f* - 🛈 breath. **p~n** *vt/i* (*haben*) 🛈 blow

Pute *f* -, -n turkey

Putsch *m* -[e]s, -e coup

Putz *m* -es plaster; (*Staat*) finery. **p~en** *vt* clean; (*Aust*) dry-clean; (*zieren*) adorn; **sich p~en** dress up; **sich** (*dat*) **die Zähne/Nase p~en** clean one's teeth/blow one's nose. **P~frau** *f* cleaner, charwoman. **p~ig** *a* 🛈 amusing, cute; (*seltsam*) odd

Puzzlespiel /'pazl-/ *nt* jigsaw

Pyramide *f* -, -n pyramid

Qq

Quacksalber *m* -s,- quack

Quadrat *nt* -[e]s, -e square. **q~isch** *a* square

quaken *vi* (*haben*) quack; <*Frosch:*> croak

Quäker(in) *m* -s,- (*f* -, -nen) Quaker

Qual *f* -, -en torment; (*Schmerz*) agony

quälen *vt* torment; (*foltern*) torture; (*bedrängen*) pester; **sich q~** torment oneself; (*leiden*) suffer; (*sich mühen*) struggle

Quälerei *f* -, -en torture

Qualifi|kation /-'tsːjoːn/ *f* -, -en qualification. **q~zieren** *vt* qualify. **q~ziert** *a* qualified; (*fähig*) competent; <*Arbeit*> skilled

Qualität *f* -, -en quality

Qualle *f* -, -n jellyfish

Qualm *m* -s [thick] smoke

qualvoll *a* agonizing

Quantum *nt* -s, -ten quantity; (*Anteil*) share, quota

Quarantäne *f* - quarantine

Quark *m* -s quark, ≈ curd cheese

Quartal *nt* -s, -e quarter

Quartett *nt* -[e]s, -e quartet

Quartier *nt* -s, -e accommodation; (*Mil*) quarters *pl*

Quarz *m* -es quartz

quasseln *vi* (*haben*) 🛈 jabber

Quaste *f* -, -n tassel

Quatsch *m* -[e]s 🛈 nonsense, rubbish; **Q~ machen** (*Unfug machen*) fool around; (*etw falsch machen*) do a silly thing. **q~en** 🛈 *vi* (*haben*) talk; <*Wasser, Schlamm:*> squelch ● *vt* talk

Quecksilber *nt* mercury

Quelle *f* -, -n spring; (*Fluss- & fig*) source

quengeln *vi* 🛈 whine

quer *adv* across, crosswise; (*schräg*) diagonally; **q~ gestreift** horizontally striped

Quere *f* - **der Q~ nach** across, crosswise; **jdm in die Q~ kommen** get in s.o.'s way

Quer|latte *f* crossbar. **Q~schiff** *nt* transept. **Q~schnitt** *m* cross-section. **q~schnittsgelähmt** *a* paraplegic. **Q~straße** *f* side-street. **Q~verweis** *m* cross-reference

quetschen vt squash; (drücken) squeeze; (zerdrücken) crush; (Culin) mash; **sich q~ in** (+ acc) squeeze into

Queue /kø:/ nt -s, -s cue

quieken vi (haben) squeal; <Maus:> squeak

quietschen vi (haben) squeal; <Tür, Dielen:> creak

Quintett nt -[e]s, -e quintet

quirlen vt mix

Quitte f -, -n quince

quittieren vt receipt <Rechnung>; sign for <Geldsumme, Sendung>; **den Dienst q~** resign

Quittung f -, -en receipt

Quiz /kvɪs/ nt -, - quiz

Quote f -, -n proportion

Rr

Rabatt m -[e]s, -e discount

Rabatte f -, -n (Hort) border

Rabattmarke f trading stamp

Rabbiner m -s,- rabbi

Rabe m -n, -n raven

Rache f - revenge, vengeance

Rachen m -s,- pharynx

rächen vt avenge; **sich r~** take revenge (**an** + dat on); <Fehler:> cost s.o. dear

Rad nt -[e]s,-̈er wheel; (Fahr-) bicycle, 🛈 bike; **Rad fahren** cycle

Radar m & nt -s radar

Radau m -s 🛈 din, racket

radeln vi (sein) 🛈 cycle

Rädelsführer m ringleader

radfahr|en* vi sep (sein) Rad fahren, s. Rad. **R~er(in)** m(f) -s,- (f -, -nen) cyclist

---
*old spelling

radier|en vt/i (haben) rub out; (Kunst) etch. **R~gummi** m eraser, rubber. **R~ung** f -, -en etching

Radieschen /-'di:sçən/ nt -s,- radish

radikal a radical, drastic

Radio nt -s, -s radio

radioaktiv a radioactive. **R~ität** f - radioactivity

Radius m -, -ien /-iən/ radius

Rad|kappe f hub-cap. **R~ler** m -s,- cyclist; (Getränk) shandy

raffen vt grab; (kräuseln) gather; (kürzen) condense

Raffin|ade f - refined sugar. **R~erie** f -, -n refinery. **R~esse** f -, -n refinement; (Schlauheit) cunning. **r~iert** a ingenious; (durchtrieben) crafty

ragen vi (haben) rise [up]

Rahm m -s (SGer) cream

rahmen vt frame. **R~** m -s,- frame; (fig) framework; (Grenze) limits pl; (einer Feier) setting

Rakete f -, -n rocket; (Mil) missile

Rallye /'rali/ nt -s, -s rally

rammen vt ram

Rampe f -, -n ramp; (Theat) front of the stage

Ramsch m -[e]s junk

ran adv = heran

Rand m -[e]s,-̈er edge; (Teller-, Gläser-, Brillen-) rim; (Zier-) border, edging; (Brief-) margin; (Stadt-) outskirts pl; (Ring) ring

randalieren vi (haben) rampage

Randstreifen m (Auto) hard shoulder

Rang m -[e]s,-̈e rank; (Theat) tier; **erster/zweiter R~** (Theat) dress/ upper circle; **ersten R~es** first-class

rangieren /raŋ'ʒi:rən/ vt shunt ● vi (haben) rank (**vor** + dat before)

Rangordnung f order of importance; (Hierarchie) hierarchy

Ranke f -, -n tendril; (Trieb) shoot

ranken (sich) vr (Bot) trail; (in die Höhe) climb

Ranzen m -s,- (Sch) satchel

ranzig a rancid

Rappe *m* -n, -n black horse

Raps *m* -es (*Bot*) rape

rar *a* rare; **er macht sich rar** ⚠ we don't see much of him. **R~ität** *f* -, -en rarity

rasant *a* fast; (*schnittig, schick*) stylish

rasch *a* quick

rascheln *vi* (*haben*) rustle

Rasen *m* -s,- lawn

rasen *vi* (*sein*) tear [along]; <*Puls:*> race; <*Zeit:*> fly; **gegen eine Mauer r~** career into a wall ● *vi* (*haben*) rave; <*Sturm:*> rage. **r~d** *a* furious; (*tobend*) raving; <*Sturm, Durst*> raging; <*Schmerz*> excruciating; <*Beifall*> tumultuous

Rasenmäher *m* lawn-mower

Rasier|apparat *m* razor. **r~en** *vt* shave; **sich r~en** shave. **R~klinge** *f* razor blade. **R~wasser** *nt* aftershave [lotion]

Raspel *f* -, -n rasp; (*Culin*) grater. **r~n** *vt* grate

Rasse *f* -, -n race. **R~hund** *m* pedigree dog

Rassel *f* -, -n rattle. **r~n** *vi* (*haben*) rattle; <*Schlüssel:*> jangle; <*Kette:*> clank

Rassendiskriminierung *f* racial discrimination

Rassepferd *nt* thoroughbred. **rassisch** *a* racial

Rassis|mus *m* - racism. **r~tisch** *a* racist

Rast *f* -, -en rest. **R~platz** *m* picnic area. **R~stätte** *f* motorway restaurant [and services]

Rasur *f* -, -en shave

Rat *m* -[e]s [piece of] advice; **sich** (*dat*) **keinen Rat wissen** not know what to do; **zu Rat[e] ziehen** = **zurate ziehen**, *s.* **zurate**

Rate *f* -, -n instalment

raten† *vt* guess; (*empfehlen*) advise ● *vi* (*haben*) guess; **jdm r~** advise s.o.

Ratenzahlung *f* payment by instalments

Rat|geber *m* -s,- adviser; (*Buch*) guide. **R~haus** *nt* town hall

ratifizier|en *vt* ratify. **R~ung** *f* -, -en ratification

Ration /ra'tsi:o:n/ *f* -, -en ration. **r~ell** *a* efficient. **r~ieren** *vt* ration

rat|los *a* helpless; **r~los sein** not know what to do. **r~sam** *pred a* advisable; prudent. **R~schlag** *m* piece of advice; **R~schläge** advice *sg*

Rätsel *nt* -s,- riddle; (*Kreuzwort-*) puzzle; (*Geheimnis*) mystery. **r~haft** *a* puzzling, mysterious. **r~n** *vi* (*haben*) puzzle

Ratte *f* -, -n rat

rau *a* rough; (*unfreundlich*) gruff; <*Klima*> harsh, raw; (*heiser*) husky; <*Hals*> sore

Raub *m* -[e]s robbery; (*Menschen-*) abduction; (*Beute*) loot, booty. **r~en** *vt* steal; abduct <*Menschen*>

Räuber *m* -s,- robber

Raub|mord *m* robbery with murder. **R~tier** *nt* predator. **R~vogel** *m* bird of prey

Rauch *m* -[e]s smoke. **r~en** *vt/i* (*haben*) smoke. **R~en** *nt* -s smoking; 'R~en verboten' 'no smoking'. **R~er** *m* -s, -smoker

Räucher|lachs *m* smoked salmon. **r~n** *vt* (*Culin*) smoke

rauf *adv* = **herauf, hinauf**

rauf|en *vt* pull ● *vr/i* (*haben*) [sich] **r~en** fight. **R~erei** *f* -,-en fight

rauh* *a* *s.* **rau**

Raum *m* -[e]s, Räume room; (*Gebiet*) area; (*Welt-*) space

räumen *vt* clear; vacate <*Wohnung*>; evacuate <*Gebäude, Gebiet, (Mil) Stellung*>; (*bringen*) put (in/auf + *acc* into/on); (*holen*) get (aus out of)

Raum|fahrer *m* astronaut. **R~fahrt** *f* space travel. **R~inhalt** *m* volume

räumlich *a* spatial

Raum|pflegerin *f* cleaner. **R~schiff** *nt* spaceship

Räumung *f* - clearing; vacating; evacuation. **R~sverkauf** *m* clearance/closing-down sale

Raupe *f* -, -n caterpillar

raus *adv* = **heraus, hinaus**

Rausch *m* -[e]s, Räusche intoxication; (*fig*) exhilaration; **einen R~haben** be drunk

rauschen *vi* (*haben*) <*Wasser, Wind:*> rush; <*Bäume Blätter:*> rustle ● *vi* (*sein*) rush [along]

Rauschgift *nt* [narcotic] drug; (*coll*) drugs *pl*. **R~süchtige(r)** *m*/*f* drug addict

räuspern (sich) *vr* clear one's throat

rausschmeißen† *vt sep* 🔲 throw out; (*entlassen*) sack

Raute *f* -, -n diamond

Razzia *f* -, -ien /-iən/ [police] raid

Reagenzglas *nt* test-tube

reagieren *vi* (*haben*) react (**auf** + *acc* to)

Reaktion /-'ts:io:n/ *f* -, -en reaction. **r~är** *a* reactionary

Reaktor *m* -s, -en /-'to:rən/ reactor

realisieren *vt* realize

Realis|mus *m* - realism. **R~t** *m* -en, -en realist. **r~tisch** *a* realistic

Realität *f* -, -en reality

Realschule *f* ≈ secondary modern school

Rebe *f* -, -n vine

Rebell *m* -en, -en rebel. **r~ieren** *vi* (*haben*) rebel. **R~ion** *f* -, -en rebellion

rebellisch *a* rebellious

Rebhuhn *nt* partridge

Rebstock *m* vine

Rechen *m* -s- rake

Rechen|aufgabe *f* arithmetical problem; (*Sch*) sum. **R~maschine** *f* calculator

recherchieren /reʃɛr'ʃi:rən/ *vt*/*i* (*haben*) investigate; (*Journ*) research

rechnen *vi* (*haben*) do arithmetic; (*schätzen*) reckon; (*zählen*) count (**zu** among; **auf** + *acc* on); **r~ mit** reckon with; (*erwarten*) expect ● *vt* calculate, work out; (*fig*) count (**zu** among). **R~** *nt* -s arithmetic

Rechner *m* -s,- calculator; (*Computer*) computer

Rechnung *f* -, -en bill; (*Comm*) invoice; (*Berechnung*) calculation; **R~ führen über** (+ *acc*) keep account of. **R~sjahr** *nt* financial year. **R~sprüfer** *m* auditor

Recht *nt* -[e]s, -e law; (*Berechtigung*) right (**auf** + *acc* to); **im R~ sein** be in the right; **R~ haben/behalten** be right; **R~ bekommen** be proved right; **jdm R~ geben** agree with s.o.; **mit** *od* **zu R~** rightly

recht *a* right; (*wirklich*) real; **ich habe keine r~e Lust** I don't really feel like it; **es jdm r~ machen** please s.o.; **jdm r~ sein** be all right with s.o. **r~ vielen Dank** many thanks

Recht|e *f* -n, -[n] right side; (*Hand*) right hand; (*Boxen*) right; **die R~e** (*Pol*) the right; **zu meiner R~en** on my right. **r~e(r,s)** *a* right; (*Pol*) right-wing; **r~e Masche** plain stitch. **R~e(r)** *m*/*f* der/die R~e the right man/woman; **R~e(s)** *nt* das R~e the right thing; **etwas R~es lernen** learn something useful; **nach dem R~en sehen** see that everything is all right

Rechteck *nt* -[e]s, -e rectangle. **r~ig** *a* rectangular

rechtfertigen *vt* justify; **sich r~en** justify oneself

recht|haberisch *a* opinionated. **r~lich** *a* legal. **r~mäßig** *a* legitimate

rechts *adv* on the right; (*bei Stoff*) on the right side; **von/nach r~** from/to the right; **zwei r~, zwei links stricken** knit two, purl two. **R~anwalt** *m*, **R~anwältin** *f* lawyer

Rechtschreibung *f* - spelling

Rechts|händer(in) *m* -s,- (*f* -, -nen) right-hander. **r~händig** *a* & *adv* right-handed. **r~kräftig** *a* legal. **R~streit** *m* law suit. **R~verkehr** *m* driving on the right. **r~widrig** *a* illegal. **R~wissenschaft** *f* jurisprudence

rechtzeitig *a* & *adv* in time

Reck *nt* -[e]s, -e horizontal bar

recken *vt* stretch

Redakteur /redak'tøːɐ̯/ *m* -s, -e editor; (*Radio, TV*) producer

Redaktion /-'tsːioːn/ *f* -, -en editing; (*Radio, TV*) production; (*Abteilung*) editorial/production department

Rede *f* -, -n speech; **zur R~ stellen** demand an explanation from; **nicht der R~ wert** not worth mentioning

reden *vi* (*haben*) talk (**von** about; **mit** to); (*eine Rede halten*) speak ● *vt* talk; speak <*Wahrheit*>. **R~sart** *f* saying

Redewendung *f* idiom

redigieren *vt* edit

Redner *m* -s,- speaker

reduzieren *vt* reduce

Reeder *m* -s,- shipowner. **R~ei** *f* -, -en shipping company

Refer|at *nt* -[e]s, -e report; (*Abhandlung*) paper; (*Abteilung*) section. **R~ent(in)** *m* -en, -en (*f* -, -nen*) speaker; (*Sachbearbeiter*) expert. **R~enz** *f* -, -en reference

Reflex *m* -es, -e reflex; (*Widerschein*) reflection. **R~ion** *f* -, -en reflection. **r~iv** *a* reflexive

Reform *f* -, -en reform. **R~ation** /-'tsːioːn/ *f* - (*Relig*) Reformation

Reform|haus *nt* health-food shop. **r~ieren** *vt* reform

Refrain /rə'frɛ̃ː/ *m* -s, -s refrain

Regal *nt* -s, -e [set of] shelves *pl*

Regatta *f* -, -ten regatta

rege *a* active; (*lebhaft*) lively; (*geistig*) alert; <*Handel*> brisk

Regel *f* -, -n rule; (*Monats-*) period. **r~mäßig** *a* regular. **r~n** *vt* regulate; direct <*Verkehr*>; (*erledigen*) settle. **r~recht** *a* real, proper ● *adv* really. **R~ung** *f* -, -en regulation; settlement

regen *vt* move; **sich r~** move; (*wach werden*) stir

Regen *m* -s,- rain. **R~bogen** *m* rainbow. **R~bogenhaut** *f* iris

Regener|ation /-'tsːioːn/ *f* - regeneration. **r~ieren** *vt* regenerate

Regen|mantel *m* raincoat. **R~schirm** *m* umbrella. **R~tag** *m* rainy day. **R~wetter** *nt* wet weather. **R~wurm** *m* earthworm

Regie /re'ʒiː/ *f* - direction; **R~ führen** direct

regier|en *vt/i* (*haben*) govern, rule; <*Monarch:*> reign [over]; (*Gram*) take. **R~ung** *f* -, -en government; (*Herrschaft*) rule; (*eines Monarchen*) reign

Regiment *nt* -[e]s, -er regiment

Region *f* -, -en region. **r~al** *a* regional

Regisseur /reʒɪ'søːɐ̯/ *m* -s, -e director

Register *nt* -s,- register; (*Inhaltsverzeichnis*) index; (*Orgel-*) stop

Regler *m* -s,- regulator

reglos *a* & *adv* motionless

regn|en *vi* (*haben*) rain; **es r~et** it is raining. **r~erisch** *a* rainy

regul|är *a* normal; (*rechtmäßig*) legitimate. **r~ieren** *vt* regulate

Regung *f* -, -en movement; (*Gefühls-*) emotion. **r~slos** *a* & *adv* motionless

Reh *nt* -[e]s, -e roe-deer; (*Culin*) venison

Rehbock *m* roebuck

reib|en† *vt* rub; (*Culin*) grate ● *vi* (*haben*) rub. **R~ung** *f* - friction. **r~ungslos** *a* (*fig*) smooth

reich *a* rich (**an** + *dat* in)

Reich *nt* -[e]s, -e empire; (*König-*) kingdom; (*Bereich*) realm

Reiche(r) *m/f* rich man/woman; **die R~en** the rich *pl*

reichen *vt* hand; (*anbieten*) offer ● *vi* (*haben*) be enough; (*in der Länge*) be long enough; **r~ bis zu** reach [up to]; (*sich erstrecken*) extend to; **mit dem Geld r~** have enough money

reich|haltig *a* extensive, large <*Mahlzeit*> substantial. **r~lich** *a* ample: <*Vorrat*> abundant. **R~tum** *m* -s, -tümer wealth (**an** + *dat* of); **R~tümer** riches. **R~weite** *f* reach; (*Techn, Mil*) range

Reif *m* -[e]s [hoar-]frost

reif *a* ripe; (*fig*) mature; **r~ für** ready for. **r~en** *vi* (*sein*) ripen; <*Wein, Käse* & *fig*> mature

Reifen *m* -s,- hoop; (*Arm-*) bangle; (*Auto-*) tyre. **R~druck** *m* tyre pressure. **R~panne** *f* puncture, flat tyre

reiflich *a* careful

Reihe *f* -, -n row; (*Anzahl & Math*) series; **der R~ nach** in turn; **wer ist an der R~?** whose turn is it? **r~n (sich)** *vr* sich r~n an (+ *acc*) follow. **R~nfolge** *f* order. **R~nhaus** *nt* terraced house

Reiher *m* -s,- heron

Reim *m* -[e]s, -e rhyme. **r~en** *vt* rhyme; **sich r~en** rhyme

rein[1] *a* pure; (*sauber*) clean; <*Unsinn, Dummheit*> sheer; **ins R~e schreiben** make a fair copy of

rein[2] *adv* = herein, hinein

Reineclaude /rɛːnəˈkloːdə/ *f* -, -n greengage

Reinfall *m* 🛈 let-down; (*Misserfolg*) flop

Rein|gewinn *m* net profit. **R~heit** *f* - purity

reinig|en *vt* clean; (*chemisch*) dry-clean. **R~ung** *f* -, -en cleaning; (*chemische*) dry-cleaning; (*Geschäft*) dry cleaner's

reinlegen *vt sep* put in; 🛈 dupe; (*betrügen*) take for a ride

reinlich *a* clean. **R~keit** *f* - cleanliness

Reis *m* -es rice

Reise *f* -, -n journey; (*See-*) voyage; (*Urlaubs-, Geschäfts-*) trip. **R~andenken** *nt* souvenir. **R~büro** *nt* travel agency. **R~bus** *m* coach. **R~führer** *m* tourist guide; (*Buch*) guide. **R~gesellschaft** *f* tourist group. **R~leiter(in)** *m(f)* courier. **r~n** *vi* (*sein*) travel. **R~nde(r)** *m/f* traveller. **R~pass** *m* passport. **R~scheck** *m* traveller's cheque. **R~veranstalter** *m* -s,- tour operator. **R~ziel** *nt* destination

Reisig *nt* -s brushwood

Reißaus *m* **R~ nehmen** 🛈 run away

Reißbrett *nt* drawing-board

reißen† *vt* tear; (*weg-*) snatch; (*töten*) kill; **Witze r~** crack jokes; **an sich** (*acc*) **r~**snatch; seize <*Macht*>; **sich r~ um** 🛈 fight for ● *vi* (*sein*) tear; <*Seil, Faden:*> break ● *vi* (*haben*) **r~ an** (+ *dat*) pull at

Reißer *m* -s,- 🛈 thriller; (*Erfolg*) big hit

Reiß|nagel *m* = R~zwecke. **R~verschluss** *m* zip [fastener]. **R~wolf** *m* shredder. **R~zwecke** *f* -, -n drawing-pin

reit|en† *vt/i* (*sein*) ride. **R~er(in)** *m* -s,- (*f* -, -nen) rider. **R~hose** *f* riding breeches *pl*. **R~pferd** *nt* saddle-horse. **R~weg** *m* bridle-path

Reiz *m* -es, -e stimulus; (*Anziehungskraft*) attraction, appeal; (*Charme*) charm. **r~bar** *a* irritable. **R~barkeit** *f* - irritability. **r~en** *vt* provoke; (*Med*) irritate; (*interessieren, locken*) appeal to, attract; arouse <*Neugier*>; (*beim Kartenspiel*) bid. **R~ung** *f* -, -en (*Med*) irritation. **r~voll** *a* attractive

rekeln (sich) *vr* stretch

Reklamation /-ˈtsiːoːn/ *f* -, -en (*Comm*) complaint

Reklam|e *f* -, -n advertising, publicity; (*Anzeige*) advertisement; (*TV, Radio*) commercial; **R~e machen** advertise (**für etw** sth). **r~ieren** *vt* complain about; (*fordern*) claim ● *vi* (*haben*) complain

Rekord *m* -[e]s, -e record

Rekrut *m* -en, -en recruit

Rek|tor *m* -s, -en /-ˈtoːrən/ (*Sch*) head[master]; (*Univ*) vice-chancellor. **R~torin** *f* -, -nen head, headmistress; vice-chancellor

Relais /rəˈlɛː/ *nt* -,- /-s, -s/ (*Electr*) relay

relativ *a* relative

Religi|on *f* -, -en religion; (*Sch*) religious education. **r~ös** *a* religious

Reling *f* -, -s (*Naut*) rail

Reliquie /reˈliːkvi̯ə/ *f* -, -n relic

rempeln *vt* jostle; (*stoßen*) push

Reneklode f -, -n greengage

Renn|bahn f race-track; (*Pferde-*) racecourse. **R~boot** nt speedboat. **r~en†** vt/i (sein) run; **um die Wette r~en** have a race. **R~en** nt -s,- race. **R~pferd** nt racehorse. **R~sport** m racing. **R~wagen** m racing car

renommiert a renowned; <*Hotel, Firma*> of repute

renovier|en vt renovate; redecorate <*Zimmer*>. **R~ung** f - renovation; redecoration

rentabel a profitable

Rente f -, -n pension; **in R~ gehen** 🚹 retire. **R~nversicherung** f pension scheme

Rentier nt reindeer

rentieren (sich) vr be profitable; (*sich lohnen*) be worth while

Rentner(in) m -s,- (f -, -nen) [old-age] pensioner

Reparatur f -, -en repair. **R~werkstatt** f repair workshop; (*Auto*) garage

reparieren vt repair, mend

Reportage /-'ta:ʒə/ f -, -n report

Reporter(in) m -s,- (f -, -nen) reporter

repräsentativ a representative (**für** of); (*eindrucksvoll*) imposing

Reprodu|ktion /-'tsjo:n/ f -, -en reproduction. **r~zieren** vt reproduce

Reptil nt -s, -ien /-iən/ reptile

Republik f -, -en republic. **r~anisch** a republican

Requisiten pl (*Theat*) properties, 🚹 props

Reservat nt -[e]s, -e reservation

Reserve f -, -n reserve; (*Mil, Sport*) reserves pl. **R~rad** nt spare wheel

reservier|en vt reserve; **r~en lassen** book. **r~t** a reserved. **R~ung** f -, -en reservation

Reservoir /rezɛr'voa:ɐ/ nt -s, -s reservoir

Residenz f -, -en residence

Resign|ation /-'tsjo:n/ f - resignation. **r~ieren** vi (*haben*) (*fig*) give up. **r~iert** a resigned

resolut a resolute

Resonanz f -, -en resonanance

Respekt /-sp-, -ʃp-/ m -[e]s respect (**vor** + dat for). **r~ieren** vt respect

respektlos a disrespectful

Ressort /rɛ'so:ɐ/ nt -s, -s department

Rest m -[e]s, -e remainder, rest; **R~e** remains; (*Essens-*) leftovers

Restaurant /rɛsto'rã:/ nt -s, -s restaurant

Restaur|ation /rɛstaura'tsjo:n/ f - restoration. **r~ieren** vt restore

Rest|betrag m balance. **r~lich** a remaining

Resultat nt -[e]s, -e result

rett|en vt save (**vor** + dat from); (*aus Gefahr befreien*) rescue; **sich r~en** save oneself; (*flüchten*) escape. **R~er** m -s,- rescuer; (*fig*) saviour

Rettich m -s, -e white radish

Rettung f -, -en rescue; (*fig*) salvation; **jds letzte R~** s.o.'s last hope. **R~sboot** nt lifeboat. **R~sdienst** m rescue service. **R~sgürtel** m lifebelt. **r~slos** adv hopelessly. **R~sring** m lifebelt. **R~swagen** m ambulance

retuschieren vt (*Phot*) retouch

Reue f - remorse; (*Relig*) repentance

Revanch|e /re'vã:ʃə/ f -, -n revenge; **R~e fordern** (*Sport*) ask for a return match. **r~ieren (sich)** vr take revenge; (*sich erkenntlich zeigen*) reciprocate (**mit** with)

Revers /re've:ɐ/ nt -,- -[s], -s/ lapel

Revier nt -s, -e district; (*Zool & fig*) territory; (*Polizei-*) [police] station

Revision f -, -en revision; (*Prüfung*) check; (*Jur*) appeal

Revolution /-'tsjo:n/ f -, -en revolution. **r~är** a revolutionary. **r~ieren** vt revolutionize

Revolver m -s,- revolver

rezen|sieren vt review. **R~sion** f -, -en review

Rezept nt -[e]s, -e prescription; (*Culin*) recipe

Rezession f -, -en recession

R-Gespräch nt reverse-charge call

Rhabarber m -s rhubarb

Rhein *m* -s Rhine. **R~land** *nt* -s
Rhineland. **R~wein** *m* hock

Rhetorik *f* - rhetoric

Rheum|a *nt* -s rheumatism.
r~atisch *a* rheumatic.
R~atismus *m* - rheumatism

Rhinozeros *nt* -[ses], -se
rhinoceros

rhyth|misch /'ryt-/ *a* rhythmic[al].
R~mus *m* -, -men rhythm

richten *vt* direct (**auf** + *acc* at);
address <*Frage*> (**an** + *acc* to); aim
<*Waffe*> (**auf** + *acc* at); (*einstellen*)
set; (*vorbereiten*) prepare;
(*reparieren*) mend; **in die Höhe r~**
raise [up]; **sich r~** be directed (**auf** +
acc at; **gegen** against); <*Blick:*> turn
(**auf** + *acc* on); **sich r~ nach** comply
with <*Vorschrift*>; fit in with <*jds
Plänen*>; (*abhängen*) depend on ● *vi*
(*haben*) **r~ über** (+ *acc*) judge

Richter *m* -s,- judge

richtig *a* right, correct; (*wirklich,
echt*) real; **das R~e** the right thing
● *adv* correctly; really; **r~ stellen**
put right <*Uhr*>; (*fig*) correct
<*Irrtum*>; **die Uhr geht r~** the clock
is right

Richtlinien *fpl* guidelines

Richtung *f* -, -en direction

riechen† *vt/i* (*haben*) smell (**nach** of;
an etw *dat* sth)

Riegel *m* -s,- bolt; (*Seife*) bar

Riemen *m* -s,- strap; (*Ruder*) oar

Riese *m* -n, -n giant

rieseln *vi* (*sein*) trickle; <*Schnee:*>
fall lightly

riesengroß *a* huge, enormous

riesig *a* huge; (*gewaltig*) enormous
● *adv* I terribly

Riff *nt* -[e]s, -e reef

Rille *f* -, -n groove

Rind *nt* -es, -er ox; (*Kuh*) cow; (*Stier*)
bull; (*R~fleisch*) beef; **R~er** cattle *pl*

Rinde *f* -, -n bark; (*Käse-*) rind;
(*Brot-*) crust

Rinderbraten *m* roast beef

Rindfleisch *nt* beef

Ring *m* -[e]s, -e ring

ringeln (sich) *vr* curl

ring|en† *vi* (*haben*) wrestle; (*fig*)
struggle (**um/nach** for) ● *vt* wring
<*Hände*>. **R~er** *m* -s,- wrestler.
R~kampf *m* wrestling match; (*als
Sport*) wrestling

rings|herum, r~um *adv* all
around

Rinn|e *f* -, -n channel; (*Dach-*) gutter.
r~en† *vi* (*sein*) run; <*Sand:*>
trickle. **R~stein** *m* gutter

Rippe *f* -, -n rib.
R~nfellentzündung *f* pleurisy

Risiko *nt* -s, -s & -ken risk

risk|ant *a* risky. **r~ieren** *vt* risk

Riss *m* -es, -e tear; (*Mauer-*) crack;
(*fig*) rift

rissig *a* cracked; <*Haut*> chapped

Rist *m* -[e]s, -e instep

Ritt *m* -[e]s, -e ride

Ritter *m* -s,- knight

Ritual *nt* -s, -e ritual

Ritz *m* -es, -e scratch. **R~e** *f* -, -n
crack; (*Fels-*) cleft; (*zwischen Betten,
Vorhängen*) gap. **r~en** *vt* scratch

Rival|e *m* -n, -n, **R~in** *f* -, -nen
rival. **R~ität** *f* -, -en rivalry

Robbe *f* -, -n seal

Robe *f* -, -n gown; (*Talar*) robe

Roboter *m* -s,- robot

robust *a* robust

röcheln *vi* (*haben*) breathe
stertorously

Rochen *m* -s,- (*Zool*) ray

Rock¹ *m* -[e]s,¨e skirt; (*Jacke*) jacket

Rock² *m* -[s] (*Mus*) rock

rodel|n *vi* (*sein/haben*) toboggan.
R~schlitten *m* toboggan

roden *vt* clear <*Land*>; grub up
<*Stumpf*>

Rogen *m* -s,- [hard] roe

Roggen *m* -s rye

roh *a* rough; (*ungekocht*) raw; <*Holz*>
bare; (*brutal*) brutal. **R~bau** *m*
-[e]s, -ten shell. **R~kost** *f* raw
[vegetarian] food. **R~ling** *m* -s, -e
brute. **R~öl** *nt* crude oil

Rohr *nt* -[e]s, -e pipe; (*Geschütz-*)
barrel; (*Bot*) reed; (*Zucker-, Bambus-*)
cane

Röhre f -, -n tube; (Radio-) valve; (Back-) oven

Rohstoff m raw material

Rokoko nt -s rococo

Rollbahn f taxiway; (Start-/ Landebahn) runway

Rolle f -, -n roll; (Garn-) reel; (Draht-) coil; (Techn) roller; (Seil-) pulley; (Lauf-) castor; (Theat) part, role; **das spielt keine R~** (fig) that doesn't matter. **r~n** vt roll; (auf-) roll up; **sich r~n** roll ● vi (sein) roll; <Flugzeug:> taxi. **R~r** m -s,- scooter

Roll|feld nt airfield. **R~kragen** m polo-neck. **R~mops** m rollmop[s] sg

Rollo nt -s, -s [roller] blind

Roll|schuh m roller-skate; **R~schuh laufen** roller-skate. **R~stuhl** m wheelchair. **R~treppe** f escalator

Rom nt -s Rome

Roman m -s, -e novel. **r~isch** a Romanesque; <Sprache> Romance

Romant|ik f - romanticism. **r~isch** a romantic

Röm|er(in) m -s,- (f -, -nen) Roman. **r~isch** a Roman

Rommé, Rommee /'rɔme:/ nt -s rummy

röntgen vt X-ray. **R~aufnahme** f, **R~bild** nt X-ray. **R~strahlen** mpl X-rays

rosa inv a, **R~** nt -[s],- pink

Rose f -, -n rose. **R~nkohl** m [Brussels] sprouts pl. **R~nkranz** m (Relig) rosary

Rosine f -, -n raisin

Rosmarin m -s rosemary

Ross nt -es,-̈er horse

Rost[1] m -[e]s, -e grating; (Kamin-) grate; (Brat-) grill

Rost[2] m -[e]s rust. **r~en** vi (haben) rust

rösten vt roast; toast <Brot>

rostfrei a stainless

rostig a rusty

rot a, **Rot** nt -s,- red; **rot werden** turn red; (erröten) go red, blush

Röte f - redness; (Scham-) blush

Röteln pl German measles sg

röten vt redden; **sich r~** turn red

rothaarig a red-haired

rotieren vi (haben) rotate

Rot|kehlchen nt -s,- robin. **R~kohl** m red cabbage

rötlich a reddish

Rotwein m red wine

Roulade /ru'la:də/ f -, -n beef olive. **R~leau** /-'lo:/ nt -s, -s [roller] blind

Routin|e /ru'ti:nə/ f -, -n routine; (Erfahrung) experience. **r~emäßig** a routine ... ● adv routinely. **r~iert** a experienced

Rowdy /'rau:di/ m -s, -s hooligan

Rübe f -, -n beet; **rote R~** beetroot

Rubin m -s, -e ruby

Rubrik f -, -en column

Ruck m -[e]s, -e jerk

ruckartig a jerky

rück|bezüglich a (Gram) reflexive. **R~blende** f flashback. **R~blick** m (fig) review (auf + acc of). **r~blickend** adv in retrospect. **r~datieren** vt (inf & pp only) backdate

Rücken m -s,- back; (Buch-) spine; (Berg-) ridge. **R~lehne** f back. **R~mark** nt spinal cord. **R~schwimmen** nt backstroke. **R~wind** m following wind; (Aviat) tail wind

rückerstatten vt (inf & pp only) refund

Rückfahr|karte f return ticket. **R~t** f return journey

Rück|fall m relapse. **R~flug** m return flight. **R~frage** f [further] query. **r~fragen** vi (haben) (inf & pp only) check (bei with). **R~gabe** f return. **r~gängig** a **r~gängig machen** cancel; break off <Verlobung>. **R~grat** nt -[e]s, -e spine, backbone. **R~hand** f backhand. **R~kehr** return. **R~lagen** fpl reserves. **R~licht** nt rear-light. **R~reise** f return journey

Rucksack m rucksack

Rück|schau f review. **R~schlag** m (Sport) return; (fig) set-back. **r~schrittlich** a retrograde.

R~seite f back; (*einer Münze*) reverse

Rücksicht f -, -en consideration. **R~nahme** f - consideration. **r~slos** a inconsiderate; (*schonungslos*) ruthless. **r~svoll** a considerate

Rück|sitz m back seat; (*Sozius*) pillion. **R~spiegel** m rear-view mirror. **R~spiel** nt return match. **R~stand** m (*Chem*) residue; (*Arbeits-*) backlog; im R~stand sein be behind. **R~ständig** a (*fig*) backward. **R~stau** m (*Auto*) tailback. **R~strahler** m -s,- reflector. **R~tritt** m resignation; (*Fahrrad*) back pedalling

rückwärt|ig a back ..., rear ... **r~s** adv backwards. **R~sgang** m reverse [gear]

Rückweg m way back

rück|wirkend a retrospective. **R~wirkung** f retrospective force; mit R~wirkung vom backdated to. **R~zahlung** f repayment

Rüde m -n, -n [male] dog

Rudel nt -s,- herd; (*Wolfs-*) pack; (*Löwen-*) pride

Ruder nt -s,- oar; (*Steuer-*) rudder; am R~ (*Naut & fig*) at the helm. **R~boot** nt rowing boat. **r~n** vt/i (*haben/sein*) row

Ruf m -[e]s, -e call; (*laut*) shout; (*Telefon*) telephone number; (*Ansehen*) reputation. **r~en†** vt/i (*haben*) call (nach for); **r~en lassen** send for

Ruf|name m forename by which one is known. **R~nummer** f telephone number. **R~zeichen** nt dialling tone

Rüge f -, -n reprimand. **r~n** vt reprimand; (*kritisieren*) criticize

Ruhe f - rest; (*Stille*) quiet; (*Frieden*) peace; (*innere*) calm; (*Gelassenheit*) composure; R~ [da]! quiet! **r~los** a restless. **r~n** vi (*haben*) rest (auf + dat on); <*Arbeit, Verkehr:*> have stopped. **R~pause** f rest, break. **R~stand** m retirement; im

R~stand retired. **R~störung** f disturbance of the peace. **R~tag** m day of rest; 'Montag R~tag' 'closed on Mondays'

ruhig a quiet; (*erholsam*) restful; (*friedlich*) peaceful; (*unbewegt, gelassen*) calm; man kann r~ darüber sprechen there's no harm in talking about it

Ruhm m -[e]s fame; (*Ehre*) glory

rühmen vt praise

ruhmreich a glorious

Ruhr f - (*Med*) dysentery

Rühr|ei nt scrambled eggs pl. **r~en** vt move; (*Culin*) stir; sich r~en move ● vi (*haben*) stir; **r~en an** (+ acc) touch; (*fig*) touch on. **r~end** a touching

Rührung f - emotion

Ruin m -s ruin. **R~e** f -, -n ruin; ruins pl (gen of). **r~ieren** vt ruin

rülpsen vi (*haben*) 🗊 belch

Rum m -s rum

Rumän|ien /-iən/ nt -s Romania. **r~isch** a Romanian

Rummel m -s 🗊 hustle and bustle; (*Jahrmarkt*) funfair

Rumpelkammer f junk-room

Rumpf m -[e]s,-̈e body, trunk; (*Schiffs-*) hull; (*Aviat*) fuselage

rund a round ● adv approximately; r~ um [a]round. **R~blick** m panoramic view. **R~brief** m circular [letter]

Runde f -, -n round; (*Kreis*) circle; (*eines Polizisten*) beat; (*beim Rennen*) lap; eine R~ Bier a round of beer

Rund|fahrt f tour. **R~frage** f poll

Rundfunk m radio; im R~ on the radio. **R~gerät** nt radio [set]

Rund|gang m round; (*Spaziergang*) walk (durch round). **r~heraus** adv straight out. **r~herum** adv all around. **r~lich** a rounded; (*mollig*) plump. **R~reise** f [circular] tour. **R~schreiben** nt circular. **r~um** adv all round. **R~ung** f -, -en curve

Runzel f -, -n wrinkle

runzlig a wrinkled

Rüpel m -s,- 🗊 lout

rupfen vt pull out; pluck <*Geflügel*>

Rüsche f -, -n frill

Ruß m -es soot

Russe m -n, -n Russian

Rüssel m -s,- (*Zool*) trunk

Russ|in f -, -nen Russian. **r~isch** a Russian. **R~isch** nt -[s] (*Lang*) Russian

Russland nt -s Russia

rüsten vi (*haben*) prepare (**zu/für** for) ● vr **sich r~** get ready

rüstig a sprightly

rustikal a rustic

Rüstung f -, -en armament; (*Harnisch*) armour. **R~skontrolle** f arms control

Rute f -, -n twig; (*Angel-, Wünschel-*) rod; (*zur Züchtigung*) birch; (*Schwanz*) tail

Rutsch m -[e]s, -e slide. **R~bahn** f slide. **R~e** f -, -n chute. **r~en** vt slide; (*rücken*) move ● vi (*sein*) slide; (*aus-, ab-*) slip; (*Auto*) skid. **r~ig** a slippery

rütteln vt shake ● vi (*haben*) **r~ an** (+ *dat*) rattle

Ss

Saal m -[e]s,Säle hall; (*Theat*) auditorium; (*Kranken-*) ward

Saat f -, -en seed; (*Säen*) sowing; (*Gesätes*) crop

sabbern vi (*haben*) 🄸 slobber; <*Baby:*> dribble; (*reden*) jabber

Säbel m -s,- sabre

Sabo|tage /zabo'ta:ʒə/ f - sabotage. **S~teur** /-'tø:ɐ̯/ m -s, -e saboteur. **s~tieren** vt sabotage

Sach|bearbeiter m expert. **S~buch** nt non-fiction book

Sache f -, -n matter, business; (*Ding*) thing; (*fig*) cause

Sach|gebiet nt (*fig*) area, field. **s~kundig** a expert. **s~lich** a factual; (*nüchtern*) matter-of-fact

sächlich a (*Gram*) neuter

Sachse m -n, -n Saxon. **S~n** nt -s Saxony

sächsisch a Saxon

Sach|verhalt m -[e]s facts pl. **S~verständige(r)** m/f expert

Sack m -[e]s,-̈e sack

Sack|gasse f cul-de-sac; (*fig*) impasse. **S~leinen** nt sacking

Sad|is|mus m - sadism. **S~t** m -en, -en sadist

säen vt/i (*haben*) sow

Safe /ze:f/ m -s, -s safe

Saft m -[e]s,-̈e juice; (*Bot*) sap. **s~ig** a juicy

Sage f -, -n legend

Säge f -, -n saw. **S~mehl** nt sawdust

sagen vt say; (*mitteilen*) tell; (*bedeuten*) mean

sägen vt/i (*haben*) saw

sagenhaft a legendary

Säge|späne mpl wood shavings. **S~werk** nt sawmill

Sahn|e f - cream. **S~ebonbon** m & nt ≈ toffee. **s~ig** a creamy

Saison /zɛ'zõ:/ f -, -s season

Saite f -, -n (*Mus, Sport*) string. **S~ninstrument** nt stringed instrument

Sakko m & nt -s, -s sports jacket

Sakrament nt -[e]s, -e sacrament

Sakristei f -, -en vestry

Salat m -[e]s, -e salad. **S~soße** f salad-dressing

Salbe f -, -n ointment

Salbei m -s & f - sage

salben vt anoint

Saldo m -s, -dos & -den balance

Salon /za'lõ:/ m -s, -s salon

salopp a casual; <*Benehmen*> informal

Salto m -s, -s somersault

Salut m -[e]s, -e salute. **s~ieren** vi (*haben*) salute

Salve f -, -n volley; (*Geschütz-*) salvo, (*von Gelächter*) burst

Salz *nt* -es, -e salt. **s~en†** *vt* salt.
  S~fass *nt* salt-cellar. **s~ig** *a* salty.
  S~kartoffeln *fpl* boiled potatoes.
  S~säure *f* hydrochloric acid

Samen *m* -s,- seed; (*Anat*) semen, sperm

Sammel|becken *nt* reservoir.
  s~n *vt/i* (*haben*) collect; (*suchen, versammeln*) gather; **sich s~n** collect; (*sich versammeln*) gather; (*sich fassen*) collect oneself.
  S~name *m* collective noun

Samm|ler(in) *m* -s,- (*f* -, -nen) collector. **S~lung** *f* -, -en collection; (*innere*) composure

Samstag *m* -s, -e Saturday. **s~s** *adv* on Saturdays

samt *prep* (+ *dat*) together with

Samt *m* -[e]s velvet

sämtlich *indef pron inv* all.
  s~e(r,s) *indef pron* all the; **s~e** Werke complete works

Sanatorium *nt* -s, -ien sanatorium

Sand *m* -[e]s sand

Sandale *f* -, -n sandal

Sand|bank *f* sandbank. **S~kasten** *m* sand-pit. **S~papier** *nt* sandpaper

sanft *a* gentle

Sänger(in) *m* -s,-(*f* -, -nen) singer

sanieren *vt* clean up; redevelop <*Gebiet*>; (*modernisieren*) modernize; make profitable <*Industrie, Firma*>; **sich s~** become profitable

sanitär *a* sanitary

Sanität|er *m* -s,- first-aid man; (*Fahrer*) ambulance man; (*Mil*) medical orderly. **S~swagen** *m* ambulance

Sanktion /zaŋk'tsi̯oːn/ *f* -, -en sanction. **s~ieren** *vt* sanction

Saphir *m* -s, -e sapphire

Sardelle *f* -, -n anchovy

Sardine *f* -, -n sardine

Sarg *m* -[e]s,-̈e coffin

Sarkasmus *m* - sarcasm

Satan *m* -s Satan; (🔲 *Teufel*) devil

Satellit *m* -en, -en satellite.
  S~enfernsehen *nt* satellite

television. **S~enschüssel** *f* satellite dish

Satin /za'tɛŋ/ *m* -s satin

Satire *f* -, -n satire

satt *a* full; <*Farbe*> rich; **s~ sein** have had enough [to eat]; **etw s~ haben** 🔳 be fed up with sth

Sattel *m* -s,-̈ saddle. **s~n** *vt* saddle.
  S~zug *m* articulated lorry

sättigen *vt* satisfy; (*Chem & fig*) saturate ● *vi* (*haben*) be filling

Satz *m* -es,-̈e sentence; (*Teil-*) clause; (*These*) proposition; (*Math*) theorem; (*Mus*) movement; (*Tennis, Zusammengehöriges*) set; (*Boden-*) sediment; (*Kaffee-*) grounds *pl*; (*Steuer-, Zins-*) rate; (*Druck-*) setting; (*Schrift-*) type; (*Sprung*) leap, bound.
  S~aussage *f* predicate.
  S~gegenstand *m* subject.
  S~zeichen *nt* punctuation mark

Sau *f* -,Säue sow

sauber *a* clean; (*ordentlich*) neat; (*anständig*) decent; **s~ machen** clean. **S~keit** *f* - cleanliness; neatness

säuberlich *a* neat

Sauce /'zoːsə/ *f* -, -n sauce; (*Braten-*) gravy

Saudi-Arabien /-i̯ən/ *nt* -s Saudi Arabia

sauer *a* sour; (*Chem*) acid; (*eingelegt*) pickled; (*schwer*) hard; **saurer Regen** acid rain

Sauerkraut *nt* sauerkraut

säuerlich *a* slightly sour

Sauerstoff *m* oxygen

saufen† *vt/i* (*haben*) drink; 🔳 booze

Säufer *m* -s,- 🔳 boozer

saugen† *vt/i* (*haben*) suck; (*staub-*) vacuum, hoover; **sich voll Wasser s~** soak up water

säugen *vt* suckle

Säugetier *nt* mammal

saugfähig *a* absorbent

Säugling *m* -s, -e infant

Säule *f* -, -n column

Saum *m* -[e]s,Säume hem; (*Rand*) edge

säumen *vt* hem; (*fig*) line

Sauna f -, -nas & -nen sauna

Säure f -, -n acidity; (*Chem*) acid

sausen vi (*haben*) rush; <*Ohren:*> buzz ● vi (*sein*) rush [along]

Saxophon, Saxofon nt -s, -e saxophone

S-Bahn f city and suburban railway

Scanner m -s,- scanner

sch int shush! (*fort*) shoo!

Schabe f -, -n cockroach

schaben vt/i (*haben*) scrape

schäbig a shabby

Schablone f -, -n stencil; (*Muster*) pattern; (*fig*) stereotype

Schach nt -s chess; S~! check! **S~brett** nt chessboard

Schachfigur f chess-man

schachmatt a s~ setzen checkmate; s~! checkmate!

Schachspiel nt game of chess

Schacht m -[e]s,-̈e shaft

Schachtel f -, -n box; (*Zigaretten-*) packet

Schachzug m move

schade a s~ sein be a pity *or* shame: zu s~ für too good for

Schädel m -s, skull. **S~bruch** m fractured skull

schaden vi (*haben*) (+ *dat*) damage; (*nachteilig sein*) hurt. **S~** m -s,-̈ damage; (*Defekt*) defect; (*Nachteil*) disadvantage. **S~ersatz** m damages pl. **S~freude** f malicious glee. **s~froh** a gloating

schädig|en vt damage, harm. **S~ung** f -, -en damage

schädlich a harmful

Schädling m -s, -e pest. **S~sbekämpfungsmittel** nt pesticide

Schaf nt -[e]s, -e sheep. **S~bock** m ram

Schäfer m -s,- shepherd. **S~hund** m sheepdog; **Deutscher S~hund** alsatian

schaffen[1]† vt create; (*herstellen*) establish; make <*Platz*>

schaffen[2] v (*reg*) ● vt manage [to do]; pass <*Prüfung*>; catch <*Zug*>; (*bringen*) take

Schaffner m -s,- conductor; (*Zug-*) ticket-inspector

Schaffung f - creation

Schaft m -[e]s,-̈e shaft; (*Gewehr-*) stock; (*Stiefel-*) leg

Schal m -s, -s scarf

Schale f -, -n skin; (*abgeschält*) peel; (*Eier-, Nuss-, Muschel-*) shell; (*Schüssel*) dish

schälen vt peel; sich s~ peel

Schall m -[e]s sound. **S~dämpfer** m silencer. **s~dicht** a soundproof. **s~en** vi (*haben*) ring out: (*nachhallen*) resound. **S~mauer** f sound barrier. **S~platte** f record, disc

schalt|en vt switch ● vi (*haben*) switch/<*Ampel:*> turn (auf + *acc* to); (*Auto*) change gear; (🄸 *begreifen*) catch on. **S~er** m -s,- switch; (*Post-, Bank-*) counter; (*Fahrkarten-*) ticket window. **S~hebel** m switch; (*Auto*) gear lever. **S~jahr** nt leap year. **S~ung** f -, -en circuit: (*Auto*) gear change

Scham f - shame; (*Anat*) private parts pl

schämen (sich) vr be ashamed

scham|haft a modest. **s~los** a shameless

Schampon nt -s shampoo. **s~ieren** vt shampoo

Schande f - disgrace, shame

schändlich a disgraceful

Schanktisch m bar

Schanze f, -, -n [ski-]jump

Schar f -, -en crowd; (*Vogel-*) flock

Scharade f -, -n charade

scharen vt um sich s~ gather round one; sich s~ um flock round. **s~weise** adv in droves

scharf a sharp; (*stark*) strong; (*stark gewürzt*) hot; <*Geruch*> pungent; <*Wind, Augen, Verstand*> keen; (*streng*) harsh; <*Galopp*> hard; <*Munition*> live; <*Hund*> fierce; s~ einstellen (*Phot*) focus; s~ sein (*Phot*) be in focus; s~ sein auf (+ *acc*) 🄸 be keen on

Schärfe *f* sharpness; strength; hotness; pungency; keenness; harshness. **s∼n** *vt* sharpen

Scharf|richter *m* executioner. **S∼schütze** *m* marksman. **S∼sinn** *m* astutenes

Scharlach *m* -s scarlet fever

Scharlatan *m* -s, -e charlatan

Scharnier *nt* -s, -e hinge

Schärpe *f* -, -n sash

scharren *vi* (*haben*) scrape; <*Huhn*> scratch ● *vt* scrape

Schaschlik *m* & *nt* -s, -s kebab

Schatten *m* -s,- shadow; (*schattige Stelle*) shade. **S∼riss** *m* silhouette. **S∼seite** *f* shady side; (*fig*) disadvantage

schattier|en *vt* shade. **S∼ung** *f* -, -en shading

schattig *a* shady

Schatz *m* -es,⸗e treasure; (*Freund, Freundin*) sweetheart

schätzen *vt* estimate; (*taxieren*) value; (*achten*) esteem; (*würdigen*) appreciate

Schätzung *f* -, -en estimate; (*Taxierung*) valuation

Schau *f* -, -en show. **S∼ bild** *nt* diagram

Schauder *m* -s shiver; (*vor Abscheu*) shudder. **s∼ haft** *a* dreadful. **s∼n** *vi* (*haben*) shiver; (*vor Abscheu*) shudder

schauen *vi* (*haben*) (*SGer, Aust*) look; **s∼, dass** make sure that

Schauer *m* -s,- shower; (*Schauder*) shiver. **S∼geschichte** *f* horror story. **s∼lich** *a* ghastly

Schaufel *f* -, -n shovel; (*Kehr-*) dustpan. **s∼n** *vt* shovel; (*graben*) dig

Schaufenster *nt* shop-window. **S∼puppe** *f* dummy

Schaukel *f* -, -n swing. **s∼n** *vt* rock ● *vi* (*haben*) rock; (*auf einer Schaukel*) swing; (*schwanken*) sway. **S∼pferd** *nt* rocking-horse. **S∼stuhl** *m* rocking-chair

Schaum *m* -[e]s foam; (*Seifen-*) lather; (*auf Bier*) froth; (*als Frisier-, Rasiermittel*) mousse

schäumen *vi* (*haben*) foam, froth; <*Seife:*> lather

Schaum|gummi *m* foam rubber. **s∼ig** *a* frothy; **s∼ig rühren** (*Culin*) cream. **S∼stoff** *m* [synthetic] foam. **S∼wein** *m* sparkling wine

Schauplatz *m* scene

schaurig *a* dreadful; (*unheimlich*) eerie

Schauspiel *nt* play; (*Anblick*) spectacle. **S∼er** *m* actor. **S∼erin** *f* actress

Scheck *m* -s, -s cheque. **S∼buch, S∼heft** *nt* cheque-book. **S∼karte** *f* cheque card

Scheibe *f* -, -n disc; (*Schieß-*) target; (*Glas-*) pane; (*Brot-, Wurst-*) slice. **S∼nwischer** *m* -s,- windscreen-wiper

Scheich *m* -s, -e & -s sheikh

Scheide *f* -, -n sheath; (*Anat*) vagina

scheid|en† *vt* separate; (*unterscheiden*) distinguish; dissolve <*Ehe*>; **sich s∼en lassen** get divorced ● *vi* (*sein*) leave; (*voneinander*) part. **S∼ung** *f* -, -en divorce

Schein *m* -[e]s, -e light; (*Anschein*) appearance; (*Bescheinigung*) certificate; (*Geld-*) note. **s∼bar** *a* apparent. **s∼en†** *vi* (*haben*) shine; (*den Anschein haben*) seem, appear

scheinheilig *a* hypocritical

Scheinwerfer *m* -s,- floodlight; (*Such-*) searchlight; (*Auto*) headlight; (*Theat*) spotlight

Scheiße *f* - (*vulg*) shit. **s∼n†** *vi* (*haben*) (*vulg*) shit

Scheit *nt* -[e]s, -e log

Scheitel *m* -s,- parting

scheitern *vi* (*sein*) fail

Schelle *f* -, -n bell. **s∼n** *vi* (*haben*) ring

Schellfisch *m* haddock

Schelm *m* -s, -e rogue

Schelte *f* - scolding

Schema *nt* -s, -mata model, pattern; (*Skizze*) diagram

Schemel *m* -s,- stool

Schenke *f* -, -n tavern

Schenkel *m* -s,- thigh

schenken *vt* give [as a present]; **jdm Vertrauen s~** trust s.o.

Scherbe *f* -, -n [broken] piece

Schere *f* -, -n scissors *pl*; (*Techn*) shears *pl*; (*Hummer-*) claw. **s~n¹†** *vt* shear; crop <*Haar*>

scheren² *vt* (*reg*) Ⓣ bother; **sich nicht s~ um** not care about

Scherenschnitt *m* silhouette

Scherereien *fpl* Ⓣ trouble *sg*

Scherz *m* -es, -e joke; **im/zum S~** as a joke. **s~en** *vi* (*haben*) joke

scheu *a* shy; <*Tier*> timid; **s~ werden** <*Pferd:*> shy

scheuchen *vt* shoo

scheuen *vt* be afraid of; (*meiden*) shun; **keine Mühe/Kosten s~** spare no effort/expense; **sich s~** be afraid (**vor** + *dat* of); shrink (**etw zu tun** from doing sth)

scheuern *vt* scrub; (*reiben*) rub; [**wund**] **s~n** chafe ● *vi* (*haben*) rub, chafe

Scheuklappen *fpl* blinkers

Scheune *f* -, -n barn

Scheusal *nt* -s, -e monster

scheußlich *a* horrible

Schi *m* -s, -er ski; **S~ fahren** *od* **laufen** ski

Schicht *f* -, -en layer; (*Geol*) stratum; (*Gesellschafts-*) class; (*Arbeits-*) shift. **S~arbeit** *f* shift work. **s~en** *vt* stack [up]

schick *a* stylish; <*Frau*> chic. **S~** *m* -[e]s style

schicken *vt/i* (*haben*) send; **s~ nach** send for

Schicksal *nt* -s, -e fate. **S~sschlag** *m* misfortune

Schieb|edach *nt* (*Auto*) sun-roof. **s~en†** *vt* push; (*gleitend*) slide; (Ⓣ *handeln mit*) traffic in; **etw s~en auf** (+ *acc*) (*fig*) put sth down to; shift <*Schuld*> on to ● *vi* (*haben*) push. **S~etür** *f* sliding door. **S~ung** *f* -, -en Ⓣ illicit deal; (*Betrug*) rigging, fixing

Schieds|gericht *nt* panel of judges; (*Jur*) arbitration tribunal. **S~richter** *m* referee; (*Tennis*) umpire; (*Jur*) arbitrator

schief *a* crooked; (*unsymmetrisch*) lopsided; (*geneigt*) slanting, sloping; (*nicht senkrecht*) leaning; <*Winkel*> oblique; (*fig*) false; suspicious ● *adv* not straight; **s~ gehen** Ⓣ go wrong

Schiefer *m* -s slate

schielen *vi* (*haben*) squint

Schienbein *nt* shin

Schiene *f* -, -n rail; (*Gleit-*) runner; (*Med*) splint. **s~n** *vt* (*Med*) put in a splint

Schieß|bude *f* shooting-gallery. **s~en†** *vt* shoot; fire <*Kugel*>; score <*Tor*> ● *vi* (*haben*) shoot, fire (**auf** + *acc* at). **S~scheibe** *f* target. **S~stand** *m* shooting-range

Schifahr|en *nt* skiing. **S~er(in)** *m(f)* skier

Schiff *nt* -[e]s, -e ship; (*Kirchen-*) nave; (*Seiten-*) aisle

Schiffahrt* *f* s. Schifffahrt

schiff|bar *a* navigable. **S~bruch** *m* shipwreck. **s~brüchig** *a* shipwrecked. **S~fahrt** *f* shipping

Schikan|e *f* -, -n harassment; **mit allen S~en** Ⓣ with every refinement. **s~ieren** *vt* harass

Schi|laufen *nt* -s skiing. **S~läufer(in)** *m(f)* -s,- (*f* -, -nen) skier

Schild¹ *m* -[e]s, -e shield

Schild² *nt* -[e]s, -er sign; (*Nummern-*) plate; (*Mützen-*) badge; (*Etikett*) label

Schilddrüse *f* thyroid [gland]

schilder|n *vt* describe. **S~ung** *f* -, -en description

Schild|kröte *f* tortoise; (*See-*) turtle. **S~patt** *nt* -[e]s tortoiseshell

Schilf *nt* -[e]s reeds *pl*

schillern *vi* (*haben*) shimmer

Schimmel *m* -s,- mould; (*Pferd*) white horse. **s~n** *vi* (*haben/sein*) go mouldy

schimmern *vi* (*haben*) gleam

Schimpanse *m* -n, -n chimpanzee

schimpf|en *vi* (*haben*) grumble (**mit** at; **über** + *acc* about); scold (**mit jdm**

s.o.) ● *vt* call. **S~wort** *nt* (*pl* -wörter) swear-word

Schinken *m* -s,- ham. **S~speck** *m* bacon

Schippe *f* -, -n shovel. **s~n** *vt* shovel

Schirm *m* -[e]s, -e umbrella; (*Sonnen-*) sunshade; (*Lampen-*) shade; (*Augen-*) visor; (*Mützen-*) peak; (*Ofen-, Bild-*) screen; (*fig: Schutz:*) shield. **S~herrschaft** *f* patronage. **S~mütze** *f* peaked cap

schizophren *a* schizophrenic. **S~ie** *f* - schizophrenia

Schlacht *f* -, -en battle

schlachten *vt* slaughter, kill

Schlacht|feld *nt* battlefield. **S~hof** *m* abattoir

Schlacke *f* -, -n slag

Schlaf *m* -[e]s sleep; im S~ in one's sleep. **S~anzug** *m* pyjamas *pl*

Schläfe *f* -, -n (*Anat*) temple

schlafen† *vi* (*haben*) sleep; **s~ gehen** go to bed; **er schläft noch** he is still asleep

schlaff *a* limp; <*Seil*> slack; <*Muskel*> flabby

Schlaf|lied *nt* lullaby. **s~los** *a* sleepless. **S~losigkeit** *f* - insomnia. **S~mittel** *nt* sleeping drug

schläfrig *a* sleepy

Schlaf|saal *m* dormitory. **S~sack** *m* sleeping-bag. **S~tablette** *f* sleeping-pill. **S~wagen** *m* sleeping-car, sleeper. **s~wandeln** *vi* (*haben/sein*) sleep-walk. **S~zimmer** *nt* bedroom

Schlag *m* -[e]s,⸚e blow; (*Faust-*) punch; (*Herz-, Puls-, Trommel-*) beat; (*einer Uhr*) chime; (*Glocken-, Gong- & Med*) stroke; (*elektrischer*) shock; (*Art*) type; **S~ e** bekommen get a beating; **S~ auf S~** in rapid succession. **S~ader** *f* artery. **S~anfall** *m* stroke. **S~baum** *m* barrier

schlagen† *vt* hit, strike; (*fällen*) fell; knock <*Loch, Nagel*> (in + *acc*

into); (*prügeln, besiegen*) beat; (*Culin*) whisk <*Eiweiß*>; whip <*Sahne*>; (*legen*) throw; (*wickeln*) wrap; **sich s~** fight ● *vi* (*haben*) beat; <*Tür:*> bang; <*Uhr:*> strike; (*melodisch*) chime; **mit den Flügeln s~** flap its wings ● *vi* (*sein*) **in etw** (*acc*) **s~** <*Blitz, Kugel:*> strike sth; **nach jdm s~** (*fig*) take after s.o.

Schlager *m* -s,- popular song; (*Erfolg*) hit

Schläger *m* -s,- racket; (*Tischtennis-*) bat; (*Golf-*) club; (*Hockey-*) stick. **S~ei** *f* -, -en fight, brawl

schlag|fertig *a* quick-witted. **S~loch** *nt* pot-hole. **S~sahne** *f* whipped cream; (*ungeschlagen*) whipping cream. **S~seite** *f* (*Naut*) list. **S~stock** *m* truncheon. **S~wort** *nt* (*pl* -worte) slogan. **S~zeile** *f* headline. **S~zeug** *nt* (*Mus*) percussion. **S~zeuger** *m* -s,- percussionist; (*in Band*) drummer

Schlamm *m* -[e]s mud. **s~ig** *a* muddy

Schlampe|e *f* -, -n 🔢 slut. **s~en** *vi* (*haben*) 🔢 be sloppy (**bei** in). **s~ig** *a* slovenly; <*Arbeit*> sloppy

Schlange *f* -, -n snake; (*Menschen-, Auto-*) queue; **S~ stehen** queue

schlängeln (sich) *vr* wind; <*Person:*> weave (**durch** through)

schlank *a* slim. **S~heitskur** *f* slimming diet

schlapp *a* tired; (*schlaff*) limp

schlau *a* clever; (*gerissen*) crafty; **ich werde nicht s~ daraus** I can't make head or tail of it

Schlauch *m* -[e]s,Schläuche tube; (*Wasser-*) hose[pipe]. **S~boot** *nt* rubber dinghy

Schlaufe *f* -, -n loop

schlecht *a* bad; (*böse*) wicked; (*unzulänglich*) poor; **s~ werden** go bad; <*Wetter:*> turn bad; **mir ist s~** I feel sick; **s~ machen** 🔢 run down. **s~gehen*** *vi sep* (*sein*) **s~ gehen**, s. **gehen**

schlecken *vt/i* (*haben*) lick (**an etw** *dat* sth); (*auf-*) lap up

Schlegel *m* -s,- (*SGer: Keule*) leg; (*Hühner-*) drumstick

schleichen† *vi* (*sein*) creep; (*langsam gehen/fahren*) crawl ● *vr* sich s~ creep. **s~d** *a* creeping

Schleier *m* -s,- veil; (*fig*) haze

Schleife *f* -, -n bow; (*Fliege*) bowtie; (*Biegung*) loop

schleifen¹ *v* (*reg*) ● *vt* drag ● *vi* (*haben*) trail, drag

schleifen²† *vt* grind; (*schärfen*) sharpen; cut <*Edelstein, Glas*>

Schleim *m* -[e]s slime; (*Anat*) mucus; (*Med*) phlegm. **s~ig** *a* slimy

schlendern *vi* (*sein*) stroll

schlenkern *vt/i* (*haben*) swing; s~ mit swing; dangle <*Beine*>

Schlepp|dampfer *m* tug. **S~e** *f* -, -n train. **s~en** *vt* drag; (*tragen*) carry; (*ziehen*) tow; **sich s~en** drag oneself; (*sich hinziehen*) drag on; **sich s~en mit** carry. **S~er** *m* -s,- tug; (*Traktor*) tractor. **S~kahn** *m* barge. **S~lift** *m* T-bar lift. **S~tau** *nt* tow-rope; **ins S~tau nehmen** take in tow

Schleuder *f* -, -n catapult; (*Wäsche-*) spin-drier. **s~n** *vt* hurl; spin <*Wäsche*> ● *vi* (*sein*) skid; **ins S~n geraten** skid. **S~sitz** *m* ejector seat

Schleuse *f* -, -n lock; (*Sperre*) sluice[-gate]. **s~n** *vt* steer

Schliche *pl* tricks

schlicht *a* plain; simple

Schlichtung *f* - settlement; (*Jur*) arbitration

Schließe *f* -, -n clasp; buckle

schließen† *vt* close (*ab-*) lock; fasten <*Kleid, Verschluss*>; (*stilllegen*) close down; (*beenden, folgern*) conclude; enter into <*Vertrag*>; **sich s~** close; **etw s~ an** (+ *acc*) connect sth to; **sich s~ an** (+ *acc*) follow ● *vi* (*haben*) close, (*den Betrieb einstellen*) close down; (*den Schlüssel drehen*) turn the key; (*enden, folgern*) conclude

Schließ|fach *nt* locker. **s~lich** *adv* finally, in the end; (*immerhin*) after all. **S~ung** *f* -, -en closure

Schliff *m* -[e]s cut; (*Schleifen*) cutting; (*fig*) polish

schlimm *a* bad

Schlinge *f* -, -n loop; (*Henkers-*) noose; (*Med*) sling; (*Falle*) snare

Schlingel *m* -s,- 🛈 rascal

schlingen† *vt* wind, wrap; tie <*Knoten*> ● *vi* (*haben*) bolt one's food

Schlips *m* -es, -e tie

Schlitten *m* -s,- sledge; (*Rodel-*) toboggan; (*Pferde-*) sleigh; **S~ fahren** toboggan

schlittern *vi* (*haben*/ *sein*) slide

Schlittschuh *m* skate; **S~ laufen** skate. **S~läufer(in)** *m(f)* -s,- (*f* -, -nen) skater

Schlitz *m* -es, -e slit; (*für Münze*) slot; (*Jacken-*) vent; (*Hosen-*) flies *pl*. **s~en** *vt* slit

Schloss *nt* -es,¨er lock; (*Vorhänge-*) padlock; (*Verschluss*) clasp; (*Gebäude*) castle; palace

Schlosser *m* -s,- locksmith; (*Auto-*) mechanic

Schlucht *f* -, -en ravine, gorge

schluchzen *vi* (*haben*) sob

Schluck *m* -[e]s, -e mouthful; (*klein*) sip

Schluckauf *m* -s hiccups *pl*

schlucken *vt/i* (*haben*) swallow

Schlummer *m* -s slumber

Schlund *m* -[e]s [back of the] throat; (*fig*) mouth

schlüpf|en *vi* (*sein*) slip; [aus dem Ei] s~en hatch. **S~er** *m* -s,- knickers *pl*. **s~rig** *a* slippery

schlürfen *vt/i* (*haben*) slurp

Schluss *m* -es,¨e end; (*S~folgerung*) conclusion; **zum S~** finally; **S~ machen** stop (**mit etw** sth); finish (**mit jdm** with s.o.)

Schlüssel *m* -s,- key; (*Schrauben-*) spanner; (*Geheim-*) code; (*Mus*) clef. **S~bein** *nt* collar-bone. **S~bund** *m* & *nt* bunch of keys. **S~loch** *nt* keyhole

Schlussfolgerung *f* conclusion

schlüssig *a* conclusive

Schluss|licht nt rear-light.
S~verkauf m sale
schmächtig a slight
schmackhaft a tasty
schmal a narrow; (dünn) thin;
(schlank) slender; (karg) meagre
schmälern vt diminish;
(herabsetzen) belittle
Schmalz¹ nt -es lard; (Ohren-) wax
Schmalz² m -es 🛈 schmaltz
Schmarotzer m -s,- parasite;
(Person) sponger
schmatzen vi (haben) eat noisily
schmausen vi (haben) feast
schmecken vi (haben) taste (nach
of); [gut] s~ taste good ● vt taste
Schmeichelei f -, -en flattery;
(Kompliment) compliment
schmeichel|haft a
complimentary, flattering. **s~n** vi
(haben) (+ dat) flatter
schmeißen† vt/i (haben) s~ [mit]
🛈 chuck
Schmeißfliege f bluebottle
schmelz|en† vt/i (sein) melt; smelt
<Erze>. **S~wasser** nt melted snow
and ice
Schmerbauch m 🛈 paunch
Schmerz m -es, -en pain; (Kummer)
grief; S~en haben be in pain. **s~en**
vt hurt; (fig) grieve ● vi (haben)
hurt, be painful. **S~ensgeld** nt
compensation for pain and suffering.
s~haft a painful. **s~los** a painless
s~stillend a pain-killing;
s~stillendes Mittel analgesic, pain-
killer. **S~tablette** f pain-killer
Schmetterball m (Tennis) smash
Schmetterling m -s, -e butterfly
schmettern vt hurl; (Tennis)
smash; (singen) sing ● vi (haben)
sound
Schmied m -[e]s, -e blacksmith
Schmiede f -, -n forge. **S~eisen**
nt wrought iron. **s~n** vt forge
Schmier|e f -, -n grease; (Schmutz)
mess. **s~en** vt lubricate; (streichen)
spread; (schlecht schreiben) scrawl
● vi (haben) smudge; (schreiben)

scrawl. **S~geld** nt 🛈 bribe. **s~ig** a
greasy; (schmutzig) grubby.
S~mittel nt lubricant
Schminke f -, -n make-up. **s~n** vt
make up; sich s~n put on make-up;
sich (dat) die Lippen s~n put on
lipstick
schmirgel|n vt sand down.
S~papier nt emery-paper
schmollen vi (haben) sulk
schmor|en vt/i (haben) braise.
S~topf m casserole
Schmuck m -[e]s jewellery;
(Verzierung) ornament, decoration
schmücken vt decorate, adorn
schmuck|los a plain. **S~stück**
nt piece of jewellery
Schmuggel m -s smuggling. **s~n**
vt smuggle. **S~ware** f contraband
Schmuggler m -s,- smuggler
schmunzeln vi (haben) smile
schmusen vi (haben) cuddle
Schmutz m -es dirt. **s~en** vi
(haben) get dirty. **s~ig** a dirty
Schnabel m -s,ˉ beak, bill; (eines
Kruges) lip; (Tülle) spout
Schnalle f -, -n buckle. **s~n** vt
strap; (zu-) buckle
schnalzen vi (haben) mit der Zunge
s~ click one's tongue
schnapp|en vi (haben) s~en nach
snap at; gasp for <Luft> ● vt snatch,
grab; (🛈 festnehmen) nab.
S~schloss nt spring lock.
S~schuss m snapshot
Schnaps m -es,ˉe schnapps
schnarchen vi (haben) snore
schnaufen vi (haben) puff, pant
Schnauze f -, -n muzzle; (eines
Kruges) lip; (Tülle) spout
schnäuzen (sich) vr blow one's
nose
Schnecke f -, -n snail; (Nackt-)
slug; (Spirale) scroll. **S~nhaus** nt
snail-shell
Schnee m -s snow; (Eier-) beaten
egg-white. **S~besen** m whisk.
S~brille f snow-goggles pl. **S~fall**
m snowfall. **S~flocke** f snowflake.
S~glöckchen nt -s,- snowdrop.
S~kette f snow chain. **S~mann**

m (*pl* **-männer**) snowman. **S~pflug** *m* snowplough. **S~schläger** *m* whisk. **S~sturm** *m* snowstorm, blizzard. **S~wehe** *f* -, **-n** snowdrift

Schneide *f* -, **-n** [cutting] edge; (*Klinge*) blade

schneiden† *vt* cut; (*in Scheiben*) slice; (*kreuzen*) cross; (*nicht beachten*) cut dead; **Gesichter s~** pull faces; **sich s~** cut oneself; (*über-*) intersect

Schneider *m* -s,- tailor. **S~in** *f* -, **-nen** dressmaker. **s~n** *vt* make <*Anzug, Kostüm*>

Schneidezahn *m* incisor

schneien *vi* (*haben*) snow; **es schneit** it is snowing

Schneise *f* -, **-n** path

schnell *a* quick; <*Auto, Tempo*> fast ● *adv* quickly; (*in s~em Tempo*) fast; (*bald*) soon; **mach s~!** hurry up! **S~igkeit** *f* - rapidity; (*Tempo*) speed. **S~kochtopf** *m* pressure-cooker. **s~stens** *adv* as quickly as possible. **S~zug** *m* express [train]

schnetzeln *vt* cut into thin strips

Schnipsel *m* & *nt* -s,- scrap

Schnitt *m* -[e]s, **-e** cut; (*Film-*) cutting; (*S~muster*) [paper] pattern; **im S~** (*durchschnittlich*) on average

Schnitte *f* -, **-n** slice [of bread]

schnittig *a* stylish; (*stromlinienförmig*) streamlined

Schnitt|lauch *m* chives *pl*. **S~muster** *nt* [paper] pattern. **S~punkt** *m* [point of] intersection. **S~wunde** *f* cut

Schnitzel *nt* -s,- scrap; (*Culin*) escalope. **s~n** *vt* shred

schnitzen *vt/i* (*haben*) carve

schnodderig *a* 🔲 brash

Schnorchel *m* -s,- snorkel

Schnörkel *m* -s,- flourish; (*Kunst*) scroll. **s~ig** *a* ornate

schnüffeln *vi* (*haben*) sniff (**an etw** *dat* sth); (🔲 *spionieren*) snoop [around]

Schnuller *m* -s,- [baby's] dummy

Schnupf|en *m* -s,- [head] cold. **S~tabak** *m* snuff

schnuppern *vt/i* (*haben*) sniff (**an etw** *dat* sth)

Schnur *f* -,⸚e string; (*Kordel*) cord; (*Electr*) flex

schnüren *vt* tie; lace [up] <*Schuhe*>

Schnurr|bart *m* moustache. **s~en** *vi* (*haben*) hum; <*Katze:*> purr

Schnürsenkel *m* [shoe-]lace

Schock *m* -[e]s, **-s** shock. **s~en** *vt* 🔲 shock. **s~ieren** *vt* shock

Schöffe *m* -n, **-n** lay judge

Schokolade *f* - chocolate

Scholle *f* -, **-n** clod [of earth]; (*Eis-*) [ice-]floe; (*Fisch*) plaice

schon *adv* already; (*allein*) just; (*sogar*) even; (*ohnehin*) anyway; **s~ einmal** before; (*jemals*) ever; **s~ immer/oft/wieder** always/often/again; **s~ deshalb** for that reason alone; **das ist s~ möglich** that's quite possible; **ja s~, aber** well yes, but

schön *a* beautiful; <*Wetter*> fine; (*angenehm, nett*) nice; (*gut*) good; (🔲 *beträchtlich*) pretty; **s~en Dank!** thank you very much!

schonen *vt* spare; (*gut behandeln*) look after. **s~d** *a* gentle

Schönheit *f* -, **-en** beauty. **S~sfehler** *m* blemish. **S~skonkurrenz** *f* beauty contest

Schonung *f* -, **-en** gentle care; (*nach Krankheit*) rest; (*Baum-*) plantation. **s~slos** *a* ruthless

Schonzeit *f* close season

schöpf|en *vt* scoop [up]; ladle <*Suppe*>; **Mut s~en** take heart. **s~erisch** *a* creative. **S~kelle** *f*. **S~löffel** *m* ladle. **S~ung** *f* -, **-en** creation

Schoppen *m* -s,- (*SGer*) ≈ pint

Schorf *m* -[e]s scab

Schornstein *m* chimney. **S~feger** *m* -s,- chimney-sweep

Schoß *m* -es,⸚e lap; (*Frack-*) tail

Schössling *m* -s, **-e** (*Bot*) shoot

Schote *f* -, **-n** pod; (*Erbse*) pea

Schotte *m* -n, **-n** Scot, Scotsman

Schotter *m* -s gravel

schott|isch *a* Scottish, Scots. **S~land** *nt* -s Scotland

schraffieren *vt* hatch

schräg *a* diagonal; (*geneigt*) sloping; **s∼ halten** tilt. **S∼strich** *m* oblique stroke

Schramme *f* -, -n scratch

Schrank *m* -[e]s,-̈e cupboard; (*Kleider-*) wardrobe; (*Akten-, Glas-*) cabinet

Schranke *f* -, -n barrier

Schraube *f* -, -n screw; (*Schiffs-*) propeller. **s∼n** *vt* screw; (*ab-*) unscrew; (*drehen*) turn. **S∼nschlüssel** *m* spanner. **S∼nzieher** *m* -s,- screwdriver

Schraubstock *m* vice

Schreck *m* -[e]s, -e fright. **S∼en** *m* -s,- fright; (*Entsetzen*) horror

Schreck|gespenst *nt* spectre. **s∼haft** *a* easily frightened; (*nervös*) jumpy. **s∼lich** *a* terrible. **S∼schuss** *m* warning shot

Schrei *m* -[e]s, -e cry, shout; (*gellend*) scream; **der letzte S∼** 🔤 the latest thing

schreib|en† *vt/i* (*haben*) write; (*auf der Maschine*) type; **richtig/falsch s∼en** spell right/wrong; **sich s∼en** <*Wort:*> be spelt; (*korrespondieren*) correspond. **S∼en** *nt* -s,- writing; (*Brief*) letter. **S∼fehler** *m* spelling mistake. **S∼heft** *nt* exercise book. **S∼kraft** *f* clerical assistant; (*für Maschineschreiben*) typist. **S∼maschine** *f* typewriter. **S∼tisch** *m* desk. **S∼ung** *f* -, -en spelling. **S∼waren** *fpl* stationery *sg*.

schreien† *vt/i* (*haben*) cry; (*gellend*) scream; (*rufen, laut sprechen*) shout

Schreiner *m* -s,- joiner

schreiten† *vi* (*sein*) walk

Schrift *f* -, -en writing; (*Druck-*) type; (*Abhandlung*) paper; **die Heilige S∼** the Scriptures *pl*. **S∼führer** *m* secretary. **s∼lich** *a* written ● *adv* in writing. **S∼sprache** *f* written language. **S∼steller(in)** *m* (-*f* -, -nen) writer. **S∼stück** *nt* document. **S∼zeichen** *nt* character

schrill *a* shrill

Schritt *m* -[e]s, -e step; (*Entfernung*) pace; (*Gangart*) walk; (*der Hose*) crotch. **S∼macher** *m* -s,- pacemaker. **s∼weise** *adv* step by step

schroff *a* precipitous; (*abweisend*) brusque; (*unvermittelt*) abrupt; <*Gegensatz*> stark

Schrot *m* & *nt* -[e]s coarse meal; (*Blei-*) small shot. **S∼flinte** *f* shotgun

Schrott *m* -[e]s scrap[-metal]; **zu S∼ fahren** 🔤 write off. **S∼platz** *m* scrap-yard

schrubben *vt/i* (*haben*) scrub

Schrull|e *f* -, -n whim; **alte S∼e** 🔤 old crone. **s∼ig** *a* cranky

schrumpfen *vi* (*sein*) shrink

schrump[e]lig *a* wrinkled

Schub *m* -[e]s,-̈e (*Phys*) thrust; (*S∼fach*) drawer; (*Menge*) batch. **S∼fach** *nt* drawer. **S∼karre** *f*, **S∼karren** *m* wheelbarrow. **S∼lade** *f* drawer

Schubs *m* -es, -e push, shove **s∼en** *vt* push, shove

schüchtern *a* shy. **S∼heit** *f* - shyness

Schuft *m* -[e]s, -e (*pej*) swine

Schuh *m* -[e]s, -e shoe. **S∼anzieher** *m* -s,- shoehorn. **S∼band** *nt* (*pl* -bänder) shoe-lace. **S∼creme** *f* shoe-polish. **S∼löffel** *m* shoehorn. **S∼macher** *m* -s,- shoemaker

Schul|abgänger *m* -s,- schoolleaver. **S∼arbeiten**, **S∼aufgaben** *fpl* homework *sg*.

Schuld *f* -, -en guilt; (*Verantwortung*) blame; (*Geld-*) debt; **S∼en machen** get into debt; **S∼ haben** be to blame (**an** + *dat* for); **jdm S∼ geben** blame s.o. ● **s∼ sein** be to blame (**an** + *dat* for). **s∼en** *vt* owe

schuldig *a* guilty (*gen* of); (*gebührend*) due; **jdm etw s∼ sein** owe s.o. sth. **S∼keit** *f* - duty

schuld|los *a* innocent. **S∼ner** *m* -s,- debtor. **S∼spruch** *m* guilty verdict

Schule *f* -, -n school; **in der/die S∼** at/to school. **s∼n** *vt* train

Schüler(in) *m* -s,- (*f* -, -nen) pupil

schul|frei *a* s~freier Tag day without school; **wir haben morgen s~frei** there's no school tomorrow. **S~hof** *m* [school] playground. **S~jahr** *nt* school year; (*Klasse*) form. **S~kind** *nt* schoolchild. **S~stunde** *f* lesson

Schulter *f* -, -n shoulder. **S~blatt** *nt* shoulder-blade

Schulung *f* - training

schummeln *vi* (*haben*) 🄴 cheat

Schund *m* -[e]s trash

Schuppe *f* -, -n scale; **S~n** *pl* dandruff *sg*. **s~n (sich)** *vr* flake [off]

Schuppen *m* -s,- shed

schürf|en *vt* mine; **sich** (*dat*) **das Knie s~en** graze one's knee ● *vi* (*haben*) **s~en nach** prospect for. **S~wunde** *f* abrasion, graze

Schürhaken *m* poker

Schurke *m* -n, -n villain

Schürze *f* -, -n apron

Schuss *m* -es,-̈e shot; (*kleine Menge*) dash

Schüssel *f* -, -n bowl; (*TV*) dish

Schuss|fahrt *f* (*Ski*) schuss. **S~waffe** *f* firearm

Schuster *m* -s,- = Schuhmacher

Schutt *m* -[e]s rubble. **S~abladeplatz** *m* rubbish dump

Schüttel|frost *m* shivering fit. **s~n** *vt* shake; **sich s~n** shake oneself/itself; (*vor Ekel*) shudder; **jdm die Hand s~n** shake s.o.'s hand

schütten *vt* pour; (*kippen*) tip; (*ver-*) spill ● *vi* (*haben*) **es schüttet** it is pouring [with rain]

Schutz *m* -es protection; (*Zuflucht*) shelter; (*Techn*) guard; **S~ suchen** take refuge. **S~anzug** *m* protective suit. **S~blech** *nt* mudguard. **S~brille** *f* goggles *pl*

Schütze *m* -n, -n marksman; (*Tor-*) scorer; (*Astr*) Sagittarius

schützen *vt* protect/(*Zuflucht gewähren*) shelter (**vor** + *dat* from) ● *vi* (*haben*) give protection/shelter (**vor** + *dat* from)

Schutz|engel *m* guardian angel. **S~heilige(r)** *m/f* patron saint

Schützling *m* -s, -e charge

schutz|los *a* defenceless, helpless. **S~mann** *m* (*pl* -männer & -leute) policeman. **S~umschlag** *m* dust-jacket

Schwaben *nt* -s Swabia

schwäbisch *a* Swabian

schwach *a* weak; (*nicht gut; gering*) poor; (*leicht*) faint

Schwäche *f* -, -n weakness. **s~n** *vt* weaken

schwäch|lich *a* delicate. **S~ling** *m* -s, -e weakling

Schwachsinn *m* mental deficiency. **s~ig** *a* mentally deficient; 🄴 idiotic

Schwager *m* -s,-̈ brother-in-law

Schwägerin *f* -, -nen sister-in-law

Schwalbe *f* -, -n swallow

Schwall *m* -[e]s torrent

Schwamm *m* -[e]s,-̈e sponge; (*SGer: Pilz*) fungus; (*essbar*) mushroom. **s~ig** *a* spongy

Schwan *m* -[e]s,-̈e swan

schwanger *a* pregnant

Schwangerschaft *f* -, -en pregnancy

Schwank *m* -[e]s,-̈e (*Theat*) farce

schwank|en *vi* (*haben*) sway; <*Boot:*> rock; (*sich ändern*) fluctuate; (*unentschieden sein*) be undecided ● (*sein*) stagger. **S~ung** *f* -, -en fluctuation

Schwanz *m* -es,-̈e tail

schwänzen *vt* 🄴 skip; **die Schule s~** play truant

Schwarm *m* -[e]s,-̈e swarm; (*Fisch-*) shoal; (🄴 *Liebe*) idol

schwärmen *vi* (*haben*) swarm; **s~ für** 🄴 adore; (*verliebt sein*) have a crush on

Schwarte *f* -, -n (*Speck-*) rind

schwarz *a* black; (🄴 *illegal*) illegal; **s~er Markt** black market; **s~ gekleidet** dressed in black; **s~ auf weiß** in black and white; **s~ sehen** (*fig*) be pessimistic; **ins S~e treffen** score a bull's-eye. **S~** *nt* -[e]s,- black. **S~arbeit** *f* moonlighting.

s~**arbeiten** vi sep (haben)
moonlight. **S~e(r)** m/f black
Schwärze f - blackness. **s~n** vt
blacken
Schwarz|fahrer m fare-dodger.
S~handel m black market (mit in).
S~händler m black marketeer.
S~markt m black market.
S~wald m Black Forest. **s~weiß**
a black and white
schwatzen, (SGer) **schwätzen** vi
(haben) chat; (klatschen) gossip;
(Sch) talk [in class] ● vt talk
Schwebe f - in der S~ (fig)
undecided. **S~bahn** f cable railway.
s~n vi (haben) float; (fig) be
undecided; <Verfahren:> be pending;
in Gefahr s~n be in danger ● (sein)
float
Schwed|e m -n, -n Swede. **S~en**
nt -s Sweden. **S~in** f -, -nen Swede.
s~isch a Swedish
Schwefel m -s sulphur
schweigen† vi (haben) be silent;
ganz zu s~ von let alone. **S~** nt -s
silence; zum **S~** bringen silence
schweigsam a silent; (wortkarg)
taciturn
Schwein nt -[e]s, -e pig; (Culin)
pork; ⊠ Schuft) swine; **S~ haben** ▣
be lucky. **S~ebraten** m roast pork.
S~efleisch nt pork. **S~erei** f -,
-en ⊠ [dirty] mess; (Gemeinheit)
dirty trick. **S~estall** m pigsty.
S~sleder nt pigskin
Schweiß m -es sweat
schweißen vt weld
Schweiz (die) - Switzerland. **S~er**
a & m -s,-, **S~erin** f -, -nen Swiss.
s~erisch a Swiss
Schwelle f -, -n threshold;
(Eisenbahn-) sleeper
schwell|en† vi (sein) swell.
S~ung f -, -en swelling
schwer a heavy; (schwierig)
difficult; (mühsam) hard; (ernst)
serious; (schlimm) bad; **3 Pfund s~**
sein weigh 3 pounds ● adv heavily;
with difficulty; (mühsam) hard;
(schlimm, sehr) badly, seriously; **s~**

krank/verletzt seriously ill/injured;
s~ hören be hard of hearing; etw s~
nehmen take sth seriously; jdm s~
fallen be hard for s.o.; es jdm s~
machen make it or things difficult
for s.o.; sich s~ tun have difficulty
(mit with); s~ zu sagen difficult or
hard to say
Schwere f - heaviness; (Gewicht)
weight; (Schwierigkeit) difficulty;
(Ernst) gravity. **S~losigkeit** f -
weightlessness
schwer|fällig a ponderous,
clumsy. **S~gewicht** nt
heavyweight. **s~hörig** a s~hörig
sein be hard of hearing. **S~kraft** f
(Phys) gravity. **s~mütig** a
melancholic. **S~punkt** m centre of
gravity; (fig) emphasis
Schwert nt -[e]s, -er sword. **S~lilie**
f iris
Schwer|verbrecher m serious
offender. **s~wiegend** a weighty
Schwester f -, -n sister; (Kranken-)
nurse. **s~lich** a sisterly
Schwieger|eltern pl parents-in-
law. **S~mutter** f mother-in-law.
S~sohn m son-in-law. **S~tochter**
f daughter-in-law. **S~vater** m
father-in-law
schwierig a difficult. **S~keit** f -,
-en difficulty
Schwimm|bad nt swimming-baths
pl. **S~becken** nt swimming-pool.
s~en† vt/i (sein/haben) swim; (auf
dem Wasser treiben) float.
S~weste f life-jacket
Schwindel m -s dizziness, vertigo;
(▣ Betrug) fraud; (Lüge) lie.
S~anfall m dizzy spell. **s~frei** a
s~frei sein have a good head for
heights. **s~n** vi (haben) lie
Schwindl|er m -s,- liar; (Betrüger)
fraud, con-man. **s~ig** a dizzy; **mir
ist** od **wird s~ig** I feel dizzy
schwing|en† vi (haben) swing;
(Phys) oscillate; (vibrieren) vibrate
● vt swing; wave <Fahne>; (drohend)
brandish. **S~ung** f -, -en oscillation;
vibration
Schwips m -es, -e einen S~ haben
▣ be tipsy

---

*old spelling

schwitzen vi (haben) sweat; **ich schwitze** I am hot

schwören† vt/i (haben) swear (**auf** + acc by)

schwul a (🔲 homosexuell) gay

schwül a close. **S~e** f - closeness

Schwung m -[e]s,⁻e swing; (Bogen) sweep; (Schnelligkeit) momentum; (Kraft) vigour. **s~los** a dull. **s~voll** a vigorous; <Bogen, Linie> sweeping; (mitreißend) spirited

Schwur m -[e]s,⁻e vow; (Eid) oath. **S~gericht** nt jury [court]

sechs inv a, **S~** f -, -en six; (Sch) ≈ fail mark. **s~eckig** a hexagonal. **s~te(r,s)** a sixth

sech|zehn inv a sixteen. **s~zehnte(r,s)** a sixteenth. **s~zig** inv a sixty. **s~zigste(r,s)** a sixtieth

See¹ m -s, -n /'ze:ən/ lake

See² f - sea; **an die/der See** to/at the seaside; **auf See** at sea. **S~fahrt** f [sea] voyage; (Schifffahrt) navigation. **S~gang** m schwerer **S~gang** rough sea. **S~hund** m seal. **s~krank** a seasick

Seele f -, -n soul

seelisch a psychological; (geistig) mental

See|macht f maritime power. **S~mann** m (pl -leute) seaman, sailor. **S~not** f in **S~not** in distress. **S~räuber** m pirate. **S~reise** f [sea] voyage. **S~rose** f water-lily. **S~sack** m kitbag. **S~stern** m starfish. **S~tang** m seaweed. **s~tüchtig** a seaworthy. **S~zunge** f sole

Segel nt -s,- sail. **S~boot** nt sailing-boat. **S~flugzeug** nt glider. **s~n** vt/i (sein/haben) sail. **S~schiff** nt sailing-ship. **S~sport** m sailing. **S~tuch** nt canvas

Segen m -s blessing

Segler m -s,- yachtsman

segnen vt bless

sehen† vt see; watch <Fernsehsendung>; **jdn/etw wieder s~** see s.o./sth again; **sich s~ lassen** show oneself ● vi (haben) see; (blicken) look (**auf** + acc at); (ragen) show (**aus** above); **gut/schlecht s~** have good/bad eyesight; **vom S~ kennen** know by sight; **s~ nach** keep an eye on; (betreuen) look after; (suchen) look for. **s~swert, s~swürdig** a worth seeing. **S~swürdigkeit** f -, -en sight

Sehne f -, -n tendon; (eines Bogens) string

sehnen (sich) vr long (**nach** for)

Sehn|sucht f - longing (**nach** for). **s~süchtig** a longing; <Wunsch> dearest

sehr adv very; (mit Verb) very much; **so s~, dass** so much that

seicht a shallow

seid s. sein¹

Seide f -, -n silk

Seidel nt -s,- beer-mug

seiden a silk ... **S~papier** nt tissue paper. **S~raupe** f silk-worm

seidig a silky

Seife f -, -n soap. **S~npulver** nt soap powder. **S~nschaum** m lather

Seil nt -[e]s, -e rope; (Draht-) cable. **S~bahn** f cable railway. **s~springen**† vi (sein) (inf & pp only) skip. **S~tänzer(in)** m(f) tightrope walker

....

sein†¹
● intransitive verb (sein)
····▸ be. **ich bin glücklich** I am happy. **er ist Lehrer/Schwede** he is a teacher/Swedish. **bist du es?** is that you? **sei still!** be quiet! **sie waren in Paris** they were in Paris. **morgen bin ich zu Hause** I shall be at home tomorrow. **er ist aus Berlin** he is or comes from Berlin
····▸ (impers + dat) **mir ist kalt/besser** I am cold/better. **ihr ist schlecht** she feels sick
····▸ (existieren) be. **es ist/sind ...** there is/are .... **es ist keine Hoffnung mehr** there is no more hope. **es sind vier davon** there are four of them. **es war einmal ein Prinz** once upon a time there was a prince
● auxiliary verb

····▶ (*zur Perfektumschreibung*) have. **er ist gestorben** he has died. **sie sind angekommen** they have arrived. **sie war dort gewesen** she had been there. **ich wäre gefallen** I would have fallen

····▶ (*zur Bildung des Passivs*) be. **wir sind gerettet worden/wir waren gerettet** we were saved

····▶ (+ *zu* + *Infinitiv*) be to be. **es war niemand zu sehen** there was no one to be seen. **das war zu erwarten** that was to be expected. **er ist zu bemitleiden** he is to be pitied. **die Richtlinien sind strengstens zu beachten** the guidelines are to be strictly followed

sein² *poss pron* his; (*Ding, Tier*) its; (*nach man*) one's; **sein Glück versuchen** try one's luck. **s~e(r,s)** *poss pron* his; (*nach man*) one's own; **das S~e tun** do one's share. **s~erseits** *adv* for his part. **s~erzeit** *adv* in those days. **s~etwegen** *adv* for his sake; (*wegen ihm*) because of him, on his account. **s~ige** *poss pron* **der/die/das s~ige** his

seins *poss pron* his; (*nach man*) one's own

seit *conj & prep* (+ *dat*) since; **s~ einiger Zeit** for some time [past]; **ich wohne s~ zehn Jahren hier** I've lived here for ten years. **s~dem** *conj* since ● *adv* since then

Seite *f* -, -n side; (*Buch-*) page; **zur S~ treten** step aside; **auf der einen/ anderen S~** (*fig*) on the one/other hand

seitens *prep* (+ *gen*) on the part of

Seiten|schiff *nt* [side] aisle. **S~sprung** *m* infidelity. **S~stechen** *nt* -s (*Med*) stitch. **S~straße** *f* side-street. **S~streifen** *m* verge; (*Autobahn-*) hard shoulder

seither *adv* since then

seit|lich *a* side ... ● *adv* at/on the side; **s~lich von** to one side of ● *prep* (+ *gen*) to one side of.

s~**wärts** *adv* on/to one side; (*zur Seite*) sideways

Sekret|är *m* -s, -e secretary; (*Schrank*) bureau. **S~ariat** *nt* -[e]s, -e secretary's office. **S~ärin** *f* -, -nen secretary

Sekt *m* -[e]s [German] sparkling wine

Sekte *f* -, -n sect

Sektor *m* -s, -en /-'to:rən/ sector

Sekunde *f* -, -n second

selber *pron* 🔢 = selbst

selbst *pron* oneself; **ich/du/er/sie s~** I myself /you yourself/ he himself/ she herself; **wir/ihr/sie s~** we ourselves/you yourselves/they themselves; **ich schneide mein Haar s~** I cut my own hair; **von s~** of one's own accord; (*automatisch*) automatically; **s~ gemacht** home-made ● *adv* even

selbständig *a* = selbstständig. **S~keit** *f* - = Selbstständigkeit

Selbst|bedienung *f* self-service. **S~befriedigung** *f* masturbation. **s~bewusst** *a* self-confident. **S~bewusstsein** *nt* self-confidence. **S~bildnis** *nt* self-portrait. **S~erhaltung** *f* self-preservation. **s~gemacht*** *a* **s~ gemacht**, **s. selbst. s~haftend** *a* self-adhesive. **S~hilfe** *f* self-help. **s~klebend** *a* self-adhesive. **S~kostenpreis** *m* cost price. **S~laut** *m* vowel. **s~los** *a* selfless. **S~mord** *m* suicide. **S~mörder(in)** *m(f)* suicide. **s~mörderisch** *a* suicidal. **S~porträt** *nt* self-portrait. **s~sicher** *a* self-assured. **s~ständig** *a* independent; self-employed <*Handwerker*>; **sich s~ständig machen** set up on one's own. **S~ständigkeit** *f* - independence. **s~süchtig** *a* selfish. **S~tanken** *nt* self-service (*for petrol*). **s~tätig** *a* automatic. **S~versorgung** *f* self-catering. **s~verständlich** *a* natural; **etw für s~ halten** take sth for granted; **das ist s~** that goes without saying; **s~!** of course! **S~verteidigung** *f* self-defence. **S~vertrauen** *nt* self-confidence. **S~verwaltung** *f* self-government

selig *a* blissfully happy; (*Relig*) blessed; (*verstorben*) late. **S~keit** *f* - bliss

Sellerie *m* -s, -s & *f* -,- celeriac; (*Stangen-*) celery

selten *a* rare ● *adv* rarely, seldom; (*besonders*) exceptionally. **S~heit** *f* -, -en rarity

seltsam *a* odd, strange. **s~erweise** *adv* oddly

Semester *nt* -s,- (*Univ*) semester

Semikolon *nt* -s, -s semicolon

Seminar *nt* -s, -e seminar; (*Institut*) department; (*Priester-*) seminary

Semmel *f* -, -n [bread] roll. **S~brösel** *pl* breadcrumbs

Senat *m* -[e]s, -e senate. **S~or** *m* -s, -en /-'to:rən/ senator

senden¹† *vt* send

sende|n² *vt* (*reg*) broadcast; (*über Funk*) transmit, send. **S~r** *m* -s,- [broadcasting] station; (*Anlage*) transmitter. **S~reihe** *f* series

Sendung *f* -, -en consignment, shipment; (*TV*) programme

Senf *m* -s mustard

senil *a* senile. **S~ität** *f* - senility

Senior *m* -s, -en /-'o:rən/ senior; **S~en** senior citizens. **S~enheim** *nt* old people's home

senken *vt* lower; bring down <*Fieber, Preise*>; bow <*Kopf*>; **sich s~** come down, fall; (*absinken*) subside

senkrecht *a* vertical. **S~e** *f* -n, -n perpendicular

Sensation /-'ts:io:n/ *f* -, -en sensation. **s~ell** *a* sensational

Sense *f* -, -n scythe

sensibel *a* sensitive

sentimental *a* sentimental

September *m* -s,- September

Serie /'ze:riə/ *f* -, -n series; (*Briefmarken*) set; (*Comm*) range. **S~nnummer** *f* serial number

seriös *a* respectable; (*zuverlässig*) reliable

Serpentine *f* -, -n winding road; (*Kehre*) hairpin bend

Serum *nt* -s,Sera serum

Service¹ /zɛr'vi:s/ *nt* -[s],- /-'vi:s[əs], -'vi:sə/ service, set

Service² /'zø:ɐvɪs/ *m* & *nt* -s /-vɪs[əs]/ (*Comm, Tennis*) service

servier|en *vt/i* (*haben*) serve. **S~erin** *f* -, -nen waitress

Serviette *f* -, -n napkin, serviette

Servus *int* (*Aust*) cheerio; (*Begrüßung*) hallo

Sessel *m* -s,- armchair. **S~bahn** *f*, **S~lift** *m* chair-lift

sesshaft *a* settled

Set /zɛt/ *nt* & *m* -[s], -s set; (*Deckchen*) place-mat

setz|en *vt* put; (*abstellen*) set down; (*hin-*) sit down <*Kind*>; move <*Spielstein*>; (*pflanzen*) plant; (*schreiben, wetten*) put; **sich s~en** sit down; (*sinken*) settle ● *vi* (*sein*) leap ● *vi* (*haben*) **s~en auf** (+ *acc*) back

Seuche *f* -, -n epidemic

seufz|en *vi* (*haben*) sigh. **S~er** *m* -s,- sigh

Sex /zɛks/ *m* -[es] sex

Sexu|alität *f* - sexuality. **s~ell** *a* sexual

sezieren *vt* dissect

Shampoo /ʃam'pu:/, **Shampoon** /ʃam'po:n/ *nt* -s shampoo

siamesisch *a* Siamese

sich *refl pron* oneself; (*mit er/sie/es*) himself/herself/itself; (*mit sie pl*) themselves; (*mit Sie*) yourself; (*pl*) yourselves; (*einander*) each other; **s~ kennen** know oneself/(*einander*) each other; **s~ waschen** have a wash; **s~** (*dat*) **die Haare kämmen** comb one's hair; **s~ wundern** be surprised; **s~ gut verkaufen** sell well; **von s~ aus** of one's own accord

Sichel *f* -, -n sickle

sicher *a* safe; (*gesichert*) secure; (*gewiss*) certain; (*zuverlässig*) reliable; sure <*Urteil*>; steady <*Hand*>; (*selbstbewusst*) self-confident; **bist du s~?** are you sure? ● *adv* safely; securely; certainly;

reliably; self-confidently;
(*wahrscheinlich*) most probably; **s~!**
certainly! **s~gehen**† *vi sep* (*sein*)
(*fig*) be sure

Sicherheit *f* - safety; (*Pol, Psych,
Comm*) security; (*Gewissheit*)
certainty; (*Zuverlässigkeit*)
reliability; (*des Urteils*) surety;
(*Selbstbewusstsein*) self-confidence.
S~sgurt *m* safety-belt; (*Auto*) seat-
belt. **S~snadel** *f* safety-pin

sicherlich *adv* certainly;
(*wahrscheinlich*) most probably

sicher|n *vt* secure; (*garantieren*)
safeguard; (*schützen*) protect; put the
safety-catch on <*Pistole*>. **S~ung** *f*
-, -en safeguard, protection;
(*Gewehr-*) safety-catch; (*Electr*) fuse

Sicht *f* - view; (*S~weite*) visibility;
auf lange S~ in the long term.
s~bar *a* visible. **S~vermerk** *m*
visa. **S~weite** *f* visibility; **außer
S~weite** out of sight

sie *pron* (*nom*) (*sg*) she; (*Ding, Tier*)
it; (*pl*) they; (*acc*) (*sg*) her; (*Ding,
Tier*) it; (*pl*) them

Sie *pron* you; **gehen/warten Sie!** go/
wait!

Sieb *nt* -[e]s, -e sieve; (*Tee-*) strainer.
s~en¹ *vt* sieve, sift

sieben² *inv a*, **S~** *f* -, -en seven.
S~sachen *fpl* 🄳 belongings.
s~te(r,s) *a* seventh

sieb|te(r,s) *a* seventh. **s~zehn** *inv*
a seventeen. **s~zehnte(r,s)** *a*
seventeenth. **s~zig** *inv a* seventy.
s~zigste(r,s) *a* seventieth

siede|n† *vt/i* (*haben*) boil.
S~punkt *m* boiling point

Siedlung *f* -, -en [housing] estate;
(*Niederlassung*) settlement

Sieg *m* -[e]s, -e victory

Siegel *nt* -s,- seal. **S~ring** *m*
signet-ring

sieg|en *vi* (*haben*) win. **S~er(in)** *m*
-s,- (*f* -, -nen) winner. **s~reich** *a*
victorious

siezen *vt* jdn s~ call s.o. 'Sie'

Signal *nt* -s, -e signal

Silbe *f* -, -n syllable

Silber *nt* -s silver. **s~n** *a* silver

Silhouette /zɪ'luɛtə/ *f* -, -n
silhouette

Silizium *nt* -s silicon

Silo *m & nt* -s, -s silo

Silvester *nt* -s New Year's Eve

Sims *m & nt* -es, -e ledge

simultan *a* simultaneous

sind *s.* sein¹

Sinfonie *f* -, -n symphony

singen† *vt/i* (*haben*) sing

Singvogel *m* songbird

sinken† *vi* (*sein*) sink; (*nieder-*) drop;
(*niedriger werden*) go down, fall; **den
Mut s~ lassen** lose courage

Sinn *m* -[e]s, -e sense; (*Denken*) mind;
(*Zweck*) point; **in gewissem S~e** in a
sense; **es hat keinen S~** it is
pointless. **S~bild** *nt* symbol

sinnlich *a* sensory; (*sexuell*) sensual;
<*Genüsse*> sensuous. **S~keit** *f* -
sensuality; sensuousness

sinn|los *a* senseless; (*zwecklos*)
pointless. **s~voll** *a* meaningful;
(*vernünftig*) sensible

Sintflut *f* flood

Siphon /'zi:fõ/ *m* -s, -s siphon

Sippe *f* -, -n clan

Sirene *f* -, -n siren

Sirup *m* -s, -e syrup; treacle

Sitte *f* -, -n custom; **S~n** manners

sittlich *a* moral. **S~keit** *f* -
morality. **S~keitsverbrecher** *m*
sex offender

sittsam *a* well-behaved; (*züchtig*)
demure

Situ|ation /-'tsɪo:n/ *f* -, -en
situation. **s~iert** *a* gut/schlecht
s~iert well/badly off

Sitz *m* -es, -e seat; (*Passform*) fit

sitzen† *vi* (*haben*) sit; (*sich befinden*)
be; (*passen*) fit; (🄳 *treffen*) hit home;
[im Gefängnis] s~ 🄳 be in jail; **s~
bleiben** remain seated; 🄳 (*Sch*) stay
or be kept down; (*nicht heiraten*) be
left on the shelf; **s~ bleiben auf** (+
dat) be left with

Sitz|gelegenheit *f* seat. **S~platz**
m seat. **S~ung** *f* -, -en session

Sizilien /-iən/ nt -s Sicily

Skala f -, -len scale; (*Reihe*) range

Skalpell nt -s, -e scalpel

skalpieren vt scalp

Skandal m -s, -e scandal. **s~ös** a scandalous

Skandinav|ien /-iən/ nt -s Scandinavia. **s~isch** a Scandinavian

Skat m -s skat

Skelett nt -[e]s, -e skeleton

Skep|sis f - scepticism. **s~tisch** a sceptical

Ski /ʃiː/ m -s, -er ski; **Ski fahren** *od* **laufen** ski. **S~fahrer(in)**, **S~läufer(in)** m(f) -s,- (f -, -nen) skier. **S~sport** m skiing

Skizz|e f -, -n sketch. **s~ieren** vt sketch

Sklav|e m -n, -n slave. **S~erei** f - slavery. **S~in** f -, -nen slave

Skorpion m -s, -e scorpion; (*Astr*) Scorpio

Skrupel m -s,- scruple. **s~los** a unscrupulous

Skulptur f -, -en sculpture

Slalom m -s, -e slalom

Slaw|e m -n, -n, **S~in** f -, -nen Slav. **s~isch** a Slav; (*Lang*) Slavonic

Slip m -s, -s briefs pl

Smaragd m -[e]s, -e emerald

Smoking m -s, -s dinner jacket

Snob m -s, -s snob. **S~ismus** m - snobbery **s~istisch** a snobbish

so adv so; (*so sehr*) so much; (*auf diese Weise*) like this/that; (*solch*) such; (🔁 *sowieso*) anyway; (🔁 *umsonst*) free; (🔁 *ungefähr*) about; **so viel** so much; **so gut/bald wie** as good/soon as; **so ein Zufall!** what a coincidence! **mir ist so, als ob** I feel as if; **so oder so** in any case; **so um zehn Mark** 🔁 about ten marks; **so?** really? ● conj (*also*) so; (*dann*) then; **so dass** = **sodass**

sobald conj as soon as

Söckchen nt -s,- [ankle] sock

Socke f -, -n sock

Sockel m -s,- plinth, pedestal

Socken m -s,- sock

sodass conj so that

Sodawasser nt soda water

Sodbrennen nt -s heartburn

soeben adv just [now]

Sofa nt -s, -s settee, sofa

sofern adv provided [that]

sofort adv at once, immediately; (*auf der Stelle*) instantly

Software /'zɔftvɛːɐ̯/ f - software

sogar adv even

sogenannt a so-called

sogleich adv at once

Sohle f -, -n sole; (*Tal-*) bottom

Sohn m -[e]s, ̈-e son

Sojabohne f soya bean

solange conj as long as

solch inv pron such; **s~ ein(e)** such a; **s~ einer/eine/eins** one/(*Person*) someone like that. **s~e(r,s)** pron such ● (*substantivisch*) **ein s~er/eine s~e/ein s~es** one/(*Person*) someone like that; **s~e** pl those; (*Leute*) people like that

Soldat m -en, -en soldier

Söldner m -s,- mercenary

Solidarität f - solidarity

solide a solid; (*haltbar*) sturdy; (*sicher*) sound; (*anständig*) respectable

Solist(in) m -en, -en (f -, -nen) soloist

Soll nt -s (*Comm*) debit; (*Produktions-*) quota

sollen†

● *auxiliary verb*

····▸ (*Verpflichtung*) be [supposed *or* meant] to. **er soll morgen zum Arzt gehen** he is [supposed] to go to the doctor tomorrow. **die beiden Flächen sollen fluchten** the two surfaces are meant to be *or* should be in alignment. **du solltest ihn anrufen** you were meant to phone him *or* should have phoned him

····▸ (*Befehl*) **du sollst sofort damit aufhören** you're to stop that at once. **er soll hereinkommen** he is to come in; (*sagen Sie es ihm*) tell him to come in

····▸ **sollte** (*subjunctive*) should; ought to. **wir sollten früher aufstehen** we ought to *or* should get up earlier. **das hätte er nicht tun/sagen sollen** he shouldn't have done/said that

····▸ (*Zukunft, Geplantes*) be to. **ich soll die Abteilung übernehmen** I am to take over the department. **du sollst dein Geld zurückbekommen** you are to *or* shall get your money back. **es soll nicht wieder vorkommen** it won't happen again. **sie sollten ihr Reiseziel nie erreichen** they were never to reach their destination

····▸ (*Ratlosigkeit*) be to; shall. **was soll man nur machen?** what is one to do?; what shall I/we do? **ich weiß nicht, was ich machen soll** I don't know what I should do *or* what to do

····▸ (*nach Bericht*) be supposed to. **er soll sehr reich sein** he is supposed *or* is said to be very rich. **sie soll geheiratet haben** they say *or* I gather she has got married

····▸ (*Absicht*) be meant *or* supposed to. **was soll dieses Bild darstellen?** what is this picture supposed to represent? **das sollte ein Witz sein** that was meant *or* supposed to be a joke

····▸ (*in Bedingungssätzen*) should. **sollte er anrufen, falls** *od* **wenn er anrufen sollte** should he *or* if he should telephone

● *intransitive verb*

····▸ (*irgendwohin gehen sollen*) be [supposed] to go. **er soll morgen zum Arzt/nach Berlin** he is [supposed] to go to the doctor/to Berlin tomorrow. **ich sollte ins Theater** I was supposed to go to the theatre

····▸ (*sonstige Wendungen*) **soll er doch!** let him! **was soll das?** what's that in aid of? ⊞

Solo *nt* -s, -los & -li solo

somit *adv* therefore, so

Sommer *m* -s,- summer. **s~lich** *a* summery; (*Sommer-*) summer ...
  ● *adv* **s~lich warm** as warm as summer. **S~sprossen** *fpl* freckles

Sonate *f* -, -n sonata

Sonde *f* -, -n probe

Sonder|angebot *nt* special offer. **s~bar** *a* odd. **S~fahrt** *f* special excursion. **S~fall** *m* special case. **s~gleichen** *adv* eine Gemeinheit s~gleichen unparalleled meanness. **S~ling** *m* -s, -e crank. **S~marke** *f* special stamp

sondern *conj* but; **nicht nur ... s~ auch** not only ... but also

Sonder|preis *m* special price. **S~schule** *f* special school

Sonett *nt* -[e]s, -e sonnet

Sonnabend *m* -s, -e Saturday. **s~s** *adv* on Saturdays

Sonne *f* -, -n sun. **s~n (sich)** *vr* sun oneself

Sonnen|aufgang *m* sunrise. **s~baden** *vi* (*haben*) sunbathe. **S~bank** *f* sun-bed. **S~blume** *f* sunflower. **S~brand** *m* sunburn. **S~brille** *f* sunglasses *pl*. **S~energie** *f* solar energy. **S~finsternis** *f* solar eclipse. **S~milch** *f* sun-tan lotion. **S~öl** *nt* sun-tan oil. **S~schein** *m* sunshine. **S~schirm** *m* sunshade. **S~stich** *m* sunstroke. **S~uhr** *f* sundial. **S~untergang** *m* sunset. **S~wende** *f* solstice

sonnig *a* sunny

Sonntag *m* -s, -e Sunday. **s~s** *adv* on Sundays

sonst *adv* (*gewöhnlich*) usually; (*im Übrigen*) apart from that; (*andernfalls*) otherwise, or [else]; **wer/was/wie/wo s~?** who/what/how/where else? **s~ niemand** no one else; **s~ noch etwas?** anything else? **s~ noch Fragen?** any more questions? **s~ jemand** *od* **wer** someone/(*fragend, verneint*) anyone else; (*irgendjemand*) [just] anyone; **s~ wo** somewhere/(*fragend, verneint*) anywhere else; (*irgendwo*) [just] anywhere. **s~ig** *a* other

sooft *conj* whenever

Sopran *m* -s, -e soprano

Sorge *f* -, -n worry (**um** about); (*Fürsorge*) care; **sich** (*dat*) **S~n machen** worry. **s~n** *vi* (*haben*) **s~n für** look after, care for; (*vorsorgen*)

provide for; (*sich kümmern*) see to;
dafür s~n, dass see *or* make sure
that ● *vr* **sich s~n** worry. **s~nfrei**
a carefree. **s~nvoll** *a* worried.
S~recht *nt* (*Jur*) custody

Sorg|falt *f* - care. **s~fältig** *a*
careful

Sorte *f* -, -n kind, sort; (*Comm*)
brand

sort|ieren *vt* sort [out]; (*Comm*)
grade. **S~iment** *nt* -[e]s, -e range

sosehr *conj* however much

Soße *f* -, -n sauce; (*Braten-*) gravy;
(*Salat-*) dressing

Souvenir /zuvə'ni:ɐ/ *nt* -s, -s
souvenir

souverän /zuvə'rɛːn/ *a* sovereign

soviel *conj* however much; **s~ ich
weiß** as far as I know ● *adv* *so viel,
s. viel

soweit *conj* as far as; (*insoweit*) [in]
so far as ● *adv* *so weit, *s.* weit

sowenig *conj* however little ● *adv*
*so wenig, *s.* wenig

sowie *conj* as well as; (*sobald*) as
soon as

sowieso *adv* anyway, in any case

sowjet|isch *a* Soviet. **S~union** *f* -
Soviet Union

sowohl *adv* **s~ ... als** *od* **wie auch
... ...** as well as ...

sozial *a* social; <*Einstellung, Beruf*>
caring. **S~arbeit** *f* social work.
S~demokrat *m* social democrat.
S~hilfe *f* social security

Sozialis|mus *m* - socialism. **S~t**
m -en, -en socialist

Sozial|versicherung *f* National
Insurance. **S~wohnung** *f* ≈
council flat

Soziologie *f* - sociology

Sozius *m* -, -se (*Comm*) partner;
(*Beifahrersitz*) pillion

Spachtel *m* -s,- & *f* -, -n spatula

Spagat *m* -[e]s, -e (*Aust*) string; **S~
machen** do the splits *pl*

Spaghetti, Spagetti *pl* spaghetti
sg

Spalier *nt* -s, -e trellis

Spalt|e *f* -, -n crack; (*Gletscher-*)
crevasse; (*Druck-*) column;

(*Orangen-*) segment. **s~en†** *vt* split.
S~ung *f* -, -en splitting; (*Kluft*)
split; (*Phys*) fission

Span *m* -[e]s,-̈e [wood] chip

Spange *f* -, -n clasp; (*Haar-*) slide;
(*Zahn-*) brace

Span|ien /-iən/ *nt* -s Spain. **S~ier**
m -s,-, **S~ierin** *f* -, -nen Spaniard.
s~isch *a* Spanish. **S~isch** *nt* -[s]
(*Lang*) Spanish

Spann *m* -[e]s instep

Spanne *f* -, -n span; (*Zeit-*) space;
(*Comm*) margin

spann|en *vt* stretch; put up
<*Leine*>; (*straffen*) tighten; (*an-*)
harness (**an** + *acc* to); **sich s~en**
tighten ● *vi* (*haben*) be too tight.
s~end *a* exciting. **S~ung** *f* -, -en
tension; (*Erwartung*) suspense;
(*Electr*) voltage

Spar|buch *nt* savings book.
S~büchse *f* money-box. **s~en** *vt/i*
(*haben*) save; (*sparsam sein*)
economize (**mit/an** + *dat* on). **S~er**
m -s,- saver

Spargel *m* -s,- asparagus

Spar|kasse *f* savings bank.
S~konto *nt* deposit account

sparsam *a* economical; <*Person*>
thrifty. **S~keit** *f* - economy; thrift

Sparschwein *nt* piggy bank

Sparte *f* -, -n branch; (*Zeitungs-*)
section; (*Rubrik*) column

Spaß *m* -es,-̈e fun; (*Scherz*) joke; **im/
aus/zum S~** for fun; **S~ machen** be
fun; <*Person:*> be joking; **viel S~!**
have a good time! **s~en** *vi* (*haben*)
joke. **S~vogel** *m* joker

Spastiker *m* -s,- spastic

spät *a* & *adv* late; **wie s~ ist es?**
what time is it? **zu s~ kommen** be
late

Spaten *m* -s,- spade

später *a* later; (*zukünftig*) future
● *adv* later

spätestens *adv* at the latest

Spatz *m* -en, -en sparrow

Spätzle *pl* (*Culin*) noodles

spazieren *vi* (*sein*) stroll; **s~ gehen**
go for a walk

Spazier|gang *m* walk; einen
S~gang machen go for a walk.
S~gänger(in) *m* -s,- (*f* -, -nen)
walker. **S~stock** *m* walking-stick
Specht *m* -[e]s, -e woodpecker
Speck *m* -s bacon. **s~ig** *a* greasy
Spedi|teur /ʃpedi'tøːɐ/ *m* -s, -e
haulage/(*für Umzüge*) removals
contractor. **S~tion** /-'tsi̯oːn/ *f* -, -en
carriage, haulage; (*Firma*) haulage/
(*für Umzüge*) removals firm
Speer *m* -[e]s, -e spear; (*Sport*)
javelin
Speiche *f* -, -n spoke
Speichel *m* -s saliva
Speicher *m* -s,- warehouse; (*dial:
Dachboden*) attic; (*Computer*)
memory. **s~n** *vt* store
Speise *f* -, -n food; (*Gericht*) dish;
(*Pudding*) blancmange. **S~eis** *nt*
ice-cream. **S~kammer** *f* larder.
S~karte *f* menu. **s~n** *vi* (*haben*)
eat ● *vt* feed. **S~röhre** *f*
oesophagus. **S~saal** *m* dining-
room. **S~wagen** *m* dining-car
Spektrum *nt* -s, -tra spectrum
Spekul|ant *m* -en, -en speculator.
s~ieren *vi* (*haben*) speculate;
s~ieren auf (+ *acc*) 🆄 hope to get
Spelze *f* -, -n husk
spendabel *a* generous
Spende *f* -, -n donation. **s~n** *vt*
donate; give <*Blut, Schatten*>; Beifall
s~n applaud. **S~r** *m* -s,- donor;
(*Behälter*) dispenser
spendieren *vt* pay for
Sperling *m* -s, -e sparrow
Sperre *f* -, -n barrier; (*Verbot*) ban;
(*Comm*) embargo. **s~n** *vt* close;
(*ver-*) block; (*verbieten*) ban; cut off
<*Strom, Telefon*>; stop <*Scheck,
Kredit*>; **s~n in** (+ *acc*) put in
<*Gefängnis, Käfig*>
Sperr|holz *nt* plywood. **S~müll** *m*
bulky refuse. **S~stunde** *f* closing
time
Spesen *pl* expenses
spezial|isieren (sich) *vr*
specialize (**auf** + *acc* in). **S~ist** *m*

-en, -en specialist. **S~ität** *f* -, -en
speciality
spicken *vt* (*Culin*) lard; **gespickt mit**
(*fig*) full of ● *vi* (*haben*) 🆄 crib (**bei**
from)
Spiegel *m* -s,- mirror; (*Wasser-,
Alkohol-*) level. **S~bild** *nt* reflection.
S~ei *nt* fried egg. **s~n** *vt* reflect;
sich **s~n** be reflected ● *vi* (*haben*)
reflect [the light]; (*glänzen*) gleam.
S~ung *f* -, -en reflection
Spiel *nt* -[e]s, -e game; (*Spielen*)
playing; (*Glücks-*) gambling; (*Schau-*)
play; (*Satz*) set; **auf dem S~ stehen**
be at stake; **aufs S~ setzen** risk.
S~automat *m* fruit machine.
S~bank *f* casino. **S~dose** *f*
musical box. **s~en** *vt/i* (*haben*)
play; (*im Glücksspiel*) gamble;
(*vortäuschen*) act; <*Roman:*> be set
(in + *dat* in); **s~en mit** (*fig*) toy with
Spieler(in) *m* -s,- (*f* -, -nen) player;
(*Glücks-*) gambler
Spiel|feld *nt* field, pitch.
S~marke *f* chip. **S~plan** *m*
programme. **S~platz** *m*
playground. **S~raum** *m* (*fig*) scope;
(*Techn*) clearance. **S~regeln** *fpl*
rules [of the game]. **S~sachen** *fpl*
toys. **S~verderber** *m* -s,-
spoilsport. **S~waren** *fpl* toys.
S~warengeschäft *nt* toyshop.
S~zeug *nt* toy; (*S~sachen*) toys *pl*
Spieß *m* -es, -e spear; (*Brat-*) spit;
skewer; (*Fleisch-*) kebab. **S~er** *m*
-s,- [petit] bourgeois. **s~ig** *a*
bourgeois
Spike[s]reifen /'ʃpaɪk[s]-/ *m*
studded tyre
Spinat *m* -s spinach
Spindel *f* -, -n spindle
Spinne *f* -, -n spider
spinn|en† *vt/i* (*haben*) spin; er
spinnt 🆄 he's crazy.
S~[en]gewebe *nt*, **S~webe** *f* -,
-n cobweb
Spion *m* -s, -e spy
Spionage /ʃpi̯o'naːʒə/ *f* - espionage,
spying. **S~abwehr** *f* counter-
espionage
spionieren *vi* (*haben*) spy
Spionin *f* -, -nen [woman] spy

Spiral|e f -, -n spiral. **s~ig** a spiral

Spirituosen pl spirits

Spiritus m - alcohol; (Brenn-) methylated spirits pl. **S~kocher** m spirit stove

spitz a pointed; (scharf) sharp; (schrill) shrill; <Winkel> acute. **S~bube** m scoundrel

Spitze f -, -n point; (oberer Teil) top; (vorderer Teil) front; (Pfeil-, Finger-, Nasen-) tip; (Schuh-, Strumpf-) toe; (Zigarren-, Zigaretten-) holder; (Höchstleistung) maximum; (Tex) lace; (⏻ Anspielung) dig; **an der S~ liegen** be in the lead

Spitzel m -s,- informer

spitzen vt sharpen; purse <Lippen>; prick up <Ohren>. **S~geschwindigkeit** f top speed

Spitzname m nickname

Spleen /ʃpliːn/ m -s, -e obsession

Splitter m -s,- splinter. **s~n** vi (sein) shatter

sponsern vt sponsor

Spore f -, -n (Biol) spore

Sporn m -[e]s, Sporen spur

Sport m -[e]s sport; (Hobby) hobby. **S~art** f sport. **S~ler** m -s,- sportsman. **S~lerin** f -, -nen sportswoman. **s~lich** a sports ...; (fair) sporting; (schlank) sporty. **S~platz** m sports ground. **S~verein** m sports club. **S~wagen** m sports car; (Kinder-) push-chair, (Amer) stroller

Spott m -[e]s mockery

spotten vi (haben) mock; **s~ über** (+ acc) make fun of; (höhnend) ridicule

spöttisch a mocking

Sprach|e f -, -n language; (Sprechfähigkeit) speech; **zur S~e bringen** bring up. **S~fehler** m speech defect. **S~labor** nt language laboratory. **s~lich** a linguistic. **s~los** a speechless

Spray /ʃpreː/ nt & m -s, -s spray. **S~dose** f aerosol [can]

Sprechanlage f intercom

sprechen† vi (haben) speak/(sich unterhalten) talk (über + acc/von

about/of); **Deutsch s~** speak German ● vt speak; (sagen) say; pronounce <Urteil>; **schuldig s~** find guilty; **Herr X ist nicht zu s~** Mr X is not available

Sprecher(in) m -s,- (f -, -nen) speaker; (Radio, TV) announcer; (Wortführer) spokesman, f spokeswoman

Sprechstunde f consulting hours pl; (Med) surgery. **S~nhilfe** f (Med) receptionist

Sprechzimmer nt consulting room

spreizen vt spread

spreng|en vt blow up; blast <Felsen>; (fig) burst; (begießen) water; (mit Sprenger) sprinkle; dampen <Wäsche>. **S~er** m -s,- sprinkler. **S~kopf** m warhead. **S~körper** m explosive device. **S~stoff** m explosive

Spreu f - chaff

Sprich|wort nt (pl -wörter) proverb. **s~wörtlich** a proverbial

Springbrunnen m fountain

spring|en† vi (sein) jump; (Schwimmsport) dive; <Ball:> bounce; (spritzen) spurt; (zer-) break; (rissig werden) crack; (SGer: laufen) run. **S~er** m -s,- jumper; (Kunst-) diver; (Schach) knight. **S~reiten** nt show-jumping

Sprint m -s, -s sprint

Spritz|e f -, -n syringe; (Injektion) injection; (Feuer-) hose. **s~en** vt spray; (be-, ver-) splash; (Culin) pipe; (Med) inject ● vi (haben) splash; <Fett:> spit ● vi (sein) splash; (hervor-) spurt. **S~er** m -s,- splash; (Schuss) dash

spröde a brittle; (trocken) dry

Sprosse f -, -n rung

Sprotte f -, -n sprat

Spruch m -[e]s,-̈e saying; (Denk-) motto; (Zitat) quotation. **S~band** nt (pl -bänder) banner

Sprudel m -s,- sparkling mineral water. **s~n** vi (haben/sein) bubble

Sprüh|dose *f* aerosol [can]. **s~en**
vt spray ● *vi* (*sein*) <*Funken:*> fly;
(*fig*) sparkle

Sprung *m* -[e]s,⸚e jump, leap;
(*Schwimmsport*) dive; (⊡ *Katzen-*)
stone's throw; (*Riss*) crack.
S~brett *nt* springboard.
S~schanze *f* ski-jump. **S~seil** *nt*
skipping-rope

Spucke *f* - spit. **s~n** *vt/i* (*haben*)
spit; (*sich übergeben*) be sick

Spuk *m* -[e]s, -e [ghostly] apparition.
s~en *vi* (*haben*) <*Geist:*> walk; in
diesem Haus **s~t** es this house is
haunted

Spülbecken *nt* sink

Spule *f* -, -n spool

Spüle *f* -, -n sink

spulen *vt* spool

spül|en *vt* rinse; (*schwemmen*) wash;
Geschirr **s~en** wash up ● *vi* (*haben*)
flush [the toilet]. **S~kasten** *m*
cistern. **S~mittel** *nt* washing-up
liquid

Spur *f* -, -en track; (*Fahr-*) lane;
(*Fährte*) trail; (*Anzeichen*) trace;
(*Hinweis*) lead

spürbar *a* noticeable

spür|en *vt* feel; (*seelisch*) sense.
S~hund *m* tracker dog

spurlos *adv* without trace

spurten *vi* (*sein*) put on a spurt

sputen (sich) *vr* hurry

Staat *m* -[e]s, -en state; (*Land*)
country; (*Putz*) finery. **s~lich** *a*
state ... ● *adv* by the state

Staatsangehörig|e(r) *m/f*
national. **S~keit** *f* - nationality

Staats|anwalt *m* state prosecutor.
S~beamte(r) *m* civil servant.
S~besuch *m* state visit.
S~bürger(in) *m(f)* national.
S~mann *m* (*pl* -**männer**) statesman.
S~streich *m* coup

Stab *m* -[e]s,⸚e rod; (*Gitter-*) bar
(*Sport*) baton; (*Mil*) staff

Stäbchen *ntpl* chopsticks

Stabhochsprung *m* pole-vault

---

*alte Schreibung

stabil *a* stable; (*gesund*) robust;
(*solide*) sturdy

Stachel *m* -s,- spine; (*Gift-*) sting;
(*Spitze*) spike. **S~beere** *f* goose-
berry. **S~draht** *m* barbed wire.
S~schwein *nt* porcupine

Stadion *nt* -s, -ien stadium

Stadium *nt* -s, -ien stage

Stadt *f* -,⸚e town; (*Groß-*) city

städtisch *a* urban; (*kommunal*)
municipal

Stadt|mitte *f* town centre.
S~plan *m* street map. **S~teil** *m*
district

Staffel *f* -, -n team; (*S~lauf*) relay;
(*Mil*) squadron

Staffelei *f* -, -en easel

Staffel|lauf *m* relay race. **s~n** *vt*
stagger; (*abstufen*) grade

Stahl *m* -s steel. **S~beton** *m*
reinforced concrete

Stall *m* -[e]s,⸚e stable; (*Kuh-*) shed;
(*Schweine-*) sty; (*Hühner-*) coop;
(*Kaninchen-*) hutch

Stamm *m* -[e]s,⸚e trunk; (*Sippe*)
tribe; (*Wort-*) stem. **S~baum** *m*
family tree; (*eines Tieres*) pedigree

stammeln *vt/i* (*haben*) stammer

stammen *vi* (*haben*) come/(*zeitlich*)
date (**von/aus** from)

stämmig *a* sturdy

Stamm|kundschaft *f* regulars
pl. **S~lokal** *nt* favourite pub

stampfen *vi* (*haben*) stamp;
<*Maschine:*> pound ● *vi* (*sein*) tramp
● *vt* pound; mash <*Kartoffeln*>

Stand *m* -[e]s,⸚e standing position;
(*Zustand*) state; (*Spiel-*) score; (*Höhe*)
level; (*gesellschaftlich*) class;
(*Verkaufs-*) stall; (*Messe-*) stand;
(*Taxi-*) rank; **auf den neuesten S~**
bringen up-date

Standard *m* -s, -s standard

Standbild *nt* statue

Ständer *m* -s,- stand; (*Geschirr-*)
rack; (*Kerzen-*) holder

Standes|amt *nt* registry office.
S~beamte(r) *m* registrar

standhaft *a* steadfast

ständig *a* constant; (*fest*) permanent

Stand|licht *nt* sidelights *pl.* **S~ort** *m* position; (*Firmen-*) location; (*Mil*) garrison. **S~punkt** *m* point of view. **S~uhr** *f* grandfather clock

Stange *f -, -n* bar; (*Holz-*) pole; (*Gardinen-*) rail; (*Hühner-*) perch; (*Zimt-*) stick; **von der S~** 🔲 off the peg

Stängel *m -s,-* stalk, stem

Stangenbohne *f* runner bean

Stanniol *nt -s* tin foil. **S~papier** *nt* silver paper

stanzen *vt* stamp; punch <*Loch*>

Stapel *m -s,-* stack, pile. **S~lauf** *m* launch[ing]. **s~n** *vt* stack *or* pile up

Star¹ *m -[e]s, -e* starling

Star² *m -[e]s* (*Med*) [**grauer**] **S~** cataract; **grüner S~** glaucoma

Star³ *m -s, -s* (*Theat, Sport*) star

stark *a* strong; <*Motor*> powerful; <*Verkehr, Regen*> heavy; <*Hitze, Kälte*> severe; (*groß*) big; (*schlimm*) bad; (*dick*) thick; (*korpulent*) stout ● *adv* (*sehr*) very much

Stärk|e *f -, -n* strength; power; thickness; stoutness; (*Größe*) size; (*Mais-, Wäsche-*) starch. **S~emehl** *nt* cornflour. **s~en** *vt* strengthen; starch <*Wäsche*>; **sich s~en** fortify oneself. **S~ung** *f -, -en* strengthening; (*Erfrischung*) refreshment

starr *a* rigid; (*steif*) stiff

starren *vi* (*haben*) stare

Starr|sinn *m* obstinacy. **s~sinnig** *a* obstinate

Start *m -s, -s* start; (*Aviat*) take-off. **S~bahn** *f* runway. **s~en** *vi* (*sein*) start; (*Aviat*) take off ● *vt* start; (*fig*) launch

Station /-'tsio:n/ *f -, -en* station; (*Haltestelle*) stop; (*Abschnitt*) stage; (*Med*) ward; **S~ machen** break one's journey. **s~är** *adv* as an inpatient. **s~ieren** *vt* station

statisch *a* static

Statist(in) *m -en, -en* (*f -, -nen*) (*Theat*) extra

Statisti|k *f -, -en* statistics *sg*; (*Aufstellung*) statistics *pl.* **s~sch** *a* statistical

Stativ *nt -s, -e* (*Phot*) tripod

statt *prep* (+ *gen*) instead of; **an seiner s~** in his place; **an Kindes s~ annehmen** adopt ● *conj* **s~ etw zu tun** instead of doing sth. **s~dessen** *adv* instead

statt|finden† *vi sep* (*haben*) take place. **s~haft** *a* permitted

Statue /'ʃta:tuə/ *f -, -n* statue

Statur *f -* build, stature

Status *m -* status. **S~symbol** *nt* status symbol

Statut *nt -[e]s, -en* statute

Stau *m -[e]s, -s* congestion; (*Auto*) [traffic] jam; (*Rück-*) tailback

Staub *m -[e]s* dust; **S~ wischen** dust; **S~ saugen** vacuum, hoover

Staubecken *nt* reservoir

staub|ig *a* dusty. **s~saugen** *vt/i* (*haben*) vacuum, hoover. **S~sauger** *m* vacuum cleaner, Hoover (P)

Staudamm *m* dam

stauen *vt* dam up; **sich s~** accumulate; <*Autos:*> form a tailback

staunen *vi* (*haben*) be amazed *or* astonished

Stau|see *m* reservoir. **S~ung** *f -, -en* congestion; (*Auto*) [traffic] jam

Steak /ʃte:k, ste:k/ *nt -s, -s* steak

stechen† *vt* stick (**in** + *acc* in); (*verletzen*) prick; (*mit Messer*) stab; <*Insekt:*> sting; <*Mücke:*> bite ● *vi* (*haben*) prick; <*Insekt:*> sting; <*Mücke:*> bite; (*mit Stechuhr*) clock in/out; **in See s~** put to sea

Stech|ginster *m* gorse. **S~kahn** *m* punt. **S~palme** *f* holly. **S~uhr** *f* time clock

Steck|brief *m* 'wanted' poster. **S~dose** *f* socket. **s~en** *vt* put; (*mit Nadel, Reißzwecke*) pin; (*pflanzen*) plant ● *vi* (*haben*) be; (*fest-*) be stuck; **s~ bleiben** get stuck; **den Schlüssel s~ lassen** leave the key in the lock

Steckenpferd *nt* hobby-horse

Steck|er *m -s,-* (*Electr*) plug. **S~nadel** *f* pin

Steg *m -[e]s, -e* foot-bridge; (*Boots-*) landing-stage; (*Brillen-*) bridge

stehen† *vi* (*haben*) stand; (*sich befinden*) be; (*still-*) be stationary; <*Maschine, Uhr:*> have stopped; **s~ bleiben** remain standing; <*Gebäude:*> be left standing; (*anhalten*) stop; <*Motor:*> stall; <*Zeit:*> stand still; **vor dem Ruin s~** face ruin; **zu jdm/etw s~** (*fig*) stand by s.o./sth; **jdm [gut] s~** suit s.o.; **sich gut s~** be on good terms; **es steht 3 zu 1** the score is 3–1. **s~d** *a* standing; (*sich nicht bewegend*) stationary; <*Gewässer:*> stagnant

Stehlampe *f* standard lamp

stehlen† *vt/i* (*haben*) steal; **sich s~** steal, creep

Steh|platz *m* standing place. **S~vermögen** *nt* stamina, staying-power

steif *a* stiff

Steig|bügel *m* stirrup. **S~eisen** *nt* crampon

steigen† *vi* (*sein*) climb; (*hochgehen*) rise, go up; <*Schulden, Spannung:*> mount; **s~ auf** (+ *acc*) climb on [to] <*Stuhl*>; climb <*Berg, Leiter*>; get on <*Pferd, Fahrrad*>; **s~ in** (+ *acc*) climb into; get in <*Auto*>; get on <*Bus, Zug*>; **s~ aus** climb out of; get out of <*Bett, Auto*>; get off <*Bus, Zug*>; **s~de Preise** rising prices

steiger|n *vt* increase; **sich s~n** increase; (*sich verbessern*) improve. **S~ung** *f* -,-en increase; improvement; (*Gram*) comparison

steil *a* steep. **S~küste** *f* cliffs *pl*

Stein *m* -[e]s, -e stone; (*Ziegel-*) brick; (*Spiel-*) piece. **S~bock** *m* ibex; (*Astr*) Capricorn. **S~bruch** *m* quarry. **S~garten** *m* rockery. **S~gut** *nt* earthenware. **s~ig** *a* stony. **s~igen** *vt* stone. **S~kohle** *f* [hard] coal. **S~schlag** *m* rock fall

Stelle *f* -, -n place; (*Fleck*) spot; (*Abschnitt*) passage; (*Stellung*) job, post; (*Behörde*) authority; **auf der S~** immediately

stellen *vt* put; (*aufrecht*) stand; set <*Wecker, Aufgabe*>; ask <*Frage*>; make <*Antrag, Forderung,*

Diagnose>; **zur Verfügung s~** provide; **lauter/leiser s~** turn up/down; **kalt/warm s~** chill/keep hot; **sich s~** [go and] stand; give oneself up (**der Polizei** to the police); **sich tot s~** pretend to be dead; **gut gestellt sein** be well off

Stellen|anzeige *f* job advertisement. **S~vermittlung** *f* employment agency. **s~weise** *adv* in places

Stellung *f* -, -en position; (*Arbeit*) job; **S~ nehmen** make a statement (**zu** on). **S~suche** *f* job-hunting

Stellvertreter *m* deputy

Stelzen *fpl* stilts. **s~** *vi* (*sein*) stalk

stemmen *vt* press; lift <*Gewicht*>

Stempel *m* -s,- stamp; (*Post-*) postmark; (*Präge-*) die; (*Feingehalts-*) hallmark. **s~n** *vt* stamp; hallmark <*Silber*>; cancel <*Marke*>

Stengel* *m* -s, *s.* **Stängel**

Steno *f* - 🔲 shorthand

Steno|gramm *nt* -[e]s, -e shorthand text. **S~grafie** *f* - shorthand. **s~grafieren** *vt* take down in shorthand ● *vi* (*haben*) do shorthand

Steppdecke *f* quilt

Steppe *f* -, -n steppe

Stepptanz *m* tap-dance

sterben† *vi* (*sein*) die (**an** + *dat* of); **im S~ liegen** be dying

sterblich *a* mortal. **S~keit** *f* - mortality

stereo *adv* in stereo. **S~anlage** *f* stereo [system]

steril *a* sterile. **s~isieren** *vt* sterilize. **S~ität** *f* - sterility

Stern *m* -[e]s, -e star. **S~bild** *nt* constellation. **S~chen** *nt* -s,- asterisk. **S~kunde** *f* astronomy. **S~schnuppe** *f* -, -n shooting star. **S~warte** *f* -, -n observatory

stets *adv* always

Steuer[1] *nt* -s,- steering-wheel; (*Naut*) helm; **am S~** at the wheel

Steuer[2] *f* -, -n tax

Steuer|bord *nt* -[e]s starboard [side]. **S~erklärung** *f* tax return. **s~frei** *a* & *adv* tax-free. **S~mann**

m (*pl* **-leute**) helmsman; (*beim Rudern*) cox. **s~n** *vt* steer; (*Aviat*) pilot; (*Techn*) control ● *vi* (*haben*) be at the wheel/(*Naut*) helm.

s~pflichtig *a* taxable. **S~rad** *nt* steering-wheel. **S~ruder** *nt* helm. **S~ung** *f* - steering; (*Techn*) controls *pl.* **S~zahler** *m* -s,- taxpayer

Stewardess /'stjuːɛdɛs/ *f* -, -en air hostess, stewardess

Stich *m* -[e]s, -e prick; (*Messer*-) stab; (*S~wunde*) stab wound; (*Bienen*-) sting; (*Mücken*-) bite; (*Schmerz*) stabbing pain; (*Näh*-) stitch; (*Kupfer*-) engraving; (*Kartenspiel*) trick

stick|en *vt/i* (*haben*) embroider. **S~erei** *f* - embroidery

Stickstoff *m* nitrogen

Stiefel *m* -s,- boot

Stief|kind *nt* stepchild. **S~mutter** *f* stepmother. **S~mütterchen** *nt* -s,- pansy. **S~sohn** *m* stepson. **S~tochter** *f* stepdaughter. **S~vater** *m* stepfather

Stiege *f* -, -n stairs *pl*

Stiel *m* -[e]s, -e handle; (*Blumen*-, *Gläser*-) stem; (*Blatt*-) stalk

Stier *m* -[e]s, -e bull; (*Astr*) Taurus

Stierkampf *m* bullfight

Stift¹ *m* -[e]s, -e pin; (*Nagel*-) tack; (*Blei*-) pencil; (*Farb*-) crayon

Stift² *nt* -[e]s, -e [endowed] foundation. **s~en** *vt* endow; (*spenden*) donate; create <*Unheil, Verwirrung*>; bring about <*Frieden*>. **S~ung** *f* -, -en foundation; (*Spende*) donation

Stil *m* -[e]s, -e style

still *a* quiet; (*reglos, ohne Kohlensäure*) still; (*heimlich*) secret; der S~e Ozean the Pacific; im S~en secretly. **S~e** *f* - quiet; (*Schweigen*) silence

Stilleben* *nt s.* Stillleben

stillen *vt* satisfy; quench <*Durst*>; stop <*Schmerzen, Blutung*>; breast-feed <*Kind*>

still|halten† *vi sep* (*haben*) keep still. **S~leben** *nt* still life

Still|schweigen *nt* silence. **S~stand** *m* standstill; zum

S~stand bringen/kommen stop.

s~stehen† *vi sep* (*haben*) stand still; (*anhalten*) stop; <*Verkehr:*> be at a standstill

Stimm|bänder *ntpl* vocal cords. **s~berechtigt** *a* entitled to vote. **S~bruch** *m* er ist im S~bruch his voice is breaking

Stimme *f* -, -n voice; (*Wahl*-) vote

stimmen *vi* (*haben*) be right; (*wählen*) vote ● *vt* tune

Stimmung *f* -, -en mood; (*Atmosphäre*) atmosphere

Stimmzettel *m* ballot-paper

stinken† *vi* (*haben*) smell/(*stark*) stink (nach of). **S~tier** *nt* skunk

Stipendium *nt* -s, -ien scholarship; (*Beihilfe*) grant

Stirn *f* -, -en forehead

stochern *vi* (*haben*) s~ in (+ *dat*) poke <*Feuer*>; pick at <*Essen*>

Stock¹ *m* -[e]s,⸚e stick; (*Ski*-) pole; (*Bienen*-) hive; (*Rosen*-) bush; (*Reb*-) vine

Stock² *m* -[e]s,- storey, floor. **S~bett** *nt* bunk-beds *pl.*

stock|en *vi* (*haben*) stop; <*Verkehr:*> come to a standstill; <*Person:*> falter. **S~ung** *f* -, -en hold-up

Stockwerk *nt* storey, floor

Stoff *m* -[e]s, -e substance; (*Tex*) fabric, material; (*Thema*) subject [matter]; (*Gesprächs*-) topic. **S~wechsel** *m* metabolism

stöhnen *vi* (*haben*) groan, moan

Stola *f* -, -len stole

Stollen *m* -s,- gallery; (*Kuchen*) stollen

stolpern *vi* (*sein*) stumble; s~ über (+ *acc*) trip over

stolz *a* proud (auf + *acc* of). **S~** *m* -es pride

stopfen *vt* stuff; (*stecken*) put; (*ausbessern*) darn ● *vi* (*haben*) be constipating

Stopp *m* -s, -s stop. **s~** *int* stop!

stoppelig *a* stubbly

stopp|en *vt* stop; (*Sport*) time ● *vi* (*haben*) stop. **S~uhr** *f* stop-watch

Stöpsel *m* -s,- plug; (*Flaschen-*) stopper

Storch *m* -[e]s,-̈e stork

Store /ʃtoːɐ:/ *m* -s, -s net curtain

stören *vt* disturb; disrupt <*Rede*>; jam <*Sender*>; (*missfallen*) bother ● *vi* (*haben*) be a nuisance

stornieren *vt* cancel

störrisch *a* stubborn

Störung *f* -, -en disturbance; disruption; (*Med*) trouble; (*Radio*) interference; **technische S~** technical fault

Stoß *m* -es,-̈e push, knock; (*mit Ellbogen*) dig; (*Hörner-*) butt; (*mit Waffe*) thrust; (*Schwimm-*) stroke; (*Ruck*) jolt; (*Erd-*) shock; (*Stapel*) stack, pile. **S~dämpfer** *m* -s,- shock absorber

stoßen† *vt* push, knock; (*mit Füßen*) kick; (*mit Kopf*) butt; (*an-*) poke, nudge; (*treiben*) thrust; **sich s~** knock oneself; **sich** (*dat*) **den Kopf s~** hit one's head ● *vi* (*haben*) push; **s~ an** (+ *acc*) knock against; (*angrenzen*) adjoin ● *vi* (*sein*) **s~ gegen** knock against; bump into <*Tür*>; **s~ auf** (+ *acc*) bump into; (*entdecken*) come across; strike <*Öl*>

Stoß|stange *f* bumper. **S~verkehr** *m* rush-hour traffic. **S~zahn** *m* tusk. **S~zeit** *f* rush-hour

stottern *vt/i* (*haben*) stutter, stammer

Str. *abbr* (**Straße**) St

Strafanstalt *f* prison

Strafe *f* -, -n punishment; (*Jur & fig*) penalty; (*Geld-*) fine; (*Freiheits-*) sentence. **s~n** *vt* punish

straff *a* tight, taut. **s~en** *vt* tighten

Strafgesetz *nt* criminal law

sträf|lich *a* criminal. **S~ling** *m* -s, -e prisoner

Straf|mandat *nt* (*Auto*) [parking/speeding] ticket. **S~porto** *nt* excess postage. **S~raum** *m* penalty area. **S~stoß** *m* penalty. **S~tat** *f* crime

---

Strahl *m* -[e]s, -en ray; (*einer Taschenlampe*) beam; (*Wasser-*) jet. **s~en** *vi* (*haben*) shine; (*funkeln*) sparkle; (*lächeln*) beam. **S~enbehandlung** *f* radiotherapy. **S~ung** *f* - radiation

Strähne *f* -, -n strand

stramm *a* tight

Strampel|höschen /-sç-/ *nt* -s,- rompers *pl*. **s~n** *vi* (*haben*) <*Baby:*> kick

Strand *m* -[e]s,-̈e beach. **s~en** *vi* (*sein*) run aground

Strang *m* -[e]s,-̈e rope

Strapaz|e *f* -, -n strain. **s~ieren** *vt* be hard on; tax <*Nerven*>

Strass *m* - & -es paste

Straße *f* -, -n road; (*in der Stadt auch*) street; (*Meeres-*) strait. **S~nbahn** *f* tram. **S~nkarte** *f* road-map. **S~nsperre** *f* road-block

Strat|egie *f* -, -n strategy. **s~egisch** *a* strategic

Strauch *m* -[e]s, Sträucher bush

Strauß¹ *m* -es, Sträuße bunch [of flowers]; (*Bukett*) bouquet

Strauß² *m* -es, -e ostrich

streben *vi* (*haben*) strive (**nach** for) ● *vi* (*sein*) head (**nach/zu** for)

Streber *m* -s,- pushy person

Strecke *f* -, -n stretch, section; (*Entfernung*) distance; (*Rail*) line; (*Route*) route

strecken *vt* stretch; (*aus-*) stretch out; (*gerade machen*) straighten; (*Culin*) thin down; **den Kopf aus dem Fenster s~** put one's head out of the window

Streich *m* -[e]s, -e prank, trick

streicheln *vt* stroke

streichen† *vt* spread; (*weg-*) smooth; (*an-*) paint; (*aus-*) delete; (*kürzen*) cut ● *vi* (*haben*) **s~ über** (+ *acc*) stroke

Streichholz *nt* match

Streich|instrument *nt* stringed instrument. **S~käse** *m* cheese spread. **S~orchester** *nt* string orchestra. **S~ung** *f* -, -en deletion; (*Kürzung*) cut

Streife *f* -, -n patrol

streifen vt brush against; (*berühren*) touch; (*verletzen*) graze; (*fig*) touch on <*Thema*>

Streifen m -s,- stripe; (*Licht-*) streak; (*auf der Fahrbahn*) line; (*schmales Stück*) strip

Streifenwagen m patrol car

Streik m -s, -s strike; in den S∼ treten go on strike. **S∼brecher** m strike-breaker, (*pej*) scab. **s∼en** vi (*haben*) strike; 🄴 refuse; (*versagen*) pack up

Streit m -[e]s, -e quarrel; (*Auseinandersetzung*) dispute. **s∼en†** vr/i (*haben*) [sich] s∼en quarrel. **S∼igkeiten** fpl quarrels. **S∼kräfte** fpl armed forces

streng a strict; <*Blick, Ton*> stern; (*rau, nüchtern*) severe; <*Geschmack*> sharp; **s∼** genommen strictly speaking. **S∼e** f - strictness; sternness; severity

Stress m -es, -e stress

streuen vt spread; (*ver-*) scatter; sprinkle <*Zucker, Salz*>; die Straßen s∼ grit the roads

streunen vi (*sein*) roam

Strich m -[e]s, -e line; (*Feder-, Pinsel-*) stroke; (*Morse-, Gedanken-*) dash. **S∼kode** m bar code. **S∼punkt** m semicolon

Strick m -[e]s, -e cord; (*Seil*) rope

strick|en vt/i (*haben*) knit. **S∼jacke** f cardigan. **S∼leiter** f rope-ladder. **S∼nadel** f knitting-needle. **S∼waren** fpl knitwear sg. **S∼zeug** nt knitting

striegeln vt groom

strittig a contentious

Stroh nt -[e]s straw. **S∼blumen** fpl everlasting flowers. **S∼dach** nt thatched roof. **S∼halm** m straw

Strolch m -[e]s, -e 🄴 rascal

Strom m -[e]s,̈-e river; (*Menschen-, Auto-, Blut-*) stream; (*Tränen-*) flood; (*Schwall*) torrent; (*Electr*) current, power; **gegen den S∼** (*fig*) against the tide. **s∼abwärts** adv downstream. **s∼aufwärts** adv upstream

strömen vi (*sein*) flow; <*Menschen, Blut:*> stream, pour

Strom|kreis m circuit. **s∼linienförmig** a streamlined. **S∼sperre** f power cut

Strömung f -, -en current

Strophe f -, -n verse

Strudel m -s,- whirlpool; (*SGer Culin*) strudel

Strumpf m -[e]s,̈-e stocking; (*Knie-*) sock. **S∼band** nt (*pl -bänder*) suspender. **S∼hose** f tights pl

Strunk m -[e]s,̈-e stalk

struppig a shaggy

Stube f -, -n room. **s∼nrein** a house-trained

Stuck m -s stucco

Stück nt -[e]s, -e piece; (*Zucker-*) lump; (*Seife*) tablet; (*Theater-*) play; (*Gegenstand*) item; (*Exemplar*) specimen; ein S∼ (*Entfernung*) some way. **S∼chen** nt -s,- [little] bit. **s∼weise** adv bit by bit; (*einzeln*) singly

Student|(in) m -en, -en (f -, -nen) student. **s∼isch** a student ...

Studie /-iə/ f -, -n study

studieren vt/i (*haben*) study

Studio nt -s, -s studio

Studium nt -s, -ien studies pl

Stufe f -, -n step; (*Treppen-*) stair; (*Raketen-*) stage; (*Niveau*) level. **s∼n** vt terrace; (*staffeln*) grade

Stuhl m -[e]s,̈-e chair; (*Med*) stools pl. **S∼gang** m bowel movement

stülpen vt put (über + acc over)

stumm a dumb; (*schweigsam*) silent

Stummel m -s,- stump; (*Zigaretten-*) butt; (*Bleistift-*) stub

Stümper m -s,- bungler

stumpf a blunt; <*Winkel*> obtuse; (*glanzlos*) dull; (*fig*) apathetic. **S∼** m -[e]s,̈-e stump

Stumpfsinn m apathy; tedium

Stunde f -, -n hour; (*Sch*) lesson

stunden vt jdm eine Schuld s∼ give s.o. time to pay a debt

Stunden|kilometer mpl kilometres per hour. **s∼lang** adv for hours. **S∼lohn** m hourly rate.

S~plan *m* timetable. **s~weise** *adv* by the hour

stündlich *a & adv* hourly

stur *a* pigheaded

Sturm *m* **-[e]s,¨-e** gale; storm; (*Mil*) assault

stürm|en *vi* (*haben*) <*Wind:*> blow hard ● *vi* (*sein*) rush ● *vt* storm; (*bedrängen*) besiege. **S~er** *m* **-s,-** forward. **s~isch** *a* stormy; <*Überfahrt*> rough

Sturz *m* **-es,¨-e** [heavy] fall; (*Preis-*) sharp drop; (*Pol*) overthrow

stürzen *vi* (*sein*) fall [heavily]; (*in die Tiefe*) plunge; <*Preise:*> drop sharply; <*Regierung:*> fall; (*eilen*) rush ● *vt* throw; (*umkippen*) turn upside down; turn out <*Speise, Kuchen*>; (*Pol*) overthrow, topple; **sich s~** throw oneself (**aus/in** + *acc* out of/into)

Sturzhelm *m* crash-helmet

Stute *f* **-, -n** mare

Stütze *f* **-, -n** support

stützen *vt* support; (*auf-*) rest; **sich s~ auf** (+ *acc*) lean on

stutzig *a* puzzled; (*misstrauisch*) suspicious

Stützpunkt *m* (*Mil*) base

Substantiv *nt* **-s, -e** noun

Substanz *f* **-, -en** substance

Subvention /-ˈtsi̯o:n/ *f* **-, -en** subsidy. **s~ieren** *vt* subsidize

Such|e *f* **-** search; **auf der S~e nach** looking for. **s~en** *vt* look for; (*intensiv*) search for; seek <*Hilfe, Rat*>; **'Zimmer gesucht'** 'room wanted' ● *vi* (*haben*) look, search (**nach** for). **S~er** *m* **-s,-** (*Phot*) viewfinder

Sucht *f* **-,¨-e** addiction; (*fig*) mania

süchtig *a* addicted. **S~e(r)** *m/f* addict

Süd *m* **-[e]s** south. **S~afrika** *nt* South Africa. **S~amerika** *nt* South America. **s~deutsch** *a* South German

Süden *m* **-s** south; **nach S~** south

Süd|frucht *f* tropical fruit. **s~lich** *a* southern; <*Richtung*> southerly ● *adv & prep* (+ *gen*) **s~lich der Stadt** south of the town. **S~pol** *m* South Pole. **s~wärts** *adv* southwards

Sühne *f* **-, -n** atonement; (*Strafe*) penalty. **s~n** *vt* atone for

Sultanine *f* **-, -n** sultana

Sülze *f* **-, -n** [meat] jelly

Summe *f* **-, -n** sum

summen *vi* (*haben*) hum; <*Biene:*> buzz ● *vt* hum

summieren (sich) *vr* add up

Sumpf *m* **-[e]s,¨-e** marsh, swamp

Sünd|e *f* **-, -n** sin. **S~enbock** *m* scapegoat. **S~er(in)** *m* **-s,-** (*f* **-, -nen**) sinner. **s~igen** *vi* (*haben*) sin

super *inv a* [!] great. **S~markt** *m* supermarket

Suppe *f* **-, -n** soup. **S~nlöffel** *m* soup-spoon. **S~nteller** *m* soup-plate. **S~nwürfel** *m* stock cube

Surf|brett /ˈsø:ɐ̯f-/ *nt* surfboard. **S~en** *nt* **-s** surfing

surren *vi* (*haben*) whirr

süß *a* sweet. **S~e** *f* **-** sweetness. **s~en** *vt* sweeten. **S~igkeit** *f* **-, -en** sweet. **s~lich** *a* sweetish; (*fig*) sugary. **S~speise** *f* sweet. **S~stoff** *m* sweetener. **S~waren** *fpl* confectionery *sg*, sweets *pl*. **S~wasser-** *pref* freshwater ...

Sylvester *nt* **-s** = **Silvester**

Symbol *nt* **-s, -e** symbol. **S~ik** *f* **-** symbolism. **s~isch** *a* symbolic

Sym|metrie *f* **-** symmetry. **s~metrisch** *a* symmetrical

Sympathie *f* **-, -n** sympathy

sympathisch *a* agreeable; <*Person*> likeable

Symptom *nt* **-s, -e** symptom. **s~atisch** *a* symptomatic

Synagoge *f* **-, -n** synagogue

synchronisieren /zynkroniˈzi:rən/ *vt* synchronize; dub <*Film*>

Syndikat *nt* **-[e]s, -e** syndicate

Syndrom *nt* **-s, -e** syndrome

synonym *a* synonymous

*old spelling

Synthese *f* -, -n synthesis

Syrien /-iən/ *nt* -s Syria

System *nt* -s, -e system. **s~atisch** *a* systematic

Szene *f* -, -n scene

Tt

Tabak *m* -s, -e tobacco

Tabelle *f* -, -n table; (*Sport*) league table

Tablett *nt* -[e]s, -s tray

Tablette *f* -, -n tablet

tabu *a* taboo. **T~** *nt* -s, -s taboo

Tacho *m* -s, -s, **Tachometer** *m* & *nt* speedometer

Tadel *m* -s,- reprimand; (*Kritik*) censure; (*Sch*) black mark. **t~los** *a* impeccable. **t~n** *vt* reprimand; censure

Tafel *f* -, -n (*Tisch, Tabelle*) table; (*Platte*) slab; (*Anschlag-, Hinweis-*) board; (*Gedenk-*) plaque; (*Schiefer-*) slate; (*Wand-*) blackboard; (*Bild-*) plate; (*Schokolade*) bar

Täfelung *f* - panelling

Tag *m* -[e]s, -e day; unter T~e underground; es wird Tag it is getting light; guten Tag! good morning/afternoon!

Tage|buch *nt* diary. **t~lang** *adv* for days

Tages|anbruch *m* daybreak. **T~ausflug** *m* day trip. **T~decke** *f* bedspread. **T~karte** *f* day ticket; (*Speise-*) menu of the day. **T~licht** *nt* daylight. **T~mutter** *f* childminder. **T~ordnung** *f* agenda. **T~rückfahrkarte** *f* day return [ticket]. **T~zeit** *f* time of the day. **T~zeitung** *f* daily [news]paper

täglich *a* & *adv* daily; zweimal t~ twice a day

tags *adv* by day; t~ zuvor/darauf the day before/after

tagsüber *adv* during the day

tag|täglich *a* daily ● *adv* every single day. **T~ung** *f* -, -en meeting; conference

Taill|e /'taljə/ *f* -, -n waist. **t~iert** /ta'ji:ɐt/ *a* fitted

Takt *m* -[e]s, -e tact; (*Mus*) bar; (*Tempo*) time; (*Rhythmus*) rhythm; im T~ in time

Taktik *f* - tactics *pl.*

takt|los *a* tactless. **T~losigkeit** *f* - tactlessness. **T~stock** *m* baton. **t~voll** *a* tactful

Tal *nt* -[e]s, -e valley

Talar *m* -s, -e robe; (*Univ*) gown

Talent *nt* -[e]s, -e talent. **t~iert** *a* talented

Talg *m* -s tallow; (*Culin*) suet

Talsperre *f* dam

Tampon /tam'põ:/ *m* -s, -s tampon

Tank *m* -s, -s tank. **t~en** *vt* fill up with <*Benzin*> ● *vi* (*haben*) fill up with petrol; (*Aviat*) refuel. **T~er** *m* -s,- tanker. **T~stelle** *f* petrol station. **T~wart** *m* -[e]s, -e petrol-pump attendant

Tanne *f* -, -n fir [tree]. **T~nbaum** *m* fir tree; (*Weihnachtsbaum*) Christmas tree. **T~nzapfen** *m* fir cone

Tante *f* -, -n aunt

Tantiemen /tan'tie:mən/ *pl* royalties

Tanz *m* -es,-e dance. **t~en** *vt/i* (*haben*) dance

Tänzer(in) *m* -s,- (*f* -, -nen) dancer

Tapete *f* -, -n wallpaper

tapezieren *vt* paper

tapfer *a* brave. **T~keit** *f* - bravery

Tarif *m* -s, -e rate; (*Verzeichnis*) tariff

tarn|en *vt* disguise; (*Mil*) camouflage. **T~ung** *f* - disguise; camouflage

Tasche *f* -, -n bag; (*Hosen-, Mantel-*) pocket. **T~nbuch** *nt* paperback. **T~ndieb** *m* pickpocket. **T~ngeld** *nt* pocket-money. **T~nlampe** *f* torch. **T~nmesser** *nt* penknife. **T~ntuch** *nt* handkerchief

Tasse *f* -, -n cup

Tastatur *f* -, -en keyboard

Tast|e *f* -, -n key; (*Druck-*) push-button. **t~en** *vi* (*haben*) feel, grope (nach for) ● *vt* key in <*Daten*>; **sich t~en** feel one's way (zu to)

Tat *f* -, -en action; (*Helden-*) deed; (*Straf-*) crime; **auf frischer Tat ertappt** caught in the act

Täter(in) *m* -s,- (*f* -, -nen) culprit; (*Jur*) offender

tätig *a* active; **t~ sein** work. **T~keit** *f* -, -en activity; (*Arbeit*) work, job

Tatkraft *f* energy

Tatort *m* scene of the crime

tätowier|en *vt* tattoo. **T~ung** *f* -, -en tattooing; (*Bild*) tattoo

Tatsache *f* fact. **T~nbericht** *m* documentary

tatsächlich *a* actual

Tatze *f* -, -n paw

Tau¹ *m* -[e]s dew

Tau² *nt* -[e]s, -e rope

taub *a* deaf; (*gefühllos*) numb

Taube *f* -, -n pigeon; dove. **T~nschlag** *m* pigeon-loft

Taub|heit *f* - deafness. **t~stumm** *a* deaf and dumb

tauch|en *vt* dip, plunge; (*unter-*) duck ● *vi* (*haben/sein*) dive/(*ein-*) plunge (in + *acc* into); (*auf-*) appear (aus out of). **T~er** *m* -s,- diver. **T~eranzug** *m* diving-suit

tauen *vi* (*sein*) melt, thaw ● *impers* **es taut** it is thawing

Tauf|becken *nt* font. **T~e** *f* -, -n christening, baptism. **t~en** *vt* christen, baptize. **T~pate** *m* godfather

taugen *vi* (*haben*) **etwas/nichts t~n** be good/no good

tauglich *a* suitable; (*Mil*) fit

Tausch *m* -[e]s, -e exchange, ⊡ swap. **t~en** *vt* exchange/(*handeln*) barter (gegen for) ● *vi* (*haben*) swap (mit etw sth; mit jdm with s.o.)

täuschen *vt* deceive, fool; betray <*Vertrauen*>; **sich t~** delude oneself; (*sich irren*) be mistaken ● *vi* (*haben*) be deceptive. **t~d** *a* deceptive; <*Ähnlichkeit*> striking

Täuschung *f* -, -en deception; (*Irrtum*) mistake; (*Illusion*) delusion

tausend *inv a* one/a thousand. **T~nt** -s, -e thousand. **T~füßler** *m* -s,- centipede. **t~ste(r, s)** *a* thousandth. **T~stel** *nt* -s,- thousandth

Tau|tropfen *m* dewdrop. **T~wetter** *nt* thaw

Taxe *f* -, -n charge; (*Kur-*) tax; (*Taxi*) taxi

Taxi *nt* -s, -s taxi, cab

Taxi|fahrer *m* taxi driver. **T~stand** *m* taxi rank

Teakholz /'ti:k-/ *nt* teak

Team /ti:m/ *nt* -s, -s team

Techni|k *f* -, -en technology; (*Methode*) technique. **T~ker** *m* -s,- technician. **t~sch** *a* technical; (*technologisch*) technological; **T~sche Hochschule** Technical University

Techno|logie *f* -, -n technology. **t~logisch** *a* technological

Teddybär *m* teddy bear

Tee *m* -s, -s tea. **T~beutel** *m* tea-bag. **T~kanne** *f* teapot. **T~löffel** *m* teaspoon

Teer *m* -s tar. **t~en** *vt* tar

Tee|sieb *nt* tea-strainer. **T~wagen** *m* [tea] trolley

Teich *m* -[e]s, -e pond

Teig *m* -[e]s, -e pastry; (*Knet-*) dough; (*Rühr-*) mixture; (*Pfannkuchen-*) batter. **T~rolle** *f* rolling-pin. **T~waren** *fpl* pasta *sg*

Teil *m* -[e]s, -e part; (*Bestand-*) component; (*Jur*) party; **zum T~** partly; **zum großen/größten T~** for the most part ● *m & nt* -[e]s (*Anteil*) share; **ich für mein[en] T~** for my part ● *nt* -[e]s, -e part; (*Ersatz-*) spare part; (*Anbau-*) unit

teil|bar *a* divisible. **T~chen** *nt* -s,- particle. **t~en** *vt* divide; (*auf-*) share out; (*gemeinsam haben*) share; (*Pol*) partition <*Land*>; **sich** (*dat*) **etw t~en** share sth; **sich t~en** divide;

(*sich gabeln*) fork; <*Meinungen:*> differ ● *vi* (*haben*) share

Teilhaber *m* -s,- (*Comm*) partner

Teilnahme *f* - participation; (*innere*) interest; (*Mitgefühl*) sympathy

teilnehm|en† *vi sep* (*haben*) t~en an (+ *dat*) take part in; (*mitfühlen*) share [in]. **T~er(in)** *m* -s,- (*f* -, -nen) participant; (*an Wettbewerb*) competitor

teil|s *adv* partly. **T~ung** *f* -, -en division; (*Pol*) partition. **t~weise** *a* partial ● *adv* partially, partly. **T~zahlung** *f* part-payment; (*Rate*) instalment. **T~zeitbeschäftigung** *f* part-time job

Teint /tɛ̃:/ *m* -s, -s complexion

Telefax *nt* fax

Telefon *nt* -s, -e [tele]phone. **T~anruf** *m*, **T~at** *nt* -[e]s, -e [tele]phone call. **T~buch** *nt* [tele]phone book. **t~ieren** *vi* (*haben*) [tele]phone

telefon|isch *a* [tele]phone ... ● *adv* by [tele]phone. **T~ist(in)** *m* -en, -en (*f* -, -nen) telephonist. **T~karte** *f* phone card. **T~nummer** *f* [tele]phone number. **T~zelle** *f* [tele]phone box

Telegraf *m* -en, -en telegraph. **T~enmast** *m* telegraph pole. **t~ieren** *vi* (*haben*) send a telegram. **t~isch** *a* telegraphic ● *adv* by telegram

Telegramm *nt* -s, -e telegram

Teleobjektiv *nt* telephoto lens

Telepathie *f* - telepathy

Teleskop *nt* -s, -e telescope

Telex *nt* -, -[e] telex. **t~en** *vt* telex

Teller *m* -s,- plate

Tempel *m* -s,- temple

Temperament *nt* -s, -e temperament; (*Lebhaftigkeit*) vivacity

Temperatur *f* -, -en temperature

Tempo *nt* -s, -s speed; T~ [T~]! hurry up!

Tendenz *f* -, -en trend; (*Neigung*) tendency

Tennis *nt* - tennis. **T~platz** *m* tennis-court. **T~schläger** *m* tennis-racket

Teppich *m* -s, -e carpet. **T~boden** *m* fitted carpet

Termin *m* -s, -e date; (*Arzt-*) appointment. **T~kalender** *m* [appointments] diary

Terpentin *nt* -s turpentine

Terrasse *f* -, -n terrace

Terrier /'tɛriɐ/ *m* -s,- terrier

Terrine *f* -, -n tureen

Territorium *nt* -s, -ien territory

Terror *m* -s terror. **t~isieren** *vt* terrorize. **T~ismus** *m* - terrorism. **T~ist** *m* -en, -en terrorist

Tesafilm (P) *m* ≈ Sellotape (P)

Test *m* -[e]s, -s & -e test

Testament *nt* -[e]s, -e will; Altes/ Neues T~ Old/New Testament. **T~svollstrecker** *m* -s,- executor

testen *vt* test

Tetanus *m* - tetanus

teuer *a* expensive; (*lieb*) dear; wie t~? how much?

Teufel *m* -s,- devil. **T~skreis** *m* vicious circle

teuflisch *a* fiendish

Text *m* -[e]s, -e text; (*Passage*) passage; (*Bild-*) caption; (*Lied-*) lyrics *pl*. **T~er** *m* -s,- copy-writer; (*Schlager-*) lyricist

Textilien /-iən/ *pl* textiles; (*Textilwaren*) textile goods

Textverarbeitungssystem *nt* word processor

Theater *nt* -s,- theatre; (🎫 *Getue*) fuss. **T~kasse** *f* box-office. **T~stück** *nt* play

Theke *f* -, -n bar; (*Ladentisch*) counter

Thema *nt* -s, -men subject

Themse *f* - Thames

Theolo|ge *m* -n, -n theologian. **T~gie** *f* - theology

theor|etisch *a* theoretical. **T~ie** *f* -, -n theory

Therapeut(in) *m* -en, -en (*f* -, -nen) therapist

Therapie *f* -, -n therapy

Thermalbad *nt* thermal bath

Thermometer *nt* -s,- thermometer

Thermosflasche (P) *f* Thermos flask (P)

Thermostat *m* -[e]s, -e thermostat

These *f* -, -n thesis

Thrombose *f* -, -n thrombosis

Thron *m* -[e]s, -e throne. **t~en** *vi* (*haben*) sit [in state]. **T~folge** *f* succession. **T~folger** *m* -s,- heir to the throne

Thunfisch *m* tuna

Thymian *m* -s thyme

ticken *vi* (*haben*) tick

tief *a* deep; (*t~ liegend, niedrig*) low; (*t~gründig*) profound; **t~er Teller** soup-plate ● *adv* deep; low; (*sehr*) deeply, profoundly; <*schlafen*> soundly. **T~** *nt* -s, -s (*Meteorol*) depression. **T~bau** *m* civil engineering. **T~e** *f* -, -n depth. **T~garage** *f* underground car park. **t~gekühlt** *a* [deep-]frozen

Tiefkühl|fach *nt* freezer compartment. **T~kost** *f* frozen food. **T~truhe** *f* deep-freeze

Tiefsttemperatur *f* minimum temperature

Tier *nt* -[e]s, -e animal. **T~arzt** *m*, **T~ärztin** *f* vet, veterinary surgeon. **T~garten** *m* zoo. **T~kreis** *m* zodiac. **T~kunde** *f* zoology. **T~quälerei** *f* cruelty to animals

Tiger *m* -s,- tiger

tilgen *vt* pay off <*Schuld*>; (*streichen*) delete; (*fig: auslöschen*) wipe out

Tinte *f* -, -n ink. **T~nfisch** *m* squid

Tipp *m* -s, -s 🖭 tip

tipp|en *vt* 🖭 type ● *vi* (*haben*) (*berühren*) touch (auf/an etw *acc* sth); (🖭 *Maschine schreiben*) type; **t~en** auf (+ *acc*) (🖭 *wetten*) bet on. **T~schein** *m* pools/lottery coupon

tipptopp *a* 🖭 immaculate

Tirol *nt* -s [the] Tyrol

Tisch *m* -[e]s, -e table; (*Schreib-*) desk; **nach T~** after the meal. **T~decke** *f* table-cloth. **T~gebet**

nt grace. **T~ler** *m* -s,- joiner; (*Möbel-*) cabinet-maker. **T~rede** *f* after-dinner speech. **T~tennis** *nt* table tennis

Titel *m* -s,- title

Toast /to:st/ *m* -[e]s, -e toast; (*Scheibe*) piece of toast. **T~er** *m* -s,- toaster

toben *vi* (*haben*) rave; <*Sturm:*> rage; <*Kinder:*> play boisterously

Tochter *f* -,- daughter. **T~gesellschaft** *f* subsidiary

Tod *m* -es death

Todes|angst *f* mortal fear. **T~anzeige** *f* death announcement; (*Zeitungs-*) obituary. **T~fall** *m* death. **T~opfer** *nt* fatality, casualty. **T~strafe** *f* death penalty. **T~urteil** *nt* death sentence

todkrank *a* dangerously ill

tödlich *a* fatal; <*Gefahr*> mortal

Toilette /toa'lɛtə/ *f* -, -n toilet. **T~npapier** *nt* toilet paper

toler|ant *a* tolerant. **T~anz** *f* - tolerance. **t~ieren** *vt* tolerate

toll *a* crazy, mad; (🖭 *prima*) fantastic; (*schlimm*) awful ● *adv* (*sehr*) very; (*schlimm*) badly. **t~kühn** *a* foolhardy. **T~wut** *f* rabies. **t~wütig** *a* rabid

Tölpel *m* -s,- fool

Tomate *f* -, -n tomato. **T~nmark** *nt* tomato purée

Tombola *f* -, -s raffle

Ton[1] *m* -[e]s clay

Ton[2] *m* -[e]s,-e tone; (*Klang*) sound; (*Note*) note; (*Betonung*) stress; (*Farb-*) shade; **der gute Ton** (*fig*) good form. **T~abnehmer** *m* -s,- pick-up. **t~angebend** *a* (*fig*) leading. **T~art** *f* tone [of voice]; (*Mus*) key. **T~band** *nt* (*pl* -bänder) tape. **T~bandgerät** *nt* tape recorder

tönen *vi* (*haben*) sound ● *vt* tint

Tonleiter *f* scale

Tonne *f* -, -n barrel, cask; (*Müll-*) bin; (*Maß*) tonne, metric ton

Topf *m* -[e]s,-e pot; (*Koch-*) pan

Topfen *m* -s (*Aust*) ≈ curd cheese

Töpferei *f* -, -en pottery

Topf|lappen *m* oven-cloth.
T∼pflanze *f* potted plant

Tor *nt* -[e]s, -e gate; (*Einfahrt*)
gateway; (*Sport*) goal

Torf *m* -s peat

torkeln *vi* (*sein/habe*) stagger

Tornister *m* -s,- knapsack; (*Sch*)
satchel

Torpedo *m* -s, -s torpedo

Torpfosten *m* goal-post

Torte *f* -, -n gateau; (*Obst-*) flan

Tortur *f* -, -en torture

Torwart *m* -s, -e goalkeeper

tot *a* dead; **tot geboren** stillborn; **sich
tot stellen** pretend to be dead

total *a* total. **T∼schaden** *m* ≈
write-off

Tote|(r) *m/f* dead man/woman;
(*Todesopfer*) fatality; **die T∼n** the
dead *pl*

töten *vt* kill

Toten|gräber *m* -s,- grave-digger.
T∼kopf *m* skull. **T∼schein** *m*
death certificate

totfahren† *vt sep* run over and kill

Toto *nt & m* -s football pools *pl*.
T∼schein *m* pools coupon

tot|schießen† *vt sep* shoot dead.
T∼schlag *m* (*Jur*) manslaughter.
t∼schlagen† *vt sep* kill

Tötung *f* -, -en killing; **fahrlässige
T∼** (*Jur*) manslaughter

Toup|et /tu'pe:/ *nt* -s, -s toupee.
t∼ieren *vt* back-comb

Tour /tu:ɐ/ *f* -, -en tour; (*Ausflug*)
trip; (*Auto-*) drive; (*Rad-*) ride;
(*Strecke*) distance; (*Techn*)
revolution; (☺ *Weise*) way

Touris|mus /tu'rɪsmʊs/ *m* -
tourism. **T∼t** *m* -en, -en tourist

Tournee /tʊr'ne:/ *f* -, -n tour

Trab *m* -[e]s trot

Trabant *m* -en, -en satellite

traben *vi* (*haben/sein*) trot

Tracht *f* -, -en [national] costume

Tradition /-'tsjo:n/ *f* -, -en
tradition. **t∼ell** *a* traditional

Trag|bahre *f* stretcher. **t∼bar** *a*
portable; <*Kleidung*> wearable

tragen† *vt* carry; (*an-/ aufhaben*)
wear; (*fig*) bear ● *vi* (*haben*) carry;
gut t∼ <*Baum:*> produce a good
crop

Träger *m* -s,- porter; (*Inhaber*)
bearer; (*eines Ordens*) holder; (*Bau-*)
beam; (*Stahl-*) girder; (*Achsel-*)
[shoulder] strap. **T∼kleid** *nt*
pinafore dress

Trag|etasche *f* carrier bag.
T∼flächenboot, T∼flügelboot
nt hydrofoil

Trägheit *f* - sluggishness; (*Faulheit*)
laziness; (*Phys*) inertia

Trag|ik *f* - tragedy. **t∼isch** *a* tragic

Tragödie /-iə/ *f* -, -n tragedy

Train|er /'trɛ:nɐ/ *m* -s,- trainer;
(*Tennis-*) coach. **t∼ieren** *vt/i*
(*haben*) train

Training /'trɛ:nɪŋ/ *nt* -s training.
T∼sanzug *m* tracksuit. **T∼s-
schuhe** *mpl* trainers

Traktor *m* -s, -en /-'to:rən/ tractor

trampeln *vi* (*haben*) stamp one's
feet ● *vi* (*sein*) trample (**auf** + *acc* on)
● *vt* trample

trampen /'trɛmpən/ *vi* (*sein*) ☺
hitch-hike

Tranchiermesser /trã'ʃi:ɐ-/ *nt*
carving-knife

Träne *f* -, -n tear. **t∼n** *vi* (*haben*)
water. **T∼ngas** *nt* tear-gas

Tränke *f* -, -n watering-place; (*Trog*)
drinking-trough. **t∼n** *vt* water
<*Pferd*>; (*nässen*) soak (**mit** with)

Trans|formator *m* -s, -en /-'to:rən/
transformer. **T∼fusion** *f* -, -en
[blood] transfusion

Transit /tran'zi:t/ *m* -s transit

Transparent *nt* -[e]s, -e banner;
(*Bild*) transparency

transpirieren *vi* (*haben*) perspire

Transport *m* -[e]s, -e transport;
(*Güter-*) consignment. **t∼ieren** *vt*
transport

Trapez *nt* -es, -e trapeze

Tratte *f* -, -n (*Comm*) draft

Traube *f* -, -n bunch of grapes;
(*Beere*) grape; (*fig*) cluster.
T∼nzucker *m* glucose

trauen *vi* (*haben*) (+ *dat*) trust ● *vt*
marry; **sich t~** dare (**etw zu tun** [to]
do sth); venture (**in** + *acc*/**aus** into/
out of)

Trauer *f* - mourning; (*Schmerz*) grief
(**um** for); **T~ tragen** be [dressed] in
mourning. **T~fall** *m* bereavement.
T~feier *f* funeral service. **t~n** *vi*
(*haben*) grieve; **t~n um** mourn [for].
T~spiel *nt* tragedy. **T~weide** *f*
weeping willow

Traum *m* -[e]s, Träume dream

Trauma *nt* -s, -men trauma

träumen *vt/i* (*haben*) dream

traumhaft *a* dreamlike; (*schön*)
fabulous

traurig *a* sad; (*erbärmlich*) sorry.
T~keit *f* - sadness

Trau|ring *m* wedding-ring.
T~schein *m* marriage certificate.
T~ung *f* -, -en wedding [ceremony]

Treff *nt* -s, -s (*Karten*) spades *pl*

treff|en† *vt* hit; <*Blitz:*> strike; (*fig:
verletzen*) hurt; (*zusammenkommen
mit*) meet; take <*Maßnahme*>; **sich
t~en** meet (**mit jdm** s.o.); **sich gut
t~en** be convenient; **es gut/schlecht
t~en** be lucky/unlucky ● *vi* (*haben*)
hit the target; **t~en auf** (+ *acc*) meet;
(*fig*) meet with. **T~en** *nt* -s,-
meeting. **T~er** *m* -s,- hit; (*Los*)
winner. **T~punkt** *m* meeting-place

treiben† *vt* drive; (*sich befassen mit*)
do; carry on <*Gewerbe*>; indulge in
<*Luxus*>; get up to <*Unfug*>; **Handel
t~** trade ● *vi* (*sein*) drift;
(*schwimmen*) float ● *vi* (*haben*) (*Bot*)
sprout. **T~** *nt* -s activity

Treib|haus *nt* hothouse.
T~hauseffekt *m* greenhouse
effect. **T~holz** *nt* driftwood.
T~riemen *m* transmission belt.
T~sand *m* quicksand. **T~stoff** *m*
fuel

trenn|bar *a* separable. **t~en** *vt*
separate/(*abmachen*) detach (**von**
from); divide, split <*Wort*>; **sich
t~en** separate; (*auseinander gehen*)
part; **sich t~en von** leave; (*fortgeben*)
part with. **T~ung** *f* -, -en

separation; (*Silben-*) division.
T~ungsstrich *m* hyphen.
T~wand *f* partition

trepp|ab *adv* downstairs. **t~auf**
adv upstairs

Treppe *f* -, -n stairs *pl*; (*Außen-*)
steps *pl*. **T~ngeländer** *nt* banisters
pl

Tresor *m* -s, -e safe

Tresse *f* -, -n braid

Treteimer *m* pedal bin

treten† *vi* (*sein*/*haben*) step;
(*versehentlich*) tread; (*ausschlagen*)
kick (**nach** at); **in Verbindung t~** get
in touch ● *vt* tread; (*mit Füßen*) kick

treu *a* faithful; (*fest*) loyal. **T~e** *f* -
faithfulness; loyalty; (*eheliche*)
fidelity. **T~händer** *m* -s,- trustee.
t~los *a* disloyal; (*untreu*) unfaithful

Tribüne *f* -, -n platform; (*Zuschauer-*
) stand

Trichter *m* -s,- funnel; (*Bomben-*)
crater

Trick *m* -s, -s trick. **T~film** *m*
cartoon. **t~reich** *a* clever

Trieb *m* -[e]s, -e drive, urge;
(*Instinkt*) instinct; (*Bot*) shoot.
T~verbrecher *m* sex offender.
T~werk *nt* (*Aviat*) engine; (*Uhr-*)
mechanism

triefen† *vi* (*haben*) drip; (*nass sein*)
be dripping (**von**/**vor** + *dat* with)

Trigonometrie *f* - trigonometry

Trikot¹ /triˈkoː/ *m* -s (*Tex*) jersey

Trikot² *nt* -s, -s (*Sport*) jersey;
(*Fußball-*) shirt

Trimester *nt* -s,- term

Trimm-dich *nt* -s keep-fit

trimmen *vt* trim; tune <*Motor*>;
sich t~ keep fit

trink|en† *vt/i* (*haben*) drink.
T~er(in) *m* -s,- (*f* -, -nen) alcoholic.
T~geld *nt* tip. **T~spruch** *m* toast

trist *a* dreary

Tritt *m* -[e]s, -e step; (*Fuß-*) kick.
T~brett *nt* step

Triumph *m* -s, -e triumph. **t~ieren**
vi (*haben*) rejoice

trocken *a* dry. **T~haube** *f* drier.
T~heit *f* -, -en dryness; (*Dürre*)
drought. **t~legen** *vt sep* change

<Baby>; drain *<Sumpf>*. **T∼milch** *f* powdered milk

trockn|en *vt/i* (*sein*) dry. **T∼er** *m* **-s,-** drier

Trödel *m* **-s** ⚄ junk. **t∼n** *vi* (*haben*) dawdle

Trödler *m* **-s,-** ⚄ slowcoach; (*Händler*) junk-dealer

Trog *m* **-[e]s,-̈e** trough

Trommel *f* **-, -n** drum. **T∼fell** *nt* ear-drum. **t∼n** *vi* (*haben*) drum

Trommler *m* **-s,-** drummer

Trompete *f* **-, -n** trumpet. **T∼r** *m* **-s,-** trumpeter

Tropen *pl* tropics

Tropf *m* **-[e]s, -e** (*Med*) drip

tröpfeln *vt/i* (*sein/haben*) drip

tropfen *vt/i* (*sein/haben*) drip. **T∼** *m* **-s,-** drop; (*fallend*) drip. **t∼weise** *adv* drop by drop

Trophäe /tro'fɛ:ə/ *f* **-, -n** trophy

tropisch *a* tropical

Trost *m* **-[e]s** consolation, comfort

tröst|en *vt* console, comfort; **sich t∼en** console oneself. **t∼lich** *a* comforting

trost|los *a* desolate; (*elend*) wretched; (*reizlos*) dreary. **T∼preis** *m* consolation prize

Trott *m* **-s** amble; (*fig*) routine

Trottel *m* **-s,-** ⚄ idiot

Trottoir /trɔ'toa:ɐ/ *nt* **-s, -s** pavement

trotz *prep* (+ *gen*) despite, in spite of. **T∼** *m* **-es** defiance. **t∼dem** *adv* nevertheless. **t∼ig** *a* defiant; stubborn

trübe *a* dull; *<Licht>* dim; *<Flüssigkeit>* cloudy; (*fig*) gloomy

Trubel *m* **-s** bustle

trüben *vt* dull; make cloudy *<Flüssigkeit>*; (*fig*) spoil; strain *<Verhältnis>* **sich t∼** *<Flüssigkeit:>* become cloudy; *<Himmel:>* cloud over; *<Augen:>* dim

Trüb|sal *f* **-** misery. **T∼sinn** *m* melancholy. **t∼sinnig** *a* melancholy

trügen† *vt* deceive ● *vi* (*haben*) be deceptive

Trugschluss *m* fallacy

Truhe *f* **-, -n** chest

Trümmer *pl* rubble *sg*; (*T∼teile*) wreckage *sg*, (*fig*) ruins

Trumpf *m* **-[e]s,-̈e** trump [card]. **t∼en** *vi* (*haben*) play trumps

Trunk *m* **-[e]s** drink. **T∼enheit** *f* **-** drunkenness; **T∼enheit am Steuer** drink-driving

Trupp *m* **-s, -s** group; (*Mil*) squad. **T∼e** *f* **-, -n** (*Mil*) unit; (*Theat*) troupe; **T∼en** troops

Truthahn *m* turkey

Tschech|e *m* **-n, -n, T∼in** *f* **-, -nen** Czech. **t∼isch** *a* Czech. **T∼oslowakei** (die) **-** Czechoslovakia

tschüs, tschüss *int* bye, cheerio

Tuba *f* **-, -ben** (*Mus*) tuba

Tube *f* **-, -n** tube

Tuberkulose *f* **-** tuberculosis

Tuch *nt* **-[e]s,-̈er** cloth; (*Hals-, Kopf-*) scarf; (*Schulter-*) shawl

tüchtig *a* competent; (*reichlich, beträchtlich*) good; (*groß*) big ● *adv* competently; (*ausreichend*) well

Tück|e *f* **-, -n** malice. **t∼isch** *a* malicious; (*gefährlich*) treacherous

Tugend *f* **-,en** virtue. **t∼haft** *a* virtuous

Tülle *f* **-, -n** spout

Tulpe *f* **-, -n** tulip

Tümmler *m* **-s,-** porpoise

Tumor *m* **-s, -en** /-'mo:rən/ tumour

Tümpel *m* **-[e]s,-** pond

Tumult *m* **-[e]s, -e** commotion; (*Aufruhr*) riot

tun† *vt* do; take *<Schritt, Blick>*; work *<Wunder>*; (*bringen*) put (**in** + *acc* into); **sich tun** happen; **jdm etwas tun** hurt s.o.; **das tut nichts** it doesn't matter ● *vi* (*haben*) act (**als ob** as if); **er tut nur so** he's just pretending; **jdm/etw gut tun** do s.o./sth. good; **zu tun haben** have things/work to do; **[es] zu tun haben mit** have to deal with. **Tun** *nt* **-s** actions *pl*

Tünche *f* **-, -n** whitewash; (*fig*) veneer. **t∼n** *vt* whitewash

Tunesien /-iən/ *nt* **-s** Tunisia

Tunfisch *m* = Thunfisch

Tunnel *m* -s,- tunnel

tupf|en *vt* dab ● *vi* (*haben*) t∼en an/
auf (+ *acc*) touch. **T∼en** *m* -s,- spot.
T∼er *m* -s,- spot; (*Med*) swab

Tür *f* -, -en door

Turban *m* -s, -e turban

Turbine *f* -, -n turbine

Türk|e *m* -n, -n Turk. **T∼ei** (die) -
Turkey. **T∼in** *f* -, -nen Turk

türkis *inv a* turquoise

türkisch *a* Turkish

Turm *m* -[e]s,¨e tower; (*Schach*) rook,
castle

Türm|chen *nt* -s,- turret. **t∼en** *vt*
pile [up]; sich t∼en pile up

Turmspitze *f* spire

turn|en *vi* (*haben*) do gymnastics.
T∼en *nt* -s gymnastics *sg*; (*Sch*)
physical education, 🚹 gym.
T∼er(in) *m* -s,- (*f* -, -nen) gymnast.
T∼halle *f* gymnasium

Turnier *nt* -s, -e tournament; (*Reit-*)
show

Turnschuhe *mpl* gym shoes;
trainers

Türschwelle *f* doorstep, threshold

Tusche *f* -, -n [drawing] ink

tuscheln *vt/i* (*haben*) whisper

Tüte *f* -, -n bag; (*Comm*) packet; (*Eis-*)
cornet; **in die T∼ blasen** 🚹 be
breathalysed

TÜV *m* - ≈ MOT [test]

Typ *m* -s, -en type; (🚹 *Kerl*) bloke.
T∼e *f* -, -n type

Typhus *m* - typhoid

typisch *a* typical (für of)

Typus *m* -, Typen type

Tyrann *m* -en, -en tyrant. **T∼ei** *f* -
tyranny. **t∼isch** *a* tyrannical.
t∼isieren *vt* tyrannize

Uu

U-Bahn *f* underground

übel *a* bad; (*hässlich*) nasty; **mir ist
ü∼** I feel sick; **jdm etw ü∼ nehmen**
hold sth against s.o. **Ü∼keit** *f* -
nausea

üben *vt/i* (*haben*) practise

über *prep* (+ *dat/acc*) over; (*höher
als*) above; (*betreffend*) about; <*Buch,
Vortrag*> on; <*Scheck, Rechnung*>
for; (*quer ü∼*) across; **ü∼ Köln
fahren** go via Cologne; **ü∼ Ostern**
over Easter; **die Woche ü∼** during
the week; **Fehler ü∼ Fehler** mistake
after mistake ● *adv* **ü∼ und ü∼** all
over; **jdm ü∼ sein** be better/(*stärker*)
stronger than s.o. ● *a* 🚹 **ü∼ sein** be
left over; **etw ü∼ sein** be fed up with
sth

überall *adv* everywhere

überanstrengen *vt insep* overtax;
strain <*Augen*>

überarbeiten *vt insep* revise; **sich
ü∼en** overwork

überbieten† *vt insep* outbid;
(*übertreffen*) surpass

Überblick *m* overall view; (*Abriss*)
summary

überblicken *vt insep* overlook;
(*abschätzen*) assess

überbringen† *vt insep* deliver

überbrücken *vt insep* (*fig*) bridge

überdies *adv* moreover

überdimensional *a* oversized

Überdosis *f* overdose

überdrüssig *a* **ü∼ sein/werden** be/
grow tired (*gen* of)

übereignen *vt insep* transfer

übereilt *a* over-hasty

übereinander *adv* one on top of/
above the other; <*sprechen*> about
each other

überein|kommen† *vi sep* (*sein*)
agree. **Ü∼kunft** *f* - agreement.

ü~stimmen *vi sep* (*haben*) agree; *<Zahlen:>* tally; *<Ansichten:>* coincide; *<Farben:>* match. **Ü~stimmung** *f* agreement

überfahren† *vt insep* run over

Überfahrt *f* crossing

Überfall *m* attack; (*Bank*-) raid

überfallen† *vt insep* attack; raid *<Bank>*; (*bestürmen*) bombard (**mit** with)

Überfluss *m* abundance; (*Wohlstand*) affluence

überflüssig *a* superfluous

überfordern *vt insep* overtax

überführ|en *vt insep* transfer; (*Jur*) convict (*gen* of). **Ü~ung** *f* transfer; (*Straße*) flyover; (*Fußgänger*-) footbridge

überfüllt *a* overcrowded

Übergabe *f* handing over; transfer

Übergang *m* crossing; (*Wechsel*) transition

übergeben† *vt insep* hand over; (*übereignen*) transfer; **sich ü~** be sick

übergehen† *vt insep* (*fig*) pass over; (*nicht beachten*) ignore; (*auslassen*) leave out

Übergewicht *nt* excess weight; (*fig*) predominance; **Ü~ haben** be overweight

über|greifen† *vi sep* (*haben*) spread (**auf** + *acc* to). **Ü~griff** *m* infringement

über|groß *a* outsize; (*übertrieben*) exaggerated. **Ü~größe** *f* outsize

überhand *adv* **ü~ nehmen** increase alarmingly

überhäufen *vt insep* inundate (**mit** with)

überhaupt *adv* (*im Allgemeinen*) altogether; (*eigentlich*) anyway; (*überdies*) besides; **ü~ nicht/nichts** not/nothing at all

überheblich *a* arrogant. **Ü~keit** *f* - arrogance

überhol|en *vt insep* overtake; (*reparieren*) overhaul. **ü~t** *a* outdated. **Ü~ung** *f* -, -en overhaul. **Ü~verbot** *nt* 'Ü~verbot' 'no overtaking'

überhören *vt insep* fail to hear; (*nicht beachten*) ignore

überirdisch *a* supernatural

überkochen *vi sep* (*sein*) boil over

überlassen† *vt insep* **jdm etw ü~** leave sth to s.o.; (*geben*) let s.o. have sth; **sich** (*dat*) **selbst ü~ sein** be left to one's own devices

Überlauf *m* overflow

überlaufen† *vi sep* (*sein*) overflow; (*Mil, Pol*) defect

Überläufer *m* defector

überleben *vt/i insep* (*haben*) survive. **Ü~de(r)** *m/f* survivor

überlegen¹ *vt sep* put over

überlegen² *v insep* ● *vt* [**sich** *dat*] **ü~** think over, consider; **es sich** (*dat*) **anders ü~** change one's mind ● *vi* (*haben*) think, reflect

überlegen³ *a* superior. **Ü~heit** *f* - superiority

Überlegung *f* -, -en reflection

überliefer|n *vt insep* hand down. **Ü~ung** *f* tradition

überlisten *vt insep* outwit

Übermacht *f* superiority

übermäßig *a* excessive

Übermensch *m* superman. **ü~lich** *a* superhuman

übermitteln *vt insep* convey; (*senden*) transmit

übermorgen *adv* the day after tomorrow

übermüdet *a* overtired

Über|mut *m* high spirits *pl*. **ü~mütig** *a* high-spirited

übernächst|e(r,s) *a* next ... but one; **ü~es Jahr** the year after next

übernächt|en *vi insep* (*haben*) stay overnight. **Ü~ung** *f* -, -en overnight stay; **Ü~ung und Frühstück** bed and breakfast

Übernahme *f* - taking over; (*Comm*) take-over

übernatürlich *a* supernatural

übernehmen† *vt insep* take over; (*annehmen*) take on; **sich ü~** overdo things; (*finanziell*) over-reach oneself

überqueren *vt insep* cross

überrasch|en *vt insep* surprise.
ü~end *a* surprising; (*unerwartet*)
unexpected. **Ü~ung** *f -*, **-en** surprise

überreden *vt insep* persuade

Überreste *mpl* remains

Überschall- *pref* supersonic

überschätzen *vt insep*
overestimate

Überschlag *m* rough estimate;
(*Sport*) somersault

überschlagen¹† *vt sep* cross
<*Beine*>

überschlagen²† *vt insep* estimate
roughly; (*auslassen*) skip; **sich ü~**
somersault; <*Ereignisse:*> happen
fast ● *a* tepid

überschneiden† (sich) *vr insep*
intersect, cross; (*zusammenfallen*)
overlap

überschreiten† *vt insep* cross;
(*fig*) exceed

Überschrift *f* heading; (*Zeitungs-*)
headline

Über|schuss *m* surplus.
ü~schüssig *a* surplus

überschwemm|en *vt insep* flood;
(*fig*) inundate. **Ü~ung** *f -*, **-en** flood

Übersee in/nach **Ü~** overseas;
aus/von **Ü~** from overseas.
Ü~dampfer *m* ocean liner.
ü~isch *a* overseas

übersehen† *vt insep* look out over;
(*abschätzen*) assess; (*nicht sehen*)
overlook, miss; (*ignorieren*) ignore

übersenden† *vt insep* send

übersetzen¹ *vi sep* (*haben/sein*)
cross [over]

übersetz|en² *vt insep* translate.
Ü~er(in) *m -s,-* (*f -*, **-nen**)
translator. **Ü~ung** *f -*, **-en**
translation

Übersicht *f* overall view; (*Abriss*)
summary; (*Tabelle*) table. **ü~lich** *a*
clear

Übersiedlung *f* move

überspielen *vt insep* (*fig*) cover up;
auf Band **ü~** tape

überstehen† *vt insep* come
through; get over <*Krankheit*>;
(*überleben*) survive

übersteigen† *vt insep* climb
[over]; (*fig*) exceed

überstimmen *vt insep* outvote

Überstunden *fpl* overtime *sg*; **Ü~**
machen work overtime

überstürz|en *vt insep* rush; **sich**
ü~en <*Ereignisse:*> happen fast.
ü~t *a* hasty

übertrag|bar *a* transferable; (*Med*)
infectious. **ü~en†** *vt insep* transfer;
(*übergeben*) assign (*dat* to); (*Techn,*
Med) transmit; (*Radio, TV*)
broadcast; (*übersetzen*) translate;
(*anwenden*) apply (auf + *acc* to) ● *a*
transferred, figurative. **Ü~ung** *f -*,
-en transfer; transmission;
broadcast; translation, application

übertreffen† *vt insep* surpass;
(*übersteigen*) exceed; **sich selbst ü~**
excel oneself

übertreib|en† *vt insep* exaggerate;
(*zu weit treiben*) overdo. **Ü~ung** *f -*,
-en exaggeration

übertreten¹† *vi sep* (*sein*) step over
the line; (*Pol*) go over/(*Relig*) convert
(zu to)

übertret|en²† *vt insep* infringe;
break <*Gesetz*>. **Ü~ung** *f -*, **-en**
infringement; breach

übertrieben *a* exaggerated

übervölkert *a* overpopulated

überwachen *vt insep* supervise;
(*kontrollieren*) monitor; (*bespitzeln*)
keep under surveillance

überwältigen *vt insep* overpower;
(*fig*) overwhelm

überweis|en† *vt insep* transfer;
refer <*Patienten*>. **Ü~ung** *f*
transfer; (*ärztliche*) referral

überwiegen† *v insep* ● *vi* (*haben*)
predominate. ● *vt* outweigh

überwind|en† *vt insep* overcome;
sich ü~en force oneself. **Ü~ung** *f*
effort

Über|zahl *f* majority. **ü~zählig** *a*
spare

überzeug|en *vt insep* convince;
sich [selbst] ü~en satisfy oneself.

ü~end *a* convincing. **Ü~ung** *f*,
-en conviction

überziehen¹† *vt sep* put on

überziehen²† *vt insep* cover;
overdraw <*Konto*>

Überzug *m* cover; (*Schicht*) coating

üblich *a* usual; (*gebräuchlich*)
customary

U-Boot *nt* submarine

übrig *a* remaining; (*andere*) other;
alles **Ü~e** [all] the rest; im **Ü~en**
besides; (*ansonsten*) apart from that;
ü~ **sein** *od* **bleiben** be left [over]; etw
ü~ **lassen** leave sth [over]; uns blieb
nichts anderes ü~ we had no choice

Übung *f* -, -en exercise; (*Üben*)
practice; **außer** *od* **aus der Ü~** out of
practice

Ufer *nt* -s,- shore; (*Fluss-*) bank

Uhr *f* -, -en clock; (*Armband-*) watch;
(*Zähler*) meter; um ein **U~** at one
o'clock; wie viel **U~** ist es? what's
the time? **U~macher** *m* -s,- watch
and clockmaker. **U~werk** *nt* clock/
watch mechanism. **U~zeiger** *m*
[clock-/watch-]hand. **U~zeit** *f* time

Uhu *m* -s, -s eagle owl

UKW *abbr* (*Ultrakurzwelle*) VHF

ulkig *a* funny; (*seltsam*) odd

Ulme *f* -, -n elm

Ultimatum *nt* -s, -ten ultimatum

Ultrakurzwelle *f* very high
frequency

Ultraschall *m* ultrasound

ultraviolett *a* ultraviolet

um *prep* (+ *acc*) [a]round; (*Uhrzeit*) at;
<*bitten*> for; <*streiten*> over; <*sich
sorgen*> about; <*betrügen*> out of;
(*bei Angabe einer Differenz*) by; um
[... herum] around, [round] about;
Tag um Tag day after day; um
seinetwillen for his sake ● *adv*
(*ungefähr*) around, about; um sein ▣
be over; <*Zeit*> be up ● *conj* um zu
to; (*Absicht*) [in order] to; zu müde,
um zu ... too tired to ...

umarm|en *vt insep* embrace, hug.
U~ung *f* -, -en embrace, hug

Umbau *m* rebuilding; conversion
(zu into). **u~en** *vt sep* rebuild;
convert (zu into)

Umbildung *f* reorganization; (*Pol*)
reshuffle

umbinden† *vt sep* put on

umblättern *v sep* ● *vt* turn [over]
● *vi* (*haben*) turn the page

umbringen† *vt sep* kill; sich u~
kill oneself

umbuchen *v sep* ● *vt* change;
(*Comm*) transfer ● *vi* (*haben*) change
one's booking

umdrehen *v sep* ● *vt* turn round/
(*wenden*) over; turn <*Schlüssel*>;
(*umkrempeln*) turn inside out; sich
u~ turn round; (*im Liegen*) turn
over ● *vi* (*haben/sein*) turn back

Umdrehung *f* turn; (*Motor-*)
revolution

umeinander *adv* around each
other; sich u~ sorgen worry about
each other

umfahren¹† *vt sep* run over

umfahren²† *vt insep* go round;
bypass <*Ort*>

umfallen† *vi sep* (*sein*) fall over;
<*Person:*> fall down

Umfang *m* girth; (*Geom*)
circumference; (*Größe*) size

umfangreich *a* extensive; (*dick*)
big

umfassen *vt insep* consist of,
comprise; (*umgeben*) surround. **u~d**
a comprehensive

Umfrage *f* survey, poll

umfüllen *vt sep* transfer

umfunktionieren *vt sep* convert

Umgang *m* [social] contact;
(*Umgehen*) dealing (mit with)

Umgangssprache *f* colloquial
language

umgeb|en† *vt/i insep* (*haben*)
surround ● *a* u~en von surrounded
by. **U~ung** *f* -, -en surroundings *pl*

umgehen† *vt insep* avoid; (*nicht
beachten*) evade; <*Straße:*> bypass

umgehend *a* immediate

Umgehungsstraße *f* bypass

umgekehrt *a* inverse;
<*Reihenfolge*> reverse; es war u~ it
was the other way round

umgraben† *vt sep* dig [over]

Umhang *m* cloak

umhauen† *vt sep* knock down; (*fällen*) chop down

umhören (sich) *vr sep* ask around

Umkehr *f* - turning back. **u~en** *v sep* ● *vi* (*sein*) turn back ● *vt* turn round; turn inside out <*Tasche*>; (*fig*) reverse

umkippen *v sep* ● *vt* tip over; (*versehentlich*) knock over ● *vi* (*sein*) fall over; <*Boot*> capsize

Umkleide|kabine *f* changing-cubicle. **u~n (sich)** *vr sep* change. **U~raum** *m* changing-room

umknicken *v sep* ● *vt* bend; (*falten*) fold ● *vi* (*sein*) bend; (*mit dem Fuß*) go over on one's ankle

umkommen† *vi sep* (*sein*) perish

Umkreis *m* surroundings *pl*; im U~ von within a radius of

umkreisen *vt insep* circle; (*Astr*) revolve around; <*Satellit*> orbit

umkrempeln *vt sep* turn up; (*von innen nach außen*) turn inside out; (*ändern*) change radically

Umlauf *m* circulation; (*Astr*) revolution. **U~bahn** *f* orbit

Umlaut *m* umlaut

umlegen *vt sep* lay *or* put down; flatten <*Getreide*>; turn down <*Kragen*>; put on <*Schal*>; throw <*Hebel*>; (*verlegen*) transfer; (🄳 *töten*) kill

umleit|en *vt sep* divert. **U~ung** *f* diversion

umliegend *a* surrounding

umpflanzen *vt sep* transplant

umranden *vt insep* edge

umräumen *vt sep* rearrange

umrechn|en *vt sep* convert. **U~ung** *f* conversion

umreißen† *vt insep* outline

Umriss *m* outline

umrühren *vt/i sep* (*haben*) stir

ums *pron* = um das

Umsatz *m* (*Comm*) turnover

umschalten *vt/i sep* (*haben*) switch over; auf Rot u~ <*Ampel:*> change to red

Umschau *f* U~ halten nach look out for

Umschlag *m* cover; (*Schutz-*) jacket; (*Brief-*) envelope; (*Med*) compress; (*Hosen-*) turn-up. **u~en†** *v sep* ● *vt* turn up; turn over <*Seite*>; (*fällen*) chop down ● *vi* (*sein*) topple over; <*Wetter:*> change; <*Wind:*> veer

umschließen† *vt insep* enclose

umschreiben *vt insep* define; (*anders ausdrücken*) paraphrase

umschulen *vt sep* retrain; (*Sch*) transfer to another school

Umschwung *m* (*fig*) change; (*Pol*) U-turn

umsehen† (sich) *vr sep* look round; (*zurück*) look back; sich u~ nach look for

umsein* *vi sep* (*sein*) um sein, *s.* um

umseitig *a & adv* overleaf

umsetzen *vt sep* move; (*umpflanzen*) transplant; (*Comm*) sell

umsied|eln *v sep* ● *vt* resettle ● *vi* (*sein*) move. **U~lung** *f* resettlement

umso *conj* ~ besser/mehr all the better/more; je mehr, ~ besser the more the better

umsonst *adv* in vain; (*grundlos*) without reason; (*gratis*) free

Umstand *m* circumstance; (*Tatsache*) fact; (*Aufwand*) fuss; (*Mühe*) trouble; unter U~en possibly; jdm U~e machen put s.o. to trouble; in andern U~en pregnant

umständlich *a* laborious; (*kompliziert*) involved

Umstands|kleid *nt* maternity dress. **U~wort** *nt* (*pl* -wörter) adverb

Umstehende *pl* bystanders

umsteigen† *vi sep* (*sein*) change

umstellen¹ *vt insep* surround

umstell|en² *vt sep* rearrange; transpose <*Wörter*>; (*anders einstellen*) reset; (*Techn*) convert; (*ändern*) change; sich u~en adjust. **U~ung** *f* rearrangement;

---

*old spelling

transposition; resetting; conversion; change; adjustment

umstritten *a* controversial; (*ungeklärt*) disputed

umstülpen *vt sep* turn upside down; (*von innen nach außen*) turn inside out

Um|sturz *m* coup. **u~stürzen** *v sep* ● *vt* overturn; (*Pol*) overthrow ● *vi* (*sein*) fall over

umtaufen *vt sep* rename

Umtausch *m* exchange. **u~en** *vt sep* change; exchange (**gegen** for)

umwechseln *vt sep* change

Umweg *m* detour; **auf U~en** (*fig*) in a roundabout way

Umwelt *f* environment. **u~freundlich** *a* environmentally friendly. **U~schutz** *m* protection of the environment

umwerfen† *vt sep* knock over; (*fig*) upset <*Plan*>

umziehen† *v sep* ● *vi* (*sein*) move ● *vt* change; **sich u~** change

umzingeln *vt insep* surround

Umzug *m* move; (*Prozession*) procession

unabänderlich *a* irrevocable; <*Tatsache*> unalterable

unabhängig *a* independent; **u~ davon, ob** irrespective of whether. **U~keit** *f* - independence

unablässig *a* incessant

unabsehbar *a* incalculable

unabsichtlich *a* unintentional

unachtsam *a* careless

unangebracht *a* inappropriate

unangenehm *a* unpleasant; (*peinlich*) embarrassing

Unannehmlichkeiten *fpl* trouble *sg*

unansehnlich *a* shabby

unanständig *a* indecent

unappetitlich *a* unappetizing

Unart *f* -, **-en** bad habit. **u~ig** *a* naughty

unauffällig *a* inconspicuous; unobtrusive

unaufgefordert *adv* without being asked

unauf|haltsam *a* inexorable. **u~hörlich** *a* incessant

unaufmerksam *a* inattentive

unaufrichtig *a* insincere

unausbleiblich *a* inevitable

unausstehlich *a* insufferable

unbarmherzig *a* merciless

unbeabsichtigt *a* unintentional

unbedenklich *a* harmless ● *adv* without hesitation

unbedeutend *a* insignificant; (*geringfügig*) slight

unbedingt *a* absolute; **nicht u~** not necessarily

unbefriedig|end *a* unsatisfactory. **u~t** *a* dissatisfied

unbefugt *a* unauthorized ● *adv* without authorization

unbegreiflich *a* incomprehensible

unbegrenzt *a* unlimited ● *adv* indefinitely

unbegründet *a* unfounded

Unbehagen *nt* unease; (*körperlich*) discomfort

unbekannt *a* unknown; (*nicht vertraut*) unfamiliar. **U~e(r)** *m/f* stranger

unbekümmert *a* unconcerned; (*unbeschwert*) carefree

unbeliebt *a* unpopular. **U~heit** *f* unpopularity

unbemannt *a* unmanned

unbemerkt *a & adv* unnoticed

unbenutzt *a* unused

unbequem *a* uncomfortable; (*lästig*) awkward

unberechenbar *a* unpredictable

unberechtigt *a* unjustified; (*unbefugt*) unauthorized

unberührt *a* untouched; (*fig*) virgin; <*Landschaft*> unspoilt

unbescheiden *a* presumptuous

unbeschrankt *a* unguarded

unbeschränkt *a* unlimited ● *adv* without limit

unbeschwert *a* carefree

unbesiegt *a* undefeated

unbespielt *a* blank

unbeständig *a* inconsistent; <*Wetter*> unsettled

unbestechlich *a* incorruptible

unbestimmt *a* indefinite: *<Alter>* indeterminate; (*ungewiss*) uncertain; (*unklar*) vague

unbestritten *a* undisputed ● *adv* indisputably

unbeteiligt *a* indifferent; **u~ an** (+ *dat*) not involved in

unbetont *a* unstressed

unbewacht *a* unguarded

unbewaffnet *a* unarmed

unbeweglich *a & adv* motionless, still

unbewohnt *a* uninhabited

unbewusst *a* unconscious

unbezahlbar *a* priceless

unbrauchbar *a* useless

und *conj* and; **und so weiter** and so on; **nach und nach** bit by bit

Undank *m* ingratitude. **u~bar** *a* ungrateful; (*nicht lohnend*) thankless. **U~barkeit** *f* ingratitude

undeutlich *a* indistinct; vague

undicht *a* leaking; **u~e Stelle** leak

Unding *nt* absurdity

undiplomatisch *a* undiplomatic

unduldsam *a* intolerant

undurch|dringlich *a* impenetrable; *<Miene>* inscrutable. **u~führbar** *a* impracticable

undurch|lässig *a* impermeable. **u~sichtig** *a* opaque; (*fig*) doubtful

uneben *a* uneven. **U~heit** *f* -, **-en** unevenness; (*Buckel*) bump

unecht *a* false; **u~er Schmuck** imitation jewellery

unehelich *a* illegitimate

uneinig *a* (*fig*) divided; [**sich** (*dat*)] **u~ sein** disagree

uneins *a* **u~ sein** be at odds

unempfindlich *a* insensitive (**gegen** to); (*widerstandsfähig*) tough; (*Med*) immune

unendlich *a* infinite; (*endlos*) endless. **U~keit** *f* - infinity

unentbehrlich *a* indispensable

unentgeltlich *a* free, *<Arbeit>* unpaid ● *adv* free of charge

unentschieden *a* undecided; (*Sport*) drawn; **u~ spielen** draw. **U~ nt -s,-** draw

unentschlossen *a* indecisive; (*unentschieden*) undecided

unentwegt *a* persistent; (*unaufhörlich*) incessant

unerfahren *a* inexperienced. **U~heit** *f* - inexperience

unerfreulich *a* unpleasant

unerhört *a* enormous; (*empörend*) outrageous

unerklärlich *a* inexplicable

unerlässlich *a* essential

unerlaubt *a* unauthorized ● *adv* without permission

unerschwinglich *a* prohibitive

unersetzlich *a* irreplaceable; *<Verlust>* irreparable

unerträglich *a* unbearable

unerwartet *a* unexpected

unerwünscht *a* unwanted; *<Besuch>* unwelcome

unfähig *a* incompetent; **u~, etw zu tun** incapable of doing sth; (*nicht in der Lage*) unable to do sth. **U~keit** *f* incompetence; inability (**zu** to)

unfair *a* unfair

Unfall *m* accident. **U~flucht** *f* failure to stop after an accident. **U~station** *f* casualty department

unfassbar *a* incomprehensible

Unfehlbarkeit *f* - infallibility

unfolgsam *a* disobedient

unförmig *a* shapeless

unfreiwillig *a* involuntary; (*unbeabsichtigt*) unintentional

unfreundlich *a* unfriendly; (*unangenehm*) unpleasant. **U~keit** *f* unfriendliness; unpleasantness

Unfriede[n] *m* discord

unfruchtbar *a* infertile; (*fig*) unproductive. **U~keit** *f* infertility

Unfug *m* **-s** mischief; (*Unsinn*) nonsense

Ungar|(in) *m* **-n, -n** (*f* -, **-nen**) Hungarian. **u~isch** *a* Hungarian. **U~n** *nt* **-s** Hungary

ungeachtet *prep* (+ *gen*) in spite of; **dessen u~** notwithstanding [this].

ungebraucht a unused

ungedeckt a uncovered; (*Sport*) unmarked; <*Tisch*> unlaid

Ungeduld f impatience. **u~ig** a impatient

ungeeignet a unsuitable

ungefähr a approximate, rough

ungefährlich a harmless

ungeheuer a enormous. **U~** nt -s,- monster

ungehorsam a disobedient. **U~** m disobedience

ungeklärt a unsolved; <*Frage*> unsettled; <*Ursache*> unknown

ungelegen a inconvenient

ungelernt a unskilled

ungemütlich a uncomfortable; (*unangenehm*) unpleasant

ungenau a inaccurate; vague. **U~igkeit** f -, -en inaccuracy

ungeniert /'ʊnʒeniːɐ̯t/ a uninhibited ● adv openly

ungenießbar a inedible; <*Getränk*> undrinkable

ungenügend a inadequate; (*Sch*) unsatisfactory

ungepflegt a neglected; <*Person*> unkempt

ungerade a <*Zahl*> odd

ungerecht a unjust. **U~igkeit** f -, -en injustice

ungern adv reluctantly

ungesalzen a unsalted

Ungeschick|lichkeit f clumsiness. **u~t** a clumsy

ungeschminkt a without make-up; <*Wahrheit*> unvarnished

ungesetzlich a illegal

ungestört a undisturbed.

ungesund a unhealthy

ungesüßt a unsweetened

ungetrübt a perfect

Ungetüm nt -s, -e monster

ungewiss a uncertain; im Ungewissen sein/lassen be/leave in the dark. **U~heit** f uncertainty

ungewöhnlich a unusual

ungewohnt a unaccustomed; (*nicht vertraut*) unfamiliar

Ungeziefer nt -s vermin

ungezogen a naughty

ungezwungen a informal; (*natürlich*) natural

ungläubig a incredulous

unglaublich a incredible, unbelievable

ungleich a unequal; (*verschieden*) different. **U~heit** f - inequality. **u~mäßig** a uneven

Unglück nt -s, -e misfortune; (*Pech*) bad luck; (*Missgeschick*) mishap; (*Unfall*) accident. **u~lich** a unhappy; (*ungünstig*) unfortunate. **u~licherweise** adv unfortunately

ungültig a invalid; (*Jur*) void

ungünstig a unfavourable; (*unpassend*) inconvenient

Unheil nt -s disaster; **U~ anrichten** cause havoc

unheilbar a incurable

unheimlich a eerie; (*gruselig*) creepy; (🔢 *groß*) terrific ● adv eerily; (🔢 *sehr*) terribly

unhöflich a rude. **U~keit** f rudeness

unhygienisch a unhygienic

Uni f -, -s 🔢 university

uni /y'niː/ inv a plain

Uniform f -, -en uniform

uninteressant a uninteresting

Union f -, -en union

universell a universal

Universität f -, -en university

Universum nt -s universe

unkenntlich a unrecognizable

unklar a unclear; (*ungewiss*) uncertain; (*vage*) vague; im U~en sein be in the dark

unkompliziert a uncomplicated

Unkosten pl expenses

Unkraut nt weed; (*coll*) weeds pl; U~ jäten weed. **U~vertilgungsmittel** nt weed-killer

unlängst adv recently

unlauter a dishonest; (*unfair*) unfair

unleserlich a illegible

unleugbar a undeniable

unlogisch a illogical

Unmenge *f* enormous amount/ (*Anzahl*) number

Unmensch *m* ⊞ brute. **u~lich** *a* inhuman

unmerklich *a* imperceptible

unmittelbar *a* immediate; (*direkt*) direct

unmöbliert *a* unfurnished

unmodern *a* old-fashioned

unmöglich *a* impossible. **U~keit** *f* - impossibility

Unmoral *f* immorality. **u~isch** *a* immoral

unmündig *a* under-age

Unmut *m* displeasure

unnatürlich *a* unnatural

unnormal *a* abnormal

unnötig *a* unnecessary

unord|entlich *a* untidy; (*nachlässig*) sloppy. **U~nung** *f* disorder; (*Durcheinander*) muddle

unorthodox *a* unorthodox ● *adv* in an unorthodox manner

unparteiisch *a* impartial

unpassend *a* inappropriate; <*Moment*> inopportune

unpersönlich *a* impersonal

unpraktisch *a* impractical

unpünktlich *a* unpunctual ● *adv* late

unrealistisch *a* unrealistic

unrecht *a* wrong ● *n* jdm u~ tun do s.o. an injustice. **U~** *nt* wrong; zu U~ wrongly; U~ haben be wrong; jdm U~ geben disagree with s.o. **u~mäßig** *a* unlawful

unregelmäßig *a* irregular

unreif *a* unripe; (*fig*) immature

unrein *a* impure; <*Luft*> polluted; <*Haut*> bad; ins U~e schreiben make a rough draft of

unrentabel *a* unprofitable

Unruh|e *f* -, -n restlessness; (*Erregung*) agitation; (*Besorgnis*) anxiety; U~en (*Pol*) unrest *sg*. **u~ig** *a* restless; (*laut*) noisy; (*besorgt*) anxious

uns *pron* (*acc/dat of* **wir**) us; (*refl*) ourselves; (*einander*) each other

unsauber *a* dirty; (*nachlässig*) sloppy

unschädlich *a* harmless

unscharf *a* blurred

unschätzbar *a* inestimable

unscheinbar *a* inconspicuous

unschlagbar *a* unbeatable

unschlüssig *a* undecided

Unschuld *f* - innocence; (*Jungfräulichkeit*) virginity. **u~ig** *a* innocent

unselbstständig, unselbständig *a* dependent ● *adv* u~ denken not think for oneself

unser *poss pron* our. **u~e(r,s)** *poss pron* ours. **u~erseits** *adv* for our part. **u~twegen** *adv* for our sake; (*wegen uns*) because of us, on our account

unsicher *a* unsafe; (*ungewiss*) uncertain; (*nicht zuverlässig*) unreliable; <*Schritte, Hand*> unsteady; <*Person*> insecure ● *adv* unsteadily. **U~heit** *f* uncertainty; unreliability; insecurity

unsichtbar *a* invisible

Unsinn *m* nonsense. **u~ig** *a* nonsensical, absurd

Unsitt|e *f* bad habit. **u~lich** *a* indecent

unsportlich *a* not sporty; (*unfair*) unsporting

uns|re(r,s) *poss pron* = unsere(r,s). **u~rige** *poss pron* der/die/das u~rige ours

unsterblich *a* immortal. **U~keit** *f* immortality

Unsumme *f* vast sum

unsympathisch *a* unpleasant; er ist mir u~ I don't like him

untätig *a* idle

untauglich *a* unsuitable; (*Mil*) unfit

unten *adv* at the bottom; (*auf der Unterseite*) underneath; (*eine Treppe tiefer*) downstairs; (*im Text*) below; hier/da u~ down here/there; nach u~ down[wards]; (*die Treppe hinunter*) downstairs; siehe u~ see below

---

*old spelling

unter *prep* (+ *dat/acc*) under; (*niedriger als*) below; (*inmitten, zwischen*) among; **u~ anderem** among other things; **u~ der Woche** during the week; **u~ sich** by themselves

Unter|arm *m* forearm. **U~bewusstsein** *nt* subconscious

unterbieten† *vt insep* undercut; beat <*Rekord*>

unterbinden† *vt insep* stop

unterbrech|en† *vt insep* interrupt; break <*Reise*>. **U~ung** *f -*, **-en** interruption, break

unterbringen† *vt sep* put; (*beherbergen*) put up

unterdessen *adv* in the meantime

Unterdrückung *f -* suppression; oppression

untere(r,s) *a* lower

untereinander *adv* one below the other; (*miteinander*) among ourselves/yourselves/themselves

unterernähr|t *a* undernourished. **U~ung** *f* malnutrition

Unterführung *f* underpass; (*Fußgänger-*) subway

Untergang *m* (*Astr*) setting; (*Naut*) sinking; (*Zugrundegehen*) disappearance; (*der Welt*) end

Untergebene(r) *m/f* subordinate

untergehen† *vi sep* (*sein*) (*Astr*) set; (*versinken*) go under; <*Schiff:*> go down, sink; (*zugrunde gehen*) disappear; <*Welt:*> come to an end

Untergeschoss *nt* basement

Untergrund *m* foundation; (*Hintergrund*) background. **U~bahn** *f* underground [railway]

unterhaken *vt sep* **jdn u~** take s.o.'s arm; **untergehakt** arm in arm

unterhalb *adv & prep* (+ *gen*) below

Unterhalt *m* maintenance

unterhalt|en† *vt insep* maintain; (*ernähren*) support; (*betreiben*) run; (*erheitern*) entertain; **sich u~en** talk; (*sich vergnügen*) enjoy oneself. **U~ung** *f -*, **-en** maintenance; (*Gespräch*) conversation; (*Zeitvertreib*) entertainment

Unter|haus *nt* (*Pol*) lower house; (*in UK*) House of Commons. **U~hemd** *nt* vest. **U~hose** *f* underpants *pl*. **u~irdisch** *a & adv* underground

Unterkiefer *m* lower jaw

unterkommen† *vi sep* (*sein*) find accommodation; (*eine Stellung finden*) get a job

Unterkunft *f -*, **-künfte** accommodation

Unterlage *f* pad; **U~n** papers

Unterlass *m* **ohne U~** incessantly

Unterlassung *f -*, **-en** omission

unterlegen *a* inferior; (*Sport*) losing; **zahlenmäßig u~** outnumbered (*dat* by). **U~e(r)** *m/f* loser

Unterleib *m* abdomen

unterliegen† *vi insep* (*sein*) lose (*dat* to); (*unterworfen sein*) be subject (*dat* to)

Unterlippe *f* lower lip

Untermiete *f* **zur U~ wohnen** be a lodger. **U~r(in)** *m(f)* lodger

unternehm|en† *vt insep* undertake; take <*Schritte*>; **etw/nichts u~en** do sth/nothing. **U~en** *nt* **-s,-** undertaking, enterprise; (*Betrieb*) concern. **U~er** *m* **-s,-** employer; (*Bau-*) contractor; (*Industrieller*) industrialist. **u~ungslustig** *a* enterprising

Unteroffizier *m* non-commissioned officer

unterordnen *vt sep* subordinate

Unterredung *f -*, **-en** talk

Unterricht *m* **-[e]s** teaching; (*Privat-*) tuition; (*U~sstunden*) lessons *pl*

unterrichten *vt/i insep* (*haben*) teach; (*informieren*) inform; **sich u~** inform oneself

Unterrock *m* slip

untersagen *vt insep* forbid

Untersatz *m* mat; (*mit Füßen*) stand; (*Gläser-*) coaster

unterscheid|en† *vt/i insep* (*haben*) distinguish; (*auseinander halten*) tell apart; **sich u~en** differ. **U~ung** *f -*, **-en** distinction

Unterschied *m* -[e]s, -e difference;
(*Unterscheidung*) distinction; **im U~**
zu ihm unlike him. **u~lich** *a*
different; (*wechselnd*) varying

unterschlag|en† *vt insep*
embezzle; (*verheimlichen*) suppress.
U~ung *f* -, -en embezzlement;
suppression

Unterschlupf *m* -[e]s shelter;
(*Versteck*) hiding-place

unterschreiben† *vt/i insep*
(*haben*) sign

Unter|schrift *f* signature; (*Bild-*)
caption. **U~seeboot** *nt* submarine

Unterstand *m* shelter

unterste(r,s) *a* lowest, bottom

unterstehen† *v insep* ● *vi* (*haben*)
be answerable (*dat* to); (*unterliegen*)
be subject (*dat* to)

unterstellen¹ *vt sep* put
underneath; (*abstellen*) store; **sich**
u~ shelter

unterstellen² *vt insep* place under
the control (*dat* of); (*annehmen*)
assume; (*fälschlich zuschreiben*)
impute (*dat* to)

unterstreichen† *vt insep*
underline

unterstütz|en *vt insep* support;
(*helfen*) aid. **U~ung** *f* -, -en support;
(*finanziell*) aid; (*regelmäßiger Betrag*)
allowance; (*Arbeitslosen-*) benefit

untersuch|en *vt insep* examine;
(*Jur*) investigate; (*prüfen*) test;
(*überprüfen*) check; (*durchsuchen*)
search. **U~ung** *f* -, -en examination;
investigation; test; check; search.
U~ungshaft *f* detention on
remand

Untertan *m* -s & -en, -en subject

Untertasse *f* saucer

Unterteil *nt* bottom (part)

Untertitel *m* subtitle

untervermieten *vt/i insep* (*haben*)
sublet

Unterwäsche *f* underwear

unterwegs *adv* on the way; (*außer*
Haus) out; (*verreist*) away

Unterwelt *f* underworld

unterzeichnen *vt insep* sign

unterziehen† *vt insep* **etw einer**
Untersuchung/Überprüfung u~
examine/ check sth; **sich einer**
Operation/Prüfung u~ have an
operation/take a test

Untier *nt* monster

untragbar *a* intolerable

untrennbar *a* inseparable

untreu *a* disloyal; (*in der Ehe*)
unfaithful. **U~e** *f* disloyalty;
infidelity

untröstlich *a* inconsolable

unübersehbar *a* obvious; (*groß*)
immense

ununterbrochen *a* incessant

unveränderlich *a* invariable;
(*gleichbleibend*) unchanging

unverändert *a* unchanged

unverantwortlich *a*
irresponsible

unverbesserlich *a* incorrigible

unverbindlich *a* non-committal;
(*Comm*) not binding ● *adv* without
obligation

unverdaulich *a* indigestible

unver|gesslich *a* unforgettable.
u~gleichlich *a* incomparable.
u~heiratet *a* unmarried.
u~käuflich *a* not for sale;
<*Muster*> free

unverkennbar *a* unmistakable

unverletzt *a* unhurt

unvermeidlich *a* inevitable

unver|mindert *a* & *adv*
undiminished. **u~mutet** *a*
unexpected

Unver|nunft *f* folly. **u~nünftig** *a*
foolish

unverschämt *a* insolent; (☐
ungeheuer) outrageous. **U~heit** *f* -,
-en insolence

unver|sehens *adv* suddenly.
u~sehrt *a* unhurt; (*unbeschädigt*)
intact

unverständlich *a*
incomprehensible; (*undeutlich*)
indistinct

unverträglich *a* incompatible;
<*Person*> quarrelsome;
(*unbekömmlich*) indigestible

---

*alte Schreibung

unver|wundbar *a* invulnerable.
u~wüstlich *a* indestructible;
<*Person, Humor*> irrepressible;
<*Gesundheit*> robust. **u~zeihlich** *a*
unforgivable

unverzüglich *a* immediate

unvollendet *a* unfinished

unvollkommen *a* imperfect;
(*unvollständig*) incomplete

unvollständig *a* incomplete

unvor|bereitet *a* unprepared.
u~hergesehen *a* unforeseen

unvorsichtig *a* careless

unvorstellbar *a* unimaginable

unvorteilhaft *a* unfavourable;
(*nicht hübsch*) unattractive

unwahr *a* untrue. **U~heit** *f* -, -en
untruth. **u~scheinlich** *a* unlikely;
(*unglaublich*) improbable; (⊞ *groß*)
incredible

unweit *adv & prep* (+ *gen*) not far

unwesentlich *a* unimportant

Unwetter *nt* -s,- storm

unwichtig *a* unimportant

unwider|legbar *a* irrefutable.
u~stehlich *a* irresistible

Unwill|e *m* displeasure. **u~ig** *a*
angry; (*widerwillig*) reluctant

unwirklich *a* unreal

unwirksam *a* ineffective

unwirtschaftlich *a* uneconomic

unwissen|d *a* ignorant. **U~heit** *f* -
ignorance

unwohl *a* unwell; (*unbehaglich*)
uneasy

unwürdig *a* unworthy (*gen* of)

Unzahl *f* vast number. **unzählig** *a*
innumerable, countless

unzerbrechlich *a* unbreakable

unzerstörbar *a* indestructible

unzertrennlich *a* inseparable

Unzucht *f* sexual offence;
gewerbsmäßige **U~** prostitution

unzüchtig *a* indecent; <*Schriften*>
obscene

unzufrieden *a* dissatisfied;
(*innerlich*) discontented. **U~heit** *f*
dissatisfaction

unzulässig *a* inadmissible

unzurechnungsfähig *a* insane.
U~keit *f* insanity

unzusammenhängend *a*
incoherent

unzutreffend *a* inapplicable;
(*falsch*) incorrect

unzuverlässig *a* unreliable

unzweifelhaft *a* undoubted

üppig *a* luxuriant; (*überreichlich*)
lavish

uralt *a* ancient

Uran *nt* -s uranium

Uraufführung *f* first performance

Urenkel *m* great-grandson; (*pl*)
great-grandchildren

Urgroß|mutter *f* great-
grandmother. **U~vater** *m* great-
grandfather

Urheber *m* -s,- originator;
(*Verfasser*) author. **U~recht** *nt*
copyright

Urin *m* -s, -e urine

Urkunde *f* -, -n certificate;
(*Dokument*) document

Urlaub *m* -s holiday; (*Mil, Admin*)
leave; auf **U~** on holiday/leave; **U~**
haben be on holiday/leave.
U~er(in) *m* -s,- (*f* -, -nen) holiday-
maker. **U~sort** *m* holiday resort

Urne *f* -, -n urn; (*Wahl-*) ballot-box

Ursache *f* cause; (*Grund*) reason;
keine **U~**! don't mention it!

Ursprung *m* origin

ursprünglich *a* original;
(*anfänglich*) initial; (*natürlich*)
natural

Urteil *nt* -s, -e judgement; (*Meinung*)
opinion; (*U~sspruch*) verdict;
(*Strafe*) sentence. **u~en** *vi* (*haben*)
judge

Urwald *m* primeval forest;
(*tropischer*) jungle

Urzeit *f* primeval times *pl*

USA *pl* USA *sg*

usw. *abbr* (**und so weiter**) etc.

utopisch *a* Utopian

Vakuum /'va:kuʊm/ *nt* -s vacuum.
v~**verpackt** *a* vacuum-packed

Vanille /va'nɪljə/ *f* - vanilla

variieren *vt/i* (*haben*) vary

Vase /'va:zə/ *f* -, -n vase

Vater *m* -s,* father. V~**land** *nt*
fatherland

väterlich *a* paternal; (*fürsorglich*)
fatherly. v~**erseits** *adv* on one's/
the father's side

Vater|schaft *f* - fatherhood; (*Jur*)
paternity. V~**unser** *nt* -s,- Lord's
Prayer

v. Chr. *abbr* (**vor Christus**) BC

Vegetar|ier(in) /vege'ta:riɐ,
-iərɪn/ *m(f)* -s,- (- , -nen) vegetarian.
v~**isch** *a* vegetarian

Veilchen *nt* -s, -n violet

Vene /'ve:nə/ *f* -, -n vein

Venedig /ve'ne:dɪç/ *nt* -s Venice

Ventil /vɛn'ti:l/ *nt* -s, -e valve.
V~**ator** *m* -s, -en /-'to:rən/ fan

verabred|en *vt* arrange; sich [mit
jdm] v~**en** arrange to meet [s.o.].
V~**ung** *f* -, -en arrangement;
(*Treffen*) appointment

verabschieden *vt* say goodbye to;
(*aus dem Dienst*) retire; pass
<*Gesetz*>; sich v~ say goodbye

verachten *vt* despise

Verachtung *f* - contempt

verallgemeinern *vt/i* (*haben*)
generalize

veränder|lich *a* changeable;
(*Math*) variable. v~**n** *vt* change;
sich v~n change; (*beruflich*) change
one's job. V~**ung** *f* change

verängstigt *a* frightened, scared

verankern *vt* anchor

veranlag|t *a* künstlerisch/
musikalisch v~t sein have an
artistic/a musical bent; **praktisch**
v~t practically minded. V~**ung** *f* -,
-en disposition; (*Neigung*) tendency;
(*künstlerisch*) bent

veranlassen *vt* (*reg*) arrange for;
(*einleiten*) institute; jdn v~ prompt
s.o. (**zu** to)

veranschlagen *vt* (*reg*) estimate

veranstalt|en *vt* organize; hold,
give <*Party*>; make <*Lärm*>. V~**er**
m -s,- organizer. V~**ung** *f* -, -en
event

verantwort|lich *a* responsible;
v~lich machen hold responsible.
V~**ung** *f* - responsibility.
v~**ungsbewusst** *a* responsible.
v~**ungslos** *a* irresponsible.
v~**ungsvoll** *a* responsible

verarbeiten *vt* use; (*Techn*)
process; (*verdauen & fig*) digest

verärgern *vt* annoy

verausgaben (sich) *vr* spend all
one's money

veräußern *vt* sell

Verb /vɛrp/ *nt* -s, -en verb

Verband *m* -[e]s,* association;
(*Mil*) unit; (*Med*) bandage; (*Wund-*)
dressing. V~**szeug** *nt* first-aid kit

verbann|en *vt* exile; (*fig*) banish.
V~**ung** *f* - exile

verbergen† *vt* hide; sich v~ hide

verbesser|n *vt* improve;
(*berichtigen*) correct. V~**ung** *f* -, -en
improvement; correction

verbeug|en (sich) *vr* bow.
V~**ung** *f* bow

verbeulen *vt* dent

verbiegen† *vt* bend

verbieten† *vt* forbid; (*Admin*)
prohibit, ban

verbillig|en *vt* reduce [in price].
v~t *a* reduced

verbinden† *vt* connect (**mit** to);
(*zusammenfügen*) join; (*verknüpfen*)
combine; (*in Verbindung bringen*)
associate; (*Med*) bandage; dress
<*Wunde*>; jdm verbunden sein (*fig*)
be obliged to s.o.

verbindlich *a* friendly; (*bindend*)
binding

---

*old spelling

Verbindung f connection;
(*Verknüpfung*) combination;
(*Kontakt*) contact; (*Vereinigung*)
association; **chemiche V~** chemical
compound; **in V~ stehen/sich in V~
setzen** be/get in touch

verbissen a grim

verbitter|n vt make bitter. **v~t** a
bitter. **V~ung** f - bitterness

verblassen vi (sein) fade

Verbleib m -s whereabouts pl

verbleit a <*Benzin*> leaded

verblüff|en vt amaze, astound.
V~ung f - amazement

verblühen vi (sein) wither, fade

verbluten vi (sein) bleed to death

verborgen vt lend

Verbot nt -[e]s, -e ban. **v~en** a
forbidden; (*Admin*) prohibited

Verbrauch m -[e]s consumption.
v~en vt use; consume
<*Lebensmittel*>; (*erschöpfen*) use up.
V~er m -s,- consumer

Verbrechen nt -s,- crime

Verbrecher m -s,- criminal

verbreit|en vt spread. **v~et** a
widespread. **V~ung** f - spread;
(*Verbreiten*) spreading

verbrenn|en† vt/i (sein) burn;
cremate <*Leiche*>. **V~ung** f -, -en
burning; cremation; (*Wunde*) burn

verbringen† vt spend

verbrühen vt scald

verbuchen vt enter

verbünd|en (sich) vr form an
alliance. **V~ete(r)** m/f ally

verbürgen vt guarantee; **sich v~
für** vouch for

Verdacht m -[e]s suspicion; **in** or **im
V~ haben** suspect

verdächtig a suspicious. **v~en** vt
suspect (gen of). **V~te(r)** m/f
suspect

verdamm|en vt condemn; (*Relig*)
damn. **v~t** a & adv ☒ damned; **v~t!**
damn!

verdampfen vt/i (sein) evaporate

verdanken vt owe (dat to)

verdau|en vt digest. **v~lich** a
digestible. **V~ung** f - digestion

Verdeck nt -[e]s, -e hood;
(*Oberdeck*) top deck

verderb|en† vi (sein) spoil;
<*Lebensmittel:*> go bad ● vt spoil; **ich
habe mir den Magen verdorben** I
have an upset stomach. **V~en** nt -s
ruin. **v~lich** a perishable;
(*schädlich*) pernicious

verdien|en vt/i (haben) earn; (fig)
deserve. **V~er** m -s,- wage-earner

Verdienst¹ m -[e]s earnings pl

Verdienst² nt -[e]s, -e merit

verdient a well-deserved

verdoppeln vt double

verdorben a spoilt, ruined;
<*Magen*> upset; (*moralisch*) corrupt;
(*verkommen*) depraved

verdreh|en vt twist; roll <*Augen*>;
(fig) distort. **v~t** a ☒ crazy

verdreifachen vt treble, triple

verdrücken vt crumple; (☒ essen)
polish off; **sich v~** ☒ slip away

Verdruss m -es annoyance

verdünnen vt dilute; **sich v~** taper
off

verdunst|en vi (sein) evaporate.
V~ung f - evaporation

verdursten vi (sein) die of thirst

veredeln vt refine; (*Hort*) graft

verehr|en vt revere; (*Relig*)
worship; (*bewundern*) admire;
(*schenken*) give. **V~er(in)** m -s,- (f -,
-nen) admirer. **V~ung** f -
veneration; worship; admiration

vereidigen vt swear in

Verein m -s, -e society; (*Sport-*) club

vereinbar a compatible. **v~en** vt
arrange. **V~ung** f -, -en agreement

vereinfachen vt simplify

vereinheitlichen vt standardize

vereinig|en vt unite; merge
<*Firmen*>; **wieder v~en** reunite;
reunify <*Land*>; **sich v~en** unite;
V~te Staaten [von Amerika] United
States sg [of America]. **V~ung** f -,
-en union; (*Organisation*)
organization

vereinzelt a isolated ● adv
occasionally

vereist a frozen; <*Straße*> icy

vereitert a septic

verenden vi (sein) die

verengen vt restrict; sich v~ narrow; <Pupille:> contract

vererb|en vt leave (dat to); (Biol & fig) pass on (dat to). **V~ung** f - heredity

verfahren† vi (sein) proceed; v~ mit deal with ● vr sich v~ lose one's way ● a muddled. **V~** nt -s,- procedure; (Techn) process; (Jur) proceedings pl

Verfall m decay; (eines Gebäudes) dilapidation; (körperlich & fig) decline; (Ablauf) expiry. **v~en**† vi (sein) decay; <Person, Sitten:> decline; (ablaufen) expire; v~en in (+ acc) lapse into; v~en auf (+ acc) hit on <Idee>

verfärben (sich) vr change colour; <Stoff:> discolour

verfass|en vt write; (Jur) draw up; (entwerfen) draft. **V~er** m -s,- author. **V~ung** f (Pol) constitution; (Zustand) state

verfaulen vi (sein) rot, decay

verfechten† vt advocate

verfehlen vt miss

verfeinde|n (sich) vr become enemies; v~t sein be enemies

verfeinern vt refine; (verbessern) improve

verfilmen vt film

verfluch|en vt curse. **v~t** a & adv 🕮 damned; v~t! damn!

verfolg|en vt pursue; (folgen) follow; (bedrängen) pester; (Pol) persecute; strafrechtlich v~en prosecute. **V~er** m -s,- pursuer. **V~ung** f - pursuit; persecution

verfrüht a premature

verfügbar a available

verfüg|en vt order; (Jur) decree ● vi (haben) v~en über (+ acc) have at one's disposal. **V~ung** f-, -en order; (Jur) decree; jdm zur V~ung stehen be at s.o.'s disposal

verführ|en vt seduce; tempt. **V~ung** f seduction; temptation

vergangen a past; (letzte) last. **V~heit** f - past; (Gram) past tense

vergänglich a transitory

vergas|en vt gas. **V~er** m -s,- carburettor

vergeb|en† vt award (an + dat to); (weggeben) give away; (verzeihen) forgive. **v~lich** a futile, vain ● adv in vain. **V~ung** f - forgiveness

vergehen† vi (sein) pass; sich v~ violate (gegen etw sth). **V~** nt -s,- offence

vergelt|en† vt repay. **V~ung** f - retaliation; (Rache) revenge

vergessen† vt forget; (liegen lassen) leave behind

vergesslich a forgetful. **V~keit** f - forgetfulness

vergeuden vt waste, squander

vergewaltig|en vt rape. **V~ung** f -, -en rape

vergießen† vt spill; shed <Tränen, Blut>

vergift|en vt poison. **V~ung** f -, -en poisoning

Vergissmeinnicht nt -[e]s, -[e] forget-me-not

vergittert a barred

verglasen vt glaze

Vergleich m -[e]s, -e comparison; (Jur) settlement. **v~bar** a comparable. **v~en**† vt compare (mit with/to)

vergnüg|en (sich) vr enjoy oneself. **V~en** nt -s,- pleasure; (Spaß) fun; viel V~en! have a good time! v~t a cheerful; (zufrieden) happy. **V~ungen** fpl entertainments

vergolden vt gild; (plattieren) gold-plate

vergraben† vt bury

vergriffen a out of print

vergrößer|n vt enlarge; <Linse:> magnify; (vermehren) increase; (erweitern) extend; expand <Geschäft>; sich v~n grow bigger; <Firma:> expand; (zunehmen) increase. **V~ung** f-, -en magnification; increase; expansion;

(*Phot*) enlargement. **V~ungsglas** *nt* magnifying glass

vergüt|en *vt* pay for; **jdm etw v~en** reimburse s.o. for sth. **V~ung** *f* -, **-en** remuneration; (*Erstattung*) reimbursement

verhaft|en *vt* arrest. **V~ung** *f* -, **-en** arrest

verhalten† (**sich**) *vr* behave; (*handeln*) act; (*beschaffen sein*) be. **V~** *nt* **-s** behaviour, conduct

Verhältnis *nt* **-ses, -se** relationship; (*Liebes-*) affair; (*Math*) ratio; **V~se** circumstances; conditions. **v~mäßig** *adv* comparatively, relatively

verhand|eln *vt* discuss; (*Jur*) try ● *vi* (*haben*) negotiate. **V~lung** *f* (*Jur*) trial; **V~lungen** negotiations

Verhängnis *nt* **-ses** fate, doom

verhärten *vt/i* (*sein*) harden

verhasst *a* hated

verhätscheln *vt* spoil

verhauen† *vt* 🄳 beat; make a mess of <*Prüfung*>

verheilen *vi* (*sein*) heal

verheimlichen *vt* keep secret

verheirat|en (**sich**) *vr* get married (mit to); **sich wieder v~en** remarry. **v~et** *a* married

verhelfen† *vi* (*haben*) **jdm zu etw v~** help s.o. get sth

verherrlichen *vt* glorify

verhexen *vt* bewitch

verhinder|n *vt* prevent; **v~t sein** be unable to come

Verhör *nt* **-s, -e** interrogation; **ins V~ nehmen** interrogate. **v~en** *vt* interrogate; **sich v~en** mishear

verhungern *vi* (*sein*) starve

verhüt|en *vt* prevent. **V~ung** *f* - prevention. **V~ungsmittel** *nt* contraceptive

verirren (**sich**) *vr* get lost

verjagen *vt* chase away

verjüngen *vt* rejuvenate

verkalkt *a* 🄳 senile

verkalkulieren (**sich**) *vr* miscalculate

Verkauf *m* sale; **zum V~** for sale. **v~en** *vt* sell; **zu v~en** for sale

Verkäufer(in) *m(f)* seller; (*im Geschäft*) shop assistant

Verkehr *m* **-s** traffic; (*Kontakt*) contact; (*Geschlechts-*) intercourse; **aus dem V~ ziehen** take out of circulation. **v~en** *vi* (*haben*) operate; (*Bus, Zug:*) run; (*Umgang haben*) associate, mix (**mit** with); (*Gast sein*) visit (**bei jdm** s.o.)

Verkehrs|ampel *f* traffic lights *pl*. **V~unfall** *m* road accident. **V~verein** *m* tourist office. **V~zeichen** *nt* traffic sign

verkehrt *a* wrong; **v~ herum** *adv* the wrong way round; (*links*) inside out

verklagen *vt* sue (**auf** + *acc* for)

verkleid|en *vt* disguise; (*Techn*) line; **sich v~en** disguise oneself; (*für Kostümfest*) dress up. **V~ung** *f* -, **-en** disguise; (*Kostüm*) fancy dress; (*Techn*) lining

verkleiner|n *vt* reduce [in size]. **V~ung** *f* - reduction

verknittern *vt/i* (*sein*) crumple

verknüpfen *vt* knot together

verkommen† *vi* (*sein*) be neglected; (*sittlich*) go to the bad; (*verfallen*) decay; <*Haus:*> fall into disrepair; <*Gegend:*> become run-down; <*Lebensmittel:*> go bad ● *a* neglected; (*sittlich*) depraved; <*Haus*> dilapidated; <*Gegend*> run-down

verkörpern *vt* embody, personify

verkraften *vt* cope with

verkrampft *a* (*fig*) tense

verkriechen† (**sich**) *vr* hide

verkrümmt *a* crooked, bent

verkrüppelt *a* crippled; <*Glied*> deformed

verkühl|en (**sich**) *vr* catch a chill. **V~ung** *f* -, **-en** chill

verkümmern *vi* (*sein*) waste/ <*Pflanze:*> wither away

verkünden *vt* announce; pronounce <*Urteil*>

verkürzen *vt* shorten; (*verringern*) reduce; (*abbrechen*) cut short; while away <*Zeit*>

Verlag *m* -[e]s, -e publishing firm

verlangen *vt* ask for; (*fordern*) demand; (*berechnen*) charge. **V~** *nt* -s desire; (*Bitte*) request

verlänger|n *vt* extend; lengthen <*Kleid*>; (*zeitlich*) prolong; renew <*Pass, Vertrag*>; (*Culin*) thin down. **V~ung** *f* -, -en extension; renewal. **V~ungsschnur** *f* extension cable

verlassen† *vt* leave; (*im Stich lassen*) desert; **sich v~ auf** (+ *acc*) rely *or* depend on ● *a* deserted. **V~heit** *f* - desolation

verlässlich *a* reliable

Verlauf *m* course; **im V~** (+ *gen*) in the course of. **v~en†** *vi* (*sein*) run; (*ablaufen*) go; **gut v~en** go [off] well ● *vr* **sich v~en** lose one's way

verlegen *vt* move; (*verschieben*) postpone; (*vor-*) bring forward; (*verlieren*) mislay; (*versperren*) block; (*legen*) lay <*Teppich, Rohre*>; (*veröffentlichen*) publish; **sich v~ auf** (+ *acc*) take up <*Beruf*>; resort to <*Bitten*> ● *a* embarrassed. **V~heit** *f* - embarrassment

Verleger *m* -s,- publisher

verleihen† *vt* lend; (*gegen Gebühr*) hire out; (*überreichen*) award, confer; (*fig*) give

verlernen *vt* forget

verletz|en *vt* injure; (*kränken*) hurt; (*verstoßen gegen*) infringe; violate <*Grenze*>. **v~end** *a* hurtful, wounding. **V~te(r)** *m/f* injured person; (*bei Unfall*) casualty. **V~ung** *f* -, -en (*Verstoß*) infringement; violation

verleugnen *vt* deny; disown <*Freund*>

verleumd|en *vt* slander; (*schriftlich*) libel. **v~erisch** *a* slanderous; libellous. **V~ung** *f* -, -en slander; (*schriftlich*) libel

verlieben (sich) *vr* fall in love (**in** + *acc* with); **verliebt sein** be in love (**in** + *acc* with)

verlier|en† *vt* lose; shed <*Laub*> ● *vi* (*haben*) lose (**an etw** *dat* sth). **V~er** *m* -s,- loser

verlob|en (sich) *vr* get engaged (**mit** to); **v~t sein** be engaged. **V~te** *f* fiancée. **V~te(r)** *m* fiancé. **V~ung** *f* -, -en engagement

verlock|en *vt* tempt. **V~ung** *f*-, -en temptation

verloren *a* lost; **v~ gehen** get lost

verlos|en *vt* raffle. **V~ung** *f* -, -en raffle; (*Ziehung*) draw

Verlust *m* -[e]s, -e loss

vermachen *vt* leave, bequeath

Vermächtnis *nt* -ses, -se legacy

vermähl|en (sich) *vr* marry. **V~ung** *f* -, -en marriage

vermehren *vt* increase; propagate <*Pflanzen*>; **sich v~** increase; (*sich fortpflanzen*) breed

vermeiden† *vt* avoid

Vermerk *m* -[e]s, -e note. **v~en** note [down]

vermessen† *vt* measure; survey <*Gelände*> ● *a* presumptuous

vermiet|en *vt* let, rent [out]; hire out <*Boot, Auto*>; **zu v~en** to let; <*Boot:*> for hire. **V~er** *m* landlord. **V~erin** *f* landlady

vermindern *vt* reduce

vermischen *vt* mix

vermissen *vt* miss

vermisst *a* missing

vermitteln *vi* (*haben*) mediate ● *vt* arrange; (*beschaffen*) find; place <*Arbeitskräfte*>

Vermittl|er *m* -s,- agent; (*Schlichter*) mediator. **V~ung** *f*-, -en arrangement; (*Agentur*) agency; (*Teleph*) exchange; (*Schlichtung*) mediation

Vermögen *nt* -s,- fortune. **v~d** *a* wealthy

vermut|en *vt* suspect; (*glauben*) presume. **v~lich** *a* probable ● *adv* presumably. **V~ung** *f* -, -en supposition; (*Verdacht*) suspicion

vernachlässigen *vt* neglect

vernehm|en† *vt* hear; (*verhören*) question; (*Jur*) examine. **V~ung** *f* -, -en questioning

---

*old spelling

verneigen (sich) *vr* bow

vernein|en *vt* answer in the negative; *(ablehnen)* reject. **v~end** *a* negative. **V~ung** *f* -, -en negative answer

vernicht|en *vt* destroy; *(ausrotten)* exterminate. **V~ung** *f* - destruction; extermination

Vernunft *f* - reason

vernünftig *a* reasonable, sensible

veröffentlich|en *vt* publish. **V~ung** *f* -, -en publication

verordn|en *vt* prescribe *(dat* for). **V~ung** *f* -, -en prescription; *(Verfügung)* decree

verpachten *vt* lease [out]

verpack|en *vt* pack; *(einwickeln)* wrap. **V~ung** *f* packaging; wrapping

verpassen *vt* miss; (🄓 *geben)* give

verpfänden *vt* pawn

verpflanzen *vt* transplant

verpfleg|en *vt* feed: sich selbst v~en cater for oneself. **V~ung** *f* - board; *(Essen)* food; Unterkunft und V~ung board and lodging

verpflicht|en *vt* oblige; *(einstellen)* engage; *(Sport)* sign; sich v~en undertake/*(versprechen)* promise **(zu** to); *(vertraglich)* sign a contract. **V~ung** *f* -, -en obligation, commitment

verprügeln *vt* beat up, thrash

Verputz *m* -es plaster. **v~en** *vt* plaster

Verrat *m* -[e]s betrayal, treachery. **v~en†** *vt* betray; give away *<Geheimnis>*

Verräter *m* -s,- traitor

verrech|nen *vt* settle; clear *<Scheck>*; sich v~nen make a mistake; *(fig)* miscalculate. **V~nungsscheck** *m* crossed cheque

verreisen *vi (sein)* go away; verreist sein be away

verrenken *vt* dislocate

verrichten *vt* perform, do

verriegeln *vt* bolt

verringer|n *vt* reduce; sich v~n decrease. **V~ung** *f* - reduction; decrease

verrost|en *vi (sein)* rust. **v~et** *a* rusty

verrückt *a* crazy, mad. **V~e(r)** *m/f* lunatic, **V~heit** *f* -, -en madness; *(Torheit)* folly

verrühren *vt* mix

verrunzelt *a* wrinkled

verrutschen *vt (sein)* slip

Vers /fɛrs/ *m* -es, -e verse

versag|en *vi (haben)* fail ● *vt* sich etw v~en deny oneself sth. **V~en** *nt* -s,- failure. **V~er** *m* -s,- failure

versalzen† *vt* put too much salt in/on; *(fig)* spoil

versamm|eln *vt* assemble. **V~lung** *f* assembly, meeting

Versand *m* -[e]s dispatch. **V~haus** *nt* mail-order firm

versäumen *vt* miss; lose *<Zeit>*; *(unterlassen)* neglect; [es] v~, etw zu tun fail to do sth

verschärfen *vt* intensify; tighten *<Kontrolle>*; increase *<Tempo>*; aggravate *<Lage>*; sich v~ intensify; increase; *<Lage:>* worsen

verschätzen (sich) *vr* sich v~ in (+ *dat)* misjudge

verschenken *vt* give away

verscheuchen *vt* shoo/*(jagen)* chase away

verschicken *vt* send; *(Comm)* dispatch

verschieb|en† *vt* move; *(aufschieben)* put off, postpone; sich v~en move, shift; *(verrutschen)* slip; *(zeitlich)* be postponed. **V~ung** *f* shift; postponement

verschieden *a* different; v~e *pl* different; *(mehrere)* various; V~es some things; *(dieses und jenes)* various things; das ist v~ it varies ● *adv* differently; v~ groß of different sizes. **v~artig** *a* diverse

verschimmel|n *vi (sein)* go mouldy. **v~t** *a* mouldy

verschlafen† *vi (haben)* oversleep ● *vt* sleep through *<Tag>*; sich v~ oversleep ● *a* sleepy

verschlagen† *vt* lose <*Seite*>; jdm
die Sprache/den Atem v~ leave s.o.
speechless/take s.o.'s breath away
● *a* sly

verschlechter|n *vt* make worse;
sich v~n get worse, deteriorate.
V~ung *f* -, -en deterioration

Verschleiß *m* -es wear and tear

verschleppen *vt* carry off;
(*entführen*) abduct; spread <*Seuche*>;
neglect <*Krankheit*>; (*hinausziehen*)
delay

verschleudern *vt* sell at a loss

verschließen† *vt* close;
(*abschließen*) lock; (*einschließen*) lock
up

verschlimmer|n *vt* make worse;
aggravate <*Lage*>; sich v~n get
worse, deteriorate. **V~ung** *f* -, -en
deterioration

verschlossen *a* reserved. **V~heit**
f - reserve

verschlucken *vt* swallow; sich v~
choke (an + *dat* on)

Verschluss *m* -es, ⸚e fastener,
clasp; (*Koffer*-) catch; (*Flaschen*-) top;
(*luftdicht*) seal; (*Phot*) shutter

verschlüsselt *a* coded

verschmelzen† *vt/i* (*sein*) fuse

verschmerzen *vt* get over

verschmutz|en *vt* soil; pollute
<*Luft*>. ● *vi* (*sein*) get dirty. **V~ung**
f - pollution

verschneit *a* snow-covered

verschnörkelt *a* ornate

verschnüren *vt* tie up

verschollen *a* missing

verschonen *vt* spare

verschossen *a* faded

verschränken *vt* cross

verschreiben† *vt* prescribe; sich
v~ make a slip of the pen

verschulden *vt* be to blame for.
V~ *nt* -s fault

verschuldet *a* v~ sein be in debt

verschütten *vt* spill; (*begraben*)
bury

verschweigen† *vt* conceal, hide

verschwend|en *vt* waste. **V~ung**
f - extravagance; (*Vergeudung*) waste

verschwiegen *a* discreet

verschwinden† *vi* (*sein*)
disappear; [mal] v~ 🔟 spend a
penny

verschwommen *a* blurred

verschwör|en† (sich) *vr*
conspire. **V~ung** *f* -, -en conspiracy

versehen† *vt* perform; hold
<*Posten*>; keep <*Haushalt*>; v~ mit
provide with; sich v~ make a
mistake. **V~** *nt* -s, - oversight;
(*Fehler*) slip; aus V~ by mistake.
v~tlich *adv* by mistake

Versehrte(r) *m* disabled person

versengen *vt* singe; (*stärker*)
scorch

versenken *vt* sink

versessen *a* keen (auf + *acc* on)

versetz|en *vt* move; transfer
<*Person*>; (*Sch*) move up;
(*verpfänden*) pawn; (*verkaufen*) sell;
(*vermischen*) blend; jdn v~en (🔟
warten lassen) stand s.o. up; jdm in
Angst/Erstaunen v~en frighten/
astonish s.o.; sich in jds Lage v~en
put oneself in s.o.'s place. **V~ung** *f*
-, -en move; transfer; (*Sch*) move to a
higher class

verseuchen *vt* contaminate

versicher|n *vt* insure; (*bekräftigen*)
affirm; jdm v~n assure s.o (dass
that). **V~ung** *f*-, -en insurance;
assurance

versiegeln *vt* seal

versiert /vɛrˈʒiːɐt/ *a* experienced

versilbert *a* silver-plated

Versmaß /ˈfɛrs-/ *nt* metre

versöhn|en *vt* reconcile; sich v~en
become reconciled. **V~ung** *f* -, -en
reconciliation

versorg|en *vt* provide, supply (mit
with); provide for <*Familie*>;
(*betreuen*) look after. **V~ung** *f* -
provision, supply; (*Betreuung*) care

verspät|en (sich) *vr* be late. **v~et**
a late; <*Zug*> delayed; <*Dank*>
belated. **V~ung** *f* - lateness; V~ung
haben be late

versperren *vt* block; bar <*Weg*>

verspiel|en *vt* gamble away. **v∼t** *a* playful

verspotten *vt* mock, ridicule

versprech|en† *vt* promise; **sich v∼en** make a slip of the tongue; **sich** (*dat*) **viel v∼en von** have high hopes of; **ein viel v∼ender Anfang** a promising start. **V∼en** *nt* **-s,-** promise. **V∼ungen** *fpl* promises

verstaatlich|en *vt* nationalize. **V∼ung** *f* - nationalization

Verstand *m* **-[e]s** mind; (*Vernunft*) reason; **den V∼ verlieren** go out of one's mind

verständig *a* sensible; (*klug*) intelligent. **v∼en** *vt* notify, inform; **sich v∼en** communicate; (*sich verständlich machen*) make oneself understood. **V∼ung** *f* - notification; communication; (*Einigung*) agreement

verständlich *a* comprehensible; (*deutlich*) clear; (*begreiflich*) understandable; **sich v∼ machen** make oneself understood. **v∼erweise** *adv* understandably

Verständnis *nt* **-ses** understanding

verstärk|en *vt* strengthen, reinforce; (*steigern*) intensify, increase; amplify <*Ton*>. **V∼er** *m* **-s,-** amplifier. **V∼ung** *f* reinforcement; increase; amplification; (*Truppen*) reinforcements *pl*

verstaubt *a* dusty

verstauchen *vt* sprain

Versteck *nt* **-[e]s, -e** hiding-place; **V∼ spielen** play hide-and-seek. **v∼en** *vt* hide; **sich v∼en** hide

verstehen† *vt* understand; (*können*) know; **falsch v∼** misunderstand; **sich v∼** understand one another; (*auskommen*) get on

versteiger|n *vt* auction. **V∼ung** *f* auction

versteinert *a* fossilized

verstell|en *vt* adjust; (*versperren*) block; (*verändern*) disguise; **sich v∼en** pretend. **V∼ung** *f* - pretence

versteuern *vt* pay tax on

verstimm|t *a* disgruntled; <*Magen*> upset; (*Mus*) out of tune. **V∼ung** *f* - ill humour; (*Magen-*) upset

verstockt *a* stubborn

verstopf|en *vt* plug; (*versperren*) block; **v∼t** blocked; <*Person*> constipated. **V∼ung** *f* **-, -en** blockage; (*Med*) constipation

verstorben *a* late, deceased. **V∼e(r)** *m/f* deceased

verstört *a* bewildered

Verstoß *m* infringement. **v∼en†** *vt* disown ● *vi* (*haben*) **v∼en gegen** contravene, infringe

verstreuen *vt* scatter

verstümmeln *vt* mutilate; garble <*Text*>

Versuch *m* **-[e]s, -e** attempt; (*Experiment*) experiment. **v∼en** *vt/i* (*haben*) try; **v∼t sein** be tempted (**zu** to). **V∼ung** *f* **-, -en** temptation

vertagen *vt* adjourn; (*aufschieben*) postpone; **sich v∼** adjourn

vertauschen *vt* exchange; (*verwechseln*) mix up

verteidig|en *vt* defend. **V∼er** *m* **-s,-** defender; (*Jur*) defence counsel. **V∼ung** *f* **-, -en** defence

verteil|en *vt* distribute; (*zuteilen*) allocate; (*ausgeben*) hand out; (*verstreichen*) spread. **V∼ung** *f* - distribution; allocation

vertief|en *vt* deepen; **v∼t sein in** (+ *acc*) be engrossed in. **V∼ung** *f* **-, -en** hollow, depression

vertikal /vɛrtiˈkaːl/ *a* vertical

vertilg|en *vt* exterminate; kill [off] <*Unkraut*>

vertippen (sich) *vr* make a typing mistake

vertonen *vt* set to music

Vertrag *m* **-[e]s,-̈e** contract; (*Pol*) treaty

vertragen† *vt* tolerate, stand; take <*Kritik, Spaß*>; **sich v∼** get on

vertraglich *a* contractual

verträglich *a* good-natured; (*bekömmlich*) digestible

vertrauen *vi* (*haben*) trust (**jdm/etw** s.o./sth; **auf** + *acc* in). **V∼** *nt* **-s** trust, confidence (**zu** in); **im V~** in confidence. **v~swürdig** *a* trustworthy

vertraulich *a* confidential; (*intim*) familiar

vertraut *a* intimate; (*bekannt*) familiar. **V~heit** *f* - intimacy; familiarity

vertreib|en† *vt* drive away; drive out <*Feind*>; (*Comm*) sell; **sich** (*dat*) **die Zeit v~en** pass the time. **V~ung** *f* -, -en expulsion

vertret|en† *vt* represent; (*einspringen für*) stand in *or* deputize for; (*verfechten*) support; hold <*Meinung*>; **sich** (*dat*) **den Fuß v~en** twist one's ankle. **V~er** *m* -s,- representative; deputy; (*Arzt-*) locum; (*Verfechter*) supporter. **V~ung** *f* -, -en representation; (*Person*) deputy; (*eines Arztes*) locum; (*Handels-*) agency

Vertrieb *m* -[e]s (*Comm*) sale

vertrocknen *vi* (*sein*) dry up

verüben *vt* commit

verunglücken *vi* (*sein*) be involved in an accident; (⚠ *missglücken*) go wrong; **tödlich v~** be killed in an accident

verunreinigen *vt* pollute; (*verseuchen*) contaminate

verursachen *vt* cause

verurteil|en *vt* condemn; (*Jur*) convict (**wegen** of); sentence (**zum Tode** to death). **V~ung** *f* - condemnation; (*Jur*) conviction

vervielfachen *vt* multiply

vervielfältigen *vt* duplicate

vervollständigen *vt* complete

verwählen (sich) *vr* misdial

verwahren *vt* keep; (*verstauen*) put away

verwahrlost *a* neglected; <*Haus*> dilapidated

Verwahrung *f* - keeping; **in V~ nehmen** take into safe keeping

verwaist *a* orphaned

verwalt|en *vt* administer; (*leiten*) manage; govern <*Land*>. **V~er** *m*

-s,- administrator; manager. **V~ung** *f* -, -en administration; management; government

verwand|eln *vt* transform, change (**in** + *acc* into) **sich v~eln** change, turn (**in** + *acc* into). **V~lung** *f* transformation

verwandt *a* related (**mit** to). **V~e(r)** *m/f* relative. **V~schaft** *f* - relationship; (*Menschen*) relatives *pl*

verwarn|en *vt* warn, caution. **V~ung** *f* warning, caution

verwechs|eln *vt* mix up, confuse; (*halten für*) mistake (**mit** for). **V~lung** *f* -, -en mix-up

verweiger|n *vt/i* (*haben*) refuse (**jdm etw** s.o sth). **V~ung** *f* refusal

Verweis *m* -es, -e reference (**auf** + *acc* to); (*Tadel*) reprimand; **v~en**† *vt* refer (**auf/an** + *acc* to); (*tadeln*) reprimand; **von der Schule v~en** expel

verwelken *vi* (*sein*) wilt

verwend|en† *vt* use; spend <*Zeit, Mühe*>. **V~ung** *f* use

verwerten *vt* utilize, use

verwesen *vi* (*sein*) decompose

verwick|eln *vt* involve (**in** + *acc* in); **sich v~eln** get tangled up. **v~elt** *a* complicated

verwildert *a* wild; <*Garten*> overgrown; <*Aussehen*> unkempt

verwinden† *vt* (*fig*) get over

verwirklichen *vt* realize

verwirr|en *vt* tangle up; (*fig*) confuse; **sich v~en** get tangled; (*fig*) become confused. **v~t** *a* confused. **V~ung** *f* - confusion

verwischen *vt* smudge

verwittert *a* weathered

verwitwet *a* widowed

verwöhn|en *vt* spoil. **v~t** *a* spoilt

verworren *a* confused

verwund|bar *a* vulnerable. **v~en** *vt* wound

verwunder|lich *a* surprising. **v~n** *vt* surprise; **sich v~n** be surprised. **V~ung** *f* - surprise

Verwund|ete(r) *m* wounded soldier; **die V~eten** the wounded *pl*. **V~ung** *f* -, -en wound

verwüst|en vt devastate, ravage.
V∼**ung** f -, -en devastation

verzählen (sich) vr miscount

verzaubern vt bewitch; (fig)
enchant; v∼ **in** (+ acc) turn into

Verzehr m -s consumption. v∼**en**
vt eat

verzeih|en† vt forgive; v∼en Sie!
excuse me! V∼**ung** f - forgiveness;
um V∼ung bitten apologize; V∼ung!
sorry! (bei Frage) excuse me!

Verzicht m -[e]s renunciation (**auf** +
acc of). v∼**en** vi (haben) do without;
v∼en auf (+ acc) give up; renounce
<Recht, Erbe>

verziehen† vt pull out of shape;
(verwöhnen) spoil; **sich v∼** lose
shape; <Holz:> warp; <Gesicht:>
twist; (verschwinden) disappear;
<Nebel:> disperse; <Gewitter:> pass
● vi (sein) move [away]

verzier|en vt decorate. V∼**ung** f -,
-en decoration

verzinsen vt pay interest on

verzöger|n vt delay; (verlangsamen)
slow down. V∼**ung** f -, -en delay

verzollen vt pay duty on; haben Sie
etwas zu v∼? have you anything to
declare?

verzweif|eln vi (sein) despair.
v∼**elt** a desperate. V∼**lung** f -
despair; (Ratlosigkeit) desperation

verzweigen (sich) vr branch [out]

Veto /'ve:to/ nt -s, -s veto

Vetter m -s, -n cousin

vgl. abbr (vergleiche) cf.

Viadukt /via'dʊkt/ nt -[e]s, -e
viaduct

Video /'vi:deo/ nt -s, -s video.
V∼**kassette** f video cassette.
V∼**recorder** /-rəkɔrdɐ/ m -s,-
video recorder

Vieh nt -[e]s livestock; (Rinder) cattle
pl; (T Tier) creature

viel pron a great deal/T a lot of; (pl)
many, T a lot of; (substantivisch)
v∼[es] much, T a lot; nicht/so/wie/
zu v∼ not/so/how/too much/ (pl)
many; v∼e pl many; das v∼e Geld
all that money ● adv much, T a lot;
v∼ mehr/weniger much more/less;

v∼ zu groß/klein much or far too
big/small; so v∼ wie möglich as
much as possible; so/zu v∼ arbeiten
work so/too much

viel|deutig a ambiguous. v∼**fach**
a multiple ● adv many times; (T oft)
frequently. V∼**falt** f - diversity,
[great] variety

vielleicht adv perhaps, maybe; (T
wirklich) really

vielmals adv very much

vielmehr adv rather; (im Gegenteil)
on the contrary

vielseitig a varied; <Person>
versatile. V∼**keit** f - versatility

vielversprechend* a viel
versprechend, s. versprechen

vier inv a, V∼ f -, -en four; (Sch) ≈
fair. V∼**eck** nt -[e]s, -e oblong,
rectangle; (Quadrat) square.
v∼**eckig** a oblong, rectangular;
square. V∼**linge** mpl quadruplets

viertel /'fɪrtəl/ inv a quarter; um v∼
neun at [a] quarter past eight; um
drei v∼ neun at [a] quarter to nine.
V∼ nt -s,- quarter; (Wein) quarter
litre; V∼ vor/nach sechs [a] quarter
to/past six. V∼**finale** nt quarter-
final. V∼**jahr** nt three months pl;
(Comm) quarter. v∼**jährlich** a &
adv quarterly. V∼**stunde** f quarter
of an hour

vier|zehn /'fɪr-/ inv a fourteen.
v∼**zehnte(r,s)** a fourteenth.
v∼**zig** inv a forty. v∼**zigste(r,s)** a
fortieth

Villa /'vɪla/ f -, -len villa

violett /vio'lɛt/ a violet

Vio|line /vio'li:nə/ f -, -n violin.
V∼**linschlüssel** m treble clef

Virus /'vi:rʊs/ nt -, -ren virus

Visier /vi'zi:ɐ/ nt -s, -e visor

Visite /vi'zi:tə/ f -, -n round; V∼
machen do one's round

Visum /'vi:zʊm/ nt -s, -sa visa

Vitamin /vita'mi:n/ nt -s, -e vitamin

Vitrine /vi'tri:nə/ f -, -n display
cabinet/(im Museum) case

Vizepräsident /'fi:tsə-/ m vice
president

Vogel *m* -s,- bird; **einen V~ haben** 🛈 have a screw loose. **V~scheuche** *f* -, -n scarecrow

Vokabeln /vo'ka:bəln/ *fpl* vocabulary *sg*

Vokal /vo'ka:l/ *m* -s, -e vowel

Volant /vo'lã:/ *m* -s, -s flounce

Volk *nt* -[e]s,-er people *sg*; (*Bevölkerung*) people *pl*

Völker|kunde *f* ethnology. **V~mord** *m* genocide. **V~recht** *nt* international law

Volks|abstimmung *f* plebiscite. **V~fest** *nt* public festival. **V~hochschule** *f* adult education classes *pl*/(*Gebäude*) centre. **V~lied** *nt* folk-song. **V~tanz** *m* folk-dance. **v~tümlich** *a* popular. **V~wirt** *m* economist. **V~wirtschaft** *f* economics *sg*. **V~zählung** *f* [national] census

voll *a* full (*von od mit* of); <*Haar*> thick; <*Erfolg, Ernst*> complete; <*Wahrheit*> whole; **v~ machen** fill up; **v~ tanken** fill up with petrol ● *adv* (*ganz*) completely; <*arbeiten*> full-time; <*auszahlen*> in full; **v~ und ganz** completely

Vollblut *nt* thoroughbred

vollende|n *vt insep* complete. **v~t** *a* perfect

Vollendung *f* completion; (*Vollkommenheit*) perfection

voller *inv a* full of

Volleyball /'vɔli-/ *m* volleyball

vollführen *vt insep* perform

vollfüllen *vt sep* fill up

Vollgas *nt* **V~ geben** put one's foot down; **mit V~** flat out

völlig *a* complete

volljährig *a* **v~ sein** (*Jur*) be of age. **V~keit** *f* - (*Jur*) majority

Vollkaskoversicherung *f* fully comprehensive insurance

vollkommen *a* perfect; (*völlig*) complete

Voll|kornbrot *nt* wholemeal bread. **V~macht** *f* -, -en authority; (*Jur*)

power of attorney. **V~mond** *m* full moon. **V~pension** *f* full board

vollständig *a* complete

vollstrecken *vt insep* execute; carry out <*Urteil*>

volltanken* *vi sep* (*haben*) **voll tanken**, *s.* **voll**

Volltreffer *m* direct hit

vollzählig *a* complete

vollziehen† *vt insep* carry out; perform <*Handlung*>; consummate <*Ehe*>; **sich v~** take place

Volt /vɔlt/ *nt* -[s],- volt

Volumen /vo'lu:mən/ *nt* -s,- volume

vom *prep* = **von dem**

von

● *preposition* (+ *dative*)

❗ Note that **von dem** can become **vom**

┈┈▸ (*räumlich*) from; (*nach Richtungen*) of. **von hier an** from here on[ward]. **von Wien aus** [starting] from Vienna. **nördlich/ südlich von Mannheim** [to the] north/south of Mannheim. **rechts/ links von mir** to the right/left of me; on my right/left

┈┈▸ (*zeitlich*) from. **von jetzt an** from now on. **von heute/morgen an** [as] from today/tomorrow; starting today/tomorrow

┈┈▸ (*zur Angabe des Urhebers, der Ursache; nach Passiv*) by. **der Roman ist von Fontane** the novel is by Fontane. **sie hat ein Kind von ihm.** she has a child by him. **er ist vom Blitz erschlagen worden** he was killed by lightning

┈┈▸ (*anstelle eines Genitivs; Zugehörigkeit, Beschaffenheit, Menge etc.*) of. **ein Stück von dem Kuchen** a piece of the cake. **einer von euch** one of you. **eine Fahrt von drei Stunden** a drive of three hours; a three-hour drive. **das Brot von gestern** yesterday's bread. **ein Tal von erstaunlicher Schönheit** a valley of extraordinary beauty

┈┈▸ (*betreffend*) about. **handeln/ wissen/erzählen** *od* **reden von ...** be/ know/talk about .... **eine Geschichte** von zwei Elefanten a story about or of two elephants

voneinander *adv* from each other; *<abhängig>* on each other

vonseiten *prep* (+ *gen*) on the part of

vonstatten *adv* v~ gehen take place

vor *prep* (+ *dat/acc*) in front of; *(zeitlich, Reihenfolge)* before; (+ *dat*) *(bei Uhrzeit)* to; *<warnen, sich fürchten>* of; *<schützen, davonlaufen>* from; *<Respekt haben>* for; **vor Angst zittern** tremble with fear; **vor drei Tagen** three days ago; **vor allen Dingen** above all ● *adv* forward; **vor und zurück** backwards and forwards

Vorabend *m* eve

voran *adv* at the front; *(voraus)* ahead; *(vorwärts)* forward. **v~gehen**† *vi sep (sein)* lead the way; *(Fortschritte machen)* make progress. **v~kommen**† *vi sep (sein)* make progress; *(fig)* get on

Vor|anschlag *m* estimate. **V~anzeige** *f* advance notice. **V~arbeiter** *m* foreman

voraus *adv* ahead *(dat* of); *(vorn)* at the front; *(vorwärts)* forward ● **im Voraus** in advance. **v~bezahlen** *vt sep* pay in advance. **v~gehen**† *vi sep (sein)* go on ahead; **jdm/etw v~gehen** precede s.o./sth. **V~sage** *f* -, -n prediction. **v~sagen** *vt sep* predict

voraussetz|en *vt sep* take for granted; *(erfordern)* require; **vorausgesetzt, dass** provided that. **V~ung** *f* -, -en assumption; *(Erfordernis)* prerequisite

voraussichtlich *a* anticipated, expected ● *adv* probably

Vorbehalt *m* -[e]s, -e reservation

vorbei *adv* past (**an jdm/etw** s.o./sth); *(zu Ende)* over. **v~fahren**† *vi sep (sein)* drive/go past. **v~gehen**† *vi sep (sein)* go past; *(verfehlen)* miss; *(vergehen)* pass; *(I besuchen)* drop in (**bei** on)

vorbereit|en *vt sep* prepare; prepare for *<Reise>*; **sich v~en** prepare [oneself] (**auf** + *acc* for). **V~ung** *f* -, -en preparation

vorbestellen *vt sep* order/*(im Theater, Hotel)* book in advance

vorbestraft *a* **v~ sein** have a [criminal] record

Vorbeugung *f* - prevention

Vorbild *nt* model. **v~lich** *a* exemplary, model ● *adv* in an exemplary manner

vorbringen† *vt sep* put forward; offer *<Entschuldigung>*

vordatieren *vt sep* post-date

Vorder|bein *nt* foreleg. **v~e(r,s)** *a* front. **V~grund** *m* foreground. **V~rad** *nt* front wheel. **V~seite** *f* front; *(einer Münze)* obverse. **v~ste(r,s)** *a* front, first. **V~teil** *nt* front

vor|drängeln (sich) *vr sep* 🚫 jump the queue. **v~drängen (sich)** *vr sep* push forward. **v~dringen**† *vi sep (sein)* advance

voreilig *a* rash

voreingenommen *a* biased, prejudiced. **V~heit** *f* - bias

vorenthalten† *vt sep* withhold

vorerst *adv* for the time being

Vorfahr *m* -en, -en ancestor

Vorfahrt *f* right of way; 'V~ beachten' 'give way'. **V~sstraße** *f* ≈ major road

Vorfall *m* incident. **v~en**† *vi sep (sein)* happen

vorfinden† *vt sep* find

Vorfreude *f* [happy] anticipation

vorführ|en *vt sep* present, show; *(demonstrieren)* demonstrate; *(aufführen)* perform. **V~ung** *f* presentation; demonstration; performance

Vor|gabe *f* *(Sport)* handicap. **V~gang** *m* occurrence; *(Techn)* process. **V~gänger(in)** *m* -s,- (*f* -, -nen) predecessor

vorgehen† *vi sep (sein)* go forward; *(voraus-)* go on ahead; *<Uhr:>* be fast; *(wichtig sein)* take precedence;

(*verfahren*) act, proceed; (*geschehen*) happen, go on. **V∼** *nt* **-s** action

vor|geschichtlich *a* prehistoric. **V∼geschmack** *m* foretaste. **V∼gesetzte(r)** *m/f* superior. **v∼gestern** *adv* the day before yesterday; **v∼gestern Abend** the evening before last

vorhaben† *vt sep* propose, intend (zu to); **etw v∼** have sth planned. **V∼** *nt* **-s,-** plan

Vorhand *f* (*Sport*) forehand

vorhanden *a* existing; **v∼ sein** exist; be available

Vorhang *m* curtain

Vorhängeschloss *nt* padlock

vorher *adv* before[hand]

vorhergehend *a* previous

vorherrschend *a* predominant

Vorher|sage *f* **-, -n** prediction: (*Wetter-*) forecast. **v∼sagen** *vt sep* predict; forecast <*Wetter*>. **v∼sehen**† *vt sep* foresee

vorhin *adv* just now

vorige(r,s) *a* last, previous

Vor|kehrungen *fpl* precautions. **V∼kenntnisse** *fpl* previous knowledge *sg*

vorkommen† *vi sep* (*sein*) happen; (*vorhanden sein*) occur; (*nach vorn kommen*) come forward; (*hervorkommen*) come out; (*zu sehen sein*) show; **jdm bekannt v∼** seem familiar to s.o.

Vorkriegszeit *f* pre-war period

vorlad|en† *vt sep* (*Jur*) summons. **V∼ung** *f* summons

Vorlage *f* model; (*Muster*) pattern; (*Gesetzes-*) bill

vorlassen† *vt sep* admit; **jdn v∼** 🔲 let s.o. pass; (*den Vortritt lassen*) let s.o. go first

Vor|lauf *m* (*Sport*) heat. **V∼läufer** *m* forerunner. **v∼läufig** *a* provisional; (*zunächst*) for the time being. **v∼laut** *a* forward. **V∼leben** *nt* past

vorleg|en *vt sep* put on <*Kette*>; (*unterbreiten*) present; (*vorzeigen*) show. **V∼er** *m* **-s,-** mat; (*Bett-*) rug

vorles|en† *vt sep* read [out]; **jdm v∼en** read to s.o. **V∼ung** *f* lecture

vorletzt|e(r,s) *a* last ... but one; **v∼es Jahr** the year before last

Vorliebe *f* preference

vorliegen† *vt sep* (*haben*) be present/(*verfügbar*) available; (*bestehen*) exist, be

vorlügen† *vt sep* lie (*dat* to)

vormachen *vt sep* put up; put on <*Kette*>; push <*Riegel*>; (*zeigen*) demonstrate; **jdm etwas v∼** (🔲 *täuschen*) kid s.o.

Vormacht *f* supremacy

vormals *adv* formerly

vormerken *vt sep* make a note of; (*reservieren*) reserve

Vormittag *m* morning; **gestern/ heute v∼** yesterday/this morning. **v∼s** *adv* in the morning

Vormund *m* **-[e]s, -munde** & **-münder** guardian

vorn *adv* at the front; **nach v∼** to the front; **von v∼** from the front/(*vom Anfang*) beginning; **von v∼ anfangen** start afresh

Vorname *m* first name

vorne *adv* = **vorn**

vornehm *a* distinguished; smart

vornehmen† *vt sep* carry out; **sich** (*dat*) **v∼, etw zu tun** plan to do sth

vornherein *adv* **von v∼herein** from the start

Vor|ort *m* suburb. **V∼rang** *m* priority, precedence (**vor** + *dat* over). **V∼rat** *m* **-[e]s, ̈e** supply, stock (**an** + *dat* of). **v∼rätig** *a* available; **v∼rätig haben** have in stock. **V∼ratskammer** *f* larder. **V∼recht** *nt* privilege. **V∼richtung** *f* device

Vorrunde *f* qualifying round

vorsagen *vt/i sep* (*haben*) recite; **jdm v∼** tell s.o. the answer

Vor|satz *m* resolution. **v∼sätzlich** *a* deliberate; (*Jur*) premeditated

Vorschau *f* preview; (*Film-*) trailer

Vorschein *m* zum V~kommen appear

Vorschlag *m* suggestion, proposal. **v~en†** *vt sep* suggest, propose

vorschnell *a* rash

vorschreiben† *vt sep* lay down; dictate (*dat* to); **vorgeschriebene Dosis** prescribed dose

Vorschrift *f* regulation; (*Anweisung*) instruction; **jdm V~en machen** tell s.o. what to do. **v~smäßig** *a* correct

Vorschule *f* nursery school

Vorschuss *m* advance

vorseh|en† *v sep* ● *vt* intend (**für/ als** for/as); (*planen*) plan; **sich v~en** be careful (**vor** + *dat* of) ● *vi* (*haben*) peep out. **V~ung** *f* - providence

Vorsicht *f* - care; (*bei Gefahr*) caution; **V~!** careful! (*auf Schild*) 'caution'. **v~ig** *a* careful; cautious. **V~smaßnahme** *f* precaution

Vorsilbe *f* prefix

Vorsitz *m* chairmanship; **den V~ führen** be in the chair. **V~ende(r)** *m/f* chairman

Vorsorge *f* V~ **treffen** take precautions; make provisions (**für** for). **v~n** *vi sep* (*haben*) provide (**für** for)

Vorspeise *f* starter

Vorspiel *nt* prelude. **v~en** *v sep* ● *vt* perform/ (*Mus*) play (*dat* for) ● *vi* (*haben*) audition

vorsprechen† *v sep* ● *vt* recite; (*zum Nachsagen*) say (*dat* to) ● *vi* (*haben*) (*Theat*) audition; **bei jdm v~** call on s.o.

Vor|sprung *m* projection; (*Fels-*) ledge; (*Vorteil*) lead (**vor** + *dat* over). **V~stadt** *f* suburb. **V~stand** *m* board [of directors]; (*Vereins-*) committee; (*Partei-*) executive

vorsteh|en† *vi sep* (*haben*) project, protrude; **einer Abteilung v~en** be in charge of a department. **V~er** *m* -s,- head

vorstell|en *vt sep* put forward <*Bein, Uhr*>; (*darstellen*) represent; (*bekanntmachen*) introduce; **sich v~en** introduce oneself; (*als*

Bewerber) go for an interview; **sich** (*dat*) **etw v~en** imagine sth. **V~ung** *f* introduction; (*bei Bewerbung*) interview; (*Aufführung*) performance; (*Idee*) idea; (*Phantasie*) imagination. **V~ungsgespräch** *nt* interview

Vorstoß *m* advance

Vorstrafe *f* previous conviction

Vortag *m* day before

vortäuschen *vt sep* feign, fake

Vorteil *m* advantage. **v~haft** *a* advantageous; flattering

Vortrag *m* -[e]s,-̈e talk; (*wissenschaftlich*) lecture. **v~en†** *vt sep* perform; (*aufsagen*) recite; (*singen*) sing; (*darlegen*) present (*dat* to)

vortrefflich *a* excellent

Vortritt *m* precedence; **jdm den V~ lassen** let s.o. go first

vorüber *adv* **v~ sein** be over; **an etw** (*dat*) **v~** past sth. **v~gehend** *a* temporary

Vor|urteil *nt* prejudice. **V~verkauf** *m* advance booking

vorverlegen *vt sep* bring forward

Vor|wahl[nummer] *f* dialling code. **V~wand** *m* -[e]s,-̈e pretext; (*Ausrede*) excuse

vorwärts *adv* forward[s]; **v~ kommen** make progress; (*fig*) get on *or* ahead

vorwegnehmen† *vt sep* anticipate

vorweisen† *vt sep* show

vorwiegend *adv* predominantly

Vorwort *nt* (*pl* -worte) preface

Vorwurf *m* reproach; **jdm Vorwürfe machen** reproach s.o. **v~svoll** *a* reproachful

Vorzeichen *nt* sign; (*fig*) omen

vorzeigen *vt sep* show

vorzeitig *a* premature

vorziehen† *vt sep* pull forward; draw <*Vorhang*>; (*lieber mögen*) prefer; favour

Vor|zimmer *nt* ante-room; (*Büro*) outer office. **V~zug** *m* preference; (*gute Eigenschaft*) merit, virtue; (*Vorteil*) advantage

vorzüglich *a* excellent

vulgär /vʊlˈgɛːɐ̯/ a vulgar ● adv in a vulgar way

Vulkan /vʊlˈkaːn/ m -s, -e volcano

Ww

Waage f -, -n scales pl; (Astr) Libra. **w~recht** a horizontal

Wabe f -, -n honeycomb

wach a awake; (aufgeweckt) alert; **w~ werden** wake up

Wach|e f -, -n guard; (Posten) sentry; (Dienst) guard duty; (Naut) watch; (Polizei-) station; **W~e halten** keep watch. **W~hund** m guard-dog

Wacholder m -s juniper

Wachposten m sentry

Wachs nt -es wax

wachsam a vigilant. **W~keit** f - vigilance

wachsen†¹ vi (sein) grow

wachs|en² vt (reg) wax. **W~figur** f waxwork

Wachstum nt -s growth

Wächter m -s,- guard; (Park-) keeper; (Parkplatz-) attendant

Wacht|meister m [police] constable. **W~posten** m sentry

wackel|ig a wobbly; <Stuhl> rickety; <Person> shaky. **W~kontakt** m loose connection. **w~n** vi (haben) wobble; (zittern) shake

Wade f -, -n (Anat) calf

Waffe f -, -n weapon; **W~n** arms

Waffel f -, -n waffle; (Eis-) wafer

Waffen|ruhe f cease-fire. **W~schein** m firearms licence. **W~stillstand** m armistice

Wagemut m daring

wagen vt risk; **es w~**, etw zu tun dare [to] do sth; **sich w~** (gehen) venture

Wagen m -s,- cart; (Eisenbahn-) carriage, coach; (Güter-) wagon; (Kinder-) pram; (Auto) car. **W~heber** m -s,- jack

Waggon /vaˈgõː/ m -s, -s wagon

Wahl f -, -en choice; (Pol, Admin) election; (geheime) ballot; **zweite W~** (Comm) seconds pl

wähl|en vt/i (haben) choose; (Pol, Admin) elect; (stimmen) vote; (Teleph) dial. **W~er(in)** m -s,- (f -, -nen) voter. **w~erisch** a choosy, fussy

Wahl|fach nt optional subject. **w~frei** a optional. **W~kampf** m election campaign. **W~kreis** m constituency. **W~lokal** nt polling-station. **w~los** a indiscriminate

Wahl|spruch m motto. **W~urne** f ballot-box

Wahn m -[e]s delusion; (Manie) mania

Wahnsinn m madness. **w~ig** a mad, insane; (🔲 unsinnig) crazy; (🔲 groß) terrible; **w~ig werden** go mad ● adv 🔲 terribly. **W~ige(r)** m/f maniac

wahr a true; (echt) real; **du kommst doch, nicht w~?** you are coming, aren't you?

während prep (+ gen) during ● conj while; (wohingegen) whereas

Wahrheit f -, -en truth. **w~sgemäß** a truthful

wahrnehm|en† vt sep notice; (nutzen) take advantage of; exploit <Vorteil>; look after <Interessen>. **W~ung** f -, -en perception

Wahrsagerin f -, -nen fortune teller

wahrscheinlich a probable. **W~keit** f - probability

Währung f -, -en currency

Wahrzeichen nt symbol

Waise f -, -n orphan. **W~nhaus** nt orphanage. **W~nkind** nt orphan

Wal m -[e]s, -e whale

---

*alte Schreibung

Wald *m* -[e]s,-̈er wood; (*groß*) forest.
w~**ig** *a* wooded

Walis|er *m* -s,- Welshman. **w~isch**
a Welsh

Wall *m* -[e]s,-̈e mound

Wallfahr|er(in) *m(f)* pilgrim. **W~t**
f pilgrimage

Walnuss *f* walnut

Walze *f* -, -n roller. **w~n** *vt* roll

Walzer *m* -s,- waltz

Wand *f* -,-̈e wall; (*Trenn-*) partition;
(*Seite*) side; (*Fels-*) face

Wandel *m* -s change

Wander|er *m* -s,-, **W~in** *f* -, -nen
hiker, rambler. **w~n** *vi* (*sein*) hike,
ramble; (*ziehen*) travel; (*gemächlich
gehen*) wander; (*ziellos*) roam.
W~schaft *f* - travels *pl*. **W~ung** *f*
-, -en hike, ramble. **W~weg** *m*
footpath

Wandlung *f* -, -en change,
transformation

Wand|malerei *f* mural. **W~tafel**
f blackboard. **W~teppich** *m*
tapestry

Wange *f* -, -n cheek.

wann *adv* when

Wanne *f* -, -n tub

Wanze *f* -, -n bug

Wappen *nt* -s,- coat of arms.
W~kunde *f* heraldry

war, wäre *s.* sein[1]

Ware *f* -, -n article; (*Comm*)
commodity; (*coll*) merchandise; **W~n**
goods. **W~nhaus** *nt* department
store. **W~nprobe** *f* sample.
W~nzeichen *nt* trademark

warm *a* warm; <*Mahlzeit*> hot; **w~**
machen heat ● *adv* warmly; **w~**
essen have a hot meal

Wärm|e *f* - warmth; (*Phys*) heat; **10
Grad W~e** 10 degrees above zero.
w~en *vt* warm; heat <*Essen,
Wasser*>. **W~flasche** *f* hot-water
bottle

Warn|blinkanlage *f* hazard
[warning] lights *pl*. **w~en** *vt/i*
(*haben*) warn (*vor* + *dat* of). **W~ung**
f -, -en warning

Warteliste *f* waiting list

warten *vi* (*haben*) wait (*auf* + *acc*
for) ● *vt* service

Wärter(in) *m* -s,- (*f* -, -nen) keeper;
(*Museums-*) attendant; (*Gefängnis-*)
warder; (*Kranken-*) orderly

Warte|raum, W~saal *m*
waiting-room. **W~zimmer** *nt* (*Med*)
waiting-room

Wartung *f* - (*Techn*) service

warum *adv* why

Warze *f* -, -n wart

was *pron* what ● *rel pron* that; **alles,
was ich brauche** all [that] I need
● *indef pron* (⊞ *etwas*) something;
(*fragend, verneint*) anything; **so was
Ärgerliches!** what a nuisance! ● *adv*
⊞ (*warum*) why; (*wie*) how

wasch|bar *a* washable.
W~becken *nt* wash-basin

Wäsche *f* - washing; (*Unter-*)
underwear

waschecht *a* colour-fast

Wäscheklammer *f* clothes-peg

waschen† *vt* wash; **sich w~** have a
wash; **W~ und Legen** shampoo and
set ● *vi* (*haben*) do the washing

Wäscherei *f* -, -en laundry

Wäsche|schleuder *f* spin-drier.
W~trockner *m* tumble-drier

Wasch|küche *f* laundry-room.
W~lappen *m* face-flannel.
W~maschine *f* washing machine.
W~mittel *nt* detergent. **W~pulver**
nt washing-powder. **W~salon** *m*
launderette. **W~zettel** *m* blurb

Wasser *nt* -s water. **W~ball** *m*
beach-ball; (*Spiel*) water polo.
w~dicht *a* watertight; <*Kleidung*>
waterproof. **W~fall** *m* waterfall.
W~farbe *f* water-colour. **W~hahn**
m tap. **W~kraft** *f* water-power.
W~kraftwerk *nt* hydroelectric
power-station. **W~leitung** *f* water-
main; **aus der W~leitung** from the
tap. **W~mann** *m* (*Astr*) Aquarius

wässern *vt* soak; (*begießen*) water
● *vi* (*haben*) water

Wasser|ski *nt* -s water-skiing.
W~stoff *m* hydrogen. **W~straße** *f*
waterway. **W~waage** *f* spirit-level

wässrig *a* watery

watscheln vi (sein) waddle

Watt nt -s,- (Phys) watt

Watt|e f - cotton wool. **w~iert** a padded; (gesteppt) quilted

WC /veˈtseː/ nt -s, -s WC

web|en vt/i (haben) weave. **W~er** m -s,- weaver. **W~stuhl** m loom

Website /webˈsaɪt/ f -s, -s web site

Wechsel m -s,- change; (Tausch) exchange; (Comm) bill of exchange. **W~geld** nt change. **w~haft** a changeable. **W~jahre** npl menopause sg. **W~kurs** m exchange rate. **w~n** vt change; (tauschen) exchange ● vi (haben) change; vary. **w~nd** a changing; varying. **W~strom** m alternating current. **W~stube** f bureau de change

weck|en vt wake [up]; (fig) awaken ● vi (haben) <Wecker:> go off. **W~er** m -s,- alarm [clock]

wedeln vi (haben) wave; mit dem Schwanz w~ wag its tail

weder conj w~ ... noch neither ... nor

Weg m -[e]s, -e way; (Fuß-) path; (Fahr-) track; (Gang) errand; sich auf den Weg machen set off

weg adv away, off; (verschwunden) gone; weg sein be away; (gegangen/ verschwunden) have gone; Hände weg! hands off!

wegen prep (+ gen) because of; (um ... willen) for the sake of; (bezüglich) about

weg|fahren† vi sep (sein) go away; (abfahren) leave. **w~fallen†** vi sep (sein) be dropped/(ausgelassen) omitted; (entfallen) no longer apply. **w~geben†** vt sep give away. **w~gehen†** vi sep (sein) leave, go away; (ausgehen) go out. **w~kommen†** vi sep (sein) get away; (verloren gehen) disappear; schlecht w~kommen 🔲 get a raw deal. **w~lassen†** vt sep let go; (auslassen) omit. **w~laufen†** vi sep (sein) run away. **w~räumen** vt sep put away; (entfernen) clear away.

w~schicken vt sep send away; (abschicken) send off. **w~tun†** vt sep put away; (wegwerfen) throw away

Wegweiser m -s,- signpost

weg|werfen† vt sep throw away. **w~ziehen†** v sep ● vt pull away ● vi (sein) move away

weh a sore; weh tun hurt; <Kopf, Rücken:> ache; jdm weh tun hurt s.o.

wehe int alas; w~ [dir/euch]! (drohend) don't you dare!

wehen vi (haben) blow; (flattern) flutter ● vt blow

Wehen fpl contractions

Wehr[1] nt -[e]s, -e weir

Wehr[2] f sich zur W~ setzen resist. **W~dienst** m military service. **W~dienstverweigerer** m -s,- conscientious objector

wehren (sich) vr resist; (gegen Anschuldigung) protest; (sich sträuben) refuse

wehr|los a defenceless. **W~macht** f armed forces pl. **W~pflicht** f conscription

Weib nt -[e]s, -er woman; (Ehe-) wife. **W~chen** nt -s,- (Zool) female. **w~lich** a feminine; (Biol) female

weich a soft; (gar) done

Weiche f -, -n (Rail) points pl

Weich|heit f - softness. **w~lich** a soft; <Charakter> weak. **W~spüler** m -s,- (Tex) conditioner. **W~tier** nt mollusc

Weide[1] f -, -n (Bot) willow

Weide[2] f -, -n pasture. **w~n** vt/i (haben) graze

weiger|n (sich) vr refuse. **W~ung** f -, -en refusal

Weihe f -, -n consecration; (Priester-) ordination. **w~n** vt consecrate; (zum Priester) ordain

Weiher m -s,- pond

Weihnacht|en nt -s & pl Christmas. **w~lich** a Christmassy. **W~sbaum** m Christmas tree. **W~slied** nt Christmas carol. **W~smann** m (pl -männer) Father Christmas. **W~stag** m erster/ zweiter W~stag Christmas Day/ Boxing Day

---

Weih|rauch *m* incense.
 W~wasser *nt* holy water

weil *conj* because; (*da*) since

Weile *f* - while

Wein *m* -[e]s, -e wine; (*Bot*) vines *pl*;
 (*Trauben*) grapes *pl*. **W~bau** *m*
 wine-growing. **W~berg** *m*
 vineyard. **W~brand** *m* -[e]s brandy

weinen *vt/i* (*haben*) cry, weep

Wein|glas *nt* wineglass. **W~karte**
 f wine-list. **W~lese** *f* grape harvest.
 W~liste *f* wine-list. **W~probe** *f*
 wine-tasting. **W~rebe** *f*, **W~stock**
 m vine. **W~stube** *f* wine-bar.
 W~traube *f* bunch of grapes;
 (*W~beere*) grape

weise *a* wise

Weise *f* -, -n way; (*Melodie*) tune

Weisheit *f* -, -en wisdom.
 W~szahn *m* wisdom tooth

weiß *a*, **W~** *nt* -,- white

weissag|en *vt/i insep* (*haben*)
 prophesy. **W~ung** *f* -, -en prophecy

Weiß|brot *nt* white bread. **W~e(r)**
 m/f white man/woman. **w~en** *vt*
 whitewash. **W~wein** *m* white wine

Weisung *f* -, -en instruction;
 (*Befehl*) order

weit *a* wide; (*ausgedehnt*) extensive;
 (*lang*) long ● *adv* widely; <*offen,*
 öffnen> wide; (*lang*) far; **von w~em**
 from a distance; **bei w~em** by far;
 w~ und breit far and wide; **ist es**
 noch w~? is it much further? **so**
 w~ wie möglich as far as possible;
 ich bin so w~ I'm ready; **w~**
 verbreitet widespread; **w~ reichende**
 Folgen far-reaching consequences

Weite *f* -, -n expanse; (*Entfernung*)
 distance; (*Größe*) width. **w~n** *vt*
 widen; stretch <*Schuhe*>

weiter *a* further ● *adv* further;
 (*außerdem*) in addition;
 (*anschließend*) then; **etw w~ tun** go
 on doing sth; **w~ nichts/niemand**
 nothing/no one else; **und so w~** and
 so on

weiter|e(r,s) *a* further; **ohne w~es**
 just like that; (*leicht*) easily

weiter|erzählen *vt sep* go on
 with; (*w~sagen*) repeat.

w~fahren† *vi sep* (*sein*) go on.
 w~geben† *vt sep* pass on. **w~hin**
 adv (*immer noch*) still; (*in Zukunft*)
 in future; (*außerdem*) furthermore;
 etw w~hin tun go on doing sth.
 w~machen *vi sep* (*haben*) carry
 on

weit|gehend *a* extensive ● *adv* to
 a large extent. **w~sichtig** *a* long-
 sighted; (*fig*) far-sighted.
 W~sprung *m* long jump.
 w~verbreitet* *a* **w~ verbreitet**, *s.*
 weit

Weizen *m* -s wheat

welch *inv pron* what; **w~ ein(e)**
 what a. **w~e(r,s)** *pron* which; **um**
 w~e Zeit? at what time? ● *rel pron*
 which; (*Person*) who ● *indef pron*
 some; (*fragend*) any; **was für w~e?**
 what sort of?

Wellblech *nt* corrugated iron

Well|e *f* -, -n wave; (*Techn*) shaft.
 W~enlänge *f* wavelength.
 W~enlinie *f* wavy line.
 W~enreiten *nt* surfing.
 W~ensittich *m* -s, -e budgerigar.
 w~ig *a* wavy

Welt *f* -, -en world; **auf der W~** in the
 world; **auf die** *od* **zur W~ kommen** be
 born. **W~all** *nt* universe.
 w~berühmt *a* world-famous.
 w~fremd *a* unworldly. **W~kugel**
 f globe. **w~lich** *a* worldly; (*nicht*
 geistlich) secular

Weltmeister|(in) *m(f)* world
 champion. **W~schaft** *f* world
 championship

Weltraum *m* space. **W~fahrer** *m*
 astronaut

Weltrekord *m* world record

wem *pron* (*dat of* **wer**) to whom

wen *pron* (*acc of* **wer**) whom

Wende *f* -, -n change. **W~kreis** *m*
 (*Geog*) tropic

Wendeltreppe *f* spiral staircase

wenden¹ *vt* (*reg*) turn ● *vi* (*haben*)
 turn [round]

wenden²† (*& reg*) *vt* turn; **sich w~**
 turn; **sich an jdn w~** turn/
 (*schriftlich*) write to s.o.

Wend|epunkt *m* (*fig*) turning-
 point. **W~ung** *f* -, -en turn;

(*Biegung*) bend; (*Veränderung*) change

wenig *pron* little; (*pl*) few; **so/zu w~** so/too little/(*pl*) few; **w~e** *pl* few ● *adv* little; (*kaum*) not much; **so w~ wie möglich** as little as possible. **w~er** *pron* less; (*pl*) fewer; **immer w~er** less and less ● *adv & conj* less. **w~ste(r,s)** least; **am w~sten** least [of all]. **w~stens** *adv* at least

wenn *conj* if; (*sobald*) when; **immer w~** whenever; **w~ nicht** *od* **außer w~** unless; **w~ auch** even though

wer *pron* who; (🔲 *jemand*) someone; (*fragend*) anyone

Werbe|agentur *f* advertising agency. **w~n†** *vt* recruit; attract <*Kunden, Besucher*> ● *vi* (*haben*) **w~n für** advertise; canvass for <*Partei*>. **W~spot** /-sp-/ *m*-**s, -s** commercial

Werbung *f* - advertising

werden†
● *intransitive verb* (*sein*)
····➤ (+ *adjective*) become; get; (*allmählich*) grow. **müde/alt/länger werden** become *or* get/grow tired/old/longer. **taub/blind/wahnsinnig werden** go deaf/blind/mad. **blass werden** become *or* turn pale. **krank werden** become *or* fall ill. **es wird warm/dunkel** it is getting warm/dark. **mir wurde schlecht/schwindlig** I began to feel sick/dizzy
····➤ (+ *noun*) become. **Arzt/Lehrer/Mutter werden** become a doctor/teacher/mother. **er will Lehrer werden** he wants to be a teacher. **was ist aus ihm geworden?** what has become of him?
····➤ **werden zu** become; turn into. **das Erlebnis wurde zu einem Albtraum** the experience became *or* turned into a nightmare. **zu Eis werden** turn into ice
● *auxiliary verb*
····➤ (*Zukunft*) will; shall. **er wird bald hier sein** he will *or* he'll soon be here. **wir werden sehen** we shall see.

es wird bald regnen it's going to rain soon
····➤ (*Konjunktiv*) **würde(n)** would. **ich würde es kaufen, wenn ...** I would buy it if .... **würden Sie so nett sein?** would you be so kind?
····➤ (*beim Passiv; pp* **worden**) be. **geliebt/geboren werden** be loved/born. **du wirst gerufen** you are being called. **er wurde gebeten** he was asked. **es wurde gemunkelt** it was rumoured. **mir wurde gesagt, dass ...** I was told that .... **das Haus ist soeben/1995 renoviert worden** the house has just been renovated/was renovated in 1995

werfen† *vt* throw; cast <*Blick, Schatten*>; **sich w~** <*Holz:*> warp

Werft *f* -, -**en** shipyard

Werk *nt* -[e]s, -e work; (*Fabrik*) works *sg*, factory; (*Trieb-*) mechanism. **W~en** *nt* -s (*Sch*) handicraft. **W~statt** *f* -,-̈**en** workshop; (*Auto-*) garage. **W~tag** *m* weekday. **w~tags** *adv* on weekdays. **w~tätig** *a* working

Werkzeug *nt* tool; (*coll*) tools *pl*

Wermut *m* -s vermouth

wert *a* **viel w~** worth a lot; **nichts w~ sein** be worthless; **jds w~ sein** be worthy of s.o. **W~** *m* -[e]s, -e value; (*Nenn-*) denomination; **im W~ von** worth. **w~en** *vt* rate

Wert|gegenstand *m* object of value. **w~los** *a* worthless. **W~minderung** *f* depreciation. **W~papier** *nt* (*Comm*) security. **W~sachen** *fpl* valuables. **w~voll** *a* valuable

Wesen *nt* -s,- nature; (*Lebe-*) being; (*Mensch*) creature

wesentlich *a* essential; (*grundlegend*) fundamental ● *adv* considerably, much

weshalb *adv* why

Wespe *f* -, -n wasp

wessen *pron* (*gen of* **wer**) whose

westdeutsch *a* West German

Weste *f* -, -n waistcoat

Westen *m* -s west

Western *m* -[s],- western

Westfalen *nt* -s Westphalia

Westindien *nt* West Indies *pl*

westlich *a* western; *<Richtung>* westerly ● *adv & prep* (+ *gen*) **w~lich [von] der Stadt** [to the] west of the town. **w~wärts** *adv* westwards

weswegen *adv* why

Wettbewerb *m* -s, -e competition

Wette *f* -, -n bet; **um die W~ laufen** race (**mit jdm** s.o.)

wetten *vt/i* (*haben*) bet (**auf** + *acc* on); **mit jdm w~** have a bet with s.o.

Wetter *nt* -s,- weather; (*Un-*) storm. **W~bericht** *m* weather report. **W~vorhersage** *f* weather forecast. **W~warte** *f* -, -n meteorological station

Wettkampf *m* contest. **W~kämpfer(in)** *m(f)* competitor. **W~lauf** *m* race. **W~rennen** *nt* race. **W~streit** *m* contest

Whisky *m* -s whisky

wichtig *a* important; **w~ nehmen** take seriously. **W~keit** *f* - importance

Wicke *f* -, -n sweet pea

Wickel *m* -s,- compress

wickeln *vt* wind; (*ein-*) wrap; (*bandagieren*) bandage; **ein Kind frisch w~** change a baby

Widder *m* -s,- ram; (*Astr*) Aries

wider *prep* (+ *acc*) against; (*entgegen*) contrary to; **w~ Willen** against one's will

widerlegen *vt insep* refute

widerlich *a* repulsive. **W~rede** *f* contradiction; **keine W~rede!** don't argue!

widerrufen† *vt/i insep* (*haben*) retract; revoke *<Befehl>*

Widersacher *m* -s,- adversary

widersetzen (sich) *vr insep* resist (**jdm/etw** s.o./sth)

widerspiegeln *vt sep* reflect

widersprechen† *vi insep* (*haben*) contradict (**jdm/etw** s.o./sth)

Widerspruch *m* contradiction; (*Protest*) protest. **w~sprüchlich** *a* contradictory. **w~spruchslos** *adv* without protest

Widerstand *m* resistance; **W~ leisten** resist. **w~sfähig** *a* resistant; (*Bot*) hardy

widerstehen† *vi insep* (*haben*) resist (**jdm/etw** s.o/sth); (*anwidern*) be repugnant (**jdm** to s.o.)

Widerstreben *nt* -s reluctance

widerwärtig *a* disagreeable

Widerwille *m* aversion, repugnance. **w~ig** *a* reluctant

widmen *vt* dedicate (*dat* to); (*verwenden*) devote (*dat* to); **sich w~en** (+ *dat*) devote oneself to. **W~ung** *f* -, -en dedication

wie *adv* how; **wie viel** how much/(*pl*) many; **um wie viel Uhr?** at what time? **wie viele?** how many? **wie ist Ihr Name?** what is your name? **wie ist das Wetter?** what is the weather like? ● *conj* as; (*gleich wie*) like; (*sowie*) as well as; (*als*) when, as; **so gut wie** as good as; **nichts wie** nothing but

wieder *adv* again; **jdn/etw w~ erkennen** recognize s.o./sth; **etw w~ verwenden/verwerten** reuse/recycle sth; **etw w~ gutmachen** make up for *<Schaden>*; redress *<Unrecht>*; (*bezahlen*) pay for sth

Wiederaufbau *m* reconstruction

wiederbekommen† *vt sep* get back. **W~belebung** *f* - resuscitation. **W~bringen†** *vt sep* bring back. **w~erkennen*** *vt sep* **w~ erkennen**, *s.* **wieder.** **w~geben†** *vt sep* give back; return; (*darstellen*) portray; (*ausdrücken, übersetzen*) render; (*zitieren*) quote. **W~geburt** *f* reincarnation

Wiedergutmachung *f* - reparation; (*Entschädigung*) compensation

wiederherstellen *vt sep* re- establish; restore *<Gebäude>*; restore to health *<Kranke>*

wiederholen *vt insep* repeat; (*Sch*) revise; **sich w~en** recur; *<Person>* repeat oneself. **w~t** *a* repeated. **W~ung** *f* -, -en repetition; (*Sch*) revision

Wieder|hören nt auf W∼hören! goodbye! **W∼käuer** m -s,- ruminant. **W∼kehr** f - return; (W∼holung) recurrence. **w∼kommen†** vi sep (sein) come back

wiedersehen* vt sep wieder sehen, s. sehen. **W∼** nt -s,- reunion; auf W∼! goodbye!

wiedervereinig|en* vt sep wieder vereinigen, s. vereinigen. **W∼ung** f reunification

wieder|verwenden* vt sep w∼ verwenden, s. wieder. **w∼verwerten*** vt sep w∼ verwerten, s. wieder

Wiege f -, -n cradle

wiegen¹† vt/i (haben) weigh

wiegen² vt (reg) rock. **W∼lied** nt lullaby

wiehern vi (haben) neigh

Wien nt -s Vienna. **W∼er** a Viennese ● m -s,- Viennese ● f -,- ≈ frankfurter. **w∼erisch** a Viennese

Wiese f -, -n meadow

Wiesel nt -s,- weasel

wieso adv why

wieviel* pron wie viel, s. wie. **w∼te(r,s)** a which; der W∼te ist heute? what is the date today?

wieweit adv how far

wild a wild; <Stamm> savage; w∼er Streik wildcat strike; w∼ wachsen grow wild. **W∼** nt -[e]s game; (Rot-) deer; (Culin) venison. **W∼e(r)** m/f savage

Wilder|er m -s,- poacher. **w∼n** vt/i (haben) poach

Wild|heger, W∼hüter m -s,- gamekeeper. **W∼leder** nt suede. **W∼nis** f - wilderness. **W∼schwein** nt wild boar. **W∼westfilm** m western

Wille m -ns will

Willenskraft f will-power

willig a willing

willkommen a welcome; w∼ heißen welcome. **W∼** nt -s welcome

wimmeln vi (haben) swarm

wimmern vi (haben) whimper

Wimpel m -s,- pennant

Wimper f -, -n [eye]lash; **W∼ntusche** f mascara

Wind m -[e]s, -e wind

Winde f -, -n (Techn) winch

Windel f -, -n nappy

winden† vt wind; make <Kranz>; in die Höhe w∼ winch up; sich w∼ wind (um round); (sich krümmen) writhe

Wind|hund m greyhound. **w∼ig** a windy. **W∼mühle** f windmill. **W∼pocken** fpl chickenpox sg. **W∼schutzscheibe** f windscreen. **W∼stille** f calm. **W∼stoß** m gust of wind. **W∼surfen** nt windsurfing

Windung f -, -en bend; (Spirale) spiral

Winkel m -s,- angle; (Ecke) corner. **W∼messer** m -s,- protractor

winken vi (haben) wave

Winter m -s,- winter. **w∼lich** a wintry; (Winter-) winter … **W∼schlaf** m hibernation; **W∼sport** m winter sports pl

Winzer m -s,- winegrower

winzig a tiny, minute

Wipfel m -s,- [tree]top

Wippe f -, -n see-saw

wir pron we; wir sind es it's us

Wirbel m -s,- eddy; (Drehung) whirl; (Trommel-) roll; (Anat) vertebra; (Haar-) crown; (Aufsehen) fuss. **w∼n** vt/i (sein/haben) whirl. **W∼säule** f spine. **W∼sturm** m cyclone. **W∼tier** nt vertebrate. **W∼wind** m whirlwind

wird s. werden

wirken vi (haben) have an effect (auf + acc on); (zur Geltung kommen) be effective; (tätig sein) work; (scheinen) seem ● vt (Tex) knit

wirklich a real. **W∼keit** f -, -en reality

wirksam a effective

Wirkung f -, -en effect. **w∼slos** a ineffective. **w∼svoll** a effective

wirr a tangled; <Haar> tousled; (verwirrt, verworren) confused

---

Wirt *m* -[e]s, -e landlord. **W~in** *f*-, -nen landlady

Wirtschaft *f* -, -en economy; (*Gast-*) restaurant; (*Kneipe*) pub. **w~en** *vi* (*haben*) manage one's finances. **w~lich** *a* economic; (*sparsam*) economical. **W~sgeld** *nt* housekeeping [money]. **W~sprüfer** *m* auditor

Wirtshaus *nt* inn; (*Kneipe*) pub

wischen *vt/i* (*haben*) wipe; wash <*Fußboden*>

wissen† *vt/i* (*haben*) know; **weißt du noch?** do you remember? **nichts w~ wollen von** not want anything to do with. **W~** *nt* -s knowledge; **meines W~s** to my knowledge

Wissenschaft *f* -, -en science. **W~ler** *m* -s,- academic; (*Natur-*) scientist. **w~lich** *a* academic; scientific

wissenswert *a* worth knowing

witter|n *vt* scent; (*ahnen*) sense. **W~ung** *f* - scent; (*Wetter*) weather

Witwe *f* -, -n widow. **W~r** *m* -s,- widower

Witz *m* -es, -e joke; (*Geist*) wit. **W~bold** *m* -[e]s, -e joker. **w~ig** *a* funny; witty

wo *adv* where; (*als*) when; (*irgendwo*) somewhere; **wo immer** wherever ● *conj* seeing that; (*obwohl*) although; (*wenn*) if

woanders *adv* somewhere else

wobei *adv* how; (*relativ*) during the course of which

Woche *f* -, -n week. **W~nende** *nt* weekend. **W~nkarte** *f* weekly ticket. **w~nlang** *adv* for weeks. **W~ntag** *m* day of the week; (*Werktag*) weekday. **w~tags** *adv* on weekdays

wöchentlich *a & adv* weekly

Wodka *m* -s vodka

wofür *adv* what ... for; (*relativ*) for which

Woge *f* -, -n wave

woher *adv* where from; **woher weißt du das?** how do you know that?

wohin *adv* where [to]; **wohin gehst du?** where are you going?

wohl *adv* well; (*vermutlich*) probably; (*etwa*) about; (*zwar*) perhaps; **w~ kaum** hardly; **sich w~ fühlen** feel well/(*behaglich*) comfortable; **jdm w~ tun** do s.o. good. **W~** *nt* -[e]s welfare, well-being; **zum W~** (+ *gen*) for the good of; **zum W~!** cheers!

Wohl|befinden *nt* well-being. **W~behagen** *nt* feeling of well-being. **W~ergehen** *nt* -s welfare. **w~erzogen** *a* well brought-up

Wohlfahrt *f* - welfare. **W~sstaat** *m* Welfare State

wohl|habend *a* prosperous, well-to-do. **w~ig** *a* comfortable. **w~schmeckend** *a* tasty

Wohlstand *m* prosperity. **W~sgesellschaft** *f* affluent society

Wohltat *f* [act of] kindness; (*Annehmlichkeit*) treat; (*Genuss*) bliss

Wohltät|er *m* benefactor. **w~ig** *a* charitable

wohl|tuend *a* agreeable. **w~tun*** *vi sep* (*haben*) **w~ tun**, *s.* wohl

Wohlwollen *nt* -s goodwill; (*Gunst*) favour. **w~d** *a* benevolent

Wohn|block *m* block of flats. **w~en** *vi* (*haben*) live; (*vorübergehend*) stay. **W~gegend** *f* residential area. **w~haft** *a* resident. **W~haus** *nt* house. **W~heim** *nt* hostel; (*Alten-*) home. **w~lich** *a* comfortable. **W~mobil** *nt* -s, -e camper. **W~ort** *m* place of residence. **W~sitz** *m* place of residence

Wohnung *f* -, -en flat; (*Unterkunft*) accommodation. **W~snot** *f* housing shortage

Wohn|wagen *m* caravan. **W~zimmer** *nt* living-room

wölb|en *vt* curve; arch <*Rücken*>. **W~ung** *f* -, -en curve; (*Archit*) vault

Wolf *m* -[e]s, ̈-e wolf; (*Fleisch-*) mincer; (*Reiß-*) shredder

Wolk|e *f* -, -n cloud. **W~enbruch** *m* cloudburst. **W~enkratzer** *m* skyscraper. **w~enlos** *a* cloudless. **w~ig** *a* cloudy

Woll|decke *f* blanket. **W~e** *f* -, -n wool

wollen†¹
● *auxiliary verb*
⸱⸱⸱➤ (*den Wunsch haben*) want to. **ich will nach Hause gehen** I want to go home. **ich wollte Sie fragen, ob …** I wanted to ask you if …
⸱⸱⸱➤ (*im Begriff sein*) be about to. **wir wollten gerade gehen** we were just about to go
⸱⸱⸱➤ (*sich in der gewünschten Weise verhalten*) will nicht refuses to. **der Motor will nicht anspringen** the engine won't *or* refuses to start
● *intransitive verb*
⸱⸱⸱➤ want to. **ob du willst oder nicht** whether you want to or not. **ganz wie du willst** just as you like
⸱⸱⸱➤ (🔲 *irgendwohin zu gehen wünschen*) **ich will nach Hause** I want to go home. **zu wem wollen Sie?** who[m] do you want to see?
⸱⸱⸱➤ (🔲 *funktionieren*) will nicht won't go. **meine Beine wollen nicht mehr** my legs are giving up 🔲
● *transitive verb*
⸱⸱⸱➤ want; (*beabsichtigen*) intend. **er will nicht, dass du ihm hilfst** he does not want you to help him. **das habe ich nicht gewollt** I never intended *or* meant that to happen

wollen² *a* woollen. **w~ig** *a* woolly. **W~sachen** *fpl* woollens.

womit *adv* what … with; (*relativ*) with which. **wonach** *adv* what … after/<*suchen*> for/<*riechen*> of; (*relativ*) after/for/of which

woran *adv* what … on/<*denken, sterben*> of; (*relativ*) on/of which; **woran hast du ihn erkannt?** how did you recognize him? **worauf** *adv* what … on/<*warten*> for; (*relativ*) on/for which; (*woraufhin*) whereupon. **woraus** *adv* what … from; (*relativ*) from which

Wort *nt* -[e]s,˝er & -e word; **jdm ins W~ fallen** interrupt s.o.

Wörterbuch *nt* dictionary

Wort|führer *m* spokesman. **w~getreu** *a* & *adv* word-for-word.

w~karg *a* taciturn. **W~laut** *m* wording

wörtlich *a* literal; (*wortgetreu*) word-for-word

wort|los *a* silent ● *adv* without a word. **W~schatz** *m* vocabulary. **W~spiel** *nt* pun, play on words

worüber *adv* what … over/<*lachen, sprechen*> about; (*relativ*) over/about which. **worum** *adv* what … round/<*bitten, kämpfen*> for; (*relativ*) round/for which; **worum geht es?** what is it about? **wovon** *adv* what … from/<*sprechen*> about; (*relativ*) from/about which. **wovor** *adv* what … in front of; <*sich fürchten*> what … of; (*relativ*) in front of which; of which. **wozu** *adv* what … to/<*brauchen, benutzen*> for; (*relativ*) to/for which; **wozu?** what for?

Wrack *nt* -s, -s wreck

wringen† *vt* wring

Wucher|preis *m* extortionate price. **W~ung** *f* -, -en growth

Wuchs *m* -es growth; (*Gestalt*) stature

Wucht *f* - force

wühlen *vi* (*haben*) rummage; (*in der Erde*) burrow ● *vt* dig

Wulst *m* -[e]s,˝e bulge; (*Fett-*) roll

wund *a* sore; **w~ reiben** chafe; **sich w~ liegen** be bedsores. **W~brand** *m* gangrene

Wunde *f* -, -n wound

Wunder *nt* -s,- wonder, marvel; (*übernatürliches*) miracle; **kein W~!** no wonder! **w~bar** *a* miraculous; (*herrlich*) wonderful. **W~kind** *nt* infant prodigy. **w~n** *vt* surprise; **sich w~n** be surprised (**über** + *acc* at). **w~schön** *a* beautiful

Wundstarrkrampf *m* tetanus

Wunsch *m* -[e]s,˝e wish; (*Verlangen*) desire; (*Bitte*) request

wünschen *vt* want; **sich** (*dat*) **etw w~** want sth; (*bitten um*) ask for sth; **jdm Glück/gute Nacht w~** wish s.o. luck/good night; **Sie w~?** can I help you? **w~swert** *a* desirable

Wunschkonzert *nt* musical request programme

wụrde, wụrde s. werden

Würde f -, -n dignity; (Ehrenrang) honour. **w~los** a undignified. **W~nträger** m dignitary. **w~voll** a dignified ● adv with dignity

wụ̈rdig a dignified; (wert) worthy

Wụrf m -[e]s,-̈e throw; (Junge) litter

Wụ̈rfel m -s,- cube; (Spiel-) dice; (Zucker-) lump. **w~n** vi (haben) throw the dice; **w~n um** play dice for ● vt throw; (in Würfel schneiden) dice. **W~zucker** m cube sugar

wụ̈rgen vt choke ● vi (haben) retch; choke (an + dat on)

Wụrm m -[e]s,-̈er worm; (Made) maggot. **w~en** vi (haben) jdn w~en ☺ rankle [with s.o.]

Wụrst f -,-̈e sausage; das ist mir W~ ☺ I couldn't care less

Wụ̈rze f -, -n spice; (Aroma) aroma

Wụrzel f -, -n root; W~n schlagen take root. **w~n** vi (haben) root

wụ̈rz|en vt season. **w~ig** a tasty; (aromatisch) aromatic; (pikant) spicy

wụ̈st a chaotic; (wirr) tangled; (öde) desolate; (wild) wild; (schlimm) terrible

Wụ̈ste f -, -n desert

Wụt f - rage, fury. **W~anfall** m fit of rage

wụ̈ten vi (haben) rage. **w~d** a furious; **w~d machen** infuriate

x /ɪks/ inv a (Math) x; ☺ umpteen. **X-Beine** ntpl knock-knees. **x-beinig, X-beinig** a knock-kneed. **x-beliebig** a ☺ any. **x-mal** adv ☺ umpteen times

Yy

Yoga /'joːga/ m & nt -[s] yoga

Zz

Zạck|e f -, -n point; (Berg-) peak; (Gabel-) prong. **z~ig** a jagged; (gezackt) serrated

zaghaft a timid; (zögernd) tentative

zäh a tough; (hartnäckig) tenacious. **z~flüssig** a viscous; <Verkehr> slow-moving. **Z~igkeit** f - toughness; tenacity

Zahl f -, -en number; (Ziffer, Betrag) figure

zahlen vt/i (haben) pay; (bezahlen) pay for; **bitte z~!** the bill please!

zählen vi (haben) count; **z~ zu** (fig) be one of/(pl) some of ● vt count; **z~ zu** add to; (fig) count among

zahlenmäßig a numerical

Zähler m -s,- meter

Zahl|grenze f fare-stage. **Z~karte** f paying-in slip. **z~los** a countless. **z~reich** a numerous; <Anzahl, Gruppe> large ● adv in large numbers. **Z~ung** f -, -en payment; **in Z~ung nehmen** take in part-exchange

Zählung f -, -en count

Zahlwort nt (pl -wörter) numeral

zahm a tame

zähmen vt tame; (fig) restrain

Zahn m -[e]s,-̈e tooth; (am Zahnrad) cog. **Z~arzt** m, **Z~ärztin** f dentist. **Z~belag** m plaque. **Z~bürste** f toothbrush. **Z~fleisch** nt gums pl. **z~los** a toothless. **Z~pasta** f -, -en

toothpaste. **Z~rad** nt cog-wheel.
Z~schmelz m enamel.
Z~schmerzen mpl toothache sg.
Z~spange f brace. **Z~stein** m
tartar. **Z~stocher** m -s,- toothpick

Zange f -, -n pliers pl; (Kneif-)
pincers pl; (Kohlen-, Zucker-) tongs
pl; (Geburts-) forceps pl

Zank m -[e]s squabble. **z~en** vr sich
z~en squabble

Zäpfchen nt -s,- (Anat) uvula;
(Med) suppository

zapfen vt tap, draw. **Z~streich** m
(Mil) tattoo

Zapf|hahn m tap. **Z~säule** f
petrol-pump

zappeln vi (haben) wriggle; <Kind:>
fidget

zart a delicate; (weich, zärtlich)
tender; (sanft) gentle. **Z~gefühl** nt
tact

zärtlich a tender; (liebevoll) loving.
Z~keit f -, -en tenderness;
(Liebkosung) caress

Zauber m -s magic; (Bann) spell.
Z~er m -s,- magician. **z~haft** a
enchanting. **Z~künstler** m
conjuror. **z~n** vi (haben) do magic;
(Zaubertricks ausführen) do
conjuring tricks ● vt produce as if
by magic. **Z~stab** m magic wand.
Z~trick m conjuring trick

Zaum m -[e]s, Zäume bridle

Zaun m -[e]s, Zäune fence

z.B. abbr (zum Beispiel) e.g.

Zebra nt -s, -s zebra. **Z~streifen** m
zebra crossing

Zeche f -, -n bill; (Bergwerk) pit

zechen vi (haben) 🗓 drink

Zeder f -, -n cedar

Zeh m -[e]s, -en toe. **Z~e** f -, -n toe;
(Knoblauch-) clove

zehn inv a, **Z~** f -, -en ten.
z~te(r,s) a tenth. **Z~tel** nt -s,-
tenth

Zeichen nt -s,- sign; (Signal) signal.
Z~setzung f - punctuation.
Z~trickfilm m cartoon

zeichn|en vt/i (haben) draw; (kenn-)
mark; (unter-) sign. **Z~ung** f -, -en
drawing

Zeige|finger m index finger. **z~n**
vt show; sich z~n appear; (sich
herausstellen) become clear ● vi
(haben) point (auf + acc to). **Z~r** m
-s,- pointer; (Uhr-) hand

Zeile f -, -n line; (Reihe) row

Zeit f -, -en time; sich (dat) Z~
lassen take one's time; es hat Z~
theres's no hurry; mit der Z~ in
time; in nächster Z~ in the near
future; zur Z~ (rechtzeitig) in time;
*(derzeit) s. zurzeit; eine Z~ lang for
a time or while

Zeit|alter nt age, era. **z~gemäß** a
modern, up-to-date. **Z~genosse** m,
Z~genossin f contemporary.
z~genössisch a contemporary.
z~ig a & adv early

zeitlich a <Dauer> in time; <Folge>
chronological. ● adv z~ begrenzt for
a limited time

zeit|los a timeless. **Z~lupe** f slow
motion. **Z~punkt** m time.
z~raubend a time-consuming.
Z~raum m period. **Z~schrift** f
magazine, periodical

Zeitung f -, -en newspaper.
Z~spapier nt newspaper

Zeit|verschwendung f waste of
time. **Z~vertreib** m pastime.
z~weise adv at times. **Z~wort** nt
(pl -wörter) verb. **Z~zünder** m time
fuse

Zelle f -, -n cell; (Telefon-) box

Zelt nt -[e]s, -e tent; (Fest-) marquee.
z~en vi (haben) camp. **Z~en** nt -s
camping. **Z~plane** f tarpaulin.
Z~platz m campsite

Zement m -[e]s cement

zen|sieren vt (Sch) mark; censor
<Presse, Film>. **Z~sur** f -, -en (Sch)
mark; (Presse-) censorship

Zentimeter m & nt centimetre.
Z~maß nt tape-measure

Zentner m -s,- [metric]
hundredweight (50 kg)

zentral a central. **Z~e** f -, -n
central office; (Partei-) headquarters

pl; (*Teleph*) exchange. **Z~heizung** *f* central heating

Zentrum *nt* -s, -tren centre

zerbrech|en† *vt/i* (*sein*) break. **z~lich** *a* fragile

zerdrücken *vt* crush

Zeremonie *f* -, -n ceremony

Zerfall *m* disintegration; (*Verfall*) decay. **z~en†** *vi* (*sein*) disintegrate; (*verfallen*) decay

zergehen† *vi* (*sein*) melt; (*sich auflösen*) dissolve

zerkleinern *vt* chop/(*schneiden*) cut up; (*mahlen*) grind

zerknüllen *vt* crumple [up]

zerkratzen *vt* scratch

zerlassen† *vt* melt

zerlegen *vt* take to pieces, dismantle; (*zerschneiden*) cut up; (*tranchieren*) carve

zerlumpt *a* ragged

zermalmen *vt* crush

zermürben *vt* (*fig*) wear down

zerplatzen *vi* (*sein*) burst

zerquetschen *vt* squash; crush

Zerrbild *nt* caricature

zerreißen† *vt* tear; (*in Stücke*) tear up; break <*Faden, Seil*> ● *vi* (*sein*) tear; break

zerren *vt* drag; pull <*Muskel*> ● *vi* (*haben*) pull (**an** + *dat* at)

zerrissen *a* torn

zerrütten *vt* ruin, wreck; shatter <*Nerven*>

zerschlagen† *vt* smash; smash up <*Möbel*>; **sich z~** (*fig*) fall through; <*Hoffnung:*> be dashed

zerschmettern *vt/i* (*sein*) smash

zerschneiden† *vt* cut; (*in Stücke*) cut up

zersplittern *vi* (*sein*) splinter; <*Glas:*> shatter ● *vt* shatter

zerspringen† *vi* (*sein*) shatter; (*bersten*) burst

Zerstäuber *m* -s,- atomizer

zerstör|en *vt* destroy; (*zunichte machen*) wreck. **Z~er** *m* -s,- destroyer. **Z~ung** *f* destruction

zerstreu|en *vt* scatter; disperse <*Menge*>; dispel <*Zweifel*>; **sich**

z~en disperse; (*sich unterhalten*) amuse oneself. **z~t** *a* absent-minded

Zertifikat *nt* -[e]s, -e certificate

zertrümmern *vt* smash [up]; wreck <*Gebäude, Stadt*>

Zettel *m* -s,- piece of paper; (*Notiz*) note; (*Bekanntmachung*) notice

Zeug *nt* -s [!] stuff; (*Sachen*) things *pl*; (*Ausrüstung*) gear; **dummes Z~** nonsense

Zeuge *m* -n, -n witness. **z~n** *vi* (*haben*) testify; **z~n von** (*fig*) show ● *vt* father. **Z~naussage** *f* testimony. **Z~nstand** *m* witness box

Zeugin *f* -, -nen witness

Zeugnis *nt* -ses, -se certificate; (*Sch*) report; (*Referenz*) reference; (*fig: Beweis*) evidence

Zickzack *m* -[e]s, -e zigzag

Ziege *f* -, -n goat

Ziegel *m* -s,- brick; (*Dach*-) tile. **Z~stein** *m* brick

ziehen† *vt* pull; (*sanfter; zücken; zeichnen*) draw; (*heraus*-) pull out; extract <*Zahn*>; raise <*Hut*>; put on <*Bremse*>; move <*Schachfigur*>; (*dehnen*) stretch; make <*Grimasse, Scheitel*>; (*züchten*) breed; grow <*Rosen*>; **nach sich z~** (*fig*) entail ● *vr* **sich z~** (*sich erstrecken*) run; (*sich verziehen*) warp ● *vi* (*haben*) pull (**an** + *dat* on/at); <*Tee, Ofen:*> draw; (*Culin*) simmer; **es zieht** there is a draught; **solche Filme z~ nicht mehr** films like that are no longer popular ● *vi* (*sein*) (*um*-) move (**nach** to); <*Menge:*> march; <*Vögel:*> migrate; <*Wolken, Nebel:*> drift

Ziehharmonika *f* accordion

Ziehung *f* -, -en draw

Ziel *nt* -[e]s, -e destination; (*Sport*) finish; (*Z~scheibe & Mil*) target; (*Zweck*) aim, goal. **z~bewusst** *a* purposeful. **z~en** *vi* (*haben*) aim (**auf** + *acc* at). **z~los** *a* aimless. **Z~scheibe** *f* target

ziemlich *a* [!] fair ● *adv* rather, fairly

Zier|de *f* -, -n ornament. **z~en** *vt* adorn

zierlich *a* dainty

Ziffer *f* -, -n figure, digit; (*Zahlzeichen*) numeral. **Z∼blatt** *nt* dial

Zigarette *f* -, -n cigarette

Zigarre *f* -, -n cigar

Zigeuner(in) *m* -s,- (*f* -, -nen) gypsy

Zimmer *nt* -s,- room. **Z∼mädchen** *nt* chambermaid. **Z∼mann** *m* (*pl* -leute) carpenter. **Z∼nachweis** *m* accommodation bureau. **Z∼pflanze** *f* house plant

Zimt *m* -[e]s cinnamon

Zink *nt* -s zinc

Zinn *m* -s tin; (*Gefäße*) pewter

Zins|en *mpl* interest *sg*; **Z∼en tragen** earn interest. **Z∼eszins** *m* -es, -en compound interest. **Z∼fuß, Z∼satz** *m* interest rate

Zipfel *m* -s,- corner; (*Spitze*) point

zirka *adv* about

Zirkel *m* -s,- [pair of] compasses *pl*; (*Gruppe*) circle

Zirkul|ation /-'tsi̯oːn/ *f* - circulation. **z∼ieren** *vi* (*sein*) circulate

Zirkus *m* -, -se circus

zirpen *vi* (*haben*) chirp

zischen *vi* (*haben*) hiss; <*Fett:*> sizzle ● *vt* hiss

Zit|at *nt* -[e]s, -e quotation. **z∼ieren** *vt/i* (*haben*) quote

Zitr|onat *nt* -[e]s candied lemon-peel. **Z∼one** *f* -, -n lemon

zittern *vi* (*haben*) tremble; (*vor Kälte*) shiver; (*beben*) shake

zittrig *a* shaky

Zitze *f* -, -n teat

zivil *a* civilian; <*Ehe, Recht*> civil. **Z∼** *nt* -s civilian clothes *pl*. **Z∼dienst** *m* community service

Zivili|sation /-'tsi̯oːn/ *f* -, -en civilization. **z∼sieren** *vt* civilize. **z∼siert** *a* civilized ● *adv* in a civilized manner

Zivilist *m* -en, -en civilian

zögern *vi* (*haben*) hesitate. **Z∼** *nt* -s hesitation. **z∼d** *a* hesitant

Zoll¹ *m* -[e]s,- inch

Zoll² *m* -[e]s,-̈e [customs] duty; (*Behörde*) customs *pl*. **Z∼abfertigung** *f* customs clearance. **Z∼beamte(r)** *m* customs officer. **z∼frei** *a* & *adv* duty-free. **Z∼kontrolle** *f* customs check

Zone *f* -, -n zone

Zoo *m* -s, -s zoo

zoologisch *a* zoological

Zopf *m* -[e]s,-̈e plait

Zorn *m* -[e]s anger. **z∼ig** *a* angry

- -

zu

● *preposition* (+ *dative*)

! Note that zu dem can become zum and zu der zur

····▶ (*Richtung*) to; (*bei Beruf*) into. **wir gehen zur Schule** we are going to school. **ich muss zum Arzt** I must go to the doctor's. **zu ... hin** towards. **er geht zum Theater/Militär** he is going into the theatre/army

····▶ (*zusammen mit*) with. **zu dem Käse gab es Wein** there was wine with the cheese. **zu etw passen** go with sth

····▶ (*räumlich; zeitlich*) at. **zu Hause** at home. **zu ihren Füßen** at her feet. **zu Ostern** at Easter. **zur Zeit** (+ *gen*) at the time of

····▶ (*preislich*) at; for. **zum halben Preis** at half price. **das Stück zu zwei Mark** at *or* for two marks each. **eine Marke zu 60 Pfennig** a 60-pfennig stamp

····▶ (*Zweck, Anlass*) for. **zu diesem Zweck** for this purpose. **zum Spaß** for fun. **zum Lesen** for reading. **zum Geburtstag bekam ich ...** for my birthday I got .... **zum ersten Mal** for the first time

····▶ (*Art und Weise*) **zu meinem Erstaunen/Entsetzen** to my surprise/horror. **zu Fuß/Pferde** on foot/horseback. **zu Dutzenden** by the dozen. **wir waren zu dritt/viert** there were three/four of us

····▶ (*Zahlenverhältnis*) to. **es steht 5 zu 3** the score is 5–3

····▶ (*Ziel, Ergebnis*) into. **zu etw werden** turn into sth

····▶ (*gegenüber*) to; towards.
freundlich/hässlich zu jdm sein be
friendly/nasty to s.o.

····▶ (*über*) on; about. **sich zu etw**
äußern to comment on sth

● *adverb*

····▶ (*allzu*) too. **zu groß/viel/weit** too
big/much/far

····▶ (*Richtung*) towards. **nach dem**
Fluss zu towards the river

····▶ (*geschlossen*) closed; (*an Schalter,*
Hahn) off. **zu sein** be closed. **Augen**
zu! close your eyes! **Tür zu!** shut the
door!

● *conjunction*

····▶ to. **etwas zu essen** something to
eat. **nicht zu glauben** unbelievable.
zu erörternde Probleme problems to
be discussed

zualler|erst *adv* first of all.
z~letzt *adv* last of all

Zubehör *nt* -s accessories *pl*

zubereit|en *vt sep* prepare.
Z~ung *f* - preparation; (*in Rezept*)
method

zubinden† *vt sep* tie [up]

zubring|en† *vt sep* spend. **Z~er** *m*
-s,- access road; (*Bus*) shuttle

Zucchini /ts:u'ki:ni/ *pl* courgettes

Zucht *f* -, -en breeding; (*Pflanzen-*)
cultivation; (*Art, Rasse*) breed; (*von*
Pflanzen) strain; (*Z~farm*) farm;
(*Pferde-*) stud

zücht|en *vt* breed; cultivate, grow
<*Rosen*>. **Z~er** *m* -s,- breeder;
grower

Zuchthaus *nt* prison

Züchtung *f* -, -en breeding;
(*Pflanzen-*) cultivation; (*Art, Rasse*)
breed; (*von Pflanzen*) strain

zucken *vi* (*haben*) twitch; (*sich z~d*
bewegen) jerk; <*Blitz:*> flash;
<*Flamme:*> flicker ● *vt* **die Achseln**
z~ shrug one's shoulders

Zucker *m* -s sugar. **Z~dose** *f*
sugar basin. **Z~guss** *m* icing.
z~krank *a* diabetic. **Z~krankheit**
f diabetes. **z~n** *vt* sugar. **Z~rohr** *nt*
sugar cane. **Z~rübe** *f* sugar beet.
Z~watte *f* candyfloss

zudecken *vt sep* cover up; (*im Bett*)
tuck up; cover <*Topf*>

zudem *adv* moreover

zudrehen *vt sep* turn off

zueinander *adv* to one another; **z~**
passen go together; **z~ halten** (*fig*)
stick together

zuerkennen† *vt sep* award (*dat* to)

zuerst *adv* first; (*anfangs*) at first

zufahr|en† *vi sep* (*sein*) **z~en auf** (+
acc) drive towards. **Z~t** *f* access;
(*Einfahrt*) drive

Zufall *m* chance; (*Zusammentreffen*)
coincidence; **durch Z~** by chance/
coincidence. **z~en†** *vi sep* (*sein*)
close, shut; **jdm z~en** <*Aufgabe:*>
fall/<*Erbe:*> go to s.o.

zufällig *a* chance, accidental ● *adv*
by chance

Zuflucht *f* refuge; (*Schutz*) shelter

zufolge *prep* (+ *dat*) according to

zufrieden *a* contented; (*befriedigt*)
satisfied; **sich z~ geben** be satisfied;
jdn z~ lassen leave s.o. in peace; **jdn**
z~ stellen satisfy s.o.; **z~ stellend**
satisfactory. **Z~heit** *f* -
contentment; satisfaction

zufrieren† *vi sep* (*sein*) freeze over

zufügen *vt sep* inflict (*dat* on); do
<*Unrecht*> (*dat* to)

Zufuhr *f* - supply

Zug *m* -[e]s,-̈e train; (*Kolonne*)
column; (*Um-*) procession; (*Mil*)
platoon; (*Vogelschar*) flock; (*Ziehen,*
Zugkraft) pull; (*Wandern, Ziehen*)
migration; (*Schluck, Luft-*) draught;
(*Atem-*) breath; (*beim Rauchen*) puff;
(*Schach-*) move; (*beim Schwimmen,*
Rudern) stroke; (*Gesichts-*) feature;
(*Wesens-*) trait

Zugabe *f* (*Geschenk*) [free] gift;
(*Mus*) encore

Zugang *m* access

zugänglich *a* accessible;
<*Mensch:*> approachable

Zugbrücke *f* drawbridge

zugeben† *vt sep* add; (*gestehen*)
admit; (*erlauben*) allow

zugehen† *vi sep* (*sein*) close; **jdm z~**
be sent to s.o.; **z~ auf** (+ *acc*) go
towards; **dem Ende z~** draw to a

close; *<Vorräte:>* run low; **auf der Party ging es lebhaft zu** the party was pretty lively

Zugehörigkeit *f* - membership

Zügel *m* -s,- rein

zugelassen *a* registered

zügel|los *a* unrestrained. **z~n** *vt* rein in; (*fig*) curb

Zuge|ständnis *nt* concession. **z~stehen†** *vt sep* grant

zügig *a* quick

Zugkraft *f* pull; (*fig*) attraction

zugleich *adv* at the same time

Zugluft *f* draught

zugreifen† *vi sep* (*haben*) grab it/ them; (*bei Tisch*) help oneself; (*bei Angebot*) jump at it; (*helfen*) lend a hand

zugrunde *adv* **z~ richten** destroy; **z~ gehen** be destroyed; (*sterben*) die; **z~ liegen** form the basis (*dat* of)

zugunsten *prep* (+ *gen*) in favour of; *<Sammlung>* in aid of

zugute *adv* **jdm/etw z~ kommen** benefit s.o./sth

Zugvogel *m* migratory bird

zuhalten† *v sep* ● *vt* keep closed; (*bedecken*) cover; **sich** (*dat*) **die Nase z~** hold one's nose

Zuhälter *m* -s,- pimp

zuhause *adv* = **zu Hause**, *s*. **Haus**. **Z~** *nt* -s,- home

zuhör|en *vi sep* (*haben*) listen (*dat* to). **Z~er(in)** *m(f)* listener

zujubeln *vi sep* (*haben*) **jdm z~** cheer s.o.

zukleben *vt sep* seal

zuknöpfen *vt sep* button up

zukommen† *vi sep* (*sein*) **z~ auf** (+ *acc*) come towards; (*sich nähern*) approach; **z~ lassen** send (**jdm** s.o.); devote *<Pflege>* (*dat* to); **jdm z~** be s.o.'s right

Zukunft *f* - future. **zukünftig** *a* future ● *adv* in future

zulächeln *vi sep* (*haben*) smile (*dat* at)

zulangen *vi sep* (*haben*) help oneself

zulassen† *vt sep* allow, permit; (*teilnehmen lassen*) admit; (*Admin*) license, register; (*geschlossen lassen*) leave closed; leave unopened *<Brief>*

zulässig *a* permissible

Zulassung *f* -, -en admission; registration; (*Lizenz*) licence

zuleide *adv* **jdm etwas z~ tun** hurt s.o.

zuletzt *adv* last; (*schließlich*) in the end

zuliebe *adv* **jdm/etw z~** for the sake of s.o./sth

zum *prep* = **zu dem**; **zum Spaß** for fun; **etw zum Lesen** sth to read

zumachen *v sep* ● *vt* close, shut; do up *<Jacke>*; seal *<Umschlag>*; turn off *<Hahn>*; (*stilllegen*) close down ● *vi* (*haben*) close, shut; (*stillgelegt werden*) close down

zumal *adv* especially ● *conj* especially since

zumindest *adv* at least

zumutbar *a* reasonable

zumute *adv* **mir ist nicht danach z~** I don't feel like it

zumut|en *vt sep* **jdm etw z~en** ask *or* expect sth of s.o.; **sich** (*dat*) **zu viel z~en** overdo things. **Z~ung** *f* - imposition

zunächst *adv* first [of all]; (*anfangs*) at first; (*vorläufig*) for the moment ● *prep* (+ *dat*) nearest to

Zunahme *f* -, -n increase

Zuname *m* surname

zünd|en *vt/i* (*haben*) ignite. **Z~er** *m* -s,- detonator, fuse. **Z~holz** *nt* match. **Z~kerze** *f* sparking-plug. **Z~schlüssel** *m* ignition key. **Z~schnur** *f* fuse. **Z~ung** *f* -, -en ignition

zunehmen† *vi sep* (*haben*) increase (**an** + *dat* in); *<Mond:>* wax; (*an Gewicht*) put on weight. **z~d** *a* increasing

Zuneigung *f* - affection

Zunft *f* -, ̈e guild

Zunge *f* -, -n tongue. **Z~nbrecher** *m* tongue-twister

zunutze *a* sich (*dat*) etw z~ machen make use of sth; (*ausnutzen*) take advantage of sth

zuoberst *adv* right at the top

zuordnen *vt sep* assign (*dat* to)

zupfen *vt/i* (*haben*) pluck (an + *dat* at); pull out <*Unkraut*>

zur *prep* = zu der; zur Schule to school; zur Zeit at present

zurate *adv* z~ ziehen consult

zurechnungsfähig *a* of sound mind

zurecht|finden† (sich) *vr sep* find one's way. **z~kommen†** *vi sep* (*sein*) cope (**mit** with); (*rechtzeitig kommen*) be in time. **z~legen** *vt sep* put out ready; sich (*dat*) eine Ausrede z~legen have an excuse all ready. **z~machen** *vt sep* get ready. **Z~weisung** *f* reprimand

zureden *vi sep* (*haben*) jdm z~ try to persuade s.o.

zurichten *vt sep* prepare; (*beschädigen*) damage; (*verletzen*) injure

zuriegeln *vt sep* bolt

zurück *adv* back; Berlin, hin und z~ return to Berlin. **z~bekommen†** *vt sep* get back. **z~bleiben†** *vi sep* (*sein*) stay behind; (*nicht mithalten*) lag behind. **z~bringen†** *vt sep* bring back; (*wieder hinbringen*) take back. **z~erstatten** *vt sep* refund. **z~fahren†** *v sep* ● *vt* drive back ● *vi* (*sein*) return, go back; (*im Auto*) drive back; (*z~weichen*) recoil. **z~finden†** *vi sep* (*haben*) find one's way back. **z~führen** *v sep* ● *vt* take back; (*fig*) attribute (**auf** + *acc* to) ● *vi* (*haben*) lead back. **z~geben†** *vt sep* give back, return. **z~geblieben** *a* retarded. **z~gehen†** *vi sep* (*sein*) go back, return; (*abnehmen*) go down; z~gehen auf (+ *acc*) (*fig*) go back to

zurückgezogen *a* secluded. **Z~heit** *f* - seclusion

zurückhalt|en† *vt sep* hold back; (*abhalten*) stop; sich z~en restrain oneself. **z~end** *a* reserved. **Z~ung** *f* - reserve

zurück|kehren *vi sep* (*sein*) return. **z~kommen†** *vi sep* (*sein*) come back, return; (*ankommen*) get back. **z~lassen†** *vt sep* leave behind; (*z~kehren lassen*) allow back. **z~legen** *vt sep* put back; (*reservieren*) keep; (*sparen*) put by; cover <*Strecke*>. **z~liegen†** *vi sep* (*haben*) be in the past; (*Sport*) be behind; das liegt lange zurück that was long ago. **z~melden (sich)** *vr sep* report back. **z~schicken** *vt sep* send back. **z~schlagen†** *v sep* ● *vi* (*haben*) hit back ● *vt* hit back; (*umschlagen*) turn back.

z~schrecken† *vi sep* (*sein*) shrink back, recoil; (*fig*) shrink (**vor** + *dat* from). **z~stellen** *vt sep* put back; (*reservieren*) keep; (*fig*) put aside; (*aufschieben*) postpone. **z~stoßen†** *v sep* ● *vt* push back ● *vi* (*sein*) reverse, back. **z~treten†** *vi sep* (*sein*) step back; (*vom Amt*) resign; (*verzichten*) withdraw. **z~weisen†** *vt sep* turn away; (*fig*) reject. **z~zahlen** *vt sep* pay back. **z~ziehen†** *vt sep* draw back; (*fig*) withdraw; sich z~ziehen withdraw; (*vom Beruf*) retire

Zuruf *m* shout. **z~en†** *vt sep* shout (*dat* to)

zurzeit *adv* at present

Zusage *f* -, -n acceptance; (*Versprechen*) promise. **z~n** *v sep* ● *vt* promise ● *vi* (*haben*) accept

zusammen *adv* together; (*insgesamt*) altogether; z~ sein be together. **Z~arbeit** *f* co-operation. **z~arbeiten** *vi sep* (*haben*) co-operate. **z~bauen** *vt sep* assemble. **z~bleiben†** *vi sep* (*sein*) stay together. **z~brechen†** *vi sep* (*sein*) collapse. **Z~bruch** *m* collapse; (*Nerven-* & *fig*) breakdown. **z~fallen†** *vi sep* (*sein*) collapse; (*zeitlich*) coincide. **z~fassen** *vt sep* summarize, sum up. **Z~fassung** *f* summary. **z~fügen** *vt sep* fit together. **z~gehören** *vi sep* (*haben*) belong together; (*z~passen*) go together. **z~gesetzt** *a* (*Gram*) compound. **z~halten†** *v sep* ● *vt* hold together; (*beisammenhalten*) keep together ● *vi* (haben) (*fig*) stick together. **Z~hang** *m* connection; (*Kontext*) context. **z~hanglos** *a* incoherent. **z~klappen** *v sep* ● *vt* fold up ● *vi* (sein) collapse. **z~kommen**† *vi sep* (sein) meet; (*sich sammeln*) accumulate. **Z~kunft** *f -,-̈e* meeting. **z~laufen**† *vi sep* (sein) gather; *<Flüssigkeit:>* collect; *<Linien:>* converge. **z~leben** *vi sep* (haben) live together. **z~legen** *v sep* ● *vt* put together; (*z~falten*) fold up; (*vereinigen*) amalgamate; pool *<Geld>* ● *vi* (haben) club together. **z~nehmen**† *vt sep* gather up; summon up *<Mut>*; collect *<Gedanken>*; **sich z~nehmen** pull oneself together. **z~passen** *vi sep* (haben) go together, match. **Z~prall** *m* collision. **z~rechnen** *vt sep* add up. **z~schlagen**† *vt sep* smash up; (*prügeln*) beat up. **z~schließen**† (**sich**) *vr sep* join together; *<Firmen:>* merge. **Z~schluss** *m* union; (*Comm*) merger

Zusammensein *nt* -s get-together

zusammensetz|en *vt sep* put together; (*Techn*) assemble; **sich z~en** sit [down] together; (*bestehen*) be made up (**aus** from). **Z~ung** *f -, -en* composition; (*Techn*) assembly; (*Wort*) compound

zusammen|stellen *vt sep* put together; (*gestalten*) compile. **Z~stoß** *m* collision; (*fig*) clash. **z~treffen**† *vi sep* (sein) meet; (*zeitlich*) coincide. **z~zählen** *vt sep* add up. **z~ziehen**† *v sep* ● *vt* draw together; (*addieren*) add up; (*konzentrieren*) mass; **sich z~ziehen** contract; *<Gewitter:>* gather ● *vi* (sein) move in together; move in (**mit** with)

Zusatz *m* addition; (*Jur*) rider; (*Lebensmittel-*) additive. **zusätzlich** *a* additional ● *adv* in addition

zuschau|en *vi sep* (haben) watch. **Z~er(in)** *m* -s,- (*f* -, -nen) spectator; (*TV*) viewer

Zuschlag *m* surcharge; (*D-Zug-*) supplement. **z~pflichtig** *a <Zug>* for which a supplement is payable

zuschließen† *v sep* ● *vt* lock ● *vi* (haben) lock up

zuschneiden† *vt sep* cut out; cut to size *<Holz>*

zuschreiben† *vt sep* attribute (*dat* to); **jdm die Schuld z~** blame s.o.

Zuschrift *f* letter; (*auf Annonce*) reply

zuschulden *adv* **sich** (*dat*) **etwas z~ kommen lassen** do wrong

Zuschuss *m* contribution; (*staatlich*) subsidy

zusehends *adv* visibly

zusein* *vi sep* (sein) zu sein, *s.* zu

zusenden† *vt sep* send (*dat* to)

zusetzen *v sep* ● *vt* add; (*einbüßen*) lose

zusicher|n *vt sep* promise. **Z~ung** *f* promise.

zuspielen *vt sep* (*Sport*) pass

zuspitzen (**sich**) *vr sep* (*fig*) become critical

Zustand *m* condition, state

zustande *adv* **z~ bringen/kommen** bring/come about

zuständig *a* competent; (*verantwortlich*) responsible

zustehen† *vi sep* (haben) **jdm z~** be s.o.'s right; *<Urlaub:>* be due to s.o.

zusteigen† *vi sep* (sein) get on; **noch jemand zugestiegen?** tickets please; (*im Bus*) any more fares please?

zustell|en *vt sep* block; (*bringen*) deliver. **Z~ung** *f* delivery

zusteuern *v sep* ● *vi* (sein) head (**auf** + *acc* for) ● *vt* contribute

zustimm|en *vi sep* (haben) agree; (*billigen*) approve (*dat* of). **Z~ung** *f* consent; approval

zustoßen† *vi sep* (sein) happen (*dat* to)

Zustrom *m* influx

Zutat *f* (*Culin*) ingredient

zuteil|en *vt sep* allocate; assign *<Aufgabe>*. **Z~ung** *f* allocation

zutiefst *adv* deeply

---

zutragen† *vt sep* carry/(*fig*) report (*dat* to); **sich z~** happen

zutrau|en *vt sep* jdm etw z~ believe s.o. capable of sth. **Z~en** *nt* -s confidence

zutreffen† *vi sep* (*haben*) be correct; **z~ auf** (+ *acc*) apply to

Zutritt *m* admittance

zuunterst *adv* right at the bottom

zuverlässig *a* reliable. **Z~keit** *f* - reliability

Zuversicht *f* - confidence. **z~lich** *a* confident

zuviel* *pron & adv* zu viel, *s.* viel

zuvor *adv* before; (*erst*) first

zuvorkommen† *vi sep* (*sein*) (+ *dat*) anticipate. **z~d** *a* obliging

Zuwachs *m* -es increase

zuwege *adv* **z~ bringen** achieve

zuweilen *adv* now and then

zuweisen† *vt sep* assign

Zuwendung *f* donation; (*Fürsorge*) care

zuwenig* *pron & adv* zu wenig, *s.* wenig

zuwerfen† *vt sep* slam <*Tür*>; jdm etw z~ throw s.o. sth

zuwider *adv* jdm z~ sein be repugnant to s.o. ● *prep* (+ *dat*) contrary to

zuzahlen *vt sep* pay extra

zuziehen† *v sep* ● *vt* pull tight; draw <*Vorhänge*>; (*hinzu-*) call in; **sich** (*dat*) **etw z~** contract <*Krankheit*>; sustain <*Verletzung*>; incur <*Zorn*> ● *vi* (*sein*) move into the area

zuzüglich *prep* (+ *gen*) plus

Zwang *m* -[e]s,ᵉ compulsion; (*Gewalt*) force; (*Verpflichtung*) obligation

zwängen *vt* squeeze

zwanglos *a* informal. **Z~igkeit** *f* - informality

Zwangsjacke *f* straitjacket

zwanzig *inv a* twenty. **z~ste(r,s)** *a* twentieth

zwar *adv* admittedly

Zweck *m* -[e]s, -e purpose; (*Sinn*) point. **z~los** *a* pointless. **z~mäßig** *a* suitable; (*praktisch*) functional

zwei *inv a*, **Z~** *f* -, -en two; (*Sch*) ≈ B. **Z~bettzimmer** *nt* twin-bedded room

zweideutig *a* ambiguous

zwei|erlei *inv a* two kinds of ● *pron* two things. **z~fach** *a* double

Zweifel *m* -s,- doubt. **z~haft** *a* doubtful; (*fragwürdig*) dubious. **z~los** *adv* undoubtedly. **z~n** *vi* (*haben*) doubt (**an etw** *dat* sth)

Zweig *m* -[e]s, -e branch. **Z~stelle** *f* branch [office]

Zwei|kampf *m* duel. **z~mal** *adv* twice. **z~reihig** *a* <*Anzug*> double-breasted. **z~sprachig** *a* bilingual

zweit *adv* **zu z~** in twos; **wir waren zu z~** there were two of us. **z~beste(r,s)** *a* second-best. **z~e(r,s)** *a* second

zweitens *adv* secondly

Zwerchfell *nt* diaphragm

Zwerg *m* -[e]s, -e dwarf

Zwickel *m* -s,- gusset

zwicken *vt/i* (*haben*) pinch

Zwieback *m* -[e]s,ᵉ rusk

Zwiebel *f* -, -n onion; (*Blumen-*)bulb

Zwielicht *nt* half-light; (*Dämmerlicht*) twilight. **z~ig** *a* shady

Zwiespalt *m* conflict

Zwilling *m* -s, -e twin; **Z~e** (*Astr*) Gemini

zwingen† *vt* force; **sich z~** force oneself. **z~d** *a* compelling

Zwinger *m* -s,- run; (*Zucht-*) kennels *pl*

zwinkern *vi* (*haben*) blink; (*als Zeichen*) wink

Zwirn *m* -[e]s button thread

zwischen *prep* (+ *dat*/*acc*) between; (*unter*) among[st]. **Z~bemerkung** *f* interjection. **z~durch** *adv* in between; (*in der Z~zeit*) in the meantime. **Z~fall** *m* incident. **Z~landung** *f* stopover. **Z~raum** *m* gap, space. **Z~wand** *f* partition. **Z~zeit** *f* in der Z~zeit in the meantime

Zwist *m* -[e]s, -e discord; (*Streit*) feud

zwitschern *vi* (*haben*) chirp

zwo *inv a* two

zwölf *inv a* twelve. **z~te(r,s)** *a* twelfth

Zylind|er *m* -s,- cylinder; (*Hut*) top hat. **z~risch** *a* cylindrical

Zyn|iker *m* -s,- cynic. **z~isch** *a* cynical. **Z~ismus** *m* - cynicism

Zypern *nt* -s Cyprus

Zypresse *f* -, -n cypress

Zyste /'tsɪːystə/ *f* -, -n cyst

English–German Dictionary

Aa

a

vor einem Vokal **an**

●*indefinite article*

····▸ ein (*m*), eine (*f*), ein (*nt*). **a problem** ein Problem. **an apple** ein Apfel. **a cat** eine Katze. **have you got a pencil?** hast du einen Bleistift? **I gave it to a beggar** ich gab es einem Bettler

! There are some cases where **a** is not translated, such as when talking about people's professions or nationalities: **she is a lawyer** sie ist Rechsanwältin. **he's an Italian** er ist Italiener

····▸ (*with 'not'*) kein (*m*), keine (*f*), kein (*nt*), keine (*pl*). **that's not a problem/not a good idea** das ist kein Problem/keine gute Idee. **there was not a chance that …** es bestand keine Möglichkeit, dass …. **she did not say a word** sie sagte kein Wort. **I didn't tell a soul** ich habe es keinem Menschen gesagt

····▸ (*per; each*) pro. **£300 a week** 300 Pfund pro Woche. **30 miles an hour** 30 Meilen pro Stunde. (*in prices*) **it costs 90p a pound** es kostet 90 Pence das Pfund.

aback *adv* **be taken ~** verblüfft sein

abandon *vt* verlassen; (*give up*) aufgeben

abate *vi* nachlassen

abattoir *n* Schlachthof *m*

abb|ey *n* Abtei *f*. **~ot** *n* Abt *m*

abbreviat|e *vt* abkürzen. **~ion** *n* Abkürzung *f*

abdicat|e *vi* abdanken. **~ion** *n* Abdankung *f*

abdom|en *n* Unterleib *m*. **~inal** *a* Unterleibs-

abduct *vt* entführen. **~ion** *n* Entführung *f*

aberration *n* Abweichung *f*; (*mental*) Verwirrung *f*

abeyance *n* **in ~** [zeitweilig] außer Kraft

abhor *vt* (*pt/pp* abhorred) verabscheuen. **~rent** *a* abscheulich

abid|e *vt* (*pt/pp* abided) (*tolerate*) aushalten; ausstehen <*person*>

ability *n* Fähigkeit *f*; (*talent*) Begabung *f*

abject *a* erbärmlich; (*humble*) demütig

ablaze *a* in Flammen

able *a* (-r, -st) fähig; **be ~ to do sth** etw tun können. **~-bodied** *a* körperlich gesund

ably *adv* gekonnt

abnormal *a* anormal; (*Med*) abnorm. **~ity** *n* Abnormität *f*. **~ly** *adv* ungewöhnlich

aboard *adv & prep* an Bord (+ *gen*)

abol|ish *vt* abschaffen. **~ition** *n* Abschaffung *f*

abominable *a*, **-bly** *adv* abscheulich

aborigines *npl* Ureinwohner *pl*

abort *vt* abtreiben. **~ion** *n* Abtreibung *f*. **~ive** *a* <*attempt*> vergeblich

about *adv* umher, herum; (*approximately*) ungefähr; **be ~** (*in circulation*) umgehen; (*in existence*) vorhanden sein; **be ~ to do sth** im Begriff sein, etw zu tun; **there was no one ~** es war kein Mensch da; **run/play ~** herumlaufen/-spielen ●*prep* um (+ *acc*) […herum]; (*concerning*) über (+ *acc*); **what is it ~?** worum geht es? <*book:*> wovon handelt es? **I know nothing ~ it** ich weiß nichts davon; **talk/know ~** reden/wissen von

about: ~-face *n*, **~-turn** *n* Kehrtwendung *f*

above *adv* oben ●*prep* über (+ *dat/ acc*); **~ all** vor allem

above: ~-board *a* legal. **~-mentioned** *a* oben erwähnt

abrasive *a* Scheuer-; *<remark>* verletzend ● *n* Scheuermittel *nt*; (*Techn*) Schleifmittel *nt*

abreast *adv* nebeneinander; **keep ~** of Schritt halten mit

abridge *vt* kürzen

abroad *adv* im Ausland; **go ~** ins Ausland fahren

abrupt *a*, **-ly** *adv* abrupt; (*sudden*) plötzlich; (*curt*) schroff

abscess *n* Abszess *m*

absence *n* Abwesenheit *f*

absent *a* abwesend; **be ~** fehlen

absentee *n* Abwesende(r) *m/f*

absent-minded *a*, **-ly** *adv* geistesabwesend; (*forgetful*) zerstreut

absolute *a*, **-ly** *adv* absolut

absorb *vt* absorbieren, aufsaugen; **~ed in** vertieft in (+ *acc*). **~ent** *a* saugfähig

absorption *n* Absorption *f*

abstain *vi* sich enthalten (**from** *gen*)

abstemious *a* enthaltsam

abstention *n* (*Pol*) [Stimm]enthaltung *f*

abstract *a* abstrakt ● *n* (*summary*) Abriss *m*

absurd *a*, **-ly** *adv* absurd. **~ity** *n* Absurdität *f*

abundan|ce *n* Fülle *f* (**of** an + *dat*). **~t** *a* reichlich

abuse[1] *vt* missbrauchen; (*insult*) beschimpfen

abus|e[2] *n* Missbrauch *m*; (*insults*) Beschimpfungen *pl*. **~ive** ausfallend

abysmal *a* 🄳 katastrophal

abyss *n* Abgrund *m*

academic *a*, **-ally** *adv* akademisch

academy *n* Akademie *f*

accelerat|e *vt/i* beschleunigen. **~ion** *n* Beschleunigung *f*. **~or** *n* (*Auto*) Gaspedal *nt*

accent *n* Akzent *m*

accept *vt* annehmen; (*fig*) akzeptieren ● *vi* zusagen. **~able** *a* annehmbar. **~ance** *n* Annahme *f*; (*of invitation*) Zusage *f*

access *n* Zugang *m*. **~ible** *a* zugänglich

accessor|y *n* (*Jur*) Mitschuldige(r) *m/f*; **~ies** *pl* (*fashion*) Accessoires *pl*; (*Techn*) Zubehör *nt*

accident *n* Unfall *m*; (*chance*) Zufall *m*; **by ~** zufällig; (*unintentionally*) versehentlich. **~al**, **-ly** *adv* zufällig; (*unintentional*) versehentlich

acclaim *vt* feiern (**as** als)

acclimatize *vt* **become ~d** sich akklimatisieren

accommodat|e *vt* unterbringen. **~ing** *a* entgegenkommend. **~ion** *n* (*rooms*) Unterkunft *f*

accompan|iment *n* Begleitung *f*. **~ist** *n* (*Mus*) Begleiter(in) *m(f)*

accompany *vt* (*pt/pp* **-ied**) begleiten

accomplice *n* Komplize/-zin *m/f*

accomplish *vt* erfüllen *<task>*; (*achieve*) erreichen. **~ed** *a* fähig. **~ment** *n* Fertigkeit *f*; (*achievement*) Leistung *f*

accord *n* **of one's own ~** aus eigenem Antrieb. **~ance** *n* **in ~ance with** entsprechend (+ *dat*)

according *adv* **~ to** nach (+ *dat*). **~ly** *adv* entsprechend

accordion *n* Akkordeon *nt*

account *n* Konto *nt*; (*bill*) Rechnung *f*; (*description*) Darstellung *f*; (*report*) Bericht *m*; **~s** *pl* (*Comm*) Bücher *pl*; **on ~ of** wegen (+ *gen*); **on no ~** auf keinen Fall; **take into ~** in Betracht ziehen, berücksichtigen ● *vi* **~ for** Rechenschaft ablegen für; (*explain*) erklären

accountant *n* Buchhalter(in) *m(f)*; (*chartered*) Wirtschaftsprüfer *m*

accumulat|e *vt* ansammeln, anhäufen ● *vi* sich ansammeln, sich anhäufen. **~ion** *n* Ansammlung *f*, Anhäufung *f*

accura|cy *n* Genauigkeit *f*. **~te** *a*, **-ly** *adv* genau

accusation *n* Anklage *f*

accusative *a & n* **~ [case]** (*Gram*) Akkusativ *m*

accuse *vt* (*Jur*) anklagen (**of** *gen*); **~ s.o. of doing sth** jdn beschuldigen, etw getan zu haben

accustom vt gewöhnen (to an + dat); grow or get ~ed to sich gewöhnen an (+ acc). ~ed a gewohnt

ace n (Cards, Sport) Ass nt

ache n Schmerzen pl ● vi weh tun, schmerzen

achieve vt leisten; (gain) erzielen; (reach) erreichen. ~ment n (feat) Leistung f

acid a sauer; (fig) beißend ● n Säure f. ~ity n Säure f. ~ rain n saurer Regen m

acknowledge vt anerkennen; (admit) zugeben; erwidern <greeting>; ~ receipt of den Empfang bestätigen (+ gen). ~ment n Anerkennung f; (of letter) Empfangsbestätigung f

acne n Akne f

acorn n Eichel f

acoustic a, -ally adv akustisch. ~s npl Akustik f

acquaint vt be ~ed with kennen; vertraut sein mit <fact>. ~ance n (person) Bekannte(r) m/f; make s.o.'s ~ance jdn kennen lernen

acquire vt erwerben

acquisit|ion n Erwerb m; (thing) Erwerbung f. ~ive a habgierig

acquit vt (pt/pp acquitted) freisprechen

acre n ≈ Morgen m

acrimonious a bitter

acrobat n Akrobat(in) m(f). ~ic a akrobatisch

across adv hinüber/herüber; (wide) breit; (not lengthwise) quer; (in crossword) waagerecht; come ~ sth auf etw (acc) stoßen; go ~ hinübergehen; bring ~ herüberbringen ● prep über (+ acc); (on the other side of) auf der anderen Seite (+ gen)

act n Tat f; (action) Handlung f; (law) Gesetz nt; (Theat) Akt m; (item) Nummer f ● vi handeln; (behave) sich verhalten; (Theat) spielen; (pretend) sich verstellen; ~ as fungieren als ● vt spielen <role>.

~ing a (deputy) stellvertretend ● n (Theat) Schauspielerei f

action n Handlung f; (deed) Tat f; (Mil) Einsatz m; (Jur) Klage f; (effect) Wirkung f; (Techn) Mechanismus m; out of ~ <machine:> außer Betrieb; take ~ handeln; killed in ~ gefallen

activate vt betätigen

activ|e a, -ly adv aktiv; on ~e service im Einsatz. ~ity n Aktivität f

act|or n Schauspieler m. ~ress n Schauspielerin f

actual a, -ly adv eigentlich; (real) tatsächlich

acupuncture n Akupunktur f

acute a scharf; <angle> spitz; <illness> akut. ~ly adv sehr

ad n ⚠ = advertisement

AD abbr (Anno Domini) n.Chr.

adamant a be ~ that darauf bestehen, dass

adapt vt anpassen; bearbeiten <play> ● vi sich anpassen. ~able a anpassungsfähig

adaptation n (Theat) Bearbeitung f

add vt hinzufügen; (Math) addieren ● vi zusammenzählen, addieren; ~ to hinzufügen zu; (fig: increase) steigern; (compound) verschlimmern. ~ up vt zusammenzählen <figures> ● vi zusammenzählen, addieren

adder n Kreuzotter f

addict n Süchtige(r) m/f

addict|ed a süchtig; ~ed to drugs drogensüchtig. ~ion n Sucht f

addition n Hinzufügung f; (Math) Addition f; (thing added) Ergänzung f; in ~ zusätzlich. ~al a, -ly adv zusätzlich

additive n Zusatz m

address n Adresse f, Anschrift f; (speech) Ansprache f ● vt adressieren (to an + acc); (speak to) anreden <person>; sprechen vor (+ dat) <meeting>. ~ee n Empfänger m

adequate a, -ly adv ausreichend

adhere vi kleben/(fig) festhalten (to an + dat)

adhesive a klebend ● n Klebstoff m

adjacent *a* angrenzend

adjective *n* Adjektiv *nt*

adjoin *vt* angrenzen an (+ *acc*). ~**ing** *a* angrenzend

adjourn *vt* vertagen (**until** auf + *acc*) ● *vi* sich vertagen. ~**ment** *n* Vertagung *f*

adjudicate *vi* (*in competition*) Preisrichter sein

adjust *vt* einstellen; (*alter*) verstellen ● *vi* sich anpassen (**to** *dat*). ~**able** *a* verstellbar. ~**ment** *n* Einstellung *f*; Anpassung *f*

ad lib *adv* aus dem Stegreif ● *vi* (*pt/pp* ad libbed) 🔲 improvisieren

administer *vt* verwalten; verabreichen <*medicine*>

administration *n* Verwaltung *f*; (*Pol*) Regierung *f*

admirable *a* bewundernswert

admiral *n* Admiral *m*

admiration *n* Bewunderung *f*

admire *vt* bewundern. ~**r** *n* Verehrer(in) *m(f)*

admission *n* Eingeständnis *nt*; (*entry*) Eintritt *m*

admit *vt* (*pt/pp* admitted) (*let in*) hereinlassen; (*acknowledge*) zugeben; ~ **to sth** etw zugeben. ~**tance** *n* Eintritt *m*. ~**tedly** *adv* zugegebenermaßen

admonish *vt* ermahnen

adolescen|ce *n* Jugend *f*, Pubertät *f*. ~**t** *a* Jugend-; <*boy, girl*> halbwüchsig ● *n* Jugendliche(r) *m/f*

adopt *vt* adoptieren; ergreifen <*measure*>; (*Pol*) annehmen <*candidate*>. ~**ion** *n* Adoption *f*

ador|able *a* bezaubernd. ~**ation** *n* Anbetung *f*

adore *vt* (*worship*) anbeten; (🔲 *like*) lieben

adorn *vt* schmücken. ~**ment** *n* Schmuck *m*

Adriatic *a & n* ~ [Sea] Adria *f*

adrift *a* **be** ~ treiben

adroit *a*, **-ly** *adv* gewandt, geschickt

adulation *n* Schwärmerei *f*

adult *n* Erwachsene(r) *m/f*

adulterate *vt* verfälschen; panschen <*wine*>

adultery *n* Ehebruch *m*

advance *n* Fortschritt *m*; (*Mil*) Vorrücken *nt*; (*payment*) Vorschuss *m*; **in** ~ im Voraus ● *vi* vorankommen; (*Mil*) vorrücken; (*make progress*) Fortschritte machen ● *vt* fördern <*cause*>; vorbringen <*idea*>; vorschießen <*money*>. ~**d** *a* fortgeschritten; (*progressive*) fortschrittlich. ~**ment** *n* Förderung *f*; (*promotion*) Beförderung *f*

advantage *n* Vorteil *m*; **take** ~ **of** ausnutzen. ~**ous** *a* vorteilhaft

adventur|e *n* Abenteuer *nt*. ~**er** *n* Abenteurer *m*. ~**ous** *a* abenteuerlich; <*person*> abenteuerlustig

adverb *n* Adverb *nt*

adverse *a* ungünstig

advert *n* 🔲 = advertisement

advertise *vt* Reklame machen für; (*by small ad*) inserieren ● *vi* Reklame machen; inserieren

advertisement *n* Anzeige *f*; (*publicity*) Reklame *f*; (*small ad*) Inserat *nt*

advertis|er *n* Inserent *m*. ~**ing** *n* Werbung *f*

advice *n* Rat *m*

advisable *a* ratsam

advis|e *vt* raten (**s.o.** jdm); (*counsel*) beraten; (*inform*) benachrichtigen; ~**e s.o. against sth** jdm von etw abraten ● *vi* raten. ~**er** *n* Berater(in) *m(f)*. ~**ory** *a* beratend

advocate[1] *n* (*supporter*) Befürworter *m*

advocate[2] *vt* befürworten

aerial *a* Luft- ● *n* Antenne *f*

aerobics *n* Aerobic *nt*

aero|drome *n* Flugplatz *m*. ~**plane** *n* Flugzeug *nt*

aerosol *n* Spraydose *f*

aesthetic *a* ästhetisch

affair *n* Angelegenheit *f*, Sache *f*; (*scandal*) Affäre *f*; **[love-]**~ [Liebes]verhältnis *nt*

affect *vt* sich auswirken auf (+ *acc*); (*concern*) betreffen; (*move*) rühren;

(*pretend*) vortäuschen. ~**ation** *n* Affektiertheit *f.* ~**ed** *a* affektiert

affection *n* Liebe *f.* ~**ate** *a*, **-ly** *adv* liebevoll

affirm *vt* behaupten

affirmative *a* bejahend ● *n* Bejahung *f*

afflict *vt* be ~ed with behaftet sein mit. ~**ion** *n* Leiden *nt*

affluen|ce *n* Reichtum *m.* ~**t** *a* wohlhabend. ~**t society** *n* Wohlstandsgesellschaft *f*

afford *vt* be able to ~ sth sich (*dat*) etw leisten können. ~**able** *a* erschwinglich

affront *n* Beleidigung *f* ● *vt* beleidigen

afloat *a* be ~ <*ship:*> flott sein; keep ~ <*person:*> sich über Wasser halten

afraid *a* be ~ Angst haben (of vor + *dat*); I'm ~ not leider nicht; I'm ~ so [ja] leider

Africa *n* Afrika *nt.* ~**n** *a* afrikanisch ● *n* Afrikaner(in) *m(f)*

after *adv* danach ● *prep* nach (+ *dat*); ~ that danach; ~ all schließlich; the day ~ tomorrow übermorgen; be ~ aus sein auf (+ *acc*) ● *conj* nachdem

after: ~**-effect** *n* Nachwirkung *f.* ~**math** *n* Auswirkungen *pl.* ~**noon** *n* Nachmittag *m;* good ~noon! guten Tag! ~**sales service** *n* Kundendienst *m.* ~**shave** *n* Rasierwasser *nt.* ~**thought** *n* nachträglicher Einfall *m.* ~**wards** *adv* nachher

again *adv* wieder; (*once more*) noch einmal; ~ and ~ immer wieder

against *prep* gegen (+ *acc*)

age *n* Alter *nt;* (*era*) Zeitalter *nt;* ~s [i] ewig; under ~ minderjährig; of ~ volljährig; two years of ~ zwei Jahre alt ● *v* (*pres p* ageing) ● *vt* älter machen ● *vi* altern; (*mature*) reifen

aged[1] *a* ~ two zwei Jahre alt

aged[2] *a* betagt ● *n* the ~ *pl* die Alten

ageless *a* ewig jung

agency *n* Agentur *f;* (*office*) Büro *nt*

agenda *n* Tagesordnung *f*

agent *n* Agent(in) *m(f);* (*Comm*) Vertreter(in) *m(f);* (*substance*) Mittel *nt*

aggravat|e *vt* verschlimmern; ([i] annoy) ärgern. ~**ion** *n* [i] Ärger *m*

aggregate *a* gesamt ● *n* Gesamtzahl *f;* (*sum*) Gesamtsumme *f*

aggress|ion *n* Aggression *f.* ~**ive** *a*, **-ly** *adv* aggressiv. ~**or** *n* Angreifer(in) *m(f)*

aggro *n* [i] Ärger *m*

aghast *a* entsetzt

agil|e *a* flink, behände; <*mind*> wendig. ~**ity** *n* Flinkheit *f,* Behändigkeit *f*

agitat|e *vt* bewegen; (*shake*) schütteln ● *vi* (*fig*) ~ for agitieren für. ~**ed** *a*, **-ly** *adv* erregt. ~**ion** *n* Erregung *f;* (*Pol*) Agitation *f*

ago *adv* vor (+ *dat*); a long time ~ vor langer Zeit; how long ~ is it? wie lange ist es her?

agony *n* Qual *f;* be in ~ furchtbare Schmerzen haben

agree *vt* vereinbaren; (*admit*) zugeben; ~ to do sth sich bereit erklären, etw zu tun ● *vi* <*people, figures:*> übereinstimmen; (*reach agreement*) sich einigen; (*get on*) gut miteinander auskommen; (*consent*) einwilligen (to in + *acc*); ~ with s.o. jdm zustimmen; <*food:*> jdm bekommen; ~ with sth (*approve of*) mit etw einverstanden sein

agreeable *a* angenehm

agreed *a* vereinbart

agreement *n* Übereinstimmung *f;* (*consent*) Einwilligung *f;* (*contract*) Abkommen *nt;* reach ~ sich einigen

agricultur|al *a* landwirtschaftlich. ~**e** *n* Landwirtschaft *f*

aground *a* gestrandet; run ~ <*ship:*> stranden

ahead *adv* straight ~ geradeaus; be ~ of s.o./sth vor jdm/etw sein; (*fig*) voraus sein; go on ~ vorgehen; get ~ vorankommen; go ~! [i] bitte! look/plan ~ vorausblicken/-planen

aid n Hilfe f; (financial)
Unterstützung f; in ∼ of zugunsten
(+ gen) ● vt helfen (+ dat)

Aids n Aids nt

aim n Ziel nt; take ∼ zielen ● vt
richten (at auf + acc); ● vi zielen (at
auf + acc); ∼ to do sth
beabsichtigen, etw zu tun. ∼less a,
-ly adv ziellos

air n Luft f; (expression) Miene f;
(appearance) Anschein m; be on the
∼ <programme:> gesendet werden;
<person:> auf Sendung sein; by ∼
auf dem Luftweg; (airmail) mit
Luftpost ● vt lüften; vorbringen
<views>

air: ∼-**conditioned** a klimatisiert.
∼-**conditioning** n Klimaanlage f.
∼**craft** n Flugzeug nt. ∼**field** n
Flugplatz m. ∼ **force** n Luftwaffe f.
∼ **freshener** n Raumspray nt.
∼**gun** n Flieger m. ∼ **hostess**
n Stewardess f. ∼ **letter** n
Aerogramm nt. ∼**line** n
Fluggesellschaft f. ∼**mail** n Luftpost
f. ∼**man** n Flieger m. ∼**plane** n
(Amer) Flugzeug nt. ∼**port** n
Flughafen m. ∼-**raid** n Luftangriff
m. ∼-**raid shelter** n
Luftschutzbunker m. ∼**ship** n
Luftschiff nt. ∼ **ticket** n Flugschein
m. ∼**tight** a luftdicht. ∼-**traffic
controller** n Fluglotse m

airy a (-ier, -iest) luftig; <manner>
nonchalant

aisle n Gang m

ajar a angelehnt

alarm n Alarm m; (device)
Alarmanlage f; (clock) Wecker m;
(fear) Unruhe f ● vt erschrecken

alas int ach!

album n Album nt

alcohol n Alkohol m. ∼**ic** a
alkoholisch ● n Alkoholiker(in) m(f).
∼**ism** n Alkoholismus m

alert a aufmerksam ● n Alarm m

algebra n Algebra f

Algeria n Algerien nt

alias n Deckname m ● adv alias

alibi n Alibi nt

alien a fremd ● n Ausländer(in) m(f)

alienate vt entfremden

alight¹ vi aussteigen (from aus)

alight² a be ∼ brennen; set ∼
anzünden

align vt ausrichten. ∼**ment** n
Ausrichtung f

alike a & adv ähnlich; (same) gleich;
look ∼ sich (dat) ähnlich sehen

alive a lebendig; be ∼ leben; be ∼
with wimmeln von

all
● adjective
····▸ (plural) alle. all [the] children alle
Kinder. all our children alle unsere
Kinder. all the books alle Bücher. all
the others alle anderen
····▸ (singular = whole) ganz. all the
wine der ganze Wein. all the town die
ganze Stadt. all my money mein
ganzes Geld; all mein Geld. all day
den ganzen Tag. all Germany ganz
Deutschland
● pronoun
····▸ (plural = all persons/things) alle.
all are welcome alle sind
willkommen. they all came sie sind
alle gekommen. are we all here? sind
wir alle da? the best pupils of all die
besten Schüler (von allen). the most
beautiful of all der/die/das schönste
von allen
····▸ (singular = everything) alles. that
is all das ist alles. all that I possess
alles, was ich besitze
····▸ all of ganz; (with plural) alle. all of
the money das ganze Geld. all of the
paintings alle Gemälde. all of you/
them Sie/sie alle
····▸ (in phrases) all in all alles in
allem. in all insgesamt. most of all
am meisten. once and for all ein für
alle Mal. not at all gar nicht
● adverb
····▸ (completely) ganz. she was all
alone sie war ganz allein. I was all
dirty ich war ganz schmutzig
····▸ (in scores) four all vier zu vier
····▸ all right (things) in Ordnung. is
everything all right? ist alles in
Ordnung? is that all right for you?
passt das Ihnen? I'm all right mir
geht es gut. did you get home all

right? sind Sie gut nach Hause gekommen? **is it all right to go in?** kann ich reingehen? **yes, all right** ja, gut. **work out all right** gut gehen; klappen ⚠

····▶ *(in phrases)* **all but** *(almost)* fast. **all at once** auf einmal. **all the better** umso besser. **all the same** *(nevertheless)* trotzdem

allege *vt* behaupten

allegiance *n* Treue *f*

allerg|ic *a* allergisch (**to** gegen). **~y** *n* Allergie *f*

alleviate *vt* lindern

alley *n* Gasse *f*; *(for bowling)* Bahn *f*

alliance *n* Verbindung *f*; *(Pol)* Bündnis *nt*

allied *a* alliiert

alligator *n* Alligator *m*

allocat|e *vt* zuteilen; *(share out)* verteilen. **~ion** *n* Zuteilung *f*

allot *vt* (*pt/pp* **allotted**) zuteilen (**s.o.** jdm)

allow *vt* erlauben; *(give)* geben; *(grant)* gewähren; *(reckon)* rechnen; *(agree, admit)* zugeben; **~ for** berücksichtigen; **~ s.o. to do sth** jdm erlauben, etw zu tun; **be ~ed to do sth** etw tun dürfen

allowance *n* [finanzielle] Unterstützung *f*; **make ~s for** berücksichtigen

alloy *n* Legierung *f*

allude *vi* anspielen (**to** auf + *acc*)

allusion *n* Anspielung *f*

ally¹ *n* Verbündete(r) *m/f*; **the Allies** *pl* die Alliierten

ally² *vt* (*pt/pp* **-ied**) verbinden; **~ oneself with** sich verbünden mit

almighty *a* allmächtig; (⚠ *big*) Riesen-. ● *n* **the A~** der Allmächtige

almond *n* *(Bot)* Mandel *f*

almost *adv* fast, beinahe

alone *a* & *adv* allein; **leave me ~** lass mich in Ruhe; **leave that ~!** lass die Finger davon! **let ~** ganz zu schweigen von

along *prep* entlang (+ *acc*); **~ the river** den Fluss entlang ● *adv* **~ with** zusammen mit; **all ~** die ganze Zeit;

come ~ komm doch; **I'll bring it ~** ich bringe es mit

alongside *adv* daneben ● *prep* neben (+ *dat*)

aloud *adv* laut

alphabet *n* Alphabet *nt*. **~ical** *a*, **-ly** *adv* alphabetisch

alpine *a* alpin; **A~** Alpen-

Alps *npl* Alpen *pl*

already *adv* schon

Alsace *n* Elsass *nt*

Alsatian *n* *(dog)* [deutscher] Schäferhund *m*

also *adv* auch

altar *n* Altar *m*

alter *vt* ändern ● *vi* sich verändern. **~ation** *n* Änderung *f*

alternate¹ *vi* [sich] abwechseln ● *vt* abwechseln

alternate² *a*, **-ly** *adv* abwechselnd; **on ~ days** jeden zweiten Tag

alternative *a* andere(r,s); **~ medicine** Alternativmedizin *f* ● *n* Alternative *f*. **~ly** *adv* oder aber

although *conj* obgleich, obwohl

altitude *n* Höhe *f*

altogether *adv* insgesamt; *(on the whole)* alles in allem

aluminium *n*, *(Amer)* **aluminum** *n* Aluminium *nt*

always *adv* immer

am *see* be

a.m. *abbr* (**ante meridiem**) vormittags

amass *vt* anhäufen

amateur *n* Amateur *m* ● *attrib* Amateur-; *(Theat)* Laien-. **~ish** *a* laienhaft

amaze *vt* erstaunen. **~d** *a* erstaunt. **~ment** *n* Erstaunen *nt*

amazing *a*, **-ly** *adv* erstaunlich

ambassador *n* Botschafter *m*

amber *n* Bernstein *m* ● *a* *(colour)* gelb

ambigu|ity *n* Zweideutigkeit *f*. **~ous** *a* **-ly** *adv* zweideutig

ambiti|on *n* Ehrgeiz *m*; *(aim)* Ambition *f*. **~ous** *a* ehrgeizig

amble *vi* schlendern

ambulance *n* Krankenwagen *m*. **~ man** *n* Sanitäter *m*

ambush n Hinterhalt m ● vt aus
dem Hinterhalt überfallen

amen int amen

amend vt ändern. ~**ment** n
Änderung f

amenities npl Einrichtungen pl

America n Amerika nt. ~**n** a
amerikanisch ● n Amerikaner(in)
m(f). ~**nism** n Amerikanismus m

amiable a nett

amicable a, -**bly** adv
freundschaftlich; <agreement>
gütlich

amid[st] prep inmitten (+ gen)

ammonia n Ammoniak nt

ammunition n Munition f

amnesty n Amnestie f

among[st] prep unter (+ dat/acc);
~ **yourselves** untereinander

amoral a amoralisch

amorous a zärtlich

amount n Menge f; (sum of money)
Betrag m; (total) Gesamtsumme f
● vi ~ **to** sich belaufen auf (+ acc);
(fig) hinauslaufen auf (+ acc)

amphibi|an n Amphibie f. ~**ous** a
amphibisch

amphitheatre n Amphitheater nt

ample a (-r, -st), -**ly** adv reichlich;
(large) füllig

amplif|ier n Verstärker m. ~**y** vt
(pt/pp -ied) weiter ausführen;
verstärken <sound>

amputat|e vt amputieren. ~**ion** n
Amputation f

amuse vt amüsieren, belustigen;
(entertain) unterhalten. ~**ment** n
Belustigung f; Unterhaltung f

amusing a amüsant

an see a

anaem|ia n Blutarmut f, Anämie f.
~**ic** a blutarm

anaesthetic n Narkosemittel nt,
Betäubungsmittel nt; **under [an]** ~ in
Narkose

anaesthetist n Narkosearzt m

analogy n Analogie f

analyse vt analysieren

analysis n Analyse f

analyst n Chemiker(in) m(f); (Psych)
Analytiker m

analytical a analytisch

anarch|ist n Anarchist m. ~**y** n
Anarchie f

anatom|ical a, -**ly** adv anatomisch.
~**y** n Anatomie f

ancest|or n Vorfahr m. ~**ry** n
Abstammung f

anchor n Anker m ● vi ankern ● vt
verankern

ancient a alt

and conj und; ~ **so on** und so weiter;
six hundred ~ **two**
sechshundertzwei; **more** ~ **more**
immer mehr; **nice** ~ **warm** schön
warm

anecdote n Anekdote f

angel n Engel m. ~**ic** a engelhaft

anger n Zorn m ● vt zornig machen

angle n Winkel m; (fig) Standpunkt
m; **at an** ~ schräg

angler n Angler m

Anglican a anglikanisch ● n
Anglikaner(in) m(f)

Anglo-Saxon a angelsächsich ● n
Angelsächsisch nt

angry a (-ier, -iest), -**ily** adv zornig;
be ~ **with** böse sein auf (+ acc)

anguish n Qual f

angular a eckig; <features> kantig

animal n Tier nt ● a tierisch

animat|e vt beleben. ~**ed** a lebhaft

animosity n Feindseligkeit f

ankle n [Fuß]knöchel m

annex[e] n Nebengebäude nt;
(extension) Anbau m

annihilate vt vernichten

anniversary n Jahrestag m

annotate vt kommentieren

announce vt bekannt geben; (over
loudspeaker) durchsagen; (at
reception) ankündigen; (Radio, TV)
ansagen; (in newspaper) anzeigen.
~**ment** n Bekanntgabe f,
Bekanntmachung f; Durchsage f;
Ansage f; Anzeige f. ~**r** n
Ansager(in) m(f)

annoy vt ärgern; (pester) belästigen; get ~ed sich ärgern. ~ance n Ärger m. ~ing a ärgerlich

annual a, **-ly** adv jährlich ● n (book) Jahresalbum nt

anonymous a, **-ly** adv anonym

anorak n Anorak m

anorexi|a n Magersucht f. ~c a be ~c an Magersucht leiden

another a & pron ein anderer/eine andere/ein anderes; (additional) noch ein(e); ~ [one] noch einer/ eine/eins; ~ time ein andermal; one ~ einander

answer n Antwort f; (solution) Lösung f ● vt antworten (s.o. jdm); beantworten <question, letter>; ~ the door/telephone an die Tür/ans Telefon gehen ● vi antworten; (Teleph) sich melden; ~ back eine freche Antwort geben. ~ing machine n (Teleph) Anrufbeantworter m

ant n Ameise f

antagonis|m n Antagonismus m. ~tic a feindselig

Antarctic n Antarktis f

antelope n Antilope f

antenatal a ~ care Schwangerschaftsfürsorge f

antenna n Fühler m; (Amer: aerial) Antenne f

anthem n Hymne f

anthology n Anthologie f

anthropology n Anthropologie f

antibiotic n Antibiotikum nt

anticipat|e vt vorhersehen; (forestall) zuvorkommen (+ dat); (expect) erwarten. ~ion n Erwartung f

anticlimax n Enttäuschung f

anticlockwise a & adv gegen den Uhrzeigersinn

antics npl Mätzchen pl

antidote n Gegengift nt

antifreeze n Frostschutzmittel nt

antipathy n Abneigung f, Antipathie f

antiquated a veraltet

antique a antik ● n Antiquität f. ~ dealer n Antiquitätenhändler m

antiquity n Altertum nt

antiseptic a antiseptisch ● n Antiseptikum nt

antisocial a asozial; [🛈] ungesellig

antlers npl Geweih nt

anus n After m

anvil n Amboss m

anxiety n Sorge f

anxious a, **-ly** adv ängstlich; (worried) besorgt; be ~ to do sth etw gerne machen wollen

any a irgendein(e); pl irgendwelche; (every) jede(r,s); pl alle; (after negative) kein(e); pl keine; ~ colour/number you like eine beliebige Farbe/Zahl; have you ~ wine/apples? haben Sie Wein/Äpfel? ● pron [irgend]einer/eine/eins; pl [irgend]welche; (some) welche(r,s); pl welche; (all) alle pl; (negative) keiner/keine/keins; pl keine; I don't want ~ of it ich will nichts davon; there aren't ~ es gibt keine ● adv noch; ~ quicker/slower noch schneller/langsamer; is it ~ better? geht es etwas besser? would you like ~ more? möchten Sie noch [etwas]? I can't eat ~ more ich kann nichts mehr essen

anybody pron [irgend]jemand; (after negative) niemand; ~ can do that das kann jeder

anyhow adv jedenfalls; (nevertheless) trotzdem; (badly) irgendwie

anyone pron = anybody

anything pron [irgend]etwas; (after negative) nichts; (everything) alles

anyway adv jedenfalls; (in any case) sowieso

anywhere adv irgendwo; (after negative) nirgendwo; <be, live> überall; <go> überallhin

apart adv auseinander; live ~ getrennt leben; ~ from abgesehen von

apartment n Zimmer nt; (flat) Wohnung f

ape n [Menschen]affe m ● vt nachäffen

aperitif n Aperitif m

apologetic a, **-ally** adv entschuldigend; be ~ sich entschuldigen

apologize vi sich entschuldigen (to bei)

apology n Entschuldigung f

apostle n Apostel m

apostrophe n Apostroph m

appal vt (pt/pp **appalled**) entsetzen. ~**ling** a entsetzlich

apparatus n Apparatur f; (Sport) Geräte pl; (single piece) Gerät nt

apparent a offenbar; (seeming) scheinbar. ~**ly** adv offenbar, anscheinend

appeal n Appell m, Aufruf m; (request) Bitte f; (attraction) Reiz m; (Jur) Berufung f ● vi appellieren (to an + acc); (ask) bitten (for um); (be attractive) zusagen (to dat); (Jur) Berufung einlegen. ~**ing** a ansprechend

appear vi erscheinen; (seem) scheinen; (Theat) auftreten. ~**ance** n Erscheinen nt; (look) Aussehen nt; to all ~ances allem Anschein nach

appendicitis n Blinddarmentzündung f

appendix n (pl **-ices**) (of book) Anhang m ● (pl **-es**) (Anat) Blinddarm m

appetite n Appetit m

appetizing a appetitlich

applau|d vt/i Beifall klatschen (+ dat). ~**se** n Beifall m

apple n Apfel m

appliance n Gerät nt

applicable a anwendbar (to auf + acc); (on form) not ~ nicht zutreffend

applicant n Bewerber(in) m(f)

application n Anwendung f; (request) Antrag m; (for job) Bewerbung f; (diligence) Fleiß m

applied a angewandt

apply vt (pt/pp **-ied**) auftragen <paint>; anwenden <force, rule> ● vi

zutreffen (to auf + acc); ~ for beantragen; sich bewerben um <job>

appoint vt ernennen; (fix) festlegen. ~**ment** n Ernennung f; (meeting) Verabredung f; (at doctor's, hairdresser's) Termin m; (job) Posten m; make an ~ment sich anmelden

appreciable a merklich; (considerable) beträchtlich

appreciat|e vt zu schätzen wissen; (be grateful for) dankbar sein für; (enjoy) schätzen; (understand) verstehen ● vi (increase in value) im Wert steigen. ~**ion** n (gratitude) Dankbarkeit f. ~**ive** a dankbar

apprehens|ion n Festnahme f; (fear) Angst f. ~**ive** a ängstlich

apprentice n Lehrling m. ~**ship** n Lehre f

approach n Näherkommen nt; (of time) Nahen nt; (access) Zugang m; (road) Zufahrt f ● vi sich nähern; <time:> nahen ● vt sich nähern (+ dat); (with request) herantreten an (+ acc); (set about) sich heranmachen an (+ acc). ~**able** a zugänglich

appropriate a angebracht, angemessen

approval n Billigung f; on ~ zur Ansicht

approv|e vt billigen ● vi ~e of sth/ s.o. mit etw/jdm einverstanden sein. ~**ing** a, **-ly** adv anerkennend

approximate a, **-ly** adv ungefähr

approximation n Schätzung f

apricot n Aprikose f

April n April m; make an ~ fool of in den April schicken

apron n Schürze f

apt a, **-ly** adv passend; be ~ to do sth dazu neigen, etw zu tun

aqualung n Tauchgerät nt

aquarium n Aquarium nt

aquatic a Wasser-

Arab a arabisch ● n Araber(in) m(f). ~**ian** a arabisch

Arabic a arabisch

arbitrary a, **-ily** adv willkürlich

arbitrat|e vi schlichten. ~**ion** n Schlichtung f

arc n Bogen m

arcade n Laubengang m; (shops) Einkaufspassage f

arch n Bogen m; (of foot) Gewölbe nt ● vt ~ its back <cat:> einen Buckel machen

archaeological a archäologisch

archaeolog|ist n Archäologe m/ -login f. ~y n Archäologie f

archaic a veraltet

archbishop n Erzbischof m

archer n Bogenschütze m. ~y n Bogenschießen nt

architect n Architekt(in) m(f). ~ural a, -ly adv architektonisch

architecture n Architektur f

archives npl Archiv nt

archway n Torbogen m

Arctic a arktisch ● n the ~ die Arktis

ardent a, -ly adv leidenschaftlich

ardour n Leidenschaft f

arduous a mühsam

are see be

area n (surface) Fläche f; (Geom) Flächeninhalt m; (region) Gegend f; (fig) Gebiet nt

arena n Arena f

Argentina n Argentinien nt

Argentin|e, ~ian a argentinisch

argue vi streiten (about über + acc); <two people:> sich streiten; (debate) diskutieren; **don't ~!** keine Widerrede! ● vt (debate) diskutieren; (reason) ~ **that** argumentieren, dass

argument n Streit m, Auseinandersetzung f; (reasoning) Argument nt; **have an** ~ sich streiten. ~**ative** a streitlustig

aria n Arie f

arise vi (pt arose, pp arisen) sich ergeben (from aus)

aristocracy n Aristokratie f

aristocrat n Aristokrat(in) m(f). ~**ic** a aristokratisch

arithmetic n Rechnen nt

arm n Arm m; (of chair) Armlehne f; ~**s** pl (weapons) Waffen pl; (Heraldry) Wappen nt ● vt bewaffnen

armament n Bewaffnung f; ~**s** pl Waffen pl

armchair n Sessel m

armed a bewaffnet; ~ **forces** Streitkräfte pl

armour n Rüstung f. ~**ed** a Panzer-

armpit n Achselhöhle f

army n Heer nt; (specific) Armee f; **join the** ~ zum Militär gehen

aroma n Aroma nt, Duft m. ~**tic** a aromatisch

arose see arise

around adv [all] ~ rings herum; **he's not** ~ er ist nicht da; **travel** ~ herumreisen ● prep um (+ acc) … herum; (approximately) gegen

arouse vt aufwecken; (excite) erregen

arrange vt arrangieren; anordnen <furniture, books>; (settle) abmachen. ~**ment** n Anordnung f; (agreement) Vereinbarung f; (of flowers) Gesteck nt; **make** ~**ments** Vorkehrungen treffen

arrest n Verhaftung f; **under** ~ verhaftet ● vt verhaften

arrival n Ankunft f; **new** ~**s** pl Neuankömmlinge pl

arrive vi ankommen; ~ **at** (fig) gelangen zu

arrogan|ce n Arroganz f. ~**t** a, -ly adv arrogant

arrow n Pfeil m

arse n (vulg) Arsch m

arson n Brandstiftung f. ~**ist** n Brandstifter m

art n Kunst f; **work of** ~ Kunstwerk nt; ~**s and crafts** pl Kunstgewerbe nt; **A**~**s** pl (Univ) Geisteswissenschaften pl

artery n Schlagader f, Arterie f

art gallery n Kunstgalerie f

arthritis n Arthritis f

artichoke n Artischocke f

article n Artikel m; (object) Gegenstand m; ~ **of clothing** Kleidungsstück nt

artificial a, -ly adv künstlich

artillery n Artillerie f

artist n Künstler(in) m(f)

artiste n (Theat) Artist(in) m(f)

artistic a, -ally adv künstlerisch

as conj (because) da; (when) als; (while) während ● prep als; **as a child/foreigner** als Kind/Ausländer ● adv **as well** auch; **as soon as** sobald; **as much as** so viel wie; **as quick as** so schnell wie du; **as you know** wie Sie wissen; **as far as I'm concerned** was mich betrifft

asbestos n Asbest m

ascend vi [auf]steigen ● vt besteigen <throne>

ascent n Aufstieg m

ascertain vt ermitteln

ash¹ n (tree) Esche f

ash² n Asche f

ashamed a beschämt; **be ~** sich schämen (of über + acc)

ashore adv an Land

ashtray n Aschenbecher m

Asia n Asien nt. **~n** a asiatisch ● n Asiat(in) m(f). **~tic** a asiatisch

aside adv beiseite

ask vt/i fragen; stellen <question>; (invite) einladen; **~ for** bitten um; verlangen <s.o.>; **~ after** sich erkundigen nach; **~ s.o. in** jdn hereinbitten; **~ s.o. to do sth** jdn bitten, etw zu tun

asleep a **be ~** schlafen; **fall ~** einschlafen

asparagus n Spargel m

aspect n Aspekt m

asphalt n Asphalt m

aspire vi **~ to** streben nach

ass n Esel m

assail vt bestürmen. **~ant** n Angreifer(in) m(f)

assassin n Mörder(in) m(f). **~ate** vt ermorden. **~ation** n [politischer] Mord m

assault n (Mil) Angriff m; (Jur) Körperverletzung f ● vt [tätlich] angreifen

assemble vi sich versammeln ● vt versammeln; (Techn) montieren

assembly n Versammlung f; (Sch) Andacht f; (Techn) Montage f. **~ line** n Fließband nt

assent n Zustimmung f

assert vt behaupten; **~ oneself** sich durchsetzen. **~ion** n Behauptung f

assess vt bewerten; (fig & for tax purposes) einschätzen: schätzen <value>. **~ment** n Einschätzung f; (of tax) Steuerbescheid m

asset n Vorteil m; **~s** pl (money) Vermögen nt; (Comm) Aktiva pl

assign vt zuweisen (to dat). **~ment** n (task) Aufgabe f

assist vt/i helfen (+ dat). **~ance** n Hilfe f. **~ant** a Hilfs- ● n Assistent(in) m(f); (in shop) Verkäufer(in) m(f)

associat|e¹ vt verbinden; (Psych) assoziieren ● vi **~ with** verkehren mit. **~ion** n Verband m

associate² a assoziiert ● n Kollege m/-gin f

assort|ed a gemischt. **~ment** n Mischung f

assum|e vt annehmen; übernehmen <office>; **~ing that** angenommen, dass

assumption n Annahme f; **on the ~** in der Annahme (that dass)

assurance n Versicherung f; (confidence) Selbstsicherheit f

assure vt versichern (s.o. jdm); **I ~ you [of that]** das versichere ich Ihnen. **~d** a sicher

asterisk n Sternchen nt

asthma n Asthma nt

astonish vt erstaunen. **~ing** a erstaunlich. **~ment** n Erstaunen nt

astray adv **go ~** verloren gehen; <person:> sich verlaufen

astride adv rittlings ● prep rittlings auf (+ dat/acc)

astrolog|er n Astrologe m/-gin f. **~y** n Astrologie f

astronaut n Astronaut(in) m(f)

astronom|er n Astronom m. **~ical** a astronomisch. **~y** n Astronomie f

astute a scharfsinnig

asylum n Asyl nt; **[lunatic] ~** Irrenanstalt f

at
● preposition

····▶ (*expressing place*) an (+ *dat*). **at
the station** am Bahnhof. **at the end**
am Ende. **at the corner** an der Ecke.
at the same place an der gleichen
Stelle

····▶ (*at s.o.'s house or shop*) bei (+ *dat*).
at Lisa's bei Lisa. **at my uncle's** bei
meinem Onkel. **at the baker's/
butcher's** beim Bäcker/Fleischer

····▶ (*inside a building*) in (+ *dat*). **at
the theatre/supermarket** im Theater/
Supermarkt. **we spent the night at a
hotel** wir übernachteten in einem
Hotel. **he is still at the office** er ist
noch im Büro

····▶ (*expressing time*) (*with clock time*)
um; (*with main festivals*) zu. **at six
o'clock** um sechs Uhr. **at midnight**
um Mitternacht. **at midday** um zwölf
Uhr mittags. **at Christmas/Easter** zu
Weihnachten/Ostern

····▶ (*expressing age*) mit. **at [the age
of] forty** mit vierzig; im Alter von
vierzig

····▶ (*expressing price*) zu. **at £2.50
[each]** zu *od* für [je] 2,50 Pfund

····▶ (*expressing speed*) mit. **at 30 m.p.h.**
mit dreißig Meilen pro Stunde

····▶ (*in phrases*) **good/bad at
languages** gut/schlecht in Sprachen.
two at a time zwei auf einmal. **at that**
(*at that point*) dabei; (*at that
provocation*) daraufhin; (*moreover*)
noch dazu

ate *see* eat
atheist *n* Atheist(in) *m(f)*
athlet|e *n* Athlet(in) *m(f)*. **~ic** *a*
sportlich. **~ics** *n* Leichtathletik *f*
Atlantic *a* & *n* the **~** [Ocean] der
Atlantik
atlas *n* Atlas *m*
atmosphere *n* Atmosphäre *f*
atom *n* Atom *nt*. **~ bomb** *n*
Atombombe *f*
atomic *a* Atom-
atrocious *a* abscheulich
atrocity *n* Gräueltat *f*
attach *vt* befestigen (**to** an + *dat*);
beimessen <*importance*> (**to** *dat*); **be
~ed to** (*fig*) hängen an (+ *dat*)
attack *n* Angriff *m*; (*Med*) Anfall *m*
● *vt/i* angreifen. **~er** *n* Angreifer *m*

attain *vt* erreichen. **~able** *a*
erreichbar
attempt *n* Versuch *m* ● *vt*
versuchen
attend *vt* anwesend sein bei; (*go
regularly to*) besuchen; (*take part in*)
teilnehmen an (+ *dat*); (*accompany*)
begleiten; <*doctor:*> behandeln ● *vi*
anwesend sein; (*pay attention*)
aufpassen; **~ to** sich kümmern um;
(*in shop*) bedienen. **~ance** *n*
Anwesenheit *f*; (*number*)
Besucherzahl *f*. **~ant** *n* Wärter(in)
m(f); (*in car park*) Wächter *m*
attention *n* Aufmerksamkeit *f*; **~!**
(*Mil*) stillgestanden! **pay ~**
aufpassen; **pay ~ to** beachten,
achten auf (+ *acc*)
attentive *a*, **-ly** *adv* aufmerksam
attic *n* Dachboden *m*
attitude *n* Haltung *f*
attorney *n* (*Amer: lawyer*)
Rechtsanwalt *m*; **power of ~**
Vollmacht *f*
attract *vt* anziehen; erregen
<*attention*>; **~ s.o.'s attention** jds
Aufmerksamkeit auf sich (*acc*)
lenken. **~ion** *n* Anziehungskraft *f*;
(*charm*) Reiz *m*; (*thing*) Attraktion *f*.
~ive *a*, **-ly** *adv* attraktiv
attribute *vt* zuschreiben (**to** *dat*)
aubergine *n* Aubergine *f*
auburn *a* kastanienbraun
auction *n* Auktion *f*, Versteigerung *f*
● *vt* versteigern. **~eer** *n*
Auktionator *m*
audaci|ous *a*, **-ly** *adv* verwegen.
~ty *n* Verwegenheit *f*; (*impudence*)
Dreistigkeit *f*
audible *a*, **-bly** *adv* hörbar
audience *n* Publikum *nt*; (*Theat,
TV*) Zuschauer *pl*; (*Radio*) Zuhörer
pl; (*meeting*) Audienz *f*
audit *n* Bücherrevision *f* ● *vt*
(*Comm*) prüfen
audition *n* (*Theat*) Vorsprechen *nt*;
(*Mus*) Vorspielen *nt*; (*for singer*)
Vorsingen *nt* ● *vi* vorsprechen;
vorspielen; vorsingen
auditor *n* Buchprüfer *m*
auditorium *n* Zuschauerraum *m*

August n August m

aunt n Tante f

au pair n ~ [girl] Au-pair-Mädchen nt

aura n Fluidum nt

auspicious a günstig; <occasion> freudig

auster|e a streng; (simple) nüchtern. ~ity n Strenge f; (hardship) Entbehrung f

Australia n Australien nt. ~n a australisch ● n Australier(in) m(f)

Austria n Österreich nt ~n a österreichisch ● n Österreicher(in) m(f)

authentic a echt, authentisch. ~ate vt beglaubigen. ~ity n Echtheit f

author n Schriftsteller m, Autor m; (of document) Verfasser m

authoritarian a autoritär

authoritative a maßgebend

authority n Autorität f; (public) Behörde f; in ~ verantwortlich

authorization n Ermächtigung f

authorize vt ermächtigen <s.o.>; genehmigen <sth>

autobiography n Autobiographie f

autograph n Autogramm nt

automatic a, -ally adv automatisch

automation n Automation f

automobile n Auto nt

autonom|ous a autonom. ~y n Autonomie f

autumn n Herbst m. ~al a herbstlich

auxiliary a Hilfs- ● n Helfer(in) m(f), Hilfskraft f

avail n to no ~ vergeblich

available a verfügbar; (obtainable) erhältlich

avalanche n Lawine f

avenge vt rächen

avenue n Allee f

average a Durchschnitts-, durchschnittlich ● n Durchschnitt m; on ~ im Durchschnitt,

durchschnittlich ● vt durchschnittlich schaffen

averse a not be ~e to sth etw (dat) nicht abgeneigt sein

avert vt abwenden

aviary n Vogelhaus nt

aviation n Luftfahrt f

avocado n Avocado f

avoid vt vermeiden; ~ s.o. jdm aus dem Weg gehen. ~able a vermeidbar. ~ance n Vermeidung f

await vt warten auf (+ acc)

awake a wach; wide ~ hellwach ● vi (pt awoke, pp awoken) erwachen

awaken vt wecken ● vi erwachen. ~ing n Erwachen nt

award n Auszeichnung f; (prize) Preis m ● vt zuerkennen (to s.o. dat); verleihen <prize>

aware a become ~ gewahr werden (of gen); be ~ that wissen, dass. ~ness n Bewusstsein nt

away adv weg, fort; (absent) abwesend; **four kilometres** ~ vier Kilometer entfernt; **play** ~ (Sport) auswärts spielen. ~ **game** n Auswärtsspiel nt

awful a, -ly adv furchtbar

awkward a schwierig; (clumsy) ungeschickt; (embarrassing) peinlich; (inconvenient) ungünstig. ~ly adv ungeschickt; (embarrassedly) verlegen

awning n Markise f

awoke(n) see awake

axe n Axt f ● vt (pres p axing) streichen

axle n (Techn) Achse f

Bb

B n (Mus) H nt

baboon n Pavian m

baby n Baby nt; (Amer 🔲) Schätzchen nt

baby: ~**ish** a kindisch. ~**-sit** vi babysitten. ~**-sitter** n Babysitter m

bachelor n Junggeselle m

back n Rücken m; (reverse) Rückseite f; (of chair) Rückenlehne f; (Sport) Verteidiger m; **at**/(Auto) in the ~ hinten; **on the** ~ auf der Rückseite; ~ **to front** verkehrt ● a Hinter- ● adv zurück; ~ **here**/**there** hier/da hinten; ~ **at home** zu Hause; **go**/**pay** ~ zurückgehen/-zahlen ● vt (support) unterstützen; (with money) finanzieren; (Auto) zurücksetzen; (Betting) [Geld] setzen auf (+ acc); (cover the back of) mit einer Verstärkung versehen ● vi (Auto) zurücksetzen. ~ **down** vi klein beigeben. ~ **in** vi rückwärts hineinfahren. ~ **out** vi rückwärts hinaus-/herausfahren; (fig) aussteigen (of aus). ~ **up** vt unterstützen; (confirm) bestätigen ● vi (Auto) zurücksetzen

back: ~**ache** n Rückenschmerzen pl. ~**biting** n gehässiges Gerede nt. ~**bone** n Rückgrat nt. ~**date** vt rückdatieren; ~**dated to** rückwirkend von. ~ **door** n Hintertür f

backer n Geldgeber m

back: ~**fire** vi (Auto) fehlzünden; (fig) fehlschlagen. ~**ground** n Hintergrund m; family ~**ground** Familienverhältnisse pl. ~**hand** n (Sport) Rückhand f. ~**handed** a <compliment> zweifelhaft

backing n (support) Unterstützung f; (material) Verstärkung f

back: ~**lash** n (fig) Gegenschlag m. ~**log** n Rückstand m (of an + dat). ~**pack** n Rucksack m. ~ **seat** n Rücksitz m. ~**side** n 🔲 Hintern m. ~**stroke** n Rückenschwimmen nt. ~**-up** n Unterstützung f; (Amer: traffic jam) Stau m

backward a zurückgeblieben; <country> rückständig ● adv rückwärts. ~**s** rückwärts; ~**s and forwards** hin und her

back yard n Hinterhof m; **not in my** ~ **yard** 🔲 nicht vor meiner Haustür

bacon n [Schinken]speck m

bacteria npl Bakterien pl

bad a (worse, worst) schlecht; (serious) schwer, schlimm; (naughty) unartig; ~ **language** gemeine Ausdrucksweise f; **feel** ~ sich schlecht fühlen; (feel guilty) ein schlechtes Gewissen haben

badge n Abzeichen nt

badger n Dachs m ● vt plagen

badly adv schlecht; (seriously) schwer; ~ **off** schlecht gestellt; ~ **behaved** unerzogen; **want** ~ sich (dat) sehnsüchtig wünschen; **need** ~ dringend brauchen

bad-mannered a mit schlechten Manieren

badminton n Federball m

bad-tempered a schlecht gelaunt

baffle vt verblüffen

bag n Tasche f; (of paper) Tüte f; (pouch) Beutel m; ~**s of** 🔲 jede Menge ● vt (🔲 reserve) in Beschlag nehmen

baggage n [Reise]gepäck nt

baggy a <clothes> ausgebeult

bagpipes npl Dudelsack m

bail n Kaution f; **on** ~ gegen Kaution ● vt ~ **s.o. out** jdn gegen Kaution freibekommen; (fig) jdm aus der Patsche helfen

bait n Köder m ● vt mit einem Köder versehen; (fig: torment) reizen

bake vt/i backen

baker n Bäcker m; ~**'s [shop]** Bäckerei f. ~**y** n Bäckerei f

baking n Backen nt. ~**-powder** n Backpulver nt

balance n (equilibrium) Gleichgewicht nt, Balance f; (scales) Waage f; (Comm) Saldo m; (outstanding sum) Restbetrag m; **[bank]** ~ Kontostand m; **in the** ~ (fig) in der Schwebe ● vt balancieren; (equalize) ausgleichen; (Comm) abschließen <books> ● vi balancieren; (fig & Comm) sich ausgleichen. ~**d** a ausgewogen

balcony n Balkon m

bald a (-er, -est) kahl; <person> kahlköpfig

bald|ly adv unverblümt. **~ness** n Kahlköpfigkeit f

ball¹ n Ball m; (Billiards, Croquet) Kugel f; (of yarn) Knäuel m & nt; on the ~ 🖫 auf Draht

ball² n (dance) Ball m

ball-bearing n Kugellager nt

ballerina n Ballerina f

ballet n Ballett nt. **~ dancer** n Balletttänzer(in) m(f)

balloon n Luftballon m; (Aviat) Ballon m

ballot n [geheime] Wahl f; (on issue) [geheime] Abstimmung f. **~-box** n Wahlurne f. **~-paper** n Stimmzettel m

ball: ~point [pen] n Kugelschreiber m. **~room** n Ballsaal m

balm n Balsam m

balmy a (-ier, -iest) a sanft

Baltic a & n the ~ [Sea] die Ostsee

bamboo n Bambus m

ban n Verbot nt ● vt (pt/pp banned) verbieten

banal a banal. **~ity** n Banalität f

banana n Banane f

band n Band nt; (stripe) Streifen m; (group) Schar f; (Mus) Kapelle f

bandage n Verband m; (for support) Bandage f ● vt verbinden; bandagieren <limb>

b. & b. abbr of bed and breakfast

bandit n Bandit m

band: ~stand n Musikpavillon m. **~wagon** n jump on the **~wagon** (fig) sich einer erfolgreichen Sache anschließen

bang n (noise) Knall m; (blow) Schlag m ● adv go ~ knallen ● int bums! peng! ● vt knallen; (shut noisily) zuknallen; (strike) schlagen auf (+ acc); ~ one's head sich (dat) den Kopf stoßen (on an + acc) ● vi schlagen; <door:> zuknallen

banger n (firework) Knallfrosch m; (🖫 sausage) Wurst f; old ~ (🖫 car) Klapperkiste f

bangle n Armreifen m

banish vt verbannen

banisters npl [Treppen]geländer nt

banjo n Banjo nt

bank¹ n (of river) Ufer nt; (slope) Hang m ● vi (Aviat) in die Kurve gehen

bank² n Bank f ● ~ on vt sich verlassen auf (+ acc)

bank account n Bankkonto nt

banker n Bankier m

bank: ~ holiday n gesetzlicher Feiertag m. **~ing** n Bankwesen nt. **~note** n Banknote f

bankrupt a bankrott; go ~ Bankrott machen ● n Bankrotteur m ● vt Bankrott machen. **~cy** n Bankrott m

banner n Banner nt; (carried by demonstrators) Transparent nt, Spruchband nt

banquet n Bankett nt

baptism n Taufe f

baptize vt taufen

bar n Stange f; (of cage) [Gitter]stab m; (of gold) Barren m; (of chocolate) Tafel f; (of soap) Stück nt; (long) Riegel m; (café) Bar f; (counter) Theke f; (Mus) Takt m; (fig: obstacle) Hindernis nt; parallel **~s** (Sport) Barren m; behind **~s** 🖫 hinter Gittern ● vt (pt/pp barred) versperren <way, door>; ausschließen <person>

barbar|ic a barbarisch. **~ity** n Barbarei f. **~ous** a barbarisch

barbecue n Grill m; (party) Grillfest nt ● vt [im Freien] grillen

barbed a ~ **wire** Stacheldraht m

barber n [Herren]friseur m

bar code n Strichkode m

bare a (-r, -st) nackt, bloß; <tree> kahl; (empty) leer; (mere) bloß

bare: ~back adv ohne Sattel. **~faced** a schamlos. **~foot** adv barfuß. **~headed** a mit unbedecktem Kopf

barely adv kaum

bargain n (agreement) Geschäft nt; (good buy) Gelegenheitskauf m; into the ~ noch dazu; make a ~ sich

einigen ● *vi* handeln; (*haggle*)
feilschen; ∼ **for** (*expect*) rechnen mit

barge *n* Lastkahn *m*; (*towed*)
Schleppkahn *m* ● *vi* ∼ **in** 🆃
hereinplatzen

baritone *n* Bariton *m*

bark[1] *n* (*of tree*) Rinde *f*

bark[2] *n* Bellen *nt* ● *vi* bellen

barley *n* Gerste *f*

bar: ∼**maid** *n* Schankmädchen *nt*.
∼**man** Barmann *m*

barmy *a* 🆃 verrückt

barn *n* Scheune *f*

barometer *n* Barometer *nt*

baron *n* Baron *m*. ∼**ess** *n* Baronin *f*

barracks *npl* Kaserne *f*

barrage *n* (*in river*) Wehr *nt*; (*Mil*)
Sperrfeuer *nt*; (*fig*) Hagel *m*

barrel *n* Fass *nt*; (*of gun*) Lauf *m*; (*of
cannon*) Rohr *nt*. ∼**-organ** *n*
Drehorgel *f*

barren *a* unfruchtbar; <*landscape*>
öde

barricade *n* Barrikade *f* ● *vt*
verbarrikadieren

barrier *n* Barriere *f*; (*across road*)
Schranke *f*; (*Rail*) Sperre *f*; (*fig*)
Hindernis *nt*

barrow *n* Karre *f*, Karren *m*

base *n* Fuß *m*; (*fig*) Basis *f*; (*Mil*)
Stützpunkt *m* ● *vt* stützen (**on** auf +
acc); **be** ∼**d on** basieren auf (+ *dat*)

base: ∼**ball** *n* Baseball *m*. ∼**less** *a*
unbegründet. ∼**ment** *n*
Kellergeschoss *nt*

bash *n* Schlag *m*; **have a** ∼! 🆃
probier es mal! ● *vt* hauen

basic *a* Grund-; (*fundamental*)
grundlegend; (*essential*) wesentlich;
(*unadorned*) einfach; **the** ∼**s** das
Wesentliche. ∼**ally** *adv*
grundsätzlich

basin *n* Becken *nt*; (*for washing*)
Waschbecken *nt*; (*for food*) Schüssel *f*

basis *n* (*pl* **-ses**) Basis *f*

bask *vi* sich sonnen

basket *n* Korb *m*. ∼**ball** *n*
Basketball *m*

Basle *n* Basel *nt*

bass *a* Bass-; ∼ **voice** Bassstimme *f*
● *n* Bass *m*; (*person*) Bassist *m*

bassoon *n* Fagott *nt*

bastard *n* 🆇 Schuft *m*

bat[1] *n* Schläger *m*; **off one's own**
∼ 🆃 auf eigene Faust ● *vt* (*pt/pp*
batted) schlagen; **not** ∼ **an eyelid**
(*fig*) nicht mit der Wimper zucken

bat[2] *n* (*Zool*) Fledermaus *f*

batch *n* (*of people*) Gruppe *f*; (*of
papers*) Stoß *m*; (*of goods*) Sendung *f*;
(*of bread*) Schub *m*

bath *n* (*pl* **-s**) Bad *nt*; (*tub*)
Badewanne *f*; ∼**s** *pl* Badeanstalt *f*;
have a ∼ baden

bathe *n* Bad *nt* ● *vt/i* baden. ∼**r** *n*
Badende(r) *m/f*

bathing *n* Baden *nt*. ∼**-cap** *n*
Bademütze *f*. ∼**-costume** *n*
Badeanzug *m*

bath: ∼**-mat** *n* Badematte *f*.
∼**room** *n* Badezimmer *nt*. ∼**-towel**
n Badetuch *nt*

battalion *n* Bataillon *nt*

batter *n* (*Culin*) flüssiger Teig *m*
● *vt* schlagen. ∼**ed** *a* <*car*>
verbeult; <*wife*> misshandelt

battery *n* Batterie *f*

battle *n* Schlacht *f*; (*fig*) Kampf *m*
● *vi* (*fig*) kämpfen (**for** um)

battle: ∼**field** *n* Schlachtfeld *nt*.
∼**ship** *n* Schlachtschiff *nt*

batty *a* 🆃 verrückt

Bavaria *n* Bayern *nt*. ∼**n** *a*
bayrisch ● *n* Bayer(in) *m(f)*

bawl *vt/i* brüllen

bay[1] *n* (*Geog*) Bucht *f*; (*Archit*) Erker
m

bay[2] *n* (*Bot*) [echter] Lorbeer *m*. ∼**-
leaf** *n* Lorbeerblatt *nt*

bayonet *n* Bajonett *nt*

bay window *n* Erkerfenster *nt*

bazaar *n* Basar *m*

BC *abbr* (**before Christ**) v. Chr.

be

(*pres* **am, are, is,** *pl* **are**; *pt* **was**,
pl **were**; *pp* **been**)

● *intransitive verb*

····▸ (*expressing identity, nature, state, age etc.*) sein. **he is a teacher** er ist Lehrer. **she is French** sie ist Französin. **he is very nice** er ist sehr nett. **I am tall** ich bin groß. **you are thirty** du bist dreißig. **it was very cold** es war sehr kalt

····▸ (*expressing general position*) sein; (*lie*) liegen; (*stand*) stehen. **where is the bank?** wo ist die Bank? **the book is on the table** das Buch liegt auf dem Tisch. **the vase is on the shelf** die Vase steht auf dem Brett

····▸ (*feel*) **I am cold/hot** mir ist kalt/heiß. **I am ill** ich bin krank. **I am well** mir geht es gut. **how are you?** wie geht es Ihnen?

····▸ (*date*) **it is the 5th today** heute haben wir den Fünften

····▸ (*go, come, stay*) sein. **I have been to Vienna** ich bin in Wien gewesen. **have you ever been to London?** bist du schon einmal in London gewesen? **has the postman been?** war der Briefträger schon da? **I've been here for an hour** ich bin seit einer Stunde hier

····▸ (*origin*) **where are you from?** woher stammen *od* kommen Sie? **she is from Australia** sie stammt *od* ist aus Australien

····▸ (*cost*) kosten. **how much are the eggs?** was kosten die Eier?

····▸ (*in calculations*) **two threes are six** zweimal drei ist *od* sind sechs

····▸ (*exist*) **there is/are** es gibt (+ *acc*). **there's no fish left** es gibt keinen Fisch mehr

● *auxiliary verb*

····▸ (*forming continuous tenses: not translated*) **I'm working** ich arbeite. **I'm leaving tomorrow** ich reise morgen [ab]. **they were singing** sie sangen. **they will be coming on Tuesday** sie kommen am Dienstag

····▸ (*forming passive*) werden. **the child was found** das Kind wurde gefunden. **German is spoken here** hier wird Deutsch gesprochen; hier spricht man Deutsch

····▸ (*expressing arrangement, obligation, destiny*) **I am to go/inform you** ich soll gehen/Sie unterrichten. **they were to fly today**

sie sollten heute fliegen. **you are to do that immediately** das sollst du sofort machen. **you are not to ...** (*prohibition*) du darfst nicht .... **they were never to meet again** (*destiny*) sie sollten sich nie wieder treffen

····▸ (*in short answers*) **Are you disappointed? — Yes I am** Bist du enttäuscht? — Ja. (*negating previous statement*) **Aren't you coming? — Yes I am!** Kommst du nicht? — Doch!

····▸ (*in tag questions*) **isn't it? wasn't she? aren't they?** *etc.* nicht wahr. **it's a beautiful house, isn't it?** das Haus ist sehr schön, nicht wahr?

beach *n* Strand *m*

bead *n* Perle *f*

beak *n* Schnabel *m*

beam *n* Balken *m*; (*of light*) Strahl *m* ● *vi* strahlen. ∼**ing** *a* [freude]strahlend

bean *n* Bohne *f*

bear¹ *n* Bär *m*

bear² *vt/i* (*pt* bore, *pp* borne) tragen; (*endure*) ertragen; gebären <*child*>; ∼ **right** sich rechts halten. ∼**able** *a* erträglich

beard *n* Bart *m*. ∼**ed** *a* bärtig

bearer *n* Träger *m*; (*of news, cheque*) Überbringer *m*; (*of passport*) Inhaber(in) *m(f)*

bearing *n* Haltung *f*; (*Techn*) Lager *nt*; **get one's** ∼**s** sich orientieren

beast *n* Tier *nt*; (🆒 *person*) Biest *nt*

beastly *a* (-ier, -iest) 🆒 scheußlich; <*person*> gemein

beat *n* Schlag *m*; (*of policeman*) Runde *f*; (*rhythm*) Takt *m* ● *vt/i* (*pt* beat, *pp* beaten) schlagen; (*thrash*) verprügeln; klopfen <*carpet*>; (*hammer*) hämmern (**on** an + *acc*); ∼ **it!** 🆒 hau ab! **it** ∼**s me** 🆒 das begreife ich nicht. ∼ **up** *vt* zusammenschlagen

beat|en *a* **off the** ∼**en track** abseits. ∼**ing** *n* Prügel *pl*

beauti|ful *a*, **-ly** *adv* schön. ∼**fy** *vt* (*pt/pp* -ied) verschönern

beauty *n* Schönheit *f*. ∼ **parlour** *n* Kosmetiksalon *m*. ∼ **spot** *n* Schönheitsfleck *m*; (*place*)

landschaftlich besonders reizvolles
Fleckchen *nt.*

beaver *n* Biber *m*

became *see* become

because *conj* weil ● *adv* ∼ of
wegen (+ *gen*)

becom|e *vt/i (pt* **became,** *pp*
become) werden. ∼**ing** *a <clothes>*
kleidsam

bed *n* Bett *nt;* (*layer*) Schicht *f;* (*of
flowers*) Beet *nt;* in ∼ im Bett; go to
∼ ins *od* zu Bett gehen; ∼ and
breakfast Zimmer mit Frühstück.
∼**clothes** *npl,* ∼**ding** *n* Bettzeug
nt. ∼**room** *n* Schlafzimmer *nt*

bedside *n* at his ∼ an seinem Bett.
∼ **lamp** *n* Nachttischlampe *f.* ∼
table *n* Nachttisch *m*

bed: ∼**sitter** *n,* ∼**sitting-room** *n*
Wohnschlafzimmer *nt.* ∼**spread** *n*
Tagesdecke *f.* ∼**time** *n* at ∼time vor
dem Schlafengehen

bee *n* Biene *f*

beech *n* Buche *f*

beef *n* Rindfleisch *nt.* ∼**burger** *n*
Hamburger *m*

bee: ∼**hive** *n* Bienenstock *m.* ∼
line *n* make a ∼-line for 🖭
zusteuern auf (+ *acc*)

been *see* be

beer *n* Bier *nt*

beet *n* (*Amer: beetroot*) Rote Bete *f;*
[*sugar*] ∼ Zuckerrübe *f*

beetle *n* Käfer *m*

beetroot *n* Rote Bete *f*

before *prep* vor (+ *dat/acc*); the day
∼ yesterday vorgestern; ∼ long bald
● *adv* vorher; (*already*) schon; never
∼ noch nie; ∼ that davor ● *conj*
(*time*) ehe, bevor. ∼**hand** *adv*
vorher, im Voraus

beg *v (pt/pp* **begged**) ● *vi* betteln ● *vt*
(*entreat*) anflehen; (*ask*) bitten (**for**
um)

began *see* begin

beggar *n* Bettler(in) *m(f);* 🖭 Kerl *m*

begin *vt/i (pt* **began,** *pp* **begun,** *pres
p* **beginning**) anfangen, beginnen; **to**
∼ with anfangs. ∼**ner** *n*
Anfänger(in) *m(f).* ∼**ning** *n* Anfang
m, Beginn *m*

begun *see* begin

behalf *n* on ∼ of im Namen von; on
my ∼ meinetwegen

behave *vi* sich verhalten; ∼ oneself
sich benehmen

behaviour *n* Verhalten *nt;* good/
bad ∼ gutes/schlechtes Benehmen *nt*

behind *prep* hinter (+ *dat/acc*); be ∼
sth hinter etw (*dat*) stecken ● *adv*
hinten; (*late*) im Rückstand; a long
way ∼ weit zurück ● *n* 🖭 Hintern
m. ∼**hand** *adv* im Rückstand

beige *a* beige

being *n* Dasein *nt;* living ∼
Lebewesen *nt;* come into ∼
entstehen

belated *a,* **-ly** *adv* verspätet

belfry *n* Glockenstube *f;* (*tower*)
Glockenturm *m*

Belgian *a* belgisch ● *n* Belgier(in)
m(f)

Belgium *n* Belgien *nt*

belief *n* Glaube *m*

believable *a* glaubhaft

believe *vt/i* glauben (**s.o.** jdm; **in** an
+ *acc*). ∼**r** *n* (*Relig*) Gläubige(r) *m/f*

belittle *vt* herabsetzen

bell *n* Glocke *f;* (*on door*) Klingel *f*

bellow *vt/i* brüllen

belly *n* Bauch *m*

belong *vi* gehören (**to** *dat*); (*be
member*) angehören (**to** *dat*). ∼**ings**
npl Sachen *pl*

beloved *a* geliebt ● *n* Geliebte(r)
m/f

below *prep* unter (+ *dat/acc*) ● *adv*
unten; (*Naut*) unter Deck

belt *n* Gürtel *m;* (*area*) Zone *f;*
(*Techn*) [Treib]riemen *m* ● *vi* (🖭
rush) rasen ● *vt* (🖭 *hit*) hauen

bench *n* Bank *f;* (*work-*) Werkbank *f*

bend *n* Biegung *f;* (*in road*) Kurve *f;*
round the ∼ 🖭 verrückt ● *v (pt/pp*
bent) ● *vt* biegen; beugen *<arm, leg>*
● *vi* sich bücken; *<thing:>* sich
biegen; *<road:>* eine Biegung
machen. ∼ **down** *vi* sich bücken. ∼
over *vi* sich vornüberbeugen

beneath *prep* unter (+ *dat/acc*); ∼
him (*fig*) unter seiner Würde ● *adv*
darunter

benefactor *n* Wohltäter(in) *m(f)*

beneficial *a* nützlich

benefit *n* Vorteil *m*; *(allowance)* Unterstützung *f*; *(insurance)* Leistung *f*; **sickness ~** Krankengeld *nt* ● *v (pt/pp* **-fited**, *pres p* **-fiting)** ● *vt* nützen (+ *dat*) ● *vi* profitieren (**from** von)

benevolen|ce *n* Wohlwollen *nt*. **~t** *a*, **-ly** *adv* wohlwollend

bent *see* **bend** ● *a* <*person*> gebeugt; *(distorted)* verbogen; (🔲 *dishonest)* korrupt; **be ~ on doing sth** darauf erpicht sein, etw zu tun ● *n* Hang *m*, Neigung *f* (**for** zu); **artistic ~** künstlerische Ader *f*

bequeath *vt* vermachen (**to** *dat)*

bereave|d *n* **the ~d** *pl* die Hinterbliebenen

beret *n* Baskenmütze *f*

Berne *n* Bern *nt*

berry *n* Beere *f*

berth *n* *(on ship)* [Schlaf]koje *f*; *(ship's anchorage)* Liegeplatz *m*; **give a wide ~ to** 🔲 einen großen Bogen machen um

beside *prep* neben (+ *dat/acc)*; **~ oneself** außer sich *(dat)*

besides *prep* außer (+ *dat)* ● *adv* außerdem

besiege *vt* belagern

best *a & n* beste(r,s); **the ~** der/die/ das Beste; **at ~** bestenfalls; **all the ~!** alles Gute! **do one's ~** sein Bestes tun; **the ~ part of a year** fast ein Jahr; **to the ~ of my knowledge** so viel ich weiß; **make the ~ of it** das Beste daraus machen ● *adv* am besten; **as ~ I could** so gut ich konnte. **~ man** *n* ≈ Trauzeuge *m*. **~seller** *n* Bestseller *m*

bet *n* Wette *f* ● *v (pt/pp* **bet** *or* **betted)** ● *vt* **~ s.o. £5** mit jdm um £5 wetten ● *vi* wetten; **~ on** [Geld] setzen auf (+ *acc)*

betray *vt* verraten. **~al** *n* Verrat *m*

better *a* besser; **get ~** sich bessern; *(after illness)* sich erholen ● *adv* besser; **~ off** besser dran; **~ not** lieber nicht; **all the ~** umso besser; **the sooner the ~** je eher, desto

besser; **think ~ of it** sich eines Besseren besinnen; **you'd ~ stay** du bleibst am besten hier ● *vt* verbessern; *(do better than)* übertreffen; **~ oneself** sich verbessern

between *prep* zwischen (+ *dat/acc)*; **~ you and me** unter uns; **~ us** *(together)* zusammen ● *adv* **[in] ~** dazwischen

beware *vi* sich in Acht nehmen (**of** vor + *dat)*; **~ of the dog!** Vorsicht, bissiger Hund!

bewilder *vt* verwirren. **~ment** *n* Verwirrung *f*

bewitch *vt* verzaubern; *(fig)* bezaubern

beyond *prep* über (+ *acc*) ... hinaus; *(further)* weiter als; **~ reach** außer Reichweite; **~ doubt** ohne jeden Zweifel; **it's ~ me** 🔲 das geht über meinen Horizont ● *adv* darüber hinaus

bias *n* Voreingenommenheit *f*; *(preference)* Vorliebe *f*; *(Jur)* Befangenheit *f* ● *vt (pt/pp* **biased)** *(influence)* beeinflussen. **~ed** *a* voreingenommen; *(Jur)* befangen

bib *n* Lätzchen *nt*

Bible *n* Bibel *f*

biblical *a* biblisch

bibliography *n* Bibliographie *f*

bicycle *n* Fahrrad *nt* ● *vi* mit dem Rad fahren

bid *n* Gebot *nt*; *(attempt)* Versuch *m* ● *vt/i (pt/pp* **bid**, *pres p* **bidding)** bieten (**for** auf + *acc)*; *(Cards)* reizen

bidder *n* Bieter(in) *m(f)*

bide *vt* **~ one's time** den richtigen Moment abwarten

big *a* (**bigger**, **biggest**) groß ● *adv* **talk ~** 🔲 angeben

bigam|ist *n* Bigamist *m*. **~y** *n* Bigamie *f*

big-headed *a* 🔲 eingebildet

bigot *n* Eiferer *m*. **~ed** *a* engstirnig

bigwig *n* 🔲 hohes Tier *nt*

bike *n* 🔲 [Fahr]rad *nt*

bikini *n* Bikini *m*

bile *n* Galle *f*

bilingual *a* zweisprachig

bilious *a* (*Med*) ~ attack
verdorbener Magen *m*

bill¹ *n* Rechnung *f*; (*poster*) Plakat *nt*;
(*Pol*) Gesetzentwurf *m*; (*Amer: note*)
Banknote *f*; ~ **of exchange** Wechsel
m ● *vt* eine Rechnung schicken (+
dat)

bill² *n* (*beak*) Schnabel *m*

billfold *n* (*Amer*) Brieftasche *f*

billiards *n* Billard *nt*

billion *n* (*thousand million*)
Milliarde *f*; (*million million*) Billion *f*

bin *n* Mülleimer *m*; (*for bread*)
Kasten *m*

bind *vt* (*pt/pp* bound) binden (to an +
acc); (*bandage*) verbinden; (*Jur*)
verpflichten; (*cover the edge of*)
einfassen. ~**ing** *a* verbindlich ● *n*
Einband *m*; (*braid*) Borte *f*; (*on ski*)
Bindung *f*

binge *n* 🗌 go on the ~ eine
Sauftour machen

binoculars *npl* [pair of] ~ Fernglas
nt

bio|chemistry *n* Biochemie *f*.
~**degradable** *a* biologisch
abbaubar

biograph|er *n* Biograph(in) *m(f)*.
~**y** *n* Biographie *f*

biological *a* biologisch

biolog|ist *n* Biologe *m*. ~**y** *n*
Biologie *f*

birch *n* Birke *f*; (*whip*) Rute *f*

bird *n* Vogel *m*; (🗌 *girl*) Mädchen *nt*;
kill two ~**s with one stone** zwei
Fliegen mit einer Klappe schlagen

Biro (P) *n* Kugelschreiber *m*

birth *n* Geburt *f*

birth: ~ **certificate** *n*
Geburtsurkunde *f*. ~**control** *n*
Geburtenregelung *f*. ~**day** *n*
Geburtstag *m*. ~**rate** *n*
Geburtenziffer *f*

biscuit *n* Keks *m*

bishop *n* Bischof *m*

bit¹ *n* Stückchen *nt*; (*for horse*) Gebiss
nt; (*Techn*) Bohreinsatz *m*; a ~ ein
bisschen; ~ **by** ~ nach und nach; a
~ **of bread** ein bisschen Brot; do
one's ~ sein Teil tun

bit² *see* bite

bitch *n* Hündin *f*; 🗷 Luder *nt*. ~**y** *a*
gehässig

bit|e *n* Biss *m*; [insect] ~ Stich *m*;
(*mouthful*) Bissen *m* ● *vt/i* (*pt* bit, *pp*
bitten) beißen; <*insect:*> stechen;
kauen <*one's nails*>. ~**ing** *a*
beißend

bitten *see* bite

bitter *a*, -**ly** *adv* bitter; ~**ly cold**
bitterkalt ● *n* bitteres Bier *nt*.
~**ness** *n* Bitterkeit *f*

bitty *a* zusammengestoppelt

bizarre *a* bizarr

black *a* (-er, -est) schwarz; be ~**and**
blue grün und blau sein ● *n* Schwarz
nt; (*person*) Schwarze(r) *m/f* ● *vt*
schwärzen; boykottieren <*goods*>

black: ~**berry** *n* Brombeere *f*.
~**bird** *n* Amsel *f*. ~**board** *n* (*Sch*)
[Wand]tafel *f*. ~**currant** *n* schwarze
Johannisbeere *f*

blacken *vt/i* schwärzen

black: ~ **eye** *n* blaues Auge *nt*.
B~ Forest *n* Schwarzwald *m*. ~
ice *n* Glatteis *nt*. ~**list** *vt* auf die
schwarze Liste setzen. ~**mail** *n*
Erpressung *f* ● *vt* erpressen.
~**mailer** *n* Erpresser(in) *m(f)*. ~
market *n* schwarzer Markt *m*. ~
out *n* have a ~**out** (*Med*) das
Bewusstsein verlieren. ~ **pudding**
n Blutwurst *f*

bladder *n* (*Anat*) Blase *f*

blade *n* Klinge *f*; (*of grass*) Halm *m*

blame *n* Schuld *f* ● *vt* die Schuld
geben (+ *dat*); no one is to ~ keiner
ist schuld daran. ~**less** *a* schuldlos

bland *a* (-er, -est) mild

blank *a* leer; <*look*> ausdruckslos
● *n* Lücke *f*; (*cartridge*) Platzpatrone
f. ~ **cheque** *n* Blankoscheck *m*

blanket *n* Decke *f*; wet ~ 🗌
Spielverderber(in) *m(f)*

blare *vt/i* schmettern

blasé *a* blasiert

blast *n* (*gust*) Luftstoß *m*; (*sound*)
Schmettern *nt*; (*of horn*) Tuten *nt*
● *vt* sprengen ● *int* 🗷 verdammt.
~**ed** *a* 🗷 verdammt

blast-off *n* (*of missile*) Start *m*

blatant *a* offensichtlich

blaze n Feuer nt ● vi brennen

blazer n Blazer m

bleach n Bleichmittel nt ● vt/i bleichen

bleak a (-er, -est) öde; (fig) trostlos

bleary-eyed a mit trüben/(on waking up) verschlafenen Augen

bleat vi blöken

bleed v (pt/pp bled) ● vi bluten ● vt entlüften <radiator>

bleep n Piepton m ● vi piepsen ● vt mit dem Piepser rufen. ~er n Piepser m

blemish n Makel m

blend n Mischung f ● vt mischen ● vi sich vermischen

bless vt segnen. ~ed a heilig; ⊠ verflixt. ~ing n Segen m

blew see **blow²**

blight n (Bot) Brand m

blind a blind; <corner> unübersichtlich; ~ man/woman Blinde(r) m/f ● n [roller] ~ Rouleau nt ● vt blenden

blind: ~ alley n Sackgasse f. ~fold a & adv mit verbundenen Augen ● n Augenbinde f ● vt die Augen verbinden (+ dat). ~ly adv blindlings. ~ness n Blindheit f

blink vi blinzeln; <light:> blinken

bliss n Glückseligkeit f. ~ful a glücklich

blister n (Med) Blase f

blitz n ⊞ Großaktion f

blizzard n Schneesturm m

bloated a aufgedunsen

blob n Klecks m

block n Block m; (of wood) Klotz m; (of flats) [Wohn]block m ● vt blockieren. ~ up vt zustopfen

blockade n Blockade f ● vt blockieren

blockage n Verstopfung f

block: ~head n ⊞ Dummkopf m. ~ letters npl Blockschrift f

bloke n ⊞ Kerl m

blonde a blond ● n Blondine f

blood n Blut nt

blood: ~-curdling a markerschütternd. ~ donor n

Blutspender m. ~ group n Blutgruppe f. ~hound n Bluthund m. ~-poisoning n Blutvergiftung f. ~ pressure n Blutdruck m. ~shed n Blutvergießen nt. ~shot a blutunterlaufen. ~ sports npl Jagdsport m. ~-stained a blutbefleckt. ~ test n Blutprobe f. ~thirsty a blutdürstig. ~-vessel n Blutgefäß nt

bloody a (-ier, -iest) blutig; ⊠ verdammt. ~-minded a ⊠ stur

bloom n Blüte f ● vi blühen

blossom n Blüte f ● vi blühen

blot n [Tinten]klecks m; (fig) Fleck m ● ~ out vt (fig) auslöschen

blotch n Fleck m. ~y a fleckig

blotting-paper n Löschpapier nt

blouse n Bluse f

blow¹ n Schlag m

blow² v (pt blew, pp blown) ● vt blasen; (fam: squander) verpulvern; ~ one's nose sich (dat) die Nase putzen ● vi blasen; <fuse:> durchbrennen. ~ away vt wegblasen ● vi wegfliegen. ~ down vt umwehen ● vi umfallen. ~ out vt (extinguish) ausblasen. ~ over vi umfallen; (fig: die down) vorübergehen. ~ up vt (inflate) aufblasen; (enlarge) vergrößern; (shatter by explosion) sprengen ● vi explodieren

blowlamp n Lötlampe f

blown see **blow²**

blowtorch n (Amer) Lötlampe f

blowy a windig

blue a (-r, -st) blau; feel ~ deprimiert sein ● n Blau nt; have the ~s deprimiert sein; out of the ~ aus heiterem Himmel

blue: ~bell n Sternhyazinthe f. ~berry n Heidelbeere f. ~bottle n Schmeißfliege f. ~ film n Pornofilm m. ~print n (fig) Entwurf m

bluff n Bluff m ● vi bluffen

blunder n Schnitzer m ● vi einen Schnitzer machen

blunt a stumpf; <person> geradeheraus. ~ly adv unverblümt, geradeheraus

blur *n* it's all a ~ alles ist verschwommen ● *vt* (*pt/pp* **blurred**) verschwommen machen; **~red** verschwommen

blush *n* Erröten *nt* ● *vi* erröten

bluster *n* Großtuerei *f*. **~y** *a* windig

boar *n* Eber *m*

board *n* Brett *nt*; (*for notices*) schwarzes Brett *nt*; (*committee*) Ausschuss *m*; (*of directors*) Vorstand *m*; on ~ an Bord; **full** ~ Vollpension *f*; ~ **and lodging** Unterkunft und Verpflegung *pl* ● *vt* einsteigen in (+ *acc*); (*Naut, Aviat*) besteigen ● *vi* an Bord gehen. ~ **up** *vt* mit Brettern verschlagen

boarder *n* Pensionsgast *m*; (*Sch*) Internatsschüler(in) *m(f)*

board: **~-game** *n* Brettspiel *nt*. **~ing-house** *n* Pension *f*. **~ing-school** *n* Internat *nt*

boast *vt* sich rühmen (+ *gen*) ● *vi* prahlen (**about** mit). **~ful** *a*, **-ly** *adv* prahlerisch

boat *n* Boot *nt*; (*ship*) Schiff *nt*

bob *vi* (*pt/pp* **bobbed**) ~ **up and down** sich auf und ab bewegen

bob-sleigh *n* Bob *m*

bodily *a* körperlich ● *adv* (*forcibly*) mit Gewalt

body *n* Körper *m*; (*corpse*) Leiche *f*; (*corporation*) Körperschaft *f*. **~guard** *n* Leibwächter *m*. **~work** *n* (*Auto*) Karosserie *f*

bog *n* Sumpf *m*

bogus *a* falsch

boil[1] *n* Furunkel *m*

boil[2] *n* bring/come to the ~ zum Kochen bringen/kommen ● *vt/i* kochen; **~ed potatoes** Salzkartoffeln *pl*. ~ **down** *vi* (*fig*) hinauslaufen (**to** auf + *acc*). ~ **over** *vi* überkochen

boiler *n* Heizkessel *m*

boiling point *n* Siedepunkt *m*

boisterous *a* übermütig

bold *a* (**-er, -est**), **-ly** *adv* kühn; (*Typ*) fett. **~ness** *n* Kühnheit *f*

bolster *n* Nackenrolle *f* ● *vt* ~ **up** Mut machen (+ *dat*)

bolt *n* Riegel *m*; (*Techn*) Bolzen *m* ● *vt* schrauben (**to** an + *acc*); verriegeln <*door*>; hinunterschlingen <*food*> ● *vi* abhauen; <*horse*:> durchgehen

bomb *n* Bombe *f* ● *vt* bombardieren

bombard *vt* beschießen; (*fig*) bombardieren

bombastic *a* bombastisch

bomber *n* (*Aviat*) Bomber *m*; (*person*) Bombenleger(in) *m(f)*

bond *n* (*fig*) Band *nt*; (*Comm*) Obligation *f*

bone *n* Knochen *m*; (*of fish*) Gräte *f* ● *vt* von den Knochen lösen <*meat*>; entgräten <*fish*>. **~-dry** *a* knochentrocken

bonfire *n* Gartenfeuer *nt*; (*celebratory*) Freudenfeuer *nt*

bonus *n* Prämie *f*; (*gratuity*) Gratifikation *f*; (*fig*) Plus *nt*

bony *a* (**-ier, -iest**) knochig; <*fish*> grätig

boo *int* buh! ● *vt* ausbuhen ● *vi* buhen

boob *n* (🖪 *mistake*) Schnitzer *m*

book *n* Buch *nt*; (*of tickets*) Heft *nt*; **keep the ~s** (*Comm*) die Bücher führen ● *vt/i* buchen; (*reserve*) [vor]bestellen; (*for offence*) aufschreiben

book: **~case** *n* Bücherregal *nt*. **~-ends** *npl* Buchstützen *pl*. **~ing-office** *n* Fahrkartenschalter *m*. **~keeping** *n* Buchführung *f*. **~let** *n* Broschüre *f*. **~maker** *n* Buchmacher *m*. **~mark** *n* Lesezeichen *nt*. **~seller** *n* Buchhändler(in) *m(f)*. **~shop** *n* Buchhandlung *f*. **~stall** *n* Bücherstand *m*

boom *n* (*Comm*) Hochkonjunktur *f*; (*upturn*) Aufschwung *m* ● *vi* dröhnen; (*fig*) blühen

boon *n* Segen *m*

boost *n* Auftrieb *m* ● *vt* Auftrieb geben (+ *dat*)

boot *n* Stiefel *m*; (*Auto*) Kofferraum *m*

booth *n* Bude *f*; (*cubicle*) Kabine *f*

booty *n* Beute *f*

booze *n* 🖪 Alkohol *m* ● *vi* 🖪 saufen

border n Rand m; (frontier) Grenze f; (in garden) Rabatte f ● vi ~ on grenzen an (+ acc). ~line case n Grenzfall m

bore¹ see bear²

bor|e² n (of gun) Kaliber nt; (person) langweiliger Mensch m; (thing) langweilige Sache f ● vt langweilen; be ~ed sich langweilen. ~edom n Langeweile f. ~ing a langweilig

born pp be ~ geboren werden ● a geboren

borne see bear²

borrow vt [sich (dat)] borgen od leihen (from von)

bosom n Busen m

boss n 🔲 Chef m ● vt herumkommandieren. ~y a herrschsüchtig

botanical a botanisch

botan|ist n Botaniker(in) m(f). ~y n Botanik f

both a & pron beide; ~[of] the children beide Kinder; ~ of them beide [von ihnen] ● adv ~ men and women sowohl Männer als auch Frauen

bother n Mühe f; (minor trouble) Ärger m ● int 🔲 verflixt! ● vt belästigen; (disturb) stören ● vi sich kümmern (about um)

bottle n Flasche f ● vt auf Flaschen abfüllen; (preserve) einmachen

bottle: ~-neck n (fig) Engpass m. ~-opener n Flaschenöffner m

bottom a unterste(r,s) ● n (of container) Boden m; (of river) Grund m; (of page, hill) Fuß m; (buttocks) Hintern m; at the ~ unten; get to the ~ of sth (fig) hinter etw (acc) kommen

bought see buy

bounce vi [auf]springen; <cheque:> 🔲 nicht gedeckt sein ● vt aufspringen lassen <ball>

bouncer n 🔲 Rausschmeißer m

bound¹ n Sprung m ● vi springen

bound² see bind ● a ~ for <ship> mit Kurs auf (+ acc); be ~ to do sth etw bestimmt machen; (obliged) verpflichtet sein, etw zu machen

boundary n Grenze f

bounds npl (fig) Grenzen pl; out of ~ verboten

bouquet n [Blumen]strauß m; (of wine) Bukett nt

bourgeois a (pej) spießbürgerlich

bout n (Med) Anfall m; (Sport) Kampf m

bow¹ n (weapon & Mus) Bogen m; (knot) Schleife f

bow² n Verbeugung f ● vi sich verbeugen ● vt neigen <head>

bow³ n (Naut) Bug m

bowel n Darm m. ~s pl Eingeweide pl

bowl¹ n Schüssel f; (shallow) Schale f

bowl² n (ball) Kugel f ● vt/i werfen. ~ over vt umwerfen

bowler n (Sport) Werfer m

bowling n Kegeln nt. ~-alley n Kegelbahn f

bowls n Bowlsspiel nt

bow-tie n Fliege f

box¹ n Schachtel f; (wooden) Kiste f; (cardboard) Karton m; (Theat) Loge f

box² vt/i (Sport) boxen

box|er n Boxer m. ~ing n Boxen nt. B~ing Day n zweiter Weihnachtstag m

box: ~-office n (Theat) Kasse f. ~-room n Abstellraum m

boy n Junge m

boycott n Boykott m ● vt boykottieren

boy: ~friend n Freund m. ~ish a jungenhaft

bra n BH m

brace n Strebe f, Stütze f; (dental) Zahnspange f; ~s npl Hosenträger mpl

bracelet n Armband nt

bracing a stärkend

bracket n Konsole f; (group) Gruppe f; (Typ) round/square ~s runde/eckige Klammern ● vt einklammern

brag vi (pt/pp bragged) prahlen (about mit)

braille n Blindenschrift f

brain n Gehirn nt; ∼s (fig)
Intelligenz f

brain: ∼less a dumm. ∼**wash** vt
einer Gehirnwäsche unterziehen.
∼**wave** n Geistesblitz m

brainy a (-ier, -iest) klug

brake n Bremse f ● vt/i bremsen.
∼**light** n Bremslicht nt

bramble n Brombeerstrauch m

branch n Ast m; (fig) Zweig m;
(Comm) Zweigstelle f; (shop) Filiale f
● vi sich gabeln

brand n Marke f ● vt (fig)
brandmarken als

brandish vt schwingen

brand-new a nagelneu

brandy n Weinbrand m

brash a nassforsch

brass n Messing nt; (Mus) Blech nt;
top ∼ 🔲 hohe Tiere pl. ∼ **band** n
Blaskapelle f

brassy a (-ier, -iest) 🔲 ordinär

brat n (pej) Balg nt

bravado n Forschheit f

brave a (-r, -st), -**ly** adv tapfer ● vt
die Stirn bieten (+ dat). ∼**ry** n
Tapferkeit f

bravo int bravo!

brawl n Schlägerei f

brawn n (Culin) Sülze f

brawny a muskulös

bray vi iahen

brazen a unverschämt

Brazil n Brasilien nt. ∼**ian** a
brasilianisch. ∼ **nut** n Paranuss f

breach n Bruch m; (Mil & fig)
Bresche f; ∼ **of contract**
Vertragsbruch m

bread n Brot nt; **slice of** ∼ **and**
butter Butterbrot nt. ∼**crumbs** npl
Brotkrümel pl; (Culin) Paniermehl
nt

breadth n Breite f

break n Bruch m; (interval) Pause f;
(interruption) Unterbrechung f; (🔲
chance) Chance f ● v (pt **broke**, pp
broken) ● vt brechen; (smash)
zerbrechen; (damage) kaputtmachen
🔲; (interrupt) unterbrechen; ∼ **one's**
arm sich (dat) den Arm brechen ● vi

brechen; <day:> anbrechen;
<storm:> losbrechen; <thing:>
kaputtgehen 🔲; <rope, thread:>
reißen; <news:> bekannt werden; **his**
voice is ∼**ing** er ist im Stimmbruch.
∼ **away** vi sich losreißen/(fig) sich
absetzen (**from** von). ∼ **down** vi
zusammenbrechen; (Techn) eine
Panne haben; <negotiations:>
scheitern ● vt aufbrechen <door>;
aufgliedern <figures>. ∼ **in** vi
einbrechen. ∼ **off** vt/i abbrechen;
lösen <engagement>. ∼ **out** vi
ausbrechen. ∼ **up** vt zerbrechen
● vi <crowd:> sich zerstreuen;
<marriage, couple:> auseinander
gehen; (Sch) Ferien bekommen

break|able a zerbrechlich. ∼**age**
n Bruch m. ∼**down** n (Techn)
Panne f; (Med) Zusammenbruch m;
(of figures) Aufgliederung f. ∼**er** n
(wave) Brecher m

breakfast n Frühstück nt

break: ∼**through** n Durchbruch m.
∼**water** n Buhne f

breast n Brust f. ∼**bone** n
Brustbein nt. ∼**feed** vt stillen. ∼
stroke n Brustschwimmen nt

breath n Atem m; **out of** ∼ außer
Atem; **under one's** ∼ vor sich (acc)
hin

breathe vt/i atmen. ∼ **in** vt/i
einatmen. ∼ **out** vt/i ausatmen

breathing n Atmen nt

breath: ∼**less** a atemlos. ∼
taking a atemberaubend

bred see **breed**

breed n Rasse f ● v (pt/pp **bred**) ● vt
züchten; (give rise to) erzeugen ● vi
sich vermehren. ∼**er** n Züchter m.
∼**ing** n Zucht f; (fig) [gute]
Lebensart f

breez|e n Lüftchen nt; (Naut) Brise
f. ∼**y** a windig

brevity n Kürze f

brew n Gebräu nt ● vt brauen;
kochen <tea>. ∼**er** n Brauer m.
∼**ery** n Brauerei f

bribe n (money) Bestechungsgeld nt
● vt bestechen. ∼**ry** n Bestechung f

brick n Ziegelstein m, Backstein m

bricklayer n Maurer m

bridal *a* Braut-

bride *n* Braut *f.* ~**groom** *n* Bräutigam *m.* ~**smaid** *n* Brautjungfer *f*

bridge[1] *n* Brücke *f*; (*of nose*) Nasenrücken *m*; (*of spectacles*) Steg *m*

bridge[2] *n* (*Cards*) Bridge *nt*

bridle *n* Zaum *m*

brief[1] *a* (-er, -est) kurz; **be ~** <*person:*> sich kurz fassen

brief[2] *n* Instruktionen *pl*; (*Jur: case*) Mandat *nt.* ~**case** *n* Aktentasche *f*

brief|ing *n* Informationsgespräch *nt.* ~**ly** *adv* kurz. ~**ness** *n* Kürze *f*

briefs *npl* Slip *m*

brigade *n* Brigade *f*

bright *a* (-er, -est), -**ly** *adv* hell; <*day*> heiter; **~ red** hellrot

bright|en *v* ~**en [up]** ● *vt* aufheitern ● *vi* sich aufheitern. ~**ness** *n* Helligkeit *f*

brilliance *n* Glanz *m*; (*of person*) Genialität *f*

brilliant *a*, -**ly** *adv* glänzend; <*person*> genial

brim *n* Rand *m*; (*of hat*) Krempe *f*

bring *vt* (*pt/pp* brought) bringen; **~ them with you** bring sie mit; **I can't ~ myself to do it** ich bringe es nicht fertig. **~ about** *vt* verursachen. **~ along** *vt* mitbringen. **~ back** *vt* zurückbringen. **~ down** *vt* herunterbringen; senken <*price*>. **~ off** *vt* vollbringen. **~ on** *vt* (*cause*) verursachen. **~ out** *vt* herausbringen. **~ round** *vt* vorbeibringen; (*persuade*) überreden; wieder zum Bewusstsein bringen <*unconscious person*>. **~ up** *vt* heraufbringen; (*vomit*) erbrechen; aufziehen <*children*>; erwähnen <*question*>

brink *n* Rand *m*

brisk *a* (-er, -est,) -**ly** *adv* lebhaft; (*quick*) schnell

bristle *n* Borste *f*

Brit|ain *n* Großbritannien *nt.* ~**ish** *a* britisch; **the ~ish** die Briten *pl*. ~**on** *n* Brite *m*/Britin *f*

Brittany *n* die Bretagne

brittle *a* brüchig, spröde

broad *a* (-er, -est) breit; <*hint*> deutlich; **in ~ daylight** am helllichten Tag. **~ beans** *npl* dicke Bohnen *pl*

broadcast *n* Sendung *f* ● *vt/i* (*pt/pp* -cast) senden. ~**er** *n* Rundfunk- und Fernsehpersönlichkeit *f.* ~**ing** *n* Funk und Fernsehen *pl*

broaden *vt* verbreitern; (*fig*) erweitern ● *vi* sich verbreitern

broadly *adv* breit; **~ speaking** allgemein gesagt

broadminded *a* tolerant

broccoli *n inv* Brokkoli *pl*

brochure *n* Broschüre *f*

broke *see* break ● *a* ☒ pleite

broken *see* break ● *a* zerbrochen, ☒ kaputt. ~**-hearted** *a* untröstlich

broker *n* Makler *m*

brolly *n* ☒ Schirm *m*

bronchitis *n* Bronchitis *f*

bronze *n* Bronze *f*

brooch *n* Brosche *f*

brood *vi* (*fig*) grübeln

broom *n* Besen *m*; (*Bot*) Ginster *m*

broth *n* Brühe *f*

brothel *n* Bordell *nt*

brother *n* Bruder *m*

brother: ~**-in-law** *n* (*pl* -s-in-law) Schwager *m.* ~**ly** *a* brüderlich

brought *see* bring

brow *n* Augenbraue *f*; (*forehead*) Stirn *f*; (*of hill*) [Berg]kuppe *f*

brown *a* (-er, -est) braun; **~ paper** Packpapier *nt* ● *n* Braun *nt* ● *vt* bräunen ● *vi* braun werden

browse *vi* (*read*) schmökern; (*in shop*) sich umsehen

bruise *n* blauer Fleck *m* ● *vt* beschädigen <*fruit*>; **~ one's arm** sich (*dat*) den Arm quetschen

brunette *n* Brünette *f*

brush *n* Bürste *f*; (*with handle*) Handfeger *m*; (*for paint, pastry*) Pinsel *m*; (*bushes*) Unterholz *nt*; (*fig: conflict*) Zusammenstoß *m* ● *vt* bürsten; putzen <*teeth*>; **~ against** streifen [gegen]; **~ aside** (*fig*) abtun.

~ off vt abbürsten. **~ up** vt/i (fig)
~ up [on] auffrischen

brusque a, **-ly** adv brüsk

Brussels n Brüssel nt. **~ sprouts**
npl Rosenkohl m

brutal a, **-ly** adv brutal. **~ity** n
Brutalität f

brute n Unmensch m. **~ force** n
rohe Gewalt f

bubble n [Luft]blase f ● vi sprudeln

buck[1] n (deer & Gym) Bock m;
(rabbit) Rammler m ● vi <horse:>
bocken

buck[2] n (Amer 🗷) Dollar m

buck[3] n pass the **~** die
Verantwortung abschieben

bucket n Eimer m

buckle n Schnalle f ● vt zuschnallen
● vi sich verbiegen

bud n Knospe f

buddy n 🗷 Freund m

budge vt bewegen ● vi sich [von der
Stelle] rühren

budget n Budget nt; (Pol)
Haushaltsplan m; (money available)
Etat m ● vi (pt/pp budgeted) **~ for**
sth etw einkalkulieren

buff a (colour) sandfarben ● n
Sandfarbe f; 🗷 Fan m ● vt polieren

buffalo n (inv or pl -es) Büffel m

buffer n (Rail) Puffer m

buffet[1] n Büfett nt; (on station)
Imbissstube f

buffet[2] vt (pt/pp buffeted) hin und
her werfen

bug n Wanze f; (🗷 virus) Bazillus m;
(🗷 device) Abhörgerät nt, 🗷 Wanze f
● vt (pt/pp bugged) 🗷 verwanzen
<room>; abhören <telephone>;
(Amer: annoy) ärgern

bugle n Signalhorn

build n (of person) Körperbau m
● vt/i (pt/pp built) bauen. **~ on** vt
anbauen (to an + acc). **~ up** vt
aufbauen ● vi zunehmen

builder n Bauunternehmer m

building n Gebäude nt. **~ site** n
Baustelle f. **~ society** n
Bausparkasse f

built see **build**. **~-in** a eingebaut.
~-in cupboard n Einbauschrank
m. **~-up area** n bebautes Gebiet nt;
(Auto) geschlossene Ortschaft f

bulb n [Blumen]zwiebel f; (Electr)
[Glüh]birne f

bulbous a bauchig

Bulgaria n Bulgarien nt

bulge n Ausbauchung f ● vi sich
ausbauchen. **~ing** a prall; <eyes>
hervorquellend

bulk n Masse f; (greater part)
Hauptteil m. **~y** a sperrig; (large)
massig

bull n Bulle m, Stier m

bulldog n Bulldogge f

bulldozer n Planierraupe f

bullet n Kugel f

bulletin n Bulletin nt

bullet-proof a kugelsicher

bullfight n Stierkampf m. **~er** n
Stierkämpfer m

bullfinch n Dompfaff m

bullock n Ochse m

bull: **~ring** n Stierkampfarena f.
~'s-eye n score a **~'s-eye** ins
Schwarze treffen

bully n Tyrann m ● vt tyrannisieren

bum n 🗷 Hintern m

bumble-bee n Hummel f

bump n Bums m; (swelling) Beule f;
(in road) holperige Stelle f ● vt
stoßen; **~ into** stoßen gegen; (meet)
zufällig treffen. **~ off** vt 🗷 um die
Ecke bringen

bumper a Rekord- ● n (Auto)
Stoßstange f

bumpy a holperig

bun n Milchbrötchen nt; (hair)
[Haar]knoten m

bunch n (of flowers) Strauß m; (of
radishes, keys) Bund m; (of people)
Gruppe f; **~ of grapes** [ganze]
Weintraube f

bundle n Bündel nt ● vt **~ [up]**
bündeln

bungalow n Bungalow m

bungle vt verpfuschen

bunk n [Schlaf]koje f. **~-beds** npl
Etagenbett nt

bunker *n* Bunker *m*

bunny *n* 🔲 Kaninchen *nt*

buoy *n* Boje *f*

buoyan|cy *n* Auftrieb *m*. ~**t** *a* be ~**t** schwimmen

burden *n* Last *f*

bureau *n* (*pl* -**x** *or* -**s**) (*desk*) Sekretär *m*; (*office*) Büro *nt*

bureaucracy *n* Bürokratie *f*

bureaucratic *a* bürokratisch

burger *n* Hamburger *m*

burglar *n* Einbrecher *m*. ~ **alarm** *n* Alarmanlage *f*

burglary *n* Einbruch *m*

burgle *vt* einbrechen in (+ *acc*); they have been ~**d** bei ihnen ist eingebrochen worden

burial *n* Begräbnis *nt*

burly *a* (-ier, -iest) stämmig

Burm|a *n* Birma *nt*. ~**ese** *a* birmanisch

burn *n* Verbrennung *f*; (*on skin*) Brandwunde *f*; (*on material*) Brandstelle *f* ● *v* (*pt/pp* **burnt** *or* **burned**) ● *vt* verbrennen ● *vi* brennen; <*food:*> anbrennen. ~ **down** *vt/i* niederbrennen

burnt *see* burn

burp *vi* 🔲 aufstoßen

burrow *n* Bau *m* ● *vi* wühlen

burst *n* Bruch *m*; (*surge*) Ausbruch *m* ● *v* (*pt/pp* **burst**) ● *vt* platzen machen ● *vi* platzen; <*bud:*> aufgehen; ~ **into tears** in Tränen ausbrechen

bury *vt* (*pt/pp* -**ied**) begraben; (*hide*) vergraben

bus *n* [Auto]bus *m*

bush *n* Strauch *m*; (*land*) Busch *m*. ~**y** *a* (-ier, -iest) buschig

busily *adv* eifrig

business *n* Angelegenheit *f*; (*Comm*) Geschäft *nt*; on ~ geschäftlich; he has no ~ er hat kein Recht (to zu); mind one's own ~ sich um seine eigenen Angelegenheiten kümmern; that's none of your ~ das geht Sie nichts an. ~**like** *a* geschäftsmäßig. ~**man** *n* Geschäftsmann *m*

bus-stop *n* Bushaltestelle *f*

bust[1] *n* Büste *f*

bust[2] *a* 🔲 kaputt; go ~ Pleite gehen ● *v* (*pt/pp* **busted** *or* **bust**) 🔲 ● *vt* kaputtmachen ● *vi* kaputtgehen

busy *a* (-ier, -iest) beschäftigt; <*day*> voll; <*street*> belebt; (*with traffic*) stark befahren; (*Amer Teleph*) besetzt; be ~ zu tun haben ● *vt* ~ **oneself** sich beschäftigen (with mit)

but *conj* aber; (*after negative*) sondern ● *prep* außer (+ *dat*); ~ **for** (*without*) ohne (+ *acc*); the last ~ one der/die/ das vorletzte; the next ~ one der/ die/das übernächste ● *adv* nur

butcher *n* Fleischer *m*, Metzger *m*; ~**'s** [shop] Fleischerei *f*, Metzgerei *f* ● *vt* [ab]schlachten

butler *n* Butler *m*

butt *n* (*of gun*) [Gewehr]kolben *m*; (*fig: target*) Zielscheibe *f*; (*of cigarette*) Stummel *m*; (*for water*) Regentonne *f* ● *vi* ~ **in** unterbrechen

butter *n* Butter *f* ● *vt* mit Butter bestreichen. ~ **up** *vt* 🔲 schmeicheln (+ *dat*)

butter: ~**cup** *a* Butterblume *f*, Hahnenfuß *m*. ~**fly** *n* Schmetterling *m*

buttocks *npl* Gesäß *nt*

button *n* Knopf *m* ● *vt* ~ **[up]** zuknöpfen. ~**hole** *n* Knopfloch *nt*

buy *n* Kauf *m* ● *vt* (*pt/pp* **bought**) kaufen. ~**er** *n* Käufer(in) *m(f)*

buzz *n* Summen *nt* ● *vi* summen

buzzer *n* Summer *m*

by *prep* (*close to*) bei (+ *dat*); (*next to*) neben (+ *dat/acc*); (*past*) an (+ *dat*) … vorbei; (*to the extent of*) um (+ *acc*); (*at the latest*) bis; (*by means of*) durch; by Mozart/Dickens von Mozart/Dickens; ~ **oneself** allein; ~ **the sea** am Meer; ~ **car/bus** mit dem Auto/Bus; ~ **sea** mit dem Schiff; ~ **day/night** bei Tag/Nacht; ~ **the hour** pro Stunde; ~ **the metre** meterweise; **six metres** ~ **four** sechs mal vier Meter; **win** ~ **a length** mit einer Länge Vorsprung gewinnen; **miss the train** ~ **a minute** den Zug um eine Minute verpassen ● *adv* ~ **and large** im Großen und Ganzen; **put** ~

beiseite legen; **go/pass** ~
vorbeigehen
bye *int* 🔲 tschüs
by: ~**-election** *n* Nachwahl *f*.
~**pass** *n* Umgehungsstraße *f*; (*Med*)
Bypass *m* ● *vt* umfahren. ~**-**
product *n* Nebenprodukt *m*.
~**stander** *n* Zuschauer(in) *m(f)*

Cc

cab *n* Taxi *nt*; (*of lorry, train*)
Führerhaus *nt*
cabaret *n* Kabarett *nt*
cabbage *n* Kohl *m*
cabin *n* Kabine *f*; (*hut*) Hütte *f*
cabinet *n* Schrank *m*; **[display]** ~
Vitrine *f*; **C**~ (*Pol*) Kabinett *nt*
cable *n* Kabel *nt*; (*rope*) Tau *nt*. ~
railway *n* Seilbahn *f*. ~
television *n* Kabelfernsehen *nt*
cackle *vi* gackern
cactus *n* (*pl* -**ti** *or* -**tuses**) Kaktus *m*
cadet *n* Kadett *m*
cadge *vt/i* 🔲 schnorren
Caesarean *a & n* ~ **[section]**
Kaiserschnitt *m*
café *n* Café *nt*
cafeteria *n*
Selbstbedienungsrestaurant *nt*
cage *n* Käfig *m*
cagey *a* 🔲 **be** ~ mit der Sprache
nicht herauswollen
cake *n* Kuchen *m*; (*of soap*) Stück *nt*.
~**d** *a* verkrustet (**with** mit)
calamity *n* Katastrophe *f*
calculat|e *vt* berechnen; (*estimate*)
kalkulieren. ~**ing** *a* (*fig*)
berechnend. ~**ion** *n* Rechnung *f*,
Kalkulation *f*. ~**or** *n* Rechner *m*
calendar *n* Kalender *m*
calf¹ *n* (*pl* **calves**) Kalb *nt*
calf² *n* (*pl* **calves**) (*Anat*) Wade *f*
calibre *n* Kaliber *nt*

call *n* Ruf *m*; (*Teleph*) Anruf *m*; (*visit*)
Besuch *m* ● *vt* rufen; (*Teleph*)
anrufen; (*wake*) wecken; ausrufen
<*strike*>; (*name*) nennen; **be** ~**ed**
heißen ● *vi* rufen; **[in *or* round]**
vorbeikommen. ~ **back** *vt*
zurückrufen ● *vi* noch einmal
vorbeikommen. ~ **for** *vt* rufen nach;
(*demand*) verlangen; (*fetch*) abholen.
~ **off** *vt* zurückrufen <*dog*>; (*cancel*)
absagen. ~ **on** *vt* bitten (**for** um);
(*appeal to*) appellieren an (+ *acc*);
(*visit*) besuchen. ~ **out** *vt* rufen;
aufrufen <*names*> ● *vi* rufen. ~ **up**
vt (*Mil*) einberufen; (*Teleph*) anrufen
call: ~**-box** *n* Telefonzelle *f*. ~**er** *n*
Besucher *m*; (*Teleph*) Anrufer *m*.
~**ing** *n* Berufung *f*. ~**-up** *n* (*Mil*)
Einberufung *f*
calm *a* (-**er**, -**est**), -**ly** *adv* ruhig ● *n*
Ruhe *f* ● *vt* ~ **[down]** beruhigen ● *vi*
~ **down** sich beruhigen. ~**ness** *n*
Ruhe *f*; (*of sea*) Stille *f*
calorie *n* Kalorie *f*
calves *npl see* **calf¹** & ²
came *see* **come**
camel *n* Kamel *nt*
camera *n* Kamera *f*
camouflage *n* Tarnung *f* ● *vt*
tarnen
camp *n* Lager *nt* ● *vi* campen; (*Mil*)
kampieren
campaign *n* Feldzug *m*; (*Comm,
Pol*) Kampagne *f* ● *vi* (*Pol*) im
Wahlkampf arbeiten
camp: ~**-bed** *n* Feldbett *nt*. ~**er** *n*
Camper *m*; (*Auto*) Wohnmobil *nt*.
~**ing** *n* Camping *nt*. ~**site** *n*
Campingplatz *m*
can¹ *n* (*for petrol*) Kanister *m*; (*tin*)
Dose *f*, Büchse *f*; **a** ~ **of beer** eine
Dose Bier

can²

pres **can**, *pt* **could**

● *auxiliary verb*
····▸ (*be able to*) können. **I can't** *or*
cannot go ich kann nicht gehen. **she**
couldn't *or* **could not go** (*was unable
to*) sie konnte nicht gehen; (*would
not be able to*) sie könnte nicht

gehen. **he could go if he had time** er könnte gehen, wenn er Zeit hätte. **if I could go** wenn ich gehen könnte. **that cannot be true** das kann nicht stimmen

····➤ (*know how to*) können. **can you swim?** können Sie schwimmen? **she can drive** sie kann Auto fahren

····➤ (*be allowed to*) dürfen. **you can't smoke here** hier dürfen Sie nicht rauchen. **can I go?** kann *od* darf ich gehen?

····➤ (*in requests*) können. **can I have a glass of water, please?** kann ich ein Glas Wasser haben, bitte? **could you ring me tomorrow?** könnten Sie mich morgen anrufen?

····➤ **could** (*expressing possibility*) könnte. **that could be so** das könnte *od* kann sein. **I could have killed him** ich hätte ihn umbringen können

Canad|a *n* Kanada *nt*. **~ian** *a* kanadisch ● *n* Kanadier(in) *m(f)*

canal *n* Kanal *m*

canary *n* Kanarienvogel *m*

cancel *vt/i* (*pt/pp* **cancelled**) absagen; abbestellen <*newspaper*>; **be ~led** ausfallen. **~lation** *n* Absage *f*

cancer *n*, & (*Astr*) **C~** Krebs *m*. **~ous** *a* krebsig

candid *a*, **-ly** *adv* offen

candidate *n* Kandidat(in) *m(f)*

candle *n* Kerze *f*. **~stick** *n* Kerzenständer *m*, Leuchter *m*

candy *n* (*Amer*) Süßigkeiten *pl*; **[piece of]** ~ Bonbon *m*

cane *n* Rohr *nt*; (*stick*) Stock *m* ● *vt* mit dem Stock züchtigen

canine *a* Hunde-. ~ **tooth** *n* Eckzahn *m*

cannabis *n* Haschisch *nt*

canned *a* Dosen-, Büchsen-

cannibal *n* Kannibale *m*. **~ism** *n* Kannibalismus *m*

cannon *n inv* Kanone *f*

cannot *see* can²

canoe *n* Paddelboot *nt*; (*Sport*) Kanu *nt*

can-opener *n* Dosenöffner *m*

can't = cannot. *See* can²

canteen *n* Kantine *f*; ~ **of cutlery** Besteckkasten *m*

canter *n* Kanter *m* ● *vi* kantern

canvas *n* Segeltuch *nt*; (*Art*) Leinwand *f*; (*painting*) Gemälde *nt*

canvass *vi* um Stimmen werben

canyon *n* Cañon *m*

cap *n* Kappe *f*, Mütze *f*; (*nurse's*) Haube *f*; (*top, lid*) Verschluss *m*

capability *n* Fähigkeit *f*

capable *a*, **-bly** *adv* fähig; **be ~ of doing sth** fähig sein, etw zu tun

capacity *n* Fassungsvermögen *nt*; (*ability*) Fähigkeit *f*; **in my ~ as** in meiner Eigenschaft als

cape¹ *n* (*cloak*) Cape *nt*

cape² *n* (*Geog*) Kap *nt*

capital *a* <*letter*> groß ● *n* (*town*) Hauptstadt *f*; (*money*) Kapital *nt*; (*letter*) Großbuchstabe *m*

capital|ism *n* Kapitalismus *m*. **~ist** *a* kapitalistisch ● *n* Kapitalist *m*. ~ **letter** *n* Großbuchstabe *m*. ~ **punishment** *n* Todesstrafe *f*

capsize *vi* kentern ● *vt* zum Kentern bringen

captain *n* Kapitän *m*; (*Mil*) Hauptmann *m* ● *vt* anführen <*team*>

caption *n* Überschrift *f*; (*of illustration*) Bildtext *m*

captivate *vt* bezaubern

captiv|e *a* **hold/take ~e** gefangen halten/nehmen ● *n* Gefangene(r) *m/f*. **~ity** *n* Gefangenschaft *f*

capture *n* Gefangennahme *f* ● *vt* gefangen nehmen; [ein]fangen <*animal*>; (*Mil*) einnehmen <*town*>

car *n* Auto *nt*, Wagen *m*; **by ~** mit dem Auto *od* Wagen

caramel *n* Karamell *m*

carat *n* Karat *nt*

caravan *n* Wohnwagen *m*; (*procession*) Karawane *f*

carbon *n* Kohlenstoff *m*; (*paper*) Kohlepapier *nt*; (*copy*) Durchschlag *m*

carbon: ~ **copy** *n* Durchschlag *m*. ~ **paper** *n* Kohlepapier *nt*

carburettor *n* Vergaser *m*

carcass *n* Kadaver *m*

card *n* Karte *f*

cardboard *n* Pappe *f*, Karton *m*. ~ **box** *n* Pappschachtel *f*; (*large*) [Papp]karton *m*

card-game *n* Kartenspiel *nt*

cardigan *n* Strickjacke *f*

cardinal *a* Kardinal- ● *n* (*Relig*) Kardinal *m*

card index *n* Kartei *f*

care *n* Sorgfalt *f*; (*caution*) Vorsicht *f*; (*protection*) Obhut *f*; (*looking after*) Pflege *f*; (*worry*) Sorge *f*; ~ of (*on letter abbr* **c/o**) bei; **take** ~ vorsichtig sein; **take into** ~ in Pflege nehmen; **take** ~ **of** sich kümmern um ● *vi* ~ **for** (*like*) mögen; (*look after*) betreuen; **I don't** ~ das ist mir gleich

career *n* Laufbahn *f*; (*profession*) Beruf *m* ● *vi* rasen

care: ~**free** *a* sorglos. ~**ful** *a*, **-ly** *adv* sorgfältig; (*cautious*) vorsichtig. ~**less** *a*, **-ly** *adv* nachlässig. ~**lessness** *n* Nachlässigkeit *f*

caretaker *n* Hausmeister *m*

car ferry *n* Autofähre *f*

cargo *n* (*pl* **-es**) Ladung *f*

Caribbean *n* the ~ die Karibik

caricature *n* Karikatur *f* ● *vt* karikieren

caring *a* <*parent*> liebevoll; <*profession, attitude*> sozial

carnation *n* Nelke *f*

carnival *n* Karneval *m*

carol *n* [**Christmas**] ~ Weihnachtslied *nt*

carp[1] *n inv* Karpfen *m*

carp[2] *vi* nörgeln

car park *n* Parkplatz *m*; (*multistorey*) Parkhaus *nt*; (*underground*) Tiefgarage *f*

carpent|er *n* Zimmermann *m*; (*joiner*) Tischler *m*. ~**ry** *n* Tischlerei *f*

carpet *n* Teppich *m*

carriage *n* Kutsche *f*; (*Rail*) Wagen *m*; (*of goods*) Beförderung *f*; (*cost*) Frachtkosten *pl*; (*bearing*) Haltung *f*

carrier *n* Träger(in) *m(f)*; (*Comm*) Spediteur *m*; ~ [**-bag**] Tragetasche *f*

carrot *n* Möhre *f*, Karotte *f*

carry *vt/i* (*pt/pp* **-ied**) tragen; **be carried away** ⊞ hingerissen sein. ~ **off** *vt* wegtragen; gewinnen <*prize*>. ~ **on** *vi* weitermachen; ~ **on with** ⊞ eine Affäre haben mit ● *vt* führen; (*continue*) fortführen. ~ **out** *vt* hinaus-/heraustragen; (*perform*) ausführen

cart *n* Karren *m*; **put the** ~ **before the horse** das Pferd beim Schwanz aufzäumen ● *vt* karren; (⊞ *carry*) schleppen

carton *n* [Papp]karton *m*; (*for drink*) Tüte *f*; (*of cream, yoghurt*) Becher *m*

cartoon *n* Karikatur *f*; (*joke*) Witzzeichnung *f*; (*strip*) Comic Strips *pl*; (*film*) Zeichentrickfilm *m*. ~**ist** *n* Karikaturist *m*

cartridge *n* Patrone *f*; (*for film*) Kassette *f*

carve *vt* schnitzen; (*in stone*) hauen; (*Culin*) aufschneiden

carving *n* Schnitzerei *f*. ~**-knife** *n* Tranchiermesser *nt*

car wash *n* Autowäsche *f*; (*place*) Autowaschanlage *f*

case[1] *n* Fall *m*; **in any** ~ auf jeden Fall; **just in** ~ für alle Fälle; **in** ~ **he comes** falls er kommt

case[2] *n* Kasten *m*; (*crate*) Kiste *f*; (*for spectacles*) Etui *nt*; (*suitcase*) Koffer *m*; (*for display*) Vitrine *f*

cash *n* Bargeld *nt*; **pay [in]** ~ [in] bar bezahlen; ~ **on delivery** per Nachnahme ● *vt* einlösen <*cheque*>. ~ **desk** *n* Kasse *f*

cashier *n* Kassierer(in) *m(f)*

cash register *n* Registrierkasse *f*

cassette *n* Kassette *f*. ~ **recorder** *n* Kassettenrecorder *m*

cast *n* (*mould*) Form *f*; (*model*) Abguss *m*; (*Theat*) Besetzung *f*; [**plaster**] ~ (*Med*) Gipsverband *m* ● *vt* (*pt/pp* **cast**) (*throw*) werfen; (*shed*) abwerfen; abgeben <*vote*>; gießen <*metal*>; (*Theat*) besetzen <*role*>. ~ **off** *vi* (*Naut*) ablegen

castle *n* Schloss *nt*; (*fortified*) Burg *f*; (*Chess*) Turm *m*

cast-offs *npl* abgelegte Kleidung *f*

castor n (wheel) [Lauf]rolle f

castor sugar n Streuzucker m

casual a, **-ly** adv (chance) zufällig; (offhand) lässig; (informal) zwanglos; (not permanent) Gelegenheits-; ~ **wear** Freizeitbekleidung f

casualty n [Todes]opfer nt; (injured person) Verletzte(r) m/f; ~ **[department]** Unfallstation f

cat n Katze f

catalogue n Katalog m ● vt katalogisieren

catapult n Katapult nt ● vt katapultieren

cataract n (Med) grauer Star m

catarrh n Katarrh m

catastroph|e n Katastrophe f. ~**ic** a katastrophal

catch n (of fish) Fang m; (fastener) Verschluss m; (on door) Klinke f; (☐ snag) Haken m ☐ ● v (pt/pp caught) ● vt fangen; (be in time for) erreichen; (travel by) fahren mit; bekommen <illness>; ~ **a cold** sich erkälten; ~ **sight of** erblicken; ~ **s.o. stealing** jdn beim Stehlen erwischen; ~ **one's finger in the door** sich (dat) den Finger in der Tür [ein]klemmen ● vi (burn) anbrennen; (get stuck) klemmen. ~ **on** vi ☐ (understand) kapieren; (become popular) sich durchsetzen. ~ **up** vt einholen ● vi aufholen; ~ **up with** einholen <s.o.>; nachholen <work>

catching a ansteckend

catch: ~**-phrase** n, ~**word** n Schlagwort nt

catchy a (-ier, -iest) einprägsam

categor|ical a, **-ly** adv kategorisch. ~**y** n Kategorie f

cater vi ~ **for** beköstigen; <firm:> das Essen liefern für <party>; (fig) eingestellt sein auf (+ acc). ~**ing** n (trade) Gaststättengewerbe nt

caterpillar n Raupe f

cathedral n Dom m, Kathedrale f

Catholic a katholisch ● n Katholik(in) m(f). **C** ~**ism** n Katholizismus m

cattle npl Vieh nt

catty a (-ier, -iest) boshaft

caught see catch

cauliflower n Blumenkohl m

cause n Ursache f; (reason) Grund m; **good** ~ gute Sache f ● vt verursachen; ~ **s.o. to do sth** jdn veranlassen, etw zu tun

caution n Vorsicht f; (warning) Verwarnung f ● vt (Jur) verwarnen

cautious a, **-ly** adv vorsichtig

cavalry n Kavallerie f

cave n Höhle f ● vi ~ **in** einstürzen

cavern n Höhle f

caviare n Kaviar m

cavity n Hohlraum m; (in tooth) Loch nt

CD abbr (compact disc) CD f; ~**-ROM** CD-ROM f

cease vt/i aufhören. ~**-fire** n Waffenruhe f. ~**less** a, **-ly** adv unaufhörlich

cedar n Zeder f

ceiling n [Zimmer]decke f; (fig) oberste Grenze f

celebrat|e vt/i feiern. ~**ed** a berühmt (for wegen). ~**ion** n Feier f

celebrity n Berühmtheit f

celery n [Stangen]sellerie m & f

cell n Zelle f

cellar n Keller m

cellist n Cellist(in) m(f)

cello n Cello nt

Celsius a Celsius

Celt n Kelte m/ Keltin f. ~**ic** a keltisch

cement n Zement m; (adhesive) Kitt m

cemetery n Friedhof m

censor n Zensor m ● vt zensieren. ~**ship** n Zensur f

census n Volkszählung f

cent n (coin) Cent m

centenary n, (Amer) **centennial** n Hundertjahrfeier f

center n (Amer) = centre

centi|grade a Celsius. ~**metre** n Zentimeter m & nt

central a, **-ly** adv zentral. ~ **heating** n Zentralheizung f. ~**ize** vt zentralisieren

centre n Zentrum nt; (middle) Mitte f ● v (pt/pp **centred**) ● vt zentrieren. **∼-forward** n Mittelstürmer m

century n Jahrhundert nt

ceramic a Keramik-

cereal n Getreide nt; (breakfast food) Frühstücksflocken pl

ceremon|ial a, -ly adv zeremoniell, feierlich ● n Zeremoniell nt. **∼ious** a, -ly adv formell

ceremony n Zeremonie f, Feier f

certain a sicher; (not named) gewiss; **for ∼** mit Bestimmtheit; **make ∼** (check) sich vergewissern (that dass); (ensure) dafür sorgen (that dass); **he is ∼ to win** er wird ganz bestimmt siegen. **∼ly** adv bestimmt, sicher; **∼ly not!** auf keinen Fall! **∼ty** n Sicherheit f, Gewissheit f; **it's a ∼ty** es ist sicher

certificate n Bescheinigung f, (Jur) Urkunde f; (Sch) Zeugnis nt

certify vt (pt/pp -ied) bescheinigen; (declare insane) für geisteskrank erklären

cf. abbr (compare) vgl.

chafe vt wund reiben

chaffinch n Buchfink m

chain n Kette f ● vt ketten (**to** an + acc). **∼ up** vt anketten

chain: ∼ reaction n Kettenreaktion f. **∼-smoker** n Kettenraucher m. **∼ store** n Kettenladen m

chair n Stuhl m; (Univ) Lehrstuhl m; (Adm) Vorsitzende(r) m/f. **∼-lift** n Sessellift m. **∼man** n Vorsitzende(r) m/f

chalet n Chalet nt

chalk n Kreide f

challeng|e n Herausforderung f, (Mil) Anruf m ● vt herausfordern; (Mil) anrufen; (fig) anfechten <statement>. **∼er** n Herausforderer m. **∼ing** a herausfordernd; (demanding) anspruchsvoll

chamber n Kammer f, **C∼ of Commerce** Handelskammer f. **∼ music** n Kammermusik f

chamber music n Kammermusik f

chamois n **∼-[leather]** Ledertuch nt

champagne n Champagner m

champion n (Sport) Meister(in) m(f); (of cause) Verfechter m ● vt sich einsetzen für. **∼ship** n (Sport) Meisterschaft f

chance n Zufall m; (prospect) Chancen pl; (likelihood) Aussicht f, (opportunity) Gelegenheit f, **by ∼** zufällig; **take a ∼** ein Risiko eingehen; **give s.o. a ∼** jdm eine Chance geben ● attrib zufällig ● vt **∼ it** es riskieren

chancellor n Kanzler m; (Univ) Rektor m

chancy a riskant

change n Veränderung f, (alteration) Änderung f, (money) Wechselgeld nt; **for a ∼** zur Abwechslung ● vt wechseln; (alter) ändern; (exchange) umtauschen (**for** gegen); (transform) verwandeln; trocken legen <baby>; **∼ one's clothes** sich umziehen; **∼ trains** umsteigen ● vi sich verändern; (**∼ clothes**) sich umziehen; (**∼ trains**) umsteigen; **all ∼!** alles aussteigen!

changeable a wechselhaft

changing-room n Umkleideraum m

channel n Rinne f, (Radio, TV) Kanal m; (fig) Weg m; **the [English] C∼** der Ärmelkanal; **the C∼ Islands** die Kanalinseln

chant vt singen; <demonstrators:> skandieren

chao|s n Chaos nt. **∼tic** a chaotisch

chap n 🗉 Kerl m

chapel n Kapelle f

chaplain n Geistliche(r) m

chapped a <skin> aufgesprungen

chapter n Kapitel nt

character n Charakter m; (in novel, play) Gestalt f, (Typ) Schriftzeichen nt; **out of ∼** uncharakteristisch; **quite a ∼** 🗉 ein Original

characteristic a, -ally adv charakteristisch (**of** für) ● n Merkmal nt

characterize *vt* charakterisieren

charge *n* (*price*) Gebühr *f*; (*Electr*) Ladung *f*; (*attack*) Angriff *m*; (*Jur*) Anklage *f*; **free of** ~ kostenlos; **be in** ~ **verantwortlich sein (of für); take** ~ **die Aufsicht übernehmen (of über + acc)** ● *vt* berechnen <*fee*>; (*Electr*) laden; (*attack*) angreifen; (*Jur*) anklagen (**with** *gen*); ~ **s.o. for sth** jdm etw berechnen

charitable *a* wohltätig; (*kind*) wohlwollend

charity *n* Nächstenliebe *f*; (*organization*) wohltätige Einrichtung *f*; **for** ~ für Wohltätigkeitszwecke

charm *n* Reiz *m*; (*of person*) Charme *f*; (*object*) Amulett *nt* ● *vt* bezaubern. ~**ing** *a*, **-ly** *adv* reizend; <*person, smile*> charmant

chart *n* Karte *f*; (*table*) Tabelle *f*

charter *n* ~ **[flight]** Charterflug *m* ● *vt* chartern; ~**ed accountant** Wirtschaftsprüfer(in) *m(f)*

chase *n* Verfolgungsjagd *f* ● *vt* jagen, verfolgen. ~ **away** *or* **off** *vt* wegjagen

chassis *n* (*pl* **chassis**) Chassis *nt*

chaste *a* keusch

chat *n* Plauderei *f*; **have a** ~ **with** plaudern mit ● *vi* (*pt/pp* **chatted**) plaudern. ~ **show** *n* Talkshow *f*

chatter *n* Geschwätz *nt* ● *vi* schwatzen; <*child*:> plappern; <*teeth*:> klappern. ~**box** *n* 🔲 Plappermaul *nt*

chatty *a* (**-ier, -iest**) geschwätzig

chauffeur *n* Chauffeur *m*

cheap *a* & *adv* (**-er, -est**), **-ly** *adv* billig. ~**en** *vt* entwürdigen

cheat *n* Betrüger(in) *m(f)*; (*at games*) Mogler *m* ● *vt* betrügen ● *vi* (*at games*) mogeln 🔲

check¹ *a* (*squared*) kariert ● *n* Karo *nt*

check² *n* Überprüfung *f*; (*inspection*) Kontrolle *f*; (*Chess*) Schach *nt*; (*Amer: bill*) Rechnung *f*; (*Amer: cheque*) Scheck *m*; (*Amer: tick*) Haken *m*; **keep a** ~ **on** kontrollieren ● *vt* [über]prüfen; (*inspect*)

kontrollieren; (*restrain*) hemmen; (*stop*) aufhalten ● *vi* **[go and]** ~ nachsehen. ~ **in** *vi* sich anmelden; (*Aviat*) einchecken ● *vt* abfertigen; einchecken. ~ **out** *vi* sich abmelden. ~ **up** *vi* prüfen, kontrollieren; ~ **up on** überprüfen

checked *a* kariert

check: ~**out** *n* Kasse *f*. ~**room** *n* (*Amer*) Garderobe *f*. ~**-up** *n* (*Med*) [Kontroll]untersuchung *f*

cheek *n* Backe *f*; (*impudence*) Frechheit *f*. ~**y** *a*, **-ily** *adv* frech

cheer *n* Beifallsruf *m*; **three** ~**s** ein dreifaches Hoch (**for** auf + *acc*); ~**s!** prost! (*goodbye*) tschüs! ● *vt* zujubeln (+ *dat*) ● *vi* jubeln. ~ **up** *vt* aufmuntern; aufheitern ● *vi* munterer werden. ~**ful** *a*, **-ly** *adv* fröhlich. ~**fulness** *n* Fröhlichkeit *f*

cheerio *int* 🔲 tschüs!

cheese *n* Käse *m*. ~**cake** *n* Käsekuchen *m*

chef *n* Koch *m*

chemical *a*, **-ly** *adv* chemisch ● *n* Chemikalie *f*

chemist *n* (*pharmacist*) Apotheker(in) *m(f)*; (*scientist*) Chemiker(in) *m(f)*; ~**'s [shop]** Drogerie *f*; (*dispensing*) Apotheke *f*. ~**ry** *n* Chemie *f*

cheque *n* Scheck *m*. ~**-book** *n* Scheckbuch *nt*. ~ **card** *n* Scheckkarte *f*

cherish *vt* lieben; (*fig*) hegen

cherry *n* Kirsche *f* ● *attrib* Kirsch-

chess *n* Schach *nt*

chess: ~**board** *n* Schachbrett *nt*. ~**-man** *n* Schachfigur *f*

chest *n* Brust *f*; (*box*) Truhe *f*

chestnut *n* Esskastanie *f*, Marone *f*; (*horse-*) [Ross]kastanie *f*

chest of drawers *n* Kommode *f*

chew *vt* kauen. ~**ing-gum** *n* Kaugummi *m*

chick *n* Küken *nt*

chicken *n* Huhn *nt* ● *attrib* Hühner- ● *a* 🔲 feige

chief *a* Haupt- ● *n* Chef *m*; (*of tribe*) Häuptling *m*. ~**ly** *adv* hauptsächlich

child *n* (*pl* ~**ren**) Kind *nt*

child: ~**birth** n Geburt f. ~**hood** n
Kindheit f. ~**ish** a kindisch. ~**less**
a kinderlos. ~**like** a kindlich. ~-
minder n Tagesmutter f

children npl see **child**

Chile n Chile nt

chill n Kälte f; (illness) Erkältung f
● vt kühlen

chilly a kühl; **I felt** ~ mich fröstelte
[es]

chime vi läuten; <clock:> schlagen

chimney n Schornstein m. ~-**pot** n
Schornsteinaufsatz m. ~-**sweep** n
Schornsteinfeger m

chin n Kinn nt

china n Porzellan nt

Chin|a n China nt. ~**ese** a
chinesisch ● n (Lang) Chinesisch nt;
the ~**ese** pl die Chinesen

chink¹ n (slit) Ritze f

chink² n Geklirr nt ● vi klirren;
<coins:> klimpern

chip n (fragment) Span m; (in china,
paintwork) angeschlagene Stelle f;
(Computing, Gambling) Chip m; ~**s**
pl (Culin) Pommes frites pl; (Amer:
crisps) Chips pl ● vt (pt/pp **chipped**)
(damage) anschlagen. ~**ped** a
angeschlagen

chirp vi zwitschern; <cricket:>
zirpen. ~**y** a 🄴 munter

chit n Zettel m

chocolate n Schokolade f; (sweet)
Praline f

choice n Wahl f; (variety) Auswahl f
● a auserlesen

choir n Chor m. ~**boy** n Chorknabe
m

choke n (Auto) Choke m ● vt
würgen; (to death) erwürgen ● vi
sich verschlucken; ~ **on** [fast]
ersticken an (+ dat)

choose vt/i (pt **chose**, pp **chosen**)
wählen; (select) sich (dat) aussuchen;
~ **to do/go** [freiwillig] tun/gehen; **as
you** ~ wie Sie wollen

choos[e]y a 🄴 wählerisch

chop n (blow) Hieb m; (Culin)
Kotelett nt ● vt (pt/pp **chopped**)
hacken. ~ **down** vt abhacken;
fällen <tree>. ~ **off** vt abhacken

chop|per n Beil nt; 🄴 (helicopter)
Hubschrauber m. ~**py** a kabbelig

chopsticks npl Essstäbchen pl

choral a Chor-

chord n (Mus) Akkord m

chore n lästige Pflicht f; [household]
~**s** Hausarbeit f

chorus n Chor m; (of song) Refrain
m

chose, chosen see **choose**

Christ n Christus m

christen vt taufen

Christian a christlich ● n
Christ(in) m(f). ~**ity** n Christentum
nt. ~ **name** n Vorname m

Christmas n Weihnachten nt. ~
card n Weihnachtskarte f. ~ **Day** n
erster Weihnachtstag m. ~ **Eve** n
Heiligabend m. ~ **tree** n
Weihnachtsbaum m

chrome n, **chromium** n Chrom nt

chronic a chronisch

chronicle n Chronik f

chrysanthemum n
Chrysantheme f

chubby a (-ier, -iest) mollig

chuck vt 🄴 schmeißen. ~ **out** vt 🄴
rausschmeißen

chuckle vi in sich (acc)
hineinlachen

chum n Freund(in) m(f)

chunk n Stück nt

church n Kirche f. ~**yard** n
Friedhof m

churn vt ~ **out** am laufenden Band
produzieren

cider n ≈ Apfelwein m

cigar n Zigarre f

cigarette n Zigarette f

cine-camera n Filmkamera f

cinema n Kino nt

cinnamon n Zimt m

circle n Kreis m; (Theat) Rang m
● vt umkreisen ● vi kreisen

circuit n Runde f; (racetrack)
Rennbahn f; (Electr) Stromkreis m.
~**ous** a ~ **route** Umweg m

circular a kreisförmig ● n
Rundschreiben nt. ~ **saw** n
Kreissäge f. ~ **tour** n Rundfahrt f

circulat|e *vt* in Umlauf setzen ● *vi* zirkulieren. **∼ion** *n* Kreislauf *m*; (*of newspaper*) Auflage *f*

circumference *n* Umfang *m*

circumstance *n* Umstand *m*; **∼s** *pl* Umstände *pl*; (*financial*) Verhältnisse *pl*

circus *n* Zirkus *m*

cistern *n* (*tank*) Wasserbehälter *m*; (*of WC*) Spülkasten *m*

cite *vt* zitieren

citizen *n* Bürger(in) *m(f)*. **∼ship** *n* Staatsangehörigkeit *f*

citrus *n* ∼ [**fruit**] Zitrusfrucht *f*

city *n* [Groß]stadt *f*

civic *a* Bürger-

civil *a* bürgerlich; <*aviation, defence*> zivil; (*polite*) höflich. **∼ engineering** *n* Hoch- und Tiefbau *m*

civilian *a* Zivil-; **in** ∼ **clothes** in Zivil ● *n* Zivilist *m*

civiliz|ation *n* Zivilisation *f*. **∼e** *vt* zivilisieren

civil: ∼servant *n* Beamte(r) *m*/ Beamtin *f*. **C∼ Service** *n* Staatsdienst *m*

claim *n* Anspruch *m*; (*application*) Antrag *m*; (*demand*) Forderung *f*; (*assertion*) Behauptung *f* ● *vt* beanspruchen; (*apply for*) beantragen; (*demand*) fordern; (*assert*) behaupten; (*collect*) abholen

clam *n* Klaffmuschel *f*

clamber *vi* klettern

clammy *a* (-ier, -iest) feucht

clamour *n* Geschrei *nt* ● *vi* ∼ **for** schreien nach

clamp *n* Klammer *f* ● *vt* [ein]spannen ● *vi* 🔲 ∼ **down on** vorgehen gegen

clan *n* Clan *m*

clang *n* Schmettern *nt*. **∼er** *n* 🔲 Schnitzer *m*

clank *vi* klirren

clap *n* **give s.o. a** ∼ jdm Beifall klatschen; ∼ **of thunder** Donnerschlag *m* ● *vt/i* (*pt/pp* **clapped**) Beifall klatschen (+ *dat*); ∼ **one's hands** [in die Hände] klatschen

clari|fication *n* Klärung *f*. **∼fy** *vt/i* (*pt/pp* -**ied**) klären

clarinet *n* Klarinette *f*

clarity *n* Klarheit *f*

clash *n* Geklirr *nt*; (*fig*) Konflikt *m* ● *vi* klirren; <*colours:*> sich beißen; <*events:*> ungünstig zusammenfallen

clasp *n* Verschluss *m* ● *vt* ergreifen; (*hold*) halten

class *n* Klasse *f*; **travel first/second** ∼ erster/zweiter Klasse reisen ● *vt* einordnen

classic *a* klassisch ● *n* Klassiker *m*. **∼al** *a* klassisch

classi|fication *n* Klassifikation *f*. **∼fy** *vt* (*pt/pp* -**ied**) klassifizieren

classroom *n* Klassenzimmer *nt*

classy *a* (-ier, -iest) 🔲 schick

clatter *n* Geklapper *nt* ● *vi* klappern

clause *n* Klausel *f*; (*Gram*) Satzteil *m*

claw *n* Kralle *f*; (*of bird of prey & Techn*) Klaue *f*; (*of crab, lobster*) Schere *f* ● *vt* kratzen

clay *n* Lehm *m*; (*pottery*) Ton *m*

clean *a* (-er, -est) sauber ● *adv* glatt ● *vt* sauber machen; putzen <*shoes, windows*>; ∼ **one's teeth** sich (*dat*) die Zähne putzen; **have sth** ∼**ed** etw reinigen lassen. ∼ **up** *vt* sauber machen

cleaner *n* Putzfrau *f*; (*substance*) Reinigungsmittel *nt*; [**dry**] ∼**'s** chemische Reinigung *f*

cleanliness *n* Sauberkeit *f*

cleanse *vt* reinigen

clear *a* (-er, -est), **-ly** *adv* klar; (*obvious*) eindeutig; (*distinct*) deutlich; <*conscience*> rein; (*without obstacles*) frei; **make sth** ∼ etw klarmachen (**to** *dat*) ● *adv* **stand** ∼ zurücktreten; **keep** ∼ **of** aus dem Wege gehen (+ *dat*) ● *vt* räumen; abräumen <*table*>; (*acquit*) freisprechen; (*authorize*) genehmigen; (*jump over*) überspringen; ∼ **one's throat** sich räuspern ● *vi* <*fog:*> sich auflösen. ∼ **away** *vt* wegräumen. ∼ **off** *vi* 🔲 abhauen. ∼ **out** *vt* ausräumen ● *vi* 🔲 abhauen. ∼ **up** *vt* (*tidy*)

aufräumen; (*solve*) aufklären ● *vi*
<*weather*>: sich aufklären

clearance *n* Räumung *f*;
(*authorization*) Genehmigung *f*;
(*customs*) [Zoll]abfertigung *f*; (*Techn*)
Spielraum *m*. ~ **sale** *n*
Räumungsverkauf *m*

clench *vt* ~ one's fist die Faust
ballen; ~ one's teeth die Zähne
zusammenbeißen

clergy *npl* Geistlichkeit *f*. ~**man** *n*
Geistliche(r) *m*

clerk *n* Büroangestellte(r) *m/f*;
(*Amer: shop assistant*) Verkäufer(in)
m(f)

clever *a* (-er, -est), -ly *adv* klug;
(*skilful*) geschickt

cliché *n* Klischee *nt*

click *vi* klicken

client *n* Kunde *m*/ Kundin *f*; (*Jur*)
Klient(in) *m(f)*

cliff *n* Kliff *nt*

climate *n* Klima *nt*

climax *n* Höhepunkt *m*

climb *n* Aufstieg *m* ● *vt* besteigen
<*mountain*>; steigen auf (+ *acc*)
<*ladder, tree*> ● *vi* klettern; (*rise*)
steigen; <*road*:> ansteigen. ~ **down**
vi hinunter-/herunterklettern; (*from
ladder, tree*) heruntersteigen; 🗉
nachgeben

climber *n* Bergsteiger *m*; (*plant*)
Kletterpflanze *f*

cling *vi* (*pt/pp* clung) sich klammern
(**to** an + *acc*); (*stick*) haften (**to** an +
dat). ~ **film** *n* Sichtfolie *f* mit
Hafteffekt

clinic *n* Klinik *f*. ~**al** *a*, -ly *adv*
klinisch

clink *vi* klirren

clip¹ *n* Klammer *f*; (*jewellery*) Klipp
m ● *vt* (*pt/pp* clipped) anklammern
(**to** an + *acc*)

clip² *n* (*extract*) Ausschnitt *m* ● *vt*
schneiden; knipsen <*ticket*>. ~**ping**
n (*extract*) Ausschnitt *m*

cloak *n* Umhang *m*. ~**room** *n*
Garderobe *f*; (*toilet*) Toilette *f*

clobber *n* 🗉 Zeug *nt* ● *vt* (🗉 *hit,
defeat*) schlagen

clock *n* Uhr *f*; (🗉 *speedometer*)
Tacho *m* ● *vi* ~ **in/out** stechen

clock: ~**wise** *a* & *adv* im
Uhrzeigersinn. ~**work** *n* Uhrwerk
nt; (*of toy*) Aufziehmechanismus *m*;
like ~**work** 🗉 wie am Schnürchen

clod *n* Klumpen *m*

clog *vt/i* (*pt/pp* clogged) ~ [up]
verstopfen

cloister *n* Kreuzgang *m*

close¹ *a* (-r, -st) nah[e] (**to** *dat*);
<*friend*> eng; <*weather*> schwül;
have a ~ **shave** 🗉 mit knapper Not
davonkommen ● *adv* nahe ● *n*
(*street*) Sackgasse *f*

close² *n* Ende *nt*; draw to a ~ sich
dem Ende nähern ● *vt* zumachen,
schließen; (*bring to an end*) beenden;
sperren <*road*> ● *vi* sich schließen;
<*shop*:> schließen, zumachen; (*end*)
enden. ~ **down** *vt* schließen;
stilllegen <*factory*> ● *vi* schließen;
<*factory*:> stillgelegt werden

closely *adv* eng, nah[e]; (*with
attention*) genau

closet *n* (*Amer*) Schrank *m*

close-up *n* Nahaufnahme *f*

closure *n* Schließung *f*; (*of factory*)
Stilllegung *f*; (*of road*) Sperrung *f*

clot *n* [Blut]gerinnsel *nt*; (🗉 *idiot*)
Trottel *m*

cloth *n* Tuch *nt*

clothe *vt* kleiden

clothes *npl* Kleider *pl*. ~**-line** *n*
Wäscheleine *f*

clothing *n* Kleidung *f*

cloud *n* Wolke *f* ● *vi* ~ **over** sich
bewölken

cloudy *a* (-ier, -iest) wolkig, bewölkt;
<*liquid*> trübe

clout *n* 🗉 Schlag *m*; (*influence*)
Einfluss *m*

clove *n* [Gewürz]nelke *f*; ~ **of garlic**
Knoblauchzehe *f*

clover *n* Klee *m*. ~ **leaf** *n* Kleeblatt
nt

clown *n* Clown *m* ● *vi* ~ [about]
herumalbern

club *n* Klub *m*; (*weapon*) Keule *f*;
(*Sport*) Schläger *m*; ~**s** *pl* (*Cards*)
Kreuz *nt*, Treff *nt*

clue n Anhaltspunkt m; (in crossword) Frage f; **I haven't a ~** 🔢 ich habe keine Ahnung

clump n Gruppe f

clumsiness n Ungeschicklichkeit f

clumsy a (-ier, -iest), **-ily** adv ungeschickt; (unwieldy) unförmig

clung see cling

clutch n Griff m; (Auto) Kupplung f; **be in s.o.'s ~es** 🔢 in jds Klauen sein ● vt festhalten; (grab) ergreifen ● vi **~ at** greifen nach

clutter n Kram m ● vt ~ **[up]** vollstopfen

c/o abbr (care of) bei

coach n [Reise]bus m; (Rail) Wagen m; (horse-drawn) Kutsche f; (Sport) Trainer m ● vt Nachhilfestunden geben (+ dat); (Sport) trainieren

coal n Kohle f

coalition n Koalition f

coal-mine n Kohlenbergwerk nt

coarse a (-r, -st), **-ly** adv grob

coast n Küste f ● vi (freewheel) im Freilauf fahren; (Auto) im Leerlauf fahren. **~er** n (mat) Untersatz m

coast: **~guard** n Küstenwache f. **~line** n Küste f

coat n Mantel m; (of animal) Fell nt; (of paint) Anstrich m; **~ of arms** Wappen nt ● vt überziehen; (with paint) streichen. **~-hanger** n Kleiderbügel m. **~-hook** n Kleiderhaken m

coating n Überzug m, Schicht f; (of paint) Anstrich m

coax vt gut zureden (+ dat)

cobble[1] n Kopfstein m; **~s** pl Kopfsteinpflaster nt

cobble[2] vt flicken. **~r** n Schuster m

cobweb n Spinnengewebe nt

cock n Hahn m; (any male bird) Männchen nt ● vt <animal:> **~ its ears** die Ohren spitzen; **~ the gun** den Hahn spannen

cockerel n [junger] Hahn m

cockney n (dialect) Cockney nt; (person) Cockney m

cock: **~pit** n (Aviat) Cockpit nt. **~roach** n Küchenschabe f. **~tail** n

Cocktail m. **~-up** n 🗵 **make a ~-up** Mist bauen (of bei)

cocky a (-ier, -iest) 🔢 eingebildet

cocoa n Kakao m

coconut n Kokosnuß f

cod n inv Kabeljau m

COD abbr (cash on delivery) per Nachnahme

coddle vt verhätscheln

code n Kode m; (Computing) Code m; (set of rules) Kodex m. **~d** a verschlüsselt

coerc|e vt zwingen. **~ion** n Zwang m

coffee n Kaffee m

coffee: **~-grinder** n Kaffeemühle f. **~-pot** n Kaffeekanne f. **~-table** n Couchtisch m

coffin n Sarg m

cogent a überzeugend

coherent a zusammenhängend; (comprehensible) verständlich

coil n Rolle f; (Electr) Spule f; (one ring) Windung f ● vt ~ **[up]** zusammenrollen

coin n Münze f ● vt prägen

coincide vi zusammenfallen; (agree) übereinstimmen

coinciden|ce n Zufall m. **~tal** a, **-ly** adv zufällig

coke n Koks m

Coke (P) n (drink) Cola f

cold a (-er, -est) kalt; **I am** or **feel ~** mir ist kalt ● n Kälte f; (Med) Erkältung f

cold: **~-blooded** a kaltblütig. **~-hearted** a kaltherzig. **~ly** adv (fig) kalt, kühl. **~ness** n Kälte f

collaborat|e vi zusammenarbeiten (with mit); **~e on sth** mitarbeiten bei etw. **~ion** n Zusammenarbeit f, Mitarbeit f; (with enemy) Kollaboration f. **~or** n Mitarbeiter(in) m(f); Kollaborateur m

collaps|e n Zusammenbruch m; Einsturz m ● vi zusammenbrechen; <roof, building> einstürzen. **~ible** a zusammenklappbar

collar n Kragen m; (for animal) Halsband nt. **~-bone** n Schlüsselbein nt

colleague n Kollege m/Kollegin f

collect vt sammeln; (fetch) abholen; einsammeln <tickets>; einziehen <taxes> ● vi sich [an]sammeln ● adv **call ~** (Amer) ein R-Gespräch führen

collection n Sammlung f; (in church) Kollekte f; (of post) Leerung f; (designer's) Kollektion f

collector n Sammler(in) m(f)

college n College nt

collide vi zusammenstoßen

colliery n Kohlengrube f

collision n Zusammenstoß m

colloquial a, **-ly** adv umgangssprachlich

Cologne n Köln nt

colon n Doppelpunkt

colonel n Oberst m

colonial a Kolonial-

colony n Kolonie f

colossal a riesig

colour n Farbe f; (complexion) Gesichtsfarbe f; (race) Hautfarbe f; **off ~** 🖪 nicht ganz auf der Höhe ● vt färben; **~ [in]** ausmalen

colour: ~-blind a farbenblind. **~ed** a farbig ● n (person) Farbige(r) m/f. **~-fast** a farbecht. **~ film** n Farbfilm m. **~ful** a farbenfroh. **~less** a farblos. **~ photo[graph]** n Farbaufnahme f. **~ television** n Farbfernsehen nt

column n Säule f; (of soldiers, figures) Kolonne f; (Typ) Spalte f; (Journ) Kolumne f

comb n Kamm m ● vt kämmen; (search) absuchen; **~ one's hair** sich (dat) [die Haare] kämmen

combat n Kampf m

combination n Kombination f

combine[1] vt verbinden ● vi sich verbinden; <people:> sich zusammenschließen

combine[2] n (Comm) Konzern m

combustion n Verbrennung f

come vi (pt came, pp come) kommen; (reach) reichen (to an + acc); **that ~ s to £10** das macht £10; **~ into money** zu Geld kommen; **~ true** wahr werden; **~ in two sizes** in zwei Größen erhältlich sein; **the years to ~** die kommenden Jahre; **how ~?** 🖪 wie das? **~ about** vi geschehen. **~ across** vi herüberkommen; 🖪 klar werden ● vt stoßen auf (+ acc).**~ apart** vi sich auseinander nehmen lassen; (accidentally) auseinander gehen. **~ away** vi weggehen; <thing:> abgehen. **~ back** vi zurückkommen. **~ by** vi vorbeikommen ● vt (obtain) bekommen. **~ in** vi hereinkommen. **~ off** vi abgehen; (take place) stattfinden; (succeed) klappen 🖪. **~ out** vi herauskommen; <book:> erscheinen; <stain:> herausgehen. **~ round** vi vorbeikommen; (after fainting) [wieder] zu sich kommen; (change one's mind) sich umstimmen lassen. **~ to** vi [wieder] zu sich kommen. **~ up** vi heraufkommen; <plant:> aufgehen; (reach) reichen (to bis); **~ up with** sich (dat) einfallen lassen

come-back n Comeback nt

comedian n Komiker m

come-down n Rückschritt m

comedy n Komödie f

comet n Komet m

comfort n Bequemlichkeit f; (consolation) Trost m ● vt trösten

comfortable a, **-bly** adv bequem

comfort station n (Amer) öffentliche Toilette f

comfy a 🖪 bequem

comic a komisch ● n Komiker m; (periodical) Comic-Heft nt

coming a kommend ● n Kommen nt

comma n Komma nt

command n Befehl m; (Mil) Kommando nt; (mastery) Beherrschung f ● vt befehlen (+ dat); kommandieren <army>

command|er n Befehlshaber m. **~ing officer** n Befehlshaber m

commemorat|e vt gedenken (+ gen). **~ion** n Gedenken nt

commence vt/i anfangen,
beginnen

commend vt loben; (*recommend*)
empfehlen (**to** dat)

comment n Bemerkung f; no ~!
kein Kommentar! ● vi sich äußern
(**on** zu); ~ **on** (*Journ*) kommentieren

commentary n Kommentar m;
[**running**] ~ (*Radio, TV*) Reportage f

commentator n Kommentator m;
(*Sport*) Reporter m

commerce n Handel m

commercial a, **-ly** adv
kommerziell ● n (*Radio, TV*)
Werbespot m

commission n (*order for work*)
Auftrag m; (*body of people*)
Kommission f; (*payment*) Provision f;
(*Mil*) [Offiziers]patent nt; **out of** ~
außer Betrieb ● vt beauftragen
<s.o.>; in Auftrag geben <thing>;
(*Mil*) zum Offizier ernennen

commit vt (*pt/pp* **committed**)
begehen; (*entrust*) anvertrauen (**to**
dat); (*consign*) einweisen (**to** in +
acc); ~ **oneself** sich festlegen;
(*involve oneself*) sich engagieren.
~**ment** n Verpflichtung f;
(*involvement*) Engagement nt. ~**ted**
a engagiert

committee n Ausschuss m,
Komitee nt

common a (**-er, -est**) gemeinsam;
(*frequent*) häufig; (*ordinary*)
gewöhnlich; (*vulgar*) ordinär ● n
Gemeindeland nt; **have in** ~
gemeinsam haben; **House of C**~**s**
Unterhaus nt

common: ~**ly** adv allgemein. **C**~
Market n Gemeinsamer Markt m.
~**place** a häufig. ~**-room** n
Aufenthaltsraum m. ~ **sense** n
gesunder Menschenverstand m

commotion n Tumult m

communal a gemeinschaftlich

communicate vt mitteilen (**to**
dat); übertragen <disease> ● vi sich
verständigen

communication n Verständigung
f; (*contact*) Verbindung f; (*message*)
Mitteilung f; ~**s** pl (*technology*)
Nachrichtenwesen nt

communicative a mitteilsam

Communion n [**Holy**] ~ das
[heilige] Abendmahl; (*Roman
Catholic*) die [heilige] Kommunion

communis|m n Kommunismus m.
~**t** a kommunistisch ● n
Kommunist(in) m(f)

community n Gemeinschaft f; **local**
~ Gemeinde f

commute vi pendeln. ~**r** n
Pendler(in) m(f)

compact a kompakt

companion n Begleiter(in) m(f).
~**ship** n Gesellschaft f

company n Gesellschaft f; (*firm*)
Firma f; (*Mil*) Kompanie f; (Ⓔ
guests) Besuch m. ~ **car** n
Firmenwagen m

comparable a vergleichbar

comparative a vergleichend;
(*relative*) relativ ● n (*Gram*)
Komparativ m. ~**ly** adv
verhältnismäßig

compare vt vergleichen (**with/to**
mit) ● vi sich vergleichen lassen

comparison n Vergleich m

compartment n Fach nt; (*Rail*)
Abteil nt

compass n Kompass m

compassion n Mitleid nt. ~**ate** a
mitfühlend

compatible a vereinbar; <drugs>
verträglich; (*Techn*) kompatibel; **be**
~ <people:> [gut] zueinander passen

compatriot n Landsmann m
/-männin f

compel vt (*pt/pp* **compelled**)
zwingen

compensat|e vt entschädigen.
~**ion** n Entschädigung f; (*fig*)
Ausgleich m

compete vi konkurrieren; (*take
part*) teilnehmen (**in** an + dat)

competen|ce n Fähigkeit f. ~**t** a
fähig

competition n Konkurrenz f;
(*contest*) Wettbewerb m; (*in
newspaper*) Preisausschreiben nt

competitive a (*Comm*)
konkurrenzfähig

competitor n Teilnehmer m; (Comm) Konkurrent m

compile vt zusammenstellen

complacen|cy n Selbstzufriedenheit f. ~**t** a, -**ly** adv selbstzufrieden

complain vi klagen (**about/of** über + acc); (formally) sich beschweren. ~**t** n Klage f; (formal) Beschwerde f; (Med) Leiden nt

complement¹ n Ergänzung f; **full** ~ volle Anzahl f

complement² vt ergänzen

complete a vollständig; (finished) fertig; (utter) völlig ● vt vervollständigen; (finish) abschließen; (fill in) ausfüllen. ~**ly** adv völlig

completion n Vervollständigung f; (end) Abschluss m

complex a komplex ● n Komplex m

complexion n Teint m; (colour) Gesichtsfarbe f

complexity n Komplexität f

complicat|e vt komplizieren. ~**ed** a kompliziert. ~**ion** n Komplikation f

compliment n Kompliment nt; ~**s** pl Grüße pl ● vt ein Kompliment machen (+ dat). ~**ary** a schmeichelhaft; (given free) Frei-

comply vi (pt/pp -ied) ~ **with** nachkommen (+ dat)

compose vt verfassen; (Mus) komponieren; **be** ~**d of** sich zusammensetzen aus. ~**r** n Komponist m

composition n Komposition f; (essay) Aufsatz m

compost n Kompost m

composure n Fassung f

compound a zusammengesetzt; <fracture> kompliziert ● n (Chem) Verbindung f; (Gram) Kompositum nt

comprehen|d vt begreifen, verstehen. ~**sible** a, -**bly** adv verständlich. ~**sion** n Verständnis nt

comprehensive a & n umfassend; ~ [**school**] Gesamtschule f. ~

insurance n (Auto) Vollkaskoversicherung f

compress vt zusammenpressen; ~**ed air** Druckluft f

comprise vt umfassen, bestehen aus

compromise n Kompromiss m ● vt kompromittieren <person> ● vi einen Kompromiss schließen

compuls|ion n Zwang m. ~**ive** a zwanghaft. ~**ory** a obligatorisch

comput|er n Computer m. ~**er game** n Computerspiel. ~**erize** vt computerisieren <data>; auf Computer umstellen <firm>. ~**literate** a mit Computern vertraut. ~**ing** n Computertechnik f

comrade n Kamerad m; (Pol) Genosse m/Genossin f

con¹ see **pro**

con² n 🅸 Schwindel m ● vt (pt/pp **conned**) 🅸 beschwindeln

concave a konkav

conceal vt verstecken; (keep secret) verheimlichen

concede vt zugeben; (give up) aufgeben

conceit n Einbildung f. ~**ed** a eingebildet

conceivable a denkbar

conceive vt (Biol) empfangen; (fig) sich (dat) ausdenken ● vi schwanger werden

concentrat|e vt konzentrieren ● vi sich konzentrieren. ~**ion** n Konzentration f

concern n Angelegenheit f; (worry) Sorge f; (Comm) Unternehmen nt ● vt (be about, affect) betreffen; (worry) kümmern; **be** ~**ed about** besorgt sein um; ~ **oneself with** sich beschäftigen mit; **as far as I am** ~**ed** was mich angeht od betrifft. ~**ing** prep bezüglich (+ gen)

concert n Konzert nt

concerto n Konzert nt

concession n Zugeständnis nt; (Comm) Konzession f; (reduction) Ermäßigung f

concise a, -**ly** adv kurz

conclude vt/i schließen

conclusion n Schluss m; in ~ abschließend, zum Schluss

conclusive a schlüssig

concoct vt zusammenstellen; (fig) fabrizieren. ~ion n Zusammenstellung f; (drink) Gebräu nt

concrete a konkret ● n Beton m ● vt betonieren

concurrently adv gleichzeitig

concussion n Gehirnerschütterung f

condemn vt verurteilen; (declare unfit) für untauglich erklären. ~ation n Verurteilung f

condensation n Kondensation f

condense vt zusammenfassen

condescend vi sich herablassen (to zu). ~ing a, -ly adv herablassend

condition n Bedingung f; (state) Zustand m; ~s pl Verhältnisse pl; on ~ that unter der Bedingung, dass ● vt (Psych) konditionieren. ~al a bedingt ● n (Gram) Konditional m. ~er n Pflegespülung f; (for fabrics) Weichspüler m

condolences npl Beileid nt

condom n Kondom nt

condominium n (Amer) ≈ Eigentumswohnung f

conduct[1] n Verhalten nt; (Sch) Betragen nt

conduct[2] vt führen; (Phys) leiten; (Mus) dirigieren. ~or n Dirigent m; (of bus) Schaffner m; (Phys) Leiter m

cone n Kegel m; (Bot) Zapfen m; (for ice-cream) [Eis]tüte f; (Auto) Leitkegel m

confectioner n Konditor m. ~y n Süßwaren pl

conference n Konferenz f

confess vt/i gestehen; (Relig) beichten. ~ion n Geständnis nt; (Relig) Beichte f

confetti n Konfetti nt

confide vt anvertrauen ● vi ~ in s.o. sich jdm anvertrauen

confidence n (trust) Vertrauen nt; (self-assurance) Selbstvertrauen nt;

(secret) Geheimnis nt; in ~ im Vertrauen. ~ **trick** n Schwindel m

confident a, -ly adv zuversichtlich; (self-assured) selbstsicher

confidential a, -ly adv vertraulich

confine vt beschränken (to auf + acc). ~**d** a (narrow) eng

confirm vt bestätigen; (Relig) konfirmieren; (Roman Catholic) firmen. ~ation n Bestätigung f; Konfirmation f; Firmung f

confiscat|e vt beschlagnahmen. ~ion n Beschlagnahme f

conflict[1] n Konflikt m

conflict[2] vi im Widerspruch stehen (with zu). ~ing a widersprüchlich

conform vi <person:> sich anpassen; <thing:> entsprechen (to dat). ~ist n Konformist m

confounded a 🄸 verflixt

confront vt konfrontieren. ~ation n Konfrontation f

confus|e vt verwirren; (mistake for) verwechseln (with mit). ~ing a verwirrend. ~ion n Verwirrung f; (muddle) Durcheinander nt

congenial a angenehm

congest|ed a verstopft; (with people) überfüllt. ~ion n Verstopfung f; Überfüllung f

congratulat|e vt gratulieren (+ dat) (on zu). ~ions npl Glückwünsche pl; ~ions! [ich] gratuliere!

congregation n (Relig) Gemeinde f

congress n Kongress m. ~man n Kongressabgeordnete(r) m

conical a kegelförmig

conifer n Nadelbaum m

conjecture n Mutmaßung f

conjunction n Konjunktion f; in ~ with zusammen mit

conjur|e vi zaubern ● vt ~e up heraufbeschwören. ~or n Zauberkünstler m

conk vi ~ out 🄸 <machine:> kaputtgehen

conker n 🄸 Kastanie f

con-man n 🄸 Schwindler m

connect *vt* verbinden (**to** mit); (*Electr*) anschließen (**to** an + *acc*); **be ~ed with** zu tun haben mit; (*be related to*) verwandt sein mit ● *vi* verbunden sein; <*train:*> Anschluss haben (**with** an + *acc*)

connection *n* Verbindung *f*; (*Rail, Electr*) Anschluss *m*; **in ~ with** in Zusammenhang mit. **~s** *npl* Beziehungen *pl*

connoisseur *n* Kenner *m*

conquer *vt* erobern; (*fig*) besiegen. **~or** *n* Eroberer *m*

conquest *n* Eroberung *f*

conscience *n* Gewissen *nt*

conscientious *a*, **-ly** *adv* gewissenhaft

conscious *a*, **-ly** *adv* bewusst; [**fully**] **~** bei [vollem] Bewusstsein; **be/become ~ of sth** sich (*dat*) etw (*gen*) bewusst sein/werden. **~ness** *n* Bewusstsein *nt*

conscript *n* Einberufene(r) *m*

consecrat|e *vt* weihen; einweihen <*church*>. **~ion** *n* Weihe *f*; Einweihung *f*

consecutive *a* aufeinanderfolgend. **-ly** *adv* fortlaufend

consent *n* Einwilligung *f*, Zustimmung *f* ● *vi* einwilligen (**to** in + *acc*), zustimmen (**to** *dat*)

consequen|ce *n* Folge *f*. **~t** *a* daraus folgend. **~tly** *adv* folglich

conservation *n* Erhaltung *f*, Bewahrung *f*. **~ist** *n* Umweltschützer *m*

conservative *a* konservativ; <*estimate*> vorsichtig. **C~** (*Pol*) *a* konservativ ● *n* Konservative(r) *m/f*

conservatory *n* Wintergarten *m*

conserve *vt* erhalten, bewahren; sparen <*energy*>

consider *vt* erwägen; (*think over*) sich (*dat*) überlegen; (*take into account*) berücksichtigen; (*regard as*) betrachten als; **~ doing sth** erwägen, etw zu tun. **~able** *a*, **-bly** *adv* erheblich

consider|ate *a*, **-ly** *adv* rücksichtsvoll. **~ation** *n* Erwägung

f; (*thoughtfulness*) Rücksicht *f*; (*payment*) Entgelt *nt*; **take into ~ation** berücksichtigen. **~ing** *prep* wenn man bedenkt (**that** dass)

consist *vi* **~ of** bestehen aus

consisten|cy *n* Konsequenz *f*; (*density*) Konsistenz *f*. **~t** *a* konsequent; (*unchanging*) gleichbleibend. **~tly** *adv* konsequent; (*constantly*) ständig

consolation *n* Trost *m*. **~ prize** *n* Trostpreis *m*

console *vt* trösten

consonant *n* Konsonant *m*

conspicuous *a* auffällig

conspiracy *n* Verschwörung *f*

constable *n* Polizist *m*

constant *a*, **-ly** *adv* beständig; (*continuous*) ständig

constipat|ed *a* verstopft. **~ion** *n* Verstopfung *f*

constituency *n* Wahlkreis *m*

constitut|e *vt* bilden. **~ion** *n* (*Pol*) Verfassung *f*; (*of person*) Konstitution *f*

constraint *n* Zwang *m*; (*restriction*) Beschränkung *f*; (*strained manner*) Gezwungenheit *f*

construct *vt* bauen. **~ion** *n* Bau *m*; (*Gram*) Konstruktion *f*; (*interpretation*) Deutung *f*; **under ~ion** im Bau

consul *n* Konsul *m*. **~ate** *n* Konsulat *nt*

consult *vt* [um Rat] fragen; konsultieren <*doctor*>; nachschlagen in (+ *dat*) <*book*>. **~ant** *n* Berater *m*; (*Med*) Chefarzt *m*. **~ation** *n* Beratung *f*; (*Med*) Konsultation *f*

consume *vt* verzehren; (*use*) verbrauchen. **~r** *n* Verbraucher *m*

consumption *n* Konsum *m*; (*use*) Verbrauch *m*

contact *n* Kontakt *m*; (*person*) Kontaktperson *f* ● *vt* sich in Verbindung setzen mit. **~ lenses** *npl* Kontaktlinsen *pl*

contagious *a* direkt übertragbar

contain *vt* enthalten; (*control*) beherrschen. **~er** *n* Behälter *m*; (*Comm*) Container *m*

contaminat|e vt verseuchen. **~ion** n Verseuchung f

contemplat|e vt betrachten; (meditate) nachdenken über (+ acc). **~ion** n Betrachtung f; Nachdenken nt

contemporary a zeitgenössisch ● n Zeitgenosse m/ -genossin f

contempt n Verachtung f; **beneath ~** verabscheuungswürdig. **~ible** a verachtenswert. **~uous** a, **-ly** adv verächtlich

content¹ n & **contents** pl Inhalt m

content² a zufrieden ● n to one's heart's **~** nach Herzenslust ● vt **~ oneself** sich begnügen (with mit). **~ed** a, **-ly** adv zufrieden

contentment n Zufriedenheit f

contest n Kampf m; (competition) Wettbewerb m. **~ant** n Teilnehmer m

context n Zusammenhang m

continent n Kontinent m

continental a Kontinental-. **~ breakfast** n kleines Frühstück nt. **~ quilt** n Daunendecke f

continual a, **-ly** adv dauernd

continuation n Fortsetzung f

continue vt fortsetzen; **~ doing** or **to do sth** fortfahren, etw zu tun; **to be ~d** Fortsetzung folgt ● vi weitergehen; (doing sth) weitermachen; (speaking) fortfahren; <weather:> anhalten

continuity n Kontinuität f

continuous a, **-ly** adv anhaltend, ununterbrochen

contort vt verzerren. **~ion** n Verzerrung f

contour n Kontur f; (line) Höhenlinie f

contracep|tion n Empfängnisverhütung f. **~tive** n Empfängnisverhütungsmittel nt

contract¹ n Vertrag m

contract² vi sich zusammenziehen. **~or** n Unternehmer m

contradict vt widersprechen (+ dat). **~ion** n Widerspruch m. **~ory** a widersprüchlich

contralto n Alt m; (singer) Altistin f

contraption n🈁 Apparat m

contrary a & adv entgegengesetzt; **~ to** entgegen (+ dat) ● n Gegenteil nt; **on the ~** im Gegenteil

contrast¹ n Kontrast m

contrast² vt gegenüberstellen (with dat) ● vi einen Kontrast bilden (with zu). **~ing** a gegensätzlich; <colour> Kontrast-

contribut|e vt/i beitragen; beisteuern <money>; (donate) spenden. **~ion** n Beitrag m; (donation) Spende f. **~or** n Beitragende(r) m/f

contrivance n Vorrichtung f

control n Kontrolle f; (mastery) Beherrschung f; (Techn) Regler m; **~s** pl (of car, plane) Steuerung f; **get out of ~** außer Kontrolle geraten ● vt (pt/pp controlled) kontrollieren; (restrain) unter Kontrolle halten; **~ oneself** sich beherrschen

controvers|ial a umstritten. **~y** n Kontroverse f

convalesce vi sich erholen. **~nce** n Erholung f

convalescent home n Erholungsheim nt

convenience n Bequemlichkeit f; **[public] ~** öffentliche Toilette f; **with all modern ~s** mit allem Komfort

convenient a, **-ly** adv günstig; **be ~ for s.o.** jdm gelegen sein, jdm passen; **if it is ~ [for you]** wenn es Ihnen passt

convent n [Nonnen]kloster nt

convention n (custom) Brauch m, Sitte f. **~al** a, **-ly** adv konventionell

converge vi zusammenlaufen

conversation n Gespräch nt; (Sch) Konversation f

conversion n Umbau m; (Relig) Bekehrung f; (calculation) Umrechnung f

convert¹ n Bekehrte(r) m/f, Konvertit m

convert² vt bekehren <person>; (change) umwandeln (into in + acc); umbauen <building>; (calculate)

umrechnen; (*Techn*) umstellen.
~**ible** *a* verwandelbar ● *n* (*Auto*)
Kabrio[lett] *nt*

convex *a* konvex

convey *vt* befördern; vermitteln
<*idea, message*>. ~**or belt** *n*
Förderband *nt*

convict¹ *n* Sträfling *m*

convict² *vt* verurteilen (**of** wegen).
~**ion** *n* Verurteilung *f*; (*belief*)
Überzeugung *f*; **previous** ~**ion**
Vorstrafe *f*

convinc|e *vt* überzeugen. ~**ing** *a*,
-**ly** *adv* überzeugend

convoy *n* Konvoi *m*

convulse *vt* **be** ~**ed** sich krümmen
(**with** vor + *dat*)

coo *vi* gurren

cook *n* Koch *m*/ Köchin *f* ● *vt/i*
kochen; **is it** ~**ed?** ist es gar? ~ **the
books** ⚏ die Bilanz frisieren.
~**book** (*Amer*) Kochbuch *nt*

cooker *n* [Koch]herd *m*; (*apple*)
Kochapfel *m*. ~**y** *n* Kochen *nt*. ~**y
book** *n* Kochbuch *nt*

cookie *n* (*Amer*) Keks *m*

cool *a* (-**er**, -**est**), -**ly** *adv* kühl ● *n*
Kühle *f* ● *vt* kühlen ● *vi* abkühlen.
~**-box** *n* Kühlbox *f*. ~**ness** *n*
Kühle *f*

coop *vt* ~ **up** einsperren

co-operat|e *vi* zusammenarbeiten.
~**ion** *n* Kooperation *f*

co-operative *a* hilfsbereit ● *n*
Genossenschaft *f*

cop *n* ⚏ Polizist *m*

cope *vi* ⚏ zurechtkommen; ~ **with**
fertig werden mit

copious *a* reichlich

copper¹ *n* Kupfer *nt* ● *a* kupfern

copper² *n* ⚏ Polizist *m*

copper beech *n* Blutbuche *f*

coppice, copse *ns* Gehölz *nt*

copy *n* Kopie *f*; (*book*) Exemplar *nt*
● *vt* (*pt/pp* -**ied**) kopieren; (*imitate*)
nachahmen; (*Sch*) abschreiben

copy: ~**right** *n* Copyright *nt*. ~**-
writer** *n* Texter *m*

coral *n* Koralle *f*

cord *n* Schnur *f*; (*fabric*) Cordsamt
m; ~**s** *pl* Cordhose *f*

cordial *a*, -**ly** *adv* herzlich ● *n*
Fruchtsirup *m*

cordon *n* Kordon *m* ● *vt* ~ **off**
absperren

corduroy *n* Cordsamt *m*

core *n* Kern *m*; (*of apple, pear*)
Kerngehäuse *nt*

cork *n* Kork *m*; (*for bottle*) Korken *m*.
~**screw** *n* Korkenzieher *m*

corn¹ *n* Korn *nt*; (*Amer: maize*) Mais
m

corn² *n* (*Med*) Hühnerauge *nt*

corned beef *n* Cornedbeef *nt*

corner *n* Ecke *f*; (*bend*) Kurve *f*;
(*football*) Eckball *m* ● *vt* (*fig*) in die
Enge treiben; (*Comm*)
monopolisieren <*market*>. ~**-stone**
n Eckstein *m*

cornet *n* (*Mus*) Kornett *nt*; (*for ice-
cream*) [Eis]tüte *f*

corn: ~**flour** *n*, (*Amer*) ~**starch** *n*
Stärkemehl *nt*

corny *a* ⚏ abgedroschen

coronation *n* Krönung *f*

coroner *n* Beamte(r) *m*, der
verdächtige Todesfälle untersucht

corporal *n* (*Mil*) Stabsunteroffizier
m

corps *n* (*pl* **corps**) Korps *nt*

corpse *n* Leiche *f*

correct *a*, -**ly** *adv* richtig; (*proper*)
korrekt ● *vt* verbessern; (*Sch, Typ*)
korrigieren. ~**ion** *n* Verbesserung *f*;
(*Typ*) Korrektur *f*

correspond *vi* entsprechen (**to**
dat); <*two things:*> sich entsprechen;
(*write*) korrespondieren. ~**ence** *n*
Briefwechsel *m*; (*Comm*)
Korrespondenz *f*. ~**ent** *n*
Korrespondent(in) *m(f)*. ~**ing** *a*, -**ly**
adv entsprechend

corridor *n* Gang *m*; (*Pol, Aviat*)
Korridor *m*

corro|de *vt* zerfressen ● *vi* rosten.
~**sion** *n* Korrosion *f*

corrugated *a* gewellt. ~ **iron** *n*
Wellblech *nt*

corrupt *a* korrupt ● *vt* korrumpieren; (*spoil*) verderben. ∼**ion** *n* Korruption *f*

corset *n* & **-s** *pl* Korsett *nt*

Corsica *n* Korsika *nt*

cosh *n* Totschläger *m*

cosmetic *a* kosmetisch ● *n* ∼s *pl* Kosmetika *pl*

cosset *vt* verhätscheln

cost *n* Kosten *pl*; ∼s *pl* (*Jur*) Kosten; **at all** ∼s um jeden Preis ● *vt* (*pt/pp* cost) kosten; **it** ∼ **me £20** es hat mich £20 gekostet ● *vt* (*pt/pp* costed) ∼ **[out]** die Kosten kalkulieren für

costly *a* (-ier, -iest) teuer

cost: ∼ **of living** *n* Lebenshaltungskosten *pl*. ∼ **price** *n* Selbstkostenpreis *m*

costume *n* Kostüm *nt*; (*national*) Tracht *f*. ∼ **jewellery** *n* Modeschmuck *m*

cosy *a* (-ier, -iest) gemütlich ● *n* (*tea-, egg-*) Wärmer *m*

cot *n* Kinderbett *nt*; (*Amer: camp bed*) Feldbett *nt*

cottage *n* Häuschen *nt*. ∼ **cheese** *n* Hüttenkäse *m*

cotton *n* Baumwolle *f*; (*thread*) Nähgarn *nt* ● *a* baumwollen ● *vi* ∼ **on** 🄸 kapieren

cotton wool *n* Watte *f*

couch *n* Liege *f*

couchette *n* (*Rail*) Liegeplatz *m*

cough *n* Husten *m* ● *vi* husten. ∼ **up** *vt/i* husten; (🄸 *pay*) blechen

cough mixture *n* Hustensaft *m*

could *see* can²

council *n* Rat *m*; (*Admin*) Stadtverwaltung *f*; (*rural*) Gemeindeverwaltung *f*. ∼ **house** *n* ≈ Sozialwohnung *f*

councillor *n* Ratsmitglied *nt*

council tax *n* Gemeindesteuer *f*

count¹ *n* Graf *m*

count² *n* Zählung *f*; **keep** ∼ zählen ● *vt/i* zählen. ∼ **on** *vt* rechnen auf (+ *acc*)

counter¹ *n* (*in shop*) Ladentisch *m*; (*in bank*) Schalter *m*; (*in café*) Theke *f*; (*Games*) Spielmarke *f*

counter² *a* Gegen- ● *vt/i* kontern

counteract *vt* entgegenwirken (+ *dat*)

counterfeit *a* gefälscht

counterfoil *n* Kontrollabschnitt *m*

counterpart *n* Gegenstück *nt*

counter-productive *a* **be** ∼ das Gegenteil bewirken

countersign *vt* gegenzeichnen

countess *n* Gräfin *f*

countless *a* unzählig

country *n* Land *nt*; (*native land*) Heimat *f*; (*countryside*) Landschaft *f*; **in the** ∼ auf dem Lande. ∼**man** *n* [**fellow**] ∼**man** Landsmann *m*. ∼**side** *n* Landschaft *f*

county *n* Grafschaft *f*

coup *n* (*Pol*) Staatsstreich *m*

couple *n* Paar *nt*; **a** ∼ **of** (*two*) zwei ● *vt* verbinden

coupon *n* Kupon *m*; (*voucher*) Gutschein *m*; (*entry form*) Schein *m*

courage *n* Mut *m*. ∼**ous** *a*, **-ly** *adv* mutig

courgettes *npl* Zucchini *pl*

courier *n* Bote *m*; (*diplomatic*) Kurier *m*; (*for tourists*) Reiseleiter(in) *m(f)*

course *n* (*Naut, Sch*) Kurs *m*; (*Culin*) Gang *m*; (*for golf*) Platz *m*; **of treatment** (*Med*) Kur *f*; **of** ∼ natürlich, selbstverständlich; **in the** ∼ **of** im Lauf[e] (+ *gen*)

court *n* Hof *m*; (*Sport*) Platz *m*; (*Jur*) Gericht *nt*

courteous *a*, **-ly** *adv* höflich

courtesy *n* Höflichkeit *f*

court: ∼ **martial** *n* (*pl* ∼s martial) Militärgericht *nt*. ∼**yard** *n* Hof *m*

cousin *n* Vetter *m*, Cousin *m*; (*female*) Kusine *f*

cove *n* kleine Bucht *f*

cover *n* Decke *f*; (*of cushion*) Bezug *m*; (*of umbrella*) Hülle *f*; (*of typewriter*) Haube *f*; (*of book, lid*) Deckel *m*; (*of magazine*) Umschlag *m*; (*protection*) Deckung *f*, Schutz *m*;

take ~ Deckung nehmen; **under separate** ~ mit getrennter Post ● *vt* bedecken; beziehen *<cushion>*; decken *<costs, needs>*; zurücklegen *<distance>*; (*Journ*) berichten über (+ *acc*); (*insure*) versichern. ~ **up** *vt* zudecken; (*fig*) vertuschen

coverage *n* (*Journ*) Berichterstattung *f* (**of** über + *acc*)

cover: ~**ing** *n* Decke *f*; (*for floor*) Belag *m*. ~**-up** *n* Vertuschung *f*

cow *n* Kuh *f*

coward *n* Feigling *m*. ~**ice** *n* Feigheit *f*. ~**ly** *a* feige

cowboy *n* Cowboy *m*; 🔲 unsolider Handwerker *m*

cower *vi* sich [ängstlich] ducken

cowshed *n* Kuhstall *m*

cox *n*, **coxswain** *n* Steuermann *m*

coy *a* (-er, -est) gespielt schüchtern

crab *n* Krabbe *f*

crack *n* Riss *m*; (*in china, glass*) Sprung *m*; (*noise*) Knall *m*; (🔲 *joke*) Witz *m*; (🔲 *attempt*) Versuch *m* ● *a* 🔲 erstklassig ● *vt* knacken *<nut, code>*; einen Sprung machen in (+ *acc*) *<china, glass>*; 🔲 reißen *<joke>*; 🔲 lösen *<problem>* ● *vi <china, glass:>* springen; *<whip:>* knallen. ~ **down** *vi* 🔲 durchgreifen

cracked *a* gesprungen; *<rib>* angebrochen; (🔲 *crazy*) verrückt

cracker *n* (*biscuit*) Kräcker *m*; (*firework*) Knallkörper *m*; [Christmas] ~ Knallbonbon *m*. ~**s** *a* **be** ~**s** 🔲 einen Knacks haben

crackle *vi* knistern

cradle *n* Wiege *f*

craft *n* Handwerk *nt*; (*technique*) Fertigkeit *f*. ~**sman** *n* Handwerker *m*

crafty *a* (-ier, -iest), **-ily** *adv* gerissen

crag *n* Felszacken *m*

cram *v* (*pt/pp* crammed) ● *vt* hineinstopfen (**into** in + *acc*); vollstopfen (**with** mit) ● *vi* (*for exams*) pauken

cramp *n* Krampf *m*. ~**ed** *a* eng

cranberry *n* (*Culin*) Preiselbeere *f*

crane *n* Kran *m*; (*bird*) Kranich *m*

crank *n* 🔲 Exzentriker *m*

crankshaft *n* Kurbelwelle *f*

crash *n* (*noise*) Krach *m*; (*Auto*) Zusammenstoß *m*; (*Aviat*) Absturz *m* ● *vi* krachen (**into** gegen); *<cars:>* zusammenstoßen; *<plane:>* abstürzen ● *vt* einen Unfall haben mit *<car>*

crash: ~**-helmet** *n* Sturzhelm *m*. ~**-landing** *n* Bruchlandung *f*

crate *n* Kiste *f*

crater *n* Krater *m*

crawl *n* (*Swimming*) Kraul *nt*; **do the** ~ kraulen; **at a** ~ im Kriechtempo ● *vi* kriechen; *<baby:>* krabbeln; ~ **with** wimmeln von

crayon *n* Wachsstift *m*; (*pencil*) Buntstift *m*

craze *n* Mode *f*

crazy *a* (-ier, -iest) verrückt; **be** ~ **about** verrückt sein nach

creak *vi* knarren

cream *n* Sahne *f*; (*Cosmetic, Med, Culin*) Creme *f* ● *a* (*colour*) cremefarben ● *vt* (*Culin*) cremig rühren. ~**y** *a* sahnig; (*smooth*) cremig

crease *n* Falte *f*; (*unwanted*) Knitterfalte *f* ● *vt* falten; (*accidentally*) zerknittern ● *vi* knittern

creat|e *vt* schaffen. ~**ion** *n* Schöpfung *f*. ~**ive** *a* schöpferisch. ~**or** *n* Schöpfer *m*

creature *n* Geschöpf *nt*

crèche *n* Kinderkrippe *f*

credibility *n* Glaubwürdigkeit *f*

credible *a* glaubwürdig

credit *n* Kredit *m*; (*honour*) Ehre *f* ● *vt* glauben; ~ **s.o. with sth** (*Comm*) jdm etw gutschreiben; (*fig*) jdm etw zuschreiben. ~**able** *a* lobenswert

credit: ~ **card** *n* Kreditkarte *f*. ~**or** *n* Gläubiger *m*

creep *vi* (*pt/pp* crept) schleichen ● *n* 🔲 fieser Kerl *m*; **it gives me the** ~**s** es ist mir unheimlich. ~**er** *n* Kletterpflanze *f*. ~**y** *a* gruselig

cremat|e *vt* einäschern. ~**ion** *n* Einäscherung *f*

crêpe *n* Krepp *m*. ~ **paper** *n* Krepppapier *nt*

crept *see* creep

crescent *n* Halbmond *m*

cress *n* Kresse *f*

crest *n* Kamm *m*; (*coat of arms*) Wappen *nt*

crew *n* Besatzung *f*; (*gang*) Bande *f*. **~ cut** *n* Bürstenschnitt *m*

crib[1] *n* Krippe *f*

crib[2] *vt/i* (*pt/pp* cribbed) 🔲 abschreiben

cricket *n* Kricket *nt*. **~er** *n* Kricketspieler *m*

crime *n* Verbrechen *nt*; (*rate*) Kriminalität *f*

criminal *a* kriminell, verbrecherisch; <*law, court*> Straf-● *n* Verbrecher *m*

crimson *a* purpurrot

crinkle *vt/i* knittern

cripple *n* Krüppel *m* ● *vt* zum Krüppel machen; (*fig*) lahmlegen. **~d** *a* verkrüppelt

crisis *n* (*pl* -ses) Krise *f*

crisp *a* (-er, -est) knusprig. **~bread** *n* Knäckebrot *nt*. **~s** *npl* Chips *pl*

criss-cross *a* schräg gekreuzt

criterion *n* (*pl* -ria) Kriterium *nt*

critic *n* Kritiker *m*. **~al** *a* kritisch. **~ally** *adv* kritisch; **~ally ill** schwer krank

criticism *n* Kritik *f*

criticize *vt* kritisieren

croak *vi* krächzen; <*frog:*> quaken

crockery *n* Geschirr *nt*

crocodile *n* Krokodil *nt*

crocus *n* (*pl* -es) Krokus *m*

crony *n* Kumpel *m*

crook *n* (*stick*) Stab *m*; (🔲 *criminal*) Schwindler *m*, Gauner *m*

crooked *a* schief; (*bent*) krumm; (🔲 *dishonest*) unehrlich

crop *n* Feldfrucht *f*; (*harvest*) Ernte *f* ● *v* (*pt/pp* cropped) ● *vt* stutzen ● *vi* **~ up** 🔲 zur Sprache kommen; (*occur*) dazwischenkommen

croquet *n* Krocket *nt*

cross *a*, **-ly** *adv* (*annoyed*) böse (**with** auf + *acc*); **talk at ~ purposes** aneinander vorbeireden ● *n* Kreuz *nt*; (*Bot, Zool*) Kreuzung *f* ● *vt* kreuzen <*cheque, animals*>; überqueren <*road*>; **~ oneself** sich bekreuzigen; **~ one's arms** die Arme verschränken; **~ one's legs** die Beine übereinander schlagen; **keep one's fingers ~ed for s.o.** jdm die Daumen drücken; **it ~ed my mind** es fiel mir ein ● *vi* (*go across*) hinübergehen/-fahren; <*lines:*> sich kreuzen. **~ out** *vt* durchstreichen

cross: **~country** *n* (*Sport*) Crosslauf *m*. **~eyed** *a* schielend; **be ~eyed** schielen. **~fire** *n* Kreuzfeuer *nt*. **~ing** *n* Übergang *m*; (*sea journey*) Überfahrt *f*. **~roads** *n* [Straßen]kreuzung *f*. **~section** *n* Querschnitt *m*. **~wise** *adv* quer. **~word** *n* **~word [puzzle]** Kreuzworträtsel *nt*

crotchety *a* griesgrämig

crouch *vi* kauern

crow *n* Krähe *f*; **as the ~ flies** Luftlinie

crowd *n* [Menschen]menge *f* ● *vi* sich drängen. **~ed** *a* [gedrängt] voll

crown *n* Krone *f* ● *vt* krönen; überkronen <*tooth*>

crucial *a* höchst wichtig; (*decisive*) entscheidend (**to** für)

crude *a* (-r, -st) primitiv; (*raw*) roh

cruel *a* (crueller, cruellest), **-ly** *adv* grausam (**to** gegen). **~ty** *n* Grausamkeit *f*

cruis|e *n* Kreuzfahrt *f* ● *vi* kreuzen; <*car:*> fahren. **~er** *n* (*Mil*) Kreuzer *m*; (*motor boat*) Kajütboot *nt*

crumb *n* Krümel *m*

crumble *vt/i* krümeln; (*collapse*) einstürzen

crumple *vt* zerknittern ● *vi* knittern

crunch *n* 🔲 **when it comes to the ~** wenn es [wirklich] drauf ankommt ● *vt* mampfen ● *vi* knirschen

crusade *n* Kreuzzug *m*; (*fig*) Kampagne *f*. **~r** *n* Kreuzfahrer *m*; (*fig*) Kämpfer *m*

crush *n* (*crowd*) Gedränge *nt* ● *vt* zerquetschen; zerknittern <*clothes*>; (*fig: subdue*) niederschlagen

crust *n* Kruste *f*

crutch *n* Krücke *f*

cry *n* Ruf *m*; (*shout*) Schrei *m*; **a far ∼ from** (*fig*) weit entfernt von ● *vi* (*pt/pp* **cried**) (*weep*) weinen; <*baby:*> schreien; (*call*) rufen

crypt *n* Krypta *f*. **∼ic** *a* rätselhaft

crystal *n* Kristall *m*; (*glass*) Kristall *nt*

cub *n* (*Zool*) Junge(s) *nt*

Cuba *n* Kuba *nt*

cubby-hole *n* Fach *nt*

cub|e *n* Würfel *m*. **∼ic** *a* Kubik-

cubicle *n* Kabine *f*

cuckoo *n* Kuckuck *m*. **∼ clock** *n* Kuckucksuhr *f*

cucumber *n* Gurke *f*

cuddl|e *vt* herzen ● *vi* **∼e up to** sich kuscheln an (+ *acc*). **∼y** *a* kuschelig

cue¹ *n* Stichwort *nt*

cue² *n* (*Billiards*) Queue *nt*

cuff *n* Manschette *f*; (*Amer: turn-up*) [Hosen]aufschlag *m*; (*blow*) Klaps *m*; **off the ∼** 🔢 aus dem Stegreif. **∼-link** *n* Manschettenknopf *m*

cul-de-sac *n* Sackgasse *f*

culinary *a* kulinarisch

culprit *n* Täter *m*

cult *n* Kult *m*

cultivate *vt* anbauen <*crop*>; bebauen <*land*>

cultural *a* kulturell

culture *n* Kultur *f*. **∼d** *a* kultiviert

cumbersome *a* hinderlich; (*unwieldy*) unhandlich

cunning *a* listig ● *n* List *f*

cup *n* Tasse *f*; (*prize*) Pokal *m*

cupboard *n* Schrank *m*

Cup Final *n* Pokalendspiel *nt*

curable *a* heilbar

curate *n* Vikar *m*; (*Roman Catholic*) Kaplan *m*

curb *vt* zügeln

curdle *vi* gerinnen

cure *n* [Heil]mittel *nt* ● *vt* heilen; (*salt*) pökeln; (*smoke*) räuchern; gerben <*skin*>

curiosity *n* Neugier *f*; (*object*) Kuriosität *f*

curious *a*, **-ly** *adv* neugierig; (*strange*) merkwürdig, seltsam

curl *n* Locke *f* ● *vt* locken ● *vi* sich locken

curly *a* (**-ier, -iest**) lockig

currant *n* (*dried*) Korinthe *f*

currency *n* Geläufigkeit *f*; (*money*) Währung *f*; **foreign ∼** Devisen *pl*

current *a* augenblicklich, gegenwärtig; (*in general use*) geläufig, gebräuchlich ● *n* Strömung *f*; (*Electr*) Strom *m*. **∼ affairs** *or* **events** *npl* Aktuelle(s) *nt*. **∼ly** *adv* zurzeit

curriculum *n* Lehrplan *m*. **∼ vitae** *n* Lebenslauf *m*

curry *n* Curry *nt & m*; (*meal*) Currygericht *nt*

curse *n* Fluch *m* ● *vt* verfluchen ● *vi* fluchen

cursory *a* flüchtig

curt *a*, **-ly** *adv* barsch

curtain *n* Vorhang *m*

curtsy *n* Knicks *m* ● *vi* (*pt/pp* **-ied**) knicksen

curve *n* Kurve *f* ● *vi* einen Bogen machen; **∼ to the right/left** nach rechts/links biegen. **∼d** *a* gebogen

cushion *n* Kissen *nt* ● *vt* dämpfen; (*protect*) beschützen

cushy *a* (**-ier, -iest**) 🔢 bequem

custard *n* Vanillesoße *f*

custom *n* Brauch *m*; (*habit*) Gewohnheit *f*; (*Comm*) Kundschaft *f*. **∼ary** *a* üblich; (*habitual*) gewohnt. **∼er** *n* Kunde *m*/Kundin *f*

customs *npl* Zoll *m*. **∼ officer** *n* Zollbeamte(r) *m*

cut *n* Schnitt *m*; (*Med*) Schnittwunde *f*; (*reduction*) Kürzung *f*; (*in price*) Senkung *f*; **∼ [of meat]** [Fleisch]stück *nt* ● *vt/i* (*pt/pp* **cut**, *pres p* **cutting**) schneiden; (*mow*) mähen; abheben <*cards*>; (*reduce*) kürzen; senken <*price*>; **∼ one's finger** sich in den Finger schneiden; **∼ s.o.'s hair** jdm die Haare schneiden; **∼ short** abkürzen. **∼ back** *vt* zurückschneiden; (*fig*) einschränken, kürzen. **∼ down** *vt* fällen; (*fig*) einschränken. **∼ off** *vt* abschneiden; (*disconnect*) abstellen; **be ~ off** (*Teleph*) unterbrochen werden. **~ out** *vt* ausschneiden; (*delete*) streichen; **be ~ out for** ⊞ geeignet sein zu. **~ up** *vt* zerschneiden; (*slice*) aufschneiden

cut-back *n* Kürzung *f*

cute *a* (**-r, -st**) ⊞ niedlich

cut glass *n* Kristall *nt*

cutlery *n* Besteck *nt*

cutlet *n* Kotelett *nt*

cut-price *a* verbilligt

cutting *a* <*remark*> bissig ● *n* (*from newspaper*) Ausschnitt *m*; (*of plant*) Ableger *m*

CV *abbr of* curriculum vitae

cycl|e *n* Zyklus *m*; (*bicycle*) [Fahr]rad *nt* ● *vi* mit dem Rad fahren. **~ing** *n* Radfahren *nt*. **~ist** *n* Radfahrer(in) *m(f)*

cylind|er *n* Zylinder *m*. **~rical** *a* zylindrisch

cynic *n* Zyniker *m*. **~al** *a*, **-ly** *adv* zynisch. **~ism** *n* Zynismus *m*

Cyprus *n* Zypern *nt*

Czech *a* tschechisch; **~ Republic** Tschechische Republik *f* ● *n* Tscheche *m*/ Tschechin *f*

Dd

dab *n* Tupfer *m*; (*of butter*) Klecks *m*

dabble *vi* **~ in sth** (*fig*) sich nebenbei mit etw befassen

dachshund *n* Dackel *m*

dad[dy] *n* ⊞ Vati *m*

daddy-long-legs *n* [Kohl]schnake *f*; (*Amer: spider*) Weberknecht *m*

daffodil *n* Osterglocke *f*, gelbe Narzisse *f*

daft *a* (**-er, -est**) dumm

dagger *n* Dolch *m*

dahlia *n* Dahlie *f*

daily *a & adv* täglich

dainty *a* (**-ier, -iest**) zierlich

dairy *n* Molkerei *f*; (*shop*) Milchgeschäft *nt*. **~ products** *pl* Milchprodukte *pl*

daisy *n* Gänseblümchen *nt*

dam *n* [Stau]damm *m* ● *vt* (*pt/pp* **dammed**) eindämmen

damage *n* Schaden *m* (**to** an + *dat*); **~s** *pl* (*Jur*) Schadenersatz *m* ● *vt* beschädigen; (*fig*) beeinträchtigen

damn *a*, *int & adv* ⊞ verdammt ● *n* **I don't care** *or* **give a ~** ⊞ ich schere mich einen Dreck darum ● *vt* verdammen. **~ation** *n* Verdammnis *f*

damp *a* (**-er, -est**) feucht ● *n* Feuchtigkeit *f*

damp|en *vt* anfeuchten; (*fig*) dämpfen. **~ness** *n* Feuchtigkeit *f*

dance *n* Tanz *m*; (*function*) Tanzveranstaltung *f* ● *vt/i* tanzen. **~ music** *n* Tanzmusik *f*

dancer *n* Tänzer(in) *m(f)*

dandelion *n* Löwenzahn *m*

dandruff *n* Schuppen *pl*

Dane *n* Däne *m*/Dänin *f*

danger *n* Gefahr *f*; **in/out of ~** in/ außer Gefahr. **~ous** *a*, **-ly** *adv* gefährlich. **~ously ill** schwer erkrankt

dangle *vi* baumeln ● *vt* baumeln lassen

Danish *a* dänisch. **~ pastry** *n* Hefeteilchen *nt*

Danube *n* Donau *f*

dare *vt/i* (*challenge*) herausfordern (**to** zu); **~ [to] do sth** [es] wagen, etw zu tun. **~devil** *n* Draufgänger *m*

daring *a* verwegen ● *n* Verwegenheit *f*

dark *a* (**-er, -est**) dunkel; **~ blue**/ **brown** dunkelblau/ -braun; **~ horse** (*fig*) stilles Wasser *nt* ● *n* Dunkelheit *f*; **after ~** nach Einbruch der Dunkelheit; **in the ~** im Dunkeln

dark|en *vt* verdunkeln ● *vi* dunkler werden. **~ness** *n* Dunkelheit *f*

dark-room *n* Dunkelkammer *f*

darling *a* allerliebst ● *n* Liebling *m*

darn *vt* stopfen

dart n Pfeil m; ~s sg (game) [Wurf]pfeil m ● vi flitzen

dash n (Typ) Gedankenstrich m; **a** ~ **of milk** ein Schuss Milch ● vi rennen ● vt schleudern. ~ **off** vi losstürzen ● vt (write quickly) hinwerfen

dashboard n Armaturenbrett nt

data npl & sg Daten pl. ~ **processing** n Datenverarbeitung f

date¹ n (fruit) Dattel f

date² n Datum nt; Ⓘ Verabredung f; **to** ~ bis heute; **out of** ~ überholt; (expired) ungültig; **be up to** ~ auf dem Laufenden sein ● vt/i datieren; (Amer Ⓘ: go out with) ausgehen mit

dated a altmodisch

dative a & n (Gram) ~ **[case]** Dativ m

daub vt beschmieren (with mit); schmieren <paint>

daughter n Tochter f. ~**-in-law** n (pl ~s-in-law) Schwiegertochter f

dawdle vi trödeln

dawn n Morgendämmerung f; **at** ~ bei Tagesanbruch ● vi anbrechen; **it** ~**ed on me** (fig) es ging mir auf

day n Tag m; ~ **by** ~ Tag für Tag; ~ **after** ~ Tag um Tag; **these** ~s heutzutage; **in those** ~s zu der Zeit

day: ~**-dream** n Tagtraum m ● vi [mit offenen Augen] träumen. ~**light** n Tageslicht nt. ~**time** n **in the** ~**time** am Tage

daze n **in a** ~ wie benommen. ~**d** a benommen

dazzle vt blenden

dead a tot; <flower> verwelkt; (numb) taub; ~ **body** Leiche f; ~ **centre** genau in der Mitte ● adv ~ **tired** todmüde; ~ **slow** sehr langsam ● n **the** ~ pl die Toten; **in the** ~ **of night** mitten in der Nacht

deaden vt dämpfen <sound>; betäuben <pain>

dead: ~ **end** n Sackgasse f. ~ **heat** n totes Rennen nt. ~**line** n [letzter] Termin m

deadly a (-ier, -iest) tödlich; (Ⓘ dreary) sterbenslangweilig

deaf a (-er, -est) taub; ~ **and dumb** taubstumm

deaf|en vt betäuben; (permanently) taub machen. ~**ening** a ohrenbetäubend. ~**ness** n Taubheit f

deal n (transaction) Geschäft nt; **whose** ~? (Cards) wer gibt? **a good** or **great** ~ eine Menge; **get a raw** ~ Ⓘ schlecht wegkommen ● v (pt/pp **dealt**) ● vt (Cards) geben; ~ **out** austeilen ● vi ~ **in** handeln mit; ~ **with** zu tun haben mit; (handle) sich befassen mit; (cope with) fertig werden mit; (be about) handeln von; **that's been dealt with** das ist schon erledigt

dealer n Händler m

dean n Dekan m

dear a (-er, -est) lieb; (expensive) teuer; (in letter) liebe(r,s)/ (formal) sehr geehrte(r,s) ● n Liebe(r) m/f ● int oh ~! oje! ~**ly** adv <love> sehr; <pay> teuer

death n Tod m; **three** ~s drei Todesfälle. ~ **certificate** n Sterbeurkunde f

deathly a ~ **silence** Totenstille f ● adv ~ **pale** totenblass

death: ~ **penalty** n Todesstrafe f. ~**-trap** n Todesfalle f

debatable a strittig

debate n Debatte f ● vt/i debattieren

debauchery n Ausschweifung f

debit n ~ **[side]** Soll nt ● vt (pt/pp **debited**) belasten; abbuchen <sum>

debris n Trümmer pl

debt n Schuld f; **in** ~ verschuldet. ~ **or** n Schuldner m

debut n Debüt nt

decade n Jahrzehnt nt

decaden|ce n Dekadenz f. ~**t** a dekadent

decaffeinated a koffeinfrei

decay n Verfall m; (rot) Verwesung f; (of tooth) Zahnfäule f ● vi verfallen; (rot) verwesen; <tooth:> schlecht werden

deceased a verstorben ● n **the** ~**d** der/die Verstorbene

deceit n Täuschung f. ~**ful** a, **-ly** adv unaufrichtig

deceive *vt* täuschen; (*be unfaithful to*) betrügen

December *n* Dezember *m*

decency *n* Anstand *m*

decent *a*, **-ly** *adv* anständig

decept|ion *n* Täuschung *f*; (*fraud*) Betrug *m*. ∼**ive** *a*, **-ly** *adv* täuschend

decide *vt* entscheiden ● *vi* sich entscheiden (**on** für)

decided *a*, **-ly** *adv* entschieden

decimal *a* Dezimal- ● *n* Dezimalzahl *f*. ∼ **point** *n* Komma *nt*

decipher *vt* entziffern

decision *n* Entscheidung *f*; (*firmness*) Entschlossenheit *f*

decisive *a* ausschlaggebend; (*firm*) entschlossen

deck¹ *vt* schmücken

deck² *n* (*Naut*) Deck *nt*; **on** ∼ an Deck; ∼ **of cards** (*Amer*) [Karten]spiel *nt*. ∼**-chair** *n* Liegestuhl *m*

declaration *n* Erklärung *f*

declare *vt* erklären; angeben <*goods*>; **anything to** ∼? etwas zu verzollen?

decline *n* Rückgang *m*; (*in health*) Verfall *m* ● *vt* ablehnen; (*Gram*) deklinieren ● *vi* ablehnen; (*fall*) sinken; (*decrease*) nachlassen

décor *n* Ausstattung *f*

decorat|e *vt* (*adorn*) schmücken; verzieren <*cake*>; (*paint*) streichen; (*wallpaper*) tapezieren; (*award medal to*) einen Orden verleihen (+ *dat*). ∼**ion** *n* Verzierung *f*; (*medal*) Orden *m*; ∼**ions** *pl* Schmuck *m*. ∼**ive** *a* dekorativ. ∼**or** *n* painter **and** ∼**or** Maler und Tapezierer *m*

decoy *n* Lockvogel *m*

decrease¹ *n* Verringerung *f*; (*in number*) Rückgang *m*

decrease² *vt* verringern; herabsetzen <*price*> ● *vi* sich verringern; <*price:*> sinken

decrepit *a* altersschwach

dedicat|e *vt* widmen; (*Relig*) weihen. ∼**ed** *a* hingebungsvoll; <*person*> aufopfernd. ∼**ion** *n* Hingabe *f*; (*in book*) Widmung *f*

deduce *vt* folgern (**from** aus)

deduct *vt* abziehen

deduction *n* Abzug *m*; (*conclusion*) Folgerung *f*

deed *n* Tat *f*; (*Jur*) Urkunde *f*

deep *a* (**-er**, **-est**), **-ly** *adv* tief; **go off the** ∼ **end** 🆃 auf die Palme gehen ● *adv* tief

deepen *vt* vertiefen

deep-freeze *n* Gefriertruhe *f*; (*upright*) Gefrierschrank *m*

deer *n inv* Hirsch *m*; (*roe*) Reh *nt*

deface *vt* beschädigen

default *n* **win by** ∼ (*Sport*) kampflos gewinnen

defeat *n* Niederlage *f*; (*defeating*) Besiegung *f*; (*rejection*) Ablehnung *f* ● *vt* besiegen; ablehnen <*motion*>; (*frustrate*) vereiteln

defect *n* Fehler *m*; (*Techn*) Defekt *m*. ∼**ive** *a* fehlerhaft; (*Techn*) defekt

defence *n* Verteidigung *f*. ∼**less** *a* wehrlos

defend *vt* verteidigen; (*justify*) rechtfertigen. ∼**ant** *n* (*Jur*) Beklagte(r) *m/f*; (*in criminal court*) Angeklagte(r) *m/f*

defensive *a* defensiv

defer *vt* (*pt/pp* **deferred**) (*postpone*) aufschieben

deferen|ce *n* Ehrerbietung *f*. ∼**tial** *a*, **-ly** *adv* ehrerbietig

defian|ce *n* Trotz *m*; **in** ∼**ce of** zum Trotz (+ *dat*). ∼**t** *a*, **-ly** *adv* aufsässig

deficien|cy *n* Mangel *m*. ∼**t** *a* mangelhaft

deficit *n* Defizit *nt*

define *vt* bestimmen; definieren <*word*>

definite *a*, **-ly** *adv* bestimmt; (*certain*) sicher

definition *n* Definition *f*; (*Phot*, *TV*) Schärfe *f*

definitive *a* endgültig; (*authoritative*) maßgeblich

deflat|e *vt* die Luft auslassen aus. ∼**ion** *n* (*Comm*) Deflation *f*

deflect *vt* ablenken

deform|ed *a* missgebildet. ∼**ity** *n* Missbildung *f*

defraud *vt* betrügen (**of** um)

defray *vt* bestreiten

defrost *vt* entfrosten; abtauen
‹fridge›; auftauen *‹food›*

deft *a* (-er, -est), **-ly** *adv* geschickt.
~ness *n* Geschicklichkeit *f*

defuse *vt* entschärfen

defy *vt* (*pt/pp* **-ied**) trotzen (+ *dat*);
widerstehen (+ *dat*) *‹attempt›*

degrading *a* entwürdigend

degree *n* Grad *m*; (*Univ*)
akademischer Grad *m*; **20 ~s** 20
Grad

de-ice *vt* enteisen

deity *n* Gottheit *f*

dejected *a*, **-ly** *adv*
niedergeschlagen

delay *n* Verzögerung *f*; (*of train,
aircraft*) Verspätung *f*; **without ~**
unverzüglich ● *vt* aufhalten;
(*postpone*) aufschieben ● *vi* zögern

delegate[1] *n* Delegierte(r) *m/f*

delegat|e[2] *vt* delegieren. **~ion** *n*
Delegation *f*

delet|e *vt* streichen. **~ion** *n*
Streichung *f*

deliberate *a*, **-ly** *adv* absichtlich;
(*slow*) bedächtig

delicacy *n* Feinheit *f*; Zartheit *f*;
(*food*) Delikatesse *f*

delicate *a* fein; *‹fabric, health›*
zart; *‹situation›* heikel;
‹mechanism› empfindlich

delicatessen *n*
Delikatessengeschäft *nt*

delicious *a* köstlich

delight *n* Freude *f* ● *vt* entzücken
● *vi* **~ in** sich erfreuen an (+ *dat*).
~ed *a* hocherfreut; **be ~ed** sich
sehr freuen. **~ful** *a* reizend

delinquent *a* straffällig ● *n*
Straffällige(r) *m/f*

deli|rious *a* **be ~rious** im Delirium
sein. **~rium** *n* Delirium *nt*

deliver *vt* liefern; zustellen *‹post,
newspaper›*; halten *‹speech›*;
überbringen *‹message›*; versetzen
‹blow›; (*set free*) befreien; **~ a baby**
ein Kind zur Welt bringen. **~y** *n*
Lieferung *f*; (*of post*) Zustellung *f*;

(*Med*) Entbindung *f*; **cash on ~y** per
Nachnahme

delta *n* Delta *nt*

deluge *n* Flut *f*; (*heavy rain*)
schwerer Guss *m*

delusion *n* Täuschung *f*

de luxe *a* Luxus-

demand *n* Forderung *f*; (*Comm*)
Nachfrage *f*; **in ~** gefragt; **on ~** auf
Verlangen ● *vt* verlangen, fordern
(**of/from** von). **~ing** *a* anspruchsvoll

demented *a* verrückt

demister *n* (*Auto*) Defroster *m*

demo *n* (*pl* **~s**) 🄴 Demonstration *f*

democracy *n* Demokratie *f*

democrat *n* Demokrat *m*. **~ic** *a*,
-ally *adv* demokratisch

demo|lish *vt* abbrechen; (*destroy*)
zerstören. **~lition** *n* Abbruch *m*

demon *n* Dämon *m*

demonstrat|e *vt* beweisen;
vorführen *‹appliance›* ● *vi* (*Pol*)
demonstrieren. **~ion** *n* Vorführung
f; (*Pol*) Demonstration *f*

demonstrator *n* Vorführer *m*;
(*Pol*) Demonstrant *m*

demoralize *vt* demoralisieren

demote *vt* degradieren

demure *a*, **-ly** *adv* sittsam

den *n* Höhle *f*; (*room*) Bude *f*

denial *n* Leugnen *nt*; **official ~**
Dementi *nt*

denim *n* Jeansstoff *m*; **~s** *pl* Jeans
pl

Denmark *n* Dänemark *nt*

denounce *vt* denunzieren;
(*condemn*) verurteilen

dens|e *a* (-r, -st), **-ly** *adv* dicht; (🄴
stupid) blöd[e]. **~ity** *n* Dichte *f*

dent *n* Delle *f*, Beule *f* ● *vt*
einbeulen; **~ed** verbeult

dental *a* Zahn-; *‹treatment›*
zahnärztlich. **~ floss** *n* Zahnseide *f*.
~ surgeon *n* Zahnarzt *m*

dentist *n* Zahnarzt *m*/-ärztin *f*. **~ry**
n Zahnmedizin *f*

denture *n* Zahnprothese *f*; **~s** *pl*
künstliches Gebiss *nt*

deny vt (pt/pp -ied) leugnen; (officially) dementieren; ~ s.o. sth jdm etw verweigern

deodorant n Deodorant nt

depart vi abfahren; (Aviat) abfliegen; (go away) weggehen/ -fahren; (deviate) abweichen (from von)

department n Abteilung f; (Pol) Ministerium nt. ~ **store** n Kaufhaus nt

departure n Abfahrt f; (Aviat) Abflug m; (from rule) Abweichung f

depend vi abhängen (on von); (rely) sich verlassen (on auf + acc); it all ~s das kommt darauf an. ~**able** a zuverlässig. ~**ant** n Abhängige(r) m/f. ~**ence** n Abhängigkeit f. ~**ent** a abhängig (on von)

depict vt darstellen

deplor|able a bedauerlich. ~**e** vt bedauern

deploy vt (Mil) einsetzen

depopulate vt entvölkern

deport vt deportieren, ausweisen. ~**ation** n Ausweisung f

depose vt absetzen

deposit n Anzahlung f; (against damage) Kaution f; (on bottle) Pfand nt; (sediment) Bodensatz m; (Geol) Ablagerung f ● vt (pt/pp deposited) legen; (for safety) deponieren; (Geol) ablagern. ~ **account** n Sparkonto nt

depot n Depot nt; (Amer: railway station) Bahnhof m

deprave vt verderben. ~**d** a verkommen

depreciat|e vi an Wert verlieren. ~**ion** n Wertminderung f; (Comm) Abschreibung f

depress vt deprimieren; (press down) herunterdrücken. ~**ed** a deprimiert. ~**ing** a deprimierend. ~**ion** n Vertiefung f; (Med) Depression f; (Meteorol) Tief nt

deprivation n Entbehrung f

deprive vt ~ s.o. of sth jdm etw entziehen. ~**d** a benachteiligt

depth n Tiefe f; in ~ gründlich; in the ~s of winter im tiefsten Winter

deputize vi ~ for vertreten

deputy n Stellvertreter m ● attrib stellvertretend

derail vt be ~ed entgleisen. ~**ment** n Entgleisung f

derelict a verfallen; (abandoned) verlassen

derisory a höhnisch; <offer> lächerlich

derivation n Ableitung f

derivative a abgeleitet ● n Ableitung f

derive vt/i (obtain) gewinnen (from aus); be ~d from <word:> hergeleitet sein aus

derogatory a abfällig

derv n Diesel[kraftstoff] m

descend vt/i hinunter-/ heruntergehen; <vehicle, lift:> hinunter-/herunterfahren; be ~ed from abstammen von. ~**ant** n Nachkomme m

descent n Abstieg m; (lineage) Abstammung f

describe vt beschreiben

descrip|tion n Beschreibung f; (sort) Art f. ~**tive** a beschreibend; (vivid) anschaulich

desecrate vt entweihen

desert¹ n Wüste f. ~ **island** verlassene Insel f

desert² vt verlassen ● vt desertieren. ~**ed** a verlassen. ~**er** n (Mil) Deserteur m. ~**ion** n Fahnenflucht f

deserv|e vt verdienen. ~**edly** adv verdientermaßen. ~**ing** a verdienstvoll

design n Entwurf m; (pattern) Muster nt; (construction) Konstruktion f; (aim) Absicht f ● vt entwerfen; (construct) konstruieren; be ~ed for bestimmt sein für

designer n Designer m; (Techn) Konstrukteur m; (Theat) Bühnenbildner m

desirable a wünschenswert; (sexually) begehrenswert

desire n Wunsch m; (longing) Verlangen nt (for nach); (sexual)

Begierde f ● vt [sich (dat)]
wünschen; (sexually) begehren

desk n Schreibtisch m; (Sch) Pult nt

desolat|e a trostlos. ~**ion** n
Trostlosigkeit f

despair n Verzweiflung f; **in** ~
verzweifelt ● vi verzweifeln

desperat|e a, **-ly** adv verzweifelt;
(urgent) dringend; **be** ~**e for**
dringend brauchen. ~**ion** n
Verzweiflung f

despicable a verachtenswert

despise vt verachten

despite prep trotz (+ gen)

despondent a niedergeschlagen

dessert n Dessert nt, Nachtisch m.
~ **spoon** n Dessertlöffel m

destination n [Reise]ziel nt; (of
goods) Bestimmungsort m

destiny n Schicksal nt

destitute a völlig mittellos

destroy vt zerstören; (totally)
vernichten. ~**er** n (Naut) Zerstörer
m

destruc|tion n Zerstörung f;
Vernichtung f. **-tive** a zerstörerisch;
(fig) destruktiv

detach vt abnehmen; (tear off)
abtrennen. ~**able** a abnehmbar.
~**ed** a ~**ed house** Einzelhaus nt

detail n Einzelheit f, Detail nt; **in** ~
ausführlich ● vt einzeln aufführen.
~**ed** a ausführlich

detain vt aufhalten; <police:> in Haft
behalten; (take into custody) in Haft
nehmen

detect vt entdecken; (perceive)
wahrnehmen. ~**ion** n Entdeckung f

detective n Detektiv m. ~ **story** n
Detektivroman m

detention n Haft f; (Sch)
Nachsitzen nt

deter vt (pt/pp deterred)
abschrecken; (prevent) abhalten

detergent n Waschmittel nt

deteriorat|e vi sich
verschlechtern. ~**ion** n
Verschlechterung f

determination n Entschlossenheit
f

determine vt bestimmen. ~**d** a
entschlossen

deterrent n Abschreckungsmittel
nt

detest vt verabscheuen. ~**able** a
abscheulich

detonate vt zünden

detour n Umweg m

detract vi ~ **from** beeinträchtigen

detriment n **to the** ~ **(of)** zum
Schaden (+ gen). ~**al** a schädlich (**to**
dat)

deuce n (Tennis) Einstand m

devaluation n Abwertung f

devalue vt abwerten <currency>

devastat|e vt verwüsten. ~**ing** a
verheerend. ~**ion** n Verwüstung f

develop vt entwickeln; bekommen
<illness>; erschließen <area> ● vi
sich entwickeln (**into** zu). ~**er** n
[property] ~**er** Bodenspekulant m

development n Entwicklung f

deviat|e vi abweichen. ~**ion** n
Abweichung f

device n Gerät nt; (fig) Mittel nt

devil n Teufel m. ~**ish** a teuflisch

devious a verschlagen

devise vt sich (dat) ausdenken

devot|e vt widmen (**to** dat). ~**ed** a,
-ly adv ergeben; <care> liebevoll; **be**
~**ed to s.o.** sehr an jdm hängen

devotion n Hingabe f

devour vt verschlingen

devout a fromm

dew n Tau m

dexterity n Geschicklichkeit f

diabet|es n Zuckerkrankheit f. ~**ic**
n Diabetiker(in) m(f)

diabolical a teuflisch

diagnose vt diagnostizieren

diagnosis n (pl -oses) Diagnose f

diagonal a, **-ly** adv diagonal ● n
Diagonale f

diagram n Diagramm nt

dial n (of clock) Zifferblatt nt; (Techn)
Skala f; (Teleph) Wählscheibe f ● vt/i
(pt/pp dialled) (Teleph) wählen; ~
direct durchwählen

dialect n Dialekt m

dialling: ~ **code** n Vorwahlnummer f. ~ **tone** n Amtszeichen nt

dialogue n Dialog m

diameter n Durchmesser m

diamond n Diamant m; (cut) Brillant m; (shape) Raute f; ~**s** pl (Cards) Karo nt

diaper n (Amer) Windel f

diarrhoea n Durchfall m

diary n Tagebuch nt; (for appointments) [Termin]kalender m

dice n inv Würfel m

dictat|e vt/i diktieren. ~**ion** n Diktat nt

dictator n Diktator m. ~**ial** a diktatorisch. ~**ship** n Diktatur f

dictionary n Wörterbuch nt

did see do

didn't = did not

die[1] n (Techn) Prägestempel m; (metal mould) Gussform f

die[2] vi (pres p dying) sterben (of an + dat); <plant, animal:> eingehen; <flower:> verwelken; **be dying to do sth** 🗉 darauf brennen, etw zu tun; **be dying for sth** 🗉 sich nach etw sehnen. ~ **down** vi nachlassen; <fire:> herunterbrennen. ~ **out** vi aussterben

diesel n Diesel m. ~ **engine** n Dieselmotor m

diet n Kost f; (restricted) Diät f; (for slimming) Schlankheitskur f; **be on a** ~ Diät leben; eine Schlankheitskur machen ● vi diät leben; eine Schlankheitskur machen

differ vi sich unterscheiden; (disagree) verschiedener Meinung sein

differen|ce n Unterschied m; (disagreement) Meinungsverschiedenheit f. ~**t** a andere(r,s); (various) verschiedene; **be** ~**t** anders sein (from als)

differential a Differenzial- ● n Unterschied m; (Techn) Differenzial nt

differentiate vt/i unterscheiden (between zwischen + dat)

differently adv anders

difficult a schwierig, schwer. ~**y** n Schwierigkeit f

diffiden|ce n Zaghaftigkeit f. ~**t** a zaghaft

dig n (poke) Stoß m; (remark) spitze Bemerkung f; (Archaeol) Ausgrabung f ● vt/i (pt/pp dug, pres p digging) graben; umgraben <garden>. ~ **out** vt ausgraben. ~ **up** vt ausgraben; umgraben <garden>; aufreißen <street>

digest vt verdauen. ~**ible** a verdaulich. ~**ion** n Verdauung f

digit n Ziffer f; (finger) Finger m; (toe) Zehe f

digital a Digital-

dignified a würdevoll

dignity n Würde f

dilapidated a baufällig

dilatory a langsam

dilemma n Dilemma nt

dilettante n Dilettant(in) m(f)

diligen|ce n Fleiß m. ~**t** a, -**ly** adv fleißig

dilute vt verdünnen

dim a (dimmer, dimmest). -**ly** adv (weak) schwach; (dark) trüb[e]; (indistinct) undeutlich; (🗉 stupid) dumm, 🗉 doof ● v (pt/pp dimmed) ● vt dämpfen

dime n (Amer) Zehncentstück nt

dimension n Dimension f; ~**s** pl Maße pl

diminutive a winzig ● n Verkleinerungsform f

dimple n Grübchen nt

din n Krach m, Getöse nt

dine vi speisen. ~**r** n Speisende(r) m/f; (Amer: restaurant) Esslokal nt

dinghy n Dinghi nt; (inflatable) Schlauchboot nt

dingy a (-ier, -iest) trübe

dining: ~-**car** n Speisewagen m. ~-**room** n Esszimmer nt. ~-**table** n Esstisch m

dinner n Abendessen nt; (at midday) Mittagessen nt; (formal) Essen nt. ~-**jacket** n Smoking m

dinosaur n Dinosaurier m

diocese n Diözese f

dip n (in ground) Senke f; (Culin) Dip m ● v (pt/pp **dipped**) vt [ein]tauchen; ~ **one's headlights** (Auto) [die Scheinwerfer] abblenden ● vi sich senken

diploma n Diplom nt

diplomacy n Diplomatie f

diplomat n Diplomat m. ~**ic** a, -**ally** adv diplomatisch

dip-stick n (Auto) Ölmessstab m

dire a (-r, -st) bitter; <consequences> furchtbar

direct a & adv direkt ● vt (aim) richten (at auf / (fig) an + acc); (control) leiten; (order) anweisen; ~ **a film/play** bei einem Film/ Theaterstück Regie führen

direction n Richtung f; (control) Leitung f; (of play, film) Regie f; ~**s** pl Anweisungen pl; ~**s for use** Gebrauchsanweisung f

directly adv direkt; (at once) sofort

director n (Comm) Direktor m; (of play, film) Regisseur m

directory n Verzeichnis nt; (Teleph) Telefonbuch nt

dirt n Schmutz m; (soil) Erde f; ~ **cheap** 🔲 spottbillig

dirty a (-ier, -iest) schmutzig

dis|ability n Behinderung f. ~**abled** a [körper]behindert

disadvantage n Nachteil m; **at a** ~ im Nachteil. ~**d** a benachteiligt

disagree vi nicht übereinstimmen (with mit); **I** ~ ich bin anderer Meinung; **oysters** ~ **with me** Austern bekommen mir nicht

disagreeable a unangenehm

disagreement n Meinungsverschiedenheit f

disappear vi verschwinden. ~**ance** n Verschwinden nt

disappoint vt enttäuschen. ~**ment** n Enttäuschung f

disapproval n Missbilligung f

disapprove vi dagegen sein; ~ **of** missbilligen

disarm vt entwaffnen ● vi (Mil) abrüsten. ~**ament** n Abrüstung f. ~**ing** a entwaffnend

disast|er n Katastrophe f; (accident) Unglück nt. ~**rous** a katastrophal

disbelief n Ungläubigkeit f; **in** ~ ungläubig

disc n Scheibe f; (record) [Schall]platte f; (CD) CD f

discard vt ablegen; (throw away) wegwerfen

discerning a anspruchsvoll

discharge[1] n Ausstoßen nt; (Naut, Electr) Entladung f; (dismissal) Entlassung f; (Jur) Freispruch m; (Med) Ausfluss m

discharge[2] vt ausstoßen; (Naut, Electr) entladen; (dismiss) entlassen; (Jur) freisprechen <accused>

disciplinary a disziplinarisch

discipline n Disziplin f ● vt Disziplin beibringen (+ dat); (punish) bestrafen

disc jockey n Diskjockey m

disclaim vt abstreiten. ~**er** n Verzichterklärung f

disclos|e vt enthüllen. ~**ure** n Enthüllung f

disco n 🔲 Disko f

discolour vt verfärben ● vi sich verfärben

discomfort n Beschwerden pl; (fig) Unbehagen nt

disconnect vt trennen; (Electr) ausschalten; (cut supply) abstellen

discontent n Unzufriedenheit f. ~**ed** a unzufrieden

discontinue vt einstellen; (Comm) nicht mehr herstellen

discord n Zwietracht f; (Mus & fig) Missklang m

discothèque n Diskothek f

discount n Rabatt m

discourage vt entmutigen; (dissuade) abraten (+ dat)

discourteous a, -**ly** adv unhöflich

discover vt entdecken. ~**y** n Entdeckung f

discreet a, -**ly** adv diskret

discretion n Diskretion f; (judgement) Ermessen nt

discriminat|e vi unterscheiden (**between** zwischen + dat); ~**e**

against diskriminieren. ~**ing** *a* anspruchsvoll. ~**ion** *n* Diskriminierung *f*

discus *n* Diskus *m*

discuss *vt* besprechen; (*examine critically*) diskutieren. ~**ion** *n* Besprechung *f*; Diskussion *f*

disdain *n* Verachtung *f*

disease *n* Krankheit *f*

disembark *vi* an Land gehen

disenchant *vt* ernüchtern

disengage *vt* losmachen

disentangle *vt* entwirren

disfigure *vt* entstellen

disgrace *n* Schande *f*; in ~ in Ungnade ● *vt* Schande machen (+ *dat*). ~**ful** *a* schändlich

disgruntled *a* verstimmt

disguise *n* Verkleidung *f*; in ~ verkleidet ● *vt* verkleiden; verstellen <*voice*>

disgust *n* Ekel *m*; in ~ empört ● *vt* anekeln; (*appal*) empören. ~**ing** *a* eklig; (*appalling*) abscheulich

dish *n* Schüssel *f*; (*shallow*) Schale *f*; (*small*) Schälchen *nt*; (*food*) Gericht *nt*. ~ **out** *vt* austeilen. ~ **up** *vt* auftragen

dishcloth *n* Spültuch *nt*

dishearten *vt* entmutigen

dishonest *a* -**ly** *adv* unehrlich. ~**y** *n* Unehrlichkeit *f*

dishonour *n* Schande *f*. ~**able** *a*, -**bly** *adv* unehrenhaft

dishwasher *n* Geschirrspülmaschine *f*

disillusion *vt* ernüchtern. ~**ment** *n* Ernüchterung *f*

disinfect *vt* desinfizieren. ~**ant** *n* Desinfektionsmittel *nt*

disinherit *vt* enterben

disintegrate *vi* zerfallen

disjointed *a* unzusammenhängend

disk *n* = disc

dislike *n* Abneigung *f* ● *vt* nicht mögen

dislocate *vt* ausrenken

dislodge *vt* entfernen

disloyal *a*, -**ly** *adv* illoyal. ~**ty** *n* Illoyalität *f*

dismal *a* trüb[e]; <*person*> trübselig

dismantle *vt* auseinander nehmen; (*take down*) abbauen

dismay *n* Bestürzung *f*. ~**ed** *a* bestürzt

dismiss *vt* entlassen; (*reject*) zurückweisen. ~**al** *n* Entlassung *f*; Zurückweisung *f*

disobedien|ce *n* Ungehorsam *m*. ~**t** *a* ungehorsam

disobey *vt/i* nicht gehorchen (+ *dat*); nicht befolgen <*rule*>

disorder *n* Unordnung *f*; (*Med*) Störung *f*. ~**ly** *a* unordentlich

disorganized *a* unorganisiert

disown *vt* verleugnen

disparaging *a*, -**ly** *adv* abschätzig

dispassionate *a*, -**ly** *adv* gelassen; (*impartial*) unparteiisch

dispatch *n* (*Comm*) Versand *m*; (*Mil*) Nachricht *f*; (*report*) Bericht *m* ● *vt* [ab]senden; (*kill*) töten

dispel *vt* (*pt/pp* dispelled) vertreiben

dispensary *n* Apotheke *f*

dispense *vt* austeilen; ~ **with** verzichten auf (+ *acc*). ~**r** *n* (*device*) Automat *m*

disperse *vt* zerstreuen ● *vi* sich zerstreuen

dispirited *a* entmutigt

display *n* Ausstellung *f*; (*Comm*) Auslage *f*; (*performance*) Vorführung *f* ● *vt* zeigen; ausstellen <*goods*>

displease *vt* missfallen (+ *dat*)

displeasure *n* Missfallen *nt*

disposable *a* Wegwerf-; <*income*> verfügbar

disposal *n* Beseitigung *f*; be at s.o.'s ~ jdm zur Verfügung stehen

dispose *vi* ~ **of** beseitigen; (*deal with*) erledigen

disposition *n* Veranlagung *f*; (*nature*) Wesensart *f*

disproportionate *a*, -**ly** *adv* unverhältnismäßig

disprove *vt* widerlegen

dispute *n* Disput *m*; (*quarrel*) Streit *m* ● *vt* bestreiten

disqualification *n* Disqualifikation *f*

disqualify *vt* disqualifizieren; ~ **s.o. from driving** jdm den Führerschein entziehen

disregard *vt* nicht beachten

disrepair *n* **fall into** ~ verfallen

disreputable *a* verrufen

disrepute *n* Verruf *m*

disrespect *n* Respektlosigkeit *f*. ~**ful** *a*, **-ly** *adv* respektlos

disrupt *vt* stören. ~**ion** *n* Störung *f*

dissatisfaction *n* Unzufriedenheit *f*

dissatisfied *a* unzufrieden

dissect *vt* zergliedern; (*Med*) sezieren. ~**ion** *n* Zergliederung *f*; (*Med*) Sektion *f*

dissent *n* Nichtübereinstimmung *f* ● *vi* nicht übereinstimmen

dissident *n* Dissident *m*

dissimilar *a* unähnlich (**to** *dat*)

dissociate *vt* ~ **oneself** sich distanzieren (**from** von)

dissolute *a* zügellos; <*life*> ausschweifend

dissolve *vt* auflösen ● *vi* sich auflösen

dissuade *vt* abbringen (**from** von)

distance *n* Entfernung *f*; **long/short** ~ lange/kurze Strecke *f*; **in the/from a** ~ in/aus der Ferne

distant *a* fern; (*aloof*) kühl; <*relative*> entfernt

distasteful *a* unangenehm

distil *vt* (*pt/pp* **distilled**) brennen; (*Chem*) destillieren. ~**lery** *n* Brennerei *f*

distinct *a* deutlich; (*different*) verschieden. ~**ion** *n* Unterschied *m*; (*Sch*) Auszeichnung *f*. ~**ive** *a* kennzeichnend; (*unmistakable*) unverwechselbar. ~**ly** *adv* deutlich

distinguish *vt*/*i* unterscheiden; (*make out*) erkennen; ~ **oneself** sich auszeichnen. ~**ed** *a* angesehen; <*appearance*> distinguiert

distort *vt* verzerren; (*fig*) verdrehen. ~**ion** *n* Verzerrung *f*; (*fig*) Verdrehung *f*

distract *vt* ablenken. ~**ion** *n* Ablenkung *f*; (*despair*) Verzweiflung *f*

distraught *a* [völlig] aufgelöst

distress *n* Kummer *m*; (*pain*) Schmerz *m*; (*poverty, danger*) Not *f* ● *vt* Kummer/Schmerz bereiten (+ *dat*); (*sadden*) bekümmern; (*shock*) erschüttern. ~**ing** *a* schmerzlich; (*shocking*) erschütternd

distribut|e *vt* verteilen; (*Comm*) vertreiben. ~**ion** *n* Verteilung *f*; Vertrieb *m*. ~**or** *n* Verteiler *m*

district *n* Gegend *f*; (*Admin*) Bezirk *m*

distrust *n* Misstrauen *nt* ● *vt* misstrauen (+ *dat*). ~**ful** *a* misstrauisch

disturb *vt* stören; (*perturb*) beunruhigen; (*touch*) anrühren. ~**ance** *n* Unruhe *f*; (*interruption*) Störung *f*. ~**ed** *a* beunruhigt; [mentally] ~**ed** geistig gestört. ~**ing** *a* beunruhigend

disused *a* stillgelegt; (*empty*) leer

ditch *n* Graben *m* ● *vt* (🄵 *abandon*) fallen lassen <*plan*>

dither *vi* zaudern

ditto *n* dito; 🄵 ebenfalls

dive *n* [Kopf]sprung *m*; (*Aviat*) Sturzflug *m*; (🄵 *place*) Spelunke *f* ● *vi* einen Kopfsprung machen; (*when in water*) tauchen; (*Aviat*) einen Sturzflug machen; (🄵 *rush*) stürzen

diver *n* Taucher *m*; (*Sport*) [Kunst]springer *m*

diverse *a* verschieden

diversify *vt*/*i* (*pt/pp* **-ied**) variieren; (*Comm*) diversifizieren

diversion *n* Umleitung *f*; (*distraction*) Ablenkung *f*

diversity *n* Vielfalt *f*

divert *vt* umleiten; ablenken <*attention*>; (*entertain*) unterhalten

divide *vt* teilen; (*separate*) trennen; (*Math*) dividieren (**by** durch) ● *vi* sich teilen

dividend *n* Dividende *f*

divine *a* göttlich

diving *n* (*Sport*) Kunstspringen *nt*. ~**-board** *n* Sprungbrett *nt*

divinity *n* Göttlichkeit *f*; (*subject*) Theologie *f*

division n Teilung f; (*separation*)
Trennung f; (*Math, Mil*) Division f;
(*Parl*) Hammelsprung m; (*line*)
Trennlinie f; (*group*) Abteilung f

divorce n Scheidung f ● vt sich
scheiden lassen von. **~d** a
geschieden; **get ~d** sich scheiden
lassen

DIY abbr of **do-it-yourself**

dizziness n Schwindel m

dizzy a (-ier, -iest) schwindlig; **I feel
~** mir ist schwindlig

do

> 3 sg pres tense **does**; pt **did**; pp
> **done**

● *transitive verb*
····▸ (*perform*) machen <*homework,
housework, exam, handstand etc*>;
tun <*duty, favour, something,
nothing*>; vorführen <*trick, dance*>;
durchführen <*test*>. **what are you
doing?** was tust od machst du? **what
can I do for you?** was kann ich für
Sie tun? **do something!** tu doch
etwas! **have you nothing better to
do?** hast du nichts Besseres zu tun?
do the washing-up /**cleaning**
abwaschen/sauber machen
····▸ (*as job*) **what does your father do?**
was macht dein Vater?; was ist dein
Vater von Beruf?
····▸ (*clean*) putzen; (*arrange*)
[zurecht]machen <*hair*>
····▸ (*cook*) kochen; (*roast, fry*) braten.
well done (*meat*) durch[gebraten]. **the
potatoes aren't done yet** die
Kartoffeln sind noch nicht richtig
durch
····▸ (*solve*) lösen <*problem, riddle*>;
machen <*puzzle*>
····▸ (🄵 *swindle*) reinlegen. **do s.o. out
of sth** jdn um etw bringen
● *intransitive verb*
····▸ (*with as or adverb*) es tun; es
machen. **do as they do** mach es wie
sie. **he can do as he likes** er kann
tun od machen, was er will. **you did
well** du hast es gut gemacht
····▸ (*get on*) vorankommen; (*in exams*)
abschneiden. **do well/badly at school**
gut/schlecht in der Schule sein. **how**

are you doing? wie geht's dir? **how
do you do?** (*formal*) guten Tag!
····▸ **will do** (*serve purpose*) es tun;
(*suffice*) [aus]reichen; (*be suitable*)
gehen. **that won't do** das geht nicht.
that will do! jetzt aber genug!
● *auxiliary verb*
····▸ (*in questions*) **do you know him?**
kennst du ihn? **what does he want?**
was will er?
····▸ (*in negation*) **I don't** or **do not wish
to take part** ich will nicht
teilnehmen. **don't be so noisy!** seid
[doch] nicht so laut!
····▸ (*as verb substitute*) **you mustn't
act as he does** du darfst nicht so wie
er handeln. **come in, do!** komm doch
herein!
····▸ (*in tag questions*) **don't you,
doesn't he** etc. nicht wahr. **you went
to Paris, didn't you?** du warst in
Paris, nicht wahr?
····▸ (*in short questions*) **Does he live in
London? — Yes, he does** Wohnt er
in London? — Ja [, stimmt]
····▸ (*for special emphasis*) **I do love
Greece** Griechenland gefällt mir
wirklich gut
····▸ (*for inversion*) **little did he know
that ...** er hatte keine Ahnung, dass
...
● *noun*

> pl **do's** or **dos**

····▸ (🄵 *celebration*) Feier f
● *phrasal verbs* ● **do away with** vt
abschaffen. ● **do for** vt 🄵: **do for
s.o.** jdn fertig machen 🄵; **be done
for** erledigt sein. ● **do in** vt (🄶 *kill*)
kaltmachen 🄶. ● **do up** vt (*fasten*)
zumachen; binden <*shoe-lace, bow-
tie*>; (*wrap*) einpacken; (*renovate*)
renovieren. ● **do with** vt: **I could do
with ...** ich brauche .... ● **do
without** vt: **do without sth** auf etw
(*acc*) verzichten; vi darauf verzichten

docile a fügsam

dock¹ n (*Jur*) Anklagebank f

dock² n Dock nt ● vi anlegen. **~er** n
Hafenarbeiter m. **~yard** n Werft f

doctor n Arzt m/ Ärztin f; (*Univ*)
Doktor m ● vt kastrieren; (*spay*)
sterilisieren

doctrine n Lehre f

document n Dokument nt. ~**ary** a Dokumentar- ● n Dokumentarbericht m; (film) Dokumentarfilm m

dodge n 🗊 Trick m, Kniff m ● vt/i ausweichen (+ dat)

dodgy a (-ier, -iest) 🗊 (awkward) knifflig; (dubious) zweifelhaft

doe n Ricke f, (rabbit) [Kaninchen]weibchen nt

does see do

doesn't = does not

dog n Hund m

dog: ~**-biscuit** n Hundekuchen m. ~**-collar** n Hundehalsband nt; (Relig 🗊) Kragen m eines Geistlichen. ~**-eared** a be ~-eared Eselsohren haben

dogged a, **-ly** adv beharrlich

dogma n Dogma nt. ~**tic** a dogmatisch

do-it-yourself n Heimwerken nt. ~ **shop** n Heimwerkerladen m

doldrums npl be in the ~ niedergeschlagen sein; <business:> daniederliegen

dole n 🗊 Stempelgeld nt; be on the ~ arbeitslos sein ● vt ~ out austeilen

doll n Puppe f ● vt 🗊 ~ oneself up sich herausputzen

dollar n Dollar m

dolphin n Delphin m

domain n Gebiet nt

dome n Kuppel m

domestic a häuslich; (Pol) Innen-; (Comm) Binnen-. ~ **animal** n Haustier nt. ~ **flight** n Inlandflug m

dominant a vorherrschend

dominat|e vt beherrschen ● vi dominieren. ~**ion** n Vorherrschaft f

domineering a herrschsüchtig

domino n (pl -es) Dominostein m; ~**es** sg (game) Domino nt

donat|e vt spenden. ~**ion** n Spende f

done see do

donkey n Esel m; ~**'s years** 🗊 eine Ewigkeit. ~**-work** n Routinearbeit f

donor n Spender(in) m(f)

don't = do not

doom n Schicksal nt; (ruin) Verhängnis nt

door n Tür f; out of ~s im Freien

door: ~**man** n Portier m. ~**mat** n [Fuß]abtreter m. ~**step** n Türschwelle f; on the ~step vor der Tür. ~**way** n Türöffnung f

dope n 🗊 Drogen pl; (🗊 information) Informationen pl; (🗊 idiot) Trottel m ● vt betäuben; (Sport) dopen

dormant a ruhend

dormitory n Schlafsaal m

dormouse n Haselmaus f

dosage n Dosierung f

dose n Dosis f

dot n Punkt m; on the ~ pünktlich. ~**-com** n Dot-com-Firma f

dote vi ~ on vernarrt sein in (+ acc)

dotted a ~ **line** punktierte Linie f; be ~ with bestreut sein mit

dotty a (-ier, -iest) 🗊 verdreht

double a & adv doppelt; <bed, chin> Doppel-; <flower> gefüllt ● n das Doppelte; (person) Doppelgänger m; ~**s** pl (Tennis) Doppel nt; ● vt verdoppeln; (fold) falten ● vi sich verdoppeln. ~ **up** vi sich krümmen (with vor + dat)

double: ~**-bass** n Kontrabass m. ~**-breasted** a zweireihig. ~**-cross** vt ein Doppelspiel treiben mit. ~**-decker** n Doppeldecker m. ~ **glazing** n Doppelverglasung f. ~ **room** n Doppelzimmer nt

doubly adv doppelt

doubt n Zweifel m ● vt bezweifeln. ~**ful** a, **-ly** adv zweifelhaft; (disbelieving) skeptisch. ~**less** adv zweifellos

dough n [fester] Teig m; (🗊 money) Pinke f. ~**nut** n Berliner [Pfannkuchen] m

dove n Taube f

dowdy a (-ier, -iest) unschick

down¹ n (feathers) Daunen pl

down² adv unten; (with movement) nach unten; go ~ hinuntergehen; come ~ herunterkommen; ~ there

da unten; £50 ~ £50 Anzahlung; ~!
(to dog) Platz! ~ with …! nieder mit
…! ● prep ~ the road/stairs die
Straße/Treppe hinunter; ~ the river
den Fluss abwärts ● vt ⚠ (drink)
runterkippen; ~ tools die Arbeit
niederlegen

down: ~**cast** a niedergeschlagen.
~**fall** n Sturz m; (ruin) Ruin m. ~
hearted a entmutigt. ~**hill** adv
bergab. ~ **payment** n Anzahlung f.
~**pour** n Platzregen m. ~**right** a &
adv ausgesprochen. ~**stairs** adv
unten; <go> nach unten ● a im
Erdgeschoss. ~**stream** adv
stromabwärts. ~**-to-earth** a
sachlich. ~**town** adv (Amer) im
Stadtzentrum. ~**ward** a nach
unten; <slope> abfallend ● adv ~[s]
abwärts, nach unten

doze n Nickerchen nt ● vi dösen. ~
off vi einnicken

dozen n Dutzend nt

Dr abbr of doctor

draft[1] n Entwurf m; (Comm) Tratte f;
(Amer Mil) Einberufung f ● vt
entwerfen; (Amer Mil) einberufen

draft[2] n (Amer) = draught

drag n in ~ ⚠ <man> als Frau
gekleidet ● vt (pt/pp dragged)
schleppen; absuchen <river>. ~ **on**
vi sich in die Länge ziehen

dragon n Drache m. ~**-fly** n Libelle
f

drain n Abfluss m; (underground)
Kanal m; **the** ~**s** die Kanalisation
● vt entwässern <land>; ablassen
<liquid>; das Wasser ablassen aus
<tank>; abgießen <vegetables>;
austrinken <glass> ● vi ~ **[away]**
ablaufen

drain|age n Kanalisation f, (of land)
Dränage f. ~**ing board** n
Abtropfbrett nt. ~**-pipe** n
Abflussrohr nt

drake n Enterich m

drama n Drama nt

dramatic a, **-ally** adv dramatisch

dramat|ist n Dramatiker m. ~**ize**
vt für die Bühne bearbeiten; (fig)
dramatisieren

drank see drink

drape n (Amer) Vorhang m ● vt
drapieren

drastic a, **-ally** adv drastisch

draught n [Luft]zug m; ~**s** sg
(game) Damespiel nt; **there is a** ~ es
zieht

draught beer n Bier nt vom Fass

draughty a zugig

draw n Attraktion f; (Sport)
Unentschieden nt; (in lottery)
Ziehung f ● v (pt drew, pp drawn)
● vt ziehen; (attract) anziehen;
zeichnen <picture>; abheben
<money>; ~ **the curtains** die
Vorhänge zuziehen/ (back) aufziehen
● vi (Sport) unentschieden spielen.
~ **back** vt zurückziehen ● vi
(recoil) zurückweichen. ~ **in** vt
einziehen ● vi einfahren. ~ **out** vt
herausziehen; abheben <money> ● vi
ausfahren. ~ **up** vt aufsetzen
<document>; herrücken <chair> ● vi
[an]halten

draw: ~**back** n Nachteil m.
~**bridge** n Zugbrücke f

drawer n Schublade f

drawing n Zeichnung f

drawing: ~**-board** n Reißbrett nt.
~**-pin** n Reißwecke f. ~**-room** n
Wohnzimmer nt

drawl n schleppende Aussprache f

drawn see draw

dread n Furcht f (of vor + dat) ● vt
fürchten. ~**ful** a, **-fully** adv
fürchterlich

dream n Traum m ● vt/i (pt/pp
dreamt or dreamed) träumen (about/
of von)

dreary a (-ier, -iest) trüb[e]; (boring)
langweilig

dregs npl Bodensatz m

drench vt durchnässen

dress n Kleid nt; (clothing) Kleidung
f ● vt anziehen; (Med) verbinden; ~
oneself, get ~ed sich anziehen ● vi
sich anziehen. ~ **up** vi sich schön
anziehen; (in disguise) sich
verkleiden (as als)

dress: ~ **circle** n (Theat) erster
Rang m. ~**er** n (furniture) Anrichte

f; (*Amer: dressing-table*) Frisiertisch *m*

dressing *n* (*Culin*) Soße *f*; (*Med*) Verband *m*

dressing: ~-**gown** *n* Morgenmantel *m*. ~-**room** *n* Ankleidezimmer *nt*; (*Theat*) [Künstler]garderobe *f*. ~-**table** *n* Frisiertisch *m*

dress: ~**maker** *n* Schneiderin *f*. ~ **rehearsal** *n* Generalprobe *f*

drew *see* draw

dried *a* getrocknet; ~ **fruit** Dörrobst *nt*

drier *n* Trockner *m*

drift *n* Abtrift *f*; (*of snow*) Schneewehe *f*; (*meaning*) Sinn *m* ● *vi* treiben; (*off course*) abtreiben; <*snow:*> Wehen bilden; (*fig*) <*person:*> sich treiben lassen

drill *n* Bohrer *m*; (*Mil*) Drill *m* ● *vt/i* bohren (**for** nach); (*Mil*) drillen

drily *adv* trocken

drink *n* Getränk *nt*; (*alcoholic*) Drink *m*; (*alcohol*) Alkohol *m* ● *vt/i* (*pt* drank, *pp* drunk) trinken. ~ **up** *vt/i* austrinken

drink|able *a* trinkbar. ~**er** *n* Trinker *m*

drinking-water *n* Trinkwasser *nt*

drip *n* Tropfen *nt*; (*drop*) Tropfen *m*; (*Med*) Tropf *m*; (⊞ *person*) Niete *f* ● *vi* (*pt/pp* dripped) tropfen

drive *n* [Auto]fahrt *f*; (*entrance*) Einfahrt *f*; (*energy*) Elan *m*; (*Psych*) Trieb *m*; (*Pol*) Aktion *f*; (*Sport*) Treibschlag *m*; (*Techn*) Antrieb *m* ● *v* (*pt* drove, *pp* driven) ● *vt* treiben; fahren <*car*>; (*Sport: hit*) schlagen; (*Techn*) antreiben; ~ **s.o. mad** ⊞ jdn verrückt machen; **what are you driving at?** ⊞ worauf willst du hinaus? ● *vi* fahren. ~ **away** *vt* vertreiben ● *vi* abfahren. ~ **off** *vt* vertreiben ● *vi* abfahren. ~ **on** *vi* weiterfahren. ~ **up** *vi* vorfahren

drivel *n* ⊞ Quatsch *m*

driven *see* drive

driver *n* Fahrer(in) *m(f)*; (*of train*) Lokführer *m*

driving: ~ **lesson** *n* Fahrstunde *f*. ~ **licence** *n* Führerschein *m*. ~ **school** *n* Fahrschule *f*. ~ **test** *n* Fahrprüfung *f*

drizzle *n* Nieselregen *m* ● *vi* nieseln

drone *n* (*sound*) Brummen *nt*

droop *vi* herabhängen

drop *n* Tropfen *m*; (*fall*) Fall *m*; (*in price, temperature*) Rückgang *m* ● *v* (*pt/pp* dropped) ● *vt* fallen lassen; abwerfen <*bomb*>; (*omit*) auslassen; (*give up*) aufgeben ● *vi* fallen; (*fall lower*) sinken; <*wind:*> nachlassen. ~ **in** *vi* vorbeikommen. ~ **off** *vt* absetzen <*person*> ● *vi* abfallen; (*fall asleep*) einschlafen. ~ **out** *vi* herausfallen; (*give up*) aufgeben

drought *n* Dürre *f*

drove *see* drive

drown *vi* ertrinken ● *vt* ertränken; übertönen <*noise*>; **be** ~**ed** ertrinken

drowsy *a* schläfrig

drudgery *n* Plackerei *f*

drug *n* Droge *f* ● *vt* (*pt/pp* drugged) betäuben

drug: ~ **addict** *n* Drogenabhängige(r) *m/f*. ~**store** *n* (*Amer*) Drogerie *f*; (*dispensing*) Apotheke *f*

drum *n* Trommel *f*; (*for oil*) Tonne *f* ● *v* (*pt/pp* drummed) ● *vi* trommeln ● *vt* ~**sth into s.o.** ⊞ jdm etw einbläuen. ~**mer** *n* Trommler *m*; (*in pop-group*) Schlagzeuger *m*. ~**stick** *n* Trommelschlegel *m*; (*Culin*) Keule *f*

drunk *see* drink ● *a* betrunken; **get** ~ sich betrinken ● *n* Betrunkene(r) *m*

drunk|ard *n* Trinker *m*. ~**en** *a* betrunken

dry *a* (drier, driest) trocken ● *vt/i* trocknen. ~ **up** *vt/i* austrocknen

dry: ~-**clean** *vt* chemisch reinigen. ~-**cleaner's** *n* (*shop*) chemische Reinigung *f*. ~**ness** *n* Trockenheit *f*

dual *a* doppelt

dual carriageway *n* ≈ Schnellstraße *f*

dubious *a* zweifelhaft

duchess *n* Herzogin *f*

duck *n* Ente *f* ● *vt* (*in water*) untertauchen ● *vi* sich ducken

duct *n* Rohr *nt*; (*Anat*) Gang *m*

dud *a* 🖬 nutzlos; <*coin*> falsch; <*cheque*> ungedeckt; (*forged*) gefälscht

due *a* angemessen; be ~ fällig sein; <*baby:*> erwartet werden; <*train:*> planmäßig ankommen; ~ **to** (*owing to*) wegen (+ *gen*); be ~ **to** zurückzuführen sein auf (+ *acc*) ● *adv* ~ **west** genau westlich

duel *n* Duell *nt*

duet *n* Duo *nt*; (*vocal*) Duett *nt*

dug *see* **dig**

duke *n* Herzog *m*

dull *a* (**-er**, **-est**) (*overcast, not bright*) trüb[e]; (*not shiny*) matt; <*sound*> dumpf; (*boring*) langweilig; (*stupid*) schwerfällig

duly *adv* ordnungsgemäß

dumb *a* (**-er**, **-est**) stumm

dummy *n* (*tailor's*) [Schneider]puppe *f*; (*for baby*) Schnuller *m*; (*Comm*) Attrappe *f*

dump *n* Abfallhaufen *m*; (*for refuse*) Müllhalde *f*, Deponie *f*; (🖬 *town*) Kaff *nt*; be down in the ~**s** 🖬 deprimiert sein ● *vt* abladen

dumpling *n* Kloß *m*

dunce *n* Dummkopf *m*

dune *n* Düne *f*

dung *n* Mist *m*

dungarees *npl* Latzhose *f*

dungeon *n* Verlies *nt*

dunk *vt* eintunken

duo *n* Paar *nt*; (*Mus*) Duo *nt*

dupe *n* Betrogene(r) *m/f* ● *vt* betrügen

duplicate¹ *n* Doppel *nt*; in ~ in doppelter Ausfertigung *f*

duplicate² *vt* kopieren; (*do twice*) zweimal machen

durable *a* haltbar

duration *n* Dauer *f*

during *prep* während (+ *gen*)

dusk *n* [Abend]dämmerung *f*

dust *n* Staub *m* ● *vt* abstauben; (*sprinkle*) bestäuben (**with** mit) ● *vi* Staub wischen

dust: ~**bin** *n* Mülltonne *f*. ~**-cart** *n* Müllwagen *m*. ~**er** *n* Staubtuch *nt*. ~**-jacket** *n* Schutzumschlag *m*. ~**man** *n* Müllmann *m*. ~**pan** *n* Kehrschaufel *f*

dusty *a* (**-ier**, **-iest**) staubig

Dutch *a* holländisch ● *n* (*Lang*) Holländisch *nt*; **the** ~ *pl* die Holländer. ~**man** *n* Holländer *m*

dutiful *a*, **-ly** *adv* pflichtbewusst

duty *n* Pflicht *f*; (*task*) Aufgabe *f*; (*tax*) Zoll *m*; be on ~ Dienst haben. ~**-free** *a* zollfrei

duvet *n* Steppdecke *f*

dwarf *n* (*pl* **-s** *or* **dwarves**) Zwerg *m*

dwell *vi* (*pt/pp* **dwelt**); ~ **on** (*fig*) verweilen bei. ~**ing** *n* Wohnung *f*

dwindle *vi* abnehmen, schwinden

dye *n* Farbstoff *m* ● *vt* (*pres p* **dyeing**) färben

dying *see* **die²**

dynamic *a* dynamisch

dynamite *n* Dynamit *nt*

dyslex|ia *n* Legasthenie *f*. ~**ic** *a* legasthenisch; be ~**ic** Legastheniker sein

Ee

each *a & pron* jede(r,s); (*per*) je; ~ **other** einander; **£1** ~ £1 pro Person; (*for thing*) pro Stück

eager *a*, **-ly** *adv* eifrig; be ~ **to do sth** etw gerne machen wollen. ~**ness** *n* Eifer *m*

eagle *n* Adler *m*

ear *n* Ohr *nt*. ~**ache** *n* Ohrenschmerzen *pl*. ~**-drum** *n* Trommelfell *nt*

earl *n* Graf *m*

early *a & adv* (**-ier**, **-iest**) früh; <*reply*> baldig; be ~ früh dran sein

earn *vt* verdienen

earnest *a*, **-ly** *adv* ernsthaft ● *n* in ~ im Ernst

earnings *npl* Verdienst *m*

ear: ~**phones** *npl* Kopfhörer *pl*. ~**ring** *n* Ohrring *m*; (*clip-on*) Ohrklips *m*. ~**shot** *n* within/out of ~shot in/ außer Hörweite

earth *n* Erde *f*; (*of fox*) Bau *m* ● *vt* (*Electr*) erden

earthenware *n* Tonwaren *pl*

earthly *a* irdisch; **be no ~ use** ⚠ völlig nutzlos sein

earthquake *n* Erdbeben *nt*

earthy *a* erdig; (*coarse*) derb

ease *n* Leichtigkeit *f* ● *vt* erleichtern; lindern <*pain*> ● *vi* <*pain:*> nachlassen; <*situation:*> sich entspannen

easily *adv* leicht, mit Leichtigkeit

east *n* Osten *m*; **to the ~ of** östlich von ● *a* Ost-, ost- ● *adv* nach Osten

Easter *n* Ostern *nt* ● *attrib* Oster-. ~ **egg** *n* Osterei *nt*

east|erly *a* östlich. ~**ern** *a* östlich. ~**ward[s]** *adv* nach Osten

easy *a* (**-ier, -iest**) leicht; **take it ~** ⚠ sich schonen; **go ~ with** ⚠ sparsam umgehen mit

easy: ~ **chair** *n* Sessel *m*. ~**going** *a* gelassen

eat *vt/i* (*pt* **ate**, *pp* **eaten**) essen; <*animal:*> fressen. ~ **up** *vt* aufessen

eatable *a* genießbar

eau-de-Cologne *n* Kölnisch Wasser *nt*

eaves *npl* Dachüberhang *m*. ~**drop** *vi* (*pt/pp* ~ **dropped**) [heimlich] lauschen

ebb *n* (*tide*) Ebbe *f* ● *vi* zurückgehen; (*fig*) verebben

ebony *n* Ebenholz *nt*

EC *abbr* (**European Community**) EG *f*

eccentric *a* exzentrisch ● *n* Exzentriker *m*

ecclesiastical *a* kirchlich

echo *n* (*pl* **-es**) Echo *nt*, Widerhall *m* ● *v* (*pt/pp* **echoed**, *pres p* **echoing**) ● *vi* widerhallen (**with** von)

eclipse *n* (*Astr*) Finsternis *f*

ecolog|ical *a* ökologisch. ~**y** *n* Ökologie *f*

economic *a* wirtschaftlich. ~**al** *a* sparsam. ~**ally** *adv* wirtschaftlich; (*thriftily*) sparsam. ~**s** *n* Volkswirtschaft *f*

economist *n* Volkswirt *m*; (*Univ*) Wirtschaftswissenschafter *m*

economize *vi* sparen (**on** an + *dat*)

economy *n* Wirtschaft *f*; (*thrift*) Sparsamkeit *f*

ecstasy *n* Ekstase *f*

ecstatic *a*, **-ally** *adv* ekstatisch

eczema *n* Ekzem *nt*

eddy *n* Wirbel *m*

edge *n* Rand *m*; (*of table, lawn*) Kante *f*; (*of knife*) Schneide *f*; **on ~** ⚠ nervös ● *vt* einfassen. ~ **forward** *vi* sich nach vorn schieben

edgy *a* ⚠ nervös

edible *a* essbar

edifice *n* [großes] Gebäude *nt*

edit *vt* (*pt/pp* **edited**) redigieren; herausgeben <*anthology, dictionary*>; schneiden <*film, tape*>

edition *n* Ausgabe *f*; (*impression*) Auflage *f*

editor *n* Redakteur *m*; (*of anthology, dictionary*) Herausgeber *m*; (*of newspaper*) Chefredakteur *m*; (*of film*) Cutter(in) *m(f)*

editorial *a* redaktionell, Redaktions- ● *n* (*Journ*) Leitartikel *m*

educate *vt* erziehen. ~**d** *a* gebildet

education *n* Erziehung *f*; (*culture*) Bildung *f*. ~**al** *a* pädagogisch; <*visit*> kulturell

eel *n* Aal *m*

eerie *a* (**-ier, -iest**) unheimlich

effect *n* Wirkung *f*, Effekt *m*; **take ~** in Kraft treten

effective *a*, **-ly** *adv* wirksam, effektiv; (*striking*) wirkungsvoll, effektvoll; (*actual*) tatsächlich. ~**ness** *n* Wirksamkeit *f*

effeminate *a* unmännlich

effervescent *a* sprudelnd

efficiency *n* Tüchtigkeit *f*; (*of machine, organization*) Leistungsfähigkeit *f*

efficient *a* tüchtig; *<machine, organization>* leistungsfähig; *<method>* rationell. **~ly** *adv* gut; *<function>* rationell

effort *n* Anstrengung *f;* make an ~ sich *(dat)* Mühe geben. **~less** *a,* **-ly** *adv* mühelos

e.g. *abbr* z.B.

egalitarian *a* egalitär

egg *n* Ei *nt.* **~-cup** *n* Eierbecher *m.* **~shell** *n* Eierschale *f*

ego *n* Ich *nt.* **~ism** *n* Egoismus *m.* **~ist** *n* Egoist *m.* **~tism** *n* Ichbezogenheit *f.* **~tist** *n* ichbezogener Mensch *m*

Egypt *n* Ägypten *nt.* **~ian** *a* ägyptisch ● *n* Ägypter(in) *m(f)*

eiderdown *n* *(quilt)* Daunendecke *f*

eigh|t *a* acht ● *n* Acht *f; (boat)* Achter *m.* **~teen** *a* achtzehn. **~teenth** *a* achtzehnte(r,s)

eighth *a* achte(r,s) ● *n* Achtel *nt*

eightieth *a* achtzigste(r,s)

eighty *a* achtzig

either *a & pron* ~ [of them] einer von [den] beiden; *(both)* beide; on ~ side auf beiden Seiten ● *adv* I don't ~ ich auch nicht ● *conj* ~ ... or entweder ... oder

eject *vt* hinauswerfen

elaborate *a,* **-ly** *adv* kunstvoll; *(fig)* kompliziert

elapse *vi* vergehen

elastic *a* elastisch. ~ **band** *n* Gummiband *nt*

elasticity *n* Elastizität *f*

elated *a* überglücklich

elbow *n* Ellbogen *m*

elder[1] *n* Holunder *m*

eld|er[2] *a* ältere(r,s) ● *n* the ~er der/ die Ältere. **~erly** *a* alt. **~est** *a* älteste(r,s) ● *n* the ~est der/die Älteste

elect *vt* wählen. **~ion** *n* Wahl *f*

elector *n* Wähler(in) *m(f).* ~ **ate** *n* Wählerschaft *f*

electric *a,* **-ally** *adv* elektrisch

electrical *a* elektrisch; ~ **engineering** Elektrotechnik *f*

electric: ~ **blanket** *n* Heizdecke *f.* ~ **fire** *n* elektrischer Heizofen *m*

electrician *n* Elektriker *m*

electricity *n* Elektrizität *f; (supply)* Strom *m*

electrify *vt* *(pt/pp* **-ied)** elektrifizieren. **~ing** *a (fig)* elektrisierend

electrocute *vt* durch einen elektrischen Schlag töten

electrode *n* Elektrode *f*

electronic *a* elektronisch. **~s** *n* Elektronik *f*

elegance *n* Eleganz *f*

elegant *a,* **-ly** *adv* elegant

elegy *n* Elegie *f*

element *n* Element *nt.* **~ary** *a* elementar

elephant *n* Elefant *m*

elevat|e *vt* heben; *(fig)* erheben. **~ion** *n* Erhebung *f*

elevator *n* *(Amer)* Aufzug *m,* Fahrstuhl *m*

eleven *a* elf ● *n* Elf *f.* **~th** *a* elfte(r,s); at the ~th hour 🄘 in letzter Minute

eligible *a* berechtigt

eliminate *vt* ausschalten

élite *n* Elite *f*

elm *n* Ulme *f*

elocution *n* Sprecherziehung *f*

elope *vi* durchbrennen 🄘

eloquen|ce *n* Beredsamkeit *f.* **~t** *a,* **~ly** *adv* beredt

else *adv* sonst; **nothing** ~ sonst nichts; **or** ~ oder; *(otherwise)* sonst; **someone/somewhere** ~ jemand/ irgendwo anders; **anyone** ~ jeder andere; *(as question)* sonst noch jemand? **anything** ~ alles andere; *(as question)* sonst noch etwas? **~where** *adv* woanders

elucidate *vt* erläutern

elusive *a* be ~ schwer zu fassen sein

emaciated *a* abgezehrt

e-mail *n* E-Mail *f.* ~ **address** *n* E-Mail-Adresse *f.* ~ **message** *n* E-Mail *f* ● *vt* per E-Mail übermitteln

<*Ergebnisse, Datei usw.*>; ~ **s.o.** jdm eine E-Mail schicken

emancipat|ed *a* emanzipiert. ~**ion** *n* Emanzipation *f*; (*of slaves*) Freilassung *f*

embankment *n* Böschung *f*; (*of railway*) Bahndamm *m*

embark *vi* sich einschiffen. ~**ation** *n* Einschiffung *f*

embarrass *vt* in Verlegenheit bringen. ~**ed** *a* verlegen. ~**ing** *a* peinlich. ~**ment** *n* Verlegenheit *f*

embassy *n* Botschaft *f*

embellish *vt* verzieren; (*fig*) ausschmücken

embezzle *vt* unterschlagen. ~**ment** *n* Unterschlagung *f*

emblem *n* Emblem *nt*

embodiment *n* Verkörperung *f*

embody *vt* (*pt/pp* **-ied**) verkörpern; (*include*) enthalten

embrace *n* Umarmung *f* ● *vt* umarmen; (*fig*) umfassen ● *vi* sich umarmen

embroider *vt* besticken; sticken <*design*> ● *vi* sticken. ~**y** *n* Stickerei *f*

embryo *n* Embryo *m*

emerald *n* Smaragd *m*

emer|ge *vi* auftauchen (**from** aus); (*become known*) sich herausstellen; (*come into being*) entstehen. ~**gence** *n* Auftauchen *nt*; Entstehung *f*

emergency *n* Notfall *m*. ~ **exit** *n* Notausgang *m*

emigrant *n* Auswanderer *m*

emigrat|e *vi* auswandern. ~**ion** *n* Auswanderung *f*

eminent *a*, **-ly** *adv* eminent

emission *n* Ausstrahlung *f*; (*of pollutant*) Emission *f*

emit *vt* (*pt/pp* **emitted**) ausstrahlen <*light, heat*>; ausstoßen <*smoke, fumes, cry*>

emotion *n* Gefühl *nt*. ~**al** *a* emotional; **become** ~**al** sich erregen

empathy *n* Einfühlungsvermögen *nt*

emperor *n* Kaiser *m*

emphasis *n* Betonung *f*

emphasize *vt* betonen

emphatic *a*, **-ally** *adv* nachdrücklich

empire *n* Reich *nt*

employ *vt* beschäftigen; (*appoint*) einstellen; (*fig*) anwenden. ~**ee** *n* Beschäftigte(r) *m/f*; (*in contrast to employer*) Arbeitnehmer *m*. ~**er** *n* Arbeitgeber *m*. ~**ment** *n* Beschäftigung *f*; (*work*) Arbeit *f*. ~**ment agency** *n* Stellenvermittlung *f*

empress *n* Kaiserin *f*

emptiness *n* Leere *f*

empty *a* leer ● *vt* leeren; ausleeren <*container*> ● *vi* sich leeren

emulsion *n* Emulsion *f*

enable *vt* ~ **s.o. to** es jdm möglich machen, zu

enact *vt* (*Theat*) aufführen

enamel *n* Email *nt*; (*on teeth*) Zahnschmelz *m*; (*paint*) Lack *m*

enchant *vt* bezaubern. ~**ing** *a* bezaubernd. ~**ment** *n* Zauber *m*

encircle *vt* einkreisen

enclos|e *vt* einschließen; (*in letter*) beilegen (**with** *dat*). ~**ure** *n* (*at zoo*) Gehege *nt*; (*in letter*) Anlage *f*

encore *n* Zugabe *f* ● *int* bravo!

encounter *n* Begegnung *f* ● *vt* begegnen (+ *dat*); (*fig*) stoßen auf (+ *acc*)

encourag|e *vt* ermutigen; (*promote*) fördern. ~**ement** *n* Ermutigung *f*. ~**ing** *a* ermutigend

encroach *vi* ~ **on** eindringen in (+ *acc*) <*land*>

encyclopaed|ia *n* Enzyklopädie *f*, Lexikon *nt*. ~**ic** *a* enzyklopädisch

end *n* Ende *nt*; (*purpose*) Zweck *m*; **in the** ~ schließlich; **at the** ~ **of May** Ende Mai; **on** ~ hochkant; **for days on** ~ tagelang; **make** ~**s meet** 🅸 [gerade] auskommen; **no** ~ **of** 🅸 unheimlich viel(e) ● *vt* beenden ● *vi* enden; ~ **up in** (🅸 *arrive at*) landen in (+ *dat*)

endanger *vt* gefährden

endeavour *n* Bemühung *f* ● *vi* sich bemühen (**to** zu)

ending n Schluss m, Ende nt; (*Gram*) Endung f

endless a, **-ly** adv endlos

endorse vt (*Comm*) indossieren; (*confirm*) bestätigen. **~ment** n (*Comm*) Indossament nt; (*fig*) Bestätigung f; (*on driving licence*) Strafvermerk m

endow vt stiften; **be ~ed with** (*fig*) haben

endurance n Durchhaltevermögen nt; **beyond ~** unerträglich

endure vt ertragen

enemy n Feind m ● attrib feindlich

energetic a tatkräftig; **be ~** voller Energie sein

energy n Energie f

enforce vt durchsetzen. **~d** a unfreiwillig

engage vt einstellen <*staff*>; (*Theat*) engagieren; (*Auto*) einlegen <*gear*> ● vi sich beteiligen (**in** an + dat); (*Techn*) ineinandergreifen. **~d** a besetzt; <*person*> beschäftigt; (*to be married*) verlobt; **get ~d** sich verloben (**to** mit). **~ment** n Verlobung f; (*appointment*) Verabredung f; (*Mil*) Gefecht nt

engaging a einnehmend

engine n Motor m; (*Naut*) Maschine f; (*Rail*) Lokomotive f; (*of jet plane*) Triebwerk nt. **~-driver** n Lokomotivführer m

engineer n Ingenieur m; (*service, installation*) Techniker m; (*Naut*) Maschinist m; (*Amer*) Lokomotivführer m. **~ing** n [mechanical] **~ing** Maschinenbau m

England n England nt

English a englisch; **the ~ Channel** der Ärmelkanal ● n (*Lang*) Englisch nt; **in ~** auf Englisch; **into ~** ins Englische; **the ~** pl die Engländer. **~man** n Engländer m. **~woman** n Engländerin f

engrav|e vt eingravieren. **~ing** n Stich m

enhance vt verschönern; (*fig*) steigern

enigma n Rätsel nt. **~tic** a rätselhaft

enjoy vt genießen; **~ oneself** sich amüsieren; **~ cooking** gern kochen; **I ~ed it** es hat mir gut gefallen/ <*food:*> geschmeckt. **~able** a angenehm, nett. **~ment** n Vergnügen nt

enlarge vt vergrößern. **~ment** n Vergrößerung f

enlist vt (*Mil*) einziehen; **~ s.o.'s help** jdn zur Hilfe heranziehen ● vi (*Mil*) sich melden

enliven vt beleben

enmity n Feindschaft f

enormity n Ungeheuerlichkeit f

enormous a, **-ly** adv riesig

enough a, adv & n genug; **be ~** reichen; **funnily ~** komischerweise

enquir|e vi sich erkundigen (**about** nach). **~y** n Erkundigung f; (*investigation*) Untersuchung f

enrage vt wütend machen

enrich vt bereichern

enrol v (*pt/pp* **-rolled**) ● vt einschreiben ● vi sich einschreiben

ensemble n (*clothing & Mus*) Ensemble nt

enslave vt versklaven

ensue vi folgen; (*result*) sich ergeben (**from** aus)

ensure vt sicherstellen; **~ that** dafür sorgen, dass

entail vt erforderlich machen; **what does it ~?** was ist damit verbunden?

entangle vt **get ~d** sich verfangen (**in** in + dat)

enter vt eintreten/ <*vehicle:*> einfahren in (+ acc); einreisen in (+ acc) <*country*>; (*register*) eintragen; sich anmelden zu <*competition*> ● vi eintreten; <*vehicle:*> einfahren; (*Theat*) auftreten; (*register as competitor*) sich anmelden; (*take part*) sich beteiligen (**in** an + dat)

enterpris|e n Unternehmen nt; (*quality*) Unternehmungsgeist m. **~ing** a unternehmend

entertain vt unterhalten; (*invite*) einladen; (*to meal*) bewirten <*guest*> ● vi unterhalten; (*have guests*) Gäste haben. **~er** n Unterhalter m. **~ment** n Unterhaltung f

enthral vt (pt/pp enthralled) be ~led gefesselt sein (by von)

enthuse vi ~ over schwärmen von

enthusias|m n Begeisterung f. ~t n Enthusiast m. ~tic a, -ally adv begeistert

entice vt locken. ~ment n Anreiz m

entire a ganz. ~ly adv ganz, völlig. ~ty n in its ~ty in seiner Gesamtheit

entitle vt berechtigen; ~d ... mit dem Titel ...; be ~d to sth das Recht auf etw (acc) haben. ~ment n Berechtigung f; (claim) Anspruch m (to auf + acc)

entrance n Eintritt m; (Theat) Auftritt m; (way in) Eingang m; (for vehicle) Einfahrt f. ~ fee n Eintrittsgebühr f

entrant n Teilnehmer(in) m(f)

entreat vt anflehen (for um)

entrust vt ~ s.o. with sth, ~ sth to s.o. jdm etw anvertrauen

entry n Eintritt m; (into country) Einreise f; (on list) Eintrag m; no ~ Zutritt/ (Auto) Einfahrt verboten

envelop vt (pt/pp enveloped) einhüllen

envelope n [Brief]umschlag m

enviable a beneidenswert

envious a, -ly adv neidisch (of auf + acc)

environment n Umwelt f

environmental a Umwelt-. ~ist n Umweltschützer m. ~ly adv ~ly friendly umweltfreundlich

envisage vt sich (dat) vorstellen

envoy n Gesandte(r) m

envy n Neid m ● vt (pt/pp -ied) ~ s.o. sth jdn um etw beneiden

epic a episch ● n Epos nt

epidemic n Epidemie f

epilep|sy n Epilepsie f. ~tic a epileptisch ● n Epileptiker(in) m(f)

epilogue n Epilog m

episode n Episode f; (instalment) Folge f

epitome n Inbegriff m

epoch n Epoche f. ~-making a epochemachend

equal a gleich (to dat); be ~ to a task einer Aufgabe gewachsen sein ● n Gleichgestellte(r) m/f ● vt (pt/pp equalled) gleichen (+ dat); (fig) gleichkommen (+ dat). ~ity n Gleichheit f

equalize vt/i ausgleichen

equally adv gleich; <divide> gleichmäßig; (just as) genauso

equat|e vt gleichsetzen (with mit). ~ion n (Math) Gleichung f

equator n Äquator m

equestrian a Reit-

equilibrium n Gleichgewicht nt

equinox n Tagundnachtgleiche f

equip vt (pt/pp equipped) ausrüsten; (furnish) ausstatten. ~ment n Ausrüstung f; Ausstattung f

equity n Gerechtigkeit f

equivalent a gleichwertig; (corresponding) entsprechend ● n Äquivalent nt; (value) Gegenwert m; (counterpart) Gegenstück nt

era n Ära f, Zeitalter nt

eradicate vt ausrotten

erase vt ausradieren; (from tape) löschen

erect a aufrecht ● vt errichten. ~ion n Errichtung f; (building) Bau m; (Biol) Erektion f

ero|de vt <water:> auswaschen; <acid:> angreifen. ~sion n Erosion f

erotic a erotisch

errand n Botengang m

erratic a unregelmäßig; <person> unberechenbar

erroneous a falsch; <belief, assumption> irrig

error n Irrtum m; (mistake) Fehler m; in ~ irrtümlicherweise

erupt vi ausbrechen. ~ion n Ausbruch m

escalat|e vt/i eskalieren. ~or n Rolltreppe f

escape n Flucht f; (from prison) Ausbruch m; have a narrow ~ gerade noch davonkommen ● vi flüchten; <prisoner:> ausbrechen;

entkommen (from aus; from s.o.
jdm); <gas:> entweichen ● vt the
name ~s me der Name entfällt mir

escapism n Eskapismus m

escort[1] n (of person) Begleiter m;
(Mil) Eskorte f

escort[2] vt begleiten; (Mil)
eskortieren

Eskimo n Eskimo m

esoteric a esoterisch

especially adv besonders

espionage n Spionage f

essay n Aufsatz m

essence n Wesen nt; (Chem, Culin)
Essenz f

essential a wesentlich;
(indispensable) unentbehrlich ● n
the ~s das Wesentliche; (items) das
Nötigste. ~ly adv im Wesentlichen

establish vt gründen; (form) bilden;
(prove) beweisen

estate n Gut nt; (possessions) Besitz
m; (after death) Nachlass m;
(housing) [Wohn]siedlung f. ~
agent n Immobilienmakler m. ~
car n Kombi[wagen] m

esteem n Achtung f ● vt
hochschätzen

estimate[1] n Schätzung f; (Comm)
[Kosten]voranschlag m; at a rough ~
grob geschätzt

estimat|e[2] vt schätzen. ~ion n
Einschätzung f

estuary n Mündung f

etc. abbr (et cetera) und so weiter,
usw.

eternal a, -ly adv ewig

eternity n Ewigkeit f

ethic|al a ethisch; (morally correct)
moralisch einwandfrei. ~s n Ethik f

Ethiopia n Äthiopien nt

ethnic a ethnisch. ~ **cleansing** n
ethnische Säuberung

etiquette n Etikette f

EU abbr (European Union) EU f

eulogy n Lobrede f

euphemis|m n Euphemismus m.
~**tic** a, -ally adv verhüllend

Euro n Euro m. ~**cheque** n
Euroscheck m

Europe n Europa nt

European a europäisch; ~ Union
Europäische Union f ● n
Europäer(in) m(f)

evacuat|e vt evakuieren; räumen
<building, area>. ~ion n
Evakuierung f; Räumung f

evade vt sich entziehen (+ dat);
hinterziehen <taxes>

evaluate vt einschätzen

evange|lical a evangelisch. ~**list**
n Evangelist m

evaporat|e vi verdunsten. ~ion n
Verdampfung f

evasion n Ausweichen nt; tax ~
Steuerhinterziehung f

evasive a, -ly adv ausweichend; be
~ ausweichen

even a (level) eben; (same, equal)
gleich; (regular) gleichmäßig;
<number> gerade; get ~ with 🔢 es
jdm heimzahlen ● adv sogar, selbst;
~ so trotzdem; not ~ nicht einmal
● vt ~ the score ausgleichen

evening n Abend m; this ~ heute
Abend; in the ~ abends, am Abend.
~ **class** n Abendkurs m

evenly adv gleichmäßig

event n Ereignis nt; (function)
Veranstaltung f; (Sport) Wettbewerb
m. ~**ful** a ereignisreich

eventual a his ~ **success** der
Erfolg, der ihm schließlich zuteil
wurde. ~**ly** adv schließlich

ever adv je[mals]; not ~ nie; for ~
für immer; hardly ~ fast nie; ~
since seitdem

evergreen n immergrüner Strauch
m/ (tree) Baum m

everlasting a ewig

every a jede(r,s); ~ **one** jede(r,s)
Einzelne; ~ **other day** jeden zweiten
Tag

every: ~**body** pron jeder[mann];
alle pl. ~**day** a alltäglich. ~ **one**
pron jeder[mann]; alle pl. ~**thing**
pron alles. ~**where** adv überall

evict vt [aus der Wohnung]
hinausweisen. ~**ion** n Ausweisung f

eviden|ce n Beweise pl; (Jur)
Beweismaterial nt; (testimony)

Aussage *f*; **give** ∼**ce** aussagen. ∼**t** *a*, **-ly** *adv* offensichtlich

evil *a* böse ● *n* Böse *nt*

evoke *vt* heraufbeschwören

evolution *n* Evolution *f*

evolve *vt* entwickeln ● *vi* sich entwickeln

ewe *n* Schaf *nt*

exact *a*, **-ly** *adv* genau; **not** ∼**ly** nicht gerade. ∼**ness** *n* Genauigkeit *f*

exaggerat|e *vt/i* übertreiben. ∼**ion** *n* Übertreibung *f*

exam *n* 🔲 Prüfung *f*

examination *n* Untersuchung *f*; (*Sch*) Prüfung *f*

examine *vt* untersuchen; (*Sch*) prüfen

example *n* Beispiel *nt* (**of** für); **for** ∼ zum Beispiel; **make an** ∼ **of** ein Exempel statuieren an (+ *dat*)

exasperat|e *vt* zur Verzweiflung treiben. ∼**ion** *n* Verzweiflung *f*

excavat|e *vt* ausschachten; (*Archaeol*) ausgraben. ∼**ion** *n* Ausgrabung *f*

exceed *vt* übersteigen. ∼**ingly** *adv* äußerst

excel *v* (*pt/pp* **excelled**) *vi* sich auszeichnen ● *vt* ∼ **oneself** sich selbst übertreffen

excellen|ce *n* Vorzüglichkeit *f*. ∼**t** *a*, **-ly** *adv* ausgezeichnet, vorzüglich

except *prep* außer (+ *dat*); ∼ **for** abgesehen von ● *vt* ausnehmen

exception *n* Ausnahme *f*. ∼**al** *a*, **-ly** *adv* außergewöhnlich

excerpt *n* Auszug *m*

excess *n* Übermaß *nt* (**of** an + *dat*); (*surplus*) Überschuss *m*; ∼**es** *pl* Exzesse *pl*

excessive *a*, **-ly** *adv* übermäßig

exchange *n* Austausch *m*; (*Teleph*) Fernsprechamt *nt*; (*Comm*) [Geld]wechsel *m*; **in** ∼ dafür ● *vt* austauschen (**for** gegen); tauschen <*places*>. ∼ **rate** *n* Wechselkurs *m*

excitable *a* [leicht] erregbar

excit|e *vt* aufregen; (*cause*) erregen. ∼**ed** *a*, **-ly** *adv* aufgeregt; **get** ∼**ed** sich aufregen. ∼**ement** *n*

Aufregung *f*; Erregung *f*. ∼**ing** *a* aufregend; <*story*> spannend

exclaim *vt/i* ausrufen

exclamation *n* Ausruf *m*. ∼ **mark** *n*, (*Amer*) ∼ **point** *n* Ausrufezeichen *nt*

exclu|de *vt* ausschließen. ∼**ding** *prep* ausschließlich (+ *gen*). ∼**sion** *n* Ausschluss *m*

exclusive *a*, **-ly** *adv* ausschließlich; (*select*) exklusiv

excrement *n* Kot *m*

excrete *vt* ausscheiden

excruciating *a* grässlich

excursion *n* Ausflug *m*

excusable *a* entschuldbar

excuse¹ *n* Entschuldigung *f*; (*pretext*) Ausrede *f*

excuse² *vt* entschuldigen; ∼ **me!** Entschuldigung!

ex-directory *a* **be** ∼ nicht im Telefonbuch stehen

execute *vt* ausführen; (*put to death*) hinrichten

execution *n* Ausführung *f*; Hinrichtung *f*

executive *a* leitend ● *n* leitende(r) Angestellte(r) *m/f*; (*Pol*) Exekutive *f*

exemplary *a* beispielhaft

exemplify *vt* (*pt/pp* **-ied**) veranschaulichen

exempt *a* befreit ● *vt* befreien (**from** von). ∼**ion** *n* Befreiung *f*

exercise *n* Übung *f*; **physical** ∼ körperliche Bewegung *f* ● *vt* (*use*) ausüben; bewegen <*horse*> ● *vi* sich bewegen. ∼ **book** *n* [Schul]heft *nt*

exert *vt* ausüben; ∼ **oneself** sich anstrengen. ∼**ion** *n* Anstrengung *f*

exhale *vt/i* ausatmen

exhaust *n* (*Auto*) Auspuff *m*; (*fumes*) Abgase *pl* ● *vt* erschöpfen. ∼**ed** *a* erschöpft. ∼**ing** *a* anstrengend. ∼**ion** *n* Erschöpfung *f*. ∼**ive** *a* (*fig*) erschöpfend

exhibit *n* Ausstellungsstück *nt*; (*Jur*) Beweisstück *nt* ● *vt* ausstellen

exhibition *n* Ausstellung *f*; (*Univ*) Stipendium *nt*. ∼**ist** *n* Exhibitionist(in) *m(f)*

exhibitor *n* Aussteller *m*

exhilarat|ing *a* berauschend. ~**ion** *n* Hochgefühl *nt*

exhume *vt* exhumieren

exile *n* Exil *nt*; (*person*) im Exil Lebende(r) *m/f* ● *vt* ins Exil schicken

exist *vi* bestehen, existieren. ~**ence** *n* Existenz *f*; **be in** ~**ence** existieren

exit *n* Ausgang *m*; (*Auto*) Ausfahrt *f*; (*Theat*) Abgang *m*

exorbitant *a* übermäßig hoch

exotic *a* exotisch

expand *vt* ausdehnen; (*explain better*) weiter ausführen ● *vi* sich ausdehnen; (*Comm*) expandieren

expans|e *n* Weite *f*. ~**ion** *n* Ausdehnung *f*; (*Techn, Pol, Comm*) Expansion *f*

expect *vt* erwarten; (*suppose*) annehmen; **I** ~ **so** wahrscheinlich

expectan|cy *n* Erwartung *f*. ~**t** *a*, -**ly** *adv* erwartungsvoll; ~**t mother** werdende Mutter *f*

expectation *n* Erwartung *f*

expedient *a* zweckdienlich

expedite *vt* beschleunigen

expedition *n* Expedition *f*

expel *vt* (*pt/pp* expelled) ausweisen (**from** aus); (*from school*) von der Schule verweisen

expenditure *n* Ausgaben *pl*

expense *n* Kosten *pl*; **business** ~**s** *pl* Spesen *pl*; **at my** ~ auf meine Kosten

expensive *a*, -**ly** *adv* teuer

experience *n* Erfahrung *f*; (*event*) Erlebnis *nt* ● *vt* erleben. ~**d** *a* erfahren

experiment *n* Versuch *m*, Experiment *nt* ● *vi* experimentieren. ~**al** *a* experimentell

expert *a*, -**ly** *adv* fachmännisch ● *n* Fachmann *m*, Experte *m*

expertise *n* Sachkenntnis *f*

expire *vi* ablaufen

expiry *n* Ablauf *m*

explain *vt* erklären

explana|tion *n* Erklärung *f*. ~**tory** *a* erklärend

explicit *a*, -**ly** *adv* deutlich

explode *vi* explodieren ● *vt* zur Explosion bringen

exploit[1] *n* [Helden]tat *f*

exploit[2] *vt* ausbeuten. ~**ation** *n* Ausbeutung *f*

exploration *n* Erforschung *f*

explore *vt* erforschen. ~**r** *n* Forschungsreisende(r) *m*

explos|ion *n* Explosion *f*. ~**ive** *a* explosiv ● *n* Sprengstoff *m*

export[1] *n* Export *m*, Ausfuhr *f*

export[2] *vt* exportieren, ausführen. ~**er** *n* Exporteur *m*

expos|e *vt* freilegen; (*to danger*) aussetzen (**to** *dat*); (*reveal*) aufdecken; (*Phot*) belichten. ~**ure** *n* Aussetzung *f*; (*Med*) Unterkühlung *f*; (*Phot*) Belichtung *f*; **24** ~**ures** 24 Aufnahmen

express *adv* <*send*> per Eilpost ● *n* (*train*) Schnellzug *m* ● *vt* ausdrücken; ~ **oneself** sich ausdrücken. ~**ion** *n* Ausdruck *m*. ~**ive** *a* ausdrucksvoll. ~**ly** *adv* ausdrücklich

expulsion *n* Ausweisung *f*; (*Sch*) Verweisung *f* von der Schule

exquisite *a* erlesen

extend *vt* verlängern; (*stretch out*) ausstrecken; (*enlarge*) vergrößern ● *vi* sich ausdehnen; <*table*:> sich ausziehen lassen

extension *n* Verlängerung *f*; (*to house*) Anbau *m*; (*Teleph*) Nebenanschluss *m*

extensive *a* weit; (*fig*) umfassend. ~**ly** *adv* viel

extent *n* Ausdehnung *f*; (*scope*) Ausmaß *nt*, Umfang *m*; **to a certain** ~ in gewissem Maße

exterior *a* äußere(r,s) ● *n* **the** ~ das Äußere

exterminat|e *vt* ausrotten. ~**ion** *n* Ausrottung *f*

external *a* äußere(r,s); **for** ~ **use only** (*Med*) nur äußerlich. ~**ly** *adv* äußerlich

extinct *a* ausgestorben; <*volcano*> erloschen. ∼**ion** *n* Aussterben *nt*

extinguish *vt* löschen. ∼**er** *n* Feuerlöscher *m*

extort *vt* erpressen. ∼**ion** *n* Erpressung *f*

extortionate *a* übermäßig hoch

extra *a* zusätzlich ● *adv* extra; (*especially*) besonders ● *n* (*Theat*) Statist(in) *m(f)*; ∼**s** *pl* Nebenkosten *pl*; (*Auto*) Extras *pl*

extract¹ *n* Auszug *m*

extract² *vt* herausziehen; ziehen <*tooth*>

extraordinary *a*, **-ily** *adv* außerordentlich; (*strange*) seltsam

extravagan|ce *n* Verschwendung *f*; **an** ∼**ce** ein Luxus *m*. ∼**t** *a* verschwenderisch

extrem|e *a* äußerste(r,s); (*fig*) extrem ● *n* Extrem *nt*; **in the** ∼**e** im höchsten Grade. ∼**ely** *adv* äußerst. ∼**ist** *n* Extremist *m*

extricate *vt* befreien

extrovert *n* extravertierter Mensch *m*

exuberant *a* überglücklich

exude *vt* absondern; (*fig*) ausstrahlen

exult *vi* frohlocken

eye *n* Auge *nt*; (*of needle*) Öhr *nt*; (*for hook*) Öse *f*; **keep an** ∼ **on** aufpassen auf (+ *acc*) ● *vt* (*pt/pp* **eyed**, *pres p* **ey[e]ing**) ansehen

eye: ∼ **brow** *n* Augenbraue *f*. ∼**lash** *n* Wimper *f*. ∼**lid** *n* Augenlid *nt*. ∼**shadow** *n* Lidschatten *m*. ∼**sight** *n* Sehkraft *f*. ∼**sore** ⊡ Schandfleck *m*. ∼**witness** *n* Augenzeuge *m*

F f

fable *n* Fabel *f*

fabric *n* Stoff *m*

fabrication *n* Erfindung *f*

fabulous *a* ⊡ phantastisch

façade *n* Fassade *f*

face *n* Gesicht *nt*; (*surface*) Fläche *f*; (*of clock*) Zifferblatt *nt*; **pull** ∼**s** Gesichter schneiden; **in the** ∼ **of** angesichts (+ *gen*); **on the** ∼ **of it** allem Anschein nach ● *vt/i* gegenüberstehen (+ *dat*); ∼ **north** <*house:*> nach Norden liegen; ∼ **the fact that** sich damit abfinden, dass

face: ∼**-flannel** *n* Waschlappen *m*. ∼**less** *a* anonym. ∼**-lift** *n* Gesichtsstraffung *f*

facet *n* Facette *f*; (*fig*) Aspekt *m*

facetious *a*, **-ly** *adv* spöttisch

facial *a* Gesichts-

facile *a* oberflächlich

facilitate *vt* erleichtern

facility *n* Leichtigkeit *f*; (*skill*) Gewandtheit *f*; ∼**ies** *pl* Einrichtungen *pl*

facsimile *n* Faksimile *nt*

fact *n* Tatsache *f*; **in** ∼ tatsächlich; (*actually*) eigentlich

faction *n* Gruppe *f*

factor *n* Faktor *m*

factory *n* Fabrik *f*

factual *a*, **-ly** *adv* sachlich

faculty *n* Fähigkeit *f*; (*Univ*) Fakultät *f*

fad *n* Fimmel *m*

fade *vi* verblassen; <*material:*> verbleichen; <*sound:*> abklingen; <*flower:*> verwelken.

fag *n* (*chore*) Plage *f*; (⊡ *cigarette*) Zigarette *f*

fail *n* **without** ∼ unbedingt ● *vi* <*attempt:*> scheitern; (*grow weak*) nachlassen; (*break down*) versagen; (*in exam*) durchfallen; ∼ **to do sth** etw nicht tun ● *vt* nicht bestehen <*exam*>; durchfallen lassen <*candidate*>; (*disappoint*) enttäuschen

failing *n* Fehler *m*

failure *n* Misserfolg *m*; (*breakdown*) Versagen *nt*; (*person*) Versager *m*

faint a (-er, -est), **-ly** adv schwach; I feel ~ mir ist schwach ● n Ohnmacht f ● vi ohnmächtig werden. **~ness** n Schwäche f

fair¹ n Jahrmarkt m; (Comm) Messe f

fair² a (-er, -est) <hair> blond; <skin> hell; <weather> heiter; (just) gerecht, fair; (quite good) ziemlich gut; (Sch) genügend; **a ~ amount** ziemlich viel ● adv **play ~** fair sein. **~ly** adv gerecht; (rather) ziemlich. **~ness** n Blondheit f; Helle f; Gerechtigkeit f; (Sport) Fairness f

fairy n Elfe f; **good/wicked ~** gute/ böse Fee f. **~ story**, **~-tale** n Märchen nt

faith n Glaube m; (trust) Vertrauen nt (in zu)

faithful a, **-ly** adv treu; (exact) genau; **Yours ~ly** Hochachtungsvoll. **~ness** n Treue f; Genauigkeit f

fake a falsch ● n Fälschung f; (person) Schwindler m ● vt fälschen; (pretend) vortäuschen

falcon n Falke m

fall n Fall m; (heavy) Sturz m; (in prices) Fallen nt; (Amer: autumn) Herbst m; **have a ~** fallen ● vi (pt fell, pp fallen) fallen; (heavily) stürzen; <night:> anbrechen; **~in love** sich verlieben; **~ back on** zurückgreifen auf (+ acc); **~ for s.o.** ⊞ sich in jdn verlieben; **~ for sth** ⊞ auf etw (acc) hereinfallen. **~ about** vi (with laughter) sich [vor Lachen] kringeln. **~ down** vi umfallen; <thing:> herunterfallen; <building:> einstürzen. **~ in** vi hineinfallen; (collapse) einfallen; (Mil) antreten; **~ in with** sich anschließen (+ dat). **~ off** vi herunterfallen; (diminish) abnehmen. **~ out** vi herausfallen; <hair:> ausfallen; (quarrel) sich überwerfen. **~ over** vi hinfallen. **~ through** vi durchfallen; <plan:> ins Wasser fallen

fallacy n Irrtum m

fallible a fehlbar

fall-out n [radioaktiver] Niederschlag m

false a falsch; (artificial) künstlich. **~hood** n Unwahrheit f. **~ly** adv falsch

false teeth npl [künstliches] Gebiss nt

falsify vt (pt/pp -ied) fälschen

falter vi zögern

fame n Ruhm m.

familiar a vertraut; (known) bekannt; **too ~** familiär. **~ity** n Vertrautheit f. **~ize** vt vertraut machen (with mit)

family n Familie f

family: ~ doctor n Hausarzt m. **~ life** n Familienleben nt. **~ planning** n Familienplanung f. **~ tree** n Stammbaum m

famine n Hungersnot f

famished a sehr hungrig

famous a berühmt

fan¹ n Fächer m; (Techn) Ventilator m

fan² n (admirer) Fan m

fanatic n Fanatiker m. **~al** a, **-ly** adv fanatisch. **~ism** n Fanatismus m

fanciful a phantastisch; (imaginative) phantasiereich

fancy n Phantasie f; I have taken a real ~ to him er hat es mir angetan ● a ausgefallen ● vt (believe) meinen; (imagine) sich (dat) einbilden; (⊞ want) Lust haben auf (+ acc); **~ that!** stell dir vor! (really) tatsächlich! **~ dress** n Kostüm nt

fanfare n Fanfare f

fang n Fangzahn m

fan heater n Heizlüfter m

fantas|ize vi fantasieren. **~tic** a fantastisch. **~y** n Fantasie f

far adv weit; (much) viel; **by ~** bei weitem; **~ away** weit weg; **as ~ as I know** soviel ich weiß; **as ~ as the church** bis zur Kirche ● a **at the ~ end** am anderen Ende; **the F~ East** der Ferne Osten

farc|e n Farce f. **~ical** a lächerlich

fare n Fahrpreis m; (money) Fahrgeld nt; (food) Kost f; **air ~** Flugpreis m

farewell int (liter) lebe wohl! ● n Lebewohl nt

far-fetched *a* weit hergeholt

farm *n* Bauernhof *m* ● *vi* Landwirtschaft betreiben ● *vt* bewirtschaften *<land>*. **~er** *n* Landwirt *m*

farm: ~house *n* Bauernhaus *nt*. **~ing** *n* Landwirtschaft *f*. **~yard** *n* Hof *m*

far: ~-reaching *a* weit reichend. **~-sighted** *a* (*fig*) umsichtig; (*Amer: long-sighted*) weitsichtig

farther *adv* weiter; **~ off** weiter entfernt

fascinat|e *vt* faszinieren. **~ing** *a* faszinierend. **~ion** *n* Faszination *f*

fascis|m *n* Faschismus *m*. **~t** *n* Faschist *m* ● *a* faschistisch

fashion *n* Mode *f*; (*manner*) Art *f*. **~able**, **-bly** *adv* modisch

fast *a & adv* (**-er**, **-est**) schnell; (*firm*) fest; *<colour>* waschecht; **be ~** *<clock:>* vorgehen; **be ~ asleep** fest schlafen

fasten *vt* zumachen; (*fix*) befestigen (**to an** + *dat*). **~er** *n*, **~ing** *n* Verschluss *m*

fastidious *a* wählerisch; (*particular*) penibel

fat *a* (**fatter**, **fattest**) dick; *<meat>* fett ● *n* Fett *nt*

fatal *a* tödlich; *<error>* verhängnisvoll. **~ity** *n* Todesopfer *nt*. **~ly** *adv* tödlich

fate *n* Schicksal *nt*. **~ful** *a* verhängnisvoll

fat-head *n* 🄸 Dummkopf *m*

father *n* Vater *m*; **F ~ Christmas** der Weihnachtsmann ● *vt* zeugen

father: ~hood *n* Vaterschaft *f*. **~in-law** *n* (*pl* **~s-in-law**) Schwiegervater *m*. **~ly** *a* väterlich

fathom *n* (*Naut*) Faden *m* ● *vt* verstehen

fatigue *n* Ermüdung *f*

fatten *vt* mästen *<animal>*

fatty *a* fett; *<foods>* fetthaltig

fatuous *a*, **-ly** *adv* albern

fault *n* Fehler *m*; (*Techn*) Defekt *m*; (*Geol*) Verwerfung *f*; **at ~** im Unrecht; **find ~ with** etwas auszusetzen haben an (+ *dat*); **it's**

your ~ du bist schuld. **~less** *a*, **-ly** *adv* fehlerfrei

faulty *a* fehlerhaft

favour *n* Gunst *f*; **I am in ~** ich bin dafür; **do s.o. a ~** jdm einen Gefallen tun ● *vt* begünstigen; (*prefer*) bevorzugen. **~able** *a*, **-bly** *adv* günstig; *<reply>* positiv

favourit|e *a* Lieblings- ● *n* Liebling *m*; (*Sport*) Favorit(in) *m(f)*. **~ism** *n* Bevorzugung *f*

fawn *a* rehbraun ● *n* Hirschkalb *nt*

fax *n* Fax *nt* ● *vt* faxen (**s.o.** jdm). **~ machine** *n* Faxgerät *nt*

fear *n* Furcht *f*, Angst *f* (**of** vor + *dat*) ● *vt/i* fürchten

fear|ful *a* besorgt; (*awful*) furchtbar. **~less** *a*, **-ly** *adv* furchtlos

feas|ibility *n* Durchführbarkeit *f*. **~ible** *a* durchführbar; (*possible*) möglich

feast *n* Festmahl *nt*; (*Relig*) Fest *nt* ● *vi* [**on**] schmausen

feat *n* Leistung *f*

feather *n* Feder *f*

feature *n* Gesichtszug *m*; (*quality*) Merkmal *nt*; (*Journ*) Feature *nt* ● *vt* darstellen

February *n* Februar *m*

fed ● *a* **be ~ up** 🄸 die Nase voll haben (**with** von)

federal *a* Bundes-

federation *n* Föderation *f*

fee *n* Gebühr *f*; (*professional*) Honorar *nt*

feeble *a* (**-r**, **-st**), **-bly** *adv* schwach

feed *n* Futter *nt*; (*for baby*) Essen *nt* ● *v* (*pt/pp* **fed**) ● *vt* füttern; (*support*) ernähren; (*into machine*) eingeben; speisen *<computer>* ● *vi* sich ernähren (**on** von)

feedback *n* Feedback *nt*

feel *v* (*pt/pp* **felt**) ● *vt* fühlen; (*experience*) empfinden; (*think*) meinen ● *vi* sich fühlen; **~ soft/hard** sich weich/hart anfühlen; **I ~ hot/ill** mir ist heiß/schlecht; **~ing** *n* Gefühl *nt*; **no hard ~ings** nichts für ungut

feet *see* **foot**

feline *a* Katzen-; (*catlike*) katzenartig

fell¹ *vt* fällen

fell² *see* **fall**

fellow *n* (🄵 *man*) Kerl *m*

fellow: ~**-countryman** *n* Landsmann *m*. ~ **men** *pl* Mitmenschen *pl*

felt¹ *see* **feel**

felt² *n* Filz *m*. ~**[-tipped] pen** *n* Filzstift *m*

female *a* weiblich ● *nt* Weibchen *nt*; (*pej: woman*) Weib *nt*

femin|ine *a* weiblich ● *n* (*Gram*) Femininum *nt*. ~**inity** *n* Weiblichkeit *f*. ~**ist** *a* feministisch ● *n* Feminist(in) *m(f)*

fenc|e *n* Zaun *m*; (🄵 *person*) Hehler *m* ● *vi* (*Sport*) fechten ● *vt* ~**e in** einzäunen. ~**er** *n* Fechter *m*. ~**ing** *n* Zaun *m*; (*Sport*) Fechten *nt*

fender *n* Kaminvorsetzer *m*; (*Naut*) Fender *m*; (*Amer: wing*) Kotflügel *m*

ferment *vi* gären ● *vt* gären lassen

fern *n* Farn *m*

feroc|ious *a* wild. ~**ity** *n* Wildheit *f*

ferry *n* Fähre *f*

fertil|e *a* fruchtbar. ~**ity** *n* Fruchtbarkeit *f*

fertilize *vt* befruchten; düngen <*land*>. ~**r** *n* Dünger *m*

fervent *a* leidenschaftlich

fervour *n* Leidenschaft *f*

festival *n* Fest *nt*; (*Mus, Theat*) Festspiele *pl*

festiv|e *a* festlich. ~**ities** *npl* Feierlichkeiten *pl*

festoon *vt* behängen (**with** mit).

fetch *vt* holen; (*collect*) abholen; (*be sold for*) einbringen

fetching *a* anziehend

fête *n* Fest *nt* ● *vt* feiern

feud *n* Fehde *f*

feudal *a* Feudal-

fever *n* Fieber *nt*. ~**ish** *a* fiebrig; (*fig*) fieberhaft

few *a* (**-er, -est**) wenige; **every** ~ **days** alle paar Tage ● *n* a ~ ein paar; **quite a** ~ ziemlich viele

fiancé *n* Verlobte(r) *m*. **fiancée** *n* Verlobte *f*

fiasco *n* Fiasko *nt*

fib *n* kleine Lüge

fibre *n* Faser *f*

fiction *n* Erfindung *f*; [*works of*] ~ Erzählungsliteratur *f*. ~**al** *a* erfunden

fictitious *a* [frei] erfunden

fiddle *n* 🄵 Geige *f*; (*cheating*) Schwindel *m* ● *vi* herumspielen (**with** mit) ● *vt* 🄵 frisieren <*accounts*>

fiddly *a* knifflig

fidelity *n* Treue *f*

fidget *vi* zappeln. ~**y** *a* zappelig

field *n* Feld *nt*; (*meadow*) Wiese *f*; (*subject*) Gebiet *nt*

field: ~ **events** *npl* Sprung- und Wurfdisziplinen *pl*. **F**~ **Marshal** *n* Feldmarschall *m*

fiendish *a* teuflisch

fierce *a* (**-r, -st**), **-ly** *adv* wild; (*fig*) heftig. ~**ness** *n* Wildheit *f*; (*fig*) Heftigkeit *f*

fiery *a* (**-ier, -iest**) feurig

fifteen *a* fünfzehn ● *n* Fünfzehn *f*. ~**th** *a* fünfzehnte(r,s)

fifth *a* fünfte(r,s)

fiftieth *a* fünfzigste(r,s)

fifty *a* fünfzig

fig *n* Feige *f*

fight *n* Kampf *m*; (*brawl*) Schlägerei *f*; (*between children, dogs*) Rauferei *f* ● *v* (*pt/pp* fought) ● *vt* kämpfen gegen; (*fig*) bekämpfen ● *vi* kämpfen; (*brawl*) sich schlagen; <*children, dogs:*> sich raufen. ~**er** *n* Kämpfer *m*; (*Aviat*) Jagdflugzeug *nt*. ~**ing** *n* Kampf *m*

figurative *a*, **-ly** *adv* bildlich, übertragen

figure *n* (*digit*) Ziffer *f*; (*number*) Zahl *f*; (*sum*) Summe *f*; (*carving, sculpture, woman's*) Figur *f*; (*form*) Gestalt *f*; (*illustration*) Abbildung *f*; **good at** ~**s** gut im Rechnen ● *vi* (*appear*) erscheinen ● *vt* (*Amer: think*) glauben

filch *vt* 🄵 klauen

file¹ *n* Akte *f*; (*for documents*) [Akten]ordner *m* ● *vt* ablegen <*documents*>; (*Jur*) einreichen

file² n (line) Reihe f; **in single ~** im Gänsemarsch

file³ n (Techn) Feile f ● vt feilen

fill n eat one's **~** sich satt essen ● vt füllen; plombieren <tooth> ● vi sich füllen. **~ in** vt auffüllen; ausfüllen <form>. **~ out** vt ausfüllen <form>. **~ up** vi sich füllen ● vt vollfüllen; (Auto) volltanken; ausfüllen <form>

fillet n Filet nt ● vt (pt/pp **filleted**) entgräten

filling n Füllung f; (of tooth) Plombe f. **~ station** n Tankstelle f

filly n junge Stute f

film n Film m ● vt/i filmen; verfilmen <book>. **~ star** n Filmstar m

filter n Filter m ● vt filtern

filth n Dreck m. **~y** a (-ier, -iest) dreckig

fin n Flosse f

final a letzte(r,s); (conclusive) endgültig ● n (Sport) Endspiel nt; **~s** pl (Univ) Abschlussprüfung f

finale n Finale nt

final|ist n Finalist(in) m(f)

final|ize vt endgültig festlegen. **~ly** adv schließlich

finance n Finanz f ● vt finanzieren

financial a, **-ly** adv finanziell

find n Fund m ● vt (pt/pp **found**) finden; (establish) feststellen; go and **~** holen; try to **~** suchen. **~ out** vt herausfinden; (learn) erfahren ● vi (enquire) sich erkundigen

fine¹ n Geldstrafe f ● vt zu einer Geldstrafe verurteilen

fine² a (-r, -st,) **-ly** adv fein; <weather> schön; he's **~** es geht ihm gut ● adv gut; cut it **~** 🅸 sich (dat) wenig Zeit lassen

finesse n Gewandtheit f

finger n Finger m ● vt anfassen

finger: ~-nail n Fingernagel m. **~print** n Fingerabdruck m. **~tip** n Fingerspitze f

finicky a knifflig; (choosy) wählerisch

finish n Schluss m; (Sport) Finish nt; (line) Ziel nt; (of product) Ausführung f ● vt beenden; (use up) aufbrauchen; **~ one's drink**

austrinken; **~ reading** zu Ende lesen ● vi fertig werden; <performance:> zu Ende sein; <runner:> durchs Ziel gehen

Finland n Finnland nt

Finn n Finne m/ Finnin f. **~ish** a finnisch

fir n Tanne f

fire n Feuer nt; (forest, house) Brand m; be on **~** brennen; catch **~** Feuer fangen; set **~** to anzünden; <arsonist:> in Brand stecken; under **~** unter Beschuss ● vt brennen <pottery>; abfeuern <shot>; schießen mit <gun>; (🅸 dismiss) feuern ● vi schießen (at auf + acc); <engine:> anspringen

fire: ~ alarm n Feuermelder m. **~ brigade** n Feuerwehr f. **~-engine** n Löschfahrzeug nt. **~ extinguisher** n Feuerlöscher m. **~man** n Feuerwehrmann m. **~place** n Kamin m. **~side** n by or at the **~side** am Kamin. **~ station** n Feuerwache f. **~wood** n Brennholz nt. **~work** n Feuerwerkskörper m; **~works** pl (display) Feuerwerk nt

firm¹ n Firma f

firm² a (-er, -est), **-ly** adv fest; (resolute) entschlossen; (strict) streng

first a & n erste(r,s); at **~** zuerst; at **~ sight** auf den ersten Blick; from the **~** von Anfang an ● adv zuerst; (firstly) erstens

first: ~ aid n erste Hilfe. **~-aid kit** n Verbandkasten m. **~-class** a erstklassig; (Rail) erster Klasse ● adv <travel> erster Klasse. **~ floor** n erster Stock; (Amer: ground floor) Erdgeschoss nt. **~ly** adv erstens. **~name** n Vorname m. **~-rate** a erstklassig

fish n Fisch m ● vt/i fischen; (with rod) angeln

fish: ~bone n Gräte f. **~erman** n Fischer m. **~ finger** n Fischstäbchen nt

fishing n Fischerei f. **~ boat** n Fischerboot nt. **~-rod** n Angel[rute] f

fish: **∼monger** n Fischhändler m.
∼y a Fisch-; (🄙 *suspicious*)
verdächtig

fission n (*Phys*) Spaltung f

fist n Faust f

fit¹ n (*attack*) Anfall m

fit² a (**fitter, fittest**) (*suitable*) geeignet;
(*healthy*) gesund; (*Sport*) fit; **∼ to eat**
essbar

fit³ n (*of clothes*) Sitz m; **be a good ∼**
gut passen ● v (*pt/pp* **fitted**) ● vi (*be
the right size*) passen ● vt anbringen
(**to** an + *dat*); (*install*) einbauen; **∼
with** versehen mit. **∼ in** vi
hineinpassen; (*adapt*) sich einfügen
(**with** in + *acc*) ● vt (*accommodate*)
unterbringen

fit|ness n Eignung f; [**physical**]
∼ness Gesundheit f; (*Sport*) Fitness
f. **∼ted** a eingebaut; <*garment*>
tailliert

fitted: **∼ carpet** n Teppichboden
m. **∼ kitchen** n Einbauküche f. **∼
sheet** n Spannlaken nt

fitting a passend ● n (*of clothes*)
Anprobe f; (*of shoes*) Weite f; (*Techn*)
Zubehörteil nt; **∼s** pl Zubehör nt

five a fünf ● n Fünf f. **∼r** n
Fünfpfundschein m

fix n (🄫 *drugs*) Fix m; **be in a ∼** 🄙 in
der Klemme sitzen ● vt befestigen
(**to** an + *dat*); (*arrange*) festlegen;
(*repair*) reparieren; (*Phot*) fixieren;
∼ a meal Essen machen

fixed a fest

fixture n (*Sport*) Veranstaltung f; **∼s
and fittings** zu einer Wohnung
gehörende Einrichtungen pl

fizz vi sprudeln

fizzle vi **∼ out** verpuffen

fizzy a sprudelnd. **∼ drink** n
Brause[limonade] f

flabbergasted a **be ∼** platt sein
🄙

flabby a schlaff

flag n Fahne f; (*Naut*) Flagge f

flag-pole n Fahnenstange f

flagrant a flagrant

flagstone n [Pflaster]platte f

flair n Begabung f

flake n Flocke f ● vi **∼ [off]**
abblättern

flamboyant a extravagant

flame n Flamme f

flan n [**fruit**] **∼** Obsttorte f

flank n Flanke f

flannel n Flanell m; (*for washing*)
Waschlappen m

flap n Klappe f; **in a ∼** 🄙 aufgeregt
● v (*pt/pp* **flapped**) vi flattern; 🄙
sich aufregen ● vt **∼ its wings** mit
den Flügeln schlagen

flare n Leuchtsignal nt. ● vi **∼ up**
auflodern; (🄙 *get angry*) aufbrausen

flash n Blitz m; **in a ∼** 🄙 im Nu ● vi
blitzen; (*repeatedly*) blinken; **∼ past**
vorbeirasen

flash: **∼back** n Rückblende f. **∼er**
n (*Auto*) Blinker m. **∼light** n (*Phot*)
Blitzlicht nt; (*Amer: torch*)
Taschenlampe f. **∼y** a auffällig

flask n Flasche f

flat a (**flatter, flattest**) flach; <*surface*>
eben; <*refusal*> glatt; <*beer*> schal;
<*battery*> verbraucht/ (*Auto*) leer;
<*tyre*> platt; (*Mus*) A **∼** As nt; B **∼** B
nt ● n Wohnung f; (🄙 *puncture*)
Reifenpanne f

flat: **∼ly** adv <*refuse*> glatt. **∼ rate**
n Einheitspreis m

flatten vt platt drücken

flatter vt schmeicheln (+ *dat*). **∼y** n
Schmeichelei f

flat tyre n Reifenpanne f

flaunt vt prunken mit

flautist n Flötist(in) m(f)

flavour n Geschmack m ● vt
abschmecken. **∼ing** n Aroma nt

flaw n Fehler m. **∼less** a tadellos;
<*complexion*> makellos

flea n Floh m

fleck n Tupfen m

fled see **flee**

flee v (*pt/pp* **fled**) ● vi fliehen (**from**
vor + *dat*) ● vt flüchten aus

fleece n Vlies nt ● vt 🄙 schröpfen

fleet n Flotte f; (*of cars*) Wagenpark
m

fleeting a flüchtig

Flemish a flämisch

flesh n Fleisch nt

flew see fly²

flex¹ vt anspannen <muscle>

flex² n (Electr) Schnur f

flexib|ility n Biegsamkeit f; (fig)
Flexibilität f. **~le** a biegsam; (fig)
flexibel

flick vt schnippen

flicker vi flackern

flier n = flyer

flight¹ n (fleeing) Flucht f

flight² n (flying) Flug m; ~ of stairs
Treppe f

flight recorder n Flugschreiber m

flimsy a (-ier, -iest) dünn; <excuse>
fadenscheinig

flinch vi zurückzucken

fling vt (pt/pp flung) schleudern

flint n Feuerstein m

flip vt/i schnippen; ~ through
durchblättern

flippant a, **-ly** adv leichtfertig

flirt n kokette Frau f ● vi flirten

flirtat|ion n Flirt m. **~ious** a
kokett

flit vi (pt/pp flitted) flattern

float n Schwimmer m; (in procession)
Festwagen m; (money) Wechselgeld
nt ● vi <thing:> schwimmen;
<person:> sich treiben lassen; (in
air) schweben

flock n Herde f; (of birds) Schwarm
m ● vi strömen

flog vt (pt/pp flogged) auspeitschen;
(🔲 sell) verkloppen

flood n Überschwemmung f; (fig)
Flut f ● vt überschwemmen

floodlight n Flutlicht nt ● vt (pt/pp
floodlit) anstrahlen

floor n Fußboden m; (storey) Stock m

floor: ~ **board** n Dielenbrett nt. ~-
polish n Bohnerwachs nt. ~ **show**
n Kabarettvorstellung f

flop n 🔲 (failure) Reinfall m; (Theat)
Durchfall m ● vi (pt/pp flopped) 🔲
(fail) durchfallen

floppy a schlapp. ~ **disc** n Diskette
f

floral a Blumen-

florid a <complexion> gerötet; <style>
blumig

florist n Blumenhändler(in) m(f)

flounder vi zappeln

flour n Mehl nt

flourish n große Geste f; (scroll)
Schnörkel m ● vi gedeihen; (fig)
blühen ● vt schwenken

flout vt missachten

flow n Fluss m; (of traffic, blood)
Strom m ● vi fließen

flower n Blume f ● vi blühen

flower: ~**bed** n Blumenbeet nt.
~**pot** n Blumentopf m. ~**y** a blumig

flown see fly²

flu n 🔲 Grippe f

fluctuat|e vi schwanken. **~ion** n
Schwankung f

fluent a, **-ly** adv fließend

fluff n Fusseln pl; (down) Flaum m.
~**y** a (-ier, -iest) flauschig

fluid a flüssig, (fig) veränderlich ● n
Flüssigkeit f

fluke n [glücklicher] Zufall m

flung see fling

fluorescent a fluoreszierend

fluoride n Fluor nt

flush n (blush) Erröten nt ● vi rot
werden ● vt spülen ● a in einer
Ebene (with mit); (🔲 affluent) gut bei
Kasse

flustered a nervös

flute n Flöte f

flutter n Flattern nt ● vi flattern

fly¹ n (pl flies) Fliege f

fly² v (pt flew, pp flown) ● vi fliegen;
<flag:> wehen; (rush) sausen ● vt
fliegen; führen <flag>

fly³ n & **flies** pl (on trousers)
Hosenschlitz m

flyer n Flieger(in) m(f); (leaflet)
Flugblatt nt

foal n Fohlen nt

foam n Schaum m; (synthetic)
Schaumstoff m ● vi schäumen

fob vt (pt/pp fobbed) ~ sth off etw
andrehen (on s.o. jdm); ~ s.o. off
jdn abspeisen (with mit)

focal n Brenn-

focus n Brennpunkt m; in ~ scharf eingestellt ● v (pt/pp **focused** or **focussed**) ● vt einstellen (on auf + acc) ● vi (fig) sich konzentrieren (on auf + acc)

fog n Nebel m

foggy a (**foggier**, **foggiest**) neblig

fog-horn n Nebelhorn nt

foible n Eigenart f

foil¹ n Folie f; (Culin) Alufolie f

foil² vt (thwart) vereiteln

foil³ n (Fencing) Florett nt

fold n Falte f; (in paper) Kniff m ● vt falten; ~ one's arms die Arme verschränken ● vi sich falten lassen; (fail) eingehen. ~ up vt zusammenfalten; zusammenklappen <chair> ● vi sich zusammenfalten/ -klappen lassen; Ⓣ <business:> eingehen

fold|er n Mappe f. ~ing a Klapp-

foliage n Blätter pl; (of tree) Laub nt

folk npl Leute pl

folk: ~**dance** n Volkstanz m. ~**song** n Volkslied nt

follow vt/i folgen (+ dat); (pursue) verfolgen; (in vehicle) nachfahren (+ dat). ~ up vt nachgehen (+ dat)

follow|er n Anhänger(in) m(f). ~**ing** a folgend ● n Folgende(s) nt; (supporters) Anhängerschaft f ● prep im Anschluss an (+ acc)

folly n Torheit f

fond a (-er, -est), **-ly** adv liebevoll; be ~ of gern haben; gern essen <food>

fondle vt liebkosen

fondness n Liebe f (for zu)

food n Essen nt; (for animals) Futter nt; (groceries) Lebensmittel pl. ~ **poisoning** n Lebensmittelvergiftung f

food poisoning n Lebensmittelvergiftung f

fool¹ n (Culin) Fruchtcreme f

fool² n Narr m; make a ~ of oneself sich lächerlich machen ● vt hereinlegen ● vi ~ around herumalbern

fool|hardy a tollkühn. ~**ish** a, **-ly** adv dumm. ~**ishness** n Dummheit f. ~**proof** a narrensicher

foot n (pl feet) Fuß m; (measure) Fuß m (30,48 cm); (of bed) Fußende nt; on ~ zu Fuß; on one's feet auf den Beinen; put one's ~ in it Ⓣ ins Fettnäpfchen treten; 7 ~ or feet 7 fuß

foot: ~**ball** n Fußball m. ~**baller** n Fußballspieler m. ~**ball pools** npl Fußballtoto nt. ~**bridge** n Fußgängerbrücke f. ~**hills** npl Vorgebirge nt. ~**hold** n Halt m. ~**ing** n Halt m. ~**lights** npl Rampenlicht nt. ~**note** n Fußnote f. ~**path** n Fußweg m. ~**print** n Fußabdruck m. ~**step** n Schritt m; **follow in s.o.'s** ~**steps** (fig) in jds Fußstapfen treten. ~**wear** n Schuhwerk nt

for

● preposition

····▶ (on behalf of; in place of; in favour of) für (+ acc). **I did it for you** ich habe es für dich gemacht. **I work for him/for a bank** ich arbeite für ihn/ für eine Bank. **be for doing sth** dafür sein, etw zu tun. **cheque/bill for £5** Scheck/Rechnung über 5 Pfund. **for nothing** umsonst. **what have you got for a cold?** was haben Sie gegen Erkältungen?

····▶ (expressing reason) wegen (+ gen); (with emotion) aus. **famous for these wines** berühmt wegen dieser Weine od für diese Weine. **he was sentenced to death for murder** er wurde wegen Mordes zum Tode verurteilt. **were it not for you/your help** ohne dich/deine Hilfe. **for fear/ love of** aus Angst vor (+ dat)/aus Liebe zu (+ dat)

····▶ (expressing purpose) (with action, meal) zu (+ dat); (with object) für (+ acc). **it's for washing the car** es ist zum Autowaschen. **we met for a discussion** wir trafen uns zu einer Besprechung. **for pleasure** zum Vergnügen. **meat for lunch** Fleisch zum Mittagessen. **what is that for?** wofür od wozu ist das? **a dish for nuts** eine Schale für Nüsse

····▶ (expressing direction) nach (+ dat); (less precise) in Richtung. **the train for Oxford** der Zug nach Oxford. **they**

were heading *or* making for London
sie fuhren in Richtung London
····▸ (*expressing time*) (*completed
process*) ... lang; (*continuing process*)
seit (+ *dat*). I lived here for two years
ich habe zwei Jahre [lang] hier
gewohnt. I have been living here for
two years ich wohne hier seit zwei
Jahren. we are staying for a week
wir werden eine Woche bleiben
····▸ (*expressing difficulty,
impossibility, embarrassment etc.*) +
dat. it's impossible/inconvenient for
her es ist ihr unmöglich/ungelegen.
it was embarrassing for our teacher
unserem Lehrer war es peinlich
● *conjunction*
····▸ denn. he's not coming for he has
no money er kommt nicht mit, denn
er hat kein Geld

forbade *see* **forbid**
forbid *vt* (*pt* **forbade**, *pp* **forbidden**)
verbieten (**s.o.** jdm). ~**ding** *a*
bedrohlich; (*stern*) streng
force *n* Kraft *f*; (*of blow*) Wucht *f*;
(*violence*) Gewalt *f*; in ~ gültig; (*in
large numbers*) in großer Zahl; come
into ~ in Kraft treten; the ~s *pl*
die Streitkräfte *pl* ● *vt* zwingen;
(*break open*) aufbrechen
forced *a* gezwungen; ~ landing
Notlandung *f*
force: ~**feed** *vt* (*pt/pp* -**fed**)
zwangsernähren. ~**ful** *a*, -**ly** *adv*
energisch
forceps *n inv* Zange *f*
forcible *a* gewaltsam
ford *n* Furt *f* ● *vt* durchwaten; (*in
vehicle*) durchfahren
fore *a* vordere(r,s)
fore: ~**arm** *n* Unterarm *m*. ~**cast**
n Voraussage *f*; (*for weather*)
Vorhersage *f* ● *vt* (*pt/pp* ~**cast**)
voraussagen, vorhersagen. ~**finger**
n Zeigefinger *m*. ~**gone** *a* be a
~**gone conclusion** von vornherein
feststehen. ~**ground** *n*
Vordergrund *m*. ~**head** *n* Stirn *f*.
~**hand** *n* Vorhand *f*
foreign *a* ausländisch; <*country*>
fremd; he is ~ er ist Ausländer. ~
currency *n* Devisen *pl*. ~**er** *n*

Ausländer(in) *m(f)*. ~ **language** *n*
Fremdsprache *f*
Foreign: ~ **Office** *n* ≈
Außenministerium *nt*. ~
Secretary *n* ≈ Außenminister *m*
fore: ~**leg** *n* Vorderbein *nt*. ~**man**
n Vorarbeiter *m*. ~**most** *a* führend
● *adv* first and ~**most** zuallererst.
~**name** *n* Vorname *m*. ~**runner** *n*
Vorläufer *m*
foresee *vt* (*pt* -**saw**, *pp* -**seen**)
voraussehen, vorhersehen. ~**able** *a*
in the ~**able future** in absehbarer
Zeit
foresight *n* Weitblick *m*
forest *n* Wald *m*. ~**er** *n* Förster *m*
forestry *n* Forstwirtschaft *f*
foretaste *n* Vorgeschmack *m*
forever *adv* für immer
forewarn *vt* vorher warnen
foreword *n* Vorwort *nt*
forfeit *n* (*in game*) Pfand *nt* ● *vt*
verwirken
forgave *see* **forgive**
forge *n* Schmiede *f* ● *vt* schmieden;
(*counterfeit*) fälschen. ~**r** *n* Fälscher
m. ~**ry** *n* Fälschung *f*
forget *vt/i* (*pt* -**got**, *pp* -**gotten**)
vergessen; verlernen <*language,
skill*>. ~**ful** *a* vergesslich.
~**fulness** *n* Vergesslichkeit *f*. ~-
me-not *n* Vergissmeinnicht *nt*
forgive *vt* (*pt* -**gave**, *pp* -**given**) ~
s.o. for sth jdm etw vergeben *od*
verzeihen
forgot(ten) *see* **forget**
fork *n* Gabel *f*; (*in road*) Gabelung *f*
● *vi* <*road:*> sich gabeln; ~ **right**
rechts abzweigen
fork-lift truck *n* Gabelstapler *m*
forlorn *a* verlassen; <*hope*> schwach
form *n* Form *f*; (*document*) Formular
nt; (*bench*) Bank *f*; (*Sch*) Klasse *f* ● *vt*
formen (**into** zu); (*create*) bilden ● *vi*
sich bilden; <*idea:*> Gestalt
annehmen
formal *a*, -**ly** *adv* formell, förmlich.
~**ity** *n* Förmlichkeit *f*; (*requirement*)
Formalität *f*
format *n* Format *nt* ● *vt*
formatieren

formation n Formation f

former a ehemalig; the ∼ der/die/das Erstere. ∼ly adv früher

formidable a gewaltig

formula n (pl -ae or -s) Formel f

formulate vt formulieren

forsake vt (pt -sook, pp -saken) verlassen

fort n (Mil) Fort nt

forth adv back and ∼ hin und her; and so ∼ und so weiter

forth: ∼coming a bevorstehend; (🖪 communicative) mitteilsam. ∼right a direkt

fortieth a vierzigste(r,s)

fortification n Befestigung f

fortify vt (pt/pp -ied) befestigen; (fig) stärken

fortnight n vierzehn Tage pl. ∼ly a vierzehntäglich ● adv alle vierzehn Tage

fortress n Festung f

fortunate a glücklich; be ∼ Glück haben. ∼ly adv glücklicherweise

fortune n Glück nt; (money) Vermögen nt. ∼-teller n Wahrsagerin f

forty a vierzig

forward adv vorwärts; (to the front) nach vorn ● a Vorwärts-; (presumptuous) anmaßend ● n (Sport) Stürmer m ● vt nachsenden <letter>. ∼s adv vorwärts

fossil n Fossil nt

foster vt fördern; in Pflege nehmen <child>. ∼-child n Pflegekind nt. ∼-mother n Pflegemutter f

fought see fight

foul a (-er, -est) widerlich; <language> unflätig; ∼ play (Jur) Mord m ● n (Sport) Foul nt ● vt verschmutzen; (obstruct) blockieren; (Sport) foulen

found[1] see find

found[2] vt gründen

foundation n (basis) Grundlage f; (charitable) Stiftung f; ∼s pl Fundament nt

founder n Gründer(in) m(f)

foundry n Gießerei f

fountain n Brunnen m

four a vier ● n Vier f

four: ∼teen a vierzehn ● n Vierzehn f. ∼teenth a vierzehnte(r,s)

fourth a vierte(r,s)

fowl n Geflügel nt

fox n Fuchs m ● vt (puzzle) verblüffen

foyer n Foyer nt; (in hotel) Empfangshalle f

fraction n Bruchteil m; (Math) Bruch m

fracture n Bruch m ● vt/i brechen

fragile a zerbrechlich

fragment n Bruchstück nt, Fragment nt

fragran|ce n Duft m. ∼t a duftend

frail a (-er, -est) gebrechlich

frame n Rahmen m; (of spectacles) Gestell nt; (Anat) Körperbau m ● vt einrahmen; (fig) formulieren; 🖪 ein Verbrechen anhängen (+ dat). ∼work n Gerüst nt; (fig) Gerippe nt

franc n (French, Belgian) Franc m; (Swiss) Franken m

France n Frankreich nt

franchise n (Pol) Wahlrecht nt; (Comm) Franchise nt

frank a, **-ly** adv offen

frankfurter n Frankfurter f

frantic a, **-ally** adv verzweifelt; außer sich (dat) (with vor)

fraternal a brüderlich

fraud n Betrug m; (person) Betrüger(in) m(f)

fray vi ausfransen

freak n Missbildung f; (person) Missgeburt f ● a anormal

freckle n Sommersprosse f

free a (freer, freest) frei; <ticket, copy, time> Frei-; (lavish) freigebig; ∼ [of charge] kostenlos; set ∼ freilassen; (rescue) befreien ● vt (pt/pp freed) freilassen; (rescue) befreien; (disentangle) freibekommen

free: ∼dom n Freiheit f. ∼hold n [freier] Grundbesitz m. ∼lance a & adv freiberuflich. ∼ly adv frei; (voluntarily) freiwillig; (generously) großzügig. **F~mason** n Freimaurer m. **~range** a **~range eggs** Landeier pl. **~ sample** n Gratisprobe f. **~style** n Freistil m. **~way** n (Amer) Autobahn f

freeze vt (pt **froze**, pp **frozen**) einfrieren; stoppen <wages> ● vi it's **~ing** es friert. **~er** n Gefriertruhe f; (upright) Gefrierschrank m. **~ing** a eiskalt ● n **below ~ing** unter Null

freight n Fracht f. **~er** n Frachter m. **~ train** n Güterzug m

French a französisch ● n (Lang) Französisch nt; **the ~** pl die Franzosen

French: **~ beans** npl grüne Bohnen pl. **~ bread** n Stangenbrot nt. **~ fries** npl Pommes frites pl. **~man** n Franzose m. **~ window** n Terrassentür f. **~woman** n Französin f

frenzy n Raserei f

frequency n Häufigkeit f; (Phys) Frequenz f

frequent[1] a, **-ly** adv häufig

frequent[2] vt regelmäßig besuchen

fresh a (-er, -est), **-ly** adv frisch; (new) neu; (cheeky) frech

freshness n Frische f

freshwater a Süßwasser-

fret vi (pt/pp **fretted**) sich grämen. **~ful** a weinerlich

fretsaw n Laubsäge f

friction n Reibung f; (fig) Reibereien pl

Friday n Freitag m

fridge n Kühlschrank m

fried see **fry**[2] ● a gebraten; **~ egg** Spiegelei nt

friend n Freund(in) m(f). **~liness** n Freundlichkeit f. **~ly** a (-ier, -iest) freundlich; **~ly with** befreundet mit. **~ship** n Freundschaft f

fright n Schreck m

frighten vt Angst machen (+ dat); (startle) erschrecken; **be ~ed** Angst haben (of vor + dat). **~ing** a Angst erregend

frightful a, **-ly** adv schrecklich

frigid a frostig; (Psych) frigide. **~ity** n Frostigkeit f; Frigidität f

frill n Rüsche f; (paper) Manschette f. **~y** a rüschenbesetzt

fringe n Fransen pl; (of hair) Pony m; (fig: edge) Rand m

frisk vi herumspringen ● vt (search) durchsuchen

frisky a (-ier, -iest) lebhaft

fritter vt **~ [away]** verplempern ▣

frivol|ity n Frivolität f. **~ous** a, **-ly** adv frivol, leichtfertig

fro see **to**

frock n Kleid nt

frog n Frosch m. **~man** n Froschmann m

frolic vi (pt/pp **frolicked**) herumtollen

from prep von (+ dat); (out of) aus (+ dat); (according to) nach (+ dat); **~ Monday** ab Montag; **~ that day** seit dem Tag

front n Vorderseite f; (fig) Fassade f; (of garment) Vorderteil nt; (sea~) Strandpromenade f; (Mil, Pol, Meteorol) Front f; **in ~ of** vor; **in** or **at the ~** vorne; **to the ~** nach vorne ● a vordere(r,s); <page, row> erste(r,s); <tooth, wheel> Vorder-

front: **~ door** n Haustür f. **~ garden** n Vorgarten m

frontier n Grenze f

frost n Frost m; (hoar-~) Raureif m; **ten degrees of ~** zehn Grad Kälte. **~bite** n Erfrierung f. **~bitten** a erfroren

frost|ed a **~ed glass** Mattglas nt. **~ing** n (Amer Culin) Zuckerguss m. **~y** a, **-ily** adv frostig

froth n Schaum m ● vi schäumen. **~y** a schaumig

frown n Stirnrunzeln nt ● vi die Stirn runzeln

froze see **freeze**

frozen see **freeze** ● a gefroren; (Culin) tiefgekühlt; **I'm ~** ▣ mir ist eiskalt. **~ food** n Tiefkühlkost f

frugal a, **-ly** adv sparsam; <meal> frugal

fruit n Frucht f; (collectively) Obst nt. **~ cake** n englischer [Tee]kuchen m

fruitful a fruchtbar

fruit: ~ **juice** n Obstsaft m. ~**less**
a, **-ly** adv fruchtlos. ~ **salad** n
Obstsalat m

fruity a fruchtig

frustrat|e vt vereiteln; (Psych)
frustrieren. ~**ion** n Frustration
f

fry vt/i (pt/pp **fried**) [in der Pfanne]
braten. ~**ing-pan** n Bratpfanne
f

fuel n Brennstoff m; (for car)
Kraftstoff m; (for aircraft) Treibstoff
m

fugitive n Flüchtling m

fulfil vt (pt/pp **-filled**) erfüllen.
~**ment** n Erfüllung f

full a & adv (-er, -est) voll; (detailed)
ausführlich; <skirt> weit; ~ **of** voll
von (+ dat), voller (+ gen); **at** ~
speed in voller Fahrt ● n **in** ~
vollständig

full: ~ **moon** n Vollmond m. ~**-
scale** a <model> in Originalgröße;
<rescue, alert> großangelegt. ~
stop n Punkt m. ~**-time** a
ganztägig ● adv ganztags

fully adv völlig; (in detail)
ausführlich

fumble vi herumfummeln (with an +
dat)

fume vi vor Wut schäumen

fumes npl Dämpfe pl; (from car)
Abgase pl

fun n Spaß m; **for** ~ aus od zum Spaß;
make ~ **of** sich lustig machen über
(+ acc); **have** ~! viel Spaß!

function n Funktion f; (event)
Veranstaltung f ● vi funktionieren;
(serve) dienen (as als). ~**al** a
zweckmäßig

fund n Fonds m; (fig) Vorrat m; ~**s**
pl Geldmittel pl ● vt finanzieren

fundamental a grundlegend;
(essential) wesentlich

funeral n Beerdigung f; (cremation)
Feuerbestattung f

funeral: ~ **march** n Trauermarsch
m. ~ **service** n Trauergottesdienst
m

funfair n Jahrmarkt m

fungus n (pl **-gi**) Pilz m

funnel n Trichter m; (on ship, train)
Schornstein m

funnily adv komisch; ~ **enough**
komischerweise

funny a (-ier, -iest) komisch

fur n Fell nt; (for clothing) Pelz m; (in
kettle) Kesselstein m. ~ **coat** n
Pelzmantel m

furious a, **-ly** adv wütend (**with auf** +
acc)

furnace n (Techn) Ofen m

furnish vt einrichten; (supply)
liefern. ~**ed** a ~ed room möbliertes
Zimmer nt. ~**ings** npl
Einrichtungsgegenstände pl

furniture n Möbel pl

further a weitere(r,s); **at the** ~ **end**
am anderen Ende; **until** ~ **notice**
bis auf weiteres ● adv weiter;
~ **off** weiter entfernt ● vt
fördern

furthest a am weitesten entfernt
● adv am weitesten

fury n Wut f

fuse¹ n (of bomb) Zünder m; (cord)
Zündschnur f

fuse² n (Electr) Sicherung f ● vt/i
verschmelzen; **the lights have**
~**d** die Sicherung [für das Licht]
ist durchgebrannt. ~**-box**
n Sicherungskasten
m

fuselage n (Aviat) Rumpf m

fuss n Getue nt; **make a** ~ **of**
verwöhnen; (caress) liebkosen ● vi
Umstände machen

fussy a (-ier, -iest) wählerisch;
(particular) penibel

futil|e a zwecklos. ~**ity** n
Zwecklosigkeit f

future a zukünftig ● n Zukunft f;
(Gram) [erstes] Futur nt

futuristic a futuristisch

fuzzy a (-ier, -iest) <hair> kraus;
(blurred) verschwommen

Gg

gabble *vi* schnell reden

gable *n* Giebel *m*

gadget *n* [kleines] Gerät *nt*

Gaelic *n* Gälisch *nt*

gag *n* Knebel *m*; (*joke*) Witz *m*; (*Theat*) Gag *m* ● *vt* (*pt/pp* **gagged**) knebeln

gaiety *n* Fröhlichkeit *f*

gaily *adv* fröhlich

gain *n* Gewinn *m*; (*increase*) Zunahme *f* ● *vt* gewinnen; (*obtain*) erlangen; ~ **weight** zunehmen ● *vi* <*clock:*> vorgehen

gait *n* Gang *m*

gala *n* Fest *nt* ● *attrib* Gala-

galaxy *n* Galaxie *f*; **the G**~ die Milchstraße

gale *n* Sturm *m*

gallant *a*, **-ly** *adv* tapfer; (*chivalrous*) galant. ~**ry** *n* Tapferkeit *f*

gall-bladder *n* Gallenblase *f*

gallery *n* Galerie *f*

galley *n* (*ship's kitchen*) Kombüse *f*; ~ **[proof]** [Druck]fahne *f*

gallon *n* Gallone *f* (= 4,5 *l*; *Amer* = 3,785 *l*)

gallop *n* Galopp *m* ● *vi* galoppieren

gallows *n* Galgen *m*

galore *adv* in Hülle und Fülle

gamble *n* (*risk*) Risiko *nt* ● *vi* [um Geld] spielen; ~ **on** (*rely*) sich verlassen auf (+ *acc*). ~**r** *n* Spieler(in) *m(f)*

game *n* Spiel *nt*; (*animals, birds*) Wild *nt*; ~**s** (*Sch*) Sport *m* ● *a* (*brave*) tapfer; (*willing*) bereit (**for** zu). ~**keeper** *n* Wildhüter *m*

gammon *n* [geräucherter] Schinken *m*

gang *n* Bande *f*; (*of workmen*) Kolonne *f*

gangling *a* schlaksig

gangrene *n* Wundbrand *m*

gangster *n* Gangster *m*

gangway *n* Gang *m*; (*Naut, Aviat*) Gangway *f*

gaol *n* Gefängnis *nt* ● *vt* ins Gefängnis sperren. ~**er** *n* Gefängniswärter *m*

gap *n* Lücke *f*; (*interval*) Pause *f*; (*difference*) Unterschied *m*

gap|e *vi* gaffen; ~**e at** anstarren. ~**ing** *a* klaffend

garage *n* Garage *f*; (*for repairs*) Werkstatt *f*; (*for petrol*) Tankstelle *f*

garbage *n* Müll *m*. ~ **can** *n* (*Amer*) Mülleimer *m*

garbled *a* verworren

garden *n* Garten *m*; **[public]** ~**s** *pl* [öffentliche] Anlagen *pl* ● *vi* im Garten arbeiten. ~**er** *n* Gärtner(in) *m(f)*. ~**ing** *n* Gartenarbeit *f*

gargle *n* (*liquid*) Gurgelwasser *nt* ● *vi* gurgeln

garish *a* grell

garland *n* Girlande *f*

garlic *n* Knoblauch *m*

garment *n* Kleidungsstück *nt*

garnet *n* Granat *m*

garnish *n* Garnierung *f* ● *vt* garnieren

garrison *n* Garnison *f*

garrulous *a* geschwätzig

garter *n* Strumpfband *nt*; (*Amer: suspender*) Strumpfhalter *m*

gas *n* Gas *nt*; (*Amer* Ⓘ: *petrol*) Benzin *nt* ● *v* (*pt/pp* **gassed**) ● *vt* vergasen ● *vi* Ⓘ schwatzen. ~ **cooker** *n* Gasherd *m*. ~ **fire** *n* Gasofen *m*

gash *n* Schnitt *m*; (*wound*) klaffende Wunde *f*

gasket *n* (*Techn*) Dichtung *f*

gas: ~ mask *n* Gasmaske *f*. ~-**meter** *n* Gaszähler *m*

gasoline *n* (*Amer*) Benzin *nt*

gasp *vi* keuchen; (*in surprise*) hörbar die Luft einziehen

gas station *n* (*Amer*) Tankstelle *f*

gastric *a* Magen-

gastronomy *n* Gastronomie *f*

gate n Tor nt; (to field) Gatter nt; (barrier) Schranke f; (at airport) Flugsteig m

gate: ~**crasher** n ungeladener Gast m. ~**way** n Tor nt

gather vt sammeln; (pick) pflücken; (conclude) folgern (**from** aus) ● vi sich versammeln; <storm.> sich zusammenziehen. ~**ing** n family ~**ing** Familientreffen nt

gaudy a (-ier, -iest) knallig

gauge n Stärke f; (Rail) Spurweite f; (device) Messinstrument nt

gaunt a hager

gauze n Gaze f

gave see give

gawky a (-ier, -iest) schlaksig

gay a (-er, -est) fröhlich; ⚅ homosexuell, ⚅ schwul

gaze n [langer] Blick m ● vi sehen; ~ **at** ansehen

GB abbr of Great Britain

gear n Ausrüstung f; (Techn) Getriebe nt; (Auto) Gang m; **change** ~ schalten

gear: ~**box** n (Auto) Getriebe nt. ~**lever** n, (Amer) ~**shift** n Schalthebel m

geese see goose

gel n Gel nt

gelatine n Gelatine f

gem n Juwel nt

gender n (Gram) Geschlecht nt

gene n Gen nt

genealogy n Genealogie f

general a allgemein ● n General m; **in** ~ im Allgemeinen. ~ **election** n allgemeine Wahlen pl

generaliz|ation n Verallgemeinerung f. ~**e** vi verallgemeinern

generally adv im Allgemeinen

general practitioner n praktischer Arzt m

generate vt erzeugen

generation n Generation f

generator n Generator m

generosity n Großzügigkeit f

generous a, -ly adv großzügig

Geneva n Genf nt

genial a, -ly adv freundlich

genitals pl [äußere] Geschlechtsteile pl

genitive a & n ~ [**case**] Genitiv m

genius n (pl -uses) Genie nt; (quality) Genialität f

genre n Gattung f, Genre nt

gent n ⚅ Herr m; **the** ~**s** sg die Herrentoilette f

genteel a vornehm

gentle a (-r, -st) sanft

gentleman n Herr m; (well-mannered) Gentleman m

gent|leness n Sanftheit f. ~**ly** adv sanft

genuine a echt; (sincere) aufrichtig. ~**ly** adv (honestly) ehrlich

geograph|ical a, -ly adv geographisch. ~**y** n Geographie f, Erdkunde f

geological a, -ly adv geologisch

geolog|ist n Geologe m/-gin f. ~**y** n Geologie f

geometr|ic(al) a geometrisch. ~**y** n Geometrie f

geranium n Geranie f

geriatric a geriatrisch ● n geriatrischer Patient m

germ n Keim m; ~**s** pl ⚅ Bazillen pl

German a deutsch ● n (person) Deutsche(r) m/f; (Lang) Deutsch nt; **in** ~ auf Deutsch; **into** ~ ins Deutsche

Germanic a germanisch

Germany n Deutschland nt

germinate vi keimen

gesticulate vi gestikulieren

gesture n Geste f

get v

pt **got**, pp **got** (Amer also **gotten**), pres p **getting**

● transitive verb

····▶ (obtain, receive) bekommen, ⚅ kriegen; (procure) besorgen; (buy) kaufen; (fetch) holen. **get a job/taxi for s.o.** jdm einen Job verschaffen/ ein Taxi besorgen. **I must get some bread** ich muss Brot holen. **get permission** die Erlaubnis erhalten. I couldn't get her on the phone ich konnte sie nicht telefonisch erreichen

····▶ (*prepare*) machen <*meal*>. **he got the breakfast** er machte das Frühstück

····▶ (*cause*) **get s.o. to do sth** jdn dazu bringen, etw zu tun. **get one's hair cut** sich (*dat*) die Haare schneiden lassen. **get one's hands dirty** sich (*dat*) die Hände schmutzig machen

····▶ **get the bus/train** (*travel by*) den Bus/Zug nehmen; (*be in time for, catch*) den Bus/Zug erreichen

····▶ **have got** (🏴 *have*) haben. **I've got a cold** ich habe eine Erkältung

····▶ **have got to do sth** etw tun müssen. **I've got to hurry** ich muss mich beeilen

····▶ (🏴 *understand*) kapieren 🏴. **I don't get it** ich kapiere nicht

● *intransitive verb*

····▶ (*become*) werden. **get older** älter werden. **the weather got worse** das Wetter wurde schlechter. **get to** kommen zu/nach <*town*>; (*reach*) erreichen. **get dressed** sich anziehen. **get married** heiraten.

● *phrasal verbs* ● **get about** *vi* (*move*) sich bewegen; (*travel*) herumkommen; (*spread*) sich verbreiten. ● **get at** *vt* (*have access*) herankommen an (+ *acc*); (🏴 *criticize*) anmachen 🏴. (*mean*) **what are you getting at?** worauf willst du hinaus? ● **get away** *vi* (*leave*) wegkommen; (*escape*) entkommen. ● **get back** *vi* zurückkommen; *vt* (*recover*) zurückbekommen; **get one's own back** sich revanchieren. ● **get by** *vi* vorbeikommen; (*manage*) sein Auskommen haben. ● **get down** *vi* heruntersteigen; **get down to** sich [heran]machen an (+ *acc*); *vt* (*depress*) deprimieren. ● **get in** *vi* (*into bus*) einsteigen; *vt* (*fetch*) hereinholen. ● **get off** *vi* (*dismount*) absteigen; (*from bus*) aussteigen; (*leave*) wegkommen; (*Jur*) freigesprochen werden; *vt* (*remove*) abbekommen. ● **get on** *vi* (*mount*) aufsteigen; (*to bus*) einsteigen; (*be on good terms*) gut auskommen (**with** mit + *dat*); (*make progress*)

Fortschritte machen; **how are you getting on?** wie geht's? ● **get out** *vi* herauskommen; (*of car*) aussteigen; **get out of** (*avoid doing*) sich drücken um; *vt* (*take out*) herausholen; herausbekommen <*cork, stain*>. ● **get over** *vi* hinübersteigen; *vt* (*fig*) hinwegkommen über (+ *acc*). ● **get round** *vi* herumkommen; **I never get round to it** ich komme nie dazu; *vt* herumkriegen; (*avoid*) umgehen. ● **get through** *vi* durchkommen. ● **get up** *vi* aufstehen

get: ~**away** *n* Flucht *f*. ~**up** *n* Aufmachung *f*

ghastly *a* (-ier, -iest) grässlich; (*pale*) blass

gherkin *n* Essiggurke *f*

ghost *n* Geist *m*, Gespenst *nt*. ~**ly** *a* geisterhaft

ghoulish *a* makaber

giant *n* Riese *m* ● *a* riesig

gibberish *n* Kauderwelsch *nt*

giblets *npl* Geflügelklein *nt*

giddiness *n* Schwindel *m*

giddy *a* (-ier, -iest) schwindlig

gift *n* Geschenk *nt*; (*to charity*) Gabe *f*; (*talent*) Begabung *f*. ~**ed** *a* begabt

gigantic *a* riesig, riesengroß

giggle *n* Kichern *nt* ● *vi* kichern

gild *vt* vergolden

gilt *a* vergoldet ● *n* Vergoldung *f*. ~**edged** *a* (*Comm*) mündelsicher

gimmick *n* Trick *m*

gin *n* Gin *m*

ginger *a* rotblond; <*cat*> rot ● *n* Ingwer *m*. ~**bread** *n* Pfefferkuchen *m*

gingerly *adv* vorsichtig

gipsy *n* = gypsy

giraffe *n* Giraffe *f*

girder *n* (*Techn*) Träger *m*

girl *n* Mädchen *nt*; (*young woman*) junge Frau *f*. ~**friend** *n* Freundin *f*. ~**ish** *a*, **-ly** *adv* mädchenhaft

gist *n* **the** ~ das Wesentliche

give *n* Elastizität *f* ● *v* (*pt* gave, *pp* given) ● *vt* geben/(*as present*) schenken (**to** *dat*); (*donate*) spenden;

<lecture> halten; <one's name>
angeben ● *vi* geben; (*yield*)
nachgeben. **~ away** *vt*
verschenken; (*betray*) verraten;
(*distribute*) verteilen. **~ back** *vt*
zurückgeben. **~ in** *vt* einreichen
● *vi* (*yield*) nachgeben. **~ off** *vt*
abgeben. **~ up** *vt/i* aufgeben; **~
oneself up** sich stellen. **~ way** *vi*
nachgeben; (*Auto*) die Vorfahrt
beachten

glacier *n* Gletscher *m*

glad *a* froh (of über + *acc*)

gladly *adv* gern[e]

glamorous *a* glanzvoll; <*film star*>
glamourös

glamour *n* [betörender] Glanz *m*

glance *n* [flüchtiger] Blick *m* ● *vi* **~
at** einen Blick werfen auf (+ *acc*). **~
up** *vi* aufblicken

gland *n* Drüse *f*

glare *n* grelles Licht *nt*; (*look*)
ärgerlicher Blick *m* ● *vi* **~ at** böse
ansehen

glaring *a* grell; <*mistake*> krass

glass *n* Glas *nt*; (*mirror*) Spiegel *m*;
~es *pl* (*spectacles*) Brille *f*. **~y** *a*
glasig

glaze *n* Glasur *f*

gleam *n* Schein *m* ● *vi* glänzen

glib *a*, **-ly** *adv* (*pej*) gewandt

glid|e *vi* gleiten; (*through the air*)
schweben. **~er** *n* Segelflugzeug *nt*.
~ing *n* Segelfliegen *nt*

glimmer *n* Glimmen *nt* ● *vi*
glimmen

glimpse *vt* flüchtig sehen

glint *n* Blitzen *nt* ● *vi* blitzen

glisten *vi* glitzern

glitter *vi* glitzern

global *a*, **-ly** *adv* global

globaliz|e *vt* globalisieren. **~ation**
n Globalisierung *f*

globe *n* Kugel *f*; (*map*) Globus *m*

gloom *n* Düsterkeit *f*; (*fig*)
Pessimismus *m*

gloomy *a* (-ier, -iest), **-ily** *adv*
düster; (*fig*) pessimistisch

glorify *vt* (*pt/pp* -ied) verherrlichen

glorious *a* herrlich; <*deed, hero*>
glorreich

glory *n* Ruhm *m*; (*splendour*) Pracht *f*
● *vi* **~ in** genießen

gloss *n* Glanz *m* ● *a* Glanz- ● *vi* **~
over** beschönigen

glossary *n* Glossar *nt*

glossy *a* (-ier, -iest) glänzend

glove *n* Handschuh *m*

glow *n* Glut *f*; (*of candle*) Schein *m*
● *vi* glühen; <*candle:*> scheinen.
~ing *a* glühend; <*account*>
begeistert

glucose *n* Traubenzucker *m*,
Glukose *f*

glue *n* Klebstoff *m* ● *vt* (*pres p*
gluing) kleben (to an + *acc*)

glum *a* (glummer, glummest), **-ly** *adv*
niedergeschlagen

glut *n* Überfluss *m* (of an + *dat*)

glutton *n* Vielfraß *m*

GM *abbr* (genetically modified); **~
crops/food** gentechnisch veränderte
Feldfrüchte/Nahrungsmittel

gnash *vt* **~ one's teeth** mit den
Zähnen knirschen

gnat *n* Mücke *f*

gnaw *vt/i* nagen (at an + *dat*)

go

3 sg pres tense **goes**; *pt* **went**;
pp **gone**

● *intransitive verb*

⋯▸ gehen; (*in vehicle*) fahren. **go by
air** fliegen. **where are you going?** wo
gehst du hin? **I'm going to France** ich
fahre nach Frankreich. **go to the
doctor's/dentist's** zum Arzt/Zahnarzt
gehen. **go to the theatre/cinema** ins
Theater/Kino gehen. **I must go to
Paris/to the doctor's** ich muss nach
Paris/zum Arzt. **go shopping**
einkaufen gehen. **go swimming**
schwimmen gehen. **go to see s.o.** jdn
besuchen [gehen]

⋯▸ (*leave*) weggehen; (*on journey*)
abfahren. **I must go now** ich muss
jetzt gehen. **we're going on Friday**
wir fahren am Freitag

⋯▸ (*work, function*) <*engine, clock*>
gehen

····▸ (*become*) werden. **go deaf** taub werden. **go mad** verrückt werden. **he went red** er wurde rot

····▸ (*pass*) <*time*> vergehen

····▸ (*disappear*) weggehen; <*coat, hat, stain*> verschwinden. **my headache/ my coat/the stain has gone** mein Kopfweh/mein Mantel/der Fleck ist weg

····▸ (*turn out, progress*) gehen; verlaufen. **everything's going very well** alles geht *od* verläuft sehr gut. **how did the party go?** wie war die Party? **go smoothly/according to plan** reibungslos/planmäßig verlaufen

····▸ (*match*) zusammenpassen. **the two colours don't go [together]** die beiden Farben passen nicht zusammen

····▸ (*cease to function*) kaputtgehen; <*fuse*> durchbrennen. **his memory is going** sein Gedächtnis lässt nach

●*auxiliary verb*

····▸ **be going to** werden + *inf.* **it's going to rain** es wird regnen. **I'm not going to** ich werde es nicht tun

●*noun*

pl **goes**

····▸ (*turn*) **it's your go** du bist jetzt an der Reihe *od* dran

····▸ (*attempt*) Versuch. **have a go at doing sth** versuchen, etw zu tun. **have another go!** versuch's noch mal!

····▸ (*energy, drive*) Energie

····▸ (*in phrases*) **on the go** auf Trab. **make a go of sth** das Beste aus etw machen

●*phrasal verbs*

●**go across** *vi* hinübergehen/-fahren; *vt* überqueren. ●**go after** *vt* (*pursue*) jagen. ●**go away** *vi* weggehen/-fahren; (*on holiday or business*) verreisen. ●**go back** *vi* zurückgehen/-fahren. ●**go back on** *vt* nicht [ein]halten <*promise*>. ●**go by** *vi* vorbeigehen/-fahren; <*time*> vergehen. ●**go down** *vi* hinuntergehen/-fahren; <*sun, ship*> untergehen; <*prices*> fallen; <*temperature, swelling*> zurückgehen. ●**go for** *vt* holen; (⚠

attack) losgehen auf (+ *acc*). ●**go in** *vi* hineingehen/-fahren; ●**go in for** *vt* teilnehmen an (+ *dat*) <*competition*>; (*take up*) sich verlegen auf (+ *acc*). ●**go off** *vi* weggehen/-fahren; <*alarm clock*> klingeln; <*alarm, gun, bomb*> losgehen; <*light*> ausgehen; (*go bad*) schlecht werden; (*leave*) gut verlaufen; *vt*: **go off sth** von etw abkommen. ●**go on** *vi* weitergehen/-fahren; <*light*> angehen; (*continue*) weitermachen; (*talking*) fortfahren; (*happen*) vorgehen. ●**go on at** *vt* ⚠ herumnörgeln an (+ *dat*). ●**go out** *vi* (*from home*) ausgehen; (*leave*) hinausgehen/-fahren; <*fire, light*> ausgehen; **go out to work/for a meal** arbeiten/essen gehen; **go out with s.o.** (⚠ *date s.o.*) mit jdm gehen ⚠. ●**go over** *vi* hinübergehen/-fahren; *vt* (*rehearse*) durchgehen. ●**go round** *vi* herumgehen/-fahren; (*visit*) vorbeigehen; (*turn*) sich drehen; (*be enough*) reichen. ●**go through** *vi* durchgehen/-fahren; *vt* (*suffer*) durchmachen; (*rehearse*) durchgehen; <*bags*> durchsuchen. ●**go through with** *vt* zu Ende machen. ●**go under** *vi* untergehen/-fahren; (*fail*) scheitern. ●**go up** *vi* hinaufgehen/-fahren; <*lift*> hochfahren; <*prices*> steigen. ●**go without** *vt*: **go without sth** auf etw (*acc*) verzichten; *vi* darauf verzichten

go-ahead *a* fortschrittlich; (*enterprising*) unternehmend ●*n* (*fig*) grünes Licht *nt*

goal *n* Ziel *nt*; (*sport*) Tor *nt*. ∼**keeper** *n* Torwart *m*. ∼**-post** *n* Torpfosten *m*

goat *n* Ziege *f*

gobble *vt* hinunterschlingen

God, god *n* Gott *m*

god: ∼**child** *n* Patenkind *nt*. ∼**daughter** *n* Patentochter *f*. ∼**dess** *n* Göttin *f*. ∼**father** *n* Pate *m*. ∼**mother** *n* Patin *f*. ∼**parents** *npl* Paten *pl*. ∼**send** *n* Segen *m*. ∼**son** *n* Patensohn *m*

goggles *npl* Schutzbrille *f*

going *a* <*price, rate*> gängig; <*concern*> gut gehend ● *n* **it is hard** ∼ es ist schwierig

gold *n* Gold *nt* ● *a* golden

golden *a* golden. ∼ **wedding** *n* goldene Hochzeit *f*

gold: ∼**fish** *n inv* Goldfisch *m*. ∼**mine** *n* Goldgrube *f*. ∼**plated** *a* vergoldet. ∼**smith** *n* Goldschmied *m*

golf *n* Golf *nt*

golf: ∼**club** *n* Golfklub *m*; (*implement*) Golfschläger *m*. ∼**course** *n* Golfplatz *m*. ∼**er** *m* Golfspieler(in) *m(f)*

gone *see* go

good *a* (better, best) gut; (*well-behaved*) brav, artig; ∼ **at** gut in (+ *dat*); **a** ∼ **deal** ziemlich viel; ∼ **morning/evening** guten Morgen/Abend ● *n* **for** ∼ für immer; **do** ∼ Gutes tun; **do s.o.** ∼ jdm gut tun; **it's no** ∼ es ist nutzlos; (*hopeless*) da ist nichts zu machen

goodbye *int* auf Wiedersehen; (*Teleph, Radio*) auf Wiederhören

good: **G**∼ **Friday** *n* Karfreitag *m*. ∼**looking** *a* gut aussehend. ∼**natured** *a* gutmütig

goodness *n* Güte *f*; **thank** ∼! Gott sei Dank!

goods *npl* Waren *pl*. ∼ **train** *n* Güterzug *m*

goodwill *n* Wohlwollen *nt*; (*Comm*) Goodwill *m*

gooey *a* Ⅰ klebrig

goose *n* (*pl* geese) Gans *f*

gooseberry *n* Stachelbeere *f*

goose: ∼**flesh** *n*, ∼**pimples** *npl* Gänsehaut *f*

gorge *n* (*Geog*) Schlucht *f* ● *vt* ∼ **oneself** sich vollessen

gorgeous *a* prachtvoll; Ⅰ herrlich

gorilla *n* Gorilla *m*

gormless *a* Ⅰ doof

gorse *n inv* Stechginster *m*

gory *a* (-ier, -iest) blutig; <*story*> blutrünstig

gosh *int* Ⅰ Mensch!

gospel *n* Evangelium *nt*

gossip *n* Klatsch *m*; (*person*) Klatschbase *f* ● *vi* klatschen

got *see* get; **have** ∼ haben; **have** ∼ **to** müssen; **have** ∼ **to do sth** etw tun müssen

Gothic *a* gotisch

gotten *see* get

goulash *n* Gulasch *nt*

gourmet *n* Feinschmecker *m*

govern *vt/i* regieren; (*determine*) bestimmen

government *n* Regierung *f*

governor *n* Gouverneur *m*; (*on board*) Vorstandsmitglied *nt*; (*of prison*) Direktor *m*; (Ⅰ *boss*) Chef *m*

gown *n* [elegantes] Kleid *nt*; (*Univ, Jur*) Talar *m*

GP *abbr of* general practitioner

grab *vt* (*pt/pp* grabbed) ergreifen; ∼ [hold of] packen

grace *n* Anmut *f*; (*before meal*) Tischgebet *nt*; **three days'** ∼ drei Tage Frist. ∼**ful** *a*, **-ly** *adv* anmutig

gracious *a* gnädig; (*elegant*) vornehm

grade *n* Stufe *f*; (*Comm*) Güteklasse *f*; (*Sch*) Note *f*; (*Amer, Sch: class*) Klasse *f*; (*Amer*) = **gradient** ● *vt* einstufen; (*Comm*) sortieren. ∼ **crossing** *n* (*Amer*) Bahnübergang *m*

gradient *n* Steigung *f*; (*downward*) Gefälle *nt*

gradual *a*, **-ly** *adv* allmählich

graduate *n* Akademiker(in) *m(f)*

graffiti *npl* Graffiti *pl*

graft *n* (*Bot*) Pfropfreis *nt*; (*Med*) Transplantat *nt*; (Ⅰ *hard work*) Plackerei *f*

grain *n* (*sand, salt, rice*) Korn *nt*; (*cereals*) Getreide *nt*; (*in wood*) Maserung *f*

gram *n* Gramm *nt*

grammar *n* Grammatik *f*. ∼ **school** *n* ≈ Gymnasium *nt*

grammatical *a*, **-ly** *adv* grammatisch

grand *a* (-er, -est) großartig

grandad *n* Ⅰ Opa *m*

grandchild n Enkelkind nt

granddaughter n Enkelin f

grandeur n Pracht f

grandfather n Großvater m. ~ **clock** n Standuhr f

grandiose a grandios

grand: ~**mother** n Großmutter f. ~**parents** npl Großeltern pl. ~ **piano** n Flügel m. ~**son** n Enkel m. ~**stand** n Tribüne f

granite n Granit m

granny n 🖽 Oma f

grant n Subvention f; (Univ) Studienbeihilfe f ● vt gewähren; (admit) zugeben; **take sth for** ~**ed** etw als selbstverständlich hinnehmen

grape n [Wein]traube f; **bunch of** ~**s** [ganze] Weintraube f

grapefruit n invar Grapefruit f

graph n grafische Darstellung f

graphic a, -**ally** adv grafisch; (vivid) anschaulich

graph paper n Millimeterpapier nt

grapple vi ringen

grasp n Griff m ● vt ergreifen; (understand) begreifen. ~**ing** a habgierig

grass n Gras nt; (lawn) Rasen m. ~**hopper** n Heuschrecke f

grassy a grasig

grate¹ n Feuerrost m; (hearth) Kamin m

grate² vt (Culin) reiben

grateful a, -**ly** adv dankbar (**to** dat)

grater n (Culin) Reibe f

gratify vt (pt/pp -**ied**) befriedigen. ~**ing** a erfreulich

gratis adv gratis

gratitude n Dankbarkeit f

gratuitous a (uncalled for) überflüssig

grave¹ a (-r, -st), -**ly** adv ernst; ~**ly ill** schwer krank

grave² n Grab nt. ~-**digger** n Totengräber m

gravel n Kies m

grave: ~**stone** n Grabstein m. ~**yard** n Friedhof m

gravity n Ernst m; (force) Schwerkraft f

gravy n [Braten]soße f

gray a (Amer) = **grey**

graze¹ vi <animal:> weiden

graze² n Schürfwunde f ● vt <car> streifen; <knee> aufschürfen

grease n Fett nt; (lubricant) Schmierfett nt ● vt einfetten; (lubricate) schmieren

greasy a (-ier, -iest) fettig

great a (-er, -est) groß; (🖽 marvellous) großartig

great: ~-**aunt** n Großtante f. **G**~ **Britain** n Großbritannien nt. ~-**grandchildren** npl Urenkel pl. ~-**grandfather** n Urgroßvater m. ~-**grandmother** n Urgroßmutter f

great|ly adv sehr. ~**ness** n Größe f

great-uncle n Großonkel m

Greece n Griechenland nt

greed n [Hab]gier f

greedy a (-ier, -iest), -**ily** adv gierig

Greek a griechisch ● n Grieche m/ Griechin f; (Lang) Griechisch nt

green a (-er, -est) grün; (fig) unerfahren ● n Grün nt; (grass) Wiese f; ~**s** pl Kohl m; **the G**~**s** pl (Pol) die Grünen pl

greenery n Grün nt

green: ~**fly** n Blattlaus f. ~**grocer** n Obst- und Gemüsehändler m. ~**house** n Gewächshaus nt

Greenland n Grönland nt

greet vt grüßen; (welcome) begrüßen. ~**ing** n Gruß m; (welcome) Begrüßung f

grew see **grow**

grey a (-er, -est) grau ● n Grau nt ● vi grau werden. ~**hound** n Windhund m

grid n Gitter nt

grief n Trauer f

grievance n Beschwerde f

grieve vi trauern (**for** um)

grill n Gitter nt; (Culin) Grill m; **mixed** ~ Gemischtes nt vom Grill ● vt/i grillen; (interrogate) [streng] verhören

grille n Gitter nt

grim a (grimmer, grimmest), **-ly** adv ernst; <determination> verbissen

grimace n Grimasse f ● vi Grimassen schneiden

grime n Schmutz m

grimy a (-ier, -iest) schmutzig

grin n Grinsen nt ● vi (pt/pp grinned) grinsen

grind n (Ⅰ hard work) Plackerei f ● vt (pt/pp ground) mahlen; (smooth, sharpen) schleifen; (Amer: mince) durchdrehen

grip n Griff m; (bag) Reisetasche f ● vt (pt/pp gripped) ergreifen; (hold) festhalten

gripping a fesselnd

grisly a (-ier, -iest) grausig

gristle n Knorpel m

grit n [grober] Sand m; (for roads) Streugut nt; (courage) Mut m ● vt (pt/pp gritted) streuen <road>

groan n Stöhnen nt ● vi stöhnen

grocer n Lebensmittelhändler m; ~'s [shop] Lebensmittelgeschäft nt. ~ies npl Lebensmittel pl

groin n (Anat) Leiste f

groom n Bräutigam m; (for horse) Pferdepfleger(in) m(f) ● vt striegeln <horse>

groove n Rille f

grope vi tasten (for nach)

gross a (-er, -est) fett; (coarse) derb; (glaring) grob; (Comm) brutto; <salary, weight> Brutto-. ~ly adv (very) sehr

grotesque a, **-ly** adv grotesk

ground¹ see grind

ground² n Boden m; (terrain) Gelände nt; (reason) Grund m; (Amer, Electr) Erde f; ~s pl (park) Anlagen pl; (of coffee) Satz m

ground: ~ **floor** n Erdgeschoss nt. ~ing n Grundlage f. ~less a grundlos. ~sheet n Bodenplane f. ~work n Vorarbeiten pl

group n Gruppe f ● vt gruppieren ● vi sich gruppieren

grouse vi Ⅰ meckern

grovel vi (pt/pp grovelled) kriechen

grow v (pt grew, pp grown) ● vi wachsen; (become) werden; (increase) zunehmen ● vt anbauen. ~ **up** vi aufwachsen; <town:> entstehen

growl n Knurren nt ● vi knurren

grown see grow. ~**up** a erwachsen ● n Erwachsene(r) m/f

growth n Wachstum nt; (increase) Zunahme f; (Med) Gewächs nt

grub n (larva) Made f; (fam: food) Essen nt

grubby a (-ier, -iest) schmuddelig

grudg|e n Groll m ● vt ~e s.o. sth jdm etw missgönnen. ~**ing** a, **-ly** adv widerwillig

gruelling a strapaziös

gruesome a grausig

gruff a, **-ly** adv barsch

grumble vi schimpfen (at mit)

grumpy a (-ier, -iest) griesgrämig

grunt n Grunzen nt ● vi grunzen

guarantee n Garantie f; (document) Garantieschein m ● vt garantieren; garantieren für <quality, success>

guard n Wache f; (security) Wächter m; (on train) ≈ Zugführer m; (Techn) Schutz m; **be on** ~ Wache stehen; **on one's** ~ auf der Hut ● vt bewachen; (protect) schützen ● vi ~ **against** sich hüten vor (+ dat). ~-**dog** n Wachhund m

guarded a vorsichtig

guardian n Vormund m

guess n Vermutung f ● vt erraten ● vi raten; (Amer: believe) glauben. ~**work** n Vermutung f

guest n Gast m. ~-**house** n Pension f

guidance n Führung f, Leitung f; (advice) Beratung f

guide n Führer(in) m(f); (book) Führer m; [Girl] G~ Pfadfinderin f ● vt führen, leiten. ~**book** n Führer m

guided a ~ **tour** Führung f

guide: ~-**dog** n Blindenhund m. ~**lines** npl Richtlinien pl

guilt n Schuld f. ~**ily** adv schuldbewusst

guilty *a* (-ier, -iest) *a* schuldig (*of gen*); <*look*> schuldbewusst; <*conscience*> schlecht

guinea-pig *n* Meerschweinchen *nt*; (*person*) Versuchskaninchen *nt*

guitar *n* Gitarre *f*. **~ist** *n* Gitarrist(in) *m(f)*

gulf *n* (*Geog*) Golf *m*; (*fig*) Kluft *f*

gull *n* Möwe *f*

gullible *a* leichtgläubig

gully *n* Schlucht *f*; (*drain*) Rinne *f*

gulp *n* Schluck *m* ● *vi* schlucken ● *vt* **~ down** hinunterschlucken

gum¹ *n* & **-s** *pl* (*Anat*) Zahnfleisch *nt*

gum² *n* Gummi[harz] *nt*; (*glue*) Klebstoff *m*; (*chewing gum*) Kaugummi *m*

gummed *see* **gum**² ● *a* <*label*> gummiert

gun *n* Schusswaffe *f*; (*pistol*) Pistole *f*; (*rifle*) Gewehr *nt*; (*cannon*) Geschütz *nt*

gun: **~fire** *n* Geschützfeuer *nt*. **~man** *n* bewaffneter Bandit *m*

gunner *n* Artillerist *m*

gunpowder *n* Schießpulver *nt*

gurgle *vi* gluckern; (*of baby*) glucksen

gush *vi* strömen; (*enthuse*) schwärmen (**over** von)

gust *n* (*of wind*) Windstoß *m*; (*Naut*) Bö *f*

gusto *n* **with ~** mit Schwung

gusty *a* böig

gut *n* Darm *m*; **~s** *pl* Eingeweide *pl*; (🔲 *courage*) Schneid *m* ● *vt* (*pt/pp* gutted) (*Culin*) ausnehmen; **~ted by fire** ausgebrannt

gutter *n* Rinnstein *m*; (*fig*) Gosse *f*; (*on roof*) Dachrinne *f*

guy *n* 🔲 Kerl *m*

guzzle *vt/i* schlingen; (*drink*) schlürfen

gym *n* 🔲 Turnhalle *f*; (*gymnastics*) Turnen *nt*

gymnasium *n* Turnhalle *f*

gymnast *n* Turner(in) *m(f)*. **~ics** *n* Turnen *nt*

gym shoes *pl* Turnschuhe *pl*

gynaecolog|ist *n* Frauenarzt *m* /-ärztin *f*. **~y** *n* Gynäkologie *f*

gypsy *n* Zigeuner(in) *m(f)*

habit *n* Gewohnheit *f*; (*Relig: costume*) Ordenstracht *f*; **be in the ~** die Angewohnheit haben (**of** zu)

habitat *n* Habitat *nt*

habitation *n* **unfit for human ~** für Wohnzwecke ungeeignet

habitual *a* gewohnt; (*inveterate*) gewohnheitsmäßig. **~ly** *adv* gewohnheitsmäßig; (*constantly*) ständig

hack¹ *n* (*writer*) Schreiberling *m*; (*hired horse*) Mietpferd *nt*

hack² *vt* hacken; **~ to pieces** zerhacken

hackneyed *a* abgedroschen

hacksaw *n* Metallsäge *f*

had *see* **have**

haddock *n inv* Schellfisch *m*

haggard *a* abgehärmt

haggle *vi* feilschen (**over** um)

hail¹ *vt* begrüßen; herbeirufen <*taxi*> ● *vi* **~ from** kommen aus

hail² *n* Hagel *m* ● *vi* hageln. **~stone** *n* Hagelkorn *nt*

hair *n* Haar *nt*; **wash one's ~** sich (*dat*) die Haare waschen

hair: **~brush** *n* Haarbürste *f*. **~cut** *n* Haarschnitt *m*; **have a ~cut** sich (*dat*) die Haare schneiden lassen. **~-do** *n* 🔲 Frisur *f*. **~dresser** *n* Friseur *m*/Friseuse *f*. **~drier** *n* Haartrockner *m*; (*hand-held*) Föhn *m*. **~pin** *n* Haarnadel *f*. **~pin bend** *n* Haarnadelkurve *f*. **~-raising** *a* haarsträubend. **~-style** *n* Frisur *f*

hairy *a* (-ier, -iest) behaart; (*excessively*) haarig; (*fam; frightening*) brenzlig

hake *n inv* Seehecht *m*

half *n* (*pl* **halves**) Hälfte *f*; **cut in** ~ halbieren; **one and a** ~ eineinhalb, anderthalb; ~ **a dozen** ein halbes Dutzend; ~ **an hour** eine halbe Stunde •*a & adv* halb; ~ **past two** halb drei; [**at**] ~ **price** zum halben Preis

half: ~-**hearted** *a* lustlos. ~-**term** *n* schulfreie Tage nach dem halben Trimester. ~-**timbered** *a* Fachwerk-. ~-**time** *n* (*Sport*) Halbzeit *f*. ~-**way** *a* the ~-**way mark/stage** die Hälfte •*adv* auf halbem Weg

halibut *n inv* Heilbutt *m*

hall *n* Halle *f*; (*room*) Saal *m*; (*Sch*) Aula *f*; (*entrance*) Flur *m*; (*mansion*) Gutshaus *nt*; ~ **of residence** (*Univ*) Studentenheim *nt*

hallmark *n* [Feingehalts]stempel *m*; (*fig*) Kennzeichen *nt* (**of** für)

hallo *int* [guten] Tag! 🔲 hallo!

hallucination *n* Halluzination *f*

halo *n* (*pl* -**es**) Heiligenschein *m*; (*Astr*) Hof *m*

halt *n* Halt *m*; **come to a** ~ stehen bleiben; <*traffic*> zum Stillstand kommen •*vi* Halt machen; ~! halt! ~**ing** *a*, *adv* -**ly** zögernd

halve *vt* halbieren; (*reduce*) um die Hälfte reduzieren

ham *n* Schinken *m*

hamburger *n* Hamburger *m*

hammer *n* Hammer *m* •*vt/i* hämmern (**at an** + *acc*)

hammock *n* Hängematte *f*

hamper *vt* behindern

hamster *n* Hamster *m*

hand *n* Hand *f*; (*of clock*) Zeiger *m*; (*writing*) Handschrift *f*; (*worker*) Arbeiter(in) *m(f)*; (*Cards*) Blatt *nt*; **on the one/other** ~ einer-/andererseits; **out of** ~ außer Kontrolle; (*summarily*) kurzerhand; **in** ~ unter Kontrolle; (*available*) verfügbar; **give s.o. a** ~ jdm behilflich sein •*vt* reichen (**to** *dat*). ~ **in** *vt* abgeben. ~ **out** *vt* austeilen. ~ **over** *vt* überreichen

hand: ~**bag** *n* Handtasche *f*. ~**book** *n* Handbuch *nt*. ~**brake** *n* Handbremse *f*. ~**cuffs** *npl* Handschellen *pl*. ~**ful** *n* Handvoll *f*; **be [quite] a** ~**ful** 🔲 nicht leicht zu haben sein

handicap *n* Behinderung *f*; (*Sport & fig*) Handikap *nt*. ~**ped** *a* **mentally/physically** ~**ped** geistig/ körperlich behindert

handkerchief *n* (*pl* ~**s** & -**chieves**) Taschentuch *nt*

handle *n* Griff *m*; (*of door*) Klinke *f*; (*of cup*) Henkel *m*; (*of broom*) Stiel *m* •*vt* handhaben; (*treat*) umgehen mit; (*touch*) anfassen. ~**bars** *npl* Lenkstange *f*

hand: ~**made** *a* handgemacht. ~**shake** *n* Händedruck *m*

handsome *a* gut aussehend; (*generous*) großzügig; (*large*) beträchtlich

hand: ~**writing** *n* Handschrift *f*. ~**written** *a* handgeschrieben

handy *a* (-**ier**, -**iest**) handlich; <*person*> geschickt; **have/keep** ~ griffbereit haben/halten

hang *vt/i* (*pt/pp* **hung**) hängen; ~ **wallpaper** tapezieren •*vt* (*pt/pp* **hanged**) hängen <*criminal*> •*n* **get the** ~ **of it** 🔲 den Dreh herauskriegen. ~ **about** *vi* sich herumdrücken. ~ **on** *vi* sich festhalten (**to** an + *dat*); (🔲 *wait*) warten. ~ **out** *vi* heraushängen; (🔲 *live*) wohnen •*vt* draußen aufhängen <*washing*>. ~ **up** *vt/i* aufhängen

hangar *n* Flugzeughalle *f*

hanger *n* [Kleider]bügel *m*

hang: ~-**glider** *n* Drachenflieger *m*. ~-**gliding** *n* Drachenfliegen *nt*. ~**man** *n* Henker *m*. ~**over** *n* 🔲 Kater *m* 🔲. ~-**up** *n* 🔲 Komplex *m*

hanker *vi* ~ **after sth** sich (*dat*) etw wünschen

hanky *n* 🔲 Taschentuch *nt*

haphazard *a*, -**ly** *adv* planlos

happen *vi* geschehen, passieren; **I** ~**ed to be there** ich war zufällig da; **what has** ~**ed to him?** was ist mit ihm los? (*become of*) was ist aus ihm geworden? **~ing** *n* Ereignis *nt*

happi|ly *adv* glücklich; (*fortunately*) glücklicherweise. **~ness** *n* Glück *nt*

happy *a* (**-ier, -iest**) glücklich. **~-go-lucky** *a* sorglos

harass *vt* schikanieren. **~ed** *a* abgehetzt. **~ment** *n* Schikane *f*; (*sexual*) Belästigung *f*

harbour *n* Hafen *m*

hard *a* (**-er, -est**) hart; (*difficult*) schwer; **~ of hearing** schwerhörig ● *adv* hart; <*work*> schwer; <*pull*> kräftig; <*rain, snow*> stark; **be ~ up** 🔲 knapp bei Kasse sein; **be ~ done by** 🔲 ungerecht behandelt werden

hard: ~back *n* gebundene Ausgabe *f*. **~board** *n* Hartfaserplatte *f*. **~-boiled** *a* hart gekocht

harden *vi* hart werden

hard-hearted *a* hartherzig

hard|ly *adv* kaum; **~ly ever** kaum [jemals]. **~ness** *n* Härte *f*. **~ship** *n* Not *f*

hard: ~ shoulder *n* (*Auto*) Randstreifen *m*. **~ware** *n* Haushaltswaren *pl*; (*Computing*) Hardware *f*. **~-wearing** *a* strapazierfähig. **~-working** *a* fleißig

hardy *a* (**-ier, -iest**) abgehärtet; <*plant*> winterhart

hare *n* Hase *m*

harm *n* Schaden *m*; **it won't do any ~** es kann nichts schaden ● *vt* **~ s.o.** jdm etwas antun. **~ful** *a* schädlich. **~less** *a* harmlos

harmonious *a*, **-ly** *adv* harmonisch

harmon|ize *vi* (*fig*) harmonieren. **~y** *n* Harmonie *f*

harness *n* Geschirr *nt*; (*of parachute*) Gurtwerk *nt* ● *vt* anschirren <*horse*>; (*use*) nutzbar machen

harp *n* Harfe *f*. **~ist** *n* Harfenist(in) *m(f)*

harpsichord *n* Cembalo *nt*

harrowing *a* grauenhaft

harsh *a* (**-er, -est**), **-ly** *adv* hart; <*voice*> rau; <*light*> grell. **~ness** *n* Härte *f*; Rauheit *f*

harvest *n* Ernte *f* ● *vt* ernten

has *see* **have**

hassle *n* 🔲 Ärger *m* ● *vt* schikanieren

haste *n* Eile *f*

hasten *vi* sich beeilen (**to** zu); (*go quickly*) eilen ● *vt* beschleunigen

hasty *a* (**-ier, -iest**), **-ily** *adv* hastig; <*decision*> voreilig

hat *n* Hut *m*; (*knitted*) Mütze *f*

hatch[1] *n* (*for food*) Durchreiche *f*; (*Naut*) Luke *f*

hatch[2] *vi* **~[out]** ausschlüpfen ● *vt* ausbrüten

hatchback *n* (*Auto*) Modell *nt* mit Hecktür

hate *n* Hass *m* ● *vt* hassen. **~ful** *a* abscheulich

hatred *n* Hass *m*

haughty *a* (**-ier, -iest**), **-ily** *adv* hochmütig

haul *n* (*loot*) Beute *f* ● *vt/i* ziehen (**on** an + *dat*)

haunt *n* Lieblingsaufenthalt *m* ● *vt* umgehen in (+ *dat*); **this house is ~ed** in diesem Haus spukt es

have

3 sg pres tense **has**; *pt and pp* **had**

● *transitive verb*

····▸ (*possess*) haben. **he has [got] a car** er hat ein Auto. **she has [got] a brother** sie hat einen Bruder. **we have [got] five minutes** wir haben fünf Minuten

····▸ (*eat*) essen; (*drink*) trinken; (*smoke*) rauchen. **have a cup of tea** eine Tasse Tee trinken. **have a pizza** eine Pizza essen. **have a cigarette** eine Zigarette rauchen. **have breakfast/dinner/lunch** frühstücken/zu Abend essen/zu Mittag essen

····▸ (*take esp. in shop, restaurant*) nehmen. **I'll have the soup/the red dress** ich nehme die Suppe/das rote Kleid. **have a cigarette!** nehmen Sie eine Zigarette!

····▸ (*get, receive*) bekommen. **I had a letter from her** ich bekam einen Brief von ihr. **have a baby** ein Baby bekommen

····▸ *(suffer)* haben *<illness, pain, disappointment>*; erleiden *<shock>*

····▸ *(organize)* **have a party** eine Party veranstalten. **they had a meeting** sie hielten eine Versammlung ab

····▸ *(take part in)* **have a game of football** Fußball spielen. **have a swim** schwimmen

····▸ *(as guest)* **have s.o. to stay** jdn zu Besuch haben

····▸ **have had it** 🅸 *<thing>* ausgedient haben; *<person>* geliefert sein. **you've had it now** jetzt ist es aus

····▸ **have sth done** etw machen lassen. **we had the house painted** wir haben das Haus malen lassen. **have a dress made** sich *(dat)* ein Kleid machen lassen. **have a tooth out** sich *(dat)* einen Zahn ziehen lassen. **have one's hair cut** sich *(dat)* die Haare schneiden lassen

●*auxiliary verb*

····▸ *(forming perfect and past perfect tenses)* haben; *(with verbs of motion and some others)* sein. **I have seen him** ich habe ihn gesehen. **he has never been there** er ist nie da gewesen. **I had gone** ich war gegangen. **if I had known ...** wenn ich gewusst hätte ...

····▸ *(in tag questions)* nicht wahr. **you've met her, haven't you?** du kennst sie, nicht wahr?

····▸ *(in short answers)* **Have you seen the film? — Yes, I have** Hast du den Film gesehen? — Ja [, stimmt]

●● **have on** *vt (be wearing)* anhaben; *(dupe)* anführen

havoc *n* Verwüstung *f*

hawk *n* Falke *m*

hawthorn *n* Hagedorn *m*

hay *n* Heu *nt*. ∼ **fever** *n* Heuschnupfen *m*. ∼**stack** *n* Heuschober *m*

hazard *n* Gefahr *f*; *(risk)* Risiko *nt* ● *vt* riskieren. ∼**ous** *a* gefährlich; *(risky)* riskant

haze *n* Dunst *m*

hazel *n* Haselbusch *m*. ∼**-nut** *n* Haselnuss *f*

hazy *a* (-ier, -iest) dunstig; *(fig)* unklar

he *pron* er

head *n* Kopf *m*; *(chief)* Oberhaupt *nt*; *(of firm)* Chef(in) *m(f)*; *(of school)* Schulleiter(in) *m(f)*; *(on beer)* Schaumkrone *f*; *(of bed)* Kopfende *nt*; ∼ **first** kopfüber ● *vt* anführen; *(Sport)* köpfen *<ball>* ● *vi* ∼ **for** zusteuern auf (+ *acc*). ∼**ache** *n* Kopfschmerzen *pl*

head|er *n* Kopfball *m*; *(dive)* Kopfsprung *m*. ∼**ing** *n* Überschrift *f*

head: ∼**lamp**, ∼**light** *n (Auto)* Scheinwerfer *m*. ∼**line** *n* Schlagzeile *f*. ∼**long** *adv* kopfüber. ∼**master** *n* Schulleiter *m*. ∼**mistress** *n* Schulleiterin *f*. ∼**-on** *a & adv* frontal. ∼**phones** *npl* Kopfhörer *m*. ∼**quarters** *npl* Hauptquartier *nt*; *(Pol)* Zentrale *f*. ∼**-rest** *n* Kopfstütze *f*. ∼**room** *n* lichte Höhe *f*. ∼**scarf** *n* Kopftuch *nt*. ∼**strong** *a* eigenwillig. ∼**way** *n* **make** ∼**way** Fortschritte machen. ∼**word** *n* Stichwort *nt*

heady *a* berauschend

heal *vt/i* heilen

health *n* Gesundheit *f*

health: ∼ **farm** *n* Schönheitsfarm *f*. ∼ **foods** *npl* Reformkost *f*. ∼**-food shop** *n* Reformhaus *nt*. ∼ **insurance** *n* Krankenversicherung *f*

healthy *a* (-ier, -iest), **-ily** *adv* gesund

heap *n* Haufen *m*; ∼**s** 🅸 jede Menge ● *vt* ∼ **[up]** häufen

hear *vt/i (pt/pp* **heard)** hören; ∼, ∼! hört, hört! **he would not** ∼ **of it** er ließ es nicht zu

hearing *n* Gehör *nt*; *(Jur)* Verhandlung *f*. ∼**-aid** *n* Hörgerät *nt*

hearse *n* Leichenwagen *m*

heart *n* Herz *nt*; *(courage)* Mut *m*; ∼**s** *pl (Cards)* Herz *nt*; **by** ∼ auswendig

heart: ∼**ache** *n* Kummer *m*. ∼**attack** *n* Herzanfall *m*. ∼**beat** *n* Herzschlag *m*. ∼**-breaking** *a*

herzzerreißend. **~-broken** *a*
untröstlich. **~burn** *n* Sodbrennen
nt. **~en** *vt* ermutigen. **~felt** *a*
herzlich[st]

hearth *n* Herd *m*; (*fireplace*) Kamin
m

heart|ily *adv* herzlich; <*eat*> viel.
~less *a*, **-ly** *adv* herzlos. **~y** *a*
herzlich; <*meal*> groß; <*person*>
burschikos

heat *n* Hitze *f*; (*Sport*) Vorlauf *m* ● *vt*
heiß machen; heizen <*room*>. **~ed**
a geheizt; <*swimming pool*> beheizt;
<*discussion*> hitzig. **~er** *n* Heizgerät
nt; (*Auto*) Heizanlage *f*

heath *n* Heide *f*

heathen *a* heidnisch ● *n* Heide *m*/
Heidin *f*

heather *n* Heidekraut *nt*

heating *n* Heizung *f*

heat wave *n* Hitzewelle *f*

heave *vt/i* ziehen; (*lift*) heben; (🔢
throw) schmeißen

heaven *n* Himmel *m.* **~ly** *a*
himmlisch

heavy *a* (-ier, -iest), **-ily** *adv* schwer;
<*traffic, rain*> stark. **~weight** *n*
Schwergewicht *nt*

heckle *vt* [durch Zwischenrufe]
unterbrechen. **~r** *n* Zwischenrufer
m

hectic *a* hektisch

hedge *n* Hecke *f*. **~hog** *n* Igel *m*

heed *vt* beachten

heel¹ *n* Ferse *f*; (*of shoe*) Absatz *m*;
down at ~ heruntergekommen

heel² *vi* **~ over** (*Naut*) sich auf die
Seite legen

hefty *a* (-ier, -iest) kräftig; (*heavy*)
schwer

height *n* Höhe *f*; (*of person*) Größe *f*.
~en *vt* (*fig*) steigern

heir *n* Erbe *m.* **~ess** *n* Erbin *f*.
~loom *n* Erbstück *nt*

held *see* hold²

helicopter *n* Hubschrauber *m*

hell *n* Hölle *f*; **go to ~!** 🔢 geh zum
Teufel! ● *int* verdammt!

hello *int* [guten] Tag! 🔢 hallo!

helm *n* [Steuer]ruder *nt*

helmet *n* Helm *m*

help *n* Hilfe *f*; (*employees*) Hilfskräfte
pl; **that's no ~** das nützt nichts ● *vt/
i* helfen (**s.o.** jdm); **~ oneself to sth**
sich (*dat*) etw nehmen; **~ yourself**
(*at table*) greif zu; **I could not ~**
laughing ich musste lachen; **it cannot**
be ~ed es lässt sich nicht ändern; **I**
can't ~ it ich kann nichts dafür

help|er *n* Helfer(in) *m(f)*. **~ful** *a*, **-ly**
adv hilfsbereit; <*advice*> nützlich.
~ing *n* Portion *f*. **~less** *a*, **-ly** *adv*
hilflos

hem *n* Saum *m* ● *vt* (*pt/pp* hemmed)
säumen; **~ in** umzingeln

hemisphere *n* Hemisphäre *f*

hem-line *n* Rocklänge *f*

hen *n* Henne *f*; (*any female bird*)
Weibchen *nt*

hence *adv* daher; **five years ~** in
fünf Jahren. **~forth** *adv* von nun
an

henpecked *a* **~ husband**
Pantoffelheld *m*

her *a* ihr ● *pron* (*acc*) sie; (*dat*) ihr

herald *vt* verkünden. **~ry** *n*
Wappenkunde *f*

herb *n* Kraut *nt*

herbaceous *a* **~ border**
Staudenrabatte *f*

herd *n* Herde *f*. **~ together** *vt*
zusammentreiben

here *adv* hier; (*to this place*) hierher;
in ~ hier drinnen; **come/bring ~**
herkommen/herbringen

hereditary *a* erblich

here|sy *n* Ketzerei *f*. **~tic** *n*
Ketzer(in) *m(f)*

herewith *adv* (*Comm*) beiliegend

heritage *n* Erbe *nt*

hero *n* (*pl* -es) Held *m*

heroic *a*, **-ally** *adv* heldenhaft

heroin *n* Heroin *nt*

hero|ine *n* Heldin *f*. **~ism** *n*
Heldentum *nt*

heron *n* Reiher *m*

herring *n* Hering *m*

hers *poss pron* ihre(r); ihrs; **a friend**
of ~ ein Freund von ihr; **that is ~**
das gehört ihr

herself *pron* selbst; (*refl*) sich; **by ~** allein

hesitant *a*, **-ly** *adv* zögernd

hesitat|e *vi* zögern. **~ion** *n* Zögern *nt*; **without ~ion** ohne zu zögern

hexagonal *a* sechseckig

heyday *n* Glanzzeit *f*

hi *int* he! (*hallo*) Tag!

hiatus *n* (*pl* **-tuses**) Lücke *f*

hibernat|e *vi* Winterschlaf halten. **~ion** *n* Winterschlaf *m*

hiccup *n* Hick *m*; (🔲 *hitch*) Panne *f*; **have the ~s** den Schluckauf haben ● *vi* hick machen

hid, hidden *see* hide²

hide *v* (*pt* hid, *pp* hidden) ● *vt* verstecken; (*keep secret*) verheimlichen ● *vi* sich verstecken

hideous *a*, **-ly** *adv* hässlich; (*horrible*) grässlich

hide-out *n* Versteck *nt*

hiding¹ *n* 🔲 **give s.o. a ~** jdn verdreschen

hiding² *n* **go into ~** untertauchen

hierarchy *n* Hierarchie *f*

high *a* (-**er**, -**est**) hoch; *attrib* hohe(r,s); <*meat*> angegangen; <*wind*> stark; (**on drugs**) high; **it's ~ time** es ist höchste Zeit ● *adv* hoch; **~ and low** überall ● *n* Hoch *nt*; (*temperature*) Höchsttemperatur *f*

high: ~brow *a* intellektuell. **~chair** *n* Kinderhochstuhl *m*. **~handed** *a* selbstherrlich. **~heeled** *a* hochhackig. **~ jump** *n* Hochsprung *m*

highlight *n* (*fig*) Höhepunkt *m*; **~s** *pl* (*in hair*) helle Strähnen *pl* ● *vt* (*emphasize*) hervorheben

highly *adv* hoch; **speak ~ of** loben; **think ~ of** sehr schätzen. **~-strung** *a* nervös

Highness *n* Hoheit *f*

high: ~ season *n* Hochsaison *f*. **~ street** *n* Hauptstraße *f*. **~ tide** *n* Hochwasser *nt*. **~way** *n* **public ~way** öffentliche Straße *f*

hijack *vt* entführen. **~er** *n* Entführer *m*

hike *n* Wanderung *f* ● *vi* wandern. **~r** *n* Wanderer *m*

hilarious *a* sehr komisch

hill *n* Berg *m*; (*mound*) Hügel *m*; (*slope*) Hang *m*

hill: ~side *n* Hang *m*. **~y** *a* hügelig

him *pron* (*acc*) ihn; (*dat*) ihm. **~self** *pron* selbst; (*refl*) sich; **by ~self** allein

hind *a* Hinter-

hind|er *vt* hindern. **~rance** *n* Hindernis *nt*

hindsight *n* **with ~** rückblickend

Hindu *n* Hindu *m* ● *a* Hindu-. **~ism** *n* Hinduismus *m*

hinge *n* Scharnier *nt*; (*on door*) Angel *f*

hint *n* Wink *m*, Andeutung *f*; (*advice*) Hinweis *m*; (*trace*) Spur *f* ● *vi* **~ at** anspielen auf (+ *acc*)

hip *n* Hüfte *f*

hip pocket *n* Gesäßtasche *f*

hippopotamus *n* (*pl* **-muses** or **-mi**) Nilpferd *nt*

hire *vt* mieten <*car*>; leihen <*suit*>; einstellen <*person*>; **~[out]** vermieten; verleihen

his *a* sein ● *poss pron* seine(r), seins; **a friend of ~** ein Freund von ihm; **that is ~** das gehört ihm

hiss *n* Zischen *nt* ● *vt/i* zischen

historian *n* Historiker(in) *m(f)*

historic *a* historisch. **~al** *a*, **-ly** *adv* geschichtlich, historisch

history *n* Geschichte *f*

hit *n* (*blow*) Schlag *m*; (🔲 *success*) Erfolg *m*; **direct ~** Volltreffer *m* ● *vt/i* (*pt/pp* hit, *pres p* hitting) schlagen; (*knock against, collide with, affect*) treffen; **~ the target** das Ziel treffen; **~ on** (*fig*) kommen auf (+ *acc*); **~ it off** gut auskommen (**with** mit); **~ one's head on sth** sich (*dat*) den Kopf an etw (*dat*) stoßen

hitch *n* Problem *nt*; **technical ~** Panne *f* ● *vt* festmachen (**to** an + *dat*); **~ up** hochziehen. **~-hike** *vi* 🔲 trampen. **~-hiker** *n* Anhalter(in) *m(f)*

hive *n* Bienenstock *m*

hoard *n* Hort *m* ● *vt* horten, hamstern

hoarding n Bauzaun m; (with advertisements) Reklamewand f

hoar-frost n Raureif m

hoarse a (-r, -st), **-ly** adv heiser. **~ness** n Heiserkeit f

hoax n übler Scherz m; (false alarm) blinder Alarm m

hobble vi humpeln

hobby n Hobby nt. **~-horse** n (fig) Lieblingsthema nt

hockey n Hockey nt

hoe n Hacke f ● vt (pres p hoeing) hacken

hog vt (pt/pp hogged) 🔲 mit Beschlag belegen

hoist n Lastenaufzug m ● vt hochziehen; hissen <flag>

hold¹ n (Naut) Laderaum m

hold² n Halt m; (Sport) Griff m; (fig: influence) Einfluss m; **get ~ of** fassen; (🔲 contact) erreichen ● v (pt/pp held) ● vt halten; <container:> fassen; (believe) meinen; (possess) haben; anhalten <breath> ● vi <rope:> halten; <weather:> sich halten. **~ back** vt zurückhalten ● vi zögern. **~ on** vi (wait) warten; (on telephone) am Apparat bleiben; **~ on to** (keep) behalten; (cling to) sich festhalten an (+ dat). **~ out** vt hinhalten ● vi (resist) aushalten. **~ up** vt hochhalten; (delay) aufhalten; (rob) überfallen

hold|all n Reisetasche f. **~er** n Inhaber(in) m(f); (container) Halter m. **~-up** n Verzögerung f; (attack) Überfall m

hole n Loch nt

holiday n Urlaub m; (Sch) Ferien pl; (public) Feiertag m; (day off) freier Tag m; **go on ~** in Urlaub fahren

holiness n Heiligkeit f

Holland n Holland nt

hollow a hohl; <promise> leer ● n Vertiefung f; (in ground) Mulde f. **~ out** vt aushöhlen

holly n Stechpalme f

holster n Pistolentasche f

holy a (-ier, -est) heilig. **H~ Ghost** or **Spirit** n Heiliger Geist m

homage n Huldigung f; **pay ~ to** huldigen (+ dat)

home n Zuhause nt (house) Haus nt; (institution) Heim nt; (native land) Heimat f ● adv **at ~** zu Hause; **come/go ~** nach Hause kommen/ gehen

home: **~ address** n Heimatanschrift f. **~ game** n Heimspiel nt. **~ help** n Haushaltshilfe f. **~land** n Heimatland nt. **~less** a obdachlos

homely a (-ier, -iest) a gemütlich; (Amer: ugly) unscheinbar

home: **~-made** a selbst gemacht. **H~ Office** n Innenministerium nt. **H~ Secretary** Innenminister m. **~sick** a **be ~sick** Heimweh haben (for nach). **~sickness** n Heimweh nt. **~ town** n Heimatstadt f. **~work** n (Sch) Hausaufgaben pl

homosexual a homosexuell ● n Homosexuelle(r) m/f

honest a, **-ly** adv ehrlich. **~y** n Ehrlichkeit f

honey n Honig m; (🔲 darling) Schatz m

honey: **~comb** n Honigwabe f. **~moon** n Flitterwochen pl; (journey) Hochzeitsreise f

honorary a ehrenamtlich; <member, doctorate> Ehren-

honour n Ehre f ● vt ehren; honorieren <cheque>. **~able** a, **-bly** adv ehrenhaft

hood n Kapuze f; (of car, pram) [Klapp]verdeck nt; (over cooker) Abzugshaube f; (Auto, Amer) Kühlerhaube f

hoof n (pl ~s or hooves) Huf m

hook n Haken m ● vt festhaken (to an + acc)

hook|ed a **~ed nose** Hakennase f; **~ed on** 🔲 abhängig von; (keen on) besessen von. **~er** n (Amer 🔲) Nutte f

hookey n **play ~** (Amer 🔲) schwänzen

hooligan n Rowdy m. **~ism** n Rowdytum nt

hooray int & n = hurrah

hoot n Ruf m; ∼s of laughter schallendes Gelächter nt ● vi <owl:> rufen; <car:> hupen; (jeer) johlen. ∼er n (of factory) Sirene f; (Auto) Hupe f

hoover n H∼ (P) Staubsauger m ● vt/i [staub]saugen

hop¹ n, & ∼s pl Hopfen m

hop² vi (pt/pp hopped) hüpfen; ∼ it! 🔟 hau ab!

hope n Hoffnung f; (prospect) Aussicht f (of auf + acc) ● vt/i hoffen (for auf + acc); I ∼ so hoffentlich

hope|ful a hoffnungsvoll; be ∼ful that hoffen, dass. ∼fully adv hoffnungsvoll; (it is hoped) hoffentlich. ∼less a, -ly adv hoffnungslos; (useless) nutzlos; (incompetent) untauglich

horde n Horde f

horizon n Horizont m

horizontal a, -ly adv horizontal. ∼ bar n Reck nt

horn n Horn nt; (Auto) Hupe f

hornet n Hornisse f

horoscope n Horoskop nt

horrible a, -bly adv schrecklich

horrid a grässlich

horrific a entsetzlich

horrify vt (pt/pp -ied) entsetzen

horror n Entsetzen nt

hors-d'œuvre n Vorspeise f

horse n Pferd nt

horse: ∼back n on ∼back zu Pferde. ∼man n Reiter m. ∼power n Pferdestärke f. ∼racing n Pferderennen nt. ∼radish n Meerrettich m. ∼shoe n Hufeisen nt

horticulture n Gartenbau m

hose n (pipe) Schlauch m ● vt ∼ down abspritzen

hosiery n Strumpfwaren pl

hospitable a, -bly adv gastfreundlich

hospital n Krankenhaus nt

hospitality n Gastfreundschaft f

host n Gastgeber m

hostage n Geisel f

hostel n [Wohn]heim nt

hostess n Gastgeberin f

hostile a feindlich; (unfriendly) feindselig

hostilit|y n Feindschaft f; ∼ies pl Feindseligkeiten pl

hot a (hotter, hottest) heiß; <meal> warm; (spicy) scharf; I am or feel ∼ mir ist heiß

hotel n Hotel nt

hot: ∼head n Hitzkopf m. ∼house n Treibhaus nt. ∼ly adv (fig) heiß, heftig. ∼plate n Tellerwärmer m; (of cooker) Kochplatte f. ∼ tap n Warmwasserhahn m. ∼-tempered a jähzornig. ∼-water bottle n Wärmflasche f

hound n Jagdhund m ● vt (fig) verfolgen

hour n Stunde f. ∼ly a & adv stündlich

house¹ n Haus nt; at my ∼ bei mir

house² vt unterbringen

house: ∼breaking n Einbruch m. ∼hold n Haushalt m. ∼holder n Hausinhaber(in) m(f). ∼keeper n Haushälterin f. ∼keeping n Hauswirtschaft f; (money) Haushaltsgeld nt. ∼plant n Zimmerpflanze f. ∼-trained a stubenrein. ∼-warming n have a ∼-warming party Einstand feiern. ∼wife n Hausfrau f. ∼work n Hausarbeit f

housing n Wohnungen pl; (Techn) Gehäuse nt

hovel n elende Hütte f

hover vi schweben. ∼craft n Luftkissenfahrzeug nt

how adv wie; ∼ do you do? guten Tag!; and ∼! und ob!

however adv (in question) wie; (nevertheless) jedoch, aber; ∼ small wie klein es auch sein mag

howl n Heulen nt ● vi heulen; <baby:> brüllen

hub n Nabe f

huddle vi ∼ together sich zusammendrängen

huff n in a ∼ beleidigt

hug n Umarmung f ● vt (pt/pp hugged) umarmen

huge *a*, **-ly** *adv* riesig

hull *n* (*Naut*) Rumpf *m*

hullo *int* = hallo

hum *n* Summen *nt*; Brummen *nt*
● *vt/i* (*pt/pp* **hummed**) summen;
<*motor:*> brummen

human *a* menschlich ● *n* Mensch *m*.
∼ **being** *n* Mensch *m*

humane *a*, **-ly** *adv* human

humanitarian *a* humanitär

humanity *n* Menschheit *f*

humble *a* (**-r**, **-st**), **-bly** *adv* demütig
● *vt* demütigen

humdrum *a* eintönig

humid *a* feucht. ∼**ity** *n* Feuchtigkeit
f

humiliat|e *vt* demütigen. ∼**ion** *n*
Demütigung *f*

humility *n* Demut *f*

humorous *a*, **-ly** *adv* humorvoll;
<*story*> humoristisch

humour *n* Humor *m*; (*mood*) Laune
f; **have a sense of** ∼ Humor haben

hump *n* Buckel *m*; (*of camel*) Höcker
m ● *vt* schleppen

hunch *n* (*idea*) Ahnung *f*

hunchback *n* Bucklige(r) *m/f*

hundred *a* **one/a** ∼ [ein]hundert
● *n* Hundert *nt*; (*written figure*)
Hundert *f*. ∼**th** *a* hundertste(r,s) ● *n*
Hundertstel *nt*. ∼**weight** *n* ≈
Zentner *m*

hung *see* hang

Hungarian *a* ungarisch ● *n*
Ungar(in) *m(f)*

Hungary *n* Ungarn *nt*

hunger *n* Hunger *m*. ∼**-strike** *n*
Hungerstreik *m*

hungry *a* (**-ier**, **-iest**), **-ily** *adv*
hungrig; **be** ∼ Hunger haben

hunt *n* Jagd *f*; (*for criminal*)
Fahndung *f* ● *vt/i* jagen; fahnden
nach <*criminal*>; ∼ **for** suchen. ∼**er**
n Jäger *m*; (*horse*) Jagdpferd *nt*.
∼**ing** *n* Jagd *f*

hurdle *n* (*Sport & fig*) Hürde *f*

hurl *vt* schleudern

hurrah, hurray *int* hurra! ● *n* Hurra
nt

hurricane *n* Orkan *m*

hurried *a*, **-ly** *adv* eilig; (*superficial*)
flüchtig

hurry *n* Eile *f*; **be in a** ∼ es eilig
haben ● *vi* (*pt/pp* **-ied**) sich beeilen;
(*go quickly*) eilen. ∼ **up** *vi* sich
beeilen ● *vt* antreiben

hurt *n* Schmerz *m* ● *vt/i* (*pt/pp* **hurt**)
weh tun (+ *dat*); (*injure*) verletzen;
(*offend*) kränken

hurtle *vi* ∼ **along** rasen

husband *n* [Ehe]mann *m*

hush *n* Stille *f* ● *vt* ∼ **up** vertuschen.
∼**ed** *a* gedämpft

husky *a* (**-ier**, **-iest**) heiser; (*burly*)
stämmig

hustle *vt* drängen ● *n* Gedränge *nt*

hut *n* Hütte *f*

hutch *n* [Kaninchen]stall *m*

hybrid *a* hybrid ● *n* Hybride *f*

hydraulic *a*, **-ally** *adv* hydraulisch

hydroelectric *a* hydroelektrisch

hydrogen *n* Wasserstoff *m*

hygien|e *n* Hygiene *f*. ∼**ic** *a*, **-ally**
adv hygienisch

hymn *n* Kirchenlied *nt*. ∼**-book** *n*
Gesangbuch *nt*

hyphen *n* Bindestrich *m*. ∼**ate** *vt*
mit Bindestrich schreiben

hypno|sis *n* Hypnose *f*. ∼**tic** *a*
hypnotisch

hypno|tism *n* Hypnotik *f*. ∼**tist** *n*
Hypnotiseur *m*. ∼**tize** *vt*
hypnotisieren

hypochondriac *n* Hypochonder *m*

hypocrisy *n* Heuchelei *f*

hypocrite *n* Heuchler(in) *m(f)*

hypodermic *a & n* ∼ [syringe]
Injektionsspritze *f*

hypothe|sis *n* Hypothese *f*. ∼**tical**
a, **-ly** *adv* hypothetisch

hyster|ia *n* Hysterie *f*. ∼**ical** *a*, **-ly**
adv hysterisch. ∼**ics** *npl*
hysterischer Anfall *m*

I i

I *pron* ich

ice *n* Eis *nt* ● *vt* mit Zuckerguss überziehen <*cake*>

ice: ~**berg** *n* Eisberg *m*. ~**box** *n* (*Amer*) Kühlschrank *m*. ~**cream** *n* [Speise]eis *nt*. ~**cube** *n* Eiswürfel *m*

Iceland *n* Island *nt*

ice: ~ **lolly** *n* Eis *nt* am Stiel. ~ **rink** *n* Eisbahn *f*

icicle *n* Eiszapfen *m*

icing *n* Zuckerguss *m*. ~ **sugar** *n* Puderzucker *m*

icon *n* Ikone *f*

icy *a* (-ier, -iest), **-ily** *adv* eisig; <*road*> vereist

idea *n* Idee *f*; (*conception*) Vorstellung *f*; **I have no** ~**!** ich habe keine Ahnung!

ideal *a* ideal ● *n* Ideal *nt*. ~**ism** *n* Idealismus *m*. ~**ist** *n* Idealist(in) *m(f)*. ~**istic** *a* idealistisch. ~**ize** *vt* idealisieren. ~**ly** *adv* ideal; (*in ideal circumstances*) idealerweise

identical *a* identisch; <*twins*> eineiig

identi|fication *n* Identifizierung *f*; (*proof of identity*) Ausweispapiere *pl*. ~**fy** *vt* (*pt/pp* **-ied**) identifizieren

identity *n* Identität *f*. ~ **card** *n* [Personal]ausweis *m*

idiom *n* [feste] Redewendung *f*. ~**atic** *a*, **-ally** *adv* idiomatisch

idiosyncrasy *n* Eigenart *f*

idiot *n* Idiot *m*. ~**ic** *a* idiotisch

idle *a* (-r, -st), **-ly** *adv* untätig; (*lazy*) faul; (*empty*) leer; <*machine*> nicht in Betrieb ● *vi* faulenzen; <*engine:*> leer laufen. ~**ness** *n* Untätigkeit *f*; Faulheit *f*

idol *n* Idol *nt*. ~**ize** *vt* vergöttern

idyllic *a* idyllisch

i.e. *abbr* (id est) d.h.

if *conj* wenn; (*whether*) ob; **as if** als ob

ignition *n* (*Auto*) Zündung *f*. ~ **key** *n* Zündschlüssel *m*

ignoramus *n* Ignorant *m*

ignoran|ce *n* Unwissenheit *f*. ~**t** *a* unwissend

ignore *vt* ignorieren

ill *a* krank; (*bad*) schlecht; **feel** ~ **at ease** sich unbehaglich fühlen ● *adv* schlecht

illegal *a*, **-ly** *adv* illegal

illegible *a*, **-bly** *adv* unleserlich

illegitimate *a* unehelich; <*claim*> unberechtigt

illicit *a*, **-ly** *adv* illegal

illiterate *a* **be** ~**te** nicht lesen und schreiben können

illness *n* Krankheit *f*

illogical *a*, **-ly** *adv* unlogisch

ill-treat *vt* misshandeln. ~**ment** *n* Misshandlung *f*

illuminat|e *vt* beleuchten. ~**ion** *n* Beleuchtung *f*

illusion *n* Illusion *f*; **be under the** ~ **that** sich (*dat*) einbilden, dass

illustrat|e *vt* illustrieren. ~**ion** *n* Illustration *f*

illustrious *a* berühmt

image *n* Bild *nt*; (*statue*) Standbild *nt*; (*exact likeness*) Ebenbild *nt*; [public] ~ Image *nt*

imagin|able *a* vorstellbar. ~**ary** *a* eingebildet

imagination *n* Fantasie *f*; (*fancy*) Einbildung *f*. ~**ive** *a*, **-ly** *adv* fantasievoll; (*full of ideas*) einfallsreich

imagine *vt* sich (*dat*) vorstellen; (*wrongly*) sich (*dat*) einbilden

imbalance *n* Unausgeglichenheit *f*

imbecile *n* Schwachsinnige(r) *m/f*; (*pej*) Idiot *m*

imitat|e *vt* nachahmen, imitieren. ~**ion** *n* Nachahmung *f*, Imitation *f*

immaculate *a*, **-ly** *adv* tadellos; (*Relig*) unbefleckt

immature *a* unreif

immediate *a* sofortig; (*nearest*) nächste(r,s). ~**ly** *adv* sofort; ~**ly**

next to unmittelbar neben ● *conj* sobald

immemorial *a* from time ∼ seit Urzeiten

immense *a*, **-ly** *adv* riesig; 🔢 enorm

immerse *vt* untertauchen

immigrant *n* Einwanderer *m*

immigration *n* Einwanderung *f*

imminent *a* be ∼ unmittelbar bevorstehen

immobile *a* unbeweglich

immodest *a* unbescheiden

immoral *a*, **-ly** *adv* unmoralisch. ∼**ity** *n* Unmoral *f*

immortal *a* unsterblich. ∼**ity** *n* Unsterblichkeit *f*. ∼**ize** *vt* verewigen

immune *a* immun (**to/from** gegen)

immunity *n* Immunität *f*

imp *n* Kobold *m*

impact *n* Aufprall *m*; (*collision*) Zusammenprall *m*; (*of bomb*) Einschlag *m*; (*fig*) Auswirkung *f*

impair *vt* beeinträchtigen

impart *vt* übermitteln (**to** *dat*); vermitteln <*knowledge*>

impartial *a* unparteiisch. ∼**ity** *n* Unparteilichkeit *f*

impassable *a* unpassierbar

impassioned *a* leidenschaftlich

impassive *a*, **-ly** *adv* unbewegt

impatien|ce *n* Ungeduld *f*. ∼**t** *a*, **-ly** *adv* ungeduldig

impeccable *a*, **-bly** *adv* tadellos

impede *vt* behindern

impediment *n* Hindernis *nt*; (*in speech*) Sprachfehler *m*

impel *vt* (*pt/pp* **impelled**) treiben

impending *a* bevorstehend

impenetrable *a* undurchdringlich

imperative *a* be ∼ dringend notwendig sein ● *n* (*Gram*) Imperativ *m*

imperceptible *a* nicht wahrnehmbar

imperfect *a* unvollkommen; (*faulty*) fehlerhaft ● *n* (*Gram*) Imperfekt *nt*. ∼**ion** *n*

Unvollkommenheit *f*; (*fault*) Fehler *m*

imperial *a* kaiserlich. ∼**ism** *n* Imperialismus *m*

impersonal *a* unpersönlich

impersonat|e *vt* sich ausgeben als; (*Theat*) nachahmen, imitieren. ∼**or** *n* Imitator *m*

impertinen|ce *n* Frechheit *f*. ∼**t** *a* frech

imperturbable *a* unerschütterlich

impetuous *a*, **-ly** *adv* ungestüm

impetus *n* Schwung *m*

implacable *a* unerbittlich

implant *vt* einpflanzen

implement[1] *n* Gerät *nt*

implement[2] *vt* ausführen

implication *n* Verwicklung *f*; ∼**s** *pl* Auswirkungen *pl*; **by** ∼ implizit

implicit *a*, **-ly** *adv* unausgesprochen; (*absolute*) unbedingt

implore *vt* anflehen

imply *vt* (*pt/pp* **-ied**) andeuten; **what are you** ∼**ing?** was wollen Sie damit sagen?

impolite *a*, **-ly** *adv* unhöflich

import[1] *n* Import *m*, Einfuhr *f*

import[2] *vt* importieren, einführen

importan|ce *n* Wichtigkeit *f*. ∼**t** *a* wichtig

importer *n* Importeur *m*

impos|e *vt* auferlegen (**on** *dat*) ● *vi* sich aufdrängen (**on** *dat*). ∼**ing** *a* eindrucksvoll

impossibility *n* Unmöglichkeit *f*

impossible *a*, **-bly** *adv* unmöglich

impostor *n* Betrüger(in) *m(f)*

impoten|ce *n* Machtlosigkeit *f*; (*Med*) Impotenz *f*. ∼**t** *a* machtlos; (*Med*) impotent

impoverished *a* verarmt

impracticable *a* undurchführbar

impractical *a* unpraktisch

imprecise *a* ungenau

impress *vt* beeindrucken; ∼ **sth [up]on s.o.** jdm etw einprägen

impression *n* Eindruck *m*; (*imitation*) Nachahmung *f*; (*edition*)

Auflage *f.* ~**ism** *n* Impressionismus *m*

impressive *a* eindrucksvoll

imprison *vt* gefangen halten; (*put in prison*) ins Gefängnis sperren

improbable *a* unwahrscheinlich

impromptu *a* improvisiert ● *adv* aus dem Stegreif

improper *a*, **-ly** *adv* inkorrekt; (*indecent*) unanständig

impropriety *n* Unkorrektheit *f*

improve *vt* verbessern; verschönern <*appearance*> ● *vi* sich bessern; ~ [up]on übertreffen. ~**ment** *n* Verbesserung *f*; (*in health*) Besserung *f*

improvise *vt/i* improvisieren

imprudent *a* unklug

impuden|ce *n* Frechheit *f.* ~**t** *a*, **-ly** *adv* frech

impuls|e *n* Impuls *m*; on [an] ~e impulsiv. ~**ive** *a*, **-ly** *adv* impulsiv

impur|e *a* unrein. ~**ity** *n* Unreinheit *f*

in *prep* in (+ *dat*/(*into*) + *acc*); **sit in the garden** im Garten sitzen; **go in the garden** in den Garten gehen; **in May** im Mai; **in 1992** [im Jahre] 1992; **in this heat** bei dieser Hitze; **in the evening** am Abend; **in the sky** am Himmel; **in the world** auf der Welt; **in the street** auf der Straße; **deaf in one ear** auf einem Ohr taub; **in the army** beim Militär; **in English/German** auf Englisch/Deutsch; **in ink/pencil** mit Tinte/Bleistift; **in a soft/loud voice** mit leiser/lauter Stimme; **in doing this, he ...** indem er das tut/tat, ... er ● *adv* (*at home*) zu Hause; (*indoors*) drinnen; **he's not in yet** er ist noch nicht da; **all in** alles inbegriffen; ([▣] *exhausted*) kaputt; **day in, day out** tagaus, tagein; **have it in for s.o.** [▣] es auf jdn abgesehen haben; **send/go in** hineinschicken/-gehen; **come/bring in** hereinkommen/-bringen ● *a* ([▣] *in fashion*) in ● *n* **the ins and outs** alle Einzelheiten *pl*

inability *n* Unfähigkeit *f*

inaccessible *a* unzugänglich

inaccura|cy *n* Ungenauigkeit *f.* ~**te** *a*, **-ly** *adv* ungenau

inac|tive *a* untätig. ~**tivity** *n* Untätigkeit *f*

inadequate *a*, **-ly** *adv* unzulänglich

inadmissible *a* unzulässig

inadvertently *adv* versehentlich

inadvisable *a* nicht ratsam

inane *a*, **-ly** *adv* albern

inanimate *a* unbelebt

inapplicable *a* nicht zutreffend

inappropriate *a* unangebracht

inarticulate *a* undeutlich; **be** ~ sich nicht gut ausdrücken können

inattentive *a* unaufmerksam

inaudible *a*, **-bly** *adv* unhörbar

inaugural *a* Antritts-

inauspicious *a* ungünstig

inborn *a* angeboren

inbred *a* angeboren

incalculable *a* nicht berechenbar; (*fig*) unabsehbar

incapable *a* unfähig; **be** ~ **of doing sth** nicht fähig sein, etw zu tun

incapacitate *vt* unfähig machen

incarnation *n* Inkarnation *f*

incendiary *a* & *n* ~ [bomb] Brandbombe *f*

incense[1] *n* Weihrauch *m*

incense[2] *vt* wütend machen

incentive *n* Anreiz *m*

incessant *a*, **-ly** *adv* unaufhörlich

incest *n* Inzest *m*, Blutschande *f*

inch *n* Zoll *m* ● *vi* ~ **forward** sich ganz langsam vorwärts schieben

incident *n* Zwischenfall *m*

incidental *a* nebensächlich; <*remark*> beiläufig; <*expenses*> Neben-. ~**ly** *adv* übrigens

incinerate *vt* verbrennen

incision *n* Einschnitt *m*

incisive *a* scharfsinnig

incite *vt* aufhetzen. ~**ment** *n* Aufhetzung *f*

inclement *a* rau

inclination *n* Neigung *f*

incline *vt* neigen; **be** ~**d to do sth** dazu neigen, etw zu tun ● *vi* sich neigen

inclu|de *vt* einschließen; (*contain*) enthalten; (*incorporate*) aufnehmen (in in + *acc*). **~ding** *prep* einschließlich (+ *gen*). **~sion** *n* Aufnahme *f*

inclusive *a* Inklusiv-; **~ of** einschließlich (+ *gen*)

incognito *adv* inkognito

incoherent *a*, **-ly** *adv* zusammenhanglos; (*incomprehensible*) unverständlich

income *n* Einkommen *nt*. **~ tax** *n* Einkommensteuer *f*

incoming *a* ankommend; <*mail, call*> eingehend

incomparable *a* unvergleichlich

incompatible *a* unvereinbar; be **~** <*people:*> nicht zueinander passen

incompeten|ce *n* Unfähigkeit *f*. **~t** *a* unfähig

incomplete *a* unvollständig

incomprehensible *a* unverständlich

inconceivable *a* undenkbar

inconclusive *a* nicht schlüssig

incongruous *a* unpassend

inconsiderate *a* rücksichtslos

inconsistent *a*, **-ly** *adv* widersprüchlich; (*illogical*) inkonsequent; be **~** <*things:*> nicht übereinstimmen

inconsolable *a* untröstlich

inconspicuous *a* unauffällig

incontinen|ce *n* Inkontinenz *f*. **~t** *a* inkontinent

inconvenien|ce *n* Unannehmlichkeit *f*; (*drawback*) Nachteil *m*. **~t** *a*, **-ly** *adv* ungünstig; be **~t for s.o.** jdm nicht passen

incorporate *vt* aufnehmen; (*contain*) enthalten

incorrect *a*, **-ly** *adv* inkorrekt

incorrigible *a* unverbesserlich

incorruptible *a* unbestechlich

increase[1] *n* Zunahme *f*; (*rise*) Erhöhung *f*; be on the **~** zunehmen

increas|e[2] *vt* vergrößern; (*raise*) erhöhen ● *vi* zunehmen; (*rise*) sich erhöhen. **~ing** *a*, **-ly** *adv* zunehmend

incredible *a*, **-bly** *adv* unglaublich

incredulous *a* ungläubig

incriminate *vt* (*Jur*) belasten

incur *vt* (*pt/pp* **incurred**) sich (*dat*) zuziehen; machen <*debts*>

incurable *a*, **-bly** *adv* unheilbar

indebted *a* verpflichtet (**to** *dat*)

indecent *a*, **-ly** *adv* unanständig

indecision *n* Unentschlossenheit *f*

indecisive *a* ergebnislos; <*person*> unentschlossen

indeed *adv* in der Tat, tatsächlich; **very much ~** sehr

indefatigable *a* unermüdlich

indefinite *a* unbestimmt. **~ly** *adv* unbegrenzt; <*postpone*> auf unbestimmte Zeit

indent *vt* (*Typ*) einrücken. **~ation** *n* Einrückung *f*; (*notch*) Kerbe *f*

independen|ce *n* Unabhängigkeit *f*; (*self-reliance*) Selbstständigkeit *f*. **~t** *a*, **-ly** *adv* unabhängig; selbstständig

indescribable *a*, **-bly** *adv* unbeschreiblich

indestructible *a* unzerstörbar

indeterminate *a* unbestimmt

index *n* Register *nt*

index: ~ card *n* Karteikarte *f*. **~ finger** *n* Zeigefinger *m*. **~-linked** *a* <*pension*> dynamisch

India *n* Indien *nt*. **~n** *a* indisch; (*American*) indianisch ● *n* Inder(in) *m(f)*; (*American*) Indianer(in) *m(f)*

Indian summer *n* Nachsommer *m*

indicat|e *vt* zeigen; (*point at*) zeigen auf (+ *acc*); (*hint*) andeuten; (*register*) anzeigen ● *vi* <*car:*> blinken. **~ion** *n* Anzeichen *nt*

indicative *n* (*Gram*) Indikativ *m*

indicator *n* (*Auto*) Blinker *m*

indifferen|ce *n* Gleichgültigkeit *f*. **~t** *a*, **-ly** *adv* gleichgültig; (*not good*) mittelmäßig

indigest|ible *a* unverdaulich; (*difficult to digest*) schwer verdaulich. **~ion** *n* Magenverstimmung *f*

indigna|nt *a*, **-ly** *adv* entrüstet, empört. **~tion** *n* Entrüstung *f*, Empörung *f*

indignity *n* Demütigung *f*

indirect *a*, **-ly** *adv* indirekt

indiscreet *a* indiskret

indiscretion *n* Indiskretion *f*

indispensable *a* unentbehrlich

indisposed *a* indisponiert

indisputable *a*, **-bly** *adv* unbestreitbar

indistinct *a*, **-ly** *adv* undeutlich

indistinguishable *a* be ~ nicht zu unterscheiden sein

individual *a*, **-ly** *adv* individuell; (*single*) einzeln ● *n* Individuum *nt*. **~ity** *n* Individualität *f*

indivisible *a* unteilbar

indoctrinate *vt* indoktrinieren

indolen|ce *n* Faulheit *f*. **~t** *a* faul

indomitable *a* unbeugsam

indoor *a* Innen-; <*clothes*> Haus-; <*plant*> Zimmer-; (*Sport*) Hallen-. **~s** *adv* im Haus, drinnen; go ~s ins Haus gehen

indulge *vt* frönen (+ *dat*); verwöhnen <*child*> ● *vi* ~ in frönen (+ *dat*). **~nce** *n* Nachgiebigkeit *f*; (*leniency*) Nachsicht *f*. **~nt** *a* [zu] nachgiebig; nachsichtig

industrial *a* Industrie-. **~ist** *n* Industrielle(r) *m*

industr|ious *a*, **-ly** *adv* fleißig. **~y** *n* Industrie *f*; (*zeal*) Fleiß *m*

inebriated *a* betrunken

inedible *a* nicht essbar

ineffective *a*, **-ly** *adv* unwirksam; <*person*> untauglich

inefficient *a* unfähig; <*organization*> nicht leistungsfähig; <*method*> nicht rationell

ineligible *a* nicht berechtigt

inept *a* ungeschickt

inequality *n* Ungleichheit *f*

inertia *n* Trägheit *f*

inescapable *a* unvermeidlich

inestimable *a* unschätzbar

inevitab|le *a* unvermeidlich. **~ly** *adv* zwangsläufig

inexact *a* ungenau

inexcusable *a* unverzeihlich

inexhaustible *a* unerschöpflich

inexpensive *a*, **-ly** *adv* preiswert

inexperience *n* Unerfahrenheit *f*. **~d** *a* unerfahren

inexplicable *a* unerklärlich

infallible *a* unfehlbar

infamous *a* niederträchtig; (*notorious*) berüchtigt

infan|cy *n* frühe Kindheit *f*; (*fig*) Anfangsstadium *nt*. **~t** *n* Kleinkind *nt*. **~tile** *a* kindisch

infantry *n* Infanterie *f*

infatuated *a* vernarrt (**with** in + *acc*)

infect *vt* anstecken, infizieren; **become ~ed** <*wound:*> sich infizieren. **~ion** *n* Infektion *f*. **~ious** *a* ansteckend

inferior *a* minderwertig; (*in rank*) untergeordnet ● *n* Untergebene(r) *m/f*

inferiority *n* Minderwertigkeit *f*. **~ complex** *n* Minderwertigkeitskomplex *m*

infern|al *a* höllisch. **~o** *n* flammendes Inferno *nt*

infertile *a* unfruchtbar

infest *vt* be **~ed with** befallen sein von; <*place*> verseucht sein mit

infidelity *n* Untreue *f*

infighting *n* (*fig*) interne Machtkämpfe *pl*

infinite *a*, **-ly** *adv* unendlich

infinitive *n* (*Gram*) Infinitiv *m*

infinity *n* Unendlichkeit *f*

inflame *vt* entzünden. **~d** *a* entzündet

inflammable *a* feuergefährlich

inflammation *n* Entzündung *f*

inflammatory *a* aufrührerisch

inflat|e *vt* aufblasen; (*with pump*) aufpumpen. **~ion** *n* Inflation *f*. **~ionary** *a* inflationär

inflexible *a* starr; <*person*> unbeugsam

inflict *vt* zufügen (**on** *dat*); versetzen <*blow*> (**on** *dat*)

influen|ce *n* Einfluss *m* ● *vt* beeinflussen. **~tial** *a* einflussreich

influenza *n* Grippe *f*

inform *vt* benachrichtigen; (*officially*) informieren; ~ s.o. of sth jdm etw mitteilen; **keep s.o.** ~ed jdn auf dem Laufenden halten ● *vi* ~ **against** denunzieren

informal *a*, **-ly** *adv* zwanglos; (*unofficial*) inoffiziell. ~ity *n* Zwanglosigkeit *f*

informant *n* Gewährsmann *m*

informat|ion *n* Auskunft *f*; **a piece of** ~ion eine Auskunft. ~ive *a* aufschlussreich; (*instructive*) lehrreich

informer *n* Spitzel *m*; (*Pol*) Denunziant *m*

infra-red *a* infrarot

infrequent *a*, **-ly** *adv* selten

infringe *vt/i* ~ [on] verstoßen gegen. ~ment *n* Verstoß *m*

infuriat|e *vt* wütend machen. ~ing *a* ärgerlich

ingenious *a* erfinderisch; <*thing*> raffiniert

ingenuity *n* Geschicklichkeit *f*

ingrained *a* eingefleischt; **be** ~ <*dirt*> tief sitzen

ingratiate *vt* ~ **oneself** sich einschmeicheln (**with** bei)

ingratitude *n* Undankbarkeit *f*

ingredient *n* (*Culin*) Zutat *f*

ingrowing *a* <*nail*> eingewachsen

inhabit *vt* bewohnen. ~ant *n* Einwohner(in) *m(f)*

inhale *vt/i* einatmen; (*Med & when smoking*) inhalieren

inherent *a* natürlich

inherit *vt* erben. ~ance *n* Erbschaft *f*, Erbe *nt*

inhibit|ed *a* gehemmt. ~ion *n* Hemmung *f*

inhospitable *a* ungastlich

inhuman *a* unmenschlich

inimitable *a* unnachahmlich

initial *a* anfänglich, Anfangs- ● *n* Anfangsbuchstabe *m*; **my** ~s meine Initialen. ~ly *adv* anfangs, am Anfang

initiat|e *vt* einführen. ~ion *n* Einführung *f*

initiative *n* Initiative *f*

inject *vt* einspritzen, injizieren. ~ion *n* Spritze *f*, Injektion *f*

injur|e *vt* verletzen. ~y *n* Verletzung *f*

injustice *n* Ungerechtigkeit *f*; **do s.o. an** ~ jdm unrecht tun

ink *n* Tinte *f*

inlaid *a* eingelegt

inland *a* Binnen- ● *adv* landeinwärts

in-laws *npl* 𝕀 Schwiegereltern *pl*

inlay *n* Einlegearbeit *f*

inlet *n* schmale Bucht *f*; (*Techn*) Zuleitung *f*

inmate *n* Insasse *m*

inn *n* Gasthaus *nt*

innate *a* angeboren

inner *a* innere(r,s). ~most *a* innerste(r,s)

innocen|ce *n* Unschuld *f*. ~t *a* unschuldig. ~tly *adv* in aller Unschuld

innocuous *a* harmlos

innovat|ion *n* Neuerung *f*. ~ive *a* innovativ. ~or *n* Neuerer *m*

innumerable *a* unzählig

inoculat|e *vt* impfen. ~ion *n* Impfung *f*

inoffensive *a* harmlos

inoperable *a* nicht operierbar

inopportune *a* unpassend

inorganic *a* anorganisch

in-patient *n* [stationär behandelter] Krankenhauspatient *m*

input *n* Input *m & nt*

inquest *n* gerichtliche Untersuchung *f* der Todesursache

inquir|e *vi* sich erkundigen (**about** nach); ~e **into** untersuchen ● *vt* sich erkundigen nach. ~y *n* Erkundigung *f*; (*investigation*) Untersuchung *f*

inquisitive *a*, **-ly** *adv* neugierig

insane *a* geisteskrank; (*fig*) wahnsinnig

insanitary *a* unhygienisch

insanity *n* Geisteskrankheit *f*

insatiable *a* unersättlich

inscription *n* Inschrift *f*

inscrutable *a* unergründlich; <*expression*> undurchdringlich

insect *n* Insekt *nt*. ~**icide** *n* Insektenvertilgungsmittel *nt*

insecur|e *a* nicht sicher; (*fig*) unsicher. ~**ity** *n* Unsicherheit *f*

insensitive *a* gefühllos; ~ **to** unempfindlich gegen

inseparable *a* untrennbar; (*people*) unzertrennlich

insert[1] *n* Einsatz *m*

insert[2] *vt* einfügen, einsetzen; einstecken <*key*>; einwerfen <*coin*>. ~**ion** *n* (*insert*) Einsatz *m*; (*in text*) Einfügung *f*

inside *n* Innenseite *f*; (*of house*) Innere(s) *nt* ● *attrib* Innen- ● *adv* innen; (*indoors*) drinnen; **go** ~ hineingehen; **come** ~ hereinkommen; ~ **out** links [herum]; **know sth** ~ **out** etw in- und auswendig kennen ● *prep* ~ **[of]** in (+ *dat*/ (*into*) + *acc*)

insight *n* Einblick *m* (**into** in + *acc*); (*understanding*) Einsicht *f*

insignificant *a* unbedeutend

insincere *a* unaufrichtig

insinuat|e *vt* andeuten. ~**ion** *n* Andeutung *f*

insipid *a* fade

insist *vi* darauf bestehen; ~ **on** bestehen auf (+ *dat*) ● *vt* ~ **that** darauf bestehen, dass. ~**ence** *n* Bestehen *nt*. ~**ent**, **-ly** *adv* beharrlich; **be** ~**ent** darauf bestehen

insole *n* Einlegesohle *f*

insolen|ce *n* Unverschämtheit *f*. ~**t** *a*, **-ly** *adv* unverschämt

insoluble *a* unlöslich; (*fig*) unlösbar

insolvent *a* zahlungsunfähig

insomnia *n* Schlaflosigkeit *f*

inspect *vt* inspizieren; (*test*) prüfen; kontrollieren <*ticket*>. ~**ion** *n* Inspektion *f*. ~**or** *n* Inspektor *m*; (*of tickets*) Kontrolleur *m*

inspiration *n* Inspiration *f*

inspire *vt* inspirieren

instability *n* Unbeständigkeit *f*; (*of person*) Labilität *f*

install *vt* installieren. ~**ation** *n* Installation *f*

instalment *n* (*Comm*) Rate *f*; (*of serial*) Fortsetzung *f*; (*Radio, TV*) Folge *f*

instance *n* Fall *m*; (*example*) Beispiel *nt*; **in the first** ~ zunächst; **for** ~ zum Beispiel

instant *a* sofortig; (*Culin*) Instant- ● *n* Augenblick *m*, Moment *m*. ~**aneous** *a* unverzüglich, unmittelbar

instant coffee *n* Pulverkaffee *m*

instantly *adv* sofort

instead *adv* statt dessen; ~ **of** statt (+ *gen*), anstelle von; ~ **of me** an meiner Stelle; ~ **of going** anstatt zu gehen

instep *n* Spann *m*, Rist *m*

instigat|e *vt* anstiften; einleiten <*proceedings*>. ~**ion** *n* Anstiftung *f*; **at his** ~**ion** auf seine Veranlassung

instil *vt* (*pt/pp* instilled) einprägen (**into s.o.** jdm)

instinct *n* Instinkt *m*. ~**ive** *a*, **-ly** *adv* instinktiv

institut|e *n* Institut *nt*. ~**ion** *n* Institution *f*; (*home*) Anstalt *f*

instruct *vt* unterrichten; (*order*) anweisen. ~**ion** *n* Unterricht *m*; Anweisung *f*; ~**ions** *pl* **for use** Gebrauchsanweisung *f*. ~**ive** *a* lehrreich. ~**or** *n* Lehrer(in) *m(f)*; (*Mil*) Ausbilder *m*

instrument *n* Instrument *nt*. ~**al** *a* Instrumental-

insubordi|nate *a* ungehorsam. ~**nation** *n* Ungehorsam *m*; (*Mil*) Insubordination *f*

insufficient *a*, **-ly** *adv* nicht genügend

insulat|e *vt* isolieren. ~**ing tape** *n* Isolierband *nt*. ~**ion** *n* Isolierung *f*

insult[1] *n* Beleidigung *f*

insult[2] *vt* beleidigen

insur|ance *n* Versicherung *f*. ~**e** *vt* versichern

intact *a* unbeschädigt; (*complete*) vollständig

intake *n* Aufnahme *f*

intangible *a* nicht greifbar

integral *a* wesentlich

integrat|e *vt* integrieren ● *vi* sich integrieren. **~ion** *n* Integration *f*

integrity *n* Integrität *f*

intellect *n* Intellekt *m*. **~ual** *a* intellektuell

intelligen|ce *n* Intelligenz *f*; (*Mil*) Nachrichtendienst *m*; (*information*) Meldungen *pl*. **~t** *a*, **-ly** *adv* intelligent

intelligible *a* verständlich

intend *vt* beabsichtigen; **be ~ed for** bestimmt sein für

intense *a* intensiv; <*pain*> stark. **~ly** *adv* äußerst; <*study*> intensiv

intensify *v* (*pt/pp* -ied) ● *vt* intensivieren ● *vi* zunehmen

intensity *n* Intensität *f*

intensive *a*, **-ly** *adv* intensiv; **be in ~ care** auf der Intensivstation sein

intent *a*, **-ly** *adv* aufmerksam; **~ on** (*absorbed in*) vertieft in (+ *acc*) ● *n* Absicht *f*

intention *n* Absicht *f*. **~al** *a*, **-ly** *adv* absichtlich

interacti|on *n* Wechselwirkung *f*. **~ve** *a* interaktiv

intercede *vi* Fürsprache einlegen (**on behalf of** für)

intercept *vt* abfangen

interchange *n* Austausch *m*; (*Auto*) Autobahnkreuz *nt*

intercom *n* [Gegen]sprechanlage *f*

intercourse *n* (*sexual*) Geschlechtsverkehr *m*

interest *n* Interesse *nt*; (*Comm*) Zinsen *pl* ● *vt* interessieren; **be ~ed** sich interessieren (**in** für). **~ing** *a* interessant. **~ rate** *n* Zinssatz *m*

interfere *vi* sich einmischen. **~nce** *n* Einmischung *f*; (*Radio, TV*) Störung *f*

interim *a* Zwischen-; (*temporary*) vorläufig

interior *a* innere(r,s), Innen- ● *n* Innere(s) *nt*

interject *vt* einwerfen. **~ion** *n* Interjektion *f*; (*remark*) Einwurf *m*

interlude *n* Pause *f*; (*performance*) Zwischenspiel *nt*

intermarry *vi* untereinander heiraten; <*different groups*> Mischehen schließen

intermediary *n* Vermittler(in) *m(f)*

intermediate *a* Zwischen-

interminable *a* endlos [lang]

intermittent *a* in Abständen auftretend

internal *a* innere(r,s); <*matter, dispute*> intern. **~ly** *adv* innerlich; <*deal with*> intern

international *a*, **-ly** *adv* international ● *n* Länderspiel *nt*; (*player*) Nationalspieler(in) *m(f)*

Internet *n* Internet *nt*; **on the ~** im Internet

internment *n* Internierung *f*

interplay *n* Wechselspiel *nt*

interpolate *vt* einwerfen

interpret *vt* interpretieren; auslegen <*text*>; deuten <*dream*>; (*translate*) dolmetschen ● *vi* dolmetschen. **~ation** *n* Interpretation *f*. **~er** *n* Dolmetscher(in) *m(f)*

interrogat|e *vt* verhören. **~ion** *n* Verhör *nt*

interrogative *a* & *n* **~ [pronoun]** Interrogativpronomen *nt*

interrupt *vt/i* unterbrechen; **don't ~!** red nicht dazwischen! **~ion** *n* Unterbrechung *f*

intersect *vi* sich kreuzen; (*Geom*) sich schneiden. **~ion** *n* Kreuzung *f*

interspersed *a* **~ with** durchsetzt mit

intertwine *vi* sich ineinanderschlingen

interval *n* Abstand *m*; (*Theat*) Pause *f*; (*Mus*) Intervall *nt*; **at hourly ~s** alle Stunde; **bright ~s** *pl* Aufheiterungen *pl*

interven|e *vi* eingreifen; (*occur*) dazwischenkommen. **~tion** *n* Eingreifen *nt*; (*Mil, Pol*) Intervention *f*

interview *n* (*Journ*) Interview *nt*; (*for job*) Vorstellungsgespräch *nt* ● *vt* interviewen; ein Vorstellungsgespräch führen mit. **~er** *n* Interviewer(in) *m(f)*

intimacy n Vertrautheit f; (sexual) Intimität f

intimate a, **-ly** adv vertraut; <friend> eng; (sexually) intim

intimidat|e vt einschüchtern. ~**ion** n Einschüchterung f

into prep in (+ acc); be ~ 🖪 sich auskennen mit; 7 ~ 21 21 [geteilt] durch 7

intolerable a unerträglich

intoleran|ce n Intoleranz f. ~**t** a intolerant

intonation n Tonfall m

intoxicat|ed a betrunken; (fig) berauscht. ~**ion** n Rausch m

intransigent a unnachgiebig

intransitive a, **-ly** adv intransitiv

intrepid a kühn, unerschrocken

intricate a kompliziert

intrigu|e n Intrige f ● vt faszinieren. ~**ing** a faszinierend

intrinsic a ~ value Eigenwert m

introduce vt vorstellen; (bring in, insert) einführen

introduct|ion n Einführung f; (to person) Vorstellung f; (to book) Einleitung f. ~**ory** a einleitend

introvert n introvertierter Mensch m

intru|de vi stören. ~**der** n Eindringling m. ~**sion** n Störung f

intuit|ion n Intuition f. ~**ive** a, **-ly** adv intuitiv

inundate vt überschwemmen

invade vt einfallen in (+ acc). ~**r** n Angreifer m

invalid¹ n Kranke(r) m/f

invalid² a ungültig

invaluable a unschätzbar; <person> unersetzlich

invariab|le a unveränderlich. ~**ly** adv immer

invasion n Invasion f

invent vt erfinden. ~**ion** n Erfindung f. ~**ive** a erfinderisch. ~**or** n Erfinder m

inventory n Bestandsliste f

invert vt umkehren. ~**ed commas** npl Anführungszeichen pl

invest vt investieren, anlegen; ~ **in** (🖪 buy) sich (dat) zulegen

investigat|e vt untersuchen. ~**ion** n Untersuchung f

invest|ment n Anlage f; be a good ~**ment** (fig) sich bezahlt machen. ~**or** n Kapitalanleger m

invidious a unerfreulich; (unfair) ungerecht

invincible a unbesiegbar

inviolable a unantastbar

invisible a unsichtbar

invitation n Einladung f

invit|e vt einladen. ~**ing** a einladend

invoice n Rechnung f ● vt ~ **s.o.** jdm eine Rechnung schicken

involuntary a, **-ily** adv unwillkürlich

involve vt beteiligen; (affect) betreffen; (implicate) verwickeln; (entail) mit sich bringen; (mean) bedeuten; be ~**d in** beteiligt sein an (+ dat); (implicated) verwickelt sein in (+ acc); get ~**d with s.o.** sich mit jdm einlassen. ~**d** a kompliziert

invulnerable a unverwundbar; <position> unangreifbar

inward a innere(r,s). ~**s** adv nach innen

iodine n Jod nt

IOU abbr Schuldschein m

Iran n der Iran

Iraq n der Irak

irascible a aufbrausend

irate a wütend

Ireland n Irland nt

iris n (Anat) Regenbogenhaut f, Iris f; (Bot) Schwertlilie f

Irish a irisch ● n the ~ pl die Iren. ~**man** n Ire m. ~**woman** n Irin f

iron a Eisen-; (fig) eisern ● n Eisen nt; (appliance) Bügeleisen nt ● vt/i bügeln

ironic[al] a ironisch

ironing n Bügeln nt; (articles) Bügelwäsche f. ~**board** n Bügelbrett nt

ironmonger n ~'s [shop] Haushaltswarengeschäft nt

irony n Ironie f

irrational a irrational

irreconcilable a unversöhnlich

irrefutable a unwiderlegbar

irregular a, **-ly** adv unregelmäßig; (against rules) regelwidrig. **~ity** n Unregelmäßigkeit f; Regelwidrigkeit f

irrelevant a irrelevant

irreparable a nicht wieder gutzumachen

irreplaceable a unersetzlich

irrepressible a unverwüstlich; be ~ <person:> nicht unterzukriegen sein

irresistible a unwiderstehlich

irresolute a unentschlossen

irrespective a ~ of ungeachtet (+ gen)

irresponsible a, **-bly** adv unverantwortlich; <person> verantwortungslos

irreverent a, **-ly** adv respektlos

irrevocable a, **-bly** adv unwiderruflich

irrigat|e vt bewässern. **~ion** n Bewässerung f

irritable a reizbar

irritant n Reizstoff m

irritat|e vt irritieren; (Med) reizen. **~ion** n Ärger m; (Med) Reizung f

is see be

Islam n der Islam. **~ic** a islamisch

island n Insel f. **~er** n Inselbewohner(in) m(f)

isolat|e vt isolieren. **~ed** a (remote) abgelegen; (single) einzeln. **~ion** n Isoliertheit f; (Med) Isolierung f

Israel n Israel nt. **~i** a israelisch ● n Israeli m/f

issue n Frage f; (outcome) Ergebnis nt; (of magazine, stamps) Ausgabe f; (offspring) Nachkommen pl ● vt ausgeben; ausstellen <passport>; erteilen <order>; herausgeben <book>; be ~d with sth etw erhalten

it
● pronoun
····▸ (as subject) er (m), sie (f), es (nt); (in impersonal sentence) es. where is the spoon? It's on the table wo ist der Löffel? Er liegt auf dem Tisch. it was very kind of you es war sehr nett von Ihnen. it's five o'clock es ist fünf Uhr

····▸ (as direct object) ihn (m), sie (f), es (nt). that's my pencil — give it to me das ist mein Bleistift — gib ihn mir.

····▸ (as dative object) ihm (m), ihr (f), ihm (nt). he found a track and followed it er fand eine Spur und folgte ihr.

····▸ (after prepositions)

> ! Combinations such as with it, from it, to it are translated by the prepositions with the prefix **da-** (**damit, davon, dazu**). Prepositions beginning with a vowel insert an 'r' (**daran, darauf, darüber**). I can't do anything with it ich kann nichts damit anfangen. don't lean on it! lehn dich nicht daran!

····▸ (the person in question) es. it's me ich bin's. is it you, Dad? bist du es, Vater? who is it? wer ist da?

Italian a italienisch ● n Italiener(in) m(f); (Lang) Italienisch nt

italics npl Kursivschrift f; in ~s kursiv

Italy n Italien nt

itch n Juckreiz m; I have an ~ es juckt mich ● vi jucken; I'm ~ing 🔲 es juckt mich (to zu). **~y** a be ~y jucken

item n Gegenstand m; (Comm) Artikel m; (on agenda) Punkt m; (on invoice) Posten m; (act) Nummer f

itinerary n [Reise]route f

its poss pron sein; (f) ihr

it's = it is, it has

itself pron selbst; (refl) sich; by ~ von selbst; (alone) allein

ivory n Elfenbein nt ● attrib Elfenbein-

ivy n Efeu m

Jj

jab n Stoß m; (📋 injection) Spritze f ● vt (pt/pp **jabbed**) stoßen

jabber vi plappern

jack n (Auto) Wagenheber m; (Cards) Bube m ● vt ~ **up** (Auto) aufbocken

jacket n Jacke f; (of book) Schutzumschlag m

jackpot n hit the ~ das große Los ziehen

jade n Jade m

jagged a zackig

jail = gaol

jam¹ n Marmelade f

jam² n Gedränge nt; (Auto) Stau m; (fam. difficulty) Klemme f ● v (pt/pp **jammed**) ● vt klemmen (**in** in + acc); stören <broadcast> ● vi klemmen

Jamaica n Jamaika nt

jangle vi klimpern ● vt klimpern mit

January n Januar m

Japan n Japan nt. ~**ese** a japanisch ● n Japaner(in) m(f); (Lang) Japanisch nt

jar n Glas nt; (earthenware) Topf m

jargon n Jargon m

jaunt n Ausflug m

jaunty a (-ier, -iest) **-ily** adv keck

javelin n Speer m

jaw n Kiefer m

jazz n Jazz m. ~**y** a knallig

jealous a, **-ly** adv eifersüchtig (of auf + acc). ~**y** n Eifersucht f

jeans npl Jeans pl

jeer vi johlen; ~ **at** verhöhnen

jelly n Gelee nt; (dessert) Götterspeise f. ~**fish** n Qualle f

jeopar|dize vt gefährden. ~**dy** n in ~**dy** gefährdet

jerk n Ruck m ● vt stoßen; (pull) reißen ● vi rucken; <limb, muscle:>

zucken. ~**ily** adv ruckweise. ~**y** a ruckartig

jersey n Pullover m; (Sport) Trikot nt; (fabric) Jersey m

jest n in ~ im Spaß

jet n (of water) [Wasser]strahl m; (nozzle) Düse f; (plane) Düsenflugzeug nt

jet: ~**-black** a pechschwarz. ~**-propelled** a mit Düsenantrieb

jetty n Landesteg m; (breakwater) Buhne f

Jew n Jude m /Jüdin f

jewel n Edelstein m; (fig) Juwel nt. ~**ler** n Juwelier m; ~**ler's [shop]** Juweliergeschäft nt. ~**lery** n Schmuck m

Jew|ess n Jüdin f. ~**ish** a jüdisch

jib vi (pt/pp **jibbed**) (fig) sich sträuben (**at** gegen)

jigsaw n ~ **[puzzle]** Puzzlespiel nt

jilt vt sitzen lassen

jingle n (rhyme) Verschen nt ● vi klimpern

jinx n 📋 it's got a ~ on it es ist verhext

jittery a 📋 nervös

job n Aufgabe f; (post) Stelle f, 📋 Job m; **be a** ~ 📋 nicht leicht sein; **it's a good** ~ **that** es ist [nur] gut, dass. ~**less** a arbeitslos

jockey n Jockei m

jocular a, **-ly** adv spaßhaft

jog n Stoß m ● v (pt/pp **jogged**) ● vt anstoßen; ~ **s.o.'s memory** jds Gedächtnis nachhelfen ● vi (Sport) joggen. ~**ging** n Jogging nt

john n (Amer 📋) Klo nt

join n Nahtstelle f ● vt verbinden (**to** mit); sich anschließen (+ dat) <person>; (become member of) beitreten (+ dat); eintreten in (+ acc) <firm> ● vi <roads:> sich treffen. ~ **in** vi mitmachen. ~ **up** vi (Mil) Soldat werden ● vt zusammenfügen

joint a, **-ly** adv gemeinsam ● n Gelenk nt; (in wood, brickwork) Fuge f; (Culin) Braten m; (📋 bar) Lokal nt

jok|e n Scherz m; (funny story) Witz m; (trick) Streich m ● vi scherzen. ~**er** n Witzbold m; (Cards) Joker m.

~ing n ~ing apart Spaß beiseite. ~ingly adv im Spaß

jolly a (-ier, -iest) lustig ● adv 🔳 sehr

jolt n Ruck m ● vt einen Ruck versetzen (+ dat) ● vi holpern

Jordan n Jordanien nt

jostle vt anrempeln

jot vt (pt/pp jotted) ~ **[down]** sich (dat) notieren

journal n Zeitschrift f; (diary) Tagebuch nt. ~**ese** n Zeitungsjargon m. ~**ism** n Journalismus m. ~**ist** n Journalist(in) m(f)

journey n Reise f

jovial a lustig

joy n Freude f. ~**ful** a, -**ly** adv freudig, froh. ~**ride** n 🔳 Spritztour f [im gestohlenen Auto]

jubil|ant a überglücklich. ~**ation** n Jubel m

jubilee n Jubiläum nt

judder vi rucken

judge n Richter m; (of competition) Preisrichter m ● vt beurteilen; (estimate) [ein]schätzen ● vi urteilen (by nach). ~**ment** n Beurteilung f; (Jur) Urteil nt; (fig) Urteilsvermögen nt

judic|ial a gerichtlich. ~**ious** a klug

jug n Kanne f; (small) Kännchen nt; (for water, wine) Krug m

juggle vi jonglieren. ~**r** n Jongleur m

juice n Saft m

juicy a (-ier, -iest) saftig; 🔳 <story> pikant

juke-box n Musikbox f

July n Juli m

jumble n Durcheinander nt ● vt ~ **[up]** durcheinander bringen. ~ **sale** n [Wohltätigkeits]basar m

jump n Sprung m; (in prices) Anstieg m; (in horse racing) Hindernis nt ● vi springen; (start) zusammenzucken; **make s.o.** ~ jdn erschrecken; ~ **at** (fig) sofort zugreifen bei <offer>; ~ **to conclusions** voreilige Schlüsse ziehen ● vt überspringen. ~ **up** vi aufspringen

jumper n Pullover m, Pulli m

jumpy a nervös

junction n Kreuzung f; (Rail) Knotenpunkt m

June n Juni m

jungle n Dschungel m

junior a jünger; (in rank) untergeordnet; (Sport) Junioren- ● n Junior m

junk n Gerümpel nt, Trödel m

junkie n 🔳 Fixer m

junk-shop n Trödelladen m

jurisdiction n Gerichtsbarkeit f

jury n the ~ die Geschworenen pl; (for competition) die Jury

just a gerecht ● adv gerade; (only) nur; (simply) einfach; (exactly) genau; ~ **as tall** ebenso groß; **I'm** ~ **going** ich gehe schon

justice n Gerechtigkeit f; **do** ~ **to** gerecht werden (+ dat)

justifiab|le a berechtigt. ~**ly** adv berechtigterweise

justi|fication n Rechtfertigung f. ~**fy** vt (pt/pp -ied) rechtfertigen

justly adv zu Recht

jut vi (pt/pp jutted) ~ **out** vorstehen

juvenile a jugendlich; (childish) kindisch ● n Jugendliche(r) m/f. ~ **delinquency** n Jugendkriminalität f

Kk

kangaroo n Känguru nt

kebab n Spießchen nt

keel n Kiel m ● vi ~ **over** umkippen; (Naut) kentern

keen a (-er, -est) (sharp) scharf; (intense) groß; (eager) eifrig, begeistert; ~ **on** 🔳 erpicht auf (+ acc); ~ **on s.o.** von jdm sehr

angetan; **be ~ to do sth** etw gerne
machen wollen. **~ly** adv tief.
~ness n Eifer m, Begeisterung f
keep n (*maintenance*) Unterhalt m;
(*of castle*) Bergfried m; **for ~s** für
immer ● v (pt/pp **kept**) ● vt behalten;
(*store*) aufbewahren; (*not throw
away*) aufheben; (*support*)
unterhalten; (*detain*) aufhalten;
freihalten <*seat*>; halten <*promise,
animals*>; führen, haben <*shop*>;
einhalten <*law, rules*>; ~ **s.o.
waiting** jdn warten lassen; ~ **sth to
oneself** etw nicht weitersagen ● vi
(*remain*) bleiben; <*food*> sich
halten; ~ **left/right** sich links/rechts
halten; ~ **on doing sth** etw
weitermachen; (*repeatedly*) etw
dauernd machen; ~ **in with** sich gut
stellen mit. ~ **up** vi Schritt halten
● vt (*continue*) weitermachen
keep|er n Wärter(in) m(f). **~ing** n
be in ~ing with passen zu
kennel n Hundehütte f; **~s** pl
(*boarding*) Hundepension f;
(*breeding*) Zwinger m
Kenya n Kenia nt
kept see **keep**
kerb n Bordstein m
kernel n Kern m
ketchup n Ketchup m
kettle n [Wasser]kessel m; **put the ~
on** Wasser aufsetzen
key n Schlüssel m; (*Mus*) Tonart f; (*of
piano, typewriter*) Taste f ● vt ~ **in**
eintasten
key: **~board** n Tastatur f; (*Mus*)
Klaviatur f. **~hole** n Schlüsselloch
nt. **~ring** n Schlüsselring m
khaki a khakifarben ● n Khaki nt
kick n [Fuß]tritt m; **for ~s** 🔲 zum
Spaß ● vt treten; ~ **the bucket** 🔲
abkratzen ● vi <*animal*>
ausschlagen
kid n (🔲 *child*) Kind nt ● vt (pt/pp
kidded) 🔲 ~ **s.o.** jdm etwas
vormachen
kidnap vt (pt/pp **-napped**) entführen.
~per n Entführer m. **~ping** n
Entführung f
kidney n Niere f

kill vt töten; 🔲 totschlagen <*time*>: ~
two birds with one stone zwei
Fliegen mit einer Klappe schlagen.
~er n Mörder(in) m(f). **~ing** n
Tötung f; (*murder*) Mord m
killjoy n Spielverderber m
kilo n Kilo nt
kilo:: **~gram** n Kilogramm nt.
~metre n Kilometer m. **~watt** n
Kilowatt nt
kilt n Schottenrock m
kind¹ n Art f; (*brand, type*) Sorte f;
what ~ of car? was für ein Auto? ~
of 🔲 irgendwie
kind² a (-er, -est) nett; ~ **to animals**
gut zu Tieren
kind|ly a (-ier, -iest) nett ● adv
netterweise; (*if you please*) gefälligst.
~ness n Güte f; (*favour*) Gefallen m
king n König m; (*Draughts*) Dame f.
~dom n Königreich nt; (*fig & Relig*)
Reich nt
king: **~fisher** n Eisvogel m. **~-
sized** a extragroß
kink n Knick m. **~y** a 🔲 pervers
kiosk n Kiosk m
kip n **have a ~** 🔲 pennen ● vi (pt/pp
kipped) 🔲 pennen
kipper n Räucherhering m
kiss n Kuss m ● vt/i küssen
kit n Ausrüstung f; (*tools*) Werkzeug
nt; (*construction ~*) Bausatz m ● vt
(pt/pp **kitted**) **~out** ausrüsten
kitchen n Küche f ● attrib Küchen-.
~ette n Kochnische f
kitchen: **~garden** n
Gemüsegarten m. **~sink** n
Spülbecken nt
kite n Drachen m
kitten n Kätzchen nt
kitty n (*money*) [gemeinsame] Kasse f
knack n Trick m, Dreh m
knead vt kneten
knee n Knie nt. **~cap** n
Kniescheibe f
kneel vi (pt/pp **knelt**) knien; ~
[down] sich [nieder]knien
knelt see **kneel**
knew see **know**
knickers npl Schlüpfer m

knife n (pl **knives**) Messer nt ● vt einen Messerstich versetzen (+ dat)

knight n Ritter m; (Chess) Springer m ● vt adeln

knit vt/i (pt/pp **knitted**) stricken; ~ **one's brow** die Stirn runzeln. **~ting** n Stricken nt; (work) Strickzeug nt. **~ting-needle** n Stricknadel f. **~wear** n Strickwaren pl

knives npl see **knife**

knob n Knopf m; (on door) Knauf m; (small lump) Beule f. **~bly** a knorrig; (bony) knochig

knock n Klopfen nt; (blow) Schlag m; **there was a ~** es klopfte ● vt anstoßen; (🄸 criticize) heruntermachen; ~ **a hole in sth** ein Loch in etw (acc) schlagen; ~ **one's head** sich (dat) den Kopf stoßen (on an + dat) ● vi klopfen. ~ **about** vt schlagen ● vi 🄸 herumkommen. ~ **down** vt herunterwerfen; (with fist) niederschlagen; (in car) anfahren; (demolish) abreißen; (🄸 reduce) herabsetzen. ~ **off** vt herunterwerfen; (🄸 steal) klauen; (🄸 complete quickly) hinhauen ● vi (🄸 cease work) Feierabend machen. ~ **out** vt ausschlagen; (make unconscious) bewusstlos schlagen; (Boxing) k.o. schlagen. ~ **over** vt umwerfen; (in car) anfahren

knock: ~-down a **~-down prices** Schleuderpreise pl. **~er** n Türklopfer m. **~-out** n (Boxing) K.O. m

knot n Knoten m ● vt (pt/pp **knotted**) knoten

know vt/i (pt **knew**, pp **known**) wissen; kennen <person>; können <language>; **get to ~** kennen lernen ● n **in the ~** 🄸 im Bild

know: ~-all n 🄸 Alleswisser m. **~-how** n 🄸 [Sach]kenntnis f. **~ing** a wissend. **~ingly** adv wissend; (intentionally) wissentlich

knowledge n Kenntnis f (of von/gen); (general) Wissen nt; (specialized) Kenntnisse pl. **~able** a **be ~able** viel wissen

knuckle n [Finger]knöchel m; (Culin) Hachse f

kosher a koscher

kudos n 🄸 Prestige nt

lab n 🄸 Labor nt

label n Etikett nt ● vt (pt/pp **labelled**) etikettieren

laboratory n Labor nt

laborious a, **-ly** adv mühsam

labour n Arbeit f; (workers) Arbeitskräfte pl; (Med) Wehen pl; **L~** (Pol) die Labourpartei ● attrib Labour- ● vi arbeiten ● vt (fig) sich lange auslassen über (+ acc). **~er** n Arbeiter m

labour-saving a arbeitssparend

lace n Spitze f; (of shoe) Schnürsenkel m ● vt schnüren

lack n Mangel m (of an + dat) ● vt I **~ the time** mir fehlt die Zeit ● vi **be ~ing** fehlen

laconic a, **-ally** adv lakonisch

lacquer n Lack m; (for hair) [Haar]spray m

lad n Junge m

ladder n Leiter f; (in fabric) Laufmasche f

ladle n [Schöpf]kelle f ● vt schöpfen

lady n Dame f; (title) Lady f

lady: ~bird n, (Amer) **~bug** n Marienkäfer m. **~like** a damenhaft

lag¹ vi (pt/pp **lagged**) ~ **behind** zurückbleiben; (fig) nachhinken

lag² vt (pt/pp **lagged**) umwickeln <pipes>

lager n Lagerbier nt

laid see **lay³**

lain see **lie²**

lake n See m

lamb n Lamm nt

lame a (-r, -st) lahm

lament n Klage f; (song) Klagelied nt ● vt beklagen ● vi klagen

laminated *a* laminiert

lamp *n* Lampe *f*; (*in street*) Laterne *f*. ~ **post** *n* Laternenpfahl *m*. ~**shade** *n* Lampenschirm *m*

lance *vt* (*Med*) aufschneiden

land *n* Land *nt*; **plot of** ~ Grundstück *nt* ● *vt/i* landen; ~ **s.o. with sth** 🔺 jdm etw aufhalsen

landing *n* Landung *f*; (*top of stairs*) Treppenflur *m*. ~**stage** *n* Landesteg *m*

land: ~**lady** *n* Wirtin *f*. ~**lord** *n* Wirt *m*; (*of land*) Grundbesitzer *m*; (*of building*) Hausbesitzer *m*. ~**mark** *n* Erkennungszeichen *nt*; (*fig*) Meilenstein *m*. ~**owner** *n* Grundbesitzer *m*. ~**scape** *n* Landschaft *f*. ~**slide** *n* Erdrutsch *m*

lane *n* kleine Landstraße *f*; (*Auto*) Spur *f*; (*Sport*) Bahn *f*; **'get in** ~**'** (*Auto*) 'bitte einordnen'

language *n* Sprache *f*; (*speech, style*) Ausdrucksweise *f*

languid *a*, **-ly** *adv* träge

languish *vi* schmachten

lanky *a* (**-ier, -iest**) schlaksig

lantern *n* Laterne *f*

lap[1] *n* Schoß *m*

lap[2] *n* (*Sport*) Runde *f*; (*of journey*) Etappe *f* ● *vi* (*pt/pp* **lapped**) plätschern (**against** gegen)

lap[3] *vt* (*pt/pp* **lapped**) ~ **up** aufschlecken

lapel *n* Revers *nt*

lapse *n* Fehler *m*; (*moral*) Fehltritt *m*; (*of time*) Zeitspanne *f* ● *vi* (*expire*) erlöschen; ~ **into** verfallen in (+ *acc*)

lard *n* [Schweine]schmalz *nt*

larder *n* Speisekammer *f*

large *a* (**-r, -st**) *& adv* groß; **by and** ~ im Großen und Ganzen; **at** ~ auf freiem Fuß. ~**ly** *adv* großenteils

lark[1] *n* (*bird*) Lerche *f*

lark[2] *n* (*joke*) Jux *m* ● *vi* ~ **about** herumalbern

laryngitis *n* Kehlkopfentzündung *f*

larynx *n* Kehlkopf *m*

laser *n* Laser *m*

lash *n* Peitschenhieb *m*; (*eyelash*) Wimper *f* ● *vt* peitschen; (*tie*) festbinden (**to** an + *acc*). ~ **out** *vi* um sich schlagen; (*spend*) viel Geld ausgeben (**on** für)

lass *n* Mädchen *nt*

lasso *n* Lasso *nt*

last *a & n* letzte(r,s); ~ **night** heute *od* gestern Nacht; (*evening*) gestern Abend; **at** ~ endlich; **for the** ~ **time** zum letzten Mal; **the** ~ **but one** der/die/das vorletzte ● *adv* zuletzt; (*last time*) das letzte Mal; **he/she went** ~ er/sie ging als Letzter/Letzte ● *vi* dauern; <*weather:*> sich halten; <*relationship:*> halten. ~**ing** *a* dauerhaft. ~**ly** *adv* schließlich, zum Schluss

latch *n* [einfache] Klinke *f*

late *a & adv* (**-r, -st**) spät; (*delayed*) verspätet; (*deceased*) verstorben; **the** ~**st news** die neuesten Nachrichten; **stay up** ~ bis spät aufbleiben; **arrive** ~ zu spät ankommen; **I am** ~ ich komme zu spät *od* habe mich verspätet; **the train is** ~ der Zug hat Verspätung. ~**comer** *n* Zuspätkommende(r) *m/f*. ~**ly** *adv* in letzter Zeit. ~**ness** *n* Zuspätkommen *nt*; (*delay*) Verspätung *f*

later *a & adv* später; ~ **on** nachher

lateral *a* seitlich

lather *n* [Seifen]schaum *m*

Latin *a* lateinisch ● *n* Latein *nt*. ~ **America** *n* Lateinamerika *nt*

latitude *n* (*Geog*) Breite *f*; (*fig*) Freiheit *f*

latter *a & n* **the** ~ der/die/das Letztere

Latvia *n* Lettland *nt*

laudable *a* lobenswert

laugh *n* Lachen *nt*; **with a** ~ lachend ● *vi* lachen (**at/about** über + *acc*); ~ **at s.o.** (*mock*) jdn auslachen. ~**able** *a* lachhaft, lächerlich

laughter *n* Gelächter *nt*

launch[1] *n* (*boat*) Barkasse *f*

launch[2] *n* Stapellauf *m*; (*of rocket*) Abschuss *m*; (*of product*) Lancierung *f* ● *vt* vom Stapel lassen <*ship*>; zu Wasser lassen <*lifeboat*>; abschießen

<*rocket*>; starten <*attack*>; (*Comm*) lancieren <*product*>

laund(e)rette *n* Münzwäscherei *f*

laundry *n* Wäscherei *f*; (*clothes*) Wäsche *f*

laurel *n* Lorbeer *m*

lava *n* Lava *f*

lavatory *n* Toilette *f*

lavender *n* Lavendel *m*

lavish *a*, **-ly** *adv* großzügig; (*wasteful*) verschwenderisch ● *vt* ∼ **sth on s.o.** jdn mit etw überschütten

law *n* Gesetz *nt*; (*system*) Recht *nt*; **study** ∼ Jura studieren; ∼ **and order** Recht und Ordnung

law: ∼**-abiding** *a* gesetzestreu. ∼ **court** *n* Gerichtshof *m*. ∼**ful** *a* rechtmäßig. ∼**less** *a* gesetzlos

lawn *n* Rasen *m*. ∼**-mower** *n* Rasenmäher *m*

lawyer *n* Rechtsanwalt *m* /-anwältin *f*

lax *a* lax, locker

laxative *n* Abführmittel *nt*

laxity *n* Laxheit *f*

lay[1] *see* lie[2]

lay[2] *vt* (*pt/pp* laid) legen; decken <*table*>; ∼ **a trap** eine Falle stellen. ∼ **down** *vt* hinlegen; festlegen <*rules, conditions*>. ∼ **off** *vt* entlassen <*workers*> ● *vi* (Ⅱ *stop*) aufhören. ∼ **out** *vt* hinlegen; aufbahren <*corpse*>; anlegen <*garden*>; (*Typ*) gestalten

lay-by *n* Parkbucht *f*

layer *n* Schicht *f*

lay: ∼**man** *n* Laie *m*. ∼**out** *n* Anordnung *f*; (*design*) Gestaltung *f*; (*Typ*) Layout *nt*

laze *vi* ∼**[about]** faulenzen

laziness *n* Faulheit *f*

lazy *a* (-ier, -iest) faul. ∼**-bones** *n* Faulenzer *m*

lead[1] *n* Blei *nt*; (*of pencil*) [Bleistift]mine *f*

lead[2] *n* Führung *f*; (*leash*) Leine *f*; (*flex*) Schnur *f*; (*clue*) Hinweis *m*, Spur *f*; (*Theat*) Hauptrolle *f*; (*distance ahead*) Vorsprung *m*; **be in the** ∼ in Führung liegen ● *vt/i* (*pt/pp* led) führen; leiten <*team*>; (*induce*)

bringen; (*at cards*) ausspielen; ∼ **the way** vorangehen; ∼ **up to sth** (*fig*) etw (*dat*) vorangehen

leader *n* Führer *m*; (*of expedition, group*) Leiter(in) *m(f)*; (*of orchestra*) Konzertmeister *m*; (*in newspaper*) Leitartikel *m*. ∼**ship** *n* Führung *f*; Leitung *f*

leading *a* führend; ∼ **lady** Hauptdarstellerin *f*

leaf *n* (*pl* leaves) Blatt *nt* ● *vi* ∼ **through sth** etw durchblättern. ∼**let** *n* Merkblatt *nt*; (*advertising*) Reklameblatt *nt*; (*political*) Flugblatt *nt*

league *n* Liga *f*

leak *n* (*hole*) undichte Stelle *f*; (*Naut*) Leck *nt*; (*of gas*) Gasausfluss *m* ● *vi* undicht sein; <*ship:*> leck sein, lecken; <*liquid:*> auslaufen; <*gas:*> ausströmen ● *vt* auslaufen lassen; ∼ **sth to s.o.** (*fig*) jdm etw zuspielen. ∼**y** *a* undicht; (*Naut*) leck

lean[1] *a* (-er, -est) mager

lean[2] *v* (*pt/pp* leaned *or* leant) ● *vt* lehnen (**against/on** an + *acc*) ● *vi* <*person*> sich lehnen (**against/on** an + *acc*); (*not be straight*) sich neigen; **be** ∼**ing against** lehnen an (+ *dat*). ∼ **back** *vi* sich zurücklehnen. ∼ **forward** *vi* sich vorbeugen. ∼ **out** *vi* sich hinauslehnen. ∼ **over** *vi* sich vorbeugen

leaning *a* schief ● *n* Neigung *f*

leap *n* Sprung *m* ● *vi* (*pt/pp* leapt *or* leaped) springen; **he leapt at it** Ⅱ er griff sofort zu. ∼ **year** *n* Schaltjahr *nt*

learn *vt/i* (*pt/pp* learnt *or* learned) lernen; (*hear*) erfahren; ∼ **to swim** schwimmen lernen

learn|ed *a* gelehrt. ∼**er** *n* Anfänger *m*; ∼**er [driver]** Fahrschüler(in) *m(f)*. ∼**ing** *n* Gelehrsamkeit *f*

lease *n* Pacht *f*; (*contract*) Mietvertrag *m* ● *vt* pachten

leash *n* Leine *f*

least *a* geringste(r,s) ● **n the** ∼ das wenigste; **at** ∼ wenigstens, mindestens; **not in the** ∼ nicht im Geringsten ● *adv* am wenigsten

leather *n* Leder *nt*

leave n Erlaubnis f; (holiday) Urlaub m; on ~ auf Urlaub; take one's ~ sich verabschieden ● v (pt/pp left) ● vt lassen; (go out of, abandon) verlassen; (forget) liegen lassen; (bequeath) vermachen (to dat); ~ it to me! überlassen Sie es mir! there is nothing left es ist nichts mehr übrig ● vi [weg]gehen/-fahren; <train, bus:> abfahren. ~ **behind** vt zurücklassen; (forget) liegen lassen. ~ **out** vt liegen lassen; (leave outside) draußen lassen; (omit) auslassen

leaves see leaf

Lebanon n Libanon m

lecherous a lüstern

lecture n Vortrag m; (Univ) Vorlesung f; (reproof) Strafpredigt f ● vi einen Vortrag/eine Vorlesung halten (on über + acc) ● vt ~ s.o. jdm eine Strafpredigt halten. ~**r** n Vortragende(r) m|f; (Univ) Dozent(in) m(f)

led see lead²

ledge n Leiste f; (shelf, of window) Sims m; (in rock) Vorsprung m

ledger n Hauptbuch nt

leech n Blutegel m

leek n Stange f Porree; ~**s** pl Porree m

left¹ see leave

left² a linke(r,s) ● adv links; <go> nach links ● n linke Seite f; on the ~ links; from/to the ~ von/nach links; the ~ (Pol) die Linke

left: ~**-handed** a linkshändig. ~**luggage [office]** n Gepäckaufbewahrung f. ~**overs** npl Reste pl. ~**-wing** a (Pol) linke(r,s)

leg n Bein nt; (Culin) Keule f; (of journey) Etappe f

legacy n Vermächtnis nt, Erbschaft f

legal a, -ly adv gesetzlich; <matters> rechtlich; <department, position> Rechts-; be ~ [gesetzlich] erlaubt sein

legality n Legalität f

legend n Legende f. ~**ary** a legendär

legible a, -bly adv leserlich

legion n Legion f

legislat|e vi Gesetze erlassen. ~**ion** n Gesetzgebung f; (laws) Gesetze pl

legislative a gesetzgebend

legitimate a rechtmäßig; (justifiable) berechtigt

leisure n Freizeit f; at your ~ wenn Sie Zeit haben. ~**ly** a gemächlich

lemon n Zitrone f. ~**ade** n Zitronenlimonade f

lend vt (pt/pp lent) leihen (s.o. sth jdm etw)

length n Länge f; (piece) Stück nt; (of wallpaper) Bahn f; (of time) Dauer f

length|en vt länger machen ● vi länger werden. ~**ways** adv der Länge nach

lengthy a (-ier, -iest) langwierig

lenien|t a, -ly adv nachsichtig

lens n Linse f; (Phot) Objektiv nt; (of spectacles) Glas nt

lent see lend

Lent n Fastenzeit f

lentil n (Bot) Linse f

leopard n Leopard m

leotard n Trikot nt

lesbian a lesbisch ● n Lesbierin f

less a, adv, n & prep weniger; ~ and ~ immer weniger

lessen vt verringern ● vi nachlassen; <value:> abnehmen

lesser a geringere(r,s)

lesson n Stunde f; (in textbook) Lektion f; (Relig) Lesung f; teach s.o. a ~ (fig) jdm eine Lehre erteilen

lest conj (liter) damit ... nicht

let vt (pt/pp let, pres p letting) lassen; (rent) vermieten; ~ alone (not to mention) geschweige denn; ~ us go gehen wir; ~ me know sagen Sie mir Bescheid; ~ oneself in for sth 🛈 sich (dat) etw einbrocken. ~ **down** vt hinunter-/herunterlassen; (lengthen) länger machen; ~ s.o. down 🛈 jdn im Stich lassen; (disappoint) jdn enttäuschen. ~ **in** vt hereinlassen. ~ **off** vt abfeuern <gun>; hochgehen lassen <firework, bomb>; (emit) ausstoßen; (excuse from) befreien

von; (*not punish*) frei ausgehen
lassen. **~ out** *vt* hinaus-/
herauslassen; (*make larger*)
auslassen. **~ through** *vt*
durchlassen. **~ up** *vi* 🔲 nachlassen
let-down *n* Enttäuschung *f*, 🔲
Reinfall *m*
lethal *a* tödlich
letharg|ic *a* lethargisch. **~y** *n*
Lethargie *f*
letter *n* Brief *m*; (*of alphabet*)
Buchstabe *m*. **~-box** *n* Briefkasten
m. **~-head** *n* Briefkopf *m*. **~ing** *n*
Beschriftung *f*
lettuce *n* [Kopf]salat *m*
let-up *n* 🔲 Nachlassen *nt*
level *a* eben; (*horizontal*)
waagerecht; (*in height*) auf gleicher
Höhe; <*spoonful*> gestrichen; **one's
~ best** sein Möglichstes ● *n* Höhe *f*;
(*fig*) Ebene *f*, Niveau *nt*; (*stage*) Stufe
f; **on the ~** 🔲 ehrlich ● *vt* (*pt/pp*
levelled) einebnen
level crossing *n* Bahnübergang *m*
lever *n* Hebel *m* ● *vt* **~ up** mit einem
Hebel anheben. **~age** *n* Hebelkraft *f*
lewd *a* (-er, -est) anstößig
liabilit|y *n* Haftung *f*; **~ies** *pl*
Verbindlichkeiten *pl*
liable *a* haftbar; **be ~ to do sth** etw
leicht tun können
liaise *vi* 🔲 Verbindungsperson sein
liaison *n* Verbindung *f*; (*affair*)
Verhältnis *nt*
liar *n* Lügner(in) *m(f)*
libel *n* Verleumdung *f* ● *vt* (*pt/pp*
libelled) verleumden. **~lous** *a*
verleumderisch
liberal *a*, **-ly** *adv* tolerant; (*generous*)
großzügig. **L~** *a* (*Pol*) liberal ● *n*
Liberale(r) *m/f*
liberat|e *vt* befreien. **~ed** *a*
<*woman*> emanzipiert. **~ion** *n*
Befreiung *f*. **~or** *n* Befreier *m*
liberty *n* Freiheit *f*; **take liberties**
sich (*dat*) Freiheiten erlauben
librarian *n* Bibliothekar(in) *m(f)*
library *n* Bibliothek *f*
Libya *n* Libyen *nt*
lice *see* **louse**

licence *n* Genehmigung *f*; (*Comm*)
Lizenz *f*; (*for TV*) ≈ Fernsehgebühr *f*;
(*for driving*) Führerschein *m*; (*for
alcohol*) Schankkonzession *f*
license *vt* eine Genehmigung/
(*Comm*) Lizenz erteilen (+ *dat*); **be
~d** <*car*:> zugelassen sein;
<*restaurant*:> Schankkonzession
haben. **~-plate** *n* (*Amer*)
Nummernschild *nt*
lick *n* Lecken *nt*; **a ~ of paint** ein
bisschen Farbe ● *vt* lecken; (🔲
defeat) schlagen
lid *n* Deckel *m*; (*of eye*) Lid *nt*
lie¹ *n* Lüge *f*; **tell a ~** lügen ● *vi* (*pt/
pp* **lied**, *pres p* **lying**) lügen; **~ to**
belügen
lie² *vi* (*pt* **lay**, *pp* **lain**, *pres p* **lying**)
liegen; **here ~s ...** hier ruht ... **~
down** *vi* sich hinlegen
lie-in *n* **have a ~** [sich] ausschlafen
lieu *n* **in ~ of** statt (+ *gen*)
lieutenant *n* Oberleutnant *m*
life *n* (*pl* **lives**) Leben *nt*; **lose one's ~**
ums Leben kommen
life: ~-boat *n* Rettungsboot *nt*. **~-
guard** *n* Lebensretter *m*. **~-jacket**
n Schwimmweste *f*. **~less** *a* leblos.
~like *a* naturgetreu. **~long** *a*
lebenslang. **~ preserver** *n* (*Amer*)
Rettungsring *m*. **~-size(d)** *a* ... in
Lebensgröße. **~time** *n* Leben *nt*; **in
s.o.'s ~time** zu jds Lebzeiten; **the
chance of a ~time** eine einmalige
Gelegenheit
lift *n* Aufzug *m*, Lift *m*; **give s.o. a ~**
jdn mitnehmen; **get a ~**
mitgenommen werden ● *vt* heben;
aufheben <*restrictions*> ● *vi* <*fog*:>
sich lichten. **~ up** *vt* hochheben
light¹ *a* (-er, -est) (*not dark*) hell; **~
blue** hellblau ● *n* Licht *nt*; (*lamp*)
Lampe *f*; **have you [got] a ~?** haben
Sie Feuer? ● *vt* (*pt/pp* **lit** *or* **lighted**)
anzünden <*fire, cigarette*>;
(*illuminate*) beleuchten. **~ up** *vi*
<*face*:> sich erhellen
light² *a* (-er, -est) (*not heavy*) leicht; **~
sentence** milde Strafe *f* ● *adv*
travel ~ mit wenig Gepäck reisen
light-bulb *n* Glühbirne *f*
lighten¹ *vt* heller machen

lighten² vt leichter machen <*load*>

lighter n Feuerzeug nt

light: ~-hearted a unbekümmert.
~house n Leuchtturm m. **~ing** n
Beleuchtung f. **~ly** adv leicht; **get
off ~ly** glimpflich davonkommen

lightning n Blitz m

lightweight a leicht ● n (*Boxing*)
Leichtgewicht nt

like¹ a ähnlich; (*same*) gleich ● prep
wie; (*similar to*) ähnlich (+ *dat*); **~
this** so; **what's he ~?** wie ist er
denn? ● conj (🟦 *as*) wie; (*Amer: as
if*) als ob

like² vt mögen; **I should/would ~** ich
möchte; **I ~ the car** das Auto gefällt
mir; **~ dancing/singing** gern
tanzen/singen ● n **~s and
dislikes** pl Vorlieben und
Abneigungen pl

like|able a sympathisch. **~lihood**
n Wahrscheinlichkeit f. **~ly** a (-ier,
-iest) & adv wahrscheinlich; **not ~ly!**
🟦 auf gar keinen Fall!

like-minded a gleich gesinnt

liken vt vergleichen (**to** mit)

like|ness n Ähnlichkeit f. **~wise**
adv ebenso

liking n Vorliebe f; **is it to your ~?**
gefällt es Ihnen?

lilac n Flieder m

lily n Lilie f

limb n Glied nt

lime n (*fruit*) Limone f; (*tree*) Linde f.
~light n **be in the ~light** im
Rampenlicht stehen

limit n Grenze f; (*limitation*)
Beschränkung f; **that's the ~!** 🟦 das
ist doch die Höhe! ● vt beschränken
(**to** auf + *acc*). **~ation** n
Beschränkung f; **~ed** a beschränkt.
~ed company Gesellschaft f mit
beschränkter Haftung

limousine n Limousine f

limp¹ n Hinken nt ● vi hinken

limp² a (-er -est), **-ly** adv schlaff

limpid a klar

line¹ n Linie f; (*length of rope, cord*)
Leine f; (*Teleph*) Leitung f; (*of
writing*) Zeile f; (*row*) Reihe f;
(*wrinkle*) Falte f; (*of business*)

Branche f; (*Amer: queue*) Schlange f;
in ~ with gemäß (+ *dat*) ● vt säumen
<*street*>

line² vt füttern <*garment*>; (*Techn*)
auskleiden

lined¹ a (*wrinkled*) faltig; <*paper*>
liniert

lined² a <*garment*> gefüttert

linen n Leinen nt; (*articles*) Wäsche f

liner n Passagierschiff nt

linesman n (*Sport*) Linienrichter m

linger vi [zurück]bleiben

lingerie n Damenunterwäsche f

linguist n Sprachkundige(r) m/f

linguistic a, **-ally** adv sprachlich

lining n (*of garment*) Futter nt;
(*Techn*) Auskleidung f

link n (*of chain*) Glied nt (*fig*)
Verbindung f ● vt verbinden; **~
arms** sich unterhaken

links n or npl Golfplatz m

lint n Verbandstoff m

lion n Löwe m; **~'s share** (*fig*)
Löwenanteil m. **~ess** n Löwin f

lip n Lippe f; (*edge*) Rand m; (*of jug*)
Schnabel m

lip: ~-reading n Lippenlesen nt. **~-
service** n **pay ~service** ein
Lippenbekenntnis ablegen (**to** zu).
~stick n Lippenstift m

liqueur n Likör m

liquid n Flüssigkeit f ● a flüssig

liquidation n Liquidation f

liquidize vt [im Mixer] pürieren.
~r n Mixer m

liquor n Alkohol m. **~ store** n
(*Amer*) Spirituosengeschäft nt

lisp n Lispeln nt ● vt/i lispeln

list¹ n Liste f ● vt aufführen

list² vi <*ship:*> Schlagseite haben

listen vi zuhören (**to** *dat*); **~ to the
radio** Radio hören. **~er** n
Zuhörer(in) m(f); (*Radio*) Hörer(in)
m(f)

listless a, **-ly** adv lustlos

lit see light¹

literacy n Lese- und
Schreibfertigkeit f

literal a wörtlich. **~ly** adv
buchstäblich

literary *a* literarisch

literate *a* be ~ lesen und schreiben können

literature *n* Literatur *f*; 🗎 Informationsmaterial *nt*

lithe *a* geschmeidig

Lithuania *n* Litauen *nt*

litre *n* Liter *m* & *nt*

litter *n* Abfall *m*; (*Zool*) Wurf *m*. ~**bin** *n* Abfalleimer *m*

little *a* klein; (*not much*) wenig ● *adv* & *n* wenig; **a** ~ ein bisschen/wenig; ~ **by** ~ nach und nach

live¹ *a* lebendig; <*ammunition*> scharf; ~ **broadcast** Live-Sendung *f*; **be** ~ (*Electr*) unter Strom stehen

live² *vi* leben; (*reside*) wohnen. ~ **on** *vt* leben von; (*eat*) sich ernähren von ● *vi* weiterleben

liveli|hood *n* Lebensunterhalt *m*. ~**ness** *n* Lebendigkeit *f*

lively *a* (-ier, -iest) lebhaft, lebendig

liver *n* Leber *f*

lives *see* life

livid *a* 🗎 wütend

living *a* lebend ● *n* earn one's ~ seinen Lebensunterhalt verdienen. ~**-room** *n* Wohnzimmer *nt*

lizard *n* Eidechse *f*

load *n* Last *f*; (*quantity*) Ladung *f*; (*Electr*) Belastung *f*; ~**s of** 🗎 jede Menge ● *vt* laden <*goods, gun*>; beladen <*vehicle*>; ~ **a camera** einen Film in eine Kamera einlegen. ~**ed** *a* beladen; (🗎 *rich*) steinreich

loaf *n* (*pl* loaves) Brot *nt*

loan *n* Leihgabe *f*; (*money*) Darlehen *nt*; **on** ~ geliehen ● *vt* leihen (*to dat*)

loath *a* be ~ to do sth etw ungern tun

loath|e *vt* verabscheuen. ~**ing** *n* Abscheu *m*

loaves *see* loaf¹

lobby *n* Foyer *nt*; (*anteroom*) Vorraum *m*; (*Pol*) Lobby *f*

lobster *n* Hummer *m*

local *a* hiesig; <*time, traffic*> Orts-; ~ **anaesthetic** örtliche Betäubung; **I'm not** ~ ich bin nicht von hier ● *n* Hiesige(r) *m/f*; (🗎 *public house*)

Stammkneipe *f*. ~ **call** *n* (*Teleph*) Ortsgespräch *nt*

locality *n* Gegend *f*

locally *adv* am Ort

locat|e *vt* ausfindig machen; **be** ~**ed** sich befinden. ~**ion** *n* Lage *f*; filmed **on** ~**ion** als Außenaufnahme gedreht

lock¹ *n* (*hair*) Strähne *f*

lock² *n* (*on door*) Schloss *nt*; (*on canal*) Schleuse *f* ● *vt* abschließen ● *vi* sich abschließen lassen. ~ **in** *vt* einschließen. ~ **out** *vt* ausschließen. ~ **up** *vt* abschließen; einsperren <*person*>

locker *n* Schließfach *nt*; (*Mil*) Spind *m*

lock: ~**out** *n* Aussperrung *f*. ~**smith** *n* Schlosser *m*

locomotive *n* Lokomotive *f*

locum *n* Vertreter(in) *m(f)*

locust *n* Heuschrecke *f*

lodge *n* (*porter's*) Pförtnerhaus *nt* ● *vt* (*submit*) einreichen; (*deposit*) deponieren ● *vi* zur Untermiete wohnen (with bei); (*become fixed*) stecken bleiben. ~**r** *n* Untermieter(in) *m(f)*

lodging *n* Unterkunft *f*; ~**s** *npl* möbliertes Zimmer *nt*

loft *n* Dachboden *m*

lofty *a* (-ier, -iest) hoch

log *n* Baumstamm *m*; (*for fire*) [Holz]scheit *nt*; **sleep like a** ~ 🗎 wie ein Murmeltier schlafen ● *vi* ~ **off** sich abmelden; ~ **on** sich anmelden

loggerheads *npl* be at ~ 🗎 sich in den Haaren liegen

logic *n* Logik *f*. ~**al** *a*, **-ly** *adv* logisch

logo *n* Symbol *nt*, Logo *nt*

loiter *vi* herumlungern

loll *vi* sich lümmeln

loll|ipop *n* Lutscher *m*. ~**y** *n* Lutscher *m*; (🗎 *money*) Moneten *pl*

London *n* London *nt* ● *attrib* Londoner. ~**er** *n* Londoner(in) *m(f)*

lone *a* einzeln. ~**liness** *n* Einsamkeit *f*

lonely *a* (-ier, -iest) einsam

lone|r n Einzelgänger m. ~**some** a einsam

long[1] a (**-er, -est**) lang; <*journey*> weit; a ~ **time** lange; a ~ **way** weit; **in the** ~ **run** auf lange Sicht; (*in the end*) letzten Endes ● adv lange; **all day** ~ den ganzen Tag; **not** ~ **ago** vor kurzem; **before** ~ bald; **no** ~**er** nicht mehr; **as** or **so** ~**as** solange; **so** ~! T tschüs!

long[2] vi ~ **for** sich sehnen nach

long-distance a Fern-; (*Sport*) Langstrecken-

longing a, **-ly** adv sehnsüchtig ● n Sehnsucht f

longitude n (*Geog*) Länge f

long: ~ **jump** n Weitsprung m. ~**lived** a langlebig. ~**-range** a (*Mil, Aviat*) Langstrecken-; <*forecast*> langfristig. ~**-sighted** a weitsichtig. ~**-sleeved** a langärmelig. ~**-suffering** a langmütig. ~**-term** a langfristig. ~ **wave** n Langwelle. ~**-winded** a langatmig

loo n T Klo nt

look n Blick m; (*appearance*) Aussehen nt; **[good]** ~**s** pl [gutes] Aussehen nt; **have a** ~ **at** sich (dat) ansehen; **go and have a** ~ sieh mal nach ● vi sehen; (*search*) nachsehen; (*seem*) aussehen; **don't** ~ sieh nicht hin; ~ **here!** hören Sie mal! ~ **at** ansehen; ~ **for** suchen; ~ **forward to** sich freuen auf (+ *acc*); ~ **in on** vorbeischauen bei; ~ **into** (*examine*) nachgehen (+ *dat*); ~ **like** aussehen wie; ~ **on to** <*room:*> gehen auf (+ *acc*). ~ **after** vt betreuen. ~ **down** vi hinuntersehen; ~ **down on s.o.** (*fig*) auf jdn herabsehen. ~ **out** vi hinaus-/heraussehen; (*take care*) aufpassen; ~ **out for** Ausschau halten nach; ~ **out!** Vorsicht! ~ **round** vi sich umsehen. ~ **up** vi aufblicken; ~ **up to s.o.** (*fig*) zu jdm aufsehen ● vt nachschlagen <*word*>

look-out n Wache f; (*prospect*) Aussicht f; **be on the** ~ **for** Ausschau halten nach

loom[1] n Webstuhl m

loom[2] vi auftauchen

loony a T verrückt

loop n Schlinge f; (*in road*) Schleife f. ~**hole** n Hintertürchen nt; (*in the law*) Lücke f

loose a (**-r, -st**), **-ly** adv lose; (*not tight enough*) locker; (*inexact*) frei; **be at a** ~ **end** nichts zu tun haben. ~ **change** n Kleingeld nt

loosen vt lockern

loot n Beute f ● vt/i plündern. ~**er** n Plünderer m

lop vt (*pt/pp* lopped) stutzen

lopsided a schief

lord n Herr m; (*title*) Lord m; **House of L**~**s** ≈ Oberhaus nt; **the L**~**'s Prayer** das Vaterunser

lorry n Last[kraft]wagen m

lose v (*pt/pp* lost) ● vt verlieren; (*miss*) verpassen ● vi verlieren; <*clock:*> nachgehen; **get lost** verloren gehen; <*person*> sich verlaufen. ~**r** n Verlierer m

loss n Verlust m; **be at a** ~ nicht mehr weiter wissen

lost see lose. ~ **property office** n Fundbüro nt

lot[1] n Los nt; (*at auction*) Posten m; **draw** ~**s** losen (for um)

lot[2] n **the** ~ alle; (*everything*) alles; **a** ~ **[of]** viel; (*many*) viele; ~**s of** eine Menge; **it has changed a** ~ es hat sich sehr verändert

lotion n Lotion f

lottery n Lotterie f. ~ **ticket** n Los nt

loud a (**-er, -est**), **-ly** adv laut; <*colours*> grell ● adv [**out**] ~ laut. ~**speaker** n Lautsprecher m

lounge n Wohnzimmer nt; (*in hotel*) Aufenthaltsraum m. ● vi sich lümmeln

louse n (*pl* lice) Laus f

lousy a (**-ier, -iest**) T lausig

lout n Flegel m, Lümmel m

lovable a liebenswert

love n Liebe f; (*Tennis*) null; **in** ~ verliebt ● vt lieben; ~ **doing sth** etw sehr gerne machen. ~**-affair** n Liebesverhältnis nt. ~ **letter** n Liebesbrief m

lovely a (**-ier, -iest**) schön

lover *n* Liebhaber *m*

love: ~ **song** *n* Liebeslied *nt*. ~ **story** *n* Liebesgeschichte *f*

loving *a*, **-ly** *adv* liebevoll

low *a* (**-er**, **-est**) niedrig; <*cloud, note*> tief; <*voice*> leise; (*depressed*) niedergeschlagen ● *adv* niedrig; <*fly, sing*> tief; <*speak*> leise ● *n* (*Meteorol*) Tief *nt*; (*fig*) Tiefstand *m*

low: ~**brow** *a* geistig anspruchslos. ~**cut** *a* <*dress*> tief ausgeschnitten

lower *a & adv see* low ● *vt* niedriger machen; (*let down*) herunterlassen; (*reduce*) senken

low: ~**-fat** *a* fettarm. ~**lands** *npl* Tiefland *nt*. ~ **tide** *n* Ebbe *f*

loyal *a*, **-ly** *adv* treu. ~**ty** *n* Treue *f*

lozenge *n* Pastille *f*

Ltd *abbr* (Limited) GmbH

lubricant *n* Schmiermittel *nt*

lubricat|e *vt* schmieren. ~**ion** *n* Schmierung *f*

lucid *a* klar. ~**ity** *n* Klarheit *f*

luck *n* Glück *nt*; **bad** ~ Pech *nt*; **good** ~**!** viel Glück! ~**ily** *adv* glücklicherweise, zum Glück

lucky *a* (**-ier**, **-iest**) glücklich; <*day, number*> Glücks-; **be** ~ Glück haben; <*thing:*> Glück bringen

lucrative *a* einträglich

ludicrous *a* lächerlich

lug *vt* (*pt/pp* lugged) 🗉 schleppen

luggage *n* Gepäck *nt*

luggage: ~**-rack** *in* Gepäckablage *f*. ~**-van** *n* Gepäckwagen *m*

lukewarm *a* lauwarm

lull *n* Pause *f* ● *vt* ~ **to sleep** einschläfern

lullaby *n* Wiegenlied *nt*

lumber *n* Gerümpel *nt*; (*Amer: timber*) Bauholz *nt* ● *vt* ~ **s.o. with sth** jdm etw aufhalsen. ~**jack** *n* (*Amer*) Holzfäller *m*

luminous *a* leuchtend

lump *n* Klumpen *m*; (*of sugar*) Stück *nt*; (*swelling*) Beule *f*; (*in breast*) Knoten *m*; (*tumour*) Geschwulst *f*; **a** ~ **in one's throat** 🗉 ein Kloß im Hals

lump: ~ **sugar** *n* Würfelzucker *m*. ~ **sum** *n* Pauschalsumme *f*

lumpy *a* (**-ier**, **-iest**) klumpig

lunacy *n* Wahnsinn *m*

lunar *a* Mond-

lunatic *n* Wahnsinnige(r) *m/f*

lunch *n* Mittagessen *nt* ● *vi* zu Mittag essen

luncheon *n* Mittagessen *nt*. ~ **voucher** *n* Essensbon *m*

lunch: ~**-hour** *n* Mittagspause *f*. ~**-time** *n* Mittagszeit *f*

lung *n* Lungenflügel *m*; ~**s** *pl* Lunge *f*

lunge *vi* sich stürzen (**at** auf + *acc*)

lurch[1] *n* **leave in the** ~ 🗉 im Stich lassen

lurch[2] *vi* <*person:*> torkeln

lure *vt* locken

lurid *a* grell; (*sensational*) reißerisch

lurk *vi* lauern

luscious *a* lecker, köstlich

lush *a* üppig

lust *n* Begierde *f*. ~**ful** *a* lüstern

lustre *n* Glanz *m*

lusty *a* (**-ier**, **-iest**) kräftig

luxuriant *a* üppig

luxurious *a*, **-ly** *adv* luxuriös

luxury *n* Luxus *m* ● *attrib* Luxus-

lying *see* lie[1], lie[2]

lynch *vt* lynchen

lyric *a* lyrisch. ~**al** *a* lyrisch; (*enthusiastic*) schwärmerisch. ~ **poetry** *n* Lyrik *f*. ~**s** *npl* [Lied]text *m*

Mm

mac *n* 🗉 Regenmantel *m*

macabre *a* makaber

macaroni *n* Makkaroni *pl*

machinations *pl* Machenschaften *pl*

machine n Maschine f ● vt (sew) mit der Maschine nähen; (Techn) maschinell bearbeiten. **~-gun** n Maschinengewehr nt

machinery n Maschinerie f

mackerel n inv Makrele f

mackintosh n Regenmantel m

mad a (madder, maddest) verrückt; (dog) tollwütig; (fam: angry) böse (at auf + acc)

madam n gnädige Frau f

madden vt (make angry) wütend machen

made see make; **~ to measure** maßgeschneidert

mad|ly adv 🔢 wahnsinnig. **~man** n Irre(r) m. **~ness** n Wahnsinn m

madonna n Madonna f

magazine n Zeitschrift f; (Mil, Phot) Magazin nt

maggot n Made f

magic n Zauber m; (tricks) Zauberkunst f ● a magisch; <word, wand> Zauber-. **~al** a zauberhaft

magician n Zauberer m; (entertainer) Zauberkünstler m

magistrate n ≈ Friedensrichter m

magnet n Magnet m. **~ic** a magnetisch. **~ism** n Magnetismus m

magnification n Vergrößerung f

magnificen|ce n Großartigkeit f. **~t** a, **-ly** adv großartig

magnify vt (pt/pp **-ied**) vergrößern; (exaggerate) übertreiben. **~ing glass** n Vergrößerungsglas nt

magnitude n Größe f; (importance) Bedeutung f

magpie n Elster f

mahogany n Mahagoni nt

maid n Dienstmädchen nt; old **~** (pej) alte Jungfer f

maiden a <speech, voyage> Jungfern-. **~ name** n Mädchenname m

mail n Post f ● vt mit der Post schicken

mail: ~bag n Postsack m. **~box** n (Amer) Briefkasten m. **~ing list** n Postversandliste f. **~man** n (Amer)

Briefträger m. **~-order firm** n Versandhaus nt

maim vt verstümmeln

main a Haupt- ● n (water, gas, electricity) Hauptleitung f

main: ~land n Festland nt. **~ly** adv hauptsächlich. **~stay** n (fig) Stütze f. **~ street** n Hauptstraße f

maintain vt aufrechterhalten; (keep in repair) instand halten; (support) unterhalten; (claim) behaupten

maintenance n Aufrechterhaltung f; (care) Instandhaltung f; (allowance) Unterhalt m

maize n Mais m

majestic a, **-ally** adv majestätisch

majesty n Majestät f

major a größer ● n (Mil) Major m; (Mus) Dur nt ● vi **~** in als Hauptfach studieren

majority n Mehrheit f; in the **~** in der Mehrzahl

major road n Hauptverkehrsstraße f

make n (brand) Marke f ● v (pt/pp **made**) ● vt machen; (force) zwingen; (earn) verdienen; halten <speech>; treffen <decision>; erreichen <destination> ● vi **~ do** vi zurechtkommen (with mit). **~ for** vi zusteuern auf (+ acc). **~ off** vi sich davonmachen (with mit). **~ out** vt (distinguish) ausmachen; (write out) ausstellen; (assert) behaupten. **~ up** vt (constitute) bilden; (invent) erfinden; (apply cosmetics to) schminken; **~ up one's mind** sich entschließen ● vi sich versöhnen; **~ up for sth** etw wieder gutmachen; **~ up for lost time** verlorene Zeit aufholen

make-believe n Phantasie f

maker n Hersteller m

make: ~ shift a behelfsmäßig ● n Notbehelf m. **~-up** n Make-up nt

maladjusted a verhaltensgestört

male a männlich ● n Mann m; (animal) Männchen nt. **~ nurse** n Krankenpfleger m. **~ voice choir** n Männerchor m

malice n Bosheit f

malicious *a*, **-ly** *adv* böswillig

malign *vt* verleumden

malignant *a* bösartig

mallet *n* Holzhammer *m*

malnutrition *n* Unterernährung *f*

malpractice *n* Berufsvergehen *nt*

malt *n* Malz *nt*

maltreat *vt* misshandeln. **~ment** *n* Misshandlung *f*

mammal *n* Säugetier *nt*

mammoth *a* riesig

man *n* (*pl* **men**) Mann *m*; (*mankind*) der Mensch; (*chess*) Figur *f*; (*draughts*) Stein *m* ● *vt* (*pt/pp* **manned**) bemannen <*ship*>; bedienen <*pump*>; besetzen <*counter*>

manage *vt* leiten; verwalten <*estate*>; (*cope with*) fertig werden mit; **~ to do sth** es schaffen, etw zu tun ● *vi* zurechtkommen; **~ on** auskommen mit. **~able** *a* <*tool*> handlich; <*person*> fügsam. **~ment** *n* Leitung *f*; **the ~ment** die Geschäftsleitung *f*

manager *n* Geschäftsführer *m*; (*of bank*) Direktor *m*; (*of estate*) Verwalter *m*; (*Sport*) [Chef]trainer *m*. **~ess** *n* Geschäftsführerin *f*. **~ial** *a* **~ial staff** Führungskräfte *pl*

managing *a* **~ director** Generaldirektor *m*

mandat|e *n* Mandat *nt*. **~ory** *a* obligatorisch

mane *n* Mähne *f*

manful *a*, **-ly** *adv* mannhaft

man: ~handle *vt* grob behandeln <*person*>. **~hole** *n* Kanalschacht *m*. **~hood** *n* Mannesalter *nt*; (*quality*) Männlichkeit *f*. **~-hour** *n* Arbeitsstunde *f*. **~-hunt** *n* Fahndung *f*

mania *n* Manie *f*. **~c** *n* Wahnsinnige(r) *m/f*

manicure *n* Maniküre *f* ● *vt* maniküren

manifest *a*, **-ly** *adv* offensichtlich

manifesto *n* Manifest *nt*

manifold *a* mannigfaltig

manipulat|e *vt* handhaben; (*pej*) manipulieren. **~ion** *n* Manipulation *f*

mankind *n* die Menschheit

manly *a* männlich

man-made *a* künstlich. **~ fibre** *n* Kunstfaser *f*

manner *n* Weise *f*; (*kind, behaviour*) Art *f*; **[good/bad] ~s** [gute/schlechte] Manieren *pl*. **~ism** *n* Angewohnheit *f*

manœuvrable *a* manövrierfähig

manœuvre *n* Manöver *nt* ● *vt/i* manövrieren

manor *n* Gutshof *m*; (*house*) Gutshaus *nt*

manpower *n* Arbeitskräfte *pl*

mansion *n* Villa *f*

manslaughter *n* Totschlag *m*

mantelpiece *n* Kaminsims *m & nt*

manual *a* Hand- ● *n* Handbuch *nt*

manufacture *vt* herstellen ● *n* Herstellung *f*. **~r** *n* Hersteller *m*

manure *n* Mist *m*

manuscript *n* Manuskript *nt*

many *a* viele ● *n* **a good/great ~** sehr viele

map *n* Landkarte *f*; (*of town*) Stadtplan *m*

maple *n* Ahorn *m*

mar *vt* (*pt/pp* **marred**) verderben

marathon *n* Marathon *m*

marble *n* Marmor *m*; (*for game*) Murmel *f*

March *n* März *m*

march *n* Marsch *m* ● *vi* marschieren ● *vt* marschieren lassen; **~ s.o. off** jdn abführen

mare *n* Stute *f*

margarine *n* Margarine *f*

margin *n* Rand *m*; (*leeway*) Spielraum *m*; (*Comm*) Spanne *f*. **~al** *a*, **-ly** *adv* geringfügig

marigold *n* Ringelblume *f*

marina *n* Jachthafen *m*

marine *a* Meeres- ● *n* Marine *f*; (*sailor*) Marineinfanterist *m*

marital *a* ehelich. **~ status** *n* Familienstand *m*

maritime *a* See-

mark[1] n (currency) Mark f

mark[2] n Fleck m; (sign) Zeichen nt; (trace) Spur f; (target) Ziel nt; (Sch) Note f ● vt markieren; (spoil) beschädigen; (characterize) kennzeichnen; (Sch) korrigieren; (Sport) decken; ~ **time** (Mil) auf der Stelle treten; (fig) abwarten. ~ **out** vt markieren

marked a, ~**ly** adv deutlich; (pronounced) ausgeprägt

market n Markt m ● vt vertreiben; (launch) auf den Markt bringen. ~**ing** n Marketing nt. ~ **research** n Marktforschung f

marking n Markierung f; (on animal) Zeichnung f

marksman n Scharfschütze m

marmalade n Orangenmarmelade f

maroon a dunkelrot

marooned a (fig) von der Außenwelt abgeschnitten

marquee n Festzelt nt

marquetry n Einlegearbeit f

marriage n Ehe f; (wedding) Hochzeit f. ~**able** a heiratsfähig

married see marry ● a verheiratet. ~ **life** n Eheleben nt

marrow n (Anat) Mark nt; (vegetable) Kürbis m

marr|y vt/i (pt/pp married) heiraten; (unite) trauen; **get** ~**ied** heiraten

marsh n Sumpf m

marshal n Marschall m; (steward) Ordner m

marshy a sumpfig

martial a kriegerisch. ~ **law** n Kriegsrecht nt

martyr n Märtyrer(in) m(f). ~**dom** n Martyrium nt

marvel n Wunder nt ● vi (pt/pp marvelled) staunen (at über + acc). ~**lous** a, -**ly** adv wunderbar

Marxis|m n Marxismus m. ~**t** a marxistisch ● n Marxist(in) m(f)

marzipan n Marzipan nt

mascot n Maskottchen nt

masculin|e a männlich ● n (Gram) Maskulinum nt. ~**ity** n Männlichkeit f

mash n ⒤, ~**ed potatoes** npl Kartoffelpüree nt

mask n Maske f ● vt maskieren

masochis|m n Masochismus m. ~**t** n Masochist m

mason n Steinmetz m. ~**ry** n Mauerwerk nt

mass[1] n (Relig) Messe f

mass[2] n Masse f ● vi sich sammeln; (Mil) sich massieren

massacre n Massaker nt ● vt niedermetzeln

massage n Massage f ● vt massieren

masseu|r n Masseur m. ~**se** n Masseuse f

massive a massiv; (huge) riesig

mass: ~ **media** npl Massenmedien pl. ~-**produce** vt in Massenproduktion herstellen. ~ **production** n Massenproduktion f

mast n Mast m

master n Herr m; (teacher) Lehrer m; (craftsman, artist) Meister m; (of ship) Kapitän m ● vt meistern; beherrschen <language>

master: ~**ly** a meisterhaft. ~-**mind** n führender Kopf m ● vt der führende Kopf sein von. ~**piece** n Meisterwerk nt. ~**y** n (of subject) Beherrschung f

mat n Matte f; (on table) Untersatz m

match[1] n Wettkampf m; (in ball games) Spiel nt; (Tennis) Match nt; (marriage) Heirat f; **be a good** ~ <colours:> gut zusammenpassen; **be no** ~ **for s.o.** jdm nicht gewachsen sein ● vt (equal) gleichkommen (+ dat); (be like) passen zu; (find sth similar) etwas Passendes finden zu ● vi zusammenpassen

match[2] n Streichholz nt. ~**box** n Streichholzschachtel f

mate[1] n Kumpel m; (assistant) Gehilfe m; (Naut) Maat m; (Zool) Männchen nt; (female) Weibchen nt ● vi sich paaren

mate[2] n (Chess) Matt nt

material n Material nt; (fabric) Stoff m; **raw** ~**s** Rohstoffe pl ● a materiell

material|ism *n* Materialismus *m*. ~**istic** *a* materialistisch. ~**ize** *vi* sich verwirklichen

maternal *a* mütterlich

maternity *n* Mutterschaft *f*. ~ **clothes** *npl* Umstandskleidung *f*. ~ **ward** *n* Entbindungsstation *f*

mathematic|al *a*, **-ly** *adv* mathematisch. ~**ian** *n* Mathematiker(in) *m(f)*

mathematics *n* Mathematik *f*

maths *n* 🛈 Mathe *f*

matinée *n* (*Theat*) Nachmittagsvorstellung *f*

matrimony *n* Ehe *f*

matron *n* (*of hospital*) Oberin *f*; (*of school*) Hausmutter *f*

matt *a* matt

matted *a* verfilzt

matter *n* (*affair*) Sache *f*; (*Phys: substance*) Materie *f*; **money** ~**s** Geldangelegenheiten *pl*; **what is the** ~? was ist los? ● *vi* wichtig sein; ~ **to s.o.** jdm etwas ausmachen; **it doesn't** ~ es macht nichts. ~**-of-fact** *a* sachlich

mattress *n* Matratze *f*

matur|e *a* reif; (*Comm*) fällig ● *vi* reifen; <*person:*> reifer werden; (*Comm*) fällig werden ● *vt* reifen lassen. ~**ity** *n* Reife *f*; (*Comm*) Fälligkeit *f*

mauve *a* lila

maximum *a* maximal ● *n* (*pl* **-ima**) Maximum *nt*. ~ **speed** *n* Höchstgeschwindigkeit *f*

---

may

    pres **may**, *pt* **might**

● *auxiliary verb*

····▸ (*expressing possibility*) können. **she may come** es kann sein, dass sie kommt; es ist möglich, dass sie kommt. **she might come** (*more distant possibility*) sie könnte kommen. **it may/might rain** es könnte regnen. **I may be wrong** vielleicht irre ich mich. **he may have missed his train** vielleicht hat er seinen Zug verpasst

····▸ (*expressing permission*) dürfen. **may I come in?** darf ich reinkommen? **you may smoke** Sie dürfen rauchen

····▸ (*expressing wish*) **may the best man win!** auf dass der Beste gewinnt!

····▸ (*expressing concession*) **he may be slow but he's accurate** mag *od* kann sein, dass er langsam ist, aber dafür ist er auch genau

····▸ **may/might as well** ebenso gut können. **we may/might as well go** wir könnten eigentlich ebensogut [auch] gehen. **we might as well give up** da können wir gleich aufgeben

---

May *n* Mai *m*

maybe *adv* vielleicht

May Day *n* der Erste Mai

mayonnaise *n* Mayonnaise *f*

mayor *n* Bürgermeister *m*. ~**ess** *n* Bürgermeisterin *f*; (*wife of mayor*) Frau Bürgermeister *f*

maze *n* Irrgarten *m*; (*fig*) Labyrinth *nt*

me *pron* (*acc*) mich; (*dat*) mir; **it's** ~ 🛈 ich bin es

meadow *n* Wiese *f*

meagre *a* dürftig

meal *n* Mahlzeit *f*, (*food*) Essen *nt*; (*grain*) Schrot *m*

mean¹ *a* (**-er**, **-est**) (*miserly*) geizig; (*unkind*) gemein; (*poor*) schäbig

mean² *a* mittlere(r,s) ● *n* (*average*) Durchschnitt *m*

mean³ *vt* (*pt/pp* **meant**) heißen; (*signify*) bedeuten; (*intend*) beabsichtigen; **I** ~ **it** das ist mein Ernst; ~ **well** es gut meinen; **be meant for** <*present:*> bestimmt sein für; <*remark:*> gerichtet sein an (+ *acc*)

meaning *n* Bedeutung *f*. ~**ful** *a* bedeutungsvoll. ~**less** *a* bedeutungslos

means *n* Möglichkeit *f*, Mittel *nt*; ~ **of transport** Verkehrsmittel *nt*; **by** ~ **of** durch; **by all** ~! aber natürlich! **by no** ~ keineswegs ● *npl* (*resources*) [Geld]mittel *pl*

meant *see* **mean³**

meantime *n* in the ∼ in der Zwischenzeit ● *adv* inzwischen

meanwhile *adv* inzwischen

measles *n* Masern *pl*

measure *n* Maß *nt*; (*action*) Maßnahme *f* ● *vt/i* messen; ∼ up to (*fig*) herankommen an (+ *acc*). ∼d *a* gemessen. ∼ment *n* Maß *nt*

meat *n* Fleisch *nt*

mechan|ic *n* Mechaniker *m*. ∼ical *a*, -ly *adv* mechanisch. ∼ical engineering Maschinenbau *m*

mechan|ism *n* Mechanismus *m*. ∼ize *vt* mechanisieren

medal *n* Orden *m*; (*Sport*) Medaille *f*

medallist *n* Medaillengewinner(in) *m(f)*

meddle *vi* sich einmischen (in in + *acc*); (*tinker*) herumhantieren (with an + *acc*)

media *see* medium ● *n pl* the ∼ die Medien *pl*

mediat|e *vi* vermitteln. ∼or *n* Vermittler(in) *m(f)*

medical *a* medizinisch; (*treatment*) ärztlich ● *n* ärztliche Untersuchung *f*. ∼ insurance *n* Krankenversicherung *f*. ∼ student *n* Medizinstudent *m*

medicat|ed *a* medizinisch. ∼ion *n* (*drugs*) Medikamente *pl*

medicinal *a* medizinisch; (*plant*) heilkräftig

medicine *n* Medizin *f*; (*preparation*) Medikament *nt*

medieval *a* mittelalterlich

mediocr|e *a* mittelmäßig. ∼ity *n* Mittelmäßigkeit *f*

meditat|e *vi* nachdenken (on über + *acc*). ∼ion *n* Meditation *f*

Mediterranean *n* Mittelmeer *nt* ● *a* Mittelmeer-

medium *a* mittlere(r,s); (*steak*) medium; of ∼ size von mittlerer Größe ● *n* (*pl* media) Medium *nt*; (*means*) Mittel *nt*

medium: ∼-sized *a* mittelgroß. ∼ wave *n* Mittelwelle *f*

medley *n* Gemisch *nt*; (*Mus*) Potpourri *nt*

meek *a* (-er, -est), -ly *adv* sanftmütig; (*unprotesting*) widerspruchslos

meet *v* (*pt/pp* met) ● *vt* treffen; (*by chance*) begegnen (+ *dat*); (*at station*) abholen; (*make the acquaintance of*) kennen lernen; stoßen auf (+ *acc*) ‹*problem*›; bezahlen ‹*bill*›; erfüllen ‹*requirements*› ● *vi* sich treffen; (*for the first time*) sich kennen lernen

meeting *n* Treffen *nt*; (*by chance*) Begegnung *f*; (*discussion*) Besprechung *f*; (*of committee*) Sitzung *f*; (*large*) Versammlung *f*

megalomania *n* Größenwahnsinn *m*

megaphone *n* Megaphon *nt*

melancholy *a* melancholisch ● *n* Melancholie *f*

mellow *a* (-er, -est) ‹*fruit*› ausgereift; ‹*sound, person*› sanft ● *vi* reifer werden

melodious *a* melodiös

melodramatic *a*, -ally *adv* melodramatisch

melody *n* Melodie *f*

melon *n* Melone *f*

melt *vt/i* schmelzen

member *n* Mitglied *nt*; (*of family*) Angehörige(r) *m/f*; M∼ of Parliament Abgeordnete(r) *m/f*. ∼ship *n* Mitgliedschaft *f*; (*members*) Mitgliederzahl *f*

memento *n* Andenken *nt*

memo *n* Mitteilung *f*

memoirs *n pl* Memoiren *pl*

memorable *a* denkwürdig

memorial *n* Denkmal *nt*. ∼ service *n* Gedenkfeier *f*

memorize *vt* sich (*dat*) einprägen

memory *n* Gedächtnis *nt*; (*thing remembered*) Erinnerung *f*; (*of computer*) Speicher *m*; from ∼ auswendig; in ∼ of zur Erinnerung an (+ *acc*)

men *see* man

menac|e *n* Drohung *f*; (*nuisance*) Plage *f* ● *vt* bedrohen. ∼ing *a*, ∼ly *adv* drohend

mend *vt* reparieren; (*patch*) flicken; ausbessern ‹*clothes*›

menfolk n pl Männer pl

menial a niedrig

menopause n Wechseljahre pl

mental a, **-ly** adv geistig; (🔲 mad) verrückt. **~ arithmetic** n Kopfrechnen nt. **~ illness** n Geisteskrankheit f

mentality n Mentalität f

mention n Erwähnung f ● vt erwähnen; **don't ~ it** keine Ursache; bitte

menu n Speisekarte f

merchandise n Ware f

merchant n Kaufmann m; (dealer) Händler m. **~ navy** n Handelsmarine f

merci|ful a barmherzig. **~fully** adv 🔲 glücklicherweise. **~less** a, **-ly** adv erbarmungslos

mercury n Quecksilber nt

mercy n Barmherzigkeit f, Gnade f; **be at s.o.'s ~** jdm ausgeliefert sein

mere a, **-ly** adv bloß

merest a kleinste(r,s)

merge vi zusammenlaufen; (Comm) fusionieren

merger n Fusion f

meringue n Baiser nt

merit n Verdienst nt; (advantage) Vorzug m; (worth) Wert m ● vt verdienen

merry a (-ier, -iest) fröhlich

merry-go-round n Karussell nt

mesh n Masche f

mesmerized a (fig) [wie] gebannt

mess n Durcheinander nt; (trouble) Schwierigkeiten pl; (something spilt) Bescherung f 🔲; (Mil) Messe f; **make a ~ of** (botch) verpfuschen ● vt **~ up** in Unordnung bringen; (botch) verpfuschen ● vi **~ about** herumalbern; (tinker) herumspielen (with mit)

message n Nachricht f; **give s.o. a ~** jdm etwas ausrichten

messenger n Bote m

Messrs n pl see **Mr**; (on letter) **~ Smith** Firma Smith

messy a (-ier, -iest) schmutzig; (untidy) unordentlich

met see **meet**

metal n Metall nt ● a Metall-. **~lic** a metallisch

metaphor n Metapher f. **~ical** a, **-ly** adv metaphorisch

meteor n Meteor m. **~ic** a kometenhaft

meteorological a Wetter-

meteorolog|ist n Meteorologe m/ -gin f. **~y** n Meteorologie f

meter[1] n Zähler m

meter[2] n (Amer) = **metre**

method n Methode f; (Culin) Zubereitung f

methodical a, **-ly** adv systematisch, methodisch

methylated a **~ spirit[s]** Brennspiritus m

meticulous a, **-ly** adv sehr genau

metre n Meter m & nt; (rhythm) Versmaß nt

metric a metrisch

metropolis n Metropole f

metropolitan a haupstädtisch; (international) weltstädtisch

mew n Miau nt ● vi miauen

Mexican a mexikanisch ● n Mexikaner(in) m(f). **Mexico** n Mexiko nt

miaow n Miau nt ● vi miauen

mice see **mouse**

micro: **~film** n Mikrofilm m. **~phone** n Mikrofon nt. **~scope** n Mikroskop nt. **~scopic** a mikroskopisch. **~wave [oven]** n Mikrowellenherd m

mid a **~ May** Mitte Mai; **in ~ air** in der Luft

midday n Mittag m

middle a mittlere(r,s); **the M~ Ages** das Mittelalter; **the ~ class[es]** der Mittelstand; **the M~ East** der Nahe Osten ● n Mitte f; **in the ~ of the night** mitten in der Nacht

middle: **~-aged** a mittleren Alters. **~-class** a bürgerlich

midge n [kleine] Mücke f

midget n Liliputaner(in) m(f)

Midlands npl **the ~** Mittelengland n

midnight n Mitternacht f

midriff n ① Taille f

midst n in the ~ of mitten in (+ dat); in our ~ unter uns

mid: ~**summer** n Hochsommer m. ~**way** adv auf halbem Wege. ~**wife** n Hebamme f. ~**winter** n Mitte f des Winters

might¹ v aux I ~ vielleicht; it ~ be true es könnte wahr sein; **he asked if** he ~ go er fragte, ob er gehen dürfte; **you** ~ **have drowned** du hättest ertrinken können

might² n Macht f

mighty a (-ier, -iest) mächtig

migraine n Migräne f

migrat|e vi abwandern; <birds:> ziehen. ~**ion** n Wanderung f; (of birds) Zug m

mike n ① Mikrofon nt

mild a (-er, -est) mild

mild|ly adv leicht; **to put it** ~**ly** gelinde gesagt. ~**ness** n Milde f

mile n Meile f (= 1,6 km); ~**s too big** ① viel zu groß

mile|age n Meilenzahl f; (of car) Meilenstand m

militant a militant

military a militärisch. ~ **service** n Wehrdienst m

milk n Milch f ● vt melken

milk: ~**man** n Milchmann m. ~ **shake** n Milchmixgetränk nt. ~ **tooth** n Milchzahn m

milky a (-ier, -iest) milchig. **M**~ **Way** n (Astr) Milchstraße f

mill n Mühle f; (factory) Fabrik f

millennium n Jahrtausend nt

milli|gram n Milligramm nt. ~**metre** n Millimeter m & nt

million n Million f; **a** ~ **pounds** eine Million Pfund. ~**aire** n Millionär(in) m(f)

mime n Pantomime f ● vt pantomimisch darstellen

mimic n Imitator m ● vt (pt/pp **mimicked**) nachahmen

mince n Hackfleisch nt ● vt (Culin) durchdrehen; **not** ~ **words** kein Blatt vor den Mund nehmen

mince: ~**meat** n Masse f aus Korinthen, Zitronat usw; **make** ~ **meat of** (fig) vernichtend schlagen. ~ **pie** n mit 'mincemeat' gefülltes Pastetchen nt

mincer n Fleischwolf m

mind n Geist m; (sanity) Verstand m; **give s.o. a piece of one's** ~ jdm gehörig die Meinung sagen; **make up one's** ~ sich entschließen; **be out of one's** ~ nicht bei Verstand sein; **have sth in** ~ etw im Sinn haben; **bear sth in** ~ an etw (acc) denken; **have a good** ~ **to** große Lust haben, zu; **I have changed my** ~ ich habe es mir anders überlegt ● vt aufpassen auf (+ acc); **I don't** ~ **the noise** der Lärm stört mich nicht; ~ **the step!** Achtung Stufe! ● vi (care) sich kümmern (about um); **I don't** ~ mir macht es nichts aus; **never** ~! macht nichts! **do you** ~ **if?** haben Sie etwas dagegen, wenn? ~ **out** vi aufpassen

mindless a geistlos

mine¹ poss pron meine(r), meins; **a friend of** ~ ein Freund von mir; **that is** ~ das gehört mir

mine² n Bergwerk nt; (explosive) Mine f ● vt abbauen; (Mil) verminen

miner n Bergarbeiter m

mineral n Mineral nt. ~ **water** n Mineralwasser nt

minesweeper n Minenräumboot nt

mingle vi ~ **with** sich mischen unter (+ acc)

miniature a Klein- ● n Miniatur f

mini|bus n Kleinbus m. ~**cab** n Kleintaxi nt

minim|al a minimal. ~**um** n (pl -ima) Minimum nt ● a Mindest-

mining n Bergbau m

miniskirt n Minirock m

minister n Minister m; (Relig) Pastor m. ~**ial** a ministeriell

ministry n (Pol) Ministerium nt

mink n Nerz m

minor a kleiner; (less important) unbedeutend ● n Minderjährige(r) m/f; (Mus) Moll nt

minority n Minderheit f

minor road n Nebenstraße f

mint¹ n Münzstätte f ● a <stamp> postfrisch; **in** ~ **condition** wie neu ● vt prägen

mint² n (herb) Minze f; (sweet) Pfefferminzbonbon m & nt

minus prep minus, weniger; (🖪 without) ohne

minute¹ n Minute f; **in a** ~ (shortly) gleich; ~**s** pl (of meeting) Protokoll nt

minute² a winzig

mirac|le n Wunder nt. ~**ulous** a wunderbar

mirror n Spiegel m ● vt widerspiegeln

mirth n Heiterkeit f

misadventure n Missgeschick nt

misapprehension n Missverständnis nt; **be under a** ~ sich irren

misbehav|e vi sich schlecht benehmen. ~**iour** n schlechtes Benehmen nt

miscalcu|late vt falsch berechnen ● vi sich verrechnen. ~**lation** n Fehlkalkulation f

miscarriage n Fehlgeburt f

miscellaneous a vermischt

mischief n Unfug m

mischievous a, -**ly** adv schelmisch; (malicious) boshaft

misconception n falsche Vorstellung f

misconduct n unkorrektes Verhalten nt; (adultery) Ehebruch m

miser n Geizhals m

miserable a, -**bly** adv unglücklich; (wretched) elend

miserly adv geizig

misery n Elend nt; (🖪 person) Miesepeter m

misfire vi fehlzünden; (go wrong) fehlschlagen

misfit n Außenseiter(in) m(f)

misfortune n Unglück nt

misgivings npl Bedenken pl

misguided a töricht

mishap n Missgeschick nt

misinform vt falsch unterrichten

misinterpret vt missdeuten

misjudge vt falsch beurteilen

mislay vt (pt/pp -**laid**) verlegen

mislead vt (pt/pp -**led**) irreführen. ~**ing** a irreführend

mismanage vt schlecht verwalten. ~**ment** n Misswirtschaft f

misnomer n Fehlbezeichnung f

misprint n Druckfehler m

misquote vt falsch zitieren

misrepresent vt falsch darstellen

miss n Fehltreffer m ● vt verpassen; (fail to hit or find) verfehlen; (fail to attend) versäumen; (fail to notice) übersehen; (feel the loss of) vermissen ● vi (fail to hit) nicht treffen. ~ **out** vt auslassen

Miss n (pl -**es**) Fräulein nt

missile n [Wurf]geschoss nt; (Mil) Rakete f

missing a fehlend; (lost) verschwunden; (Mil) vermisst; **be** ~ fehlen

mission n Auftrag m; (Mil) Einsatz m; (Relig) Mission f

missionary n Missionar(in) m(f)

misspell vt (pt/pp -**spelt** or -**spelled**) falsch schreiben

mist n Dunst m; (fog) Nebel m; (on window) Beschlag m ● vi ~ **up** beschlagen

mistake n Fehler m; **by** ~ aus Versehen ● vt (pt **mistook**, pp **mistaken**); ~ **for** verwechseln mit

mistaken a falsch; **be** ~ sich irren. ~**ly** adv irrtümlicherweise

mistletoe n Mistel f

mistress n Herrin f; (teacher) Lehrerin f; (lover) Geliebte f

mistrust n Misstrauen nt ● vt misstrauen (+ dat)

misty a (-**ier**, -**iest**) dunstig; (foggy) neblig; (fig) unklar

misunderstand vt (pt/pp -**stood**) missverstehen. ~**ing** n Missverständnis nt

misuse¹ vt missbrauchen

misuse² n Missbrauch m

mitigating a mildernd

mix n Mischung f ● vt mischen ● vi
sich mischen; ∼ **with** (associate with)
verkehren mit. ∼ **up** vt mischen;
(muddle) durcheinander bringen;
(mistake for) verwechseln (**with** mit)

mixed a gemischt; be ∼ up
durcheinander sein

mixer n Mischmaschine f; (Culin)
Küchenmaschine f

mixture n Mischung f; (medicine)
Mixtur f; (Culin) Teig m

mix-up n Durcheinander nt;
(confusion) Verwirrung f; (mistake)
Verwechslung f

moan n Stöhnen nt ● vi stöhnen;
(complain) jammern

mob n Horde f; (rabble) Pöbel m; (॒
gang) Bande f ● vt (pt/pp **mobbed**)
herfallen über (+ acc); belagern
<celebrity>

mobile a beweglich ● n Mobile nt;
(telephone) Handy nt. ∼ **home** n
Wohnwagen m. ∼ **phone** n Handy
nt

mobility n Beweglichkeit f

mock a Schein- ● vt verspotten.
∼**ery** n Spott m

mock-up n Modell nt

mode n [Art und] Weise f; (fashion)
Mode f

model n Modell nt; (example)
Vorbild nt; [fashion] ∼ Mannequin
nt ● a Modell-; (exemplary) Muster-
● v (pt/pp **modelled**) ● vt formen,
modellieren; vorführen <clothes>
● vi Mannequin sein; (for artist)
Modell stehen

moderate[1] vt mäßigen

moderate[2] a mäßig; <opinion>
gemäßigt. ∼**ly** adv mäßig; (fairly)
einigermaßen

moderation n Mäßigung f; in ∼
mit Maß[en]

modern a modern. ∼**ize** vt
modernisieren. ∼ **languages** npl
neuere Sprachen pl

modest a bescheiden; (decorous)
schamhaft. ∼**y** n Bescheidenheit f

modif|**ication** n Abänderung f. ∼**y**
vt (pt/pp **-fied**) abändern

moist a (-er, -est) feucht

moisten vt befeuchten

moistur|**e** n Feuchtigkeit f. ∼**izer**
n Feuchtigkeitscreme f

molar n Backenzahn m

mole[1] n Leberfleck m

mole[2] n (Zool) Maulwurf m

molecule n Molekül nt

molest vt belästigen

mollify vt (pt/pp **-ied**) besänftigen

mollycoddle vt verzärteln

molten a geschmolzen

mom n (Amer fam) Mutti f

moment n Moment m, Augenblick
m; at the ∼ im Augenblick,
augenblicklich. ∼**ary** a
vorübergehend

momentous a bedeutsam

momentum n Schwung m

monarch n Monarch(in) m(f). ∼**y** n
Monarchie f

monastery n Kloster nt

Monday n Montag m

money n Geld nt

money: ∼-**box** n Sparbüchse f. ∼-
lender n Geldverleiher m. ∼ **order**
n Zahlungsanweisung f

mongrel n Promenadenmischung f

monitor n (Techn) Monitor m ● vt
überwachen <progress>; abhören
<broadcast>

monk n Mönch m

monkey n Affe m

mono n Mono nt

monogram n Monogramm nt

monologue n Monolog m

monopol|**ize** vt monopolisieren.
∼**y** n Monopol nt

monosyllable n einsilbiges Wort
nt

monotone n in a ∼ mit monotoner
Stimme

monoton|**ous** a, -**ly** adv eintönig,
monoton; (tedious) langweilig. ∼**y** n
Eintönigkeit f, Monotonie f

monster n Ungeheuer nt; (cruel
person) Unmensch m

monstrosity n Monstrosität f

monstrous a ungeheuer;
(outrageous) ungeheuerlich

month *n* Monat *m*. ~**ly** *a & adv* monatlich ● *n* (*periodical*) Monatszeitschrift *f*

monument *n* Denkmal *nt*. ~**al** *a* (*fig*) monumental

moo *n* Muh *nt* ● *vi* (*pt/pp* mooed) muhen

mood *n* Laune *f*; **be in a good/bad** ~ gute/schlechte Laune haben

moody *a* (-ier, -iest) launisch

moon *n* Mond *m*; **over the** ~ 🔲 überglücklich

moon: ~**light** *n* Mondschein *m*. ~**lighting** *n* 🔲 ≈ Schwarzarbeit *f*. ~**lit** *a* mondhell

moor[1] *n* Moor *nt*

moor[2] *vt* (*Naut*) festmachen ● *vi* anlegen

mop *n* Mopp *m*; ~ **of hair** Wuschelkopf *m* ● *vt* (*pt/pp* mopped) wischen. ~ **up** *vt* aufwischen

moped *n* Moped *nt*

moral *a*, **-ly** *adv* moralisch, sittlich; (*virtuous*) tugendhaft ● *n* Moral *f*; ~**s** *pl* Moral *f*

morale *n* Moral *f*

morality *n* Sittlichkeit *f*

morbid *a* krankhaft; (*gloomy*) trübe

more *a*, *adv & n* mehr; (*in addition*) noch; **a few** ~ noch ein paar; **any** ~ noch etwas; **once** ~ noch einmal; ~ **or less** mehr oder weniger; **some** ~ **tea?** noch etwas Tee? ~ **interesting** interessanter; ~ [**and** ~] **quickly** [immer] schneller

moreover *adv* außerdem

morgue *n* Leichenschauhaus *nt*

morning *n* Morgen *m*; **in the** ~ morgens, am Morgen; (*tomorrow*) morgen früh

Morocco *n* Marokko *nt*

moron *n* 🔲 Idiot *m*

morose *a*, **-ly** *adv* mürrisch

morsel *n* Happen *m*

mortal *a* sterblich; (*fatal*) tödlich ● *n* Sterbliche(r) *m/f*. ~**ity** *n* Sterblichkeit *f*. ~**ly** *adv* tödlich

mortar *n* Mörtel *m*

mortgage *n* Hypothek *f* ● *vt* hypothekarisch belasten

mortuary *n* Leichenhalle *f*; (*public*) Leichenschauhaus *nt*; (*Amer: undertaker's*) Bestattungsinstitut *nt*

mosaic *n* Mosaik *nt*

Moscow *n* Moskau *nt*

mosque *n* Moschee *f*

mosquito *n* (*pl* -es) [Stech]mücke *f*, Schnake *f*; (*tropical*) Moskito *m*

moss *n* Moos *nt*. ~**y** *a* moosig

most *a* der/die/das meiste; (*majority*) die meisten; **for the** ~ **part** zum größten Teil ● *adv* am meisten; (*very*) höchst; **the** ~ **interesting day** der interessanteste Tag; ~ **unlikely** höchst unwahrscheinlich ● *n* das meiste; ~ **of them** die meisten [von ihnen]; **at [the]** ~ höchstens; ~ **of the time** die meiste Zeit. ~**ly** *adv* meist

MOT *n* ≈ TÜV *m*

motel *n* Motel *nt*

moth *n* Nachtfalter *m*; [**clothes-**] ~ Motte *f*

mothball *n* Mottenkugel *f*

mother *n* Mutter *f*

mother: ~**hood** *n* Mutterschaft *f*. ~**-in-law** *n* (*pl* ~**s-in-law**) Schwiegermutter *f*. ~**land** *n* Mutterland *nt*. ~**ly** *a* mütterlich. ~**-of-pearl** *n* Perlmutter *f*. ~**-to-be** *n* werdende Mutter *f*

mothproof *a* mottenfest

motif *n* Motiv *nt*

motion *n* Bewegung *f*; (*proposal*) Antrag *m*. ~**less** *a*, **-ly** *adv* bewegungslos

motivat|e *vt* motivieren. ~**ion** *n* Motivation *f*

motive *n* Motiv *nt*

motor *n* Motor *m*; (*car*) Auto *nt* ● *a* Motor-; (*Anat*) motorisch ● *vi* [mit dem Auto] fahren

motor: ~**bike** *n* 🔲 Motorrad *nt*. ~ **boat** *n* Motorboot *nt*. ~ **car** *n* Auto *nt*, Wagen *m*. ~**cycle** *n* Motorrad *nt*. ~**cyclist** *n* Motorradfahrer *m*. ~**ing** *n* Autofahren *nt*. ~**ist** *n* Autofahrer(in) *m(f)*. ~ **vehicle** *n* Kraftfahrzeug *nt*. ~**way** *n* Autobahn *f*

mottled *a* gesprenkelt

motto n (pl **-es**) Motto nt

mould¹ n (fungus) Schimmel m

mould² n Form f ● vt formen (**into** zu). **~ing** n (Archit) Fries m

mouldy a schimmelig; (🔲 worthless) schäbig

mound n Hügel m; (of stones) Haufen m

mount n (animal) Reittier nt; (of jewel) Fassung f; (of photo, picture) Passepartout nt ● vt (get on) steigen auf (+ acc); (on pedestal) montieren auf (+ acc); besteigen <horse>; fassen <jewel>; aufziehen <photo, picture> ● vi aufsteigen; <tension:> steigen. **~ up** vi sich häufen; (add up) sich anhäufen

mountain n Berg m

mountaineer n Bergsteiger(in) m(f). **~ing** n Bergsteigen nt

mountainous a bergig, gebirgig

mourn vt betrauern ● vi trauern (**for** um). **~er** n Trauernde(r) m/f. **~ful** a, **-ly** adv trauervoll. **~ing** n Trauer f

mouse n (pl **mice**) Maus f. **~trap** n Mausefalle f

moustache n Schnurrbart m

mouth¹ vt **~** sth etw lautlos mit den Lippen sagen

mouth² n Mund m; (of animal) Maul nt; (of river) Mündung f

mouth: ~ful n Mundvoll m; (bite) Bissen m. **~-organ** n Mundharmonika f. **~wash** n Mundwasser nt

movable a beweglich

move n Bewegung f; (fig) Schritt m; (moving house) Umzug m; (in board game) Zug m; **on the ~** unterwegs; **get a ~ on** 🔲 sich beeilen ● vt bewegen; (emotionally) rühren; (move along) rücken; (in board game) ziehen; (take away) wegnehmen; wegfahren <car>; (rearrange) umstellen; (transfer) versetzen <person>; verlegen <office>; (propose) beantragen; **~ house** umziehen ● vi sich bewegen; (move house) umziehen; **don't ~!** stillhalten! (stop) stillstehen! **~ along** vt/i weiterrücken. **~ away**

vt/i wegrücken; (move house) wegziehen. **~ in** vi einziehen. **~ off** vi <vehicle:> losfahren. **~ out** vi ausziehen. **~ over** vt/i [zur Seite] rücken. **~ up** vi aufrücken

movement n Bewegung f; (Mus) Satz m; (of clock) Uhrwerk nt

movie n (Amer) Film m; **go to the ~s** ins Kino gehen

moving a beweglich; (touching) rührend

mow vt (pt **mowed**, pp **mown** or **mowed**) mähen

mower n Rasenmäher m

MP abbr see **Member of Parliament**

Mr n (pl **Messrs**) Herr m

Mrs n Frau f

Ms n Frau f

much a, adv & n viel; **as ~ as** so viel wie; **~ loved** sehr geliebt

muck n Mist m; (🔲 filth) Dreck m. **~ about** vi herumalbern; (tinker) herumspielen (**with** mit). **~ out** vt ausmisten. **~ up** vt 🔲 vermasseln; (make dirty) schmutzig machen

mucky a (**-ier, -iest**) dreckig

mud n Schlamm m

muddle n Durcheinander nt; (confusion) Verwirrung f ● vt **~ [up]** durcheinander bringen

muddy a (**-ier, -iest**) schlammig; <shoes> schmutzig

mudguard n Kotflügel m; (on bicycle) Schutzblech nt

muffle vt dämpfen

muffler n Schal m; (Amer, Auto) Auspufftopf m

mug¹ n Becher m; (for beer) Bierkrug m; (🔲 face) Visage f; (🔲 simpleton) Trottel m

mug² vt (pt/pp **mugged**) überfallen. **~ger** n Straßenräuber m. **~ging** n Straßenraub m

muggy a (**-ier, -iest**) schwül

mule n Maultier nt

mulled a **~ wine** Glühwein m

multi: ~coloured a vielfarbig, bunt. **~lingual** a mehrsprachig. **~national** a multinational

multiple *a* vielfach; *(with pl)* mehrere ● *n* Vielfache(s) *nt*

multiplication *n* Multiplikation *f*

multiply *v (pt/pp* -**ied)** ● *vt* multiplizieren **(by** mit) ● *vi* sich vermehren

multistorey *a* ~ **car park** Parkhaus *nt*

mum *n* 🇬🇧 Mutti *f*

mumble *vt/i* murmeln

mummy[1] *n* 🇬🇧 Mutti *f*

mummy[2] *n (Archaeol)* Mumie *f*

mumps *n* Mumps *m*

munch *vt/i* mampfen

municipal *a* städtisch

munitions *npl* Kriegsmaterial *nt*

mural *n* Wandgemälde *nt*

murder *n* Mord *m* ● *vt* ermorden. ~**er** *n* Mörder *m.* ~**ess** *n* Mörderin *f.* ~**ous** *a* mörderisch

murky *a* (-**ier, -iest)** düster

murmur *n* Murmeln *nt* ● *vt/i* murmeln

muscle *n* Muskel *m*

muscular *a* Muskel-; *(strong)* muskulös

museum *n* Museum *nt*

mushroom *n* [essbarer] Pilz *m*, *esp* Champignon *m* ● *vi (fig)* wie Pilze aus dem Boden schießen

mushy *a* breiig

music *n* Musik *f*; *(written)* Noten *pl*; **set to** ~ vertonen

musical *a* musikalisch ● *n* Musical *nt.* ~ **box** *n* Spieldose *f.* ~ **instrument** *n* Musikinstrument *nt*

musician *n* Musiker(in) *m(f)*

music-stand *n* Notenständer *m*

Muslim *a* mohammedanisch ● *n* Mohammedaner(in) *m(f)*

must *v aux (nur Präsens)* müssen; *(with negative)* dürfen ● *n a* ~ 🇬🇧 ein Muss *nt*

mustard *n* Senf *m*

musty *a* (-**ier, -iest)** muffig

mute *a* stumm

mutilat|e *vt* verstümmeln. ~**ion** *n* Verstümmelung *f*

mutin|ous *a* meuterisch. ~**y** *n* Meuterei *f* ● *vi (pt/pp* -**ied)** meutern

mutter *n* Murmeln *nt* ● *vt/i* murmeln

mutton *n* Hammelfleisch *nt*

mutual *a* gegenseitig; (🇬🇧 *common)* gemeinsam. ~**ly** *adv* gegenseitig

muzzle *n (of animal)* Schnauze *f*; *(of firearm)* Mündung *f*; *(for dog)* Maulkorb *m*

my *a* mein

myself *pron* selbst; *(refl)* mich; **by** ~ allein; **I thought to** ~ ich habe mir gedacht

mysterious *a,* -**ly** *adv* geheimnisvoll; *(puzzling)* mysteriös, rätselhaft

mystery *n* Geheimnis *nt*; *(puzzle)* Rätsel *nt*; ~ **[story]** Krimi *m*

mysti|c[al] *a* mystisch. ~**cism** *n* Mystik *f*

mystified *a* **be** ~ vor einem Rätsel stehen

mystique *n* geheimnisvoller Zauber *m*

myth *n* Mythos *m*; (🇬🇧 *untruth)* Märchen *nt*. ~**ical** *a* mythisch; *(fig)* erfunden

mythology *n* Mythologie *f*

Nn

nab *vt (pt/pp* **nabbed)** 🇬🇧 erwischen

nag[1] *n (horse)* Gaul *m*

nag[2] *vt/i (pp/pp* **nagged)** herumnörgeln **(s.o.** an jdm)

nail *n (Anat, Techn)* Nagel *m*; **on the** ~ 🇬🇧 sofort ● *vt* nageln **(to** an + *acc)*

nail: ~-**brush** *n* Nagelbürste *f.* ~-**file** *n* Nagelfeile *f.* ~ **scissors** *npl* Nagelschere *f.* ~ **varnish** *n* Nagellack *m*

naïve *a,* -**ly** *adv* naiv. ~**ty** *n* Naivität *f*

naked *a* nackt; *<flame>* offen; with the ~ eye mit bloßem Auge. **~ness** *n* Nacktheit *f*

name *n* Name *m*; *(reputation)* Ruf *m*; by ~ dem Namen nach; by the ~ of namens; call s.o. ~s ⊞ jdn beschimpfen ● *vt* nennen; *(give a name to)* einen Namen geben (+ *dat*); *(announce publicly)* den Namen bekannt geben von. **~less** *a* namenlos. **~ly** *adv* nämlich

name: **~-plate** *n* Namensschild *nt*. **~sake** *n* Namensvetter *m*/ Namensschwester *f*

nanny *n* Kindermädchen *nt*

nap *n* Nickerchen *nt*

napkin *n* Serviette *f*

nappy *n* Windel *f*

narcotic *n* *(drug)* Rauschgift *nt*

narrat|e *vt* erzählen. **~ion** *n* Erzählung *f*

narrative *n* Erzählung *f*

narrator *n* Erzähler(in) *m(f)*

narrow *a* (-er, -est) schmal; *(restricted)* eng; *<margin, majority>* knapp; have a ~ escape mit knapper Not davonkommen ● *vi* sich verengen. **~-minded** *a* engstirnig

nasal *a* nasal; *(Med & Anat)* Nasen-

nasty *a* (-ier, -iest) übel; *(unpleasant)* unangenehm; *(unkind)* boshaft; *(serious)* schlimm

nation *n* Nation *f*; *(people)* Volk *nt*

national *a* national; *<newspaper>* überregional; *<campaign>* landesweit ● *n* Staatsbürger(in) *m(f)*

national: ~ **anthem** *n* Nationalhymne *f*. **N~ Health Service** *n* staatlicher Gesundheitsdienst *m*. **N~ Insurance** *n* Sozialversicherung *f*

nationalism *n* Nationalismus *m*

nationality *n* Staatsangehörigkeit *f*

national|ization *n* Verstaatlichung *f*. **~ize** *vt* verstaatlichen

native *a* einheimisch; *(innate)* angeboren ● *n* Eingeborene(r) *m/f*; *(local inhabitant)* Einheimische(r) *m/f*; a ~ of Vienna ein gebürtiger Wiener

native: ~ **land** *n* Heimatland *nt*. ~ **language** *n* Muttersprache *f*

natter *vi* ⊞ schwatzen

natural *a*, **-ly** *adv* natürlich; ~[-coloured] naturfarben

natural: ~ **gas** *n* Erdgas *nt*. ~ **history** *n* Naturkunde *f*

naturalist *n* Naturforscher *m*

natural|ization *n* Einbürgerung *f*. **~ize** *vt* einbürgern

nature *n* Natur *f*; *(kind)* Art *f*; by ~ von Natur aus. ~ **reserve** *n* Naturschutzgebiet *nt*

naughty *a* (-ier, -iest), **-ily** *adv* unartig; *(slightly indecent)* gewagt

nausea *n* Übelkeit *f*

nautical *a* nautisch. ~ **mile** *n* Seemeile *f*

naval *a* Marine-

nave *n* Kirchenschiff *nt*

navel *n* Nabel *m*

navigable *a* schiffbar

navigat|e *vi* navigieren ● *vt* befahren *<river>*. **~ion** *n* Navigation *f*

navy *n* [Kriegs]marine *f* ● *a* ~ [blue] marineblau

near *a* (-er, -est) nah[e]; the ~est bank die nächste Bank ● *adv* nahe; draw ~ sich nähern ● *prep* nahe an (+ *dat/acc*); in der Nähe von

near: **~by** *a* nahe gelegen, nahe liegend. **~ly** *adv* fast, beinahe; not **~ly** bei weitem nicht. **~ness** *n* Nähe *f*. ~ **side** *n* Beifahrerseite *f*. **~-sighted** *a* (*Amer*) kurzsichtig

neat *a* (-er, -est), **-ly** *adv* adrett; *(tidy)* ordentlich; *(clever)* geschickt; *(undiluted)* pur. **~ness** *n* Ordentlichkeit *f*

necessarily *adv* notwendigerweise; not ~ nicht unbedingt

necessary *a* nötig, notwendig

necessit|ate *vt* notwendig machen. **~y** *n* Notwendigkeit *f*; work from **~y** arbeiten, weil man es nötig hat

neck *n* Hals *m*; ~ and ~ Kopf an Kopf

necklace *n* Halskette *f*

neckline n Halsausschnitt m

née a ~ X geborene X

need n Bedürfnis nt; (misfortune) Not f; be in ~ of brauchen; in case of ~ notfalls; if ~ be wenn nötig; there is a ~ for es besteht ein Bedarf an (+ dat); there is no ~ for that das ist nicht nötig ● vt brauchen; you ~ not go du brauchst nicht zu gehen; ~ I come? muss ich kommen? I ~ to know ich muss es wissen

needle n Nadel f

needless a, -ly adv unnötig; ~ to say selbstverständlich, natürlich

needlework n Nadelarbeit f

needy a (-ier, -iest) bedürftig

negation n Verneinung f

negative a negativ ● n Verneinung f; (photo) Negativ nt

neglect n Vernachlässigung f ● vt vernachlässigen; (omit) versäumen (to zu). ~ed a verwahrlost. ~ful a nachlässig

negligen|ce n Nachlässigkeit f. ~t a, -ly adv nachlässig

negligible a unbedeutend

negotiat|e vt aushandeln; (Auto) nehmen <bend> ● vi verhandeln. ~ion n Verhandlung f. ~or n Unterhändler(in) m(f)

Negro a Neger- ● n (pl -es) Neger m

neigh vi wiehern

neighbour n Nachbar(in) m(f). ~hood n Nachbarschaft f. ~ing a Nachbar-. ~ly a [gut]nachbarlich

neither a & pron keine(r, s) [von beiden] ● adv ~... nor weder ... noch ● conj auch nicht

neon n Neon nt

nephew n Neffe m

nepotism n Vetternwirtschaft f

nerve n Nerv m; (🔲 courage) Mut m; (🔲 impudence) Frechheit f. ~-racking a nervenaufreibend

nervous a, -ly adv (afraid) ängstlich; (highly strung) nervös; (Anat, Med) Nerven-. ~ breakdown n Nervenzusammenbruch m. ~ness Ängstlichkeit f

nervy a (-ier, -iest) nervös; (Amer: impudent) frech

nest n Nest nt ● vi nisten

nestle vi sich schmiegen (against an + acc)

net¹ n Netz nt; (curtain) Store m

net² a netto; <salary, weight> Netto-

netball n ≈ Korbball m

Netherlands npl the ~ die Niederlande pl

nettle n Nessel f

network n Netz nt

neurolog|ist n Neurologe m/ -gin f. ~y n Neurologie f

neur|osis n (pl -oses) Neurose f. ~otic a neurotisch

neuter a (Gram) sächlich ● n (Gram) Neutrum nt ● vt kastrieren; (spay) sterilisieren

neutral a neutral ● n in ~ (Auto) im Leerlauf. ~ity n Neutralität f

never adv nie, niemals; (🔲 not) nicht; ~ mind macht nichts; well I ~! ja so was! ~-ending a endlos

nevertheless adv dennoch, trotzdem

new a (-er, -est) neu

new: ~comer n Neuankömmling m. ~fangled a (pej) neumodisch. ~-laid a frisch gelegt

newly adv frisch. ~-weds npl Jungverheiratete pl

new: ~ moon n Neumond m. ~ness n Neuheit f

news n Nachricht f; (Radio, TV) Nachrichten pl; piece of ~ Neuigkeit f

news: ~agent n Zeitungshändler m. ~ bulletin n Nachrichtensendung f. ~letter n Mitteilungsblatt nt. ~paper n Zeitung f; (material) Zeitungspapier nt. ~reader n Nachrichtensprecher(in) m(f)

New: ~ Year's Day n Neujahr nt. ~ Year's Eve n Silvester nt. ~ Zealand n Neuseeland nt

next a & n nächste(r, s); who's ~? wer kommt als Nächster dran? the ~ best das nächstbeste; ~ door nebenan; my ~ of kin mein nächster

Verwandter; **~ to nothing** fast gar nichts; **the week after ~** übernächste Woche ● *adv* als Nächstes; **~ to** neben

nib *n* Feder *f*

nibble *vt/i* knabbern (**at** an + *dat*)

nice *a* (**-r, -st**) nett; *<day, weather>* schön; *<food>* gut; *<distinction>* fein. **~ly** *adv* nett; (*well*) gut

niche *n* Nische *f*; (*fig*) Platz *m*

nick *n* Kerbe *f*; (🎛 *prison*) Knast *m*; (🎛 *police station*) Revier *nt*; **in good ~** 🎛 in gutem Zustand ● *vt* einkerben; (*steal*) klauen; (🎛 *arrest*) schnappen

nickel *n* Nickel *nt*; (*Amer*) Fünfcentstück *nt*

nickname *n* Spitzname *m*

nicotine *n* Nikotin *nt*

niece *n* Nichte *f*

Nigeria *n* Nigeria *nt*. **~n** *a* nigerianisch ● *n* Nigerianer(in) *m(f)*

night *n* Nacht *f*; (*evening*) Abend *m*; **at ~** nachts

night: **~-club** *n* Nachtklub *m*. **~-dress** *n* Nachthemd *nt*. **~fall** *n* **at ~fall** bei Einbruch der Dunkelheit. **~-gown** *n*, 🎛 **~ie** *n* Nachthemd *nt*

nightingale *n* Nachtigall *f*

night: **~-life** *n* Nachtleben *nt*. **~ly** *a* nächtlich ● *adv* jede Nacht. **~mare** *n* Albtraum *m*. **~-time** *n* **at ~-time** bei Nacht

nil *n* null

nimble *a* (**-r, -st**), **-bly** *adv* flink

nine *a* neun ● *n* Neun *f*. **~teen** *a* neunzehn. **~teenth** *a* neunzehnte(r, s)

ninetieth *a* neunzigste(r, s)

ninety *a* neunzig

ninth *a* neunte(r, s)

nip *vt* kneifen; (*bite*) beißen; **~ in the bud** (*fig*) im Keim ersticken ● *vi* (🎛 *run*) laufen

nipple *n* Brustwarze *f*; (*Amer: on bottle*) Sauger *m*

nitwit *n* 🎛 Dummkopf *m*

no *adv* nein ● *n* (*pl* **noes**) Nein *nt* ● *a* kein(e); (*pl*) keine; **in no time** [sehr] schnell; **no parking/smoking**

Parken/Rauchen verboten; **no one** = nobody

nobility *n* Adel *m*

noble *a* (**-r, -st**) edel; (*aristocratic*) adlig. **~man** *n* Adlige(r) *m*

nobody *pron* niemand, keiner ● *n* **a ~** ein Niemand *m*

nocturnal *a* nächtlich; *<animal, bird>* Nacht-

nod *n* Nicken *nt* ● *v* (*pt/pp* **nodded**) ● *vi* nicken ● *vt* **~ one's head** mit dem Kopf nicken

noise *n* Geräusch *nt*; (*loud*) Lärm *m*. **~less** *a*, **-ly** *adv* geräuschlos

noisy *a* (**-ier, -iest**), **-ily** *adv* laut; *<eater>* geräuschvoll

nomad *n* Nomade *m*. **~ic** *a* nomadisch; *<life, tribe>* Nomaden-

nominal *a*, **-ly** *adv* nominell

nominat|e *vt* nominieren, aufstellen; (*appoint*) ernennen. **~ion** *n* Nominierung *f*; Ernennung *f*

nominative *a & n* (*Gram*) **~[case]** Nominativ *m*

nonchalant *a*, **-ly** *adv* nonchalant; *<gesture>* lässig

nondescript *a* unbestimmbar; *<person>* unscheinbar

none *pron* keine(r)/keins; **~ of it/this** nichts davon ● *adv* **~ too** nicht gerade; **~ too soon** [um] keine Minute zu früh; **~ the less** dennoch

nonentity *n* Null *f*

non-existent *a* nicht vorhanden

non-fiction *n* Sachliteratur *f*

nonplussed *a* verblüfft

nonsens|e *n* Unsinn *m*. **~ical** *a* unsinnig

non-smoker *n* Nichtraucher *m*

non-stop *adv* ununterbrochen; *<fly>* nonstop

non-swimmer *n* Nichtschwimmer *m*

non-violent *a* gewaltlos

noodles *npl* Bandnudeln *pl*

noon *n* Mittag *m*; **at ~** um 12 Uhr mittags

noose *n* Schlinge *f*

nor *adv* noch ● *conj* auch nicht

Nordic *a* nordisch

norm *n* Norm *f*

normal *a* normal. **~ity** *n* Normalität *f*. **~ly** *adv* normal; (*usually*) normalerweise

north *n* Norden *m*; **to the ~ of** nördlich von ● *a* Nord-, nord- ● *adv* nach Norden

north: N~ America *n* Nordamerika *nt*. **~-east** *a* Nordost- ● *n* Nordosten *m*

norther|ly *a* nördlich. **~n** *a* nördlich. **N~n Ireland** *n* Nordirland *nt*

north: N~ Pole *n* Nordpol *m*. **N~ Sea** *n* Nordsee *f*. **~ward[s]** *adv* nach Norden. **~-west** *a* Nordwest- ● *n* Nordwesten *m*

Nor|way *n* Norwegen *nt*. **~wegian** *a* norwegisch ● *n* Norweger(in) *m(f)*

nose *n* Nase

nosebleed *n* Nasenbluten *nt*

nostalg|ia *n* Nostalgie *f*. **~ic** *a* nostalgisch

nostril *n* Nasenloch *nt*

nosy *a* (-ier, -iest) Ⓘ neugierig

not
● *adverb*
····▸ nicht. **I don't know** ich weiß nicht. **isn't she pretty?** ist sie nicht hübsch?
····▸ **not** a kein. **he is not a doctor** er ist kein Arzt. **she didn't wear a hat** sie trug keinen Hut. **there was not a person to be seen** es gab keinen Menschen zu sehen. **not a thing** gar nichts. **not a bit** kein bisschen
····▸ (*in elliptical phrases*) **I hope not** ich hoffe nicht. **of course not** natürlich nicht. **not at all** überhaupt nicht; (*in polite reply to thanks*) keine Ursache; gern geschehen. **certainly not!** auf keinen Fall! **not I** ich nicht
····▸ **not ... but ...** nicht ... sondern .... **it was not a small town but a big one** es war keine kleine Stadt, sondern eine große

notab|le *a* bedeutend; (*remarkable*) bemerkenswert. **~ly** *adv* insbesondere

notation *n* Notation *f*; (*Mus*) Notenschrift *f*

notch *n* Kerbe *f*

note *n* (*written comment*) Notiz *f*, Anmerkung *f*; (*short letter*) Briefchen *nt*, Zettel *m*; (*bank* **~**) Banknote *f*, Schein *m*; (*Mus*) Note *f*; (*sound*) Ton *m*; (*on piano*) Taste *f*; **half/whole ~** (*Amer*) halbe/ganze Note *f*; **of ~** von Bedeutung; **make a ~ of** notieren ● *vt* beachten; (*notice*) bemerken (**that** dass)

notebook *n* Notizbuch *nt*

noted *a* bekannt (**for** für)

note: ~paper *n* Briefpapier *nt*. **~worthy** *a* beachtenswert

nothing *n, pron & adv* nichts; **for ~** umsonst; **~ but** nichts als; **~ much** nicht viel; **~ interesting** nichts Interessantes

notice *n* (*on board*) Anschlag *m*, Bekanntmachung *f*; (*announcement*) Anzeige *f*; (*review*) Kritik *f*; (*termination of lease, employment*) Kündigung *f*; **give [in one's] ~** kündigen; **give s.o. ~** jdm kündigen; **take no ~!** ignoriere es! ● *vt* bemerken. **~able** *a*, **-bly** *adv* merklich. **~-board** *n* Anschlagbrett *nt*

noti|fication *n* Benachrichtigung *f*. **~fy** *vt* (*pt/pp* **-ied**) benachrichtigen

notion *n* Idee *f*

notorious *a* berüchtigt

notwithstanding *prep* trotz (+ *gen*) ● *adv* trotzdem, dennoch

nought *n* Null *f*

noun *n* Substantiv *nt*

nourish *vt* nähren. **~ing** *a* nahrhaft. **~ment** *n* Nahrung *f*

novel *a* neu[artig] ● *n* Roman *m*. **~ist** *n* Romanschriftsteller(in) *m(f)*. **~ty** *n* Neuheit *f*

November *n* November *m*

novice *n* Neuling *m*; (*Relig*) Novize *m*/Novizin *f*

now *adv & conj* jetzt; **~ [that]** jetzt, wo; **just ~** gerade, eben; **right ~** sofort; **~ and again** hin und wieder; **now, now!** na, na!

nowadays *adv* heutzutage

nowhere *adv* nirgendwo, nirgends

nozzle *n* Düse *f*

nuance *n* Nuance *f*

nuclear *a* Kern-. ~ **deterrent** *n* nukleares Abschreckungsmittel *nt*

nucleus *n* (*pl* **-lei**) Kern *m*

nude *a* nackt ● *n* (*Art*) Akt *m*; **in the** ~ nackt

nudge *vt* stupsen

nud|ist *n* Nudist *m*. ~**ity** *n* Nacktheit *f*

nuisance *n* Ärgernis *nt*; (*pest*) Plage *f*; **be a** ~ ärgerlich sein

null *a* ~ **and void** null und nichtig

numb *a* gefühllos, taub ● *vt* betäuben

number *n* Nummer *f*; (*amount*) Anzahl *f*; (*Math*) Zahl *f* ● *vt* nummerieren; (*include*) zählen (**among** zu). ~**-plate** *n* Nummernschild *nt*

numeral *n* Ziffer *f*

numerical *a*, **-ly** *adv* numerisch; **in** ~ **order** zahlenmäßig geordnet

numerous *a* zahlreich

nun *n* Nonne *f*

nurse *n* [Kranken]schwester *f*; (*male*) Krankenpfleger *m*; **children's** ~ Kindermädchen *nt* ● *vt* pflegen

nursery *n* Kinderzimmer *nt*; (*Hort*) Gärtnerei *f*; [**day**] ~ Kindertagesstätte *f*. ~ **rhyme** *n* Kinderreim *m*. ~ **school** *n* Kindergarten *m*

nursing *n* Krankenpflege *f*. ~ **home** *n* Pflegeheim *nt*

nut *n* Nuss *f*; (*Techn*) [Schrauben]mutter *f*; (🔲 *head*) Birne *f* 🔲; **be** ~**s** 🔲 spinnen 🔲. ~**crackers** *npl* Nussknacker *m*. ~**meg** *n* Muskat *m*

nutrient *n* Nährstoff *m*

nutrit|ion *n* Ernährung *f*. ~**ious** *a* nahrhaft

nutshell *n* Nussschale *f*; **in a** ~ (*fig*) kurz gesagt

nylon *n* Nylon *nt*

Oo

O *n* (*Teleph*) null

oak *n* Eiche *f*

OAP *abbr* (**old-age pensioner**) Rentner(in) *m(f)*

oar *n* Ruder *nt*. ~**sman** *n* Ruderer *m*

oasis *n* (*pl* **oases**) Oase *f*

oath *n* Eid *m*; (*swear-word*) Fluch *m*

oatmeal *n* Hafermehl *nt*

oats *npl* Hafer *m*; (*Culin*) [**rolled**] ~ Haferflocken *pl*

obedien|ce *n* Gehorsam *m*. ~**t** *a*, **-ly** *adv* gehorsam

obey *vt/i* gehorchen (+ *dat*); befolgen <*instructions, rules*>

obituary *n* Nachruf *m*; (*notice*) Todesanzeige *f*

object¹ *n* Gegenstand *m*; (*aim*) Zweck *m*; (*intention*) Absicht *f*; (*Gram*) Objekt *nt*; **money is no** ~ Geld spielt keine Rolle

object² *vi* Einspruch erheben (**to** gegen); (*be against*) etwas dagegen haben

objection *n* Einwand *m*; **have no** ~ nichts dagegen haben. ~**able** *a* anstößig; <*person*> unangenehm

objectiv|e *a*, **-ly** *adv* objektiv ● *n* Ziel *nt*. ~**ity** *n* Objektivität *f*

objector *n* Gegner *m*

obligation *n* Pflicht *f*; **without** ~ unverbindlich

obligatory *a* obligatorisch; **be** ~ Vorschrift sein

oblig|e *vt* verpflichten; (*compel*) zwingen; (*do a small service*) einen Gefallen tun (+ *dat*). ~**ing** *a* entgegenkommend

oblique *a* schräg; <*angle*> schief; (*fig*) indirekt

obliterate *vt* auslöschen

oblivion *n* Vergessenheit *f*

oblivious *a* **be** ~ sich (*dat*) nicht bewusst sein (**of** *gen*)

oblong *a* rechteckig ● *n* Rechteck *nt*

obnoxious *a* widerlich

oboe *n* Oboe *f*

obscen|e *a* obszön. **~ity** *n* Obszönität *f*

obscur|e *a* dunkel; (*unknown*) unbekannt ● *vt* verdecken; (*confuse*) verwischen. **~ity** *n* Dunkelheit *f*; Unbekanntheit *f*

observa|nce *n* (*of custom*) Einhaltung *f*. **~nt** *a* aufmerksam. **~tion** *n* Beobachtung *f*; (*remark*) Bemerkung *f*

observatory *n* Sternwarte *f*

observe *vt* beobachten; (*say, notice*) bemerken; (*keep, celebrate*) feiern; (*obey*) einhalten. **~r** *n* Beobachter *m*

obsess *vt* **be ~ed by** besessen sein von. **~ion** *n* Besessenheit *f*; (*persistent idea*) fixe Idee *f*. **~ive** *a*, **-ly** *adv* zwanghaft

obsolete *a* veraltet

obstacle *n* Hindernis *nt*

obstina|cy *n* Starrsinn *m*. **~te** *a*, **-ly** *adv* starrsinnig; <*refusal*> hartnäckig

obstruct *vt* blockieren; (*hinder*) behindern. **~ion** *n* Blockierung *f*; Behinderung *f*; (*obstacle*) Hindernis *nt*. **~ive** *a* **be ~ive** Schwierigkeiten bereiten

obtain *vt* erhalten. **~able** *a* erhältlich

obtrusive *a* aufdringlich; <*thing*> auffällig

obtuse *a* begriffsstutzig

obvious *a*, **-ly** *adv* offensichtlich, offenbar

occasion *n* Gelegenheit *f*; (*time*) Mal *nt*; (*event*) Ereignis *nt*; (*cause*) Anlass *m*, Grund *m*; **on the ~ of** anlässlich (+ *gen*)

occasional *a* gelegentlich. **~ly** *adv* gelegentlich, hin und wieder

occult *a* okkult

occupant *n* Bewohner(in) *m(f)*; (*of vehicle*) Insasse *m*

occupation *n* Beschäftigung *f*; (*job*) Beruf *m*; (*Mil*) Besetzung *f*; (*period*) Besatzung *f*. **~al** *a* Berufs-.

~al therapy *n* Beschäftigungstherapie *f*

occupier *n* Bewohner(in) *m(f)*

occupy *vt* (*pt/pp* **occupied**) besetzen <*seat, (Mil) country*>; einnehmen <*space*>; in Anspruch nehmen <*time*>; (*live in*) bewohnen; (*fig*) bekleiden <*office*>; (*keep busy*) beschäftigen

occur *vi* (*pt/pp* **occurred**) geschehen; (*exist*) vorkommen, auftreten; **it ~red to me that** es fiel mir ein, dass. **~rence** *n* Auftreten *nt*; (*event*) Ereignis *nt*

ocean *n* Ozean *m*

o'clock *adv* **[at] 7 ~ [um] 7 Uhr**

octagonal *a* achteckig

October *n* Oktober *m*

octopus *n* (*pl* **-puses**) Tintenfisch *m*

odd *a* (**-er, -est**) seltsam, merkwürdig; <*number*> ungerade; (*not of set*) einzeln; **forty ~** über vierzig; **~ jobs** Gelegenheitsarbeiten *pl*; **the ~ one out** die Ausnahme; **at ~ moments** zwischendurch

odd|ity *n* Kuriosität *f*. **~ly** *adv* merkwürdig; **~ly enough** merkwürdigerweise **~ment** *n* (*of fabric*) Rest *m*

odds *npl* (*chances*) Chancen *pl*; **at ~** uneinig; **~ and ends** Kleinkram *m*

ode *n* Ode *f*

odious *a* widerlich

odour *n* Geruch *m*. **~less** *a* geruchlos

of

● *preposition*

····▸ (*indicating belonging, origin*) von (+ *dat*); genitive. **the mother of twins** die Mutter von Zwillingen. **the mother of the twins** die Mutter der Zwillinge *or* von den Zwillingen. **the Queen of England** die Königin von England. **a friend of mine** ein Freund von mir. **a friend of the teacher's** ein Freund des Lehrers. **the brother of her father** der Bruder ihres Vaters. **the works of Shakespeare** Shakespeares Werke. **it was nice of him** es war nett von ihm

····▶ (*made of*) aus (+ *dat*). **a dress of cotton** ein Kleid aus Baumwolle

····▶ (*following number*) **five of us** fünf von uns. **the two of us** wir zwei. **there were four of us waiting** wir waren vier, die warteten

····▶ (*followed by number, description*) von (+ *dat*). **a girl of ten** ein Mädchen von zehn Jahren. **a distance of 50 miles** eine Entfernung von 50 Meilen. **a man of character** ein Mann von Charakter. **a woman of exceptional beauty** eine Frau von außerordentlicher Schönheit. **a person of strong views** ein Mensch mit festen Ansichten

❗ of is not translated after measures and in some other cases: **a pound of apples** ein Pfund Äpfel; **a cup of tea** eine Tasse Tee; **a glass of wine** ein Glas Wein; **the city of Chicago** die Stadt Chicago; **the fourth of January** der vierte Januar

off *prep* von (+ *dat*); ~ **the coast** vor der Küste; **get** ~ **the ladder/bus** von der Leiter/aus dem Bus steigen ● *adv* weg; <*button, lid, handle*> ab; <*light*> aus; <*brake*> los; <*machine*> abgeschaltet; <*tap*> zu; (*on appliance*) 'off' 'aus'; **2 kilometres** ~ 2 Kilometer entfernt; **a long way** ~ weit weg; (*time*) noch lange hin; ~ **and on** hin und wieder; **with his hat/coat** ~ ohne Hut/Mantel; **20%** ~ 20% Nachlass; **be** ~ (*leave*) [weg]gehen; (*Sport*) starten; <*food:*> schlecht sein; **be well** ~ gut dran sein; (*financially*) wohlhabend sein; **have a day** ~ einen freien Tag haben

offal *n* (*Culin*) Innereien *pl*

offence *n* (*illegal act*) Vergehen *nt*; **give/take** ~ Anstoß erregen/nehmen (**at** an + *dat*)

offend *vt* beleidigen. ~**er** *n* (*Jur*) Straftäter *m*

offensive *a* anstößig; (*Mil, Sport*) offensiv ● *n* Offensive *f*

offer *n* Angebot *nt*; **on (special)** ~ im Sonderangebot ● *vt* anbieten (**to** *dat*);

leisten <*resistance*>; ~ **to do sth** sich anbieten, etw zu tun. ~**ing** *n* Gabe *f*

offhand *a* brüsk; (*casual*) lässig

office *n* Büro *nt*; (*post*) Amt *nt*

officer *n* Offizier *m*; (*official*) Beamte(r) *m*/ Beamtin *f*; (*police*) Polizeibeamte(r) *m*/-beamtin *f*

official *a* offiziell, amtlich ● *n* Beamte(r) *m*/ Beamtin *f*; (*Sport*) Funktionär *m*. ~**ly** *adv* offiziell

officious *a*, **-ly** *adv* übereifrig

off-licence *n* Wein und Spirituosenhandlung *f*

off-load *vt* ausladen

off-putting *a* 🔲 abstoßend

offset *vt* (*pt/pp* **-set**, *pres p* **-setting**) ausgleichen

offshoot *n* Schössling *m*; (*fig*) Zweig *m*

offshore *a* Offshore-

offside *a* (*Sport*) abseits

offspring *n* Nachwuchs *m*

offstage *adv* hinter den Kulissen

off-white *a* fast weiß

often *adv* oft; **every so** ~ von Zeit zu Zeit

oh *int* oh! ach! **oh dear!** o weh!

oil *n* Öl *nt*; (*petroleum*) Erdöl *nt* ● *vt* ölen

oil: ~**field** *n* Ölfeld *nt*. ~**-painting** *n* Ölgemälde *nt*. ~ **refinery** *n* [Erd]ölraffinerie *f*. ~**-tanker** *n* Öltanker *m*. ~ **well** *n* Ölquelle *f*

oily *a* (**-ier, -iest**) ölig

ointment *n* Salbe *f*

OK *a & int* 🔲 in Ordnung; okay ● *adv* (*well*) gut ● *vt* (*auch* **okay**) (*pt/pp* **okayed**) genehmigen

old *a* (**-er, -est**) alt; (*former*) ehemalig

old: ~ **age** *n* Alter *nt*. ~**-age pensioner** *n* Rentner(in) *m(f)*. ~ **boy** *n* ehemaliger Schüler. ~**-fashioned** *a* altmodisch. ~ **girl** *n* ehemalige Schülerin *f*

olive *n* Olive *f*; (*colour*) Oliv *nt* ● *a* olivgrün. ~ **oil** *n* Olivenöl *nt*

Olympic *a* olympisch ● *n* **the** ~**s** die Olympischen Spiele *pl*

omelette *n* Omelett *nt*

ominous *a* bedrohlich

omission n Auslassung f; (failure to do) Unterlassung f

omit vt (pt/pp **omitted**) auslassen; ~ **to do sth** es unterlassen, etw zu tun

omnipotent a allmächtig

on prep auf (+ dat/(on to) + acc); (on vertical surface) an (+ dat/(on to) + acc); (about) über (+ acc); **on Monday** [am] Montag; **on Mondays** montags; **on the first of May** am ersten Mai; **on arriving** als ich ankam; **on one's finger** am Finger; **on the right/left** rechts/links; **on the Rhine** am Rhein; **on the radio/television** im Radio/Fernsehen; **on the bus/train** im Bus/Zug; **go on the bus/train** mit dem Bus/Zug fahren; **on me** (with me) bei mir; **it's on me** 🖪 das spendiere ich ● adv (further on) weiter; (switched on) an; <brake> angezogen; <machine> angeschaltet; (on appliance) **'on'** 'ein'; **with/without his hat/coat on** mit/ohne Hut/Mantel; **be on** <film:> laufen; <event:> stattfinden; **be on at** 🖪 bedrängen (zu to); **it's not on** 🖪 das geht nicht; **on and on** immer weiter; **on and off** hin und wieder; **and so on** und so weiter

once adv einmal; (formerly) früher; **at ~** sofort; (at the same time) gleichzeitig; **~ and for all** ein für alle Mal ● conj wenn; (with past tense) als

oncoming a **~ traffic** Gegenverkehr m

one a ein(e); (only) einzig; **not ~** kein(e); **~ day/evening** eines Tages/Abends ● n Eins f ● pron eine(r)/eins; (impersonal) man; **which ~** welche(r,s); **~ another** einander; **~ by ~** einzeln; **~ never knows** man kann nie wissen

one: ~-parent family n Einelternfamilie f. **~self** pron selbst; (refl) sich; **by ~self** allein. **~-sided** a einseitig. **~-way** a <street> Einbahn-; <ticket> einfach

onion n Zwiebel f

onlooker n Zuschauer(in) m(f)

only a einzige(r,s); **an ~ child** ein Einzelkind nt ● adv & conj nur; **~ just** gerade erst; (barely) gerade noch

onset n Beginn m; (of winter) Einsetzen nt

onward[s] adv vorwärts; **from then ~** von der Zeit an

ooze vi sickern

opaque a undurchsichtig

open a, **-ly** adv offen; **be ~** <shop:> geöffnet sein; **in the ~ air** im Freien ● n **in the ~** im Freien ● vt öffnen, aufmachen; (start, set up) eröffnen ● vi sich öffnen; <flower:> aufgehen; <shop:> öffnen, aufmachen; (be started) eröffnet werden. **~ up** vt öffnen, aufmachen

open day n Tag m der offenen Tür

opener n Öffner m

opening n Öffnung f; (beginning) Eröffnung f; (job) Einstiegsmöglichkeit f. **~ hours** npl Öffnungszeiten pl

open: ~-minded a aufgeschlossen. **~ sandwich** n belegtes Brot nt

opera n Oper f. **~-house** n Opernhaus nt. **~-singer** n Opernsänger(in) m(f)

operate vt bedienen <machine, lift>; betätigen <lever, brake>; (fig: run) betreiben ● vi (Techn) funktionieren; (be in action) in Betrieb sein; (Mil & fig) operieren; **~ [on]** (Med) operieren

operatic a Opern-

operation n (see operate) Bedienung f; Betätigung f; Operation f; **in ~** (Techn) in Betrieb; **come into ~** (fig) in Kraft treten; **have an ~** (Med) operiert werden. **~al** a be **~al** in Betrieb sein; <law:> in Kraft sein

operative a wirksam

operator n (user) Bedienungsperson f; (Teleph) Vermittlung f

operetta n Operette f

opinion n Meinung f; **in my ~** meiner Meinung nach. **~ated** a rechthaberisch

opponent n Gegner(in) m(f)

opportun|e *a* günstig. **~ist** *n* Opportunist *m*

opportunity *n* Gelegenheit *f*

oppos|e *vt* Widerstand leisten (+ *dat*); (*argue against*) sprechen gegen; **be ~ed to sth** gegen etw sein; **as ~ed to** im Gegensatz zu. **~ing** *a* gegnerisch

opposite *a* entgegengesetzt; <*house, side*> gegenüberliegend; **~ number** (*fig*) Gegenstück *nt*; **the ~ sex** das andere Geschlecht ● *n* Gegenteil *nt* ● *adv* gegenüber ● *prep* gegenüber (+ *dat*)

opposition *n* Widerstand *m*; (*Pol*) Opposition *f*

oppress *vt* unterdrücken. **~ion** *n* Unterdrückung *f*. **~ive** *a* tyrannisch; <*heat*> drückend

opt *vi* **~ for** sich entscheiden für

optical *a* optisch

optician *n* Optiker *m*

optimis|m *n* Optimismus *m*. **~t** *n* Optimist *m*. **~tic** *a*, **-ally** *adv* optimistisch

optimum *a* optimal

option *n* Wahl *f*; (*Comm*) Option *f*. **~al** *a* auf Wunsch erhältlich; <*subject*> wahlfrei

opu|lence *n* Prunk *m*. **~lent** *a* prunkvoll

or *conj* oder; (*after negative*) noch; **or [else]** sonst; **in a year or two** in ein bis zwei Jahren

oral *a*, **-ly** *adv* mündlich; (*Med*) oral ● *n* Mündliche(s) *nt*

orange *n* Apfelsine *f*, Orange *f*; (*colour*) Orange *nt* ● *a* orangefarben

oratorio *n* Oratorium *nt*

oratory *n* Redekunst *f*

orbit *n* Umlaufbahn *f* ● *vt* umkreisen

orchard *n* Obstgarten *m*

orches|tra *n* Orchester *nt*. **~tral** *a* Orchester-. **~trate** *vt* orchestrieren

ordeal *n* (*fig*) Qual *f*

order *n* Ordnung *f*; (*sequence*) Reihenfolge *f*; (*condition*) Zustand *m*; (*command*) Befehl *m*; (*in restaurant*) Bestellung *f*; (*Comm*) Auftrag *m*; (*Relig, medal*) Orden *m*; **out of ~** <*machine*> außer Betrieb; **in ~ that** damit; **in ~ to help** um zu helfen ● *vt* (*put in ~*) ordnen; (*command*) befehlen (+ *dat*); (*Comm, in restaurant*) bestellen; (*prescribe*) verordnen

orderly *a* ordentlich; (*not unruly*) friedlich ● *n* (*Mil, Med*) Sanitäter *m*

ordinary *a* gewöhnlich, normal

ore *n* Erz *nt*

organ *n* (*Biol & fig*) Organ *nt*; (*Mus*) Orgel *f*

organic *a*, **-ally** *adv* organisch; (*without chemicals*) biodynamisch; <*crop*> biologisch angebaut; <*food*> Bio-. **~ farming** *n* biologischer Anbau *m*

organism *n* Organismus *m*

organist *n* Organist *m*

organization *n* Organisation *f*

organize *vt* organisieren; veranstalten <*event*>. **~r** *n* Organisator *m*; Veranstalter *m*

orgy *n* Orgie *f*

Orient *n* Orient *m*. **o~al** *a* orientalisch ● *n* Orientale *m*/ Orientalin *f*

orientation *n* Orientierung *f*

origin *n* Ursprung *m*; (*of person, goods*) Herkunft *f*

original *a* ursprünglich; (*not copied*) original; (*new*) originell ● *n* Original *nt*. **~ity** *n* Originalität *f*. **~ly** *adv* ursprünglich

originate *vi* entstehen

ornament *n* Ziergegenstand *m*; (*decoration*) Verzierung *f*. **~al** *a* dekorativ

ornate *a* reich verziert

ornithology *n* Vogelkunde *f*

orphan *n* Waisenkind *nt*, Waise *f*. **~age** *n* Waisenhaus *nt*

orthodox *a* orthodox

ostensible *a*, **-bly** *adv* angeblich

ostentat|ion *n* Protzerei *f* 🔲. **~ious** *a* protzig 🔲

osteopath *n* Osteopath *m*

ostrich *n* Strauß *m*

other *a*, *pron* & *n* andere(r,s); **the ~ [one]** der/die/das andere; **the ~ two** die zwei anderen; **no ~s** sonst keine;

any ~ **questions?** sonst noch
Fragen? **every ~ day** jeden zweiten
Tag; **the ~ day** neulich; **the ~
evening** neulich abends; **someone/
something or ~** irgendjemand/-etwas
● *adv* anders; **~ than him** außer
ihm; **somehow/somewhere or ~**
irgendwie/irgendwo

otherwise *adv* sonst; (*differently*)
anders

ought *v aux* **I/we ~ to stay** ich
sollte/wir sollten eigentlich bleiben;
he ~ not to have done it er hätte es
nicht machen sollen

ounce *n* Unze *f* (*28, 35 g*)

our *a* unser

ours *poss pron* unsere(r,s); **a friend of
~** ein Freund von uns; **that is ~** das
gehört uns

ourselves *pron* selbst; (*refl*) uns; **by
~** allein

out *adv* (*not at home*) weg; (*outside*)
draußen; (*not alight*) aus;
(*unconscious*) bewusstlos; **be ~**
<*sun:*> scheinen; <*flower*> blühen;
<*workers*> streiken; <*calculation:*>
nicht stimmen; (*Sport*) aus sein; (*fig:
not feasible*) nicht infrage kommen;
~ and about unterwegs; **have it ~
with s.o.** 🔢 jdn zur Rede stellen; **get
~!** 🔢 raus! **~ with it!** 🔢 heraus
damit! ● *prep* **~ of** aus (+ *dat*); **go ~
(of) the door** zur Tür hinausgehen;
be ~ of bed/ the room nicht im
Bett/im Zimmer sein; **~ of breath/
danger** außer Atem/Gefahr; **~ of
work** arbeitslos; **nine ~ of ten** neun
von zehn; **be ~ of sugar** keinen
Zucker mehr haben

outboard *a* **~ motor**
Außenbordmotor *m*

outbreak *n* Ausbruch *m*

outbuilding *n* Nebengebäude *nt*

outburst *n* Ausbruch *m*

outcast *n* Ausgestoßene(r) *m/f*

outcome *n* Ergebnis *nt*

outcry *n* Aufschrei *m* [der
Entrüstung]

outdated *a* überholt

outdo *vt* (*pt* **-did**, *pp* **-done**)
übertreffen, übertrumpfen

outdoor *a* <*life, sports*> im Freien;
~ swimming pool Freibad *nt*

outdoors *adv* draußen; **go ~** nach
draußen gehen

outer *a* äußere(r,s)

outfit *n* Ausstattung *f*; (*clothes*)
Ensemble *nt*; (🔢 *organization*)
Laden *m*

outgoing *a* ausscheidend; <*mail*>
ausgehend; (*sociable*) kontaktfreudig;
~s *npl* Ausgaben *pl*

outgrow *vi* (*pt* **-grew**, *pp* **-grown**)
herauswachsen aus

outing *n* Ausflug *m*

outlaw *n* Geächtete(r) *m/f* ● *vt*
ächten

outlay *n* Auslagen *pl*

outlet *n* Abzug *m*; (*for water*)
Abfluss *m*; (*fig*) Ventil *nt*; (*Comm*)
Absatzmöglichkeit *f*

outline *n* Umriss *m*; (*summary*)
kurze Darstellung *f* ● *vt* umreißen

outlive *vt* überleben

outlook *n* Aussicht *f*; (*future
prospect*) Aussichten *pl*; (*attitude*)
Einstellung *f*

outmoded *a* überholt

outnumber *vt* zahlenmäßig
überlegen sein (+ *dat*)

out-patient *n* ambulanter Patient
m

outpost *n* Vorposten *m*

output *n* Leistung *f*; Produktion *f*

outrage *n* Gräueltat *f*; (*fig*) Skandal
m; (*indignation*) Empörung *f*. **~ous**
a empörend

outright[1] *a* völlig, total; <*refusal*>
glatt

outright[2] *adv* ganz; (*at once*) sofort;
(*frankly*) offen

outset *n* Anfang *m*

outside[1] *a* äußere(r,s); **~ wall**
Außenwand *f* ● *n* Außenseite *f*; **from
the ~** von außen; **at the ~** höchstens

outside[2] *adv* außen; (*out of doors*)
draußen; **go ~** nach draußen gehen
● *prep* außerhalb (+ *gen*); (*in front
of*) vor (+ *dat/acc*)

outsider *n* Außenseiter *m*

outsize *a* übergroß

outskirts *npl* Rand *m*

outspoken *a* offen; **be** ~ kein Blatt vor den Mund nehmen

outstanding *a* hervorragend; (*conspicuous*) bemerkenswert; (*Comm*) ausstehend

outstretched *a* ausgestreckt

outvote *vt* überstimmen

outward *a* äußerlich; ~ **journey** Hinreise *f* ● *adv* nach außen. ~**ly** *adv* nach außen hin, äußerlich. ~**s** *adv* nach außen

outwit *vt* (*pt/pp* **-witted**) überlisten

oval *a* oval ● *n* Oval *nt*

ovation *n* Ovation *f*

oven *n* Backofen *m*

over *prep* über (+ *acc/dat*); ~ **dinner** beim Essen; ~ **the phone** am Telefon; ~ **the page** auf der nächsten Seite ● *adv* (*remaining*) übrig; (*ended*) zu Ende; ~ **again** noch einmal; ~ **and** ~ immer wieder; ~ **here/there** hier/da drüben; **all** ~ (*everywhere*) überall; **it's all** ~ es ist vorbei; **I ache all** ~ mir tut alles weh

overall[1] *n* Kittel *m*; ~**s** *pl* Overall *m*

overall[2] *a* gesamt; (*general*) allgemein ● *adv* insgesamt

overbalance *vi* das Gleichgewicht verlieren

overbearing *a* herrisch

overboard *adv* (*Naut*) über Bord

overcast *a* bedeckt

overcharge *vt* ~ **s.o.** jdm zu viel berechnen ● *vi* zu viel verlangen

overcoat *n* Mantel *m*

overcome *vt* (*pt* **-came**, *pp* **-come**) überwinden; **be** ~ **by** überwältigt werden von

overcrowded *a* überfüllt

overdo *vt* (*pt* **-did**, *pp* **-done**) übertreiben; (*cook too long*) zu lange kochen; ~ **it** (🄘 *do too much*) sich übernehmen

overdose *n* Überdosis *f*

overdraft *n* [Konto]überziehung *f*; **have an** ~ sein Konto überzogen haben

overdue *a* überfällig

overestimate *vt* überschätzen

overflow[1] *n* Überschuss *m*; (*outlet*) Überlauf *m*

overflow[2] *vi* überlaufen

overgrown *a* <*garden*> überwachsen

overhang[1] *n* Überhang *m*

overhang[2] *vt/i* (*pt/pp* **-hung**) überhängen (über + *acc*)

overhaul[1] *n* Überholung *f*

overhaul[2] *vt* (*Techn*) überholen

overhead[1] *adv* oben

overhead[2] *a* Ober-; (*ceiling*) Decken-. ~**s** *npl* allgemeine Unkosten *pl*

overhear *vt* (*pt/pp* **-heard**) mit anhören <*conversation*>

overheat *vi* zu heiß werden

overjoyed *a* überglücklich

overland *a & adv* auf dem Landweg; ~ **route** Landroute *f*

overlap *vi* (*pt/pp* **-lapped**) sich überschneiden

overleaf *adv* umseitig

overload *vt* überladen

overlook *vt* überblicken; (*fail to see, ignore*) übersehen

overnight[1] *adv* über Nacht; **stay** ~ übernachten

overnight[2] *a* Nacht-; ~ **stay** Übernachtung *f*

overpass *n* Überführung *f*

overpay *vt* (*pt/pp* **-paid**) überbezahlen

overpopulated *a* übervölkert

overpower *vt* überwältigen. ~**ing** *a* überwältigend

overpriced *a* zu teuer

overrated *a* überbewertet

overreact *vi* überreagieren. ~**ion** *n* Überreaktion *f*

overriding *a* Haupt-

overrule *vt* ablehnen; **we were** ~**d** wir wurden überstimmt

overrun *vt* (*pt* **-ran**, *pp* **-run**, *pres p* **-running**) überrennen; überschreiten <*time*>; **be** ~ **with** überlaufen sein von

overseas[1] *adv* in Übersee; **go** ~ nach Übersee gehen

overseas[2] *a* Übersee-

oversee vt (pt -saw, pp -seen) beaufsichtigen

overshadow vt überschatten

overshoot vt (pt/pp -shot) hinausschießen über (+ acc)

oversight n Versehen nt

oversleep vi (pt/pp -slept) [sich] verschlafen

overstep vt (pt/pp -stepped) überschreiten

overt a offen

overtake vt/i (pt -took, pp -taken) überholen

overthrow vt (pt -threw, pp -thrown) (Pol) stürzen

overtime n Überstunden pl ● adv work ~ Überstunden machen

overtired a übermüdet

overture n (Mus) Ouvertüre f; ~s pl (fig) Annäherungsversuche pl

overturn vt umstoßen ● vi umkippen

overweight a übergewichtig; be ~ Übergewicht haben

overwhelm vt überwältigen. ~ing a überwältigend

overwork n Überarbeitung f ● vt überfordern ● vi sich überarbeiten

overwrought a überreizt

ow|e vt schulden/ (fig) verdanken ([to] s.o. jdm); ~e s.o. sth jdm etw schuldig sein. ~ing to prep wegen (+ gen)

owl n Eule f

own[1] a & pron eigen; it's my ~ es gehört mir; a car of my ~ mein eigenes Auto; on one's ~ allein; get one's ~ back 🔢 sich revanchieren

own[2] vt besitzen; I don't ~ it es gehört mir nicht. ~ up vi es zugeben

owner n Eigentümer(in) m(f), Besitzer(in) m(f); (of shop)Inhaber(in) m(f). ~ship n Besitz m

oxygen n Sauerstoff m

oyster n Auster f

Pp

pace n Schritt m; (speed) Tempo nt; keep ~ with Schritt halten mit ● vi ~ up and down auf und ab gehen. ~-maker n (Sport & Med) Schrittmacher m

Pacific a & n the ~ [Ocean] der Pazifik

pacifist n Pazifist m

pacify vt (pt/pp -ied) beruhigen

pack n Packung f; (Mil) Tornister m; (of cards) [Karten]spiel nt; (gang) Bande f; (of hounds) Meute f; (of wolves) Rudel nt; a ~ of lies ein Haufen Lügen ● vt/i packen; einpacken <article>; be ~ed (crowded) [gedrängt] voll sein. ~ up vt einpacken ● vi 🔢 <machine:> kaputtgehen

package n Paket nt. ~ holiday n Pauschalreise f

packet n Päckchen nt

packing n Verpackung f

pact n Pakt m

pad n Polster nt; (for writing) [Schreib]block m ● vt (pt/pp padded) polstern

padding n Polsterung f; (in written work) Füllwerk nt

paddle[1] n Paddel nt ● vt (row) paddeln

paddle[2] vi waten

paddock n Koppel f

padlock n Vorhängeschloss nt ● vt mit einem Vorhängeschloss verschließen

paediatrician n Kinderarzt m /-ärztin f

pagan a heidnisch ● n Heide m/ Heidin f

page[1] n Seite f

page[2] n (boy) Page m ● vt ausrufen <person>

paid *see* pay ● *a* bezahlt; **put ~ to** 🔲 zunichte machen

pail *n* Eimer *m*

pain *n* Schmerz *m*; **be in ~** Schmerzen haben; **take ~s** sich (*dat*) Mühe geben; **~ in the neck** 🔲 Nervensäge *f*

pain: ~ful *a* schmerzhaft; (*fig*) schmerzlich. **~killer** *n* schmerzstillendes Mittel *nt*. **~less** *a*, **-ly** *adv* schmerzlos

painstaking *a* sorgfältig

paint *n* Farbe *f* ● *vt/i* streichen; <*artist:*> malen. **~brush** *n* Pinsel *m*. **~er** *n* Maler *m*; (*decorator*) Anstreicher *m*. **~ing** *n* Malerei *f*; (*picture*) Gemälde *nt*

pair *n* Paar *nt*; **~ of trousers** Hose *f* ● *vi* **~ off** Paare bilden

pajamas *n pl* (*Amer*) Schlafanzug *m*

Pakistan *n* Pakistan *nt*. **~i** *a* pakistanisch ● *n* Pakistaner(in) *m(f)*

pal *n* Freund(in) *m(f)*

palace *n* Palast *m*

palatable *a* schmackhaft

palate *n* Gaumen *m*

palatial *a* palastartig

pale *a* (**-r, -st**) blass ● *vi* blass werden. **~ness** *n* Blässe *f*

Palestin|e *n* Palästina *nt*. **~ian** *a* palästinensisch ● *n* Palästinenser(in) *m(f)*

palette *n* Palette *f*

palm *n* Handfläche *f*; (*tree, symbol*) Palme *f* ● *vt* **~ sth off on s.o.** jdm etw andrehen. **P~ Sunday** *n* Palmsonntag *m*

palpable *a* tastbar; (*perceptible*) spürbar

palpitations *npl* Herzklopfen *nt*

paltry *a* (**-ier, -iest**) armselig

pamper *vt* verwöhnen

pamphlet *n* Broschüre *f*

pan *n* Pfanne *f*; (*saucepan*) Topf *m*; (*of scales*) Schale *f*

panacea *n* Allheilmittel *nt*

pancake *n* Pfannkuchen *m*

panda *n* Panda *m*

pandemonium *n* Höllenlärm *m*

pane *n* [Glas]scheibe *f*

panel *n* Tafel *f*, Platte *f*; **~ of experts** Expertenrunde *f*; **~ of judges** Jury *f*. **~ling** *n* Täfelung *f*

pang *n* **~s of hunger** Hungergefühl *nt*; **~s of conscience** Gewissensbisse *pl*

panic *n* Panik *f* ● *vi* (*pt/pp* **panicked**) in Panik geraten. **~-stricken** *a* von Panik ergriffen

panoram|a *n* Panorama *nt*. **~ic** *a* Panorama-

pansy *n* Stiefmütterchen *nt*

pant *vi* keuchen; <*dog:*> hecheln

panther *n* Panther *m*

panties *npl* [Damen]slip *m*

pantomime *n* [zu Weihnachten aufgeführte] Märchenvorstellung *f*

pantry *n* Speisekammer *f*

pants *npl* Unterhose *f*; (*woman's*) Schlüpfer *m*; (*trousers*) Hose *f*

pantyhose *n* (*Amer*) Strumpfhose *f*

paper *n* Papier *nt*; (*newspaper*) Zeitung *f*; (*exam ~*) Testbogen *m*; (*exam*) Klausur *f*; (*treatise*) Referat *nt*; **~s** *pl* (*documents*) Unterlagen *pl*; (*for identification*) [Ausweis]papiere *pl* ● *vt* tapezieren

paper: ~back *n* Taschenbuch *nt*. **~-clip** *n* Büroklammer *f*. **~weight** *n* Briefbeschwerer *m*. **~work** *n* Schreibarbeit *f*

par *n* (*Golf*) Par *nt*; **on a ~** gleichwertig (**with** *dat*)

parable *n* Gleichnis *nt*

parachut|e *n* Fallschirm *m* ● *vi* [mit dem Fallschirm] abspringen. **~ist** *n* Fallschirmspringer *m*

parade *n* Parade *f*; (*procession*) Festzug *m* ● *vt* (*show off*) zur Schau stellen

paradise *n* Paradies *nt*

paradox *n* Paradox *nt*. **~ical** *a*, paradox

paraffin *n* Paraffin *nt*

paragraph *n* Absatz *m*

parallel *a* & *adv* parallel ● *n* (*Geog*) Breitenkreis *m*; (*fig*) Parallele *f*

paralyse *vt* lähmen; (*fig*) lahmlegen

paralysis *n* (*pl* **-ses**) Lähmung *f*

paranoid a [krankhaft] misstrauisch

parapet n Brüstung f

paraphernalia n Kram m

parasite n Parasit m, Schmarotzer m

paratrooper n Fallschirmjäger m

parcel n Paket nt

parch vt austrocknen; **be ~ed** <person:> einen furchtbaren Durst haben

parchment n Pergament nt

pardon n Verzeihung f; (Jur) Begnadigung f; **~?** 🆃 bitte? **I beg your ~** wie bitte? (sorry) Verzeihung! ● vt verzeihen; (Jur) begnadigen

parent n Elternteil m; **~s** pl Eltern pl. **~al** a elterlich

parenthesis n (pl -ses) Klammer f

parish n Gemeinde f. **~ioner** n Gemeindemitglied nt

park n Park m ● vt/i parken

parking n Parken nt; **'no ~'** 'Parken verboten'. **~-lot** n (Amer) Parkplatz m. **~-meter** n Parkuhr f. **~ space** n Parkplatz m

parliament n Parlament nt. **~ary** a parlamentarisch

parochial a Gemeinde-; (fig) beschränkt

parody n Parodie f ● vt (pt/pp -ied) parodieren

parole n **on ~** auf Bewährung

parquet n **~ floor** Parkett nt

parrot n Papagei m

parsley n Petersilie f

parsnip n Pastinake f

parson n Pfarrer m

part n Teil m; (Techn) Teil nt; (area) Gegend f; (Theat) Rolle f; (Mus) Part m; **spare ~** Ersatzteil nt; **for my ~** meinerseits; **on the ~ of** vonseiten (+ gen); **take s.o.'s ~** für jdn Partei ergreifen; **take ~ in** teilnehmen an (+ dat) ● adv teils ● vt trennen; scheiteln <hair> ● vi <people:> sich trennen; **~ with** sich trennen von

partial a Teil-; **be ~ to** mögen. **-ly** adv teilweise

particip|ant n Teilnehmer(in) m(f). **~ate** vi teilnehmen (**in** an + dat). **~ation** n Teilnahme f

particle n Körnchen nt; (Phys) Partikel nt; (Gram) Partikel f

particular a besondere(r,s); (precise) genau; (fastidious) penibel; **in ~** besonders. **~ly** adv besonders. **~s** npl nähere Angaben pl

parting n Abschied m; (in hair) Scheitel m

partition n Trennwand f; (Pol) Teilung f ● vt teilen

partly adv teilweise

partner n Partner(in) m(f); (Comm) Teilhaber m. **~ship** n Partnerschaft f; (Comm) Teilhaberschaft f

partridge n Rebhuhn nt

part-time a & adv Teilzeit-; **be** or **work ~** Teilzeitarbeit machen

party n Party f, Fest nt; (group) Gruppe f; (Pol, Jur) Partei f

pass n Ausweis m; (Geog, Sport) Pass m; (Sch) ≈ ausreichend; **get a ~** bestehen ● vt vorbeigehen/-fahren an (+ dat); (overtake) überholen; (hand) reichen; (Sport) abgeben, abspielen; (approve) annehmen; (exceed) übersteigen; bestehen <exam>; machen <remark>; fällen <judgement>; (Jur) verhängen <sentence>; **~ the time** sich (dat) die Zeit vertreiben; **~ one's hand over sth** mit der Hand über etw (acc) fahren ● vi vorbeigehen/-fahren; (get by) vorbeikommen; (overtake) überholen; <time:> vergehen; (in exam) bestehen; **~ away** vi sterben. **~ down** vt herunterreichen; (fig) weitergeben. **~ out** vi ohnmächtig werden. **~ round** vt herumreichen. **~ up** vt heraufreichen; (🆃 miss) vorübergehen lassen

passable a <road> befahrbar; (satisfactory) passabel

passage n Durchgang m; (corridor) Gang m; (voyage) Überfahrt f; (in book) Passage f

passenger n Fahrgast m; (Naut, Aviat) Passagier m; (in car) Mitfahrer m. **~ seat** n Beifahrersitz m

passer-by n (pl **-s-by**) Passant(in) m(f)

passion n Leidenschaft f. **~ate** a, **-ly** adv leidenschaftlich

passive a passiv ● n Passiv nt

pass: ~port n [Reise]pass m. **~word** n Kennwort nt; (Mil) Losung f

past a vergangene(r,s); (former) ehemalig; **that's all ~** das ist jetzt vorbei ● n Vergangenheit f ● prep an (+ dat) ... vorbei; (after) nach; **at ten ~ two** um zehn nach zwei ● adv vorbei; **go ~** vorbeigehen

pasta n Nudeln pl

paste n Brei m; (adhesive) Kleister m; (jewellery) Strass m ● vt kleistern

pastel n Pastellfarbe f, (drawing) Pastell nt ● attrib Pastell-

pastime n Zeitvertreib m

pastry n Teig m; **cakes and ~ies** Kuchen und Gebäck

pasture n Weide f

pasty n Pastete f

pat n Klaps m; (of butter) Stückchen nt ● vt (pt/pp patted) tätscheln; **~ s.o. on the back** jdm auf die Schulter klopfen

patch n Flicken m; (spot) Fleck m; **not a ~ on** 🔢 gar nicht zu vergleichen mit ● vt flicken. **~ up** vt [zusammen]flicken; beilegen <quarrel>

patchy a ungleichmäßig

patent n Patent nt ● vt patentieren. **~ leather** n Lackleder nt

paternal a väterlich

path n (pl **-s**) [Fuß]weg m, Pfad m; (orbit, track) Bahn f; (fig) Weg m

pathetic a mitleiderregend; <attempt> erbärmlich

patience n Geduld f; (game) Patience f

patient a, **-ly** adv geduldig ● n Patient(in) m(f)

patio n Terrasse f

patriot n Patriot(in) m(f). **~ic** a patriotisch. **~ism** n Patriotismus m

patrol n Patrouille f ● vt/i patrouillieren [in (+ dat)]; <police:>

auf Streife gehen/fahren [in (+ dat)]. **~ car** n Streifenwagen m

patron n Gönner m; (of charity) Schirmherr m; (of the arts) Mäzen m; (customer) Kunde m/Kundin f; (Theat) Besucher m. **~age** n Schirmherrschaft f

patroniz|e vt (fig) herablassend behandeln. **~ing** a, **-ly** adv gönnerhaft

patter n (speech) Gerede nt

pattern n Muster nt

paunch n [Schmer]bauch m

pause n Pause f ● vi innehalten

pave vt pflastern; **~ the way** den Weg bereiten (for dat). **~ment** n Bürgersteig m

paw n Pfote f; (of large animal) Pranke f, Tatze f

pawn¹ n (Chess) Bauer m; (fig) Schachfigur f

pawn² vt verpfänden. **~ broker** n Pfandleiher m

pay n Lohn m; (salary) Gehalt nt; **be in the ~ of** bezahlt werden von ● v (pt/pp **paid**) ● vt bezahlen; zahlen <money>; **~ s.o. a visit** jdm einen Besuch abstatten; **~ s.o. a compliment** jdm ein Kompliment machen ● vi zahlen; (be profitable) sich bezahlt machen; (fig) sich lohnen; **~ for sth** etw bezahlen. **~ back** vt zurückzahlen. **~ in** vt einzahlen. **~ off** vt abzahlen <debt> ● vi (fig) sich auszahlen

payable a zahlbar; **make ~ to** ausstellen auf (+ acc)

payment n Bezahlung f; (amount) Zahlung f

pea n Erbse f

peace n Frieden m; **for my ~ of mind** zu meiner eigenen Beruhigung

peace|ful a, **-ly** adv friedlich. **~maker** n Friedensstifter m

peach n Pfirsich m

peacock n Pfau m

peak n Gipfel m; (fig) Höhepunkt m. **~ed cap** n Schirmmütze f. **~ hours** npl Hauptbelastungszeit f; (for traffic) Hauptverkehrszeit f

peal n (of bells) Glockengeläut nt; ∼s of laughter schallendes Gelächter nt

peanut n Erdnuss f

pear n Birne f

pearl n Perle f

peasant n Bauer m

peat n Torf m

pebble n Kieselstein m

peck n Schnabelhieb m; (kiss) flüchtiger Kuss m ● vt/i picken/(nip) hacken (at nach)

peculiar a eigenartig, seltsam; ∼ to eigentümlich (+ dat). ∼ity n Eigenart f

pedal n Pedal nt ● vt fahren <bicycle> ● vi treten

pedantic a, -ally adv pedantisch

pedestal n Sockel m

pedestrian n Fußgänger(in) m(f) ● a (fig) prosaisch. ∼ crossing n Fußgängerüberweg m. ∼ precinct n Fußgängerzone f

pedigree n Stammbaum m ● attrib <animal> Rasse-

pedlar n Hausierer m

peek vi 🔲 gucken

peel n Schale f ● vt schälen; ● vi <skin:> sich schälen; <paint:> abblättern. ∼ings npl Schalen pl

peep n kurzer Blick m ● vi gucken. ∼-hole n Guckloch nt

peer¹ vi ∼ at forschend ansehen

peer² n Peer m; his ∼s pl seinesgleichen

peg n (hook) Haken m; (for tent) Pflock m, Hering m; (for clothes) [Wäsche]klammer f; off the ∼ 🔲 von der Stange

pejorative a, -ly adv abwertend

pelican n Pelikan m

pellet n Kügelchen nt

pelt¹ n (skin) Pelz m, Fell nt

pelt² vt bewerfen ● vi ∼ [down] <rain:> [hernieder]prasseln

pelvis n (Anat) Becken nt

pen¹ n (for animals) Hürde f

pen² n Federhalter m; (ballpoint) Kugelschreiber m

penal a Straf-. ∼ize vt bestrafen; (fig) benachteiligen

penalty n Strafe f; (fine) Geldstrafe f; (Sport) Strafstoß m; (Football) Elfmeter m

penance see penny

pence see penny

pencil n Bleistift m ● vt (pt/pp pencilled) mit Bleistift schreiben. ∼-sharpener n Bleistiftspitzer m

pendulum n Pendel nt

penetrat|e vt durchdringen; ∼e into eindringen in (+ acc). ∼ing a durchdringend. ∼ion n Durchdringen nt

penfriend n Brieffreund(in) m(f)

penguin n Pinguin m

penicillin n Penizillin nt

peninsula n Halbinsel f

penis n Penis m

penitentiary n (Amer) Gefängnis nt

pen: ∼knife n Taschenmesser nt. ∼-name n Pseudonym nt

penniless a mittellos

penny n (pl pence; single coins pennies) Penny m; (Amer) Centstück nt; the ∼'s dropped 🔲 der Groschen ist gefallen

pension n Rente f; (of civil servant) Pension f. ∼er n Rentner(in) m(f); Pensionär(in) m(f)

pensive a nachdenklich

pent-up a angestaut

penultimate a vorletzte(r,s)

people npl Leute pl, Menschen pl; (citizens) Bevölkerung f; the ∼ das Volk; English ∼ die Engländer; ∼ say man sagt; for four ∼ für vier Personen ● vt bevölkern

pepper n Pfeffer m; (vegetable) Paprika m

pepper: ∼mint n Pfefferminz nt; (Bot) Pfefferminze f. ∼pot n Pfefferstreuer m

per prep pro; ∼ cent Prozent nt

percentage n Prozentsatz m; (part) Teil m

perceptible a wahrnehmbar

percept|ion n Wahrnehmung f. ∼ive a feinsinnig

perch[1] *n* Stange *f* ● *vi* <*bird*:> sich niederlassen

perch[2] *n inv* (*fish*) Barsch *m*

percussion *n* Schlagzeug *nt*. **~instrument** *n* Schlaginstrument *nt*

perennial *a* <*problem*> immer wiederkehrend ● *n* (*Bot*) mehrjährige Pflanze *f*

perfect[1] *a* perfekt, vollkommen; (🔲 *utter*) völlig ● *n* (*Gram*) Perfekt *nt*

perfect[2] *vt* vervollkommnen. **~ion** *n* Vollkommenheit *f*; **to ~ion** perfekt

perfectly *adv* perfekt; (*completely*) vollkommen, völlig

perforated *a* perforiert

perform *vt* ausführen; erfüllen <*duty*>; (*Theat*) aufführen <*play*>; spielen <*role*> ● *vi* (*Theat*) auftreten; (*Techn*) laufen. **~ance** *n* Aufführung *f*; (*at theatre, cinema*) Vorstellung *f*; (*Techn, Sport*) Leistung *f*. **~er** *n* Künstler(in) *m(f)*

perfume *n* Parfüm *nt*; (*smell*) Duft *m*

perhaps *adv* vielleicht

perilous *a* gefährlich

perimeter *n* [äußere] Grenze *f*; (*Geom*) Umfang *m*

period *n* Periode *f*; (*Sch*) Stunde *f*; (*full stop*) Punkt *m* ● *attrib* <*costume*> zeitgenössisch; <*furniture*> antik. **~ic** *a*, **-ally** *adv* periodisch. **~ical** *n* Zeitschrift *f*

peripher|al *a* nebensächlich. **~y** *n* Peripherie *f*

perish *vi* <*rubber*:> verrotten; <*food*:> verderben; (*liter: die*) ums Leben kommen. **~able** *a* leicht verderblich. **~ing** *a* (🔲 *cold*) eiskalt

perjur|e *vt* **~e oneself** einen Meineid leisten. **~y** *n* Meineid *m*

perk[1] *n* 🔲 [Sonder]vergünstigung *f*

perk[2] *vi* **~ up** munter werden

perm *n* Dauerwelle *f* ● *vt* **~ s.o.'s hair** jdm eine Dauerwelle machen

permanent *a* ständig; <*job, address*> fest. **~ly** *adv* ständig; <*work, live*> dauernd, permanent; <*employed*> fest

permissible *a* erlaubt

permission *n* Erlaubnis *f*

permit[1] *vt* (*pt/pp* **-mitted**) erlauben (*s.o.* jdm)

permit[2] *n* Genehmigung *f*

perpendicular *a* senkrecht ● *n* Senkrechte *f*

perpetual *a*, **-ly** *adv* ständig, dauernd

perpetuate *vt* bewahren; verewigen <*error*>

perplex *vt* verblüffen. **~ed** *a* verblüfft

persecut|e *vt* verfolgen. **~ion** *n* Verfolgung *f*

perseverance *n* Ausdauer *f*

persevere *vi* beharrlich weitermachen

Persia *n* Persien *nt*

Persian *a* persisch; <*cat, carpet*> Perser-

persist *vi* beharrlich weitermachen; (*continue*) anhalten; <*view*:> weiter bestehen; **~ in doing sth** dabei bleiben, etw zu tun. **~ence** *n* Beharrlichkeit *f*. **~ent** *a*, **-ly** *adv* beharrlich; (*continuous*) anhaltend

person *n* Person *f*; **in ~** persönlich

personal *a*, **-ly** *adv* persönlich. **~ hygiene** *n* Körperpflege *f*

personality *n* Persönlichkeit *f*

personify *vt* (*pt/pp* **-ied**) personifizieren, verkörpern

personnel *n* Personal *nt*

perspective *n* Perspektive *f*

persp|iration *n* Schweiß *m*. **~ire** *vi* schwitzen

persua|de *vt* überreden; (*convince*) überzeugen. **~sion** *n* Überredung *f*; (*powers of ~sion*) Überredungskunst *f*

persuasive *a*, **-ly** *adv* beredsam; (*convincing*) überzeugend

pertinent *a* relevant (**to** für)

perturb *vt* beunruhigen

peruse *vt* lesen

pervers|e *a* eigensinnig. **~ion** *n* Perversion *f*

pervert[1] *vt* verdrehen; verführen <*person*>

pervert[2] *n* Perverse(r) *m*

pessimis|m *n* Pessimismus *m*. **~t**
n Pessimist *m*. **~tic** *a*, **-ally** *adv*
pessimistisch

pest *n* Schädling *m*; (🔲 *person*)
Nervensäge *f*

pester *vt* belästigen

pesticide *n*
Schädlingsbekämpfungsmittel *nt*

pet *n* Haustier *nt*; (*favourite*) Liebling
m ● *vt* (*pt/pp* **petted**) liebkosen

petal *n* Blütenblatt *nt*

peter *vi* ~ **out** allmählich aufhören

petition *n* Bittschrift *f*

pet name *n* Kosename *m*

petrified *a* vor Angst wie
versteinert

petrol *n* Benzin *nt*

petroleum *n* Petroleum *nt*

petrol: **~pump** *n* Zapfsäule *f*. **~
station** *n* Tankstelle *f*. **~ tank** *n*
Benzintank *m*

petticoat *n* Unterrock *m*

petty *a* (**-ier, -iest**) kleinlich. **~
cash** *n* Portokasse *f*

petulant *a* gekränkt

pew *n* [Kirchen]bank *f*

pharmaceutical *a*
pharmazeutisch

pharmac|ist *n* Apotheker(in) *m(f)*.
~y *n* Pharmazie *f*; (*shop*) Apotheke *f*

phase *n* Phase *f* ● *vt* ~ **in/out**
allmählich einführen/abbauen

Ph.D. (*abbr of* **Doctor of Philosophy**)
Dr. phil.

pheasant *n* Fasan *m*

phenomen|al *a* phänomenal. **~on**
n (*pl* **-na**) Phänomen *nt*

philharmonic *n* (*orchestra*)
Philharmoniker *pl*

Philippines *npl* Philippinen *pl*

philistine *n* Banause *m*

philosoph|er *n* Philosoph *m*.
~ical *a*, **-ly** *adv* philosophisch. **~y**
n Philosophie *f*

phlegmatic *a* phlegmatisch

phobia *n* Phobie *f*

phone *n* Telefon *nt*; be on the ~
Telefon haben; (*be phoning*)
telefonieren ● *vt* anrufen ● *vi*
telefonieren. **~ back** *vt/i*

zurückrufen. **~ book** *n*
Telefonbuch *nt*. **~ box** *n*
Telefonzelle *f*. **~ card** *n*
Telefonkarte *f*. **~-in** *n* (*Radio*)
Hörersendung *f*. **~ number** *n*
Telefonnummer *f*

phonetic *a* phonetisch. **~s** *n*
Phonetik *f*

phoney *a* (**-ier, -iest**) falsch; (*forged*)
gefälscht

photo *n* Foto *nt*, Aufnahme *f*.
~copier *n* Fotokopiergerät *nt*.
~copy *n* Fotokopie *f* ● *vt*
fotokopieren

photogenic *a* fotogen

photograph *n* Fotografie *f*,
Aufnahme *f* ● *vt* fotografieren

photograph|er *n* Fotograf(in) *m(f)*.
~ic *a*, **-ally** *adv* fotografisch. **~y** *n*
Fotografie *f*

phrase *n* Redensart *f* ● *vt*
formulieren. **~-book** *n*
Sprachführer *m*

physical *a*, **-ly** *adv* körperlich

physician *n* Arzt *m*/ Ärztin *f*

physic|ist *n* Physiker(in) *m(f)*. **~s**
n Physik *f*

physiotherap|ist *n*
Physiotherapeut(in) *m(f)*. **~y** *n*
Physiotherapie *f*

physique *n* Körperbau *m*

pianist *n* Klavierspieler(in) *m(f)*;
(*professional*) Pianist(in) *m(f)*

piano *n* Klavier *nt*

pick¹ *n* Spitzhacke *f*

pick² *n* Auslese *f*; take one's ~ sich
(*dat*) aussuchen ● *vt/i* (*pluck*)
pflücken; (*select*) wählen, sich (*dat*)
aussuchen; **~ and choose**
wählerisch sein; **~ a quarrel** einen
Streit anfangen; **~ holes in** 🔲
kritisieren; **~ at one's food** im
Essen herumstochern. **~ on** *vt*
wählen; (🔲 *find fault with*)
herumhacken auf (+ *dat*). **~ up** *vt*
in die Hand nehmen; (*off the ground*)
aufheben; hochnehmen <*baby*>;
(*learn*) lernen; (*acquire*) erwerben;
(*buy*) kaufen; (*Teleph*) abnehmen
<*receiver*>; auffangen <*signal*>;
(*collect*) abholen; aufnehmen
<*passengers*>; <*police:*> aufgreifen

<criminal>; sich holen *<illness>*; 🟦
aufgabeln *<girl>*; ~ **oneself up**
aufstehen ● *vi* (*improve*) sich
bessern

pickaxe *n* Spitzhacke *f*

picket *n* Streikposten *m*

pickle *n* (*Amer: gherkin*) Essiggurke
f; ~**s** *pl* [Mixed] Pickles *pl* ● *vt*
einlegen

pick: ~**pocket** *n* Taschendieb *m*.
~**-up** *n* (*truck*) Lieferwagen *m*

picnic *n* Picknick *nt* ● *vi* (*pt/pp*
-nicked) picknicken

picture *n* Bild *nt*; (*film*) Film *m*; **as
pretty as a ~** bildhübsch; **put s.o. in
the ~** (*fig*) jdn ins Bild setzen ● *vt*
(*imagine*) sich (*dat*) vorstellen

picturesque *a* malerisch

pie *n* Pastete *f*, (*fruit*) Kuchen *m*

piece *n* Stück *nt*; (*of set*) Teil *nt*; (*in
game*) Stein *m*; (*Journ*) Artikel *m*; **a
~ of bread/paper** ein Stück Brot/
Papier; **a ~ of news/advice** eine
Nachricht/ein Rat; **take to ~s**
auseinander nehmen ● *vt* ~ **together**
zusammensetzen; (*fig*)
zusammenstückeln. ~**meal** *adv*
stückweise

pier *n* Pier *m*; (*pillar*) Pfeiler *m*

pierc|e *vt* durchstechen. ~**ing** *a*
durchdringend

pig *n* Schwein *nt*

pigeon *n* Taube *f*. ~**-hole** *n* Fach *nt*

piggy|back *n* **give s.o. a ~back** jdn
huckepack tragen. ~ **bank** *n*
Sparschwein *nt*

pigheaded *a* 🟦 starrköpfig

pigment *n* Pigment *nt*

pig: ~**skin** *n* Schweinsleder *nt*.
~**sty** *n* Schweinestall *m*. ~**tail** *n* 🟦
Zopf *m*

pilchard *n* Sardine *f*

pile¹ *n* (*of fabric*) Flor *m*

pile² *n* Haufen *m* ● *vt* ~ **sth on to sth**
etw auf etw (*acc*) häufen. ~ **up** *vt*
häufen ● *vi* sich häufen

piles *npl* Hämorrhoiden *pl*

pile-up *n* Massenkarambolage *f*

pilgrim *n* Pilger(in) *m(f)*. ~**age** *n*
Pilgerfahrt *f*, Wallfahrt *f*

pill *n* Pille *f*

pillar *n* Säule *f*. ~**-box** *n*
Briefkasten *m*

pillow *n* Kopfkissen *nt*. ~**case** *n*
Kopfkissenbezug *m*

pilot *n* Pilot *m*; (*Naut*) Lotse *m* ● *vt*
fliegen *<plane>*; lotsen *<ship>*. ~
light *n* Zündflamme *f*

pimple *n* Pickel *m*

pin *n* Stecknadel *f*; (*Techn*) Bolzen *m*,
Stift *m*; (*Med*) Nagel *m*; **I have ~s
and needles in my leg** 🟦 mein Bein
ist eingeschlafen ● *vt* (*pt/pp* **pinned**)
anstecken (**to/on** an + *acc*); (*sewing*)
stecken; (*hold down*) festhalten

pinafore *n* Schürze *f*. ~ **dress** *n*
Kleiderrock *m*

pincers *npl* Kneifzange *f*; (*Zool*)
Scheren *pl*

pinch *n* Kniff *m*; (*of salt*) Prise *f*; **at a
~** 🟦 zur Not ● *vt* kneifen, zwicken;
(*fam; steal*) klauen; ~ **one's finger**
sich (*dat*) den Finger klemmen ● *vi*
<shoe:> drücken

pine¹ *n* (*tree*) Kiefer *f*

pine² *vi* ~ **for** sich sehnen nach

pineapple *n* Ananas *f*

ping-pong *n* Tischtennis *nt*

pink *a* rosa

pinnacle *n* Gipfel *m*; (*on roof*)
Turmspitze *f*

pin: ~**point** *vt* genau festlegen.
~**stripe** *n* Nadelstreifen *m*

pint *n* Pint *nt* (*0,57 l, Amer: 0,47 l*)

pioneer *n* Pionier *m* ● *vt*
bahnbrechende Arbeit leisten für

pious *a*, **-ly** *adv* fromm

pip¹ *n* (*seed*) Kern *m*

pip² *n* (*sound*) Tonsignal *nt*

pipe *n* Pfeife *f*; (*for water, gas*) Rohr
nt ● *vt* in Rohren leiten; (*Culin*)
spritzen

pipe: ~**dream** *n* Luftschloss *nt*.
~**line** *n* Pipeline *f*; **in the ~line** 🟦
in Vorbereitung

piping *a* ~ **hot** kochend heiß

pirate *n* Pirat *m*

piss *vi* 🗙 pissen

pistol *n* Pistole *f*

piston *n* (*Techn*) Kolben *m*

pit n Grube f; (for orchestra) Orchestergraben m

pitch¹ n (steepness) Schräge f; (of voice) Stimmlage f; (of sound) [Ton]höhe f; (Sport) Feld nt; (of street trader) Standplatz m; (fig: degree) Grad m ● vt werfen; aufschlagen <tent> ● vi fallen

pitch² n (tar) Pech nt. ~**black** a pechschwarz. ~**dark** a stockdunkel

piteous a erbärmlich

pitfall n (fig) Falle f

pith n (Bot) Mark nt; (of orange) weiße Haut f

pithy a (-ier, -iest) (fig) prägnant

piti|ful a bedauernswert. ~**less** a mitleidslos

pittance n Hungerlohn m

pity n Mitleid nt, Erbarmen nt; [what a] ~! [wie] schade! take ~ on sich erbarmen über (+ acc) ● vt bemitleiden

pivot n Drehzapfen m ● vi sich drehen (on um)

pizza n Pizza f

placard n Plakat nt

placate vt beschwichtigen

place n Platz m; (spot) Stelle f; (town, village) Ort m; (🅱 house) Haus nt; out of ~ fehl am Platze; take ~ stattfinden ● vt setzen; (upright) stellen; (flat) legen; (remember) unterbringen 🅱; ~ an order eine Bestellung aufgeben; be ~d (in race) sich platzieren. ~**mat** n Set nt

placid a gelassen

plague n Pest f ● vt plagen

plaice n inv Scholle f

plain a (-er, -est) klar; (simple) einfach; (not pretty) nicht hübsch; (not patterned) einfarbig; <chocolate> zartbitter; in ~ clothes in Zivil ● adv (simply) einfach ● n Ebene f. ~**ly** adv klar, deutlich; (simply) einfach; (obviously) offensichtlich

plait n Zopf m ● vt flechten

plan n Plan m ● vt (pt/pp planned) planen; (intend) vorhaben

plane¹ n (tree) Platane f

plane² n Flugzeug nt; (Geom & fig) Ebene f

plane³ n (Techn) Hobel m ● vt hobeln

planet n Planet m

plank n Brett nt; (thick) Planke f

planning n Planung f

plant n Pflanze f; (Techn) Anlage f; (factory) Werk nt ● vt pflanzen; (place in position) setzen; ~ oneself sich hinstellen. ~**ation** n Plantage f

plaque n [Gedenk]tafel f; (on teeth) Zahnbelag m

plaster n Verputz m; (sticking ~) Pflaster nt; ~ [of Paris] Gips m ● vt verputzen <wall>; (cover) bedecken mit

plastic n Kunststoff m, Plastik nt ● a Kunststoff-, Plastik-; (malleable) formbar, plastisch

plastic surgery n plastische Chirurgie f

plate n Teller m; (flat sheet) Platte f; (with name, number) Schild nt; (gold and silverware) vergoldete/ versilberte Ware f; (in book) Tafel f ● vt (with gold) vergolden; (with silver) versilbern

platform n Plattform f; (stage) Podium nt; (Rail) Bahnsteig m; ~ 5 Gleis 5

platinum n Platin nt

platitude n Plattitüde f

plausible a plausibel

play n Spiel nt; [Theater]stück nt; (Radio) Hörspiel nt; (TV) Fernsehspiel nt; ~ on words Wortspiel nt ● vt/i spielen; ausspielen <card>; ~ safe sichergehen. ~ **down** vt herunterspielen. ~ **up** vi 🅱 Mätzchen machen

play: ~**er** n Spieler(in) m(f). ~**ful** a, -**ly** adv verspielt. ~**ground** n Spielplatz m; (Sch) Schulhof m. ~**group** n Kindergarten m

playing: ~**card** n Spielkarte f. ~**field** n Sportplatz m

play: ~**mate** n Spielkamerad m. ~**thing** n Spielzeug nt. ~**wright** n Dramatiker m

plc *abbr* (public limited company) ≈ GmbH

plea *n* Bitte *f*; **make a ~ for** bitten um

plead *vi* flehen (**for** um); **~ guilty** sich schuldig bekennen; **~ with s.o.** jdn anflehen

pleasant *a* angenehm; *<person>* nett. **~ly** *adv* angenehm; *<say, smile>* freundlich

pleas|e *adv* bitte ● *vt* gefallen (+ *dat*); **~e s.o.** jdm eine Freude machen; **~e oneself** tun, was man will. **~ed** *a* erfreut; **be ~ed with/ about sth** sich über etw (*acc*) freuen. **~ing** *a* erfreulich

pleasure *n* Vergnügen *nt*; (*joy*) Freude *f*; **with ~** gern[e]

pleat *n* Falte *f* ● *vt* fälteln

pledge *n* Versprechen *nt* ● *vt* verpfänden; versprechen

plentiful *a* reichlich

plenty *n* eine Menge; (*enough*) reichlich; **~ of money/people** viel Geld/viele Leute

pliable *a* biegsam

pliers *npl* [Flach]zange *f*

plight *n* [Not]lage *f*

plinth *n* Sockel *m*

plod *vi* (*pt/pp* **plodded**) trotten; (*work*) sich abmühen

plonk *n* Ⅰ billiger Wein *m*

plot *n* Komplott *nt*; (*of novel*) Handlung *f*; **~ of land** Stück *nt* Land ● *vt* einzeichnen ● *vi* ein Komplott schmieden

plough *n* Pflug *m* ● *vt/i* pflügen

ploy *n* Ⅰ Trick *m*

pluck *n* Mut *m* ● *vt* zupfen; rupfen *<bird>*; pflücken *<flower>*; **~ up courage** Mut fassen

plucky *a* (**-ier, -iest**) tapfer, mutig

plug *n* Stöpsel *m*; (*wood*) Zapfen *m*; (*cotton wool*) Bausch *m*; (*Electr*) Stecker *m*; (*Auto*) Zündkerze *f*; (Ⅰ *advertisement*) Schleichwerbung *f* ● *vt* zustopfen; (Ⅰ *advertise*) Schleichwerbung machen für. **~ in** *vt* (*Electr*) einstecken

plum *n* Pflaume *f*

plumage *n* Gefieder *nt*

plumb|er *n* Klempner *m*. **~ing** *n* Wasserleitungen *pl*

plume *n* Feder *f*

plump *a* (**-er, -est**) mollig, rundlich ● *vt* **~ for** wählen

plunge *n* Sprung *m*; **take the ~** Ⅰ den Schritt wagen ● *vt/i* tauchen

plural *a* pluralisch ● *n* Mehrzahl *f*, Plural *m*

plus *prep* plus (+ *dat*) ● *a* Plus- ● *n* Pluszeichen *nt*; (*advantage*) Plus *nt*

plush[y] *a* luxuriös

ply *vt* (*pt/pp* **plied**) ausüben *<trade>*; **~ s.o. with drink** jdm ein Glas nach dem anderen eingießen. **~wood** *n* Sperrholz *nt*

p.m. *adv* (*abbr of* post meridiem) nachmittags

pneumatic *a* pneumatisch. **~ drill** *n* Presslufthammer *m*

pneumonia *n* Lungenentzündung *f*

poach *vt* (*Culin*) pochieren; (*steal*) wildern. **~er** *n* Wilddieb *m*

pocket *n* Tasche *f*; **be out of ~** [an einem Geschäft] verlieren ● *vt* einstecken. **~-book** *n* Notizbuch *nt*; (*wallet*) Brieftasche *f*. **~-money** *n* Taschengeld *nt*

pod *n* Hülse *f*

poem *n* Gedicht *nt*

poet *n* Dichter(in) *m(f)*. **~ic** *a* dichterisch

poetry *n* Dichtung *f*

poignant *a* ergreifend

point *n* Punkt *m*; (*sharp end*) Spitze *f*; (*meaning*) Sinn *m*; (*purpose*) Zweck *m*; (*Electr*) Steckdose *f*; **~s** *pl* (*Rail*) Weiche *f*; **~ of view** Standpunkt *m*; **good/bad ~s** gute/schlechte Seiten; **what is the ~?** wozu? **the ~ is** es geht darum; **up to a ~** bis zu einem gewissen Grade; **be on the ~ of doing sth** im Begriff sein, etw zu tun ● *vt* richten (**at** auf + *acc*); ausfugen *<brickwork>* ● *vi* deuten (**at/to** auf + *acc*); (*with finger*) mit dem Finger zeigen. **~ out** *vt* zeigen auf (+ *acc*); **~ sth out to s.o.** jdn auf etw (*acc*) hinweisen

point-blank *a* aus nächster Entfernung; (*fig*) rundweg

point|ed *a* spitz; *<question>* gezielt. **~less** *a* zwecklos, sinnlos

poise *n* Haltung *f*

poison *n* Gift *nt* ● *vt* vergiften. **~ous** *a* giftig

poke *n* Stoß *m* ● *vt* stoßen; schüren *<fire>*; *(put)* stecken

poker¹ *n* Schüreisen *nt*

poker² *n* *(Cards)* Poker *nt*

poky *a* (-ier, -iest) eng

Poland *n* Polen *nt*

polar *a* Polar-. **~bear** *n* Eisbär *m*

Pole *n* Pole *m*/Polin *f*

pole¹ *n* Stange *f*

pole² *n* *(Geog, Electr)* Pol *m*

pole-vault *n* Stabhochsprung *m*

police *npl* Polizei *f*

police: **~man** *n* Polizist *m*. **~ station** *n* Polizeiwache *f*. **~woman** *n* Polizistin *f*

policy¹ *n* Politik *f*

policy² *n* *(insurance)* Police *f*

Polish *a* polnisch

polish *n* *(shine)* Glanz *m*; *(for shoes)* [Schuh]creme *f*; *(for floor)* Bohnerwachs *m*; *(for furniture)* Politur *f*; *(for silver)* Putzmittel *nt*; *(for nails)* Lack *m*; *(fig)* Schliff *m* ● *vt* polieren; bohnern *<floor>*. **~ off** *vt* 🄴 verputzen *<food>*; erledigen *<task>*

polite *a*, **-ly** *adv* höflich. **~ness** *n* Höflichkeit *f*

politic|al *a*, **-ly** *adv* politisch. **~ian** *n* Politiker(in) *m(f)*

politics *n* Politik *f*

poll *n* Abstimmung *f*; *(election)* Wahl *f*; [opinion] **~** [Meinungs]umfrage *f*

pollen *n* Blütenstaub *m*, Pollen *m*

polling: **~-booth** *n* Wahlkabine *f*. **~-station** *n* Wahllokal *nt*

pollut|e *vt* verschmutzen. **~ion** *n* Verschmutzung *f*

polo *n* Polo *nt*. **~-neck** *n* Rollkragen *m*

polystyrene *n* Polystyrol *nt*; *(for packing)* Styropor (P) *nt*

polythene *n* Polyäthylen *nt*. **~ bag** *n* Plastiktüte *f*

pomp *n* Pomp *m*

pompous *a*, **-ly** *adv* großspurig

pond *n* Teich *m*

ponder *vi* nachdenken

ponderous *a* schwerfällig

pony *n* Pony *nt*. **~-tail** *n* Pferdeschwanz *m*

poodle *n* Pudel *m*

pool *n* [Schwimm]becken *nt*; *(pond)* Teich *m*; *(of blood)* Lache *f*; *(common fund)* [gemeinsame] Kasse *f*; **~s** *pl* [Fußball]toto *nt* ● *vt* zusammenlegen

poor *a* (-er, -est) arm; *(not good)* schlecht; in **~** health nicht gesund. **~ly** *a* be **~ly** krank sein ● *adv* ärmlich; *(badly)* schlecht

pop¹ *n* Knall *m* ● *v* (*pt/pp* popped) ● *vt* (🄴 *put*) stecken (in in + *acc*) ● *vi* knallen; *(burst)* platzen. **~ in** *vi* 🄴 reinschauen. **~ out** *vi* 🄴 kurz rausgehen

pop² *n* 🄴 Popmusik *f*, Pop *m* ● *attrib* Pop-

popcorn *n* Puffmais *m*

pope *n* Papst *m*

poplar *n* Pappel *f*

poppy *n* Mohn *m*

popular *a* beliebt, populär; *<belief>* volkstümlich. **~ity** *n* Beliebtheit *f*, Popularität *f*

populat|e *vt* bevölkern. **~ion** *n* Bevölkerung *f*

porcelain *n* Porzellan *nt*

porch *n* Vorbau *m*; *(Amer)* Veranda *f*

porcupine *n* Stachelschwein *nt*

pore *n* Pore *f*

pork *n* Schweinefleisch *nt*

porn *n* 🄴 Porno *m*

pornograph|ic *a* pornographisch. **~y** *n* Pornographie *f*

porridge *n* Haferbrei *m*

port¹ *n* Hafen *m*; *(town)* Hafenstadt *f*

port² *n* *(Naut)* Backbord *nt*

port³ *n* *(wine)* Portwein *m*

portable *a* tragbar

porter *n* Portier *m*; *(for luggage)* Gepäckträger *m*

porthole *n* Bullauge *nt*

portion *n* Portion *f*; *(part, share)* Teil *nt*

portrait *n* Porträt *nt*

portray vt darstellen. ~**al** n Darstellung f

Portug|al n Portugal nt. ~**uese** a portugiesisch ● n Portugiese m/ -giesin f

pose n Pose f ● vt aufwerfen <*problem*>; stellen <*question*> ● vi posieren; (*for painter*) Modell stehen

posh a 🅸 feudal

position n Platz m; (*posture*) Haltung f; (*job*) Stelle f; (*situation*) Lage f, Situation f; (*status*) Stellung f ● vt platzieren; ~ **oneself** sich stellen

positive a, -**ly** adv positiv; (*definite*) eindeutig; (*real*) ausgesprochen ● n Positiv nt

possess vt besitzen. ~**ion** n Besitz m; ~**ions** pl Sachen pl

possess|ive a Possessiv-; **be** ~**ive about s.o.** zu sehr an jdm hängen

possibility n Möglichkeit f

possib|le a möglich. ~**ly** adv möglicherweise; **not** ~**ly** unmöglich

post¹ n (*pole*) Pfosten m

post² n (*place of duty*) Posten m; (*job*) Stelle f

post³ n (*mail*) Post f; **by** ~ mit der Post ● vt aufgeben <*letter*>; (*send by* ~) mit der Post schicken; **keep s.o.** ~**ed** jdn auf dem Laufenden halten

postage n Porto nt

postal a Post-. ~ **order** n ≈ Geldanweisung f

post: ~**-box** n Briefkasten m. ~**card** n Postkarte f; (*picture*) Ansichtskarte f. ~**code** n Postleitzahl f. ~**-date** vt vordatieren

poster n Plakat nt

posterity n Nachwelt f

posthumous a, -**ly** adv postum

post: ~**man** n Briefträger m. ~**mark** n Poststempel m

post-mortem n Obduktion f

post office n Post f

postpone vt aufschieben; ~ **until** verschieben auf (+ acc). ~**ment** n Verschiebung f

postscript n Nachschrift f

posture n Haltung f

pot n Topf m; (*for tea, coffee*) Kanne f; ~**s of money** 🅸 eine Menge Geld

potato n (pl -**es**) Kartoffel f

potent a stark

potential a, -**ly** adv potenziell ● n Potenzial nt

pot: ~**-hole** n Höhle f; (*in road*) Schlagloch nt. ~**-shot** n **take a** ~**-shot at** schießen auf (+ acc)

potter n Töpfer(in) m(f). ~**y** n Töpferei f; (*articles*) Töpferwaren pl

potty a (-**ier**, -**iest**) 🅸 verrückt ● n Töpfchen nt

pouch n Beutel m

poultry n Geflügel nt

pounce vi zuschlagen; ~ **on** sich stürzen auf (+ acc)

pound¹ n (*money & 0,454 kg*) Pfund nt

pound² vi <*heart:*> hämmern; (*run heavily*) stampfen

pour vt gießen; einschenken <*drink*> ● vi strömen; (*with rain*) gießen. ~ **out** vi ausströmen ● vt ausschütten; einschenken <*drink*>

pout vi einen Schmollmund machen

poverty n Armut f

powder n Pulver nt; (*cosmetic*) Puder m ● vt pudern

power n Macht f; (*strength*) Kraft f; (*Electr*) Strom m; (*nuclear*) Energie f; (*Math*) Potenz f. ~ **cut** n Stromsperre f. ~**ed** a betrieben (**by** mit); ~**ed by electricity** mit Elektroantrieb. ~**ful** a mächtig; (*strong*) stark. ~**less** a machtlos. ~**-station** n Kraftwerk nt

practicable a durchführbar, praktikabel

practical a, -**ly** adv praktisch. ~ **joke** n Streich m

practice n Praxis f; (*custom*) Brauch m; (*habit*) Gewohnheit f; (*exercise*) Übung f; (*Sport*) Training nt; **in** ~ (*in reality*) in der Praxis; **out of** ~ außer Übung; **put into** ~ ausführen

practise vt üben; (*carry out*) praktizieren; ausüben <*profession*> ● vi üben; <*doctor:*> praktizieren. ~**d** a geübt

praise n Lob nt ● vt loben.
  ~worthy a lobenswert

pram n Kinderwagen m

prank n Streich m

prawn n Garnele f, Krabbe f

pray vi beten. **~er** n Gebet nt

preach vt/i predigen. **~er** n
  Prediger m

pre-arrange vt im Voraus
  arrangieren

precarious a, **-ly** adv unsicher

precaution n Vorsichtsmaßnahme
  f

precede vt vorangehen (+ dat)

preceden|ce n Vorrang m. **~t** n
  Präzedenzfall m

preceding a vorhergehend

precinct n Bereich m; (traffic-free)
  Fußgängerzone f, (Amer: district)
  Bezirk m

precious a kostbar; <style> preziös
  ● adv Ⓔ **~ little** recht wenig

precipice n Steilabfall m

precipitation n (Meteorol)
  Niederschlag m

precis|e a, **-ly** adv genau. **~ion** n
  Genauigkeit f

precocious a frühreif

pre|conceived a vorgefasst.
  ~conception n vorgefasste
  Meinung f

predator n Raubtier nt

predecessor n Vorgänger(in) m(f)

predicat|e n (Gram) Prädikat nt.
  ~ive a, **-ly** adv prädikativ

predict vt voraussagen. **~able** a
  voraussehbar; <person>
  berechenbar. **~ion** n Voraussage f

predomin|ant a vorherrschend.
  ~antly adv hauptsächlich,
  überwiegend. **~ate** vi vorherrschen

preen vt putzen

prefab n Ⓔ [einfaches] Fertighaus
  nt. **~ricated** a vorgefertigt

preface n Vorwort nt

prefect n Präfekt m

prefer vt (pt/pp preferred) vorziehen;
  I **~ to walk** ich gehe lieber zu Fuß; I
  ~ wine ich trinke lieber Wein

prefera|ble a be **~ble** vorzuziehen
  sein (to dat). **~bly** adv vorzugsweise

preferen|ce n Vorzug m. **~tial** a
  bevorzugt

pregnan|cy n Schwangerschaft f.
  ~t a schwanger; <animal> trächtig

prehistoric a prähistorisch

prejudice n Vorurteil nt; (bias)
  Voreingenommenheit f ● vt
  einnehmen (against gegen). **~d** a
  voreingenommen

preliminary a Vor-

prelude n Vorspiel nt

premature a vorzeitig; <birth>
  Früh-. **~ly** adv zu früh

premeditated a vorsätzlich

premier a führend ● n (Pol)
  Premier[minister] m

premiere n Premiere f

premises npl Räumlichkeiten pl;
  on the **~** im Haus

premium n Prämie f; be at a **~**
  hoch im Kurs stehen

premonition n Vorahnung f

preoccupied a [in Gedanken]
  beschäftigt

preparation n Vorbereitung f;
  (substance) Präparat nt

preparatory a Vor-

prepare vt vorbereiten; anrichten
  <meal> ● vi sich vorbereiten (for auf
  + acc); **~d** to bereit zu

preposition n Präposition f

preposterous a absurd

prerequisite n Voraussetzung f

Presbyterian a presbyterianisch
  ● n Presbyterianer(in) m(f)

prescribe vt vorschreiben; (Med)
  verschreiben

prescription n (Med) Rezept nt

presence n Anwesenheit f,
  Gegenwart f, **~ of mind**
  Geistesgegenwart f

present[1] a gegenwärtig; be **~**
  anwesend sein; (occur) vorkommen
  ● n Gegenwart f; (Gram) Präsens nt;
  at **~** zurzeit; for the **~** vorläufig

present[2] n (gift) Geschenk nt

present[3] vt überreichen; (show)
  zeigen; vorlegen <cheque>;

(*introduce*) vorstellen; ~ **s.o. with sth** jdm etw überreichen. ~**able** *a* be ~**able** sich zeigen lassen können

presentation *n* Überreichung *f*

presently *adv* nachher; (*Amer: now*) zurzeit

preservation *n* Erhaltung *f*

preservative *n* Konservierungsmittel *nt*

preserve *vt* erhalten; (*Culin*) konservieren; (*bottle*) einmachen ● *n* (*Hunting & fig*) Revier *nt*; (*jam*) Konfitüre *f*

preside *vi* den Vorsitz haben (**over** bei)

presidency *n* Präsidentschaft *f*

president *n* Präsident *m*; (*Amer: chairman*) Vorsitzende(r) *m/f*. ~**ial** *a* Präsidenten-; <*election*> Präsidentschafts-

press *n* Presse *f* ● *vt/i* drücken; drücken auf (+ *acc*) <*button*>; pressen <*flower*>; (*iron*) bügeln; (*urge*) bedrängen; ~ **for** drängen auf (+ *acc*); be ~**ed for time** in Zeitdruck sein. ~ **on** *vi* weitergehen/-fahren; (*fig*) weitermachen

press: ~ **cutting** *n* Zeitungsausschnitt *m*. ~**ing** *a* dringend

pressure *n* Druck *m*. ~**-cooker** *n* Schnellkochtopf *m*

pressurize *vt* Druck ausüben auf (+ *acc*). ~**d** *a* Druck-

prestig|e *n* Prestige *nt*. ~**ious** *a* Prestige-

presumably *adv* vermutlich

presume *vt* vermuten

presumpt|ion *n* Vermutung *f*; (*boldness*) Anmaßung *f*. ~**uous** *a*, **-ly** *adv* anmaßend

pretence *n* Verstellung *f*; (*pretext*) Vorwand *m*

pretend *vt* (*claim*) vorgeben; ~ **that** so tun, als ob; ~ **to be** sich ausgeben als

pretentious *a* protzig

pretext *n* Vorwand *m*

pretty *a* (**-ier, -iest**), ~**ily** *adv* hübsch ● *adv* (𝕀 *fairly*) ziemlich

prevail *vi* siegen; <*custom*:> vorherrschen; ~ **on s.o. to do sth** jdn dazu bringen, etw zu tun

prevalen|ce *n* Häufigkeit *f*. ~**t** *a* vorherrschend

prevent *vt* verhindern, verhüten; ~ **s.o. [from] doing sth** jdn daran hindern, etw zu tun. ~**ion** *n* Verhinderung *f*, Verhütung *f*. ~**ive** *a* vorbeugend

preview *n* Voraufführung *f*

previous *a* vorhergehend; ~ **to** vor (+ *dat*). ~**ly** *adv* vorher, früher

prey *n* Beute *f*; **bird of** ~ Raubvogel *m*

price *n* Preis *m* ● *vt* (*Comm*) auszeichnen. ~**less** *a* unschätzbar; (*fig*) unbezahlbar

prick *n* Stich *m* ● *vt/i* stechen

prickl|e *n* Stachel *m*; (*thorn*) Dorn *m*. ~**y** *a* stachelig; <*sensation*> stechend

pride *n* Stolz *m*; (*arrogance*) Hochmut *m* ● *vt* ~ **oneself on** stolz sein auf (+ *acc*)

priest *n* Priester *m*

prim *a* (**primmer, primmest**) prüde

primarily *adv* hauptsächlich, in erster Linie

primary *a* Haupt-. ~ **school** *n* Grundschule *f*

prime¹ *a* Haupt-; (*first-rate*) erstklassig

prime² *vt* scharf machen <*bomb*>; grundieren <*surface*>

Prime Minister *n* Premierminister(in) *m(f)*

primitive *a* primitiv

primrose *n* gelbe Schlüsselblume *f*

prince *n* Prinz *m*

princess *n* Prinzessin *f*

principal *a* Haupt- ● *n* (*Sch*) Rektor(in) *m(f)*

principally *adv* hauptsächlich

principle *n* Prinzip *nt*, Grundsatz *m*; **in/on** ~ im/aus Prinzip

print *n* Druck *m*; (*Phot*) Abzug *m*; **in** ~ gedruckt; (*available*) erhältlich; **out of** ~ vergriffen ● *vt* drucken; (*write in capitals*) in Druckschrift schreiben; (*Computing*) ausdrucken;

(*Phot*) abziehen. **~ed matter** *n*
Drucksache *f*

print|er *n* Drucker *m*. **~ing** *n*
Druck *m*

printout *n* (*Computing*) Ausdruck *m*

prior *a* frühere(r,s); **~ to** vor (+ *dat*)

priority *n* Priorität *f*, Vorrang *m*

prise *vt* **~ open/up** aufstemmen/
hochstemmen

prison *n* Gefängnis *nt*. **~er** *n*
Gefangene(r) *m/f*

privacy *n* Privatsphäre *f*; **have no ~**
nie für sich sein

private *a*, **-ly** *adv* privat;
(*confidential*) vertraulich; <*car,
secretary, school*> Privat- ● *n* (*Mil*)
[einfacher] Soldat *m*; **in ~** privat;
(*confidentially*) vertraulich

privation *n* Entbehrung *f*

privilege *n* Privileg *nt*. **~d** *a*
privilegiert

prize *n* Preis *m* ● *vt* schätzen

pro *n* Ⓘ Profi *m*; **the ~s and cons**
das Für und Wider

probability *n* Wahrscheinlichkeit *f*

probable *a*, **-bly** *adv*
wahrscheinlich

probation *n* (*Jur*) Bewährung *f*

probe *n* Sonde *f*; (*fig: investigation*)
Untersuchung *f*

problem *n* Problem *nt*; (*Math*)
Textaufgabe *f*. **~atic** *a*
problematisch

procedure *n* Verfahren *nt*

proceed *vi* gehen; (*in vehicle*)
fahren; (*continue*) weitergehen/
-fahren; (*speaking*) fortfahren; (*act*)
verfahren

proceedings *npl* Verfahren *nt*;
(*Jur*) Prozess *m*

proceeds *npl* Erlös *m*

process *n* Prozess *m*; (*procedure*)
Verfahren *nt*; **in the ~** dabei ● *vt*
verarbeiten; (*Admin*) bearbeiten;
(*Phot*) entwickeln

procession *n* Umzug *m*, Prozession
f

proclaim *vt* ausrufen

proclamation *n* Proklamation *f*

procure *vt* beschaffen

prod *n* Stoß *m* ● *vt* stoßen

prodigy *n* **[infant] ~** Wunderkind *nt*

produce¹ *n* landwirtschaftliche
Erzeugnisse *pl*

produce² *vt* erzeugen, produzieren;
(*manufacture*) herstellen; (*bring out*)
hervorholen; (*cause*) hervorrufen;
inszenieren <*play*>; (*Radio, TV*)
redigieren. **~r** *n* Erzeuger *m*,
Produzent *m*; Hersteller *m*; (*Theat*)
Regisseur *m*; (*Radio, TV*)
Redakteur(in) *m(f)*

product *n* Erzeugnis *nt*, Produkt *nt*.
~ion *n* Produktion *f*; (*Theat*)
Inszenierung *f*

productiv|e *a* produktiv; <*land,
talks*> fruchtbar. **~ity** *n*
Produktivität *f*

profession *n* Beruf *m*. **~al** *a*, **-ly**
adv beruflich; (*not amateur*) Berufs-;
(*expert*) fachmännisch; (*Sport*)
professionell ● *n* Fachmann *m*;
(*Sport*) Profi *m*

professor *n* Professor *m*

proficien|cy *n* Können *nt*. **~t** *a* **be
~t in** beherrschen

profile *n* Profil *nt*; (*character study*)
Porträt *nt*

profit *n* Gewinn *m*, Profit *m* ● *vi* **~
from** profitieren von. **~able** *a*, **-bly**
adv gewinnbringend; (*fig*)
nutzbringend

profound *a*, **-ly** *adv* tief

program (*Amer & Computing*) *n*
Programm *nt* ● *vt* (*pt/pp*
programmed) programmieren

programme *n* Programm *nt*;
(*Radio, TV*) Sendung *f*. **~r** *n*
(*Computing*) Programmierer(in) *m(f)*

progress¹ *n* Vorankommen *nt*; (*fig*)
Fortschritt *m*; **in ~** im Gange; **make
~** (*fig*) Fortschritte machen

progress² *vi* vorankommen; (*fig*)
fortschreiten. **~ion** *n* Folge *f*;
(*development*) Entwicklung *f*

progressive *a* fortschrittlich. **~ly**
adv zunehmend

prohibit *vt* verbieten (**s.o.** jdm).
~ive *a* unerschwinglich

project¹ *n* Projekt *nt*; (*Sch*) Arbeit *f*

project² vt projizieren <film>;
(plan) planen ● vi (jut out) vorstehen

projector n Projektor m

prolific a fruchtbar; (fig) produktiv

prologue n Prolog m

prolong vt verlängern

promenade n Promenade f ● vi
spazieren gehen

prominent a vorstehend;
(important) prominent; (conspicuous)
auffällig

promiscuous a be ~ous häufig
den Partner wechseln

promis|e n Versprechen nt ● vt/i
versprechen (s.o. jdm). ~ing a viel
versprechend

promot|e vt befördern; (advance)
fördern; (publicize) Reklame machen
für; **be ~ed** (Sport) aufsteigen. ~ion
n Beförderung f; (Sport) Aufstieg m;
(Comm) Reklame f

prompt a prompt, unverzüglich;
(punctual) pünktlich ● adv pünktlich
● vt/i veranlassen (to zu); (Theat)
soufflieren (+ dat). ~er n Souffleur
m/Souffleuse f. ~ly adv prompt

prone a **be** or **lie** ~ auf dem Bauch
liegen; **be ~ to** neigen zu

pronoun n Fürwort nt, Pronomen nt

pronounce vt aussprechen;
(declare) erklären. ~d a ausgeprägt;
(noticeable) deutlich. ~ment n
Erklärung f

pronunciation n Aussprache f

proof n Beweis m; (Typ)
Korrekturbogen m. ~-reader n
Korrektor m

prop¹ n Stütze f ● vt (pt/pp propped)
~ **against** lehnen an (+ acc). ~ **up** vt
stützen

prop² n (Theat ⊞) Requisit nt

propaganda n Propaganda f

propel vt (pt/pp propelled)
[an]treiben. ~ler n Propeller m

proper a, -ly adv richtig; (decent)
anständig

property n Eigentum nt; (quality)
Eigenschaft f; (Theat) Requisit nt;
(land) [Grund]besitz m; (house) Haus
nt

prophecy n Prophezeiung f

prophesy vt (pt/pp -ied)
prophezeien

prophet n Prophet m. ~ic a
prophetisch

proportion n Verhältnis nt; (share)
Teil m; ~s pl Proportionen;
(dimensions) Maße. ~al a, -ly adv
proportional

proposal n Vorschlag m; (of
marriage) [Heirats]antrag m

propose vt vorschlagen; (intend)
vorhaben; einbringen <motion> ● vi
einen Heiratsantrag machen

proposition n Vorschlag m

proprietor n Inhaber(in) m(f)

propriety n Korrektheit f;
(decorum) Anstand m

prose n Prosa f

prosecut|e vt strafrechtlich
verfolgen. ~ion n strafrechtliche
Verfolgung f; **the ~ion** die Anklage.
~or n [Public] **P~or** Staatsanwalt m

prospect n Aussicht f

prospect|ive a (future) zukünftig.
~or n Prospektor m

prospectus n Prospekt m

prosper vi gedeihen, florieren;
<person> Erfolg haben. ~ity n
Wohlstand m

prosperous a wohlhabend

prostitut|e n Prostituierte f. ~ion
n Prostitution f

prostrate a ausgestreckt

protagonist n Kämpfer m; (fig)
Protagonist m

protect vt schützen (from vor +
dat); beschützen <person>. ~ion n
Schutz m. ~ive a Schutz-; (fig)
beschützend. ~or n Beschützer m

protein n Eiweiß nt

protest¹ n Protest m

protest² vi protestieren

Protestant a protestantisch ● n
Protestant(in) m(f)

protester n Protestierende(r) m/f

prototype n Prototyp m

protrude vi [her]vorstehen

proud a, -ly adv stolz (of auf + acc)

prove vt beweisen ● vi ~ **to be** sich
erweisen als

proverb *n* Sprichwort *nt*

provide *vt* zur Verfügung stellen; spenden *<shade>*; **∼ s.o. with sth** jdn mit etw versorgen *od* versehen ● *vi* **∼ for** sorgen für

provided *conj* **∼ [that]** vorausgesetzt [dass]

providen|ce *n* Vorsehung *f.* **∼tial** *a* be **∼tial** ein Glück sein

provinc|e *n* Provinz *f*; *(fig)* Bereich *m.* **∼ial** *a* provinziell

provision *n* Versorgung *f (of* mit); **∼s** *pl* Lebensmittel *pl.* **∼al** *a*, **-ly** *adv* vorläufig

provocat|ion *n* Provokation *f.* **∼ive** *a*, **-ly** *adv* provozierend; *(sexually)* aufreizend

provoke *vt* provozieren; *(cause)* hervorrufen

prow *n* Bug *m*

prowl *vi* herumschleichen

proximity *n* Nähe *f*

pruden|ce *n* Umsicht *f.* **∼t** *a*, **-ly** *adv* umsichtig; *(wise)* klug

prudish *a* prüde

prune¹ *n* Backpflaume *f*

prune² *vt* beschneiden

pry *vi (pt/pp* pried) neugierig sein

psalm *n* Psalm *m*

psychiatric *a* psychiatrisch

psychiatr|ist *n* Psychiater(in) *m(f).* **∼y** *n* Psychiatrie *f*

psychic *a* übersinnlich

psycho|analysis *n* Psychoanalyse *f.* **∼analyst** *n* Psychoanalytiker(in) *m(f)*

psychological *a*, **-ly** *adv* psychologisch; *<illness>* psychisch

psycholog|ist *n* Psychologe *m/* -login *f.* **∼y** *n* Psychologie *f*

P.T.O. *abbr* (please turn over) b.w.

pub *n* 🔢 Kneipe *f*

puberty *n* Pubertät *f*

public *a*, **-ly** *adv* öffentlich; make **∼** publik machen ● *n* the **∼** die Öffentlichkeit

publican *n* [Gast]wirt *m*

publication *n* Veröffentlichung *f*

public: ∼ holiday *n* gesetzlicher Feiertag *m.* **∼ house** *n* [Gast]wirtschaft *f*

publicity *n* Publicity *f*; *(advertising)* Reklame *f*

publicize *vt* Reklame machen für

public: ∼ school *n* Privatschule *f*; *(Amer)* staatliche Schule *f.* **∼- spirited** *a* be **∼-spirited** Gemeinsinn haben

publish *vt* veröffentlichen. **∼er** *n* Verleger(in) *m(f)*; *(firm)* Verlag *m.* **∼ing** *n* Verlagswesen *nt*

pudding *n* Pudding *m*; *(course)* Nachtisch *m*

puddle *n* Pfütze *f*

puff *n (of wind)* Hauch *m*; *(of smoke)* Wölkchen *nt* ● *vt* blasen, pusten; **∼ out** ausstoßen. ● *vi* keuchen; **∼ at** paffen an (+ *dat) <pipe>*. **∼ed** *a (out of breath)* aus der Puste. **∼ pastry** *n* Blätterteig *m*

pull *n* Zug *m*; *(jerk)* Ruck *m*; *(🔢 influence)* Einfluss *m* ● *vt* ziehen; ziehen an (+ *dat) <rope>*; **∼ a muscle** sich *(dat)* einen Muskel zerren; **∼ oneself together** sich zusammennehmen; **∼ one's weight** tüchtig mitarbeiten; **∼ s.o.'s leg** 🔢 jdn auf den Arm nehmen. **∼ down** *vt* herunterziehen; *(demolish)* abreißen. **∼ in** *vt* hereinziehen ● *vi (Auto)* einscheren. **∼ off** *vt* abziehen; 🔢 schaffen. **∼ out** *vt* herausziehen ● *vi (Auto)* ausscheren. **∼ through** *vt* durchziehen ● *vi (recover)* durchkommen. **∼ up** *vt* heraufziehen; ausziehen *<plant>* ● *vi (Auto)* anhalten

pullover *n* Pullover *m*

pulp *n* Brei *m*; *(of fruit)* [Frucht]fleisch *nt*

pulpit *n* Kanzel *f*

pulse *n* Puls *m*

pulses *npl* Hülsenfrüchte *pl*

pummel *vt (pt/pp* pummelled) mit den Fäusten bearbeiten

pump *n* Pumpe *f* ● *vt* pumpen; 🔢 aushorchen. **∼ up** *vt (inflate)* aufpumpen

pumpkin *n* Kürbis *m*

pun *n* Wortspiel *nt*

punch[1] *n* Faustschlag *m*; (*device*) Locher *m* ● *vt* boxen; lochen <*ticket*>; stanzen <*hole*>

punch[2] *n* (*drink*) Bowle *f*

punctual *a*, **-ly** *adv* pünktlich. **~ity** *n* Pünktlichkeit *f*

punctuat|e *vt* mit Satzzeichen versehen. **~ion** *n* Interpunktion *f*

puncture *n* Loch *nt*; (*tyre*) Reifenpanne *f* ● *vt* durchstechen

punish *vt* bestrafen. **~able** *a* strafbar. **~ment** *n* Strafe *f*

punt *n* (*boat*) Stechkahn *m*

puny *a* (-ier, -iest) mickerig

pup *n* = puppy

pupil *n* Schüler(in) *m(f)*; (*of eye*) Pupille *f*

puppet *n* Puppe *f*; (*fig*) Marionette *f*

puppy *n* junger Hund *m*

purchase *n* Kauf *m*; (*leverage*) Hebelkraft *f* ● *vt* kaufen. **~r** *n* Käufer *m*

pure *a* (-r, -st,) **-ly** *adv* rein

purge *n* (*Pol*) Säuberungsaktion *f* ● *vt* reinigen

puri|fication *n* Reinigung *f*. **~fy** *vt* (*pt/pp* -ied) reinigen

puritanical *a* puritanisch

purity *n* Reinheit *f*

purple *a* [dunkel]lila

purpose *n* Zweck *m*; (*intention*) Absicht *f*; (*determination*) Entschlossenheit *f*; on ~ absichtlich. **~ful**, *a*, **-ly** *adv* entschlossen. **~ly** *adv* absichtlich

purr *vi* schnurren

purse *n* Portemonnaie *nt*; (*Amer: handbag*) Handtasche *f*

pursue *vt* verfolgen; (*fig*) nachgehen (+ *dat*). **~r** *n* Verfolger *m*

pursuit *n* Verfolgung *f*; Jagd *f*; (*pastime*) Beschäftigung *f*

pus *n* Eiter *m*

push *n* Stoß *m*; get the ~ 🔲 hinausfliegen ● *vt/i* schieben; (*press*) drücken; (*roughly*) stoßen. ~ **off** *vt* hinunterstoßen ● *vi* (🔲 *leave*) abhauen. ~ **on** *vi* (*continue*) weitergehen/-fahren; (*with activity*)

weitermachen. ~ **up** *vt* hochschieben; hochtreiben <*price*>

push: **~-button** *n* Druckknopf *m*. **~-chair** *n* [Kinder]sportwagen *m*

pushy *a* 🔲 aufdringlich

puss *n*, **pussy** *n* Mieze *f*

put *vt* (*pt/pp* put, *pres p* putting) tun; (*place*) setzen; (*upright*) stellen; (*flat*) legen; (*express*) ausdrücken; (*say*) sagen; (*estimate*) schätzen (**at** auf + *acc*); ~ **aside** *or* **by** beiseite legen ● *vi* ~ **to sea** auslaufen ● *a* **stay** ~ dableiben. ~ **away** *vt* wegräumen. ~ **back** *vt* wieder hinsetzen/ -stellen/-legen; zurückstellen <*clock*>. ~ **down** *vt* hinsetzen/ -stellen/-legen; (*suppress*) niederschlagen; (*kill*) töten; (*write*) niederschreiben; (*attribute*) zuschreiben (**to** *dat*). ~ **forward** *vt* vorbringen; vorstellen <*clock*>. ~ **in** *vt* hineinsetzen/-stellen/-legen; (*insert*) einstecken; (*submit*) einreichen ● *vi* ~ **in for** beantragen. ~ **off** *vt* ausmachen <*light*>; (*postpone*) verschieben; ~ **s.o. off** jdn abbestellen; (*disconcert*) jdn aus der Fassung bringen. ~ **on** *vt* anziehen <*clothes, brake*>; sich (*dat*) aufsetzen <*hat*>; (*Culin*) aufsetzen; anmachen <*light*>; aufführen <*play*>; annehmen <*accent*>; ~ **on weight** zunehmen. ~ **out** *vt* hinaussetzen/ -stellen/-legen; ausmachen <*fire, light*>; ausstrecken <*hand*>; (*disconcert*) aus der Fassung bringen; ~ **s.o./oneself out** jdm/sich Umstände machen. ~ **through** *vt* durchstecken; (*Teleph*) verbinden (**to** mit). ~ **up** *vt* errichten <*building*>; aufschlagen <*tent*>; aufspannen <*umbrella*>; anschlagen <*notice*>; erhöhen <*price*>; unterbringen <*guest*> ● *vi* (*at hotel*) absteigen in (+ *dat*); ~ **up with sth** sich (*dat*) etw bieten lassen

putrid *a* faulig

putty *n* Kitt *m*

puzzl|e *n* Rätsel *nt*; (*jigsaw*) Puzzlespiel *nt* ● *vt* it **~es me** es ist mir rätselhaft. **~ing** *a* rätselhaft

pyjamas *npl* Schlafanzug *m*

pylon n Mast m
pyramid n Pyramide f
python n Pythonschlange f

Qq

quack n Quaken nt; (doctor) Quacksalber m ● vi quaken
quadrangle n Viereck nt; (court) Hof m
quadruped n Vierfüßer m
quadruple a vierfach ● vt vervierfachen ● vi sich vervierfachen
quaint a (-er, -est) malerisch; (odd) putzig
quake n 🔲 Erdbeben nt ● vi beben; (with fear) zittern
qualif|ication n Qualifikation f; (reservation) Einschränkung f. **~ied** a qualifiziert; (trained) ausgebildet; (limited) bedingt
qualify v (pt/pp -ied) ● vt qualifizieren; (entitle) berechtigen; (limit) einschränken ● vi sich qualifizieren
quality n Qualität f; (characteristic) Eigenschaft f
qualm n Bedenken pl
quantity n Quantität f, Menge f; in ~ in großen Mengen
quarantine n Quarantäne f
quarrel n Streit m ● vi (pt/pp quarrelled) sich streiten. **~some** a streitsüchtig
quarry[1] n (prey) Beute f
quarry[2] n Steinbruch m
quart n Quart nt
quarter n Viertel nt; (of year) Vierteljahr nt; (Amer) 25-Cent-Stück nt; **~s** pl Quartier nt; at [a] ~ to six um Viertel vor sechs ● vt vierteln; (Mil) einquartieren (on bei). **~-final** n Viertelfinale nt

quarterly a & adv vierteljährlich
quartet n Quartett nt
quartz n Quarz m
quay n Kai m
queasy a I feel ~ mir ist übel
queen n Königin f; (Cards, Chess) Dame f
queer a (-er, -est) eigenartig; (dubious) zweifelhaft; (ill) unwohl
quell vt unterdrücken
quench vt löschen
query n Frage f; (question mark) Fragezeichen nt ● vt (pt/pp -ied) infrage stellen; reklamieren <bill>
quest n Suche f (for nach)
question n Frage f; (for discussion) Thema nt; out of the ~ ausgeschlossen; the person in ~ die fragliche Person ● vt infrage stellen; ~ s.o. jdn ausfragen; <police:> jdn verhören. **~able** a zweifelhaft. **~ mark** n Fragezeichen nt
questionnaire n Fragebogen m
queue n Schlange f ● vi ~ [up] Schlange stehen, sich anstellen (for nach)
quibble vi Haarspalterei treiben
quick a (-er, -est), **-ly** adv schnell; be ~! mach schnell! ● adv schnell. **~en** vt beschleunigen ● vi sich beschleunigen
quick: ~sand n Treibsand m. **~-tempered** a aufbrausend
quid n inv 🔲 Pfund nt
quiet a (-er, -est), **-ly** adv still; (calm) ruhig; (soft) leise; keep ~ about 🔲 nichts sagen von ● n Stille f; Ruhe f
quiet|en vt beruhigen ● vi ~en down ruhig werden. **~ness** n Stille f; Ruhe f
quilt n Steppdecke f. **~ed** a Stepp-
quintet n Quintett nt
quirk n Eigenart f
quit v (pt/pp quitted or quit) ● vt verlassen; (give up) aufgeben; ~ doing sth aufhören, etw zu tun ● vi gehen
quite adv ganz; (really) wirklich; ~ [so]! genau! ~ a few ziemlich viele
quits a quitt

quiver *vi* zittern

quiz *n* Quiz *nt* ● *vt* (*pt/pp* **quizzed**) ausfragen. **~zical** *a*, **-ly** *adv* fragend

quota *n* Anteil *m*; (*Comm*) Kontingent *nt*

quotation *n* Zitat *nt*; (*price*) Kostenvoranschlag *m*; (*of shares*) Notierung *f*. **~ marks** *npl* Anführungszeichen *pl*

quote *n* ⚑ = quotation; **in ~s** in Anführungszeichen ● *vt/i* zitieren

rabbi *n* Rabbiner *m*; (*title*) Rabbi *m*

rabbit *n* Kaninchen *nt*

rabid *a* fanatisch; <*animal*> tollwütig

rabies *n* Tollwut *f*

race¹ *n* Rasse *f*

race² *n* Rennen *nt*; (*fig*) Wettlauf *m* ● *vi* [am Rennen] teilnehmen; <*athlete, horse*:> laufen; (⚑ *rush*) rasen ● *vt* um die Wette laufen mit; an einem Rennen teilnehmen lassen <*horse*>

race: ~course *n* Rennbahn *f*. **~horse** *n* Rennpferd *nt*. **~track** *n* Rennbahn *f*

racial *a*, **-ly** *adv* rassisch; <*discrimination*> Rassen-

racing *n* Rennsport *m*; (*horse-*) Pferderennen *nt*. **~ car** *n* Rennwagen *m*. **~ driver** *n* Rennfahrer *m*

racis|m *n* Rassismus *m*. **~t** *a* rassistisch ● *n* Rassist *m*

rack¹ *n* Ständer *m*; (*for plates*) Gestell *nt* ● *vt* **~ one's brains** sich (*dat*) den Kopf zerbrechen

rack² *n* **go to ~ and ruin** verfallen; (*fig*) herunterkommen

racket *n* (*Sport*) Schläger *m*; (*din*) Krach *m*; (*swindle*) Schwindelgeschäft *nt*

racy *a* (**-ier, -iest**) schwungvoll; (*risqué*) gewagt

radar *n* Radar *m*

radian|ce *n* Strahlen *nt*. **~t** *a*, **-ly** *adv* strahlend

radiat|e *vt* ausstrahlen ● *vi* <*heat*:> ausgestrahlt werden; <*roads*:> strahlenförmig ausgehen. **~ion** *n* Strahlung *f*

radiator *n* Heizkörper *m*; (*Auto*) Kühler *m*

radical *a*, **-ly** *adv* radikal ● *n* Radikale(r) *m/f*

radio *n* Radio *nt*; **by ~** über Funk ● *vt* funken <*message*>

radio|active *a* radioaktiv. **~activity** *n* Radioaktivität *f*

radish *n* Radieschen *nt*

radius *n* (*pl* **-dii**) Radius *m*, Halbmesser *m*

raffle *n* Tombola *f*

raft *n* Floß *nt*

rafter *n* Dachsparren *m*

rag *n* Lumpen *m*; (*pej: newspaper*) Käseblatt *nt*

rage *n* Wut *f*; **all the ~** ⚑ der letzte Schrei ● *vi* rasen

ragged *a* zerlumpt; <*edge*> ausgefranst

raid *n* Überfall *m*; (*Mil*) Angriff *m*; (*police*) Razzia *f* ● *vt* überfallen; (*Mil*) angreifen; <*police*> eine Razzia durchführen in (+ *dat*); (*break in*) eindringen in (+ *acc*). **~er** *n* Eindringling *m*; (*of bank*) Bankräuber *m*

rail *n* Schiene *f*; (*pole*) Stange *f*; (*hand~*) Handlauf *m*; (*Naut*) Reling *f*; **by ~** mit der Bahn

railings *npl* Geländer *nt*

railroad *n* (*Amer*) = railway

railway *n* [Eisen]bahn *f*. **~ station** *n* Bahnhof *m*

rain *n* Regen *m* ● *vi* regnen

rain: ~bow *n* Regenbogen *m*. **~coat** *n* Regenmantel *m*. **~fall** *n* Niederschlag *m*

rainy *a* (**-ier, -iest**) regnerisch

raise n (Amer) Lohnerhöhung f ● vt
erheben; (upright) aufrichten; (make
higher) erhöhen; (lift) [hoch]heben;
aufziehen <child, animal>;
aufwerfen <question>; aufbringen
<money>

raisin n Rosine f

rake n Harke f, Rechen m ● vt
harken, rechen

rally n Versammlung f; (Auto) Rallye
f; (Tennis) Ballwechsel m ● vt
sammeln

ram n Schafbock m ● vt (pt/pp
rammed) rammen

rambl|e n Wanderung f ● vi
wandern; (in speech) irrereden. ∼**er**
n Wanderer m; (rose) Kletterrose f.
∼**ing** a weitschweifig; <club>
Wander-

ramp n Rampe f; (Aviat) Gangway f

rampage¹ n be/go on the ∼
randalieren

rampage² vi randalieren

ramshackle a baufällig

ran see run

ranch n Ranch f

random a willkürlich; a ∼ sample
eine Stichprobe ● n at ∼ aufs
Geratewohl; <choose> willkürlich

rang see ring²

range n Serie f, Reihe f; (Comm)
Auswahl f, Angebot nt (of an + dat);
(of mountains) Kette f; (Mus) Umfang
m; (distance) Reichweite f; (for
shooting) Schießplatz m; (stove)
Kohlenherd m ● vi reichen; ∼ from
... to gehen von ... bis. ∼**r** n
Aufseher m

rank n (row) Reihe f; (Mil) Rang m;
(social position) Stand m; the ∼ **and
file** die breite Masse ● vt/i einstufen;
∼ **among** zählen zu

ransack vt durchwühlen; (pillage)
plündern

ransom n Lösegeld nt; hold s.o. to
∼ Lösegeld für jdn fordern

rape n Vergewaltigung f ● vt
vergewaltigen

rapid a, **-ly** adv schnell. ∼**ity** n
Schnelligkeit f

rapist n Vergewaltiger m

raptur|e n Entzücken nt. ∼**ous** a,
-ly adv begeistert

rare¹ a (-r, -st), **-ly** adv selten

rare² a (Culin) englisch gebraten

rarefied a dünn

rarity n Seltenheit f

rascal n Schlingel m

rash¹ n (Med) Ausschlag m

rash² a (-er, -est), **-ly** adv voreilig

rasher n Speckscheibe f

raspberry n Himbeere f

rat n Ratte f; (🄸 person) Schuft m;
smell a ∼ 🄸 Lunte riechen

rate n Rate f; (speed) Tempo nt; (of
payment) Satz m; (of exchange) Kurs
m; ∼**s** pl (taxes) ≈ Grundsteuer f; **at
any** ∼ auf jeden Fall; **at this** ∼ auf
diese Weise ● vt einschätzen; ∼
among zählen zu ● vi ∼ **as** gelten
als

rather adv lieber; (fairly) ziemlich;
∼! und ob!

rating n Einschätzung f; (class)
Klasse f; (sailor) [einfacher] Matrose
m; ∼**s** pl (Radio, TV) ≈
Einschaltquote f

ratio n Verhältnis nt

ration n Ration f ● vt rationieren

rational a, **-ly** adv rational. ∼**ize**
vt/i rationalisieren

rattle n Rasseln nt; (of windows)
Klappern nt; (toy) Klapper f ● vi
rasseln; klappern ● vt rasseln mit

raucous a rau

rave vi toben; ∼ **about** schwärmen
von

raven n Rabe m

ravenous a heißhungrig

ravine n Schlucht f

raving a ∼ **mad** 🄸 total verrückt

ravishing a hinreißend

raw a (-er, -est) roh; (not processed)
Roh-; <skin> wund; <weather>
nasskalt; (inexperienced) unerfahren;
get a ∼ **deal** 🄸 schlecht
wegkommen. ∼ **materials** npl
Rohstoffe pl

ray n Strahl m

razor n Rasierapparat m. ∼ **blade** n
Rasierklinge f

re *prep* betreffs (+ *gen*)

reach *n* Reichweite *f*; (*of river*) Strecke *f*; **within/out of** ~ in/außer Reichweite ● *vt* erreichen; (*arrive at*) ankommen in (+ *dat*); (~ *as far as*) reichen bis zu; kommen zu <*decision, conclusion*>; (*pass*) reichen ● *vi* reichen (**to** bis zu); ~ **for** greifen nach

react *vi* reagieren (**to** auf + *acc*)

reaction *n* Reaktion *f*. ~**ary** *a* reaktionär

reactor *n* Reaktor *m*

read *vt/i* (*pt/pp* **read**) lesen; (*aloud*) vorlesen (**to** *dat*); (*Univ*) studieren; ablesen <*meter*>. ~ **out** *vt* vorlesen

readable *a* lesbar

reader *n* Leser(in) *m(f)*; (*book*) Lesebuch *nt*

readily *adv* bereitwillig; (*easily*) leicht

reading *n* Lesen *nt*; (*Pol, Relig*) Lesung *f*

readjust *vt* neu einstellen ● *vi* sich umstellen (**to** auf + *acc*)

ready *a* (-ier, -iest) fertig; (*willing*) bereit; (*quick*) schnell; **get** ~ sich fertig machen; (*prepare to*) sich bereitmachen

ready: ~**-made** *a* fertig. ~**-to-wear** *a* Konfektions-

real *a* wirklich; (*genuine*) echt; (*actual*) eigentlich ● *adv* (*Amer* 🄸) echt. ~ **estate** *n* Immobilien *pl*

realis|m *n* Realismus *m*. ~**t** *n* Realist *m*. ~**tic** *a*, **-ally** *adv* realistisch

reality *n* Wirklichkeit *f*

realization *n* Erkenntnis *f*

realize *vt* einsehen; (*become aware*) gewahr werden; verwirklichen <*hopes, plans*>; einbringen <*price*>

really *adv* wirklich; (*actually*) eigentlich

realm *n* Reich *nt*

realtor *n* (*Amer*) Immobilienmakler *m*

reap *vt* ernten

reappear *vi* wiederkommen

rear¹ *a* Hinter-; (*Auto*) Heck- ● *n* the ~ der hintere Teil; **from the** ~ von hinten

rear² *vt* aufziehen ● *vi* ~ [**up**] <*horse:*> sich aufbäumen

rearrange *vt* umstellen

reason *n* Grund *m*; (*good sense*) Vernunft *f*; (*ability to think*) Verstand *m*; **within** ~ in vernünftigen Grenzen ● *vi* argumentieren; ~ **with** vernünftig reden mit. ~**able** *a* vernünftig; (*not expensive*) preiswert. ~**ably** *adv* (*fairly*) ziemlich

reassur|ance *n* Beruhigung *f*; Versicherung *f*. ~**e** *vt* beruhigen; ~**e s.o. of sth** jdm etw (*gen*) versichern

rebel¹ *n* Rebell *m*

rebel² *vi* (*pt/pp* **rebelled**) rebellieren. ~**lion** *n* Rebellion *f*. ~**lious** *a* rebellisch

rebound¹ *vi* abprallen

rebound² *n* Rückprall *m*

rebuild *vt* (*pt/pp* **-built**) wieder aufbauen

rebuke *n* Tadel *m* ● *vt* tadeln

recall *n* Erinnerung *f* ● *vt* zurückrufen; abberufen <*diplomat*>; (*remember*) sich erinnern an (+ *acc*)

recant *vi* widerrufen

recap *vt/i* 🄸 = recapitulate

recapitulate *vt/i* zusammenfassen; rekapitulieren

recapture *vt* wieder gefangen nehmen <*person*>; wieder einfangen <*animal*>

reced|e *vi* zurückgehen. ~**ing** *a* <*forehead, chin*> fliehend

receipt *n* Quittung *f*; (*receiving*) Empfang *m*; ~**s** *pl* (*Comm*) Einnahmen *pl*

receive *vt* erhalten, bekommen; empfangen <*guests*>. ~**r** *n* (*Teleph*) Hörer *m*; (*of stolen goods*) Hehler *m*

recent *a* kürzlich erfolgte(r,s). ~**ly** *adv* vor kurzem

receptacle *n* Behälter *m*

reception *n* Empfang *m*; ~ [**desk**] (*in hotel*) Rezeption *f*. ~**ist** *n* Empfangsdame *f*

receptive a aufnahmefähig; ~ **to** empfänglich für

recess n Nische f; (holiday) Ferien pl

recession n Rezession f

recharge vt [wieder] aufladen

recipe n Rezept nt

recipient n Empfänger m

recital n (of poetry, songs) Vortrag m; (of instrumental music) Konzert nt

recite vt aufsagen; (before audience) vortragen

reckless a, **-ly** adv leichtsinnig; (careless) rücksichtslos. ~**ness** n Leichtsinn m; (carelessness) Rücksichtslosigkeit f

reckon vt rechnen; (consider) glauben ● vi ~ **on/with** rechnen mit

reclaim vt zurückfordern; zurückgewinnen <land>

reclin|e vi liegen. ~**ing seat** n Liegesitz m

recluse n Einsiedler(in) m(f)

recognition n Erkennen nt; (acknowledgement) Anerkennung f; **in** ~ als Anerkennung (**of** gen)

recognize vt erkennen; (know again) wieder erkennen; (acknowledge) anerkennen

recoil vi zurückschnellen; (in fear) zurückschrecken

recollect vt sich erinnern an (+ acc). ~**ion** n Erinnerung f

recommend vt empfehlen. ~**ation** n Empfehlung f

recon|cile vt versöhnen; ~**cile oneself to** sich abfinden mit. ~**ciliation** n Versöhnung f

reconnaissance n (Mil) Aufklärung f

reconnoitre vi (pres p **-tring**) auf Erkundung ausgehen

reconsider vt sich (dat) noch einmal überlegen

reconstruct vt wieder aufbauen; rekonstruieren <crime>

record[1] vt aufzeichnen; (register) registrieren; (on tape) aufnehmen

record[2] n Aufzeichnung f; (Jur) Protokoll nt; (Mus) [Schall]platte f; (Sport) Rekord m; ~**s** pl Unterlagen

pl; **off the** ~ inoffiziell; **have a [criminal]** ~ vorbestraft sein

recorder n (Mus) Blockflöte f

recording n Aufnahme f

re-count[1] vt nachzählen

re-count[2] n (Pol) Nachzählung f

recover vt zurückbekommen ● vi sich erholen. ~**y** n Wiedererlangung f; (of health) Erholung f

recreation n Erholung f; (hobby) Hobby nt. ~**al** a Freizeit-; **be** ~**al** erholsam sein

recruit n (Mil) Rekrut m; **new** ~ (member) neues Mitglied nt; (worker) neuer Mitarbeiter m ● vt rekrutieren; anwerben <staff>. ~**ment** n Rekrutierung f; Anwerbung f

rectang|le n Rechteck nt. ~**ular** a rechteckig

rectify vt (pt/pp **-ied**) berichtigen

rector n Pfarrer m; (Univ) Rektor m. ~**y** n Pfarrhaus nt

recur vi (pt/pp **recurred**) sich wiederholen; <illness:> wiederkehren

recurren|ce n Wiederkehr f. ~**t** a wiederkehrend

recycle vt wieder verwerten

red a (**redder, reddest**) rot ● n Rot nt

redd|en vt röten ● vi rot werden. ~**ish** a rötlich

redecorate vt renovieren; (paint) neu streichen; (wallpaper) neu tapezieren

redeem vt einlösen; (Relig) erlösen

redemption n Erlösung f

red: ~**-haired** a rothaarig. ~**-handed** a **catch s.o.** ~**-handed** jdn auf frischer Tat ertappen. ~ **herring** n falsche Spur f. ~**-hot** a glühend heiß. ~ **light** n (Auto) rote Ampel f. ~**ness** n Röte f

redo vt (pt **-did**, pp **-done**) noch einmal machen

redouble vt verdoppeln

red tape n Ⓔ Bürokratie f

reduc|e vt verringern, vermindern; (in size) verkleinern; ermäßigen <costs>; herabsetzen <price, goods>; (Culin) einkochen lassen. ~**tion** n

Verringerung f; (in price)
Ermäßigung f; (in size)
Verkleinerung f

redundan|cy n
Beschäftigungslosigkeit f. ~t a
überflüssig; **make** ~t entlassen; **be
made** ~t beschäftigungslos werden

reed n [Schilf]rohr nt; ~s pl Schilf
nt

reef n Riff nt

reek vi riechen (**of** nach)

reel n Rolle f, Spule f ● vi (stagger)
taumeln ● vt ~ **off** (fig)
herunterrasseln

refectory n Refektorium nt; (Univ)
Mensa f

refer v (pt/pp referred) ● vt
verweisen (**to** an + acc); übergeben,
weiterleiten <matter> (**to** an + acc)
● vi ~ **to** sich beziehen auf (+ acc);
(mention) erwähnen; (concern)
betreffen; (consult) sich wenden an
(+ acc); nachschlagen in (+ dat)
<book>; **are you** ~ring **to me?**
meinen Sie mich?

referee n Schiedsrichter m;
(Boxing) Ringrichter m; (for job)
Referenz f ● vt/i (pt/pp refereed)
Schiedsrichter/Ringrichter sein (bei)

reference n Erwähnung f; (in book)
Verweis m; (for job) Referenz f; **with**
~ **to** in Bezug auf (+ acc); **make [a]**
~ **to** erwähnen. ~ **book** n
Nachschlagewerk nt

referendum n Volksabstimmung f

refill¹ vt nachfüllen

refill² n (for pen) Ersatzmine f

refine vt raffinieren. ~d a fein,
vornehm. ~ment n Vornehmheit f;
(Techn) Verfeinerung f. ~ry n
Raffinerie f

reflect vt reflektieren; <mirror:>
[wider]spiegeln; **be** ~ed **in** sich
spiegeln in (+ dat) ● vi nachdenken
(**on** über + acc). ~ion n Reflexion f;
(image) Spiegelbild nt; **on** ~ion nach
nochmaliger Überlegung. ~or n
Rückstrahler m

reflex n Reflex m

reflexive a reflexiv

reform n Reform f ● vt reformieren
● vi sich bessern

refrain¹ n Refrain m

refrain² vi ~ **from doing sth** etw
nicht tun

refresh vt erfrischen. ~ing a
erfrischend. ~ments npl
Erfrischungen pl

refrigerat|e vt kühlen. ~or n
Kühlschrank m

refuel vt/i (pt/pp -fuelled) auftanken

refuge n Zuflucht f; **take** ~ Zuflucht
nehmen

refugee n Flüchtling m

refund¹ n **get a** ~ sein Geld
zurückbekommen

refund² vt zurückerstatten

refusal n (see refuse¹) Ablehnung f;
Weigerung f

refuse¹ vt ablehnen; (not grant)
verweigern; ~ **to do sth** sich
weigern, etw zu tun ● vi ablehnen;
sich weigern

refuse² n Müll m

refute vt widerlegen

regain vt wiedergewinnen

regal a, -**ly** adv königlich

regard n (heed) Rücksicht f; (respect)
Achtung f; ~**s** pl Grüße pl; **with** ~
to in Bezug auf (+ acc) ● vt ansehen,
betrachten (**as** als). ~ing prep
bezüglich (+ gen). ~less adv ohne
Rücksicht (**of** auf + acc)

regatta n Regatta f

regime n Regime nt

regiment n Regiment nt. ~al a
Regiments-

region n Region f; **in the** ~ **of** (fig)
ungefähr. ~al a, -**ly** adv regional

register n Register nt; (Sch)
Anwesenheitsliste f ● vt
registrieren; (report) anmelden;
einschreiben <letter>; aufgeben
<luggage> ● vi (report) sich
anmelden

registrar n Standesbeamte(r) m

registration n Registrierung f;
Anmeldung f. ~ **number** n
Autonummer f

registry office n Standesamt nt

regret n Bedauern nt ● vt (pt/pp
regretted) bedauern. ~**fully** adv mit
Bedauern

regrettab|le a bedauerlich. ~**ly**
adv bedauerlicherweise

regular a, **-ly** adv regelmäßig;
(usual) üblich ● n (in pub)
Stammgast m; (in shop)
Stammkunde m. ~**ity** n
Regelmäßigkeit f

regulat|e vt regulieren. ~**ion** n
(rule) Vorschrift f

rehears|al n (Theat) Probe f. ~**e** vt
proben

reign n Herrschaft f ● vi herrschen,
regieren

rein n Zügel m

reindeer n inv Rentier nt

reinforce vt verstärken. ~**ment** n
Verstärkung f; send ~**ments**
Verstärkung schicken

reiterate vt wiederholen

reject vt ablehnen. ~**ion** n
Ablehnung f

rejects npl (Comm) Ausschussware
f

rejoic|e vi (liter) sich freuen. ~**ing**
n Freude f

rejoin vt sich wieder anschließen (+
dat); wieder beitreten (+ dat) <club,
party>

rejuvenate vt verjüngen

relapse n Rückfall m ● vi einen
Rückfall erleiden

relate vt (tell) erzählen; (connect)
verbinden

relation n Beziehung f; (person)
Verwandte(r) m/f. ~**ship** n
Beziehung f; (link) Verbindung f;
(blood tie) Verwandtschaft f; (affair)
Verhältnis nt

relative n Verwandte(r) m/f ● a
relativ; (Gram) Relativ-. ~**ly** adv
relativ, verhältnismäßig

relax vt lockern, entspannen ● vi
sich lockern, sich entspannen.
~**ation** n Entspannung f. ~**ing** a
entspannend

relay[1] vt (pt/pp **-layed**) weitergeben;
(Radio, TV) übertragen

relay[2] n. ~ **[race]** n Staffel f

release n Freilassung f, Entlassung
f; (Techn) Auslöser m ● vt freilassen;
(let go of) loslassen; (Techn)
auslösen; veröffentlichen
<information>

relent vi nachgeben. ~**less** a, **-ly**
adv erbarmungslos; (unceasing)
unaufhörlich

relevan|ce n Relevanz f. ~**t** a
relevant (to für)

reliab|ility n Zuverlässigkeit f. ~**le**
a, **-ly** adv zuverlässig

relian|ce n Abhängigkeit f (on von).
~**t** a angewiesen (on auf + acc)

relic n Überbleibsel nt; (Relig)
Reliquie f

relief n Erleichterung f; (assistance)
Hilfe f; (replacement) Ablösung f;
(Art) Relief nt

relieve vt erleichtern; (take over
from) ablösen; ~ of entlasten von

religion n Religion f

religious a religiös

relinquish vt loslassen; (give up)
aufgeben

relish n Genuss m; (Culin) Würze f
● vt genießen

reluctan|ce n Widerstreben nt. ~**t**
a widerstrebend; be ~**t** zögern (to
zu). ~**tly** adv ungern, widerstrebend

rely vi (pt/pp **-ied**) ~ on sich
verlassen auf (+ acc); (be dependent
on) angewiesen sein auf (+ acc)

remain vi bleiben; (be left) übrig
bleiben. ~**der** n Rest m. ~**ing** a
restlich. ~**s** npl Reste pl; **[mortal]**
~**s** [sterbliche] Überreste pl

remand n on ~ in
Untersuchungshaft ● vt ~ in
custody in Untersuchungshaft
schicken

remark n Bemerkung f ● vt
bemerken. ~**able** a, **-bly** adv
bemerkenswert

remarry vi wieder heiraten

remedy n [Heil]mittel nt (for gegen);
(fig) Abhilfe f ● vt (pt/pp **-ied**)
abhelfen (+ dat); beheben <fault>

remember vt sich erinnern an (+
acc); ~ to do sth daran denken, etw
zu tun ● vi sich erinnern

remind vt erinnern (of an + acc). **~er** n Andenken nt; (letter, warning) Mahnung f

reminisce vi sich seinen Erinnerungen hingeben. **~nces** npl Erinnerungen pl. **~nt** a be ~nt of erinnern an (+ acc)

remnant n Rest m

remorse n Reue f. **~ful** a, **-ly** adv reumütig. **~less** a, **-ly** adv unerbittlich

remote a fern; (isolated) abgelegen; (slight) gering. **~ control** n Fernsteuerung f; (for TV) Fernbedienung f

remotely adv entfernt; **not ~** nicht im Entferntesten

removable a abnehmbar

removal n Entfernung f; (from house) Umzug m. **~ van** n Möbelwagen m

remove vt entfernen; (take off) abnehmen; (take out) herausnehmen

render vt machen; erweisen <service>; (translate) wiedergeben; (Mus) vortragen

renegade n Abtrünnige(r) m/f

renew vt erneuern; verlängern <contract>. **~al** n Erneuerung f; Verlängerung f

renounce vt verzichten auf (+ acc)

renovat|e vt renovieren. **~ion** n Renovierung f

renown n Ruf m. **~ed** a berühmt

rent n Miete f ● vt mieten; (hire) leihen; **~ [out]** vermieten; verleihen. **~al** n Mietgebühr f; Leihgebühr f

renunciation n Verzicht m

reopen vt/i wieder aufmachen

reorganize vt reorganisieren

rep n Ⓔ Vertreter m

repair n Reparatur f; **in good/bad ~** in gutem/schlechtem Zustand ● vt reparieren

repatriate vt repatriieren

repay vt (pt/pp -paid) zurückzahlen; **~ s.o. for sth** jdm etw zurückzahlen. **~ment** n Rückzahlung f

repeal n Aufhebung f ● vt aufheben

repeat n Wiederholung f ● vt/i wiederholen; **~ after me** sprechen Sie mir nach. **~ed** a, **-ly** adv wiederholt

repel vt (pt/pp repelled) abwehren; (fig) abstoßen. **~lent** a abstoßend

repent vi Reue zeigen. **~ance** n Reue f. **~ant** a reuig

repercussions npl Auswirkungen pl

repertoire, repertory n Repertoire nt

repetit|ion n Wiederholung f. **~ive** a eintönig

replace vt zurücktun; (take the place of) ersetzen; (exchange) austauschen. **~ment** n Ersatz m

replay n (Sport) Wiederholungsspiel nt; **[action] ~** Wiederholung f

replenish vt auffüllen <stocks>; (refill) nachfüllen

replica n Nachbildung f

reply n Antwort f (to auf + acc) ● vt/i (pt/pp replied) antworten

report n Bericht m; (Sch) Zeugnis nt; (rumour) Gerücht nt; (of gun) Knall m ● vt berichten; (notify) melden; **~ s.o. to the police** jdn anzeigen ● vi berichten (on über + acc); (present oneself) sich melden (to bei). **~er** n Reporter(in) m(f)

reprehensible a tadelnswert

represent vt darstellen; (act for) vertreten, repräsentieren. **~ation** n Darstellung f

representative a repräsentativ (of für) ● n Bevollmächtigte(r) m/(f); (Comm) Vertreter(in) m(f); (Amer, Pol) Abgeordnete(r) m/f

repress vt unterdrücken. **~ion** n Unterdrückung f. **~ive** a repressiv

reprieve n Begnadigung f; (fig) Gnadenfrist f ● vt begnadigen

reprimand n Tadel m ● vt tadeln

reprint[1] n Nachdruck m

reprint[2] vt neu auflegen

reprisal n Vergeltungsmaßnahme f

reproach n Vorwurf m ● vt Vorwürfe pl machen (+ dat). **~ful** a, **-ly** adv vorwurfsvoll

reproduc|e vt wiedergeben, reproduzieren ● vi sich fortpflanzen.

∼tion *n* Reproduktion *f*; (*Biol*) Fortpflanzung *f*

reptile *n* Reptil *nt*

republic *n* Republik *f*. **∼an** *a* republikanisch ● *n* Republikaner(in) *m(f)*

repugnan|ce *n* Widerwille *m*. **∼t** *a* widerlich

repuls|ion *n* Widerwille *m*. **∼ive** *a* abstoßend, widerlich

reputable *a* <*firm*> von gutem Ruf; (*respectable*) anständig

reputation *n* Ruf *m*

request *n* Bitte *f* ● *vt* bitten

require *vt* (*need*) brauchen; (*demand*) erfordern; **be ∼d to do sth** etw tun müssen. **∼ment** *n* Bedürfnis *nt*; (*condition*) Erfordernis *nt*

resale *n* Weiterverkauf *m*

rescue *n* Rettung *f* ● *vt* retten. **∼r** *n* Retter *m*

research *n* Forschung *f* ● *vt* erforschen; (*Journ*) recherchieren. **∼er** *n* Forscher *m*; (*Journ*) Rechercheur *m*

resem|blance *n* Ähnlichkeit *f*. **∼ble** *vt* ähneln (+ *dat*)

resent *vt* übel nehmen; einen Groll hegen gegen <*person*>. **∼ful** *a*, **-ly** *adv* verbittert. **∼ment** *n* Groll *m*

reservation *n* Reservierung *f*; (*doubt*) Vorbehalt *m*; (*enclosure*) Reservat *nt*

reserve *n* Reserve *f*; (*for animals*) Reservat *nt*; (*Sport*) Reservespieler(in) *m(f)* ● *vt* reservieren; <*client:*> reservieren lassen; (*keep*) aufheben; sich (*dat*) vorbehalten <*right*>. **∼d** *a* reserviert

reservoir *n* Reservoir *nt*

reshuffle *n* (*Pol*) Umbildung *f* ● *vt* (*Pol*) umbilden

residence *n* Wohnsitz *m*; (*official*) Residenz *f*; (*stay*) Aufenthalt *m*

resident *a* ansässig (**in** + *dat*); <*housekeeper, nurse*> im Haus wohnend ● *n* Bewohner(in) *m(f)*; (*of street*) Anwohner *m*. **∼ial** *a* Wohn-

residue *n* Rest *m*; (*Chem*) Rückstand *m*

resign *vt* **∼ oneself to** sich abfinden mit ● *vi* kündigen; (*from public office*) zurücktreten. **∼ation** *n* Resignation *f*; (*from job*) Kündigung *f*; Rücktritt *m*. **∼ed** *a*, **-ly** *adv* resigniert

resilient *a* federnd; (*fig*) widerstandsfähig

resin *n* Harz *nt*

resist *vt/i* sich widersetzen (+ *dat*), (*fig*) widerstehen (+ *dat*). **∼ance** *n* Widerstand *m*. **∼ant** *a* widerstandsfähig

resolut|e *a*, **-ly** *adv* entschlossen. **∼ion** *n* Entschlossenheit *f*; (*intention*) Vorsatz *m*; (*Pol*) Resolution *f*

resolve *n* Entschlossenheit *f*; (*decision*) Beschluss *m* ● *vt* beschließen; (*solve*) lösen

resort *n* (*place*) Urlaubsort *m*; **as a last ∼** wenn alles andere fehlschlägt ● *vi* **∼ to** (*fig*) greifen zu

resound *vi* widerhallen

resource *n* **∼s** *pl* Ressourcen *pl*. **∼ful** *a* findig

respect *n* Respekt *m*, Achtung *f* (**for** vor + *dat*); (*aspect*) Hinsicht *f*; **with ∼ to** in Bezug auf (+ *acc*) ● *vt* respektieren, achten

respect|able *a*, **-bly** *adv* ehrbar; (*decent*) anständig; (*considerable*) ansehnlich. **∼ful** *a*, **-ly** *adv* respektvoll

respective *a* jeweilig. **∼ly** *adv* beziehungsweise

respiration *n* Atmung *f*

respite *n* [Ruhe]pause *f*; (*delay*) Aufschub *m*

respond *vi* antworten; (*react*) reagieren (**to** auf + *acc*)

response *n* Antwort *f*; Reaktion *f*

responsibility *n* Verantwortung *f*; (*duty*) Verpflichtung *f*

responsib|le *a* verantwortlich; (*trustworthy*) verantwortungsvoll. **∼ly** *adv* verantwortungsbewusst

rest[1] *n* Ruhe *f*; (*holiday*) Erholung *f*; (*interval & Mus*) Pause *f*; **have a ∼**

eine Pause machen; (*rest*) sich ausruhen ● *vt* ausruhen; (*lean*) lehnen (on an/auf + *acc*) ● *vi* ruhen; (*have a rest*) sich ausruhen

rest² *n* the ~ der Rest; (*people*) die Übrigen *pl* ● *vi* it ~s with you es ist an Ihnen (**to** zu)

restaurant *n* Restaurant *nt*, Gaststätte *f*

restful *a* erholsam

restive *a* unruhig

restless *a*, **-ly** *adv* unruhig

restoration *n* (*of building*) Restaurierung *f*

restore *vt* wiederherstellen; restaurieren <*building*>

restrain *vt* zurückhalten; ~ oneself sich beherrschen. ~**ed** *a* zurückhaltend. ~**t** *n* Zurückhaltung *f*

restrict *vt* einschränken; ~ to beschränken auf (+ *acc*). ~**ion** *n* Einschränkung *f*; Beschränkung *f*. ~**ive** *a* einschränkend

rest room *n* (*Amer*) Toilette *f*

result *n* Ergebnis *nt*, Resultat *nt*; (*consequence*) Folge *f*; **as a** ~ als Folge (**of** *gen*) ● *vi* sich ergeben (**from** aus); ~ **in** enden in (+ *dat*); (*lead to*) führen zu

resume *vt* wieder aufnehmen ● *vi* wieder beginnen

résumé *n* Zusammenfassung *f*

resumption *n* Wiederaufnahme *f*

resurrect *vt* (*fig*) wieder beleben. ~**ion** *n* the R ~**ion** (*Relig*) die Auferstehung

resuscitat|e *vt* wieder beleben. ~**ion** *n* Wiederbelebung *f*

retail *n* Einzelhandel *m* ● *a* Einzelhandels- ● *adv* im Einzelhandel ● *vt* im Einzelhandel verkaufen ● *vi* ~ **at** im Einzelhandel kosten. ~**er** *n* Einzelhändler *m*

retain *vt* behalten

retaliat|e *vi* zurückschlagen. ~**ion** *n* Vergeltung *f*; **in** ~**ion** als Vergeltung

retarded *a* zurückgeblieben

reticen|ce *n* Zurückhaltung *f*. ~**t** *a* zurückhaltend

retina *n* Netzhaut *f*

retinue *n* Gefolge *nt*

retire *vi* in den Ruhestand treten; (*withdraw*) sich zurückziehen. ~**d** *a* im Ruhestand. ~**ment** *n* Ruhestand *m*

retiring *a* zurückhaltend

retort *n* scharfe Erwiderung *f*; (*Chem*) Retorte *f* ● *vt* scharf erwidern

retrace *vt* ~ one's steps denselben Weg zurückgehen

retrain *vt* umschulen ● *vi* umgeschult werden

retreat *n* Rückzug *m*; (*place*) Zufluchtsort *m* ● *vi* sich zurückziehen

retrial *n* Wiederaufnahmeverfahren *nt*

retrieve *vt* zurückholen; (*from wreckage*) bergen; (*Computing*) wieder auffinden

retrograde *a* rückschrittlich

retrospect *n* in ~ rückblickend. ~**ive** *a*, **-ly** *adv* rückwirkend; (*looking back*) rückblickend

return *n* Rückkehr *f*; (*giving back*) Rückgabe *f*; (*Comm*) Ertrag *m*; (*ticket*) Rückfahrkarte *f*; (*Aviat*) Rückflugschein *m*; **by** ~ **[of post]** postwendend; **in** ~ dafür; **in** ~ **for** für; **many happy** ~**s!** herzlichen Glückwunsch zum Geburtstag! ● *vt* zurückgehen/-fahren; (*come back*) zurückkommen ● *vt* zurückgeben; (*put back*) zurückstellen/-legen; (*send back*) zurückschicken

return ticket *n* Rückfahrkarte *f*; (*Aviat*) Rückflugschein *m*

reunion *n* Wiedervereinigung *f*; (*social gathering*) Treffen *nt*

reunite *vt* wieder vereinigen

reuse *vt* wieder verwenden

rev *n* (*Auto* Ⓘ) Umdrehung *f* ● *vt/i* ~ **[up]** den Motor auf Touren bringen

reveal *vt* zum Vorschein bringen; (*fig*) enthüllen. ~**ing** *a* (*fig*) aufschlussreich

revel *vi* (*pt/pp* revelled) ~ **in sth** etw genießen

revelation *n* Offenbarung *f*, Enthüllung *f*

revenge *n* Rache *f*; (*fig & Sport*) Revanche *f* ● *vt* rächen

revenue *n* [Staats]einnahmen *pl*

revere *vt* verehren. **~nce** *n* Ehrfurcht *f*

Reverend *a* the **~** X Pfarrer X; (*Catholic*) Hochwürden X

reverent *a*, **-ly** *adv* ehrfürchtig

reversal *n* Umkehrung *f*

reverse *a* umgekehrt ● *n* Gegenteil *nt*; (*back*) Rückseite *f*; (*Auto*) Rückwärtsgang *m* ● *vt* umkehren; (*Auto*) zurücksetzen ● *vi* zurücksetzen

revert *vi* **~** to zurückfallen an (+ *acc*)

review *n* Rückblick *m* (of auf + *acc*); (*re-examination*) Überprüfung *f*; (*Mil*) Truppenschau *f*; (*of book, play*) Kritik *f*, Rezension *f* ● *vt* zurückblicken auf (+ *acc*); überprüfen <*situation*>; rezensieren <*book, play*>. **~er** *n* Kritiker *m*, Rezensent *m*

revis|e *vt* revidieren; (*for exam*) wiederholen. **~ion** *n* Revision *f*; (*for exam*) Wiederholung *f*

revival *n* Wiederbelebung *f*

revive *vt* wieder beleben; (*fig*) wieder aufleben lassen ● *vi* wieder aufleben

revolt *n* Aufstand *m* ● *vi* rebellieren ● *vt* anwidern. **~ing** *a* widerlich, eklig

revolution *n* Revolution *f*; (*Auto*) Umdrehung *f*. **~ary** *a* revolutionär. **~ize** *vt* revolutionieren

revolve *vi* sich drehen; **~ around** kreisen um

revolv|er *n* Revolver *m*. **~ing** *a* Dreh-

revue *n* Revue *f*; (*satirical*) Kabarett *nt*

revulsion *n* Abscheu *m*

reward *n* Belohnung *f* ● *vt* belohnen. **~ing** *a* lohnend

rewrite *vt* (*pt* rewrote, *pp* rewritten) noch einmal [neu] schreiben; (*alter*) umschreiben

rhetoric *n* Rhetorik *f*. **~al** *a* rhetorisch

rheumatism *n* Rheumatismus *m*, Rheuma *nt*

Rhine *n* Rhein *m*

rhinoceros *n* Nashorn *nt*, Rhinozeros *nt*

rhubarb *n* Rhabarber *m*

rhyme *n* Reim *m* ● *vt* reimen ● *vi* sich reimen

rhythm *n* Rhythmus *m*. **~ic[al]** *a*, **-ally** *adv* rhythmisch

rib *n* Rippe *f*

ribbon *n* Band *nt*; (*for typewriter*) Farbband *nt*

rice *n* Reis *m*

rich *a* (-er, -est), **-ly** *adv* reich; <*food*> gehaltvoll; (*heavy*) schwer ● *n* **the ~** *pl* die Reichen; **~es** *pl* Reichtum *m*

ricochet *vi* abprallen

rid *vt* (*pt/pp* rid, *pres p* ridding) befreien (of von); **get ~ of** loswerden

riddance *n* good **~**! auf Nimmerwiedersehen!

ridden *see* ride

riddle *n* Rätsel *nt*

riddled *a* **~ with** durchlöchert mit

ride *n* Ritt *m*; (*in vehicle*) Fahrt *f*; **take s.o. for a ~** 🎳 jdn reinlegen ● *v* (*pt* rode, *pp* ridden) ● *vt* reiten <*horse*>; fahren mit <*bicycle*> ● *vi* reiten; (*in vehicle*) fahren. **~r** *n* Reiter(in) *m(f)*; (*on bicycle*) Fahrer(in) *m(f)*

ridge *n* Erhebung *f*; (*on roof*) First *m*; (*of mountain*) Grat *m*, Kamm *m*

ridicule *n* Spott *m* ● *vt* verspotten, spotten über (+ *acc*)

ridiculous *a*, **-ly** *adv* lächerlich

riding *n* Reiten *nt* ● *attrib* Reit-

riff-raff *n* Gesindel *nt*

rifle *n* Gewehr *nt* ● *vt* plündern; **~ through** durchwühlen

rift *n* Spalt *m*; (*fig*) Riss *m*

rig *n* Ölbohrturm *m*; (*at sea*) Bohrinsel *f* ● *vt* (*pt/pp* rigged) **~ out** ausrüsten; **~ up** aufbauen

right *a* richtig; (*not left*) rechte(r,s); **be ~** <*person:*> Recht haben;

<clock:> richtig gehen; **put ~** wieder in Ordnung bringen; *(fig)* richtig stellen; **that's ~!** das stimmt! ● *adv* richtig; *(directly)* direkt; *(completely)* ganz; *(not left)* rechts; *<go>* nach rechts; **~ away** sofort ● *n* Recht *nt*; *(not left)* rechte Seite *f*; **on the ~** rechts; **from/to the ~** von/nach rechts; **be in the ~** Recht haben; **by ~s** eigentlich; **the R~** *(Pol)* die Rechte. **~ angle** *n* rechter Winkel *m*

rightful *a*, **-ly** *adv* rechtmäßig

right-handed *a* rechtshändig

rightly *adv* mit Recht

right-wing *a* *(Pol)* rechte(r,s)

rigid *a* starr; *(strict)* streng. **~ity** *n* Starrheit *f*; Strenge *f*

rigorous *a*, **-ly** *adv* streng

rigour *n* Strenge *f*

rim *n* Rand *m*; *(of wheel)* Felge *f*

rind *n* *(on fruit)* Schale *f*; *(on cheese)* Rinde *f*; *(on bacon)* Schwarte *f*

ring¹ *n* Ring *m*; *(for circus)* Manege *f*; **stand in a ~** im Kreis stehen ● *vt* umringen

ring² *n* Klingeln *nt*; **give s.o. a ~** *(Teleph)* jdn anrufen ● *v* *(pt* **rang**, *pp* **rung)** ● *vt* läuten; **~ [up]** *(Teleph)* anrufen ● *vi* *<bells:>* läuten; *<telephone:>* klingeln. **~ back** *vt/i* *(Teleph)* zurückrufen

ring: ~leader *n* Rädelsführer *m.* **~road** *n* Umgehungsstraße *f*

rink *n* Eisbahn *f*

rinse *n* Spülung *f*; *(hair colour)* Tönung *f* ● *vt* spülen

riot *n* Aufruhr *m*; **~s** *pl* Unruhen *pl*; **run ~** randalieren ● *vi* randalieren. **~er** *n* Randalierer *m.* **~ous** *a* aufrührerisch; *(boisterous)* wild

rip *n* Riss *m* ● *vt/i* *(pt/pp* **ripped)** zerreißen; **~ open** aufreißen. **~ off** *vt* 🔟 neppen

ripe *a* *(-r, -st)* reif

ripen *vi* reifen ● *vt* reifen lassen

ripeness *n* Reife *f*

rip-off *n* 🔟 Nepp *m*

ripple *n* kleine Welle *f*

rise *n* Anstieg *m*; *(fig)* Aufstieg *m*; *(increase)* Zunahme *f*; *(in wages)* Lohnerhöhung *f*; *(in salary)* Gehaltserhöhung *f*; **give ~ to** Anlass geben zu ● *vi* *(pt* **rose**, *pp* **risen)** steigen; *<ground:>* ansteigen; *<sun, dough:>* aufgehen; *<river:>* entspringen; *(get up)* aufstehen; *(fig)* aufsteigen **(to** zu). **~r** *n* **early ~r** Frühaufsteher *m*

rising *a* steigend; *<sun>* aufgehend ● *n* *(revolt)* Aufstand *m*

risk *n* Risiko *nt*; **at one's own ~** auf eigene Gefahr ● *vt* riskieren

risky *a* *(-ier, -iest)* riskant

rite *n* Ritus *m*

ritual *a* rituell ● *n* Ritual *nt*

rival *a* rivalisierend ● *n* Rivale *m*/ Rivalin *f*. **~ry** *n* Rivalität *f*; *(Comm)* Konkurrenzkampf *m*

river *n* Fluss *m*

rivet *n* Niete *f* ● *vt* [ver]nieten; **~ed by** *(fig)* gefesselt von

road *n* Straße *f*; *(fig)* Weg *m*

road: ~map *n* Straßenkarte *f*. **~safety** *n* Verkehrssicherheit *f*. **~side** *n* Straßenrand *m*. **~way** *n* Fahrbahn *f*. **~works** *npl* Straßenarbeiten *pl*. **~worthy** *a* verkehrssicher

roam *vi* wandern

roar *n* Gebrüll *nt*; **~s of laughter** schallendes Gelächter *nt* ● *vi* brüllen; *(with laughter)* schallend lachen. **~ing** *a* *<fire>* prasselnd; **do a ~ing trade** 🔟 ein Bombengeschäft machen

roast *a* gebraten, Brat-; **~ beef/pork** Rinder-/Schweinebraten *m* ● *n* Braten *m* ● *vt/i* braten; rösten *<coffee, chestnuts>*

rob *vt* *(pt/pp* **robbed)** berauben **(of** *gen)*; ausrauben *<bank>*. **~ber** *n* Räuber *m*. **~bery** *n* Raub *m*

robe *n* Robe *f*; *(Amer: bathrobe)* Bademantel *m*

robin *n* Rotkehlchen *nt*

robot *n* Roboter *m*

robust *a* robust

rock¹ *n* Fels *m*; **on the ~s** *<ship>* aufgelaufen; *<marriage>* kaputt; *<drink>* mit Eis

rock² *vt/i* schaukeln

rock³ n (Mus) Rock m

rockery n Steingarten m

rocket n Rakete f

rocking: ~**-chair** n Schaukelstuhl m. ~**-horse** n Schaukelpferd nt

rocky a (-ier, -iest) felsig; (unsteady) wackelig

rod n Stab m; (stick) Rute f; (for fishing) Angel[rute] f

rode see ride

rodent n Nagetier nt

rogue n Gauner m

role n Rolle f

roll n Rolle f; (bread) Brötchen nt; (list) Liste f; (of drum) Wirbel m ● vi rollen; be ~ing in money 🔢 Geld wie Heu haben ● vt rollen; walzen <lawn>; ausrollen <pastry>. ~ **over** vi sich auf die andere Seite rollen. ~ **up** vt aufrollen; hochkrempeln <sleeves> ● vi 🔢 auftauchen

roller n Rolle f; (lawn, road) Walze f; (hair) Lockenwickler m. ~ **blind** n Rollo nt. ~**-coaster** n Berg-und-Talbahn f. ~**-skate** n Rollschuh m

rolling-pin n Teigrolle f

Roman a römisch ● n Römer(in) m(f)

romance n Romantik f; (love-affair) Romanze f; (book) Liebesgeschichte f

Romania n Rumänien nt. ~**n** a rumänisch ● n Rumäne m/-nin f

romantic a, -**ally** adv romantisch. ~**ism** n Romantik f

Rome n Rom nt

romp vi [herum]tollen

roof n Dach nt; (of mouth) Gaumen m ● vt ~ **[over]** überdachen. ~**-top** n Dach nt

rook n Saatkrähe f; (Chess) Turm m

room n Zimmer nt; (for functions) Saal m; (space) Platz m. ~**y** a geräumig

roost n Hühnerstange f

root¹ n Wurzel f; take ~ anwachsen ● vi Wurzeln schlagen. ~ **out** vt (fig) ausrotten

root² vi ~ **about** wühlen; ~ **for s.o.** 🔢 für jdn sein

rope n Seil nt; know the ~**s** 🔢 sich auskennen. ~ **in** vt 🔢 einspannen

rose¹ n Rose f; (of watering-can) Brause f

rose² see rise

rostrum n Podium nt

rosy a (-ier, -iest) rosig

rot n Fäulnis f; (🔢 nonsense) Quatsch m ● vi (pt/pp rotted) [ver]faulen

rota n Dienstplan m

rotary a Dreh-; (Techn) Rotations-

rotat|e vt drehen ● vi sich drehen; (Techn) rotieren. ~**ion** n Drehung f; in ~**ion** im Wechsel

rote n by ~ auswendig

rotten a faul; 🔢 mies; <person> fies

rough a (-er, -est) rau; (uneven) uneben; (coarse, not gentle) grob; (brutal) roh; (turbulent) stürmisch; (approximate) ungefähr ● adv sleep ~ im Freien übernachten ● vt ~ **it** primitiv leben. ~ **out** vt im Groben entwerfen

roughage n Ballaststoffe pl

rough draft n grober Entwurf m

rough|ly adv (see rough) rau; grob; roh; ungefähr. ~**ness** n Rauheit f

rough paper n Konzeptpapier nt

round a (-er, -est) rund ● n Runde f; (slice) Scheibe f; do one's ~**s** seine Runde machen ● prep um (+ acc); ~ **the clock** rund um die Uhr ● adv all ~ ringsherum; ask s.o. ~ jdn einladen ● vt biegen um <corner>. ~ **off** vt abrunden. ~ **up** vt aufrunden; zusammentreiben <animals>; festnehmen <criminals>

roundabout a ~ route Umweg m ● n Karussell nt; (for traffic) Kreisverkehr m

round trip n Rundreise f

rous|e vt wecken; (fig) erregen. ~**ing** a mitreißend

route n Route f; (of bus) Linie f

routine a, -**ly** adv routinemäßig ● n Routine f; (Theat) Nummer f

row¹ n (line) Reihe f

row² vt/i rudern

row³ n 🔢 Krach m ● vi 🔢 sich streiten

rowdy a (-ier, -iest) laut

rowing boat n Ruderboot nt

royal a, **-ly** adv königlich

royalt|y n Königtum nt; (persons) Mitglieder pl der königlichen Familie; **-ies** pl (payments) Tantiemen pl

rub vt (pt/pp **rubbed**) reiben; (polish) polieren; **don't ~ it in** 🔲 reib es mir nicht unter die Nase. **~ off** vt abreiben ● vi abgehen. **~ out** vt ausradieren

rubber n Gummi m; (eraser) Radiergummi m. **~ band** n Gummiband nt

rubbish n Abfall m, Müll m; (🔲 nonsense) Quatsch m; (🔲 junk) Plunder m. **~ bin** n Abfalleimer m. **~ dump** n Abfallhaufen m; (official) Müllhalde f

rubble n Trümmer pl

ruby n Rubin m

rudder n [Steuer]ruder nt

rude a (-r, -st), **-ly** adv unhöflich; (improper) unanständig. **~ness** n Unhöflichkeit f

rudimentary a elementar; (Biol) rudimentär

ruffian n Rüpel m

ruffle vt zerzausen

rug n Vorleger m, [kleiner] Teppich m; (blanket) Decke f

rugged a <coastline> zerklüftet

ruin n Ruine f; (fig) Ruin m ● vt ruinieren

rule n Regel f; (control) Herrschaft f; (government) Regierung f; (for measuring) Lineal nt; **as a ~** in der Regel ● vt regieren, herrschen über (+ acc); (fig) beherrschen; (decide) entscheiden; ziehen <line> ● vi regieren, herrschen. **~ out** vt ausschließen

ruled a <paper> liniert

ruler n Herrscher(in) m(f); (measure) Lineal nt

ruling a herrschend; <factor> entscheidend; (Pol) regierend ● n Entscheidung f

rum n Rum m

rumble n Grollen nt ● vi grollen; <stomach:> knurren

rummage vi wühlen; **~ through** durchwühlen

rumour n Gerücht nt ● vt **it is ~ed that** es geht das Gerücht, dass

rump n Hinterteil nt. **~ steak** n Rumpsteak nt

run n Lauf m; (journey) Fahrt f; (series) Serie f, Reihe f; (Theat) Laufzeit f; (Skiing) Abfahrt f; (enclosure) Auslauf m; (Amer: ladder) Laufmasche f; **~ of bad luck** Pechsträhne f; **be on the ~** flüchtig sein; **in the long ~** auf lange Sicht ● v (pt **ran**, pp **run**, pres p **running**) ● vi laufen; (flow) fließen; <eyes:> tränen; <bus:> verkehren; <butter, ink:> zerfließen; <colours:> [ab]färben; (in election) kandidieren ● vt laufen lassen; einlaufen lassen <bath>; (manage) führen, leiten; (drive) fahren; eingehen <risk>; (Journ) bringen <article>; **~ one's hand over sth** mit der Hand über etw (acc) fahren. **~ away** vi weglaufen. **~ down** vi hinunter-/ herunterlaufen; <clockwork:> ablaufen; <stocks:> sich verringern ● vt (run over) überfahren; (reduce) verringern; (🔲 criticize) heruntermachen. **~ in** vi hinein-/ hereinlaufen. **~ off** vi weglaufen ● vt abziehen <copies>. **~ out** vi hinaus-/herauslaufen; <supplies, money:> ausgehen; **I've ~ out of sugar** ich habe keinen Zucker mehr. **~ over** vt überfahren. **~ up** vi hinauf-/heraufplaufen; (towards) hinlaufen ● vt machen <debts>; auflaufen lassen <bill>; (sew) schnell nähen

runaway n Ausreißer m

run-down a <area> verkommen

rung[1] n (of ladder) Sprosse f

rung[2] see **ring**[2]

runner n Läufer m; (Bot) Ausläufer m; (on sledge) Kufe f. **~ bean** n Stangenbohne f. **~-up** n Zweite(r) m/f

running a laufend; <water> fließend; **four times ~** viermal nacheinander

● *n* Laufen *nt*; (*management*) Führung *f*, Leitung *f*; **be/not be in the ~** eine/keine Chance haben

runny *a* flüssig

run: **~-up** *n* (*Sport*) Anlauf *m*; (*to election*) Zeit *f* vor der Wahl. **~way** *n* Start- und Landebahn *f*

rupture *n* Bruch *m* ● *vt/i* brechen

rural *a* ländlich

ruse *n* List *f*

rush¹ *n* (*Bot*) Binse *f*

rush² *n* Hetze *f*; **in a ~** in Eile ● *vi* sich hetzen; (*run*) rasen; <*water:*> rauschen ● *vt* hetzen, drängen. **~-hour** *n* Hauptverkehrszeit *f*, Stoßzeit *f*

Russia *n* Russland *nt*. **~n** *a* russisch ● *n* Russe *m*/Russin *f*; (*Lang*) Russisch *nt*

rust *n* Rost *m* ● *vi* rosten

rustle *vi* rascheln ● *vt* rascheln mit; (*Amer*) stehlen <*cattle*>. **~ up** *vt* 🄴 improvisieren

rustproof *a* rostfrei

rusty *a* (-ier, -iest) rostig

rut *n* Furche *f*

ruthless *a*, **-ly** *adv* rücksichtslos. **~ness** *n* Rücksichtslosigkeit *f*

rye *n* Roggen *m*

Ss

sabbath *n* Sabbat *m*

sabotage *n* Sabotage *f* ● *vt* sabotieren

sachet *n* Beutel *m*; (*scented*) Kissen *nt*

sack *n* Sack *m*; **get the ~** 🄴 rausgeschmissen werden ● *vt* 🄴 rausschmeißen

sacred *a* heilig

sacrifice *n* Opfer *nt* ● *vt* opfern

sacrilege *n* Sakrileg *nt*

sad *a* (sadder, saddest) traurig: <*loss, death*> schmerzlich. **~den** *vt* traurig machen

saddle *n* Sattel *m* ● *vt* satteln; **~ s.o. with sth** 🄴 jdm etw aufhalsen

sadist *n* Sadist *m*. **~ic** *a*, **-ally** *adv* sadistisch

sad|ly *adv* traurig; (*unfortunately*) leider. **~ness** *n* Traurigkeit *f*

safe *a* (-r, -st) sicher; <*journey*> gut; (*not dangerous*) ungefährlich; **~ and sound** gesund und wohlbehalten ● *n* Safe *m*. **~guard** *n* Schutz *m* ● *vt* schützen. **~ly** *adv* sicher; <*arrive*> gut

safety *n* Sicherheit *f*. **~-belt** *n* Sicherheitsgurt *m*. **~-pin** *n* Sicherheitsnadel *f*. **~-valve** *n* [Sicherheits]ventil *nt*

sag *vi* (*pt/pp* sagged) durchhängen

saga *n* Saga *f*; (*fig*) Geschichte *f*

said *see* say

sail *n* Segel *nt*; (*trip*) Segelfahrt *f* ● *vi* segeln; (*on liner*) fahren; (*leave*) abfahren (**for** nach) ● *vt* segeln mit

sailing *n* Segelsport *m*. **~-boat** *n* Segelboot *nt*. **~-ship** *n* Segelschiff *nt*

sailor *n* Seemann *m*; (*in navy*) Matrose *m*

saint *n* Heilige(r) *m/f*. **~ly** *a* heilig

sake *n* **for the ~ of ...** um ... (*gen*) willen; **for my/your ~** um meinet-/deinetwillen

salad *n* Salat *m*. **~-dressing** *n* Salatsoße *f*

salary *n* Gehalt *nt*

sale *n* Verkauf *m*; (*event*) Basar *m*; (*at reduced prices*) Schlussverkauf *m*; **for ~** zu verkaufen

sales|man *n* Verkäufer *m*. **~woman** *n* Verkäuferin *f*

saliva *n* Speichel *m*

salmon *n* Lachs *m*

saloon *n* Salon *m*; (*Auto*) Limousine *f*; (*Amer: bar*) Wirtschaft *f*

salt *n* Salz *nt* ● *a* salzig; <*water, meat*> Salz- ● *vt* salzen; (*cure*) pökeln; streuen <*road*>. **~-cellar** *n* Salzfass *nt*. **~ water** *n* Salzwasser *nt*. **~y** *a* salzig

salute n (Mil) Gruß m ● vt/i (Mil) grüßen

salvage n (Naut) Bergung f ● vt bergen

salvation n Rettung f; (Relig) Heil nt

same a & pron **the ~** der/die/das gleiche; (pl) die gleichen; (identical) der-/die-/dasselbe; (pl) dieselben ● adv **the ~** gleich; **all the ~** trotzdem

sample n Probe f; (Comm) Muster nt ● vt probieren; kosten <food>

sanatorium n Sanatorium nt

sanction n Sanktion f ● vt sanktionieren

sanctuary n (Relig) Heiligtum nt; (refuge) Zuflucht f; (for wildlife) Tierschutzgebiet nt

sand n Sand m ● vt ~ **[down]** [ab]schmirgeln

sandal n Sandale f

sand: ~bank n Sandbank f. **~paper** n Sandpapier nt. **~-pit** n Sandkasten m

sandwich n; Sandwich m ● vt ~**ed between** eingeklemmt zwischen

sandy a (-ier, -iest) sandig; <beach, soil> Sand-; <hair> rotblond

sane a (-r, -st) geistig normal; (sensible) vernünftig

sang see **sing**

sanitary a hygienisch; <system> sanitär. **~ napkin** n (Amer), **~ towel** n [Damen]binde f

sanitation n Kanalisation und Abfallbeseitigung pl

sanity n [gesunder] Verstand m

sank see **sink**

sap n (Bot) Saft m ● vt (pt/pp sapped) schwächen

sarcas|m n Sarkasmus m. **~tic** a, **-ally** adv sarkastisch

sardine n Sardine f

sash n Schärpe f

sat see **sit**

satchel n Ranzen m

satellite n Satellit m. **~ television** n Satellitenfernsehen nt

satin n Satin m

satire n Satire f

satirical a, **-ly** adv satirisch

satir|ist n Satiriker(in) m(f)

satisfaction n Befriedigung f; **to my ~** zu meiner Zufriedenheit

satisfactory a, **-ily** adv zufrieden stellend

satisfy vt (pp/pp -ied) befriedigen; zufrieden stellen <customer>; (convince) überzeugen; **be ~ied** zufrieden sein. **~ing** a befriedigend; <meal> sättigend

saturate vt durchtränken; (Chem & fig) sättigen

Saturday n Samstag m

sauce n Soße f; (cheek) Frechheit f. **~pan** n Kochtopf m

saucer n Untertasse f

saucy a (-ier, -iest) frech

Saudi Arabia n Saudi-Arabien n

sauna n Sauna f

saunter vi schlendern

sausage n Wurst f

savage a wild; (fierce) scharf; (brutal) brutal ● n Wilde(r) m/f. **~ry** n Brutalität f

save n (Sport) Abwehr f ● vt retten (from vor + dat); (keep) aufheben; (not waste) sparen; (collect) sammeln; (avoid) ersparen; (Sport) verhindern <goal> ● vi ~ **[up]** sparen

saver n Sparer m

saving n (see **save**) Rettung f; Sparen nt; Ersparnis f; **~s** pl (money) Ersparnisse pl

savour n Geschmack m ● vt auskosten. **~y** a würzig

saw¹ see **see¹**

saw² n Säge f ● vt/i (pt sawed, pp sawn or sawed) sägen

saxophone n Saxophon nt

say n Mitspracherecht nt; **have one's ~** seine Meinung sagen ● vt/i (pt/pp said) sagen; sprechen <prayer>; **that is to ~** das heißt; **that goes without ~ing** das versteht sich von selbst. **~ing** n Redensart f

scab n Schorf m; (pej) Streikbrecher m

scaffolding n Gerüst nt

scald vt verbrühen

scale¹ n (of fish) Schuppe f

scale² n Skala f; (Mus) Tonleiter f; (ratio) Maßstab m ● vt (climb) erklettern. **~ down** vt verkleinern

scales npl (for weighing) Waage f

scalp n Kopfhaut f

scamper vi huschen

scan n (Med) Szintigramm nt ● v (pt/pp **scanned**) ● vt absuchen; (quickly) flüchtig ansehen; (Med) szintigraphisch untersuchen

scandal n Skandal m; (gossip) Skandalgeschichten pl. **~ize** vt schockieren. **~ous** a skandalös

Scandinavia n Skandinavien nt. **~n** a skandinavisch ● n Skandinavier(in) m(f)

scanner n Scanner m

scanty a (-ier, -iest), **-ily** adv spärlich; <clothing> knapp

scapegoat n Sündenbock m

scar n Narbe f

scarc|e a (-r, -st) knapp; **make oneself ~e** 🛇 sich aus dem Staub machen. **~ely** adv kaum. **~ity** n Knappheit f

scare n Schreck m; (panic) [allgemeine] Panik f ● vt Angst machen (+ dat); **be ~d** Angst haben (of vor + dat)

scarf n (pl **scarves**) Schal m; (square) Tuch nt

scarlet a scharlachrot

scary a unheimlich

scathing a bissig

scatter vt verstreuen; (disperse) zerstreuen ● vi sich zerstreuen. **~ed** a verstreut; <showers> vereinzelt

scatty a (-ier, -iest) 🛇 verrückt

scene n Szene f; (sight) Anblick m; (place of event) Schauplatz m; **behind the ~s** hinter den Kulissen

scenery n Landschaft f; (Theat) Szenerie f

scenic a landschaftlich schön

scent n Duft m; (trail) Fährte f; (perfume) Parfüm nt. **~ed** a parfümiert

sceptic|al a, **-ly** adv skeptisch. **~ism** n Skepsis f

schedule n Programm nt; (of work) Zeitplan m; (timetable) Fahrplan m; **behind ~** im Rückstand; **according to ~** planmäßig ● vt planen

scheme n Programm nt; (plan) Plan m; (plot) Komplott nt ● vi Ränke schmieden

schizophrenic a schizophren

scholar n Gelehrte(r) m/f. **~ly** a gelehrt. **~ship** n Gelehrtheit f; (grant) Stipendium nt

school n Schule f; (Univ) Fakultät f ● vt schulen

school: ~boy n Schüler m. **~girl** n Schülerin f. **~ing** n Schulbildung f. **~master** n Lehrer m. **~mistress** n Lehrerin f. **~teacher** n Lehrer(in) m(f)

scien|ce n Wissenschaft f. **~tific** a wissenschaftlich. **~tist** n Wissenschaftler m

scissors npl Schere f; **a pair of ~** eine Schere

scoff¹ vi **~ at** spotten über (+ acc)

scoff² vt 🛇 verschlingen

scold vt ausschimpfen

scoop n Schaufel f; (Culin) Portionierer m; (Journ) Exklusivmeldung f ● vt **~ out** aushöhlen; (remove) auslöffeln

scooter n Roller m

scope n Bereich m; (opportunity) Möglichkeiten pl

scorch vt versengen. **~ing** a glühend heiß

score n [Spiel]stand m; (individual) Punktzahl f; (Mus) Partitur f; (Cinema) Filmmusik f; **on that ~** was das betrifft ● vt erzielen; schießen <goal>; (cut) einritzen ● vi Punkte erzielen; (Sport) ein Tor schießen; (keep score) Punkte zählen. **~r** n Punktezähler m; (of goals) Torschütze m

scorn n Verachtung f ● vt verachten. **~ful** a, **-ly** adv verächtlich

Scot n Schotte m/Schottin f

Scotch *a* schottisch ● *n* (*whisky*) Scotch *m*

Scot|land *n* Schottland *nt*. **~s, ~tish** *a* schottisch

scoundrel *n* Schurke *m*

scour *vt* (*search*) absuchen; (*clean*) scheuern

scout *n* (*Mil*) Kundschafter *m*; [Boy] S~ Pfadfinder *m*

scowl *n* böser Gesichtsausdruck *m* ● *vi* ein böses Gesicht machen

scram *vi* 🄵 abhauen

scramble *n* Gerangel *nt* ● *vi* klettern; ~ **for** sich drängen nach. **~d egg[s]** *n*[*pl*] Rührei *nt*

scrap[1] *n* (🄵 *fight*) Rauferei *f* ● *vi* sich raufen

scrap[2] *n* Stückchen *nt*; (*metal*) Schrott *m*; **~s** *pl* Reste; **not a** ~ kein bisschen ● *vt* (*pt/pp* scrapped) aufgeben

scrapbook *n* Sammelalbum *nt*

scrape *vt* schaben; (*clean*) abkratzen; (*damage*) [ver]schrammen. ~ **through** *vi* gerade noch durchkommen. ~ **together** *vt* zusammenkriegen

scrappy *a* lückenhaft

scrapyard *n* Schrottplatz *m*

scratch *n* Kratzer *m*; **start from** ~ von vorne anfangen; **not be up to** ~ zu wünschen übrig lassen ● *vt/i* kratzen; (*damage*) zerkratzen

scrawl *n* Gekrakel *nt* ● *vt/i* krakeln

scream *n* Schrei *m* ● *vt/i* schreien

screech *n* Kreischen *nt* ● *vt/i* kreischen

screen *n* Schirm *m*; (*Cinema*) Leinwand *f*; (*TV*) Bildschirm *m* ● *vt* schützen; (*conceal*) verdecken; vorführen <*film*>; (*examine*) überprüfen; (*Med*) untersuchen

screw *n* Schraube *f* ● *vt* schrauben. ~ **up** *vt* festschrauben; (*crumple*) zusammenknüllen; zusammenkneifen <*eyes*>; (🗷 *bungle*) vermasseln

screwdriver *n* Schraubenzieher *m*

scribble *n* Gekritzel *nt* ● *vt/i* kritzeln

script *n* Schrift *f*; (*of speech, play*) Text *m*; (*Radio, TV*) Skript *nt*; (*of film*) Drehbuch *nt*

scrounge *vt/i* schnorren. **~r** *n* Schnorrer *m*

scrub[1] *n* (*land*) Buschland *nt*, Gestrüpp *nt*

scrub[2] *vt/i* (*pt/pp* scrubbed) schrubben

scruff *n* **by the** ~ **of the neck** beim Genick

scruffy *a* (-ier, -iest) vergammelt

scrum *n* Gedränge *nt*

scruple *n* Skrupel *m*

scrupulous *a*, **-ly** *adv* gewissenhaft

scuffle *n* Handgemenge *nt*

sculpt|or *n* Bildhauer(in) *m(f)*. **~ure** *n* Bildhauerei *f*; (*piece of work*) Skulptur *f*, Plastik *f*

scum *n* Schmutzschicht *f*; (*people*) Abschaum *m*

scurry *vi* (*pt/pp* -ied) huschen

scuttle[1] *vt* versenken <*ship*>

scuttle[2] *vi* schnell krabbeln

sea *n* Meer *nt*, See *f*; **at** ~ auf See; **by** ~ mit dem Schiff. **~food** *n* Meeresfrüchte *pl*. **~gull** *n* Möwe *f*

seal[1] *n* (*Zool*) Seehund *m*

seal[2] *n* Siegel *nt* ● *vt* versiegeln; (*fig*) besiegeln. ~ **off** *vt* abriegeln

sea-level *n* Meeresspiegel *m*

seam *n* Naht *f*; (*of coal*) Flöz *nt*

seaman *n* Seemann *m*; (*sailor*) Matrose *m*

seance *n* spiritistische Sitzung *f*

search *n* Suche *f*; (*official*) Durchsuchung *f* ● *vt* durchsuchen; absuchen <*area*> ● *vi* suchen (**for** nach). **~ing** *a* prüfend, forschend

search: ~light *n* [Such]scheinwerfer *m*. **~party** *n* Suchmannschaft *f*

sea: ~sick *a* seekrank. **~side** *n* **at/to the ~side** am/ans Meer

season *n* Jahreszeit *f*; (*social, tourist, sporting*) Saison *f* ● *vt* (*flavour*) würzen. **~al** *a* Saison-. **~ing** *n* Gewürze *pl*

season ticket *n* Dauerkarte *f*

seat n Sitz m; (place) Sitzplatz m; (bottom) Hintern m; **take a ~** Platz nehmen ● vt setzen; (have seats for) Sitzplätze bieten (+ dat); **remain ~ed** sitzen bleiben. **~-belt** n Sicherheitsgurt m; **fasten one's ~-belt** sich anschnallen

sea: ~weed n [See]tang m. **~worthy** a seetüchtig

seclu|ded a abgelegen. **~sion** n Zurückgezogenheit f

second a zweite(r,s); **on ~ thoughts** nach weiterer Überlegung ● n Sekunde f; (Sport) Sekundant m; **~s** pl (goods) Waren zweiter Wahl ● adv (in race) an zweiter Stelle ● vt unterstützen <proposal>

secondary a zweitrangig; (Phys) Sekundär-. **~ school** n höhere Schule f

second: ~-best a zweitbeste(r,s). **~ class** adv <travel, send> zweiter Klasse. **~-class** a zweitklassig

second hand n (on clock) Sekundenzeiger m

second-hand a gebraucht ● adv aus zweiter Hand

secondly adv zweitens

second-rate a zweitklassig

secrecy n Heimlichkeit f

secret a geheim; <agent, police> Geheim-; <drinker, lover> heimlich ● n Geheimnis nt

secretarial a Sekretärinnen-; <work, staff> Sekretariats-

secretary n Sekretär(in) m(f)

secretive a geheimtuerisch

secretly adv heimlich

sect n Sekte f

section n Teil m; (of text) Abschnitt m; (of firm) Abteilung f; (of organization) Sektion f

sector n Sektor m

secular a weltlich

secure a, **-ly** adv sicher; (firm) fest; (emotionally) geborgen ● vt sichern; (fasten) festmachen; (obtain) sich (dat) sichern

securit|y n Sicherheit f; (emotional) Geborgenheit f; **~ies** pl Wertpapiere pl

sedan n (Amer) Limousine f

sedate a, **-ly** adv gesetzt

sedative a beruhigend ● n Beruhigungsmittel nt

sediment n [Boden]satz m

seduce vt verführen

seduct|ion n Verführung f. **~ive** a, **-ly** adv verführerisch

see v (pt saw, pp seen) ● vt sehen; (understand) einsehen; (imagine) sich (dat) vorstellen; (escort) begleiten; **go and ~** nachsehen; (visit) besuchen; **~ you later!** bis nachher! **~ing** that da ● vi sehen; (check) nachsehen; **~ about** sich kümmern um. **~ off** vt verabschieden; (chase away) vertreiben; **~ through** vt (fig) durchschauen <person>

seed n Samen m; (of grape) Kern m; (fig) Saat f; (Tennis) gesetzter Spieler m; **go to ~** Samen bilden; (fig) herunterkommen. **~ed** a (Tennis) gesetzt

seedy a (-ier, -iest) schäbig; <area> heruntergekommen

seek vt (pt/pp sought) suchen

seem vi scheinen

seen see see¹

seep vi sickern

seethe vi **~ with anger** vor Wut schäumen

see-through a durchsichtig

segment n Teil m; (of worm) Segment nt; (of orange) Spalte f

segregat|e vt trennen. **~ion** n Trennung f

seize vt ergreifen; (Jur) beschlagnahmen; **~ s.o. by the arm** jdn am Arm packen. **~ up** vi (Techn) sich festfressen

seldom adv selten

select a ausgewählt; (exclusive) exklusiv ● vt auswählen; aufstellen <team>. **~ion** n Auswahl f

self n (pl selves) Ich nt

self: ~-assurance n Selbstsicherheit f. **~-assured** a selbstsicher. **~-catering** n Selbstversorgung f. **~-centred** a egozentrisch. **~-confidence** n

Selbstbewusstsein *nt*,
Selbstvertrauen *nt*. **~-confident** *a*
selbstbewusst. **~-conscious** *a*
befangen. **~-contained** *a* <*flat*>
abgeschlossen. **~-control** *n*
Selbstbeherrschung *f*. **~-defence** *n*
Selbstverteidigung *f*; (*Jur*) Notwehr
f. **~-employed** selbstständig. **~-
esteem** *n* Selbstachtung *f*. **~-
evident** *a* offensichtlich. **~-
indulgent** *a* maßlos. **~-interest** *n*
Eigennutz *m*

self|ish *a*, **-ly** *adv* egoistisch,
selbstsüchtig. **~less** *a*, **-ly** *adv*
selbstlos

self: **~-pity** *n* Selbstmitleid *nt*. **~-
portrait** *n* Selbstporträt *nt*. **~-
respect** *n* Selbstachtung *f*. **~-
righteous** *a* selbstgerecht. **~-
sacrifice** *n* Selbstaufopferung *f*. **~-
satisfied** *a* selbstgefällig. **~-
service** *n* Selbstbedienung *f*
● *attrib* Selbstbedienungs-. **~-
sufficient** *a* selbstständig

sell *v* (*pt/pp* **sold**) ● *vt* verkaufen; **be
sold out** ausverkauft sein ● *vi* sich
verkaufen. **~ off** *vt* verkaufen

seller *n* Verkäufer *m*

Sellotape (P), *n* ≈ Tesafilm (P) *m*

sell-out *n* **be a ~** ausverkauft sein;
(🄴 *betrayal*) Verrat sein

selves *see* **self**

semester *n* (*Amer*) Semester *nt*

semi|breve *n* (*Mus*) ganze Note *f*.
~circle *n* Halbkreis *m*. **~circular**
a halbkreisförmig. **~colon** *n*
Semikolon *nt*. **~-detached** *a* & *n* **~-
detached [house]**
Doppelhaushälfte *f*. **~-final** *n*
Halbfinale *nt*

seminar *n* Seminar *nt*

senat|e *n* Senat *m*. **~or** *n* Senator
m

send *vt/i* (*pt/pp* **sent**) schicken; **~ for**
kommen lassen <*person*>; sich (*dat*)
schicken lassen <*thing*>. **~er** *n*
Absender *m*. **~-off** *n*
Verabschiedung *f*

senile *a* senil

senior *a* älter; (*in rank*) höher ● *n*
Ältere(r) *m/f*; (*in rank*)

Vorgesetzte(r) *m/f*. **~ citizen** *n*
Senior(in) *m(f)*

seniority *n* höheres Alter *nt*; (*in
rank*) höherer Rang *m*

sensation *n* Sensation *f*; (*feeling*)
Gefühl *nt*. **~al** *a*, **-ly** *adv*
sensationell

sense *n* Sinn *m*; (*feeling*) Gefühl *nt*;
(*common ~*) Verstand *m*; **make ~**
Sinn ergeben ● *vt* spüren. **~less** *a*,
-ly *adv* sinnlos; (*unconscious*)
bewusstlos

sensible *a*, **-bly** *adv* vernünftig;
<*suitable*> zweckmäßig

sensitiv|e *a*, **-ly** *adv* empfindlich;
(*understanding*) einfühlsam. **~ity** *n*
Empfindlichkeit *f*

sensual *a* sinnlich. **-ity** *n*
Sinnlichkeit *f*

sensuous *a* sinnlich

sent *see* **send**

sentence *n* Satz *m*; (*Jur*) Urteil *nt*;
(*punishment*) Strafe *f* ● *vt*
verurteilen

sentiment *n* Gefühl *nt*; (*opinion*)
Meinung *f*; (*sentimentality*)
Sentimentalität *f* **~al** *a* sentimental.
~ality *n* Sentimentalität *f*

sentry *n* Wache *f*

separable *a* trennbar

separate[1] *a*, **-ly** *adv* getrennt,
separat

separat|e[2] *vt* trennen ● *vi* sich
trennen. **~ion** *n* Trennung *f*

September *n* September *m*

septic *a* vereitert

sequel *n* Folge *f*; (*fig*) Nachspiel *nt*

sequence *n* Reihenfolge *f*

serenade *n* Ständchen *nt* ● *vt* **~**
s.o. jdm ein Ständchen bringen

seren|e *a*, **-ly** *adv* gelassen. **~ity** *n*
Gelassenheit *f*

sergeant *n* (*Mil*) Feldwebel *m*; (*in
police*) Polizeimeister *m*

serial *n* Fortsetzungsgeschichte *f*;
(*Radio, TV*) Serie *f*. **~ize** *vt* in
Fortsetzungen veröffentlichen/
(*Radio, TV*) senden

series *n inv* Serie *f*

serious *a*, **-ly** *adv* ernst; <*illness,
error*> schwer. **~ness** *n* Ernst *m*

sermon *n* Predigt *f*

servant *n* Diener(in) *m(f)*

serve *n* (*Tennis*) Aufschlag *m* ● *vt* dienen (+ *dat*); bedienen <*customer, guest*>; servieren <*food*>; verbüßen <*sentence*>; **it ~s you right!** das geschieht dir recht! ● *vi* dienen; (*Tennis*) aufschlagen

service *n* Dienst *m*; (*Relig*) Gottesdienst *m*; (*in shop, restaurant*) Bedienung *f*; (*transport*) Verbindung *f*; (*maintenance*) Wartung *f*; (*set of crockery*) Service *nt*; (*Tennis*) Aufschlag *m*; **~s** *pl* Dienstleistungen *pl*; (*on motorway*) Tankstelle und Raststätte *f*; **in the ~s** beim Militär; **out of/in ~** <*machine:*> außer/in Betrieb ● *vt* (*Techn*) warten

service: **~ area** *n* Tankstelle und Raststätte *f*. **~ charge** *n* Bedienungszuschlag *m*. **~man** *n* Soldat *m*. **~ station** *n* Tankstelle *f*

serviette *n* Serviette *f*

servile *a* unterwürfig

session *n* Sitzung *f*

set *n* Satz *m*; (*of crockery*) Service *nt*; (*of cutlery*) Garnitur *f*; (*TV, Radio*) Apparat *m*; (*Math*) Menge *f*; (*Theat*) Bühnenbild *nt*; (*Cinema*) Szenenaufbau *m*; (*of people*) Kreis *m* ● *a* (*ready*) fertig, bereit; (*rigid*) fest; <*book*> vorgeschrieben; **be ~ on doing sth** entschlossen sein, etw zu tun ● *v* (*pt/pp* **set**, *pres p* **setting**) ● *vt* setzen; (*adjust*) einstellen; stellen <*task, alarm clock*>; festsetzen, festlegen <*date, limit*>; aufgeben <*homework*>; zusammenstellen <*questions*>; [ein]fassen <*gem*>; einrichten <*bone*>; legen <*hair*>; decken <*table*> ● *vi* <*sun:*> untergehen; (*become hard*) fest werden. **~ back** *vt* zurücksetzen; (*hold up*) aufhalten; (🄴 *cost*) kosten. **~ off** *vi* losgehen; (*in vehicle*) losfahren ● *vt* auslösen <*alarm*>; explodieren lassen <*bomb*>. **~ out** *vi* losgehen; (*in vehicle*) losfahren ● *vt* auslegen; (*state*) darlegen. **~ up** *vt* aufbauen; (*fig*) gründen

settee *n* Sofa *nt*, Couch *f*

setting *n* Rahmen *m*; (*surroundings*) Umgebung *f*

settle *vt* (*decide*) entscheiden; (*agree*) regeln; (*fix*) festsetzen; (*calm*) beruhigen; (*pay*) bezahlen ● *vi* sich niederlassen; <*snow, dust:*> liegen bleiben; (*subside*) sich senken; <*sediment:*> sich absetzen. **~ down** *vi* sich beruhigen; (*permanently*) sesshaft werden. **~ up** *vi* abrechnen

settlement *n* (*see* **settle**) Entscheidung *f*; Regelung *f*; Bezahlung *f*; (*Jur*) Vergleich *m*; (*colony*) Siedlung *f*

settler *n* Siedler *m*

set-up *n* System *nt*

seven *a* sieben. **~teen** *a* siebzehn. **~teenth** *a* siebzehnte(r,s)

seventh *a* siebte(r,s)

seventieth *a* siebzigste(r,s)

seventy *a* siebzig

several *a* & *pron* mehrere, einige

sever|e *a* (**-r, -st,**) **-ly** *adv* streng; <*pain*> stark; <*illness*> schwer. **~ity** *n* Strenge *f*; Schwere *f*

sew *vt/i* (*pt* **sewed**, *pp* **sewn** or **sewed**) nähen

sewage *n* Abwasser *nt*

sewer *n* Abwasserkanal *m*

sewing *n* Nähen *nt*; (*work*) Näharbeit *f*. **~ machine** *n* Nähmaschine *f*

sewn *see* **sew**

sex *n* Geschlecht *nt*; (*sexuality, intercourse*) Sex *m*. **~ist** *a* sexistisch

sexual *a*, **-ly** *adv* sexuell. **~ intercourse** *n* Geschlechtsverkehr *m*

sexuality *n* Sexualität *f*

sexy *a* (**-ier, -iest**) sexy

shabby *a* (**-ier, -iest**), **-ily** *adv* schäbig

shack *n* Hütte *f*

shade *n* Schatten *m*; (*of colour*) [Farb]ton *m*; (*for lamp*) [Lampen]schirm *m*; (*Amer: window-blind*) Jalousie *f* ● *vt* beschatten

shadow *n* Schatten *m* ● *vt* (*follow*) beschatten

shady a (-ier, -iest) schattig; (🔲 *disreputable*) zwielichtig

shaft n Schaft m; (*Techn*) Welle f; (*of light*) Strahl m; (*of lift*) Schacht m

shaggy a (-ier, -iest) zottig

shake n Schütteln nt ● v (*pt* shook, *pp* shaken) ● vt schütteln; (*shock*) erschüttern; ~ hands with s.o. jdm die Hand geben ● vi wackeln; (*tremble*) zittern. ~ off vt abschütteln

shaky a (-ier, -iest) wackelig; <*hand, voice*> zittrig

shall v aux we ~ see wir werden sehen; what ~ I do? was soll ich machen?

shallow a (-er, -est) seicht; <*dish*> flach; (*fig*) oberflächlich

sham a unecht ● n Heuchelei f ● vt (*pt/pp* shammed) vortäuschen

shambles n Durcheinander nt

shame n Scham f; (*disgrace*) Schande f; be a ~ schade sein; what a ~! wie schade!

shame|ful a, -ly adv schändlich. ~less a, -ly adv schamlos

shampoo n Shampoo nt ● vt schamponieren

shan't = shall not

shape n Form f; (*figure*) Gestalt f ● vt formen (into zu). ~less a formlos; <*clothing*> unförmig

share n [An]teil m; (*Comm*) Aktie f ● vt/i teilen. ~holder n Aktionär(in) m(f)

shark n Hai[fisch] m

sharp a (-er, -est), -ly adv scharf; (*pointed*) spitz; (*severe*) heftig; (*sudden*) steil; (*alert*) clever; (*unscrupulous*) gerissen ● adv scharf; (*Mus*) zu hoch; at six o'clock ~ Punkt sechs Uhr ● n (*Mus*) Kreuz nt. ~en vt schärfen; [an]spitzen <*pencil*>

shatter vt zertrümmern; (*fig*) zerstören; ~ed <*person.*> erschüttert; (🔲 *exhausted*) kaputt ● vi zersplittern

shave n Rasur f; have a ~ sich rasieren ● vt rasieren ● vi sich rasieren. ~r n Rasierapparat m

shawl n Schultertuch nt

she pron sie

shears npl [große] Schere f

shed¹ n Schuppen m

shed² vt (*pt/pp* shed, *pres p* shedding) verlieren; vergießen <*blood, tears*>; ~ light on Licht bringen in (+ *acc*)

sheep n inv Schaf nt. ~-dog n Hütehund m

sheepish a, -ly adv verlegen

sheer a rein; (*steep*) steil; (*transparent*) hauchdünn

sheet n Laken nt, Betttuch nt; (*of paper*) Blatt nt; (*of glass, metal*) Platte f

shelf n (*pl* shelves) Brett nt, Bord nt; (*set of shelves*) Regal nt

shell n Schale f; (*of snail*) Haus nt; (*of tortoise*) Panzer m; (*on beach*) Muschel f; (*Mil*) Granate f ● vt pellen; enthülsen <*peas*>; (*Mil*) [mit Granaten] beschießen. ~ out vi 🔲 blechen

shellfish n inv Schalentiere pl; (*Culin*) Meeresfrüchte pl

shelter n Schutz m; (*air-raid ~*) Luftschutzraum m ● vt schützen (from vor + *dat*) ● vi sich unterstellen. ~ed a geschützt; <*life*> behütet

shelve vt auf Eis legen; (*abandon*) aufgeben

shelving n (*shelves*) Regale pl

shepherd n Schäfer m ● vt führen

sherry n Sherry m

shield n Schild m; (*for eyes*) Schirm m; (*Techn & fig*) Schutz m ● vt schützen (from vor + *dat*)

shift n Verschiebung f; (*at work*) Schicht f ● vt rücken; (*take away*) wegnehmen; (*rearrange*) umstellen; schieben <*blame*> (on to auf + *acc*) ● vi sich verschieben; (🔲 *rush*) rasen

shifty a (-ier, -iest) (*pej*) verschlagen

shimmer n Schimmer m ● vi schimmern

shin n Schienbein nt

shine n Glanz m ● v (*pt/pp* shone) ● vi leuchten; (*reflect light*) glänzen;

<sun.> scheinen ● *vt* ~ **a light on** beleuchten

shingle *n* (*pebbles*) Kiesel *pl*

shiny *a* (-ier, -iest) glänzend

ship *n* Schiff *nt* ● *vt* (*pt/pp* **shipped**) verschiffen

ship: ~**building** *n* Schiffbau *m*. ~**ment** *n* Sendung *f*. ~**per** *n* Spediteur *m*. ~**ping** *n* Versand *m*; (*traffic*) Schifffahrt *f*. ~**shape** *a* & *adv* in Ordnung. ~**wreck** *n* Schiffbruch *m*. ~**wrecked** *a* schiffbrüchig. ~**yard** *n* Werft *f*

shirt *n* [Ober]hemd *nt*; (*for woman*) Hemdbluse *f*

shit *n* (*vulg*) Scheiße *f* ● *vi* (*pt/pp* **shit**) (*vulg*) scheißen

shiver *n* Schauder *m* ● *vi* zittern

shoal *n* (*fish*) Schwarm *m*

shock *n* Schock *m*; (*Electr*) Schlag *m*; (*impact*) Erschütterung *f* ● *vt* einen Schock versetzen (+ *dat*); (*scandalize*) schockieren. ~**ing** *a* schockierend; (🛈 *bad*) fürchterlich

shoddy *a* (-ier, -iest) minderwertig

shoe *n* Schuh *m*; (*of horse*) Hufeisen *nt* ● *vt* (*pt/pp* **shod**, *pres p* **shoeing**) beschlagen *<horse>*

shoe: ~**horn** *n* Schuhanzieher *m*. ~-**lace** *n* Schnürsenkel *m*. ~-**string** *n* **on a** ~-**string** 🛈 mit ganz wenig Geld

shone *see* **shine**

shoo *vt* scheuchen ● *int* sch!

shook *see* **shake**

shoot *n* (*Bot*) Trieb *m*; (*hunt*) Jagd *f* ● *v* (*pt/pp* **shot**) ● *vt* schießen; (*kill*) erschießen; drehen *<film>* ● *vi* schießen. ~ **down** *vt* abschießen. ~ **out** *vi* (*rush*) herausschießen. ~ **up** *vi* (*grow*) in die Höhe schießen/ *<prices:>* schnellen

shop *n* Laden *m*, Geschäft *nt*; (*workshop*) Werkstatt *f*; **talk** ~ 🛈 fachsimpeln ● *vi* (*pt/pp* **shopped**, *pres p* **shopping**) einkaufen; **go** ~**ping** einkaufen gehen

shop: ~ **assistant** *n* Verkäufer(in) *m(f)*. ~**keeper** *n* Ladenbesitzer(in) *m(f)*. ~-**lifter** *n* Ladendieb *m*. ~-**lifting** *n* Ladendiebstahl *m*

shopping *n* Einkaufen *nt*; (*articles*) Einkäufe *pl*; **do the** ~ einkaufen. ~ **bag** *n* Einkaufstasche *f*. ~ **centre** *n* Einkaufszentrum *nt*. ~ **trolley** *n* Einkaufswagen *m*

shop-window *n* Schaufenster *nt*

shore *n* Strand *m*; (*of lake*) Ufer *nt*

short *a* (-er, -est) kurz; *<person>* klein; (*curt*) schroff; **a** ~ **time ago** vor kurzem; **be** ~ **of ...** zu wenig ... haben; **be in** ~ **supply** knapp sein ● *adv* kurz; (*abruptly*) plötzlich; (*curtly*) kurz angebunden; **in** ~ kurzum; ~ **of** (*except*) außer; **go** ~ Mangel leiden

shortage *n* Mangel *m* (**of** an + *dat*); (*scarcity*) Knappheit *f*

short: ~**bread** *n* ≈ Mürbekekse *pl*. ~ **circuit** *n* Kurzschluss *m*. ~**coming** *n* Fehler *m*. ~ **cut** *n* Abkürzung *f*

shorten *vt* [ab]kürzen; kürzer machen *<garment>*

short: ~**hand** *n* Kurzschrift *f*, Stenographie *f*. ~**list** *n* engere Auswahl *f*

short|ly *adv* in Kürze; ~**ly before/ after** kurz vorher/danach. ~**ness** *n* Kürze *f*; (*of person*) Kleinheit *f*

shorts *npl* Shorts *pl*

short: ~-**sighted** *a* kurzsichtig. ~-**sleeved** *a* kurzärmelig. ~ **story** *n* Kurzgeschichte *f*. ~-**tempered** *a* aufbrausend. ~-**term** *a* kurzfristig. ~ **wave** *n* Kurzwelle *f*

shot *see* **shoot** ● *n* Schuss *m*; (*pellets*) Schrot *m*; (*person*) Schütze *m*; (*Phot*) Aufnahme *f*; (*injection*) Spritze *f*; (🛈 *attempt*) Versuch *m*; **like a** ~ 🛈 sofort. ~**gun** *n* Schrotflinte *f*. ~-**put** *n* (*Sport*) Kugelstoßen *nt*

should *v aux* **you** ~ **go** du solltest gehen; **I** ~ **have seen him** ich hätte ihn sehen sollen; **I** ~ **like** ich möchte; **this** ~ **be enough** das müsste eigentlich reichen; **if he** ~ **be there** falls er da sein sollte

shoulder *n* Schulter *f* ● *vt* schultern; (*fig*) auf sich (*acc*) nehmen. ~-**blade** *n* Schulterblatt *nt*

shout *n* Schrei *m* ● *vt/i* schreien. ~ **down** *vt* niederschreien

shouting n Geschrei nt

shove n Stoß m ● vt stoßen; (🔲 put) tun ● vi drängeln. ∼ **off** vi 🔲 abhauen

shovel n Schaufel f ● vt (pt/pp **shovelled**) schaufeln

show n (display) Pracht f; (exhibition) Ausstellung f, Schau f; (performance) Vorstellung f; (Theat, TV) Show f; **on** ∼ ausgestellt ● v (pt **showed**, pp **shown**) ● vt zeigen; (put on display) ausstellen; vorführen <film> ● vi sichtbar sein; <film:> gezeigt werden. ∼ **in** vt hereinführen. ∼ **off** vi 🔲 angeben ● vt vorführen; (flaunt) angeben mit. ∼ **up** vi [deutlich] zu sehen sein; (🔲 arrive) auftauchen ● vt deutlich zeigen; (🔲 embarrass) blamieren

shower n Dusche f; (of rain) Schauer m; **have a** ∼ duschen ● vt ∼ **with** überschütten mit ● vi duschen

show-jumping n Springreiten nt

shown see **show**

show: ∼**-off** n Angeber(in) m(f). ∼**room** n Ausstellungsraum m

showy a protzig

shrank see **shrink**

shred n Fetzen m; (fig) Spur f ● vt (pt/pp **shredded**) zerkleinern; (Culin) schnitzeln. ∼**der** n Reißwolf m; (Culin) Schnitzelwerk nt

shrewd a (-er, -est), **-ly** adv klug. ∼**ness** n Klugheit f

shriek n Schrei m ● vt/i schreien

shrill a, **-y** adv schrill

shrimp n Garnele f, Krabbe f

shrink vi (pt **shrank**, pp **shrunk**) schrumpfen; <garment:> einlaufen; (draw back) zurückschrecken (**from** vor + dat)

shrivel vi (pt/pp **shrivelled**) verschrumpeln

Shrove n ∼ **Tuesday** Fastnachtsdienstag m

shrub n Strauch m

shrug n Achselzucken nt ● vt/i (pt/ pp **shrugged**) ∼ [one's shoulders] die Achseln zucken

shrunk see **shrink**

shudder n Schauder m ● vi schaudern; (tremble) zittern

shuffle vi schlurfen ● vt mischen <cards>

shun vt (pt/pp **shunned**) meiden

shunt vt rangieren

shut v (pt/pp **shut**, pres p **shutting**) ● vt zumachen, schließen ● vi sich schließen; <shop:> schließen, zumachen. ∼ **down** vt schließen; stilllegen <factory> ● vi schließen. ∼ **up** vt abschließen; (lock in) einsperren ● vi 🔲 den Mund halten

shutter n [Fenster]laden m; (Phot) Verschluss m

shuttle n (Tex) Schiffchen nt

shuttle service n Pendelverkehr m

shy a (-er, -est), **-ly** adv schüchtern; (timid) scheu. ∼**ness** n Schüchternheit f

siblings npl Geschwister pl

Sicily n Sizilien nt

sick a krank; <humour> makaber; **be** ∼ (vomit) sich übergeben; **be** ∼ **of sth** 🔲 etw satt haben; **I feel** ∼ mir ist schlecht

sick|ly a (-ier, -iest) kränklich. ∼**ness** n Krankheit f; (vomiting) Erbrechen nt

side n Seite f; **on the** ∼ (as sideline) nebenbei; ∼ **by** ∼ nebeneinander; (fig) Seite an Seite; **take** ∼s Partei ergreifen (**with** für) ● attrib Seiten- ● vi ∼ **with** Partei ergreifen für

side: ∼**board** n Anrichte f. ∼**-effect** n Nebenwirkung f. ∼**lights** npl Standlicht nt. ∼**line** n Nebenbeschäftigung f. ∼**-show** n Nebenattraktion f. ∼**-step** vt ausweichen (+ dat). ∼**walk** n (Amer) Bürgersteig m. ∼**ways** adv seitwärts

siding n Abstellgleis nt

siege n Belagerung f; (by police) Umstellung f

sieve n Sieb nt ● vt sieben

sift vt sieben; (fig) durchsehen

sigh n Seufzer m ● vi seufzen

sight n Sicht f; (faculty) Sehvermögen nt; (spectacle) Anblick

m; (*on gun*) Visier *nt*; **∼s** *pl*
Sehenswürdigkeiten *pl*; **at first ∼** auf
den ersten Blick; **lose ∼ of** aus dem
Auge verlieren; **know by ∼** vom
Sehen kennen ● *vt* sichten

sightseeing *n* **go ∼** die
Sehenswürdigkeiten besichtigen

sign *n* Zeichen *nt*; (*notice*) Schild *nt*
● *vt/i* unterschreiben; <*author,
artist:*> signieren. **∼ on** *vi* (*as
unemployed*) sich arbeitslos melden;
(*Mil*) sich verpflichten

signal *n* Signal *nt* ● *vt/i* (*pt/pp*
signalled) signalisieren; **∼ to s.o.**
jdm ein Signal geben

signature *n* Unterschrift *f*; (*of
artist*) Signatur *f*

significan|ce *n* Bedeutung *f*. **∼t** *a*,
-ly *adv* (*important*) bedeutend

signify *vt* (*pt/pp* **-ied**) bedeuten

signpost *n* Wegweiser *m*

silence *n* Stille *f*; (*of person*)
Schweigen *nt* ● *vt* zum Schweigen
bringen. **∼r** *n* (*on gun*)
Schalldämpfer *m*; (*Auto*) Auspufftopf
m

silent *a*, **-ly** *adv* still; (*without
speaking*) schweigend; **remain ∼**
schweigen

silhouette *n* Silhouette *f*; (*picture*)
Schattenriss *m* ● *vt* **be ∼d** sich als
Silhouette abheben

silicon *n* Silizium *nt*

silk *n* Seide *f* ● *attrib* Seiden-

silky *a* (**-ier, -iest**) seidig

sill *n* Sims *m* & *nt*

silly *a* (**-ier, -iest**) dumm, albern

silver *a* silbern; <*coin, paper*> Silber-
● *n* Silber *nt*

silver: ∼-plated *a* versilbert.
∼ware *n* Silber *nt*

similar *a*, **-ly** *adv* ähnlich. **∼ity** *n*
Ähnlichkeit *f*

simmer *vi* leise kochen, ziehen ● *vt*
ziehen lassen

simple *a* (**-r, -st**) einfach; <*person*>
einfältig. **∼-minded** *a* einfältig

simplicity *n* Einfachheit *f*

simpli|fication *n* Vereinfachung *f*.
∼fy *vt* (*pt/pp* **-ied**) vereinfachen

simply *adv* einfach

simulate *vt* vortäuschen; (*Techn*)
simulieren

simultaneous *a*, **-ly** *adv*
gleichzeitig

sin *n* Sünde *f* ● *vi* (*pt/pp* **sinned**)
sündigen

since
● *preposition*
····▸ seit (+ *dat*). **he's been living here
since 1991** er wohnt* seit 1991 hier. **I
had been waiting since 8 o'clock** ich
wartete* [schon] seit 8 Uhr. **since
seeing you** seit ich dich gesehen
habe. **how long is it since your
interview?** wie lange ist es seit
deinem Vorstellungsgespräch?
● *adverb*
····▸ seitdem. **I haven't spoken to her
since** seitdem habe ich mit ihr nicht
gesprochen. **the house has been
empty ever since** das Haus steht
seitdem leer. **he has since remarried**
er hat danach wieder geheiratet.
long since vor langer Zeit
● *conjunction*
····▸ seit. **since she has been living in
Germany** seit sie in Deutschland
wohnt*. **since they had been in
London** seit sie in London waren*.
how long is it since he left? wie
lange ist es her, dass er weggezogen
ist? **it's a year since he left** es ist ein
Jahr her, dass er weggezogen ist
····▸ (*because*) da. **since she was ill, I
had to do it** da sie krank war,
musste ich es tun

! *Note the different tenses in
German

sincere *a* aufrichtig; (*heartfelt*)
herzlich. **∼ly** *adv* aufrichtig; **Yours
∼ly** Mit freundlichen Grüßen

sincerity *n* Aufrichtigkeit *f*

sinful *a* sündhaft

sing *vt/i* (*pt* **sang**, *pp* **sung**) singen

singe *vt* (*pres p* **singeing**) versengen

singer *n* Sänger(in) *m(f)*

single *a* einzeln; (*one only*) einzig;
(*unmarried*) ledig; <*ticket*> einfach;
<*room, bed*> Einzel- ● *n* (*ticket*)
einfache Fahrkarte *f*; (*record*) Single

f; **~s** *pl* (*Tennis*) Einzel *nt* ● *vt* **~ out** auswählen

single: ~-handed *a & adv* allein. **~ parent** *n* Alleinerziehende(r) *m/f*

singly *adv* einzeln

singular *a* eigenartig; (*Gram*) im Singular ● *n* Singular *m*

sinister *a* finster

sink *n* Spülbecken *nt* ● *v* (*pt* **sank**, *pp* **sunk**) ● *vi* sinken ● *vt* versenken <*ship*>; senken <*shaft*>. **~ in** *vi* einsinken; (🗉 *be understood*) kapiert werden

sinner *n* Sünder(in) *m(f)*

sip *n* Schlückchen *nt* ● *vt* (*pt/pp* **sipped**) in kleinen Schlucken trinken

siphon *n* (*bottle*) Siphon *m*. **~ off** *vt* mit einem Saugheber ablassen

sir *n* mein Herr; **S~** (*title*) Sir; **Dear S~s** Sehr geehrte Herren

siren *n* Sirene *f*

sister *n* Schwester *f*; (*nurse*) Oberschwester *f*. **~-in-law** *n* Schwägerin *f*

sit *v* (*pt/pp* **sat**, *pres p* **sitting**) ● *vi* sitzen; (*sit down*) sich setzen; <*committee:*> tagen ● *vt* setzen; machen <*exam*>. **~ back** *vi* sich zurücklehnen. **~ down** *vi* sich setzen. **~ up** *vi* [aufrecht] sitzen; (*rise*) sich aufsetzen; (*not slouch*) gerade sitzen

site *n* Gelände *nt*; (*for camping*) Platz *m*; (*Archaeol*) Stätte *f*

sitting *n* Sitzung *f*; (*for meals*) Schub *m*

situat|e *vt* legen; **be ~ed** liegen. **~ion** *n* Lage *f*; (*circumstances*) Situation *f*; (*job*) Stelle *f*

six *a* sechs. **~teen** *a* sechzehn. **~teenth** *a* sechzehnte(r,s)

sixth *a* sechste(r,s)

sixtieth *a* sechzigste(r,s)

sixty *a* sechzig

size *n* Größe *f*

sizzle *vi* brutzeln

skate *n* Schlittschuh *m* ● *vi* Schlittschuh laufen. **~r** *n* Eisläufer(in) *m(f)*

skating *n* Eislaufen *nt*. **~-rink** *n* Eisbahn *f*

skeleton *n* Skelett *nt*. **~ key** *n* Dietrich *m*

sketch *n* Skizze *f*; (*Theat*) Sketch *m* ● *vt* skizzieren

sketchy *a* (**-ier, -iest**), **-ily** *adv* skizzenhaft

ski *n* Ski *m* ● *vi* (*pt/pp* **skied**, *pres p* **skiing**) Ski fahren *or* laufen

skid *n* Schleudern *nt* ● *vi* (*pt/pp* **skidded**) schleudern

skier *n* Skiläufer(in) *m(f)*

skiing *n* Skilaufen *nt*

skilful *a*, **-ly** *adv* geschickt

skill *n* Geschick *nt*. **~ed** *a* geschickt; (*trained*) ausgebildet

skim *vt* (*pt/pp* **skimmed**) entrahmen <*milk*>

skimp *vt* sparen an (+ *dat*)

skimpy *a* (**-ier, -iest**) knapp

skin *n* Haut *f*; (*on fruit*) Schale *f* ● *vt* (*pt/pp* **skinned**) häuten; schälen <*fruit*>

skin: ~-deep *a* oberflächlich. **~-diving** *n* Sporttauchen *nt*

skinny *a* (**-ier, -iest**) dünn

skip¹ *n* Container *m*

skip² *n* Hüpfer *m* ● *v* (*pt/pp* **skipped**) *vi* hüpfen; (*with rope*) seilspringen ● *vt* überspringen

skipper *n* Kapitän *m*

skipping-rope *n* Sprungseil *nt*

skirmish *n* Gefecht *nt*

skirt *n* Rock *m* ● *vt* herumgehen um

skittle *n* Kegel *m*

skive *vi* 🗉 blaumachen

skull *n* Schädel *m*

sky *n* Himmel *m*. **~light** *n* Dachluke *f*. **~scraper** *n* Wolkenkratzer *m*

slab *n* Platte *f*; (*slice*) Scheibe *f*; (*of chocolate*) Tafel *f*

slack *a* (**-er, -est**) schlaff, locker; <*person*> nachlässig; (*Comm*) flau ● *vi* bummeln

slacken *vi* sich lockern; (*diminish*) nachlassen ● *vt* lockern; (*diminish*) verringern

slain *see* **slay**

slam v (pt/pp **slammed**) ● vt zuschlagen; (put) knallen 🔲; (🔲 criticize) verreißen ● vi zuschlagen

slander n Verleumdung f ● vt verleumden

slang n Slang m. **~y** a salopp

slant n Schräge f; on the **~** schräg ● vt abschrägen; (fig) färben <report> ● vi sich neigen

slap n Schlag m ● vt (pt/pp **slapped**) schlagen; (put) knallen 🔲 ● adv direkt

slapdash a 🔲 schludrig

slash n Schlitz m ● vt aufschlitzen; [drastisch] reduzieren <prices>

slat n Latte f

slate n Schiefer m ● vt 🔲 heruntermachen; verreißen <performance>

slaughter n Schlachten nt; (massacre) Gemetzel nt ● vt schlachten; abschlachten <men>

Slav a slawisch ● n Slawe m/ Slawin f

slave n Sklave m/ Sklavin f ● vi **~** [away] schuften

slavery n Sklaverei f

slay vt (pt **slew**, pp **slain**) ermorden

sledge n Schlitten m

sleek a (-er, -est) seidig; (well-fed) wohlgenährt

sleep n Schlaf m; go to **~** einschlafen; put to **~** einschläfern ● v (pt/pp **slept**) ● vi schlafen ● vt (accommodate) Unterkunft bieten für. **~er** n Schläfer(in) m(f); (Rail) Schlafwagen m; (on track) Schwelle f

sleeping: **~-bag** n Schlafsack m. **~-pill** n Schlaftablette f

sleep: **~less** a schlaflos. **~-walking** n Schlafwandeln nt

sleepy a (-ier, -iest), **-ily** adv schläfrig

sleet n Schneeregen m

sleeve n Ärmel m; (for record) Hülle f. **~less** a ärmellos

sleigh n [Pferde]schlitten m

slender a schlank; (fig) gering

slept see **sleep**

slew see **slay**

slice n Scheibe f ● vt in Scheiben schneiden

slick a clever

slid|e n Rutschbahn f; (for hair) Spange f; (Phot) Dia nt ● v (pt/pp **slid**) ● vi rutschen ● vt schieben. **~ing** a gleitend; <door, seat> Schiebe-

slight a (-er, -est), **-ly** adv leicht; <importance> gering; <acquaintance> flüchtig; (slender) schlank; not in the **~est** nicht im Geringsten; **~ly** better ein bisschen besser ● vt kränken, beleidigen ● n Beleidigung f

slim a (**slimmer**, **slimmest**) schlank; <volume> schmal; (fig) gering ● vi eine Schlankheitskur machen

slim|e n Schleim m. **~y** a schleimig

sling n (Med) Schlinge f ● vt (pt/pp **slung**) 🔲 schmeißen

slip n (mistake) Fehler m, 🔲 Patzer m; (petticoat) Unterrock m; (paper) Zettel m; give s.o. the **~** 🔲 jdm entwischen; **~** of the tongue Versprecher m ● v (pt/pp **slipped**) ● vi rutschen; (fall) ausrutschen; (go quickly) schlüpfen ● vt schieben; **~** s.o.'s mind jdm entfallen. **~ away** vi sich fortschleichen. **~ up** vi 🔲 einen Schnitzer machen

slipper n Hausschuh m

slippery a glitschig; <surface> glatt

slipshod a schludrig

slip-up n 🔲 Schnitzer m

slit n Schlitz m ● vt (pt/pp **slit**) aufschlitzen

slither vi rutschen

slog n [hard] **~** Schinderei f ● vi (pt/pp **slogged**) schuften

slogan n Schlagwort nt; (advertising) Werbespruch m

slop|e n Hang m; (inclination) Neigung f ● vi sich neigen. **~ing** a schräg

sloppy a (-ier, -iest) schludrig; (sentimental) sentimental

slosh vi 🔲 schwappen

slot n Schlitz m; (TV) Sendezeit f ● v (pt/pp **slotted**) ● vt einfügen ● vi sich einfügen (**in** in + acc)

slot-machine n Münzautomat m; (for gambling) Spielautomat m

slouch vi sich schlecht halten

slovenly a schlampig

slow a (-er, -est), **-ly** adv langsam; be ~ <clock:> nachgehen; in ~ motion in Zeitlupe ● adv langsam ● vt verlangsamen ● vi ~ down, ~ up langsamer werden. **~ness** n Langsamkeit f

sludge n Schlamm m

slug n Nacktschnecke f

sluggish a, **-ly** adv träge

sluice n Schleuse f

slum n Elendsviertel nt

slumber n Schlummer m ● vi schlummern

slump n Sturz m ● vi fallen; (crumple) zusammensacken; <prices:> stürzen; <sales:> zurückgehen

slung see sling

slur vt (pt/pp slurred) undeutlich sprechen

slurp vt/i schlürfen

slush n [Schnee]matsch m; (fig) Kitsch m

slut n Schlampe f 🗉

sly a (-er, -est), **-ly** adv verschlagen ● n on the ~ heimlich

smack n Schlag m, Klaps m ● vt schlagen ● adv 🗉 direkt

small a (-er, -est) klein ● adv chop up ~ klein hacken ● n ~ of the back Kreuz nt

small: ~ **ads** npl Kleinanzeigen pl. ~ **change** n Kleingeld nt. **~pox** n Pocken pl. ~ **talk** n leichte Konversation f

smart a (-er, -est), **-ly** adv schick; (clever) schlau, clever; (brisk) flott; (Amer 🗉: cheeky) frech ● vi brennen

smarten vt ~ **oneself up** mehr auf sein Äußeres achten

smash n Krach m; (collision) Zusammenstoß m; (Tennis) Schmetterball m ● vt zerschlagen; (strike) schlagen; (Tennis) schmettern ● vi zerschmettern; (crash) krachen (**into** gegen). **~ing** a 🗉 toll

smear n verschmierter Fleck m; (Med) Abstrich m; (fig) Verleumdung f ● vt schmieren; (coat) beschmieren (**with** mit); (fig) verleumden ● vi schmieren

smell n Geruch m; (sense) Geruchsinn m ● v (pt/pp smelt or smelled) ● vt riechen; (sniff) riechen an (+ dat) ● vi riechen (**of** nach)

smelly a (-ier, -iest) übel riechend

smelt see smell

smile n Lächeln nt ● vi lächeln; ~ **at** anlächeln

smirk vi feixen

smith n Schmied m

smock n Kittel m

smog n Smog m

smoke n Rauch m ● vt/i rauchen; (Culin) räuchern. **~less** a rauchfrei; <fuel> rauchlos

smoker n Raucher m; (Rail) Raucherabteil nt

smoking n Rauchen nt; 'no ~' 'Rauchen verboten'

smoky a (-ier, -iest) verraucht; <taste> rauchig

smooth a (-er, -est), **-ly** adv glatt ● vt glätten. ~ **out** vt glatt streichen

smother vt ersticken; (cover) bedecken; (suppress) unterdrücken

smoulder vi schwelen

smudge n Fleck m ● vt verwischen ● vi schmieren

smug a (smugger, smuggest), **-ly** adv selbstgefällig

smuggl|e vt schmuggeln. **~er** n Schmuggler m. **~ing** n Schmuggel m

snack n Imbiss m. **~-bar** n Imbissstube f

snag n Schwierigkeit f, 🗉 Haken m

snail n Schnecke f; at a ~'s pace im Schneckentempo

snake n Schlange f

snap n Knacken nt; (photo) Schnappschuss m ● attrib <decision> plötzlich ● v (pt/pp snapped) ● vi [entzwei]brechen; ~ **at** (bite) schnappen nach; (speak sharply) [scharf] anfahren ● vt zerbrechen;

snappy a (-ier, -iest) (*say*) fauchen; (*Phot*) knipsen. **~ up** vt wegschnappen

snapshot n Schnappschuss m

snare n Schlinge f

snarl vi [mit gefletschten Zähnen] knurren

snatch n (*fragment*) Fetzen pl ● vt schnappen; (*steal*) klauen; entführen <*child*>; **~ sth from s.o.** jdm etw entreißen

sneak n ⚏ Petze f ● vi schleichen; (⚏ *tell tales*) petzen ● vt (*take*) mitgehen lassen ● vi **~ in/out** sich hinein-/hinausschleichen

sneakers npl (*Amer*) Turnschuhe pl

sneer vi höhnisch lächeln; (*mock*) spotten

sneeze n Niesen nt ● vi niesen

snide a ⚏ abfällig

sniff vi schnüffeln ● vt schnüffeln an (+ *dat*)

snigger vi [boshaft] kichern

snip n Schnitt m ● vt/i **~ [at]** schnippeln an (+ *dat*)

snippet n Schnipsel m; (*of information*) Bruchstück nt

snivel vi (*pt/pp* snivelled) flennen

snob n Snob m. **~bery** n Snobismus m. **~bish** a snobistisch

snoop vi ⚏ schnüffeln

snooty a ⚏ hochnäsig

snooze n Nickerchen nt ● vi dösen

snore vi schnarchen

snorkel n Schnorchel m

snort vi schnauben

snout n Schnauze f

snow n Schnee m ● vi schneien; **~ed under with** (*fig*) überhäuft mit

snow: ~ball n Schneeball m. **~drift** n Schneewehe f. **~drop** n Schneeglöckchen nt. **~fall** n Schneefall m. **~flake** n Schneeflocke f. **~man** n Schneemann m. **~plough** n Schneepflug m

snub n Abfuhr f ● vt (*pt/pp* snubbed) brüskieren

snub-nosed a stupsnasig

snuffle vi schnüffeln

snug a (snugger, snuggest) behaglich, gemütlich

snuggle vi sich kuscheln (**up to** an + *acc*)

so adv so; **so am I** ich auch; **so I see** das sehe ich; **that is so** das stimmt; **so much the better** umso besser; **if so** wenn ja; **so as to** um zu; **so long!** ⚏ tschüs! ● pron **I hope so** hoffentlich; **I think so** ich glaube schon; **I'm afraid so** leider ja; **so saying/doing, he/she** ... indem er/sie das sagte/tat, ... ● conj (*therefore*) also; **so that** damit; **so what!** na und! **so you see** wie du siehst

soak vt nass machen; (*steep*) einweichen; (⚏ *fleece*) schröpfen ● vi weichen; <*liquid*:> sickern. **~ up** vt aufsaugen

soaking a & adv **~ [wet]** patschnass ⚏

soap n Seife f. **~ opera** n Seifenoper f. **~ powder** n Seifenpulver nt

soapy a (-ier, -iest) seifig

soar vi aufsteigen; <*prices*:> in die Höhe schnellen

sob n Schluchzer m ● vi (*pt/pp* sobbed) schluchzen

sober a, **-ly** adv nüchtern; (*serious*) ernst; <*colour*> gedeckt. **~ up** vi nüchtern werden

so-called a sogenannt

soccer n ⚏ Fußball m

sociable a gesellig

social a gesellschaftlich; (*Admin, Pol, Zool*) sozial

socialis|m n Sozialismus m. **~t** a sozialistisch ● n Sozialist m

socialize vi [gesellschaftlich] verkehren

socially adv gesellschaftlich; **know ~** privat kennen

social: ~ security n Sozialhilfe f. **~ worker** n Sozialarbeiter(in) m(f)

society n Gesellschaft f; (*club*) Verein m

sociolog|ist n Soziologe m. **~y** n Soziologie f

sock n Socke f; (kneelength) Kniestrumpf m

socket n (of eye) Augenhöhle f; (of joint) Gelenkpfanne f; (wall plug) Steckdose f

soda n Soda nt; (Amer) Limonade f. ~ **water** n Sodawasser nt

sodden a durchnässt

sofa n Sofa nt. ~ **bed** n Schlafcouch f

soft a (-er, -est), -**ly** adv weich; (quiet) leise; (gentle) sanft; (🛈 silly) dumm. ~ **drink** n alkoholfreies Getränk nt

soften vt weich machen; (fig) mildern ● vi weich werden

soft: ~ **toy** n Stofftier nt. ~**ware** n Software f

soggy a (-ier, -iest) aufgeweicht

soil¹ n Erde f, Boden m

soil² vt verschmutzen

solar a Sonnen-

sold see sell

soldier n Soldat m ● vi ~ **on** [unbeirrbar] weitermachen

sole¹ n Sohle f

sole² n (fish) Seezunge f

sole³ a einzig. ~**ly** adv einzig und allein

solemn a, -**ly** adv feierlich; (serious) ernst

solicitor n Rechtsanwalt m/ -anwältin f

solid a fest; (sturdy) stabil; (not hollow, of same substance) massiv; (unanimous) einstimmig; (complete) ganz

solidarity n Solidarität f

solidify vi (pt/pp -ied) fest werden

solitary a einsam; (sole) einzig

solitude n Einsamkeit f

solo n Solo nt ● a Solo-; <flight> Allein- ● adv solo. ~**ist** n Solist(in) m(f)

solstice n Sonnenwende f

soluble a löslich

solution n Lösung f

solvable a lösbar

solve vt lösen

solvent n Lösungsmittel nt

sombre a dunkel; <mood> düster

some a & pron etwas; (a little) ein bisschen; (with pl noun) einige; (a few) ein paar; (certain) manche(r,s); (one or the other) [irgend]ein; ~ **day** eines Tages; **I want** ~ ich möchte etwas/ (pl) welche; **will you have** ~ **wine?** möchten Sie Wein? **do** ~ **shopping** einkaufen

some: ~**body** pron & n jemand; (emphatic) irgendjemand. ~**how** adv irgendwie. ~**one** pron & n = somebody

somersault n Purzelbaum m 🛈; (Sport) Salto m; **turn a** ~ einen Purzelbaum schlagen/einen Salto springen

something pron & adv etwas; (emphatic) irgendetwas; ~ **different** etwas anderes; ~ **like this** so etwas [wie das]

some: ~**time** adv irgendwann ● a ehemalig. ~**times** adv manchmal. ~**what** adv ziemlich. ~**where** adv irgendwo; <go> irgendwohin

son n Sohn m

song n Lied nt. ~**bird** n Singvogel m

son-in-law n (pl ~s-in-law) Schwiegersohn m

soon adv (-er, -est) bald; (quickly) schnell; **too** ~ zu früh; **as** ~ **as possible** so bald wie möglich; ~**er or later** früher oder später; **no** ~**er had I arrived than ...** kaum war ich angekommen, da ...; **I would** ~**er stay** ich würde lieber bleiben

soot n Ruß m

sooth|e vt beruhigen; lindern <pain>. ~**ing** a, -**ly** adv beruhigend; lindernd

sophisticated a weltgewandt; (complex) hoch entwickelt

sopping a & adv ~ [**wet**] durchnässt

soppy a (-ier, -iest) 🛈 rührselig

soprano n Sopran m; (woman) Sopranistin f

sordid a schmutzig

sore a (-r, -st) wund; (painful) schmerzhaft; **have a** ~ **throat**

Halsschmerzen haben ● *n* wunde
Stelle *f*. ~**ly** *adv* sehr

sorrow *n* Kummer *m*

sorry *a* (-ier, -iest) (*sad*) traurig;
(*wretched*) erbärmlich; **I am** ~ es tut
mir Leid; **she is** *or* **feels** ~ **for him** er
tut ihr Leid; **I am** ~ **to say** leider; ~!
Entschuldigung!

sort *n* Art *f*, (*brand*) Sorte *f*; **he's a
good** ~ 🆃 er ist in Ordnung ● *vt*
sortieren. ~ **out** *vt* sortieren; (*fig*)
klären

sought *see* **seek**

soul *n* Seele *f*

sound[1] *a* (-er, -est) gesund; (*sensible*)
vernünftig; (*secure*) solide;
(*thorough*) gehörig ● *adv* **be** ~
asleep fest schlafen

sound[2] *n* (*strait*) Meerenge *f*

sound[3] *n* Laut *m*; (*noise*) Geräusch
nt; (*Phys*) Schall *m*; (*Radio, TV*) Ton
m; (*of bells, music*) Klang *m*; **I don't
like the** ~ **of it** 🆃 das hört sich nicht
gut an ● *vi* [er]tönen; (*seem*) sich
anhören ● *vt* (*pronounce*)
aussprechen; schlagen <*alarm*>;
(*Med*) abhorchen <*chest*>

soundly *adv* solide; <*sleep*> fest;
<*defeat*> vernichtend

soundproof *a* schalldicht

soup *n* Suppe *f*

sour *a* (-er, -est) sauer; (*bad-
tempered*) griesgrämig, verdrießlich

source *n* Quelle *f*

south *n* Süden *m*; **to the** ~ **of**
südlich von ● *a* Süd-, süd- ● *adv*
nach Süden

south: **S**~ **Africa** *n* Südafrika *nt*.
S~ **America** *n* Südamerika *nt*. ~
east *n* Südosten *m*

southerly *a* südlich

southern *a* südlich

southward[s] *adv* nach Süden

souvenir *n* Andenken *nt*, Souvenir
nt

Soviet *a* <*History*> sowjetisch; ~
Union Sowjetunion *f*

sow[1] *n* Sau *f*

sow[2] *vt* (*pt* sowed, *pp* sown *or*
sowed) säen

soya *n* ~ **bean** Sojabohne *f*

spa *n* Heilbad *nt*

space *n* Raum *m*; (*gap*) Platz *m*;
(*Astr*) Weltraum *m* ● *vt* ~ **[out]** [in
Abständen] verteilen

space: ~**craft** *n* Raumfahrzeug *nt*.
~**ship** *n* Raumschiff *nt*

spacious *a* geräumig

spade *n* Spaten *m*; (*for child*)
Schaufel *f*; ~**s** *pl* (*Cards*) Pik *nt*

Spain *n* Spanien *nt*

span[1] *n* Spanne *f*; (*of arch*)
Spannweite *f* ● *vt* (*pt/pp* spanned)
überspannen; umspannen <*time*>

span[2] *see* **spick**

Span|iard *n* Spanier(in) *m(f)*. ~**ish**
a spanisch ● *n* (*Lang*) Spanisch *nt*;
the ~**ish** *pl* die Spanier

spank *vt* verhauen

spanner *n* Schraubenschlüssel *m*

spare *a* (*surplus*) übrig; (*additional*)
zusätzlich; <*seat, time*> frei; <*room*>
Gäste-; <*bed, cup*> Extra- ● *n* (*part*)
Ersatzteil *nt* ● *vt* ersparen; (*not hurt*)
verschonen; (*do without*) entbehren;
(*afford to give*) erübrigen. ~ **wheel**
n Reserverad *nt*

sparing *a*, -**ly** *adv* sparsam

spark *n* Funke *nt*. ~**[ing]-plug** *n*
(*Auto*) Zündkerze *f*

spark|le *n* Funkeln *nt* ● *vi* funkeln.
~**ing** *a* funkelnd; <*wine*> Schaum-

sparrow *n* Spatz *m*

sparse *a* spärlich. ~**ly** *adv* spärlich;
<*populated*> dünn

spasm *n* Anfall *m*; (*cramp*) Krampf
m. ~**odic** *a*, -**ally** *adv* sporadisch

spastic *a* spastisch [gelähmt] ● *n*
Spastiker(in) *m(f)*

spat *see* **spit**[2]

spatter *vt* spritzen; ~ **with**
bespritzen mit

spawn *n* Laich *m* ● *vt* (*fig*)
hervorbringen

speak *v* (*pt* spoke, *pp* spoken) ● *vi*
sprechen (**to** mit) ~**ing**! (*Teleph*) am
Apparat! ● *vt* sprechen; sagen
<*truth*>. ~ **up** *vi* lauter sprechen; ~
up for oneself seine Meinung äußern

speaker *n* Sprecher(in) *m(f)*; (*in
public*) Redner(in) *m(f)*; (*loudspeaker*)
Lautsprecher *m*

spear n Speer m ● vt aufspießen

spec n on ~ 🔲 auf gut Glück

special a besondere(r,s), speziell.
~**ist** n Spezialist m; (Med) Facharzt
m/-ärztin f. ~**ity** n Spezialität f

special|ize vi sich spezialisieren
(in auf + acc). ~**ly** adv speziell;
(particularly) besonders

species n Art f

specific a bestimmt; (precise)
genau; (Phys) spezifisch. ~**ally** adv
ausdrücklich

specification n & ~**s** pl genaue
Angaben pl

specify vt (pt/pp -ied) [genau]
angeben

specimen n Exemplar nt; (sample)
Probe f; (of urine) Urinprobe f

speck n Fleck m

speckled a gesprenkelt

spectacle n (show) Schauspiel nt;
(sight) Anblick m. ~**s** npl Brille f

spectacular a spektakulär

spectator n Zuschauer(in) m(f)

speculat|e vi spekulieren. ~**ion** n
Spekulation f. ~**or** n Spekulant m

sped see speed

speech n Sprache f; (address) Rede
f. ~**less** a sprachlos

speed n Geschwindigkeit f;
(rapidity) Schnelligkeit f ● vi (pt/pp
sped) schnell fahren ● (pt/pp
speeded) (go too fast) zu schnell
fahren. ~ **up** (pt/pp speeded up)
● vt/i beschleunigen

speed: ~**boat** n Rennboot nt.
~**ing** n Geschwindigkeitsü-
berschreitung f. ~ **limit** n
Geschwindigkeitsbeschränkung f

speedometer n Tachometer m

speedy a (-ier, -iest), **-ily** adv
schnell

spell¹ n Weile f; (of weather) Periode
f

spell² v (pt/pp spelled or spelt) ● vt
schreiben; (aloud) buchstabieren;
(fig: mean) bedeuten ● vi richtig
schreiben; (aloud) buchstabieren. ~
out vt buchstabieren; (fig) genau
erklären

spell³ n Zauber m; (words)
Zauberspruch m. ~**bound** a wie
verzaubert

spelling n (of a word) Schreibweise
f; (orthography) Rechtschreibung f

spelt see spell²

spend vt/i (pt/pp spent) ausgeben;
verbringen <time>

spent see spend

sperm n Samen m

sphere n Kugel f; (fig) Sphäre f

spice n Gewürz nt; (fig) Würze f

spicy a würzig, pikant

spider n Spinne f

spik|e n Spitze f; (Bot, Zool) Stachel
m; (on shoe) Spike m. ~**y** a stachelig

spill v (pt/pp spilt or spilled) ● vt
verschütten ● vi überlaufen

spin v (pt/pp spun, pres p spinning)
● vt drehen; spinnen <wool>;
schleudern <washing> ● vi sich
drehen

spinach n Spinat m

spindl|e n Spindel f. ~**y** a
spindeldürr

spin-drier n Wäscheschleuder f

spine n Rückgrat nt; (of book)
[Buch]rücken m; (Bot, Zool) Stachel
m. ~**less** a (fig) rückgratlos

spin-off n Nebenprodukt nt

spinster n ledige Frau f

spiral a spiralig ● n Spirale f ● vi
(pt/pp spiralled) sich hochwinden. ~
staircase n Wendeltreppe f

spire n Turmspitze f

spirit n Geist m; (courage) Mut m;
~**s** pl (alcohol) Spirituosen pl; in low
~**s** niedergedrückt. ~ **away** vt
verschwinden lassen

spirited a lebhaft; (courageous)
beherzt

spiritual a geistig; (Relig) geistlich

spit¹ n (for roasting) [Brat]spieß m

spit² n Spucke f ● vt/i (pt/pp spat,
pres p spitting) spucken; <cat:>
fauchen; <fat:> spritzen; **it's ~ting
with rain** es tröpfelt

spite n Boshaftigkeit f; in ~ of trotz
(+ gen) ● vt ärgern. ~**ful** a, **-ly** adv
gehässig

splash n Platschen nt; (🔲 drop) Schuss m; ~ **of colour** Farbfleck m ● vt spritzen; ~ **s.o. with sth** jdn mit etw bespritzen ● vi spritzen. ~ **about** vi planschen

splendid a herrlich, großartig

splendour n Pracht f

splint n (Med) Schiene f

splinter n Splitter m ● vi zersplittern

split n Spaltung f; (Pol) Bruch m; (tear) Riss m ● v (pt/pp **split**, pres p **splitting**) ● vt spalten; (share) teilen; (tear) zerreißen ● vi sich spalten; (tear) zerreißen; ~ **on s.o.** 🔲 jdn verpfeifen. ~ **up** vt aufteilen ● vi <couple:> sich trennen

splutter vi prusten

spoil n ~**s** pl Beute f ● v (pt/pp **spoilt** or **spoiled**) ● vt verderben; verwöhnen <person> ● vi verderben. ~**sport** n Spielverderber m

spoke¹ n Speiche f

spoke², **spoken** see **speak**

spokesman n Sprecher m

sponge n Schwamm m ● vt abwaschen ● vi ~ **on** schmarotzen bei. ~**bag** n Waschbeutel m. ~**cake** n Biskuitkuchen m

sponsor n Sponsor m; (godparent) Pate m/Patin f ● vt sponsern

spontaneous a, **-ly** adv spontan

spoof n 🔲 Parodie f

spooky a (-ier, -iest) 🔲 gespenstisch

spool n Spule f

spoon n Löffel m ● vt löffeln. ~**ful** n Löffel m

sporadic a, **-ally** adv sporadisch

sport n Sport m ● vt [stolz] tragen. ~**ing** a sportlich

sports: ~ **car** n Sportwagen m. ~ **coat** n, ~ **jacket** n Sakko m. ~**man** n Sportler m. ~**woman** n Sportlerin f

sporty a (-ier, -iest) sportlich

spot n Fleck m; (place) Stelle f (dot) Punkt m; (drop) Tropfen m; (pimple) Pickel m; ~**s** pl (rash) Ausschlag m; **on the** ~ auf der Stelle ● vt (pt/pp **spotted**) entdecken

spot: ~ **check** n Stichprobe f. ~**less** a makellos; (🔲 very clean) blitzsauber. ~**light** n Scheinwerfer m; (fig) Rampenlicht nt

spotted a gepunktet

spouse n Gatte m/Gattin f

spout n Schnabel m, Tülle f ● vi schießen (**from** aus)

sprain n Verstauchung f ● vt verstauchen

sprang see **spring²**

sprawl vi sich ausstrecken

spray¹ n (of flowers) Strauß m

spray² n Sprühnebel m; (from sea) Gischt m; (device) Spritze f; (container) Sprühdose f; (preparation) Spray nt ● vt spritzen; (with aerosol) sprühen

spread n Verbreitung f; (paste) Aufstrich m; (🔲 feast) Festessen nt ● v (pt/pp **spread**) ● vt ausbreiten; streichen <butter, jam>; bestreichen <bread, surface>; streuen <sand, manure>; verbreiten <news, disease>; verteilen <payments> ● vi sich ausbreiten. ~ **out** vt ausbreiten; (space out) verteilen ● vi sich verteilen

spree n 🔲 **go on a shopping** ~ groß einkaufen gehen

sprightly a (-ier, -iest) rüstig

spring¹ n Frühling m ● attrib Frühlings-

spring² n (jump) Sprung m; (water) Quelle f; (device) Feder f; (elasticity) Elastizität f ● v (pt **sprang**, pp **sprung**) ● vi springen; (arise) entspringen (**from** dat) ● vt ~ **sth on s.o.** jdn mit etw überfallen

spring: ~**cleaning** n Frühjahrsputz m. ~**time** n Frühling m

sprinkl|e vt sprengen; (scatter) streuen; bestreuen <surface>. ~**ing** n dünne Schicht f

sprint n Sprint m ● vi rennen; (Sport) sprinten. ~**er** n Kurzstreckenläufer(in) m(f)

sprout n Trieb m; [**Brussels**] ~**s** pl Rosenkohl m ● vi sprießen

sprung see **spring²**

spud n ▯ Kartoffel f

spun see spin

spur n Sporn m; (*stimulus*) Ansporn m; on the ~ of the moment ganz spontan ● vt (pt/pp spurred) ~ [on] (fig) anspornen

spurn vt verschmähen

spurt n (*Sport*) Spurt m; put on a ~ spurten ● vi spritzen

spy n Spion(in) m(f) ● vi spionieren; ~ on s.o. jdm nachspionieren. ● vt (▯ see) sehen

spying n Spionage f

squabble n Zank m ● vi sich zanken

squad n Gruppe f; (*Sport*) Mannschaft f

squadron n (*Mil*) Geschwader nt

squalid a, -ly adv schmutzig

squall n Bö f ● vi brüllen

squalor n Schmutz m

squander vt vergeuden

square a quadratisch; <*metre, mile*> Quadrat-; <*meal*> anständig; all ~ ▯ quitt ● n Quadrat nt; (*area*) Platz m; (*on chessboard*) Feld nt ● vt (*settle*) klären; (*Math*) quadrieren

squash n Gedränge nt; (*drink*) Fruchtsaftgetränk nt; (*Sport*) Squash nt ● vt zerquetschen; (*suppress*) niederschlagen. ~y a weich

squat a gedrungen ● vi (pt/pp squatted) hocken; ~ in a house ein Haus besetzen. ~ter n Hausbesetzer m

squawk vi krächzen

squeak n Quieken nt; (*of hinge, brakes*) Quietschen nt ● vi quieken; quietschen

squeal n Kreischen nt ● vi kreischen

squeamish a empfindlich

squeeze n Druck m; (*crush*) Gedränge nt ● vt drücken; (*to get juice*) ausdrücken; (*force*) zwängen

squiggle n Schnörkel m

squint n Schielen nt ● vi schielen

squirm vi sich winden

squirrel n Eichhörnchen nt

squirt n Spritzer m ● vt/i spritzen

St abbr (**Saint**) St.; (**Street**) Str.

stab n Stich m; (▯ *attempt*) Versuch m ● vt (pt/pp stabbed) stechen; (*to death*) erstechen

stability n Stabilität f

stable¹ a (-r, -st) stabil

stable² n Stall m; (*establishment*) Reitstall m

stack n Stapel m; (*of chimney*) Schornstein m ● vt stapeln

stadium n Stadion nt

staff n (*stick & Mil*) Stab m ● (& pl) (*employees*) Personal nt; (*Sch*) Lehrkräfte pl ● vt mit Personal besetzen. ~-room n (*Sch*) Lehrerzimmer nt

stag n Hirsch m

stage n Bühne f; (*in journey*) Etappe f; (*in process*) Stadium nt; by or in ~s in Etappen ● vt aufführen; (*arrange*) veranstalten

stagger vi taumeln ● vt staffeln <*holidays*>; versetzt anordnen <*seats*>; I was ~ed es hat mir die Sprache verschlagen. ~ing a unglaublich

stagnant a stehend; (fig) stagnierend

stagnate vi (fig) stagnieren

stain n Fleck m; (*for wood*) Beize f ● vt färben; beizen <*wood*>; ~ed glass farbiges Glas nt. ~less a <*steel*> rostfrei

stair n Stufe f; ~s pl Treppe f. ~case n Treppe f

stake n Pfahl m; (*wager*) Einsatz m; (*Comm*) Anteil m; be at ~ auf dem Spiel stehen ● vt ~ a claim to sth Anspruch auf etw (*acc*) erheben

stale a (-r, -st) alt; <*air*> verbraucht. ~mate n Patt nt

stalk¹ n Stiel m, Stängel m

stall n Stand m; ~s pl (*Theat*) Parkett nt ● vi <*engine:*> stehen bleiben; (fig) ausweichen ● vt abwürgen <*engine*>

stalwart a treu ● n treuer Anhänger m

stamina n Ausdauer f

stammer n Stottern nt ● vt/i stottern

stamp n Stempel m; (postage ~)
[Brief]marke f ● vt stempeln;
(impress) prägen; (put postage on)
frankieren ● vi stampfen. ~ **out** vt
[aus]stanzen; (fig) ausmerzen

stampede n wilde Flucht f ● vi in
Panik fliehen

stance n Haltung f

stand n Stand m; (rack) Ständer m;
(pedestal) Sockel m; (Sport) Tribüne
f; (fig) Einstellung f ● v (pt/pp **stood**)
● vi stehen; (rise) aufstehen; (be
candidate) kandidieren; (stay valid)
gültig bleiben; ~ **still** stillstehen; ~
firm (fig) festbleiben; ~ **to reason**
logisch sein; ~ **in for** vertreten; ~
for (mean) bedeuten ● vt stellen;
(withstand) standhalten (+ dat);
(endure) ertragen; vertragen
<climate>; (put up with) aushalten;
haben <chance>; ~ **s.o. a beer** jdm
ein Bier spendieren; **I can't ~ her** 🔲
ich kann sie nicht ausstehen. ~ **by**
vi daneben stehen; (be ready) sich
bereithalten ● vt ~ **by s.o.** (fig) zu
jdm stehen. ~ **down** vi (retire)
zurücktreten. ~ **out** vi
hervorstehen; (fig) herausragen. ~
up vi aufstehen; ~ **up for** eintreten
für; ~ **up to** sich wehren gegen

standard a Normal- ● n Maßstab
m; (Techn) Norm f; (level) Niveau nt;
(flag) Standarte f; ~**s** pl (morals)
Prinzipien pl. ~**ize** vt
standardisieren; (Techn) normen

stand-in n Ersatz m

standing a (erect) stehend;
(permanent) ständig ● n Rang m;
(duration) Dauer f. ~**-room** n
Stehplätze pl

stand: ~**offish** a distanziert.
~**point** n Standpunkt m. ~**still** n
Stillstand m; **come to a** ~**still** zum
Stillstand kommen

stank see **stink**

staple¹ a Grund-

staple² n Heftklammer f ● vt heften.
~**r** n Heftmaschine f

star n Stern m; (asterisk) Sternchen
nt; (Theat, Sport) Star m ● vi (pt/pp
starred) die Hauptrolle spielen

starboard n Steuerbord nt

starch n Stärke f ● vt stärken. ~**y** a
stärkehaltig; (fig) steif

stare n Starren nt ● vt starren; ~ **at**
anstarren

stark a (-er, -est) scharf; <contrast>
krass

starling n Star m

start n Anfang m, Beginn m;
(departure) Aufbruch m; (Sport)
Start m; **from the** ~ von Anfang an;
for a ~ erstens ● vi anfangen,
beginnen; (set out) aufbrechen;
<engine:> anspringen; (Auto, Sport)
starten; (jump) aufschrecken; **to** ~
with zuerst ● vt anfangen, beginnen;
(cause) verursachen; (found)
gründen; starten <car, race>; in
Umlauf setzen <rumour>. ~**er** n
(Culin) Vorspeise f; (Auto, Sport)
Starter m. ~**ing-point** n
Ausgangspunkt m

startle vt erschrecken

starvation n Verhungern nt

starve vi hungern; (to death)
verhungern ● vt verhungern lassen

state n Zustand m; (Pol) Staat m; ~
of play Spielstand m; **be in a** ~
<person:> aufgeregt sein ● attrib
Staats-, staatlich ● vt erklären;
(specify) angeben

stately a (-ier, -iest) stattlich. ~
home n Schloss nt

statement n Erklärung f; (Jur)
Aussage f; (Banking) Auszug m

statesman n Staatsmann m

static a statisch; **remain** ~
unverändert bleiben

station n Bahnhof m; (police) Wache
f; (radio) Sender m; (space, weather)
Station f; (Mil) Posten m; (status)
Rang m ● vt stationieren; (post)
postieren. ~**ary** a stehend; **be** ~**ary**
stehen

stationery n Briefpapier nt;
(writing materials) Schreibwaren pl

station-wagon n (Amer)
Kombi[wagen] m

statistic n statistische Tatsache f.
~**al** a, **-ly** adv statistisch. ~**s** n &
pl Statistik f

statue n Statue f

stature n Statur f; (fig) Format nt

status n Status m, Rang m

statut|e n Statut nt. ~**ory** a gesetzlich

staunch a (-er, -est), **-ly** adv treu

stave vt ~ **off** abwenden

stay n Aufenthalt m ● vi bleiben; (reside) wohnen; ~ **the night** übernachten. ~ **behind** vi zurückbleiben. ~ **in** vi zu Hause bleiben; (Sch) nachsitzen. ~ **up** vi <person:> aufbleiben

steadily adv fest; (continually) stetig

steady a (-ier, -iest) fest; (not wobbly) stabil; <hand> ruhig; (regular) regelmäßig; (dependable) zuverlässig

steak n Steak nt

steal vt/i (pt stole, pp stolen) stehlen (from dat). ~ **in/out** vi sich hinein-/hinausstehlen

stealthy a heimlich

steam n Dampf m ● vt (Culin) dämpfen, dünsten ● vi dampfen. ~ **up** vi beschlagen

steam engine n Dampfmaschine f; (Rail) Dampflokomotive f

steamer n Dampfer m

steamy a dampfig

steel n Stahl m

steep a, **-ly** adv steil; (🄸 exorbitant) gesalzen

steeple n Kirchturm m

steer vt/i (Auto) lenken; (Naut) steuern; ~ **clear of s.o./sth** jdm/ etw aus dem Weg gehen. ~**ing** n (Auto) Lenkung f. ~**ing-wheel** n Lenkrad nt

stem¹ n Stiel m; (of word) Stamm m

stem² vt (pt/pp stemmed) eindämmen; stillen <bleeding>

stench n Gestank m

stencil n Schablone f

step n Schritt m; (stair) Stufe f; ~**s** pl (ladder) Trittleiter f; in ~ im Schritt; ~ **by** ~ Schritt für Schritt; **take** ~**s** (fig) Schritte unternehmen ● vi (pt/pp stepped) treten; ~ **in** (fig) eingreifen. ~ **up** vt (increase) erhöhen, steigen; verstärken <efforts>

step: ~**brother** n Stiefbruder m. ~**child** n Stiefkind nt. ~**daughter** n Stieftochter f. ~**father** n Stiefvater m. ~**ladder** n Trittleiter f. ~**mother** n Stiefmutter f. ~**sister** n Stiefschwester f. ~**son** n Stiefsohn m

stereo n Stereo nt; (equipment) Stereoanlage f. ~**phonic** a stereophon

stereotype n stereotype Figur f

steril|e a steril. ~**ize** vt sterilisieren

sterling a Sterling-; (fig) gediegen ● n Sterling m

stern¹ a (-er, -est), **-ly** adv streng

stern² n (of boat) Heck nt

stew n Eintopf m; in a ~ 🄸 aufgeregt ● vt/i schmoren; ~**ed fruit** Kompott nt

steward n Ordner m; (on ship, aircraft) Steward m. ~**ess** n Stewardess f

stick¹ n Stock m; (of chalk) Stück nt; (of rhubarb) Stange f; (Sport) Schläger m

stick² v (pt/pp stuck) ● vt stecken; (stab) stechen; (glue) kleben; (🄸 put) tun; (🄸 endure) aushalten ● vi stecken; (adhere) kleben, haften (to an + dat); (jam) klemmen; ~ **at it** 🄸 dranbleiben; ~ **up for** 🄸 eintreten für; **be stuck** nicht weiterkönnen; <vehicle:> festsitzen, festgefahren sein; <drawer:> klemmen; **be stuck with sth** 🄸 etw am Hals haben. ~ **out** vi abstehen; (project) vorstehen ● vt hinausstrecken; herausstrecken <tongue>

sticker n Aufkleber m

sticking plaster n Heftpflaster nt

sticky a (-ier, -iest) klebrig; (adhesive) Klebe-

stiff a (-er, -est), **-ly** adv steif; <brush> hart; <dough> fest; (difficult) schwierig; <penalty> schwer; **be bored** ~ 🄸 sich zu Tode langweilen. ~**en** vt steif machen ● vi steif werden. ~**ness** n Steifheit f

stifl|e *vt* ersticken; *(fig)*
unterdrücken. **~ing** *a* be **~ing** zum
Ersticken sein

still *a* still; *<drink>* ohne
Kohlensäure; **keep ~** stillhalten;
stand ~ stillstehen ● *adv* noch;
(emphatic) immer noch;
(nevertheless) trotzdem; **~ not** immer
noch nicht

stillborn *a* tot geboren

still life *n* Stillleben *nt*

stilted *a* gestelzt, geschraubt

stimulant *n* Anregungsmittel *nt*

stimulat|e *vt* anregen. **~ion** *n*
Anregung *f*

stimulus *n* (*pl* **-li**) Reiz *m*

sting *n* Stich *m*; *(from nettle,
jellyfish)* Brennen *nt*; *(organ)* Stachel
m ● *v* (*pt/pp* **stung**) ● *vt* stechen ● *vi*
brennen; *<insect:>* stechen

stingy *a* (**-ier, -iest**) geizig, 🔲
knauserig

stink *n* Gestank *m* ● *vi* (*pt* **stank**, *pp*
stunk) stinken (**of** nach)

stipulat|e *vt* vorschreiben. **~ion** *n*
Bedingung *f*

stir *n* *(commotion)* Aufregung *f* ● *v*
(*pt/pp* **stirred**) *vt* rühren ● *vi* sich
rühren

stirrup *n* Steigbügel *m*

stitch *n* Stich *m*; *(Knitting)* Masche
f; *(pain)* Seitenstechen *nt*; **be in ~es**
🔲 sich kaputtlachen ● *vt* nähen

stock *n* Vorrat *m* (**of** an + *dat*); *(in
shop)* [Waren]bestand *m*; *(livestock)*
Vieh *nt*; *(lineage)* Abstammung *f*;
(Finance) Wertpapiere *pl*; *(Culin)*
Brühe *f*; *(plant)* Levkoje *f*; **in/out of
~** vorrätig/nicht vorrätig; **take ~**
(fig) Bilanz ziehen ● *a* Standard- ● *vt*
<shop:> führen; auffüllen *<shelves>*.
~ up *vi* sich eindecken (**with** mit)

stock: ~broker *n* Börsenmakler *m*.
S~ Exchange *n* Börse *f*

stocking *n* Strumpf *m*

stock: ~market *n* Börse *f*. **~-
taking** *n* (*Comm*) Inventur *f*

stocky *a* (**-ier, -iest**) untersetzt

stodgy *a* pappig [und schwer
verdaulich]

stoke *vt* heizen

stole, stolen *see* **steal**

stomach *n* Magen *m*. **~-ache** *n*
Magenschmerzen *pl*

stone *n* Stein *m*; *(weight)* 6,35kg ● *a*
steinern; *<wall, Age>* Stein- ● *vt* mit
Steinen bewerfen; entsteinen
<fruit>. **~-cold** *a* eiskalt. **~-deaf** *n*
🔲 stocktaub

stony *a* steinig

stood *see* **stand**

stool *n* Hocker *m*

stoop *n* **walk with a ~** gebeugt gehen
● *vi* sich bücken

stop *n* Halt *m*; *(break)* Pause *f*; *(for
bus)* Haltestelle *f*; *(for train)* Station
f; *(Gram)* Punkt *m*; *(on organ)*
Register *nt*; **come to a ~** stehen
bleiben; **put a ~ to sth** etw
unterbinden ● *v* (*pt/pp* **stopped**) ● *vt*
anhalten, stoppen; *(switch off)*
abstellen; *(plug, block)* zustopfen;
(prevent) verhindern; **~ s.o. doing
sth** jdn daran hindern, etw zu tun; **~
doing sth** aufhören, etw zu tun; **~
that!** hör auf damit! ● *vi* anhalten;
(cease) aufhören; *<clock:>* stehen
bleiben ● *int* halt!

stop: ~gap *n* Notlösung *f*. **~over** *n*
(Aviat) Zwischenlandung *f*

stoppage *n* Unterbrechung *f*;
(strike) Streik *m*

stopper *n* Stöpsel *m*

stop-watch *n* Stoppuhr *f*

storage *n* Aufbewahrung *f*; *(in
warehouse)* Lagerung *f*; *(Computing)*
Speicherung *f*

store *n* *(stock)* Vorrat *m*; *(shop)*
Laden *m*; *(department ~)* Kaufhaus
nt; *(depot)* Lager *nt*; **in ~** auf Lager;
be in ~ for s.o. *(fig)* jdm bevorstehen
● *vt* aufbewahren; *(in warehouse)*
lagern; *(Computing)* speichern. **~-
room** *n* Lagerraum *m*

storey *n* Stockwerk *nt*

stork *n* Storch *m*

storm *n* Sturm *m*; *(with thunder)*
Gewitter *nt* ● *vt/i* stürmen. **~y** *a*
stürmisch

story *n* Geschichte *f*; *(in newspaper)*
Artikel *m*; ((🔲 *lie*) Märchen *nt*

stout *a* (-er, -est) beleibt; (*strong*) fest

stove *n* Ofen *m*; (*for cooking*) Herd *m*

stow *vt* verstauen. **~away** *n* blinder Passagier *m*

straggl|e *vi* hinterherhinken. **~er** *n* Nachzügler *m*. **~y** *a* strähnig

straight *a* (-er, -est) gerade; (*direct*) direkt; (*clear*) klar; <*hair*> glatt; <*drink*>; pur; **be ~** (*tidy*) in Ordnung sein ● *adv* gerade; (*directly*) direkt, geradewegs; (*clearly*) klar; **~ away** sofort; **~ on** *or* **ahead** geradeaus; **~ out** (*fig*) geradeheraus; **sit/stand up ~** gerade sitzen/stehen

straighten *vt* gerade machen; (*put straight*) gerade richten ● *vi* gerade werden; **~ [up]** <*person:*> sich aufrichten. **~ out** *vt* gerade biegen

straightforward *a* offen; (*simple*) einfach

strain *n* Belastung *f*; **~s** *pl* (*of music*) Klänge *pl* ● *vt* belasten; (*overexert*) überanstrengen; (*injure*) zerren <*muscle*>; (*Culin*) durchseihen; abgießen <*vegetables*>. **~ed** *a* <*relations*> gespannt. **~er** *n* Sieb *nt*

strait *n* Meerenge *f*; **in dire ~s** in großen Nöten

strand[1] *n* (*of thread*) Faden *m*; (*of hair*) Strähne *f*

strand[2] *vt* **be ~ed** festsitzen

strange *a* (-r, -st) fremd; (*odd*) seltsam, merkwürdig. **~ly** *adv* seltsam, merkwürdig; **~ enough** seltsamerweise. **~r** *n* Fremde(r) *m/f*

strangle *vt* erwürgen; (*fig*) unterdrücken

strap *n* Riemen *m*; (*for safety*) Gurt *m*; (*to grasp in vehicle*) Halteriemen *m*; (*of watch*) Armband *nt*; (*shoulder ~*) Träger *m* ● *vt* (*pt/pp* **strapped**) schnallen

strapping *a* stramm

strategic *a*, **-ally** *adv* strategisch

strategy *n* Strategie *f*

straw *n* Stroh *nt*; (*single piece, drinking*) Strohhalm *m*; **that's the last ~** jetzt reicht's aber

strawberry *n* Erdbeere *f*

stray *a* streunend ● *n* streunendes Tier *nt* ● *vi* sich verirren; (*deviate*) abweichen

streak *n* Streifen *m*; (*in hair*) Strähne *f*; (*fig: trait*) Zug *m*

stream *n* Bach *m*; (*flow*) Strom *m*; (*current*) Strömung *f*; (*Sch*) Parallelzug *m* ● *vi* strömen

streamline *vt* (*fig*) rationalisieren. **~d** *a* stromlinienförmig

street *n* Straße *f*. **~car** *n* (*Amer*) Straßenbahn *f*. **~lamp** *n* Straßenlaterne *f*

strength *n* Stärke *f*; (*power*) Kraft *f*; **on the ~ of** auf Grund (+ *gen*). **~en** *vt* stärken; (*reinforce*) verstärken

strenuous *a* anstrengend

stress *n* (*emphasis*) Betonung *f*; (*strain*) Belastung *f*; (*mental*) Stress *m* ● *vt* betonen; (*put a strain on*) belasten. **~ful** *a* stressig ⚠

stretch *n* (*of road*) Strecke *f*; (*elasticity*) Elastizität *f*; **at a ~** ohne Unterbrechung; **have a ~** sich strecken ● *vt* strecken; (*widen*) dehnen; (*spread*) ausbreiten; fordern <*person*>; **~ one's legs** sich (*dat*) die Beine vertreten ● *vt* sich erstrecken; (*become wider*) sich dehnen; <*person:*> sich strecken. **~er** *n* Tragbahre *f*

strict *a* (-er, -est), **-ly** *adv* streng; **~ly speaking** streng genommen

stride *n* [großer] Schritt *m*; **take sth in one's ~** mit etw gut fertig werden ● *vi* (*pt* **strode**, *pp* **stridden**) [mit großen Schritten] gehen

strident *a*, **-ly** *adv* schrill; <*colour*> grell

strife *n* Streit *m*

strike *n* Streik *m*; (*Mil*) Angriff *m*; **be on ~** streiken ● *v* (*pt/pp* **struck**) ● *vt* schlagen; (*knock against, collide with*) treffen; anzünden <*match*>; stoßen auf (+ *acc*) <*oil, gold*>; abbrechen <*camp*>; (*impress*) beeindrucken; (*occur to*) einfallen (+ *dat*); **~ s.o. a blow** jdm einen Schlag versetzen ● *vi* treffen; *<lightning:>* einschlagen; *<clock:>* schlagen; *(attack)* zuschlagen; *<workers:>* streiken

striker *n* Streikende(r) *m/f*

striking *a* auffallend

string *n* Schnur *f*; *(thin)* Bindfaden *m*; *(of musical instrument, racket)* Saite *f*; *(of bow)* Sehne *f*; *(of pearls)* Kette *f*; the ∼s *(Mus)* die Streicher *pl*; pull ∼s 🗉 seine Beziehungen spielen lassen ● *vt (pt/pp* strung*)* *(thread)* aufziehen *<beads>*

stringent *a* streng

strip *n* Streifen *m* ● *v (pt/pp* stripped*)* ● *vt* ablösen; ausziehen *<person, clothes>*; abziehen *<bed>*; abbeizen *<wood, furniture>*; auseinander nehmen *<machine>*; *(deprive)* berauben *(of gen)*; ∼ sth off sth etw von etw entfernen ● *vi (undress)* sich ausziehen

stripe *n* Streifen *m*. ∼d *a* gestreift

stripper *n* Stripperin *f*; *(male)* Stripper *m*

strive *vi (pt* strove, *pp* striven*)* sich bemühen (to zu); ∼ for streben nach

strode *see* stride

stroke¹ *n* Schlag *m*; *(of pen)* Strich *m*; *(Swimming)* Zug *m*; *(style)* Stil *m*; *(Med)* Schlaganfall *m*; ∼ of luck Glücksfall *m*

stroke² ● *vt* streicheln

stroll *n* Bummel *m* 🗉 ● *vi* bummeln 🗉. ∼er *n (Amer: pushchair)* [Kinder]sportwagen *m*

strong *a (-er, -est)*, -ly *adv* stark; *(powerful, healthy)* kräftig; *(severe)* streng; *(sturdy)* stabil; *(convincing)* gut

strong: ∼hold *n* Festung *f*; *(fig)* Hochburg *f*. ∼-room *n* Tresorraum *m*

strove *see* strive

struck *see* strike

structural *a*, -ly *adv* baulich

structure *n* Struktur *f*; *(building)* Bau *m*

struggle *n* Kampf *m*; with a ∼ mit Mühe ● *vt* kämpfen; ∼ to do sth sich abmühen, etw zutun

strum *v (pt/pp* strummed*)* ● *vt* klimpern auf (+ *dat*) ● *vi* klimpern

strung *see* string

strut¹ *n* Strebe *f*

strut² *vi (pt/pp* strutted*)* stolzieren

stub *n* Stummel *m*; *(counterfoil)* Abschnitt *m*. ∼ out *vt (pt/pp* stubbed*)* ausdrücken *<cigarette>*

stubble *n* Stoppeln *pl*

stubborn *a*, -ly *adv* starrsinnig; *<refusal>* hartnäckig

stubby *a*, *(-ier, -iest)* kurz und dick

stuck *see* stick². ∼-up *a* 🗉 hochnäsig

stud *n* Nagel *m*; *(on clothes)* Niete *f*; *(for collar)* Kragenknopf *m*; *(for ear)* Ohrstecker *m*

student *n* Student(in) *m(f)*; *(Sch)* Schüler(in) *m(f)*

studio *n* Studio *nt*; *(for artist)* Atelier *nt*

studious *a* lerneifrig; *(earnest)* ernsthaft

stud|y *n* Studie *f*; *(room)* Arbeitszimmer *nt*; *(investigation)* Untersuchung *f*; ∼ies *pl* Studium *nt* ● *v (pt/pp* studied*)* ● *vt* studieren; *(examine)* untersuchen ● *vi* lernen; *(at university)* studieren

stuff *n* Stoff *m*; *(🗉 things)* Zeug *nt* ● *vt* vollstopfen; *(with padding, Culin)* füllen; ausstopfen *<animal>*; *(cram)* [hinein]stopfen. ∼ing *n* Füllung *f*

stuffy *a (-ier, -iest)* stickig; *(old-fashioned)* spießig

stumbl|e *vi* stolpern; ∼e across zufällig stoßen auf (+ *acc*). ∼ing-block *n* Hindernis *nt*

stump *n* Stumpf *m* ● ∼ up *vt/i* 🗉 blechen. ∼ed *a* 🗉 überfragt

stun *vt (pt/pp* stunned*)* betäuben

stung *see* sting

stunk *see* stink

stunning *a* 🗉 toll

stunt *n* 🗉 Kunststück *nt*

stupendous *a*, -ly *adv* enorm

stupid *a* dumm. ∼ity *n* Dummheit *f*. ∼ly *adv* dumm; ∼ly [enough] dummerweise

sturdy a (-ier, -iest) stämmig; <furniture> stabil; <shoes> fest

stutter n Stottern nt ● vt/i stottern

sty n (pl sties) Schweinestall m

style n Stil m; (fashion) Mode f; (sort) Art f; (hair~) Frisur f; **in ~** in großem Stil

stylish a, -ly adv stilvoll

stylist n Friseur m/ Friseuse f. **~ic** a, -ally adv stilistisch

suave a (pej) gewandt

subconscious a, -ly adv unterbewusst ● n Unterbewusstsein nt

subdivi|de vt unterteilen. **~sion** n Unterteilung f

subdue vt unterwerfen. **~d** a gedämpft; <person> still

subject[1] a be ~ **to** sth etw (dat) unterworfen sein ● n Staatsbürger(in) m(f); (of ruler) Untertan m; (theme) Thema nt; (of investigation) Gegenstand m; (Sch) Fach nt; (Gram) Subjekt nt

subject[2] vt unterwerfen (**to** dat); (expose) aussetzen (**to** dat)

subjective a, -ly adv subjektiv

subjunctive n Konjunktiv m

sublime a, -ly adv erhaben

submarine n Unterseeboot nt

submerge vt untertauchen; **be ~d** unter Wasser stehen ● vi tauchen

submission n Unterwerfung f

submit v (pt/pp -mitted, pres p -mitting) ● vt vorlegen (**to** dat); (hand in) einreichen ● vi sich unterwerfen (**to** dat)

subordinate[1] a untergeordnet ● n Untergebene(r) m/f

subordinate[2] vt unterordnen (**to** dat)

subscribe vi spenden; ~ **to** (fig); abonnieren <newspaper>. **~r** n Spender m; Abonnent m

subscription n (to club) [Mitglieds]beitrag m; (to newspaper) Abonnement nt; **by ~** mit Spenden; <buy> im Abonnement

subsequent a, -ly adv folgend; (later) später

subside vi sinken; <ground:> sich senken; <storm:> nachlassen

subsidiary a untergeordnet ● n Tochtergesellschaft f

subsid|ize vt subventionieren. **~y** n Subvention f

substance n Substanz f

substandard a unzulänglich; <goods> minderwertig

substantial a solide; <meal> reichhaltig; (considerable) beträchtlich. **~ly** adv solide; (essentially) im Wesentlichen

substitut|e n Ersatz m; (Sport) Ersatzspieler(in) m(f) ● vt ~**e A for B** B durch A ersetzen ● vi ~**e for s.o.** jdn vertreten. **~ion** n Ersetzung f

subterranean a unterirdisch

subtitle n Untertitel m

subtle a (-r, -st), -tly adv fein; (fig) subtil

subtract vt abziehen, subtrahieren. **~ion** n Subtraktion f

suburb n Vorort m. **~an** a Vorort-. **~ia** n die Vororte pl

subway n Unterführung f; (Amer: railway) U-Bahn f

succeed vi Erfolg haben; <plan:> gelingen; (follow) nachfolgen (+ dat); **I ~ed** es ist mir gelungen; **he ~ed in escaping** es gelang ihm zu entkommen ● vt folgen (+ dat)

success n Erfolg m. **~ful** a,-ly adv erfolgreich

succession n Folge f; (series) Serie f; (to title, office) Nachfolge f; (to throne) Thronfolge f; **in ~** hintereinander

successive a aufeinander folgend

successor n Nachfolger(in) m(f)

succumb vi erliegen (**to** dat)

such
● adjective
····▸ (of that kind) solch. **such a book** ein solches Buch; so ein Buch ⚇. **such a person** ein solcher Mensch; so ein Mensch ⚇. **such people** solche Leute. **such a thing** so etwas. **no such example** kein solches

Beispiel. **there is no such thing** so etwas gibt es nicht; das gibt es gar nicht. **there is no such person** eine solche Person gibt es nicht. **such writers as Goethe and Schiller** Schriftsteller wie Goethe und Schiller

····▸ (*so great*) solch; derartig. **I've got such a headache!** ich habe solche Kopfschmerzen! **it was such fun!** das machte solchen Spaß! **I got such a fright that** ... ich bekam einen derartigen *od* 🖃 so einen Schrecken, dass ...

····▸ (*with adjective*) so. **such a big house** ein so großes Haus. **he has such lovely blue eyes** er hat so schöne blaue Augen. **such a long time** so lange

● *pronoun*

····▸ **as such** als solcher/solche/ solches. **the thing as such** die Sache als solche. (*strictly speaking*) **this is not a promotion as such** dies ist im Grunde genommen keine Beförderung

····▸ **such is: such is life** so ist das Leben. **such is not the case** das ist nicht der Fall

┊···▸ **such as** wie [zum Beispiel]

suchlike *pron* 🖃 dergleichen

suck *vt/i* saugen; lutschen <*sweet*>. ~ **up** *vt* aufsaugen ● *vi* ~ **up to s.o.** 🖃 sich bei jdm einschmeicheln

suction *n* Saugwirkung *f*

sudden *a*, **-ly** *adv* plötzlich; (*abrupt*) jäh ● *n* **all of a** ~ auf einmal

sue *vt* (*pres p* **suing**) verklagen (**for** auf + *acc*) ● *vi* klagen

suede *n* Wildleder *nt*

suet *n* [Nieren]talg *m*

suffer *vi* leiden (**from** an + *dat*) ● *vt* erleiden; (*tolerate*) dulden

suffice *vi* genügen

sufficient *a*, **-ly** *adv* genug, genügend; **be** ~ genügen

suffocat|e *vt/i* ersticken. ~**ion** *n* Ersticken *nt*

sugar *n* Zucker *m* ● *vt* zuckern; (*fig*) versüßen. ~ **basin**, ~**-bowl** *n* Zuckerschale *f*. ~**y** *a* süß; (*fig*) süßlich

suggest *vt* vorschlagen; (*indicate, insinuate*) andeuten. ~**ion** *n* Vorschlag *m*; Andeutung *f*; (*trace*) Spur *f*. ~**ive** *a*, **-ly** *adv* anzüglich

suicidal *a* selbstmörderisch

suicide *n* Selbstmord *m*

suit *n* Anzug *m*; (*woman's*) Kostüm *nt*; (*Cards*) Farbe *f*; (*Jur*) Prozess *m* ● *vt* (*adapt*) anpassen (**to** *dat*); (*be convenient for*) passen (+ *dat*); (*go with*) passen zu; <*clothing:*> stehen (*s.o. jdm*); **be** ~**ed for** geeignet sein für; ~ **yourself!** wie du willst!

suit|able *a* geeignet; (*convenient*) passend; (*appropriate*) angemessen; (*for weather, activity*) zweckmäßig. ~**ably** *adv* angemessen; zweckmäßig

suitcase *n* Koffer *m*

suite *n* Suite *f*; (*of furniture*) Garnitur *f*

sulk *vi* schmollen. ~**y** *a* schmollend

sullen *a*, **-ly** *adv* mürrisch

sultry *a* (**-ier**, **-iest**) <*weather*> schwül

sum *n* Summe *f*; (*Sch*) Rechenaufgabe *f* ● *vt/i* (*pt/pp* **summed**) ~ **up** zusammenfassen; (*assess*) einschätzen

summar|ize *vt* zusammenfassen. ~**y** *n* Zusammenfassung *f* ● *a*, **-ily** *adv* summarisch; <*dismissal*> fristlos

summer *n* Sommer *m*. ~**time** *n* Sommer *m*

summery *a* sommerlich

summit *n* Gipfel *m*. ~ **conference** *n* Gipfelkonferenz *f*

summon *vt* rufen; holen <*help*>; (*Jur*) vorladen

summons *n* (*Jur*) Vorladung *f* ● *vt* vorladen

sumptuous *a*, **-ly** *adv* prunkvoll; <*meal*> üppig

sun *n* Sonne *f* ● *vt* (*pt/pp* **sunned**) ~ oneself sich sonnen

sun: ~**bathe** *vi* sich sonnen. ~**-bed** *n* Sonnenbank *f*. ~**burn** *n* Sonnenbrand *m*

Sunday *n* Sonntag *m*

sunflower *n* Sonnenblume *f*

sung *see* sing

sunglasses *npl* Sonnenbrille *f*

sunk *see* sink

sunny *a* (-ier, -iest) sonnig

sun: ~**rise** *n* Sonnenaufgang *m.* ~**roof** *n* (*Auto*) Schiebedach *nt.* ~**set** *n* Sonnenuntergang *m.* ~**shade** *n* Sonnenschirm *m.* ~**shine** *n* Sonnenschein *m.* ~**stroke** *n* Sonnenstich *m.* ~**-tan** *n* [Sonnen]bräune *f.* ~**-tanned** *a* braun [gebrannt]. ~**-tan oil** *n* Sonnenöl *nt*

super *a* 🔲 prima, toll

superb *a* erstklassig

superficial a, -ly *adv* oberflächlich

superfluous *a* überflüssig

superintendent *n* (*of police*) Kommissar *m*

superior *a* überlegen; (*in rank*) höher ● *n* Vorgesetzte(r) *m/f.* ~**ity** *n* Überlegenheit *f*

superlative *a* unübertrefflich ● *n* Superlativ *m*

supermarket *n* Supermarkt *m*

supernatural *a* übernatürlich

supersede *vt* ersetzen

superstiti|on *n* Aberglaube *m.* ~**ous** *a*, **-ly** *adv* abergläubisch

supervis|e *vt* beaufsichtigen; überwachen <*work*>. ~**ion** *n* Aufsicht *f*; Überwachung *f.* ~**or** *n* Aufseher(in) *m(f)*

supper *n* Abendessen *nt*

supple *a* geschmeidig

supplement *n* Ergänzung *f*; (*addition*) Zusatz *m*; (*to fare*) Zuschlag *m*; (*book*) Ergänzungsband *m*; (*to newspaper*) Beilage *f* ● *vt* ergänzen. ~**ary** *a* zusätzlich

supplier *n* Lieferant *m*

supply *n* Vorrat *m*; **supplies** *pl* (*Mil*) Nachschub *m* ● *vt* (*pt/pp* **-ied**) liefern; ~ **s.o. with sth** jdn mit etw versorgen

support *n* Stütze *f*; (*fig*) Unterstützung *f* ● *vt* stützen; (*bear weight of*) tragen; (*keep*) ernähren; (*give money to*) unterstützen; (*speak in favour of*) befürworten; (*Sport*)

Fan sein von. ~**er** *n* Anhänger(in) *m(f)*; (*Sport*) Fan *m*

suppose *vt* annehmen; (*presume*) vermuten; (*imagine*) sich (*dat*) vorstellen; **be** ~**d to do sth** etw tun sollen; **not be** ~**d to** 🔲 nicht dürfen; **I** ~ **so** vermutlich. ~**dly** *adv* angeblich

supposition *n* Vermutung *f*

suppress *vt* unterdrücken. ~**ion** *n* Unterdrückung *f*

supremacy *n* Vorherrschaft *f*

supreme *a* höchste(r,s); <*court*> oberste(r,s)

sure *a* (-r, -st) sicher; **make** ~ sich vergewissern (**of** *gen*); (*check*) nachprüfen ● *adv* (*Amer* 🔲) klar; ~ **enough** tatsächlich. ~**ly** *adv* sicher; (*for emphasis*) doch; (*Amer: gladly*) gern

surf *n* Brandung *f*

surface *n* Oberfläche *f* ● *vi* (*emerge*) auftauchen

surfboard *n* Surfbrett *nt*

surfing *n* Surfen *nt*

surge *n* (*of sea*) Branden *nt*; (*fig*) Welle *f* ● *vi* branden; ~ **forward** nach vorn drängen

surgeon *n* Chirurg(in) *m(f)*

surgery *n* Chirurgie *f*; (*place*) Praxis *f*; (*room*) Sprechzimmer *nt*; (*hours*) Sprechstunde *f*; **have** ~ operiert werden

surgical *a*, **-ly** *adv* chirurgisch

surly *a* (-ier, -iest) mürrisch

surname *n* Nachname *m*

surpass *vt* übertreffen

surplus *a* überschüssig ● *n* Überschuss *m* (**of** an + *dat*)

surpris|e *n* Überraschung *f* ● *vt* überraschen; **be** ~**ed** sich wundern (**at** über + *acc*). ~**ing** *a*, **-ly** *adv* überraschend

surrender *n* Kapitulation *f* ● *vi* sich ergeben; (*Mil*) kapitulieren ● *vt* aufgeben

surround *vt* umgeben; (*encircle*) umzingeln; ~**ed by** umgeben von. ~**ing** *a* umliegend. ~**ings** *npl* Umgebung *f*

surveillance *n* Überwachung *f*; **be under ~** überwacht werden

survey[1] *n* Überblick *m*; (*poll*) Umfrage *f*; (*investigation*) Untersuchung *f*; (*of land*) Vermessung *f*; (*of house*) Gutachten *nt*

survey[2] *vt* betrachten; vermessen <*land*>; begutachten <*building*>. **~or** *n* Landvermesser *m*; Gutachter *m*

survival *n* Überleben *nt*; (*of tradition*) Fortbestand *m*

surviv|e *vt* überleben ● *vi* überleben; <*tradition:*> erhalten bleiben. **~or** *n* Überlebende(r) *m/f*; **be a ~or** nicht unterzukriegen sein

susceptible *a* empfänglich/ (*Med*) anfällig (**to** für)

suspect[1] *vt* verdächtigen; (*assume*) vermuten; **he ~s nothing** er ahnt nichts

suspect[2] *a* verdächtig ● *n* Verdächtige(r) *m/f*

suspend *vt* aufhängen; (*stop*) [vorläufig] einstellen; (*from duty*) vorläufig beurlauben. **~ders** *npl* (*Amer: braces*) Hosenträger *pl*

suspense *n* Spannung *f*

suspension *n* (*Auto*) Federung *f*. **~ bridge** *n* Hängebrücke *f*

suspici|on *n* Verdacht *m*; (*mistrust*) Misstrauen *nt*; (*trace*) Spur *f*. **~ous** *a*, **-ly** *adv* misstrauisch; (*arousing suspicion*) verdächtig

sustain *vt* tragen; (*fig*) aufrechterhalten; erhalten <*life*>; erleiden <*injury*>

sustenance *n* Nahrung *f*

swagger *vi* stolzieren

swallow[1] *vt/i* schlucken. **~ up** *vt* verschlucken; verschlingen <*resources*>

swallow[2] *n* (*bird*) Schwalbe *f*

swam *see* swim

swamp *n* Sumpf *m* ● *vt* überschwemmen

swan *n* Schwan *m*

swank *vi* 🅴 angeben

swap *n* 🅴 Tausch *m* ● *vt/i* (*pt/pp* swapped) 🅴 tauschen (**for** gegen)

swarm *n* Schwarm *m* ● *vi* schwärmen; **be ~ing with** wimmeln von

swat *vt* (*pt/pp* swatted) totschlagen

sway *vi* schwanken; (*gently*) sich wiegen ● *vt* (*influence*) beeinflussen

swear *v* (*pt* swore, *pp* sworn) ● *vt* schwören ● *vi* schwören (**by** auf + *acc*); (*curse*) fluchen. **~-word** *n* Kraftausdruck *m*

sweat *n* Schweiß *m* ● *vi* schwitzen

sweater *n* Pullover *m*

Swed|e *n* Schwede *m*/Schwedin *f*. **~en** *n* Schweden *nt*. **~ish** *a* schwedisch

sweep *n* Schornsteinfeger *m*; (*curve*) Bogen *m*; (*movement*) ausholende Bewegung *f* ● *v* (*pt/pp* swept) ● *vt* fegen, kehren ● *vi* (*go swiftly*) rauschen; <*wind:*> fegen

sweeping *a* ausholend; <*statement*> pauschal; <*changes*> weit reichend

sweet *a* (**-er, -est**) süß; **have a ~ tooth** gern Süßes mögen ● *n* Bonbon *m* & *nt*; (*dessert*) Nachtisch *m*

sweeten *vt* süßen

sweet: ~heart *n* Schatz *m*. **~ness** *n* Süße *f*. **~ pea** *n* Wicke *f*. **~-shop** *n* Süßwarenladen *m*

swell *n* Dünung *f* ● *v* (*pt* swelled, *pp* swollen *or* swelled) ● *vi* [an]schwellen; <*wood:*> aufquellen ● *vt* anschwellen lassen; (*increase*) vergrößern. **~ing** *n* Schwellung *f*

swelter *vi* schwitzen

swept *see* sweep

swerve *vi* einen Bogen machen

swift *a* (**-er, -est**), **-ly** *adv* schnell

swig *n* 🅴 Schluck *m*

swim *n* **have a ~** schwimmen ● *vi* (*pt* swam, *pp* swum) schwimmen; **my head is ~ming** mir dreht sich der Kopf. **~mer** *n* Schwimmer(in) *m(f)*

swimming *n* Schwimmen *nt*. **~-baths** *npl* Schwimmbad *nt*. **~-pool** *n* Schwimmbecken *nt*; (*private*) Swimmingpool *m*

swimsuit *n* Badeanzug *m*

swindle *n* Schwindel *m*, Betrug *m* ● *vt* betrügen. **~r** *n* Schwindler *m*

swine n (pej) Schwein nt

swing n Schwung m; (shift) Schwenk m; (seat) Schaukel f; **in full ~** in vollem Gange ● (pt/pp **swung**) ● vi schwingen; (on swing) schaukeln; (dangle) baumeln; (turn) schwenken ● vt schwingen; (influence) beeinflussen

swipe n ⊞ Schlag m ● vt ⊞ knallen; (steal) klauen

swirl n Wirbel m ● vt/i wirbeln

Swiss a Schweizer, schweizerisch ● n Schweizer(in) m(f); **the ~** pl die Schweizer. **~ roll** n Biskuitrolle f

switch n Schalter m; (change) Wechsel m; (Amer, Rail) Weiche f ● vt wechseln; (exchange) tauschen ● vi wechseln; **~ to** umstellen auf (+ acc). **~ off** vt ausschalten; abschalten <engine>. **~ on** vt einschalten

switchboard n [Telefon]zentrale f

Switzerland n die Schweiz

swivel v (pt/pp **swivelled**) ● vt drehen ● vi sich drehen

swollen see swell

swoop n (by police) Razzia f ● vi ~ **down** herabstoßen

sword n Schwert nt

swore see swear

sworn see swear

swot n ⊞ Streber m ● vt (pt/pp **swotted**) ⊞ büffeln

swum see swim

swung see swing

syllable n Silbe f

syllabus n Lehrplan m; (for exam) Studienplan m

symbol n Symbol nt (of für). **~ic** a, **-ally** adv symbolisch **~ism** n Symbolik f. **~ize** vt symbolisieren

symmetr|ical a, **-ly** adv symmetrisch. **~y** n Symmetrie f

sympathetic a, **-ally** adv mitfühlend; (likeable) sympathisch

sympathize vi mitfühlen

sympathy n Mitgefühl nt; (condolences) Beileid nt

symphony n Sinfonie f

symptom n Symptom nt

synagogue n Synagoge f

synchronize vt synchronisieren

synonym n Synonym nt. **~ous** a, **-ly** adv synonym

synthesis n (pl **-ses**) Synthese f

synthetic a synthetisch

Syria n Syrien nt

syringe n Spritze f

syrup n Sirup m

system n System nt. **~atic** a, **-ally** adv systematisch

Tt

tab n (projecting) Zunge f; (with name) Namensschild nt; (loop) Aufhänger m; **pick up the ~** ⊞ bezahlen

table n Tisch m; (list) Tabelle f; **at [the] ~** bei Tisch. **~-cloth** n Tischdecke f. **~spoon** n Servierlöffel m

tablet n Tablette f; (of soap) Stück nt

table tennis n Tischtennis nt

tabloid n kleinformatige Zeitung f; (pej) Boulevardzeitung f

taciturn a wortkarg

tack n (nail) Stift m; (stitch) Heftstich m; (Naut & fig) Kurs m ● vt festnageln; (sew) heften ● vi (Naut) kreuzen

tackle n Ausrüstung f ● vt angehen <problem>; (Sport) angreifen

tact n Takt m, Taktgefühl nt. **~ful** a, **-ly** adv taktvoll

tactic|al a, **-ly** adv taktisch. **~s** npl Taktik f

tactless a, **-ly** adv taktlos. **~ness** n Taktlosigkeit f

tag n (label) Schild nt ● vi (pt/pp **tagged**) ~ **along** mitkommen

tail n Schwanz m; **~s** pl (tailcoat) Frack m; **heads or ~s?** Kopf oder

Zahl? ● *vt* (🔢 *follow*) beschatten ● *vi*
~ **off** zurückgehen

tail: ~**back** *n* Rückstau *m*. ~ **light**
n Rücklicht *nt*

tailor *n* Schneider *m*. ~-**made** *a*
maßgeschneidert

taint *vt* verderben

take *v* (*pt* took, *pp* taken) ● *vt*
nehmen; (*with one*) mitnehmen; (*take
to a place*) bringen; (*steal*) stehlen;
(*win*) gewinnen; (*capture*)
einnehmen; (*require*) brauchen; (*last*)
dauern; (*teach*) geben; machen
<*exam, subject, holiday,
photograph*>; messen <*pulse,
temperature*>; ~ **sth to the cleaner's**
etw in die Reinigung bringen; **be** ~**n
ill** krank werden; ~ **sth calmly** etw
gelassen aufnehmen ● *vi* <*plant*:>
angehen; ~ **after s.o.** jdm
nachschlagen; (*in looks*) jdm ähnlich
sehen; ~ **to** (*like*) mögen; (*as a habit*)
sich (*dat*) angewöhnen. ~ **away** *vt*
wegbringen; (*remove*) wegnehmen;
(*subtract*) abziehen; 'to ~ away' 'zum
Mitnehmen'. ~ **back** *vt*
zurücknehmen; (*return*)
zurückbringen. ~ **down** *vt*
herunternehmen; (*remove*)
abnehmen; (*write down*)
aufschreiben. ~ **in** *vt*
hineinnehmen; (*bring indoors*)
hereinholen; (*to one's home*)
aufnehmen; (*understand*) begreifen;
(*deceive*) hereinlegen; (*make smaller*)
enger machen. ~ **off** *vt* abnehmen;
ablegen <*coat*>; sich (*dat*) ausziehen
<*clothes*>; (*deduct*) abziehen; (*mimic*)
nachmachen ● *vi* (*Aviat*) starten. ~
on *vt* annehmen; (*undertake*)
übernehmen; (*engage*) einstellen; (*as
opponent*) antreten gegen. ~ **out** *vt*
hinausbringen; (*for pleasure*)
ausgehen mit; ausführen <*dog*>;
(*remove*) herausnehmen; (*withdraw*)
abheben <*money*>; (*from library*)
ausleihen; ~ **it out on s.o.** 🔢 seinen
Ärger an jdm auslassen. ~ **over** *vt*
hinüberbringen; übernehmen <*firm,
control*> ● *vi* ~ **over from s.o.** jdn
ablösen. ~ **up** *vt* hinaufbringen;
annehmen <*offer*>; ergreifen
<*profession*>; sich (*dat*) zulegen

<*hobby*>; in Anspruch nehmen
<*time*>; einnehmen <*space*>;
aufreißen <*floorboards*>; ~ **sth up
with s.o.** mit jdm über etw (*acc*)
sprechen

take: ~-**away** *n* Essen *nt* zum
Mitnehmen; (*restaurant*) Restaurant
nt mit Straßenverkauf. ~-**off** *n*
(*Aviat*) Start *m*, Abflug *m*. ~-**over** *n*
Übernahme *f*

takings *npl* Einnahmen *pl*

talcum *n* ~ **[powder]** Körperpuder
m

tale *n* Geschichte *f*

talent *n* Talent *nt*

talk *n* Gespräch *nt*; (*lecture*) Vortrag
m ● *vi* reden, sprechen (**to/with** mit)
● *vt* reden; ~ **s.o. into sth** jdn zu etw
überreden. ~ **over** *vt* besprechen

talkative *a* gesprächig

tall *a* (-er, -est) groß; <*building, tree*>
hoch. ~ **story** *n* übertriebene
Geschichte *f*

tally *vi* übereinstimmen

tame *a* (-r, -st), -**ly** *adv* zahm; (*dull*)
lahm 🔢 ● *vt* zähmen. ~**r** *n*
Dompteur *m*

tamper *vi* ~ **with** sich (*dat*) zu
schaffen machen an (+ *dat*)

tampon *n* Tampon *m*

tan *a* gelbbraun ● *n* Gelbbraun *nt*;
(*from sun*) Bräune *f* ● *v* (*pt/pp*
tanned) ● *vt* gerben <*hide*> ● *vi*
braun werden

tang *n* herber Geschmack *m*; (*smell*)
herber Geruch *m*

tangible *a* greifbar

tangle *n* Gewirr *nt*; (*in hair*)
Verfilzung *f* ● *vt* ~ **[up]** verheddern
● *vi* sich verheddern

tank *n* Tank *m*; (*Mil*) Panzer *m*

tanker *n* Tanker *m*; (*lorry*)
Tank[last]wagen *m*

tantrum *n* Wutanfall *m*

tap *n* Hahn *m*; (*knock*) Klopfen *nt*; **on**
~ zur Verfügung ● *v* (*pt/pp* tapped)
● *vt* klopfen an (+ *acc*); anzapfen
<*barrel, tree*>; erschließen
<*resources*>; abhören <*telephone*>
● *vi* klopfen. ~-**dance** *n*

Stepp[tanz] *m* ● *vi* Stepp tanzen, steppen

tape *n* Band *nt*; (*adhesive*) Klebstreifen *m*; (*for recording*) Tonband *nt* ● *vt* mit Klebstreifen zukleben; (*record*) auf Band aufnehmen

tape-measure *n* Bandmaß *nt*

taper *vi* sich verjüngen

tape recorder *n* Tonbandgerät *nt*

tar *n* Teer *m* ● *vt* (*pt/pp* tarred) teeren

target *n* Ziel *nt*; (*board*) [Ziel]scheibe *f*

tarnish *vi* anlaufen

tarpaulin *n* Plane *f*

tart¹ *a* (-er, -est) sauer

tart² *n* ≈ Obstkuchen *m*; (*individual*) Törtchen *nt*; (🗷 *prostitute*) Nutte *f* ● *vt* ~ **oneself up** 🔟 sich auftakeln

tartan *n* Schottenmuster *nt*; (*cloth*) Schottenstoff *m*

task *n* Aufgabe *f*; **take s.o. to** ~ jdm Vorhaltungen machen. ~ **force** *n* Sonderkommando *nt*

tassel *n* Quaste *f*

taste *n* Geschmack *m*; (*sample*) Kostprobe *f* ● *vt* kosten, probieren; schmecken <*flavour*> ● *vi* schmecken (of nach). ~**ful** *a*, -ly *adv* (*fig*) geschmackvoll. ~**less** *a*, -ly *adv* geschmacklos

tasty *a* (-ier, -iest) lecker

tat *see* tit²

tatters *npl* in ~s in Fetzen

tattoo *n* Tätowierung *f* ● *vt* tätowieren

tatty *a* (-ier, -iest) schäbig; <*book*> zerfleddert

taught *see* teach

taunt *n* höhnische Bemerkung *f* ● *vt* verhöhnen

taut *a* straff

tawdry *a* (-ier, -iest) billig und geschmacklos

tax *n* Steuer *f* ● *vt* besteuern; (*fig*) strapazieren. ~**able** *a* steuerpflichtig. ~**ation** *n* Besteuerung *f*

taxi *n* Taxi *nt* ● *vi* (*pt/pp* taxied, *pres p* taxiing) <*aircraft*:> rollen. ~

driver *n* Taxifahrer *m*. ~ **rank** *n* Taxistand *m*

taxpayer *n* Steuerzahler *m*

tea *n* Tee *m*. ~**bag** *n* Teebeutel *m*. ~**break** *n* Teepause *f*

teach *vt/i* (*pt/pp* taught) unterrichten; ~ **s.o. sth** jdm etw beibringen. ~**er** *n* Lehrer(in) *m(f)*. ~**ing** *n* Unterrichten *nt*

tea: ~**cloth** *n* (*for drying*) Geschirrtuch *nt*. ~**cup** *n* Teetasse *f*

teak *n* Teakholz *nt*

team *n* Mannschaft *f*; (*fig*) Team *nt*; (*of animals*) Gespann *nt*

teapot *n* Teekanne *f*

tear¹ *n* Riss *m* ● *v* (*pt* tore, *pp* torn) ● *vt* reißen; (*damage*) zerreißen; ~ **oneself away** sich losreißen ● *vi* [zer]reißen; (*run*) rasen. ~ **up** *vt* zerreißen

tear² *n* Träne *f*. ~**ful** *a* weinend. ~**fully** *adv* unter Tränen. ~**gas** *n* Tränengas *nt*

tease *vt* necken

tea: ~**set** *n* Teeservice *nt*. ~ **shop** *n* Café *nt*. ~**spoon** *n* Teelöffel *m*

teat *n* Zitze *f*; (*on bottle*) Sauger *m*

tea-towel *n* Geschirrtuch *nt*

technical *a* technisch; (*specialized*) fachlich. ~**ity** *n* technisches Detail *nt*; (*Jur*) Formfehler *m*. ~**ly** *adv* technisch; (*strictly*) streng genommen. ~ **term** *n* Fachausdruck *m*

technician *n* Techniker *m*

technique *n* Technik *f*

technological *a*, -ly *adv* technologisch

technology *n* Technik *f*

teddy *n* ~ [bear] Teddybär *m*

tedious *a* langweilig

tedium *n* Langeweile *f*

teenage *a* Teenager-; ~ **boy/girl** Junge *m*/Mädchen *nt* im Teenageralter. ~**r** *n* Teenager *m*

teens *npl* **the** ~ die Teenagerjahre *pl*

teeter *vi* schwanken

teeth *see* tooth

teeth|e *vi* zahnen. **~ing troubles**
npl (*fig*) Anfangsschwierigkeiten *pl*

teetotal *a* abstinent. **~ler** *n*
Abstinenzler *m*

telecommunications *npl*
Fernmeldewesen *nt*

telegram *n* Telegramm *nt*

telegraph pole *n* Telegrafenmast
m

telephone *n* Telefon *nt*; **be on the
~** Telefon haben; (*be telephoning*)
telefonieren ● *vt* anrufen ● *vi*
telefonieren

telephone: ~ booth *n*, **~ box** *n*
Telefonzelle *f*. **~ directory** *n*
Telefonbuch *nt*. **~ number** *n*
Telefonnummer *f*

telephoto *a* **~ lens** Teleobjektiv *nt*

telescop|e *n* Teleskop *nt*, Fernrohr
nt. **~ic** *a* (*collapsible*) ausziehbar

televise *vt* im Fernsehen
übertragen

television *n* Fernsehen *nt*; **watch ~**
fernsehen; **~ [set]** Fernseher *m* ▣

tell *vt/i* (*pt/pp* **told**) sagen (**s.o.** jdm);
(*relate*) erzählen; (*know*) wissen;
(*distinguish*) erkennen; **~ the time**
die Uhr lesen; **time will ~** das wird
man erst sehen; **his age is beginning
to ~** sein Alter macht sich
bemerkbar. **~ off** *vt* ausschimpfen

telly *n* ▣ = **television**

temp *n* ▣ Aushilfssekretärin *f*

temper *n* (*disposition*) Naturell *nt*;
(*mood*) Laune *f*; (*anger*) Wut *f*; **lose
one's ~** wütend werden ● *vt* (*fig*)
mäßigen

temperament *n* Temperament *nt*.
~al *a* temperamentvoll; (*moody*)
launisch

temperate *a* gemäßigt

temperature *n* Temperatur *f*; **have
or run a ~** Fieber haben

temple[1] *n* Tempel *m*

temple[2] *n* (*Anat*) Schläfe *f*

tempo *n* Tempo *nt*

temporary *a*, **-ily** *adv*
vorübergehend; <*measure, building*>
provisorisch

tempt *vt* verleiten; (*Relig*)
versuchen; herausfordern <*fate*>;

(*entice*) [ver]locken; **be ~ed versucht
sein (to zu)**. **~ation** *n* Versuchung
f. **~ing** *a* verlockend

ten *a* zehn

tenaci|ous *a*, **-ly** *adv* hartnäckig.
~ty *n* Hartnäckigkeit *f*

tenant *n* Mieter(in) *m(f)*; (*Comm*)
Pächter(in) *m(f)*

tend *vi* **~ to do sth** dazu neigen, etw
zu tun

tendency *n* Tendenz *f*; (*inclination*)
Neigung *f*

tender *a* zart; (*loving*) zärtlich;
(*painful*) empfindlich. **~ly** *adv*
zärtlich. **~ness** *n* Zartheit *f*;
Zärtlichkeit *f*

tendon *n* Sehne *f*

tenner *n* ▣ Zehnpfundschein *m*

tennis *n* Tennis *nt*. **~-court** *n*
Tennisplatz *m*

tenor *n* Tenor *m*

tense *a* (**-r, -st**) gespannt ● *vt*
anspannen <*muscle*>

tension *n* Spannung *f*

tent *n* Zelt *nt*

tentative *a*, **-ly** *adv* vorläufig;
(*hesitant*) zaghaft

tenterhooks *npl* **be on ~** wie auf
glühenden Kohlen sitzen

tenth *a* zehnte(r,s) ● *n* Zehntel *nt*

tenuous *a* schwach

tepid *a* lauwarm

term *n* Zeitraum *m*; (*Sch*) ≈ Halbjahr
nt; (*Univ*) ≈ Semester *nt*; (*expression*)
Ausdruck *m*; **~s** *pl* (*conditions*)
Bedingungen *pl*; **in the short/long ~**
kurz-/langfristig; **be on good/bad ~s**
gut/nicht gut miteinander
auskommen

terminal *a* End-; (*Med*) unheilbar
● *n* (*Aviat*) Terminal *m*; (*of bus*)
Endstation *f*; (*on battery*) Pol *m*;
(*Computing*) Terminal *nt*

terminat|e *vt* beenden; lösen
<*contract*>; unterbrechen
<*pregnancy*> ● *vi* enden

terminology *n* Terminologie *f*

terminus *n* (*pl* **-ni**) Endstation *f*

terrace *n* Terrasse *f*; (*houses*)
Häuserreihe *f*. **~d house** *n*
Reihenhaus *nt*

terrain n Gelände nt

terrible a, **-bly** adv schrecklich

terrific a 🔢 (*excellent*) sagenhaft; (*huge*) riesig

terri|fy vt (pt/pp **-ied**) Angst machen (+ dat); be ∼**fied** Angst haben. ∼**fying** a Furcht erregend

territorial a Territorial-

territory n Gebiet nt

terror n [panische] Angst f; (*Pol*) Terror m. ∼**ism** n Terrorismus m. ∼**ist** n Terrorist m. ∼**ize** vt terrorisieren

terse a, **-ly** adv kurz, knapp

test n Test m; (*Sch*) Klassenarbeit f; **put to the** ∼ auf die Probe stellen ● vt prüfen; (*examine*) untersuchen (**for** auf + acc)

testament n Testament nt

testify v (pt/pp **-ied**) ● vt beweisen; ∼ **that** bezeugen, dass ● vi aussagen

testimonial n Zeugnis nt

testimony n Aussage f

test-tube n Reagenzglas nt

tether n be at the end of one's ∼ am Ende seiner Kraft sein ● vt anbinden

text n Text m. ∼**book** n Lehrbuch nt

textile a Textil- ● n ∼**s** pl Textilien pl

texture n Beschaffenheit f; (*Tex*) Struktur f

Thai a thailändisch. ∼**land** n Thailand nt

Thames n Themse f

than conj als

thank vt danken (+ dat); ∼ **you** [very much] danke [schön]. ∼**ful** a, **-ly** adv dankbar. ∼**less** a undankbar

thanks npl Dank m; ∼! 🔢 danke! ∼ **to** dank (+ dat or gen)

that

pl **those**

● *adjective*

⸱⸱⸱➤ der (m), die (f), das (nt), die (pl); (*just seen or experienced*) dieser (m), diese (f), dieses (nt), diese (pl). **I'll never forget that day** den Tag werde ich nie vergessen. **I liked that house** dieses Haus hat mir gut gefallen

● *pronoun*

⸱⸱⸱➤ der (m), die (f), das (nt), die (pl). **that is not true** das ist nicht wahr. **who is that in the garden?** wer ist das [da] im Garten? **I'll take that** ich nehme den/die/das. **I don't like those** die mag ich nicht. **is that you?** bist du es? **that is why** deshalb

⸱⸱⸱➤ **like that** so. **don't be like that!** sei doch nicht so! **a man like that** ein solcher Mann; so ein Mann 🔢

⸱⸱⸱➤ (*after prepositions*) da …. **after that** danach. **with that** damit. **apart from that** außerdem

⸱⸱⸱➤ (*relative pronoun*) der (m), die (f), das (nt), die (pl). **the book that I'm reading** das Buch, das ich lese. **the people that you got it from** die Leute, von denen du es bekommen hast. **everyone that I know** jeder, den ich kenne. **that is all that I have** das ist alles, was ich habe

● *adverb*

⸱⸱⸱➤ so. **he's not that stupid** so blöd ist er [auch wieder] nicht. **it wasn't that bad** so schlecht war es auch nicht. **a nail about that long** ein etwa so langer Nagel

⸱⸱⸱➤ (*relative adverb*) der (m), die (f), das (nt), die (pl). **the day that I first met her** der Tag, an dem ich sie zum ersten Mal sah. **at the speed that he was going** bei der Geschwindigkeit, die er hatte

● *conjunction*

⸱⸱⸱➤ dass. **I don't think that he'll come** ich denke nicht, dass er kommt. **we know that you're right** wir wissen, dass du Recht hast. **I'm so tired that I can hardly walk** ich bin so müde, dass ich kaum gehen kann

⸱⸱⸱➤ **so that** (*purpose*) damit; (*result*) sodass. **he came earlier so that they would have more time** er kam früher, damit sie mehr Zeit hatten. **it was late, so that I had to catch the bus** es war spät, sodass ich den Bus nehmen musste

thatch n Strohdach nt. ∼**ed** a strohgedeckt

thaw n Tauwetter nt ● vt/i auftauen; it's ~ing es taut

the def art der/die/das; (pl) die; **play ~ piano/violin** Klavier/Geige spielen ● adv ~ **more** ~ **better** je mehr, desto besser; **all** ~ **better** umso besser

theatre n Theater nt; (Med) Operationssaal m

theatrical a Theater-; (showy) theatralisch

theft n Diebstahl m

their a ihr

theirs poss pron ihre(r), ihrs; **a friend of** ~ ein Freund von ihnen; **those are** ~ die gehören ihnen

them pron (acc) sie; (dat) ihnen

theme n Thema nt

themselves pron selbst; (refl) sich; **by** ~ allein

then adv dann; (at that time in past) damals; **by** ~ bis dahin; **since** ~ seitdem; **before** ~ vorher; **from** ~ **on** von da an; **now and** ~ dann und wann; **there and** ~ auf der Stelle ● a damalig

theology n Theologie f

theoretical a, **-ly** adv theoretisch

theory n Theorie f; **in** ~ theoretisch

therap|ist n Therapeut(in) m(f). **~y** n Therapie f

there adv da; (with movement) dahin, dorthin; **down/up** ~ da unten/oben; ~ **is/are** da ist/sind; (in existence) es gibt ● int ~, ~! nun, nun!

there: ~abouts adv da [in der Nähe]; **or ~abouts** (roughly) ungefähr. **~fore** adv deshalb, also

thermometer n Thermometer nt

Thermos (P) n ~ **[flask]** Thermosflasche (P) f

thermostat n Thermostat m

these see **this**

thesis n (pl **-ses**) Dissertation f; (proposition) These f

they pron sie; ~ **say** (generalizing) man sagt

thick a (**-er**, **-est**), **-ly** adv dick; (dense) dicht; <liquid> dickflüssig; (🔢 stupid) dumm ● adv dick ● n in the ~ of mitten in (+ dat). **~en** vt dicker machen; eindicken <sauce> ● vi dicker werden; <fog:> dichter werden; <plot:> komplizierter werden. **~ness** n Dicke f; (density) Dichte f; (of liquid) Dickflüssigkeit f

thief n (pl **thieves**) Dieb(in) m(f)

thigh n Oberschenkel m

thimble n Fingerhut m

thin a (**thinner**, **thinnest**), **-ly** adv dünn ● adv dünn ● v (pt/pp **thinned**) ● vt verdünnen <liquid> ● vi sich lichten

thing n Ding nt; (subject, affair) Sache f; ~**s** pl (belongings) Sachen pl; **for one** ~ erstens; **just the** ~! genau das Richtige! **how are** ~**s**? wie geht's? **the latest** ~ 🔢 der letzte Schrei

think vt/i (pt/pp **thought**) denken (**about/of** an + acc); (believe) meinen; (consider) nachdenken; (regard as) halten für; **I** ~ **so** ich glaube schon; **what do you** ~ **of it**? was halten Sie davon? ~ **over** vt sich (dat) überlegen. ~ **up** vt sich (dat) ausdenken

third a dritte(r,s) ● n Drittel nt. **~ly** adv drittens. **~-rate** a drittrangig

thirst n Durst m. ~**y** a, **-ily** adv durstig; **be** ~**y** Durst haben

thirteen a dreizehn. ~**th** a dreizehnte(r,s)

thirtieth a dreißigste(r,s)

thirty a dreißig

this a (pl **these**) diese(r,s); (pl) diese; ~ **one** diese(r,s) da; **I'll take** ~ ich nehme diesen/diese/ dieses; ~ **evening/morning** heute Abend/ Morgen; **these days** heutzutage ● pron (pl **these**) das, dies[es]; (pl) die, diese; ~ **and that** dies und das; ~ **or that** dieses oder das da; **like** ~ so; ~ **is Peter** das ist Peter; (Teleph) hier [spricht] Peter; **who is** ~? wer ist das? (Teleph, Amer) wer ist am Apparat?

thistle n Distel f

thorn n Dorn m

thorough a gründlich

thoroughbred n reinrassiges Tier nt; (horse) Rassepferd nt

thorough|ly *adv* gründlich; (*completely*) völlig; (*extremely*) äußerst. **~ness** *n* Gründlichkeit *f*

those *see* **that**

though *conj* obgleich, obwohl; **as ~** als ob ● *adv* 🔲 doch

thought *see* **think** ● *n* Gedanke *m*; (*thinking*) Denken *nt*. **~ful** *a*, **-ly** *adv* nachdenklich; (*considerate*) rücksichtsvoll. **~less** *a*, **-ly** *adv* gedankenlos

thousand *a* one/a **~** [ein]tausend ● *n* Tausend *nt*. **~th** *a* tausendste(r,s) ● *n* Tausendstel *nt*

thrash *vt* verprügeln; (*defeat*) [vernichtend] schlagen

thread *n* Faden *m*; (*of screw*) Gewinde *nt* ● *vt* einfädeln; auffädeln <*beads*>. **~bare** *a* fadenscheinig

threat *n* Drohung *f*; (*danger*) Bedrohung *f*

threaten *vt* drohen (+ *dat*); (*with weapon*) bedrohen; **~ s.o. with sth** jdm etw androhen ● *vi* drohen. **~ing** *a*, **-ly** *adv* drohend; (*ominous*) bedrohlich

three *a* drei. **~fold** *a* & *adv* dreifach

thresh *vt* dreschen

threshold *n* Schwelle *f*

threw *see* **throw**

thrift *n* Sparsamkeit *f*. **~y** *a* sparsam

thrill *n* Erregung *f*; 🔲 Nervenkitzel *m* ● *vt* (*excite*) erregen; **be ~ed with** sich sehr freuen über (+ *acc*). **~er** *n* Thriller *m*. **~ing** *a* erregend

thrive *vi* (*pt* **thrived** *or* **throve**, *pp* **thrived** *or* **thriven**) gedeihen (**on** bei); <*business:*> florieren

throat *n* Hals *m*; **cut s.o.'s ~** jdm die Kehle durchschneiden

throb *n* Pochen *nt* ● *vi* (*pt/pp* **throbbed**) pochen; (*vibrate*) vibrieren

throes *npl* **in the ~ of** (*fig*) mitten in (+ *dat*)

throne *n* Thron *m*

throttle *vt* erdrosseln

through *prep* durch (+ *acc*); (*during*) während (+ *gen*); (*Amer: up to & including*) bis einschließlich ● *adv* durch; **wet ~** durch und durch nass;

read sth ~ etw durchlesen ● *a* <*train*> durchgehend; **be ~** (*finished*) fertig sein; (*Teleph*) durch sein

throughout *prep* **~ the country** im ganzen Land; **~ the night** die Nacht durch ● *adv* ganz; (*time*) die ganze Zeit

throve *see* **thrive**

throw *n* Wurf *m* ● *vt* (*pt* **threw**, *pp* **thrown**) werfen; schütten <*liquid*>; betätigen <*switch*>; abwerfen <*rider*>; (🔲 *disconcert*) aus der Fassung bringen; 🔲 geben <*party*>; **~ sth to s.o.** jdm etw zuwerfen. **~ away** *vt* wegwerfen. **~ out** *vt* hinauswerfen; (**~** *away*) wegwerfen; verwerfen <*plan*>. **~ up** *vt* hochwerfen ● *vi* sich übergeben

throw-away *a* Wegwerf-

thrush *n* Drossel *f*

thrust *n* Stoß *m*; (*Phys*) Schub *m* ● *vt* (*pt/pp* **thrust**) stoßen; (*insert*) stecken

thud *n* dumpfer Schlag *m*

thug *n* Schläger *m*

thumb *n* Daumen *m* ● *vt* **~ a lift** 🔲 per Anhalter fahren. **~tack** *n* (*Amer*) Reißzwecke *f*

thump *n* Schlag *m*; (*noise*) dumpfer Schlag *m* ● *vt* schlagen ● *vi* hämmern; <*heart:*> pochen

thunder *n* Donner *m* ● *vi* donnern. **~clap** *n* Donnerschlag *m*. **~storm** *n* Gewitter *nt*. **~y** *a* gewittrig

Thursday *n* Donnerstag *m*

thus *adv* so

thwart *vt* vereiteln; **~ s.o.** jdm einen Strich durch die Rechnung machen

tick¹ *n* **on~** 🔲 auf Pump

tick² *n* (*sound*) Ticken *nt*; (*mark*) Häkchen *nt*; (🔲 *instant*) Sekunde *f* ● *vi* ticken ● *vt* abhaken. **~ off** *vt* abhaken; 🔲 rüffeln

ticket *n* Karte *f*; (*for bus, train*) Fahrschein *m*; (*Aviat*) Flugschein *m*; (*for lottery*) Los *nt*; (*for article deposited*) Schein *m*; (*label*) Schild *nt*; (*for library*) Lesekarte *f*; (*fine*) Strafzettel *m*. **~ collector** *n*

Fahrkartenkontrolleur *m*. ~ **office** *n* Fahrkartenschalter *m*; (*for entry*) Kasse *f*

tick|le *n* Kitzeln *nt* ● *vt/i* kitzeln. ~**lish** *a* kitzlig

tidal *a* ~ **wave** Flutwelle *f*

tide *n* Gezeiten *pl*; (*of events*) Strom *m*; **the** ~ **is** in/out es ist Flut/Ebbe ● *vt* ~ **s.o. over** jdm über die Runden helfen

tidiness *n* Ordentlichkeit *f*

tidy *a* (-ier, -iest), -**ily** *adv* ordentlich ● *vt* ~ [**up**] aufräumen

tie *n* Krawatte *f*; Schlips *m*; (*cord*) Schnur *f*; (*fig: bond*) Band *nt*; (*restriction*) Bindung *f*; (*Sport*) Unentschieden *nt*; (*in competition*) Punktgleichheit *f* ● *v* (*pres p tying*) ● *vt* binden; machen <*knot*> ● *vi* (*Sport*) unentschieden spielen; (*have equal scores, votes*) punktgleich sein. ~ **up** *vt* festbinden; verschnüren <*parcel*>; fesseln <*person*>; **be** ~**d up** (*busy*) beschäftigt sein

tier *n* Stufe *f*; (*of cake*) Etage *f*; (*in stadium*) Rang *m*

tiger *n* Tiger *m*

tight *a* (-er, -est), -**ly** *adv* fest; (*taut*) straff; <*clothes*> eng; <*control*> streng; (🇬🇧 *drunk*) blau ● *adv* fest

tighten *vt* fester ziehen; straffen <*rope*>; anziehen <*screw*>; verschärfen <*control*> ● *vi* sich spannen

tightrope *n* Hochseil *nt*

tights *npl* Strumpfhose *f*

tile *n* Fliese *f*; (*on wall*) Kachel *f*; (*on roof*) [Dach]ziegel *m* ● *vt* mit Fliesen auslegen; kacheln <*wall*>; decken <*roof*>

till¹ *prep & conj* = **until**

till² *n* Kasse *f*

tilt *n* Neigung *f* ● *vt* kippen; [zur Seite] neigen <*head*> ● *vi* sich neigen

timber *n* [Nutz]holz *nt*

time *n* Zeit *f*; (*occasion*) Mal *nt*; (*rhythm*) Takt *m*; ~**s** (*Math*) mal; **at** ~**s** manchmal; ~ **and again** immer wieder; **two at a** ~ zwei auf einmal; **on** ~ pünktlich; **in** ~ rechtzeitig;

(*eventually*) mit der Zeit; **in no** ~ im Handumdrehen; **in a year's** ~ in einem Jahr; **behind** ~ verspätet; **behind the** ~**s** rückständig; **for the** ~ **being** vorläufig; **what is the** ~? wie spät ist es? wie viel Uhr ist es? **did you have a nice** ~? hat es dir gut gefallen? ● *vt* stoppen <*race*>; **be well** ~**d** gut abgepaßt sein

time: ~ **bomb** *n* Zeitbombe *f*. ~**less** *a* zeitlos. ~**ly** *a* rechtzeitig. ~-**switch** *n* Zeitschalter *m*. ~-**table** *n* Fahrplan *m*; (*Sch*) Stundenplan *m*

timid *a*, -**ly** *adv* scheu; (*hesitant*) zaghaft

timing *n* (*Sport, Techn*) Timing *nt*

tin *n* Zinn *nt*; (*container*) Dose *f* ● *vt* (*pt/pp* **tinned**) in Dosen konservieren. ~ **foil** *n* Stanniol *nt*; (*Culin*) Alufolie *f*

tinge *n* Hauch *m*

tingle *vi* kribbeln

tinker *vi* herumbasteln (**with** *an* + *dat*)

tinkle *n* Klingeln *nt* ● *vi* klingeln

tinned *a* Dosen-

tin opener *n* Dosenöffner *m*

tinsel *n* Lametta *nt*

tint *n* Farbton *m* ● *vt* tönen

tiny *a* (-ier, -iest) winzig

tip¹ *n* Spitze *f*

tip² *n* (*money*) Trinkgeld *nt*; (*advice*) Rat *m*, 🇬🇧 Tipp *m*; (*for rubbish*) Müllhalde *f* ● *v* (*pt/pp* **tipped**) ● *vt* (*tilt*) kippen; (*reward*) Trinkgeld geben (**s.o.** jdm) ● *vi* kippen. ~ **out** *vt* auskippen. ~ **over** *vt/i* umkippen

tipped *a* Filter-

tipsy *a* 🇬🇧 beschwipst

tiptoe *n* **on** ~ auf Zehenspitzen

tiptop *a* 🇬🇧 erstklassig

tire *vt/i* ermüden. ~**d** *a* müde; **be** ~**d of sth** etw satt haben; ~**d out** [völlig] erschöpft. ~**less** *a*, -**ly** *adv* unermüdlich. ~**some** *a* lästig

tiring *a* ermüdend

tissue *n* Gewebe *nt*; (*handkerchief*) Papiertaschentuch *nt*

tit *n* (*bird*) Meise *f*

titbit *n* Leckerbissen *m*

title n Titel m

to
● *preposition*
····▸ *(destinations: most cases)* zu (+ *dat*). **go to work/the station** zur Arbeit/zum Bahnhof gehen. **from house to house** von Haus zu Haus. **go/come to s.o.** zu jdm gehen/ kommen
····▸ *(with name of place or points of compass)* nach. **to Paris/Germany** nach Paris/Deutschland. **to Switzerland** in die Schweiz. **from East to West** von Osten nach Westen. **I've never been to Berlin** ich war noch nie in Berlin
····▸ *(to cinema, theatre, bed)* in (+ *acc*). **to bed with you!** ins Bett mit dir!
····▸ *(to wedding, party, university, the toilet)* auf (+ *acc*).
····▸ *(up to)* bis zu (+ *dat*). **to the end** bis zum Schluss. **to this day** bis heute. **5 to 6 pounds** 5 bis 6 Pfund
····▸ *<give, say, write>* + *dat*. **give/say sth to s.o.** jdm etw geben/sagen. **she wrote to him/the firm** sie hat ihm/an die Firma geschrieben
····▸ *<address, send, fasten>* an (+ *acc*). **she sent it to her brother** sie schickte es an ihren Bruder
····▸ *(in telling the time)* vor. **five to eight** fünf vor acht. **a quarter to ten** Viertel vor zehn
● *before infinitive*
····▸ *(after modal verb) (not translated).* **I want to go** ich will gehen. **he is learning to swim** er lernt schwimmen. **you have to** du musst [es tun]
····▸ *(after adjective)* zu. **it is easy to forget** es ist leicht zu vergessen
····▸ *(expressing purpose, result)* um … zu. **he did it to annoy me** er tat es, um mich zu ärgern. **she was too tired to go** sie war zu müde um zu gehen
● *adverb*
····▸ **be to** *<door, window>* angelehnt sein. **pull a door to** eine Tür anlehnen
····▸ **to and fro** hin und her

toad n Kröte f

toast n Toast m ● vt toasten *<bread>*; *(drink a ~ to)* trinken auf (+ *acc*). **~er** n Toaster m

tobacco n Tabak m. **~nist's [shop]** n Tabakladen m

toboggan n Schlitten m ● vi Schlitten fahren

today n & adv heute; **~ week** heute in einer Woche

toddler n Kleinkind nt

toe n Zeh m; *(of footwear)* Spitze f ● vt **~ the line** spuren. **~nail** n Zehennagel m

toffee n Karamell m & nt

together adv zusammen; *(at the same time)* gleichzeitig

toilet n Toilette f. **~ bag** n Kulturbeutel m. **~ paper** n Toilettenpapier nt

toiletries npl Toilettenartikel pl

token n Zeichen nt; *(counter)* Marke f; *(voucher)* Gutschein m ● attrib symbolisch

told see tell ● a **all ~** insgesamt

tolerable a, **-bly** adv erträglich; *(not bad)* leidlich

toleran|ce n Toleranz f. **~t** a, **-ly** adv tolerant

tolerate vt dulden, tolerieren; *(bear)* ertragen

toll n Gebühr f; *(for road)* Maut f *(Aust)*; **death ~** Zahl f der Todesopfer

tomato n *(pl* **-es**) Tomate f

tomb n Grabmal nt

tombstone n Grabstein m

tom-cat n Kater m

tomorrow n & adv morgen; **~ morning** morgen früh; **the day after ~** übermorgen; **see you ~!** bis morgen!

ton n Tonne f; **~s of** 🔲 jede Menge

tone n Ton m; *(colour)* Farbton m ● vt **~** down dämpfen; *(fig)* mäßigen. **~ up** vt kräftigen; straffen *<muscles>*

tongs npl Zange f

tongue n Zunge f; **~ in cheek** 🔲 nicht ernst

tonic n Tonikum nt; (for hair) Haarwasser nt; (fig) Wohltat f; ~ [water] Tonic nt

tonight n & adv heute Nacht; (evening) heute Abend

tonne n Tonne f

tonsil n (Anat) Mandel f. ~**litis** n Mandelentzündung f

too adv zu; (also) auch; ~ much/little zu viel/zu wenig

took see take

tool n Werkzeug nt; (for gardening) Gerät nt

tooth n (pl teeth) Zahn m

tooth: ~**ache** n Zahnschmerzen pl. ~**brush** n Zahnbürste f. ~**less** a zahnlos. ~**paste** n Zahnpasta f. ~**pick** n Zahnstocher m

top¹ n (toy) Kreisel m

top² n oberer Teil m; (apex) Spitze f; (summit) Gipfel m; (Sch) Erste(r) m/f; (top part or half) Oberteil nt; (head) Kopfende nt; (of road) oberes Ende nt; (upper surface) Oberfläche f; (lid) Deckel m; (of bottle) Verschluss m; (garment) Top m; at the/on ~ oben; on ~ of oben auf (+ dat/acc); on ~ of that (besides) obendrein; from ~ to bottom von oben bis unten ● a oberste(r,s); (highest) höchste(r,s); (best) beste(r,s) ● vt (pt/pp topped) an erster Stelle stehen auf (+ dat) <list>; (exceed) übersteigen; (remove the ~ of) die Spitze abschneiden von. ~ up vt nachfüllen, auffüllen

top: ~ hat n Zylinder[hut] m. ~-heavy a kopflastig

topic n Thema nt. ~al a aktuell

topple vt/i umstürzen

torch n Taschenlampe f; (flaming) Fackel f

tore see tear¹

torment¹ n Qual f

torment² vt quälen

torn see tear¹ ● a zerrissen

torpedo n (pl -es) Torpedo m ● vt torpedieren

torrent n reißender Strom m. ~**ial** a <rain> wolkenbruchartig

tortoise n Schildkröte f. ~**shell** n Schildpatt nt

tortuous a verschlungen; (fig) umständlich

torture n Folter f; (fig) Qual f ● vt foltern; (fig) quälen

toss vt werfen; (into the air) hochwerfen; (shake) schütteln; (unseat) abwerfen; mischen <salad>; wenden <pancake>; ~ a coin mit einer Münze losen ● vi ~ and turn (in bed) sich [schlaflos] im Bett wälzen

tot¹ n kleines Kind nt; (🄙 of liquor) Gläschen nt

tot² vt (pt/pp totted) ~ up 🄙 zusammenzählen

total a gesamt; (complete) völlig, total ● n Gesamtzahl f; (sum) Gesamtsumme f ● vt (pt/pp totalled); (amount to) sich belaufen auf (+ acc)

totalitarian a totalitär

totally adv völlig, total

totter vi taumeln

touch n Berührung f; (sense) Tastsinn m; (Mus) Anschlag m; (contact) Kontakt m; (trace) Spur f; (fig) Anflug m; get/be in ~ sich in Verbindung setzen/in Verbindung stehen (with mit) ● vt berühren; (get hold of) anfassen; (lightly) tippen auf/an (+ acc); (brush against) streifen [gegen]; (fig: move) rühren; anrühren <food, subject>; don't ~ that! fass das nicht an! ● vi sich berühren; ~ on (fig) berühren. ~ down vi (Aviat) landen. ~ up vt ausbessern

touch|ing a rührend. ~y a empfindlich

tough a (-er, -est) zäh; (severe, harsh) hart; (difficult) schwierig; (durable) strapazierfähig

toughen vt härten; ~ up abhärten

tour n Reise f, Tour f; (of building, town) Besichtigung f; (Theat, Sport) Tournee f; (of duty) Dienstzeit f ● vt fahren durch ● vi herumreisen

touris|m n Tourismus m, Fremdenverkehr m. ~t n Tourist(in) m(f) ● attrib Touristen-. ~t office n Fremdenverkehrsbüro nt

tournament n Turnier nt

tour operator *n* Reiseveranstalter *m*

tousle *vt* zerzausen

tow *n* give s.o./a car a ~ jdn/ein Auto abschleppen ● *vt* schleppen; ziehen *<trailer>*

toward[s] *prep* zu (+ *dat*); (*with time*) gegen (+ *acc*); (*with respect to*) gegenüber (+ *dat*)

towel *n* Handtuch *nt*. ~**ling** *n* (*Tex*) Frottee *nt*

tower *n* Turm *m* ● *vi* ~ **above** überragen. ~ **block** *n* Hochhaus *nt*. ~**ing** *a* hoch aufragend

town *n* Stadt *f.* ~ **hall** *n* Rathaus *nt*

tow-rope *n* Abschleppseil *nt*

toxic *a* giftig

toy *n* Spielzeug *nt* ● *vi* ~ **with** spielen mit; stochern in (+ *dat*) *<food>*. ~**shop** *n* Spielwarengeschäft *nt*

trace *n* Spur *f* ● *vt* folgen (+ *dat*); (*find*) finden; (*draw*) zeichnen; (*with tracing-paper*) durchpausen

track *n* Spur *f*; (*path*) [unbefestigter] Weg *m*; (*Sport*) Bahn *f*; (*Rail*) Gleis *nt*; **keep** ~ **of** im Auge behalten ● *vt* verfolgen. ~ **down** *vt* aufspüren; (*find*) finden

tracksuit *n* Trainingsanzug *m*

tractor *n* Traktor *m*

trade *n* Handel *m*; (*line of business*) Gewerbe *nt*; (*business*) Geschäft *nt*; (*craft*) Handwerk *nt*; **by** ~ von Beruf ● *vt* tauschen; ~ **in** (*give in part exchange*) in Zahlung geben ● *vi* handeln (**in** mit)

trade mark *n* Warenzeichen *nt*

trader *n* Händler *m*

trade: ~ **union** *n* Gewerkschaft *f.* ~ **unionist** *n* Gewerkschaftler(in) *m(f)*

trading *n* Handel *m*

tradition *n* Tradition *f.* ~**al** *a*, **-ly** *adv* traditionell

traffic *n* Verkehr *m*; (*trading*) Handel *m*

traffic: ~ **circle** *n* (*Amer*) Kreisverkehr *m.* ~ **jam** *n* [Verkehrs]stau *m.* ~ **lights** *npl* [Verkehrs]ampel *f.* ~ **warden** *n* ≈ Hilfspolizist *m*; (*woman*) Politesse *f*

tragedy *n* Tragödie *f*

tragic *a*, **-ally** *adv* tragisch

trail *n* Spur *f*; (*path*) Weg *m*, Pfad *m* ● *vi* schleifen; *<plant:>* sich ranken ● *vt* verfolgen, folgen (+ *dat*); (*drag*) schleifen

trailer *n* (*Auto*) Anhänger *m*; (*Amer: caravan*) Wohnwagen *m*; (*film*) Vorschau *f*

train *n* Zug *m*; (*of dress*) Schleppe *f* ● *vt* ausbilden; (*Sport*) trainieren; (*aim*) richten auf (+ *acc*); erziehen *<child>*; abrichten/(*to do tricks*) dressieren *<animal>*; ziehen *<plant>* ● *vi* eine Ausbildung machen; (*Sport*) trainieren. ~**ed** *a* ausgebildet

trainee *n* Auszubildende(r) *m/f*; (*Techn*) Praktikant(in) *m(f)*

train|er *n* (*Sport*) Trainer *m*; (*in circus*) Dompteur *m*; ~**ers** *pl* Trainingsschuhe *pl.* ~**ing** *n* Ausbildung *f*; (*Sport*) Training *nt*; (*of animals*) Dressur *f*

trait *n* Eigenschaft *f*

traitor *n* Verräter *m*

tram *n* Straßenbahn *f*

tramp *n* Landstreicher *m* ● *vi* stapfen; (*walk*) marschieren

trample *vt/i* trampeln

trance *n* Trance *f*

tranquil *a* ruhig. ~**lity** *n* Ruhe *f*

tranquillizer *n* Beruhigungsmittel *nt*

transaction *n* Transaktion *f*

transcend *vt* übersteigen

transfer¹ *n* (*see* **transfer²**) Übertragung *f*; Verlegung *f*; Versetzung *f*; Überweisung *f*; (*Sport*) Transfer *m*; (*design*) Abziehbild *nt*

transfer² *v* (*pt/pp* **transferred**) ● *vt* übertragen; verlegen *<firm, prisoners>*; versetzen *<employee>*; überweisen *<money>*; (*Sport*) transferieren ● *vi* [über]wechseln; (*when travelling*) umsteigen

transform *vt* verwandeln. ~**ation** *n* Verwandlung *f.* ~**er** *n* Transformator *m*

transfusion *n* Transfusion *f*

transistor *n* Transistor *m*

transit n Transit m; (of goods) Transport m; **in** ~ <goods> auf dem Transport

transition n Übergang m. ~**al** a Übergangs-

translat|e vt übersetzen. ~**ion** n Übersetzung f. ~**or** n Übersetzer(in) m(f)

transmission n Übertragung f

transmit vt (pt/pp **transmitted**) übertragen. ~**ter** n Sender m

transparen|cy n (Phot) Dia nt. ~**t** a durchsichtig

transplant[1] n Verpflanzung f, Transplantation f

transplant[2] vt umpflanzen; (Med) verpflanzen

transport[1] n Transport m

transport[2] vt transportieren. ~**ation** n Transport m

transpose vt umstellen

trap n Falle f; (🔲 mouth) Klappe f; **pony and** ~ Einspänner m ● vt (pt/pp **trapped**) [mit einer Falle] fangen; (jam) einklemmen; **be** ~**ped** festsitzen; (shut in) eingeschlossen sein. ~**door** n Falltür f

trash n Schund m; (rubbish) Abfall m; (nonsense) Quatsch m. ~**can** n (Amer) Mülleimer m. ~**y** a Schund-

trauma n Trauma nt. ~**tic** a traumatisch

travel n Reisen nt ● v (pt/pp **travelled**) ● vi reisen; (go in vehicle) fahren; <light, sound:> sich fortpflanzen; (Techn) sich bewegen ● vt bereisen; fahren <distance>. ~ **agency** n Reisebüro nt. ~ **agent** n Reisebürokaufmann m

traveller n Reisende(r) m/f; (Comm) Vertreter m; ~**s** pl (gypsies) Zigeuner pl. ~**'s cheque** n Reisescheck m

trawler n Fischdampfer m

tray n Tablett nt; (for baking) [Back]blech nt; (for documents) Ablagekorb m

treacher|ous a treulos; (dangerous, deceptive) tückisch. ~**y** n Verrat m

tread n Schritt m; (step) Stufe f; (of tyre) Profil nt ● v (pt **trod**, pp **trodden**) ● vi (walk) gehen; ~ **on/in** treten auf/ in (+ acc) ● vt treten

treason n Verrat m

treasure n Schatz m ● vt in Ehren halten. ~**r** n Kassenwart m

treasury n Schatzkammer f; **the T**~ das Finanzministerium

treat n [besonderes] Vergnügen nt ● vt behandeln; ~ **s.o. to sth** jdm etw spendieren

treatment n Behandlung f

treaty n Vertrag m

treble a dreifach; ~ **the amount** dreimal so viel ● n (Mus) Diskant m; (voice) Sopran m ● vt verdreifachen ● vi sich verdreifachen

tree n Baum m

trek n Marsch m ● vi (pt/pp **trekked**) latschen

trellis n Gitter nt

tremble vi zittern

tremendous a, **-ly** adv gewaltig; (🔲 excellent) großartig

tremor n Zittern nt; [earth] ~ Beben nt

trench n Graben m; (Mil) Schützengraben m

trend n Tendenz f; (fashion) Trend m. ~**y** a (**-ier, -iest**) 🔲 modisch

trepidation n Beklommenheit f

trespass vi ~ **on** unerlaubt betreten

trial n (Jur) [Gerichts]verfahren nt, Prozess m; (test) Probe f; (ordeal) Prüfung f; **be on** ~ auf Probe sein; (Jur) angeklagt sein (**for** wegen); **by** ~ **and error** durch Probieren

triang|le n Dreieck nt; (Mus) Triangel m. ~**ular** a dreieckig

tribe n Stamm m

tribunal n Schiedsgericht nt

tributary n Nebenfluss m

tribute n Tribut m; **pay** ~ Tribut zollen (**to** dat)

trick n Trick m; (joke) Streich m; (Cards) Stich m; (feat of skill) Kunststück nt ● vt täuschen, 🔲 hereinlegen

trickle vi rinnen

trick|ster n Schwindler m. ~**y** a
(-ier, -iest) a schwierig

tricycle n Dreirad nt

tried see try

trifl|e n Kleinigkeit f; (Culin) Trifle
nt. ~**ing** a unbedeutend

trigger n Abzug m; (fig) Auslöser m
● vt ~ [**off**] auslösen

trim a (trimmer, trimmest) gepflegt
● n (cut) Nachschneiden nt;
(decoration) Verzierung f; (condition)
Zustand m ● vt schneiden; (decorate)
besetzen. ~**ming** n Besatz m;
~**mings** pl (accessories) Zubehör nt;
(decorations) Verzierungen pl

trio n Trio nt

trip n Reise f; (excursion) Ausflug m
● v (pt/pp tripped) ● vt ~ s.o. up
jdm ein Bein stellen ● vi stolpern
(on/over über + acc)

tripe n Kaldaunen pl; (nonsense)
Quatsch m

triple a dreifach ● vt verdreifachen
● vi sich verdreifachen

triplets npl Drillinge pl

triplicate n in ~ in dreifacher
Ausfertigung

tripod n Stativ nt

tripper n Ausflügler m

trite a banal

triumph n Triumph m ● vi
triumphieren (over über + acc).
~**ant** a, -**ly** adv triumphierend

trivial a belanglos. ~**ity** n
Belanglosigkeit f

trod, trodden see tread

trolley n (for food) Servierwagen m;
(for shopping) Einkaufswagen m; (for
luggage) Kofferkuli m; (Amer: tram)
Straßenbahn f

trombone n Posaune f

troop n Schar f; ~**s** pl Truppen pl

trophy n Trophäe f; (in competition)
≈ Pokal m

tropic|s npl Tropen pl. ~**al** a
tropisch; <fruit> Süd-

trot n Trab m ● vi (pt/pp trotted)
traben

trouble n Ärger m; (difficulties)
Schwierigkeiten pl; (inconvenience)
Mühe f, (conflict) Unruhe f; (Med)
Beschwerden pl; (Techn) Probleme
pl; **get into** ~ Ärger bekommen; **take**
~ sich (dat) Mühe geben ● vt
(disturb) stören; (worry)
beunruhigen ● vi sich bemühen. ~-
maker n Unruhestifter m. ~**some**
a schwierig; <flies, cough> lästig

trough n Trog m

troupe n Truppe f

trousers npl Hose f

trousseau n Aussteuer f

trout n inv Forelle f

trowel n Kelle f

truant n play ~ die Schule
schwänzen

truce n Waffenstillstand m

truck n Last[kraft]wagen m; (Rail)
Güterwagen m

trudge vi latschen

true a (-r, -st) wahr; (loyal) treu;
(genuine) echt; **come** ~ in Erfüllung
gehen; **is that** ~? stimmt das?

truly adv wirklich; (faithfully) treu;
Yours ~ mit freundlichen Grüßen

trump n (Cards) Trumpf m ● vt
übertrumpfen

trumpet n Trompete f. ~**er** n
Trompeter m

truncheon n Schlagstock m

trunk n [Baum]stamm m; (body)
Rumpf m; (of elephant) Rüssel m; (for
travelling) [Übersee]koffer m; (Amer:
of car) Kofferraum m; ~**s** pl
Badehose f

trust n Vertrauen nt; (group of
companies) Trust m; (organization)
Treuhandgesellschaft f; (charitable)
Stiftung f ● vt trauen (+ dat),
vertrauen (+ dat); (hope) hoffen ● vi
vertrauen (in/to auf + acc)

trustee n Treuhänder m

trust|ful a, -**ly** adv, ~**ing** a
vertrauensvoll. ~**worthy** a
vertrauenswürdig

truth n (pl -s) Wahrheit f. ~**ful** a,
-**ly** adv ehrlich

try n Versuch m ● v (pt/pp tried) ● vt
versuchen; (sample, taste) probieren;

(*be a strain on*) anstrengen; (*Jur*) vor Gericht stellen; verhandeln <*case*> ● *vi* versuchen; (*make an effort*) sich bemühen. ~ **on** *vt* anprobieren; aufprobieren <*hat*>. ~ **out** *vt* ausprobieren

trying *a* schwierig

T-shirt *n* T-Shirt *nt*

tub *n* Kübel *m*; (*carton*) Becher *m*; (*bath*) Wanne *f*

tuba *n* (*Mus*) Tuba *f*

tubby *a* (-ier, -iest) rundlich

tube *n* Röhre *f*; (*pipe*) Rohr *nt*; (*flexible*) Schlauch *m*; (*of toothpaste*) Tube *f*; (*Rail* 🔟) U-Bahn *f*

tuberculosis *n* Tuberkulose *f*

tubular *a* röhrenförmig

tuck *n* Saum *m*; (*decorative*) Biese *f* ● *vt* (*put*) stecken. ~ **in** *vt* hineinstecken; ~ **s.o. in** *or* **up** jdn zudecken ● *vi* (🔟 *eat*) zulangen

Tuesday *n* Dienstag *m*

tuft *n* Büschel *nt*

tug *n* Ruck *m*; (*Naut*) Schleppdampfer *m* ● *v* (*pt/pp* tugged) ● *vt* ziehen ● *vi* zerren (**at** *an* + *dat*)

tuition *n* Unterricht *m*

tulip *n* Tulpe *f*

tumble *n* Sturz *m* ● *vi* fallen. ~**down** *a* verfallen. ~**-drier** *n* Wäschetrockner *m*

tumbler *n* Glas *nt*

tummy *n* 🔟 Bauch *m*

tumour *n* Tumor *m*

tumult *n* Tumult *m*

tuna *n* Thunfisch *m*

tune *n* Melodie *f*; out of ~ <*instrument*> verstimmt ● *vt* stimmen; (*Techn*) einstellen. ~ **in** *vt* einstellen; ● *vi* ~ **in to a station** einen Sender einstellen. ~ **up** *vi* (*Mus*) stimmen

tuneful *a* melodisch

Tunisia *n* Tunesien *nt*

tunnel *n* Tunnel *m* ● *vi* (*pt/pp* tunnelled) einen Tunnel graben

turban *n* Turban *m*

turbine *n* Turbine *f*

turbulen|ce *n* Turbulenz *f*. ~**t** *a* stürmisch

turf *n* Rasen *m*; (*segment*) Rasenstück *nt*

Turk *n* Türke *m*/Türkin *f*

turkey *n* Truthahn *m*

Turk|ey *n* die Türkei. ~**ish** *a* türkisch; **the** ~**ish** die Türken

turmoil *n* Aufruhr *m*; (*confusion*) Durcheinander *nt*

turn *n* (*rotation*) Drehung *f*; (*bend*) Kurve *f*; (*change of direction*) Wende *f*; (*Theat*) Nummer *f*; (🔟 *attack*) Anfall *m*; **do s.o. a good** ~ jdm einen guten Dienst erweisen; **take** ~**s** sich abwechseln; **in** ~ der Reihe nach; **out of** ~ außer der Reihe; **it's your** ~ du bist an der Reihe ● *vt* drehen; (~ *over*) wenden; (*reverse*) umdrehen; (*Techn*) drechseln <*wood*>; ~ **the page** umblättern; ~ **the corner** um die Ecke biegen ● *vi* sich drehen; (~ *round*) sich umdrehen; <*car*:> wenden; <*leaves*:> sich färben; <*weather*:> werden; (*become*) werden; ~ **right/left** nach rechts/links abbiegen; ~ **to s.o.** sich an jdn wenden. ~ **away** *vt* abweisen ● *vi* sich abwenden. ~ **down** *vt* herunterschlagen <*collar*>; herunterdrehen <*heat, gas*>; leiser stellen <*sound*>; (*reject*) ablehnen; abweisen <*person*>. ~ **in** *vt* einschlagen <*edges*> ● *vi* <*car*:> einbiegen; (🔟 *go to bed*) ins Bett gehen. ~ **off** *vt* zudrehen <*tap*>; ausschalten <*light, radio*>; abstellen <*water, gas, engine, machine*> ● *vi* abbiegen. ~ **on** *vt* aufdrehen <*tap*>; einschalten <*light, radio*>; anstellen <*water, gas, engine, machine*>. ~ **out** *vt* (*expel*) vertreiben, 🔟 hinauswerfen; ausschalten <*light*>; abdrehen <*gas*>; (*produce*) produzieren; (*empty*) ausleeren; [gründlich] aufräumen <*room, cupboard*> ● *vi* (*go out*) hinausgehen; (*transpire*) sich herausstellen. ~ **over** *vt* umdrehen. ~ **up** *vt* hochschlagen <*collar*>; aufdrehen <*heat, gas*>; lauter stellen <*sound, radio*> ● *vi* auftauchen

turning *n* Abzweigung *f*. ~**-point** *n* Wendepunkt *m*

turnip *n* weiße Rübe *f*

turn: ~**out** *n* (*of people*) Beteiligung *f*. ~**over** *n* (*Comm*) Umsatz *m*; (*of staff*) Personalwechsel *m*. ~**pike** *n* (*Amer*) gebührenpflichtige Autobahn *f*. ~**table** *n* Drehscheibe *f*; (*on record player*) Plattenteller *m*. ~**up** *n* [Hosen]aufschlag *m*

turquoise *a* türkis[farben] ● *n* (*gem*) Türkis *m*

turret *n* Türmchen *nt*

turtle *n* Seeschildkröte *f*

tusk *n* Stoßzahn *m*

tutor *n* [Privat]lehrer *m*

tuxedo *n* (*Amer*) Smoking *m*

TV *abbr of* **television**

tweed *n* Tweed *m*

tweezers *npl* Pinzette *f*

twelfth *a* zwölfter(r,s)

twelve *a* zwölf

twentieth *a* zwanzigste(r,s)

twenty *a* zwanzig

twice *adv* zweimal

twig *n* Zweig *m*

twilight *n* Dämmerlicht *nt*

twin *n* Zwilling *m* ● *attrib* Zwillings-

twine *n* Bindfaden *m*

twinge *n* Stechen *nt*; ~ **of conscience** Gewissensbisse *pl*

twinkle *n* Funkeln *nt* ● *vi* funkeln

twin town *n* Partnerstadt *f*

twirl *vt/i* herumwirbeln

twist *n* Drehung *f*; (*curve*) Kurve *f*; (*unexpected occurrence*) überraschende Wendung *f* ● *vt* drehen; (*distort*) verdrehen; (🇬🇧 *swindle*) beschummeln; ~ **one's ankle** sich (*dat*) den Knöchel verrenken ● *vi* sich drehen; <*road:*> sich winden. ~**er** *n* 🇬🇧 Schwindler *m*

twit *n* 🇬🇧 Trottel *m*

twitch *n* Zucken *nt* ● *vi* zucken

twitter *n* Zwitschern *nt* ● *vi* zwitschern

two *a* zwei

two: ~**faced** *a* falsch. ~**piece** *a* zweiteilig. ~**way** *a* ~**way traffic** Gegenverkehr *m*

tycoon *n* Magnat *m*

tying *see* **tie**

type *n* Art *f*, Sorte *f*; (*person*) Typ *m*; (*printing*) Type *f* ● *vt* mit der Maschine schreiben, 🇬🇧 tippen ● *vi* Maschine schreiben, 🇬🇧 tippen. ~**writer** *n* Schreibmaschine *f*. ~**written** *a* maschinegeschrieben

typical *a*, **-ly** *adv* typisch (**of** für)

typify *vt* (*pt/pp* **-ied**) typisch sein für

typing *n* Maschineschreiben *nt*

typist *n* Schreibkraft *f*

tyrannical *a* tyrannisch

tyranny *n* Tyrannei *f*

tyrant *n* Tyrann *m*

tyre *n* Reifen *m*

Uu

ugl|iness *n* Hässlichkeit *f*. ~**y** *a* (**-ier, -iest**) hässlich; (*nasty*) übel

UK *abbr see* **United Kingdom**

ulcer *n* Geschwür *nt*

ultimate *a* letzte(r,s); (*final*) endgültig; (*fundamental*) grundlegend, eigentlich. ~**ly** *adv* schließlich

ultimatum *n* Ultimatum *nt*

ultraviolet *a* ultraviolett

umbrella *n* [Regen]schirm *m*

umpire *n* Schiedsrichter *m* ● *vt/i* Schiedsrichter sein (bei)

umpteen *a* 🇬🇧 zig. ~**th** *a* 🇬🇧 zigste(r,s)

unable *a* **be** ~ **to do sth** etw nicht tun können

unabridged *a* ungekürzt

unaccompanied *a* ohne Begleitung; <*luggage*> unbegleitet

unaccountable *a* unerklärlich

unaccustomed *a* ungewohnt; **be** ~ **to sth** etw (*acc*) nicht gewohnt sein

unaided *a* ohne fremde Hilfe

unanimous *a*, **-ly** *adv* einmütig; <*vote, decision*> einstimmig

unarmed *a* unbewaffnet

unassuming *a* bescheiden

unattended *a* unbeaufsichtigt

unauthorized *a* unbefugt

unavoidable *a* unvermeidlich

unaware *a* be ~ of sth sich (*dat*) etw (*gen*) nicht bewusst sein. ~s *adv* catch s.o. ~s jdn überraschen

unbearable *a*, **-bly** *adv* unerträglich

unbeat|able *a* unschlagbar. ~en *a* ungeschlagen; <*record*> ungebrochen

unbelievable *a* unglaublich

unbiased *a* unvoreingenommen

unblock *vt* frei machen

unbolt *vt* aufriegeln

unbreakable *a* unzerbrechlich

unbutton *vt* aufknöpfen

uncalled-for *a* unangebracht

uncanny *a* unheimlich

unceasing *a* unaufhörlich

uncertain *a* (*doubtful*) ungewiss; <*origins*> unbestimmt; be ~ nicht sicher sein. ~ty *n* Ungewissheit *f*

unchanged *a* unverändert

uncharitable *a* lieblos

uncle *n* Onkel *m*

uncomfortable *a*, **-bly** *adv* unbequem; feel ~ (*fig*) sich nicht wohl fühlen

uncommon *a* ungewöhnlich

uncompromising *a* kompromisslos

unconditional *a*, ~ly *adv* bedingungslos

unconscious *a* bewusstlos; (*unintended*) unbewusst; be ~ of sth sich (*dat*) etw (*gen*) nicht bewusst sein. ~ly *adv* unbewusst

unconventional *a* unkonventionell

uncooperative *a* nicht hilfsbereit

uncork *vt* entkorken

uncouth *a* ungehobelt

uncover *vt* aufdecken

undecided *a* unentschlossen; (*not settled*) nicht entschieden

undeniable *a*, **-bly** *adv* unbestreitbar

under *prep* unter (+ *dat/acc*); ~ it darunter; ~ there da drunter; ~ repair in Reparatur; ~ construction im Bau; ~ age minderjährig ● *adv* darunter

undercarriage *n* (*Aviat*) Fahrwerk *nt*, Fahrgestell *nt*

underclothes *npl* Unterwäsche *f*

undercover *a* geheim

undercurrent *n* Unterströmung *f*; (*fig*) Unterton *m*

underdog *n* Unterlegene(r) *m*

underdone *a* nicht gar; (*rare*) nicht durchgebraten

underestimate *vt* unterschätzen

underfed *a* unterernährt

underfoot *adv* am Boden

undergo *vt* (*pt* -went, *pp* -gone) durchmachen; sich unterziehen (+ *dat*) <*operation, treatment*>

undergraduate *n* Student(in) *m(f)*

underground[1] *adv* unter der Erde; <*mining*> unter Tage

underground[2] *a* unterirdisch; (*secret*) Untergrund- ● *n* (*railway*) U-Bahn *f*. ~ car park *n* Tiefgarage *f*

undergrowth *n* Unterholz *nt*

underhand *a* hinterhältig

underlie *vt* (*pt* -lay, *pp* -lain, *pres p* -lying) zugrunde liegen (+ *dat*)

underline *vt* unterstreichen

underlying *a* eigentlich

undermine *vt* (*fig*) unterminieren, untergraben

underneath *prep* unter (+ *dat/acc*) ● *adv* darunter

underpants *npl* Unterhose *f*

underpass *n* Unterführung *f*

underprivileged *a* unterprivilegiert

underrate *vt* unterschätzen

undershirt *n* (*Amer*) Unterhemd *nt*

understand *vt/i* (*pt/pp* -stood) verstehen; I ~ that ... (*have heard*) ich habe gehört, dass ... ~able *a* verständlich. ~ably *adv* verständlicherweise

understanding *a* verständnisvoll ● *n* Verständnis *nt*; (*agreement*)

Vereinbarung *f*; **reach an ~** sich
verständigen

understatement *n* Untertreibung
f

undertake *vt* (*pt* **-took**, *pp* **-taken**)
unternehmen; **~ to do sth** sich
verpflichten, etw zu tun

undertaker *n* Leichenbestatter *m*;
[firm of] ~s Bestattungsinstitut *n*

undertaking *n* Unternehmen *nt*;
(*promise*) Versprechen *nt*

undertone *n* (*fig*) Unterton *m*; **in an
~** mit gedämpfter Stimme

undervalue *vt* unterbewerten

underwater[1] *a* Unterwasser-

underwater[2] *adv* unter Wasser

underwear *n* Unterwäsche *f*

underweight *a* untergewichtig; **be
~** Untergewicht haben

underworld *n* Unterwelt *f*

undesirable *a* unerwünscht

undignified *a* würdelos

undo *vt* (*pt* **-did**, *pp* **-done**)
aufmachen; (*fig*) ungeschehen
machen

undone *a* offen; (*not accomplished*)
unerledigt

undoubted *a* unzweifelhaft. **~ly**
adv zweifellos

undress *vt* ausziehen; **get ~ed** sich
ausziehen ● *vi* sich ausziehen

undue *a* übermäßig

unduly *adv* übermäßig

unearth *vt* ausgraben; (*fig*) zutage
bringen. **~ly** *a* unheimlich; **at an
~ly hour** 🄸 in aller Herrgottsfrühe

uneasy *a* unbehaglich

uneconomic *a*, **-ally** *adv*
unwirtschaftlich

unemployed *a* arbeitslos ● *npl* **the
~** die Arbeitslosen

unemployment *n* Arbeitslosigkeit
f

unending *a* endlos

unequal *a* unterschiedlich;
<*struggle*> ungleich. **~ly** *adv*
ungleichmäßig

unequivocal *a*, **-ly** *adv* eindeutig

unethical *a* unmoralisch; **be ~**
gegen das Berufsethos verstoßen

uneven *a* uneben; (*unequal*)
ungleich; (*not regular*)
ungleichmäßig; <*number*> ungerade

unexpected *a*, **-ly** *adv* unerwartet

unfair *a*, **-ly** *adv* ungerecht, unfair.
~ness *n* Ungerechtigkeit *f*

unfaithful *a* untreu

unfamiliar *a* ungewohnt;
(*unknown*) unbekannt

unfasten *vt* aufmachen; (*detach*)
losmachen

unfavourable *a* ungünstig

unfeeling *a* gefühllos

unfit *a* ungeeignet; (*incompetent*)
unfähig; (*Sport*) nicht fit; **~ for work**
arbeitsunfähig

unfold *vt* auseinander falten,
entfalten; (*spread out*) ausbreiten
● *vi* sich entfalten

unforeseen *a* unvorhergesehen

unforgettable *a* unvergesslich

unforgivable *a* unverzeihlich

unfortunate *a* unglücklich;
(*unfavourable*) ungünstig;
(*regrettable*) bedauerlich; **be ~**
<*person*:> Pech haben. **~ly** *adv*
leider

unfounded *a* unbegründet

unfurl *vt* entrollen

unfurnished *a* unmöbliert

ungainly *a* unbeholfen

ungrateful *a*, **-ly** *adv* undankbar

unhappiness *n* Kummer *m*

unhappy *a* unglücklich; (*not
content*) unzufrieden

unharmed *a* unverletzt

unhealthy *a* ungesund

unhurt *a* unverletzt

unification *n* Einigung *f*

uniform *a*, **-ly** *adv* einheitlich ● *n*
Uniform *f*

unify *vt* (*pt/pp* **-ied**) einigen

unilateral *a*, **-ly** *adv* einseitig

unimaginable *a* unvorstellbar

unimportant *a* unwichtig

uninhabited *a* unbewohnt

unintentional *a*, **-ly** *adv*
unabsichtlich

union *n* Vereinigung *f*; (*Pol*) Union *f*;
(*trade ~*) Gewerkschaft *f*

unique *a* einzigartig. **~ly** *adv* einmalig

unison *n* in ~ einstimmig

unit *n* Einheit *f*; (*Math*) Einer *m*; (*of furniture*) Teil *nt*, Element *nt*

unite *vt* vereinigen ● *vi* sich vereinigen

united *a* einig. **U~ Kingdom** *n* Vereinigtes Königreich *nt*. **U~ Nations** *n* Vereinte Nationen *pl*. **U~ States [of America]** *n* Vereinigte Staaten *pl* [von Amerika]

unity *n* Einheit *f*; (*harmony*) Einigkeit *f*

universal *a*, **-ly** *adv* allgemein

universe *n* [Welt]all *nt*, Universum *nt*

university *n* Universität *f* ● *attrib* Universitäts-

unjust *a*, **-ly** *adv* ungerecht

unkind *a*, **-ly** *adv* unfreundlich; (*harsh*) hässlich

unknown *a* unbekannt

unlawful *a*, **-ly** *adv* gesetzwidrig

unleaded *a* bleifrei

unleash *vt* (*fig*) entfesseln

unless *conj* wenn … nicht; ~ **I am mistaken** wenn ich mich nicht irre

unlike *prep* im Gegensatz zu (+ *dat*)

unlikely *a* unwahrscheinlich

unlimited *a* unbegrenzt

unload *vt* entladen; ausladen <*luggage*>

unlock *vt* aufschließen

unlucky *a* unglücklich; <*day, number*> Unglücks-; **be** ~ Pech haben; <*thing*:> Unglück bringen

unmarried *a* unverheiratet. ~ **mother** *n* ledige Mutter *f*

unmask *vt* (*fig*) entlarven

unmistakable *a*, **-bly** *adv* unverkennbar

unnatural *a*, **-ly** *adv* unnatürlich; (*not normal*) nicht normal

unnecessary *a*, **-ily** *adv* unnötig

unnoticed *a* unbemerkt

unobtainable *a* nicht erhältlich

unobtrusive *a*, **-ly** *adv* unaufdringlich; <*thing*> unauffällig

unofficial *a*, **-ly** *adv* inoffiziell

unpack *vt/i* auspacken

unpaid *a* unbezahlt

unpleasant *a*, **-ly** *adv* unangenehm

unplug *vt* (*pt/pp* **-plugged**) den Stecker herausziehen von

unpopular *a* unbeliebt

unprecedented *a* beispiellos

unpredictable *a* unberechenbar

unprepared *a* nicht vorbereitet

unpretentious *a* bescheiden

unprofitable *a* unrentabel

unqualified *a* unqualifiziert; (*fig: absolute*) uneingeschränkt

unquestionable *a* unbezweifelbar; <*right*> unbestreitbar

unravel *vt* (*pt/pp* **-ravelled**) entwirren; (*Knitting*) aufziehen

unreal *a* unwirklich

unreasonable *a* unvernünftig

unrelated *a* unzusammenhängend; **be** ~ nicht verwandt sein; <*events*:> nicht miteinander zusammenhängen

unreliable *a* unzuverlässig

unrest *n* Unruhen *pl*

unrivalled *a* unübertroffen

unroll *vt* aufrollen ● *vi* sich aufrollen

unruly *a* ungebärdig

unsafe *a* nicht sicher

unsatisfactory *a* unbefriedigend

unsavoury *a* unangenehm; (*fig*) unerfreulich

unscathed *a* unversehrt

unscrew *vt* abschrauben

unscrupulous *a* skrupellos

unseemly *a* unschicklich

unselfish *a* selbstlos

unsettled *a* ungeklärt; <*weather*> unbeständig; <*bill*> unbezahlt

unshakeable *a* unerschütterlich

unshaven *a* unrasiert

unsightly *a* unansehnlich

unskilled *a* ungelernt; <*work*> unqualifiziert

unsociable *a* ungesellig

unsophisticated *a* einfach

unsound *a* krank, nicht gesund; <*building*> nicht sicher; <*advice*>

unzuverlässig; <*reasoning*> nicht stichhaltig

unstable *a* nicht stabil; (*mentally*) labil

unsteady *a*, **-ily** *adv* unsicher; (*wobbly*) wackelig

unstuck *a* come ~ sich lösen; (🔲 *fail*) scheitern

unsuccessful *a*, **-ly** *adv* erfolglos; be ~ keinen Erfolg haben

unsuitable *a* ungeeignet; (*inappropriate*) unpassend; (*for weather, activity*) unzweckmäßig

unthinkable *a* unvorstellbar

untidiness *n* Unordentlichkeit *f*

untidy *a*, **-ily** *adv* unordentlich

untie *vt* aufbinden; losbinden <*person, boat, horse*>

until *prep* bis (+ *acc*); not ~ erst; ~ the evening bis zum Abend ● *conj* bis; not ~ erst wenn; (*in past*) erst als

untold *a* unermesslich

untrue *a* unwahr; that's ~ das ist nicht wahr

unused¹ *a* unbenutzt; (*not utilized*) ungenutzt

unused² *a* be ~ to sth etw nicht gewohnt sein

unusual *a*, **-ly** *adv* ungewöhnlich

unveil *vt* enthüllen

unwanted *a* unerwünscht

unwelcome *a* unwillkommen

unwell *a* be *or* feel ~ sich nicht wohl fühlen

unwieldy *a* sperrig

unwilling *a*, **-ly** *adv* widerwillig; be ~ to do sth etw nicht tun wollen

unwind *v* (*pt/pp* unwound) ● *vt* abwickeln ● *vi* sich abwickeln; (🔲 *relax*) sich entspannen

unwise *a*, **-ly** *adv* unklug

unworthy *a* unwürdig

unwrap *vt* (*pt/pp* -wrapped) auswickeln; auspacken <*present*>

unwritten *a* ungeschrieben

up *adv* oben; (*with movement*) nach oben; (*not in bed*) auf; <*road*> aufgerissen; <*price*> gestiegen; be up for sale zu verkaufen sein; up there

da oben; up to (*as far as*) bis; time's up die Zeit ist um; what's up? 🔲 was ist los? what's he up to? 🔲 was hat er vor? I don't feel up to it ich fühle mich dem nicht gewachsen; go up hinaufgehen; come up heraufkommen ● *prep* be up on sth [oben] auf etw (*dat*) sein; up the mountain oben am Berg; (*movement*) den Berg hinauf; be up the tree oben im Baum sein; up the road die Straße entlang; up the river stromaufwärts; go up the stairs die Treppe hinaufgehen

upbringing *n* Erziehung *f*

update *vt* auf den neuesten Stand bringen

upgrade *vt* aufstufen

upheaval *n* Unruhe *f*; (*Pol*) Umbruch *m*

uphill *a* (*fig*) mühsam ● *adv* bergauf

uphold *vt* (*pt/pp* upheld) unterstützen; bestätigen <*verdict*>

upholster *vt* polstern. ~y *n* Polsterung *f*

upkeep *n* Unterhalt *m*

upmarket *a* anspruchsvoll

upon *prep* auf (+ *dat/acc*)

upper *a* obere(r,s) <*deck, jaw, lip*> Ober-; have the ~ hand die Oberhand haben ● *n* (*of shoe*) Obermaterial *nt*

upper class *n* Oberschicht *f*

upright *a* aufrecht

uprising *n* Aufstand *m*

uproar *n* Aufruhr *m*

upset¹ *vt* (*pt/pp* upset, *pres p* upsetting) umstoßen; (*spill*) verschütten; durcheinander bringen <*plan*>; (*distress*) erschüttern; <*food:*> nicht bekommen (+ *dat*); get ~ about sth sich über etw (*acc*) aufregen

upset² *n* Aufregung *f*; have a stomach ~ einen verdorbenen Magen haben

upshot *n* Ergebnis *nt*

upside down *adv* verkehrt herum; turn ~ umdrehen

upstairs¹ *adv* oben; <*go*> nach oben

upstairs² *a* im Obergeschoss

upstart n Emporkömmling m

upstream adv stromaufwärts

uptake n slow on the ~ schwer von Begriff; be quick on the ~ schnell begreifen

upturn n Aufschwung m

upward a nach oben; <*movement*> Aufwärts-; ~ **slope** Steigung f ● adv ~[s] aufwärts, nach oben

uranium n Uran nt

urban a städtisch

urge n Trieb m, Drang m ● vt drängen; ~ **on** antreiben

urgen|cy n Dringlichkeit f. ~**t** a, -**ly** adv dringend

urine n Urin m, Harn m

us pron uns; **it's us** wir sind es

US[A] abbr USA pl

usable a brauchbar

usage n Brauch m; (of word) [Sprach]gebrauch m

use[1] n (see use[2]) Benutzung f; Verwendung f; Gebrauch m; **be [of] no ~** nichts nützen; **it is no ~** es hat keinen Zweck; **what's the ~?** wozu?

use[2] vt benutzen <*implement, room, lift*>; verwenden <*ingredient, method, book, money*>; gebrauchen <*words, force, brains*>; ~ **[up]** aufbrauchen

used[1] a gebraucht; <*towel*> benutzt; <*car*> Gebraucht-

used[2] pt **be ~ to sth** an etw (acc) gewöhnt sein; **get ~ to** sich gewöhnen an (+ acc); **he ~ to say** er hat immer gesagt; **he ~ to live here** er hat früher hier gewohnt

useful a nützlich. ~**ness** n Nützlichkeit f

useless a nutzlos; (not usable) unbrauchbar; (pointless) zwecklos

user n Benutzer(in) m(f)

usher n Platzanweiser m; (in court) Gerichtsdiener m

usherette n Platzanweiserin f

USSR abbr (History) UdSSR f

usual a üblich. ~**ly** adv gewöhnlich

utensil n Gerät nt

utility a Gebrauchs-

utilize vt nutzen

utmost a äußerste(r,s), größte(r,s) ● n **do one's ~** sein Möglichstes tun

utter[1] a, -**ly** adv völlig

utter[2] vt von sich geben <*sigh, sound*>; sagen <*word*>

U-turn n (fig) Kehrtwendung f; 'no ~s' (Auto) 'Wenden verboten'

Vv

vacan|cy n (job) freie Stelle f; (room) freies Zimmer nt; 'no ~**cies**' 'belegt'. ~**t** a frei; <*look*> [gedanken]leer

vacate vt räumen

vacation n (Univ & Amer) Ferien pl

vaccinat|e vt impfen. ~**ion** n Impfung f

vaccine n Impfstoff m

vacuum n Vakuum nt, luftleerer Raum m ● vt saugen. ~ **cleaner** n Staubsauger m

vagina n (Anat) Scheide f

vague a (-r, -st), -**ly** adv vage; <*outline*> verschwommen

vain a (-er, -est) eitel; <*hope, attempt*> vergeblich; **in** ~ vergeblich. ~**ly** adv vergeblich

valiant a, -**ly** adv tapfer

valid a gültig; <*claim*> berechtigt; <*argument*> stichhaltig; <*reason*> triftig. ~**ity** n Gültigkeit f

valley n Tal nt

valour n Tapferkeit f

valuable a wertvoll. ~**s** npl Wertsachen pl

valuation n Schätzung f

value n Wert m; (usefulness) Nutzen m ● vt schätzen. ~ **added tax** n Mehrwertsteuer f

valve n Ventil nt; (Anat) Klappe f; (Electr) Röhre f

van n Lieferwagen m

vandal n Rowdy m. ~**ism** n mutwillige Zerstörung f. ~**ize** vt demolieren

vanilla n Vanille f

vanish vi verschwinden

vanity n Eitelkeit f

vapour n Dampf m

variable a unbeständig; (Math) variabel; (adjustable) regulierbar

variant n Variante f

variation n Variation f; (difference) Unterschied m

varied a vielseitig; <diet:> abwechslungsreich

variety n Abwechslung f; (quantity) Vielfalt f; (Comm) Auswahl f; (type) Art f; (Bot) Abart f; (Theat) Varieté nt

various a verschieden. ~**ly** adv unterschiedlich

varnish n Lack m ● vt lackieren

vary v (pt/pp -ied) ● vi sich ändern; (be different) verschieden sein ● vt [ver]ändern; (add variety to) abwechslungsreicher gestalten

vase n Vase f

vast a riesig; <expanse> weit. ~**ly** adv gewaltig

vat n Bottich m

VAT abbr (value added tax) Mehrwertsteuer f, MwSt.

vault¹ n (roof) Gewölbe nt; (in bank) Tresor m; (tomb) Gruft f

vault² n Sprung m ● vt/i ~ [over] springen über (+ acc)

VDU abbr (visual display unit) Bildschirmgerät nt

veal n Kalbfleisch nt ● attrib Kalbs-

veer vi sich drehen; (Auto) ausscheren

vegetable n Gemüse nt; ~**s** pl Gemüse nt ● attrib Gemüse-; <oil, fat> Pflanzen-

vegetarian a vegetarisch ● n Vegetarier(in) m(f)

vegetation n Vegetation f

vehement a, -**ly** adv heftig

vehicle n Fahrzeug nt

veil n Schleier m ● vt verschleiern

vein n Ader f; (mood) Stimmung f; (manner) Art f

velocity n Geschwindigkeit f

velvet n Samt m

vending-machine n [Verkaufs]automat m

vendor n Verkäufer(in) m(f)

veneer n Furnier nt; (fig) Tünche f. ~**ed** a furniert

venerable a ehrwürdig

Venetian a venezianisch. **v**~**blind** n Jalousie f

vengeance n Rache f; with a ~ gewaltig

Venice n Venedig nt

venison n (Culin) Reh(fleisch) nt

venom n Gift nt; (fig) Hass m. ~**ous** a giftig

vent n Öffnung f

ventilat|e vt belüften. ~**ion** n Belüftung f; (installation) Lüftung f. ~**or** n Lüftungsvorrichtung f; (Med) Beatmungsgerät nt

ventriloquist n Bauchredner m

venture n Unternehmung f ● vt wagen ● vi sich wagen

venue n (for event) Veranstaltungsort m

veranda n Veranda f

verb n Verb nt. ~**al** a, -**ly** adv mündlich; (Gram) verbal

verbose a weitschweifig

verdict n Urteil nt

verge n Rand m ● vi ~ on (fig) grenzen an (+ acc)

verify vt (pt/pp -ied) überprüfen; (confirm) bestätigen

vermin n Ungeziefer nt

vermouth n Wermut m

versatil|e a vielseitig. ~**ity** n Vielseitigkeit f

verse n Strophe f; (of Bible) Vers m; (poetry) Lyrik f

version n Version f; (translation) Übersetzung f; (model) Modell nt

versus prep gegen (+ acc)

vertical a, -**ly** adv senkrecht ● n Senkrechte f

vertigo n (Med) Schwindel m

verve n Schwung m

very *adv* sehr; ~ **much** sehr; (*quantity*) sehr viel; ~ **probably** höchstwahrscheinlich; **at the** ~ **most** allerhöchstens ● *a* (*mere*) bloß; **the** ~ **first** der/die/das allererste; **the** ~ **thing** genau das Richtige; **at the** ~ **end/beginning** ganz am Ende/Anfang; **only a** ~ **little** nur ein ganz kleines bisschen

vessel *n* Schiff *nt*; (*receptacle & Anat*) Gefäß *nt*

vest *n* [Unter]hemd *nt*; (*Amer: waistcoat*) Weste *f*

vestige *n* Spur *f*

vestry *n* Sakristei *f*

vet *n* Tierarzt *m* /-ärztin *f* ● *vt* (*pt/pp* **vetted**) überprüfen

veteran *n* Veteran *m*

veterinary *a* tierärztlich. ~ **surgeon** *n* Tierarzt *m* /-ärztin *f*

veto *n* (*pl* **-es**) Veto *nt*

VHF *abbr* (**very high frequency**) UKW

via *prep* über (+ *acc*)

viable *a* lebensfähig; (*fig*) realisierbar; <*firm*> rentabel

viaduct *n* Viadukt *nt*

vibrat|e *vi* vibrieren. ~**ion** *n* Vibrieren *nt*

vicar *n* Pfarrer *m*. ~**age** *n* Pfarrhaus *nt*

vice[1] *n* Laster *nt*

vice[2] *n* (*Techn*) Schraubstock *m*

vice[3] *a* Vize-; ~ **chairman** stellvertretender Vorsitzender *m*

vice versa *adv* umgekehrt

vicinity *n* Umgebung *f*; **in the** ~ **of** in der Nähe von

vicious *a*, **-ly** *adv* boshaft; <*animal*> bösartig

victim *n* Opfer *nt*. ~**ize** *vt* schikanieren

victor *n* Sieger *m*

victor|ious *a* siegreich. ~**y** *n* Sieg *m*

video *n* Video *nt*; (*recorder*) Videorecorder *m* ● *attrib* Video-

video: ~ **cassette** *n* Videokassette *f*. ~ **game** *n* Videospiel *nt*. ~ **recorder** *n* Videorecorder *m*

Vienn|a *n* Wien *nt*. ~**ese** *a* Wiener

view *n* Sicht *f*; (*scene*) Aussicht *f*, Blick *m*; (*picture, opinion*) Ansicht *f*; **in my** ~ **meiner** Ansicht nach; **in** ~ **of** angesichts (+ *gen*); **be on** ~ besichtigt werden können ● *vt* sich (*dat*) ansehen; besichtigen <*house*>; (*consider*) betrachten ● *vi* (*TV*) fernsehen. ~**er** *n* (*TV*) Zuschauer(in) *m(f)*

view: ~**finder** *n* (*Phot*) Sucher *m*. ~**point** *n* Standpunkt *m*

vigilan|ce *n* Wachsamkeit *f*. ~**t** *a*, **-ly** *adv* wachsam

vigorous *a*, **-ly** *adv* kräftig; (*fig*) heftig

vigour *n* Kraft *f*; (*fig*) Heftigkeit *f*

vile *a* abscheulich

villa *n* (*for holidays*) Ferienhaus *nt*

village *n* Dorf *nt*. ~**r** *n* Dorfbewohner(in) *m(f)*

villain *n* Schurke *m*; (*in story*) Bösewicht *m*

vindicat|e *vt* rechtfertigen. ~**ion** *n* Rechtfertigung *f*

vindictive *a* nachtragend

vine *n* Weinrebe *f*

vinegar *n* Essig *m*

vineyard *n* Weinberg *m*

vintage *a* erlesen ● *n* (*year*) Jahrgang *m*. ~ **car** *n* Oldtimer *m*

viola *n* (*Mus*) Bratsche *f*

violat|e *vt* verletzen; (*break*) brechen; (*disturb*) stören; (*defile*) schänden. ~**ion** *n* Verletzung *f*; Schändung *f*

violen|ce *n* Gewalt *f*; (*fig*) Heftigkeit *f*. ~**t** *a* gewalttätig; (*fig*) heftig. ~**tly** *adv* brutal; (*fig*) heftig

violet *a* violett ● *n* (*flower*) Veilchen *nt*

violin *n* Geige *f*, Violine *f*. ~**ist** *n* Geiger(in) *m(f)*

VIP *abbr* (**very important person**) Prominente(r) *m/f*

viper *n* Kreuzotter *f*

virgin *a* unberührt ● *n* Jungfrau *f*. ~**ity** *n* Unschuld *f*

viril|e *a* männlich. ~**ity** *n* Männlichkeit *f*

virtual *a* a ~ ... praktisch ein ... ~**ly** *adv* praktisch

virtu|e n Tugend f; (advantage) Vorteil m; **by** or **in ~e of** auf Grund (+ gen)

virtuoso n (pl -si) Virtuose m

virtuous a tugendhaft

virus n Virus nt

visa n Visum nt

visibility n Sichtbarkeit f; (Meteorol) Sichtweite f

visible a, -bly adv sichtbar

vision n Vision f; (sight) Sehkraft f; (foresight) Weitblick m

visit n Besuch m ● vt besuchen; besichtigen <town, building>. ~**or** n Besucher(in) m(f); (in hotel) Gast m; **have ~ors** Besuch haben

visor n Schirm m; (Auto) [Sonnen]blende f

vista n Aussicht f

visual a, -ly adv visuell. ~ **display unit** n Bildschirmgerät nt

visualize vt sich (dat) vorstellen

vital a unbedingt notwendig; (essential to life) lebenswichtig. ~**ity** n Vitalität f. ~**ly** adv äußerst

vitamin n Vitamin nt

vivaci|ous a, -ly adv lebhaft. ~**ty** n Lebhaftigkeit f

vivid a, -ly adv lebhaft; <description> lebendig

vocabulary n Wortschatz m; (list) Vokabelverzeichnis nt; **learn ~** Vokabeln lernen

vocal a, -ly adv stimmlich; (vociferous) lautstark

vocalist n Sänger(in) m(f)

vocation n Berufung f. ~**al** a Berufs-

vociferous a lautstark

vodka n Wodka m

vogue n Mode f

voice n Stimme f ● vt zum Ausdruck bringen

void a leer; (not valid) ungültig; ~ **of** ohne ● n Leere f

volatile a flüchtig; <person> sprunghaft

volcanic a vulkanisch

volcano n Vulkan m

volley n (of gunfire) Salve f; (Tennis) Volley m

volt n Volt nt. ~**age** n (Electr) Spannung f

voluble a, -bly adv redselig; <protest> wortreich

volume n (book) Band m; (Geom) Rauminhalt m; (amount) Ausmaß nt; (Radio, TV) Lautstärke f

voluntary a, -ily adv freiwillig

volunteer n Freiwillige(r) m/f ● vt anbieten; geben <information> ● vi sich freiwillig melden

vomit n Erbrochene(s) nt ● vt erbrechen ● vi sich übergeben

voracious a gefräßig; <appetite> unbändig

vot|e n Stimme f; (ballot) Abstimmung f; (right) Wahlrecht nt ● vi abstimmen; (in election) wählen. ~**er** n Wähler(in) m(f)

vouch vi ~ **for** sich verbürgen für. ~**er** n Gutschein m

vowel n Vokal m

voyage n Seereise f; (in space) Reise f, Flug m

vulgar a vulgär, ordinär. ~**ity** n Vulgarität f

vulnerable a verwundbar

vulture n Geier m

Ww

wad n Bausch m; (bundle) Bündel nt. ~**ding** n Wattierung f

waddle vi watscheln

wade vi waten

wafer n Waffel f

waffle¹ vi 🄵 schwafeln

waffle² n (Culin) Waffel f

waft vt/i wehen

wag v (pt/pp wagged) ● vt wedeln mit ● vi wedeln

wage n, & ~**s** pl Lohn m

wager n Wette f

wagon n Wagen m; (Rail) Waggon m

wail n [klagender] Schrei m ● vi heulen; (lament) klagen

waist n Taille f. **~coat** n Weste f. **~line** n Taille f

wait n Wartezeit f; lie in ~ for auflauern (+ dat) ● vi warten (for auf + acc); (at table) servieren; ~ on bedienen ● vt ~ one's turn warten, bis man an der Reihe ist

waiter n Kellner m; ~! Herr Ober!

waiting: **~-list** n Warteliste f. **~-room** n Warteraum m; (doctor's) Wartezimmer nt

waitress n Kellnerin f

waive vt verzichten auf (+ acc)

wake¹ n Totenwache f ● v (pt woke, pp woken) ~ [up] ● vt [auf]wecken ● vi aufwachen

wake² n (Naut) Kielwasser nt; in the ~ of im Gefolge (+ gen)

Wales n Wales nt

walk n Spaziergang m; (gait) Gang m; (path) Weg m; go for a ~ spazieren gehen ● vi gehen; (not ride) laufen, zu Fuß gehen; (ramble) wandern; **learn to ~** laufen lernen ● vt ausführen <dog>. **~ out** vi hinausgehen; <workers:> in den Streik treten; ~ **out on s.o.** jdn verlassen

walker n Spaziergänger(in) m(f); (rambler) Wanderer m/Wanderin f

walking n Gehen nt; (rambling) Wandern nt. **~-stick** n Spazierstock m

wall n Wand f; (external) Mauer f; **drive s.o. up the ~** 🔲 jdn auf die Palme bringen ● vt ~ **up** zumauern

wallet n Brieftasche f

wallflower n Goldlack m

wallop vt (pt/pp walloped) 🔲 schlagen

wallow vi sich wälzen; (fig) schwelgen

wallpaper n Tapete f ● vt tapezieren

walnut n Walnuss f

waltz n Walzer m ● vi Walzer tanzen

wander vi umherwandern, 🔲 bummeln; (fig: digress) abschweifen. ~ **about** vi umherwandern

wangle vt 🔲 organisieren

want n Mangel m (of an + dat); (hardship) Not f; (desire) Bedürfnis nt ● vt wollen; (need) brauchen; ~ **[to have] sth** etw haben wollen; ~ **to do sth** etw tun wollen; **I ~ you to go** ich will, dass du gehst; **it ~s painting** es müsste gestrichen werden ● vi **he doesn't ~ for anything** ihm fehlt es an nichts. **~ed** a <criminal> gesucht

war n Krieg m; **be at ~** sich im Krieg befinden

ward n [Kranken]saal m; (unit) Station f; (of town) Wahlbezirk m; (child) Mündel nt ● vt ~ **off** abwehren

warden n (of hostel) Heimleiter(in) m(f); (of youth hostel) Herbergsvater m; (supervisor) Aufseher(in) m(f)

warder n Wärter(in) m(f)

wardrobe n Kleiderschrank m; (clothes) Garderobe f

warehouse n Lager nt; (building) Lagerhaus nt

wares npl Waren pl

war: **~fare** n Krieg m. **~like** a kriegerisch

warm a (-er, -est), **-ly** adv warm; <welcome> herzlich; **I am ~** mir ist warm ● vt wärmen. ~ **up** vt aufwärmen ● vi warm werden; (Sport) sich aufwärmen. **~-hearted** a warmherzig

warmth n Wärme f

warn vt warnen (of vor + dat). **~ing** n Warnung f; (advance notice) Vorwarnung f; (caution) Verwarnung f

warp vt verbiegen ● vi sich verziehen

warrant n (for arrest) Haftbefehl m; (for search) Durchsuchungsbefehl m ● vt (justify) rechtfertigen; (guarantee) garantieren

warranty n Garantie f

warrior n Krieger m

warship n Kriegsschiff nt

wart n Warze f

wartime n Kriegszeit f

wary a (-ier, -iest), **-ily** adv vorsichtig; (suspicious) misstrauisch

was see be

wash n Wäsche f; (Naut) Wellen pl; have a ∼ sich waschen ● vt waschen; spülen <dishes>; aufwischen <floor>; ∼ one's hands sich (dat) die Hände waschen ● vi sich waschen. ∼ out vt auswaschen; ausspülen <mouth>. ∼ up vt/i abwaschen, spülen ● vi (Amer) sich waschen

washable a waschbar

wash-basin n Waschbecken nt

washer n (Techn) Dichtungsring m; (machine) Waschmaschine f

washing n Wäsche f. ∼-machine n Waschmaschine f. ∼-powder n Waschpulver nt. ∼-up n Abwasch m; do the ∼-up abwaschen, spülen. ∼-up liquid n Spülmittel nt

wasp n Wespe f

waste n Verschwendung f; (rubbish) Abfall m; ∼s pl Öde f ● a <product> Abfall- ● vt verschwenden ● vi ∼ away immer mehr abmagern

waste: ∼ful a verschwenderisch. ∼ land n Ödland nt. ∼ paper n Altpapier nt. ∼-paper basket n Papierkorb m

watch n Wache f; (timepiece) [Armband]uhr f ● vt beobachten; sich (dat) ansehen <film, match>; (keep an eye on) achten auf (+ acc); ∼ television fernsehen ● vi zusehen. ∼ out vi Ausschau halten (for nach); (be careful) aufpassen

watch: ∼-dog n Wachhund m. ∼ful a, -ly adv wachsam. ∼man n Wachmann m

water n Wasser nt; ∼s pl Gewässer nt ● vt gießen <garden, plant>; (dilute) verdünnen ● vi <eyes:> tränen; my mouth was ∼ing mir lief das Wasser im Munde zusammen. ∼ down vt verwässern

water: ∼-colour n Wasserfarbe f; (painting) Aquarell nt. ∼cress n Brunnenkresse f. ∼fall n Wasserfall m

watering-can n Gießkanne f

water: ∼-lily n Seerose f. ∼ logged a be ∼logged <ground:> unter Wasser stehen. ∼ polo n Wasserball m. ∼proof a wasserdicht. ∼-skiing n Wasserskilaufen nt. ∼tight a wasserdicht. ∼way n Wasserstraße f

watery a wässrig

watt n Watt nt

wave n Welle f; (gesture) Handbewegung f; (as greeting) Winken nt ● vt winken mit; (brandish) schwingen; wellen <hair>; ∼ one's hand winken ● vi winken (to dat); <flag:> wehen. ∼length n Wellenlänge f

waver vi schwanken

wavy a wellig

wax n Wachs nt; (in ear) Schmalz nt ● vt wachsen. ∼works n Wachsfigurenkabinett nt

way n Weg m; (direction) Richtung f; (respect) Hinsicht f; (manner) Art f; (method) Art und Weise f; ∼s pl Gewohnheiten pl; on the ∼ auf dem Weg (to nach/zu); (under way) unterwegs; a little/long ∼ ein kleines/ganzes Stück; a long ∼ off weit weg; this ∼ hierher; (like this) so; which ∼ in welche Richtung; (how) wie; by the ∼ übrigens; in some ∼s in gewisser Hinsicht; either ∼ so oder so; in this ∼ auf diese Weise; in a ∼ in gewisser Weise; lead the ∼ vorausgehen; make ∼ Platz machen (for dat); 'give ∼' (Auto) 'Vorfahrt beachten'; go out of one's ∼ (fig) sich (dat) besondere Mühe geben (to zu); get one's [own] ∼ seinen Willen durchsetzen ● adv weit; ∼ behind weit zurück. ∼ in n Eingang m

way out n Ausgang m; (fig) Ausweg m

WC abbr WC nt

we pron wir

weak a (-er, -est), **-ly** adv schwach; <liquid> dünn. ∼en vt schwächen ● vi schwächer werden. ∼ling n

Schwächling *m*. **~ness** *n* Schwäche
f

wealth *n* Reichtum *m*; (*fig*) Fülle *f*
(of an + *dat*.). **~y** *a* (-ier, -iest) reich

weapon *n* Waffe *f*

wear *n* (*clothing*) Kleidung *f*; *~* and
tear Abnutzung *f*, Verschleiß *m* ● *v*
(*pt* wore, *pp* worn) ● *vt* tragen;
(*damage*) abnutzen; **what shall I ~?**
was soll ich anziehen? ● *vi* sich
abnutzen; (*last*) halten. **~ off** *vi*
abgehen; <*effect:*> nachlassen. **~
out** *vt* abnutzen; (*exhaust*)
erschöpfen ● *vi* sich abnutzen

weary *a* (-ier, -iest), **-ily** *adv* müde

weather *n* Wetter *nt*; **in this ~** bei
diesem Wetter; **under the ~** 🔲 nicht
ganz auf dem Posten ● *vt* abwettern
<*storm*>; (*fig*) überstehen

weather: ~-beaten *a* verwittert;
wettergegerbt <*face*>. **~ forecast** *n*
Wettervorhersage *f*

weave[1] *vi* (*pt/pp* weaved) sich
schlängeln (**through** durch)

weave[2] *n* (*Tex*) Bindung *f* ● *vt* (*pt*
wove, *pp* woven) weben. **~r** *n* Weber
m

web *n* Netz *nt*. **~site** *n* Website *f*

wed *vt/i* (*pt/pp* wedded) heiraten.
~ding *n* Hochzeit *f*

wedding: ~ day *n* Hochzeitstag *m*.
~ dress *n* Hochzeitskleid *nt*. **~
ring** *n* Ehering *m*, Trauring *m*

wedge *n* Keil *m* ● *vt* festklemmen

Wednesday *n* Mittwoch *m*

wee *a* 🔲 klein ● *vi* Pipi machen

weed *n* & **~s** *pl* Unkraut *nt* ● *vt/i*
jäten. **~ out** *vt* (*fig*) aussieben

weedkiller *n*
Unkrautvertilgungsmittel *nt*

weedy *a* 🔲 spillerig

week *n* Woche *f*. **~day** *n*
Wochentag *m*. **~end** *n* Wochenende
nt

weekly *a* & *adv* wöchentlich ● *n*
Wochenzeitschrift *f*

weep *vi* (*pt/pp* wept) weinen

weigh *vt/i* wiegen. **~ down** *vt* (*fig*)
niederdrücken. **~ up** *vt* (*fig*)
abwägen

weight *n* Gewicht *nt*; **put on/lose ~**
zunehmen/abnehmen

weight-lifting *n* Gewichtheben *nt*

weighty *a* (-ier, -iest) schwer;
(*important*) gewichtig

weir *n* Wehr *nt*.

weird *a* (-er, -est) unheimlich;
(*bizarre*) bizarr

welcome *a* willkommen; **you're ~!**
nichts zu danken! **you're ~ to (have)
it** das können Sie gerne haben ● *n*
Willkommen *nt* ● *vt* begrüßen

weld *vt* schweißen. **~er** *n*
Schweißer *m*

welfare *n* Wohl *nt*; (*Admin*)
Fürsorge *f*. **W ~ State** *n*
Wohlfahrtsstaat *m*

well[1] *n* Brunnen *m*; (*oil* ~) Quelle *f*

well[2] *adv* (better, best) gut; **as ~**
auch; **as ~ as** (*in addition*) sowohl
... als auch; **~ done!** gut gemacht!
● *a* gesund; **he is not ~** es geht ihm
nicht gut; **get ~ soon!** gute
Besserung! ● *int* nun, na

well: ~-behaved *a* artig. **~-being**
n Wohl *nt*

wellingtons *npl* Gummistiefel *pl*

well: ~-known *a* bekannt. **~-off** *a*
wohlhabend; **be ~-off** gut dransein.
~-to-do *a* wohlhabend

Welsh *a* walisisch ● *n* (*Lang*)
Walisisch *nt*; **the ~** *pl* die Waliser.
~man *n* Waliser *m*

went *see* go

wept *see* weep

were *see* be

west *n* Westen *m*; **to the ~ of**
westlich von ● *a* West-, west- ● *adv*
nach Westen. **~erly** *a* westlich.
~ern *a* westlich ● *n* Western *m*

West: ~ Germany *n*
Westdeutschland *nt*. **~ Indian** *a*
westindisch ● *n* Westinder(in) *m(f)*.
~ Indies *npl* Westindische Inseln
pl

westward[s] *adv* nach Westen

wet *a* (wetter, wettest) nass; <🔲
person> weichlich, lasch; **'~ paint'**
'frisch gestrichen' ● *vt* (*pt/pp* wet or
wetted) nass machen

whack *vt* 🔊 schlagen. **~ed** *a* 🔊 kaputt

whale *n* Wal *m*

wharf *n* Kai *m*

what
● *pronoun*
····▶ (*in questions*) was. **what is it?** was ist das? **what do you want?** was wollen Sie? **what is your name?** wie heißen Sie? **what?** (🔊 *say that again*) wie?; was? **what is the time?** wie spät ist es? (*indirect*) **I didn't know what to do** ich wusste nicht, was ich machen sollte

❗ The equivalent of a preposition with **what** in English is a special word in German beginning with *wo-* (*wor-* before a vowel): **for what? what for?** = wofür? wozu? **from what?** wovon? **on what?** worauf? worüber? **under what?** worunter? **with what?** womit? etc. **what do you want the money for?** wozu willst du das Geld? **what is he talking about?** wovon redet er?

····▶ (*relative pronoun*) was. **do what I tell you** tu, was ich dir sage. **give me what you can** gib mir, so viel du kannst. **what little I know** das bisschen, das ich weiß. **I don't agree with what you are saying** ich stimme dem nicht zu, was Sie sagen

····▶ (*in phrases*) **what about me?** was ist mit mir? **what about a cup of coffee?** wie wäre es mit einer Tasse Kaffee? **what if she doesn't come?** was ist, wenn sie nicht kommt? **what of it?** was ist dabei?

● *adjective*
····▶ (*asking for selection*) welcher (*m*), welche (*f*), welches (*nt*), welche (*pl*). **what book do you want?** welches Buch willst du haben? **what colour are the walls?** welche Farbe haben die Wände? **I asked him what train to take** ich habe ihn gefragt, welchen Zug ich nehmen soll

····▶ (*asking how much/many*) **what money does he have?** wie viel Geld hat er? **what time is it?** wie spät ist

es? **what time does it start?** um wie viel Uhr fängt es an?

····▶ **what kind of ...?** was für [ein(e)]? **what kind of man is he?** was für ein Mensch ist er?

····▶ (*in exclamations*) was für (+ *nom*). **what a fool you are!** was für ein Dummkopf du doch bist! **what cheek/luck!** was für eine Frechheit/ein Glück! **what a huge house!** was für ein riesiges Haus! **what a lot of people!** was für viele Leute!

whatever *a* [egal] welche(r,s) ● *pron* was ... auch; **~ is it?** was ist das bloß? **~ he does** was er auch tut; **nothing ~** überhaupt nichts

whatsoever *pron & a* ≈ **whatever**

wheat *n* Weizen *m*

wheel *n* Rad *nt*; (*pottery*) Töpferscheibe *f*; (*steering* **~**) Lenkrad *nt*; **at the ~** am Steuer ● *vt* (*push*) schieben ● *vi* kehrtmachen; (*circle*) kreisen

wheel: ~barrow *n* Schubkarre *f*. **~chair** *n* Rollstuhl *m*. **~clamp** *n* Parkkralle *f*

when *adv* wann; **the day ~** der Tag, an dem ● *conj* wenn; (*in the past*) als; (*although*) wo ... doch; **~ swimming/reading** beim Schwimmen/Lesen

whenever *conj & adv* [immer] wenn; (*at whatever time*) wann immer; **~ did it happen?** wann ist das bloß passiert?

where *adv & conj* wo; **~ [to]** wohin; **~ [from]** woher

whereabouts¹ *adv* wo

whereabouts² *n* Verbleib *m*; (*of person*) Aufenthaltsort *m*

whereas *conj* während; (*in contrast*) wohingegen

whereupon *adv* worauf[hin]

wherever *conj & adv* wo immer; (*to whatever place*) wohin immer; (*from whatever place*) woher immer; (*everywhere*) überall wo; **~ possible** wenn irgend möglich

whether *conj* ob

which

●*adjective*

····➤ (*in questions*) welcher (*m*), welche (*f*), welches (*nt*), welche (*pl*). **which book do you need?** welches Buch brauchst du? **which one?** welcher/welche/welches? **which ones?** welche? **which one of you did it?** wer von euch hat es getan? **which way?** (*which direction*) welche Richtung?; (*where*) wohin?; (*how*) wie?

····➤ (*relative*) **he always comes at one, at which time I'm having lunch/by which time I've finished** er kommt immer um ein Uhr; dann esse ich gerade zu Mittag/bis dahin bin ich schon fertig

●*pronoun*

····➤ (*in questions*) welcher (*m*), welche (*f*), welches (*nt*), welche (*pl*). **which is which?** welcher/welche/welches ist welcher/welche/welches? **which of you?** wer von euch?

····➤ (*relative*) der (*m*), die (*f*), das (*nt*), die (*pl*); (*genitive*) dessen (*m, nt*), deren (*f, pl*); (*dative*) dem (*m, nt*), der (*f*), denen (*pl*); (*referring to a clause*) was. **the book which I gave you** das Buch, das ich dir gab. **the trial, the result of which we are expecting** der Prozess, dessen Ergebnis wir erwarten. **the house of which I was speaking** das Haus, von dem *od* wovon ich redete. **after which** wonach; nach dem. **on which** worauf; auf dem. **the shop opposite which we parked** der Laden, gegenüber dem wir parkten. **everything which I tell you** alles, was ich dir sage

whichever *a & pron* [egal] welche(r,s); ~ **it is** was es auch ist

while *n* Weile *f*; **a long** ~ lange; **be worth** ~ sich lohnen; **it's worth my** ~ es lohnt sich für mich ●*conj* während; (*as long as*) solange; (*although*) obgleich ●*vt* ~ **away** sich (*dat*) vertreiben

whilst *conj* während

whim *n* Laune *f*

whimper *vi* wimmern; <*dog:*> winseln

whine *vi* winseln

whip *n* Peitsche *f*; (*Pol*) Einpeitscher *m* ●*vt* (*pt/pp* **whipped**) peitschen; (*Culin*) schlagen. ~**ped cream** *n* Schlagsahne *f*

whirl *vt/i* wirbeln. ~**pool** *n* Strudel *m*. ~**-wind** *n* Wirbelwind *m*

whirr *vi* surren

whisk *n* (*Culin*) Schneebesen *m* ●*vt* (*Culin*) schlagen

whisker *n* Schnurrhaar *nt*

whisky *n* Whisky *m*

whisper *n* Flüstern *nt* ●*vt/i* flüstern

whistle *n* Pfiff *m*; (*instrument*) Pfeife *f* ●*vt/i* pfeifen

white *a* (**-r, -st**) weiß ●*n* Weiß *nt*; (*of egg*) Eiweiß *nt*; (*person*) Weiße(r) *m/f*

white: ~ **coffee** *n* Kaffee *m* mit Milch. ~-**collar worker** *n* Angestellte(r) *m*. ~ **lie** *n* Notlüge *f*

whiten *vt* weiß machen ●*vi* weiß werden

whiteness *n* Weiß *nt*

Whitsun *n* Pfingsten *nt*

whiz[z] *vi* (*pt/pp* **whizzed**) zischen. ~-**kid** *n* 𝕀 Senkrechtstarter *m*

who *pron* wer; (*acc*) wen; (*dat*) wem ●*rel pron* der/die/das, (*pl*) die

whoever *pron* wer [immer]; ~ **he is** wer er auch ist; ~ **is it?** wer ist das bloß?

whole *a* ganz; <*truth*> voll ●*n* Ganze(s) *nt*; **as a** ~ als Ganzes; **on the** ~ im Großen und Ganzen; **the** ~ **of Germany** ganz Deutschland

whole: ~**food** *n* Vollwertkost *f*. ~-**hearted** *a* rückhaltlos. ~**meal** *a* Vollkorn-

wholesale *a* Großhandels- ●*adv* en gros; (*fig*) in Bausch und Bogen. ~**r** *n* Großhändler *m*

wholly *adv* völlig

whom *pron* wen; **to** ~ wem ●*rel pron* den/die/das, (*pl*) die; (*dat*) dem/der/dem, (*pl*) denen

whopping *a* 𝕀 Riesen-

whore *n* Hure *f*

whose *pron* wessen; ~ **is that?** wem gehört das? ●*rel pron* dessen/deren/dessen, (*pl*) deren

why *adv* warum; *(for what purpose)* wozu; *that's* ~ darum

wick *n* Docht *m*

wicked *a* böse; *(mischievous)* frech, boshaft

wicker *n* Korbgeflecht *nt* ● *attrib* Korb-

wide *a* (-r, -st) weit; *(broad)* breit; *(fig)* groß ● *adv* weit; *(off target)* daneben; ~ **awake** hellwach; **far and** ~ weit und breit. ~**ly** *adv* weit; *<known, accepted>* weithin; *<differ>* stark

widen *vt* verbreitern; *(fig)* erweitern ● *vi* sich verbreitern

widespread *a* weit verbreitet

widow *n* Witwe *f.* ~**ed** *a* verwitwet. ~**er** *n* Witwer *m*

width *n* Weite *f*; *(breadth)* Breite *f*

wield *vt* schwingen; ausüben *<power>*

wife *n* (*pl* **wives**) [Ehe]frau *f*

wig *n* Perücke *f*

wiggle *vi* wackeln ● *vt* wackeln mit

wild *a* (-er, -est), -**ly** *adv* wild; *<animal>* wild lebend; *<flower>* wild wachsend; *(furious)* wütend ● *adv* wild; *run* ~ frei herumlaufen ● *n in* **the** ~ **wild; the** ~**s** *pl* die Wildnis *f*

wilderness *n* Wildnis *f*; *(desert)* Wüste *f*

wildlife *n* Tierwelt *f*

will¹
● *auxiliary verb*

  past **would**

••••▶ *(expressing the future)* werden. **she will arrive tomorrow** sie wird morgen ankommen. **he will be there by now** er wird jetzt schon da sein

••••▶ *(expressing intention)* (*present tense*) **will you go?** gehst du? **I promise I won't do it again** ich verspreche, ich machs nicht noch mal

••••▶ *(in requests)* **will/would you please tidy up?** würdest du bitte aufräumen? **will you be quiet!** willst du ruhig sein!

••••▶ *(in invitations)* **will you have/ would you like some wine?** wollen Sie/möchten Sie Wein?

••••▶ *(negative: refuse to)* nicht wollen. **they won't help me** sie wollen mir nicht helfen. **the car won't start** das Auto will nicht anspringen

••••▶ *(in tag questions)* nicht wahr. **you'll be back soon, won't you?** du kommst bald wieder, nicht wahr? **you will help her, won't you?** du hilfst ihr doch, nicht wahr?

••••▶ *(in short answers)* **Will you be there? — Yes I will** Wirst du da sein? — Ja

will² *n* Wille *m*; *(document)* Testament *nt*

willing *a* willig; *(eager)* bereitwillig; **be** ~ bereit sein. ~**ly** *adv* bereitwillig; *(gladly)* gern. ~**ness** *n* Bereitwilligkeit *f*

willow *n* Weide *f*

will-power *n* Willenskraft *f*

wilt *vi* welk werden, welken

wily *a* (-ier, -iest) listig

win *n* Sieg *m* ● *v* (*pt/pp* **won**; *pres p* **winning**) ● *vt* gewinnen; bekommen *<scholarship>* ● *vi* gewinnen; (*in battle*) siegen. ~ **over** *vt* auf seine Seite bringen

wince *vi* zusammenzucken

winch *n* Winde *f* ● *vt* ~ **up** hochwinden

wind¹ *n* Wind *m*; ([!] *flatulence*) Blähungen *pl* ● *vt* ~ **s.o.** jdm den Atem nehmen

wind² *v* (*pt/pp* **wound**) ● *vt* (*wrap*) wickeln; *(move by turning)* kurbeln; aufziehen *<clock>* *vi* *<road:>* sich winden. ~ **up** *vt* aufziehen *<clock>*; schließen *<proceedings>*

wind: ~ **instrument** *n* Blasinstrument *nt*. ~**mill** *n* Windmühle *f*

window *n* Fenster *nt*; *(of shop)* Schaufenster *nt*

window: ~**box** *n* Blumenkasten *m*. ~**-cleaner** *n* Fensterputzer *m*. ~**pane** *n* Fensterscheibe *f*. ~**shopping** *n* Schaufensterbummel *m*. ~**-sill** *n* Fensterbrett *nt*

windpipe *n* Luftröhre *f*

windscreen *n*, (*Amer*) **windshield** *n* Windschutzscheibe *f*. **~-wiper** *n* Scheibenwischer *m*

wind surfing *n* Windsurfen *nt*

windy *a* (-ier, -iest) windig

wine *n* Wein *m*

wine: ~-bar *n* Weinstube *f*. **~ glass** *n* Weinglas *nt*. **~-list** *n* Weinkarte *f*

winery *n* (*Amer*) Weingut *nt*

wine-tasting *n* Weinprobe *f*

wing *n* Flügel *m*; (*Auto*) Kotflügel *m*; **~s** *pl* (*Theat*) Kulissen *pl*

wink *n* Zwinkern *nt*; **not sleep a ~** kein Auge zutun ● *vi* zwinkern; <*light:*> blinken

winner *n* Gewinner(in) *m(f)*; (*Sport*) Sieger(in) *m(f)*

winning *a* siegreich; <*smile*> gewinnend. **~-post** *n* Zielpfosten *m*. **~s** *npl* Gewinn *m*

wint|er *n* Winter *m*. **~ry** *a* winterlich

wipe *n* give sth a ~ etw abwischen ● *vt* abwischen; aufwischen <*floor*>; (*dry*) abtrocknen. **~ out** *vt* (*cancel*) löschen; (*destroy*) ausrotten. **~ up** *vt* aufwischen

wire *n* Draht *m*

wiring *n* [elektrische] Leitungen *pl*

wisdom *n* Weisheit *f*; (*prudence*) Klugheit *f*. **~ tooth** *n* Weisheitszahn *m*

wise *a* (-r, -st), **-ly** *adv* weise; (*prudent*) klug

wish *n* Wunsch *m* ● *vt* wünschen; **~ s.o. well** jdm alles Gute wünschen; **I ~ you could stay** ich wünschte, du könntest hier bleiben ● *vi* sich (*dat*) etwas wünschen. **~ful** *a* **~ful thinking** Wunschdenken *nt*

wistful *a*, **-ly** *adv* wehmütig

wit *n* Geist *m*, Witz *m*; (*intelligence*) Verstand *m*; (*person*) geistreicher Mensch *m*; **be at one's ~s' end** sich (*dat*) keinen Rat mehr wissen

witch *n* Hexe *f*. **~craft** *n* Hexerei *f*

with *prep* mit (+ *dat*); **~ fear/cold** vor Angst/Kälte; **~ it** damit; **I'm going ~ you** ich gehe mit; **take it ~ you** nimm es mit; **I haven't got it ~ me** ich habe es nicht bei mir

withdraw *v* (*pt* **-drew**, *pp* **-drawn**) ● *vt* zurückziehen; abheben <*money*> ● *vi* sich zurückziehen. **~al** *n* Zurückziehen *nt*; (*of money*) Abhebung *f*; (*from drugs*) Entzug *m*

wither *vi* [ver]welken

withhold *vt* (*pt/pp* **-held**) vorenthalten (**from s.o.** jdm)

within *prep* innerhalb (+ *gen*) ● *adv* innen

without *prep* ohne (+ *acc*); **~ my noticing it** ohne dass ich es merkte

withstand *vt* (*pt/pp* **-stood**) standhalten (+ *dat*)

witness *n* Zeuge *m*/ Zeugin *f* ● *vt* Zeuge/Zeugin sein (+ *gen*); bestätigen <*signature*>

witticism *n* geistreicher Ausspruch *m*

witty *a* (-ier, -iest) witzig, geistreich

wives *see* wife

wizard *n* Zauberer *m*

wizened *a* verhutzelt

wobb|le *vi* wackeln. **~ly** *a* wackelig

woke, woken *see* wake[1]

wolf *n* (*pl* wolves) Wolf *m*

woman *n* (*pl* women) Frau *f*. **~izer** *n* Schürzenjäger *m*

womb *n* Gebärmutter *f*

women *npl see* woman

won *see* win

wonder *n* Wunder *nt*; (*surprise*) Staunen *nt* ● *vt/i* sich fragen; (*be surprised*) sich wundern; **I ~ da frage ich mich**; **I ~ whether she is ill** ob sie wohl krank ist? **~ful** *a*, **-ly** *adv* wunderbar

won't = will not

wood *n* Holz *nt*; (*forest*) Wald *m*; **touch ~!** unberufen!

wood: ~ed *a* bewaldet. **~en** *a* Holz-; (*fig*) hölzern. **~pecker** *n* Specht *m*. **~wind** *n* Holzbläser *pl*. **~work** *n* (*wooden parts*) Holzteile *pl*; (*craft*) Tischlerei *f*. **~worm** *n* Holzwurm *m*

wool *n* Wolle *f* ● *attrib* Woll-. **~len** *a* wollen

woolly *a* (-ier, -iest) wollig; *(fig)* unklar

word *n* Wort *nt*; *(news)* Nachricht *f*; by ~ of mouth mündlich; have a ~ with sprechen mit; have ~s einen Wortwechsel haben. ~ing *n* Wortlaut *m*. ~ **processor** *n* Textverarbeitungssystem *nt*

wore *see* wear

work *n* Arbeit *f*; *(Art, Literature)* Werk *nt*; ~s *pl (factory, mechanism)* Werk *nt*; at ~ bei der Arbeit; out of ~ arbeitslos ● *vi* arbeiten; *<machine, system:>* funktionieren; *(have effect)* wirken; *(study)* lernen; it won't ~ *(fig)* es klappt nicht ● *vt* arbeiten lassen; bedienen *<machine>*; betätigen *<lever>*. ~ **off** *vt* abarbeiten. ~ **out** *vt* ausrechnen; *(solve)* lösen ● *vi* gut gehen, 🇬🇧 klappen. ~ **up** *vt* aufbauen; sich *(dat)* holen *<appetite>*; get ~ed up sich aufregen

workable *a (feasible)* durchführbar

worker *n* Arbeiter(in) *m(f)*

working *a* berufstätig; *<day, clothes>* Arbeits-; be in ~ order funktionieren. ~ **class** *n* Arbeiterklasse *f*

work: ~**man** *n* Arbeiter *m*; *(craftsman)* Handwerker *m*. ~**manship** *n* Arbeit *f*. ~**shop** *n* Werkstatt *f*

world *n* Welt *f*; in the ~ auf der Welt; think the ~ of s.o. große Stücke auf jdn halten. ~**ly** *a* weltlich; *<person>* weltlich gesinnt. ~**-wide** *a & adv* weltweit

worm *n* Wurm *m*

worn *see* wear ● *a* abgetragen. ~**out** *a* abgetragen; *<carpet>* abgenutzt; *<person>* erschöpft

worried *a* besorgt

worry *n* Sorge *f* ● *v (pt/pp* worried) ● *vt* beunruhigen; *(bother)* stören ● *vi* sich beunruhigen, sich *(dat)* Sorgen machen. ~**ing** *a* beunruhigend

worse *a & adv* schlechter; *(more serious)* schlimmer ● *n* Schlechtere(s) *nt*; Schlimmere(s) *nt*

worsen *vt* verschlechtern ● *vi* sich verschlechtern

worship *n* Anbetung *f*; *(service)* Gottesdienst *m* ● *vt (pt/pp* -shipped) anbeten

worst *a* schlechteste(r,s); *(most serious)* schlimmste(r,s) ● *adv* am schlechtesten; am schlimmsten ● *n* the ~ das Schlimmste

worth *n* Wert *m*; £10's ~ of petrol Benzin für £10 ● *a* be ~ £5 £5 wert sein; be ~ it *(fig)* sich lohnen. ~**less** *a* wertlos. ~**while** *a* lohnend

worthy *a* würdig

would *v aux* I ~ do it ich würde es tun, ich täte es; ~ you go? würdest du gehen? he said he ~n't er sagte, er würde es nicht tun; what ~ you like? was möchten Sie?

wound[1] *n* Wunde *f* ● *vt* verwunden

wound[2] *see* wind[2]

wove, woven *see* weave[2]

wrangle *n* Streit *m*

wrap *n* Umhang *m* ● *vt (pt/pp* wrapped) ~ [up] wickeln; einpacken *<present>* ● *vi* ~ up warmly sich warm einpacken. ~**per** *n* Hülle *f*. ~**ping** *n* Verpackung *f*

wrath *n* Zorn *m*

wreath *n (pl* -s) Kranz *m*

wreck *n* Wrack *nt* ● *vt* zerstören; zunichte machen *<plans>*; zerrütten *<marriage>*. ~**age** *n* Wrackteile *pl*; *(fig)* Trümmer *pl*

wren *n* Zaunkönig *m*

wrench *n* Ruck *m*; *(tool)* Schraubenschlüssel *m*; be a ~ *(fig)* weh tun ● *vt* reißen; ~ sth from s.o. jdm etw entreißen

wrestle *vi* ringen. ~**er** *n* Ringer *m*. ~**ing** *n* Ringen *nt*

wretch *n* Kreatur *f*. ~**ed** *a* elend; *(very bad)* erbärmlich

wriggle *n* Zappeln *nt* ● *vi* zappeln; *(move forward)* sich schlängeln; ~ out of sth 🇬🇧 sich vor etw *(dat)* drücken

wring *vt (pt/pp* wrung) wringen; *(~ out)* auswringen; umdrehen *<neck>*; ringen *<hands>*

wrinkle *n* Falte *f*; (*on skin*) Runzel *f*
● *vt* kräuseln ● *vi* sich kräuseln,
sich falten. **~d** *a* runzlig

wrist *n* Handgelenk *nt*. **~-watch** *n*
Armbanduhr *f*

write *vt/i* (*pt* wrote, *pp* written, *pres p*
writing) schreiben. **~ down** *vt*
aufschreiben. **~ off** *vt* abschreiben;
zu Schrott fahren <*car*>

write-off *n* ≈ Totalschaden *m*

writer *n* Schreiber(in) *m(f)*; (*author*)
Schriftsteller(in) *m(f)*

writhe *vi* sich winden

writing *n* Schreiben *nt*;
(*handwriting*) Schrift *f*; in **~**
schriftlich. **~-paper** *n*
Schreibpapier *nt*

written *see* write

wrong *a*, **-ly** *adv* falsch; (*morally*)
unrecht; (*not just*) ungerecht; be **~**
nicht stimmen; <*person:*> Unrecht
haben; what's **~**? was ist los? ● *adv*
falsch; go **~** <*person:*> etwas falsch
machen; <*machine:*> kaputtgehen;
<*plan:*> schief gehen ● *n* Unrecht *nt*
● *vt* Unrecht tun (+ *dat*). **~ful** *a*
ungerechtfertigt. **~fully** *adv*
<*accuse*> zu Unrecht

wrote *see* write

wrung *see* wring

wry *a* (-er, -est) ironisch; <*humour*>
trocken

Xx

Xmas *n* 🛈 Weihnachten *nt*

X-ray *n* (*picture*) Röntgenaufnahme *f*;
~s *pl* Röntgenstrahlen *pl* ● *vt*
röntgen; durchleuchten <*luggage*>

Yy

yacht *n* Jacht *f*; (*for racing*)
Segeljacht *f*. **~ing** *n* Segeln *nt*

yank *vt* 🛈 reißen

Yank *n* 🛈 Ami *m* 🛈

yap *vi* (*pt/pp* yapped) <*dog:*>
kläffen

yard¹ *n* Hof *m*; (*for storage*) Lager *nt*

yard² *n* Yard *nt* (= *0,91 m*)

yarn *n* Garn *nt*; (🛈 *tale*) Geschichte
f

yawn *n* Gähnen *nt* ● *vi* gähnen

year *n* Jahr *nt*; (*of wine*) Jahrgang *m*;
for **~s** jahrelang. **~ly** *a & adv*
jährlich

yearn *vi* sich sehnen (**for** nach).
~ing *n* Sehnsucht *f*

yeast *n* Hefe *f*

yell *n* Schrei *m* ● *vi* schreien

yellow *a* gelb ● *n* Gelb *nt*

yelp *vi* jaulen

yes *adv* ja; (*contradicting*) doch ● *n*
Ja *nt*

yesterday *n & adv* gestern; **~'s**
paper die gestrige Zeitung; **the day**
before ~ vorgestern

yet *adv* noch; (*in question*) schon;
(*nevertheless*) doch; **as ~** bisher; **not**
~ noch nicht; **the best ~** das bisher
beste ● *conj* doch

Yiddish *n* Jiddisch *nt*

yield *n* Ertrag *m* ● *vt* bringen;
abwerfen <*profit*> ● *vi* nachgeben;
(*Amer, Auto*) die Vorfahrt
beachten

yoga *n* Yoga *m*

yoghurt *n* Joghurt *m*

yoke *n* Joch *nt*; (*of garment*) Passe
f

yolk *n* Dotter *m*, Eigelb *nt*

you *pron* du; (*acc*) dich; (*dat*) dir; (*pl*)
ihr; (*acc, dat*) euch; (*formal*) (*nom &*
acc, sg & pl) Sie; (*dat, sg & pl*) Ihnen;
(*one*) man; (*acc*) einen; (*dat*) einem;

all of ∼ ihr/Sie alle; **I know** ∼ ich
kenne dich/euch/Sie; **I'll give** ∼
the money ich gebe dir/euch/Ihnen
das Geld; **it does** ∼ **good** es tut
einem gut; **it's bad for** ∼ es ist
ungesund

young *a* (**-er, -est**) jung ● *npl*
(*animals*) Junge *pl*; **the** ∼ die Jugend
f. ∼**ster** *n* Jugendliche(r) *m/f*;
(*child*) Kleine(r) *m/f*

your *a* dein; (*pl*) euer; (*formal*)
Ihr

yours *poss pron* deine(r), deins; (*pl*)
eure(r), euers; (*formal, sg & pl*)
Ihre(r), Ihr[e]s; **a friend of** ∼ ein
Freund von dir/Ihnen/euch; **that is**
∼ das gehört dir/Ihnen/euch

yourself *pron* (*pl* **-selves**) selbst;
(*refl*) dich; (*dat*) dir; (*pl*) euch;
(*formal*) sich; **by** ∼ allein

youth *n* (*pl* **-s**) Jugend *f*; (*boy*)
Jugendliche(r) *m*. ∼**ful** *a* jugendlich.
∼ **hostel** *n* Jugendherberge *f*

Yugoslavia *n* Jugoslawien *nt*

zero *n* Null *f*

zest *n* Begeisterung *f*

zigzag *n* Zickzack *m* ● *vi* (*pt/pp*
-zagged) im Zickzack laufen/ (*in
vehicle*) fahren

zinc *n* Zink *nt*

zip *n* ∼ **[fastener]** Reißverschluss *m*
● *vt* ∼ **[up]** den Reißverschluss
zuziehen an (+ *dat*)

zip code *n* (*Amer*) Postleitzahl *f*

zipper *n* Reißverschluss *m*

zodiac *n* Tierkreis *m*

zone *n* Zone *f*

zoo *n* Zoo *m*

zoological *a* zoologisch

zoolog|ist *n* Zoologe *m*/gin *f*. ∼**y** *n*
Zoologie *f*

zoom *vi* sausen. ∼ **lens** *n*
Zoomobjektiv *nt*

Zz

zeal *n* Eifer *m*

zealous *a*, **-ly** *adv* eifrig

zebra *n* Zebra *nt*. ∼ **crossing** *n*
Zebrastreifen *m*

German irregular verbs

1st, 2nd, and 3rd person present are given after the infinitive, and past subjunctive after the past indicative, where there is a change of vowel or any other irregularity.

Compound verbs are only given if they do not take the same forms as the corresponding simple verb, e.g. *befehlen*, or if there is no corresponding simple verb, e.g. *bewegen*.

An asterisk (*) indicates a verb which is also conjugated regularly.

Infinitive	Past tense	Past participle
abwägen	wog (wöge) ab	abgewogen
ausbedingen	bedang (bedänge) aus	ausbedungen
backen (du bäckst, er bäckt)	buk (büke)	gebacken
befehlen (du befiehlst, er befiehlt)	befahl (beföhle, befähle)	befohlen
beginnen	begann (begänne)	begonnen
beißen (du/er beißt)	biss (bisse)	gebissen
bergen (du birgst, er birgt)	barg (bärge)	geborgen
bewegen²	bewog (bewöge)	bewogen
biegen	bog (böge)	gebogen
bieten	bot (böte)	geboten
binden	band (bände)	gebunden
bitten	bat (bäte)	gebeten
blasen (du/er bläst)	blies	geblasen
bleiben	blieb	geblieben
bleichen*	blich	geblichen
braten (du brätst, er brät)	briet	gebraten
brechen (du brichst, er bricht)	brach (bräche)	gebrochen
brennen	brannte (brennte)	gebrannt
bringen	brachte (brächte)	gebracht
denken	dachte (dächte)	gedacht
dreschen (du drischst, er drischt)	drosch (drösche)	gedroschen
dringen	drang (dränge)	gedrungen

Infinitive	Past tense	Past participle
dürfen (ich/er darf, du darfst)	durfte (dürfte)	gedurft
empfehlen (du empfiehlst, er empfiehlt)	empfahl (empföhle)	empfohlen
erlöschen (du erlischst, er erlischt)	erlosch (erlösche)	erloschen
erschrecken (du	erschrak (erschäke)	erschrocken

erschrickst, er erschrickt)

Infinitive	Past tense	Past participle
erwägen	erwog (erwöge)	erwogen
essen (du/er isst)	aß (äße)	gegessen
fahren (du fährst, er fährt)	fuhr (führe)	gefahren
fallen (du fällst, er fällt)	fiel	gefallen
fangen (du fängst, er fängt)	fing	gefangen
fechten (du fichtst, er ficht)	focht (föchte)	gefochten
finden	fand (fände)	gefunden
flechten (du flichtst, er flicht)	flocht (flöchte)	geflochten
fliegen	flog (flöge)	geflogen
fliehen	floh (flöhe)	geflohen
fließen (du/er fließt)	floss (flösse)	geflossen
fressen (du/er frisst)	fraß (fräße)	gefressen
frieren	fror (fröre)	gefroren
gären*	gor (göre)	gegoren
gebären (du gebierst, sie gebiert)	gebar (gebäre)	geboren
geben (du gibst, er gibt)	gab (gäbe)	gegeben
gedeihen	gedieh	gediehen
gehen	ging	gegangen
gelingen	gelang (gelänge)	gelungen
gelten (du giltst, er gilt)	galt (gölte, gälte)	gegolten
genesen (du/er genest)	genas (genäse)	genesen
genießen (du/er genießt)	genoss (genösse)	genossen
geschehen (es geschieht)	geschah (geschähe)	geschehen
gewinnen	gewann (gewönne, gewänne)	gewonnen
gießen (du/er gießt)	goss (gösse)	gegossen
gleichen	glich	geglichen
gleiten	glitt	geglitten
glimmen	glomm (glömme)	geglommen
graben (du gräbst, er gräbt)	grub (grübe)	gegraben
greifen	griff	gegriffen

Infinitive	Past tense	Past participle
haben (du hast, er hat)	hatte (hätte)	gehabt
halten (du hältst, er hält)	hielt	gehalten
hängen²	hing	gehangen
hauen	haute	gehauen
heben	hob (höbe)	gehoben
heißen (du/er heißt)	hieß	geheißen
helfen (du hilfst, er hilft)	half (hülfe)	geholfen
kennen	kannte (kennte)	gekannt
klingen	klang (klänge)	geklungen
kneifen	kniff	gekniffen
kommen	kam (käme)	gekommen
können (ich/er kann, du kannst)	konnte (könnte)	gekonnt
kriechen	kroch (kröche)	gekrochen
laden (du lädst, er lädt)	lud (lüde)	geladen

lassen (du/er lässt)	ließ	gelassen
laufen (du läufst, er läuft)	lief	gelaufen
leiden	litt	gelitten
leihen	lieh	geliehen
lesen (du/er liest)	las (läse)	gelesen
liegen	lag (läge)	gelegen
lügen	log (löge)	gelogen
mahlen	mahlte	gemahlen
meiden	mied	gemieden
melken	molk (mölke)	gemolken
messen (du/er misst)	maß (mäße)	gemessen
misslingen	misslang (misslänge)	misslungen
mögen (ich/er mag, du magst)	mochte (möchte)	gemocht
müssen (ich/er muss, du musst)	musste (müsste)	gemusst
nehmen (du nimmst, er nimmt)	nahm (nähme)	genommen
nennen	nannte (nennte)	genannt
pfeifen	pfiff	gepfiffen
preisen (du/er preist)	pries	gepriesen
raten (du rätst, er rät)	riet	geraten
reiben	rieb	gerieben
reißen (du/er reißt)	riss	gerissen
reiten	ritt	geritten
rennen	rannte (rennte)	gerannt
riechen	roch (röche)	gerochen
ringen	rang (ränge)	gerungen
rinnen	rann (ränne)	geronnen

Infinitive	Past tense	Past participle
rufen	rief	gerufen
salzen* (du/er salzt)	salzte	gesalzen
saufen (du säufst, er säuft)	soff (söffe)	gesoffen
saugen*	sog (söge)	gesogen
schaffen[1]	schuf (schüfe)	geschaffen
scheiden	schied	geschieden
scheinen	schien	geschienen
scheißen (du/er scheißt)	schiss	geschissen
schelten (du schiltst, er schilt)	schalt (schölte)	gescholten
scheren[1]	schor (schöre)	geschoren
schieben	schob (schöbe)	geschoben
schießen (du/er schießt)	schoss (schösse)	geschossen
schlafen (du schläfst, er schläft)	schlief	geschlafen
schlagen (du schlägst, er schlägt)	schlug (schlüge)	geschlagen
schleichen	schlich	geschlichen
schleifen[2]	schliff	geschliffen
schließen (du/er schießt)	schloss (schlösse)	geschlossen
schlingen	schlang (schlänge)	geschlungen

schmeißen (du/er schmeißt)	schmiss (schmisse)	geschmissen
schmelzen (du/er schmilzt)	schmolz (schmölze)	geschmolzen
schneiden	schnitt	geschnitten
schrecken* (du schrickst, er schrickt)	schrak (schräke)	geschreckt
schreiben	schrieb	geschrieben
schreien	schrie	geschrie[e]n
schreiten	schritt	geschritten
schweigen	schwieg	geschwiegen
schwellen (du schwillst, er schwillt)	schwoll (schwölle)	geschwollen
schwimmen	schwamm (schwömme)	geschwommen
schwinden	schwand (schwände)	geschwunden
schwingen	schwang (schwänge)	geschwungen
schwören	schwor (schwüre)	geschworen
sehen (du siehst, er sieht)	sah (sähe)	gesehen
sein (ich bin, du bist, er ist, wir sind, ihr seid, sie sind)	war (wäre)	gewesen

Infinitive	Past tense	Past participle
senden[1]	sandte (sendete)	gesandt
sieden	sott (sötte)	gesotten
singen	sang (sänge)	gesungen
sinken	sank (sänke)	gesunken
sitzen (du/er sitzt)	saß (säße)	gesessen
sollen (ich/er soll, du sollst)	sollte	gesollt
spalten*	spaltete	gespalten
spinnen	spann (spönne, spänne)	gesponnen
sprechen (du sprichst, er spricht)	sprach (spräche)	gesprochen
sprießen (du/er sprießt)	spross (sprösse)	gesprossen
springen	sprang (spränge)	gesprungen
stechen (du stichst, er sticht)	stach (stäche)	gestochen
stehen	stand (stünde, stände)	gestanden
stehlen (du stiehlst, er stiehlt)	stahl (stähle)	gestohlen
steigen	stieg	gestiegen
sterben (du stirbst, er stirbt)	starb (stürbe)	gestorben
stinken	stank (stänke)	gestunken
stoßen (du/er stößt)	stieß	gestoßen
streichen	strich	gestrichen
streiten	stritt	gestritten
tragen (du trägst, er trägt)	trug (trüge)	getragen
treffen (du triffst, er trifft)	traf (träfe)	getroffen
treiben	trieb	getrieben
treten (du trittst, er tritt)	trat (träte)	getreten
triefen*	troff (tröffe)	getroffen

trinken	trank (tränke)	getrunken
trügen	trog (tröge)	getrogen
tun (du tust, er tut)	tat (täte)	getan
verderben (du verdirbst, er verdirbt)	verdarb (verdürbe)	verdorben
vergessen (du/er vergisst)	vergaß (vergäße)	vergessen
verlieren	verlor (verlöre)	verloren
verzeihen	verzieh	verziehen
wachsen[1] (du/er wächst)	wuchs (wüchse)	gewachsen
waschen (du wäschst, er wäscht)	wusch (wüsche)	gewaschen
wenden[2]*	wandte (wendete)	gewandt
werben (du wirbst, er wirbt)	warb (würbe)	geworben

Infinitive	Past tense	Past participle
werden (du wirst, er wird)	wurde (würde)	geworden
werfen (du wirfst, er wirft)	warf (würfe)	geworfen
wiegen[1]	wog (wöge)	gewogen
winden	wand (wände)	gewunden
wissen (ich/er weiß, du weißt)	wusste (wüsste)	gewusst
wollen (ich/er will, du willst)	wollte	gewollt
wringen	wrang (wränge)	gewrungen
ziehen	zog (zöge)	gezogen
zwingen	zwang (zwänge)	gezwungen

German
Grammar

WILLIAM ROWLINSON

Acknowledgements

The author wishes to thank Harry Ferrar for his meticulous reading of the manuscript and his many useful suggestions, and the editorial staff of Oxford University Press for their continued support, advice, and encouragement.

Contents

TRANSLATION PROBLEMS *236*

GLOSSARY OF GRAMMATICAL TERMS *251*

I Verbs

TENSE FORMATION

There are three types of German verb, *weak* (completely regular), *strong* (irregular, though tending to follow certain patterns), and *mixed* (partly strong, partly weak). All German verbs have infinitives ending **-en** (or occasionally just **-n**), so it is not possible to tell from the infinitive of a verb whether it is weak, strong, or mixed.

The tenses of German verbs are either simple, in which case the verb is a single word, or compound, in which case the verb is formed with part of one of the three auxiliary (helping) verbs, **haben**, **sein**, and **werden**, together with the past participle or the infinitive:

> simple tense: **ich sage**, *I say*
> compound tenses: **ich habe gesagt**, *I have said*
> **ich werde sagen**, *I shall say*

Apart from the formation of their past participles, all verbs follow the same pattern in their compound tenses.

Weak verbs

The vast majority of German verbs are weak and follow a single pattern. Their past tense is formed by adding **-te** to their stem (the infinitive minus its **-(e)n** ending), and their past participle is formed **ge . . . t**:

> **sagen**, *to say*
> **ich sage**, *I say*
> **ich sagte**, *I said*
> **ich habe gesagt**, *I have said*

▶ The complete tense formation of a weak (regular) verb is given on pp. 5–7, with the verb endings printed in bold.

▶ Some weak verbs have an infinitive ending **-eln** or **-ern** rather than **-en**. Their endings are dealt with on p. 13.

▶ Some verbs have no **ge-** in their past participle. See p. 14 (Verbs ending **-ieren** and **-eien**) and p. 34 (Inseparable Prefixes).

Strong verbs

Strong verbs change their stem vowels in the past tense and (often) in their past participle, and sometimes in parts of the present as well. They may also change the consonant after that vowel. Their past participles are formed **ge . . . en**.

> **singen**, *to sing*
> **ich singe**, *I sing*
> **ich sang**, *I sang*
> **ich habe gesungen**, *I have sung*

▶ The endings of strong verbs are regular. The complete tense formation of a strong verb is given on pp. 7–9, with the verb endings printed in bold.

▶ The modal verbs, **lassen**, and **werden** have two past participles used in differing circumstances. See pp. 66–7.

▶ There is a list of all German strong and mixed verbs showing their vowel changes on pp. 73–85.

Mixed verbs

There are only nine mixed verbs: **bringen**, *to bring*, **denken**, *to think*, **haben**, *to have*, **kennen**, *to know*, **nennen**, *to name*, **rennen**, *to run*, **senden**, *to send*, **wenden**, *to turn*, and **wissen**, *to know*. They take weak verb endings, but also change their

stem vowel (and sometimes the following consonant) like
strong verbs:

> **bringen**, *to bring*
> **ich bringe**, *I bring*
> **ich brachte**, *I brought*
> **ich habe gebracht**, *I have brought*

▶ The complete tense formation of a mixed verb is given on pp.
9–11, with the verb endings printed in bold. Mixed verbs and
their vowel changes are included in the list of Irregular Verbs
on pp. 73–85.

Simple-tense formation

The simple tenses are the present and past tenses and the
present and past subjunctive.

To form each simple tense a fixed set of endings is added to
the verb's stem. The stem is its infinitive minus **-en** (or **-n**).
The ending of the verb corresponds to the subject of the verb:

> **ich sage**, *I say*
> **er sagt**, *he says*
> **wir sagen**, *we say*

The endings are different for strong verbs on the one hand and
for weak and mixed verbs on the other. See conjugation tables,
p. 5 onwards.

Compound-tense formation

Compound tenses are formed, as in English, from the past
participle or the infinitive of the verb, used with an auxiliary
verb. The auxiliary verbs in German are **haben**, *to have*, **sein**,
to be, and **werden**, *to become*. The compound tenses and their
formation are as follows:

perfect tense:
   present of **haben** + PAST PARTICIPLE: **er hat gesagt,**
   he has said

pluperfect tense:
   past of **haben** + PAST PARTICIPLE: **er hatte gesagt,** *he
   had said*

future tense:
   present of **werden** + INFINITIVE: **er wird sagen,** *he will say*

conditional tense:
   past subjunctive of **werden** + INFINITIVE: **er würde
   sagen,** *he would say*

future perfect tense:
   future of **haben** + PAST PARTICIPLE: **er wird gesagt
   haben,** *he will have said*

conditional perfect tense:
   conditional of **haben** + PAST PARTICIPLE: **er würde
   gesagt haben,** *he would have said*

perfect subjunctive:
   present subjunctive of **haben** + PAST PARTICIPLE: **er
   habe gesagt,** *he has said/may have said*

pluperfect subjunctive:
   past subjunctive of **haben** + PAST PARTICIPLE: **er hätte
   gesagt,** *he had said/might have said*

Transitive verbs form their past compound tenses with
haben. Intransitive verbs of motion and the verbs **sein,** *to be,*
werden, *to become,* and **bleiben,** *to remain,* use the auxiliary
sein instead of **haben** in compound tenses:

> **er ist gewesen,** *he has been*
> **er war geworden,** *he had become*
> **er wird geblieben sein,** *he will have remained*

With some verbs that use **sein** the 'motion' idea may not be
immediately obvious. There is a list of these verbs on p. 16.

The past subjunctive is often substituted for the conditional, and the pluperfect subjunctive is very frequently substituted for the conditional perfect. See p. 24.

▶ For the position of the past participle in the sentence see pp. 217–18.

CONJUGATION OF WEAK VERBS

This is the regular pattern for the active form of most German verbs. For the forms of the passive see p. 29.

In all tenses **sie** (*she*), **es** (*it*), **man** (*one*), and singular nouns are followed by the **er** form of the verb; plural nouns are followed by the **sie** (*they*) form.

infinitive	**sagen**, *to say*
present participle	**sagend**, *saying*
past participle	**gesagt**, *said*
imperative	sag(**e**), *say* (**du** *form*)
	sag**en** wir, *let's say*
	sag**t**, *say* (**ihr** *form*)
	sag**en** Sie, *say* (**Sie** form)

Simple tenses

present tense, *I say, I am saying*	ich sag**e**	wir sag**en**
	du sag**st**	ihr sag**t**
	Sie sag**en**[1]	
	er sag**t**	sie sag**en**
past tense, *I said, I was saying*	ich sag**te**	wir sag**ten**
	du sag**test**	ihr sag**tet**
	Sie sag**ten**[1]	
	er sag**te**	sie sag**ten**

---

[1] The polite form of *you* in both singular and plural is **Sie**. See p. 133.

present subjunctive, *I say, I may say*	ich sag**e**		wir sag**en**
	du sag**est**		ihr sag**et**
		Sie sag**en**[1]	
	er sag**e**		sie sag**en**
past subjunctive, *I said, I might say*	ich sag**te**		wir sag**ten**
	du sag**test**		ihr sag**tet**
		Sie sag**ten**[1]	
	er sag**te**		sie sag**ten**

Compound tenses

perfect tense, *I said, I have said, I have been saying*	ich **habe** gesagt		wir **haben** gesagt
	du **hast** gesagt		ihr **habt** gesagt
		Sie **haben** gesagt[1]	
	er **hat** gesagt		sie **haben** gesagt
pluperfect tense, *I had said, I had been saying*	ich **hatte** gesagt		wir **hatten** gesagt
	du **hattest** gesagt		ihr **hattet** gesagt
		Sie **hatten** gesagt[1]	
	er **hatte** gesagt		sie **hatten** gesagt
future tense, *I shall[2] say, I shall[2] be saying*	ich **werde** sagen		wir **werden** sagen
	du **wirst** sagen		ihr **werdet** sagen
		Sie **werden** sagen[1]	
	er **wird** sagen		sie **werden** sagen
conditional tense, *I should[3] say, I should[3] be saying*	ich **würde** sagen		wir **würden** sagen
	du **würdest** sagen		ihr **würdet** sagen
		Sie **würden** sagen[1]	
	er **würde** sagen		sie **würden** sagen
future perfect tense, *I shall[2] have said, I shall[2] have been saying*	ich **werde** gesagt **haben**		wir **werden** gesagt **haben**
	du **wirst** gesagt **haben**		ihr **werdet** gesagt **haben**
		Sie **werden** gesagt **haben**[1]	
	er **wird** gesagt **haben**		sie **werden** gesagt **haben**

[1] The polite form of *you* in both singular and plural is **Sie**. See p. 133.

[2] In English we often use *will* here.

[3] In English we often use *would* here.

conditional perfect tense, *I should[1] have said, I should[1] have been saying*	ich **würde** gesagt **haben**	wir **würden** gesagt **haben**
	du **würdest** gesagt **haben**	ihr **würdet** gesagt **haben**
	Sie **würden** gesagt **haben**[2]	
	er **würde** gesagt **haben**	sie **würden** gesagt **haben**
perfect subjunctive, *I have said, I may have said*	ich **habe** gesagt	wir **haben** gesagt
	du **habest** gesagt	ihr **habet** gesagt
	Sie **haben** gesagt[2]	
	er **habe** gesagt	sie **haben** gesagt
pluperfect subjunctive, *I had said, I might have said*	ich **hätte** gesagt	wir **hätten** gesagt
	du **hättest** gesagt	ihr **hättet** gesagt
	Sie **hätten** gesagt[2]	
	er **hätte** gesagt	sie **hätten** gesagt

CONJUGATION OF STRONG VERBS

This is the regular pattern of endings for the active form of German strong verbs. As well as adding these endings, strong verbs also change their vowel (and sometimes the following consonant) in the past participle, throughout the past tense, and (sometimes) in the **du** and **er** forms of the present and the imperative. These changes are listed in the Irregular Verb list on pp. 73–85. For the forms of the passive see p. 29.

In all tenses **sie** (*she*), **es** (*it*), **man** (*one*), and singular nouns are followed by the **er** form of the verb; plural nouns are followed by the **sie** form.

infinitive	**fangen**, *to catch*
present participle	**fangend**, *catching*
past participle	**gefangen**, *caught*
imperative	**fang(e)**, *catch* (**du** form)[3]

---

[1] In English we often use *would* here.

[2] The polite form of *you* in both singular and plural is **Sie**. See page 133.

[3] Verbs like **fangen** that take an umlaut in the **du** and **er** forms of the present tense do not use it in the imperative. See p. 26.

fangen wir, *let's catch*
fangt, *catch* (**ihr** form)
fangen Sie, *catch* (**Sie** form)

Simple tenses

present tense,	ich fange		wir fangen
I catch, I am catching	du fängst		ihr fangt
		Sie fangen[1]	
	er fängt		sie fangen
past tense,	ich fing		wir fingen
I caught, I was	du fingst		ihr fingt
catching		Sie fingen[1]	
	er fing		sie fingen
present subjunctive,	ich fange		wir fangen
I catch, I may catch	du fangest		ihr fanget
		Sie fangen[1]	
	er fange		sie fangen
past subjunctive,	ich finge		wir fingen
I caught, I might	du fingest		ihr finget
catch		Sie fingen[1]	
	er finge		sie fingen

Compound tenses

perfect tense,	ich **habe** gefangen		wir **haben** gefangen
I caught, I have	du **hast** gefangen		ihr **habt** gefangen
caught, I have been		Sie **haben** gefangen[1]	
catching	er **hat** gefangen		sie **haben** gefangen
pluperfect tense,	ich **hatte** gefangen		wir **hatten** gefangen
I had caught, I had	du **hattest** gefangen		ihr **hattet** gefangen
been catching		Sie **hatten** gefangen[1]	
	er **hatte** gefangen		sie **hatten** gefangen

---

[1] The polite form of *you* in both singular and plural is **Sie**. See p. 133.

future tense, *I shall[1] catch, I shall[1] be catching*	ich **werde** fangen	wir **werden** fangen
	du **wirst** fangen	ihr **werdet** fangen
	Sie **werden** fangen[2]	
	er **wird** fangen	sie **werden** fangen
conditional tense, *I should[3] catch, I should[3] be catching*	ich **würde** fangen	wir **würden** fangen
	du **würdest** fangen	ihr **würdet** fangen
	Sie **würden** fangen[2]	
	er **würde** fangen	sie **würden** fangen
future perfect tense, *I shall[1] have caught, I shall[1] have been catching*	ich **werde** gefangen **haben**	wir **werden** gefangen **haben**
	du **wirst** gefangen **haben**	ihr **werdet** gefangen **haben**
	Sie **werden** gefangen **haben**[2]	
	er **wird** gefangen **haben**	sie **werden** gefangen **haben**
conditional perfect tense, *I should[3] have caught, I should[3] have been catching*	ich **würde** gefangen **haben**	wir **würden** gefangen **haben**
	du **würdest** gefangen **haben**	ihr **würdet** gefangen **haben**
	Sie **würden** gefangen **haben**[2]	
	er **würde** gefangen **haben**	sie **würden** gefangen **haben**
perfect subjunctive, *I have caught, I may have caught*	ich **habe** gefangen	wir **haben** gefangen
	du **habest** gefangen	ihr **habet** gefangen
	Sie **haben** gefangen[2]	
	er **habe** gefangen	sie **haben** gefangen
pluperfect subjunctive, *I had caught, I might have caught*	ich **hätte** gefangen	wir **hätten** gefangen
	du **hättest** gefangen	ihr **hättet** gefangen
	Sie **hätten** gefangen[2]	
	er **hätte** gefangen	sie **hätten** gefangen

CONJUGATION OF MIXED VERBS

This is the regular pattern for the active form of mixed verbs. For the forms of the passive see p. 29.

---

[1] In English we often use *will* here.
[2] The polite form of *you* in both singular and plural is **Sie**. See page 133.
[3] In English we often use *would* here.

In all tenses **sie** (*she*), **es** (*it*), **man** (*one*), and singular nouns are followed by the **er** form of the verb; plural nouns are followed by the **sie** form.

infinitive	kenn**en**, *to know*
present participle	kenn**end**, *knowing*
past participle	**gekannt**, *known*
imperative	kenn**(e)**, *know* (**du** form)
	kenn**en** wir, *let's know*
	kenn**t**, *know* (**ihr** form)
	kenn**en** Sie, *know* (**Sie** form)

Simple tenses

present tense,	ich kenn**e**		wir kenn**en**
I know	du kenn**st**		ihr kenn**t**
		Sie kenn**en**[1]	
	er kenn**t**		sie kenn**en**
past tense,	ich kann**te**		wir kann**ten**
I knew	du kann**test**		ihr kann**tet**
		Sie kann**ten**[1]	
	er kann**te**		sie kann**ten**
present subjunctive,	ich kenn**e**		wir kenn**en**
I know, I may know	du kenn**est**		ihr kenn**et**
		Sie kenn**en**[1]	
	er kenn**e**		sie kenn**en**
past subjunctive,	ich kenn**te**		wir kenn**ten**
I knew, I might	du kenn**test**		ihr kenn**tet**
know		Sie kenn**ten**[1]	
	er kenn**te**		sie kenn**ten**

---

[1] The polite form of *you* in both singular and plural is **Sie**. See p. 133.

Compound tenses

perfect tense, *I knew, I have known*	ich **habe** gekannt	wir **haben** gekannt
	du **hast** gekannt	ihr **habt** gekannt
	Sie **haben** gekannt[1]	
	er **hat** gekannt	sie **haben** gekannt
pluperfect tense, *I had known*	ich **hatte** gekannt	wir **hatten** gekannt
	du **hattest** gekannt	ihr **hattet** gekannt
	Sie **hatten** gekannt[1]	
	er **hatte** gekannt	sie **hatten** gekannt
future tense, *I shall know*	ich **werde** kennen	wir **werden** kennen
	du **wirst** kennen	ihr **werdet** kennen
	Sie **werden** kennen[1]	
	er **wird** kennen	sie **werden** kennen
conditional tense, *I would know*	ich **würde** kennen	wir **würden** kennen
	du **würdest** kennen	ihr **würdet** kennen
	Sie **würden** kennen[1]	
	er **würde** kennen	sie **würden** kennen
future perfect tense, *I shall have known*	ich **werde** gekannt **haben**	wir **werden** gekannt **haben**
	du **wirst** gekannt **haben**	ihr **werdet** gekannt **haben**
	Sie **werden** gekannt **haben**[1]	
	er **wird** gekannt **haben**	sie **werden** gekannt **haben**
conditional perfect tense, *I would have known*	ich **würde** gekannt **haben**	wir **würden** gekannt **haben**
	du **würdest** gekannt **haben**	ihr **würdet** gekannt **haben**
	Sie **würden** gekannt **haben**[1]	
	er **würde** gekannt **haben**	sie **würden** gekannt **haben**
perfect subjunctive, *I have known, I may have known*	ich **habe** gekannt	wir **haben** gekannt
	du **habest** gekannt	ihr **habet** gekannt
	Sie **haben** gekannt[1]	
	er **habe** gekannt	sie **haben** gekannt
pluperfect subjunctive, *I had known, I might have known*	ich **hätte** gekannt	wir **hätten** gekannt
	du **hättest** gekannt	ihr **hättet** gekannt
	Sie **hätten** gekannt[1]	
	er **hätte** gekannt	sie **hätten** gekannt

[1] The polite form of *you* in both singular and plural is **Sie**. See p. 133.

Minor irregularities in verbs

Almost all these changes are made to make the verb easier to pronounce.

■ Verbs ending **-den** or **-ten**

Weak verbs ending **-den** or **-ten** always add an extra **e** before an ending that doesn't already begin with **e**:

> **reden**, *to speak*: **du redest**, *you speak*
> **antworten**, *to answer*: **ihr antwortetet**, *you answered*
> **blenden**, *to dazzle*: **es hat geblendet**, *it has dazzled*

Strong verbs ending **-den** or **-ten** do the same, except in the **du** form of the past tense:

> **finden**, *to find*: **du findest**, *you find*
> **bitten**, *to ask*: **ihr batet**, *you asked*

but

> **du fandst**, *you found*
> **du batst**, *you asked*

In speech the **e** is often omitted in the **du** form of the present (of both weak and strong verbs):

> **du antwortst nicht!**, *you're not answering*

■ Verbs ending in **-[**CONSONANT**]men** and **-[**CONSONANT**]nen**

Verbs (they are all weak) with a consonant followed by **m** or **n** at the end of their stem add an extra **e** before an ending that doesn't already begin with **e**, but only if this would otherwise be impossible to pronounce:

> **atmen**, *to breathe*: **du atmest**, *you breathe*
> **regnen**, *to rain*: **es regnete**, *it was raining*

but

> **lernen**, *to learn*: **du lernst**, *you learn* (an extra **e** is not necessary for pronunciation)

■ Weak verbs ending **-eln** and **-ern**

The **n** is removed from the infinitive to form the stem and normal endings are then added to this; however, the **e** of the stem may be omitted with verbs ending **-eln** (usually) and **-ern** (sometimes) in the **ich** form of the present and the **du** form of the imperative:

> **angeln**, *to fish*: **ich ang(e)le gern**, *I like fishing*
> **rudern**, *to row*: **ich rud(e)re lieber**, *I prefer rowing*
> **schmeicheln**, *to flatter*: **schmeich(e)le mir nicht!**, *don't flatter me*

Plural endings of these verbs have no **e**:

> **wir angeln**, *we fish*
> **ihr rudert**, *you row*

■ Verbs whose stem ends in an **s** sound

All verbs whose stems end **-s**, **-ß**, **-z**, or **-x** lose the **s** in the ending of the **du** form of the present:

> **hexen**, *to bewitch*: **du hext**
> **heizen**, *to heat*: **du heizt**
> **schießen**, *to shoot*: **du schießt**

In strong verbs with these stems the ending of the **du** form of the past tense is **-est**:

> **du schossest**, *you shot* (in spoken German **du schosst** is also found)

Note that none of this applies to the stem-ending **-sch**, which has quite regular verb endings after it:

> **wischen**, *to wipe*: **du wischst**

■ Verbs whose stem ends in a vowel or **h**

With both weak and strong verbs whose stems end in a vowel or **h**, the **e** of an **-en** ending disappears in spoken German (and sometimes in printed German too, especially in poetry):

> **einsehen**, *to understand* : „**Das sehn Sie nicht ein**", *'You don't understand that'*

This also applies to infinitives, and to the **-en** ending of the past participles of strong verbs:

> „**Das wollen Sie nicht einsehn**", *'You don't want to understand it'*
> „**Das haben Sie nicht eingesehn**", *'You didn't understand it'*

It does not apply to the past of weak verbs, where a **t** comes before the **-en** ending:

> **bauen**, *build*: **wir bauten; sie bauten**

■ Verbs ending **-ieren** and **-eien**

Verbs ending **-ieren** and **-eien** have no **ge-** in their past participle. They are all weak:

> **ich habe ihn schon informiert**, *I've already informed him*
> **das hat sie prophezeit**, *she prophesied that*

▶ Inseparable verbs also form past participles without **ge-**. See p. 34.

■ Loss of **-e** endings

☐ In spoken German the **-e** ending of the **ich** form of the present almost always disappears:

> „**Ja, ich geh schon**", **sage ich**, *'Yes, all right, I'm going'*, *I say*

☐ In spoken German the **-e** ending of the **du** form of the imperative almost always disappears in both weak and strong verbs:

> „**Komm gut nach Hause**", **sagte sie**, *'Get home safely'*, *she said*

This applies also to strong verbs that simply add an umlaut to their vowel in the **du** form of the present: in the imperative they do not add the umlaut, but they may take an **e**:

> **fahren**, *to go*
> **du fährst**, *you go*
> **fahr/fahre schneller!**, *go faster!*

However, strong verbs that actually change their vowel in the **du** form of the present (as opposed to simply adding an umlaut) also change it in the **du** form of the imperative. They can never take an **e**:

> **helfen**, *to help*
> **du hilfst**, *you help*
> **hilf mir!**, *help me!*

□ The final **e** of verbs ending in **-eln, -ern** is never dropped if they have already dropped the **e** of their stem (see p. 13). Nor is it dropped with verbs ending **-[**CONSONANT**]men** or **-[**CONSONANT**]nen**, whose stem is unpronounceable without an ending:

> **atmen**, *to breathe*: **atme!**

□ In spoken German the **-e** of the ending of the **ich** and **er** forms of weak verbs in the past tense often disappears before a vowel. This is written with an apostrophe:

> „**Na also, ich sagt' es schon**", *'There you are, I told you so'*

COMPOUND TENSES

▶ For the formation of the compound tenses see p. 3.

Compound tenses formed with sein

Virtually all transitive verbs and reflexive verbs form their past compound tenses with **haben**. So do most intransitive verbs.

However, three groups of intransitive verbs use **sein**:

■ Verbs expressing motion, involving change of place

> **er ist heute gefahren**, *he left today*
> **sie ist in das Zimmer getanzt**, *she danced into the room*

If the verb simply expresses the action, rather than change of place, **haben** is usually used:

> **ich habe heute viel geritten**, *I've ridden a lot today*
> **wir haben gestern abend im „Astoria" getanzt**, *we went dancing at the Astoria last night*

■ Verbs expressing change of state

> **sie ist aufgewacht**, *she woke up*
> **Großmutter ist gestorben**, *grandmother has died*
> **du bist aber groß geworden**, *you have got big*

In this group are included verbs meaning *to happen* (**geschehen, passieren, vorkommen, vorgehen**).

Werden, *to become*, also takes **sein** when it is used to form the passive:

> **ich bin gefragt worden**, *I have been asked*

See Passive, p. 29.

■ The following verbs, where the idea of 'motion' or of 'change of state' seems doubtful or non-existent

> **begegnen** (+ DAT), *meet* (also **sich begegnen**, *meet one another*)
> **bleiben**, *remain*
> **gelingen**, *succeed* (**es ist mir gelungen**, *I succeeded*); also **misslingen**, *fail*
> **glücken**, succeed (**es ist mir geglückt**, *I succeeded*); also **missglücken**, *fail*
> **sein**, *be*

'Motion' verbs used transitively

Some verbs of motion that are normally intransitive and take sein can also be used transitively. They then take **haben**.

> **hat er dein Mofa gefahren?**, *has he ridden your moped?*

A very few verbs that take **sein** when used intransitively, or that are compounded from verbs that take **sein**, continue to use **sein** when they are used transitively. They are

> **loswerden**, *get rid of*
> **eingehen**, *take on*
> **Gefahr laufen**, *run a risk*
> **eine Strecke gehen**, *go some distance*

> **bist du diese Katze immer noch nicht losgeworden?**, *have you still not got rid of that cat?*

USE OF TENSES

The present tense

There is only one form of the present tense in German, corresponding to both the present simple and the present continuous in English. So **ich gehe** translates both *I go* and *I am going*. There is no possible translation of *I am going* using the present participle in German. If the continuing nature of the action needs to be stressed, **(gerade) dabei sein** is used:

> **ich bin gerade dabei, die letzten Worte zu schreiben**, *I'm just writing the last words*

General uses of the present tense

■ As in English the present is used not just to indicate what is going on at the moment:

> **ich stricke einen Pulli**, *I'm knitting a pullover*

but also what habitually occurs:

zum Frühstück esse ich nur Müsli, *I eat only muesli at breakfast*

■ It can also be used, again as in English, to indicate a future:

ich komme gleich, *I'm coming (I'll come) right away*

This use is more frequent than in English, partly because German has no equivalent to the English form *I'm going to . . .* It is especially used when an adverb already shows that the event is in the future:

kommst du morgen?, *are you coming tomorrow?* (**wirst du morgen kommen?** *asks about intention: are you going to (do you intend to) come tomorrow?*). See uses of the future tense, p. 22.

■ German uses the present as a past narrative tense (the 'historic present') at least as frequently as English:

Acht Gestalten, die Gesichter hinter Tüchern und Wollmützen versteckt, **schlendern** langsam zum Haus Nummer 128. Dann ein Krachen! Die Eingangstür **splittert**, mit einem Brecheisen **knacken** die Vermummten das Schloss. Für die Nachbarn ein klarer Fall: Hier **sind** Einbrecher am Werk. Die Polizei, die Minuten später am Tatort **erscheint, denkt** ähnlich. Großräumig **werden** die umliegenden Straßen **gesichert**, die übrigen Beamten **observieren** das Haus. Nach und nach **marschieren** immer mehr Männer in das leer stehende Haus am Gereonswall, einige **haben** sogar ihren Hund dabei.

(Express)

Eight figures with their faces hidden behind scarves and woolly hats strolled slowly up to number 128. Then came a crash. The entrance door splintered—the disguised figures were breaking the lock with a crowbar. For the neighbours it was perfectly clear—burglars were at work here. The police, who appeared at the scene of the crime moments later, thought the same thing. The

> *surrounding streets were made secure over a wide area,*
> *the remaining officers took up watch on the house.*
> *Gradually more and more men trooped into the empty*
> *house in Gereonswall. Some even had their dogs with*
> *them.*

English would be unlikely to continue with the historic present
for so long, and through so many verbs. It would either use the
past throughout, as above, or if the passage started in the
historic present it would probably change back to the past at
'*For the neighbours it was perfectly clear . . .*'

Special uses of the present tense

■ Present tense with **seit** (*for*; *since*, preposition) and **seitdem**
(*since then*, adverb)

□ With the prepositions *for* and *since*, when an action or state
which started in the past is still going on in the present, English
uses the perfect continuous ('*I have been doing*'); German—
exactly like French in these circumstances—uses a present tense.

> **sie wäscht seit anderthalb Stunden ab**, *she's been*
> *washing up for an hour and a half*
> **ich warte seit zwanzig nach eins**, *I've been waiting*
> *since twenty past one*

However, where a series of actions is referred to (as opposed
to one continuing one), a perfect is used, as in English:

> **seit Anfang Juli hat es jeden Tag geregnet**, *it's*
> *rained every single day since the beginning of July*

and the perfect is normally always used where the statement is
negative:

> **ich habe sie seit vier Wochen nicht mehr**
> **gesehen**, *I haven't seen her for four weeks*

□ Exactly the same rules apply to the adverb **seitdem**, *since (then)*:

> **und seitdem warte ich hier**, *and since then I've*
> *been waiting here*

> **seitdem hat es jeden Tag geregnet,** *it's rained every day since*
>
> **ich habe sie seitdem nicht mehr gesehen,**
>   *I haven't seen her since*

■ Present tense with **seitdem** or **seit** (*since*, conjunction)

After the conjunction **seitdem**, *since*, the present tense in German in the **seitdem** clause *always* corresponds to the past continuous in English:

> **ich habe kein einziges Wort mit ihr gewechselt, seitdem sie hier wohnt,** *I haven't exchanged a single word with her since she's been living here*

Seit is also used as a conjunction, though less commonly than **seitdem**.

▶ See also **seit** + past tense, p. 21.

▶ For a fuller treatment of the conjunctions **seitdem** and **seit** see pp. 199–200.

■ Present tense with **kommen**

With **kommen** + infinitive (= *come in order to do something*), German uses a present where English uses a perfect:

> **ich komme, euch zu warnen,** *I've come to warn you*

The past tense and the perfect tense

The past tense

■ In written narrative, the German past tense corresponds exactly to the English past:

> **Das Transportflugzeug stürzte in der Nacht zum Mittwoch kurz nach dem Start von Ramstein nach Frankfurt über einem Wald ab und explodierte.**
>   *(Berliner Zeitung)*
> *Shortly after leaving Ramstein for Frankfurt on Tuesday night the aircraft came down over a wood and exploded.*

■ In spoken narrative, both the past tense and the perfect are used with little or no difference in meaning. See p. 22, The narrative perfect.

■ The past tense is used with **seit** (*since*; *for*) and **seitdem** (*since*, conjunction; *since then*, adverb):

> **ich wartete seit zwanzig nach eins**, *I'd been waiting since twenty past one*
>
> **seitdem sie hier wohnte, hatte ich kein einziges Wort mit ihr gewechselt**, *I hadn't exchanged a single word with her since she'd been living here*

Where English uses the pluperfect continuous (= *I had been doing*) with these expressions, German uses the past tense.

▶ See also **seit** + present tense, p. 20.

▶ For a fuller treatment of the conjunctions **seitdem** and **seit** see pp. 199–200.

The perfect tense

■ The perfect tense has two main uses in German: as a 'true' perfect and as a past narrative tense.

□ The 'true' perfect (= *I have done*)

As often in English, the true perfect is used to speak of something that happened in the past and has some bearing on what is being talked about in the present:

> **hast du meine Pralinen gegessen?**, *have you eaten my chocolates?*

However, German uses the perfect in this way much more rigorously than English does:

> **Bismarck hat die Grundlagen des heutigen deutschen Staats gelegt**, *Bismarck laid the foundations of the present German state*

Where English uses a perfect continuous, a perfect is used in German:

> **was hast du gemacht?**, *what have you been doing?*
> **ich habe gelesen; ich habe auch ferngesehen**,
> *I've been reading; I've been watching television too*

□ The narrative perfect

In conversation and letter-writing English usually uses the past as the narrative tense: in German the perfect is commoner. It is especially predominant in south Germany (and Austria and Switzerland). However, the past tense is also in quite common use, especially in north Germany, and especially with **haben** and **sein**, the modals, and some of the commoner strong verbs (e.g. **kommen, gehen**). Perfect and past tenses will frequently be found mixed within the same sentence, and in most cases either is entirely acceptable. If in doubt, use the perfect.

> **er kam gestern (ist gestern gekommen) und wollte**
> **wissen, was hier zu tun war — ich hab ihm sofort**
> **das Auto gezeigt (zeigte ihm sofort das Auto)**, *he*
> *came yesterday and wanted to know what was to be*
> *done—I showed him the car straight away*

Where English uses the past continuous to describe a state of affairs, German tends to use a past tense rather than a perfect, though here too the perfect is by no means impossible:

> **es regnete, und so hab ich meinen Schirm**
> **mitgenommen**, *it was raining, and so I took my umbrella*

The future tense

The future is used much less frequently than in English and the present is usually substituted for it if an adverb with a future meaning is used:

> **ich seh dich morgen**, *I'll see you tomorrow*

This also applies if there is an adverb clause with a future meaning:

**wenn Sie das zu Ende geschrieben haben, bin
ich schon längst weg**, *when you've finished
writing that I'll be long gone*

■ The future may express firm intention:

**ich werd dich morgen sehen, du kannst dich darauf
verlassen**, *I will see you tomorrow, you can rely on it*

■ The future (and more frequently the future perfect) may
express probability, as they sometimes do in English:

**ich bekomme keine Antwort — er wird nicht da
sein**, *I'm getting no reply, he's probably not in*

sie wird den Bus wieder verpasst haben, *she'll
have missed her bus again*

■ The future (and the present) are used as alternatives to the
imperative (see p. 27):

**du wirst sofort nach Hause gehen! (du gehst
sofort nach Hause!)**, *go home immediately!*

The conditional and conditional perfect tenses

■ The conditional is normally found in the main clause of an
'if' sentence ('*if he came I would go*'). The same is true of the
conditional perfect. Where these tenses appear in sentences
without an 'if' clause, an 'if' clause is generally to be
understood:

das würde ich nicht machen! [wenn ich du wäre], *I
wouldn't do that! (if I were you)*

**das würde sie sonst nicht tun [wenn das nicht der Fall
wäre]**, *otherwise she wouldn't do it (if that were not the
case)*

There are three basic types of 'if' sentence:

□ 'it may happen'

**wenn er anruft, fahre ich heute noch (werde ich
heute noch fahren)**, *if he phones I'll go today*

The **wenn** clause has a present, the main clause has a present or a future.

□ 'it might happen'

> **wenn er anrufen würde, würde ich heute noch fahren**, *if he phoned I'd go today*

Both clauses have a conditional (American usage has '*would phone*' in the 'if' clause, exactly parallel to the German). In formal German the past subjunctive may be used in the 'if' clause and, if the verb is strong, in the main clause also:

> **wenn er anriefe, führe ich heute noch**

The apparently past-tense '*phoned*' in English is actually a remnant of our past subjunctive.

In spoken German **sollen** is often used in the **wenn** clause (**wenn er anrufen sollte**).

▶ For the forms of the past subjunctive see pp. 5–11.

□ 'it might have happened but it didn't'

> **wenn er angerufen hätte, wäre ich heute noch gefahren**, *if he'd phoned* (American: '*would have phoned*'), *I'd have gone today*

Both clauses normally have a pluperfect subjunctive. The conditional perfect is sometimes found in the main clause (**würde . . . gefahren sein**).

▶ For the forms of the pluperfect subjunctive see pp. 5–11.

■ In all three types normal order (rather than inversion) is occasionally found in the main clause:

> **wenn er anrufen würde, ich würde heute noch fahren**

■ In all three types, if the 'if' clause comes first, the word **wenn** may be entirely omitted, the verb placed at the head of its clause, and **so** or **dann** (*then*) inserted at the head of the main clause:

> **ruft er heute an, (so/dann) werde ich heute fahren**
> **hätte er angerufen, (so/dann) wäre ich heute**
> **noch gefahren**

So is more literary than **dann**. Both may be omitted and in modern journalism often are; beware of attempting to read such sentences as questions!

■ **Wer**, *anyone who*, and **wenn nicht**, *unless*

Wer is really the equivalent of '**wenn jemand**' and follows the same rules as **wenn** used in 'if' sentences:

> **wer das gesagt hätte, hätte gelügt**, *anyone who*
> *said that would have been lying* (= **wenn jemand**
> **das gesagt hätte, hätte er gelügt**)

Wenn nicht also follows the same rules as **wenn**. Notice the position of the **nicht**:

> **wenn er nicht Geld genug hat, wird er zu Hause**
> **bleiben**, *unless he has enough money he'll stay at home*

THE IMPERATIVE

The imperative is used to give orders or instructions or to express requests.

Formation of the imperative

The imperative has four forms, which are based on the **du**, **wir**, **ihr**, and **Sie** forms of the present tense of the verb, with the verb first and the subject always following in the case of the **wir** and **Sie** forms. The **du** form of the imperative ends in **-e** rather than **-st**.

> **mache (du)!**, *make!*
> **machen wir!**, *let's make!*
> **macht (ihr)!**, *make!*
> **machen Sie!**, *make!*

The subject is usually dropped with the **du** and **ihr** forms, unless the sense is '*you* do it, not someone else'. The final **-e** of the **du** form is often omitted, especially in speech.
The exclamation mark is much more common with the imperative in German than in English, though not absolutely obligatory.

■ Strong verbs with a complete vowel change (not just an added umlaut) in the **du** and **er** forms of the present also make this change in the **du** form of the imperative. The final **-e** is never used with these verbs:

> **geben: du gibst; gib!**
> **fahren: du fährst; fahr(e)!**

Nehmen and **treten**, which also make consonant changes in the **du** and **er** forms of the present, make the same changes in the imperative: **nimm!**; **tritt!**

Sehen (imperative normally **sieh!**) has the form **siehe!** when giving a reference:

> **siehe Kapitel 3**, *see chapter 3*

■ **Sein** has irregular imperative forms: **sei (du)**, **seien wir**, **seid (ihr)**, **seien Sie**. The **du** forms of the (highly uncommon) imperative of **werden** and **wissen** are **werde!** and **wisse!**

■ Third-person commands (*let him/her/it/them . . .*) are expressed by using the present tense of **sollen**, the imperative of **lassen**, or (more literary) the present subjunctive of the verb:

> **er soll sofort kommen! / lass ihn sofort kommen! / er komme sofort!**, *he is to to come immediately*

▶ For the present subjunctive see pp. 5–11.

Alternatives to the imperative

■ The forms **wollen wir machen**, **wir wollen machen**, and **lass(t) uns machen** are frequent alternatives to **machen wir**.

■ **Wollen Sie bitte . . .** is much used as a polite form of command or request:

> **wollen Sie bitte Platz nehmen!**, *would you sit down please*

■ Official language often uses an infinitive or (in military commands) a past participle for the imperative:

> **nicht hinauslehnen!**, *don't lean out*
> **stillgestanden!**, *attention!*

■ A future tense may also be used as an imperative (see p. 23), as may a present tense with future meaning:

> **du machst es gleich!**, *you'll do it now!*

■ The impersonal passive (see p. 71) may also be used with an imperative sense:

> **hier wird nicht geraucht!**, *no smoking here!*

REFLEXIVE VERBS

Reflexive verbs are verbs whose direct or indirect object is the same as their subject (*he dries himself*; *she allows herself a chocolate*). In German they consist of a simple verb followed by the reflexive pronoun in the accusative or dative.

■ The reflexive pronouns

Apart from **sich**, they are the same as the ordinary accusative and dative object pronouns. Here is the present tense of two reflexive verbs showing all the reflexive pronouns in the accusative and dative:

sich trocknen, *dry oneself*	**sich erlauben**, *allow oneself (something)*
ich trockne **mich**	ich erlaube **mir**
du trocknest **dich**	du erlaubst **dir**
er trocknet **sich**	er erlaubt **sich**
wir trocknen **uns**	wir erlauben **uns**

ihr trocknet **euch**	ihr erlaubt **euch**
Sie trocknen **sich**	Sie erlauben **sich**
sie trocknen **sich**	sie erlauben **sich**

Notice that **sich** does not have a captital letter in the **Sie** (*you*) form.

☐ The reflexive pronoun corresponding to **man** is **sich**.

☐ Reflexive verbs form their compound past tenses with **haben**.

☐ The reflexive pronoun normally stands in the same position as other pronouns, in normal order immediately after the verb. In an infinitive phrase it comes first:

> **Sie werden gebeten, sich sofort in die Halle zu begeben**, *you are asked to make your way into the hall immediately*

■ Rec procal pronouns (*each other*)

Reflexive pronouns in the plural—**uns, euch, sich**—as well as meaning *(to) ourselves, (to) yourselves, (to) themselves*, can also mean *(to) one another* or *(to) each other*. This includes **sich** when it refers to **man** with a plural meaning (*we, you, people, etc.*):

> **wir sehen uns übermorgen**, *we'll see each other the day after tomorrow*
> **sie begegnen sich jeden Abend**, *they bump into each other every evening*
> **man muss sich lieben**, *we must love one another*

If ambiguity might arise, **selbst** is added where the pronoun is reflexive and **gegenseitig** where it is reciprocal:

> **sie fragten sich selbst, ob . . .** , *they asked themselves whether . . .*
> **sie fragten sich gegenseitig, ob . . .** , *they asked each other whether . . .*

Instead of the reciprocal pronoun **einander** may be used:

wir sehen einander übermorgen, *we'll see each other the day after tomorrow*

It is less common than **sich**, except after a preposition, where it must be used. It is always written as one word with the preposition:

seid nett zueinander!, *be nice to each other*

■ A German reflexive verb may correspond to a English one:

du musst dich waschen, *you must wash yourself*

but often it does not:

du hast dich verfahren, *you've taken the wrong road*
das bilden Sie sich ein, *you're just imagining that*

■ Reflexive verbs are occasionally used in German where English uses a passive (see p. 32):

das lässt sich machen, *that can be done*
das erklärt sich leicht, *that's easily explained*

■ The dative of the reflexive pronoun is often used with the sense of *for me* (etc.) to show involvement:

das werd ich mir auch besorgen, *I'll get myself that too*
das musst du dir ansehen, *you must have a look at that*
das kann ich mir denken, *I can well believe that*

▶ See also Pronouns, pp. 132–3.

THE PASSIVE

The passive forms of the tenses are those where the subject of the verb experiences the action rather than performs it (active: *he helped*; passive: *he was helped*).

Formation of the passive

The passive in English is formed with parts of the verb *to be* plus the past participle; in German it is formed in a similar way using parts of the verb **werden**, *to become*, plus the past participle:

> **es wird preiswert verkauft**, *it is being sold at a bargain price*
>
> **es wurde überall anerkannt**, *it was recognized everywhere*

■ The tenses of the passive are:

present passive	**es wird gemacht**, *it is done*
past passive	**es wurde gemacht**, *it was done*
perfect passive	**es ist gemacht worden**, *it has been done*
pluperfect passive	**es war gemacht worden**, *it had been done*
future passive	**es wird gemacht werden**, *it will be done*
conditional passive	**es würde gemacht werden**, *it would be done*

The past participle form of **werden** used when forming the passive is **worden**, not **geworden**:

> **er ist von seiner Firma belohnt worden**, *he was rewarded by his firm*

■ The following tenses and verb forms are virtually never used in the passive:

future perfect (**es wird gemacht worden sein**, *it will have been done*)

conditional perfect (**es würde gemacht worden sein**, *it would have been done*—the pluperfect subjunctive is used instead of this—see p. 24)

imperative

present participle

■ Where subjunctive forms of the passive are needed, **werden** is put into its equivalent subjunctive tense:

> **es wird gemacht → es werde gemacht** (present subjunctive passive)

■ With a passive verb in English *by* indicates either the 'doer' of the action or the instrument used. In German **von** is used for the person doing the action, **durch** for the instrument used:

> **er ist von seiner Frau ermordet worden**, *he was murdered by his wife*
>
> **er ist durch Gift ermordet worden**, *he was killed by poison*

but note

> **sie ist von einem Bus überfahren worden**, *she was run over by a bus*

—in this sentence the bus is seen as the 'doer' of the action, not as an instrument.

■ The ordinary past participle of a verb when used as an adjective always has a passive meaning, as in English:

> **eine längst vergessene Zeit**, *a long-forgotten time* (the time has *been* forgotten)

■ In English, the indirect object of an active verb may be made into the subject of the corresponding passive verb:

> *Adrian gave me the book→ I was given the book by Adrian*

This is impossible in German. *I was given the book* can be translated using **man**:

> **man gab mir das Buch** (literally: *someone gave me the book*)

but if the 'doer' is mentioned ('*by Adrian*') the active form has to be used in German:

> **Adrian gab mir das Buch**

In the same way, verbs which take the dative in German cannot be used in the passive. *I was helped by Adrian* must become active:

> **Adrian hat mir geholfen**

There *is* an impersonal passive equivalent:

> **es wurde mir von Adrian geholfen** (literally: *it was helped to me by Adrian*)

—but this is clumsy and little used, and should be avoided.

► For the passive infinitive see p. 45.

Alternatives to the passive with werden

The passive, whilst not being largely avoided as it is in French, is used in German less frequently than in English. This is especially true of the future passive.

■ **Man** (*one, people*) is frequently used instead:

> **man hat mich angerufen**, *I was phoned up*

■ Sometimes a reflexive verb is used:

> **es hat sich als falsch erwiesen**, *it has been proved false*
>
> **das erklärt sich dadurch, dass** . . . , *that is explained by the fact that . . .*
>
> **das lässt sich machen**, *that can be done*

■ When the passive conveys a state rather than an action **sein** is used instead of **werden**:

> **sie war gut dafür geeignet**, *she was well suited to it*
>
> **der Brief ist auf Englisch geschrieben**, *the letter is written in English* (but: **er wurde letzte Woche von mir geschrieben**, *it was written by me last week*)

COMPOUND VERBS

Compound verbs follow the same pattern of tense-endings as simple verbs. They are formed by adding a prefix to the simple verb. This prefix may be either separable (**auf-, an-, zu-,** etc.), or inseparable (**er-, be-, ver-,** etc.), or sometimes separable, sometimes inseparable according to the meaning of the verb (**um-, unter-, durch-,** etc.).

Separable prefixes

Most prefixes are separable, and most separable prefixes can also be used as parts of speech in their own right, usually prepositions (**aus**steigen), but occasionally adverbs (**davon**laufen), nouns (**teil**nehmen), adjectives (**frei**sprechen). A verb with a separable prefix always has the stress on the prefix.

Position of the prefix

■ A separable prefix is found attached to its verb in the infinitive:

> **ich muß aufstehen**, *I have to get up*
> **dürfen wir weggehen?**, *may we go away?*

If the infinitive is used with **zu**, the **zu** is inserted between prefix and verb:

> **ich versuche aufzustehen**, *I'm trying to get up*

■ The prefix also remains attached in the present participle:

> **die aufgehende Sonne**, *the rising sun*

■ Once the verb is used in any of its tenses, however, the prefix separates from it and moves to the end of the clause:

> **ich stehe früh auf**, *I get up early*
> **ich stand auf**, *I got up*
> **geh sofort weg!**, *go away at once!*

If the verb itself is at the end of the clause (as is the case in subordinate order) the prefix and verb join up again:

> **ich weiß nicht, wann wir heute abfahren**, *I don't know when we're leaving today*

■ In the past participle the **ge-** appears between prefix and verb:

> **der Zug ist schon abgefahren**, *the train has already left*

Inseparable prefixes

The prefixes **be-**, **emp-**, **ent-**, **er-**, **ge-**, **miss-**, **ver-**, **zer-** are always inseparable. The only difference between verbs with these prefixes and simple verbs is that they have no **ge-** in their past participle:

verstehen, *to understand*: **ich habe verstanden**

Inseparable prefixes do not exist as independent words (unlike most separable prefixes). They never take the stress, which always goes on the verb itself.

Prefixes that may be either separable or inseparable

The prefixes **durch-**, **hinter-**, **über-**, **um-**, **unter-**, **voll-**, **wider-**, **wieder-** are separable with some verbs, inseparable with others. Whether they are being used separably or inseparably can immediately be distinguished in speech by where the main accent is—on the prefix or on the stem of the verb.

Often the same verb has different meanings according to whether the prefix is separable or inseparable. Quite frequently the separable version of the verb will have a literal meaning, the inseparable version a figurative one:

übersetzen (sep.), *ferry across*
übersetzen (insep.), *translate*

This is not, however, always the case: if in any doubt, check in the dictionary.

Double prefixes

■ A separable prefix followed by an inseparable one separates, but the verb has no **ge-** in its past participle:

zubereiten, *to prepare*
er bereitet das Mittagessen zu, *he's preparing lunch*

> **er versucht, das Mittagessen zuzubereiten**, *he's trying*
> *to prepare lunch*
> **er hat das Mittagessen zubereitet**, *he's prepared lunch*

■ With the verb **missverstehen**, *to misunderstand* (which has a
double inseparable prefix), the prefixes do not separate, and
there is no **ge-** in the past participle; however, in the infinitive
with **zu** the **miss-** behaves like a separable prefix:
misszuverstehen, and the stress throughout is on **miss-**:

> **sie <u>miss</u> versteht mich immer**, *she always*
> *misunderstands me*
> **um mich nicht <u>miss</u> zuverstehen . . .** , *so as not to*
> *misunderstand me . . .*

■ The separable prefixes **hin-** and **her-** in their literal
meanings imply respectively motion away from and motion
towards the speaker. As well as being added to simple verbs
they may also be added to compound verbs, producing a
double separable prefix. This behaves like a single separable
prefix:

> **er kommt herauf**, *he's coming up*
> **er ist heraufgekommen**, *he came up*
> **er braucht nicht heraufzukommen**, *he doesn't*
> *need to come up*

■ The separable prefix **wieder-** is the equivalent of the English
prefix *re-*. Attached to a verb with a separable prefix, it stands
alone when the prefix is separated from its verb:

> **wiederherstellen**, *to restore*
> **ich stelle es wieder her**, *I'm restoring it*
> **stell es wieder her!**, *restore it*
> **sobald du es wiederherstellst . . .** , *as soon as*
> *you restore it*
> **man hat es wiederhergestellt**, *they've restored it*
> **man versucht es wiederherzustellen**, *they're*
> *trying to restore it*

Somewhat similarly, in the compound verb **loswerden** the **los** only joins the verb in its infinitive and past participle:

> **ich muss es loswerden**, *I must get rid of it*
> **wenn du es endlich los wirst . . .** , *if you're finally getting rid of it . . .*

PARTICIPLES

The present participle

Formation of the present participle

The present participle (in English, the *-ing* part of the verb) is formed in German for all verbs by adding **-d** to the infinitive:

> **machen**, *to make* : **machend**, *making*
> **gehen**, *to go* : **gehend**, *going*

Sein, *to be*, and **haben**, *to have*, have no present participles.

Uses of the present participle

The present participle is most commonly found as an adjective in German, standing immediately in front of a noun:

> **das wartende Auto**, *the waiting car*

It can, in this position, form the last element of a phrase that may be considerably longer than would be possible in front of the noun in English:

> **das reglos in der Hüppertstraße vor den großen Toren der Militärkaserne wartende Auto**, *the car, waiting motionless before the great gates of the military barracks in the Hüppertstraße*

In this position it also substitutes for the infinitive:

> **ein bei dieser Dunkelheit kaum zu sehendes Auto**, *a car scarcely to be seen in this darkness*

Note that the present participle has a passive meaning ('a car to *be* seen') in this construction.

■ Many present participles have come to be treated as adjectives and can be used after verbs such as **sein** or **werden** just as adjectives can. They can equally be used as adverbs. They include

> **auffallend**, *striking*
> **aufregend**, *exciting*
> **reizend**, *charming*
> **empörend**, *shocking*

and noun + present participle combinations such as

> **bahnbrechend**, *pioneering*
> **teilnehmend**, *compassionate*

> **ich finde sie ganz reizend und überraschend schön,**
> *I find her quite charming and astonishingly beautiful*

The past participle

Formation of the past participle

Past participles of weak verbs are formed by adding **ge-** to the beginning and **-t** to the end of the stem of the verb:

> **machen**, *to make* → **gemacht**, *made*
> **wandern**, *to hike* → **gewandert**, *hiked*

There is an extra **-e** in the past-participle ending of verbs whose infinitives end **-ten** and **-den**:

> **antworten**, *to answer* → **geantwortet**, *answered*
> **senden**, *to send* → **gesendet**, *sent*

Past participles of strong verbs are formed by adding **ge-** to the beginning and **-en** to the end of the stem of the verb, often with a vowel change and sometimes with a consonant change as well:

> **braten**, *to roast* →**gebraten**, *roasted*
> **bleiben**, *to stay*→**geblieben**, *stayed*
> **leiden**,*to suffer*→**gelitten**, *suffered*

▶ The modals and **werden** and **lassen** have two past participles. See p. 30 (**werden**) and p. 66 (modals and **lassen**).

▶ Verbs ending **-eien** and **-ieren** and verbs with inseparable prefixes have no **ge-** in the past participle. For further details see pp. 14 and 34.

▶ For all past participles of strong verbs see the Irregular Verb list, pp. 73–85.

Uses of the past participle

■ The past participle is used to form all the past compound tenses. It is always placed at the end of its clause. See pp. 217–18.

■ The past participle is used with **werden** or **sein** to form the passive. See p. 29.

■ The past participle may be used adjectivally; it then agrees with a following noun, takes an adverb qualification, etc., just like any other adjective:

> **ein verlorener Gegenstand**, *a lost object*
> **ich bin völlig erschöpft**, *I'm completely exhausted*

Like the present participle it may be found, with the appropriate adjective ending, standing before its noun at the end of an adjective phrase. This may sometimes be extremely long:

> **ich muss mich für Ihren gestern per Fax in unserem**
> **Münchener Büro erhaltenen Brief herzlich**
> **bedanken**, *I must thank you cordially for your letter,*
> *received yesterday by fax in our Munich office*

This construction is extremely common in books, newspapers, and letters, but almost never found in spoken German.

■ The past participle may be used in an adjective phrase standing separately from its noun. It usually (but not necessarily) stands at the end of the phrase:

> **auf seinen Regenschirm gestützt, trat er ins Restaurant**, *leaning on his umbrella, he came into the restaurant*
>
> **gequält von einer Schar ihrer Enkelkinder, saß die alte Dame ruhig vorm Ofen und strickte**, *tormented by a crowd of her grandchildren the old lady sat by the stove calmly knitting*

■ The past participle is occasionally used as an imperative. See p. 27.

■ After the verb **kommen**, *to come*, German uses the past participle of a motion verb where English uses the present participle:

> **sie kommt gelaufen**, *she comes running*
> **du kamst herbeigeeilt**, *you came hurrying up*

THE SUBJUNCTIVE

The subjunctive expresses doubt, uncertainty, disagreement, and scarcely exists any longer in English (*if I were you*; *if that be so*; *would that he were* are some of the few remaining examples of it). In German, though some of its forms are literary or affected, it is still in constant use in both the written and spoken language.

Its main use is in reported matter, in order to disclaim personal responsibility for what is being said, or at least to distance oneself from it. The subjunctive is much used in newspaper reports. It is by no means obligatory when reporting speech, however, and indeed is rarely used when the reporting verb (**er sagt, er meint**, etc.) is in the present and related tenses (see p. 40).

Formation of the subjunctive

The subjunctive has four forms, present, past (sometimes called the imperfect), perfect, and pluperfect. Their grammatical names do NOT indicate their function—the past subjunctive is not a past tense.

▶ For the subjunctive forms of weak verbs see pp. 5–7.

▶ For the subjunctive forms of strong verbs see pp. 7–9.

▶ For the subjunctive forms of mixed verbs see pp. 9–11.

■ The future subjunctive is little used. It is formed with the present subjunctive of **werden** + infinitive:

ich werde gehen	**wir werden gehen**
du werdest gehen	**ihr werdet gehen**
er werde gehen	**sie werden gehen**

■ There is an almost never used future perfect subjunctive, formed with the present subjunctive of **werden** + the perfect infinitive:

ich werde gegangen sein, etc.

■ The present subjunctive of **sein** is irregular:

ich sei	**wir seien**
du sei(e)st	**ihr seiet**
er sei	**sie seien**

The subjunctive in reported speech

The subjunctive is used in indirect speech largely as a distancing device ('this is what she said, it may or may not be true, I'm not responsible for it'). It is what is said, not the 'saying' verb, that goes into the subjunctive.

If the 'saying' verb is in the present, future, or imperative, the verb that follows is not put into the subjunctive. The same applies if the 'saying' verb is in the perfect but refers to something said in the immediate past.

If it is in any past tense the following verb will normally be in the subjunctive. In German (but not in English) the tense of the subjunctive depends on the tense of the *original direct speech*.

Choice of subjunctive tense in reported speech

■ If the original speech was in the present, the present subjunctive is used to report it (or the past subjunctive, see below). This tense sequence is different from English:

> **sie sagte, dass er gehe**, *she said he was going* (her actual words were 'er geht')

■ If the original speech was in a past tense, the perfect subjunctive is used to report it (or the pluperfect subjunctive, see below). This too does not correspond to English tenses:

> **sie sagte, dass er gegangen sei**, *she said he had gone* (her actual words were 'er ist gegangen')

■ If the original speech was in the future or conditional, the conditional is used to report it, unless it is in the **er** form, in which case the future subjunctive may be used:

> **sie sagte, dass du gehen würdest**, *she said you would go* (her actual words were 'du wirst gehen')

but: **sie sagte, dass er gehen werde/würde**, *she said he would go* (her actual words were 'er wird gehen')

■ Many forms of the present and perfect subjunctive are not obviously subjunctive; in such cases the past subjunctive should be used instead of the present subjunctive, and the pluperfect subjunctive instead of the perfect subjunctive:

> **sie sagte, dass ich es hätte**, *she said I had it* (**habe** would not be obviously subjunctive)
>
> **sie sagte, dass ich es gemacht hätte**, *she said I had done it* (**gemacht habe** would not be obviously subjunctive)

This substitution may sometimes be made even when the other tense is clearly subjunctive (especially in the spoken language, and especially by north Germans), and it is almost always made to avoid the **du** and **ihr** forms of the present subjunctive, which are little used in spoken German.

Also avoided are past subjunctives of strong verbs except the most common ones (e.g. **wäre**, **hätte**, **würde**, and the modals). Especially shunned are the irregular past subjunctives (see Irregular Verb list, pp. 73–85).

Dropped dass

In all the above examples the **dass** may be dropped, with normal instead of subordinate word order after the 'saying' word:

sie sagte, ich hätte es gemacht

This form without **dass** is actually the more common, except after a negative (**sie sagte nicht, dass** . . .). Newspaper reports will frequently drop the saying verb as well, after an initial indication of who was speaking. Inserts like '*he added*', '*she continued*', '*it went on*' are often necessary in English to show that reported speech continues: in German the subjunctive demonstrates this clearly:

> **Nach Angaben der Meteorologen in Dahlem gingen bei dem Gewitter auch bis zu fünf Zentimeter große Hagelkörner nieder. In Zehlendorf seien** [not **sind**, so this is also part of the report . . .] **23 Liter Niederschlag je Quadratmeter gemessen worden.**
>
> *(Der Tagesspiegel)*

> *According to information received from the Dahlem weather-forecasters, hailstones up to five centimetres in size also fell during this storm. In Zehlendorf precipitation of 23 litres per square metre was measured, it is claimed.*

'Saying' verbs

All verbs introducing reported matter count as 'saying' verbs. The following is a list of such verbs that may not be obviously of this kind at first glance:

ahnen, *suspect*	**erklären**, *explain*
annehmen, *assume*	**erwarten**, *expect*
denken, *think*	**fragen**, *ask*

fühlen, *feel*	**sich einbilden**, *imagine (falsely)*
fürchten, *fear*	**sich vorstellen**, *imagine*
hoffen, *hope*	**träumen**, *dream*
hören, *hear*	**wünschen**, *wish*
meinen, *think*	**zweifeln**, *doubt*
schreiben, *write*	

Other uses of the subjunctive

■ The past subjunctive of **werden (würde)** plus the infinitive is used to form the conditional tense; in the case of **sein**, **haben**, the modals, and some of the commoner strong verbs a past subjunctive is often used instead of a conditional:

> **ich würde sein / ich wäre**, *I would be*

■ The past and pluperfect subjunctive are used in 'if' sentences. See Conditional, p. 24.

■ The subjunctive is used in some set third-person commands (**Gott sei Dank!**, *thank God*; **es lebe die Republik!**, *long live the Republic!*). Otherwise third-person commands are expressed by the present of **sollen** or by the imperative of **lassen**:

> **er soll das tun / lass ihn das tun**, *let him do it*

▶ See Imperative, p. 25.

■ The past subjunctive is frequently used in conversation to tone down a suggestion, to make it more polite:

> **ich weiß, wie das zu schaffen wäre**, *I know how that might be managed*
> **das wären dreizehn Mark fünfzig**, *that will be DM 13.50*
> **wäre Ihnen das recht?**, *would that be all right?*
> **wären Sie damit zufrieden?**, *are you happy with that then?*

English has a variety of strategies for this ('*might*', future for present, '*would*', '*then*', etc.).

Note the similar use, when telephoning, of

> **ich hätte gern mit Herrn X gesprochen**, *could I
> possibly speak to Herr X?*

■ Subjunctive after **als ob / als wenn**, *as if*

The subjunctive is correctly used after **als ob** and **als wenn**
(though in casual speech it may not be). There is a difference in
meaning according to the tense used:

> **sie sah aus, als ob sie nicht ganz vertrauenswürdig
> sei**, *she looked as if she wasn't completely reliable* (and
> it turned out she wasn't!)
>
> **sie sah aus, als ob sie nicht ganz vertrauenswürdig
> wäre**, *she looked as if she wasn't completely reliable*
> (but it turned out she was)

There is a similar difference between perfect and pluperfect
subjunctives (both = *had been*).

The **ob** or **wenn** may be dropped, with inverted instead of
subordinate word order after **als**. This is more literary:

> **sie sah aus, als sei sie nicht ganz
> vertrauenswürdig**

■ The subjunctive is also found after **damit** and **(so)dass**,
meaning *so that*. This is a very literary use. More usual is the
addition of **können**:

> **halt die Leiter, damit er das Bild aufhängen kann
> (aufhänge)**, *hold the ladder, so that he can (may)
> hang the picture*

Similarly with **damit . . . nicht**, *lest*. Here **können** is not used:

> **halt die Leiter, damit sie nicht fällt (falle)**, *hold
> the ladder, so it doesn't fall*

■ The subjunctive is sometimes used after **nicht dass**, *not
that*, **ohne dass**, *without*, **anstatt dass**, *instead of*, and **zu**
ADJECTIVE . . . **als dass**, *too* ADJECTIVE *to*. It gives a less
brusque meaning:

nicht, dass Sie zu alt wären . . ., *not that you're too old . . .*

(rather more polite than **nicht, dass Sie zu alt sind . . .**)

The subjunctive tenses found are the past and pluperfect.

THE INFINITIVE

Infinitives of German verbs end in **-en** or occasionally just **-n**, and correspond to the English *to . . .* form of the verb:

> **machen,** *to make*
> **handeln,** *to act*
> **tun,** *to do*

The infinitive is the 'name' of the verb: it is really a sort of noun and can be used as such, then being given a capital letter like all nouns. Infinitives used as nouns are neuter:

> **das Rauchen ist sicher gefährlich,** *smoking (to smoke) is certainly dangerous*

English often uses the *-ing* form of the verb in this case.

■ Infinitives stand at the end of the clause:

> **ich hoffe, morgen in die Stadt zu fahren,** *I hope to go into town tomorrow*

▶ See Word Order, p. 224.

■ When they have a dependent infinitive, the modal verbs (**dürfen, können, mögen, müssen, sollen, wollen**) use their own infinitive instead of their past participle in past compound tenses. The same applies to **lassen, sehen,** and **hören,** and a few other verbs. See pp. 66–7 and 68–9.

■ The infinitive in German has perfect and passive forms:

> **gemacht haben,** *to have made*
> **gemacht werden,** *to be made*
> **gemacht worden sein,** *to have been made*

These forms are used exactly as their English equivalents are:

> **er hofft, bis dann den Versuch gemacht zu haben**, *he hopes to have made the attempt by then*

The infinitive with and without zu

Infinitives usually follow ('depend on') another verb, and as in English they are joined to it by **zu**, *to* or by nothing at all:

> **ich versuche zu schwimmen**, *I'm trying to swim*
> **ich muss schwimmen**, *I must swim*

Whether **zu** is used or not depends on the head verb, not on the infinitive, and it doesn't vary—it is always **versuchen** + **zu** + infinitive, **müssen** + infinitive.

■ Most verbs in fact take **zu**. Only the following do not:

□ The modal verbs: **dürfen, können, mögen, müssen, sollen, wollen**. See p. 60 onwards.

□ **sehen**, *to see*
hören, *to hear*
fühlen, *to feel*
spüren, *to feel, to perceive*

> **ich sah ihn kommen**, *I saw him coming*

Again, English uses the *-ing* form of the verb here.

With these verbs a '**wie . . .** ' clause is normally substituted if the infinitive would be in any way qualified:

> **ich sah, wie er langsam um die Ecke kam**, *I saw him coming slowly round the corner*

□ **finden**, *to find* (only + **stehen** or **liegen**, *to find standing/lying*)

> **ich fand meine Socken auf dem Tisch liegen**, *I found my socks lying on the table*

□ **heißen**, *to bid, to tell . . . to* (literary use)

> **er hieß mich gehen**, *he bade me go (he told me to go)*

□ **lassen**, *to let; to make* (see p. 68)

■ **bleiben, gehen, kommen, schicken, haben** are used without **zu** with certain infinitives, as follows.

□ **bleiben** + 'situation' verb:

> **sitzen bleiben**, *to stay seated*
> **stehen bleiben**, *to remain standing*
> etc.

□ **gehen, kommen, schicken**, in cases where the interest is entirely focused on the dependent verb:

> **du gehst aber jetzt schlafen!**, *you really are going to bed now!*
> **kommst du heute abend tanzen?**, *are you coming dancing tonight?*
> **sie hat mich einkaufen geschickt**, *she sent me shopping*

□ **haben**, meaning *to have something kept or stored somewhere*:

> **ich habe meine Schuhe im Schrank liegen**, *I've got my shoes in the cupboard*

■ Three verbs sometimes take **zu**, sometimes not: **helfen**, *to help*; **lehren**, *to teach*; **lernen**, *to learn*.

With these verbs an unqualified infinitive has no **zu**, a qualified one has **zu**:

> **sie hilft mir abwaschen**, *she's helping me wash up*
> **hilf mir, dieses schmutzige Geschirr abzuwaschen**, *help me wash up these dirty dishes*

With **lehren** and **lernen** a 'wie . . . ' clause is often substituted in the latter case:

> **sie lehrte mich, wie man Geschirr abwäscht**, *she taught me (how) to wash dishes*

■ After **sein**, **zu** + the infinitive has a passive meaning in German:

> **es war niemand zu sehen**, *there was nobody to be seen* (not '*to see*')
>
> **ist Herr Meyer zu sprechen, bitte?**, *can I speak to Herr Meyer please?* (*is Herr M. to be spoken to?*)

■ After parts of speech other than verbs, the infinitive is used with **zu**:

> **das ist schwer zu sagen**, *that's difficult to say*
>
> **ich sehe keine Möglichkeit, das zu tun**, *I can see no possibility of doing that*
>
> **arbeiten ist besser, als im Liegestuhl zu liegen**, *working is better than lying in a deckchair*

In the last case (after **als**) the infinitive is occasionally found without **zu**.

■ Where the sense allows it the infinitive may also be preceded by **um . . . zu**, meaning *in order to*. Notice the word order (**um** always starts the phrase):

> **ich bin hier, um meine Rechte und die meiner Mitbürger zu verlangen**, *I am here in order to demand my rights and those of my fellow citizens*

An adjective with **zu . . .**, *too*, or **. . . genug**, *enough*, is also followed by **um . . . zu** + infinitive, not just **zu**:

> **er ist alt genug (zu jung), um besser zu wissen**, *he's old enough (too young) to know better*

▶ For the use of the infinitive as an imperative see Imperative, p. 27.

▶ For the use of the comma with the infinitive see Punctuation, p. 231.

OBJECT OF THE VERB

Verbs in German may be followed by a direct (accusative) object, an indirect (dative) object, a preposition plus object, or a combination of these.

Verbs with the accusative

Most verbs taking an accusative object ('transitive' verbs) correspond exactly to English verbs and present no problems. But note

■ **sprechen** means *to speak to* and takes an accusative:

> **darf ich ihn sprechen, bitte?**, *may I speak to him please?*

(**Sprechen mit** + dative can also be used in this sense.)

■ **fragen, lehren, kosten,** and **nennen** (and its more formal equivalent, **heißen**) have two accusative objects:

> **es kostete mich 300 Mark**, *it cost me DM 300*
> **sie lehrte mich Computerwissenschaft**, *she taught me computer science*
> **frag mich das nicht!**, *don't ask me that*
> **er nannte (hieß) mich einen Dummkopf**, *he called me a fool* (the second accusative here is technically a complement)

Verbs with the dative

■ Some verbs that are transitive in English take a dative (indirect) object in German. Such verbs are

auffallen, *to strike*	**gefallen**, *to please*
begegnen, *to meet*	**gehorchen**, *to obey*
danken, *to thank*	**gleichen**, *to equal;*
dienen, *to serve*	*to resemble*
drohen, *to threaten*	**gratulieren**, *to*
folgen, *to follow*	*congratulate*

helfen, *to help*
imponieren, *to impress*
kündigen, *to sack*
Leid tun: das tut mir Leid, *I'm sorry*
(miss)trauen, *to (dis)trust*
nutzen/nützen, *to benefit; to help*
passen, *to suit; to fit*

raten, *to advise*
schaden, *to harm*
schmeicheln, *to flatter*
stehen, *to suit*
trotzen, *to defy*
versichern, *to assure (somebody)*
wehtun (das tut mir weh), *to hurt*

es hat mir sehr gefallen, *it pleased me a lot*
sie ist mir begegnet, *she met (= ran into) me*

Note that **begegnen** and **folgen** are verbs of motion without a direct object and so form their past compound tenses with **sein**.

■ In addition to the above list, most verbs with the following prefixes take the dative: **bei-, ein-, ent-, entgegen-, nach-, vor-, wider-, zu-:**

> **sie rief mir nach,** *she called after me*
> **er stand mir bei,** *he stood by me*

But note that **nachahmen** and **nachmachen**, both meaning *to imitate*, take the accusative.

■ The verbs **erlauben**, *to allow*, **glauben**, *to believe*, **verzeihen**, *to forgive*, **verbieten**, *to forbid*, and **befehlen**, *to order*, have an accusative if the object is a thing:

> **das glaube ich,** *I believe that*
> **man erlaubt nichts,** *nothing is allowed*

. . . but a dative if the object is a person:

> **ich glaube ihr nicht,** *I don't believe her*
> **man erlaubte ihm, gleich zu fahren,** *they allowed him to go straight away*

With **antworten**, *to answer*, a personal object is in the dative, but for an impersonal object **auf** + the accusative is used:

ich will dir sofort antworten, *I want to answer you straight away*

ich habe auf deinen Brief schon geantwortet, *I've already answered your letter*

■ A small number of reflexive verbs take a direct object that is not their reflexive pronoun; the reflexive in this case is a dative:

das kann ich mir denken, *I can imagine that*

The dative reflexive differs from the accusative only in the **mir** and **dir** forms (see p. 27).

Most such verbs are reflexive forms of verbs in the list on pp. 49–50. The following verbs, where the reflexive pronoun is dative, are not:

sich einbilden, *to imagine (wrongly)*
sich vornehmen, *to make up one's mind to*
sich vorstellen, *to imagine, to visualize*

stell dir das vor!, *just imagine that!*

▶ Many impersonal verbs also take a dative. See pp. 70–2.

▶ For dative indicating possession see p. 88.

Verbs followed by a preposition

Most prepositions may be used after verbs. Some verbs take more than one preposition, with different meanings.

The preposition that follows a German verb often differs from that used with the equivalent English verb and must be learned with the verb.

Dative or accusative?

For the case used with literal meanings of prepositions that can take either dative or accusative see pp. 159–60. The case with figurative meanings of these prepositions varies according to the preposition used:

■ **an:** meaning *in respect of, from, by, in connection with*: dative

> **es fehlt mir am notwendigen Geld,** *I lack the necessary money*
>
> **ich leide an der Grippe,** *I'm suffering from flu*
>
> **ich erkannte ihn an seiner Stimme,** *I recognized him by his voice*
>
> **das hasse ich an deinem Bruder,** *that's what I hate about your brother*

meaning *in the (mental) direction of*: accusative

> **ich erinnere mich an ihn,** *I remember him*
>
> **denk an mich,** *think of me*
>
> **glaubst du an Gott?,** *do you believe in God?*

■ **auf:** normally accusative, but note **beruhen auf** + DAT, *be based on*, **bestehen auf** + DAT, *insist on*

■ **in:** dative

■ **über:** normally accusative, but note **brüten über** + DAT, *to brood on*, **stehen über** + DAT, *to have mastered (a topic)*

■ **unter:** dative

■ **vor:** dative

▶ The rules above apply equally to prepositions used after adjectives and after nouns.

▶ For the prepositions used with individual verbs see the list on pp. 53–60.

Verb + preposition + -ing

English often makes the *-ing* form of the verb into the object of the preposition:

> *I insist on them going with you*
> *I insist on going with you*

In the first type of example above, where *going* has a different subject from *insist*, German uses the preposition compounded with **da-** followed by a clause beginning **dass:**

> **ich bestehe darauf, dass sie mit euch mitfahren**
> (literally: *I insist on it, that . . .*)

In the second type of example above, where both *insist* and *going* have the same subject, an infinitive phrase may be used instead of the **dass** clause:

> **ich bestehe darauf, mit euch mitzufahren**

or: **ich bestehe darauf, dass ich mit euch mitfahre**

If the preposition begins with a vowel, as above, **dar-** and not **da-** is added.

Verbs followed by the genitive

A small number of German verbs, mostly reflexive, are followed by the genitive. They are found mainly in literary or legal language. The commonest are

> **anklagen**, *to accuse of*
> **berauben**, *to rob of*
> **sich entsinnen**, *to recollect*
> **sich erbarmen**, *to take pity on*
> **sich erfreuen**, *to enjoy* (e.g. health)
> **sich erinnern**, *to remember* (more commonly: **an** + ACC)
> **sich rühmen**, *to boast*
> **sich schämen**, *to be ashamed of* (more commonly: **wegen** + GEN)
> **sich vergewissern**, *to make sure of*
> **versichern**, *to assure of*
> **sich versichern**, *to secure*
>
> **ich kann Sie meiner Hilfe versichern**, *I can assure you of my help*

ALPHABETICAL LIST OF VERB CONSTRUCTIONS

The list includes the commonest verbs taking the dative and the genitive and the commonest verb + preposition constructions (with their case).

abhängen von + DAT	*be dependent on*
achten auf + ACC	*look after*
Acht geben auf + ACC	*pay attention to*
sich amüsieren über + ACC	*laugh at*
angeln nach + DAT	*fish for*
sich ängstigen um + ACC	*be anxious about*
anklagen + GEN	*accuse of*
sich anpassen + DAT	*adapt oneself to*
anspielen auf + ACC	*allude to*
antworten + DAT	*answer (somebody)*
antworten auf + ACC	*answer (something)*
anwenden auf + ACC	*apply to*
sich ärgern über + ACC	*get annoyed with*
auffallen + DAT	*strike (= occur to)*
auffallen an + DAT	*be striking about*
aufhören mit + DAT	*stop (doing)*
aufpassen auf + ACC	*keep an eye on*
ausschauen nach + DAT	*look out for*
ausweichen + DAT	*get out of the way of*
basieren auf + DAT	*be based on*
bauen auf + ACC	*build on*
sich bedanken für + ACC	*thank for*
befehlen + DAT	*order (somebody)*
befördern zu + DAT	*promote (to the post/rank of)*
begegnen + DAT	*meet*
beitragen zu + DAT	*contribute to*
sich beklagen bei + DAT	*complain to*
sich beklagen über + ACC	*complain about*
beneiden um + ACC	*envy (something)*
berauben + GEN	*rob (somebody) of*
beruhen auf + DAT	*be based on*
beruhigen über + ACC	*reassure about*
sich beschäftigen mit + DAT	*occupy oneself with*
sich beschränken auf + ACC	*restrict oneself to*
sich beschweren bei + DAT	*complain to*
sich beschweren über + ACC	*complain about*

bestehen auf + DAT	*insist on*
bestehen aus + DAT	*consist of*
bestehen in + DAT	*consist in*
sich beteiligen an + DAT	*participate in*
beten um + ACC	*pray for*
betteln um + ACC	*beg for*
sich bewerben um + ACC	*apply for*
sich beziehen auf + ACC	*refer to*
bitten um + ACC	*ask for*
danken + DAT	*thank*
denken an + ACC	*think of*
denken über + ACC or	*think of (= have an opinion of)*
von + DAT	
sich (DAT) denken	*imagine*
dienen + DAT	*serve*
dienen zu + DAT	*be (used) for*
drohen + DAT	*threaten*
sich drücken vor + DAT	*get out of*
dürsten nach + DAT	*thirst for*
sich (DAT) einbilden	*imagine (wrongly)*
eingehen auf + ACC	*agree to*
sich einsetzen für + ACC	*do what one can for*
einverstanden sein mit + DAT	*be in agreement with*
es ekelt (mich) vor + DAT	*. . . disgusts (me)*
entkommen + DAT	*escape from*
sich entscheiden für + ACC	*decide in favour of*
sich entschließen zu + DAT	*decide on*
sich entschuldigen bei + DAT	*apologize to*
sich entsinnen + GEN	*recollect*
sich erbarmen + GEN	*take pity on*
sich erfreuen + GEN	*enjoy (e.g. health)*
sich erholen von + DAT	*recover from*
erinnern an + ACC	*remind*
sich erinnern an + ACC	*remember*
erkennen an + DAT	*recognize by*
erkranken an + DAT	*become ill with*

sich erkundigen über + ACC or **nach** + DAT	*enquire about*
erlauben + DAT	*allow (somebody)*
ernennen zu + DAT	*appoint (to the post of)*
erröten über + ACC	*blush at*
erschrecken vor + DAT	*be scared by*
erschrecken über + ACC	*be shocked at*
sich erstrecken auf + ACC	*include*
erzählen über + ACC or **von** + DAT	*tell about*
es fehlt an + DAT	*there's a lack of*
fischen nach + DAT	*fish for (e.g. compliments)*
flehen um + ACC	*plead for*
fliehen vor + DAT	*flee from*
folgen + DAT	*follow*
fragen nach + DAT, **um** + ACC, or **über** + ACC	*ask for*
sich freuen auf + ACC	*look forward to*
sich freuen über + ACC	*be pleased at*
sich fürchten vor + DAT	*be afraid of*
gebrauchen zu + DAT	*use for*
gefallen + DAT	*please*
gefallen an + DAT	*be pleasing about*
gehorchen + DAT	*obey*
gehören + DAT	*belong to*
es geht um + ACC	*it's a matter of*
gelingen + DAT	*succeed*
genügen + DAT	*be enough for*
sich gewöhnen an + ACC	*get used to*
glauben + DAT	*believe (somebody)*
glauben an + ACC	*believe in*
gleichen + DAT	*equal*
graben nach + DAT	*dig for*
gratulieren + DAT	*congratulate*
greifen nach + DAT	*reach for*
halten für + ACC	*consider*

halten von + DAT	*think of; hold an opinion of*
handeln von + DAT	*be about*
es handelt sich um + ACC	*it's a question of*
hassen an + DAT	*hate about*
helfen + DAT	*help*
herrschen über + ACC	*rule over*
hinweisen auf + ACC	*refer to*
hoffen auf + ACC	*hope for*
hören über + ACC or **von** + DAT	*hear about*
sich hüten vor + DAT	*be on guard against*
imponieren + DAT	*impress*
sich interessieren für + ACC	*be interested in*
interessiert sein an + DAT	*be interested in*
sich irren in + DAT	*be mistaken about*
kämpfen um + ACC	*fight for*
kennen an + DAT	*know by*
klagen über + ACC	*grumble about*
kommen zu + DAT	*get around to*
konkurrieren um + ACC	*compete for*
sich konzentrieren auf + ACC	*concentrate on*
sich kümmern um + ACC	*care about*
kündigen + DAT	*sack*
lachen über + ACC	*laugh at*
lauern auf + ACC	*lie in wait for*
leben von + DAT	*live on*
leiden an + DAT or **unter** + DAT	*suffer from*
Leid tun + DAT (**es tut mir Leid**)	*be sorry*
lesen über + ACC or **von** + DAT	*read about*
misstrauen + DAT	*distrust*
nachdenken über + ACC	*think about*
nachgeben + DAT	*give way to; give more to*
neigen zu + DAT	*be prone to*
nutzen/nützen + DAT	*benefit; help*
passen + DAT	*suit; fit*
raten + DAT	*advise*
reagieren auf + ACC	*react to*

rechnen auf + ACC	*count on*
rechnen mit + DAT	*reckon with*
reden von + DAT	*talk about*
reden über + ACC	*say unpleasant things about*
reichen + DAT	*be enough for*
retten vor + DAT	*rescue from*
riechen nach + DAT	*smell of*
sich rühmen + GEN	*boast*
sagen über + ACC or **von** + DAT	*say about*
sagen zu + DAT	*say to*
schaden + DAT	*harm*
schicken nach + DAT	*send for*
schießen auf + ACC	*shoot at*
schimpfen über + ACC	*grumble at*
schimpfen auf + ACC	*swear at*
schlagen nach + DAT	*hit out at*
schmecken + DAT	*taste good to*
schmecken nach + DAT	*taste of*
schmeicheln + DAT	*flatter*
schreiben über + ACC or **von** + DAT	*write about*
schützen vor + DAT	*protect from*
schwärmen für + ACC or **von** + DAT	*be mad/crazy about*
sehen nach + DAT	*look like*
sich sehnen nach + DAT	*long for*
sorgen für + ACC	*look after*
sich sorgen um + ACC	*worry about*
sprechen über + ACC or **von** + DAT	*speak about*
stehen + DAT	*suit*
sterben an + DAT	*die of (e.g. a disease)*
sterben vor + DAT	*be dying of (e.g. boredom)*
strahlen vor + DAT	*beam with*
streben nach + DAT	*strive for*
streiken um + ACC	*strike for*

sich streiten um + ACC	*quarrel over*
sich streiten über + ACC	*quarrel about*
sich stürzen auf + ACC	*rush at*
suchen nach + DAT	*look for*
tasten nach + DAT	*grope for*
sich täuschen über + ACC	*be mistaken about*
sich täuschen in + DAT	*be mistaken in (somebody)*
teilnehmen an + DAT	*take part in*
telefonieren mit + DAT	*telephone*
telefonieren nach + DAT	*telephone for*
trauen + DAT	*trust*
trauern um + ACC	*mourn for*
träumen von + DAT	*dream about*
trinken auf + ACC	*drink to*
trotzen + DAT	*defy*
überreden zu + DAT	*talk into having*
sich umsehen nach + DAT	*look out for*
sich unterhalten über + ACC	*talk about*
sich verabschieden von + DAT	*say goodbye to*
verbieten + DAT	*forbid (somebody)*
verfügen über + ACC	*have at one's disposal*
sich vergewissern + GEN	*make sure of*
verlangen nach + DAT	*crave for; ask to see*
verlängern um + ACC	*extend by*
sich verlassen auf + ACC	*rely on*
sich verrechnen um + ACC	*make a mistake of*
versichern + DAT	*assure (somebody)*
versichern + GEN	*assure . . . of (something)*
sich versichern + GEN	*make certain of*
sich verstecken vor + DAT	*hide from*
verstehen unter + DAT	*understand by*
sich verstehen mit + DAT	*get on with (somebody)*
vertrauen + DAT	*trust*
verzeihen + DAT	*forgive*
verzichten auf + ACC	*renounce*
vorangehen + DAT	*go ahead of*

vorbeigehen an + DAT	*go past*
sich vorbereiten auf + ACC	*prepare for*
sich (DAT) **vornehmen**	*make one's mind up*
vorstehen + DAT	*be in charge of*
sich (DAT) **vorstellen**	*imagine; visualize*
wählen zu + DAT	*elect (to the office of)*
warnen vor + DAT	*warn of*
warten auf + ACC	*wait for*
wehtun + DAT	*hurt*
sich weiden an + DAT	*gloat over*
sich wenden an + ACC	*turn to*
werben um + ACC	*court*
weitergeben an + ACC	*pass on to*
widersprechen + DAT	*contradict*
widerstehen + DAT	*resist*
wissen über + ACC or **von** + DAT	*know about*
sich wundern über + ACC	*be surprised at*
zählen auf + ACC	*count on*
zählen unter + DAT or **zu** + DAT	*number among*
sich zanken um + ACC	*quarrel over*
zielen auf + ACC	*aim at*
zittern vor + DAT	*tremble with*
zugrunde gehen an + DAT	*be ruined by*
zusehen + DAT	*watch (somebody)*
zustimmen + DAT	*agree with*

THE MODAL VERBS AND LASSEN

The modal verbs (auxiliary verbs of 'mood' like *can, must, will* in English) always have a dependent infinitive:

darf ich Ihnen helfen?, *may I help you?*

Even if this infinitive is occasionally not expressed (**darf ich?**, *may I?*), it is virtually always implied. The only exception to this is some uses of **mögen**: see p. 62.

The modal verbs in German are

> **dürfen**, *may* (permission)
> **können**, *can*
> **mögen**, *may* (possibility)
> **müssen**, *must*
> **sollen**, *is to*
> **wollen**, *want*

The meanings given above are in fact not really adequate.
These verbs have a number of different meanings and shades of
meaning in different uses of their various tenses. These are
explained below.

dürfen

■ The basic meaning of **dürfen** is *to be allowed to*; it can also
express quite strong possibility. The English equivalent, in both
meanings, is often *may* in the present:

> **darf ich Ihnen etwas sagen?**, *may I tell you something?*
> **das darf wohl sein**, *that may well be so*

. . . *could* in the past:

> **ich durfte zum ersten Mal reisen**, *I could (= was
> allowed to) travel for the first time*

. . . and *might* in the past subjunctive:

> **dürfte ich noch ein Stück Torte nehmen?**, *might I
> possibly take another piece of gateau?*
> **das dürfte wahr sein**, *that might well be true*

In the negative, English uses *mustn't = is not allowed to*:

> **das darf ich nicht essen**, *I mustn't (I'm not allowed
> to) eat that*

■ Note also:

> **was darf es sein?**, *can I help you?; what shall it be?* (in
> shops, bars)
> **ich darf Ihnen sagen, dass . . .**, *I am able to tell you that . . .*

können

■ Basically **können** corresponds to *can* or *is able to* in the present:

> **kannst du mitfahren?**, *can you come with us?*

... and *could* or *was able to* in the past:

> **sie konnte nicht kommen**, *she couldn't come*

■ **Können** also expresses possibility:

> **das kann sein**, *that may be*
> **das kann nicht sein**, *that's not possible*
> **sie kann jeden Moment kommen**, *she may come at any moment*

The past subjunctive expresses remoter possibility:

> **das könnte ich vielleicht tun**, *I might perhaps do that*

■ It is frequently used colloquially for **dürfen**, just as English uses *can* for *may*:

> **kann ich mitkommen?**, *can/may I come with you?*

■ Note also:

> **er kann Italienisch**, *he speaks Italian*
> **dafür kann ich nichts**, *it's not my fault (I can't do anything about it)*

mögen

■ **Mögen** means both *to like*:

> **das mag ich nicht**, *I don't like that*
> **ich mag nicht**, *I don't like to*
> **möchten Sie noch Zucker?**, *would you like some more sugar?*

... and *to be likely*, usually expressed by *may* in English:

> **das mag sein**, *that may be*

In the past this becomes, in English, *may (well) have been* or *must have been*:

> **er mochte fünfzig sein,** *he must have been (may well have been) fifty*

■ **Mögen** also means *to want,* with a weaker, more polite sense than **wollen**:

> **ich mochte nicht,** *I didn't want to*

The past subjunctive, **ich möchte,** *I should like,* is much politer than **ich will,** *I want*:

> **ich möchte etwas länger bleiben,** *I should like to stay a little longer*
> **ich möchte Kaffee bitte,** *I should like coffee please*

This is the form of **mögen** in most frequent use.

■ The past subjunctive also expresses polite doubt or disagreement:

> **man möchte vielleicht dagegen einwenden . . . ,** *one might just possibly say, on the other hand . . .*

■ The past subjunctive is also used to give polite indirect commands:

> **sagen Sie ihr, sie möchte hereinkommen,** *tell her to please come in*

müssen

■ The basic meaning of **müssen** is *must = to have to*:

> **du musst alles aufessen,** *you must eat everything up*

In the negative, this becomes *don't have to* in English:

> **du musst das nicht essen,** *you don't have to eat that*

(*You mustn't eat that!* is correctly **das darfst du nicht essen!** (or **das sollst du nicht essen!**); however, in conversation **du**

musst das nicht essen is also used in this meaning, with a
weaker stress on the **musst** than in the '*don't have to*' meaning.)

■ **Müssen** is also used to mean *must* or *to have to* expressing
inevitability:

> **muss das sein?**, *is that really necessary?*
> **sie muss bald hier sein**, *she's bound to be (she has*
> *to be) here soon*

■ **Müssen** in the past subjunctive means *ought to be*, where
there is no sense of duty (where there is, **sollte** is used):

> **es müsste gehen**, *it ought to be possible*
> **das Haus müsste irgendwo hier sein**, *the house*
> *ought to be somewhere around here*

■ **Haben zu** also exists, meaning *to have to*, where this means
to be in possession of something, to which something must be done:

> **ich habe ein Auto zu verkaufen**, *I have a car to sell*
> but: **ich muss mein Auto verkaufen**, *I have to sell my car*

sollen

■ The basic meaning is *is to* or *is supposed to*, expressing intention:

> **sie soll heute kommen**, *she's to come (supposed to be*
> *coming) today*
> **sie sollte gestern kommen**, *she was supposed to be*
> *coming yesterday*
> **was soll das heißen?**, *what's that supposed (intended) to*
> *mean?*
> **du sollst dein Geld bekommen**, *you're going to get (you're*
> *to get) your money*
> **ihr wisst, dass ihr das nicht tun sollt**, *you know you*
> *shouldn't (are not supposed to) be doing that*

■ **Sollen** also means *to be supposed to* in the sense of '*people say*
that':

er soll reich sein, *he's supposed to be rich*
es soll bis fünf Verletzte gegeben haben, *reports say that up to five people were injured*

■ In the past and pluperfect subjunctive it means *ought to/should* and *ought to have/should have*, expressing moral duty:

das solltest du nicht machen, *you ought not to (shouldn't) do that*
das hätte er nicht tun sollen, *he ought not to (shouldn't) have done that*

■ It is used to express a command or wish, especially in the third person:

er soll ein bisschen warten, *let him wait a bit*

■ It can also be used, like **mögen** (see p. 63), in indirect commands:

sagen Sie ihr, sie soll hereinkommen, *tell her to come in*

wollen

■ The basic meaning of **wollen** is *to want* or *will*:

er will gehen, *he wants to go*
es will nicht funktionieren, *it won't (= refuses to) work*
willst du was?, *do you want something?* (much less polite than **möchtest du etwas?**)

■ **Wollen** also sometimes means *to need*:

das will sehr viel Zeit, *that needs a great deal of time*

■ It frequently means *to be about to*, expressing intention:

das will ich sofort machen, *I'll do that straight away* (stronger than '**das werde ich . . .**')
ich wollte gerade sagen . . . , *I was just going to say . . .*

■ It can form a polite alternative to the imperative:

wollen wir gehen?, *let's go*
wollen Sie bitte Platz nehmen, *would you please take a seat*

■ It can mean *to claim*, or, in the negative, *not to admit*:

er will ein Millionär sein, *he claims to be a millionaire*
kein Mensch will es gemacht haben, *nobody admits they did it*

▶ For **lassen** + an infinitive meaning *to get something done* or *to have something done*, see p. 68.

Formation and use of the modals

▶ The modals are irregular, mixed verbs. For their conjugation see the Irregular Verb list, pp. 73–85.

■ Infinitives dependent on the modals are used without **zu**:

das will ich sofort erklären, *I'll explain that straight away*

■ The modals can also be used without a dependent infinitive:

du musst nicht, *you don't have to*
das mag ich nicht so sehr, *I'm not too keen on that*
ganz wie du willst, *just as you like*

■ Verbs of motion are very often dropped after the modals, especially in spoken German:

ich will nach Berlin, *I want to go to Berlin*

With **mögen** this can only be done after the past subjunctive, **möchte**.

In the case of separable-prefix verbs, the prefix is not dropped:

ich muss weg (= weggehen), *I must be off*
möchtest du mit? (= mitkommen), *would you like to come with us?*

■ Past participles of the modals

The modal verbs all have two past participles, one formed
ge . . . t, the other identical with the infinitive. The infinitive
form is used where the modal has a dependent infinitive (which
is more usually the case):

> **Du hast nicht fahren können? — Ich habe leider nicht
> gekonnt**, *You weren't able to go?—I'm sorry, I couldn't*

▶ **Lassen** and, sometimes, **sehen** and **hören** behave similarly.
See pp. 68 and 69.

■ Modals in compound tenses in subordinate clauses

When two infinitives come together at the end of a subordinate
clause, an auxiliary verb stands before them, not after as you
would expect. Where this happens it is usually a modal in a
compound tense that is involved:

> **ich weiß, dass du nicht gestern hast fahren
> können**, *I know you couldn't go yesterday*

Notice that this applies not just with **haben** and **sein** used to
form past compound tenses, but also with **werden** in the future
and conditional tenses of modals:

> **ich hoffe, dass du nicht wirst spielen müssen**,
> *I hope you won't have to play*

This whole construction tends to be avoided in conversation
(e.g. by using the past tense for the perfect).

■ The modals can be used with a perfect infinitive (past
participle plus **haben/sein**), as they can in English. Notice the
change in meaning this produces:

	sie hat es sagen müssen, *she had to say it*
but:	**sie muss es gesagt haben**, *she must have said it*
	sie haben es machen sollen, *they were supposed to do it*
but:	**sie sollen es gemacht haben**, *they're supposed to have
done it*

> **sie haben es tun können,** *they have been able to do it*

but: **sie können es getan haben,** *they may have done it*

■ A modal, as in English, may be followed by a passive infinitive (past participle plus **werden**):

> **es muss getan werden,** *it must be done*

or by another modal:

> **das musst du aber machen können,** *you really must be able to do that*

Lassen and similar verbs

■ **Lassen** has two principal meanings—*to let*:

> **er ließ sie entkommen,** *he let them escape*

. . . and *to make, to cause to, to have (something done)*:

> **ich lasse mir die Haare schneiden,** *I'm going to have my hair cut*
> **sie ließ uns holen,** *she sent for us (had us fetched)*

■ Like the modal verbs, **lassen** takes a following infinitive without **zu**. Also like the modals, **lassen** has two past participles. They are **gelassen** and **lassen**. The latter is used when **lassen** appears with the infinitive of another verb:

> **ich habe mir die Haare schneiden lassen,** *I've had my hair cut*

■ The reflexive form **sich lassen** means *can be* + past participle. It is followed by an active infinitive in German, with a passive sense:

> **das lässt sich machen,** *that can be done*
> **es lässt sich nicht leugnen, dass . . . ,** *it cannot be denied that . . .*

■ The past participles of **fallen lassen**, *to drop*, and **liegen lassen**, *to leave (lying about)*, are found both with and without **ge-**; the form without **ge-** is the more usual:

wo hast du es denn liegen (ge)lassen?, *where did you leave it then?*

Sehen, hören, heißen, fühlen

■ The rules about infinitives and past participles that apply to **lassen** (infinitives without **zu**; two past-participle forms) also apply to **sehen** and **hören**, where the construction with the infinitive form of the past participle is fairly frequent, especially in written German:

ich habe ihn kommen hören, *I heard him coming*

They also apply to the literary verb **heißen**, *to bid* :

er hieß mich eintreten, *he bade me enter*

■ **Fühlen** takes an infinitive without **zu**; it also has a second past participle in the infinitive form, but this is usually avoided by using **wie**:

ich fühlte mein Herz höher schlagen, *I felt my heart beat faster*
ich habe gefühlt, wie mein Herz höher schlug, *I felt my heart beat faster* (**ich habe mein Herz höher schlagen fühlen** is possible but stilted)

▶ For more on these and similar verbs see pp. 46–7.
▶ For **helfen**, **lehren**, and **lernen** with and without **zu**, see p. 47.

IMPERSONAL VERBS

Impersonal verbs are verbs whose subject is, in English, *there* or a non-specific *it*. In German this is **es**:

es ist kein Geld im Safe, *there's no money in the safe*
es regnet, *it's raining*

Impersonal verbs corresponding to English 'it . . .'

With all verbs in this group **es** is seen as a true subject, corresponding to the English *it*. If something other than **es** is put in front of the verb, the **es** is placed after the verb like any normal subject:

> **heute regnet es**, *today it's raining*
> **mich ärgert es, dass . . .** , *it annoys me that . . .*

The **es** also stays in subordinate order:

> **ich weiß nicht, ob es heute regnen wird**, *I don't know if it's going to rain today*

This group includes:

■ Most weather verbs. These have an impersonal *it* (**es**) as subject:

> **es regnet**, *it's raining*
> **es schneit**, *it's snowing*
> **es zieht**, *it's draughty*
> —and very many others

■ Verbs with an impersonal subject and a personal object, either accusative or (more often) dative, sometimes reflexive, for example:

> **es ärgert mich**, *it annoys me*
> **es ist mir recht**, *it's OK by me*
> **es scheint mir**, *it seems to me*
> **es handelt sich um**, *it's a question of*

■ **Es ist** or **es sind** + noun or pronoun. German has a fixed order: normal order with nouns, inversion with pronouns:

> **es ist meine Schwester**, *it's my sister*
> **Sie sind es!**, *it's you!*

Impersonal verbs with a postponed subject (usually corresponding to English 'there . . . ')

With these verbs **es** simply functions as a substitute for the real subject, which is being held back until after the verb to give it more importance. This **es** usually corresponds to the English *there*. Very many verbs can be made impersonal in this way:

> **es bleibt jetzt sehr wenig Zeit**, *there's very little time left now*

☐ If the real subject is plural, so is the verb:

> **es stehen viele Autos auf dem Parkplatz**, *there are a lot of cars (standing) in the car park*

☐ If an adverb appears before the verb in this construction, the **es** simply disappears (there is no need for it, as the real subject now takes its normal third place in inverted order):

> **heute stehen viele Autos auf dem Parkplatz**, *there are many cars in the car park today* (compare: **heute regnet es**)

The **es** also disappears in subordinate order, for the same reason:

> **ich weiß schon, dass heute viele Autos auf dem Parkplatz stehen**, *I'm quite aware that there are a lot of cars in the car park today*

▶ For the appropriate translation of *there is* see pp. 72–3.

☐ The real subject may be a clause. Where the real subject is a clause English uses *it* rather than *there* for the 'postponing' subject:

> **es ist wahr, dass er das nie gesagt hat**, *it is true that he never said that* (real subject: *that he never said that*)
>
> **wahr ist, dass er das nie gesagt hat**
>
> **es steht in meiner Zeitung, dass . . .** , *it says in my paper that . . .*
>
> **in meiner Zeitung steht, dass. . .**

☐ With this construction in the passive, no real subject need be expressed at all:

> **es wird hier gebaut / hier wird gebaut**, *there's construction work taking place here*

Impersonal verbs corresponding to an English personal verb

Many German impersonal verbs are the equivalent of ordinary English personal verbs. Among the commonest verbs of this kind are:

> **es fehlt mir an** (+ DAT), *I lack*
> **es geht mir** (**gut**, etc.), *I'm* (*well*, etc.)
> **es gelingt mir**, *I succeed*
> **es tut mir Leid**, *I'm sorry*
> **es freut mich**, *I'm glad*

With verbs in this group the **es** is retained after the verb if anything else is placed first in the sentence:

> **mir geht es gut heute**, *I feel well today*

But note the following exceptions, where the **es** very often disappears, especially in written German:

> **es ist mir** (**kalt**, etc.), *I'm* (*cold*, etc.)
> **es wird mir** (**kalt**, etc.), *I'm getting* (*cold*, etc.)
> **es ist mir, als ob . . . / es kommt mir vor, als ob . . .** ,
>   *I feel as if . . .*
> **es ist mir schlecht/übel**, *I feel sick*
> **es friert mich**, *I feel cold*
> **es wundert mich, dass . . .** , *I'm surprised that . . .*
>
> **mir ist (es) furchtbar warm hier**, *I feel terribly hot here*

In spoken German the **es** is often retained as . . . **s**:

> **mich frierts**, *I'm cold*

There is, there are

The English expression *there is / there are* corresponds to the German **es ist / es sind**, though German likes to substitute a more precise verb if possible (**es steht, es liegt**, etc.).

However, where existence rather than position is to be expressed, **es gibt** is used instead, meaning *there is, there are*. The **es** is always kept in this construction, the verb is always singular, and it is followed by an accusative:

> **es ist kein einziges Glas im Schrank,** *there isn't a single glass in the cupboard*
> **es gibt keine Gläser mehr,** *there aren't any glasses left*

Es ist / es sind loses the **es** in inverted or subordinate order.

ALPHABETICAL LIST OF IRREGULAR VERBS

This list includes all strong and mixed verbs in modern usage.

■ Compound verbs should be looked up under their simple form.

■ Where an irregular present-tense **er** form is given, the same irregularity will occur in the **du** form.

■ Irregular past subjunctives are given in brackets after the past tense.

■ An asterisk before the past participle indicates a verb whose past compound tenses are formed with **sein** when the verb is used intransitively.

▶ For the complete formation of the present and past tenses given here, see pp. 8 and 10.

▶ Past compound tenses and passive tenses are regular (except for the past participle form, given below). For their formation, see pp. 8 and 11 (past compound tenses) and p. 29 (passive tenses).

▶ Future and conditional tenses are regular. For their formation, see pp. 9 and 11.

▶ Present and future subjunctives are regular (except the present subjunctive of **sein**, see p. 40). For their formation see pp. 8 and 10 (present subjunctive) and p. 40 (future subjunctive).

▶ Perfect and pluperfect subjunctives are regular (except for the past participle form, given below). For their formation, see pp. 9 and 121.

▶ Past subjunctives are regular except as shown below, in brackets after the past tense. For their formation see pp. 8 and 10.

infinitive	meaning	present, er form, if irregular	past (er form; + past subjunctive if irregular)	past participle (* = sein)
backen	*bake*	backt/bäckt	backte	gebacken
befehlen	*command*	befiehlt	befahl (beföhle)	befohlen
beginnen	*begin*		begann	begonnen
beißen	*bite*		biss	gebissen
bergen	*save*	birgt	barg	geborgen
bersten	*burst*	birst	barst	*geborsten
biegen	*bend*		bog	gebogen
bieten	*offer*		bot	geboten
binden	*tie*		band	gebunden
bitten	*ask*		bat	gebeten
blasen	*blow*	bläst	blies	geblasen
bleiben	*stay*		blieb	*geblieben
braten	*roast*	brät	briet	gebraten
brechen	*break*	bricht	brach	gebrochen
brennen	*burn*		brannte (brennte)	gebrannt
bringen	*bring*		brachte	gebracht
denken	*think*		dachte	gedacht

infinitive	meaning	present, **er** form, if irregular	past (**er** form; + past subjunctive if irregular)	past participle (* = **sein**)
dreschen	*thresh*	drischt	drosch	gedroschen
dringen	*be urgent*		drang	gedrungen
dürfen	*be allowed*	ich/er darf	durfte	gedurft/dürfen
empfehlen	*recommend*	empfiehlt	empfahl (empföhle)	empfohlen
erlöschen	*die out*	erlischt	erlosch	*erloschen
erschrecken	*be startled*[1]	erschrickt	erschrak	*erschrocken
essen	*eat*	isst	aß	gegessen
fahren	*travel*	fährt	fuhr	*gefahren
fallen	*fall*	fällt	fiel	*gefallen
fangen	*catch*	fängt	fing	gefangen
fechten	*fence*	ficht	focht	gefochten
finden	*find*		fand	gefunden
flechten	*plait*	flicht	flocht	geflochten
fliegen	*fly*		flog	*geflogen
fliehen	*flee*		floh	*geflohen
fließen	*flow*		floss	*geflossen
fressen	*eat (of animals)*	frisst	fraß	gefressen

frieren	freeze		fror	gefroren
gebären	bear (child)	gebärt/gebiert	gebar	geboren
geben	give	gibt	gab	gegeben
gedeihen	prosper		gedieh	*gediehen
gehen	go		ging	*gegangen
gelingen	succeed		gelang	*gelungen
gelten	be valid	gilt	galt (gölte)	gegolten
genesen	recover		genas	*genesen
genießen	enjoy		genoss	genossen
geschehen	happen	geschieht	geschah	*geschehen
gewinnen	win		gewann (gewönne)	gewonnen
gießen	pour		goss	gegossen
gleichen	resemble		glich	geglichen
gleiten	slip		glitt	*geglitten
graben	dig	gräbt	grub	gegraben
greifen	grasp		griff	gegriffen
haben	have	du hast; er hat	hatte	gehabt
halten	hold	hält	hielt	gehalten

---

[1] In the sense of *to startle* erschrecken is weak.

infinitive	meaning	present, **er** form, if irregular	past (**er** form; + past subjunctive if irregular)	past participle (* = **sein**)
hauen	*hit*		haute	gehaut/
				gehauen
hängen[1]	*hang*		hing	gehangen
heben	*raise*		hob	gehoben
heißen	*be called*		hieß	geheißen
helfen	*help*	hilft	half (hülfe)	geholfen
kennen	*know*		kannte (kennte)	gekannt
klingen	*sound*		klang	geklungen
kneifen	*pinch*		kniff	gekniffen
kommen	*come*		kam	*gekommen
können	*can*	ich/er kann	konnte	gekonnt/können
kriechen	*crawl*		kroch	*gekrochen
laden	*load*	lädt	lud	geladen
lassen	*let*	lässt	ließ	gelassen/lassen
laufen	*run*	läuft	lief	*gelaufen
leiden	*put up with*		litt	gelitten
leihen	*lend*		lieh	geliehen

lesen	*read*	liest	las	gelesen
liegen	*lie*		lag	gelegen
lügen	*tell lies*		log	gelogen
mahlen	*grind*		mahlte	gemahlen
meiden	*avoid*		mied	gemieden
melken[2]	*milk*	milkt	molk	gemolken
messen	*measure*	misst	maß	gemessen
misslingen	*fail*		misslang	*misslungen
mögen	*like*	ich/er mag	mochte	gemocht/mögen
müssen	*must*	ich/er muss	musste	gemusst/müssen
nehmen	*take*	nimmt	nahm	genommen
nennen	*name*		nannte (nennte)	genannt
pfeifen	*whistle*		pfiff	gepfiffen
preisen	*praise*		pries	gepriesen
quellen	*gush*	quillt	quoll	*gequollen
raten	*advise*	rät	riet	geraten
reiben	*rub*		rieb	gerieben

[1] **Hängen** is strong when intransitive, weak when transitive.
[2] **Melken** is very frequently weak.

infinitive	meaning	present, **er** form, if irregular	past (**er** form; + past subjunctive if irregular	past participle (* = sein)
reißen	*tear*		riss	gerissen
reiten	*ride*		ritt	*geritten
rennen	*run*		rannte (rennte)	*gerannt
riechen	*smell*		roch	gerochen
ringen	*struggle*		rang	gerungen
rinnen	*run*		rann	*geronnen
rufen	*call*		rief	gerufen
salzen	*salt*		salzte	gesalzen
saufen	*drink heavily*	säuft	soff	gesoffen
saugen[1]	*suck*		sog	gesogen
schaffen	*create*[2]		schuf	geschaffen
scheiden	*separate*		schied	*geschieden
scheinen	*seem*		schien	geschienen
scheißen	*shit*		schiss	geschissen
schelten	*scold*	schilt	schalt (schölte)	gescholten
scheren	*trim*		schor	geschoren
schieben	*push*		schob	geschoben

schließen	shoot		schoss	geschossen
schinden	ill-treat		schindete	geschunden
schlafen	sleep	schläft	schlief	geschlafen
schlagen	hit	schlägt	schlug	geschlagen
schleichen	creep		schlich	*geschlichen
schleifen	sharpen		schliff	geschliffen
schleißen[3]	strip		schliss	geschlissen
schließen	shut		schloss	geschlossen
schlingen	loop		schlang	geschlungen
schmeißen	fling		schmiss	geschmissen
schmelzen	melt	schmilzt	schmolz	*geschmolzen
schneiden	cut		schnitt	geschnitten
schreiben	write		schrieb	geschrieben
schreien	shout		schrie	geschrie(e)n
schreiten	step		schritt	*geschritten
schweigen	be silent		schwieg	geschwiegen

[1] **Saugen** is usually weak.
[2] In the sense of *to manage* **schaffen** is weak.
[3] **Schleißen** and its compounds are often weak.

infinitive	meaning	present, **er** form, if irregular	past (**er** form; + past subjunctive if irregular)	past participle (* = sein)
schwellen	*swell*[1]	schwillt	schwoll	*geschwollen
schwimmen	*swim*		schwamm (schwömme)	*geschwommen
schwinden	*dwindle*		schwand	*geschwunden
schwingen	*swing*		schwang	*geschwungen
schwören	*swear*		schwor (schwüre)	geschworen
sehen	*see*	sieht	sah	gesehen
sein	*be*	ich bin; du bist; er ist; wir/sie sind; ihr seid	war	*gewesen
senden	*send*[2]		sandte (sendete)	gesandt
singen	*sing*		sang	gesungen
sinken	*sink*		sank	*gesunken
sinnen	*think*		sann	gesonnen
sitzen	*sit*		saß	gesessen
sollen	*is to*	ich/er soll	sollte	gesollt/sollen
spalten	*split*		spaltete	gespaltet/gespalten

speien	*spew forth*		spie	gespie(e)n
spinnen	*spin*		spann (spönne)	gesponnen
sprechen	*speak*	spricht	sprach	gesprochen
sprießen	*sprout*		spross	*gesprossen
springen	*jump*		sprang	*gesprungen
stechen	*stab*	sticht	stach	gestochen
stehen	*stand*		stand (stünde)	gestanden
stehlen	*steal*	stiehlt	stahl	gestohlen
steigen	*climb*		stieg	*gestiegen
sterben	*die*	stirbt	starb (stürbe)	*gestorben
stinken	*stink*		stank	gestunken
stoßen	*push*	stößt	stieß	gestoßen
streichen	*stroke*		strich	gestrichen
streiten	*quarrel*		stritt	gestritten
tragen	*carry*	trägt	trug	getragen
treffen	*meet*	trifft	traf	getroffen

[1] In the transitive sense of *to fill (a sail)* **schwellen** is weak.
[2] In the sense of *to broadcast* **senden** is weak.

Infinitive	meaning	present, **er** form, if irregular	past (**er** form; + past subjunctive if irregular)	past participle (* = **sein**)
treiben	*drive*		trieb	getrieben
treten	*step*	tritt	trat	*getreten
trinken	*drink*		trank	getrunken
trügen	*deceive*		trog	getrogen
tun	*do*	ich tue; du tust; er/ihr tut; wir/sie tun	tat	getan
verderben	*spoil*	verdirbt	verdarb (verdürbe)	*verdorben
verdrießen	*annoy*		verdross	verdrossen
vergessen	*forget*	vergisst	vergaß	vergessen
verlieren	*lose*		verlor	verloren
verlöschen	*go out*	verlischt	verlosch	*verloschen
wachsen	*grow*	wächst	wuchs	*gewachsen
waschen	*wash*	wäschst	wusch	gewaschen
weben[1]	*weave*		wob	gewoben
weichen	*budge*		wich	*gewichen
weisen	*point*		wies	gewiesen

wenden[2]	turn	wendet	wandte (wendete)	gewandt
werben	advertise	wirbt	warb (würbe)	geworben
werden	become	du wirst; er wird	wurde	*geworden/worden
werfen	throw	wirft	warf (würfe)	geworfen
wiegen	weigh[3]		wog	gewogen
winden	wind		wand	gewunden
wissen	know	ich/er weiß	wusste	gewusst
wollen	want	ich/er will	wollte	gewollt/wollen
zeihen	indict		zieh	geziehen
ziehen	pull		zog	gezogen
zwingen	force		zwang	gezwungen

---

1 Weben is usually weak in modern German.
2 Wenden may also be weak.
3 Wiegen is weak when it means to rock.

| Articles

Articles are words like *a* and *the*. In German the form of the article changes according to the gender and case of the noun following and according to whether the noun is singular or plural. For noun cases see p. 96.

FORMATION OF ARTICLES

The forms of the definite article (**der**, *the*) and indefinite article (**ein**, *a*) are as follows, shown here with a masculine noun **der Mann**, *man*, a feminine noun **die Frau**, *woman*, a neuter noun **das Buch**, *book*, and a plural noun **die Leute**, *people*:

Definite article: **der**, *the*

	SINGULAR			PLURAL
	masculine	*feminine*	*neuter*	
nominative	der Mann	die Frau	das Buch	die Leute
accusative	den Mann	die Frau	das Buch	die Leute
genitive	des Mannes	der Frau	des Buches	der Leute
dative	dem Mann	der Frau	dem Buch	den Leuten

■ Following the pattern of **der** are: **dieser**, *this/that*; **welcher**, *which*; **jener**, *that*; **jeder**, *every*; **mancher**, *many a*:

dieser, *this, that*

	SINGULAR			PLURAL
	masculine	*feminine*	*neuter*	
nominative	dieser	diese	dieses	diese
accusative	diesen	diese	dieses	diese
genitive	dieses	dieser	dieses	dieser
dative	diesem	dieser	diesem	diesen

▶ **Jener** is uncommon in modern German. For *that* **dieser** or, in speech, an emphasized **der** is used. See Demonstrative Adjectives, p.115.

▶ The definite article often compounds with certain prepositions to form a single word. So **zu + dem = zum**. See p. 161.

▶ For the noun endings in the genitive singular and dative plural, see pp. 97–9.

Indefinite article: **ein**, *a*

	SINGULAR			PLURAL
	masculine	*feminine*	*neuter*	
nominative	ein Mann	eine Frau	ein Buch	keine Leute
accusative	einen Mann	eine Frau	ein Buch	keine Leute
genitive	eines Mannes	einer Frau	eines Buches	keiner Leute
dative	einem Mann	einer Frau	einem Buch	keinen Leuten

■ Following the pattern of **ein** are: **kein**, *no* (used above for the plural forms, since **ein** has no plural) and the possessive adjectives: **mein**, *my*; **dein**, *your*; **sein**, *his/its*; **ihr**, *her/their*; **unser**, *our*; **euer**, *your*; **Ihr**, *your*.

■ **Unser** (sometimes) and **euer** (always) lose the final **e** of their stem when they have an ending: **eure Bücher**.

▶ For **kein** see p. 153.

▶ For the possessives see p. 115.

USING THE ARTICLES

Articles are used in a number of places in German where we would omit them in English.

■ The definite article is used with abstract nouns much more frequently than in English, especially when the noun is generalized:

> **die Eifersucht ist keine Tugend**, *jealousy is no virtue* (jealousy in general)

but: **das klingt wie Eifersucht**, *that sounds like jealousy*
        (a bit of jealousy)

Abstract nouns usually lose their definite article after the
prepositions **durch**, *through*, **gegen**, *against*, **ohne**, *without*, and
über, *about*.

■ The definite article, with added emphasis in speech, is used
instead of the demonstrative **jener**, to mean *that*:

   ich möchte *den* Kuchen, bitte, *I'd like that cake, please*

■ The definite article is used with a noun in the genitive where
in English no article would be used:

   der Klang der Musik, *the sound of music*

Spoken German usually prefers **von** to the genitive; no article is
then necessary:

   der Klang von Musik

■ The definite article is often used instead of the possessive
with parts of the body and with clothes:

   hebt die Hand!, *put your hand up!*
   zieh das Hemd aus, *take your shirt off*

A dative to indicate the person concerned may be added . . .

   möchtest du dir die Hände waschen?, *would you
      like to wash your hands?*

. . . and must be added when someone other than the subject of
the sentence owns the piece of clothing or the part of the body
referred to:

   sie drückte mir die Hand, *she pressed my hand*

□ This construction cannot be used when the part of the body
is the subject:

   deine Hand ist sehr klein, *your hand is very small*

□ The alternative construction with the possessive as in
English, though less frequent, is entirely possible:

zieh dein Hemd aus, *take your shirt off*

■ The definite article is used with geographical names in the following instances:

☐ Before feminine names of countries:

wir fahren in die Schweiz, *we're travelling to Switzerland*

It is also used with the very few masculine and plural country names. See pp. 93 and 176. The article is dropped in addresses, however: **Schweiz** on the envelope, not **die Schweiz**.

☐ Before geographical names with adjectives (English usage varies here):

das neue Deutschland, *the new Germany*
das schöne Italien, *beautiful Italy*

The same applies to proper names:

der doofe Fritz, *daft Fritz*

☐ Before names of mountains, lakes, streets:

die Zugspitze; der Comer See, *Lake Como;* **die Bismarckstraße**

■ The definite article is used with months, seasons, parts of the day, meals:

am Vormittag, *in the morning*
der Mai ist gekommen, *May is here*
im Sommer nimmt man das Frühstück draußen, *in summer we eat breakfast outside*

■ A definite (not an indefinite) article is used in expressions of price + quantity like *seven marks a kilo*:

sieben Mark das Kilo, *seven marks a kilo*
drei Mark das Stück, *three marks apiece*

Pro, *per,* may also be used in this way. See Prepositions, p. 178.

■ A definite article may be used, familiarly, before proper names:

> **hast du den Günter gesehen?**, *have you seen Günter?*

OMISSION OF THE ARTICLES

■ The article is omitted in many prepositional phrases where we would expect it in English:

> **zu Ende**, *at an end*
> **bei Ausbruch des Krieges**, *at the outbreak of war*
> **nach längerer Zeit**, *after quite a long time*

And note **Anfang**, **Mitte**, and **Ende** with months, where both article and preposition are omitted:

> **sie kommt Anfang September**, *she's coming at the beginning of September*

■ The indefinite article is not used after **sein**, *to be* (or **werden**, *to become*, or **bleiben**, *to remain*) + a profession or nationality:

> **er wird Computerwissenschaftler**, *he's going to be a computer scientist*
> **sie ist Amerikanerin**, *she's an American*

It *is* used, though, if there is an adjective in front of the noun:

> **er ist ein bekannter Schriftsteller**, *he's a well-known writer*

■ The indefinite article is not used after **als**, *as (a)*:

> **ich als Engländer weiß, dass. . .** , *I as an Englishman know that . . .*
> **er arbeitet als Maurer**, *he's working as a builder*

I Nouns

All nouns in German are spelled with a capital letter.

GENDER OF NOUNS

English has three genders: masculine, feminine, and neuter (*he, she, it*). German also has three, but whereas in English gender virtually always corresponds logically to the sex of the noun, this is not the case in German. Most nouns denoting male people and animals are in fact masculine in German, most of those denoting females are feminine; but names of inanimate objects may be masculine, feminine, or neuter. Unlike English nouns, German nouns usually make their gender obvious by means of the article and (sometimes) the adjectives in front of them.

The rules for gender in German are far from watertight—there are exceptions to most of them.

Masculine groups

■ Masculine are: names of males; days, months, seasons; points of the compass; makes of car:

> **der Mann,** *man,* **der Montag,** *Monday,* **der Januar,** *January,* **der Sommer,** *summer,* **der Norden,** *north,* **der Opel**

■ Nouns indicating a 'doer', ending **-er**, are masculine:

> **der Gärtner,** *gardener,* **der Sänger,** *singer*

By analogy, so are most 'doing' instruments: **der Computer,** *computer,* **der Wecker,** *alarm.*

■ Nouns ending **-ich**, **-ig**, **-ling** are masculine:

> **der Fittich**, *wing*, **der Honig**, *honey*, **der Lehrling**, *apprentice*

■ Nouns ending **-ismus**, **-ist**, and **-ant** are masculine. These are all of foreign origin:

> **der Kapitalismus**, *capitalism*, **der Bassist**, *bass guitarist*, **der Protestant**, *protestant*

Feminine groups

■ Feminine are: names of females; names of ships, makes of aeroplane; numbers as nouns; German rivers (exceptions: **der Rhein, der Main, der Neckar, der Inn, der Lech**). Non-German rivers ending **-a** or **-e** are also feminine; others are masculine:

> **die Frau**, *woman*, **die Scharnhorst**, **die Boeing**, **die Sieben**, *(the) seven*, **die Donau**, *Danube*, **die Wolga**, *Volga*, **die Themse**, *Thames*

■ Feminine forms of traders, workers, and many animals are made by adding **-in**:

> **die Gärtnerin**, *gardener*, **die Sängerin**, *singer*, **die Hündin**, *bitch*

Often an umlaut is added where this is possible (as in **Hund → Hündin** above).

■ Nouns ending **-ei**, **-ie**, **-ion**, **-heit**, **-keit**, **-schaft**, **-tät**, **-ung** are feminine (these are mostly abstract nouns):

> **die Gärtnerei**, *gardening*, **die Chemie**, *chemistry*, **die Nation**, *nation*, **die Klugheit**, *cleverness*, **die Einigkeit**, *unity*, **die Errungenschaft**, *achievement*, **die Rarität**, *rarity*, **die Regierung**, *government*

■ Nouns ending **-a** and most (though beware, not all!) nouns ending **-e** are feminine:

> **die Tuba**, *tuba*, **die Klippe**, *cliff*

Neuter groups

■ Neuter are: names of continents, countries, towns, and the German Länder (common exceptions: **die Bundesrepublik Deutschland**, *the Federal Republic*, **die Vereinigten Staaten** (pl.), *the United States*, **die Schweiz**, *Switzerland*, **die Türkei**, *Turkey*, **die Tschechoslowakei**, *Czechoslovakia*):

> **(das) Europa**, *Europe*, **(das) Deutschland**, *Germany*,
> **(das) Köln**, *Cologne*, **(das) Bayern**, *Bavaria*

Country names that are not neuter always have the article. *To* is **nach** with neuter countries, **in** with masculines, feminines, and plurals.

■ Neuter are names of metals (exceptions: **die Bronze**, *bronze*, **der Stahl**, *steel*); chemicals; letters of the alphabet; fractions:

> **das Eisen**, *iron*, **das Dioxin**, *dioxin*, **das A**, *A*, **das Drittel**, *third*

■ The names of the young of humans and animals are neuter:

> **das Kind**, *child*, **das Baby**, *baby*, **das Lamm**, *lamb*,
> **das Kalb**, *calf*, **das Junge** (adjectival noun), *cub*

■ Neuter are nouns ending **-lein** and **-chen**. These indicate diminutives:

> **das Fräulein**, *girl*, **das Mädchen**, *girl*

■ Nouns ending **-tum** and **-um** are neuter (exceptions: **der Reichtum**, *wealth*, **der Irrtum**, *mistake*):

> **das Eigentum**, *property*, **das Zentrum**, *centre*

■ Infinitives (and other parts of speech) used as nouns are neuter:

> **das Lachen**, *laughing*

■ Foreign nouns ending **-ment**, **-fon**, **-ett** are neuter:

> **das Experiment**, *experiment*, **das Mikrofon**,
> *microphone*, **das Parkett**, *(theatre) stalls*

■ Most (but beware, by no means all!) nouns beginning **Ge-** or ending **-nis** are neuter:

> **das Gebäude**, *building*, **das Geheimnis**, *secret*

Gender of compound nouns

Compound nouns have the same gender as the last element of which they are composed:

> **die Stadt**, *town*→**die Großstadt**, *city*
> **das Haus**, *house*→**das Rathaus**, *town hall*
> **der Baum**, *tree*→**der Apfelbaum**, *apple tree*

■ **Teil**, *part* is masculine, but some of its compounds are masculine, some neuter:

der Vorteil, *advantage*	**das Urteil**, *verdict*
der Nachteil, *disadvantage*	**das Gegenteil**, *opposite*
der Anteil, *share*	**das Abteil**, *compartment*

■ **Meter** and its metric-measurement compounds (**Kilometer, Zentimeter**, etc.) though officially neuter are usually treated as masculine.

Nouns with different genders, depending on meaning

der Band, *volume, book*	**die Band**, *band, group*	**das Band**, *tape, ribbon*
der Bund, *union*		**das Bund**, *bundle*
der Erbe, *heir*		**das Erbe**, *inheritance*
der Gehalt, *capacity*		**das Gehalt**, *salary*
der Golf, *gulf, bay*		**das Golf**, *golf*
der Gummi, *eraser*		**das Gummi**, *rubber*
der Heide, *heathen*	**die Heide**, *heath*	
der Hut, *hat*	**die Hut**, *protection*	
der Junge, *boy*		**das Junge**, *cub*

der Kiefer, jaw	die Kiefer, pine	
der Kunde, customer	die Kunde, news	
der Leiter, leader, head	die Leiter, ladder	
	die Mark, mark (coin)	das Mark, marrow
der Messer, surveyor		das Messer, knife
der Militär, military man		das Militär, the military
der Moment, moment		das Moment, factor
der Otter, otter	die Otter, adder	
der Pack, package		das Pack, mob
der Schild, shield		das Schild, sign (board)
der See, lake	die See, sea	
	die Steuer, tax	das Steuer, rudder
der Stift, peg, drawing-pin		das Stift, foundation
der Tau, dew		das Tau, rope
der Tor, fool		das Tor, goal, gate
der Verdienst, earnings		das Verdienst, service
der Weise, sage	die Weise, manner, way	

Gender traps!

The following nouns have genders that look unlikely:

das Fräulein, girl	das Mitglied, member
die Geisel, hostage	die Person, person
das Genie, genius	die Wache, guard, sentry
das Mädchen, girl	die Waise, orphan

CASE OF NOUNS

Nouns and pronouns are used in four cases in German: the nominative, the accusative, the genitive, and the dative.

■ The nominative is used for the subject of the sentence, and also for the complement of the verbs **sein**, *to be*, **werden**, *to become*, **bleiben**, *to remain*, **heißen**, *to be called*, and a few others.

> **der Hund bellte**, *the dog barked*
> **der Hund ist ein Dackel**, *the dog is a dachshund*

■ The accusative is used for the direct object, and after some prepositions (see p. 160). It is also used for definite adverbial expressions of time (see p. 212):

> **er streichelte den Hund**, *he stroked the dog*
> **er ging rund um den Hund**, *he walked around the dog*
> **sie kommt nächsten Mittwoch**, *she's coming next Wednesday*

■ The genitive is the case which shows possession. It is also used after some prepositions (see p. 160), and for indefinite adverbial expressions of time (see p. 213).

> **der Hund meines Mannes**, *my husband's dog*
> **anstatt des Hundes**, *instead of the dog*
> **eines Tages wird es passieren**, *one day it will happen*

In English a genitive may be placed in front of another noun to show possession:

> *Peter's car; my parents' house*

This is only possible in German with personal names (there is no apostrophe); otherwise the genitive follows the noun:

> **Peters Auto; das Haus meiner Eltern**

■ The dative is the indirect-object case; with some verbs the only object is in the dative (see pp. 49–50). It is also used after many prepositions (see pp. 159 and 160) and with many adjectives (see pp. 110–1):

sie gab dem Hund mein Abendessen, *she gave my supper to the dog*

mit dem Hund, *with the dog*

der Hund ist seinem Frauchen sehr gehorsam, *the dog is very obedient to his mistress*

Case changes in nouns

The case of a noun is indicated largely by the preceding article (see p. 86). Nouns also make the following case changes, however:

■ Almost all masculine nouns which form their plural in **-n** or **-en** also add this ending to all cases of the singular except the nominative:

der Russe, *Russian*

	singular	*plural*
nominative	**der Russe**	**die Russen**
accusative	**den Russen**	**die Russen**
genitive	**des Russen**	**der Russen**
dative	**dem Russen**	**den Russen**

Do not be surprised to hear these nouns used without the **-(e)n** in the singular in conversation.

☐ Nouns ending **-or** add **-en** in the plural only. Their genitive singular adds **-s**. The stress moves to the **o** in the plural:

der Professor: genitive singular, **des Professors**
plural, **die Professoren**

☐ **Herr** adds **-n** throughout the singular (**Herrn**), **-en** in the plural (**Herren**).

☐ Seven masculine nouns ending **-e** add **-ns** instead of **-n** in the genitive singular:

der Name, *name*

	singular	*plural*
nominative	**der Name**	**die Namen**
accusative	**den Namen**	**die Namen**
genitive	**des Namens**	**der Namen**
dative	**dem Namen**	**den Namen**

The other nouns in this group are: **der Buchstabe,** *letter*, **der Friede,** *peace*, **der Funke,** *spark*, **der Gedanke,** *thought*, **der Glaube,** *belief*, and **der Wille,** *will*. All except **der Buchstabe** may occasionally be found with the **-n** in the nominative too:

> **der Friede** or **der Frieden,** *peace*

One neuter, **das Herz,** *heart*, also behaves in this way; it stays as **das Herz** in the accusative, however.

■ All other masculine nouns and neuter nouns add **-s** or **-es** in the genitive singular. The extra **e** is obligatory with nouns already ending in an 's' sound. It is also frequently found with monosyllables and with nouns with their stress on the last syllable:

> **der Gipfel,** *peak*: genitive singular, **des Gipfels**
> **der Schuss,** *shot*: genitive singular, **des Schusses**
> **der Baum,** *tree*: genitive singular, **des Baum(e)s**
> **das Geschenk,** *present*: genitive singular, **des Geschenk(e)s**

Neuter nouns ending **-nis** add **-ses** in the genitive:

> **das Gefängnis,** *prison*: genitive singular, **des Gefängnisses**

The genitive sounds rather formal in spoken German. Very frequently **von** + dative is substituted:

> **das Haus meiner Eltern→das Haus von meinen Eltern,** *my parents' house*

■ Personal names, both masculine and feminine, add **-s** in the genitive:

Peters Auto; Lauras Auto; Mutters Auto; Kohls Auto

If the name already ends in an 's' sound (**-s, -ß, -x, -z**) it simply adds an apostrophe for the genitive, or, occasionally in written German, **-ens**:

Hans' Auto or **Hansens Auto**

More frequently **von** is used:

das Auto von Hans

Titles in the genitive, except **Herr**, are not declined:

Kanzler Kohls Außenminister, *Chancellor Kohl's Foreign Minister*
Herrn Schmidts Nase, *Herr Schmidt's nose*

■ Masculine and neuter monosyllables formerly added **-e** to their dative singular. This **e** can still be found in some common expressions: **nach Hause**, *home*; **zu Hause**, *at home*; **auf dem Lande**, *in the country.*

■ All nouns except those with plural **-s** or already ending **-n** add **-n** to their dative plural:

der Mann: nominative plural, **die Männer**
            dative plural, **den Männern**

■ Adjectives being used as nouns take a capital letter and the appropriate gender; they still change according to case as if they were adjectives (see Adjectives as nouns, pp. 109–10):

der Reisende, *the (male) traveller*
ein Reisender, *a (male) traveller*

■ A noun in apposition goes into the same case as the noun it stands in apposition to:

er war früher bei Robotron, der größten Firma in dieser Stadt, *he used to be with Robotron, the biggest firm in that town* (**Robotron** is in the dative—after **bei**—so **Firma** is also in the dative)

PLURAL OF NOUNS

There are no watertight rules for the formation of the plural in German. As a very general rule, most masculine nouns have plural ⁼e, most feminines -(e)n, most neuters ⁼er. However, the plural really has to learned with the noun. The following are indications of what a plural is likely to be, rather than rules: there are numerous exceptions.

Plural of masculine nouns

Basically ⁼e.

However, about 50 just add **-e** and do not modify. Among the commonest that do not modify are:

der Arm, *arm*	**der Punkt**, *point*
der Hund, *dog*	**der Ruf**, *cry*
der Laut, *sound*	**der Schuh**, *shoe*
der Monat, *month*	**der Tag**, *day*
der Ort, *place*	**der Versuch**, *attempt*
der Pfad, *path*	

In addition:

- Nouns ending **-el**, **-en**, **-er** → no ending, some modify
- The following → ⁼er (**-er** in the case of **Geist**)

der Geist, *spirit*	**der Rand**, *edge*
der Gott, *God*	**der Reichtum**, *wealth* (pl. *riches*)
der Irrtum, *mistake*	**der Strauch**, *shrub*
der Mann, *man*	**der Wald**, *forest*
der Mund, *mouth*	**der Wurm**, *worm*

- Nouns ending **-e** → **-n**

Many nouns in this category also add the **-n** in the singular. See pp. 97–8.

Additionally, a group of about 50 masculines not ending **-e** form their plural with **-en**. Many of these do not add the **-en** in the singular (e.g. **der Staat**, *state*, **der See**, *lake*, **der Schmerz**, *pain*, **der Vetter**, *cousin*).

Plural of feminine nouns

Basically **-(e)n**.

All feminine nouns of more than one syllable form their plural this way, except **die Mutter (¨)**, *mother*, **die Tochter (¨)**, *daughter*, and nouns ending **-nis**, which double their **s** and add **e**:

> **die Kenntnis**, *(piece of) knowledge*: plural, **die Kenntnisse**

In addition:

■ About 30 monosyllables form their plural with **¨e**. Some of the commoner are

die Frucht, *fruit*	**die Nuss**, *nut*
die Hand, *hand*	**die Stadt**, *town*
die Kuh, *cow*	**die Wand**, *wall*
die Maus, *mouse*	**die Wurst**, *sausage*
die Nacht, *night*	

■ Nouns ending **-in** double their **n** before adding **-en**:

> **die Gärtnerin**, *gardener*: plural, **die Gärtnerinnen**

Modern journalistic usage is to spell this plural with a capital **I** in the middle of the word to produce a unisex version of the otherwise strongly masculine-looking **-er** form:

> **die BürgerInnen**, *male and female citizens*

Plural of neuter nouns

Basically **¨er**.

Neuters with plural **-er** always modify if possible. In addition:

■ Neuter nouns ending **-el**, **-en**, **-er** → no change (exception: **das Kloster (¨)**, *monastery*)

- Nouns ending **-lein, -chen**→no change

- Nouns ending **-nis**→**-nisse**

    das Ereignis, *event*: plural, **die Ereignisse**

- The following five nouns→**-(e)n**

    das Auge, *eye,* **das Bett,** *bed,* **das Ende,** *end,* **das Hemd,** *shirt,* **das Ohr,** *ear*

These neuters add the **-(e)n** in the plural only.

- About 50 monosyllables→**-e**

Among the commonest are:

das Bein, *leg*	**das Recht,** *right*
das Boot, *boat*	**das Schaf,** *sheep*
das Brot, *loaf*	**das Schiff,** *ship*
das Fest, *festival*	**das Schwein,** *pig*
das Gleis, *rail*	**das Spiel,** *game*
das Haar, *hair*	**das Stück,** *piece*
das Heft, *exercise book*	**das Tier,** *animal*
das Jahr, *year*	**das Tor,** *goal*
das Meer, *sea*	**das Zelt,** *tent*
das Paar, *pair*	**das Ziel,** *aim*
das Pferd, *horse*	

Plural of nouns of foreign origin

Where these have been assimilated into the language over many years they follow the rules and indications above; new and relatively new foreign nouns take **-s.** Some hover, e.g. **der Balkon,** *balcony* (pl.: **-s** or **-e**).

Most foreign nouns ending **-o** take **-s**; those ending **-a** usually change it to **-en** in the plural (**das Drama,** *drama,* **die Dramen; die Firma,** *firm,* **die Firmen**—but **das Komma,** *comma,* **die Kommas**).

Plural of compound nouns

Compound nouns have the same plural as the last element of which they are composed.

die Stadt (¨e), *city*, so: **die Hauptstadt** (¨e), *capital*

Compounds of **-mann** form their plural with **-leute**:

der Kaufmann, *merchant*: plural, **die Kaufleute**

Exceptions: **der Schneemann** (¨er), *snowman*, **der Staatsmann** (¨er), *statesman*. And notice **der Ehemann**, *husband*: plural, **die Ehemänner** = *husbands*; plural, **die Eheleute** = *married couples*.

Nouns with different plurals for different meanings

das Band, *bond* (**die Bande**); *tape* (**die Bänder**)
die Bank, *bench* (**die Bänke**); *bank* (**die Banken**)
der Block, *alliance* (**die Blöcke**); *pad of paper, block of flats* (**die Blocks**)
die Mutter, *mother* (**die Mütter**); *(tech.) nut* (**die Muttern**)
der Strauß, *ostrich* (**die Strauße**); *bunch of flowers* (**die Sträuße**)
das Wort, *word* (**die Worte**, *connected words*; **die Wörter**, *unconnected words*)

Nouns with no singular form

The following nouns only occur in the plural:

die Leute, *people*
die Ferien, *holidays*
die Eltern, *parents*
die Großeltern, *grandparents*

Other nouns are substituted for a singular: **die Person**, *person*; **der Ferientag**, *day off*; **der Vater**, *father*, **die Mutter**, *mother*, etc. **Der Elternteil** exists for *parent*, but is literary and clumsy.

Singular for plural

■ The following nouns are singular in German and plural in English:

die Brille, *spectacles*	**das Mittelalter**, *the Middle*
der Dank, *thanks*	*Ages*
das Feuerwerk, *fireworks*	**die Schere**, *scissors*
die Hose, *trousers*	**die Treppe**, *stairs*
der Inhalt, *contents*	**die Umgebung**, *surroundings*
der Lohn, *wages*	**die Zange**, *tongs*

Many of the above have plurals with the sense of 'more than one set of':

> **zwei Treppen hoch**, *up two flights of stairs*

■ The following nouns are singular in English and plural in German:

die Kosten, *cost*	**(die) Weihnachten**, *Christmas*
die Möbel, *furniture*	**(die) Ostern**, *Easter*
die Noten, *(sheet) music*	**(die) Pfingsten**, *Whitsun*
die Zinsen, *interest*	

When the three in the right-hand column are the subject of a sentence, however, they are used with a singular verb:

> **bald kommt Weihnachten**, *Christmas will soon be here*

■ Masculine and neuter nouns used as expressions of quantity do not pluralize:

> **zwei Glas Wein**, *two glasses of wine*

Feminine expressions of quantity do:

> **zwei Flaschen Wein**, *two bottles of wine*

Note that *of* is not translated after expressions of quantity.

I Adjectives

In German, an adjective standing in front of a noun adds endings to show whether that noun is singular or plural, what its gender is, and what case it stands in. The endings the adjective adds depend on what sort of article is standing before it. In general, the more the article tells you about the noun, the less the adjective does.

Adjectives only add an ending if they stand in front of a noun—adjectives standing after the verb remain unchanged. Where two or more adjectives stand in front of a noun they both take the same ending.

ADJECTIVE ENDINGS

Adjectives after der

The adjective endings following the definite article **der**, *the*, are as follows:

SINGULAR

	masculine	*feminine*	*neuter*
nom.	der rot**e** Hut, *the red hat*	die rot**e** Lampe, *the red lamp*	das rot**e** Buch, *the red book*
acc.	den rot**en** Hut	die rot**e** Lampe	das rot**e** Buch
gen.	des rot**en** Hut(e)s	der rot**en** Lampe	des rot**en** Buch(e)s
dat.	dem rot**en** Hut	der rot**en** Lampe	dem rot**en** Buch

PLURAL

nom.	die rot**en** Autos, *the red cars*
acc.	die rot**en** Autos
gen.	der rot**en** Autos
dat.	den rot**en** Autos

■ Like adjectives after **der** are adjectives after: **welcher**, *which*; **irgendwelcher**, *some . . . or other*; **dieser**, *this/that*; **jener**, *that*; **jeder**, *every*; **mancher**, *many a*.

Adjectives after ein

The adjective endings following the indefinite article **ein**, *a*, are as follows:

	SINGULAR		
	masculine	*feminine*	*neuter*
nom.	ein rot**er** Hut, a red hat	eine rot**e** Lampe, a red lamp	ein rot**es** Buch, a red book
acc.	einen rot**en** Hut	eine rot**e** Lampe	ein rot**es** Buch
gen.	eines rot**en** Hut(e)s	einer rot**en** Lampe	eines rot**en** Buch(e)s
dat.	einem rot**en** Hut	einer rot**en** Lampe	einem rot**en** Buch

	PLURAL
nom.	keine rot**en** Autos, no red cars
acc.	keine rot**en** Autos
gen.	keiner rot**en** Autos
dat.	keinen rot**en** Autos

■ Like adjectives after **ein** are adjectives after: **kein**, *no*; **irgendein**, *some . . . or other*; and the possessives **mein**, *my*, **dein**, *your*, **sein**, *his, its*, **ihr**, *her, their*, **unser**, *our*, **euer**, *your*, **Ihr**, *your*. Do not be tempted to add **unser** and **euer** to the 'der' group because they end in **-er**!

■ **Irgendein** has no plural form: **irgendwelche** (see p. 151) is used instead.

Adjectives without an article

Adjectives standing in front of a noun but with no preceding article take the following endings. These give much of the information about gender, case, and number that would otherwise be given by the article:

	SINGULAR		
	masculine	*feminine*	*neuter*
nom.	weißer Wein,	frische Milch,	neues Geld,
	white wine	*fresh milk*	*new money*
acc.	weißen Wein	frische Milch	neues Geld
gen.	weißen Wein(e)s	frischer Milch	neuen Geld(e)s
dat.	weißem Wein	frischer Milch	neuem Geld

	PLURAL	
nom.	junge Leute,	
	young people	
acc.	junge Leute	
gen.	junger Leute	
dat.	jungen Leuten	

■ Notice the **-en** genitive form of masculine and neuter singular. In fact, the genitive forms are usually avoided if possible, often by using **von**, *of*.

■ The above endings are used on an adjective that follows an indeclinable word or phrase like

> **ein bisschen**, *a little*
> **ein paar**, *a few*
> **lauter**, *nothing but*
> **mehr/weniger**, *more/less*
> **-lei** words such as **allerlei**, *all kinds of*, **derlei**, *such kinds of*

They are also used after names in the genitive:

> **Mutters neues Kleid**, *mother's new dress*

and after numbers:

> **zwei junge Leute**, *two young people*

Adjectives without endings

■ Adjectives when they do not stand before a noun do not have endings:

die Milch ist frisch, *the milk is fresh*

■ Adjectives ending in **-a** and those formed from town names by the addition of **-er** have no further endings:

eine prima Idee, *a great idea*
ein lila Sofa, *a purple sofa*
die Berliner Luft, *the Berlin air*

Adjectives after indefinites

Indefinite pronoun + adjective

After **nichts**, *nothing*, **(et)was**, *something*, **allerlei**, *all kinds of*, and other indefinite pronouns an adjective has a capital letter. It takes the ending **-es** in the nominative and accusative and the ending **-em** in the dative (the genitive is rarely found):

hier ist etwas Gutes, *here's something good*
hast du nichts Interessanteres?, *have you nothing more interesting?*
mit allerlei Gutem, *with all kinds of good things*

■ If the adjective is itself an indefinite it takes the ending but no capital:

etwas anderes, *something different*

■ With **alles** the endings differ: nominative and accusative: **alles Neue**, *everything new*; dative: **allem Neuen**.

Indefinite adjective + adjective + noun

This construction is almost always found in the plural. With the indefinite adjectives

bestimmte, *certain*   **mehrere**, *several*
einige, *some*   **verschiedene**, *various*
einzelne, *individual*   **viele**, *many*
folgende, *the following*   **wenige**, *few*
gewisse, *certain*

—and other less common indefinites—endings on both the

indefinite and the adjective are the same: they are, and behave like, two adjectives, their endings determined by what, if anything, stands in front of them:

> **viele alte Leute,** *many old people*
> **die wenigen jungen Leute,** *the few young people*

However, **alle/sämtliche,** *all,* **beide,** *both,* **solche,** *such,* and **manche,** *many,* are followed by an adjective declined as after the plural **die:**

> **alle guten Leute,** *all good people*

Adjectives losing an e

■ Adjectives ending **-el** (always) and **-en, -er** (sometimes) drop the **e** when they have an ending:

> **übel: eine üble Laune,** *a bad mood*
> **finster: ein finst(e)rer Mensch,** *a sinister person*

The **e** of the comparative **-er** ending is never dropped, however:

> **ein schönerer Tag als gestern,** *a finer day than yesterday*

■ An **e** preceded by **-au** or **-eu** is always dropped if the adjective has an ending:

> **sauer: eine saure Miene,** *a cross look*
> **teuer: ein teures Getränk,** *an expensive drink*

■ The adjective **hoch** loses its **c** when it has an ending:

> **ein hoher Turm,** *a high tower*

ADJECTIVES AS NOUNS

All adjectives can be used as nouns, as can present and past participles. They have a capital letter and the adjective endings they would have if they were followed, according to the sense, by **Mann,** *man,* **Frau,** *woman,* or **Ding,** *thing:*

> **ein Reisender**, *a (male) traveller ('travelling man')*
> **eine Reisende**, *a (female) traveller ('travelling woman')*
> **das Gute und das Böse**, *good and evil ('good thing',*
> *'evil thing')*

If they have a qualifying adjective it takes the same ending that they have:

> **mit diesem müden Reisenden**, *with this tired traveller*

If the adjective has an actual noun that it can refer back to it does not take a capital:

> **ein kleines Glas und ein großes**, *a small glass and*
> *a large one*

Der Beamte, *official*, formed from an old past participle, behaves like an adjective. **Der Junge**, *boy*, originally from the adjective **jung**, *young*, now behaves like a noun; **das Junge**, *cub*, however, still behaves as an adjective.

ADJECTIVES WITH THE DATIVE

Many adjectives can be used with a dative noun or pronoun in German, almost always corresponding to *to* + noun or pronoun in English. The dative noun or pronoun usually stands before the adjective.

The commonest such adjectives are:

ähnlich, *similar*	**gehorsam**, *obedient*
(un)angenehm, *(dis)agreeable*	**(gut, übel) gesinnt**, *(well,*
(un)begreiflich, *(in)comprehensible*	*badly) disposed*
behilflich, *helpful*	**gleich**, *all the same*
(un)bekannt, *(un)familiar,*	**lästig**, *troublesome*
(un)known	**leicht**, *easy*
dankbar, *grateful*	**nah(e)**, *near*
egal, *all the same*	**nützlich**, *useful*
ergeben, *devoted*	**peinlich**, *embarrassing*
fremd, *unknown*	**schuldig**, *in debt*

schwer, *difficult*   **unmöglich**, *impossible*
(un)treu, *(un)faithful*   **unterlegen**, *inferior*
überlegen, *superior*   **unzugänglich**, *inaccessible*

> **das ist vielen Leuten unbegreiflich**, *that is incomprehensible to many people*
> **wie kann ich Ihnen behilflich sein?**, *how can I help (be helpful to) you?*

ADJECTIVES WITH THE GENITIVE

In literary German a few adjectives are found with a preceding genitive. **Bewusst**, *aware*, **gewiss**, *certain*, **sicher**, *sure*, **würdig**, *worthy*, are the commonest of these; in everyday German **von** + dative is used instead.

COMPARATIVE AND SUPERLATIVE OF ADJECTIVES

Formation of the comparative and superlative

There are two different ways to form the comparative and superlative of adjectives in English, according to the length of the adjective:

> *long: longer* (comparative), *longest* (superlative)
> *extensive: more extensive* (comparative), *most extensive* (superlative)

German forms the comparative and superlative in one way only, with the two endings **-er** (comparative) and **-(e)st** (superlative). There is no equivalent to the English use of *more*, *most* with longer adjectives.

Normal adjective endings are added to a comparative or superlative adjective standing in front of a noun.

■ Example: **leicht**, *easy*

□ Comparative: **leichter**.

> **es ist leichter, als es war**, *it's easier than it was*
> **das ist eine leichtere Aufgabe**, *that's an easier job*

□ Superlative, before a noun or an understood noun: **leichtest-**.

> **das ist die leichteste Aufgabe**, *that's the easiest job*
> **diese Aufgabe ist die leichteste**, *this job is (the) easiest (job)*

□ Superlative, standing alone: **am leichtesten**

> **das Leben ist in den Ländern des Westens am leichtesten**, *life is easiest in the countries of the West*

In the second type of superlative we are comparing aspects of one thing (here, aspects of life) rather than, as in the first one, several things (several jobs).

The extra **e** in the superlative is used (as above) where the word would be difficult or impossible to pronounce without it.

■ Comparative adjectives whose stem ends **-el**, **-en**, or **-er** usually drop the **e** in their stem when they have a further ending:

> **dunkel**, *dark*: **die dunkleren Abende**, *the darker evenings*

■ The adjectives listed below modify their vowel in the comparative and superlative, thus:

> **alt**, *old*: comparative: **älter**, superlative: **ältest-**

alt, *old*	**krank**, *sick*
arm, *poor*	**kurz**, *short*
dumm, *stupid*	**lang**, *long*
grob, *coarse*	**scharf**, *sharp*
hart, *hard*	**schwach**, *weak*
jung, *young*	**schwarz**, *black*
kalt, *cold*	**stark**, *strong*
klug, *clever*	**warm**, *warm*

Modification is optional for:

blass, *pale*   **nass**, *wet*
fromm, *pious*   **rot**, *red*
gesund, *healthy*   **schmal**, *narrow*
glatt, *smooth*

■ The following adjectives have irregular comparatives and/or superlatives:

	comparative	*superlative*
groß, *big*	größer	größt-
gut, *good*	besser	best-
hoch, *high*	höher	höchst-
nah, *near*	näher	nächst-
viel, *much*	mehr	meist-

Mehr, *more*, and **weniger**, *less*, do not take endings:

> **du hast mehr Geld, er hat weniger Geld**, *you have more money, he has less money*

■ The following adjectives, which are always used in front of a noun and never stand alone, have only comparative and superlative forms. In each case the superlative is formed by addng -st to the comparative form:

> **äußer-**, *outer* (**äußerst-**, *outermost*)
> **hinter-**, *back* (**hinterst-**, *hindmost*)
> **inner-**, *inner* (**innerst-**, *innermost*)
> **mittler-**, *middle* (**mittlerst-**, *most central*)
> **nieder-**, *inferior* (**niederst-**, *most inferior*)
> **ober-**, *upper* (**oberst-**, *uppermost*)
> **unter-**, *lower* (**unterst-**, *lowest*)
> **vorder-**, *front* (**vorderst-**, *foremost*)

■ Past participles used as adjectives form their comparative with **mehr** and their superlative with **am meisten** or **meist-**:

> **dies ist das am meisten gekaufte Waschpulver / das meistgekaufte Waschpulver**, *this is the most (frequently) purchased washing powder*

Using the comparative and superlative

■ After a comparison *than* is **als**; after expressions of equality (and after negated expressions of equality) *as* is **wie**:

> **er ist älter als ich**, *he's older than I am*
> **er ist (nicht) so alt wie sie**, *he's (not) as old as she is*

In conversation **wie** ('**älter wie ich**') is very often also heard in the first type of sentence above.

Than ever after a comparative is **denn je**:

> **es ist teurer denn je**, *it's dearer than ever*

■ *More and more* is **immer** + comparative:

> **die Fragen werden immer schwieriger . . .** , *the questions get more and more difficult . . .*
> **. . . und immer länger**, *. . . and longer and longer*

■ *The more . . . the more* is **je . . . desto**:

> **je länger ich warte, desto kälter werd ich**, *the longer I wait the colder I get*

The word order of the main clause is always **desto** + comparative, followed by inverted order. **Umso** may be used instead of **desto**.

■ With quite a number of common adjectives a comparative can be used to mean '*fairly . . .*':

> **eine längere Zeit**, *a fairly long time*
> **eine jüngere Dame**, *a relatively young lady*

■ In English, *most* can mean simply '*extremely*', in which case it corresponds to the superlative adverbs **höchst** (not used with monosyllables) or **äußerst**:

> **das ist äußerst nett von Ihnen**, *that's most kind of you*
> **es war höchst unangenehm**, *it was most unpleasant*

DEMONSTRATIVE ADJECTIVES

Demonstrative adjectives (*this, that* in English) stand in exactly the same relationship to nouns as definite and indefinite articles do. They are in fact sometimes known as demonstrative articles.

The demonstrative adjectives in German are **dieser**, *this*, *that*, and **jener**, *that*. They both decline like **der** (see pp. 86–7).

■ **Jener** is uncommon in modern German. **Dieser** is used for both *this* and *that*. Where a differentiation has to be made an emphasized **der** is used for *that* in speech:

> **darf ich *den* Kuchen haben, bitte?**, *may I have that cake please?*

■ **Da** (or **dort**) may be added after the noun, in which case the **der** and the **da** have equal stress:

> **ja, den Kuchen da (dort)**, *yes, that cake*

▶ **Dieser, jener**, and **der** can also be used as pronouns (= *this one, that one*). See Demonstrative Pronouns, pp. 137–8.

POSSESSIVE ADJECTIVES

The possessive adjectives are

> **mein**, *my*
> **dein**, *your*
> **sein**, *his; its*
> **ihr**, *her*
> **unser**, *our*
> **euer**, *your*
> **Ihr**, *your* (polite form)
> **ihr**, *their*
>
> **das ist mein Freund**, *that is my friend*

They all decline like **ein** (see p. 87); their endings are determined by the gender and case of the noun that follows them.

■ When **unser** and **euer** have an ending the **e** of the stem is frequently dropped. This is especially the case with **euer**:

> **das ist eure Mutter?**, *that's your mother?*

In the forms **unseren** and **unserem**, **eueren** and **euerem** the second **e** is often dropped instead, especially in spoken German:

> **wir kamen mit unserm Vater**, *we came with our father*

■ **Euer** with a capital is used for *Your* in titles:

> **Eure Majestät**, *Your Majesty*
> **Eure Eminenz**, *Your Eminence*

■ The genitive forms of the possessive pronoun (singular: **dessen, deren, dessen**; plural: **deren**) are used instead of the possessive adjective where it is necessary to avoid ambiguity:

> **sie fuhr mit Ilse und ihrem Freund**, *she was travelling with her friend, and with Ilse*
> **sie fuhr mit Ilse und deren Freund**, *she was travelling with Ilse and her (Ilse's) friend* (**deren** is feminine, to agree with **Ilse**)

▶ *My, your, his, her, our, their* are possessive adjectives and stand in front of a noun. *Mine, yours, his, hers, ours, theirs* are possessive pronouns and stand alone. Don't confuse them! For the possessive pronouns in German see pp. 135–7.

THE INTERROGATIVE ADJECTIVE

The interrogative adjective is **welcher**, *which*:

> **welche Jacke ist deine?**, *which jacket is yours?*
> **welchen Jungen meinst du?**, *which boy do you mean?*

Welcher declines like **der**. See p. 86.

■ As well as beginning a direct question, **welcher** + noun can introduce an indirect question, with subordinate order:

> **ich weiß nicht mehr, welche Jacke ich anhatte**,
> *I don't remember which jacket I had on*

■ In older and literary German **welch** without any ending is the equivalent of **was für**:

> **welch eine (was für eine) Schande!**, *what a disgrace!*

▶ **Welcher** can stand alone without a noun as an interrogative pronoun (= *which one*, see p. 144) or as a relative pronoun (= *which* or *that*, see pp. 139–40).

INDEFINITE ADJECTIVES

Indefinite adjectives, as a group, include in English such words as *several, such, each, every*. In German almost all of them can be used both as adjectives and as pronouns and so they are more conveniently grouped together. A complete alphabetical list of all common indefinites, with both their adjective and their pronoun uses, can be found on pp. 144–58.

I Adverbs

Adverbs describe or modify a verb:

> **sie singt schön**, *she sings beautifully*

or an adjective:

> **sie hat eine unwahrscheinlich schöne Stimme**,
> *she has an incredibly beautiful voice*

or another adverb:

> **sie singt unwahrscheinlich schön**, *she sings*
> *incredibly beautifully*

or very occasionally a preposition or a conjunction:

> **oben im Apfelbaum**, *up in the apple tree*
> **mitten in der Rede**, *in the middle of the speech*
> **selbst wenn er das getan hat . . .** , *even if he's*
> *done that . . .*

ADVERB FORMATION

Most adjectives in German can be used unchanged, with no
endings, as adverbs. Quite a few adverbs exist only as adverbs,
however (**völlig**, *completely*; **unten**, *downstairs*; **außerdem**,
besides, etc.).

Adverbs ending -weise

Many adverbs are formed from a noun (or occasionally an
adjective + **-er**) + **weise**. For example:

from nouns:

> **teilweise**, *partly*
> **zeitweise**, *temporarily*
> **beispielsweise**, *for example*
> **ausnahmsweise**, *as an exception*

from adjectives:

> **glücklicherweise**, *luckily*
> **komischerweise**, *funnily enough*

A few of them may also be used as adjectives:

> **eine teilweise Senkung**, *a partial reduction*

Gern

The adverb **gern**, *gladly*, may be used with verbs to mean '*like*':

> **ich hab dich gern**, *I like you*
> **ich esse gern Blumenkohl**, *I like cauliflower*
> **ich bin gern in Berlin**, *I like (being in) Berlin*

With **gern haben**, **gern** goes to the end of the sentence; in the expression **ich hätte gern**, *I should like*, **gern** always follows the verb; otherwise it stands in the normal position for a 'manner' adverb. See Word Order, p. 221.

Gern may have an **-e**, **gerne**, especially when standing alone:

> **Kommst du mit? — Ja, gerne**, *Are you coming along?—Yes, with pleasure*

▶ **Gern** has an irregular comparative and superlative: see p. 121.

Hier and da

These two adverbs can only be used to mean *here* and *there* when no motion is involved. When motion is involved **hierher** and **dahin** must be used:

> **sie steht da**, *she's standing there*
> **sie geht dahin**, *she's going there*
>
> **er bleibt hier**, *he's staying here*
> **er kommt hierher**, *he's coming here*

The **hin** or **her** can split off like a separable prefix:

> **da geht sie wieder hin**, *she's off there again*

The above also applies to **dort/dorthin**, *(to) there* (a more precisely localized place than **da**) and the question adverb **wo/wohin**, *(to) where*:

> **wo bist du?**, *where are you?*
> **wohin gehst du? / wo gehst du hin?**, *where are you going (to)?*

A similar use of **hin** for motion (though without the possibility of splitting off) is found with:

> **irgendwo/irgendwohin**, *somewhere or other*
> **überall/überallhin**, *everywhere*

Woher, *from where*, **irgendwoher**, *from somewhere or other*, and **überallher**, *from everywhere*, do not present a problem, since the *from* is obligatory in English.

COMPARATIVE AND SUPERLATIVE OF ADVERBS

Adverbs, like adjectives, form their comparative with the ending **-er** and their superlative with **-(e)st**.

■ Example: **leicht**, *easily*

□ Comparative: **leichter**

> **es lässt sich leichter machen**, *it can be done more easily*

□ Superlative: **am leichtesten**

das lässt sich am leichtesten machen, *that can be
done most easily*

The extra **e** in the superlative is used (as above) where the
word would be difficult or impossible to pronounce without it.

The superlative adverb form is identical with that of the
adjective when standing alone. See p. 112.

■ Adjectives that modify their vowel in the comparative and
superlative also modify when used as adverbs. See list, p. 112.

Oft, *often*, also modifies (**öfter, am öftesten**), though
häufiger, *more frequently*, and **am häufigsten**, *most frequently*,
tend to be used instead.

■ The following adverbs have irregular comparatives and
superlatives:

	comparative	*superlative*
bald, *soon*	eher	am ehesten
gern, *gladly*	lieber	am liebsten

▶ For adjectives with irregular comparatives and superlatives
(most of which can also be used as adverbs), see p. 113.

■ A group of superlative adverbs ending **-stens** correspond
(generally) to the English *at (the)* + superlative. The
commonest are:

frühstens, *at the earliest*	**nächstens**, *soon*
höchstens, *at most*	**spätestens**, *at the latest*
letztens, *recently*	**strengstens**, *most strictly*
meistens, *mostly*	**wärmstens**, *most warmly*
mindestens, *at least*	**wenigstens**, *at least*

The common spoken form **zumindestens**, *at least*, is a mixture
of **mindestens**, included above, and the adverb **zumindest**, *at
least*.

▶ For **erstens**, *firstly*, etc., see Numbers, p. 206.

■ *Than* after a comparative adverb is **als**, *as* after an expression
of equality is **wie**:

er macht es leichter als ich, *he does it more easily than I (do)*

er macht es genau so leicht wie früher, *he does it just as easily as he used to*

This is similar to the constructions used with adjectives (see p. 114).

▶ For the order of adverbs and their position in the sentence, see Word Order, p. 221.

ALPHABETICAL LIST OF ADVERBIAL PARTICLES

Adverbial particles—words like **mal, doch, ja**—are much used, especially in spoken German, to give flavour to the language. There are English equivalents, but English relies more on differences of intonation and emphasis and uses particles much less freely. So they can rarely be translated directly from German into English. The following list gives the main adverbial particles with their basic meaning and examples of their use in various related meanings.

aber, *but*

■ adds emphasis

das war aber ausgezeichnet, *that was really outstanding*

Du hast es schon wieder verloren? — Aber nein!, *You've lost it again?—No, of course I haven't*

allerdings, *admittedly*

■ *however, though* (concedes)

ihr Auto will ich kaufen, allerdings muss der Preis vernünftiger sein, *I intend to buy her car, though the price will have to be more reasonable*

■ agrees strongly with what is seen as obvious

> **Es wird schwer sein — Ja, allerdings**, *It'll be hard—Well yes, of course*

Freilich is used with the same meaning in both instances. **Zwar** (see also p. 131) can be used with the first meaning above.

auch, *also*

■ *even*

> **auch du würdest es tun können**, *even you would be able to do it*
> **auch nicht meine Mutter würde so was sagen**, *even my mother wouldn't say something like that*
> **auch wenn er schreibt, werde ich kein Wort sagen**, *even if he writes I won't say a word*

■ *either* (with a negative)

> **sie macht es auch nicht**, *she won't do it either*
> **ich auch nicht**, *me neither*

■ correcting something that should have been obvious

> **das hat er auch nicht gesagt**, *but that's not what he said*

■ concessive *-ever*, with **wer, was, wie, wann** (producing *whoever, whatever, however, whenever*)

> **wie groß es auch sein mag, werden wir es gern liefern**, *however large it may be we'll gladly deliver it*

Note the position of **auch**.

■ emphasis

> **das musst du auch tun**, *you really will have to do that, too*

denn, *then*

■ *then* (the English concessive *then*)

> **gehst du denn?**, *are you going, then?*

Then = *if that's the case* is **dann**:

> **dann gehe ich!**, *then (in that case) I'm going*

So is *then* = *at that point in time* or *next*:

> **sie ging dann**, *then she went*

In north Germany **denn** is often—confusingly—misused for **dann**.

■ in **es sei denn, dass**, *unless*, and **geschweige denn**, *much less, let alone*

> **ich hole ihn vom Bahnhof ab, es sei denn, dass mein Auto wieder kaputt ist**, *I'll fetch him from the station, unless my car's broken down again*
> **Rad fahren kann sie nicht, geschweige denn reiten**, *she can't ride a bike, let alone a horse*

doch, *yet*

■ *none the less, even so*

> **wir haben ihn gewarnt, aber er ist doch darauf getreten**, *we warned him, but he stepped on it just the same*

Doch has stress in this use.

■ in a statement with question intonation, = **nicht wahr**

> **du fliegst doch heute morgen?**, *your plane goes this morning, doesn't it?*

■ *surely* (with a negative)

> **du fliegst doch nicht mit dieser Fluglinie?**, *you're surely not flying with that airline?*

■ *oh yes* (contradicting a negative statement or question, = French *si*)

> **Du fliegst nicht heute — Doch!**, *You're not flying today—Oh yes I am*

It is sometimes strengthened with **ja** in this use: **ja doch!**

■ with the imperative, = *come on (now)*

> **sei doch vernünftig!**, *come on, be reasonable*

■ with **mal**, conveys encouragement

> **tus doch mal!**, *go on, do it!*

eben, *just*

■ *just now*

> **sie ist eben angekommen**, *she has just arrived*

Gerade can be used with the same meaning; **soeben** is stronger, = *this very minute*.

■ *just = exactly*

> **eben das meinte ich**, *that's just (exactly) what I meant*
> **ja, eben**, *yes, exactly*

This is also the meaning of **eben-** in compounds: **ebendeshalb**, *that's exactly why*.

■ expressing resignation

> **dann eben nicht**, *well then, we won't*
> **das ist eben kalter Kaffee**, *that's just water under the bridge then*

In south Germany **halt** is used in this sense.

eigentlich, *really*

■ *in point of fact*

**es ist eigentlich viel schwerer als ich gedacht
habe,** *really (in fact) it's much harder than I thought*

The strengthening '*really*' is **wirklich**:

es ist wirklich schwer!, *it's <u>really</u> difficult!*

Similarly, as adjectives **wirklich** means *real = true*,
eigentlich means *real = fundamental*:

der wirkliche Unterschied, *the real (true) difference*
der eigentliche Unterschied, *the real difference (the
actual difference, in point of fact)*

einmal, *once*

▶ See **mal**, pp. 127–83.

etwa, *about*

■ *approximately*

etwa zehn Sekunden, *approximately ten seconds*

■ *by any chance, really*

hast du etwa Geld?, *do you have money, by any
chance?*
bist du etwa müde?, *are you perhaps tired?*
du willst doch nicht etwa sagen, dass . . . , *you
don't really mean to say that . . .*

Don't confuse with **etwas**, *some, somewhat*:

hast du etwas Geld?, *have you some money?*
du bist etwas müde, *you're a bit tired*

freilich, *admittedly*

▶ See **allerdings**, pp. 122–3.

gerade, *just*

▶ See **eben**, p. 125.

ja, *certainly*

■ *of course*

> **du wirst ihn ja kennen**, *you'll know him of course*
> **das weißt du ja schon**, *of course, you know that already*

■ underlining a fact, = *why!* or *really*

> **du bist ja schon da!**, *why, you're here already!*
> **das ist ja blöd**, *that really is stupid*
> **es ist ja direkt unglaublich**, *it's actually totally incredible*

■ concessive *of course*

> **sie ist ja furchtbar nett, aber . . .** , *she's awfully nice, of course, but . . .*

■ *indeed* (= *nay*)

> **er ist wohlhabend, ja sogar reich**, *he's well off, indeed you could even say (nay) rich*

mal; einmal, *once*

Mal is the more common in the spoken language in almost all cases. If **einmal** means literally *once* (i.e. *not twice*), the stress moves to the first syllable.

■ *one day, some day, sometime or other*

> **ich werde Sie (ein)mal in Deutschland besuchen**, *I'll visit you in Germany one day*
> **es war einmal ein Riese**, *once upon a time there was a giant*
> **irgendeinmal**, *some time or other*

■ *for once*

> **ich will mal einen Kaffee trinken**, *I'll have a coffee
> for once*
> **(ein)mal zur Abwechslung**, *just once for a change*

■ with an exclamation or after **wollen**, = *just*

> **sei du (ein)mal ruhig!**, *you just be quiet!*
> **Augenblick mal!**, *just a moment*
> **lass mal sehen!**, *let's (just) have a look*
> **wir wollen mal sehen**, *we'll just have a look*

■ with **noch**, = *again*

> **tus noch (ein)mal**, *do it again*

Noch (ein)mal implies the repetition of a specific action;
wieder, *again*, is more general

> **sie ist wieder da**, *she's back again*

■ **nun (ein)mal** expresses resigned acceptance

> **die Sache ist nun (ein)mal so**, *that's the way things are*

noch, *yet*

■ *still, yet* (time)

> **bist du noch da?**, *are you still here?*
> **er ist noch nicht dreizehn**, *he's not yet thirteen*

Immer is used to strengthen **noch**, before it (**immer noch**) or
after (**noch immer**).

■ *left*

> **wie viel Geld hast du noch?**, *how much money have
> you left?*

■ *more, further*

> **noch zwei Glas Wein, bitte**, *two more glasses of
> wine, please*

noch kleiner, *even smaller*
was noch?, *what else?*

nur, *only*

- *only*

    man kann nur lachen, *you can only (you've got to) laugh*
    nur einmal, *only once*

- *just (especially after exclamations)*

    nur langsam!, *just do it slowly*
    sehen Sie nur!, *just look!*
    wenn ich nur bitten darf, *if I may just ask*

schon, *already*

- *already, yet*

    sie ist schon da, *she's already there*
    ist sie schon da gewesen?, *has she been there yet?*

- *as early as*

    er wird schon morgen hier sein, *he'll be here as early as tomorrow*

- *even*

    schon das war zu viel, *even that was too much*

- *certainly, I'm sure*

    er wird schon kommen, *he'll certainly come*
    das stimmt schon, *I'm sure that's true*
    ich glaube schon, *I think so*

- with **weil** and **wegen**, = *if only because*

    ich darf nicht mitkommen, schon weil es so spät anfängt, *I can't come with you, if only because it begins so late*

weiter, *further*

- *further*

    das Haus liegt etwas weiter entfernt, *the house is a bit further away*

- *else*, when **weiter** is used with **nichts** or in a question

    und weiter nichts, *and nothing else (nothing further)*
    was ist weiter zu tun?, *what else is there to do?*

Sonst is an alternative to **weiter** in this meaning.

- *on*

    sprich mal weiter, *just go on speaking*

- **weiter nicht** = *not that*

    das ist weiter nicht schlimm, *that doesn't matter very much (that's not that bad)*

wirklich, *really*

▶ See **eigentlich**, pp. 125–6.

wohl, *indeed*

- *indeed, certainly*

    das kann man wohl sagen, *you can certainly say that*

The **wohl** is moderately stressed.

- *probably*

    sie wird wohl jetzt zu Hause sein, *she's probably home by now*

The **wohl** is not stressed.

- *full well*

    das weißt du wohl, *you know very well*

The **wohl** is moderately stressed.

■ *admittedly*

> **ich war wohl dafür verantwortlich, habe aber trotzdem nichts getan,** *I was indeed responsible for it, but in spite of that I did nothing*

The **wohl** is moderately stressed.

■ **wohl aber** = *but on the other hand*

> **ich kenne ihn nicht, wohl aber seinen Bruder,** *I don't know him, but I do know his brother*

The **wohl** is strongly stressed.

zwar, *admittedly*

■ *admittedly*

> **der ist zwar langsam, aber nicht faul,** *admittedly he's slow, but not lazy*

▶ For this meaning see also **allerdings,** pp. 122–3.

■ **und zwar** = *and furthermore* (introduces an extra phrase to clarify or extend)

> **er kommt immer früh an, und zwar gegen sieben,** *he always arrives early—about seven in fact*

I Pronouns

PERSONAL PRONOUNS

The basic use of the four cases of personal pronouns is similar to that of nouns. See p. 96.

Forms of the personal pronouns

The subject (nominative) pronouns are:

singular	*plural*
ich, *I*	**wir**, *we*
du, *you*	**ihr**, *you*
Sie, *you* (polite form)	
er, *he*; **sie**, *she*; **es**, *it*	**sie**, *they*

The direct object (accusative) pronouns are:

singular	*plural*
mich, *me*	**uns**, *us*
dich, *you*	**euch**, *you*
Sie, *you* (polite form)	
ihn, *him*; **sie**, *her*; **es**, *it*	**sie**, *them*

The indirect object (dative) pronouns are:

singular	*plural*
mir, *to me*	**uns**, *to us*
dir, *to you*	**euch**, *to you*
Ihnen, *to you* (polite form)	
ihm, *to him/to it*; **ihr**, *to her*	**ihnen**, *to them*

The reflexive pronouns are:

singular	*plural*
mich (accusative), *myself*;	**uns**, *(to) ourselves*
mir (dative), *to myself*	

dich (accusative), *yourself;*   **euch,** *(to)* yourselves
dir (dative), *to yourself*
sich, *(to) yourself/-selves* (polite form)
sich, *(to) him-/her-/itself*   **sich,** *(to) themselves*

■ The polite pronoun **Sie,** *you,* is both singular and plural. It always has a capital in all forms except the reflexive **sich.**

■ The familiar forms **du** and **ihr** are used to friends, relatives, colleagues, children, and animals. The plural form **ihr** is used both for more than one 'du' and for a mixed group of **du**'s and **Sie**'s. Teachers use **Sie** to students in the last three forms of the Gymnasium, equivalent to the English sixth form. Using **du** to someone one is on **Sie** terms with, without their permission, is rude.

> **wollen wir uns duzen?,** *shall we start using 'du' to each other?*

■ Pronouns agree in gender with the noun they refer to:

> **wo ist mein Bleistift? — ah, ich hab ihn,** *where's my pencil?—ah, I've got it*

However, **sie** is usually used to refer to **(das) Mädchen,** *girl,* and **(das) Fräulein,** *girl, Miss.*

■ The indefinite pronoun **man,** *one,* has the accusative and dative forms **einen** and **einem.** Its reflexive form is **sich,** its possessive **sein.** See pp. 153–4.

■ Genitive of the personal pronoun (*of me,* etc.).

The forms are:

> **meiner,** *of me;* **deiner,** *of you;* **seiner,** *of him, of it;*
> **ihrer,** *of her, of them;* **unser,** *of us;* **euer,** *of you*

They sound literary and are usually avoided as follows:

☐ Prepositions that take the genitive may be used with the dative instead.

☐ Verbs that can take the genitive (e.g. **sich erinnern**) always have a preferable alternative construction (e.g. **sich erinnern an** + accusative).

☐ Adjectives that take the genitive use **dessen**, *of that*, instead of **seiner**, and **derselben**, *of the same*, instead of **ihrer**.

Virtually the only time the genitive personal pronoun is used in modern German is with the adjectives **sicher**, *sure*, and **würdig**, *worthy*, which take a preceding genitive and have no alternative construction:

> **bist du seiner ganz sicher?**, *are you quite sure of him?*

Es as anticipatory object

A number of verbs insert the pronoun **es** as an anticipatory object into their main clause when they have a clause beginning **dass**, or an infinitive phrase, as their real object:

> **ich kann es nicht ertragen, dass er immer so spät kommt**, *I can't stand him always coming so late*
> **sie hat es fertig gebracht, ihr Visum zu bekommen**, *she has managed to get her visa*

This is obligatory with the following verbs:

ablehnen, *to refuse*	**genießen**, *to enjoy*
aushalten, *to endure*	**lassen**, *to refrain from*
erreichen, *to manage*	**lieben**, *to love*
ertragen, *to endure*	**unterlassen**, *to omit*
fertig bringen, *to manage*	**verstehen**, *to know how to*

Es is also always used with expressions such as **es eilig haben**, *to be in a hurry*, **es satt haben**, *to be sick of*, **es nötig haben**, *to need*, where the **es** forms part of the verbal phrase:

> **ich habe es eilig**, *I'm in a hurry*
> **ich habe es eilig, nach Hause zu kommen**, *I'm in a hurry to get home*

In addition to the list above there are many other verbs with which an anticipatory **es** may occasionally be found.

Reflexive pronouns

These are used where the direct or indirect object of the verb is the same as the subject. In addition:

■ In German a reflexive pronoun is used after a preposition to refer back to the subject of the sentence:

> **diese Zeit hat sie jetzt hinter sich**, *she's got those days behind her now*
> **sie hatte nur zehn Mark bei sich**, *she only had ten marks with her*

■ A dative reflexive is used in the phrase **vor sich hin**, *to oneself*, usually with a verb of speaking:

> **er redete vor sich hin**, *he was talking to himself*

▶ See also Reflexive Verbs, p. 27.

POSSESSIVE PRONOUNS

In German there are several forms of the possessive pronoun (in English: *mine, yours, hers,* etc.). The most common form is **meiner** (etc.), declined like **dieser**:

	masculine	*feminine*	*neuter*	*plural*
nominative	meiner, *mine*	meine	mein(e)s	meine
accusative	meinen	meine	mein(e)s	meine
genitive	meines	meiner	meines	meiner
dative	meinem	meiner	meinem	meinen

The forms corresponding to **meiner** for the other persons are:

deiner, etc., *yours*
Ihrer, etc., *yours* (polite form)
seiner, etc., *his; its own*
uns(e)rer, etc., *ours*
eu(e)rer, etc., *yours*
ihrer, etc., *hers; theirs*

■ In the neuter nominative and accusative the **–e** is usually dropped in **meins, deins, seins, ihrs, Ihrs**.

■ **Eu(e)rer** (usually) and **uns(e)rer** (sometimes) lose the final **e** of their stem when they have an ending:

> **eure sind besser als uns(e)re**, *yours are better than ours*

■ The following forms are also found:

☐　**mein**, *mine*
dein, *yours*
sein, *his; its own*
unser, *ours*
euer, *yours*

These take no endings, are formal or poetic, and can only be used after the verb **sein**:

> **mein Herz ist dein**, *my heart is yours*

They are never used after **es/das ist**. Furthermore, '**ihr**', *hers/theirs*, and '**Ihr**', *yours* (polite form) don't exist.

☐　**der meine, die meine, das meine**, *mine*
der deine, die deine, das deine, *yours*
etc.

In this form of the possessive pronoun **mein-** etc. is treated as an adjective after the definite article. It is rather less common than the first form given above (**meiner** etc.), especially in spoken German.

☐ The form **der meinige, der deinige**, etc., where **meinig-** etc. is also an adjective, is also found. It sounds a little old-fashioned.

■ The English genitive form *of mine* (etc.) is **von mir** (etc.):

> **die sind Bekannte von mir**, *they're acquaintances of mine*

DEMONSTRATIVE PRONOUNS

Demonstrative pronouns single out ('demonstrate') particular people or things. The demonstrative pronouns in German are **dieser**, *this (one)*, **der** or **jener**, *that (one)*, **derjenige**, *the one*, and **wer**, *the one who*. **Dieser** and **jener** are identical in form with the demonstrative adjectives **dieser** and **jener** (see p. 86).

Dieser, jener, der

Except in the special meaning of *the former*, **jener** has dropped out of common use. **Dieser** may be used for both *this one* and *that one*:

> **geben Sie mir dieses bitte**, *give me that (this), please*

Frequently **der**, emphasized in speech and sometimes followed by **da**, *there*, is used for *that one* (plural: *those*):

> **stellen sie es zu denen (da) bitte**, *put it with those, please*

As a demonstrative pronoun **der** is declined like the relative pronoun **der** (see p. 139). **Dieser** and **jener** are declined like the definite article **der** (see p. 86).

The form **dies** is often found, especially in conversation, instead of **dieses** (neuter nominative and accusative):

> **dies ist aber wunderschön**, *this one is really marvellous*

■ For *this one*, *that one* after a preposition the compounds with **da(r)-** are used:

> **legen Sie es bitte darunter**, *put it under that (one),*
> *please*

In this use, where **da-** = *this one/that one*, the stress in spoken German goes on the 'da'. Compare **da-** = *it*, p. 162.

■ The demonstrative spoken without stress is often used in conversation instead of **er**, *he*, **sie**, *she/they*, and **es**, *it*. It is particularly useful to distinguish **sie**, *they*, from **Sie**, *you*:

> **die sind wirklich hässlich**, *they're really ugly* (**sie**
> would be ambiguous in speech!)

The neuter forms **das** and (less common) **dies**, unstressed, are alternatives to **es** used with **sein**, *to be*, postponing the real subject; they are used with both a singular and a plural verb:

> **das (dies) ist meine Mutter, und das (dies) sind**
> **meine Schwestern**, *that's my mother and those*
> *are my sisters*

■ **Dieser** and **jener** also mean, respectively, *the latter* and *the former*. They are used in these meanings without the rather literary sound that 'the latter' and 'the former' have in English:

> **was Hans und seinen Bruder betrifft: dieser ist**
> **schon bei der Bundeswehr gewesen, jener hat**
> **seinen Militärdienst noch nicht abgeleistet**, *as far*
> *as Hans and his brother are concerned, the latter has*
> *(Hans's brother has) been in the army, the former has*
> *(Hans has) not yet done his national service*

Derjenige

The demonstrative pronoun **derjenige** (fem.: **diejenige**, neut.: **dasjenige**) means *the one*. Both parts of the word decline, the second part as an adjective after the definite article. **Derjenige** is usually followed by the relative **der**:

> **ich suche denjenigen, den er mitgebracht hat**,
> *I'm looking for the one he brought with him*

Derjenige is literary; in conversation the demonstrative **der** is used instead:

> **ich suche den, den er mitgebracht hat**

Wer

Wer is the equivalent of '**derjenige, der**'. It refers to people and has the general meaning of *anybody who, those who, the one who*. It always stands at the head of the sentence.

> **wer schon bezahlt hat, darf daran teilnehmen,**
> *anyone who has already paid may take part*

Distinguish **wer** followed by subordinate order, meaning *anybody who*, from **wer** introducing a question, meaning *who?*:

> **wer hat schon bezahlt?**, *who's already paid?*

RELATIVE PRONOUNS

Relative pronouns introduce a subordinate clause within the sentence and usually relate it back to a noun in the main clause. In English they are *who, whom, whose, which, that, what*.

The relative pronouns in German are **der** and **welcher**, which are identical in meaning and can refer to either people (*who*, etc.; *that*) or things (*which*; *that*). They introduce subordinate order, sending the verb to the end of the clause.

There is a third relative, **was** (*what*), which introduces a noun clause (see pp. 141–2). **Was** is invariable; the forms of **der** and **welcher** are as follows:

der

	masculine	*feminine*	*neuter*	*plural*
nominative	der	die	das	die
accusative	den	die	das	die
genitive	dessen	deren	dessen	deren
dative	dem	der	dem	denen

welcher

	masculine	*feminine*	*neuter*	*plural*
nominative	welcher	welche	welches	welche
accusative	welchen	welche	welches	welche
dative	welchem	welcher	welchem	welchen

☐ **Welcher** has no genitive forms and is less frequently used than **der**. For **welcher** as an interrogative adjective introducing a subordinate clause, see p. 117.

☐ **Welcher** can't be used after indefinite pronouns referring to people (**niemand**, *nobody*, **jemand**, *somebody*, etc.):

> **kennen Sie jemand, der das tun könnte?**, *do you know anybody who could do that?*

☐ Beware! Distinguish carefully the relative **das**, *that*, referring back to a neuter noun, from the conjunction **dass**, *that*, introducing a clause and not referring back to any noun.

☐ Relatives can be omitted in English: *the man (that) you're speaking to*, but not in German.

■ Relatives agree in gender and number with the noun or pronoun they refer back to; but their case depends on their function in the clause they introduce. So:

> **der Mann, den Sie eingestellt haben, ist ein alter Freund von mir**, *the man that you have appointed is an old friend of mine*

Den is singular and masculine, because **der Mann**, to which it refers back, is singular and masculine. **Den** is accusative, however, because in the clause it introduces it is the object of **eingestellt haben**.

☐ Exactly the same rule applies to the genitive relative:

> **der Mann, dessen Tochter Sie eingestellt haben, ist ein alter Freund von mir**, *the man whose daughter you have appointed is an old friend of mine*

Dessen is masculine because **Mann** is masculine (and in spite of the fact that it stands before the feminine word **Tochter**).

☐ Where a thing rather than a person is referred to with a genitive, English often uses *of which* after the noun. German still uses **dessen/deren** and does not change the normal word order:

> **dieses Buch, dessen Anfang Sie vorgelesen haben**, *that book, the beginning of which (whose beginning) you read out*

■ A relative may follow a preposition. It stands in the case that normally follows that preposition:

> **der Herr, mit dem du sprichst . . .** , *the man you're speaking to* (literally, *with whom you're speaking*)
>
> **der Herr, mit dessen Frau du sprichst . . .** , *the man whose wife you're speaking to* (literally, *with whose wife you're speaking*)

In English the preposition may stand either in front of the relative (*to whose wife you're speaking*), or, less clumsily, at the end of the clause (*whose wife you're speaking to*). Only the first of these two is possible in German.

☐ A less common alternative to preposition plus relative is a compound formed with **wo-** plus the preposition: **von dem→wovon**. This form can only be used to refer to things. Before a preposition beginning with a vowel an **r** is inserted: **auf dem→worauf**.

> **der Stuhl, worauf du sitzt, gehörte meinen Großeltern**, *the chair you're sitting on belonged to my grandparents*

In conversation **auf dem** would be more likely.

■ **Was** is used

☐ (= *which*) to refer back to a clause:

> **er ist gewählt worden, was ich kaum glauben
> kann,** *he has been elected, which (something) I can
> hardly believe*

☐ (= *what*) at the beginning of the sentence, to introduce a
noun clause:

> **was ich kaum glauben kann, ist die Tatsache,
> dass . . . ,** *what I can scarcely believe, is the fact
> that . . .*

☐ (= *that*; *which*) as the relative after the indefinite pronouns
alles, *everything*, **nichts**, *nothing*, **das**, *that*, **vieles**, *much*,
weniges, *little*, and usually after **etwas**, *something*, and
folgendes, *the following*:

> **fast alles, was er sagt, ist Unsinn,** *nearly
> everything (that) he says is nonsense*

☐ (= *that*) as the relative after neuter adjectival nouns:

> **das ist das Beste, was du je getan hast**, *that's the
> best thing you've ever done*

Was is not used after a preposition; **wo(r)-** + preposition is
substituted:

> **alles, woraus unsere Produkte hergestellt
> sind**, *everything that our products are made
> from*

Was may of course introduce a question as well, either direct
or indirect:

> **was meinst du?**, *what do you mean?*
> **ich weiß nicht, was du meinst**, *I don't know what
> you mean*

▶ For **wer** as combined demonstrative and relative (= *the one
who*) see p. 139.

INTERROGATIVE PRONOUNS

The interrogative pronouns in English are *who?*, *what?*, and *which?* In German they are **wer?**, *who?*, **was?**, *what?*, and **welcher?**, *which?*. **Wer** and **was** decline as follows:

nominative	wer?	was?
accusative	wen?	was?
genitive	wessen?	wessen?
dative	wem?	

They may be used in both direct and indirect questions:

wer sagt das?, *who says so?*
ich weiß nicht, was er gesagt hat, *I don't know what he said*
wessen Kugelschreiber hast du da?, *whose pen have you got there?*
ich weiß nicht, wem er gehört, *I don't know who it belongs to*

■ **Was** has no dative and its genitive is little used.

■ Both **wer** and **was** have no plural forms, though they may have a plural meaning, and with the verb **sein** they may take a plural verb form:

wer sind diese Dummköpfe?, *who are these idiots?*

With other verbs this is impossible: **alles** is added instead where a plural has to be indicated:

wer kommt denn alles?, *who is/are coming then?*

■ After a preposition **was** is not normally used, especially in written German; **wo(r)-** + preposition is substituted:

womit schreibst du?, *what are you writing with?*

The extra **-r** is used before a preposition beginning with a vowel.

The compounds **wohin** and **woher** are used to ask about motion towards and away from:

wohin gehst du?, *where are you going (to)?*
woher kommst du?, *where have you come from?*

NB: with **durch**: **wodurch** = *by what means*, **durch was** = *through what* (motion).

■ *Which (one)?* is **welcher?**, used as a pronoun:

Hol mir meinen Mantel! — Welchen?, *Get me my coat—Which one?*

▶ *Which* can also be an interrogative adjective (*which book?*). In this case it is **welcher**. See pp. 116–7.

ALPHABETICAL LIST OF INDEFINITE PRONOUNS AND ADJECTIVES

Indefinite pronouns (*somebody, something, anybody*, etc. in English) all take the third person (**er** form) of the verb in German, as they do in English. The forms of object pronouns, reflexives, possessives corresponding to the indefinite pronouns are also third-person masculine forms (**ihn**, **sich**, **sein**, and their plurals).

jeder erinnert sich an seine Vergangenheit,
everyone remembers his (their) past

Indefinites all have a small letter in German. Some indefinites only function as pronouns, most can also be used as adjectives.

The genitive forms of the indefinites are in most cases rare, problematic, or unused. They are best avoided (use **von** or rephrase the sentence) except in the specific cases mentioned below.

The alphabetical list includes all common indefinite pronouns and adjectives.

■ **alles**, *everything*; *anything*; **alle**, *all*; *everybody*; **sämtlich**, *all*; *complete*

☐ **Alles** and **alle** decline like **dieses** and **diese** (see p. 86). As in English, **alle**, *all*, can either itself be the subject of the sentence, or stand after the verb with a personal pronoun as subject:

> **alles ist möglich**, *everything is possible*
> **alle waren da / sie waren alle da**, *they were all there*
> **alle vier waren da / sie waren alle vier da**, *all four were there*

In the spoken language the neuter singular **alles** is used to mean *nothing but* or *entirely*:

> **das waren alles Parteimitglieder**, *they were every one of them party members*

and, also in the spoken language, **alle** is used as an adjective to mean '*all gone*':

> **das Bier ist alle**, *we've run out of beer*

☐ As an adjective (*all*), **all** takes no endings and stands in front of the article (or possessive or demonstrative):

> **all die Soldaten**, *all (of) the soldiers*
> **trotz all deines Geldes**, *in spite of all your money*

If there is no article (or possessive or demonstrative) following, it declines like **dieser**:

> **alle Leute wissen das — alle intelligenten Leute**, *everybody knows that—all intelligent people*

☐ The adjective **sämtlich** means *complete*:

> **Shakespeares sämtliche Werke**, *Shakespeare's complete works*

It is also very commonly used to mean *all* as an adjective, especially in the plural:

die sämtlichen Soldaten, *all the soldiers*
dein sämtliches Geld, *all your money*

Preceded by an article (or a possessive or demonstrative adjective) **sämtlich** behaves as an adjective; otherwise an adjective after it takes **-en**:

sämtliche intelligenten Leute, *all intelligent people*

□ Note that **ganz** can also translate *all* where it means *whole*:

die ganze Zeit, *all the time* (= the whole time)

■ **ander**, *other*, **ein and(e)rer**, *somebody else*, **der and(e)re**, *the other one*

Ander declines as an adjective; when it has an ending it often drops the **e** of the stem:

ein andrer wüsste das nicht, *anybody else wouldn't know that*
alles andere, *everything else*

It often follows numbers rather than standing in front of them:

die zwei anderen Kinder, *the other two children* (**die anderen zwei** is possible, however)

Where *other* means *more* it is **noch**:

eine andere Flasche Wein, *another bottle of wine* (a different one—there's something wrong with this one)
noch eine Flasche Wein, *another bottle of wine* (a further one—we've finished this one)

■ **anders**, *different(ly)*; *else*

□ **Anders** is invariable and is used after **sein** or as an adverb:

die Sache ist ganz anders, *the matter is quite different*
das musst du anders machen, *you'll have to do that differently*

In front of a noun *different* is **ander-**:

> **eine andere Sache**, *a different matter*

☐ **Anders** is also used to mean *else* after **jemand** and **niemand, wer** and **wo**. It is invariable; in the case of **wo** it often joins up:

> **das war niemand anders als sein Onkel**, *it was no one else but (none other than) his uncle*
> **wo kann es anders sein?**, *where else can it be?*
> **es muss woanders sein**, *it must be somewhere else*

■ **beide**, *both*; *two*

☐ **Beide** declines like **dieser** (see p. 86) when it stands alone:

> **sie sind beide da / beide sind da**, *they are both there*

After a definite article it declines as an adjective. Note the different word order: *both the* is **die beiden**:

> **die beiden Studenten**, *both the students; the two students*

Die beiden is a very common alternative to **die zwei** for *the two*. **Beide** is the normal word used with personal pronouns:

> **wir beide**, *the two of us*

Einer von beiden means *one or other (of them)*; **keiner von beiden** means *neither of them*:

> **keiner von beiden will es tun**, *neither of them wants to do it*

Beide may be strengthened with **alle: alle beide**, *both of you, both of us*, etc.:

> **ihr seid alle beide eingeladen**, *both of you are invited*

☐ **Beides** can also be used as a neuter (often as an alternative to **beide**)—it is singular and invariable and is found in places where in English a plural would be used. It takes a singular verb except when used with **sein** and a plural noun:

> **ich habe beides gesehen**, *I've seen both (of them)*
> **beides wäre möglich**, *both (either) would be possible*
> **es waren beides Parteimitglieder / beides waren Parteimitglieder**, *they were both party members* (compare **alles**, p. 145)

■ **ein**, *one*; **einer**, *one*; *someone*

□ As well as being the indefinite article (see p. 87), **ein** can be a pronoun, when it declines like **dieses** (see p. 86). Its masculine form **einer** is used to refer to people when gender is not specified:

> **einer von uns muss es tun**, *one of us must do it*
> **einer muss es tun**, *someone must do it*

The **e** of the nominative and accusative **eines** is often dropped:

> **eins von beiden**, *one of the two*

Ein(e)s often means *one thing*:

> **eins muss ich sagen**, *there's one thing I've got to say*

▶ **Einen** and **einem** substitute for the non-existent accusative and dative of **man**. See p. 153.

□ **Ein**, *one*, can also be used as an adjective, when it takes adjective endings:

> **er kam in dem einen Auto an, fuhr in dem anderen ab**, *he arrived in (the) one car and left in the other*

□ The compounded form **unsereiner** means *the likes of us, people of our sort*. It declines like the pronoun **einer** and has no plural or genitive singular. The neuter **unsereins** is used in spoken German for either sex:

> **unsereins** (less colloquial: **unsereiner**) **fährt nicht erster Klasse**, *our sort don't go first class*

■ **ein bisschen**, *a bit*; *a little* (in south Germany almost always: **ein bissel**); **ein paar**, *a few*

Normally invariable:

> **er ist ein bisschen verrückt**, *he's a bit mad*
> **mit ein bisschen Geld kann man alles machen**,
> *with a bit of money you can do anything*
> **mit ein paar Leuten**, *with a few people*

but *the little bit* is **das bisschen**, *the few* is **die paar**, which change according to case:

> **mit dem bisschen Geld, das ich noch habe**, *with the little bit of money I still have*
> **mit den paar Leuten, die noch mit mir sprechen**, *with the few people who still speak to me*

The words **bisschen** and **paar** are always spelled with a small letter in these constructions.

▶ See also **einige**, *a few*, below, and **wenige**, *(very) few*, p. 158.

■ **einige**, *some, a few*

☐ **Einige** is usually plural; it is declined like plural **diese** (see p. 86). It can be used as a pronoun or an adjective:

> **einige waren Deutsche**, *some (a few) were Germans*
> **einige Journalisten standen vorm Rathaus**, *a few journalists were standing in front of the town hall*

▶ **Einige** means *a few*; *the few* is **die wenigen** or **die paar** (see this page, above). *Few* (= *very few*) is **wenige**: see p. 158.

☐ **Einige** is occasionally found in the singular: **einiger, einige, einiges**. It is used both as a pronoun and as an adjective:

> **einiges bleibt noch**, *some of it is still left*
> **vor einiger Zeit**, *some time ago*

- **ein paar**, *a few*
▶ See **ein bisschen**, p. 149.

- **etwas**, *something, anything; somewhat; some*; **nichts**, *nothing*

☐ **Etwas** as a pronoun means *something* or *anything*:

> **ich muss dir etwas zeigen**, *I must show you something*

In conversation the pronoun **etwas** is very often shortened to **was**:

> **können Sie mir was zeigen?**, *can you show me anything?*

So etwas means *that sort of thing, something like that*:

> **haben Sie so etwas wie dieses, aber in Rot?**, *have you got something like this, only in red?*
> **nein, so was führen wir nicht**, *no, we don't keep that sort of thing*

So was is also used as an exclamation:

> **na, so was!**, *well, would you believe it!*

☐ **Nichts** means *not . . . anything* as well as *nothing*:

> **ich kann Ihnen nichts zeigen**, *I can't show you anything*

Qualifying adverbs, e.g. **gar/durchaus**, *at all*, **sonst**, *else*, precede it:

> **hier ist gar nichts**, *there's nothing at all here*
> **ich habe sonst nichts**, *I've nothing else*

▶ **Nichts** and **(et)was** may be followed by a neuter adjective with a capital letter (**nichts Gutes**, *nothing good*): see p. 108.

☐ **Etwas** can also be used adjectivally:

> **ich habe gerade etwas Zeit**, *I have some (a little) time at the moment*

and, often, as an adverb:

> **er ist etwas geizig**, *he's somewhat (a bit) mean*

■ **irgend(et)was, irgendjemand, irgendein,** etc.

□ **Irgend** adds the sense of '*or other*' or '*at all*' when joined to another indefinite: **irgend(et)was,** *something or other, anything at all*; **irgendjemand,** *someone or other, anyone at all*:

> **hast du irgendetwas gesehen?,** *did you see anything (at all)?*
>
> **irgendjemand muss es getan haben,** *somebody or other (<u>somebody</u>) must have done it*
>
> **du musst irgendwas tun,** *you must do <u>something</u>*

□ **Irgend** joins up with the following, forming adverbs:

> **wann: irgendwann,** *some time or other*
> **wie: irgendwie,** *somehow, anyhow*
> **wo: irgendwo,** *somewhere or other*
> **wohin: irgendwohin,** *(to) somewhere or other*
> **woher: irgendwoher,** *from somewhere or other*
>
> **wir werden uns irgendwann wiedersehen,** *we'll see each other again sometime (or other)*

□ **Irgend** joins up with the following, forming adjectives:

> **ein: irgendein,** *some . . . or other*
> **welcher: irgendwelcher,** *some . . . or other*
>
> **das muss irgendeinen Sinn haben,** *that must have some (sort of) meaning*

Irgendein declines like **ein,** the indefinite article (see p. 87).

Irgendwelcher declines like **dieser** (see p. 86); it is mainly used before abstract nouns and as the plural of **irgendein** (**ein** has no plural):

> **habt ihr irgendwelche Schwierigkeiten damit gehabt?,** *did you have any difficulties with it?*

□ **Irgendeiner** and **irgendwelcher** are pronoun forms of **irgendein** and **irgendwelche.** They are declined like **dieser** (see p. 86) and mean *someone or other.*

irgendeiner wird da sein, *someone or other will be there*

■ **jeder**, *everyone*; *every*, *each*, **jedermann**, *everyone*

□ **Jeder** is declined like **dieser**:

jeder weiß, wie groß es ist, *everyone knows how big it is*

It is very frequently used as an adjective, declined in the same way:

jeder Zehnjährige weiß, wie groß es ist, *every ten-year-old knows how big it is*

It is occasionally used in the plural:

jede zehn Sekunden, *every ten seconds*

It can also be used after **ein**, to form **ein jeder**, *each and every one*. Here it behaves as an adjective after **ein**:

er begrüßte einen jeden persönlich, *he greeted each and every one personally*

□ **Jedermann** is an alternative to **jeder**. It is much less common, can only be used as a pronoun, is singular, and takes an ending only in the genitive:

dieses Gericht ist nicht jedermanns Sache, *this dish isn't to everyone's liking*

■ **jemand**, *somebody*; **niemand**, *nobody*

These decline as follows:

nominative	**jemand**	**niemand**
accusative	**jemand** or **jemanden**	**niemand** or **niemanden**
genitive	**(jemand(e)s)**	**(niemand(e)s)**
dative	**jemand** or **jemandem**	**niemand** or **niemandem**

Both forms of the accusative and dative are common in speech; the form with the ending is more usual in writing. The genitive is little used.

Somebody else, nobody else is **sonst jemand, sonst niemand**.

▶ For **jemand/niemand Schönes**, *someone/no one beautiful*, see Adjectives, p. 108.

▶ See also **irgendjemand**, p. 151.

■ **keiner**, *no one*; **kein**, *no*

☐ As a pronoun **keiner** declines like **dieser** (see p. 86). It is more precise than **niemand**, often being the equivalent of *none, not one*:

> **keiner weiß, wie er aussieht**, *no one knows what he looks like*
>
> **keiner von uns hat ihn gesehen**, *none of us (not a single one of us) has seen him*

☐ As an adjective **kein** declines like **ein**: see p. 87. It is always used instead of **nicht ein** except

to stress the *one*:

> **nicht ein Pfennig Geld**, *not one penny, not a single penny*

when **nicht** and **ein** are split for stylistic emphasis:

> **einen Tiroler Hut hab ich nicht!**, *I don't <u>possess</u> a Tyrolean hat*

after **wenn**:

> **ich hätte es nicht gesagt, wenn Sie nicht einen Tiroler Hut getragen hätten**, *I wouldn't have said it if you hadn't been wearing a Tyrolean hat*

before **sondern** ('*not this but that*'):

> **das ist nicht ein Tiroler Hut, sondern ein bayrischer**, *that's not a Tyrolean hat, it's Bavarian*

■ **man**, *one, we, you, they, people in general*

Man is a subject pronoun, taking the **er** form of the verb. It corresponds to the English *one*, but whereas spoken English

avoids *one* as formal (using *we*, *they*, *people* . . . instead),
German uses **man** quite informally, much as French uses *on*.

Man has the reflexive **sich** and the possessive **sein**; it has no
cases other than the nominative, borrowing **einen** for
accusative, **einem** for dative, and avoiding the genitive.

> **man sagt, dass . . .** , *people say that*
> **man kratzt sich nicht in der Öffentlichkeit**, *one
> does not scratch in public*
> **dort kann es einem zu warm werden**, *it can get
> too hot for you there*

The possessive **sein** cannot be used to refer to **man** as part
of the subject—the rather cumbersome '**das man hat**' has to
be used instead:

> **die Ideen, die man hat, sind oft am Anfang nicht
> ganz klar**, *one's ideas are often not entirely clear to
> start with*

■ **manch**e, *many*; **mancher**, *many a*

□ **Manche** is plural; it is declined like plural **diese** (see p. 86).
It is often identical in meaning with **viele** (see pp. 156–7).
Manche . . . manche means *some (people) . . . some (people)*:

> **manche sagen Ja, manche dagegen sagen Nein**,
> *some say yes, some on the other hand say no*

The singular, **mancher**, *many a one*, is a little old-fashioned:

> **mancher wäre auch dieser Meinung**, *many a one
> (many people) would also be of this opinion*

□ **Mancher** is also used as an adjective, also declined like
dieser. An adjective following it behaves like an adjective
following **dieser**. **Mancher** quite often has a (meaningless) **so**
in front of it:

> **manche Frauen sind nicht deiner Meinung**, *many
> women wouldn't agree with you*
> **so mancher brave Mann**, *many an honest man*

Manch can be used without an ending before **ein**:

> **manch eine Frau,** *many a woman*

This too is rather old-fashioned.

■ **mehrere,** *several*

Mehrere is only found in the plural. It declines like an ordinary adjective, and a second adjective after it takes the same ending as **mehrere**:

> **mehrere ungewöhnliche Tatsachen,** *several unusual facts*

■ **nichts,** *nothing*

► See **etwas**, p. 150.

■ **niemand,** *no one*

► See **jemand**, p. 152.

■ **sämtlich,** *all*

► See **alles**, p. 145.

■ **solch,** *such*; **so ein,** *such a*

□ In the singular **solch** is most frequently used as an adjective. The word order is different from the English:

> **ein solcher Film zieht ein großes Publikum an,** *such a film attracts a large audience*

□ In conversation **so ein** is frequently substituted for **ein solcher**:

> **hast du je so einen Film gesehen?,** *have you ever seen a film like that?*

So is always used after **kein**:

> **das war kein so hervorragender Film,** *that wasn't such a terrific film*

□ **Solch ein** is also found, but is not common in speech:

solch ein hervorragender Film, *such an outstanding film*

In this construction **solch** is invariable.

☐ The pronoun form of **solch** is **solcher**, declined like **dieser** (see p. 86):

den Film als solchen fand ich nicht so hervorragend, *I didn't find the film as such so terrific*

This form is also used as an adjective in the plural (since the **ein** of **ein solcher** and **so ein** has no plural form):

solche Filme interessieren mich nicht, *such films (films like that) don't interest me*

It is occasionally used in the singular (**so** is commoner):

bei solchem schlechten Wetter bleibe ich zu Hause, *in such bad weather I stay at home*

▶ For **so etwas** see **etwas**, p. 150.

■ **unsereiner**, *people of our sort*

▶ See **einer**, p. 148.

■ **viel**, *much*; **viele**, *many*

☐ As a pronoun **viel** is declined:

	singular	plural
nominative	**viel** or **vieles**	**viele**
accusative	**viel** or **vieles**	**viele**
genitive		**vieler**
dative	**viel** or **vielem**	**vielen**

nicht viele denken wie du, *not many think like you*
viel(es), was du sagst, ist unverständlich, *much that (of what) you say is incomprehensible*

The form without an ending is sometimes said to be the more general, but often there seems to be little difference between the two forms. There is no genitive singular.

☐ **Viel** is also used, much more commonly, as an adjective standing without an article in front of a noun. In this case it takes no endings in the singular and the endings shown above in the plural:

> **wie viel Geld hast du?**, *how much money have you?*
> **ich habe so viel Zeit**, *I've so much time*
> **nicht viele Engländer kommen zu uns**, *not many English visit us*

Viel can also be used as an adjective after an article, in which case it takes normal adjective endings:

> **die vielen guten Weine, die man hier kaufen kann**, *the many good wines one can buy here*

☐ An adjective following **viel** in the singular behaves as an adjective without an article (see pp. 106–7):

> **mit sehr viel schlechtem Wein**, *with a very great deal of bad wine*

After **viele** in the plural it behaves like an adjective after another adjective (see p. 108–9):

> **viele ältere Engländer**, *many elderly English*

☐ **Soviel** is written as one word when it is a conjunction (= *as far as*), but as two when it means *so much*:

> **soviel ich weiß, hat er nicht so viel Theater gesehen**, *as far as I know he hasn't seen very much theatre*

▶ **Viel** has an irregular comparative and superlative (**mehr**, **meist**). See p. 113.

■ **welcher**, *some*; *any*

Welcher is declined like **dieser** (see p. 86):

> **wir haben keinen Kaffee mehr, hast du welchen?**, *we've no coffee left, have you any?*

It refers back to the last-stated noun and is especially common in spoken German.

▶ **Welcher** can also be an interrogative pronoun (see pp. 143–4), an interrogative adjective (see pp. 116–17), and a relative pronoun or adjective (see pp. 139–40).

▶ See also **irgendwelcher**, p. 151.

■ **wenig**, *little*; **wenige**, *few*

For the basic form and use of **wenig**, see **viel**, pp. 156–7: everything stated there about **viel** (except the sections on the comparative and superlative) also applies to **wenig**.

☐ **ein wenig**, *a little*, is invariable:

> **wir haben nur ein wenig Zeit**, *we only have a little time*

A very little is **ein klein wenig** (the **klein** is also invariable):

> **ein (ganz) klein wenig Zucker, bitte**, *(just) a very little sugar, please*

I Prepositions

Prepositions—words like *in, on, over*—stand in front of a noun or pronoun to relate it to the rest of the sentence:

> **er ging direkt in sein Zimmer**, *he went straight into his room* (preposition: **in**, *into*)

Prepositions can also stand in front of a verb—*without singing*. In English this part of the verb is usually the *-ing* form. In German most prepositions cannot be followed by a verb, and the sentence has to be reconstructed (see Translation Problems, *-ing*, pp. 139–40). Those that can be followed by a verb use the infinitive with **zu**:

> **ohne zu singen**, *without singing*
> **um zu singen**, *in order to sing*

CASE WITH PREPOSITIONS

Prepositions in German are followed by nouns or pronouns in the accusative, the genitive, or the dative.

■ The dative is the case found most frequently after a preposition. In general, if you are not sure what case a preposition takes and are not in a position to look it up, use the dative. The following nine very common prepositions always take the dative, and there are many others:

aus, *out of*	**mit**, *with*
außer, *except; outside*	**nach**, *after; to*
bei, *near; with; at the*	**seit**, *since*
house of	**von**, *from; of*
gegenüber, *opposite*	**zu**, *to*
(follows noun)	

■ Seven prepositions always take the accusative:

bis, *until*	**für**, *for*
durch, *through*	**gegen**, *against; towards*
entlang, *along* (following	**ohne**, *without*
its noun; otherwise	**um**, *round*
dative)	

There are also a very small number of less common prepositions that always take the accusative.

■ Four common prepositions take the genitive:

(an)statt, *instead of*	**während**, *during*
trotz, *in spite of*	**wegen**, *because of*

Prepositions ending **-seits** (e.g. **diesseits**, *this side of*) and **-halb** (e.g. **innerhalb**, *inside*) can take the genitive, but are more often found followed by **von** + the dative.

A large number of uncommon prepositions and prepositional phrases, including many legal ones, also take the genitive.

■ A group of prepositions take the accusative if motion towards is implied and the dative if not. The prepositions in this group are:

an, *on; at*	**über**, *over*
auf, *on*	**unter**, *under; among*
in, *in*	**vor**, *in front of*
hinter, *behind*	**zwischen**, *between*
neben, *near; beside*	

The only prepositions outside this group that commonly imply motion towards are **zu** and **nach**, with which the case is always dative. So apart from **zu** and **nach**, if a preposition implies motion towards, as a general rule use the accusative.

■ **An**, **auf**, **über**, and **vor**, and less frequently other prepositions, can be used with a figurative meaning after verbs (e.g. **bestehen auf**, *insist on*). In such cases **vor** always takes the dative, **auf** and **über** usually take the accusative, and **an** varies (see pp. 51–2). For more detail on individual prepositions see the Alphabetical List, pp. 163–87. For preposition and case with individual verbs, Oxford Reference: *German Verbs* should be consulted.

■ Where two prepositions joined by **und** or **oder** stand before the same noun it takes the case of the last one:

> **du kommst mit oder ohne deine Schwester?**, *are you coming with or without your sister?*

CONTRACTED FORMS OF PREPOSITIONS

Many prepositions can combine with a following definite article to produce a contraction:

> **wir gehen zum (= zu *dem*) Laden**, *we're going to the shop*

■ Contractions are not used

where the article is stressed (meaning *that*):

> **wir gehen zu *dem* Laden**, *we're going to that shop*

where the noun has an adjective clause that particularizes it:

> **wir gehen zu dem Laden, wo wir immer einkaufen**, *we're going to the shop where we always shop* (i.e. that particular shop)

■ Apart from the above cases the following contracted forms are almost always preferred to the non-contracted forms:

am (an dem)	**vom (von dem)**
beim (bei dem)	**zum (zu dem)**
im (in dem)	**zur (zu der)**
ins (in das)	

In addition, the following contractions are very frequent indeed in spoken German and are very often found in modern printed German:

ans (an das)	übern (über den)
aufs (auf das)	übers (über das)
außerm (außer dem)	ums (um das)
durchs (durch das)	unterm (unter dem)
fürs (für das)	untern (unter den)
hinterm (hinter dem)	unters (unter das)
hintern (hinter den)	vorm (vor dem)
hinters (hinter das)	vors (vor das)
überm (über dem)	

Other contracted forms may be heard in spoken German:

> **tus aufn Tisch**, *put it on the table*

DA + PREPOSITIONS

Da may be prefixed to most prepositions, giving the meaning 'preposition + *it*':

> **von**, *from* → **davon**, *from it*: **was hast du davon?**, *what do you get from it?*

If the preposition begins with a vowel an extra **r** is inserted: **daraus**.

■ These combined forms are only used to refer to things.

■ The prepositions **außer, bis, gegenüber, ohne, seit** do not have **da**- forms; nor do prepositions that take the genitive.

In questions prepositions combine with **wo** in the same way to give the meaning 'preposition + *what*':

> **wovon?**, *of what?*
>
> **worüber?**, *about what?*
>
> **worüber sprichst du?**, *what are you talking about?*

▶ See Interrogative Pronouns, pp. 143–4.

▶ **Wo** combinations can also be used as relatives. See Relative Pronouns, p. 141.

ALPHABETICAL LIST OF GERMAN PREPOSITIONS AND THEIR USE

The use of prepositions differs considerably from language to language. Below we give an alphabetical list of all common German prepositions, and many less common ones, with their main and subsidiary meanings, their cases, and their use. Where a preposition has a number of meanings, the principal meaning is given first, with other meanings following in alphabetical order.

In addition, on pp. 188–94 there is an alphabetical list of English prepositions with their various German equivalents, for cross-reference to the German list.

ab, *from* (time); *from . . . on* (place)

+ dative

> **ab morgen**, *from tomorrow*
> **ab Mainz fuhr der Zug noch langsamer**, *from Mainz on the train went even more slowly*

an, *at*

+ dative (no motion, or motion within) or accusative (motion towards)

at (dative)

> **es ist jemand an der Tür**, *there's someone at the door*
> **er unterrichtet an der Kantschule**, *he teaches at the Kantschule*
> **am Wochenende**, *at the weekend*

at (accusative)

> **er klopfte an die Tür**, *he knocked at the door*

about (dative)

> **das gefällt mir an ihm,** *that's what I like about him*
>
> **was ist daran komisch?,** *what's funny about it?*
>
> **das Schlimmste an der ganzen Sache ist . . . ,** *the worst thing about the whole business is . . .*

by (dative)

> **du erkennst mich an meinem rosa Anorak,** *you'll recognize me by my pink anorak*

of; in respect of (dative)

> **ein Mangel an Geld,** *a lack of money*
>
> **ein großer Aufwand an Zeit,** *a great expenditure of time*
>
> **sie ist reich an Ideen,** *she is rich in (= in respect of) ideas*

on (= *up against*; dative)

> **Frankfurt am Main,** . . . *on the River Main*
>
> **am Ufer des Sees,** *on the bank of the lake*
>
> **der Spiegel hängt an der langen Wand,** *the mirror hangs on the long wall*
>
> **sie gingen am Strand entlang,** *they walked along on the beach*

on (but not literally *on top of*, and no motion towards; dative)

> **er arbeitet an einem neuen Buch,** *he's working on a new book*
>
> **am Sonntag,** *on Sunday*
>
> **am zweiten Februar,** *on the second of February*

on(to) (often, a vertical surface; accusative)

> **schreib es an die Tafel,** *write it on the board*
>
> **er lehnte es an die Wand,** *he leant it on (against) the wall*

to (accusative)

> **an die Arbeit!**, *to work!*
>
> **sie schickte ein Weihnachtsgeschenk an ihre Mutter**, *she sent a Christmas present to her mother*

(an)statt, *instead of*

+ genitive

> **er kam anstatt seines Sohnes**, *he came instead of his son*

Sometimes takes dative instead of genitive, and must do when the noun has no article or adjective in front of it:

> **anstatt Protesten**, *instead of protests*

auf, *on(to)*

+ dative (no motion, or motion within) or accusative (motion towards)

on (dative)

> **es ist so viel Verkehr auf der Straße**, *there's so much traffic on the road*
>
> **sie stand eine Zeitlang auf dem Marktplatz**, *she stood for a time on (in) the market square*

on(to) (accusative)

> **er ging auf die Straße hinaus**, *he went out onto the street*
>
> **sie legte sich auf das Bett**, *she lay down on the bed*

at (accusative)

> **sie machte es auf meinen Wunsch (meine Bitte)**, *she did it at my wish (my request)*

for (+ future time; accusative)

> **sie kommt auf eine Woche**, *she's coming for a week*

in

> **der Vogel saß auf einem Baum**, *the bird was sitting in a tree*
>
> **auf keine Weise**, *in no way*
>
> **auf Englisch**, *in English*
>
> **auf jeden Fall**, *come what may* (= *in any possible case*)

of (accusative)

> **ich habe keine Hoffnung (keine Aussicht) auf eine Antwort**, *I've no hope (no prospect) of an answer*
>
> **sie war immer eifersüchtig (neidisch, stolz) auf mich**, *she was always jealous (envious, proud) of me*

to (accusative)

> **die Antwort auf meine Frage**, *the answer to my question*
>
> **du hast kein Recht auf einen Pass**, *you have no right to a passport*

aus, *out of*

+ dative

out of

> **er stieg aus dem Auto**, *he got out of the car*
>
> **trink nicht aus der Flasche!**, *don't drink out of the bottle*
>
> **sie tat es aus Stolz**, *she did it out of pride*

from

> **aus welcher Richtung kommt der Wind?**, *which direction is the wind coming from?*

Woher kommst du?—Aus Bremen, *Where are you from?—From Bremen*

made of

ein Tisch aus Holz, *a table made of wood*

außer, *except*

+ dative

except; apart from

ich habe kein Karo außer dem As, *I haven't a diamond except (apart from) the ace*

außer uns war niemand da, *nobody was there except us*

beyond

seine Treue ist außer Zweifel, *his loyalty is beyond doubt*

out of

diese Bahn ist außer Betrieb, *this tram is out of service*

seine Kinder waren außer Kontrolle, *his children were out of control*

ich bin außer Atem, *I'm out of breath*

außerhalb, *outside*

+ genitive

er wohnt außerhalb der Stadt, *he lives outside the town*

Often takes **von** + dative instead of genitive:

er wohnt außerhalb von der Stadt

bei, *at the house of*

+ dative

at the house of

>**Sahne kannst du beim Bäcker kaufen**, *you can buy cream at the baker's*
>
>**bei uns (zu Hause)**, *at our house; at home*
>
>**wir sind bei Kaisers eingeladen**, *we're invited to the Kaisers'*

To the house of is **zu** (**bei** can't be used with a verb of motion):

>**wir gehen zu Kaisers**, *we're going to the Kaisers'*

at

>**beim Frühstück**, *at breakfast*
>
>**bei der Arbeit**, *at work*
>
>**bei der bloßen Idee**, *at the very idea*
>
>**bei nächster Gelegenheit**, *at the next opportunity*

by; near

>**bleib bei mir!**, *stay by me*
>
>**sie saß beim Feuer**, *she sat by the fire*
>
>**Gräfelfing bei München**, *Gräfelfing near Munich*

for (= in spite of)

>**bei allen seiner Tugenden ist er kein liebenswerter Mensch**, *for all his virtues he's not a lovable person*
>
>**bei alledem**, *for all that*

in

>**bei gutem Wetter**, *in fine weather*
>
>**bei schlechter Laune**, *in a bad mood*

with

>**bei Norddeutschen ist der Fall anders**, *with north Germans the case is different*

**bei diesen Preisen kann man sich kaum was
leisten**, *with prices like these you can hardly afford
anything*

beiderseits, *on both sides of*

+ genitive

beiderseits der Straße, *on both sides of the street*

Often takes **von** + dative instead of genitive:

beiderseits von der Straße

betreffend, *with regard to*

+ accusative; commercial German; less common; usually
follows noun or pronoun

Ihr Fax betreffend . . ., *with regard to your fax . . .*

bis, *until*; *as far as*

+ accusative

until

bis jetzt habe ich nichts gesehen, *I've seen
nothing until now*
warte nur bis nächsten Frühling, *just wait until
next spring*
bis Sonnabend!, *see you on* (= *goodbye until*)
Saturday

When a noun with an article follows **bis**, **bis zu** + dative is used:

bis zum dritten Oktober, *until the third of October*
geh bis zur Kreuzung, *go on until (go as far as) the
crossroads*

The negative of **bis**, *not until*, is **erst** + **um**, **erst an**, etc.:

    erst um drei Uhr, *not until three o'clock*
    erst am dritten Mai, *not until the third of May*

by

    bis übermorgen ist es fertig, *it'll be ready by the day after tomorrow*

bis auf, *except (for)*

+ accusative

    wir sind alle durchgefallen bis auf die drei Mädchen, *we all failed except (for) the three girls*

dank, *thanks to*

+ dative (occasionally genitive); less common

    dank Ihrer Hilfe bin ich heute noch am Leben, *thanks to your help I am still alive today*

diesseits, *on this side of*

+ genitive

    diesseits des Flusses, *on this side of the river*

Often takes **von** + dative instead of genitive:

    diesseits vom Fluss

durch, *through; by*

+ accusative

through

    sie watete durch den Bach, *she waded through the stream*
    sie marschierten durch die Stadt, *they marched through the town*
    es kam durch das Fenster, *it came through the window*

by

du hast es durch deine Briefe klargemacht,
you've made it clear by your letters
er ist durch Schnee aufgehalten worden, *he was
held up by snow*

By is **durch** in passive constructions where a thing is referred to as
the cause; where it is a person, **von** is used. See Passive, pp. 30–1.

eingerechnet, *including*

+ accusative; less common; usually follows noun or pronoun

die zwei Flaschen Wein (mit) eingerechnet,
including the two bottles of wine

entlang, *along*

+ accusative; usually follows noun or pronoun—takes dative if
it precedes

sie schlenderte die Straße entlang, *she strolled
along the road*
entlang dem Kanal, *along the canal*

entsprechend, *corresponding to*

+ dative; commercial German; less common; usually follows a
noun or pronoun

unseren Erwartungen entsprechend,
corresponding to our expectations

für, *for*

+ accusative

ich habe die Blumen für dich gebracht, *I've
brought the flowers for you*

ich habe sie am Bahnhof für zehn Mark gekauft,
I bought them for ten marks at the station

das ist sehr leicht für mich, *that's very easy for me*

Was für ein means *what sort of*. The **für** does not affect the case of **ein**: the **ein** declines according to its job in the sentence:

mit was für einem Kuli schreibst du?, *what sort of a ballpoint are you writing with?*

gegen, *against*

+ accusative

against

er war immer gegen die EG, *he was always against the EC*

er lehnte die Leiter gegen die Mauer, *he leant the ladder against the wall*

hätten Sie etwas dagegen, wenn wir etwas später essen würden?, *would you have anything against our eating a little later?*

es geschah gegen alle unsere Hoffnungen, *it happened against all our hopes*

about (with numbers)

gegen dreihundert Soldaten, *about 300 soldiers*

compared to

gegen dich bin ich nichts, *I'm nothing compared to you*

for (= *in exchange for*)

das bekommen Sie nur gegen Bargeld, *you only get that for ready cash*

towards (usually with time)

gegen fünf Uhr, *towards five o'clock*

gegenüber, *opposite*

+ dative; follows a pronoun, usually follows a noun

opposite

> **die Sparkasse liegt dem Kino gegenüber
> (gegenüber dem Kino)**, *the savings bank is
> opposite the cinema*

compared to

> **dir gegenüber bin ich ein Anfänger**, *I'm a beginner
> compared to you*

towards

> **unsere Haltung gegenüber den neuen
> Bundesländern**, *our attitude towards the new
> federal states*

gemäß; zufolge, *in accordance with*

both: + dative; formal; less common; usually follow noun or
pronoun

> **Ihren Befehlen gemäß / zufolge**, *in accordance
> with your commands*

hinter, *behind*; *beyond*

+ dative (no motion, or motion within) or accusative (motion
towards)

behind (dative)

> **der Garten liegt hinter dem Haus**, *the garden is
> behind the house*
> **du darfst hier hinter dem Haus spielen**, *you can
> play here behind the house*
> **aber nicht hinter dem Zaun!**, *but not beyond the
> fence!*

behind (accusative)

> **geh schnell hinter die Mauer!**, *get behind the wall quickly*

in, *in; into*

+ dative (no motion, or motion within) or accusative (motion towards)

in (dative)

> **wir essen immer im Wohnzimmer**, *we always eat in the living-room*
> **er lief im Wohnzimmer umher**, *he ran about in the living-room*
> **im Winter**, *in winter*
> **im Januar**, *in January*
> **in fünf Minuten**, *in five minutes*

into (accusative)

> **er lief schnell ins Wohnzimmer**, *he ran quickly into the living-room*
> **sie tanzten bis tief in die Nacht hinein**, *they danced deep into the night*

to (accusative)

> **gehen wir in die Kirche oder ins Kino?**, *shall we go to church or to the cinema?*
> **in die Vereinigten Staaten**, *to the USA* (only non-neuter names of countries; see pp. 176–7)

innerhalb, *inside; within*

+ genitive

> **innerhalb des Schlosses**, *inside the castle*

Often takes **von** + dative instead of genitive:

innerhalb vom Schloss

. . . and must take **von** when the noun has no article or adjective before it:

innerhalb von drei Stunden, *within three hours*

jenseits, *on the other side of; beyond*

+ genitive

jenseits des Todes, *beyond death*

Often takes **von** + dative instead of genitive:

jenseits vom Tod

laut, *according to*

+ dative or genitive; less common; newspaper and TV language

laut unseren (unsrer) letzten Meldungen,
according to our latest reports

mit, *with*

+ dative

with

Obsttorte mit Schlagsahne, *fruit flan with whipped cream*
ich bin mit meinem Mann gekommen, *I'm here with my husband*
kommst du mit?, *are you coming with us/me?*
iss das mit deiner Gabel!, *eat it with your fork*

at

mit 60 km/h (= Stundenkilometern) fahren, *to travel at 60 k.p.h.*
mit 18 (Jahren), *at eighteen*

by

> **fährst du mit dem Bus?**, *are you going by bus?*
> **es kam mit der Post**, *it came by post*

nach, *after*

+ dative

after

> **nach deinem Examen**, *after your exam*
> **nach der Schule**, *after school*
> **er kam uns nach**, *he came after us* (**nachkommen**)
> **ein Tag nach dem anderen**, *one day after another*
> **zwanzig nach vier**, *twenty past* (= *after*) *four*

according to

> **nach Shakespeare**, *according to Shakespeare*
> **nach Geschmack**, *according to taste*
> **nach meiner Uhr ist es schon drei**, *by* (= *according to*) *my watch it's already three*
> **meiner Meinung nach**, *in* (= *according to*) *my opinion* (note position of **nach** in this set phrase)

for

> **die Sehnsucht (der Wunsch, das Verlangen, die Suche) nach politischer Macht**, *the longing (the wish, the craving, the search) for political power*

to (with countries, towns, continents)

> **wir fahren nach England**, *we're travelling to England*
> **eine Reise nach Berlin**, *a journey to Berlin*
> **nächstes Jahr gehts nach Australien**, *next year we're off to Australia*

But before countries used with the definite article (i.e. feminine ones, plus the very few plural or masculine ones) **in** is used:

in die Türkei, *to Turkey*
in die USA, *to the USA* (**nach** *is also found*)
in den Jemen, *to the Yemen*

Spoken north German extends this use of **nach** = *to* to many other places:

er ist nach der Bushaltestelle gelaufen, *he walked to the bus stop*

to the (with compass points, directions)

nach Süden (also **in den**), *to the south*
nach rechts, *to the right*
nach oben, *to the top; upstairs*

towards

sie sah nach der offenen Tür, *she looked towards the open door*
er ging langsam nach dem Fluss zu, *he went slowly towards the river*
nach Hause, *(to) home*

neben, *beside*; *next to*

+ dative (no motion, or motion within) or accusative (motion towards)

beside (dative)

er saß dicht neben mir, *he was sitting right beside (next to) me*
sie ging neben mir auf der Straße, *she was walking beside me on the street* (no motion relative to me)

beside (accusative)

er setzte sich dicht neben mich, *he sat down right beside me*
stell die Flasche neben die anderen, *put the bottle beside (next to) the others*

besides (dative)

> **neben den Butterbroten brauchen wir auch Wein,**
> *besides (as well as) the sandwiches we need wine too*

oberhalb, *above*

+ genitive; less common

> **oberhalb der Berghütte,** *above the mountain hut*

Often takes **von** + dative instead of genitive:

> **oberhalb von der Berghütte**

ohne, *without*

+ accusative

> **ohne Hoffnung,** *without hope*
> **ohne Hut,** *without a hat*
> **ohne seinen Hut,** *without his hat*

The indefinite article (but not possessives, etc.) is omitted after **ohne**.

per, *per*, *by*; pro, *per*

+ accusative; less common

> **per Luftpost,** *by airmail*
> **dreimal pro Woche,** *three times a (per) week*

Neither of these prepositions takes an article, so the accusative that follows them is usually hidden.

seit, *since*

+ dative

since

> **er ist hier seit Montag,** *he's been here since Monday*

ich habe sie seit Ostern nicht mehr gesehen,
    I haven't seen her again since Easter

for

seit zwei Monaten, *for three months*
seit einiger Zeit, *for some time*

■ Note the tenses used with **seit:**

du isst seit einer Stunde, *you've been eating for an hour*

du isst seit halb eins, *you've been eating since 12.30*

For an action or state starting in the past and going on to the present, **seit** + present tense is used (the English is the perfect continuous). **Seit** can have either of its two meanings.

With a negative, or a series of actions, the perfect is used, as in English:

du hast seit einer Stunde nichts gegessen, *you haven't eaten anything for an hour*

seit halb eins hast du drei Brötchen und vier Bockwürste gegessen, *since half past twelve you've eaten three rolls and four sausages*

□ The above also applies to an action starting before some point in the past and continuing to that point. This produces **seit** + the past tense:

er war seit einer Stunde dort, *he had been there for an hour*

The English tense here is the pluperfect. With a negative or a series of actions the German also uses the pluperfect:

er war seit Weihnachten dreimal in Frankfurt gewesen, *he had been to Frankfurt three times since Christmas*

statt, *instead of*

+ genitive (shortened form of **anstatt**; identical in use)

▶ See **anstatt**, p. 165.

trotz, *in spite of*

+ genitive

> **er kam trotz des Regens**, *he came in spite of the rain*

Often takes dative instead of genitive, and must do when the noun has no article or adjective in front of it:

> **trotz Karten und Briefen**, *in spite of cards and letters*

And note the datives in **trotz allem**, *in spite of everything*, and **trotzdem**, *in spite of that*.

über, *over; above*

+ dative (no motion, or motion within) or accusative (motion towards)

over; above (dative)

> **das Bild hängt über dem Fernseher**, *the picture hangs over the television*
> **Wasservögel kreisten über dem See**, *waterfowl were circling above (over) the lake*

over (accusative)

> **wir fahren hier über die Bahn**, *here we go over the railway*
> **über eine halbe Stunde**, *over half an hour*
> **über Weihnachten**, *over Christmas*
> **ein Wettlauf über 1000 Meter**, *a race over 1000 metres*

about (accusative)

> **ich muss darüber nachdenken,** *I must think about that*
> **wissen Sie etwas über Raupen?,** *do you know*
>> *anything about caterpillars?*
> **er hielt einen Vortrag über Raupen,** *he gave a*
>> *lecture about caterpillars*

via (accusative)

> **fahren Sie über Hamburg?,** *are you going via*
>> *Hamburg?*
> **er ist über die Autobahn gekommen,** *he came via*
>> *(along) the motorway*

um, *round; around*

+ accusative

(a)round

> **sie kam um die Ecke,** *she came round the corner*
> **um 1900,** *around 1900*

Um is often strengthened by adding **rings** or **rund** before it
or **herum** after it (or both):

> **rund um die Stadt herum lief eine Mauer,** *right*
>> *round the town ran a wall*

at (with clock times)

> **um sieben Uhr,** *at seven o'clock*
> **um Mittag,** *at noon*

▶ See Time, p. 208.

by

> **ich muss den Termin um eine Woche verschieben,** *I*
>> *have to postpone the appointment by a week*
> **es ist um drei Meter länger als das andere,** *it's*
>> *longer by three metres than the other one*

for

> **der Kampf um das tägliche Brot**, *the fight for one's daily bread*
> **wir spielen nicht um Geld**, *we're not playing for money*
> **eine Bitte um Hilfe**, *a request for help*
> **ich habe Angst um mein Leben**, *I fear for my life*

for the sake of (**um** + genitive + **willen**)

> **um Himmels willen tu das nicht!**, *don't do it, for heaven's sake!*

unter, *below*; *under*

+ dative (no motion, or motion within) or accusative (motion towards)

below; *under* (dative)

> **wir wohnen unter Schmidts**, *we live below the Schmidts*
> **sie tanzten unter freiem Himmel**, *they danced under the open sky*

below; *under* (accusative)

> **wir setzten uns unter eine Eiche**, *we sat down under an oak*

among (dative)

> **wir sind unter Freunden**, *we're among friends*

among (accusative)

> **du gehst nicht oft genug unter Leute in deinem Alter**, *you don't mix with (go among) people of your own age enough*

given (dative)

> **unter diesen Umständen**, *in (= given) these circumstances*
> **unter einer Bedingung**, *on (= given) one condition*

under (= *at less than*; dative)

> **unter hundert Mark verkauf ichs nicht!**, *I'm not selling it under 100 DM*

unterhalb, *below*

+ genitive; less common

> **er wohnt irgendwo unterhalb der Kantstraße**, *he lives somewhere below Kantstraße*

Sometimes takes **von** + dative instead of genitive:

> **unterhalb von der Kantstraße**

von, *from*

+ dative

from

> **ich habe das Geld von meinem Vater erhalten**, *I received the money from my father*
> **gehst du jetzt von hier weg?**, *are you going away from here now?*
> **von Morgen bis in die Nacht**, *from morning till night*
> **von hier aus kannst du drei Grafschaften sehen**, *from (up) here you can see three counties*
> **von mir aus kannst du es sofort tun**, *from my point of view (as far as I'm concerned) you can do it straight away*

about

> **was hältst du davon?**, *what do you think about it?*
> **ich schwärme (bin begeistert) von deinem neuen Auto**, *I'm mad about your new car*

by (in passive constructions)

> **es ist schon von der Putzfrau gemacht worden**, *it has already been done by the cleaning lady* (see Passive, pp. 30–1)

of

> **der Geruch von Zwiebeln**, *the smell of onions*
> **der Prinz von Dänemark**, *the Prince of Denmark*
> **ein Kind von vier Jahren**, *a child of four*
> **das ist furchtbar nett von Ihnen**, *that's awfully
>   kind of you*

Von (= *of*) is also very frequently used instead of the genitive in
spoken German; the genitive is seen as literary or affected:

> **die Tante meines Freundes → die Tante von
>   meinem Freund**, *my friend's aunt*

vor, *in front of*

+ dative (no motion, or motion within) or accusative (motion
towards)

in front of (dative)

> **draußen vorm Haus stand eine Straßenlaterne**,
>   *outside in front of the house stood a streetlamp*
> **er ging zwei Schritte vor mir**, *he walked two paces
>   in front of me* (no motion relative to me)

in front of (accusative)

> **stell dein Auto vor die Polizeiwache**, *leave your
>   car in front of the police station*

before (dative)

> **vor Sonnenuntergang**, *before sunset*
> **vor dem letzten Krieg**, *before the last war*
> **zehn Minuten vor zehn**, *ten to* (= *before*) *ten*

of (= *in the face of*; *as a consequence of*)

> **sie stirbt vor Hunger**, *she's dying of hunger*
> **ich habe Angst vor Stieren**, *I'm afraid of bulls*
> **vor Stieren muß man immer auf der Hut sein**,
>   *you must always beware of bulls*

> **da war keine Warnung vor Stieren**, *there was no warning of bulls*

with; for (with emotions; dative)

> **er strahlte vor Freude**, *he beamed with joy*
> **ich konnte vor Aufregung nicht denken**, *I couldn't think for excitement*

während, *during*

+ genitive

during

> **es geschah während des Kriegs**, *it happened during the war*

Sometimes takes dative instead of genitive, and must do when the noun has no article or adjective in front of it:

> **während drei Jahren**, *for three years*

wegen, *because of*

+ genitive; in literary German may follow its noun

because of

> **wir sind nur wegen des guten Wetters hier**, *we're only here because of the fine weather*

on . . . 's account

> **tu das nicht wegen meines Mannes!**, *don't do it on my husband's account*

Sometimes takes dative instead of genitive, and must do with a pronoun or when the noun has no article or adjective in front of it:

> **tu das nicht wegen mir!**, *don't do it on my account!*
> **bloß wegen ein paar Leuten**, *just because of a few people*

The compound forms **meinetwegen, deinetwegen**, etc. are also used instead of **wegen mir**, **wegen dir**, etc.

Von wegen + dative is used in colloquial German to mean *about*:

> **erzähl mir nichts von wegen Lohnsteuer!**, *don't talk to me about income tax!*

wider, *against*

+ accusative; less common; literary

> **ich tat es wider Willen**, *I did it against my will*

zu, *to*

+ dative

to

> **ich fahre zu meiner Tante in Ostfriesland**, *I'm going to my aunt in Ostfriesland*
> **ich fahre zum Flughafen**, *I'm driving to the airport*
> **du gehst zu Bett!**, *you're going to bed now*
> **er geht zur Schule**, *he goes to school*
> **du bist zum Abendessen eingeladen**, *you're invited to supper*
> **kommen Sie zur Sache!**, *come to the point!*

at

> **zu Ostern und zu Weihnachten**, *at Easter and Christmas*
> **zu Hause**, *at home*
> **die da zu drei Mark, bitte**, *those at three marks, please*
> **der Römer zu Frankfurt**, *the Römer (town-hall) at Frankfurt*

for

> **meine Neigung (Freundschaft, Liebe) zu Ihnen**, *my liking (friendship, love) for you*

bist du zum Essen fertig?, *are you ready to eat*
   (= for eating)?
zum zweiten Mal, *for the second time*
was kriegst du zu Weihnachten (deinem
   Geburtstag)?, *what are you getting for Christmas*
   (your birthday)?

zufolge, *in accordance with*

▶ See **gemäß**, p. 173.

zuliebe, *for the sake of*

+ dative; less common; follows noun or pronoun

tu es mir zuliebe, *do it for my sake*

zwischen, *between*

+ dative (no motion, or motion within) or accusative (motion
towards)

between (dative)

sie stand zwischen mir und ihrem Bruder, *she*
   was standing between her brother and me
sie ging zwischen mir und ihrem Bruder, *she was*
   walking between her brother and me (no motion
   relative to us)

between (accusative)

das Auto fuhr zwischen die Eingangssäulen und
   in die große Garage, *the car drove between the*
   entrance pillars and into the big garage

CROSS-REFERENCE LIST OF ENGLISH PREPOSITIONS

Prepositions presenting problems of translation are listed. These prepositions are cross-referenced to the list of German prepositions starting on p. 163. It is dangerous to take a German meaning from the list that follows without subsequently checking its usage in the German list.

about
  an, 164
  über, 181
  von, 183
  with numbers, **gegen**, 172

above
  oberhalb, 178
  über, 180

according to
  laut, 175
  nach, 176

after
  nach, 176

against
  gegen, 172
  wider, 186

along
  entlang, 171

among
  unter, 182

apart from
  außer, 167

around
  um, 181

as . . . as in comparisons
  so . . . wie. See p. 114.

as far as
  bis, 169

as well as
  neben, 178

at
  an, 163
  auf, 165
  bei, 168
  mit, 175
  zu, 186
  with clock times, **um**, 181

at the house of
  bei, 168

because of
  wegen, 185

before
  vor, 184

behind
  hinter, 173–4

below
  unter, 182
  unterhalb, 183

beside
  neben, 177

besides
  neben, 178

between
  zwischen, 187

instead of
  (an)statt, 165

into
  in, 174

made of
  aus, 167

near
  bei, 168

next to
  neben, 177

not until
  see **bis,** 169–70

of
  von, 184
  = *in the face of,* **vor,** 184–5

on
  auf, 165
  = *up against,* **an,** 164
  = *given,* **unter,** 182
  non-literal, **an,** 164

on . . . 's account
  wegen, 185

on both sides of
  beiderseits, 169

on the other side of
  jenseits, 175

on this side of
  diesseits, 170

on(to)
  an, 164
  auf, 165

| Conjunctions

Conjunctions are joining-words. They may join nouns or pronouns:

> **sie oder ihr Hund**, *she or her dog* (conjunction: **oder**)

or phrases:

> **ein sehr aufgeregter und doch noch arbeitender Beamter**, *an official, very excited and yet still working* (conjunction: **und**)

or two or more main clauses:

> **er singt, aber er kann nicht spielen**, *he sings, but he can't play* (conjunction: **aber**)

A conjunction like this that can join two main clauses together is called a coordinating conjunction.

Some conjunctions introduce subordinate clauses:

> **ich tue es, sobald ich das Geld habe**, *I'll do it as soon as I have the money* (conjunction: **sobald**)

This sort of conjunction is called a subordinating conjunction.

COORDINATING CONJUNCTIONS

In German there are six common coordinating conjunctions. When these conjunctions introduce a clause they are followed by normal word order—i.e. subject, verb, rest of sentence. See Word Order, p. 215.

They are:

aber, *but*	**oder**, *or*
allein, *only; but*	**sondern**, *but (on the contrary)*
denn, *for*	**und**, *and*

Nearly all other conjunctions are subordinating conjunctions (see p. 197).

- **Aber** can also be an adverb, meaning *however*:

> **ihr Zug war verspätet, sie ist aber angekommen**, *her train was late; she's arrived, however, (or, but she's arrived)*

- **Allein** explains why something didn't happen:

> **ich hatte mitfahren wollen, allein ich war erkältet**, *I had wanted to go with them, only (but) I had a cold*

It is rather literary: **aber** is usually used in this sense in spoken German.

- **Oder** is also used in *either . . . or* sentences: **entweder . . . oder**:

> **entweder bezahlt er die Rechnung oder er bekommt die Sachen nicht**, *either he pays the bill or he doesn't get the goods*
> **entweder Sie bezahlen oder ich rufe die Polizei**, *either you pay or I call the police*

Note the two possible word orders in the **entweder** half of the sentence. There is a difference in tone: inversion after **entweder**, no threat; normal order after **entweder**, threat!

The opposite of **entweder . . . oder** is **weder . . . noch**, *neither . . . nor*. Both **weder** and **noch** are adverbs, and both must be followed by inversion:

> **weder bezahle ich noch werden Sie die Polizei rufen**, *I shall neither pay, nor will you call the police*

- **Sondern** always follows a negative and has the sense of a correction: '*not this but, on the contrary, that*'. Compare:

> **das ist nicht wahr, sondern (es ist) falsch**, *that's not true, but false*
> **das ist nicht wahr, aber es ist interessant**, *that's not true, but it's interesting*

Not only . . . but also is **nicht nur . . . sondern auch**:

> **nicht nur ist es furchtbar einfach, sondern man kann es jetzt auch sehr preiswert bekommen**, *not only is it very easy, but you can now also get it very cheaply*

Nicht nur is an adverb, followed by inversion; **sondern** is a coordinating conjunction followed by normal order; and the **auch** stands as an adverb later in the second clause.

SUBORDINATING CONJUNCTIONS

Apart from the conjunctions listed above all others are subordinating: they send the verb to the end of the clause. See Word Order, p. 222.

If the clause introduced by a subordinating conjunction stands first in the sentence, the main-clause verb stands immediately after it. See Word Order, p. 216.

Question words (**wo, wann**, etc.) can also be used as subordinating conjunctions in order to introduce indirect questions:

> **wann kommt er?**, *when is he coming?*
> **ich frage mich, wann er kommt**, *I wonder when he's coming*

Problems of some subordinating conjunctions

■ **Als, wenn, wann**, *when*

□ **Als** is only used to mean '*when, on one occasion in the past*':

> **als er anrief, wusste ich sofort, wer es war**, *when he phoned I knew straight away who it was*

□ **Wenn** means *when* in the present and future:

> **wenn er anruft, werde ich ihm die Wahrheit sagen**, *when he phones I'll tell him the truth*

However, **wenn** can also mean *if*; if there is ambiguity, use **sobald**, *as soon as*, for *when*:

> **sobald er anruft, werde ich ihm die Wahrheit sagen**

☐ **Wenn** is also used to mean '*when, on more than one occasion in the past*'. If there is ambiguity in this sense of **wenn**, use **sooft**, *as often as*:

> **er rief an, wenn er konnte / sooft er konnte,** *he phoned when(ever) he could*

☐ **Wann** is the question word *when*, also used in indirect questions:

> **wann ruft er an?,** *when is he phoning?*
> **ich weiß nicht, wann er anruft,** *I don't know when he's phoning*

☐ After time expressions (*the day when . . .* , *the moment when . . .*), **als** and **wenn** may be used for *when*, but **wo** is also frequently found:

> **der Tag, als er ankam / wo er ankam,** *the day when he arrived*

■ **Bis**, *until*; **erst als**, **erst wenn**, *not until*

Bis is both a preposition and a subordinating conjunction:

> **bis morgen,** *until tomorrow* (preposition)
> **bis wir kommen,** *until we come* (conjunction)

▶ See pp. 169–70 for **bis** as a preposition.

☐ The negative of **bis** the conjunction (*not until*) is **erst als** or **erst wenn** (see p. 197 for the difference between **als** and **wenn**):

> **erst wenn wir kommen, wird er fahren dürfen,** *not until we come will he be allowed to leave*
> **erst als wir kamen, durfte er fahren,** *not until we came was he allowed to leave*

Notice what happens when the 'not until' clause stands second in the sentence:

> **er wird erst fahren dürfen, wenn wir kommen,**
> *he will not be allowed to leave until we come*

☐ **Bis** can also mean *by the time that*:

> **bis du kommst, habe ich alles aufgegessen,** *by
> the time you come I'll have eaten everything*

■ **Seit(dem),** *since*

Seitdem is the conjunction corresponding to the preposition **seit,** *since.* **Seit** can also be used as a conjunction, but **seitdem** is more common.

The tenses used with **seit(dem)** are the same in all respects as those used with **seit** the preposition (see Prepositions, pp. 178–9):

☐ Events start in the past, continue to present . . .

Both clauses are in the present tense in German (both perfect in English):

> **seitdem ich hier wohne, bin ich viel glücklicher,**
> *since I've been living here I've been much happier*

With a negative main clause, the main clause is in the perfect, the **seitdem** clause in the present tense (both perfect in English):

> **seitdem ich hier wohne, habe ich keinen
> Menschen gesehen,** *since I've been living here I've
> seen no one*

☐ Events start in the past, continue to the point in the past we are talking about . . .

Both clauses are in the past tense in German (both pluperfect in English):

> **seitdem ich dort wohnte, war ich viel glücklicher,**
> *since I'd been living there, I'd been much happier*

With a negative main clause, the main clause is in the pluperfect, the **seitdem** clause in the past tense (both pluperfect in English):

seitdem ich dort wohnte, hatte ich keinen Menschen gesehen, *since I'd been living here I'd seen no one*

Numbers, Time, Measurements

CARDINAL NUMBERS

The cardinal numbers are

0	null	19	neunzehn
1	ein (eins when counting)	20	zwanzig
2	zwei (often zwo in speech)	21	einundzwanzig
3	drei	22	zweiundzwanzig ...
4	vier	30	dreißig
5	fünf	40	vierzig
6	sechs	50	fünfzig
7	sieben	60	sechzig
8	acht	70	siebzig
9	neun	80	achtzig
10	zehn	90	neunzig
11	elf	100	(ein)hundert
12	zwölf	101	(ein)hundert(und)eins ...
13	dreizehn	200	zweihundert ...
14	vierzehn	1000	(ein)tausend
15	fünfzehn	1001	tausendeins ...
16	sechzehn	2000	zweitausend ...
17	siebzehn	1000 000	eine Million ...
18	achtzehn	1000 000 000	eine Milliarde

■ Number punctuation

□ There are no commas between numbers in German; instead a space is left. This space is often (but not always) omitted with units of thousands:

9000 but **10 000**

Very occasionally numbers are found printed with full stops instead of spaces.

☐ Telephone numbers are split up into (and spoken in) pairs:

> **54 78 34, vierundfünfzig achtundsiebzig**
> **vierunddreißig**

☐ The centuries (except millennia) are counted in hundreds:

> **im Jahre neunzehnhundertneunundneunzig**, *in 1999*
>
> but: **im Jahre zweitausend**, *in 2000*

☐ Numbers up to but not including **eine Million** are written as a single word:

> **zwei Millionen**
> **dreihundertsiebentausendneunhundertneunundneunzig**,
> *2,307,999*

Such monster written forms are avoided wherever possible; a space or hyphen is sometimes found after **-tausend**.

■ **Ein** has an **-s** when counting, in arithmetic, and when used after a noun (**Zimmer eins**, *room one*); otherwise it declines like the indefinite article. At the end of compounds, however (**hunderteins** etc.), it has the **-s** form even when standing before a noun. Unlike the indefinite article, **ein** = *one* is stressed in spoken German.

One can be a pronoun, in which case it is **einer, eine, ein(e)s**, declined like **dieser** (see Indefinites, p. 148):

> **nimm ein(e)s von den beiden!**, *take one of the two*

■ As well as their numerical-adjective forms above, **das Hundert** and **das Tausend** are also nouns, used in such contexts as **viele Tausende** (sometimes written **tausende**) **von Menschen**, *many thousands of people*. **Die Million** and **die Milliarde** only have noun forms. They both take a plural **-(e)n**; this plural form is also used when counting.

■ Note the colloquial form **zig-**, *umpteen*: **zighundert**, *umpteen hundred*, **zigtausend**, *umpteen thousand*.

■ Indeclinable forms in **-er** are used in the following cases; the nouns are masculine:

> **ein Fünfziger**, *a 50-mark note*
> **ein Dreiundneunziger**, *a '93 wine*
> **in den achtziger Jahren**, *in the eighties*

ORDINAL NUMBERS

Ordinal numbers (*first, second, third,* etc.) are formed by adding **-t** to the cardinal number (up to and including **neunzehnt-**, *nineteenth*) or **-st** (from **zwanzigst-**, *twentieth*, on). **Erst-**, *first*, **dritt-**, *third*, **siebt-**, *seventh*, and **acht-**, *eighth*, are irregular.

> **erst-**
> **zweit-** (often **zwot-** in conversation, by analogy with **zwo**)
> **dritt-**
> **viert-** ...
> **sechst-**
> **siebt-** (**siebent-** exists but sounds old-fashioned)
> **acht-**
> **neunt-** ...
> **zwanzigst-**
> **einundzwanzigst-** ...
> **dreißigst-** ...
> **(ein)hundertst-**
> **(ein)hundert(und)erst-** ...
> **millionst-**

■ Ordinals are adjectives. They always have endings.

■ Ordinals compound with superlatives:

> **das zweitkleinste Bundesland**, *the second smallest Federal State*

They also form adverbs with **-ens**:

> **drittens**, *thirdly*

See p. 206.

■ The German order with **erst-** (and **letzt-**) used with a cardinal number is often the reverse of the English:

> **die drei ersten (letzten) Wagen**, *the first (last) three coaches*

The English order (**die ersten drei**) is also possible.

■ To abbreviate ordinals a full stop or occasionally **(s)t-** is used, thus:

> **zweite: 2.; II.; 2te**
> **zwanzigste: 20.; XX.; 20ste**

Roman numerals + full stop are used for the names of kings:

> **Heinrich V.**, *Heinrich V*

■ The ordinals are used with **zu** and without any ending to mean *in . . . s*:

> **zu zweit,** *in twos*; **zu dritt**, *in threes*, etc.

In ones is **einzeln**.

FRACTIONS

Fractions are formed by adding **-el** to the ordinal. They have a small letter as (indeclinable) adjectives, a capital as (neuter) nouns. Whole number + fraction is frequently written as a single word:

> **ein achtel Liter**, *an eighth of a litre*
> **ein Viertel Leberwurst**, *a quarter of liver sausage*
> **Viertel vor eins**, *a quarter to one*
> **eineinviertel**, *one and a quarter*

> **das Ganze**, *the whole*
> **ein halb / die Hälfte**, ½
> **ein drittel / Drittel**, ⅓
> **ein viertel / Viertel**, ¼
> **ein hundertstel / Hundertstel**, ¹⁄₁₀₀

> **drei siebtel / Siebtel**, ⅜
> **anderthalb / ein(und)einhalb**, 1½
> **zweieinhalb**, 2½

Compounds of **-halb** (**anderthalb**, etc.) take no endings.

■ **Halb** and **Hälfte**

ein halb- = *half a*

> **ein halbes Dutzend Eier**, *half a dozen eggs*

die Hälfte = *half (of)*

> **die Hälfte meines Vermögens**, *half my money*

halb = *half (adverb)*

> **meine Arbeit is nur halb fertig**, *my work is only
> half finished*

■ Decimals are written (and spoken) with a comma rather
than a decimal point:

> **11,704: elf Komma sieben null vier**, or
> **elfkommasiebennullvier**, *11·704*

■ The basic mathematical signs are:

+	**und; plus**	÷	**(geteilt) durch**
–	**weniger; minus**	^{2}	**hoch zwei**
×	**mal**	%	**Prozent**

> **zwanzig durch fünf (ist) gleich vier**, *twenty
> divided by five equals (is) four*
> **drei hoch zwei (ist) gleich neun**, *three squared
> equals (is) nine*
> **sieben Prozent**, *seven per cent*

NUMERICAL COMPOUNDS

■ **einfach**, *simple*
> **zweifach**, *double* (also **doppelt**)
> **dreifach**, *triple*, etc.

These are ordinary adjectives.

- **einmal**, *once*
  zweimal, *twice*
  dreimal, *three times*, etc.
  x-mal, zigmal, *umpteen times*

- **erstens**, *firstly*
  zweitens, *secondly*
  drittens, *thirdly*, etc.

- **einerlei**, *one kind of* (also: *the same kind of; identical*)
  zweierlei, *two kinds of*
  dreierlei, *three kinds of*, etc.

These are invariable adjectives.

Note the idiomatic use of **einerlei**:

> **es ist mir einerlei**, *it's all the same to me*

TIME AND DATE

Time of day

> **wie spät ist es?; wie viel Uhr ist es?**, *what time is it?*
>
> **haben Sie die richtige Uhrzeit bitte?**, *do you have the right time please?* (more polite)

es ist ein Uhr, *one o'clock*
> **fünf (Minuten) nach eins**, *five past one*
> **Viertel nach eins**, *quarter past one*
> **fünfundzwanzig (Minuten) nach eins / fünf vor halb zwei**, *twenty-five past one*
> **halb zwei**, *half past one* (NB: not '*half past two*'!)
> **Viertel vor zwei**, *quarter to two*
> **eine Minute vor zwei**, *a minute to two*
> **zwei Uhr**, *two o'clock*
> **fünf vor (nach) zwölf**, *five to (past) twelve*

Mittag, *twelve noon*
Mitternacht, *midnight*

The forms **viertel (auf) drei** and **drei viertel (auf) drei** for *quarter past two* and *quarter to three* (etc.) are sometimes heard in south Germany, constructed on the same look-ahead principle as **halb drei**.

■ There are no equivalents to a.m. and p.m. in German. To be specific use:

vormittags, *in the morning*
nachmittags, *in the afternoon*
abends, *in the evening*
nachts, *at night*

■ Units of clock time

die Sekunde, *second*
die Minute, *minute*
die Stunde, *hour*
eine halbe Stunde, *half an hour*
eine Viertelstunde, *a quarter of an hour,*
eine Dreiviertelstunde, *three-quarters of an hour*

The 24-hour clock

The 24-hour clock is much more common in Germany than here, being used for virtually all official and semi-official times; the 12-hour clock is standard in conversation, however.

es ist ein Uhr fünfzehn, *01.15*
ein Uhr dreißig, *01.30*
ein Uhr fünfundvierzig, *01.45*
dreizehn Uhr, *13.00*
vierundzwanzig Uhr, *24.00* (24 as opposed to 00 is only normally used for midnight exactly)
null Uhr eins, *00.01*

Expressions with time of day

■ **ab**, *from*

> **ab sieben Uhr**, *from seven (on)*

■ **bis**, *by*

> **bis elf Uhr sind wir da**, *we'll be there by eleven*

Bis also means *until*—the context makes clear which:

> **das Restaurant hat von Mittag bis drei auf**, *the restaurant's open from twelve to three*

See Prepositions, pp. 169–70.

■ **gegen; ungefähr um**, *at about*

> **der Zug kommt ungefähr um Mittag (gegen Mittag) an**, *the train comes in at about 12 o'clock*

Ungefähr um is to be preferred, since **gegen** is ambiguous—it could mean '*towards*', i.e. *just before* (clearer: **kurz vor**). **Um . . . herum**, *about*, is also common in spoken German.

■ **Punkt; genau; gerade**, *exactly*

> **es ist Punkt/genau/gerade eins**, *it's exactly one o'clock*
> **es ist genau/gerade ein Uhr zwanzig**, *it's exactly twenty past one*
> **es ist genau halb**, *it's exactly half past*

■ **um**, *at*

> **um wie viel Uhr fährt der Zug?**, *what time does the train go?*
> **um sieben Uhr**, *at seven o'clock*

Note also: **Schlag zwei**, *on (at) the stroke of two.*

■ **vorbei**, *past*

> **es ist Mitternacht vorbei**, *it's past midnight*

Note the position of **vorbei**.

Days, months, seasons

- **Sonntag**, *Sunday*
  Montag, *Monday*
  Dienstag, *Tuesday*
  Mittwoch, *Wednesday*
  Donnerstag, *Thursday*
  Freitag, *Friday*
  Sonnabend (north Germany), **Samstag** (south
    Germany), *Saturday*

Days of the week are masculine.

> **Was ist heute für ein Tag?—Heute ist Montag,**
> *What day is it?—It's Monday*

- **Januar**, *January*
  Februar, *February*
  März, *March*
  April, *April*
  Mai, *May*
  Juni, *June*
  Juli, *July*
  August, *August*
  September, *September*
  Oktober, *October*
  November, *November*
  Dezember, *December*

Months are masculine.

- **der Frühling**, *spring*
  der Sommer, *summer*
  der Herbst, *autumn*
  der Winter, *winter*

Seasons are normally used with the definite article.

- **vorgestern**, *the day before yesterday*
  gestern, *yesterday*

heute, *today*
morgen, *tomorrow*
übermorgen, *the day after tomorrow*

■ **gestern Morgen, gestern früh**, *yesterday morning*
gestern Nachmittag, *yesterday afternoon*
gestern Abend, *last night* (= *yesterday evening*)

heute Nacht, *last night* (= *during the night*)
heute früh, heute Morgen, heute Vormittag, *this morning*
heute Nachmittag, *this afternoon*
heute Abend, *tonight* (= *this evening*)
heute Nacht, *tonight* (= *during the night*)

morgen früh, *tomorrow morning* (*tomorrow early* is **morgen ganz früh**)
morgen Nachmittag, *tomorrow afternoon*
morgen Abend, *tomorrow evening*

Note the ambiguity in **heute Nacht**, *last night* or *tonight*. The context makes the meaning clear.

■ **vor drei Monaten**, *three months ago*
vorletzte Woche, *the week before last*
gestern vor einer Woche, gestern vor acht (NB!) **Tagen**, *a week ago yesterday*
heute in einer Woche, heute über acht Tage, *a week today*
übernächste Woche, *the week after next*
in drei Monaten, *in three months time*

■ **lange vorher**, *long before*
ein Jahr vorher, *a year before*
am Tag vorher, tags zuvor, *the day before*
am folgenden Tag, tags darauf, *the day after*
ein Jahr danach, *a year after*
lange danach, *long after*

The date

> **der Wievielte ist heute?, den Wievielten haben wir heute?**, *what's the date today?*
> **heute ist der erste Januar**, *today's the first of January*
> **heute ist der Erste**, *today's the first*
> **wir fahren Sonnabend den Sechsten**, *we go on Saturday the sixth*

Length of time

■ **lang(e)**, *for* (time completed, normally in the past)

> **wie lange war er dort?**, *how long was he there?*
> **er war drei Wochen (lang) dort**, *he was there (for) three weeks*
> **er war stundenlang (tagelang, wochenlang, etc.) dort**, *he was there (for) hours (days, weeks, etc.)*

Lang(e) may be omitted, except in the question and where it forms part of the word. The **-e** is often dropped. Note **eine Zeit lang**, *for a time*.

■ **auf, für**, *for* (time intended)

> **(auf) wie lange ist er hier?**, *how long is he here (for)?*
> **er ist auf drei Wochen hier**, *he's here for three weeks*

Though this construction normally refers to future time, it can be set back into the past, still conveying the intention:

> **er war auf drei Wochen dort**, *he was there for three weeks* (he intended to stay that long)

Auf is followed by the accusative. **Für** may be used instead of **auf**. It is slightly less common.

- **seit,** *for* (time started in the past, continuing into the present)

> **seit wie lange ist er hier?,** *how long has he been here?*
>
> **er ist hier seit drei Wochen,** *he's been here for three weeks*

▶ For tenses with **seit** see p. 179.

Definite time expressions

Definite expressions of time stand in the accusative, or take a preposition, usually **an** or **in** + dative:

> **den ganzen Tag (Morgen, Nachmittag,** etc.), *all day (morning, afternoon,* etc.)
>
> **jeden Tag,** *every day*
>
> **alle drei Tage,** *every third day*
>
> **diesen Freitag, dieses Jahr,** *this Friday, this year*
>
> **nächsten Freitag,** *next Friday* (= the coming Friday)
>
> **den nächsten Tag, am nächsten Tag,** *next day* (= the day following)
>
> **am Freitag,** *on Friday*
>
> **im Januar,** *in January*
>
> **im Frühling,** *in spring*
>
> **am Abend,** *in the evening*
>
> **am Tag,** *by day*
>
> **dreimal am Tag (in der Woche),** *three times a day (a week)*
>
> **in der Nacht,** *by night, in the night*
>
> **im Jahre 1999,** *in 1999* (or just **1999**—but NOT 'in 1999')
>
> **im siebzehnten Jahrhundert,** *in the 17th century*
>
> **n. Chr. (= nach Christus),** *AD*
>
> **v. Chr. (= vor Christus),** *BC*

Folgend, *following,* **letzt,** *last,* **vorig, vergangen,** *previous,* may be used in the same way as **nächst.**

No preposition is used with **Anfang, Mitte, Ende**:

> **er kommt Anfang (Mitte, Ende) Mai**, *he's coming
> at the beginning (in the middle, at the end) of May*

Indefinite time expressions

Indefinite expressions of time stand in the genitive:

> **eines Tages**, *one day*
> **eines Abends**, *one evening*
> **eines Montags**, *one Monday*
> **morgens, vormittags**, *in the morning*
> **nachmittags**, *in the afternoon*
> **abends**, *in the evening*
> **wochentags**, *on weekdays*
> **sonntags**, *on Sundays*

By analogy: **eines Nachts**, *one night*, **nachts**, *at night*—in
spite of the fact that **Nacht** is feminine!

MEASUREMENTS

> **welche Maße hat die Küche?**, *what are the
> kitchen's measurements?*
> **die Küche ist 3,20 Meter (drei Meter zwanzig,
> or—more technically—dreikommazweinull
> Meter) lang, 2,10 Meter breit und 2,20 Meter
> hoch**, *the kitchen is 3·2 metres long, 2·1 metres
> wide, and 2·2 metres high*
>
> **3,20 (Meter) mal 2,10 mal 2;20**, *3·2 metres by 2·1
> by 2·2*
>
> **welche Größe haben Sie (tragen Sie)?**, *what size
> are you (do you take)?*
> **ich habe (trage) Größe 13**, *I'm (I take) size 13*
> **wie viel wiegst du?**, *what do you weigh?*
> **ich wiege einhundertdreißig Kilo**, *I weigh 130 kg.*

wie groß sind Sie?, *how tall are you?*

ich bin ein Meter neunzig groß, *I'm 1·9 metres tall*

drei Meter tief, drei Meter dick, *three metres deep, three metres thick*

das Thermometer steht auf zwei (Grad), *the thermometer is at (on) two degrees*

2000 cm³ (zweitausend Kubikzentimeter), *2000 cc*

|Word Order

WORD ORDER IN MAIN CLAUSES

There are two types of word order in main clauses in German, *normal order*, in which the subject comes first, the verb second, and then the rest of the clause third; and *inverted order*, in which something other than the subject comes first, the verb second, the subject (usually) third, and then the rest of the clause fourth.

Normal and inverted order

■ In both normal and inverted order the verb is firmly fixed as the second grammatical element in the clause. Subject, object, adverb, or adverb clause may precede the verb in a German sentence, but only one of these.

□ Normal order, subject first, verb second:

> **der junge Mann stand um halb neun sehr böse**
> **vorm Kino,** *the young man was standing outside*
> *the cinema at half past eight in a very bad temper*

□ Inverted order, verb second, subject third:

> **furchtbar böse stand der junge Mann um halb**
> **neun vorm Kino**
> **um halb neun stand der junge Mann furchtbar**
> **böse vorm Kino**
> **vorm Kino stand der junge Mann um halb neun**
> **furchtbar böse**

In each of these instances the verb is the second grammatical element in the sentence; in each instance one (and only one!) adverb phrase stands in front of it and the subject stands after it.

The first element in inverted order may be an entire subordinate clause (itself in subordinate order, see p. 222); it will be followed by a comma, with the main-clause verb next and then the main-clause subject:

> **wenn du so spät ankommst** (subordinate clause)**, bin** (main-clause verb) **ich** (main-clause subject) **natürlich böse**, *if you arrive so late naturally I'm cross*

■ A coordinating conjunction may introduce a second or subsequent main clause to the sentence, followed by normal order:

> **er war furchtbar böse, denn der Film hatte schon angefangen**, *he was in a very bad temper, for the film had already started*

The coordinating conjunction **denn** (see p. 195) is here followed by normal order: subject, verb, rest of sentence.

■ There may be two or more main clauses joined by **und** or **oder** where, as in English, the subject is understood from the first:

> **er lief ins Wohnzimmer, nahm seinen Rechner in die Hand und lief wieder hinaus**, *he ran into the living room, picked up his calculator, and ran out again*

This is in fact normal order: the **er** from the first **er lief** is understood before **nahm** and again before the second **lief**.

In German the subject can be understood *only* in its normal position in front of the verb. If there is something else standing in front of the verb in the second or third clause of a sentence like the one above, the subject, in this case **er**, must be expressed:

> **er lief ins Wohnzimmer, nahm seinen Rechner in die Hand und ohne weiteres lief er hinaus**, *. . . and without further ado ran out* (in German the subject **er** must be there if **ohne weiteres** stands before the verb)

■ The following, standing at the head of a clause, are not felt to be part of it; they have a comma after them and do not affect subsequent word order:

☐ **ja** and **nein**

> **nein, das glaube ich nicht**, *no, I don't believe it*

☐ exclamations (which may have either a comma or an exclamation mark)

> **ach, ich habe meinen Schlüssel vergessen**, *oh, I've forgotten my key*

☐ names of people addressed

> **Günter, dich meinte ich nicht**, *Günter, I didn't mean you*

☐ **er sagte,** and other verbs introducing indirect speech, but not followed by **dass**:

> **er sagte, er wollte sofort bezahlen**, *he said he wanted to pay right away*

See p. 42.

☐ summing-up expressions, for example

> **das heißt**, *that is*
> **im Gegenteil**, *on the contrary*
> **ehrlich gesagt**, *to be honest*
> **unter uns**, *between ourselves*
> **wie gesagt**, *as I said*
> **wissen Sie**, *you know*
>
> **unter uns, ich konnte sie nie leiden**, *between ourselves, I never liked her*

Position of the parts of the verb in compound tenses

■ In past compound tenses the auxiliary verb stays in the second position, but the past participle goes to the end of the clause:

> **er hatte sehr lang gewartet**, *he had waited for a very long time*

■ With future and conditional tenses the auxiliary verb stays in second position, and the infinitive goes to the end:

> **sie wird sicher bald kommen**, *she's sure to turn up soon*

■ With future perfect and conditional perfect tenses the order at the end of the clause is past participle, then infinitive:

> **er wird sehr lange gewartet haben**, *he will have been waiting a very long time*

Position of the prefix with separable verbs

■ In simple tenses of separable verbs the separable prefix goes to the end of the clause:

> **der Film fing vor zwanzig Minuten an**, *the film started twenty minutes ago*

■ In compound tenses of such verbs the prefix and the past participle or the prefix and the infinitive both go to the end of the clause and join up:

> **der Film hat schon angefangen**, *the film has already started*
>
> **der Film wird bald anfangen**, *the film will soon start*

▶ See Separable Prefixes, p. 33, and Double Prefixes, pp. 34–6.

Position of the verb in direct questions

In direct questions the verb is placed either first, or, if there is a question word to introduce the question, immediately after this:

> **bleibst du noch lange hier vorm Kino stehen?**, *are you going to stay standing here in front of the cinema for much longer?*

wo bist du denn geblieben?, *where have you been, then?*

As in English a statement with the appropriate intonation may be used as a question. The verb is then second:

du kommst rein?, *(are) you coming in?*

Position of the verb in commands

In commands the verb is usually placed first in the sentence. If the subject is expressed it follows the verb:

komm schnell rein, wir verpassen den Film!, *come on in quickly, we're missing the film*
sei du mal ruhig!, *(you) just be quiet!*

Position of the subject

■ In statements the subject is normally first or third, though object pronouns after the verb may displace a noun subject to fourth position:

noch lange ruhte sich der alte Großvater in der Küche aus, *for some time yet the old grandfather stayed resting in the kitchen*

Here the reflexive direct object is third, the noun subject fourth.

Putting something other than the subject first in a statement usually gives extra emphasis to whatever is put first.

zum allerletzten Mal wiederhole ich die Frage, *I shall repeat the question for the very last time*

■ In questions the subject is second or (if there is a question word) third, immediately after the verb. As in statements, an object pronoun after the verb may stand before a noun subject.

Position of the object

■ Objects usually come early in the sentence after the verb. In normal order a pronoun object comes directly after the verb:

> **er nahm sich schnell noch etwas von dem schmackhaften Eintopf**, *he quickly helped himself to some more of the tasty stew*

The **sich** (indirect object) comes straight after the verb; the short adverb **schnell**, however, comes before the long direct object **noch etwas von dem schmackhaften Eintopf**.

■ If there is more than one object

☐ pronoun objects always precede noun objects:

> **schick mir eine Karte!**, *send me a card*

☐ with two pronoun objects the accusative comes first:

> **schick sie mir!**, *send it to me*

☐ with two noun objects the dative comes first:

> **schick Karen die Karte!**, *send Karen the card*

This is identical with the most common (though not the only possible) order of objects in English.

Position of the complement

The complement of such verbs as **sein**, *to be*, **werden**, *to become*, and **bleiben**, *to remain*, goes as late in the clause as possible:

> **sie ist sicher dieses Jahr zum ersten Mal Karnevalsprinzessin**, *she's certainly going to be carnival princess this year, for the first time*

Position of adverbs

■ The normal order of adverbs is *time—reason—manner—place*:

> **er fährt sofort mit dem Auto nach Hildesheim**,
> *he's going right away by car to Hildesheim*
>
> **er fährt heute zu ihrer Hochzeit nach
> Hildesheim,** *he's going to Hildesheim today for
> (because of) her wedding*

If there are two adverbs of the same kind the more general
one comes first:

> **er fuhr letztes Jahr am einundzwanzigsten
> August nach Hildesheim**, *last year he went to
> Hildesheim, on the twenty-first of August*

A time adverb will often precede a noun object:

> **er hat gestern sein Auto verkauft**, *he sold his car
> yesterday*

The order and position of adverbs is, however, far from rigid:
moving one to a position late in the sentence gives it additional
importance:

> **er hat sein Auto gestern verkauft** *(he sold it yesterday,
> he can't have sold it today, whatever you say)*

Generally speaking, in German the strong, important position
in the sentence is at the end.

■ Negative adverbs (**nicht, nie**, etc.) stand in front of the
word or words they are negating:

> **das habe ich nie wirklich gesagt**, *I never really
> said that*

If they negate the action of the verb they stand as near the end
as possible:

> **das habe ich wirklich nie gesagt**, *I really never said that.*

▶ See also **kein**, p. 153.

WORD ORDER IN SUBORDINATE CLAUSES

A subordinate clause may be introduced by a subordinating conjunction (any conjunction except the six coordinating ones, see p. 195), or by a relative pronoun (see p. 139). All parts of the clause stay in main-clause order except the verb, which moves to the very end of the clause.

> normal order: **ich habe nicht genug Geld**, *I haven't enough money*
>
> subordinate order: **ich tue es, weil ich nicht genug Geld habe**, *I'm doing it because I haven't enough money*

■ In subordinate order a separable verb recombines with its prefix at the end of the clause:

> normal order: **ich gehe in zwanzig Minuten fort**, *I'm going out in twenty minutes*
>
> subordinate order: **ich tue es, weil ich in zwanzig Minuten fortgehe**, *I'm doing it because I'm going out in twenty minutes*

▶ See p. 33.

■ If there is a past participle or an infinitive at the end of the clause the verb goes beyond these, right at the end:

> **ein Mann muss tun, was ein Mann tun muss**, *a man's got to do what a man's got to do*

However, if there are two or more infinitive forms at the end of the clause the verb will stand immediately before and not after these:

> **damals hat ein Mann tun müssen, was ein Mann hat tun müssen**, *in those days a man had to do what a man had to do*

▶ See p. 67.

■ If there are two subordinate clauses joined by **und** (or **oder** or **sondern**), the verb goes to the end in both:

> **ich tue es, weil ich fortgehen muss und nicht**
> **sehr viel Zeit habe,** *I'm doing it because I'm going*
> *out and (I) haven't got very much time*

If two subordinate clauses share the same verb, it goes at the
end of the second one:

> **ich tue es, weil ich in die Stadt fahren und fürs**
> **Wochenende einkaufen muss,** *I'm doing it because I*
> *have to go into town and shop for the weekend*

■ If one subordinate clause is embedded in another, they must
both have subordinate order:

> **ich frage mich, ob das Auto, das ich letzte**
> **Woche gekauft habe, wirklich so viel wert ist,**
> *I'm wondering if the car I bought last week is really*
> *worth that much*

Don't be tempted to say or write ' . . . ist wirklich so viel wert'.

■ Either subordinate or inverted order may be used for
exclamatory clauses:

> **was für blöde Sachen er geredet hat! / was hat er**
> **für blöde Sachen geredet!,** *what rubbish he talked!*

■ Subordinate order is not always adhered to in spoken
German: phrases tend to be added after the verb:

> **ich bin ganz sicher, dass alles klappen wird mit**
> **deinem Examen,** *I'm quite sure everything'll go*
> *well with your exam*

There is an increasing tendency for this to occur in written
German as well.

INFINITIVE PHRASES

Infinitives used in a phrase go at the end of that phrase:

> **seine Hoffung, am gleichen Tag nach Mannheim**
> **zu fahren, ging nicht in Erfüllung,** *his hope of*
> *going to Mannheim the same day was not realized*

Position of infinitives without zu

■ Infinitives without **zu** are included in the clause, at the end:

> **ich muss heute fahren**, *I've got to go today*

There, they go before a past participle:

> **er hatte an diesem Tag fahren müssen**, *he had had to go on that day*

. . . before an infinitive that forms part of the future and conditional tenses:

> **ich werde heute fahren müssen**, *I'm going to have to go today*

. . . and before the verb in subordinate order:

> **ich weiß, dass du fahren musst**, *I know you've got to go*

Position of infinitives with zu

■ Infinitives with **zu** are placed at the end of a clause. If they have other qualifications such as adverbs or objects they form a phrase of their own, marked off from the clause by a comma (see Punctuation, p. 231).

> **er versucht zu arbeiten**, *he's trying to work*
> **sie hat versucht, ihr Auto zu verkaufen**, *she's been trying to sell her car*

■ Where an infinitive depends on a separable verb the infinitive may go before or after the prefix:

> **er fing zu arbeiten an / er fing an zu arbeiten**, *he began to work*

If the infinitive is qualified it usually goes after the prefix:

> **er fing an, regelmäßig an seinem Auto zu arbeiten**, *he began to work on his car regularly*

■ In subordinate order with a verb in a simple tense, a short infinitive phrase with **zu** is enclosed within the clause:

> **ich weiß, dass sie es zu verkaufen versucht**, *I know she's trying to sell it*
>
> **ich weiß, dass sie ihr Auto zu verkaufen versucht**, or **. . . dass sie versucht, ihr Auto zu verkaufen**, *I know she's trying to sell her car*

A longer infinitive phrase stands outside the clause:

> **ich weiß, dass sie versucht, diesen alten, klapprigen Trabant zu verkaufen**, *I know she's trying to sell that beat-up old Trabant*

■ In subordinate order with a verb in a compound tense, the infinitive stands outside the clause:

> **ich weiß, dass sie versucht hat, es zu verkaufen**, *I know she's been trying to sell it*

■ Infinitives preceded by **um . . . zu**, *in order to,* **ohne . . . zu**, *without . . . -ing*, and **(an)statt zu**, *instead of . . . -ing*, are always placed outside the clause:

> **ich bin hier, um mein Auto zu verkaufen**, *I'm here (in order) to sell my car*

OTHER PHRASES ETC. NORMALLY STANDING OUTSIDE THE CLAUSE

■ Apart from infinitives with **zu** + further qualification, the following types of phrases usually stand outside the clause:

□ question tags, like **nicht wahr?, ja?, oder?** (corresponding to *isn't it?, aren't you?, or is it?*, etc.)

> **du bleibst hier, oder?**, *you're staying here—aren't you?* (open question)
>
> **du bleibst hier, nicht? / nicht wahr? / ja?**, *you're staying here, aren't you?* (I'm pretty sure you are)

☐ phrases beginning **wie** and **als**, forming the second part of a comparison

> **du hast es genau so schwierig gefunden wie ich**, *you found it just as difficult as I did (as me)*
>
> **nein, ich habe es viel schwieriger gefunden als du**, *no, I found it a lot more difficult than you (did)*

Where **als** and **wie** simply mean *as* or *like*, functioning as a sort of equals sign, the phrase they introduce does not stand outside the clause:

> **das haben sie mir als Deutscher sagen wollen?**, *you meant to say that to me, as a German?*
>
> **das kann selbst ein Dummkopf wie ich verstehen**, *even an idiot like me can understand that*

☐ phrases beginning **sondern** and **außer**

> **sie hat es nicht gemacht, sondern ich**, *it wasn't she who did it, but me (I)*
>
> **ich habe nichts gelesen außer einem Krimi**, *I read nothing except a detective story*

Sondern phrases have a comma before them (see Punctuation, pp. 229–30).

☐ **oder nicht**, and sometimes other phrases beginning **oder**

> **wird er kommen oder nicht?**, *is he going to come or not?*
>
> **möchtest du Erdbeeren essen oder die Torte?**, *would you like strawberries or the gateau?*

■ A relative clause stands outside the main clause when it refers back to a noun or pronoun standing immediately before a part of the verb at the end of the clause:

> **er hat schnell das Geld genommen, das ich ihm angeboten habe**, *he quickly took the money I was offering him*

but: **das Geld, das ich ihm angeboten habe, hat er schnell genommen**

I Punctuation and Spelling

CAPITAL LETTERS

■ All nouns and other words used as nouns have a capital letter:

> **der Mann**, *the man*
> **das Lachen**, *laughing* (verbal noun)
> **der Reisende**, *the traveller* (present participle used as noun)

■ Pronouns:

□ The polite **Sie** and its other forms (**Ihnen, Ihr-**—but not the reflexive form **sich**) always have a capital.

■ Adjectives made from town names by adding **-er** have a capital:

> **der Kölner Dom**, *Cologne cathedral*

■ Adjectives in geographical and other names have a capital:

> **das Rote Meer**, *the Red Sea*
> **Deutsche Bundesbahn**, *German Railways*

■ Adjectives after indefinites have a capital:

> **etwas Grünes**, *something green*
> **alles Gute!**, *all the best!*

but indefinites themselves do not take a capital:

> **etwas anderes**, *something different*

▶ See p. 108.

■ Adjectives referring to countries take a small letter as adjectives, a capital as the name of the language:

> **die deutsche Sprache**, *the German language*
> **sie spricht Englisch**, *she speaks English*
> **auf Englisch**, *in English*

■ A capital is frequently used in German in mid-sentence after a colon.

■ Cardinal numbers have a small letter, except **Million, Milliarde**, and sometimes **Hundert, Tausend** (see p. 202). Fractions are written with either a capital or a small letter (see pp. 204–5).

Ordinal numbers used as adjectives have small letters, but notice:

> **Friedrich der Zweite**, *Friedrich II*

■ Nouns not used as nouns have a small letter:

> **die Schuld**, *guilt*: **du bist daran schuld**, *it's your fault*
> **das Paar**, *pair*: **ein paar Sachen**, *a few things*
> **das Recht**, *right*: **es ist mir recht**, *it's all right by me*

Das bisschen, *bit*, is now only ever used with a small letter:

> **ein bisschen Zucker**, *a little sugar*
> **kein bisschen Zucker**, *no sugar at all*
> **das klein bisschen Zucker**, *the small amount of sugar* (note the invariable **klein**)

THE COMMA

The use of commas is largely a matter of individual style in English. In German, however, commas are used according to fixed rules that must be followed.

■ Commas are used in lists to divide off items (but not before the **und** at the end):

> **er ist jung, schön, reich und gesund**, *he's young, handsome, rich, and healthy*

■ Commas are not used between two adjectives if the second is felt to form a single concept with its noun:

> **ein schöner, saftiger Schinken**, *a nice juicy ham*
> **ein schöner westfälischer Schinken**, *a nice Westphalian ham*

■ A comma is used before and/or after each subordinate clause to separate it from the main clause:

> **Ich weiß, dass er kommen wird.** *I know he'll come.*
> **Wenn er kommt, werden wir essen**. *When he comes we'll eat.*
> **Die Leute, die kommen werden, sind mir bekannt**. *The people who're coming are known to me.*

The comma comes before, not after, the subordinating conjunction.

■ Commas are not used before **und** or **oder** introducing a new main clause:

> **Er isst hier oder auch manchmal isst er im Restaurant.** *He eats here, or sometimes in a restaurant*
> **Er kam und wir aßen.** *He came and we ate.*

■ Commas are always placed before the other coordinating conjunctions (**aber, sondern, denn, allein**—see p. 195), whether they introduce a clause or a phrase:

> **Ich klopfte, aber niemand antwortete.** *I knocked but no one answered.*
> **Es ist nicht rot, sondern weiß.** *It is not red, but white.*

■ Unlike English, German does not separate adverb phrases with commas:

> **Er stand wie immer mit Blumen vor der Tür.** *He was standing, with flowers as always, at the door.*

Adjective phrases, however, are often given commas:

> **Er betrachtete, grün vor Neid, das Auto, das ich gerade gekauft hatte.** *He looked, green with envy, at the car I had just bought.*

■ Commas are placed round appositional phrases and before a phrase beginning **und zwar**:

> **Herr Schmidt, unser neuer Chef, ist heute erschienen, und zwar um acht Uhr.** *Herr Schmidt, our new boss, turned up today, and, would you believe it, at eight o'clock.*

■ Commas are sometimes used to join two main clauses, where the equivalent English would correctly have a semicolon. This occurs particularly where the second clause begins with **trotzdem**, *in spite of that*, **unterdessen**, *meanwhile*, and **statt dessen**, *instead*:

> **Es regnet, trotzdem wollen wir wandern.** *It's raining; in spite of that we're still going walking.*

■ A comma is used where we would use a decimal point:

> **2,3** *2·3*

It is not used in large numbers, which are written with spaces where English uses commas:

> **1999 777** *1,999,777*

▶ See Numbers, p. 201.

■ Commas are used with infinitive phrases as follows.

□ An infinitive phrase consisting only of **zu** + infinitive has no comma before it:

> **Sie versucht zu singen.** *She tries to sing.*

□ One that is longer than just **zu** + infinitive usually has a comma:

> **Sie versucht, den ganzen Ring auswendig zu lernen.** *She's trying to learn the whole of the Ring by heart.*

□ There is always a comma where the infinitive is a complement after **sein**:

> **Ihr einziges Streben ist, zu singen.** *Her only aspiration is to sing.*

□ There is no comma, however long the infinitive phrase, after the verbs **brauchen**, *to need*, **haben**, *to have*, **sein**, *to be*, **scheinen**, *to seem*, and **pflegen**, *to be accustomed*:

> **Jetzt brauchst du kein einziges Wort mehr zu sagen.** *Now you don't need to say a single word more.*

THE COLON

The colon marks an amplification or explanation of what has gone before. English may use a colon or a dash for this. In German the clause following a colon very frequently starts with a capital letter:

> **Etwas muß ich aber erklären: Das Haus ist nicht zu verkaufen.** *One thing I must make clear, however—the house is not for sale.*

The colon is also used to introduce direct speech after a verb of saying:

> **Sie sagte: „Komm gut nach Hause!"** *She said,*
> *'Get home safely.'*

THE HYPHEN

A hyphen is used to represent part of a compound, to avoid clumsy repetition:

> **Radio- und Fernsehgeräte** (= **Radiogeräte und**
> **Fernsehgeräte**), *radio and television sets*

It is also occasionally used, for clarity, to break up very long compound words.

THE DASH

This usually indicates a pause, often for thought (*dash* = **der Gedankenstrich**). It may also be used instead of three dots to suspend the sense. It is sometimes used to separate two passages of direct speech within the same paragraph.

INVERTED COMMAS

The opening set of inverted commas is placed on the line in German. Both sets are printed the opposite way round from English. German uses double inverted commas for direct speech, whereas English more and more frequently uses single:

> **„Das ist nicht wahr",** **sagte er**. *'That's not true', he*
> *said.*

French guillemets (also printed the 'wrong' way round) are sometimes found:

> **»Das ist nicht wahr!«**

For speech within speech single inverted commas are used: **,** **'**.

THE EXCLAMATION MARK

The exclamation mark is used much more than in English. In none of the following cases is it obligatory, however. It is very frequently used . . .

■ after exclamations

> **Au! Das kann nicht sein!** *Oh, that can't be true!*

■ after imperatives

> **Steh auf!** *Stand up.*

■ in public notices and admonitions, where English would not punctuate at all

> **Das Betreten der Baustelle ist verboten!** *Keep out*
> **Nicht hinauslehnen!** *Do not lean out of the window*

■ sometimes at the start of letters, where English uses a comma

> **Liebe Gisela!** *Dear Gisela,*
> **Sehr geehrte Damen und Herren!** *Dear Sir or Madam,*

A comma is nowadays more common in German in this case.

FULL STOP

The full stop is used to end a sentence, and to indicate abbreviations. However, it is only used for abbreviations if what is normally said aloud for that abbreviation is the words for which it stands, not the letters of the abbreviation:

> **d.h.** (spoken: **das heißt**), *i.e.*

but: **DB** (= **Deutsche Bahn**, *German Railways*)

> **PKW** (sometimes **Pkw**; = **Personenkraftwagen**, *passenger vehicle; car*)

Notice that **usw.** (= **und so weiter**, *etc.*) has only one full stop.

A full stop is used to abbreviate an ordinal number (including its adjective ending):

> **am 20. August (am zwanzigsten August)**, *on the 20th of August*

EMPHASIS

In older printed material this is shown by spaced printing:

> **Ich möchte d e n** . *I want that one.*

This has now been largely replaced by italics, as in English:

> **Ich möchte *den*.**

SPELLING PECULIARITIES

■ Syllable division

In German a word broken at the end of a line divides according to syllables: **kom-for-ta-bel**, *com-fort-able*. This is, however, largely a matter for printers, since we almost never split a word when writing by hand.

■ ß

The use of **ß** is purely a written distinction: even though it is sometimes called '**das scharfe S**', there is *no* difference in pronunciation between **ß** and **ss**.

ß is nowadays only used after a long vowel:

> **die Füße**, *feet* (long **ü**)

but: **die Flüsse**, *rivers* (short **ü**)

> **das Maß**, *measure* (long **a**)

but: **nass**, *wet* (short **a**)

der Schoß, *lap* (long **o**)

but: **das Schloss,** *castle* (short **o**)

With proper names usage varies and has to be learned individually (the musicians, for instance, are Johann Strauß and Richard Strauss).

If ß is not available (e.g. on a keyboard) use **ss**; **sz** used for ß is old-fashioned. ß has no capital form—where a word is printed entirely in capitals **SS** is used. In Switzerland ß is often not used at all (the up-market **Neue Zürcher Zeitung** always uses **ss** only).

I Translation Problems

The following list is alphabetical. It includes items not treated in the body of the grammar, or treated in a number of different places and more conveniently brought together here. Reference is made throughout to the places in the body of the grammar where more detail may be found.

Translation problems not covered here should be tackled via the Index, or via the various alphabetical lists in the Grammar:

AS

■ As a conjunction expressing time (= *when*) *as* is **wie** or **indem**. **Wie** is the more colloquial; **indem** is only used where both actions occur literally at the same time:

> **wie ich aus dem Bus stieg, begegnete ich ihr vorm Rathaus**, *as (when) I got off the bus I ran into her in front of the town hall*
>
> **wie/indem ich aus dem Bus stieg, verrenkte ich mir den Fuß**, *as I got off the bus I twisted my ankle*

■ As a conjunction expressing manner (= *like*) *as* must be **wie**:

> **wie Sie sehen, habe ich mir den Fuß verrenkt**, *as you see, I've sprained my ankle*

■ In comparisons of equality (*as . . . as*), the first *as* is **so**, the second **wie**:

> **er ist genauso unsicher wie ich**, *he's just as unsure as I (am)*

The negative of this construction is **nicht so . . . wie**, *not as . . . as*:

> **er ist nicht so unsicher wie ich**, *he's not as unsure as I (am)*

As can also be a conjunction introducing a complete clause in a comparison of equality; it is still **wie**:

> **sie macht es fast so gut, wie ich es gemacht habe**, *she does it almost as well as I did it*

■ As a conjunction expressing cause (= *since*), *as* is **da**:

> **da er nicht hier ist, werde ich es selber machen**, *as he's not here I'll do it myself*

■ Meaning '*in the capacity of*', *as* is **als**:

> **ich als Fachmann kann Ihnen versichern, dass . . .** , *I, as an expert, can assure you that . . .*

▶ *As if* is **als ob** or **als wenn**. See p. 44.

FOR

■ Conjunction, **denn**:

> **du musst es tun, denn wir werden sonst keine Gelegenheit finden**, *you must do it, for we shan't find any opportunity otherwise*

Denn is slightly less formal than *for* is in English. As in English the **denn** *(for)* clause can't start the sentence.

■ Preposition with time (for other prepositional uses of *for* consult pp. 190–1):

☐ A completed period in the past— **lang**, or a time expression in the accusative:

    er war drei Jahre lang im Jemen, *he was in the Yemen for three years*

    er musste einen ganzen Monat warten, *he had to wait for a whole month*

☐ A period starting in the present or the future— **auf** + ACC or **für**:

    ich bin auf/für drei Wochen hier, *I'm here for three weeks*

☐ An intended period in the past— **auf** + ACC or **für**:

    sie kam auf/für drei Jahre nach Deutschland, *she came to Germany for three years* (no statement of how long she stayed)

☐ A period in the past stretching up to the present— **seit** + present tense:

    sie ist seit drei Wochen hier, *she's been here for three weeks*

▶ See pp. 178–9 for tenses used.

☐ A period in the distant past stretching up to the point in the past that we are speaking of— **seit** + past tense:

    er war seit drei Jahren im Jemen, als . . . , *he had been in the Yemen for three years, when . . .*

▶ See pp. 178–9 for tenses used.

IF

■ *If* introducing a clause of possibility is **wenn**:

    wenn du kommst, bring es mit, *if you come bring it with you*

It may also introduce a shortened version of this kind of clause:

    wenn überhaupt, *if at all*
    wenn möglich, *if possible*

■ Introducing an indirect question, *if (= whether)* is **ob**:

> **ich weiß nicht, ob ich es mitbringen kann**, *I don't know if I can bring it with me*

-ING

The *-ing* form of the verb in English corresponds basically to the present participle in German (see pp. 36–7), but it is used in ways in English that are not always paralleled in German.

■ There is no German equivalent to the English continuous tenses (*I am waiting*, etc.). The equivalent simple or compound tense must be used:

> **ich esse**, *I'm eating*
> **ich aß**, *I was eating*
> **ich habe gegessen**, *I have been eating*

■ When two actions are going on at the same time, the *-ing* phrase is translated by a clause introduced by **indem**:

> **indem sie auf das Auto wartete, dachte sie an Hans**, *waiting for the car she thought of Hans*

Auf das Auto wartend, dachte sie . . . is not impossible, but much rarer than in English.

■ When two actions occur consecutively, the *-ing* phrase is translated by a second main clause:

> **er machte die Tür auf und stieg aus dem Auto**, *opening the door, he got out of the car*

■ Where the English present participle is used as a noun, German uses a verbal noun (the infinitive with a capital letter):

> **Warten is so langweilig**, *waiting is so boring*
> **wir haben keine Zeit zum Tennisspielen**, *we've no time for playing tennis*

■ When the English *-ing* form is the equivalent of *to* + infinitive, **zu** + infinitive is used in German:

> **sie begann zu weinen**, *she began crying (= began to cry)*
>
> **danach zu schicken, wäre das einfachste**, *sending for it (= to send for it) would be easiest*

■ With the verbs *to see, to hear, to feel* (and many others) English can make a present participle depend on the object *(I hear her returning)*. A similar construction is possible in German with **hören, sehen**, and a limited number of other verbs; in German a dependent infinitive without **zu** is used:

> **ich höre sie zurückkommen**, *I hear her returning*

▶ See pp. 46–7.

■ *Instead of* + *-ing* and *without* + *-ing* are translated by **anstatt**, *instead of*, and **ohne**, *without*, + **zu** + infinitive:

> **ohne zu sprechen**, *without speaking*
> **anstatt Rad zu fahren**, *instead of cycling*

■ *By . . . -ing* is translated as **indem** + clause or **dadurch, dass** + clause:

> **er ist uns entkommen, indem er ein Motorboot gestohlen hat / er ist uns dadurch entkommen, dass er ein Motorboot gestohlen hat**, *he got away from us by stealing a motorboat*

A similar construction to **dadurch, dass** is used when a verb that takes a preposition is followed by *-ing*:

bestehen auf, *to insist on*
> **ich bestehe darauf, dass ich mitkomme**, *I insist on coming with you*
> **ich bestehe darauf, dass er mitkommt**, *I insist on him coming with you*

▶ See pp. 52–3.

ONLY

■ As an adjective after an article, **einzig**:

> **das ist das einzige Geschenk, das ich bekommen habe**, *it's the only present I got*

■ As an adjective before an article, **nur**:

> **nur das Baby war da**, *only the baby was there*

■ Before a pronoun, **allein** or **nur**. **Allein** follows its pronoun, **nur** precedes it:

> **sie allein war da / nur sie war da**, *only she was there*

■ As a time adverb, **erst**:

> **erst als sie die Tür aufmachte**, *only when she opened the door*
> **erst nach dem Abendessen**, *only after supper*
> **erst jetzt verstehe ich**, *only now do I understand*
> **die Bank macht erst um zehn auf**, *the bank only opens at ten*

▶ For **erst als/wenn**, *only when*, see Until, p. 249.

■ Otherwise, as an adverb, *only* is **nur**:

> **nur langsam machte sie die Tür auf**, *she opened the door only slowly*
> **wenn sie das nur früher gesagt hätte**, *if only she had said that earlier*

■ As a conjunction, *only* is **allein** or **aber**:

> **ich hätte es getan, allein/aber ich wollte nicht**, *I'd have done it, only I didn't want to*

▶ *Not only . . . but also* is **nicht nur . . . sondern auch**. See p. 194.

PUT

The translation of the verb *to put* depends on the position in which whatever is 'put' finally ends up.

- **stellen** *(to place)*: the object stands in a vertical position

  > **stellen Sie die Flaschen dorthin**, *put the bottles down there*

- **legen** *(to lay)*: the object lies horizontally

  > **legen Sie die Platte dorthin**, *put the disc down there*

- **stecken** *(to stick)*: the object is put into something

  > **stecken Sie den Brief in den Kasten**, *put the letter into the letterbox*

- **setzen** *(to set)*: the object is put into a sitting position; this is also the verb used for many non-literal meanings of *put*

  > **er setzte ihr das Baby auf den Schoß**, *he put the baby on her lap*
  >
  > **setzen Sie ihren Namen dorthin bitte**, *put your name there please*
  >
  > **man hat den Lift außer Betrieb gesetzt**, *they've put the lift out of action*

- **Tun**, *to do*, is much used in the spoken (but not the written) language for all senses of *to put*:

  > **tun Sie sie dorthin**, *put them down there*

Observe the difference between **legen**, *to lay = to put into a lying position*, and the strong verb **liegen**, *to lie = to be in a lying position*. Similarly, **setzen**, *to set = to put into a sitting position*, and **sitzen** (strong), *to sit = to be in a sitting position*.

SINCE

- Preposition indicating time: **seit**

  > **seit Sonntag**, *since Sunday*

er ist seit letzter Woche hier, *he's been here since last week*

▶ For tense with **seit**, preposition, see pp. 178–9.

■ Conjunction indicating time: **seitdem** or **seit**

seitdem er hier ist, habe ich nur Ärger mit ihm, *since he's been here I've been having nothing but trouble with him*

▶ For tenses with **seit(dem)**, see pp. 199–200.

■ Conjunction indicating reason: **da**

da er aber hier ist, muss ich mich irgendwie damit abfinden, *since he's here, though, I'll have to put up with it somehow*

SO

■ **So** translated **so**:

☐ = *to such a degree*

ich bin so müde, dass ich nicht mehr gehen kann, *I'm so tired (that) I can't walk any further*

☐ = *therefore*

er war nicht da, so musste ich allein gehen, *he wasn't there, so I had to go alone*

☐ = *thus*

so hätte man eigentlich gedacht, *so one might in fact have thought*

☐ before an adjective (note the position of the article in German)

nach einer so langen Reise, *after so long a journey*

☐ in a negative comparison

> **sie ist nicht so alt wie ich**, *she's not so old as I (am)*

■ *So* translated **also:**

☐ = *for that reason*

> **morgen hab ich Geburtstag, also musst du dich darauf vorbereiten**, *tomorrow's my birthday, so you must get ready for it*

☐ summing up (= *then*)

> **das ist es also**, *so that's it*

■ *So* as object of verb: **es**

> **ich hätte es gesagt, wenn . . .** *I'd have said so, if . . .*

The **es** must come after the verb. If you wish to invert, use **das:**

> **das hat er sehr langsam getan**, *he did so very slowly*

Verbs of thinking and hoping have nothing at all:

> **ja, ich denke**, *yes, I think so*

■ *So much the* + adjective: **umso** + adjective:

> **umso besser**, *so much the better*

■ *So as to*: **um . . . zu**

> **du solltest laufen, um nicht kalt zu werden**, *you should run so as not to get cold*

■ *Something so* + adjective: **so etwas** + adjectival noun

> **so etwas Schönes**, *something so beautiful*

SO THAT

So that is **damit** or **sodass**.

■ **Damit** means '*with the intention that*':

> **ich habe den Regenschirm mitgebracht, damit
> du trocken bleibst**, *I've brought the umbrella, so
> that you'll stay dry*

In literary German the subjunctive is sometimes found after **damit**.

- **Sodass** means '*with the result that*':

> **es hat furchtbar geregnet, sodass ich den
> Regenschirm aufspannen musste**, *it rained
> dreadfully, so (that) I had to put the umbrella up*

As in English, the **so** can move into the main clause:

> **es hat so furchtbar geregnet, dass ich den
> Regenschirm aufspannen musste**, *it rained so
> dreadfully that I had to put the umbrella up*

THAT

That has four different grammatical uses in English, each
translated differently into German.

- It may be a demonstrative pronoun:

> **gib mir das dort**, *give me that*
> **das ist aber schön!**, *that's really nice*

Dies(es) could equally be used, or less commonly **jenes**. See
pp. 137–8 for more detail.

- It may be a demonstrative adjective:

> **ich hätte gern *den* Kuchen, bitte**, *I should like that
> cake please*

Diesen Kuchen could equally be used, or less commonly
jenen Kuchen. See p. 115 for more detail.

- It may be a relative pronoun:

> **das Geschenk, das du mitgebracht hast**, *the
> present that you brought*
> **der Mann, den ich geschickt habe**, *the man that I sent*

Welches, welchen would also be possible. See pp. 139–40 for more detail.

■ It may be a conjunction:

> **ich weiß, dass es nicht sehr leicht ist,** *I know that it's not very easy*

This is **dass**, with subordinate order.

Don't confuse **ich weiß, dass . . .** with **das Geschenk, das . . . .** **Dass** introduces a noun clause, here the object of **ich weiß**, telling us what 'I know'—**dass** is a conjunction. **Das** introduces an adjective clause, telling us more about a specific noun, here **das Geschenk**, *the present*. **Das** is neuter because **das Geschenk** is neuter—**das** is a relative pronoun.

THERE

There in German is either **da** or **dort**. **Dort** indicates a quite precise place, **da** is more general:

> **da ist jemand,** *there's somebody there*
> **er ist dort auf der Terrasse,** *he's there on the terrace*

■ *There* with a motion verb

There used with a motion verb must be **dahin** or **dorthin**, *to there*:

> **ich fahre morgen dahin,** *I'm going there tomorrow*

With other adverbs of place German makes a similar distinction between 'motion towards' and 'no motion towards', by using **nach**:

> **ich bin unten,** *I'm downstairs*
> **kommen Sie nach unten,** *come downstairs*

▶ See pp. 119–20.

■ *There is, there are*

There is, there are in German is **es ist, es sind**. Very often, however, German prefers a more specific verb like **es steht**, *there stands*, **es liegt**, *there lies*. These agree, as **sein** does, with the noun in the nominative that stands after them, and not with the **es**, producing the odd-looking plurals **es stehen**, *there stand*, **es liegen**, *there lie*, etc.

When existence rather than position is being spoken of **es gibt** + accusative is used for *there is, there are*. The verb stays in the singular:

> **es gibt viele Leute, die das sagen**, *there are a lot of people who say that*

▶ See pp. 72–3.

TO LIKE

The basic translation of *to like* is **gern haben** ('*to have gladly*'):

> **hast du Kinder gern?**, *do you like children?*
> **ich hätte gern zwei Stück Kuchen**, *I should like two pieces of cake*

■ Where English follows *to like* with the *-ing* form of the verb, German uses that verb + **gern**:

> **fährst du gern Ski?**, *do you like skiing?*

Especially with verbs of eating and drinking, but also with other verbs, German uses this construction where English simply uses *to like* + object:

> **sie trinkt gern Milch**, *she likes milk*
> **isst du gern Kartoffelsalat?**, *do you like potato salad?*
> **ich höre gern Brahms**, *I like Brahms*

■ The impersonal verb **es gefällt mir** indicates an immediate rather than a lasting impression:

> **Das Bild? Ja, es gefällt mir**, *That picture? Yes, I like it*

■ **Mögen** also means *to like* (amongst other things); the present tense is used particularly for people:

> **ich mag sie nicht so sehr**, *I don't like her all that much*

This construction is more common in the negative.

The past subjunctive, **möchte**, *would like*, used as a conditional, is very common indeed:

> **ich möchte noch Kaffee bitte**, *I should like some more coffee, please*
> **möchten Sie was kaufen?**, *would you like (do you want) to buy something?*

Gern may be added to **möchte** with little if any change to the meaning. **Ich möchte gern** is particularly used when buying things in shops:

> **ich möchte gern drei Pfund Pflaumen bitte**, *I should like three pounds of plums please*

▶ See p. 119 for the position of **gern** in the sentence, and further details.

▶ For **mögen** see pp. 62–3.

UNTIL

■ Preposition, followed by an adverb or an adverbial phrase— **bis**:

> **bis drei Uhr**, *until three o'clock*
> **bis morgen**, *until tomorrow (see you tomorrow)*

■ Preposition, followed by a noun or pronoun— **bis** + second preposition, usually **zu**:

> **bis zum Letzten des Monats**, *until the last of the month*
> **bis auf weiteres**, *until further notice*

- Negative preposition, *not until*— **erst** (*only*) + a preposition:

    > **erst am Letzten des Monats**, *not until (only on) the last of the month*
    > **erst um Mitternacht**, *not until midnight*
    > **erst nach dem Krieg**, *not until after the war*

- Conjunction— **bis**:

    > **bis es repariert wird, müssen Sie irgendwie ohne auskommen**, *until it's repaired you must manage without it somehow*

- Negative conjunction, *not until*— **erst als, erst wenn**:

    > **erst wenn sie es erklären**, *not until they explain it*
    > **erst als sie es erklärt hatten**, *not until they'd explained it*

The difference between **erst wenn** and **erst als** is the same as that between the simple conjunctions **wenn** and **als** (see p. 197).

▶ See also **bis**, pp. 198–9.

WHEN

- *When* in German as a question word is **wann**. This is used in both direct and indirect questions:

    > **wann kommt sie zurück?**, *when is she coming back?*
    > **ich weiß nicht, wann sie zurückkommt**, *I don't know when she's coming back*

- *When* as a conjunction, referring to one occasion in the past, is **als**:

    > **ich war da, als sie zurückkam**, *I was there when she came back*

Referring to the present, the future, or to more than one occasion in the past, it is **wenn**:

ich war immer da, wenn sie zurückkam, I was
always there when she came back

■ **Wo** is frequently used for *when* after expressions of time:

am Tag, wo sie zurückkam, war ich da, I was
there on the day when she came back

▶ See pp. 197–8 for more detail.

WHICH

Which is both a question word (referring to both people and
things) and a relative (referring to things).

■ In questions, as an adjective used with a noun it is **welcher**:

welche Sorte möchten Sie?, which kind would you
like?

Similarly in indirect questions:

ich weiß nicht, welche Sorte ich möchte, I don't
know which kind I want

▶ See p. 116–17.

■ As a pronoun in questions it is **welcher**:

Welches? Das dort im Schaufenster, Which? That
one in the window

▶ See p. 144.

■ As a relative pronoun it is **der** or **welcher**:

das Sofa, auf dem (auf welchem) du sitzt, the
sofa which you're sitting on

▶ See pp. 139–42.

Glossary of Grammatical Terms

Abstract Noun The name of something that is not a concrete object or person. Words such as *difficulty, hope, discussion* are abstract nouns.

Accusative The direct object case in German. See Case.

Active See Passive.

Adjectival Noun An adjective used as if it were a noun: *the good, the bad, and the really horrid. Good, bad, horrid* are adjectives used as nouns (with the definite article *the*).

Adjective A word describing a noun. *A big, blue, untidy painting—big, blue, untidy* are adjectives describing the noun *painting*.

Adverb A word that describes or modifies (i) a verb: *he did it gracefully* (adverb: *gracefully*), or (ii) an adjective: *a disgracefully large helping* (adverb: *disgracefully*), or (iii) another adverb: *she skated extraordinarily gracefully* (adverbs: *extraordinarily, gracefully*).

Agreement In German, adjectives agree with nouns when they stand in front of them, verbs agree with subject nouns or pronouns, pronouns agree with nouns, etc. This is a way of showing that something refers to or goes with something else. Agreement is by number (showing whether something is singular or plural), by gender (showing whether something is masculine, feminine, or neuter), and by case (showing whether something is nominative, accusative, genitive, or dative). For instance: **mit diesen grünen Socken**, *with these green socks*: **mit** must be followed by the dative, so that the noun that follows it (**die Socke**, *sock*, plural **Socken**) has to be in the dative; **dies-** adds its dative plural ending **-en** to agree with **Socken**, and so does **grün**.

Apposition Two nouns or noun phrases used together, the second one giving further information about the first: *the station master, a big man with a moustache, came in. A big man with a moustache* is in apposition to *the station master*.

Articles The little words like *a* and *the* that stand in front of nouns. In English, *the* is the definite article (it defines a particular item in a category: *the hat you've got on*); *a* or *an* is the indefinite article (it doesn't specify which item in a category: *wear a hat*, any hat).

Auxiliary Verb A verb used to help form a compound tense. In *I am walking, he has walked*, the auxiliary verbs are *to be (am)* and *to have (has)*.

Cardinal Number A number used in counting (*one, two, three, four*, etc.). Compare with Ordinal (Number).

Case Nouns, pronouns, adjectives, and articles show 'case' in German. This is an indication of the role they are playing within the sentence. There are four cases: the nominative, which is the case in which the subject of the sentence stands; the accusative, which is the case in which the direct object stands; the genitive, which shows possession; and the dative, which is the case in which the indirect object stands. The last three cases are also used after prepositions. Case still exists in English pronouns (nominative: *he*, accusative: *him*, genitive: *his*) but has almost disappeared otherwise.

Clause A self-contained section of a sentence containing a full verb: *He came in and was opening his mail when the lights went out*—'he came in', 'and (he) was opening his mail', 'when the lights went out' are clauses.

Comparative With adjectives and adverbs, the form produced (in English) by adding *-er* or prefixing '*more*': *bigger, more difficult, more easily*.

Complement The equivalent to an object with verbs such as *to be, to become*. The complement refers back to the subject and stands (correctly) in the nominative: *George became an engine driver. It is I. Engine driver* and *I* are complements.

Compound Noun Noun formed from two or more separate words, e.g. **das Dampfbügeleisen**, *steam-iron*—both English and German words are compound nouns. English often inserts a hyphen into compound nouns, especially if they are long. German does this only rarely, so some German compounds are very long indeed.

Compound Tense Tense of a verb formed by a part of that verb preceded by an auxiliary verb (*am, have, shall,* etc.): *am walking; have walked; shall walk.*

Compound Verb Verb formed by the addition of a prefix (*un-, over-, de-, dis-,* etc.) to another verb. Simple verbs: *wind, take;* compound verbs: *unwind, overtake.* German has many compound verbs. See Prefix.

Conditional Perfect Tense The tense used to express what might have happened (if something else had occurred) and formed in English with *should have* (*I should have walked, we should have walked*) or *would have* (*you would have walked, he would have walked, they would have walked*).

Conditional Tense The tense used to express what might happen (if something else occurred) and formed in English with *should* (*I should walk, we should walk*) or *would* (*you would walk, he would walk, they would walk*).

Conjugation The pattern which a type of verb follows. For instance, a regular verb in English is conjugated like this: infinitive, *to walk;* present, *I walk, he walks;* past, *he walked;* perfect, *he has walked,* etc.

Conjunction A word like *and, but, when, because* that starts a clause and joins it to the rest of the sentence.

Consonant A letter representing a sound that can only be used in conjunction with a vowel. In German, the vowels are **a, ä, e, i, o, ö, u, ü,** and (used only very occasionally) **y**. All the other letters of the alphabet are consonants.

Coordinating Conjunction A conjunction that joins two or more main clauses. Alternatively it may join two or more nouns or pronouns, or two or more phrases.

Dative The indirect object case in German. English has no dative case—we use *to* with the noun or pronoun instead. See Case.

Declension The system of endings used in German on an article, adjective, or noun to indicate case, gender, and number.

Definite Article See Articles.

Demonstrative Adjective An adjective that is used to point out a particular thing: *I'll have that cake*; *this cake is terrible*; *give me those cakes—that, this, those* are demonstrative adjectives.

Demonstrative Article Alternative name for Demonstrative Adjective.

Demonstrative Pronoun A pronoun that is used to point out a particular thing: *I'll have that*; *this is terrible*; *give me those—that, this, those* are demonstrative pronouns.

Direct Object The noun or pronoun that experiences the action of the verb: *he hits me*, direct object: *me*. See also Indirect Object.

Direct Question The simple form of the question, as put. Direct question: *Who are you?* Indirect question: *She asked me who I was. Who I was* is the indirect question. See Indirect Question.

Ending See Stem.

Feminine See Gender.

First Person See Third Person.

Future Perfect Tense The tense used to express what, at some future time, will be a past occurrence. Formed in English with *shall have* (*I shall have walked, we shall have walked*) and *will have* (*you will have walked, he will have walked, they will have walked*).

Future Tense The tense used to express a future occurrence and formed in English with *shall* (*I shall walk, we shall walk*) or *will* (*you will walk, he will walk, they will walk*).

Gender In German, a noun or pronoun may be masculine, feminine, or neuter: this is known as the gender of the noun or pronoun. The gender may correspond to the sex of the thing named, or may not. In English gender only shows in pronouns (*he, she, it,* etc.) and corresponds to the sex of the thing named. See Agreement.

Genitive One of the four cases in German: the genitive shows possession. The genitive is found in English, usually formed with *-s*: *Joan's book*; *his book*; *whose book*. See Case.

Historic Present Present tense used to relate past events, often in order to make the narrative more vivid: *So then I go into the kitchen and what do I see?*

Imperative The form of the verb that expresses a command. In English it is usually the same as the infinitive without *to*: infinitive, *to walk*, imperative, *walk!*

Imperfect Subjunctive In German, alternative name for the Past Subjunctive. See Subjunctive.

Imperfect Tense In German, alternative name for the Past Tense. See Past Tense.

Impersonal Verb A verb whose subject is an unspecific *it* or *there*: *it is raining*; *there's no need for that*.

Indefinite Adjective An adjective such as *each, such, some, other, every, several* that does not specify identifiable people or objects.

Indefinite Article See Articles.

Indefinite Pronoun A pronoun such as *somebody, anybody, something, anything, everybody, nobody* that does not specify identifiable people or objects.

Indirect Object The noun or pronoun at which the direct object is aimed. In English it either has or can have *to* in front of it: *I passed it (to) him,* indirect object *(to) him; I gave her my address (I gave my address to her),* indirect object *(to) her.* In these examples *it* and *my address* are direct objects. In German as in English some verbs take an indirect object only.

Indirect Question A question (without a question mark) in a subordinate clause. It is introduced by some such expression as *I wonder if . . . , do you know where . . . , I'll tell him when . . . , he's asking who . . .* Direct question: *When is he coming?* Indirect question: *I don't know when he's coming.*

Infinitive The basic part of the verb from which other parts are derived. In English, it is normally preceded by *to: to walk, to run.*

Inseparable Prefix See Prefix.

Inseparable Verb A compound verb consisting of a simple verb with an inseparable prefix. See Prefix.

Interrogative The question form of the verb.

Interrogative Adjective A question word (in English *which . . . ?* or *what . . . ?*) used adjectivally with a following noun: *which book do you mean?*

Interrogative Adverb An adverb that introduces a direct question, in English *why?, when?, how?,* etc. In indirect questions the same words function as conjunctions, joining the question to the main clause. *Why do you say that?*—direct question, *why* is an interrogative adverb; *I don't know why you say that*—indirect question, *why* is a conjunction.

Interrogative Pronoun A pronoun that asks a question, in English *who?* and *what?*

Intransitive Of verbs: having no direct object.

Irregular Verb In German, a verb that does not follow the standard pattern of a regular (also called a 'weak') verb. See Strong Verb; Mixed Verb.

Main Clause A clause within a sentence that could stand on its own and still make sense. For example: *He came in when he* *was ready. He came in* is a main clause (it makes sense standing on its own); *when he was ready* is a subordinate clause (it can't stand on its own and still make sense).

Masculine See Gender.

Mixed Verb In German, a verb that both changes its vowel in the past (like a strong verb) and also adds characteristic endings (like a weak verb). See Strong Verb; Weak Verb.

Modal Verbs (literally 'verbs of mood'). These are the auxiliary verbs (other than *have* and *be*) that always appear with a dependent infinitive: *I can walk, I must walk, I will walk*—*can, must, will* are modal verbs.

Neuter See Gender.

Nominative One of the four cases in German. The nominative is the case the subject of the sentence stands in. See Case.

Noun A word that names a person or thing. *Peter, box, glory, indecision* are nouns.

Noun Clause A clause that is the equivalent of a noun within the sentence: *I don't want to catch whatever you've got* (*whatever you've got* is a clause for which we might substitute a noun, e.g. *measles*).

Number With nouns, pronouns, etc.—the state of being either singular or plural. See Agreement.

Object See Direct Object; Indirect Object.

Ordinal (Number) A number such as *first, second, third, fourth*, normally used adjectivally referring to one thing in a series.

Passive The basic tenses of a verb are active. Passive tenses are the set of tenses that are used in order to make the person or thing experiencing the action of the verb (normally the object) into the subject of the verb. Active (basic tense): *I discover it*, passive: *it is discovered (by me)*; active: *he ate them*, passive: *they were eaten (by him)*.

Passive Infinitive The passive form of the infinitive, where the implied subject suffers the action of the verb. In English: active infinitive, *to eat*; passive infinitive, *to be eaten*. The perfect infinitive can also be put into the passive: perfect infinitive, active: *to have eaten*; perfect infinitive, passive, *to have been eaten*.

Past Continuous, Perfect Continuous In English, the past tenses formed using *-ing*, implying that something was or has been continuing to occur: past continuous: *I was walking*, perfect continuous: *I have been walking*.

Past Participle The part of the verb used to form compound past tenses. In English, it usually ends in *-ed*. Verb: *to walk*; past participle: *walked*; perfect tense: *I have walked*.

Past Tense In German, the tense used in written narrative and, for some verbs, in speech as well; often the equivalent to the English past tense: **ich machte**, *I made*.

Perfect Continuous See Past Continuous.

Perfect Infinitive The past form of the infinitive, formed in English from *to have* + past participle: *to have walked*.

Perfect Tense The past tense that, in English, is formed by using *have* + past participle: *I have walked*. The German perfect is usually formed in the same way (**haben** + past participle), but its use is not quite the same.

Personal Pronouns Subject and object pronouns referring to people or things (*he, him, she, her, it*, etc.).

Phrasal Verb In English, a verb made by combining a simple verb with a preposition or adverb: *run out, jump up, stand down*. English phrasal verbs often correspond to German separable verbs. See Separable Verbs.

Phrase A self-contained section of a sentence that does not contain a full verb. *Being late as usual, he arrived at a quarter past eleven*: *at a quarter past eleven* is a phrase; present and past participles are not full verbs, so *being late as usual* is also a phrase. Compare Clause.

Pluperfect Continuous In English, the equivalent tense to the pluperfect using *had been* + *-ing*, implying that something had been going on (when something else happened), e.g.: *I had been walking for an hour, when . . .*

Pluperfect Tense The past tense that, in English, is formed by using *had* + past participle: *I had walked*. The German pluperfect is usually formed and used in the same way (with the past tense of **haben** + past participle).

Possessive Adjective An adjective that indicates possession; in English, *my, your, her*, etc.: *that is my book*.

Possessive Article Alternative name for Possessive Adjective.

Possessive Pronoun A pronoun that indicates possession; in English, *mine, yours, hers*, etc.: *that book is mine*.

Prefix In German, a short addition to the beginning of a verb. This may form an integral part of the verb (it is then called an inseparable prefix and the verb an inseparable verb), or it may in certain circumstances separate off (it is then a separable prefix and the verb a separable verb). German separable verbs quite often correspond to English phrasal verbs: **aufstehen**, *to stand up*; **ich stehe auf**, *I stand up*.

Preposition A word like *in, over, near, across* that stands in front of a noun or pronoun relating it to the rest of the sentence.

Present Continuous See Present Tense.

Present Participle The part of the verb that in English ends in *-ing*: *to walk*: present participle, *walking*.

Present Tense The tense of the verb that refers to things now happening regularly (simple present: *I walk*), or happening at the moment (present continuous: *I am walking*).

Pronoun A word such as *he, she, which, mine* that stands instead of a noun (usually already mentioned).

Question See Direct Question; Indirect Question.

Reciprocal Pronoun A pronoun like *each other, one another* which implies that one inflicts the verb's action on the other member of a plural subject and not on oneself. *They shot themselves* is a reflexive verb; *they shot each other* is a reciprocal verb.

Reflexive Pronoun See Reflexive Verb.

Reflexive Verb A verb whose object is the same as its subject: *he likes himself, she can dress herself. Himself, herself* are reflexive pronouns.

Relative Pronoun A pronoun that introduces a subordinate clause and at the same time allows that clause to function as an adjective or noun. In English the relative pronouns are *who(m), which, whose, that,* and *what. Tell me what you know!*: *what you know* is a noun clause and the direct object of *tell me.* It is introduced by the relative pronoun *what. That's the lad who stole my wallet*: *who stole my wallet* is an adjectival clause describing *lad.* It is introduced by the relative pronoun *who.*

Second Person See Third Person.

Separable Prefix See Prefix.

Separable Verb A verb formed from a simple verb and a separable prefix. See Prefix.

Simple Tense A one-word tense of a verb: *I walk, I run* (as opposed to a compound tense: *I am walking, I was running*).

Stem The part of a verb to which endings indicating tense, person, etc. are added. Verb: *to walk*: stem, *walk-*: *he walk-s, he walk-ed,* etc.

Strong Verb In German, an irregular verb, showing its past tense by a vowel change.

Subject (of verb, clause, or sentence) The noun or pronoun that initiates the action of the verb: *George walked*, subject: *George*; *he hit George*, subject: *he.*

Subjunctive In German, a set of tenses that express doubt or unlikelihood. The subjunctive still exists in only a few expressions in English: *If I were you* [but I'm not], *I'd go now* (*I were* is subjunctive—the normal past tense is *I was*).

Subordinate Clause A clause in a sentence that depends, in order to make sense, on a main clause. See Main Clause.

Subordinating Conjunction A conjunction that introduces a subordinate clause.

Superlative With adjectives and adverbs, the form produced by adding *-est* or prefixing '*most*': *biggest, most difficult, most easily*.

Tense The form of a verb that indicates when the action takes place (e.g. present tense: *I walk*; past tense: *I walked*).

Third Person *He, she, it, they* (and their derivatives, like *him, his, her, their*), or any noun, or any indefinite or demonstrative pronoun. The first person is *I* or *we* (and their derivatives), the second person is *you* (and its derivatives).

Transitive Of verbs: having a direct object.

Umlaut The only accent used in German: the two dots ('diaeresis') placed over the vowels **a, o, u**, to indicate a change in the way they are pronounced.

Verb The word that tells you what the subject of the clause does: *he goes*; *she dislikes me*; *have you eaten it?*; *they know nothing*—*goes, dislikes, have eaten, know* are verbs.

Verbal Noun Part of the verb (in English, usually the present participle) used as a noun: *smoking is bad for you*: verbal noun, *smoking*.

Vowel A letter representing a sound that can be pronounced by itself without the addition of other sounds. In German, the vowels are **a, ä, e, i, o, ö, u, ü**, and (used only very occasionally) **y**.

Weak Verb The name given to a regular verb in German—one that follows the standard verb pattern.

| Index

English prepositions should be looked up in the alphabetical list on page 188.

Irregular verbs should be looked up in the alphabetical list on page 73.

Verb constructions (preposition, case) should be looked up in the alphabetical list of verbs on page 53.

Definitions of grammatical terms will be found in the glossary on page 251.

Also available from Oxford University Press

Oxford Take off in German
Language learning course with almost 5 hours of audio
Book and 4 cassettes 0–19–860275–8
Book and 4 CDs 0–19–860294–4
Book only 0–19–860295–2

Oxford Take off in German Dictionary
0–19–860332–0
(available in UK only)

Pocket Oxford-Duden German Dictionary
The ideal dictionary for higher examinations
0–19–860280–4

The Oxford Colour German Dictionary Plus
Colour headwords throughout
0–19–864561–9
0–19–864561–1 (US edition)

The Oxford Starter German Dictionary
Designed for absolute beginners
0–19–860329–0

Oxford German Verbpack
0–19–860339–8

Oxford German Wordpack
0–19–860336–3